Feminist Biblical Interpretation

Feminist Biblical Interpretation

A Compendium of Critical Commentary on the
Books of the Bible and Related Literature

Edited by   Luise Schottroff and Marie-Theres Wacker

With the cooperation of Claudia Janssen and Beate Wehn
Martin Rumscheidt, editor of the American Edition

Translated by   Lisa E. Dahill, Everett R. Kalin, Nancy Lukens,
Linda M. Maloney, Barbara Rumscheidt (†),
Martin Rumscheidt, and Tina Steiner

WILLIAM B. EERDMANS PUBLISHING COMPANY
GRAND RAPIDS, MICHIGAN / CAMBRIDGE, U.K.

Originally published in German under the title *Kompendium Feministische Bibelauslegung,*
2nd corrected edition, Gütersloh: Chr. Kaiser Gütersloher Verlagshaus, 1999.
Edited by Luise Schottroff and Marie-Theres Wacker, with the collaboration
of Claudia Janssen and Beate Wehn.

Published 2012 by
Wm. B. Eerdmans Publishing Co.
2140 Oak Industrial Drive N.E., Grand Rapids, Michigan 49505 /
P.O. Box 163, Cambridge CB3 9PU U.K.

Printed in the United States of America

18 17 16 15 14 13 12   7 6 5 4 3 2 1

Library of Congress Cataloging-in-Publication Data

Kompendium Feministische Bibelauslegung. English.
  Feminist biblical interpretation: a compendium of critical
  commentary on the books of the Bible and related literature /
  edited by Luise Schottroff and Marie-Theres Wacker with the
  cooperation of Claudia Janssen and Beate Wehn;
  Martin Rumscheidt, editor of the American edition;
  translated by Lisa E. Dahill . . . [et al.].
      p.   cm.
  Includes index.
  ISBN 978-0-8028-6097-2 (pbk.: alk. paper)
  1. Bible — Feminist criticism. I. Schottroff, Luise. II. Wacker, Marie-Theres.
  III. Rumscheidt, Martin. IV. Title.

BS521.4.K6513   2012
220.6082 — dc23

                                    2012016867

www.eerdmans.com

Contents

Contents

Contents

Preface of the Editors to the First German Edition

I

It is no exaggeration to assert that in the last two decades the approaches, questions, and conclusions of feminist interpretation of the Bible have gained increasingly in plausibility and dissemination throughout the world. This is so not only in the domain of practical education but also in that of university scholarship. There have never been as many women qualified in theology and exegesis as there are now advancing feminist interpretation of the Bible through diverse methods and highly differentiated foci of interest. Frequently their points of departure are specific themes or else biblical texts that appear promising in relation to questions of particular relevance to women. It has been clear for a long time, however, that what is at issue here is not simply biblical texts that deal with women or "favored topics" of feminist theology. Critical feminist analysis has to be brought to bear on the books of the Bible and on the Bible as a whole.

Two works have appeared in the United States that make this wide-ranging endeavor visible and draw it together. *The Women's Bible Commentary,* edited by Carol Newsom and Sharon Ringe, 1992, comprises contributions by women who live and teach in North America. All books of the Protestant Christian Bible are addressed in short commentaries; in addition, there are two historical, informational survey articles and two contributions dealing with selected early Jewish and Christian writings. The two-volume work *Searching the Scriptures,* edited by Elisabeth Schüssler Fiorenza and published in 1993/94, offers, in its first volume, foundational essays on method and hermeneutics. The second volume contains brief commentaries on every New Testament book, and a wide range of other early Christian literature and early Jewish writings not part of the Hebrew Bible. The contributors to this work are drawn from five continents in accordance with the overall concept of this project: to document and advance the pluriform range of the women-specific engagement with the Bible.

Sometime in mid-1995 the two editors of the present work, Luise Schottroff for the New Testament and Marie-Theres Wacker for the Old Testament, wrote to a group of about thirty women in the German-speaking world and invited them to work with us in planning and producing a compendium of feminist biblical interpretation. All of them were known to us and active in the work of feminist exegesis, be it in postgraduate studies or in full-time academic teaching positions. The response was overwhelming: after the first phase of correspondence, nearly half of the writings to be addressed were "claimed." In addition, we received numerous suggestions of other women who were interested in the project or who should be sounded out about it. In cooperation with Barbara Heller of the Evangelische Akademie Hofgeismar and Ruth Habermann of the Evangelische Akademie Bad Boll and with the generous financial assistance of Gütersloher Verlagshaus, two symposia were arranged, for the spring and the fall of 1996. At each symposium, six authors presented their contributions for discussion, with about twenty-five authors present. Other additional interested women and men also took part. These two very intense symposia allowed the authors to get to know one another, support one another with critique, and make decisions about further work on related questions and topics. But chiefly the symposia were an opportunity for the participants to be involved from the very outset in carrying this project forward, to give it shape and to influence its direction, to work together in clarifying or, at least, making manageable the numerous emerging hermeneutical questions.

II

The specific profile of the "compendium" was worked out at the symposia.

As a decidedly *feminist* project, it seeks to present women-centered exegetical work on the Bible. For that reason, the team of authors consists exclusively of women who relate themselves more explicitly than is the case in *The Women's Bible Commentary* to one of the by now numerous and diverse feminist exegetical points of departure. On this point, the compendium is perhaps more akin to *Searching the Scriptures*. The clearly desired plurality in method and feminist hermeneutic marks every contributor individually, but all share the conviction that Christian anti-Judaism, Western colonialism, and all forms of racism have to be opposed at the same time misogyny is.

Furthermore, the compendium wishes to signal its women-centeredness and its feminism in noting that the contributors are especially concerned to provide bibliographical documentation of the feminist discussion of their respective writings. Works of traditional exegesis are only sparsely referred to and involve in general only commentaries worthy of commendation, as well as, of course, the monographs and articles actually used in the contributed essay. It was decided not to recite again what is known as "introductory knowledge," such as the date or authorship of each writing. Greater detail is provided about such basic information only for little-known or relatively inaccessible writings.

Since this is a project of *contextual* interpretation of the Bible, we found it necessary to be consciously attentive to the context wherein the project itself was born and to its anticipated readership. The compendium came into being in Germany and wishes, in distinction particularly from the North American works mentioned earlier, to give visibility to the labor of the feminist exegetes of the German-speaking world whose number has grown noticeably in recent years. Our work appears as a publication in Germany. Since it is published by a firm whose program is one of Christian theology, it is expected that in Germany it will be primarily German-speaking Christian women and men who will pick it up. We do hope nonetheless to reach other readers also. Almost all the authors themselves also belong to one of the "great" Christian churches. This corresponds yet again to the way scholarship is structured in the German-speaking world and how it separates theological faculties along confessional lines as contrasted, for example, to the Anglo-Saxon world and its departments of religion where women of different denominations and religions study and do research together and often next to "atheists" interested in religion.

We editors do not at all intend to leave the impression that we view our context, as just depicted, as something "natural." It was clearly a matter of course for us to go beyond it at least selectively and symbolically. We are pleased that we could involve authors from East Asia and Latin America and that a few women who "straddle" the boundaries between Europe and North America are on the team. We rejoice that the palette of Christian-feminist approaches to reality has become quite broad and that a number of such "boundary straddlers" are found in the pages of this book. We made a particular effort to involve Jewish feminist scholars of the Bible. Here German history caught up with us very quickly. In the context of the Federal Republic of Germany, Jewish women must experience being particularly co-opted when a group of Christian feminist women theologians invites their participation in a common project of biblical interpretation. Some Jewish women used this argument to turn down the invitation. So much the greater our joy when we were able to win over Athalya Brenner and Marianne Wallach-Faller, two high-profile scholars, for the project. The sudden and tragic death of Marianne Wallach-Faller in January 1997 came as a hard blow. She was not able to commit to paper her commentary on Malachi. In her memory, the present Christian feminist contribution on that prophet intentionally includes Jewish traditions of interpretation and refers in a pointedly critical way to crucial manifestations of Christian anti-Judaism.[1]

A feminist interpretation of the *Bible:* that is what this work is meant to be. But even among Christians, what the word "Bible" comprises is not altogether un-

1. In memory of M. Wallach-Faller, cf. Marianne Wallach-Faller, *Die Frau im Tallit. Judentum feministisch gelesen,* ed. Doris Brodbeck and Yvonne Domhardt (Zurich, 2000).

ambiguous. The canon of the Protestant Reformation differs from that of the Roman Catholic Church in that the latter includes seven writings in addition to the books of the Hebrew Bible: 1 and 2 Maccabees, Baruch, Judith, Tobit, Sirach, Wisdom, as well as the Greek expansions of Daniel and Esther. The sequence of the biblical writings also differs in the two canons. And, of course, Judaism and Christianity exhibit a marked difference on the understanding of "canon." The whole question of the canon has its own explosive force for Christian feminist theology insofar as the history of the canon is entangled in the history of how women were rendered invisible and excluded from the churches' decision-making and governing bodies. As a way of redressing this, there now exist anthologies of texts, such as Rosemary Radford Ruether's *Womanguides,* published in 1985, where excerpts from biblical writings are juxtaposed with texts from ancient Oriental history of religion and with selections from the traditions of nonbiblical religions with the intent of creating a new canon grounded in feminist theology.

While *The Women's Bible Commentary* does not take up this matter, *Searching the Scriptures* takes a position by rendering the boundaries of the canon fluid. Numerous noncanonical writings of early Judaism and of early Christian communities are included in that commentary. The order of chapters in the commentary volume does not follow the traditional sequence of books found in the Bible. It is more the genre of texts that dictated the order. The writings of the Hebrew Bible are completely absent; the reason for this was initially a matter of organization in that an intended cooperation with a Jewish editor could not be arranged. But that absence can also be read as a reminder of the explosive question of the common Jewish and Christian part of the Bible between Christian abandonment and Christian co-opting of it.

The feminist discussion of the canon is not silenced in the compendium but cannot be settled either in the circle of the contributors. For that reason, we name the problem and advance the discussion somewhat pragmatically. All writings that are part of the widest Christian canon are addressed in short commentaries. We were concerned to find authors for those books where uncharted feminist territory, apart from brief references in *The Women's Bible Commentary,* had to be entered. Most of the noncanonical literary works we chose to include came about as a result of a proposal by an author who was ready to work on the suggested text or had already completed preliminary studies of it. The order of essays is, at it were, in layers: the writings of the Old/First Testament in the choice and order of the Protestant churches are followed by the seven writings added in the Roman Catholic biblical canon. However, the expansions to Daniel and Esther are addressed within the context of Daniel and Esther. Four further early Jewish writings were chosen; these are followed by the books of the New Testament and a series of selected early Christian pieces of literature. The latter provide insight into women's history of biblical times, into the emergence of certain images of women, as well as into theological developments.

In naming the groups of texts in question, we did not insist on standardization. This holds especially for the names of the two parts of the Christian Bible. The designation "Old Testament" for the first part of the Christian Bible next to the "New Testament" can be misread as anti-Jewish and derogatory: the New surpasses the Old or annuls it. That designation needs to be problematized for that reason. The proposal to speak of the "Hebrew Bible" leaps too easily over the question of the Christian canon in that it takes into view only those books that were written in Hebrew. An alternate designation caught the attention of many: the "First Testament"; it seeks to stress the dignity of the never-abrogated covenant of God with the Jewish people. Yet, it too is not free of being misunderstood particularly when coupled with the corresponding concept of the "Second Testament." Does not a "second" testament overtake once again a "first" testament? The designation of the New Testament as the "Christian Testament" is problematic as well since it threatens to exclude the "First" Testament from the Christian canon. In the compendium, these names are used one next to the other in order to create sensitivity for the already mentioned problem of the relation between Judaism and Christianity. Related to this is the question of the name of God. Throughout the Hebrew Bible the instruction is found to pronounce the four consonants of God's name YHWH, the so-called Tetragrammaton, as "Adonai," my Lord, my Lords, or also as "shema," THE Name. Is exegetical language to dismiss this and speak of "Yahweh"? On the other hand, though, can feminist women reading the Bible with more than two decades of critiquing patriarchy on their backs, repeat the names "my Lord," "Adonai," *kyrios* (LXX and NT)? The women of the Marburg project "Hedwig Jahnow" have suggested[2] writing "GOD," a word that, contrary to the Tetragrammaton YHWH, can be pronounced directly. In addition, it does not call into question the monotheistic confession of those who pronounce this name, and also calls to mind the Tetragrammaton through the use of capital letters. Numerous authors have taken up this suggestion for their essays in the compendium. But in this matter too we have not imposed majority opinions on one another; every contributor decided herself.

Finally, as befits a "compendium," our authors have developed a coherent feminist reading of their respective writing, highlighted the primary foci of feminist research in that writing, and added a bibliography of women-specific substance to their contributions. In this way, the work mirrors the feminist discussion process especially in the German-speaking world and also stimulates it. And it gives an overview of feminist interpretation of the Bible in conversation with international research and discussion.

The readership we have primarily in mind are people with theological training, working in congregational settings, in adult education, and in the school sys-

---

2. See Hedwig Jahnow et al., *Feministische Hermeneutik und Erstes Testament. Analysen und Interpretationen* (Stuttgart: W. Kohlhammer Verlag, 1994).

tem. The overall structure of this work, its language and the way it intensifies the problem, appears to be most appropriate to that "target group." But, of course, students of theology, people interested in feminist interpretation of the Bible, professional colleagues, and the curious are invited wholeheartedly to study, browse, leaf through, immerse themselves in, and critique our work.

III

Last but not least, we express gratitude.

We thank all the contributors for their willingness to work together, for their ability to take criticism, and for their patience during the long birthing process of the compendium. Thanks also to the women who planned the gatherings in Hofgeismar and Bad Boll, to Barbara Heller and Ruth Habermann for their hospitality and competent accompaniment. But thank you also to those to whose time-intensive and indefatigable behind-the-scene work the compendium owes its present shape: Pauleen Cusack, Elisabeth Frey, Helga Gewecke, Gabriele Merks-Leinen, and Birgit Springer, who translated some of the essays initially written in various languages; to Sonja Strube, who prepared the index of authors for the German edition and without whom the index of women's names would not have become reality. Thank you to Stefanie Kurzenknabe, Stefanie Müller, Annemarie Oesterle, Ute Ochtendung, and Sandra Schröers for proofreading throughout the various phases of this project. Thank you to Dr. Claudia Janssen and Beate Wehn, who from the very start inserted themselves in this endeavor with an infectious enthusiasm and offered important and valuable help for the New Testament part. In their hands also lay the editorial preparation and standardization of the entire manuscript, all the way to the final diskette formatting. Thank you to Gütersloher Verlagshaus for taking charge of the project; we want to mention Ms. Ulrike von Essen, who initiated the project and then assisted in planning it; Ms. Christel Gehrmann, who skillfully organized the conversations on how concretely to realize this endeavor; Ms. Linda Opgen-Rhein for her well-done work on the cover design; Mr. Johannes Lüers and his coworkers in the production department who, above all, magnanimously and promptly dealt with even late submissions in the final phase of printing.

As the first to have read the entire work, we wish all our readers as much pleasure and profit as we had ourselves!

Luise Schottroff and Marie-Theres Wacker
Kassel and Cologne, June 1998

Preface of the Editors to the Second German Edition

After five months, the *Compendium of Feminist Interpretation of the Bible* is already going into its second edition. Editors and contributors alike rejoice in the numerous positive reviews in journals and radio discussions as well as in the fine reception accorded the work since its appearance in the autumn of last year. No substantive changes were made to the new edition; misprints were corrected, proper names in the Bible were standardized, and, as much as possible, the short biographies of the contributors updated.

At the beginning of December 1998, the symposium "Feminist Interpretation of the Bible" was held at the Catholic Faculty of Theology of the University of Münster. There the compendium was presented to a broad public from the university milieu, to ecclesiastical and community-based women's organizations, and to other interested groups. The exchange between the contributors and editors present and others who attended the symposium touched on first impressions of the text, the questions it raised, and what new perspectives it opened up. We express gratitude to the Ministerium für Schule und Weiterbildung, Wissenschaft und Forschung of Nordrhein-Westfalen for its financial support of this event; it particularly helped the contributors to reflect, on the basis of this work, on the present condition of feminist exegesis in its placement between feminist theory, theologically responsible interpretation of the Bible in its methodological plurality, and practical communication. We also envisioned future projects.

The circle of the compendium's contributors does not see itself as a closed entity. We explicitly encourage theologians, desirous to specialize in feminist exegesis, to get in touch with us.

LUISE SCHOTTROFF AND MARIE-THERES WACKER
Kassel and Münster, February 1999

Editors' Preface to the American Edition

The *Kompendium feministische Bibelauslegung*, the first edition of which appeared in the fall of 1998 and which went into a second edition just months later, presented for the first time a large compilation of feminist exegetical perspectives in the German language areas. The fact that a third, unrevised edition followed in 2007, this time as an inexpensive study edition, demonstrates that in the meantime it has found recognition as a standard work of feminist exegesis. In the foreword to the first German edition we describe the context that led us to undertake the project, and the intentions that directed us as editors and as authors. In the following we wish to sketch several important developments and shifts in the discourse that have occurred in Europe since the book was first published.[1]

With regard to method, at the time of their first publication the essays in the *Kompendium* were already ahead of mainstream exegesis with its historical-critical-oriented methodology in that they increasingly took up "alternative" approaches. Meanwhile, it has been confirmed that of all historical methods used, those that allow biblical texts to be connected back to their contemporary historical context and are related to social processes are especially fruitful for feminist inquiry. However, a particular emphasis in recent publications has not been so much on historical methods, but on text-oriented or reading-oriented ones, especially with regard to the original further development of narratological and intertextual approaches. One factor here is certainly the significant growth of the number of German-speaking feminist exegetical scholars working in academia, many of whom regularly attend the congresses of the Society of Biblical Literature (SBL). Their networks in Europe have also become stronger and more interconnected. In the context of the European Society of Women Doing Research in Theology

1. See also Marie-Theres Wacker, "Feminist Criticism and Related Aspects," in *The Oxford Handbook of Biblical Studies,* ed. John W. Rogerson and Judith M. Lieu (Oxford, 2006), 634-54; Marie-Theres Wacker, "Challenges and Opportunities in Feminist Theology and Biblical Studies in Europe," *Journal of Feminist Studies in Religion* 25, no. 2 (2009): 117-21.

(ESWTR), a project has just been launched to bundle the results of women-specific exegesis and biblical interpretation by women in a grand total of twenty volumes. It will be published simultaneously in German, English, Italian, and Spanish.[2] The first volume on the Torah appeared in 2010.[3]

The sensitization with regard to Christian anti-Semitism that grew out of discussions in the 1980s, in feminist theology and exegesis as in other circles, led to numerous feminist-motivated studies in the past decade that decisively approached the Jesus movement as an internal Jewish movement, and the Second Testament writings as writings of early Judaism. Many of the authors of the *Kompendium,* notably Protestant authors, were involved in the translation of the *Bibel in gerechter Sprache* (literally, "just language" or, more familiar to English readers, "inclusive language Bible"), first published in 2006,[4] which evolved out of the Bible studies held during the gatherings of the German biennial Protestant *Kirchentag.* This new Bible translation attempts not only to make women visible in the biblical texts and in their world, but also to place the writings of the Second Testament decidedly into their Jewish context, overcoming anti-Jewish clichés of traditional Bible translation, above all that of Luther. In the same time period, in part reinforced by the events of September 11, the demand for a Jewish-Christian-Muslim dialogue among women increased enormously. One can safely assume that conversation about common traditions in the Holy Scriptures (Tanakh, Bible, Koran) will receive even more attention.

Granted, even in the foreword to the first edition of the *Kompendium,* we had written that the work must combat Western colonialism as well as misogyny along with Christian anti-Judaism. However, the methods and perspectives of genuinely anticolonial or postcolonial biblical interpretation are still largely unknown in German exegesis and theology. Yet the efforts made in this context to pay conscious attention to "voices" from the Southern Hemisphere have also increased, particularly among women. We ourselves learned a lot in this process. Today we know that it was naïve of us, in describing the Christian canon, to claim that we based our work on the *Kompendium* on the "most extensive form of the canon." In making this claim we recognized neither the fact that the canon of the Orthodox churches, which is based on the Septuagint, is more extensive than that of the Roman Catholic canon, nor that the canon of the Ethiopian church even includes books in its Holy Scriptures that Western Christianity locates far outside the canon, for example, the book of Enoch. However, we still lack a compendium of feminist biblical interpretation with such a broad perspective!

The developments mentioned so far can be described as a concrete manifesta-

2. Irmtraud Fischer et al., eds., *The Bible and Women: An Encyclopedia of Exegesis and Cultural History* (Atlanta and Leiden, 2011).

3. Irmtraud Fischer and Mercedes Navarro Puerto, eds., *Torah* (Atlanta and Leiden, 2010).

4. Ulrike Bail et al., eds., *Bibel in gerechter Sprache,* 3rd ed. (Gütersloh, 2007). See www.sbl-site.org/publications/article.aspx?ArticleId=760-764 for description and discussion.

tion of the insight that the many kinds of profound differences among women must be accounted for, and that every attempt to make statements about "women" or in the name of "women" must be rejected as naïve or imperialistic, because they disregard concrete contexts and concrete experiences. This insight has profoundly influenced the women writers of the *Kompendium*, and this insight led feminist theology and exegesis in the German-speaking world already in the early 1990s to accept as plausible the terminological and factual distinction between biological "sex" and cultural "gender." This distinction provided the opportunity to discuss cultural differences among women appropriately under the rubric of "gender," yet at the same time to retain biological "sex" as somehow still common to all women, without having to problematize it further.

Several major developments in the sex/gender debate entered the feminist theology and exegesis discussion in the German language area only after the publication of the *Kompendium*, for example, the idea that the distinction between "sex" and "gender," when elaborated further along the lines of social constructivism or deconstruction, can lead to the questioning of such a distinction itself; that the construction of "sex," too, is culturally conditioned; and that the binary sex/gender system in particular represents a powerful cultural norm with far-reaching consequences for society and individuals that can be the subject of critical study. Some of the *Kompendium* authors have entered into this debate in the meantime, for example, writing about constructions of the body in biblical texts or biblical symbolism of the body. Others have taken up impulses from masculinity studies or queer theory for their exegetical work.

But this debate has still further substantial far-reaching implications, of course. Without being able to presuppose stable definitions of essence, subject, or identity, it has also become more difficult to define even what is "feminist," especially on a global scale. For feminist exegesis this means recognizing a diverse array of interpretive possibilities and options whose "feminist" common denominator is not established a priori. The authors of the *Kompendium* themselves are not bound to a common "definition" of "feminism." However, the fundamental principles mentioned in the original preface — combating Western colonialism as well as misogyny along with Christian anti-Judaism — may still be regarded as a kind of political minimum on which the authors agree — a minimum standard that has not become outdated even in the age of deconstruction!

This translation is based on the German text of the first and second editions of the *Kompendium*, published in 1998 and 1999, respectively. It includes updated material, first of all in the short biographies of the individual women authors, who now report on their current areas of research and also refer to their recent publications. Secondly, the authors had the opportunity to add to their bibliographies titles that have appeared since 1998 and that they consider important. Since the more recent U.S. publications are not listed in every case, they should be named here: *The Women's Bible Commentary* appeared in late 1998 in an expanded edition that now also includes a selection of Greek-Jewish texts, above all, those belonging to the Roman Catholic biblical canon.[5] Athalya Brenner published a second series of her *Feminist Companion to the (Hebrew) Bible;*[6] this project was continued by Amy-Jill Levine and others to include the Second Testament. The most recent work to mention is *The Queer Bible Commentary.*[7]

Thus, after a long process, the *Kompendium* now appears in English translation. We have many people to thank for the completion of this project, above all, its editor, Prof. Dr. Martin Rumscheidt. From the beginning it was he who made this volume possible by his persistence and vision, coordinating, translating, offering advice, and carrying it through to the end. We thank the William B. Eerdmans Publishing Company for its patient participation in this process. We know what a wealth of knowledge and persistence translating requires, so we offer very special thanks to each of the volume's translators: Lisa Dahill, Everett Kalin, Nancy Lukens, Linda Maloney, the late Barbara Rumscheidt, Martin Rumscheidt, and Tina Steiner. In the last phase of manuscript preparation, especially in formatting the bibliographies, the assistance of Stephanie Feder and Daniela Abels in Münster was a great help.

LUISE SCHOTTROFF AND MARIE-THERES WACKER
Kassel and Münster, March 2010

Translated by NANCY LUKENS

5. Carol A. Newsom and Sharon H. Ringe, eds., *The Women's Bible Commentary,* expanded ed. (Louisville, 1998).

6. Athalya Brenner, ed., *A Feminist Companion to the (Hebrew) Bible,* 2nd ser. (Sheffield, 1998-2001).

7. Deryn Guest et al., eds., *The Queer Bible Commentary* (London, 2006).

Preface by the Editor of the English Language Edition

Many moons ago, at an annual meeting of the American Academy of Religion and the Society of Biblical Literature, one of the German editors of *Kompendium feministische Bibelauslegung,* Professor Luise Schottroff, and I met with Mr. William B. Eerdmans Jr. to discuss the possibility of having this major work published in English translation. No decision was made at that time. A number of months later, having gathered more information and assessments, Mr. Eerdmans decided to support the project. Since then, he has accompanied our work with patience, encouragement, and energy. The translators and editors on both sides of the Atlantic are deeply grateful to him for that.

Since its first publication in Germany, the *Kompendium* has seen two further editions, a signal of the significant attention it has aroused. While there exist numerous publications of feminist theological and hermeneutical studies of the Bible and of its individual writings, the *Kompendium* is the only work thus far to address every book of the Bible; it also addresses books of the Apocrypha and several extrabiblical contemporary writings. In many ways, by engaging existing feminist biblical research, this translation extends the dialogue and opens it to further exploration. In addition, a number of biblical writings are addressed here by feminist theological and hermeneutical approaches for the first time and thus introduced into the evocative and provocative feminist discussion. By the same token, this volume challenges secular feminist criticism to engage with biblical feminist theology.

Concurrently with writing the *Kompendium,* many of its authors were involved in a project to prepare a translation of the Bible that was sensitive to post-Shoah conversations between Jews and Christians and to the issue of gender justice. The Bible's pervasive vision of justice is the undertone of that translation, as its title seeks to communicate: *Bibel in gerechter Sprache.*[1] It endeavors to do justice

---

1. (Gütersloh: Gütersloher Verlagshaus, 2006), 1st and 2nd eds. Fifty-two translators from Germany, Austria, Switzerland, the Netherlands, and the United States of America were involved in this project.

in a number of ways following these aims: to be as faithful as possible to the original languages of the Bible, to hallow the proper name of God in the Bible by offering several possibilities of rendering it, to make women visible in texts that intend to include them but rarely ever name them explicitly, to take seriously that Jesus was a Jew and that he lived in the tradition of Jewish religion and was faithful to the Torah, to avoid anti-Judaistic interpretations, and finally to be highly attentive to the social conditions of life in biblical times. All these aims guide the biblical interpretations presented in *Feminist Biblical Interpretation,* several authors of which actually use their translations of biblical verses from *Bibel in gerechter Sprache* in their essays.

Two additional distinct, albeit closely related, dimensions should be explicitly mentioned. One is the question that prodded the team of scholars who launched this project: What do or what can writings in and around the Bible really tell us about the day-to-day existence of women? In answer the authors have unearthed voices in the texts that resist the androcentrism, patriarchy, and misogyny present in the Bible. The second is that of women today who, bearing the debilitating burden of continuing and flourishing forms of patriarchy, turn to these scriptural texts to see if they might discover there traces or suggestions of a freedom they may find in the here and now. And so this work intends to address not only the scholarly community with its specific concerns but also all who search the Scriptures for an alternative and resisting reality.

The SBL Handbook of Style for Ancient Near Eastern, Biblical, and Early Christian Studies[2] presents two ways of transliterating Hebrew texts: the *academic* and the *general-purpose* style. In accordance with the German editors and their clearly stated conviction that "Christian anti-Judaism, Western colonialism, and all forms of racism have to be opposed at the same time misogyny is" (p. xiii above), it was decided to use the academic style in the English language edition as a way to honor Jewish tradition. In this context I wish to express profound gratitude to Dr. Nicole Ruane of Portsmouth, New Hampshire, who readily accepted the task of preparing the transliteration of the Hebrew terminology for this book. How often have teachers of systematic theology (like this editor) been rescued by scholars with Dr. Ruane's competence! Thank you, Nicole.

Similar gratitude is owed to others, and I wish to name several persons specifically for their participation in bringing this project to fruition. The initial plan that Barbara and Martin Rumscheidt would undertake the translation was defeated by Barbara's untimely death not long after we had begun our work. The willingness of Lisa E. Dahill, Everett Kalin, Nancy Lukens, Linda Maloney, and Tina Steiner literally salvaged the project. For their enthusiasm and their labor I owe them a gratitude that cannot be "translated" into words. With heartfelt thanks I note the assistance of Luise Schottroff, Marie-Theres Wacker, and many of their

---

2. (Peabody, Mass.: Hendrickson, 1999).

sister authors who read and commented on the translated texts of their chapters, clarifying meaning and underlying intention, thereby helping us provide a translation as faithful as any translation can be to the original text. Two persons deserve thanks for an important but tedious part of scholarly translation: the preparation of bibliographies. Since every chapter includes its own literature section, this task required much research work. Professor Wacker engaged Ms. Daniela Abels and Ms. Stephanie Feder of the Westfälische Wilhelms-Universität Münster to undertake the requisite labor. To Ms. Abels and Ms. Feder the editor of the present edition is profoundly grateful, as well as to Professor Wacker for making these two women available for that component. And much gratitude is due to Mr. William B. Eerdmans for his generous financial support for their work. Often authors and editors cannot completely imagine how they tax the gifts and energies of those persons who through the labor of copy editing turn a written text into "literature." I draw on a folksy expression from Canada's Newfoundland and Labrador to express respect and endless gratitude to Mr. Tom Raabe, our copy editor at Wm. B. Eerdmans Publishing Company, and to Ms. Jenny Hoffman for her guidance over the years this translation was in the making: I behold your work and, accordingly, humbly bow to you.

Finally, I acknowledge, deeply moved, the generosity of Luise Schottroff and Marie-Theres Wacker in joining with me to dedicate *Feminist Biblical Interpretation: A Compendium of Critical Commentary on the Books of the Bible and Related Literature* to the memory of Barbara Rumscheidt — *aleha hashalom*.

MARTIN RUMSCHEIDT
Dover, N.H., November 2010

Genesis 1–11: The Primordial History

Helen Schüngel-Straumann

Prefatory Note on the Hermeneutical Approach

My exegetical work is committed to the historical-critical method, sharpened by a specifically feminist perspective. This critique is aimed especially at the androcentrism of previous commentaries; that is, it opposes the de facto masculine standard that has been and is still being applied in interpreting this material. Related to this is the fact that the Bible has always been read and interpreted *selectively*, often abusing the Bible to fortify the bastions of male dominance. It is thus absolutely essential to distinguish between the biblical texts themselves and their *impact* throughout the history of their reception. By reception history I mean all forms of use and adaptation of biblical texts, not only in exegetical or scholarly contexts, but also in art, liturgy, and literature, as well as in the more narrowly theological uses, for example, by the church fathers. Often the reception history of certain biblical motifs — in the present context the motif of the first woman comes to mind — has resulted in more negative readings than with the biblical narrative itself. This does not mean, however, that the biblical texts, which undeniably originated in a patriarchal society, should be excluded from feminist critical view. Here, too, it is important to avoid thinking in polarities such as positive biblical texts versus negative reception history.

The Fateful Reduction of the Primordial History in Christian Tradition to "Woman" and "the Fall"

In roughly two thousand years of traditional interpretation, the statements of the first eleven chapters of Genesis have been significantly narrowed to certain themes that have played a dominant role in *Christian* theology: first, the role of woman, particularly her second-class status and her subordination to man, and second, the fixation on the so-called Fall (Gen 3), in which woman has been foregrounded as the more active party, as so-called seductress. These two problems have to a great extent defined the so-called Christian image of woman, routinely assigning to the female half of humanity the heavier burden vis-à-vis the question of evil and thereby acquitting men from facing it. Many women have also internalized this narrowing interpretation. This is made worse by the fact that several First Testament writers incorporated such views, which had already formed in antiquity, into their work, and by passing them on to the church fathers, they defined the entire Middle Ages. By contrast, Jewish tradition largely ignored this misogynist reception. Thus, by valuing the Second Testament narratives over those of the First Testament, Christian tradition framed a far more negative image of women than did postbiblical Jewish tradition.

In light of these selective readings, primordial history must now be explored *holistically*. It is a complex that was largely taken over in its given sequence from the world of Oriental antiquity. The individual narratives are considerably older than the Bible, and the span from creation to the flood was a given for *all* biblical writers. The most interesting question for us today is how these writers use this inherited material, change it, and adapt it to their own faith context. In pursuing this question I will focus on the image of human being.

Primordial history can stand on its own as a separate complex from the later story of the people of Israel, which begins with Sarah and Abraham (Gen 12). Its statements are intended to address issues of humanity, specifically everything that played a role before and beyond tangible history. For example: Where do human beings come from? What is human being? What determines human destiny? Why is there evil if God created a good world? Why are there conflicts among people, between man and woman, between brothers, between human beings and their environment? And so forth. All these questions relating to humankind are of course fundamental to any theology. This explains why the first chapters of Genesis have always played a prominent role in biblical commentaries.

The Older Part of Primordial History (Genesis 2–11)

The source to which historical-critical scholars have attributed the older portions of Genesis 1–11, the so-called Jahwist (J), is adamantly questioned by many today, especially in dating his material. It does appear certain, however, that the more narrative parts attributed to him are older than the later chapters of the priestly writings (P) written in exile and afterward, and that the J narratives can be assumed to have been written down in the so-called kings era of Israel (tenth to sixth centuries B.C.E.).

What can be attributed to the Jahwist are the two chapters about the creation of the garden and of human being, the creation of woman, and the violation of God's commandment (Gen 2–3); the story of Cain and Abel as well as that of

Lamech and his wives Ada and Zillah (Gen 4); the mythical story of the sons of the gods and the daughters of humans (Gen 6:1-4); the older parts of the story of the flood (Gen 6–9); and, after the flood, the story of the building of the tower of Babel (Gen 11).

The exegetical direction taken since the Hellenistic period has affected women negatively because this is when precisely those texts that assign a special role to women or to one woman, namely, Genesis 2 and 3, as well as 6:1-4, from primordial history, were singled out for commentary.

In Genesis 3, the woman is positioned in the center of the action and plays the active role, while the man in this narrative is completely passive. In Genesis 6:1-4, to be sure, the women are seen as passive, but in later commentaries they have become active seductresses (see below). Predecessors to the traditional Christian practice of singling out Genesis 3 of all texts as hard evidence for the so-called Fall can be found in commentaries on this story from late antiquity. In the First Testament of the Bible itself, this connection is made only once, in Sirach 25:24:

> Woman is the origin of sin,
> and it is through her that we all die. (NEB)

This sentence, which is quoted in all subsequent commentaries, clearly refers to Genesis 3. For Roman Catholic and Orthodox tradition, this sentence belongs to the canon of Holy Scripture, whereas the Reformed churches regard the book of Sirach as apocryphal. Sirach is also absent from the Jewish canon.

Thus the misogynist thread connecting Genesis 3 with Sirach 25:24, which is then woven into the late post-Pauline letter 1 Timothy (2:8-15), is a particularly Catholic problem. The fact that there is not a single allusion to the woman of Genesis 3 in the entire rest of the First Testament, even among the prophets, who reflect so often on guilt and sin, should give us pause. The identification of woman and sin (most often in the context of sexuality and the body) thus does not originate in the Genesis texts at all, but results from a tendentious interpretation that was adopted and expanded upon by Christian tradition, especially that of ascetic movements, throughout history.

Complicating the Christian image of woman is the fact that exegetes as early as the second century introduced the typological juxtaposition of Eve-Mary, in analogy to the Pauline typology Adam-Christ. In the process Eve as sinful woman came to be positioned as a foil to the perfection of Mary (see Leisch-Kiesl 1992, 40ff. for documentation from the early centuries). This pattern, too, was more influential in the Roman Catholic Church than in the Reformed churches, which do not assign such an exemplary role to Mary. The situation is different still in the development of Jewish commentaries, which make no such juxtaposition between Eve and Mary but do set her against Lilith, Adam's first wife, who plays the negative role (see Ruether 1985, 123ff.; Levinson 1992, 67-71), while Eve enjoys high regard as the "mother of all living beings." Since Jewish theology does not speak of a "fall" of or of "original sin," it is almost entirely free of the drastically negative evolutions of the figure of Eve that dominate Christian theology.

Genesis 2 and 3

These two chapters of Genesis belong together. They are closely related in content; numerous key terms and wordplays, which are partially lost in translation, also unite the two chapters. To be sure, these narratives of the primordial history must not be read as historically factual statements. Christian tradition did so to a great extent up until the historical-critical method became prevalent. Early Christian scholars took great pains to harmonize the numerous discrepancies and contradictions in the narratives. However, Genesis 2 and 3 were never intended to represent a historical sequence. Instead, the two chapters should be read concurrently as *parallel* stories. Genesis 2 describes how God planned the creation of man and woman; that is, it shows the divine intention for human beings to live together as partners. Genesis 3, by contrast, describes human reality as it actually is. The moment one looks for a "before" and "after" (e.g., an "original state" of human being), one misses the intended point of the story entirely.

The biblical narrator clearly has a special interest in woman, for he tells about the creation of woman as a separate act, whereas ancient Near Eastern sources do not. What is more, the presumed sources for the biblical narratives spoke only of the creation of humankind *('ādām)*. This *'ādām* (earthling) is made from *'ădāmâ* (earth) and must return to it in the end, that is, must die. *'Ādām* is put into the garden and is driven out of the garden at the end of the story. Thus the skeletal narrative focuses on *'ādām* (human being) as a species. If *'ādām* were not every human being, man and woman, then woman would be immortal — an absurd idea! The words *'ādām* and *'ădāmâ* constitute the first pun in Genesis 2–3. The second, a play on *'îš* and *'iššâ*, occurs in the center of Genesis 2 in the account of the creation of woman.

God constructs a woman out of the *'ādām*, a creature obviously still incomplete or androgynous. This is the beginning of sexual difference in humankind, *'îš* and *'iššâ*. The climax of this text is the poetic line in 2:23, the formulaic claim of relatedness: "This, finally, is bone of my bone and flesh of my flesh!" With these words *'ādām* expresses joy in having found a partner who is a peer. Just as the Song of Songs describes how God intends unself-conscious intimacy between man and woman to look, here the Jahwist conveys how the life of man and woman in God's good creation should look. There is no statement about marriage here. This is a fundamental description of human beings as partners in an ideal relationship. The numerous parallels to the Song of Songs, including the garden metaphors, were first identified by Phyllis Trible. In the perspective of the narrative's male author, of course, *'ādām* becomes a man the moment the woman is added to the picture. This can cause misreadings of the biblical narrative itself.

In Christian tradition, the concepts of "rib" and "helpmate" were especially introduced to document woman's second-class status and inferiority. These views are not supported by the Hebrew text. The masculine concept *'ēzer kĕnegdô* (a help to correspond to him) signifies not a subordinate helper in the sense of a maid, but precisely a specially *qualified* source of support. The masculine *'ēzer*, in almost half of its biblical occurrences, refers to the assistance God gives that humankind alone cannot provide. Neither does *'ēzer* refer to woman's role in procreation, as in Augustine's reading (*De Genesi ad litteram* 11.5). Rather it connotes very substantial help for humankind as a species (cf. Schüngel-Straumann 1989b, 30-31).

Genesis 3 then describes things as they really are. Trust between the sexes has been ruptured; human beings are not doing justice to their relationship with God, nor with one another. The expression of this rupture comes by way of "shame," which signifies something much more basic than sexual self-consciousness before the other. Here the author makes a pun on the root *'ārôm/'ārûm* (naked/clever), which occurs in both chapters. Chapter 2 ends with the comment that the humans are naked *('ārôm/'ārûm)* but are not ashamed before one another. Then in Genesis 3 they are ashamed before one another — and before God! — and they hide. Genesis 3:1 introduces the serpent, who begins a dialogue with the woman. The serpent is more clever (naked?) than all the beasts of the field. It promises the woman cleverness, but later on the only thing the human beings discover is their nakedness (Gen 3:7). Thus the serpent wraps itself around the concepts *'ārôm/'ārûm* by misleading the woman, literally "deceiving" her.

There have been numerous attempts to explain the serpent — a symbol of wisdom as well as a symbol for cults — which First Testament authors frowned upon. According to the text, it is a *creature,* not a devilish oppositional force as later readings would have it. The serpent represents the force that again and again makes Israel listen to other voices than YHWH's, whenever they present their interests cleverly enough.

The question of the role of woman is more difficult. Why does the biblical author have the woman carry on a discussion with the serpent *alone?* Where is the man? All the common traditional interpretations — that the woman is more easily tempted, more susceptible to sin, and more fleshly — must be rejected. Ancient Near Eastern iconography also shows that the author put the woman, not the man, under the tree. The association is frequently made between tree and woman, tree and goddess. And the act of offering food is a matter for women; they are the nurturers. Thus we see that the Jahwist was beholden to certain formal rules. He had *no choice* but to put the woman under the tree. This has nothing to do with a greater affinity of woman for sin. At first, the connotation is value-neutral. Thus the Jahwist gives no explanation for evil in Genesis 3 — nor does the entire Bible.

He demonstrates the fact that evil is in the world, but he does not attribute guilt as misogynist commentaries have done.

Genesis 3:14-19 raises a special problem in the form of the etiological descriptions of how things really were, that is, the statements about the serpent, the woman, and human beings. It is a fateful mistake to interpret these poetic lines as "punishments," as has been and still is the case. The result of the human violation of God's command is their exile by God from the garden, analogous to God's placing the first human creature in the garden (Gen 2:8; 3:23-24). The author describes etiologically in these sentences what he sees happening in his own time: toilsome and often fruitless labor in the fields, woman's painful experience of pregnancy and childbirth, and then the domination of man over woman. The author's choice of words shows that these conditions were *not* willed by God. Genesis 2 describes the way God intended the relationship between man and woman to be. The author expresses unequivocally that this intended relationship has been perverted, trust ruptured, and instead of joy in one another's company, there is domination of the one by the other.

The way the lines about the woman are translated already gives cause for misreadings. Often they are rendered in the form of *commands,* as if God had given instructions to be obeyed: "In pain you shall bring forth children, yet your desire shall be for your husband, and he shall rule over you!" Today it is accepted without question among biblical scholars, male and female, that these sentences are etiological descriptions of a state of being, not commands. Thus they should be rendered in the present or future tense: "He rules over you" or "He will rule over you." The first line about "pains" during childbirth, which still leads many women today to internalize every humiliation relating to sexuality as a punishment they deserve because of the "Fall," is totally nonexistent in the text. Genesis 3:16 merely mentions "toil," using exactly the same word that elsewhere describes human labor and the toil associated with it. To translate it with "pain" is to read unwarranted meaning into the text. Though childbirth is undeniably associated with pain, this is not mentioned in the text. Most translations of this passage are typical of the strictly male perspective of the outsider. This perspective ignores the ambivalence in the very experience of childbirth as women know it — namely, pain *and* joy.

Finally, something must be said about the naming of the human being, especially the woman, in the creation story. Besides the gender-differentiated words *'îš* and *'iššâ,* Genesis 2–3 contain only one other word for woman, namely, *ḥawwâ* (derived from *ḥay,* life, "mother of all living things") at the end of chapter 3. This characterization has no foundation in the text because the account of the first human birth follows only in Genesis 4:1. There the word *ḥawwâ,* which is later repeated in connection with Eve, is more justified. Since this name occurs nowhere else in the entire Hebrew Bible, it is likely a later addition. However, it is precisely here that Jewish interpretations looked for reason to elevate the first woman to the "mother of all living things." This intertwining of chapters 3 and 4 through use of the name for the first woman shows the close connection between the two stories of misdeeds. In other places, too, they are closely associated with one another by content and terminology. At the end of Genesis 4:1-16 we see the same kind of exile as at the end of Genesis 3; Cain is driven out of the field, in fact he is even cursed, whereas neither of the human beings in Genesis 3 is cursed but only the serpent (Gen 3:14). Thus Genesis 4 can be seen as an intensification of Genesis 3.

The Male Acts of Violence in Genesis 4–11

The Jahwist author follows the story of the so-called Fall immediately with the story of Cain and Abel, and with it the story of the first murder. In the course of the rest of primordial history he shows a succession of acts of male violence, beginning with Genesis 4. As soon as two men engage in competitive behavior with one another, one murders the other. For the author, the human state of fallenness into sin is such a comprehensive phenomenon that he cannot demonstrate it conclusively in a *single* narrative, but needs various starting points to circumscribe the different nuances. And it is here in Genesis 4 that a word for "sin" first occurs in the Hebrew Bible. It is interesting, after all, that such a term is absent in Genesis 3, even though Hebrew has over a dozen concepts for guilt and sin. Not until Genesis 4:7 do we find a reference to resisting this sin. Significantly, it comes in the form of God's warning to Cain, that is, not to kill his brother. "Sin" here is something demonic that lurks, waiting for the person to fall for it. Cain is challenged to resist it, which in the end he does not do, or even try to do. Sin here is equated with an act of violence against one's brother.

In Genesis 4:23-24, in describing Lamech, the text escalates violence almost endlessly as Lamech sings the praises of his vengeance. Finally, the rebellion against God finds yet another variant in Genesis 11:1-9 with the story of the building of the tower of Babel. Here the point is to "make a name for ourselves" (11:4) and to become independent of God. The men who build the tower plan a special kind of uprising against God. It is possible that this last story in the Jahwist narrative shows that humankind was in no way different or better after the flood (see below) than before.

Women do not figure into any of these accounts except as mothers, wives, and daughters of the men named. In Genesis 6:1-4 it is a different matter.

Genesis 6:1-4

Immediately prior to the flood narrative, the Jahwist inserted what is likely an ancient mythical piece that tells of a relationship between the "sons of the gods" and earthly women. These (sexual) relationships do not meet the narrator's approval; they serve as an etiological explanation for a certain sort of hero or giant who, given his size or strength, apparently has a special connection to "heaven." Women play a strictly passive role in these four brief verses, which are obviously meant to show the increasingly fallen state of sinfulness if even the "heavenly ones" participate in it.

What is interesting for a feminist interpretation, beyond this short biblical text itself, is the reception it has experienced in numerous apocryphal narratives. In the last centuries before the common era, there was an extreme heightening of interest in all kinds of heavenly beings (angels) (cf. Tobit), and this short narrative led to numerous apocryphal writings and commentaries that describe in most glowing colors the relationship of "angels" with earthly women. Since they cannot be quoted at length here, we will briefly summarize the very different perspective of these writings and the far more negative view of women they convey. While the women in Genesis 6:1-4 were strictly passive as victims of the sons of the gods — more specifically victims of rape — in the apocryphal narratives the women become more and more the active parties. It is they who seduce the heavenly ones to descend from their heights and strike them dumb with their beauty (cf. the especially drastic wording in 1 Enoch 6–11). In addition, the texts present value judgments throughout. There is another aspect as well: the angels are made "impure" by the earthly women; sexual desire is identified with earthly women, and this desire ultimately brings evil into the world. All these texts, which are influenced by Hellenism, reveal a strong dualistic opposition between spirit and flesh that does not exist in the Hebrew Bible. In these commentaries, the daughters of humankind in Genesis 6:1-4 represent the flesh, lower human nature, sexual desire, evil.

These numerous writings of the Hellenistic-Roman era were adopted by Second Testament writers, especially Paul, as well as by more than a few church fathers later on. They stem from groups of male ascetics and reflect a typical male fear of sexuality that is projected onto the heavenly sphere. Because the tendentious bias of these writings has had such disastrous results — a subterranean current leads from here to the fifteenth-century "witch hunts" *(Hexenhammer)* — it is crucial to take up these texts and investigate them further (cf. Küchler 1986).

The Flood

In the older variant of the flood narrative in the J source, one can still detect traces of the Oriental sources. Thus there are incongruities in the narrative, which become understandable in view of the long period over which they evolved. Common among Oriental accounts is the motif of the gods sending a flood as punishment for human misbehavior. However, in the J source, the *reason* for punishment is more closely associated with the human being. In his introduction to the biblical flood narrative (Gen 6:5-7), the author very clearly emphasizes that human beings are *responsible* for their actions and their consequences.

In these three verses the concept 'ādām is used four times to mean human-kind *(die Menschheit)*. First, there is reference to their wickedness, then YHWH recalls the creation of human beings. Thus in Genesis 2 and 3, 'ādām as a collective term includes every human being that is distinct from the animal world, women and men and of course children as well. Everything that is human must drown in the flood. If 'ādām only included men, as a later misreading claimed again and again (see below on Gen 1), women would not have died in the flood, which is as absurd as the idea that in Genesis 3 only the men were mortal (cf. 3:19). Thus no distinction at all is made in the biblical text between human beings — neither regarding their spoiled state nor for the resulting consequences; all are equally at fault, all die in the same manner.

Things become somewhat more complicated with the image of God. At the end of the flood YHWH promises never again to allow such a catastrophe to befall humankind, no matter how they behave (Gen 8:21-22). YHWH, who speaks after the flood, appears completely transformed, yet people have remained the same, and have learned nothing from the catastrophe. This change (8:1) can be traced through the religious history of prebiblical flood narratives, especially the Gilgamesh Epic. Thus in the Gilgamesh narrative it is the god of storms and nations, Enlil, who inspires the flood and sets it in motion. In the end, however, it is the great mother goddess Ishtar, herself also a creator of human beings, who cannot bear to see that "her" people have been drowned. She breaks out in a loud lament at the end of the flood (Gilgamesh Epic, tablet 11). In the end a sacrifice is offered as in the biblical story, but Ishtar prevents Enlil, who caused the flood, from enjoying the sacrifice. The Jahwist combines in the one YHWH figure, the only deity, features that had been spread over diverse divine beings in the ancient Near Eastern narratives. The "simple" characters in the polytheistic context become a "complex" character in the one God YHWH who changes from Enlil to Ishtar (cf. Keel 1989).

In moving toward monotheism, an attempt is made to combine the diverse characteristics of a polytheistic world in this *one* YHWH. The side of the Sumerian-Akkadian mother deity that is sympathetic to humankind thus constitutes the merciful side of YHWH. The significance of this for the flood story is that in the end the maternal aspect wins out in the struggle, which this text implies must be carried out within the very person of YHWH. Thus J is well on the way to a holistic view of God in which masculine and feminine features are combined, whereas in other cultures they are spread over several deities. It would not do justice to the substance of the narratives to see God in the Jahwist story of primordial history as a purely masculine God — even though YHWH is always spoken of in grammatically masculine forms. Just as the Jahwist is moving toward a holistic image of humankind, he is (8:2) also attempting to balance the features of male and female deities, which he only achieves with a certain unevenness.

Primordial History in the Priestly Writings, Especially Genesis 1:1-2, 4a

"P" as Frame Narrative and Corrective

The Genesis 1–11 primordial history narrative contains parts written later than the Jahwist's work. Among the priestly portions that are especially easily recognized and dated because of its stereotypical language, its love of numbers (genealogies), and its systematic structure is, above all, the well-known creation text at the beginning of the Bible, Genesis 1. The P source originated in the Babylonian exile (587-538 B.C.E.), a time of extreme insecurity in which people sought to gain a new consciousness of their faith and their tradition. The fact that Genesis 1 introduces the entire Hebrew Bible is indicative of its significance as a frame for the entire Pentateuch, the five books of Moses. Since it can be assumed that the priestly text is based on familiarity with the earlier material, we can also assume that conscious corrections were made to the conception of humankind and of God.

Genesis 1 contains other elements besides the creation of humankind (see below) that are of interest to feminist exegesis. In Genesis 1:2, for example, the grammatically feminine concept *rûaḥ* (spirit-power; *Geistkraft*) is introduced to name the spirit-power of God that was present before and during the creation. It is inadvisable to think of Genesis 1 as *the* biblical creation story; numerous psalms and other poetic texts contain older conceptualizations of the creation than the commonly known "creation by the word" (cf. Pss 33; 104) central to Genesis 1 (cf. the thorough discussion of this in Schüngel-Straumann 1992).

The Image of Humankind of Genesis 1

The Genesis 1 account is written according to a clear scheme. The writers thought it important to spread the eight or more acts of creation over six days; after all, the climax of the account is not the creation of humankind, but the Sabbath. God rests on the seventh day. The whole text is shaped by its movement toward this conclusion.

What is said about the creation of humankind as man and woman is decisive for the image of humankind and for a feminist exegesis. That will therefore be the focus of the following comments, although other aspects (e.g., ecological statements) also enter into the biblical story for the first time in Genesis 1 (cf. Zenger 1987).

On the last day, humankind is created along with the beasts of the field. Quite fundamentally, Genesis 1:26-28 offers a *theological* explanation for the place of humankind in creation, the relation between God and humans and relations among humans. In contrast to other works, here God's decision to create human beings is specifically named ("Let us make humankind . . . ," v. 26). This resolve already indicates the purpose of creation, namely, dominion over all that had been created previously. The core of the narrative is the three-line poetic middle section in verse 27, which reports the implementation of this decision:

> So God created humankind in his image,
>> in the image of God he created him;
>> male and female he created them.

Gender difference is articulated precisely at the center of this poignant passage. Thus gender difference is an integral part of God's good creation and is expressed with the adjectives "male" and "female." As in Genesis 2, where we are told in vivid terms that it is not good for *'ādām,* the human being, to be alone, here, too, a single sentence directly connects the differentiation of the sexes with the fact of human beings' creation in the image of God (9:6). Humankind as a species, in its male and female forms, is in God's image. The writers of Genesis 1 would certainly have not understood any attempt to separate humankind into spirit *(Geist)* and soul, for example, or to limit the text to the soul alone, as is typical in Christian anthropology.

The third section (v. 28) brings blessing to humankind as created. It articulates the place and task of humankind against the background of ancient Near Eastern concepts of humanity. Humans are to *have dominion,* namely, as God's representatives, as do the ancient Near Eastern kings. According to the ideal of the good shepherd, who leads and guides his people, humankind as God's representatives are to bear responsibility for the rest of creation, as God does for the world as a whole. Thus humankind has a *task,* as in Genesis 2. Work and tasks are part of the good creation, not a punishment. But if humans are only allowed dominion over the rest of creation — and according to P they must not even kill animals but eat a vegetarian diet — then the implicit and explicit message is this: humans must not dominate other humans; God *alone* is to have dominion over human beings. Beyond the shadow of a doubt, this also eliminates the domination of man over woman, for both man and woman have dominion over or guide the rest of creation. Quite obviously this means that neither sex may presume to lord it over the other. In this respect P is saying something quite similar to the older Genesis 3 narrative: when man dominates woman, this goes *counter* to creation; it is a perversion of the original order of creation. Only P says it even more pointedly. Since this source has no sin narrative, this programmatic statement about the relations of the sexes moves into the center of the message about creation of human beings in the image of God. In using the term "human," "man" *(der Mensch),* one often loses sight of the fact that it refers to *both* sexes. The leadership function is transferred by God to both, man and woman. The German word *herrschen* (rule) makes this difficult to recognize because its very root, *Herr* (lord, master, mister, gentleman), points only to men. But if man *alone* rules the world, the result is a topsy-turvy order of things, a perversion of what was originally intended.

In the priestly writings among the narratives of origins (Gen 5 and 9, for example), which return to the theme of creation in the image of God, it is as clear as in Genesis 1 that this applies to *all* human beings, and that it is not lost even after the flood. In the central sentence, Genesis 9:6, where humankind *('ādām)* is forbidden to shed human blood, the text refers expressly back to the creation of humankind as in the image of God. In this sentence the concept *'ādām* occurs three times. If it applied only to men, men would be allowed to kill women! The most terrible form of domination over another human being, murder, is forbidden here by recalling the message that humankind bears the image of God.

How was it possible for the message of woman being made in God's image to be weakened again and again, even denied to a certain extent, throughout the history of Christian biblical interpretation, even into the twentieth century? In the late First Testament period commentators already began to restrict the concept of *'ādām* as it occurs in Genesis 1 to mean both sexes, narrowing it to signify man as *male*. In early Jewish commentaries (e.g., in the various biographies of Adam and Eve), which were republished again and again in the common era, *'ādām* was often read as a proper name (Adam), leading to a completely one-sided understanding of the texts of the history of origins in which *'ādām* always means human being, humankind as collective entity. Such reconceptions also played a role in the translation of these texts into Greek; the popular Hellenistic view is that "human" in its fullest sense really only means man as male. So, statements made about man and woman alike have often been understood as applying only to man as male. Thus the statements about creation in the image of God were seen as early as the pre-Christian era as applying only to man as male. "Image" in its fullest sense can only mean "human" in its fullest sense, and that, it was said, applies only to man as male.

A number of apocryphal texts (for sources, see Schüngel-Straumann 1989b, especially 54-78) offer vivid and wordy explanations why women are supposedly *not* made in the image of God, or possibly are made in the image only when seen together with the man, while the man is seen as in the image of God in his own right. Other apocryphal writers demand of woman that she cover her head with a veil, the veil serving to cover for the fact that she lacks God's image. Such traditions of late antiquity are reflected in Paul's elaborate explanations in 1 Corinthians 11, where he establishes clear second-class status for women, subordinates them to men, and asserts that they bear a lesser degree of God's image. The veil, too, appears in this text (1 Cor 11:5-6). The fact that such a clear statement as the one in Genesis 1 about man and woman being made in God's image was later interpreted with such misogynist bias is a subject in dire need of more thorough feminist research.

The Intrinsic Value of First Testament Messages versus the Later Interpretations

Even though the biblical texts contain numerous aspects that feminist exegetes today must consider with a critical eye because they *all* arose out of a patriarchal society, one must avoid going behind the texts themselves when they clearly assert equality of the sexes. And when many Second Testament writers working in the context of misogynist readings of the Genesis texts in late antiquity weaken even the clear assertions of woman's creation in the image of God and demand woman's subordination to man, one must reject and correct such interpretations. The problem in Christian interpretation has been and often still is the fact that in general, the Second Testament is valued more highly than the assertions of the Hebrew Bible. This explains how statements by Second Testament writers who were grossly misled about the place and role of women could be considered valid for almost two thousand years, were thought of as "the will of God," and were internalized in people's minds and lives.

The thorny task of reworking the misogynist history of the reception of the primordial history narrative is therefore far from completed — in many places it has not even begun. This task is just as important as developing new feminist conceptualizations of one's own.

LITERATURE

Børresen, Kari Elisabeth, ed. 1991. *The Image of God: Gender Models in Judaeo-Christian Tradition.* Oslo.

Gössmann, Elisabeth. 1991. "Anthropologie." In *Wörterbuch der feministischen Theologie,* edited by Elisabeth Gössmann et al., 16-22. Gütersloh.

―――, ed. 1985. *Eva Gottes Meisterwerk. Archiv für philosophie- und theologiegesschichtliche Frauenforschung.* Vol. 2. Munich.

Keel, Othmar. 1989. "Jahwe in der Rolle der Muttergottheit." *Orientierung* 53:89-92.

Küchler, Max. 1986. *Schweigen, Schmuck und Schleier. Drei neutestamentliche Vorschriften zur Verdrängung der Frauen auf dem Hintergrund einer frauenfeindlichen Exegese des Alten Testaments im antiken Judentum.* Novum Testamentum et Orbis Antiquus, vol. 1. Fribourg and Göttingen.

Leisch-Kiesl, Monika. 1992. *Eva als Andere. Eine exemplarische Untersuchung zu Frühchristentum und Mittelalter.* Cologne.

Levinson, Pnina Navè. 1992. *Eva und ihre Schwestern. Perspektiven einer jüdisch-feministischen Theologie.* Gütersloh.

Meyers, Carol. 1988. *Discovering Eve: Ancient Israelite Women in Context.* New York.

Ruether, Rosemary Radford. 1985. *Womanguides.* Boston.

―――. 1987. *Frauenbilder — Gottesbilder.* Gütersloh.

Schneider, Theodor, ed. 1989. *Mann und Frau — Grundproblem theologischer Anthropologie.* Quaestiones disputatae, vol. 121. Freiburg.

Schroer, Silvia. 1987. *In Israel gab es Bilder. Nachrichten von darstellender Kunst im Alten Testament.* Orbis Biblicus et Orientalis, vol. 74. Fribourg and Göttingen.

Schüngel-Straumann, Helen. 1989a. "Mann und Frau in den Schöpfungstexten von Gen 1–3 unter Berücksichtigung der innerbiblischen Wirkungsgeschichte." In *Mann und Frau — Grundproblem theologischer Anthropologie*, edited by Theodor Schneider, 142-66. Quaestiones disputatae, vol. 121. Freiburg.

―――. 1989b. *Die Frau am Anfang. Eva und die Folgen*. Freiburg. 2nd ed. Münster, 1997.

―――. 1991a. "Bibel." In *Wörterbuch feministische Theologie*, edited by Elisabeth Gössmann et al., 49-54. Gütersloh.

―――. 1991b. "Eva." In *Wörterbuch feministische Theologie*, edited by Elisabeth Gössmann et al., 90-95. Gütersloh.

―――. 1991c. "Geist." In *Wörterbuch feministische Theologie*, edited by Elisabeth Gössmann et al., 146-47. Gütersloh.

―――. 1991d. "Gottebenbildlichkeit." In *Wörterbuch feministische Theologie*, edited by Elisabeth Gössmann et al., 173-77. Gütersloh.

―――. 1992. *Rûah bewegt die Welt. Gottes schöpferische Lebenskraft in der Krisenzeit des Exils*. Stuttgarter Bibelstudien, vol. 151. Stuttgart.

―――. 1996. *"Denn Gott bin ich, und kein Mann." Gottesbilder im Ersten Testament — feministisch betrachtet*. Mainz.

―――. 1997. *Die Frau am Anfang. Eva und die Folgen*. 2nd ed. Münster.

Trible, Phyllis. 1978. "Gegen das patriarchalische Prinzip in Bibelinterpretationen." In *Frauenbefreiung. Biblische und theologische Argumente*, edited by Elisabeth Moltmann-Wendel, 93-117. Munich.

Westermann, Claus. 1974. *Genesis 1–11*. Biblischer Kommentar, vol. 1, 1. Neukirchen.

Zenger, Erich. 1987. *Gottes Bogen in den Wolken. Untersuchungen zu Komposition und Theologie der priesterschriftlichen Urgeschichte*. 2nd ed. Stuttgarter Bibelstudien, vol. 112. Stuttgart.

For Further Reading

Schüngel-Straumann, Helen. 1998. "'From a Woman Sin Had Its Beginning, and Because of Her We All Die' (Sir 25:24)." *Theology Digest* 45:203-12.

―――. 1999a. "Der Mensch als Bild Gottes in Gen 1. Frauenfeindliche Erblasten aufarbeiten." In *Gleichstellung der Geschlechter und die Kirchen*, edited by Denise Buser and Adrian Loretan, 71-86. Fribourg.

―――. 1999b. "Paritätische Modelle von männlich und weiblich am Anfang der Bibel." In *The Crisis of Israelite Religion*, edited by Bob Becking et al., 183-93. Oudtestamentische Studiën, vol. 42. Leiden.

―――. 2002. "Feministische Exegese ausgewählter Beispiele aus der Urgeschichte. Rückblick auf ein Vierteljahrhundert feministische Auslegung von Gen 2 und 3." In *Congress Volume Basel 2001*, edited by André Lemaire, 205-23. Supplements to Vetus Testamentum, vol. 92. Leiden.

―――. 2004. "Eva, die Frau am Anfang." In *Geschlechterstreit am Beginn der europäischen Moderne*, edited by Gisela Engel et al., 28-37. Königstein.

―――. 2010. "Die biblische Paradieserzählung als 'Gründungsmythos' der Geschlechter." In *Paradies. Topographien der Sehnsucht*, edited by Claudia Benthien and Manuela Gerlof, 99-114. Cologne.

Translated by Nancy Lukens

Genesis 12–50: The Story of Israel's Origins as a Women's Story

Irmtraud Fischer

Preliminary Reflections

The Bible is a book that comes to us from a patriarchal culture. The majority of texts were written, extended, and interpreted by men from their predominantly androcentric perspective. If there are texts that show convincing signs of possibly having been produced by women, they too do not tend to break the framework of society constituted by patriarchy. According to Athalya Brenner (Brenner and van Dijk-Hemmes 1993, 1-13), one has to probe which texts, under the *given* presuppositions of the androcentric view of the world, actually show opposition to it and express authentic voices of women. In other words, in the Bible there are no "feminist texts" in the narrow sense of the word. There are only — or under these circumstances, one should say even — texts that prove that the patriarchal worldview was never without fissures. Under these premises, it makes little sense to search the Bible only for utterances that are to legitimize the struggle for liberation and agency of women today — and one has to consider that not even today all women think this is a necessary and legitimate struggle. Feminist exegesis of the Bible does not probe only the Bible itself but also what the androcentric tradition of exegesis and scholarship has made of the texts.

Overview

Scholarship subdivides Genesis 12–50 into the following parts: *Abraham* narrative, *Isaac* narrative, *Jacob* narrative, and *Joseph* narrative. This terminology already suggests that we are faced with stories of *men* that write *men's* history. But if one looks closely at the biblical evidence, a fundamentally different picture appears: almost every other text in the so-called Abraham narrative has a main character that is an important female protagonist. The so-called Isaac narrative consists of actualizing retellings from the Abraham-Sarah stories, the rest are Rebekah stories.

From Genesis 29 onward, the narratives deal considerably more with the women Rachel and Leah than with their father. And yet, this part of Genesis is called "Jacob-Laban narrative." The narratives in Genesis 34; 35:16-22a; and 38, which foreground the separate tribes of Israel that formed from the group of their "brothers," are told as women stories revolving around Dinah, Rachel, Bilhah, and Tamar. Still, the whole textual cluster from Genesis 12 to Genesis 36 and 38 is termed in theological jargon as the stories of the *fathers,* or the *patriarchs.* Since nothing in the textual evidence of Genesis merits such terminology, it seems to stem from those who perceive the Bible as narrowly androcentric and who, by choosing such language, impose a mode of reading that renders women invisible. It is therefore better to speak of the *(primordial) parent* narratives (PPN): the so-called fathers are the *parents* of Israel!

To grasp the meaning of what these stories tell us about women, one should not only search the text for women protagonists carrying the plot. But because of the length restriction, the discussion will focus on these women. Largely I will follow the order of the canonical text. Matching the narrative genre of Genesis, I will present a narrative of feminist scholarship of the specific texts, based on my earlier publications (Fischer 1994 and, for a wider audience, Fischer 2005).

Sarah, Hagar, and Abraham

The genealogy that charts the generations from Shem to Terah constitutes the link between earliest history and the history of Israel (Gen 11:10-25). It consists only of male names, but the summary after each generation reads: "he bore sons and *daughters.*" It is therefore consistent that the narrative of the genealogy of Terah (Gen 11:26-32) mentions four men and three women: Abram, Nahor, Haran, and Lot and Sarai, Milcah, and Iscah. Sarai, Abram's wife, is infertile. It is specifically emphasized in 11:31 that she came with the family on the journey to Haran, while at the beginning of chapter 12, which deals with Abram's exodus and the journey to the Promised Land, the woman is made invisible, and the nephew Lot is explicitly mentioned.

Sarai's Abandonment

The first real story that follows the note-like introduction is that of Sarai's abandonment (12:10-20). To escape famine, the couple travels toward Egypt. At the border Abram loses courage. He fears that the Egyptians are sexually volatile and thus could kill him to get to his beautiful wife. The threatening scene he imagines for himself culminates in verse 12: "Then they will kill me, but they will let you live." So he speaks to Sarai and tries to convince her to pretend that she is his sister. It is telling that the narrator presents the concerns of the man. The fact that he does not allow the woman to answer shows his particular viewpoint of the events. Sarai is the victim; her consent is absent. She remains mute. Upon arrival in Egypt, the worries of the man are shown to be unfounded and his strategies of problem solving unsuitable. *Because* he pretends his wife is his sister, the Egyptians find her a desirable woman (cf. vv. 18f.) — not violently grabbed by any ordinary person but accepted into the house of the pharaoh with all the conventions of the dowry. On the completion of the first plot sequence (v. 16a), the narrator remarks: "Abram was well done by at her expense" (Crüsemann 1978, 74-75). There is just one who disagrees with this treatment of her: YHWH, who enters the plot in opposition to the pharaoh "because of Sarai, Abram's wife" (v. 17b). Pharaoh's demand for an account does not lay blame on Sarai but on the patriarch. He himself is responsible for the blunder by abandoning her (and thereby putting her in the way of danger!). Without asking for his presents back, the pharaoh, in a gesture of stately condescension, exiles the abashed man and his wife (vv. 19-20).

This version of the abandonment story belonged presumably to the oldest Southern cycle of narratives of the primordial parents, consisting of complete single narratives. In the later literary context (12:6-9) one reads this story of *Sarai's abandonment* as the *abandonment of the double promise of a land* that Abram leaves without God's instruction, *and of progeny* by abandoning the potential mother. One thing is certain: even though the language suggests that the patriarch is the one to whom the so-called promise to the "fathers" is directly addressed, he cannot fulfill it with any woman. The promise is not given to the father alone but to the married couple, Abram and Sarai.

Childlessness and Emancipation with Divine Approval

In the final version of Genesis the problem of the couple's childlessness is initially discussed in reference to the affected male. When God reaffirms the promise, Abram asks, "What will you give me, for I continue childless?" (15:2). Infertility is thus not treated predominantly here as a female problem, but as a male problem. Genesis 16:1-6 looks at childlessness from Sarai's perspective. She bears him no child, but she has an Egyptian slave woman named Hagar. Instead of submitting to fate, Sarai actively engages to change the situation. According to the words that the narrator puts into her mouth, her primary concern is not their child together but a child for herself (16:2). She thus seeks refuge in the often documented socio-hierarchical compensatory practice of the ancient Orient of substitute bearing of children by the slave woman for the main wife. In addition to the exploitation of labor of this woman on the lowest rung of the social ladder, her sexuality is exploited. Hagar is not asked at all for her consent. Abram obeys his wife's order, goes to her slave woman, and she becomes pregnant. The narrator subtly hints at the ensuing conflict between the three: for the couple Hagar has no name. She is arrested in her low social status even when she gets pregnant for her mistress. Hagar, however, perceives her status in the social hierarchy differently when pregnant (Bal, van Dijk-Hemmes, and van Ginneken 1988, 46). The position of her mistress is not uncontested anymore. Yet Sarai does not put herself on the same level as her slave woman. She tries to solve the problem by addressing her equal. The man who obediently followed her order denies all competence for resolving the conflict, thereby abandoning the mother of his child to her mistress's harsh oppression. Hagar ends her oppression by deciding to flee. When she rests by a well in the desert, she encounters — according to the oldest version of this story — a messenger, who legitimizes her flight and promises freedom for herself and her son. The name Ishmael that she is to give to her child is a name to commemorate her liberation from oppression. Hagar names then the god and the well of the encounter (16:13f.). Her experience of God becomes the founding legend of a holy site.

The basic narrative of Genesis 16 (= 16bn, composed of vv. 1-2, 4-8, and 11-14) undergoes three further redactions in the course of the literary-historical development of the PPN: the first extension (v. 9) changes the narrative of the woman's deliverance into a "text of terror" (Trible 1984). In accordance with ancient Oriental law concerning slaves, the messenger sends the escaped woman back to her oppression. The (exilic) editor needs this command to return in order to tell the story of how Hagar and Ishmael are driven away again in 21:8-14. He exacerbates the oppression by ordering the slave woman to deliver herself into her mistress's hands (plural) in submission, whereas 16:6, in the basic narrative, had spoken of "being in her hand" (singular). Hagar's return is not told but assumed in 21:8-14. Thus, the dual oppression is taken up in this second tale of terror.

The incorporation of a version suggested by the priestly writings (16:3 and 15-16) introduces a further change. In it is a genealogical note stating that Ishmael is Abram's legitimate, firstborn son. The result of this priestly redaction (Rp) is that in Genesis 16 Hagar does not have to return to her harsh mistress and that her child is born under the guardianship of his father and recognized as his lawful son. The latest redaction gives Hagar a promise that is in no way inferior to the promises to descendants that in terms of their linguistic form are given exclusively to fathers — and not to mothers (16:10; cf. 15:5; 22:17; 32:12).

A Son for Sarah

According to Genesis 16bn, Sarai's attempt to get a son through her slave woman fails. The couple is not human enough to grant the pregnant woman the necessary room for life. When Sarah and Abraham go beyond their fertile age, they still are childless: the story of 18:1-15, which belongs to the same literary layer as 16bn, tells us of the turning point. The visit of the three men in the tent at Mamre is meant initially only for the husband. Abraham offers these guests hospitality and conducts a conversation of few words with them that more and more concentrates on Sarah. At the climax, it is the One for whom nothing is impossible (v. 14) who speaks, promising a son, not for Abraham but "for Sarah" (v. 10). When Sarah, who is still hidden in the tent, hears this promise, all she can do is to laugh in a realistic appraisal of her situation. Only when she realizes in the dialogue *who* it is who speaks and gives the promise does her doubt disappear and faith take its place. The discussion around her laughter (vv. 13-15) should not be interpreted as a reproach by the One who makes the promise. Sarah's laughter is foregrounded because it resonates in the name of her son Isaac (cf. 21:6-7). What started as a visit among men and a conversation with Abraham ended as an encounter between God and the woman Sarah.

But the redaction inserted by the priestly writing (P) into Genesis disenfranchises the primarily feminine experience of the promise of birth and the naming of the son in favor of the father. Chapter 17, which in the final version of Genesis is read before the older narrative of Genesis 18, makes Sarah's encounter with God look like a derivative experience mediated by her husband. In addition to the covenant — including the sign of circumcision that excludes women (Plaskow 1991) — Abram is given a new name: Abraham, "Father of Multitudes." He is also charged to change Sarai's name to Sarah, "(Ruling) Lady." Abram is renamed by God, Sarai by her husband. The man is thus given the power of defining over his wife. The promise to Sarah in 17:16 is no less than that given to the patriarch, but is given to the man and not directly to the woman. Through the inclusion of the passages from the priestly writings, Abraham becomes the intermediary between God and Sarah. Women are included in God's community only because and through and with their men — not as individual subjects.

Abandonment Again

In the canonical order of the Genesis material, Abraham abandons Sarah again in the year in which she is to become pregnant. In its original version, Genesis 20 narrates that Abimelech, the king of Gerar, sends for Sarah and takes her into his harem. In a dream sent by God, the foreign ruler is informed that he has taken a married woman into his house — and not, as Abraham had indicated, his unmarried sister (vv. 2-3). Threatening death, God, who is partial in Sarah's favor, orders her return (v. 7). Abimelech obeys immediately — just like the pharaoh in 12:17-20 — and is healed from the already effected punishment of infertility (20:17b-18). It is no coincidence that the note of the barrenness of all the women in Abimelech's household comes at the end of the episode. It prepares the reader for the immediately following report of Sarah's pregnancy and Isaac's birth (21:1-3). With the retrospective narrative technique of 20:18, the possibility of God's promise of a son to be fulfilled with another man than Abraham is decidedly excluded.

Genesis 20 is also edited later to enhance the image of the infamous patriarch, who at that time is already famous for his fear of God. The denial of their marriage is now also attributed to the woman (v. 5). She is changed from victim to accomplice, and the lie of being siblings becomes a (half-)truth (v. 12). God's death threat cannot be averted by the return of the woman but solely by the prayer of the patriarch, who has been elevated to the level of prophet (cf. the inserts in 20:7a, 17a). This later layer also smoothes over the inglorious story of the expulsion of Hagar and Ishmael in 21:8-14. Abraham feels sorry for his son. Only God's promise to make this son also into a nation persuades Abraham to part with Ishmael and his mother (21:11-13).

The Expulsion of Hagar and Her Son

The original story of expulsion, 21:8-10, 14-21, like Genesis 16, sketches a harsh image of the arch-parents. At the celebration of Isaac's weaning, Sarah realizes that her son is not the firstborn and thus not the main heir. She sees to it that Abraham drives Hagar and her son away. In the course of the big feast that the husband puts on for Sarah and Isaac, he sends Hagar and her son into the desert with one day's ration of water and bread. When the child almost dies of thirst, an angel from heaven rescues Hagar from despair and her son from dying. The mother Hagar receives a promise for her son of the same magnitude as the promise to the "fathers" (21:18; cf. 17:20)

Abraham's Two Sons

The story of Hagar's expulsion, of the son's near-death, and of their rescue has been treated in exegetical discussion as trivial literature — as a sentimental little tale of a mother's trouble with a crying child where God has to get involved. The twin narrative to this "tale," which bears the same plot structure and in parts corresponds word for word to it (cf. the synopsis in Fischer 2005), is the story of Abraham being commanded to sacrifice Isaac. But unlike the former, this story has been interpreted as the devastating tragedy of unconditional obedience toward an incomprehensible God.

Genesis 22, the story of the binding of Isaac, is what made the image of Abraham as it is found in tradition in the first place. Through its history of interpretation in Judaism as well as Christianity, Genesis 22 has become one of the central texts of the whole Bible. Originally it was meant to be seen together with Genesis 21:8-14: Abraham has abandoned all the people around him. Twice he abandons his wife Sarah through the denial of their married relationship (12:10-16; 20). He also abandons Hagar, the mother of his child, the first time when she is pregnant and he withdraws his support (Gen 16), and the second time together with his firstborn, Ishmael, whom he sends away from his house never to see again and puts in fatal harm's way (21:8-21). Now he has only this one son, the only son that he loves, Isaac (22:2). And this son, following God's order, he is to sacrifice with his own hands. The story is about the testing of Abraham, not about the sacrifice of Isaac (22:1). In commanding Abraham to do this, God imposes on Abraham what he had imposed on people around him, particularly on women: to be cut off from the flow of life. The death of an old man would follow the normal course of life. But if God wants to touch Abraham, he has to touch all he has left for his future: his son. Like Ishmael, Isaac is rescued in the last minute by an angel and is saved from death (21:17; 22:11). Abraham passes the test: father and son are allowed to live on like the desperate Hagar and Ishmael, who had been threatened by death of thirst.

Sarah's Burial Place

Where is Sarah in this story? After all, Isaac, who is to be sacrificed, is also *her* son. Yet, she remains invisible. Her experiences of abandonment have filled her cup of suffering to the brim. But she is also an accomplice in the expulsion of Hagar and Ishmael. Her own son, like Ishmael before him, is in deadly peril. But Sarah does not have to be tested any more. A Jewish tradition (cf. Brock 1974; 1984) explains that Sarah's death follows immediately after this story because of shock at the events in Moriah. Genesis 23, a story that draws on the records of Sarah's death and burial in the Priestly source (vv. 1-2 and 19), presents the female ancestor of the first generation as the first heir of the Promised Land seeing that she is buried on the first piece of land that Abraham buys there. In her grave at Machpelah all the mothers and fathers of Israel are buried, with the exception of Rachel and Joseph (Gen 25:9-10; 35:27-29; 47:29-31; 50:5-14). For all intents and purposes, the burial site of the ancestors of the people is the grave of a woman.

The Rebekah Cycle

The ancestress is dead. Her son is not yet married. So the old patriarch sends his servant to his relative in his country of origin to fetch a woman from there for Isaac (Gen 24).

Rebekah in the Succession from Abraham and Sarah

Abraham imposes only one condition on the servant's assignment: the woman must be willing to leave her country, her relatives, and her family, as he himself once did (24:5-8; cf. 12:1-4a). When the servant arrives in the town of Nahor, he sits down by the well, which in ancient Oriental towns was the meeting place for women. He finds what he is looking for in Rebekah, whose introduction in the narrative is constructed like an appearance. "Behold, Rebekah came out" (v. 15). Rebekah is not only the woman who matches the patriarchal ideals that the servant obviously understands to be the criteria for God's choice (vv. 14, 42-44). She is the woman of the right family to which the genealogy in 22:20-24 had already pointed: the family tree of Milcah and Nahor culminates in 22:23a in the brief note of conception (!) of Rebekah. Her story is made to be parallel to that of Abraham because she, like him, leaves her people, her relatives, and her family and announces her decision with "I will go" (24:58), just like Abraham, who in days gone by followed God's voice and left (cf. 12:4). Not Isaac but Rebekah is portrayed as the adequate link in the promise of the Abrahamic line. This becomes clear in the bridal blessing for Rebekah: "May your offspring gain possession of the gates of their foes" (24:60), which is almost the exact wording of the last promise to Abraham after his successful test in 22:17. Isaac, on the other hand, is linked with the tradition of Abraham's failure when he, like his father before him, lies to Abimelech saying that his wife is his sister (26:1-11).

Rivalries between Peoples and a Complicated Pregnancy

The so-called Isaac cycle is really a Rebekah cycle. Frettlöh (1994) showed that Rebekah is not portrayed as the ideal, pure, and submissive bride in Genesis 24. At the very first encounter of the couple (24:62-67), the woman takes leadership. The man remains passive and regards Rebekah as a mother substitute (v. 67). She is the active one. When she becomes pregnant, she asks YHWH for clarity about the complications during her pregnancy; this she does without her husband (25:21-23). The word given to her is an oracle about peoples and the twins she is carrying and how the second-born will dominate the older one (25:22f.). The story of the origin of two peoples is composed unambiguously as a story of the genuinely female experiences of pregnancy and birth.

The Mother Determines Who Will Receive the Blessing

God's words to Rebekah explain why she favors her younger son and the contrast that presents to the socially legitimized norm of preferring the firstborn Esau by the father (25:28). Isaac is presented in the story of the deceit in Genesis 27 as a tricked, albeit suspicious, old man. Rebekah firmly holds the reins and guides the plot according to her own designs (cf. Willi-Plein 1989, 328ff. for a reading of Gen 27 as a Rebekah narrative). But in a patriarchal culture the mother who knows the circumstances cannot give the blessing that legitimizes the family's progression. So she orders her favorite son, Jacob, to obtain the patriarchal blessing through trickery. Rebekah prepares everything for this to happen, and she assumes full responsibility (27:13). The narrator tells this story of trickery not without irony: the blessing that Isaac is supposedly giving his favorite son defines the subordinate son from the mother whereas the one who has the claim to predominance is defined by the father (27:29). The facts are exactly opposite. When the deceit becomes apparent, father and favorite son can only cry, shaken deeply. But YHWH endorses the blessing and thus supports Rebekah's choice (28:10-17).

In the Mother's Home: Leah and Rachel, Bilhah and Zilpah

To rescue Jacob from the persecution of the deceived, Rebekah sends him to her own family. There he will find refuge, and there he is to wait until she calls him back (27:43-45). What is tragic about the mother who had managed to make her son into the main heir, is that she herself had to send him away from her never to see him again.

When Jacob arrives at the dwelling place of his mother's relatives, he meets his cousin Rachel at a well, watering the sheep of her father. Jacob takes over her work for her — not only at times but for seven long years in lieu of the bridal price that he, a refugee without means, cannot generate in any other way. As in Genesis 24:28-30, the suitor is introduced to the family by the bride (29:12-13). The romantic scene is interrupted by the narrator, who informs the reader that Laban has *two* daughters (29:16). The older, Leah, has tender eyes (not weak, as in Butting 1987), and the younger, Rachel, is beautiful. The outer appearance counts when the women are introduced. But *the younger brother,* who had pretended to be the older (Gen 27), falls in love with *the younger sister.* In the morning after the wedding night, Jacob discovers, in shock — like his father's and brother's shock earlier — that his father-in-law had given him the older sister under the pretense that she was the younger one. This intrigue costs the woman much (like the abandonment narratives). Jacob, who cannot get rid of the woman he did not want, hates her (29:31) because of her father's deed.

The Women Founders of Israel

For that reason, YHWH shows compassion to the dejected woman and makes her womb fertile. He does not do so for Rachel: she remains infertile. Leah's births describe the whole tragedy of an unloved woman who loves her husband: the first three children get names that express the hope of caring attention. Only the name of the fourth expresses thanks to YHWH, who compensates for her isolation by giving her children (29:31-35).

The first conversation between Jacob and his favorite wife is portrayed by the narrator as a hefty marital argument (30:1-3). Rachel wants children. The attention of the husband that her sister longs for, is securely hers. Like Sarah before her, she resorts to the surrogate birthing by her slave woman (cf. Fischer 1994, 91-102). Rachel, however, in contrast to Sarah's treatment of Hagar, manages to integrate Bilhah into the family. Bilhah has the name and rank of a maid in the eyes of the chief wife. She bears two sons for Jacob, whom Rachel names in such a way as to express her own life experience. The second child's name interprets the entire narrative, which is disconcerting in that it shows women as being exclusively preoccupied with bearing children. This has earned the First Testament the accusation that it degrades women to "birth machines." "Naphtali" receives its meaning from the sisters' wrestling over God, thereby building up the house of the one who wrestled with God, "Israel." Corresponding to the twelve tribes, twelve sons *have* to be born in one generation if one wants to read the founding history of Israel as a family history — rather than a history of a ruling dynasty. In this literary genre, vital sexuality and fertile women found the nation. Jacob appears next to the active women as a passive "means to an end." This becomes apparent in the birth legend for Issachar, 30:14-18: Leah sells Rachel some mandrakes that Reuben had brought her for the price of one night with Jacob. The sexuality of the man becomes the object of exchange between the women. The price, which the man accepts unquestioningly, explains the reasons why Leah does not become pregnant anymore (29:35): Jacob no longer goes to her. This one night with him brings her another pregnancy. After she named the children born to her slave woman with names expressing good luck and happiness (Gad, Asher), thereby asserting her stature among women (30:11-12), the name Issachar once again expresses thankfulness to God. And now Jacob also stays with her; this is expressed by the name of her last son, Zebulun (30:19-20).

The Importance of Daughters

Leah's vital power seemingly ebbing away, she bears a daughter as her last child. The usual note of conception of sons and the explanation for the name giving are missing in Dinah's case. Daughters do not count in a society that generally constructs its genealogy in terms of male descendants. To determine that in the three generations of the primordial parents so few women were born is to read the biblical text fundamentalistically. Daughters are silently passed over (cf. Archer 1990, 18). Dinah's birth notice in its position as an appendix suggests that it is a secondary addition. In the final text, however, it is tantamount to a marginalization of female descendants.

The PPN do not know a *general* denigration of daughters. In the branch of the family that remained on the eastern side of the Jordan, daughters and the female line count almost exclusively. Rebekah also does not run to her father's house but into the "mother's house" (Gen 24:28; cf. Meyers 1991). This fact should not be (mis)interpreted as matriarchal structures in that society; it is conditioned by the origin of the mothers of Israel in that branch of the family. Women can be found in all genealogies of the primordial parent narratives, even though the emphasis rests on men. In the whole composition of these narratives, peoples are represented through the kinship between sons of a father, between brothers, but the mixing of two groups of peoples is represented in every case through marriage. The "genealogy" of the whole of Israel (Gen 12–35), as well as that of the Edomites in Genesis 36, is constructed according to this pattern. As a result, women are given more weight than men: the pale son of the primordial parents of the southern region, Isaac, is "given in marriage" to Rebekah, the strong ancestress of the northern region. The descendants of Esau even emigrate to the country of origin of the two women Oholibamah (36:2, 18) and Timna (36:12, 22), where they settle in the region of the women, Seir (36:9, 20). Two of the tribal territories of Edom are named after these two women (36:40-41) who enable Esau's integration into Seir.

Marriage Contract and Territorial Borders

Through his wives, Jacob is also integrated into the household of his mother. As a refugee, in the time approaching his marriage, he does not live patrilocally (in the house of his father) according to custom but in the house of his future wives' father. He works there as a shepherd. When conflict arises about the wealth of the herd, he, having worked twenty years as a servant, thinks about going home, which eventually his God also calls him to do. To do so he has to obtain his wives' consent (31:4). Rachel and Leah's speech shows for the first time solidarity between them (cf. Schmidt 1989, 36) as well as their agreement with Jacob's plan but by no means indicates a submissive stance from them. With self-confidence they say to their husband: the wealth belongs to "*us* and to our children" (31:16) — and in no way to "you." The two women for once agree in the opposition to their father. When the family leaves Laban's house, Rachel steals the teraphim, the household gods (31:19). The angry search for the gods brings Rachel into mortal danger, but she averts this through her cunning (31:30-35). With the teraphim, Rachel evidently takes away the legitimacy of the clan: after this, no sons go there to find women for themselves. Moreover, Rachel constitutes with this the importance of her own genealogy, as the story of Joseph ultimately corroborates (cf. Spanier 1992, 405).

Before the final separation, Laban, whose daughters had not left his house at marriage but only now, sets a condition for the marriage contract: Jacob is not allowed to oppress either of the women and he must not bring another woman into the marriage. The contract serves to safeguard the daughters and appears of the same order as the one governing the division of territory (31:44–32:1).

Rachel's Life Force

The twelfth son of the family, the children of which are defined through their mothers (35:22b-26), is already born by the time the family reaches their destination in Canaan (35:16-20). During the journey, contractions take Rachel by surprise. She gives birth to her second child, into which she pours all her vital energy, and then she dies. She calls him Ben-Oni, "son of my life-force" (Schäfer-Bossert 1994, 122). The change of name by the father to Benjamin is not to be interpreted as depreciation of women's life force. Jacob noticeably favors specifically Rachel's sons among the brothers (Gen 37; 43). Rachel, who thought she would die without children (plural, 30:1), dies at the moment she has children (plural). Her tomb — in contrast to the cave at Machpelah — has a historical effect outside Genesis (1 Sam 10:2; Jer 31:15; Matt 2:18).

Structural and Physical Violence against Women

Many of the so-called stories of division about the separation of the genealogically segmentary lines of descent from that of Israel, the main line, also report violence against women. The narratives of Hagar (Gen 16; 21:8-14) also belong to that group of stories.

Lot's Daughters

Lot, Abraham's nephew, had a fight with his uncle over resources; he leaves and goes his own way (Gen 13). He offers his two virgin daughters to the men of Sodom for collective rape (Gen 19:8). This seems to him a suitable strategy to protect the two *male* guests from violent sexual degradation. That both women escape unscathed has to do with the godly nature of the two visitors who are able to avert the danger. In a similar situation, the concubine of the Levite in Judges 19 does not even survive her ordeal. Seifert (1994, 56-65; cf. also Rashkow 1994) argues on the basis of the attempts to exonerate incestuous fathers made to this very day, that Lot's sexual violence against his daughters continues in 19:30-38: Lot, who because of his inebriation allegedly caused by his daughters is declared innocent (19:33, 35), is — read with a hermeneutics of suspicion — the rapist of his daughters. The absence of the mother, who when she looked back had turned into a pillar of salt (19:26), is a further argument for reading the story as one of incest. Moreover, the presence of wine, a typical cultural good, and localization of the event in a deserted setting also support this reading. The two women, who are defined through their relationship to their father, become pregnant and give birth to two sons who bear names that hint at their incestuous origin: Ben-ammi, meaning "son of my relative," and Moab, "from father" (19:37-38). The interpretation of Genesis 19 as a hushed-up story of incest makes much sense. Reservations are in place insofar as the story of Sodom is told with unambiguously negative judgments whereas the story of Lot's daughters is completely void of such judgments. Also, it needs to be remembered that Genesis speaks clearly when it comes to sexual coercion.

Bilhah

Genesis 35:22 deals with the incest of Reuben with Bilhah, the concubine of his father Jacob. There is no indication that the woman consented. This emphasizes the narrative technique in Genesis where the victims of sexual violence remain speechless (cf. 12:10-16; 16:1-6; 34). In the blessing of the tribes, Genesis 49:3-4, only Reuben is made responsible for the breaking of the taboo, and he is excluded from the main inheritance of the promised line. Genesis 34 and 38 tend to approach the blessing of the tribes in a fashion similar to Genesis 49: Simeon and Levi, Jacob's second- and third-born sons, are excluded because of their extreme revenge on the Shechemites. It falls to Leah's fourth-born, Judah, whose story is narrated in Genesis 38. The stories about exclusion from and the receiving of the promised heritage are all narrated as stories of women.

Dinah

When Dinah wants to go out to Shechem to see the daughters of the region (34:1), she is seen by the son of the local prince, Shechem, who rapes her. The only daughter, who seeks female companionship, falls into the brutal "company" of a man. As the subsequent plot shows, Shechem does not fit the stereotype of the rapist. After his crime, he feels attracted to the woman and is willing to pay any dowry. Jacob and his sons regard this attack against the woman as a violation of the honor of the family, and with cunning present circumcision as a condition for the wedding (34:14). When Shechem submits to this, Simeon and Levi fall on him, kill him, and take Dinah, who obviously had already been taken into his household, back to the family (34:26). The brothers are interested only in revenge, not in the well-being of their sister. She remains a silent victim of the brutal men around her.

This story also undergoes redaction later. It is turned into an — albeit inglorious — example for the prohibition of mixed marriages. Now the rapist is no longer the sole negotiator; his father is too. And the condition of circumcision is applied collectively, not only to the potential bridegroom. Both brothers take revenge after the circumcision; they kill the entire male population of Shechem and take women and children captive. In this version, the violence done to the woman has become just a minor detail of the story. In the prayer of the Simeonite woman Judith (Jth 9:2-6), the rape of Dinah appears as a symbolic story for the defilement of the temple (cf. Standhartinger 1994, 108ff.). What the revenge of Simeon did not achieve is accomplished later by his daughter Judith: to safeguard the people from the incursion of the noncircumcised upon them (→ Judith).

Tamar

The story that accounts for the continuation of the promised line in the house of Judah also begins with injustice toward a woman. But Tamar does not remain in the role of the victim but, as her own fate changes, becomes the founder of the house of Judah from which the Davidic line of kings arises (Ruth).

Genesis 38 starts with the narration of the marriage between Judah and a daughter of Shua whose name is not given. She bears three sons and names them in the tradition of her mother-in-law Leah (38:3-5; cf. 29:32-35). But the first attempt at founding the house of Judah happens in the city of deceit (Chezib, 38:5). For his firstborn, Er, Judah chooses a woman named Tamar. When Er dies he orders his second son, Onan, to honor the duty of raising the offspring for his brother, according to Deuteronomy 25:5, and to marry the widow. Although Onan exploits the woman's sexuality (Jeansonne 1990, 102), he denies her an offspring that would integrate her alone into the patriarchal family of the deceased brother and assure her the position of the mother of the main heir. YHWH lets this son die as well (Gen 38:10). With the excuse that the third son is too young, Judah sends Tamar back to the house of her parents. There she is to wait for the marriage to her brother-in-law (= levirate marriage). Judah commits injustice toward his daughter-in-law in many ways. He bars her from the provision that is legally hers through the levirate marriage and blames her for the death of his two sons. He refuses to give her his only remaining son, Shelah. Thus he also denies her the advantages of widowhood that would have allowed her to marry a freely chosen husband from outside the family. When Shelah reaches adulthood, he is not given to Tamar as a husband. Therefore, she takes off her widow's clothes, veils herself to be unrecognizable, and sleeps by the gate of Enaim (well of the twins) with her father-in-law. As pledge for the payment for the "prostitute," she cleverly bargains for the outer signs of his identity, his seal, staff, and cord. Because she immediately returns home and resumes her widowhood, the messenger sent to take payment to her fails to find the supposed prostitute. For Judah, the threefold pledge that unquestionably identifies his person is lost. He fears disgrace (38:23). When the patriarch hears that his daughter-in-law is pregnant, he suddenly emphasizes that he has not let her out of the levirate marriage. Right away, he calls for the death penalty — without speaking to her. Tamar sends the three items of the pledge to the man who wanted to condemn her to a lifelong, unprotected widowhood. They show that he is an adulterer of the levirate marriage. He has to admit publicly that

Tamar is more in the right than he (38:26) and that he committed injustice by withholding his third son from her. The birth of Tamar's twins is told to parallel that of Rebekah (38:27-30; cf. Gen 25:24-26). Thus, her sons, who take the place of the two deceased, continue the genealogical line after Jacob through Judah — on to the woman, who is to inscribe herself into the feminine-defined genealogy of Israel through her unconventional actions, Ruth (Ruth 4:11).

Women in the Joseph Narrative

Ruth and Tamar are portrayed as positive "seductresses," but the wife of Potiphar is portrayed negatively in Genesis 39. Joseph's conduct is exemplary, but she is typecast as "foreign" and "foolish" (Niditch 1992, 25; → Proverbs). In the framework of Genesis, this story can be read as a variation of the abandonment narratives but with reversed gender roles: the young man Joseph is abandoned by his brothers. In the foreign land he is coveted by a powerful woman. As a man, however, he escapes the sexual abuse — unlike his ancestresses and his sister Dinah. The woman takes revenge for the rejection and accuses him of sexual advances and thus ruins the early career of the one who saves Israel from starvation.

Aseneth, Joseph's wife and daughter of a priest from On, is mentioned only twice very briefly in Genesis (for contrast, → Joseph and Aseneth). She bears the two sons, Manasseh and Ephraim, who, contrary to the prepriestly tradition of the PPN, are named by the father (41:50-52). In the list of settlers in Genesis 46:20, she is mentioned as an exemplary daughter-in-law who legitimates exogamic marriages. Next to the women Leah, Zilpah, Rachel, and Bilhah, the androcentric list (46:5-27) contains the daughter Dinah (46:15) and the granddaughter Serah (46:17) exemplarily. The number of persons is determined exclusively by the men, but the women mentioned show that a small but complete nation moves to Egypt. Joseph's story, in contrast to the PPN, is a classic male story. Butting showed that Queen Esther is the female pendant to his political function and power (1994, 69; → Esther).

Summary

The primordial parent narratives tell stories of nations and tribes in the literary genre of family narratives. That means that the story of Israel's origin is told in large part as a woman's narrative, as a story of women, who never break down the patriarchal system in which they live but with their powerful actions prick many holes in it. In these actions they often have the God of Israel on their side. Israel does not write the beginning of its history as legends of holy people. Realistically appraising the reality of a male-dominated society, this story addresses also violence against women.

It follows from the literary genre of the family narrative that the sphere of men's and women's lives is restricted to the small circle of relatives. In this literary form the family *is* the political public of the nation and the surrounding peoples. Today, the gender of women is defined through their role in the family — and thus in the private space of the home — while that of men is defined through the (political) public. For the interpretation of the PPN it is therefore quite telling that one held the female gender to be congruent with its stereotypical roles and did not look any further for depth dimensions in the narratives of women. One found what one already knew and wanted to preserve since the sphere of women's lives corresponded in the PPN to the prescriptive sphere of women in patriarchal culture: they are concerned primarily with their children and husbands, they fight with one another, and they are often dealing with God. But the men in those narratives also are not doing anything different. For that reason, no corresponding gender perceptions could be found for the stories of men in the PPN that are set just as exclusively in the small circle of the family (with the exception of Gen 14). Hence, one was forced to look behind the "private" for another dimension of meaning, and it was found in the political dimension of the history of the peoples. The exegetic tradition that trivializes the stories of women in the PPN and reads them in a fundamentalist way looks at the men stories differently. The narratives of men are examined in the historic-critical mode and interpreted as highly theological history of the origin of Israel and its neighbors. Such an exegetical tradition has to be judged as sexist. It applies double standards to the two genders. Feminist exegesis needs to guard against treading in those worn-out paths: the mothers of Israel are no "little matrons." They are the founders of Israel.

LITERATURE

Archer, Léonie J. 1990. *Her Price Is Beyond Rubies.* Journal for the Study of the Old Testament: Supplement Series, vol. 60. Sheffield.

Bach, Alice. 1993. "Breaking Free of the Biblical Frame-Up: Uncovering the Woman in Genesis 39." In *A Feminist Companion to Genesis,* edited by Athalya Brenner, 318-42. Feminist Companion to the Bible, vol. 2. Sheffield.

Bal, Mieke, Fokkelien van Dijk-Hemmes, and Grietje van Ginneken. 1988. *Und Sara lachte. . . .* Münster.

Baumgart, Norbert C. 1999. *Die Umkehr des Schöpfergottes. Zu Komposition und religionsgeschichtlichem Hintergrund von Gen 5–9.* Herders biblische Studien, vol. 22. Freiburg.

Brenner, Athalya. 1985. *The Israelite Woman.* Journal for the Study of the Old Testament: Supplement Series, vol. 21. Sheffield.

Brenner, Athalya, and Fokkelien van Dijk-Hemmes. 1993. *On Gendering Biblical Texts.* Biblical Interpretation Series, vol. 1. Leiden.

Brock, Sebastian. 1974. "Sarah and the Aqedah." *Muséon: Revue d'études orientales* 87:67-77.

————. 1984. "Genesis 22: Where Was Sarah?" *Expository Times* 96:14-17.

Bucher-Gillmayr, Susanne. 1994. "Eine textlinguistische Untersuchung zu Gen 24." Ph.D. diss., Innsbruck.

Butting, Klara. 1987. "Rachel und Leah." *Texte und Kontexte* 33:25-54.

————. 1994. *Die Buchstaben werden sich noch wundern*. Berlin.

Crüsemann, Frank. 1978. "'Er aber soll dein Herr sein' (Genesis 3,16)." In *Als Mann und Frau geschaffen*, edited by F. Crüsemann and H. Thyen, 15-106. Kennzeichen, vol. 2. Gelnhausen.

Fischer, Irmtraud. 1994. *Die Erzeltern Israels*. Beihefte zur Zeitschrift für die alttestamentliche Wissenschaft, vol. 222. Berlin.

————. 1995. "Den Frauen der Kochtopf — den Männern die hohe Politik?" *Christliche-Pädagogische Blätter* 108:134-38.

————. 2005. *Women Who Wrestled with God: Biblical Stories of Israel's Beginnings*. Translated from the second German edition into English by Linda M. Maloney. Collegeville, Minn.

Frettlöh, Magdalene L. 1994. "Isaak und seine Mütter." *Evangelische Theologie* 54:427-52.

Gössmann, Elisabeth, ed. 2000. *Eva-Gottes Meisterwerk*. Archiv für philosophie- und theologiegeschichtliche Frauenforschung, vol. 2, 2. Enlarged ed. Munich.

Herwig, Rachel Monika. 1994. *Die jüdische Mutter*. Darmstadt.

Jeansonne, Sharon Pace. 1990. *The Women of Genesis*. Minneapolis.

Kvam, Kirsten E., Linda S. Schearing, and Valerie H. Ziegler, eds. 1999. *Eve and Adam: Jewish, Christian, and Muslim Readings on Genesis and Gender*. Bloomington, Ind.

Meyers, Carol. 1991. "To Her Mother's House." In *The Bible and the Politics of Genesis: Festschrift for Norman K. Gottwald*, edited by David Jobling et al., 39-51. Cleveland.

Niditch, Susan. 1992. "Genesis." In *The Women's Bible Commentary*, edited by Carol A. Newsom and Sharon H. Ringe, 10-25. London and Louisville.

Plaskow, Judith. 1991. *Standing Again at Sinai: Judaism from a Feminist Perspective*. San Francisco.

Rashkow, Ilona. 1994. "Daughters and Fathers in Genesis . . . ; or, What Is Wrong with This Picture?" In *A Feminist Companion to Exodus*, edited by Athalya Brenner, 22-36. Sheffield.

Schäfer-Bossert, Stefanie. 1994. "Den Männern die Macht und der Frau die Trauer?" In *Feministische Hermeneutik und Erstes Testament*, edited by Hedwig Jahnow et al., 106-25. Stuttgart.

Schmidt, Eva Renate. 1989. "1. Mose 29–31. Vom Schwesternstreit zur Solidarität." In *Feministisch gelesen*, vol. 2, edited by Eva Renate Schmidt, 29-39. Stuttgart.

Scholz, Susanne. 1997. "Rape Plots: A Feminist Cultural Study of Genesis 34." Ph.D. diss., Union Theological Seminary, New York.

Schottroff, Luise, Marie-Theres Wacker, and Sylvia Schroer. 1998. *Feminist Interpretation: The Bible in Women's Perspective*. Minneapolis.

Schüngel-Straumann, Helen. 1984. "Tamar." *Bibel und Kirche* 39:148-57.

————. 1989. *Die Frau am Anfang. Eva und die Folgen*. Freiburg; 3rd ed. Münster, 1999.

————. 2002a. *Feministische Auslegung ausgewählter Beispiele aus der Urgeschichte. Rückblick auf ein Vierteljahrhundert feministische Auslegung von Gen 2 und 3*. International Society for the Study of the Old Testament 5, Basle 2001. Tagungsband. Leiden.

———. 2002b. *Anfänge feministischer Exegese. Gesammelte Beiträge.* Münster.

Seifert, Elke. 1994. "Lot und seine Töchter." In *Feministische Hermeneutik und Erstes Testament,* edited by Hedwig Jahnow et al., 48-66. Stuttgart.

Spanier, Kitziah. 1992. "Rachel's Theft of the Teraphim: Her Struggle for Family Privacy." *Vetus Testamentum* 42:404-12.

Standhartinger, Angela. 1994. "'Um zu sehen die Töchter des Landes.' Die Perspektive Dinas in der jüdisch-hellenistischen Diskussion um Gen 34." In *Religious Propaganda and Missionary Competition in the New Testament World: Festschrift for Dieter Georgi,* edited by Lukas Bormann et al., 89-116. Supplements to Novum Testamentum, vol. 74. Leiden.

Trible, Phyllis. 1984. *Texts of Terror.* Philadelphia.

Van Dijk-Hemmes, Fokkelien. 1989. "Tamar and the Limits of Patriarchy: Between Rape and Seduction." In *Anti-Covenant,* edited by Mieke Bal, 135-56. Journal for the Study of the Old Testament: Supplement Series, vol. 81. Sheffield.

Wacker, Marie-Theres. 1989. "1. Mose 16 und 21: Hagar die Befreite." In *Feministisch gelesen,* vol. 1, edited by Eva Renate Schmidt et al., 25-32. Stuttgart.

West, Ramona Faze. 1987. *Ruth: A Retelling of Genesis 38?* Ann Arbor, Mich.

Willi-Plein, Ina. 1989. "Genesis 27 als Rebekkageschichte." *Theologische Zeitschrift* 45:315-34.

Translated by Tina Steiner

Exodus: The Meaning of Liberation from "His" Perspective

Susanne Scholz

Introduction: Androcentrism in the Book of Exodus

Through the centuries Exodus has inspired the imagination of female and male theologians, writers, artists, musicians, and laypeople. The story of the exodus of the people of Israel from slavery in Egypt, of the miracle at the Red Sea, of the feeding with manna and quails, of the revelation in the burning thornbush, of the ten plagues, and of the dance around the golden calf is one of the most well-known stories of the Hebrew Bible. The figure of Moses as the savior from hardship and as God's trusted servant is known even to those who otherwise have very little knowledge of the Bible.

Within Christian and theological circles this book also plays a particular role. Renowned scholars of the forties and fifties like Martin Noth and Gerhard von Rad found in the book important theological and historical statements about the history of Israel. In the sixties and seventies Latin American and black American liberation theologians used the motif of the exodus for their work. Feminist theologians also found the story of the exodus from Egypt evocative of the situation of women in churches. Mary Daly, for example, was speaking in 1972 about an exodus from a sexist religion that women had to venture.

For these reasons it is surprising that feminist biblical scholars hesitated to look at this book of the Bible. The recourse to the story of the exodus and liberation of the people of Israel is evidently burdened with difficulties as soon as the text is analyzed in light of feminist exegetical considerations. Generally, feminist interpreters had made it their task to look at the role of women in biblical texts. A favored method to do this was to highlight biblical women in order to categorize them in historical, literary, and theological ways. However, the book of Exodus does not contain many female characters. Only the first two chapters and a few additional remarks in the middle section of the book mention women. Feminist literature thus concentrates primarily on those chapters and shows little interest in the book otherwise.

In the following, the whole book of Exodus will be read from a feminist perspective. Existing feminist research results of text passages will be included. In this I will foreground the increasingly prominent insight of recent years that women within biblical literature need to be understood as male constructs in order to demonstrate the presence of oppressive structures like sexism, racism, ethnocentrism, class discrimination, and imperialism (Exum in Brenner 1994; Weems 1992). I treat the book of Exodus as a literary composition characterized by an androcentric point of view (cf. Praetorius 1991). The forty chapters can be divided into two main parts. The narrative of the first part establishes Moses as the leader of Israel (1:1–18:27). The second part describes how God is recognized as the savior of the people of Israel (19:1–40:38). I chose a literary method that reads the biblical text in its final version. In view of the many attempts to date and locate Exodus in the history of Israel, I want to refer the reader to the important analysis by Whitelam (1996). His study shows how biblical scholars have been influenced in their description of the history of Israel by their own historical situation. Therefore, according to Whitelam, we do not have reliable dates.

Exodus 1:1–18:27: The Appointment of Moses as Leader of the People of Israel

There are four subdivisions. These narrate, respectively, Moses' birth, his calling to be a leader, Israel's flight from Egypt, and the grumbling of the Israelites about Moses.

Exodus 1:1–2-25: Circumstances of Moses' Birth and His Early Years

Seven literary sections, in chiastic order, tell of the circumstances of the birth of Moses and of his early years (cf. Boadt 1995): 1:1-7 offers a short summary of the situation (A); 1:8-14 narrates the reversal of the situation (B); 1:15-21 tells of threatening danger (C); 1:22–2:10 narrates the circumstances of Moses' birth (D); 2:11-15 mentions another danger (C′); 2:16-22 shows a reversal of the situation (B′); and 2:23-25 summarizes the situation (A′). Moses' birth is at the center of the whole section. Moses is surrounded by many different women who save him and other sons.

1:1-7 (A)   The first verses of the book of Exodus connect the sequence of events with those of Joseph and his brothers in Genesis. After relating that Jacob had moved to Egypt to be near his son Joseph, the verses narrate the death of his family and the many descendants. The wives, daughters, and women of Joseph and his brothers are not mentioned. Male pronouns and verbs show who is important in the perspective of the narrative.

1:8-14 (B) However, the situation of the Israelites changes very soon. After a period of harmonious living together in Egypt, they are persecuted. When a different pharaoh takes the reign, who has not heard of Joseph, they are subjected to slavery. The ruler is motivated by fear of the other, and he looks with suspicion at the high birthrate of the Israelites, which he fears will threaten his own people (1:9). Therefore he decrees that the Israelites be made slaves. Yet, the birthrate of the Israelites keeps on growing (1:12). As a result, the Egyptian slaveholders treat them worse and make them work under "harsh demands" (1:13-14). The Israelites seem to endure their fate in silence. As passive victims they endure the violence and build Egyptian cities. The king's position of power is made clear in the text by direct speech (1:9-10). He speaks while the Israelites are represented through indirect speech.

1:15-21 (C) Since the birthrate does not drop after the enslavement of the Israelites, the pharaoh thinks of another measure. He speaks to the midwives Shiphrah and Puah; it is unclear grammatically whether they are of Hebrew or Egyptian origin. But for the first time two women are mentioned. They are given names, which positions them in the foreground, while the mighty king remains nameless. A nameless king is positioned opposite two named midwives.

Feminist interpreters highlight this imbalance, which favors the midwives (Ellmenreich 1988). However, Shiphrah and Puah only fulfill typical female roles. They look after and rescue children. From an androcentric perspective, this is exactly the task women are meant to carry out. Even though the midwives appear in an important function, their activities do not challenge typical female roles. So long as they remain in their prescribed feminine roles, the androcentric writer allows them to trick the pharaoh.

By foregrounding the two midwives the narrator also underlines his contempt for the pharaoh because even women can trick him. His order to let live all the female babies testifies to his underestimation not only of the midwives but also of the "daughters." Because of this underestimation of the weakest links, the strongest adversary of the pharaoh is born and saved. This is the main irony of the androcentric narrative.

The midwives exploit the pharaoh's prejudices relating to the ethnic difference between Hebrew and Egyptian women in order to justify their actions. The pharaoh accepts these assumptions as reality, and thus they win the upper hand. This use of national, ethnic, and gendered categories serves to describe the weakness of the pharaoh, who cannot prevent the birth of his adversary. A critique of such categories is not offered by the androcentric narrator (Weems 1992).

1:22–2:10 (D) Feminist exegetes agree that this passage occupies a central position. Altogether, twelve women assist Moses in the first part of his life and make sure that he survives (Siebert-Hommes in Brenner 1994). At the moment of his birth he already has to thank four women for his existence: the two midwives Shiphrah and Puah, his mother, and his sister. Further, eight women help him before he reaches manhood. One is the daughter of the pharaoh, who does not obey her father's command but raises Moses. In 2:16-22 the daughters of the priest of Midian assist him. One of the daughters, Zipporah, marries him.

The third attempt by the pharaoh to control the high birthrate of the Israelites is told within the narrative of the birth of Moses. The literary ordering of this passage positions the son, the sister, and the mother around the daughter of the pharaoh. She is the frame around the newborn Moses, who stands in the middle of the narrative (Siebert-Hommes 1992):

Introduction: Wedding of the parents (2:1)
A Birth of the *son* (2:2)
  B *Mother* gives up her child (2:3)
    C *Sister* watches (2:4)
      D *Daughter* of the pharaoh sees the basket (2:5)
        E *Moses* as newborn baby (2:6a)
      D′ *Daughter* of the pharaoh shows mercy (2:6b)
    C′ *Sister* negotiates (2:7-8)
  B′ *Mother* nurses (2:9)
A′ *Son* is adopted (2:10)

This diagram of the literary structure by Siebert-Hommes shows that this passage starts and ends with Moses. All the women are concerned with his well-being. Their presence protects him from the danger of the pharaoh. Whereas the midwives in 1:15-21 were identified by their names, the women here remain nameless. Their relationship to men defines them. The daughter of the pharaoh is mentioned, but only through her father, who also remains without a name. Her social and ethnic status is more important than her name. Only the male newborn is named.

The Hebrew text contains an interesting detail that fudges the identity of the mother and the daughter of the pharaoh. In 2:10a the daughter is explicitly mentioned as "Pharaoh's daughter." The mother is mentioned with the personal pronoun "she" in the Hebrew text. In 2:10b it says word for word that "Moses is for her a son." In this half-verse it is grammatically possible that the personal pronoun "her" refers to the mother, because she is referred to as "her" in the previous verse. 2:10c and 2:10d also use only the pronoun "she" and do not mention directly the "daughter of the pharaoh." From a literary perspective, Moses' mother and the daughter of the pharaoh are the same in their care for Moses.

Even when this observation is not incorporated, the name Moses and its explanation suggest that such an interpretation is permissible. If one assumes that the daughter of the pharaoh gives Moses his name (2:10e), it can only be understood in a figurative sense, because the explanation of the name does not directly refer to her. She herself does not fetch the basket from the water; one of her slave women does and brings it to her (2:5). Indirectly, also, Moses' mother is rescuing her son out of the water because by putting the basket into the water she creates the circumstances for his rescue (2:3). For the androcentric narrator it is thus immaterial which woman rescues Moses. In a sense they are all participating in the rescue.

Another detail in relation to Moses' name points to the androcentrism of the text. Most of the time it is assumed that Pharaoh's daughter names Moses because the name makes sense only in Egyptian and because it is similar to the names Tutmose, Amose, or Ramose. Yet, within the book of Exodus the name is explained by a Hebrew etymology, which does not cohere with the grammatical rules of Hebrew verbs. Because an active participle constitutes the name Moses, it means "one, who moves out." The giving of the name thus hints already in 2:10 at Moses' future role as savior (Exum 1983), and the achievement of the rescue by the women is marginalized.

The multitude of women in the first chapters of the book of Exodus prompted feminist interpreters to highlight and emphasize the significance of women in the continuation of the history of Israel. Without the women, there would not have been an exodus from Egypt; therefore their brave acts of defiance help the whole nation (cf., e.g., Ellmenreich 1988; Exum 1983; Gebhardt 1989; Siebert-Hommes 1998). This positive interpretation is contradicted by the fact that the women characters enter the picture only in their concern about sons, or rather about one son. Their activities pave the way for the main male protagonist Moses to assume his position and to accept his task. When the moment arrives in which Moses does not need the child care and education provided by the women, they disappear from the narrative.

In addition, many feminist exegetes see 1:22–2:10 as an example of women achieving their goal by working together in solidarity (Aratangi 1990; Kerscher 1995; Tapia 1991). Despite ethnic, religious, and social differences, the women in 1:22–2:10 pull together and place the well-being of the newborn at the center, so that Moses can escape from the brutal order. At the same time, one needs to problematize this example, for the women are described in typical female roles, which are not challenged in the androcentric narrative.

2:11-15 (C′) From now on, the way Moses fares occupies center stage in the narrative. Moses has grown up and he goes to his "brothers" to see how they are doing. How Moses knows that the Israelites are his "brothers" is not explained in the text. When he witnesses an Egyptian foreman beating an Israelite, he kills the foreman secretly. Shortly after this, when he tries to mediate for a peaceful solution between two Israelites, they reject him. They perceive him to be an Egyptian who killed his own countryman and now presumes to exhort them as "fellow men" to peaceful interaction. Moses fears the consequences of his deed. He is situated in a no-man's-land. He flees Egypt when the pharaoh tries to kill him. Two Israelite men doubt for the first time Moses' claim that he is their leader. Egyptian and Israelite men determine the plot.

2:16-22 (B′) Moses flees to Midian, where he rests near a well. And as is typical for the genre of "scene of betrothal" (Alter 1981), he meets his future wife Zipporah there. When the seven daughters of the priest of Midian come to the well, he helps them to draw water and water the sheep. They invite him to their home and intro-duce him to their father as an "Egyptian" man (2:19). Subsequently Reuel, who is otherwise mentioned by the name of Jethro, offers him his daughter as wife (2:21b). The next verse covers at least nine months in that it says that Zipporah bore him a son. Father Moses calls him Gershom, "because I have become an alien (*gēr*) in a foreign land" (2:22). The mother remains in the background. Everything concerns Moses, even the name of his son.

2:23-25 (A′) Like the beginning of this unit, the conclusion also offers a sum-mary. The king who is responsible for the Israelites' enslavement dies. The men and women of Israel sigh and cry out to God. Then God remembers the covenant with the so-called patriarchs Abraham, Isaac, and Jacob. The matriarchs Sarah, Rebekah, Rachel, and Leah are not mentioned. From an androcentric perspective, only the men count.

The portrayal of the situation of the Israelites in Egypt frames the account of Moses' birth and his flight to Midian. This literary structure thus emphasizes the sig-nificance of Moses. The next unit follows from this with the same central concern.

Exodus 3:1–6:30: The Calling of Moses to Leadership and His Objections

3:1–4:17 Fourteen times the Hebrew root "to see" is mentioned in this passage. It is the key word connecting the previous section of the text with the scene of Mo-ses' calling. As God "saw" the sons of Israel in 2:25, so Moses sees the burning bush in 3:2. Other repetitions also connect this passage to the previous one. The names Abraham, Isaac, and Jacob occur in the summarizing comment in 2:24 as well as in the speech by God in 3:6 (see also 3:15, 16; 4:5). In addition, the Hebrew root *yd*ʿ (to observe) is repeated in 2:25 and in 3:7. The latter verse also explains what has been left unmentioned in 2:25, which says God "observed" without specifying what is observed. In 3:7 God observes the *suffering* of the people of Israel. A further repeti-tion is made through the Hebrew root ʿ*nh* (which here means to oppress) in 1:11 and 3:7. This repetition also links the passage 3:1–4:17 to the whole previous sec-tion, 1:1–2:25.

God calls Moses to be the leader of the Israelites in order to guide them to a country flowing with milk and honey (3:14-22). In this speech the women of Israel are mentioned. They are supposed to ask their Egyptian mistresses for jewelry and clothes to robe the sons and daughters of Israel (3:22). After the women were described as mothers and caregivers for babies, they are now associated with jewelry. Here they merit only a brief remark, as the speech mainly deals with Moses.

Moses immediately realizes the obstacles of his calling and tries five times to convince God to change his mind (3:11, 13; 4:1, 10, and 13). Five times God answers him (3:12, 14-22; 4:2-9, 11-12, 14-17). One answer is particularly important from a theological perspective. It explains God's name: "I shall be what I shall be" (3:14). A few verses earlier God tried to calm Moses with "I am with you" (3:12). A few verses later God promises: "I will be with your speech and [Aaron's] speech" (4:15). God promises Moses to be with him whenever he is needed. But Moses remains suspicious and doubts the promise. He thinks of three further objections, whereupon God becomes angry (4:14) and simply orders Moses what to do. God appoints Moses as messenger for God above Aaron (4:16). A hierarchical solution ends the debate.

However, the reference to God's name embodies an image of God that transcends androcentrism. Although the narrator generally speaks of God only in masculine pronouns and verbs, the definition in 3:14 does not contain a gender-specific label. Moreover, the idea of God presented here is not static and unchanging but rather conceived in dynamic and fluid terms because, according to Hebrew grammar, the forms of verbs do not allow for unambiguous fixation of tense. Therefore, the name of God in 3:14 can be translated in the present tense: "I am what I am." A combination of present and future tense is also possible: "I am what I will be," or the other way around: "I will be what I am." The first-person singular is not gender-specific in Hebrew. For this reason the relative pronoun in 3:14 can be read as either "she" or "he."

4:18-27 After receiving his calling, Moses decides to move to Egypt with his wife and son. His father-in-law encourages him to go, but his wife does not say a word. A further word from God instructs Moses to tell the pharaoh that he should let the Israelites go, because Israel is God's "firstborn son." Should the pharaoh refuse to let them go, God will kill the firstborn sons of Egypt. Because of the many repetitions and doublings in this section, historical-critical biblical scholars assumed different sources. Particularly 4:24-26 was considered a secondary insert, because of its puzzling content (Derby 1989; Lehane 1996; Reis 1991; Schneemann 1989). On the other hand, Zipporah speaks here for the first and only time (4:25). She is the one who acts decisively, and it is through her acting that Moses survives. By transmitting only an incomprehensible fragment, the androcentric narrator pushes Zipporah's significance to the margins.

4:27–6:30 Aaron supports his brother when Moses convinces the people with the help of signs (4:27-31). But the negotiations with the pharaoh only lead to harder conditions. Finally God calls Moses to his task again (6:2-9). The words "to know" (6:7) and "Abraham, Isaac, and Jacob" (6:8) link this section to the first account of Moses receiving his calling (3:1–4:17). After receiving this repeated calling, Aaron and Moses go to the pharaoh again to ask for the release of the Israelites (6:13).

Moses' authority is supported by the genealogy of his forefathers (6:14-25). This list of ancestors legitimates Moses' calling as the leader of the people of Israel. All his male ancestors are mentioned, but the list also contains some women mentioned in their roles as wives, mothers, and daughters. They are worth mentioning only because of their relationship to men. Jochebed, Moses' mother, appears (6:20), but not his sister or Zipporah. Instead Aaron's wife Elisheba is mentioned (6:23), as well as Putiel's daughters, one of whom marries Eleazar and bears him a son (6:25).

God's summons, in which God sends Moses to the pharaoh, frames the list of ancestors. Moses' objection, however, dominates the whole section to the last sentence (3:1–6:30). In 6:30 Moses rejects his task again: "Since I am a poor speaker, why would Pharaoh listen to me?" As if it had been spoken into the wind, no reply is forthcoming; God answers no longer. The next section continues to deal with the negotiations between Moses and the pharaoh.

Exodus 7:1–15:21: The Victory over Egypt and the Songs of Praise of Moses and Miriam

7:1–13:16 Pharaoh pays attention to Moses only after ten plagues have afflicted nature and people in Egypt. The plagues can be subdivided into three groups of three plagues each, while the last plague stands on its own (Plaut 1981). The severity of the plagues increases with each new plague: from the first group (bloody water, frogs, gnats) to the second group (flies, diseased livestock, festering boils on animals and people) to the third group (thunder and hail, locusts, and darkness) and on to the last, worst plague, in which God kills the firstborn males.

The duel between Pharaoh and Moses rests on the fact that God steadfastly hardens Pharaoh's heart (4:21; 7:3). During nine plagues Pharaoh does not let the people of Israel go (7:22; 8:15, 28; 9:7). After the tenth plague God softens the heart of Pharaoh (11:1) so that he "may know" God (7:17; 8:6[Eng. 10]). The death of all the firstborn males is required before Pharaoh relents (12:31). The power struggle between Moses and Aaron, on one side, and the magicians and mighty of Pharaoh's court, on the other, finally comes to an end. While the Israelites sit in their houses and celebrate the Passover for the first time, the Egyptians cry out in their suffering (12:29-30). The male firstborn of poor and rich are killed (11:5). The plague affects animals and human beings (11:5). At the same time, the men of Israel celebrate the Passover (12:3-11). Men being liberated and being killed are the center of events.

13:17–14:31   The narrative follows the exodus of the people from Egypt into the desert. As a pillar of cloud and fire, God guides the Israelites, who emigrate with "a mixed crowd" (12:38). The people reach the sea. The Egyptian army poses a threat. In fear the people cry out to God and accuse Moses: "Better for us to serve the Egyptians than to die in the wilderness" (14:12). God does not speak to the people directly but addresses Moses to explain what he has to do (14:15). Moses' special powers and the powers of nature enable the Israelites to escape. When the army tries to follow through the Red Sea, the waves converge above them. The dead soldiers on the shore convince the people of God's might, and they believe in him and "his servant" Moses (14:31).

15:1-21   The victory is followed by Moses' hymn of victory (15:1-18), which is followed by a short song by Miriam (15:21), who here is called a "prophetess" (15:20). Burns regards this title as a later addition because it is not mentioned in any of the other biblical verses that mention her (Burns 1987).

Feminist biblical scholars emphasize particularly the significance of this song by Miriam (e.g., Anderson and da Silva Gorgulho 1989; Brooke 1994; Lüneburg 1988; Wacker 1988). It is regarded as one of the oldest songs in the Hebrew Bible. Burns (1987), for example, sees this song as preserving a liturgical tradition that celebrates God as godly warrior. Janzen (1992) thinks it might have preceded the song of Moses, because it mentions the event of 14:16-30, whereas the song of Moses comes in response to the reaction of the people in 14:31. Wacker points to another interesting detail. She translates Miriam's song as follows: "Sing to the Lord / exalted is he / horse and chariot / has he thrown into the sea!" Instead of "horseman" (*rōkĕbô*) she reads "chariot" (*rikĕbô*). Her interpretation solves the ethical problem of Miriam rejoicing in the death of the Egyptian soldiers. Miriam, in this version, rejoices only in the destruction of the war equipment, whereas the song of Moses overtly celebrates the death of the enemies.

The mentioning of Miriam at such an important stage of the narrative led women exegetes to follow the literary traces of Miriam in the Hebrew Bible. Miriam appears in Numbers 12:1-15; 20:1; 26:59; Deuteronomy 24:8-9; 1 Chronicles 6:3; and Micah 6:4. On occasion, Miriam is portrayed as the equal of Moses and Aaron in leadership (Trible 1989). She therefore became an important figure to identify with for many Jewish women and Christian women (cf. Langer, Leistner, and Moltmann-Wendel 1982; Adelman 1986).

But within an interpretation that identifies the androcentric point of view of the book of Exodus, Miriam appears in a different light. She is the leader of those women who celebrate the destruction of the enemies' army as God's triumph in one verse, while Moses sings eighteen long verses to the salvation wrought by God. Moreover, Exodus 15:20 mentions Miriam as Aaron's sister and thus hides the fact that she is also Moses' sister. Her familial ties to Moses, whose rescue she also helped effect, remains unmentioned. Miriam appears as a marginal figure, which only underscores the central position of Moses all the more.

Exodus 15:22–18:27: The Israelites' Murmuring against Moses and His Leadership

15:22–17:7   After the events at the Red Sea, Moses leads the people through the desert. Three times they resist his leadership because of lack of food (15:22-26; 16:1-36; 17:1-7; cf. also Num 14:1-4; 17:6-11). In all three stories Moses mediates between the people and God. To begin with, the Israelites reach Marah, but the water is not drinkable (Exod 15:22-26). When the Israelites were in slavery (2:23), and later at the Red Sea (14:10), they cried directly to God, but now they turn to Moses and no longer to God (15:24). Through Moses, God gives the first legal statutes to the people in the form of a condition and introduces himself as a healing God (15:26). This is linked to the threat that the people will become ill if they do not keep these instructions. There is no reaction by the people to the condition given them.

In the second episode, which takes place in the desert of Sin (16:1-12), the people accuse Moses and Aaron of bad leadership again (16:2-3). Once again the people directly address Moses and Aaron. After that God speaks only to Moses (16:4). Moses and Aaron explain to the people the laborious procedure of when to collect the bread. Moses' speech of defense against the complaints of the people (16:8; cf. 16:7) results in God showing himself conciliatory (16:12).

After the threatening famine is averted by the gift of manna, the Israelites grumble for a third time (17:1-7). In Rephidim they lack water. Again the people accuse Moses and not God. But Moses points out that their protest against him is also a protest against God. At every turn, God's intervention serves to strengthen Moses' authority. After the people criticize Moses' leadership again (17:3) and Moses "cries" to God (17:4), God advises him to perform a miracle in front of the elders (masculine plural, 17:5-6). When Moses strikes the rock and water gushes forth, the people stop their complaining.

17:8-16   Moses' leadership gets undisputed recognition in this section of the narrative. In the battle with the Amalekites the men of Israel are victorious because Moses lifts his arms. He gets help from Aaron and Hur, who support his arms, and from Joshua, who leads the battle. The plot is dominated by men.

18:1-27   The visit of his father-in-law Jethro follows abruptly. Twice within the narrative, indirect speech hints that Zipporah, Moses' wife, and Gershom and Eliezer, his sons, are also present (18:2, 5). Jethro's direct speech also emphasizes their presence (18:6). But Moses kisses and greets only his father-in-law (18:7). After Jethro has praised God for the rescue of the people (18:10-11), Aaron and the other elders meet for a meal. Zipporah and her sons are not mentioned again. The report of Jethro's departure also seems to suggest that he is alone (18:27). The focus of the narrative is Moses and his work. Jethro's advice is directed solely to him. Selected men are to help share the responsibilities of Moses (18:25-26).

Exodus 19:1–40:38: The Acknowledgment of God as the Rescuer of the People of Israel

After Moses has been established as the undisputed leader of the people in the first part of the book, the second main part describes in four sections the acknowledgment of God as the Rescuer of the people of Israel.

Exodus 19:1–24:18: The Arrival of the People at Sinai and God's Revelation

19:1-25   When the Israelites reach Mount Sinai, Moses ascends "to God" and receives God's words (19:3-6). Similar to Deuteronomy 32:11, God appears here in the image of the eagle tending its young. God is offering a covenant to the people of Israel to be a holy people (Exod 19:6). Judith Plaskow uses this verse as the starting point of developing a Jewish-feminist theology that explicitly includes women in the event at Sinai. Thus the significance of the event is fundamentally changed (Plaskow 1990).

Moses discusses God's offer with the elders (masculine plural) of the people. The elders and the people accept the covenant. Following this, God promises Moses that God will appear in a cloud and speak to Moses so that the people will have "faith in" Moses always (19:9). As in the last section, Moses' personality also plays an important and central role in the main part of the narrative.

To prepare for the announced revelation, God orders the people to hallow themselves. According to Moses' words, this means that the men are not allowed to touch women for three days prior to the event (19:15). This verse makes clear that the term "people" refers to the men of Israel only and that Moses excludes the women of Israel from the encounter with God.

20:1-21   When God is revealed in a cloud on Sinai with lightning and thunder and the sound of a trumpet (19:16), the men of Israel are not allowed to approach all the way. Only Moses can come close. He receives the Ten Commandments, which use male pronouns exclusively (cf. Deut 5:6-21). Because of this grammatical androcentrism, Brenner doubts that women are included as addressees of the Ten Commandments (Brenner 1994, 255-58). Although daughters and slave women are allowed explicitly to rest on the Sabbath, wives remain unmentioned (Exod 20:10). Yes, the mother is to be honored, but she is named only after the father (20:12). The male addressee is advised not to covet the neighbor's (male singular) "wife, slave, slave girl, ox, donkey, or anything that belongs to him" (20:17). The reverse scenario that speaks of the assets of the female neighbor (female singular) is not mentioned. The Decalogue therefore does not represent an equal order of society, but presupposes slavery, misogyny, and class discrimination as the basic components of the common life of society.

The hierarchies expressed in these commandments are also reflected in the reaction of the people to the revelation. The Israelites run away and plead with Moses to talk to God so that they will not "die" (20:19). The people have accepted Moses in his role as leader, but they are still frightened by God.

20:22–23:19 The so-called book of the covenant contains regulations that deal with property, theft, and rules for protection. Many of these rules express the androcentrism of this old work of law. The rights of the Hebrew male and female slaves are particularly telling in this regard (21:2-11), even though Gruber sees in them the origins of the Jewish matrilineal system (Gruber 1995). Women appear here as wives of slaves, either brought along by a slave into slavery or else given to a slave by the slave owner (21:3-4). In the latter, the wife and children belong to the owner when he releases the slave. If the slave does not want to leave his family behind, he has to remain "for life" (21:6). According to Gruber, this rule shows that the identity of the children is determined by the mother and not the father. But it also shows that slavery is presupposed as a social and economic institution. Women are represented as slaves throughout, men as slaves and slave owners.

The regulations include the case when a father sells his daughter as a slave (21:7). She is not allowed to be set free like other slaves. If the master no longer likes a slave purchased under these circumstances, he has to redeem her because he is not allowed to sell her as he likes (21:8). However, he can designate her for his son (21:9). If he buys another female slave, he has to see to the needs of the first slave (21:10-11). This law represents the man as an autonomous subject who rules over women in slavery. He sells and buys; he decides and feeds. Although the law posits certain limits on him, he is the decision maker, whereas the women are seen as possible slaves throughout.

The laws do not criticize or question slavery, but they legitimize a social order of inequality and oppression. The consequences of such a view are exemplified in 21:20-21. The law punishes a slave owner only when he beats his male or female slaves to death. If they live for one or two days after the assault, he only has to pay a fine (cf. also 21:26-27). Therefore the law supports the rights of the slave owner and disadvantages the slave.

The androcentric outlook is apparent in other regulations too. If a woman miscarries because she has been hurt in an argument between her husband and another man, it is the husband who decides the amount of the fine to be paid, not the woman herself (21:22). The seduction of a young woman by a man is not seen as an issue in which she has the right at least to speak and be heard; it is a matter only between her father and the man. Similarly, the laws around sexual assault (e.g., Deut 22:22-29) also show that the woman herself is not heard. The book of the covenant also legislates the death penalty for "sorceresses" (Exod 22:18), for sexual acts with animals (22:19), and for those who worship other gods (22:20). Interestingly, it does not mention male magicians.

But some laws do protect women and children who adjust to the androcentric social order. If they lose father or husband through death, they will receive social assistance. God threatens the men of Israel to heed this law because God will listen to the "cries" of widows and orphans (22:22). If the men contravene this law, they themselves may die and their own wives will be widowed and their children orphaned. Since from an androcentric perspective only men have a say, this law codex represents only Israelite men as subjects under the commandments of God. If the women of Israel submit to this order, they in turn will receive protection.

Poverty is accepted as a social given in the book of the covenant. It does not suggest drastic measures to abolish poverty but only criticizes usury (22:25) and emphasizes the rights of the poor (23:3, 6; cf. Pixley 1987, who differs here).

23:20-33 The epilogue to the book of the covenant makes plain the problematical nature of the androcentric point of view. In this passage, God promises the people that they will arrive successfully in the land if they keep the covenant, and also announces the "eradication" of the other people who already live there and the "terror" they will face (23:23, 27). "I shall drive them out little by little until you have grown numerous enough to take possession of the country" (23:30; cf. also 23:31; 33:2). This text tells of a militant politics of extermination in the name of God. The androcentric view thus combines with other tendencies that stabilize hierarchies and the politics of violence (cf. Warrior 1991).

24:1-18 The people unanimously accept the ordinances (24:3). Subsequently Moses erects an altar on which young men sacrifice offerings to give thanks (24:5). Moses then seals the covenant (24:8). Together with the men Aaron, Nadab and Abihu, and seventy of the elders (masculine plural), Moses again ascends the mountain where they encounter (r'h) God (24:10). The verb r'h points to God seeing in 2:25 and to Moses seeing in 3:2. The people do not flee anymore from God as they did in 20:19, but acknowledge God as their rescuer. After they have eaten and quenched their thirst, Moses departs from them. After the seventh day, God appears to him in fire (24:18). Moses remains on the mountain for forty days and nights.

Exodus 25:1–31:18: Endeavors to Institutionalize the Presence of God

During those forty days and nights Moses receives detailed instructions about the building of the tabernacle. The priesthood that Aaron and his sons administer is also legislated (chapters 28 and 29). God's presence in Israel requires meticulous regulations so that the men and women of Israel "will know that I am the LORD their God who brought them out of Egypt" (29:46).

Exodus 32:1–34:35: The People of Israel Doubt

The people do not see Moses return from the mountain (32:1). To assure themselves of God's presence in their midst, the Israelites, with Aaron's help, cast a golden calf from their women's, sons', and daughters' gold (32:2). Again women are mentioned explicitly in connection with jewelry (32:2). First God's (32:7-11) and then Moses' anger (32:19-21) reestablish the proposed order. Moses commands the sons of Levi to kill three thousand men (32:27-28), and God strikes the people (32:34). The punishment is enormous. Apart from the killing of three thousand on Moses' orders, the narrative does not give a number for God's punishment (32:35). When God speaks to Moses again (33:1–34:28), he is given the second tablets of the law (34:29).

Exodus 35:1–40:38: The Presence of God Becomes Institutionalized

The tumult caused by the golden calf has ceased. In a last step Moses institutionalizes the presence of God. He orders the construction of the tabernacle. In 35:20-29 women as well as men contribute to the making of the tabernacle. The word "woman" is mentioned four times in that passage: 35:22, 25, 26, 29. Women give their jewelry and hand-woven cloths. According to 38:8, women bring their mirrors for the crafting of the altar. Görg sees in this passage the traces of an old life-giving cult that was maintained particularly by women (Görg 1984). The giving of mirrors might suggest (at least temporary) "cultic chastity" of these women (Wacker 1995). The narrator mentions the women again only in an androcentric perspective, which reinforces typical gender roles. The explicit reference to women here shows once again that other passages where they are not mentioned simply include them by implication.

The conclusion of the tabernacle's construction is described in detail. Similar to Genesis 2:2 where God completes creation, here in Exodus 40:33 it says: "So Moses completed the work." The central role of Moses in the rescue of the people of Israel and their recognition of God could hardly have been expressed more powerfully. Afterward, at the close of the book, the "glory of God" fills the tabernacle in order to accompany Israel in its journey through the desert.

A Concluding Observation: Feminist Quintessence

The description of the androcentric outlook makes it plain that it is problematic to view Exodus as a story of liberation. My observations show that the narrative serves the creation and stabilization of manifold social hierarchies and forms of oppression.

First, the few women are represented in typical roles. They care for children, they own jewelry, and they appear in socially weak positions. Exceptions like Miriam and Zipporah remain on the margins of the literary composition. The typical roles for women are further entrenched by God's speeches. In the narrative, God speaks to the males of Israel.

Second, the social laws and regulations show how questionable it is to interpret Exodus as a story of liberation. The laws governing male and female slaves, the death penalty, the relationships with foreign tribes, and the violent and bloody confrontations with the people of Egypt all stabilize a repressive and hierarchically organized concept of society. Liberation from such a concept is not part of the vision of Exodus.

Third, the image of God in this text does not liberate; it instills fear even in the Israelites (e.g., 20:19). God commands, decides, becomes angry, punishes even when there are hints of a less authoritarian and hierarchical image in the text (3:14). God does not communicate directly with the Israelites but speaks only to Moses. God does set the Israelites free from slavery but then orders their submission to his reign. The reaction by the people to such a God is telling: they do not dare any more to call to God directly as they did during their time of oppression (2:23) but complain to Moses (15:22–17:7). Only when the people accept the laws do they recognize God as their rescuer through chosen representatives (24:1-18).

Fourth, it is not the liberation that occupies the center of the narrative but Moses. The events stabilize the faith of the people in him as well as in God (4:16; 14:31). The well-being of the people depends on both of them, and Moses occupies the central position between God and the people.

But to uncover the androcentrism of the book of Exodus does not mean that this biblical text is superfluous for feminist Christians. As long as contemporary societies are structured androcentrically and Western culture is influenced by biblical images and stories, Exodus will represent an important source for theological reflection. In the debates on this text and its gender roles, societal structures and rules, its image of God, and the position of Moses, feminist theologians can contribute to the clarification of contemporary questions. It is for that reason that women engaged in feminist theology and Christians have in the book of Exodus a not to be neglected source in their search for theologically responsible discourse and actions.

LITERATURE

Adelman, Penina V. 1986. *Miriam's Well: Rituals for Jewish Women around the Year*. New York.

Alter, Robert. 1981. *The Art of Biblical Narrative*. New York.

Anderson, Ana Flora, and Gilberto da Silva Gorgulho. 1989. "Mirjam and Her Companions." In *The Future of Liberation Theology*, edited by Marc H. Ellis and Otto Maduro, 205-19. Festschrift for Gustavo Gutiérrez. Maryknoll, N.Y.

Aratangi, Canny. 1990. "Born into a Living Hope: The Role of the Midwives Shiprah and Puah; Exodus 1:15-21." *Pacific Journal of Theology* 4:41-44.

Bergant, Dianne. 1987. "Exodus as a Paradigm in Feminist Theology." In *Exodus — a Lasting Paradigm*, edited by Bas van Iersel et al., 100-106. Edinburgh.

Boadt, Lawrence. 1995. "Divine Wonders Never Cease: The Birth of Moses in God's Plan of Exodus." In *Preaching Biblical Texts: Expositions by Jewish and Christian Scholars*, edited by Frederick C. Holmgren and Herman E. Schaalman, 46-61. Grand Rapids.

Brazilian Pastoral Workers. 1991. "Miriam." *Estudos Biblicos* 29:37-39.

Brenner, Athalya, ed. 1994. *A Feminist Companion to Exodus to Deuteronomy*. Sheffield.

Brooke, George J. 1994. "A Long-Lost Song of Miriam." *Biblical Archaeology Review* 20:62-65.

Burns, Rita. 1987. *Has the Lord Indeed Spoken Only through Moses? A Study of the Biblical Portrait of Miriam*. Atlanta.

Daly, Mary. 1972. "The Women's Movement: An Exodus Community." *Religious Education* 67:327-35.

Derby, Josiah. 1989. "Why Did God Want to Kill Moses?" *Jewish Bible Quarterly* 18:222-29.

Dreyfus, Stanley A. 1995. "The Burning Bush through the Eyes of Midrash: God's Word Then and Now." In *Preaching Biblical Texts: Expositions by Jewish and Christian Scholars*, edited by Frederick C. Holmgren and Herman E. Schaalman, 62-75. Grand Rapids.

Ellmenreich, Renate. 1988. "2. Mose 1,15-21. Pua und Schiphra — zwei Frauen im Widerstand." In *Feministisch gelesen*, edited by Eva Renate Schmidt, Mieke Korenhof, and Renate Jost, 1:39-44. Stuttgart.

Exum, J. Cheryl. 1983. "You Shall Let Every Daughter Live: A Study of Exodus 1:8–2:10." *Semeia* 28:63-82.

Fretheim, Terence E. 1991. "The Plagues as Ecological Signs of Historical Disaster." *Journal of Biblical Literature* 110:385-96.

Gebhardt, Esther. 1989. "2. Mose 2,1-10. Frauen für das Leben." In *Feministisch gelesen*, edited by Eva Renate Schmidt, Mieke Korenhof, and Renate Jost, 2:55-62. Stuttgart.

Görg, Manfred. 1984. "Der Spiegeldienst der Frauen (Ex. 38,8)." *Biblische Notizen* 23:9-13.

Gruber, Mayer I. 1995. "Matrilineal Determination of Jewishness: Biblical and Near Eastern Roots." In *Pomegranates and Golden Bells: Studies in Biblical and Near Eastern Ritual, Law, and Literature*, edited by David P. Wright, David Noel Freedman, and Avi Hurvitz, 437-43. Festschrift for Jacob Milgrom. Winona Lake, Ind.

Heister, Maria-Sybilla. 1986. *Frauen in der biblischen Glaubensgeschichte*. 2nd ed. Göttingen.

Janzen, J. Gerald. 1992. "Song of Moses, Song of Mirjam: Who Is Seconding Whom?" *Catholic Biblical Quarterly* 54:211-20.

John, Cresy, et al. 1991. "An Asian Feminist Perspective, the Exodus Story (Exodus 1:8-22; 2:1-10): An Asian Group Work." In *Voices from the Margin: Interpreting the Bible in the Third World*, edited by Rasiah S. Sugirtharajah, 267-79. Maryknoll, N.Y.

Kerscher, Kristina. 1995. "God's First Instrument of Liberation." *Bible Today* 33:359-63.

Langer, Heidemarie, Herta Leistner, and Elisabeth Moltmann-Wendel. 1982. *Mit Mirjam durch das Schilfmeer. Frauen bewegen die Kirche.* Stuttgart.

Lehane, Terry John. 1996. "Zipporah and the Passover." *Jewish Biblical Quarterly* 24:46-50.

Lüneburg, Elisabeth. 1988. "2. Moses 15,20f. Schlagt die Trommeln, tanzt und fürchtet euch nicht!" In *Feministisch gelesen*, edited by Eva Renate Schmidt, Mieke Korenhof, and Renate Jost, 1:45-52. Stuttgart.

Pixley, George V. 1987. *On Exodus: A Liberation Perspective.* Maryknoll, N.Y.

Plaskow, Judith. 1990. *Standing Again at Sinai: Judaism from a Feminist Perspective.* New York.

———. 1992. *Und wieder stehen wir am Sinai. Eine jüdisch-feministische Theologie.* Fribourg and Luzern.

Plaut, Gunther. 1981. *The Torah: A Modern Commentary.* New York.

Praetorius, Ina. 1991. "Androzentrismus." In *Wörterbuch der feministischen Theologie*, edited by Elisabeth Gössmann et al., 14-15. Gütersloh.

Raboteau, Albert J. 1994. "African-Americans, Exodus, and the American Israel." In *African-American Christianity: Essays in History*, edited by Paul E. Johnson, 1-17. Berkeley.

Reis, Tamarkin Pamela. 1991. "The Bridegroom of Blood: A New Reading." *Judaism* 159, no. 40:324-31.

Schneemann, Gisela. 1989. "Die Deutung and Bedeutung der Beschneidung nach Exodus 4,24-26." *Communio viatorum* 32, no. 1-2:21-37.

Setel, Drorah O'Donnell. 1992. "Exodus." In *The Women's Bible Commentary*, edited by Carol A. Newsom and Sharon H. Ringe, 26-35. London and Louisville.

Siebert-Hommes, Jopie. 1988. "Twelve Women in Exodus 1 and 2: The Role of Daughters and Sons in the Stories concerning Moses." In *Amsterdamse Cahiers voor Exegese en Bijbelse Theologie* 12:47-58.

———. 1992. "Die Geburtsgeschichte des Mose innerhalb des Erzählzusammenhangs von Exodus I und II." *Vetus Testamentum* 42:398-404.

———. 1998. *Let the Daughters Live! The Literary Architecture of Exodus 1–2 as a Key for Interpretation.* Leiden.

Tapia, Elizabeth S. 1991. "The Story of Shiphrah and Puah: Disobedient or Subservient Women?" *CTC Bulletin* 10:44-45.

Trible, Phyllis. 1989. "Subversive Justice: Tracing the Miriamic Traditions." In *Justice and the Holy*, edited by Douglas A. Knight and Peter J. Paris, 99-109. Festschrift for Walter Harrelson. Atlanta.

Wacker, Marie-Theres. 1988. "Miriam. Kritischer Mut einer Prophetin." In *Zwischen Ohnmacht und Befreiung. Biblische Frauengestalten*, edited by Karin Walter, 44-52. Freiburg.

———. 1995. "'Religionsgeschichte Israels' oder 'Theologie des Alten Testaments' — (k)eine Alternative?" *Jahrbuch für biblische Theologie* 10:129-55.

Warrior, Robert Allen. 1991. "A Native American Perspective: Canaanites, Cowboys and

Indians." In *Voices from the Margin: Interpreting the Bible in the Third World,* edited by Rasiah S. Sugirtharajah, 287-95. Maryknoll, N.Y.

Weber, Beat. 1990. "'Jede Tochter aber sollt ihr am Leben lassen!' — Beobachtungen zu Ex 1,15–2,10 und seinem Kontext aus literaturwissenschaftlicher Perspektive." *Biblische Notizen* 55:47-76.

Weems, Renita J. 1992. "The Hebrew Women Are Not Like the Egyptian Women: The Ideology of Race, Gender and Sexual Reproduction in Exodus 1." *Semeia* 59:25-34.

Whitelam, Keith W. 1996. *The Invention of Ancient Israel.* London and New York.

Willi-Plein, Ina. 1988. *Das Buch vom Auszug. 2. Mose (Exodus).* Neukirchen-Vluyn.

———. 1991. "Ort und literarische Funktion der Geburtsgeschichte des Mose." *Vetus Testamentum* 41:110-18.

Translated by Tina Steiner

Leviticus: The ABC of Creation

Gerburgis Feld

The general attitude of so-called introductions to commentaries on the book of Leviticus is an attestation to the strangeness and resistant character of this book. There is talk of lack of historical substance, lack of prophetic force, the absence of poetry, and monotonous, boring casuistry. Thematically, too, this book is not readily accessible to modern readers: priests who behave like butchers, have houses torn down and sick people set apart; men and women who bring sacrifices because of simple biological processes or who have to die for sins that we cannot discern or understand. In short, this is *a violent, even a bloodthirsty, book.* Leviticus is apparently the least-read and most unattractive book in the Bible, at least for First World Christians. From a feminist perspective it seems "unredeemable," since women appear only as *objects* of cultic-legal purity prescriptions (concerning the regulation of sexual intercourse and marriage, as well as specifically female matters including birth and menstruation). Only one woman is mentioned by name (Shulamith, at 24:11), so that here the feminist search for traces of hidden or forgotten women's traditions appears to hit a wall.

This superficial impression of the book's insignificance and minimal authority is frequently affirmed in the aporiae of scholarly literature. Simply allowing the "strangeness of the book" to stand seems to be an appropriate way out of this dilemma of scholarly imponderability and cultural-historical alienations, not only as regards certain ideas and phenomena in Leviticus, but also with respect to the literary and theological claims of the book. But what is gained by this, apart from a hermeneutical refuge, especially in view of the accusation of anti-Judaism that is directed at feminist scholars, among others? What needs to be done, rather, is to apprehend and evaluate the overarching issue inherent in the book: the question of the *compatibility of the human being and God,* in everyday life as well as in worship. This issue demands, besides the acknowledgment of Leviticus as possibly a compositional unity, among other things also the examination and appreciation of the continued influence of certain of its ideas, that is, the notions of sacrifice and purity, in the modern world.

The answer to this question lies in the priestly concept of holiness and purity and of cultic sacrifice. In a first step, therefore, we will describe this concept and its possible meanings for Leviticus, in order thereafter to take up anew the question of the literary composition of the book and its contents. This, finally, will enable us to look again at the texts of Leviticus 12, 15, and 18, which are central for women. This study rests on the insights of social anthropology as well as recent approaches to literary criticism. Our goal is to present some observations on cultural-historical developments and to see how they are comparable with "Levitical" themes.

A priori: The title of the book, taken over from Greek usage *(to levitikon)*, must be understood as synonymous with "priestly/cultic." In rabbinic tradition Leviticus is called the "Torah of the Priests" *(tôrat hakkōhănîm)*, which names its essential characteristic. In origin, Leviticus is attributed to the correspondingly named "Priestly source" (= P), which — according to the dominant current opinion — was composed in the exilic/postexilic period (sixth to fifth century B.C.E.).

The Concepts of Holiness and Purity

The epitome of holiness is YHWH. He is "the Holy One of Israel" (thirty-six times in the First Testament, e.g., Isa 6, and elsewhere). Predominant in Leviticus is the priestly-cultic usage of the adjective *qādôš*, "holy"; that is, everything that belongs to the sphere of the Holy One and serves his cult is holy (Lev 23:15-20). The contrary concept is the common (10:10) or unclean/impure (15:31). On the other hand, it is striking that YHWH's statements about himself, "I am holy" (11:44, and frequently), are connected with statements about the holiness of the people. YHWH's holiness is the standard and impulse for human beings to avoid every kind of uncleanness and to be clean, or pure, in order to be able to approach YHWH's holiness and purity. In Israel this led to a scale of social levels of value; around YHWH, the Holy One, are grouped, at increasing distances:

1. The priests, who are tasked with distinguishing between the holy and the common and instructing the Israelites (10:10);
2. The land and the people God has chosen, who stand out as a community of priests over against the other nations (20:26); and
3. Individual Israelites.

This compact characterization is also reflected in the structure of the book: surrounded by two literary complexes concerned with the sphere of the Holy that is localized in the cult, with sacrifices and feasts (1–10: regulations for the priests and the cult; 16–27: regulations for all Israel, the Day of Atonement, etc.), there stands in the center of the book (11–15) the so-called Purity Torah, which applies to individual Israelites in their daily lives, in the preparation and eating of food, and in fundamental daily actions and events such as sickness, sexuality and love, giving birth and dying.

Modern readers find it difficult to comprehend why precisely these basic features of human existence should be the object of purity regulations. If we keep in mind the overall concept, it becomes clear that Leviticus uses the terms "clean"/ "pure" *(ṭāhôr)* and "unclean"/"impure" *(ṭāmē')* functionally. This serves, first of all, the evaluation of the *cultic eligibility* of a person, an animal, or an object, that is, its categorization as regards possible contact with the Holy.

It is true that uncleanness/impurity can be transmitted to people and objects through touch, which is why such contact is to be avoided (11:43-44), and is warned against (13:45), but the condition of uncleanness *(ṭum'â)* can be ended — that is, changed, or changed back, to a condition of cleanness *(ṭohŏrâ)* through a number of means (e.g., washing, separating, distance in time). Here there is a clear distinction between temporary uncleanness, for example, as a result of sickness or in the case of menstruation, and permanent uncleanness: the latter leads, for animals or objects, to a strict prohibition against eating or using them, and for human beings, to exclusion from the community of Israel (18:29).

How did the attributes of clean or unclean come to be ascribed to certain animals, objects, or people? History of religion, ethnology, and sociology offer different kinds of explanations. The demonistic explanation, which, beginning from a particular religio-ethnological understanding of taboos, interpreted the First Testament purity laws as relics of magical ideas, no longer appears acceptable. But it is still unthinkingly applied to explain the prescriptions regarding human genitalia and sexual practices (cf. Feld 1996, 35).

Ethnological and social-anthropological studies have eliminated the demonistic explanation. The British anthropologist Mary Douglas, in her study *Purity and Danger* (1966), made it clear that notions of cleanness and uncleanness are by no means characteristic only of so-called primitive societies; rather, this is a universal concept that can be explained by a general rule. According to Douglas, cleanness or purity is the result of the cultural concept of a particular society whose social needs are regulated by purity codes. The symbol of this social cosmos of the group is the body, its microcosm. The concern of the Israelites "for the integrity, unity, and purity of the physical body" is, according to Douglas, "an expression of the threatened boundaries of their political community" (1966, 164). Against this background a repugnance for bodily impurity reflected Israel's antipathy toward mixing with foreign peoples; the command not to eat certain animals was an expression of separation from the neighboring peoples for whom these animals were regarded as cultic objects or the matter for sacrifices.

Consequently, the purity codes are, on the one hand, an expression of the social instability of the exiled community, and become, on the other hand, especially in the diaspora situation, instances of Jewish discovery of identity. In the Israelite system of classification, purity or cleanness was equated with completeness and normality, while impurity or uncleanness meant incompleteness and abnormality. Death and the dead were regarded on this scale of values as the extreme of uncleanness, the greatest abnormality. Therefore contact with the corpses of people or animals represented the highest degree of uncleanness.

Symbolic interpretations have described this polar scheme of purity and impurity in terms of the fundamental polarity of life and death. Impure and unclean are those who have the aura of death about them in some way. A leper is going through a slow process of dying; excretions are regarded as the loss of the juices of life and bring one close to death. The same is true of genital bleeding (15:5, 25-26). Among animals, those above all are unclean that, because they eat carrion or are reptilian, are close to the materials of death (11:11-20). In this model the notion of impurity rests on fear of the mysterious life force of blood and the eerie power of death.

The demand that the people be holy — "you are to be holy" — and YHWH's own statement, "for I, your God, am holy," are part of a complex model of relationship between the people Israel and its God. It rests, on the one hand, on YHWH's election and liberation of the people, and on the other hand on the identification and naming of this God as "holy," which may mean something like "powerful, transcendent, beyond moral challenge," and that likewise connotes, for the Priestly authors, "clean, pure."

The translation of *qādôš* as "own" (Wegner 1992, 40) serves to clarify this relationship structure. The holy is what belongs to the deity, God's property. The path to it is cultic purity, and it requires a process of separation and of sorting out everything that cannot be the deity's property. But the human being who desires to be holy cannot exist of itself and for itself. Human beings eat and drink, love and copulate, fall ill, give birth, and die: problematic situations in the life of every individual in which boundary crossings — of oneself and the body of the other — become unavoidable. Consequently, these themes are central to the purity codes. However, they also have a special accent inasmuch as they link the complex of purity with the theme of sacrifice.

The Concept of Cultic Sacrifice

In modernity, sacrifice means self-negation, self-surrender, or, in certain economic or social structures, the squandering of innocent human life, or even animal or plant life. The original character of sacrifice as *gift/donation* to a deity, a higher and significant Other, in the sense of preserving or restoring cosmic unity and communication with that Other, has faded into the background. Marcel Mauss has identified this kind of interaction between the human and God as a form of exchange, of gift and countergift, *gift exchange*. Still more: In thanks for the gift, what has been given by the deity, the human is obligated to sacrifice, to give part of the gift back to its originator: "They [the gods] are in fact the true owners of the things and goods of the world. Exchange with them was the most necessary, and failure to exchange was the most dangerous thing" (Mauss 1994, 43).

In Leviticus, too, we find traces of this original type of sacrifice. Blood and fat — symbols of the central organs of life — are reserved for YHWH and denied to humans (17:10-16, and elsewhere). The blood is poured out or sprinkled on the altar; the fat is burned. Leviticus 17:11 lends precision: "For the life of the flesh is in the blood; and I have given it to you." What originally belonged to YHWH is given back to him; he is nourished and appeased. This is expressed also in the basic meaning of the word *minḥâ* for the grain offering (2:1). First of all, *minḥâ* means the food itself (7:9, and frequently), but then also the gift or the tribute presented to a powerful person, a deity, to put him or her in a good mood. In addition, we regularly find at the end of the directions for sacrifice the remark: "an offering by fire for a pleasing odor for YHWH" (2:16, and frequently). This points to the idea that parts of the sacrifice rise up to God as a sign of the effort, the spirit of the one sacrificing.

In Leviticus 17:11b we find clear evidence of a second stage of development of the idea of sacrifice: "for making atonement for your lives on the altar." Thus Leviticus 4–5 focus on the so-called guilt offering and sin offerings *(ḥaṭṭā't and 'āšām)* to atone for inadvertent sins. This aspect of "removal of guilt" then culminates in the ritual of the great Day of Atonement (Lev 16). Responsibility for this new form of communication with God in the sacrificial cult is assigned not only to political and economic changes in Israel, but especially to the theological developments in diaspora Judaism: the Priestly concept of cultic piety is supported by monolatry/monotheism: YHWH is understood to be the sole giver of the gift (liberation from slavery in Egypt; the gift of the land and its fruitfulness) given to the people Israel. This gift is so radical that it cannot ultimately be reciprocated; that is, the human being cannot maintain the form of gift exchange either economically or morally. The consequence is that the sacrifice assumes the function of atonement for the sins of the people. This aspect is virulent especially in chapters 17–26, the so-called Holiness Code. Here, on the one hand, we find polemic against the other gods, said to be nothing, and, on the other, YHWH reappears here, even more intensively, as a speaking "I" who appoints clear contractual conditions for communication with his people. With full consistency he threatens that, if his commandments are not kept, "I will not smell your pleasing odors" (26:31) — which, in the mind of the Priestly author, means an end to communication.

In this Priestly concept of sacrifice, women are disadvantaged in a number of ways:

1. We may suppose that the YHWH cult in Jerusalem permitted no goddesses or female priests. The professional cultic personnel at the sanctuary is drawn

from the Aaronic priesthood. Women appear here only as family members; their cultic activities are restricted by the suppression of private family sacrifices in favor of the atoning sacrifices. With the prescription that only "every male among the priests" may eat of the flesh of the sin offering (6:29, and frequently), the common meal is separated from the sacrificial ceremony and given over to the specialists. In this way the family, with its private sacrifices, is made dependent on the sanctuary as the institutional place of atonement, and so also the laity are made dependent on the priests, and the women on the men, since women are at the lowest rung of the sacrificial hierarchy. Leviticus 15:14, 29 suggest the same thing.

The priestly concept of sacrifice leads ultimately to a centralization of the cult at the sanctuary, the place where contact with the profane/unclean is forbidden, and to its concentration in the ritual of the great Day of Atonement (Lev 16), which is intended both to cleanse the sanctuary and to atone for the sins of the people. The demand for purity and holiness, to be accomplished before the sacrificial action is undertaken, also presumes an act of separation that imitates God's act in creation (*bādāl*, "distinguish, set apart"; cf. Lev 10:10; 11:47; 20:25 with Gen 1:14, 18). Here again, the priests are in a privileged position.

2. The link between holiness and ritual purity evoked by the cult also affects those sacrificing, as well as the material of the sacrifice (Lev 7:19-21), and again emphasizes the higher value of everything male:[1] the purity prescriptions for the priests include even the female members of their families, especially those who, in the patriarchal family system, are directly subject to the head of the family, namely, the wife and daughter, and demand their sexual purity, that is, chastity. A priest may not marry a prostitute, a widow, or a divorced woman (21:7-8, 13-14). Only in this way can his fatherhood be assured and an inherited priesthood established. If a priest's daughter becomes a prostitute, she is to be punished with death because she "profanes her father" (21:9).

3. The aspects of violence and death inherent in sacrifice are reemphasized through an evaluation of blood in the sense of social hierarchy: the blood associated with killing brings protection to the person, supports the covenant with God, and brings atonement, whereas the blood associated with menstruation and giving birth is rejected as polluting.

In Leviticus 1:2 we are struck by the use of the word *'ādām* for the person offering sacrifice. While everywhere else the one sacrificing is referred to as *'îš*, here, at the very beginning of the book, a connotation is constructed, coupling the first person created, *'ādām*, with the earth *('ădāmâ)* and blood *(dām)* as the instances

---

1. Female animals were accepted only for personal sacrifices (4:32), never for those made in the name of the whole community.

crucial to the creation. Those sacrificing thus stand in a series with *'ādām;* they are part of the creation regarded as unity and harmony. The sacrifice itself acquires the character of something that preserves and restores creation.

The Overall Composition of Leviticus

So-called source criticism falls into a vicious circle here. On the one hand there is consensus that the text belongs to P, while on the other hand Leviticus is the very text that has created controversy about the unity of P. Suggested solutions regarding the literary origins of the book have been sought either in a still more difficult definition of that source or in a recourse to P as a stage of redactional revision, but seldom with an eye to a literary unity of the book. Setting aside a diachronic perspective, the most recent studies give an impression of what kind of sense this text makes if we inquire about its "canonical intention."

1. Christopher H. Smith (1996) takes as the starting point for his study the increased questioning of the so-called Holiness Code. He says that the obvious contextual links in Leviticus (to Exodus and Numbers) allow us to assume a continuous body of legal material extending over several books. For Leviticus this means that chapters 17–26, which are perceived as a literary unit, must be linked to the textual unit of chapters 1–16. In addition, the literary unity of the book is formally indicated both by the repetition of certain formulaic expressions that mark off thematic sections and by the shifts between the genre-specific legal and narrative sections. This yields a structure in seven units, with the narrative units (chapters 8–10; 16; 24:10-23) related to one another and serving as structural indicators for the legal portions (chapters 1–7; 11–15; 17:1–24:9; 25–27):

Legal	Narrative	Theme	Function
1–7		sacrifice	
	8–10	*death of Aaron's sons*	negative example
11–15		purity	
	16	*cleansing of the sanctuary and atonement for the people*	linking the themes of purity and holiness
17:1–24:9		holiness	
	24:10-23	*stoning of a blasphemer*	negative example
25–27		redemption	

Smith's analysis has some aspects that agree with our observations about functionality. (1) The legal sections, each concluded with a narrative unit, treat the central Priestly ideas: sacrifice, purity, holiness. Each of these themes is supplemented by a concrete example of application, in narrative form: not following the rules of the *sacrificial* cult leads to the deaths of Nadab and Abihu; not achieving *purity* and *holiness* requires atonement on the great Day of Atonement; not recognizing YHWH's *holiness* leads to the death of the blasphemer. (2) Chapter 16, the ritual of the Day of Atonement, constitutes the center of the seven parts. This structural weight is in accord with the function of the chapter as a connecting link between the Purity Torah and the Holiness Code, as well as with the centering of P's theology on the aspect of atonement. (3) Smith attributes to the narrative in 24:10-23, usually interpreted as an interruption of the Holiness Code, a bridge function between the laws on sanctification of daily life and the cult in 17:1–24:9 and the social laws that follow in 25–27, based on the holiness of the land. This thesis is confirmed by:

a. The Egyptian lineage of the one who blasphemes God (24:10). This points to Egypt as the symbol of the "historically" experienced (23:43) and impending, threatened exile (26:43). (The threefold affirmation that the blasphemer is an "Israelite woman's son" points to the patriarchal orientation of the Israelite tribal society; this maternal descent is inadequate for the man to be integrated into the tribe.)
b. The means and method of "punishment." By imposing hands, as with sacrificial animals (1:4) and the scapegoat (16:21), the Israelites identify themselves with YHWH's judgment and thus obtain atonement for themselves by committing themselves, simultaneously, to hallow YHWH's name.

The symbolic number seven as a structural mark in the text should lead us, in my opinion, to suppose that Leviticus was composed in analogy to the "first" creation account (= P). Genesis 1:1–2:4a reveals both a frame and an internal structure (cf. Zenger 1983, 71-80), in which the frame is constituted by the category of "time" and the internal structure is organized by the perspective of "life." For a comparison, see the table on page 59. In midrashic fashion, Leviticus develops how the Priestly authors imagine the realization and maintenance of creation and communication with God, in daily life as in worship.

2. Mary Douglas posits, in her study "Poetic Structure in Leviticus" (1995), that Leviticus can be understood as an independent theological tractate. Each part of the book, she says, is interwoven in the structure of the whole and contributes to the development of the overall movement of the book; likewise, the beginning and end of the text correspond. This leads her to posit a *ring composition* and to attribute different theological weight to certain parts. The concentric structure of the textual pattern is said to show that chapter 19 is the real turning point and thus the theological climax of the ring composition, while the Purity Torah in chapters 11–15 functions as the center or mirror point for the holiness emphasized in the ex-

Genesis			Leviticus	
"Time"	First Day	Day and Night (1:3-5)	First Part (1–7)	Sacrifices govern the course of the day
"Life"	Second/ Third Days	Creation of the space for life (1:6-13)	Second/ Third Parts (8–10; 11–15)	Material maintenance of the living space in the sacrificial cult and in everyday life
"Time"	Fourth Day	Days and Years/ Annual festivals (1:14-19)	Fourth Part (16)	Annual ritual of the great Day of Atonement
"Life"	Fifth/ Sixth Days	Creation of living creatures (1:20-31)	Fifth/Sixth Parts (17–24:9)	Sanctification of life on the social and cultic levels
"Time"	Seventh Day	Week/rhythm of work and rest (2:2-3)	Seventh Part (25–27)	Holy years; 25:2: time of rest for the land

position: "In this structure impurity enters the reasoning by the *via negativa* and is clearly subordinate to the positive view of the theistic universe against which it is balanced" (Douglas 1995, 255). Her position is confirmed by the structuring of the Holiness Code in Leviticus 17–26, in which chapter 19 — in its form as well as its content — takes the central position: formally shaped by the style of the Decalogue, in its content it presents a kind of compendium, with a series of rules for behavior in relations between people. The high point of this program is the command to love the neighbor. But who is the neighbor? In Leviticus 19:17-18 the word "neighbor" *(rē'eh)* is used in analogy to "brother," "fellow Israelite," and "sons of the people." In 19:34 the commandment is applied to strangers *(gērîm)*. While both Jewish and Christian interpreters have put forth their utmost efforts to determine who was first to establish this commandment of love for other human beings, the fact that the formulation of this verse apparently excludes women was evidently not considered worthy of reflection. The more appropriate question would be who really lives out this commandment of love for the neighbor/fellow human being.

Leviticus 19, as the condensed middle of a composition made up of concentric circles, makes transparent the correspondence of the Priestly ideas of sacrifice, purity, and holiness. The *righteousness* or *justice* that is the focus here appears equivalent to the purity in the sacrificial cult that is the subject of the first part of the book and to the holiness of the land and the resulting codification of social laws at its end. Thus uncleanness or impurity can only be equivalent to unrighteousness or injustice. The integration of the sacrificial cult and the Purity Torah in an overarching system sustained by the principle of "righteousness" ultimately relativizes the power of the priesthood and exalts the practical-ethical competencies of the people. Leviticus 19:2 names the gathered community (ʿēdâ) of the Israelites as the addressee of this collection of laws. Accordingly, women are by no means excluded from the attribution of competence just described. Rather, their opportunities to develop that competence are circumscribed by the evaluation of the aspects of women's lives developed in a patriarchal context. Here again the idea of cultic purity comes into play: it serves to disadvantage women in the system of sacrifices, purity, and holiness we have described.

Women's Cultic Uncleanness

Leviticus emphasizes two forms of cultic uncleanness or impurity in connection with the female sex: (1) the biological processes of menstruation and birth (12; 15:19-30) and (2) illegitimate sexual relations (18:7-23; 20:8-21).

Since a consideration of these texts isolated from their context often creates the impression of a fundamental and, above all, arbitrary devaluation of female sexuality and physicality, we should first inquire about the leading theological motif in the larger text units to which the individual texts belong.

Leviticus 11–15 can be divided by the introductory formulae ("and YHWH spoke to . . ." [11:1, and elsewhere]) and concluding formulae ("this is the law pertaining to . . ." [11:46, and elsewhere]) into six thematic sections:

1.	(a)	11:1-23	Distinction: edible/nonedible animals
	(b)	11:24-25	Contact with carrion
2.		12	Birth
3.	(a)	13:1-46	Leprosy in humans
	(b)	13:47-59	Leprosy in clothing
4.		14:1-32	Purification rituals in cases of leprosy in humans
5.		14:33-57	Leprosy in houses
6.		15	Genital secretions

Thus far no persuasive structural principle has been demonstrated beyond the thematic designation as a Purity Torah.

If we consider Mary Douglas's proposal, the principle of *boundary crossing* recommends itself. Everything that crosses over the boundaries of the criteria of normality and completeness that are recognized in the Israelite system of order is unclean. Consumption of food, as the first and most important process for guaranteeing human survival, represents crossing the boundary of one's own body, to which foreign matter is added. Since this cannot be avoided, at least the matter that becomes part of the body must be *clean*: only animals that correspond to their own specific system of order (e.g., 11:3, those that chew the cud and have cloven hooves) are "clean." But the birds and kinds of insects (11:13-19) and small creatures (11:20) that are altogether "normal" within their own phylum and yet are declared unclean are all flesh-eating animals. The privilege of eating flesh was, according to Genesis 9:3, conceded only to human beings; that is, these animals do not act in conformity to the sphere that has been assigned to them. The instance that here leads to a declaration of uncleanness is an anomaly in view of a crossing of boundaries between nature (= animal) and culture (= human being).

When a human being is born, the boundaries of the mother's body are crossed as the child is brought forth. This theme is followed by that of the giving and taking of nourishment, because this guarantees the survival of the human race through procreation. At the same time, however, this sequence reflects the symbolism of a separation between external and internal, between the self and the exterior world: taking nourishment is a process that breaks through the boundaries of the body from outside to inside, while the reverse is true of birth.

If these prescriptions guarantee the fundamental — quasi-material — forms of maintaining human life, Leviticus 13–14 in turn attends again to the disruption of bodily boundaries from without: leprosy makes all the personal, bodily (skin and clothing), and material (house) integuments/boundaries fragile, blemished, in short, incomplete and abnormal, and therefore unclean. This is again an expression of the contrast between nature and culture: the possible physical deformities of a leper destroy his or her "human" appearance; the person affected is to stay "outside the camp" (13:46), to "wear torn clothes and let the hair of his head be disheveled" (13:45); these are the external signs by which one can recognize someone who is no longer part of the human cultural world. Leprosy in clothing and houses is caused by plants and mold, that is, things belonging to the realm of nature that here break into the human world, the culture.

Leviticus 15 explains the fluids that come from within the body, whether pathological or normal features of physical nature, as unclean, in line with the symbolism of external and internal thus described.

The overarching criterion for distinguishing between clean and unclean, and the structural principle of the textual unit Leviticus 11–15, is consequently *boundary crossing:* between external and internal, normal and abnormal, culture and nature.

Leviticus 12

The shortest chapter in Leviticus concerns the uncleanness of a woman after childbirth and the prescriptions that must be followed for her purification. These include, first of all, a waiting period of seven days after the birth of a boy (v. 2) and fourteen days after the birth of a girl (v. 5), during which the woman is *ṭāmē'*, in the first stage of the purification process. Then follows "her time of blood purification" (v. 4), thirty-three days in the first case and sixty-six days in the second

(v. 5). This yields a total of forty or eighty days of *ṭum'â*, during which the woman "shall not touch any holy thing, or come into the sanctuary" (v. 4). Afterward, at the end of the waiting period, a burnt offering and a sin offering are to be brought; what is sacrificed, according to verse 8, is determined by the woman's economic circumstances. There is no requirement for a purifying bath.

While the cultic consequences for a woman in the status of *ṭum'â*, as described in verse 4, basically follow from the Priestly concept of the cult and purity, there seems to be no satisfactory explanation for the discrepancy between the periods of purification after the birth of a male or a female child. The culture's higher valuation of the male sex, which also appears in the equivalent sums suggested for men and women in Leviticus 27:2-7, or the idea of YHWH as representative of male power/holiness, may have led to the idea of a "double uncleanness" after the birth of a girl.

Leviticus 12:7 says: "He [the priest] shall offer it before YHWH, and make atonement on her behalf; then she shall be clean from her flow of blood." The Hebrew formulation *māqôr dāmêhā*, frequently rendered "flow of blood," should be translated literally as "source/fountain of blood." *Māqôr* is used primarily in poetic texts, where it refers to the source of life and happiness (Ps 36:10; Prov 10:11) or of wisdom (Prov 18:4), or to God as the source of living water (Jer 2:13). This positive coloring of the use of the word makes it unlikely that a connotation of death is connected with blood. Rather, *māqôr* is associated with a geological fountain and thus with the equation water = life. The text thus resumes an association that was already hinted at in Leviticus 12:2, where we read "if a woman brings forth seed. . . ." This usage recalls the P creation account and links the woman's womb with the womb of the earth. The expressions "bring forth seed" and "source/fountain of blood" thus combine to form a metaphor: the woman giving birth as womb/fountain of life.

The association of postpartum secretions with uncleanness can thus no longer be explained on the basis of resentment toward the female body, but rather in terms of the principle of *boundary crossing*, already alluded to several times. The association with the geological fountain makes this clear: the fluid emerging and running over crosses existing boundaries, those of the self and the external world. Whitekettle (1996) points to a further symbolic congruence between Leviticus and the P primal history: starting from the image of the woman's uterus as a fountain and the highly symbolic numbers seven and forty (in Leviticus as in Genesis), he suggests that the length of the menstrual or postpartum uncleanness is determined by the length of the geological processes described in the P accounts of the creation and flood. Thus as an orderly world was created from chaos in seven days, and later returns in forty days into chaos and in the same length of time is renewed, so the woman's uterus is returned to its original state after seven days, in the case of menstruation and the first stage after birth, and in forty days in the second stage after birth. The uterus that has become useless to the reproductive system is restored, after the expiration of this period of time, to its full functionality.

The sin and burnt offerings required at the end of the purification process are a *"rite of passage"* (Petermann 1996, 55). The burnt offering is in thanksgiving for the gift given, the child; the sin offering affords atonement *(kipper)* for purification and makes access to the holy possible again. Thus, through the whole process the woman is restored to a cult-capable status.

That the woman, as the *Einheitsübersetzung* (of the Bible) has it, is to spend "the time of her purification at home" (vv. 4, 5) is not in the Hebrew text [English translations generally say only that she is not to enter the sanctuary. — Trans.]. What has happened here is that the concept of *niddâ*, used in verse 2 to explain her status as *ṭum'â*, has been applied to a social reality supposed to lie behind the text.

Leviticus 15

This concentrically structured chapter focuses on cultic uncleanness caused by genital secretions: verse 18, which attributes uncleanness to heterosexual intercourse, is surrounded by symmetric series of regulations concerning both male and female normal and abnormal secretions. The man's emission of semen (vv. 16-17: seminal emission; v. 18: in coitus) causes uncleanness, just as do a woman's menstruation (vv. 19-24) and all unhealthy secretions (vv. 2-12, 25-27) from the genitalia of men or women. Those who have the secretions are unclean, and everything that comes into contact with them, both human and material, is contaminated and can transfer that condition to third parties. For lesser uncleanness, caused by seminal emission or secondarily acquired, for example, by sitting on a contaminated object, the condition of uncleanness endures until evening. Objects are cleaned with water. Pollution and sexual intercourse require those affected to bathe afterward. In a higher degree of uncleanness (unhealthy secretions of men or women; sexual contact with a menstruating woman), another seven days must elapse before complete purification. After the designated period, those affected are to bring a sin offering and a burnt offering, which will return them to the condition of *ṭohŏrâ*.

Contamination takes place through contact. But while every kind of physical contact with a woman experiencing genital bleeding leads to uncleanness, for a man whose genitals are unhealthy this is restricted to touching his body (= penis, v. 7), saliva (v. 8), and unwashed hands (v. 11). For a woman, sources of contamination also include objects that have touched another, already contaminated, object (v. 23). The menstruating woman's *ṭum'â* is separately qualified as *niddâ* — a term whose basic meaning only refers to the secretion of menstrual blood. Interpreting this as derived from a "memory of a spatial separation of those menstruating" (Petermann 1996, 50) or those giving birth is dubious in light of the sparse attestation of the texts supporting it and also should be regarded as a transfer to the biblical text of the universality and formal agreement of menstruation rituals asserted by traditional ethnologies (cf. Feld 1996, 34).

To conclude the process of purification, both men and women bring their sacrifice to the priest at the opening of the Tent of Meeting. The regulations correspond in their essentials to those for the sacrifice to be offered after a birth (12:6-8). The man is required, in addition, to "come before the LORD" (15:14), a formula that is used, in 15:15 and 15:30, for the sacrificial actions that can be carried out only by the priest. The absence of this indication in the woman's sacrifice is hard to interpret. At any rate, it is certain that both men and women are not regarded here as patients, but as active participants in the cult.

Leviticus 18 and 20

The leading theme of chapters 17–26 is "holiness," which is made the responsibility of the community in the central chapter 19. This "catechism" is surrounded by laws that assert that any form of sexuality outside its legitimate place, the monogamous nuclear family, is the cause of cultic uncleanness and a danger to the survival of Israel. Leviticus 18 thus links sexuality with the question of remaining in the land, and Leviticus 20, which also prescribes punishments corresponding to individual sexual laws, associates it with the "correct" worship of God. From a formal point of view the subsequent ordinances are directed to all Israelites, but in the patriarchal context of Israel they are addressed primarily to men. Hence women are regarded as forbidden sexual objects if they are the legal property of another man who, as husband or father, is entitled to control and dispose of the sexual and reproductive functions of these women. The fact that the daughters of the nuclear family remain unmentioned can be interpreted on the basis of the legal situation thus sketched as a logical omission: the daughter "belongs to her father, and if he uses her — his property — sexually, that does not destroy the peace within the family, at least not as long as the daughter is unmarried" (Seifert 1997, 222). Or else it may be that the regard for paternal authority and integrity is so high that an explicit mention of this prohibition would almost be equivalent to an insult and undermining of it (Frymer-Kensky 1992).

The androcentric character of the sexual laws is culturally conditioned. In addition, the laws reflect the Priestly notion of the organizational structure of creation: as long as sexuality has regard for the principle of boundary crossing (here in the case of family structures), it is literally creative; everything else is a falling back into chaos, and only the death of the delinquent can rectify it (20:18!).

"And God Saw That It Was Good"

From a cultural-historical perspective, Leviticus — which is so often dismissed as a substratum of an archaic culture — is a highly vivid document. The "strangeness" of these cultic regulations, so often invoked, is relativized in view of the tenacity of "Levitical" ideas in modern society, especially as regards many taboos surrounding the female body (cf. Feld 1996, passim).

1. Leviticus is evidence of the interplay of sexuality and power — that is, in the form of cultic disqualification — with its vast implications, especially for women, in the patriarchal context.[2] Modern forms of this phenomenon are found in the struggles, enduring even today, over the liturgical roles of women, especially in the Roman Catholic Church, or, for example, in the debate over abortion, which has been taken out of the hands of women and subjected to arguments reflecting issues of social control.

2. The supposed time-context in which the book originated points to a phenomenon that can repeatedly be seen in history and politics: the "tragedy of proximity." Israel reacts to the nearness of (and control by) a different culture, something that appeared, during the exile, as an existential threat, with a politics of cultural and religious exclusion. This is a tried and true method of acting, by no means overcome in our world, but whose fatal consequences, when there is a corresponding ability to put it into effect through political or even military means, can be observed every day.

3. Historically as well as theologically, "a positive reception of the cultic laws in the sense of a Christian reappropriation" (Petermann 1996, 58) appears impossible. However, the following implications of the Priestly concepts of sacrifice, purity, and holiness are worthy of consideration:

   a. Whereas today the female body in particular is given a commercial function, Leviticus perceives human bodiliness as an aspect of religious culture. While the sexual laws require control of sexual behavior, they at the same time emphasize the indispensable value, in light of creation theology, of sexuality as an essential part of life (for the priestly office as well!).

   b. In view of the actual existence of a "culture of sacrifice" in modern societies — especially in politics, ecology, and individual lives — the institution of atonement in the Priestly cult (e.g., sin offerings and guilt offerings) can be seen to have an exculpatory and liberating function.

   c. The Priestly concept of purity is grounded in the longing for holiness in the full expression of life; our civilized world's "quest for purity" has taken on the character of a threat to creation.

The quest for closeness to God leads to the exclusion of everything that appears incompatible with God. The formula "and God saw that it was good" in the

---

2. For older Jewish interpretations, cf. Mishnah *Niddah* 7.4; Babylonian Talmud *Ketubbot* 61a; Babylonian Talmud *Berakhot* 24a, and frequently elsewhere; recall the ritual of "churching of women" after childbirth, practiced in Roman Catholic Christianity until 1964.

P creation account does *not* follow explicitly the account of the creation of human beings (Gen 1:26-28), but is made to comment on God's entire creative work: "God saw everything that he had made, and indeed, it was very good" (Gen 1:31). It is the human role to make sure that the creation remains good. Leviticus, however, shows how the Priestly authors spelled creation: Leviticus is their *ABC of Creation*.

LITERATURE

Douglas, Mary. 1966. *Purity and Danger*. London.

—————. 1995. "Poetic Structure in Leviticus." In *Pomegranates and Golden Bells: Studies in Biblical, Jewish, and Near Eastern Ritual Law and Literature in Honor of Jacob Milgrom*, edited by David P. Wright, David Noel Freedman, and Avi Hurvitz, 239-56. Winona Lake, Ind.

Eilberg-Schwartz, Howard. 1990. *The Savage in Judaism: An Anthropology of Israelite Religion and Ancient Judaism*. Bloomington, Ind.

Feld, Gerburgis. 1996. "'Wie es eben Frauen ergeht' (Gen 31,35). Kulturgeschichtliche Überlieferungen zum Umgang mit der Menstruation der Frau in Gesellschaft und Theologie." In *Von der Wurzel getragen. Christlich-feministische Exegese in Auseinandersetzung mit Antijudaismus*, edited by Luise Schottroff and Marie-Theres Wacker, 29-41. Leiden, New York, and Cologne.

Frymer-Kensky, Tikva. 1992. "Sex and Sexuality." In *The Anchor Bible Dictionary*, 5:1144-46. New York.

Mauss, Marcel. 1994. *Die Gabe. Form und Funktion des Austauschs in archaischen Gesellschaften*. 2nd ed. Frankfurt.

Petermann, Batmartha Ina Johanne. 1996. "Machen Geburt und Monatsblutung die Frau 'unrein'? Zur Revisionsbedürftigkeit eines mißverstandenen Diktums." In *Von der Wurzel getragen. Christlich-feministische Exegese in Auseinandersetzung mit Antijudaismus*, edited by Luise Schottroff and Marie-Theres Wacker, 43-60. Leiden, New York, and Cologne.

Schottroff, Luise, and Marie-Theres Wacker, eds. 1996. *Von der Wurzel getragen. Christlich-feministische Exegese in Auseinandersetzung mit Antijudaismus*. Leiden, New York, and Cologne.

Seifert, Elke. 1997. *Vater und Tochter im Alten Testament. Eine ideologiekritische Untersuchung zur Verfügungsgewalt von Vätern über ihre Töchter*. Neukirchen-Vluyn.

Smith, Christopher H. 1996. "The Literary Structure of Leviticus." *Journal for the Study of the Old Testament* 70:17-32.

Staubli, Thomas. 1996. *Die Bücher Levitikus, Numeri*. Neuer Stuttgarter Kommentar, Altes Testament, vol. 3. Stuttgart.

Wegner, Judith Romney. 1992. "Leviticus." In *The Women's Bible Commentary*, edited by Carol A. Newsom and Sharon H. Ringe, 36-44. London and Louisville.

Whitekettle, Richard. 1996. "Levitical Thought and the Female Reproductive Cycle: Wombs, Wellsprings, and the Primeval World." *Vetus Testamentum* 46:376-91.

Zenger, Erich. 1983. *Gottes Bogen in den Wolken. Untersuchungen zu Komposition und Theologie der priesterschriftlichen Urgeschichte*. Stuttgarter Bibelstudien, vol. 112. Stuttgart.

For Further Reading

Ellens, Deborah L. 2008. *Women in the Sex Texts of Leviticus and Deuteronomy.* New York.

Erbele-Küster, Dorothea. 2008. *Körper und Geschlecht. Studien zu Leviticus 12 und 15.* Wissenschaftliche Monographien zum Alten and Neuen Testament, vol. 121. Neukirchen-Vluyn.

Milgrom, Jacob. 2000. *Leviticus 17–22.* New York.

———. 2001. *Leviticus 23–27.* New York.

Wasserfall, Rahel R., ed. 1999. *Women and Water: Menstruation in Jewish Law and Life.* Hanover, N.H., and London.

Translated by Linda M. Maloney

Numbers: On Boundaries

Ursula Rapp

What Kind of Text Is the Book of Numbers and How Can We Still Read It Today?

The book of Numbers is not a historical work describing the desert wandering according to scientific historical standards. Its intent is to make important statements for its own time, packaged in legal texts and stories from Israel's earliest period. Its present is the exilic and postexilic period, when people attempted to organize anew, socially as well as in other respects (and at a later time around the new temple). The interests of Priestly writers dominate the composition of the book. We find a *social project* reflecting the ideas and values of Priestly circles, in which the cult and the categories of (im)purity play essential roles (→ Leviticus).

Within the framework of a feminist reading of these texts, I will inquire about the position of women within this social construct, where they are shown their place, where they may appear and where not, and how and in what contexts sexuality is spoken of at all. Feminism is an attitude toward realities that looks not only at women, but also at society as a whole. If I work with selected texts that concern themselves with women, I intend, starting from there, to throw a spotlight on other texts in the book of Numbers to show that mechanisms, structures, and categories that force women to the margins, the boundaries of the social system, are also at work in other spheres and affect other groups. This can serve as an example of the truth that sexism is inseparable from other social and religious exclusions.

Since Numbers is concerned with group identity and self-definition, the question of the exclusion of others, strangers, those not tolerated, is absolutely central. Sharp boundaries are drawn between what has its place, what may be, and what may not be. And what may not be is always that which a society would not or could not accept (Valtink 1996, 7). This system finds its concrete manifestation today in a Eurocentric, androcentric Europe (or North America) and a corresponding Christian theology, politics, and economy. What was deadly for "the stranger" in the book of Numbers is just as deadly today. The consequences are revealed, now as then, in wars and — today more than then — in economic and ecological catastrophes.

The interests of the Priestly circles are in the foreground; therefore, orders of rank within society are important. In this sense we are dealing with a patriarchal system in which different orders are subtly interleaved and interdependent. Consequently, the oppression and exclusion of women are always connected also with the oppression and exclusion of other groups, whether ethnicities, races, or religions. To understand the argumentation and interests of the texts, I will be using the historical-critical method, with a focus on narrative analysis.

Since I must work only with examples chosen from the text, I would like at this point to give a short overview of the content of Numbers. One can see from commentaries and introductory works why this book is located, within the Pentateuch, after Leviticus and before Deuteronomy. The stage is Sinai (1:1–10:10) and then the continued journey toward the Promised Land as far as Jericho (36:13). Numbers is made up of narratives about the journey, but a variety of legal texts and directives has been inserted in it (chapters 5; 6; 8; 9:1-14; 10:1-10; 15; 18; 19; 27:1-11; 28–30; 33:50–36:13). Almost all the texts clearly reveal the desire to establish an order of rank (the naming of heads of families in 1:4; 7:2; 36:1, and frequently; the separation of the Levites in chapters 8 and 35 and the exaltation of the Aaronides in chapter 18; the authority of Moses, chapters 12; 16–17), to prescribe organization and divisions (chapters 1–4; 10:1-10; 26–27; 33–34), to answer the question of who belongs to the camp or the community (un/cleanness in chapters 5 and 19), and to achieve certainty.

Numbers 5:11-31: The Control of Female Sexuality

The first extended text in the book of Numbers devoted to a woman deals with the ordeal of a woman suspected of adultery. The text addresses essential aspects under which women were regarded, although from a negative perspective. This is about a biblically established role for women (that of wife), their sexuality, and their social legitimacy. Adultery was socially unacceptable and intolerable (Camp 1985, 114), and was subject to corresponding taboos and fears. At the same time, we have here the only biblical legal decision made by means of a magical act.

The Priestly attitude toward the adulteress is clear from certain observations we can make about the text. In the passages where the woman is the subject (vv. 12, 13, 14, 19, 20, 22, 27, 28, 29, 31), the text reveals a certain logic. These statements can be divided into three categories differing in time. The first are those describing the possible adultery: she goes astray or turns aside (vv. 12, 19, 20, 29) and is unfaithful (vv. 12, 27). The second and third group describe the consequences, with the latter pertaining to the results of the ritual. In the second category the issue is only whether the woman is unclean/defiled or not (vv. 13, 14, 19, 20, 27, 28, 29), and the consequences of the ritual are either that she is immune (vv. 19, 28) and can conceive (more) children (v. 28), or that she suffers the consequences of the bitter water, becomes an execration among her people (v. 27), and must bear her iniquity (v. 31). While there is no positively formulated alternative to the woman's adultery, the consequences of her action represent alternatives: defiled/undefiled and fruitful/unfruitful, that is, an execration. This makes it clear that the issue is not damage to the man's property relations in the juridical sense. The problem is shifted to the realm of priestly power and is to be resolved within the priestly schema of *clean and unclean, "within and without"* (cf. 5:1-4; 6:1-21; 9:1-14; 12; 19). The fact that, if she is declared guilty, the woman becomes an execration for the whole people (5:21, 27) reveals the idea that individuals' violations of law affect the whole society (as regards adultery, cf. Bach 1993, 35, 47). This extension serves to establish social control over individual misbehavior (Be'er 1994, 157).

The text begins with two different starting points: in verses 12-13, 14 it is not clear what the (original) occasion must be: the woman's act or the man's jealousy or mistrust, which does not presuppose the former. This observation cannot simply be reduced to the fact that there are no witnesses (v. 13). It is about the man's fear (on this, cf. Bach 1993, 31, 35, 46) that his wife may be unfaithful to him, and this fear determines what happens next. This is about whether and how *the woman's sexuality can be controlled.* The formulation in verses 19, 20 is given a quite literal translation in the NRSV: "You [have not] turned aside to uncleanness while under your husband's authority . . . you have gone astray while under your husband's authority" (cf. Bach 1993, 37). The man's interest in keeping a grip on his wife's sexuality combines here with the Priestly effort, through the categories of cleanness/uncleanness, to control as many aspects of society as possible (here marriage and adultery). The priest appears here likewise as the agent of male interests (Bach 1993, 40). The adulteress is not stoned (as, e.g., in Deut 22:22-29), but receives a punishment that, within this system, is equivalent to death (cf. Bach 1993, 36, 42, 45). She is banned from the camp, from the community. Women's sexual desire is understood to be against the rules and a betrayal of the social order (Bach 1993, 32).

Against the two representatives of their own power and interests, the husband and the priest, the woman is quite unable to defend herself or to influence events in any way. This is not about her innocence; the emphasis is on her guilt (Num 5:19-22, 27), which is much more fully described than her (always possible) acquittal (Bach 1993, 40-41).

Numbers 12:1-16: Miriam, the Prophet Denounced

But Not in Our Midst

Numbers 12:1-16 presents a reflection on the state of authority in Israel. Miriam and Aaron, she taking the lead (she is mentioned first in v. 1, and the verb is in the third-person feminine singular), criticize Moses' marriage to a Cushite woman (Butting 2001, 53-55; Fischer 2002, 73-74; Rapp 2002, 64-80). But the point of their reproof is in verse 2, in the question of prophetic legitimation and authority (Schüngel-Straumann 1982, 499; 1984, 255). Miriam lays claim to the same prophetic competency as Moses (Wacker 1988, 48; cf. Exod 15:20, where she is called a prophet). This illuminates the subject under two aspects: one Priestly (namely, the uncleanness of a non-Israelite woman; cf. Num 31), and the other prophetic (Trible 1994, 175).

Miriam is absolutely central to the text and occasions most of the action. God's action is entirely directed to Miriam (hears her in v. 2; speaks to her [and Aaron] in vv. 4, 6; comes to her and calls her [and Aaron] in v. 4) (Rapp 2002, 55-59). All the verbs of motion that dominate verses 4-10 are connected with her, when she is not herself the subject. The same is true of the people's waiting and setting out in verses 15-16. Aaron's and Moses' speeches are also on her account (vv. 11, 13). The only things not related to Miriam are the statements that Moses had taken a Cushite woman as his wife (v. 1) and that the people had camped in the wilderness of Paran (v. 16). So what happens in this text is fundamentally about Miriam (Rapp 2002, 117-18).

Certain distinct actions are attributed to Miriam: she speaks (vv. 1, 2); she goes out of the camp (vv. 4, 5), following God's call; she has leprosy (v. 10); she is shut out of the camp and brought in again (v. 15). She shares certain actions with Aaron (vv. 1, 2, 4, 5). The leprosy and exclusion from, and bringing into, the camp apply to her alone — that is, not the deeds themselves, but the consequences surrounding the theme of exclusion and the question of who/what should or may belong to the community. *From that point of view, Miriam stands for an aspect that is not allowed any place in the community* (otherwise frequently expressed in the categories of uncleanness/cleanness: 5:1-4; 6:1-21, or sin: 15; 31:32-36, and frequently).

In most passages we can observe a clear time sequence for the individual actions, but at some points this schema is broken up. A reference to the past (v. 1), a repetition (vv. 4 and 5), and a simultaneity of three events (vv. 9, 10) slow the text and demand attention at those points where Moses' marriage is at issue, where Miriam and Aaron are to go out, and where God's wrath departs, the cloud lifts, and Miriam is leprous. What is important is that she must leave the camp not because of her leprosy, but because God has banned her from the Tent of Meeting, and this because of what she had said about the Cushite woman. *Hence it is not merely the critique of Moses that is central to the text, but also the encounter with God and the question of how to deal with those who criticize.* (In other passages they are threatened with death; that is, they have no place in the community: Numbers 11, had Moses not intervened and changed God's mind; 14:21-23, 27-30: the determination that the first wilderness generation must die there; 16:1-50: Korah, Dathan, and Abiram.) In Numbers 12 they are to be treated as temporary lepers (Lev 14:1-32).

Here leprosy is a consequence of God's burning wrath. Elsewhere in Numbers that wrath falls on the whole nation, or a whole generation (Num 11:1, 10, 33; 25:3;

32:10, 13), but never on an individual person. Wrath is always kindled when some-one questions God's power, but not that of Moses. From this point of view Miriam is a double exception. But the fact that God's wrath is kindled shows that *her offense is something that fundamentally calls into question the whole constitution of the community of God.* Likewise, leprosy is not a common divine punishment; it is primarily something that excludes, is unclean or makes unclean, and must be cleansed by a priest. These observations underscore again that the critique of Moses is a serious matter, indeed equivalent to a critique of God, and must never occur within the community (Rapp 2002, 112-15; Bachmann 2009, 330-33). Her uncleanness puts Miriam on the same footing as the Cushite woman; both are outside the society (Trible 1994, 177).

Groups of Prophetic Women?

This does not say that the story simply relates an episode from the life of Miriam. It is, however, possible that certain ideas and interests associated with Miriam manifest themselves in this story. There is said to be reference in Numbers 12 to an older Miriam story that arose during the period of the monarchy in Judah and is found in verses 1 (without "and Aaron"), 4, 5, 9, 10, 12-16 (for a close reading, see Rapp 2002, 123-47).

Appeal to the authority of Moses is most likely attributable, during the time of the monarchy, to the highest judicial authority in Jerusalem (Crüsemann 1992, 120). It is therefore possible that Miriam, or the group behind her, had criticized the misuse of power by this institution made up of priests, Levites, and heads of families. We can no longer determine what constituted that misuse of power. (Miriam also appears in Num 20 in a context of such misuse. For an attempt to view Miriam as the representative of the priests and Moses as representative of the Levites, cf. Burns 1987, 59, and frequently. For another theory, see Fischer, 2002, 77-79; Rapp 2002, 178-93.)

Understanding the text in this way, one could say that after the collapse of the monarchy and its institutions there was no way to begin again. The text contains a new interpretation and so sets up a confrontation with "false prophets" (male and female). It is possible that Miriam is symbolic of women prophets in general (cf. Exod 15:20).

Women prophets first appear in the late monarchical period in Judah, and then in the Babylonian exile alongside male prophets; they are a central theme in the conflict over true and false prophecy. Ezekiel 13:17-21 mentions groups of women prophets who do not prophesy explicitly in the name of YHWH. Independently of that, there were evidently women prophets who, after 587 B.C.E., were so influential in Judah that in the eyes of Priestly groups (so Ezekiel) they represented dangerous competition (Jost 1994, 63-64; cf. also Kessler 1996).

Numbers 20:1-13: The Death of Miriam

And That We Hear Anything at All about It . . .

The fact that there is any account at all of Miriam's death shows that she was a significant person, an important figure in Israelite tradition. It is striking, however, that this brief notice of her death appears suddenly and with no link to the surrounding text. It is possible that a longer text about her death and burial has been silenced and forgotten (Schüngel-Straumann 1982, 499). Burns (1987, 116-19) emphasizes that 20:1b, the death notice, comes from a later redactor than the Priestly source who took care that the three leading figures of Moses, Aaron, and Miriam die at the last three stations of the wilderness journey. That is why Miriam's death is not told at 13:26-29, where there is also mention of Kadesh. Nevertheless, the tradition of the tomb in Kadesh is very old; it is attributed to the Jahwist (Burns 1987, 119) and sometimes is even regarded as historically plausible (Schüngel-Straumann 1984, 247).

Miriam's death is neither associated with a sin nor attributed to divine punishment, which is unique within the wilderness journey. She leads the people until the end of their desert wandering, practically as long as Moses and Aaron; she is therefore just as important as they are (cf. Mic 6:4).

And Her Death Is Not the End . . .

The vocabulary in Numbers 20 shows that the report of Miriam's death is set within three major thematic contexts: *death* ("die," vv. 1, 4, 26, 28; "burial," v. 1; "succumb," vv. 3, 29; "be gathered to the ancestors" [literally: to the people], vv. 24, 26); *being led up from Egypt* ("bring," vv. 4, 5, 12; "lead up," v. 5); and *failure of the male leadership elite* ("not trusting in God and not showing God's holiness," v. 12; "rebelling against God's command," v. 24). The narrative segments of the text speak only of the theme of death (vv. 1, 24), whereas within the speeches of the people (vv. 3-5) and God (vv. 12, 24-26) it is clear that *death threatens through the lack of water and thus also because of their location in the wilderness (vv. 3-5) and because of the illegitimate actions of the leading group (vv. 12, 24-26).*

The further sequence of actions shows us a logical progression of individual acts that affect one another. The exception is a caesura in the text: Miriam's death and the lack of water (vv. 1, 2) can also be seen as simultaneous events. That is, as long as Miriam was alive there was water (cf. Babylonian Talmud, *Ta'anit* 9a; for the connection of Miriam with water, cf. Exod 2:3-8; 15:20-21), life was not threatened by death, and the people were not tormented by the fear of death. Likewise, as long as Miriam was alive, Aaron and Moses did not commit sin and fulfilled their offices. If we were to formulate a countertheme to that of death, as stated above, it would be as follows: as long as Miriam lives, both the provision of water (and thus of life) in the desert and the correctness of the leadership elite are guaranteed. In other words: *Miriam represents life in the desert* (Trible 1994, 180 comes to the same conclusion) *and a sinless leadership* (Butting 2001, 67-70; Fischer 2002, 80-82; Rapp 2002, 274-81, 323-26).

Still more: In Numbers 20 the account of the march, which had ceased abruptly in chapter 17, begins again. At the end of Numbers 17, at verses 27 and 28 (Eng. 12 and 13), the people's fear of death is expressed in almost the same words as in 20:3-4. Of course, there the issue was not the dangers of the desert, but the encounter with God. Numbers 18, then, gives orders about who may approach the sanctuary, and when and how, so as not to die in the process (i.e., instructions for right worship), and Numbers 19 describes the process of purification after touching a corpse, which was just as unclean and dangerous as an encounter with God. The connection between Miriam and chapter 19 is visible in the sacrificial gifts (v. 6), which were also to be used for purifying lepers (Lev 14:4), flowing water for the purification of anyone who has touched a corpse (Num 19:11-13), and seven days of separation, as prescribed for Miriam in chapter 12 (Trible 1994, 178-79).

In this context, can Miriam's death be regarded as appeasing or consoling? Can this be a statement that death is not to be understood fundamentally as punishment?

If we compare the brief notice of Miriam's death with the account of Aaron's death (vv. 22-29), we notice some differences; the most important of these is probably that Aaron has a successor while Miriam does not. Thus, while the derivation of the priestly office (Aaron) from the wilderness period is meant to assure Israel of its continuity, stability, and fundamental significance, it must be clear, in contrast, that Miriam does not represent any office, since she did not receive a successor from God, and in the present time of the Priestly redactor no one could appeal to her. This statement is underscored by a reminiscence that expresses the distance from God in Miriam's death: Miriam dies in the valley, as would be known from the location of Kadesh, while Aaron dies on a mountain, in fact on its summit, a place that in itself suggests closeness to God (cf. Exod 19, with Moses' continual ascent and descent, and frequently elsewhere). God announces Aaron's death three times (Num 20:24, 26 [2x]).

The divine authority behind Aaron and his ministry (for other pro-Aaronide texts see 3:6; 18, and elsewhere) is completely lacking for Miriam. Thus the redactors of the text had *no interest in Miriam,* or only a negative one, namely, to undercut the group(s) that appealed to her for support (Rapp 2002, 261-62, 325-26).

Two observations on the text favor a late-exilic, or rather early postexilic, origin (for a later dating, see Rapp 2002, 320-22). One is that the priestly office evidently required some strengthening, which was entirely possible at that time, since there was no temple. The second follows from the first: if we assume that Israel's society in the first years after the exile was not yet organized, so that its institutions and authorities had to establish themselves, it may be true that women had more freedom in their social roles and religious practices (Schroer 1998, 137). The more important it was, then, to set limits precisely on those groups that were attempting to establish themselves. One such may have been a company of women prophets or women priests who appealed to Miriam or derived their social functions from hers.

Miriam, a "Fence Sitter"

According to Numbers 20, Miriam is a marginal figure. Four margins or borders are mentioned: the border between wandering in the wilderness (which, according to 14:33-34, was punishment for grumbling) and continuing the march; the border between wilderness wandering and entry into the land, and thus between a peaceful and a warlike existence (the first military clash is in Num 21!); the border on which Kadesh lies; and the border between life and death (survival in the wilderness, errors of the leadership elite) — thus historical, geographical, and human boundaries. In this sense Miriam can be understood as a person who found herself between different spheres, a boundary walker or "fence sitter."

Numbers 25:1-18: The Construction of the Stranger/Other

The text of Numbers 25 gives essential information about concepts and schemata used to construct an ideology and a legitimation for social structures. Traditional studies of the text pose literary-critical questions that are hard to justify, and focus primarily on two themes: the Baal of Peor, or rather the cult represented by this god, and the eternal covenant with the priestly line of the Aaronides. Baal of Peor appears to have been one of the non-Israelite fertility gods (in my opinion, the thesis sometimes advanced about a burial cult and ancestor worship is unsustainable). The priestly covenant is an essential element of the text's statement, and I will return to it later.

To better understand a broader dimension of the text, we need to keep in mind Moses' history with Midian. After he had murdered an Egyptian slaveowner, it was in Midian that he first found shelter from those who pursued him for the murder (Exod 2:15). There he first met God (Exod 3), and there he married Zipporah, a Midianite woman (Exod 2:18-22). His father-in-law, a priest (Exod 2:16; 3:1), led the Israelites through the wilderness for a long time (Num 10:29-32), and he also gave Moses suggestions about the organization of the people (Exod 18:13-27). That is, Israel was structured according to a Midianite social order. Numbers 10:29 represents a break in this very close relationship, since there Moses' brother-in-law rejects his offer to adhere to faith in God. We may conclude from this that the "Moses religion" was not all that attractive. So Midian missed its chance to join (peacefully) with Israel, but it was also not occupied. Numbers 25 speaks of an event with heavy consequences, for this is the beginning of an enmity and the start of Israel's war with Midian (Num 31). That war was also Moses' last action before he died (31:2)!

Exclusion and Killing

The text weaves together two stories. The first is the narrative of how Israelite men had sexual relations with Moabite women and then worshiped the Moabites' god, Baal of Peor. God then orders Moses to impale the chiefs of the Moabites before him, their faces to the sun. But Moses does nothing of the kind; he instead orders the judges in Israel to kill only the men who accepted blame (vv. 1-5). The second story is about Zimri, an Israelite who "brought the Midianite woman Cozbi to his brothers while 'they' [apparently the assembled community] were weeping at the entrance of the tent of meeting." Phinehas the priest then took the initiative and murdered Zimri and Cozbi in her chamber, which brought an end to the plague (what kind it was is not stated) (vv. 6-8b, 14-15).

These two stories are linked at four points, each of which has to do with *death and killing*: verse 8: through murder, Phinehas ended the plague that had befallen the Israelites; verse 9: the plague killed 24,000 people; verses 10-13: God's speech says it was the murder that soothed his wrath and thus founded the eternal covenant with the priestly tribe of the Aaronides; verses 16-18: God's speech calls on Moses to kill the Midianites because of the business with Baal of Peor and Cozbi, who was murdered on the day of the plague.

Apart from proper names (Israel, Israelites, Midian, YHWH, Baal of Peor) and terms relating to descent or membership ("daughters," "daughter," "sons," "son," "father," "house," "the people"), scarcely any words are repeated in the text. Thus descent and membership in the family or nation are important to the text. They establish oppositions, and at the same time they structure the text in sections: verses 1-5, the *daughters* of Moab and Israel, or the people; verses 6-13, the Israelites (Hebrew "sons/children of Israel") and the *Midianite woman;* verses 14-15, Zimri and *Cozbi* as son and daughter of their fathers and tribes; verse 18, God's final speech, which explicitly sets aside such contrasts and yet builds on them.

That is, *the delimiting of Israel–Moab/Midian is a central theme of the text and is expressed through hereditary relationships and the contrast between man and woman, with the foreign always expressed by the woman or women.*

The only person whose descent is clearly stated, but as an *absolute,* with no opposite, is the *priest* Phinehas. His position evidently does not require definition in terms of an Other. Another thing that distinguishes Phinehas is that he is the only one of the leadership elite who in some sense acts according to God's instruction, while the assembled community apparently "only" stands by and weeps. What is shocking is that God's command legitimates the murder.

The only synonymous words in the text have to do with killing (v. 4c: "impale"; v. 5a: "kill"; v. 8b: "pierce"; v. 11c: "consume"; vv. 14, 15, 17, 18: "slay," "kill"). On the narrative level only one verb is used in the active voice, describing Phinehas's deed (v. 8b). The remaining "verbs of killing" in the narrative text are formulated in the passive (v. 14a: "the slain Israelite"; v. 14b: "who was killed"; v. 15a: "the Midianite woman who was killed"). All the other verbs that speak of killing appear in the speeches. These speeches, however, all proceed "from top to bottom"; they are the commands of a higher-up to a person lower on the ladder (God to Moses or Moses to the judges). The result is that killing proceeds from the more powerful, since even Phinehas, as a priest with whom God makes an everlasting covenant, is more powerful than just any Israelite (so the Hebrew formulation is to be understood). *Power is thus expressed in this text through violent killing.*

Numbers 25 constructs the separation of Israel from Moab/Midian, and thus the Stranger, the Other, in terms of the category of gender (adultery and the story of Cozbi and Zimri; for the connection between separation/exclusion and sexuality, see 5:1-4, 12-31). This is connected to the question of who claims *the power to decide about life and death* (God, Moses, and priests!).

In addition, this theme of division and separation is interwoven with the legitimation of the Aaronide priesthood. It inserts itself into all these aspects and thus is, alongside God, *the* power in the text: Phinehas forces himself into the intimate relationship between two people and thus claims for himself the power to define what sexual conduct is allowed and what is not. He also represents the "right" worship, for even if there is no explicit contrast drawn with the celebrations in verse 2, he is allied with God (the right one) and makes decisions about life and death.

The image for what is foreign is the women of the other nation. It is nothing new that especially women, and indeed those of a different ethnicity, stand for "the Other" (Moab/Midian). But it is important to make this clear, even in central biblical texts. This text is central because it sets Israel apart, because it thus defines and establishes (group) identity and because it gives preeminence to a single authority. In this text women represent the foreign cult (Moabites) and sexuality (the Midianite Cozbi). The text rejects both, because — within the system — each is deadly and unclean.

The assembly of the whole community (v. 6) and the priestly class are regarded as legal institutions in the postexilic period (Crüsemann 1992, 126ff.). Inasmuch as the former resists the divine command to kill, it stands for those who did not pursue the extermination of Midian and thus the exclusion of the Other as vehemently as did the priestly class.

Numbers 27:1-11 and 36:1-13: Being a Daughter Is Not a Strong Lobbying Position

Numbers 27 and 36 are connected because in both cases the issue is the right of inheritance of the daughters of Zelophehad. Chapter 36 is often regarded as an expansion and specification of chapter 27, but in fact it weakens the point of Numbers 27.

A Gentle Inquiry and Its Sociopolitical Consequences?

In Numbers 27:4 the daughters of Zelophehad petition for their inheritance (*'ăḥuzzâ*), which certainly refers to land. This follows both from the meaning of the word *'ăḥuzzâ* and from the context of Numbers 26, which is about the division of the land. Ownership of land also implied rights that may likewise have been of interest to the daughters. The reason for the accounting in chapter 26, after all, was not only the division of the land, but also the ordering of the society as such. (Other texts concerned with this ordering are, e.g., chapters 1; 2; 3:14-39; 10:1-10, 11-36.)

We can discern four important points in the daughters' argument. They emphasize (1) the death of their father, mentioning it twice, and emphasize (2) that he had no sons (this is also said twice). But (3) no personal interests are alluded to, and (4) they distance their father, and thus themselves, from the rebellion of the Korahites (Num 16; see Sterring 1994, 88-89).

Their main argument is that the name of their father must not "be taken away." Since this formulation is unique in the First Testament, we can only guess at its meaning: it is possible that it points to patrilineal inheritance (26:52-56). The name of the father is retained when the daughters are empowered to inherit land in the same way accorded to sons.

Why do the daughters mention the "company of Korah"? Current commentaries say this is because the Korahites had lost their right to inherit the land by their rebellion against Moses and Aaron (much like Miriam in Num 12). That is improbable, if only because Korah belonged to the tribe of Levi, who did not inherit any part of the land in any case (18:20-24, and frequently). Korah's crime was that he attacked the divine order by questioning Moses and Aaron. The daughters of Zelophehad might be accused of something similar, and therefore they distance themselves from that incident and its consequences (Sterring 1994, 90). Their primary difference from the Korahites, however, is that they do not question Moses' authority; rather, they lay claim to it on behalf of their interest. They really do act intelligently.

The general law formulated in verses 8-11 (according to which God approves the daughters' position) makes it clear that brothers (of the deceased and his father, vv. 9-10) are the group within the family who have primacy in inheritance.

When a man dies without sons, his wife, who is identified within the First Testament's social laws as a widow and the poorest of the poor, has no resources, but the daughter takes precedence over all other male members of the family.

A Clash between Men and Women

A comparison with chapter 36 clarifies the daughters' right of inheritance. The arguments of the Gileadite heads of families — that is, the families to which Zelophehad belonged — reveal a great deal. (1) They emphasize the authority of the law (v. 2), but point out some distinctions within it. Whereas *God commanded Moses* to divide the land by lots, Moses *was commanded BY God* to give Zelophehad's inheritance to his daughters. The second law seems not to have been given so directly, and to be less essential. (2) They point out that the distribution of the land takes place by lot, and therefore should not be meddled with (vv. 2, 3). (3) They draw boundaries between the tribes. The words *maṭṭeh* and *šebeṭ* do not appear in Numbers 27, and they apply to the drawing of boundaries between one's own tribe and the others, to whom nothing is to be surrendered (vv. 3, 4). (4) The family heads' problem is not that a name will be taken away, but rather the land (vv. 3, 4). This presumes that the property of a woman goes to her husband as soon as she marries. The variant, well attested in the Bible, by which a man marries into his wife's tribe (cf. Ezra 2:61; Neh 7:61-64), is not considered (Sterring 1994, 93).

These two texts also attest that the rules for women's rights and property extant in the postexilic period in the Jewish colony at Elephantine in Egypt did not apply to Palestine, or at least that attempts to apply them failed (contra Eskenazi 1992, 31-32).

While the family heads argue with authority, the status quo, and the division of property, but do not make any explicit demands, the interest of Zelophehad's daughters is in the concrete case, a situation that demands a resolution (so also Sakenfeld 1992, 51). They are not afraid of losing their property to another tribe, but of losing it to their own, although in contrast to their uncles they do not construct an opposing party. Sterring sees features in the behavior of the family heads that are typical of a patriarchal society: they act as soon as their own status and security are endangered (1994, 94). *The actual condition corresponds to the divine order (which also is central in chapter 26), and in the eyes of the family heads it is being called into question by the daughters of Zelophehad.* (For the importance of the order, cf. the enumeration in chapters 1; 2; 3:14-29, and frequently elsewhere, or in 7:1-88; 8:1-4.)

Chapter 36 concludes in shocking fashion: the family heads win, and the general law is that daughters who have no brothers must marry their cousins (v. 11), even though in verse 6 God had still insisted that they might marry "whom they think best." But that puts us back at the beginning of chapter 27: it is not the brothers of the deceased who inherit, but their sons. The women's hope for a right to participate in decisions and management, still a reality in 27:11, is thus destroyed. *Patrilineal inheritance is made the rule, and the final verse (36:13) claims God as the authority for this.*

Numbers 30:2-17 (1-16): Controlling Women's Religious Practices

Numbers 30 concerns itself with the question of when women's vows are valid and when they are not. However, we find no instructions for women about when, for what purpose, and in what form they may make a vow; instead, there are *laws for men* who, as fathers and husbands, may annul their daughters' or wives' vows. It may be that in the postexilic period vows were a common form of religious practice (cf. 6:1-21; 15:1-10).

We can observe the following about women's religious and social reality: (1) It was part of women's religious practice to make vows (cf. also Hannah in 1 Sam 1:11; Num 6:2 makes it clear that women, too, could make Nazirite vows); but (2) in doing so, the women remained completely under the control of their "supervisory" men, their fathers or husbands, whom they apparently had to inform about their intentions (Num 30:5, 6, 8, 9, 12, 13 [4, 5, 7, 8, 11, 12]). The text reveals something about this: while women are the subjects of religious actions, which gives the impression that they enjoyed self-determination, the text formulates laws for men, and not a single instruction for women. This is about how *men should exercise control over women.* (3) Nothing is said about the fact *that* they have this position of power, since that is presumed as a matter of course.

Numbers 31:1-54: War, Uncleanness/Cleanness, and What Women Have to Do with It

This chapter describes one of the first wars conducted by Israel. When, in what follows, the terms "just war" and "holy war" are used, it is because the First Testament has no comprehensive term for these struggles, and yet it does legitimate the killing. A reason is given for the war; it has a goal (e.g., extermination of undesirable, economic "demands") that is justified, and then the injustice and insanity of war are pushed into the background. This way of proceeding is by no means unique to ancient Israel and is not intended here to emphasize the violence of the First Testament scriptures. Rather, this is about pointing to a facet of ancient (and modern) war strategy that defends the interests of the victors and does not ask about the losers and the slaughtered.

Numbers 31 follows thematically on Numbers 25: the key words "Midian," "Midianites," and "Baal of Peor" are taken up again (31:2, 3, 7, 9, 15-17), and God's command to Moses (25:17-18) is carried out. But in addition, Midian's attempt to have Israel cursed by the seer Balaam (Num 22–24) is given as a reason for the war (31:16: the Midianite women in Num 25 were acting on Balaam's advice). The strict *division between "us" and "them,"* so noticeable in Numbers 25, is likewise characteristic of chapter 31 (Niditch 1993, 44, and elsewhere). In the first part, verses 1-24, the Israelites are regularly distinguished from Midian (vv. 2, 9) or Balaam and Baal of Peor (v. 16).

This is a war text; it already envisions well-organized troops with divisions of thousands and hundreds, embedded in a clearly hierarchical society of priests, commanders, soldiers, and civilian population (Niditch 1993, 48). Phinehas, the priest already known to us from Numbers 25 as a murderer, leads the murderous army (31:7-8), not with the implements of war, but with those of the temple (v. 6). The war is thus declared to be a *holy war* and is understood as a "just war" (for the significance and legitimation of war, cf. 32:2-27; Niditch 1993, 41-42). But it is burdened by a certain ambivalence: although justified, killing and contact with the dead still make one unclean, and the soldiers have to carry out some precisely described washings (31:19-24).

The foci of the text can be perceived in the use of the word *kōl* (all, every one). It appears very frequently in verses 1-24, but then not again until verse 52. *Kōl* appears in connection with *war and killing* (vv. 4, 7, 9, 10, 11, 15, 17, 18) and also *purity/cleanness* (vv. 19, 20, 23), both areas of boundary drawing. In war and killing, the separation between "us" and "the others" comes to light, since the others are to be eliminated. But these two themes also melt into one another because the men become unclean through killing, and because in cases of uncleanness/cleanness the issue is who may belong to the camp and who may not. This connection appears clearly again when we consider why, out of the whole Midianite population, only the virginal young women are not to be murdered. The question of who is to be killed is not about the logic of war, but about purity. Deuteronomy 21:10-14 tells how Israelites are to deal with captured women. There it is unimportant whether the woman is a virgin or not; she must only submit to a "transitional rite." Numbers 31 draws the security fence much tighter. The woman must be a virgin, because she might already be "soiled" by a non-Israelite, and just to be really sure, she should not even have reached the age of puberty. That is also the reason why male children are not to be left alive. As adult men they would bring foreign (polluting) seed into Israel (Niditch 1993, 50-51).

Texts about women in the book of Numbers address areas that are central to a patriarchal social system. They concern the question of who and what is not accepted in the group. The question of the category of uncleanness/cleanness (Num 5; 12) and the foreign (Num 25; 31) is treated within the Priestly context. Strict ordinances run through the whole book and are intended to secure the system; they push women to the margins, restricting them to the role of wives (Num 5; 30) or daughters (Num 30), but in every case they are men's dependents. Numbers is also aware of women as critics (Num 12; 20; 27; 36). Thus women stand at the margins, or outside the order. These observations come to a focus in the text that tells of Miriam's death; there the boundaries are very clear: women on the margins, an unpleasant, despised place, but with a good view.

LITERATURE

Bach, Alice. 1993. "Good to the Last Drop: Viewing the Sotah (Numbers 5:11-31) as the Glass Half Empty and Wondering How to View It Half Full." In *The New Literary Criticism and the Hebrew Bible*, edited by J. Cheryl Exum and David J. A. Clines, 26-54. Journal for the Study of the Old Testament: Supplement Series, vol. 143. Sheffield.

Be'er, Ilana. 1994. "Blood Discharge: On Female Im/Purity in the Priestly Code and in Biblical Narrative." In *A Feminist Companion to Exodus to Deuteronomy*, edited by Athalya Brenner, 152-64. Sheffield.

Brenner, Athalya, ed. 1994. *A Feminist Companion to Exodus to Deuteronomy*. Sheffield.

Burns, Rita J. 1987. *Has the Lord Indeed Spoken Only through Moses? A Study of the Biblical Portrait of Miriam*. Society of Biblical Literature Dissertation Series, vol. 84. Atlanta.

Camp, Claudia V. 1985. *Wisdom and the Feminine in the Book of Proverbs*. Sheffield.

Crüsemann, Frank. 1992. *Die Tora. Theologie und Sozialgeschichte des alttestamentlichen Gesetzes*. Munich.

Eskenazi, Tamara. 1992. "Out from the Shadows: Biblical Women in the Post-exilic Era." *Journal for the Study of the Old Testament* 54:25-43.

Jost, Renate. 1994. "Die Töchter deines Volkes prophezeien." In *Für Gerechtigkeit streiten. Theologie im Alltag einer bedrohten Welt*, edited by Dorothee Sölle, 59-64. Gütersloh.

Kessler, Rainer. 1996. "Mirjam und die Prophetie der Perserzeit." In *Gott an den Rändern. Sozialgeschichtliche Perspektiven auf die Bibel*, edited by Ulrike Bail and Renate Jost, 64-72. Festschrift for Willy Schottroff. Gütersloh.

Niditch, Susan. 1993. "War, Women and Defilement in Numbers 31." *Semeia* 61:39-57.

Sakenfeld, Katharine Doob. 1992. "Numbers." In *The Women's Bible Commentary*, edited by Carol A. Newsom and Sharon H. Ringe, 45-51. London and Louisville.

Schroer, Silvia. 1995. "Auf dem Weg zu einer feministischen Rekonstruktion der Geschichte Israels." In *Feministische Exegese. Forschungsbeiträge zur Bibel aus der Perspektive von Frauen*, edited by Luise Schottroff, Silvia Schroer, and Marie-Theres Wacker, 81-172. Darmstadt.

———. 1998. *Feminist Interpretation: The Bible in Women's Perspective*. Translated by Barbara Rumscheidt and Martin Rumscheidt. Minneapolis: Fortress.

Schüngel-Straumann, Helen. 1982. "Frauen im Alten Testament." *Der evangelische Erzieher* 34:496-506.

———. 1984. "Frauen in der Bibel." In *Christ in der Gegenwart* 36:239, 247, 255, 271, 279, 287, 295, 303, 311, 319, 327, 343.

Sterring, Ankie. 1994. "The Will of the Daughters." In *A Feminist Companion to Exodus to Deuteronomy*, edited by Athalya Brenner, 88-99. Sheffield.

Trible, Phyllis. 1994. "Bringing Miriam out of the Shadows." In *A Feminist Companion to Exodus to Deuteronomy*, edited by Athalya Brenner, 166-86. Sheffield.

Valtink, Eveline. 1996. "Feministisch-christliche Identität und Antijudaismus." In *Von der*

Wurzel getragen. Christlich-feministische Exegese in Auseinandersetzung mit Antijudaismus, edited by Luise Schottroff and Marie-Theres Wacker, 1-26. Leiden.
Wacker, Marie-Theres. 1988. "Mirjam. Kritischer Mut einer Prophetin." In *Zwischen Ohnmacht und Befreiung. Biblische Frauengestalten,* edited by Karin Walter, 44-52. Freiburg, Basel, and Vienna.

FOR FURTHER READING

Ackerman, Susan. 2002. "Why Is Miriam Also among the Prophets? (and Is Zipporah among the Priests?)." *Journal of Biblical Literature* 121, no. 1:47-80.
Bachmann, García Mercedes. 2009. "Mirjam als politische Führungsfigur beim Exodus." In *Tora. Die Bibel und die Frauen. Eine exegetisch-kulturgeschichtliche Enzyklopädie,* edited by Irmtraud Fischer, Mercedes Navarro-Puerto, and Andrea Taschl-Erber, vol. 1, 1, 305-46. Stuttgart (forthcoming in English).
Butting, Klara. 2001. *Prophetinnen gefragt: Die Bedeutung der Prophetinnen im Kanon aus Tora und Prophetie. Erev-Rav-Hefte: Biblisch-feministische Texte.* Vol. 3. Knesebeck.
Camp, Claudia V. 2003. "Over Her Dead Body: The Estranged Woman and the Price of the Promised Land." *Journal of Northwest Semitic Languages* 29:1-13.
Fischer, Irmtraud. 2002. *Gotteskünderinnen: Zu einer geschlechterfairen Deutung des Phänomens der Prophetie und der Prophetinnen der hebräischen Bibel.* Stuttgart.
Mbuwayesango, Dora R. 2003. "Can Daughters Be Sons? The Daughters of Zelophehad in Patriarchal and Imperial Society." In *Relating to the Text: Interdisciplinary and Form-Critical Insights on the Bible,* edited by Timothy Sandoval and Carleen Mandolfo, 251-62. Journal for the Study of the Old Testament: Supplement Series, vol. 384. London and New York.
Rapp, Ursula. 2002. *Mirjam: Eine feministisch-rhetorische Lektüre der Mirjamtexte in der hebräischen Bibel.* Beihefte zur Zeitschrift für die alttestamentliche Wissenschaft, vol. 317. Berlin.
Shemesh, Yael. 2007. "A Gender Perspective on the Daughters of Zelophehad: Bible, Talmudic Midrash, and Modern Feminist Midrash." *Biblical Interpretation* 15, no. 1:80-109.

Translated by Linda M. Maloney

Deuteronomy: Rights and Justice for Women in the Law

Angelika Engelmann

General Remarks and Setting the Mood

Deuteronomy has been called the center of the Old Testament (Gerhard von Rad), and Frank Crüsemann dubs the Deuteronomic law (Deut 12–26) the core of the biblical canon (1992, 310). Its content centers on these principal themes: the one chosen people is to have only one place of worship for the one God, YHWH. These central ideas of so-called cult centralization, unity of worship, and purity of cult played a prominent role especially from the late royal period in Israel's history onward.

This description raises the question whether the aims of Deuteronomy were undisputed and a matter of general consensus in the community, or whether there were other voices and movements as well. Where and how did those people react who found these centralizing ideas to be a restriction of religious diversity? Matriarchal feminists have attempted an answer, contrasting the (masculine) history of monotheism with the (feminine) history of remembrance and return to the religion of the Great Goddess (especially Weiler 1989).

These central themes of Deuteronomy, especially in relation to biblical monotheism, on the one hand, and the nonmonotheistic religious forms in biblical Israel and its surrounding world, on the other, have thus far been only occasional objects of feminist theological discussion and research (cf. Wacker 1991c and the bibliography listed there). Marie-Theres Wacker (1991a, 17-18) has given a detailed overview of the state of discussion of monotheism itself.

The fifth book of Moses is complete in itself, but thus far there have been only a few preliminary successes in attempting to discover its "internal principles of organization and subdivision" (Crüsemann 1992, 239). The book is stylized as a discourse by Moses, and consequently it is placed between the books that tell of the wilderness wandering (Numbers) and the entry into the land (Joshua). This ordering corresponds to the book's internal aim; Moses offers a great formal retrospect and prospect. The composition and thematic anchoring of Deuteronomy in the two great corpuses of the Pentateuch and the Deuteronomistic Historical Work is in itself revealing of its outstanding significance.

However, as for its origins, we cannot premise either Mosaic authorship or a dating of the book to Israel's early years. The title "Deuteronomy" indicates that this fifth book of Moses is a *mišnê hattôrâ*, a copy. According to Deuteronomy 17:18, when the king has ascended the throne he is to cause a copy (LXX here uses the word *deuteronomium*) of the book preserved by the Levitical priests to be prepared. But the Deuteronomy we have is not simply a copy of a law book preserved in that or any other way; a comparison between it and, for example, the Book of the Covenant (Exod 21–23) makes it clear that Deuteronomy is not an expansion or development of an existing corpus of laws, but something new. Why was it apparently necessary, at a particular historical moment, to create an altogether new work? And when was that? Scholarly literature on this set of problems (although it has taken scarcely any account of feminist questions) is very extensive and controversial (cf. Crüsemann 1992, 235 n. 2). In this essay I will primarily follow Crüsemann's research because, on the one hand, it is well grounded, and on the other hand, it does not ignore feminist questions. In general I will assume that a basic text of Deuteronomy, including the Deuteronomic law in Deuteronomy 12–26, stems from the northern kingdom and was brought to Jerusalem in 722 B.C.E. There it played an authoritative role in King Josiah's reform. Other scholarship assumes that the Deuteronomic law itself was composed at that time (on this cf. Crüsemann 1992, 251-52).

A general division of Deuteronomy reveals a clear structure: the major section, the Deuteronomic law (12–26), is surrounded by the groups of introductory discourses (1–11) and concluding discourses (27–30); Deuteronomy 31–34 then constitutes a conclusion to the whole of the Pentateuch, the Torah.

Patriarchy and Deuteronomy

At least since Elisabeth Schüssler Fiorenza's book *Bread Not Stone* (1984, xi), it has been axiomatic in feminist theology that "the Bible is not only written in the words of men but also serves to legitimate patriarchal power and oppression." Under that premise, with regard to Deuteronomy as a whole and the Deuteronomic law in particular, there arise such questions as the following: For whom are these laws meant? Who formulated them? When and why were they proposed? Why was it apparently necessary to formulate the family laws in particular in such detail?

A comparison to the Book of the Covenant proves interesting. There we find only one relevant law (Exod 22:15-16[Eng. 16-17]), which is mentioned in relation to restitution. When a daughter is raped, her father is entitled to damages from the rapist if he refuses to marry her. This law alone illustrates not only patriarchal thinking and acting, but also how women are objects and not subjects in legal texts (on this, see also Frymer-Kensky 1992, 54).

But against this background it is striking that in Deuteronomy women are described differently, namely, as subjects as well as objects. Frank Crüsemann has shown that women's legal position in Deuteronomy is quite varied (1992, 291ff., and also Crüsemann and Thyen 1978, 21ff.). It is true that the legal texts reflect a male world: the legal machinery is almost exclusively in men's hands and the texts address themselves to men and make them the subjects of the law. The legal texts in which women are explicitly mentioned show them to be legally dependent throughout their lives, first on their fathers and then on their husbands. In only a few cases — for example, as widow or as mother — are they in any position to act independently before the law. Nevertheless, the legal position of women should not be derived solely from these texts in which women appear explicitly. Feminist linguistics has made us aware of the phenomenon of inclusive language (cf. Pusch 1990, 43). If we are to determine the legal position of women in the Hebrew Bible in general and in Deuteronomy in particular, we must always ask whether women are included in the texts in question or not. Crüsemann has proposed a working hypothesis for Deuteronomy:

> Women are not excluded from every text that speaks of men; rather, they are everywhere *included in the meaning* of the inclusive language of the legal and cultic texts, unless they are explicitly excluded or, because of other circumstances, do not come within the scope of the text. The important language of Deuteronomy that addresses the free, landowning men as "you," "thou," as representatives of the people as a whole, does not relegate women to the groups that are not addressed — such as Levites, priests, foreigners, and slaves — but instead includes them in the "you" being addressed. Thus, the Exodus and the ownership of the Land, and so the broad scope of the deuteronomic Torah, belongs to them, too. (Crüsemann 1992, 94)

Deuteronomy has a striking interest in determining matters of marriage and family law. One reason for this could be that Deuteronomy was intended, on the one hand, to address the urban conditions of the late royal period, when a dissolution of the ancient tribal customs was in progress and there was a corresponding need to have interfamilial conflicts decided by the court of the elders, meeting in public at the gate of the city or town. This massive reduction of the rights of the paterfamilias then signified a previously unknown legal security for all those who were subject to patriarchal power — women and children, for example. In interfamilial and sexual conflicts these laws protected them from the legal violence of the husband/father, since the public court was responsible for all such conflicts. At the same time, and on the other hand, however, these laws supported the Deuteronomic interest in cultic purity and unity (cf. Crüsemann and Thyen 1978, 23-24, and Crüsemann 1992, 299-300).

Hence a critique of patriarchy in Deuteronomy begins both within the family and in the public social sphere. It cannot be clearly determined, nor has it been investigated as regards individual historical periods, whether, for example, the public sphere of the elders at the gate was exclusively male at all times. It was in particular the elders of the congregations who, in their political and judicial function as local officials, were responsible for the preservation of both divine and civil law. According to what is said in the book of Judges, Deborah (Judg 4–5) was also part of that group. In a different way Huldah, for example (2 Kings 22), exercised a public office. The task of the elders, as leaders and representatives of the people, was certainly not restricted to men, if we consider the importance of Miriam (Exod 15:20; Num 12; Mic 6:4) as a leader alongside Moses. Unfortunately, this thematic area has not yet been the object of First Testament study to an adequate extent, and a one-sided attribution of public offices and leadership functions to men remains an issue open to discussion even today.

Deuteronomy 1–11

Chapters 1–3 are made up of a speech by Moses, a grand historical retrospective from Horeb to the entry into the land from the territory east of the Jordan, and a warning to keep the commandments. What is especially interesting here is that the first commandment is joined to the second, and the prohibition of images from Exodus 20:4-5 is thus augmented by an essential idea. The command in Deuteronomy 4:16 that prohibits making an image of God is made concrete by the specification that no image of any kind of creature may be made, either male or female. Here the same words are used for male and female as in Genesis 1:27. Of course, there it is said that the human being is made in the image of God, male and female. Thus in Deuteronomy the idea that God cannot be imaged in any expressive form, whether male or female, is very clearly sharpened.

In the introductory discourse in Deuteronomy 1–3 we encounter the theological purpose that extends through 2 Kings and that, because of its orientation to Deuteronomy, is called Deuteronomistic: YHWH has led the people, but the people were fearful and disobedient and did not believe. So YHWH's wrath was enkindled, and he acted accordingly.

Chapters 5–11 begin a second introductory speech whose subject is the election of Israel through YHWH's love; further warnings then follow. A text of special interest is the repetition of the Decalogue from Exodus 20:2-17 in Deuteronomy 5:6-21. The most significant deviation from Exodus 20 here is the extended grounding given the Sabbath commandment, through a recollection of life in Egypt and the exodus, whereas in Exodus 20 the Sabbath rest is founded on the seventh day of creation, the day on which the Creator rested (cf. Deut 5:15 with Exod 20:11). For an in-depth examination of research on the Decalogue by First Testament scholars, see Crüsemann 1992, 408-9, and other works cited below.

The Decalogue has had a more profound influence in the history of Christian theology than almost any other text of the Hebrew Bible, affecting ethics and catechetics. It is just this exalted significance that needs to be called into question; we offer here, simply by way of suggestion, three notes. Absent from the Decalogue are certain essential basic themes of the rest of the Torah: for example, protection of the weak in society and of marginal groups deprived of rights, and behavior toward nature, the animals and plants. Deuteronomy 10:12-22 posits a clearly partisan attitude toward the weak (namely, orphans, widows, and strangers). Thus it is clear even within Deuteronomy that the Decalogue does not encompass all the essential themes of social ethics. Jewish exegesis and tradition have therefore, for this reason in particular, maintained a certain skepticism toward the special place of the Decalogue in Christian theology. Finally, matriarchal-feminist criticism (but not only that) has been piqued by the Decalogue's structure of prohibition and command, so that complete reversals have been proposed as woman-relevant interpretations of the text: for example, Elga Sorge's "Ten Permissions" (Sorge 1987).

These restrictive remarks are by no means intended to devalue the Decalogue; they are only pointers to expansions and an exposure of interests relevant to the issue of the "canon within the canon." "God's will is found in the Torah; it is formulated in the fullness of the commandments given at Sinai. The ten words are only their beginning. They are something special, as a human head is something special. But if it is separated from the rest of the body, they are both dead. And something like that has often been done to the Decalogue" (Crüsemann 1995, 44).

In Judaism, the *"shema' Israel"* in Deuteronomy 6:4-9, together with Deuteronomy 11:13-21, Numbers 15:37-41, and various blessings, make up the text that is brought to mind daily in morning and evening prayer. It is a central word of faith. Here commandment has become prayer, and this reveals the Jewish understanding of tradition, according to which it is not doctrine but life that is the foundation of community. In Judaism, women are not obligated to study Scripture, and yet "that 'Hear, O Israel,' . . . has become the spiritual guiding word of the Jewish people throughout the centuries" (Goodman-Thau 1989, 65). The Jewish theologian Eveline Goodman-Thau expresses it this way: "When we recite the *shema',* we grasp the uniqueness of every human being and the unity between man and woman, since both were created as God's image (Gen 1:27; 5:2). We are able to express this unity and so become part of revelation" (Goodman-Thau 1989, 65). In the Talmud there is a discussion between men about whether women should recite the *shema'* or not, or whether they are capable of doing it. But in any case, women have prayed it in every age (Levinson 1992, 131). Likewise, there is a discussion about the inclusion or exclusion of women from the Sabbath commandment: daughters and virgins should keep it, but the participation of married women is unclear.

Deuteronomy 12–26

The Deuteronomic law in chapters 12–26 is the center of the book. However, the biblical outline scheme for the many laws, ordinances, and directions in this corpus is not clearly evident in all cases. It is certainly true that the techniques by which the material in ancient Near Eastern law codes was arranged do not correspond to modern principles of legal organization (Lohfink 1977, 66). But given the abundance of material, we can select only a few themes, and even those can be addressed only in general terms.

The following selection is primarily concerned with the laws that explicitly or implicitly speak thematically about women. This does not adequately attend to the principle referred to above, according to which women are always included where they are not explicitly excluded, but given the breadth of the themes, this seems the best way to proceed. However, the decision to begin with a brief look at the laws concerning offices in Deuteronomy 16:18–18:22 is directly related to that basic principle: we want to test them to see to what extent they can be understood inclusively.

The Laws for Offices

Norbert Lohfink (1977, 65ff.) has produced an impressive redaction-critical exposition of how we can demonstrate, behind the individual laws for offices (Deut 16:18–17:13: rules for judges, officials; 17:14-20: rules for the king; 18:1-8: rules for the priests; 18:9-22: rules for prophets), an overarching system of law. The principal authorities are placed in relationship to one another by a clearly conceived principle. Judges and officials, the king, the priests, and the prophets are the exponents of secular and spiritual power. It is possible that a principal redaction of this part of the Deuteronomic law was intended to shape an overall system of laws for the leading authorities in Israel, and so presented a proposal for a constitution. That proposal seems to have been more a theoretical concept, a utopian theory, than a description of the existing reality (Lohfink 1977, 68). It is interesting to inquire of this process, when Israel gave itself a kind of fundamental law: What was the position of women in that society? In which offices and functions would we encounter them? They were probably not considered in the context of the laws for office, but are to be thought of as the wives, respectively, of the judges, officials, kings, priests, and prophets. But especially with regard to the prophetic office we can demonstrate that women also exercised it: for example, Miriam, Deborah, Huldah. Huldah in particular is a clear example of the acceptance of women in leadership functions. In connection with the discovery of the law during the renovations in the temple, 2 Kings 22 reports that King Josiah sought advice from *her,* a woman, and her alone, about what the discovery of this law might mean.

It is still a worthwhile task to undertake a closer investigation of the history of female participation in the public offices recorded by the Bible in Israel's history.

Rights for the Weak and the Poor

Some laws mention orphans and widows, as well as foreigners, with the intention that in certain situations these groups are to be accorded special care or attention. Interesting in this connection are the laws in Deuteronomy 24:17-18, 19, 20-22. In all three of these laws the phrase "you were a slave in Egypt" gives the reason why the rights of orphans and foreigners may not be bent, and a widow's garment may not be taken as security. The sheaves forgotten in the fields and the olives still hanging in the trees after the first beating are also to be set aside for the foreigners, orphans, and widows. Israel, which is addressed by these laws, is not to forget that it was enslaved in Egypt and is to remember YHWH's redeeming deed. Here we find protective laws formulated for those in need of protection, corresponding to the theological intent of Deuteronomy 10:12-22: YHWH does justice for the orphans and widows and loves the foreigner, giving them food and clothing. Above all, childless widows who could not return to their parents' house had, for the most part, a very difficult life, and therefore they required special protection. In Deuteronomy, as well as in Exodus 22:21(22), this need for protection is formulated as a religious obligation.

Deuteronomy 24:6 belongs in this same context. It is forbidden to take both millstones in pledge. Women, including also slave women, needed their handmills to bake bread, and if they had to give them in pledge they would starve. Life is equated with the ability to provide for life's needs.

The system of the social safety net (Crüsemann 1992, 269) is here made visible. Problem groups in that society, including widows and orphans, but also all those whose task was to see to people's material needs, are to be protected so that they can live. We should refer briefly to a very different law here, because it mentions a woman by name as a monitory example of false dealing. In Deuteronomy 24:8-9 it is demanded that in cases of leprosy the rules prescribed by the priests are to be followed exactly, and one is to act according to the corresponding ordinances. Further, the text recalls Miriam in Numbers 12:10-15: she was punished by YHWH with leprosy. Numbers 12 is not an unproblematic text; we can see in it, among other things, leadership rivalries between Miriam and Moses. But as far as the law in Deuteronomy 24:8-9 is concerned, that view of Miriam has long become irrelevant; she is cited for the purpose of illustrating what will happen to anyone who does not follow the orders of the priests regarding certain purity regulations. The recollection of Miriam serves as a warning. This is a misuse of women's history, even if the necessity of purity regulations is by no means disputed. What interests are concealed behind this set of justifications?

Laws regarding Adultery and Sexual Assault

The laws in Deuteronomy regarding sexuality give us good insights into the laws concerning families and marriage in the late royal period and clearly reflect patriarchal conditions.

This is immediately apparent in the law concerning adultery in Deuteronomy 22:22: "If a man is caught lying with the wife of another man, both of them shall die." What is interesting here is that only the familial state of the woman is indicated. It makes no difference whether the man is married or not; he can only violate someone else's marriage. The law provides for the punishment of both parties to adultery, but the betrayed husband is forbidden to impose punishment himself. Here Deuteronomy assumes a locus of decision making that is different, for example, from Proverbs 6:32-35, which at least suggests the possibility that the betrayed husband could consider taking payment as reparation. According to Deuteronomy, the public court alone can pass judgment and carry out the sentence (Crüsemann 1992, 299). The woman is protected in a sense: in such a case she is not subject to the arbitrary decision of her husband. Autonomous or lynch "justice" is not proposed. However, it remains an open question whether the rule that the sentence of death is to be pronounced and carried out not by the husband, but by the elders at the gate, represents an act of justice toward the woman. In contrast, the decision of the betrayed husband according to Proverbs 6:32-35 at least offers some wiggle room or, better, openness to life.

Four laws concerning family and marriage in Deuteronomy deal with the themes of calumny of a young woman and rape of a virgin (on this see Locher 1986). The very number of these laws and the distinctions among the cases show that there was need for or interest in some regulation in this area. On the one hand, there is an association with the high degree of value accorded to women in tradition, observable elsewhere in the ancient Near East as well; on the other hand, it is precisely young women and virgins who are the subject of special laws. Who was served by these laws and who had an interest in writing them? The law in Deuteronomy 22:13-21 is especially revealing. It describes the case of a man who comes to dislike his wife and wants to get rid of her. He brings charges against her, saying that at the time of the marriage she was not a virgin. Two solutions are provided: First, the woman's parents are to contest the charge by bringing the proof of virginity, presenting the bloody sheet from the wedding night before the elders at the gate, publicly, thus convicting the husband of lying. Then the elders are to punish the husband and impose a fine on him, roughly double the bride-price, to be paid to the woman's father. The woman has to remain with her husband. He may not divorce her. In the other case, namely, that the husband's assertion is true or the proof cannot be produced, the woman is to be stoned at the door of her father's house by the men of the place because, while she was living in that house as her father's daughter, she did not remain a virgin.

The law regards the woman simply as an object and in both cases rules without reference to her about how the rights of the father or the husband can be upheld or protected. In the first case the subsequent public proof of her virginity at the time of her marriage is already degrading in itself, and it means that the woman is exposed, with no opportunity to defend herself or to prevent this from happening. Afterward, she must also stay with a husband who is anxious to get rid of her. Is this not further punishment for her, since her life with this man under these circumstances can scarcely be a happy one? In the other case, if there is some problem in proving her virginity, she is threatened with the death penalty. So, no matter whether a husband's charge is true or not, the woman is the one who suffers, in the literal sense of the words. Here patriarchal relationships are revealed in a way that is especially oppressive of women.

In her study, Locher mentions that the law does not address what happens to the innocent victims of rape (Locher 1986, 233). Crüsemann evaluates this law differently; he emphasizes that "the mere fact that the patriarchal power of the husband over his wife is broken by the rights of her family of origin, and by the possibility that he himself may experience severe punishment and loss of honor, is highly important. Not only sexual offenses, but sexual calumny will be tried in the public courts" (Crüsemann 1992, 298-99). Not a word is said about the fact that the punishment of the woman is very unequal to what the husband must bear in case his calumny is refuted. From the woman's perspective the law in Deuteronomy 22:13-21 may represent progress in comparison to the fathers' choices that are justified in Genesis 38:24 or Genesis 34. Nevertheless, the amount of dishonor and degradation that women must take upon themselves according to Deuteronomy 22:13-21 is such that the historical development in this regard from Israel's early period to the royal era is very difficult to interpret in a positive sense.

Three laws concern the rape of a betrothed or unbetrothed young woman. Deuteronomy 22:23-24 describes a situation in the city. A man rapes a betrothed woman; both are to be stoned outside the city: the woman because she was inside the city and did not call for help, and so had not offered any audible resistance. The man must die because he "violated his neighbor's wife." The two reasons given once again reveal the unequal situation of women and men. Still, the next law, in Deuteronomy 22:25-27, is interesting. It concerns the same deed: a man rapes a betrothed woman. But it happens in a different environment: not in the city, but in the country, where she cannot call anyone to her aid. In this case only the rapist must die, for the woman had no chance of defending herself. It is explicitly emphasized that she has no guilt that deserves death. This judgment is, of course, correct, but not a word is said about the injustice and suffering imposed on the woman. She and her rights do not occupy the attention of the lawgiver. In a further law, Deuteronomy 22:28-29, the case of sexual assault is again described. If the woman is not yet betrothed when she is raped, the man must pay her father, as compensation, the usual brideprice, and must marry her. He may not give her a writ of divorce; she has to live with her rapist for the rest of her life. This law is similar to the one in Exodus 22:15(16). There, however, the father of the woman can refuse to give his daughter to the rapist, and he still has a claim to compensation, to the amount of the bride-price. Neither in the Deuteronomistic formulation nor in Exodus 22 is the woman's situation considered. Similarly to Deuteronomy 22:13-21, the legal decision addresses the interests of the man (the rapist), the husband, or the father. In all these laws the woman is the object and not the subject of the process.

Thus, even if these family laws are a restriction on unlimited patriarchal power or paternal exercise of power, we must still insist in conclusion that rape and calumny are not clearly described as what they are: namely, injustice toward women. It is precisely this injury to their dignity and their honor that is not addressed by the laws. Injustice is named only in relation to the respective male family members whose property the woman is considered to be: father, husband, or wife of the neighbor. This perspective reveals androcentric thinking in a patriarchal society.

Divorce

In Israel a man had the right to end his marriage and give his wife a letter of divorce. The woman could then enter into a new marriage. Deuteronomy 24:1-4 establishes regulations for cases of remarriage. If the woman's second marriage ends, either because the husband has also given her a letter of divorce or because she has been widowed, the first husband may not marry that woman again. Sexual intercourse with the other husband has made her taboo for him. This law also reflects only male ideas. There is no consideration or mention of what it would mean for a woman if she were to marry her first husband again after having previously received a letter of divorce from him because she had become distasteful to him.

Levirate Marriage

Levirate marriage, or marriage between brother-in-law and sister-in-law, was the obligatory marriage of a childless widow to her brother-in-law, or possibly another of her late husband's relatives, in order to preserve the patrilineal line of descent, that is, the right of inheritance from the deceased. Ultimately, the levirate law thus also included the obligation to care for the childless woman. One problem with the levirate system seems to have been refusal by the male family member to beget offspring for the deceased. Genesis 38 may represent a model for women. There we find a very eventful and clever story about how the widowed Tamar, through her cunning and intelligence, bested her father-in-law when he tried to refuse her the levirate right. However, in practice the application of the levirate law seems in most cases to have presented more difficulty than the Tamar story indicates. Almost all the passages related to the levirate system are concerned with how to deal with the refusal of the men in question or the difficulties arising for women in trying to obtain their rights.

In Deuteronomy 25:5-6, marriage with a brother-in-law is presented as a normal law, by no means in contradiction to the prohibition of incest in Leviticus 18:16. Deuteronomy 25:7-10 deals in astonishing fashion with the refusal of the brother-in-law to fulfill his duty. The widow has the right to make a complaint before the elders at the gate and to accuse him there. Then the elders are to summon him and speak with him. If he continues to refuse, the woman can punish him with a ritual of shaming. In the presence of the elders — that is, in public — she is to take the shoe from his foot, spit in his face, and reproach him with the accusation that the house he has thus inherited is to be called a "barefoot house." What is interesting in this law is that the woman, as agent, while she cannot ultimately obtain her rights (different from Gen 38), can make the injustice public. The lawmaker is counting on the pressure of public opinion and the fear of exposure.

Rights of Inheritance

The patrilineal succession of inheritance and patrilocal family structures are the background for the law in Deuteronomy 21:15-17 concerning the inheritance rights of the firstborn, which are inviolable. The text depicts the concrete and perhaps not unusual case of a man with two wives, one of whom he loves and one he does not. The man may not neglect the inheritance rights of the firstborn, even if he is the son of the unloved wife, for "he is the first issue of his virility." The inheritance is not affected by the relationship the man has to the mothers of his sons; the order of begetting determines the rank regarding inheritance. This law may be a critique of, for example, Genesis 25:29-34, where the firstborn sells his birthright to his younger brother.

Laws Related to War

The broad field of war and military service yields some interesting laws that emphasize the great value of marriage. Deuteronomy 20:7 gives a rule that a man who is betrothed to a woman but has not yet married her is free from military service. He could be killed. This emphasizes the evaluation of marriage as superior to the necessities of war in certain cases.

Very similarly, Deuteronomy 24:5 says a man who has just married is to be free from military service for a year. These laws reveal the great significance of marriage, which was linked to the expectation of children.

Two laws mention women as the spoils of war. According to Deuteronomy 20:14, women, children, and animals are all legitimate booty, the gift of YHWH; they can be seized and enjoyed. With regard to a woman as booty, Deuteronomy 21:10-14 prescribes that the man may marry her if she pleases him, once she has laid aside the garb of a captive and mourned one month for her mother and father. But if she should cease to please him, he may not treat her or sell her as a slave; he must set her free. This law regulates the rights of a foreign woman in a surprising manner. Once a woman who was a prisoner of war has become an Israelite wife according to law, she is also due the letter of divorce, and she can go wherever she wants. Her husband must grant her that right.

Laws of Taboo

Deuteronomic law contains prohibitions associated with sexual taboos. Deuteronomy 25:11-12 clarifies a case in which two men are grappling with one another and the wife of one of them comes to the aid of her husband. The law prescribes that if she should take hold of the sexual organs of the other man, her hand is to be cut off. This harsh punishment of the woman with mutilation shows that the somewhat dangerous help given by the wife is less important than the possibility that she could take hold of a man's sexual organs. What kinds of fears or experiences lie behind this law?

Deuteronomy 23:1 (22:30; cf. Gen 9:21-29) is also about male feelings of shame. This says no one may lift up the hem of his father's garment so as to see his sexual organs. At the same time, this law formulates the taboo of the father's marriage. It is forbidden for a son to marry his mother or stepmother. In 1 Kings 2:17-21, in contrast, this is presumed, and is regarded as legally possible.

Two other laws (Deut 22:5 and Deut 23:18-19) are given the theological foundation "it is abhorrent to YHWH" or "YHWH hates it." Deuteronomy 22:5 forbids women to wear men's garments and men to wear women's garments. Was there an actual need for this law because the author feared the weakening of the externally evident role images of women and men? It remains an open question whether this law refers to transvestites or to the influence of Phoenician cultic practices (see Nielsen 1995, ad loc.). In Deuteronomy 23:17-18 it is forbidden for Israelite women and men to be *qĕdēšâ* (prostitutes). Such are not to enter the temple, and no wages of a prostitute could be brought into the temple. These legal provisions are apparently formulated because there were existing practices against which Deuteronomy wished to establish barriers. These are generally discussed under the rubric of "cultic prostitution," but such an institution has been sharply questioned in recent scholarship (cf., e.g., Frevel 1995, 643ff., and van der Toorn 1989, 193ff.). As regards the (female) *qĕdēšôt*, in the royal period such servants of God seem to have functioned alongside the priests in the context of the cult. They seem to have had roles in the sacrifices and probably were part of the staff of the temple. Possibly that was the reason they did not have families of their own and so may have been regarded as sexually available. By no means are they accurately described as prostitutes, even though we encounter that association, in a pejorative sense, in various biblical contexts (on this see Wacker 1996, 282-83). Deuteronomy 23:18-19 thus rejects "foreign" personnel at the temple and points toward a cultic purity that, historically speaking, never existed in this form.

The Asherah

The law in Deuteronomy 16:21 forbids anyone to plant or set up a sacred tree as an image of Asherah near the temple. Probably the prohibition refers to an existing state of things at the high altar of the temple at the time the law was written (Frevel 1995, 164-210). This opens up the extensive topic of the confrontation with the Asherah. The word "Asherah," on the one hand, is the name of a goddess, and, on the other, is a cultic object, usually a sacred tree, that could have been cut or carved for cultic purposes and was, together with stone *(maṣṣebet)* and altar, part of the standard inventory of a cultic high place. However, it would seem that the Asherah or Asherim did not play a part in the cult at the open-air sanctuaries, but rather in the political centers and central sanctuaries, including the temple in Jerusalem (1 Kings 15:13). In the books of Kings, we find traces indicating that at least in the southern kingdom an Asherah cult existed alongside the cult of YHWH for as long as three hundred years (on this cf. Schroer 1994, 17-18; Wacker 1991b, 140-41; Braulik 1991, 106-7).

Frevel, in his extensive investigation of Deuteronomy 16:21 (1995, 164-209), has attempted to show that the prohibition there is not a general forbidding of the cult of Asherah, but rather an attempt to force Asherah's importance to the margins and to break up an existing couple-relationship between YHWH and Asherah in the official cult. Independently of that interpretation, Deuteronomy 16:21 is an interesting and important indication of an aspect of Israel's religious history. We can also see a connection between the rejection of Asherah and the process by which women were forced out of cultic-religious functions (on this, see Wacker 1991b, 149).

Generational Questions

One interesting question concerns the pedagogical duties within the family and in the public arena. The law in Deuteronomy 21:18-21 seems like a description of problems parents have in bringing up a "stubborn and rebellious son," but the actual background appears to be generational conflict. If the mother and father can no longer communicate with their son and are making no headway, the conflict is to be brought before the public, represented by the elders at the gate, for settlement. This can extend even to the stoning of the son by the men of the city. This law seems intended to regulate relationships in which sons rebel against their — perhaps elderly — parents, or when communication between them has been broken off. The theme of generational conflict appears in several places and is also the background, for example, for Exodus 20:12 and parallels, Deuteronomy 5:16, or Proverbs 19:18. As for the question of pedagogical duties, this law mentions both mother and father equally as being responsible for their son. Likewise, he has duties to both of them (cf. also Lev 19:3).

Both father and mother have duties regarding the upbringing of their children, but the father also has a catechetical responsibility for the son, according to Deuteronomy 6:20-25, Exodus 13:14-16, and elsewhere. The father teaches the son Israel's fundamental confessions. This raises the question: What about mothers and daughters? Were daughters also taught in the same way, and what catechetical tasks did mothers fulfill (cf. Prov 31:1)?

Deuteronomy 27–34

The last chapters of Deuteronomy contain both the final discourses (Deut 27–30), corresponding to the opening discourses in Deuteronomy 1–11, and the conclusion to the whole Pentateuch (Deut 31–34). The final discourses are about the blessing that follows from keeping the commandments and the curses that ensue if they are not kept. Particularly in the curses in Deuteronomy 27:15ff., some of the commandments of the Deuteronomic law are repeated and the assembly is called upon to confirm the curse, for example, in 27:20: "Cursed be anyone who lies with his father's wife, because he has violated his father's rights. All the people shall say 'Amen!'" But there are also prohibitions of broader extent, especially in the sexual realm, that were not addressed in the Deuteronomic law (e.g., no sexual relations with a half-sister or mother-in-law). The content of the final discourses is an assertion that the law is good and can be fulfilled.

The promises of blessing in Deuteronomy 28:1-14 present a clear illustration of how the "you" being addressed includes women: Deuteronomy 28:4 reads: "Blessed shall be the fruit of your womb. . . ." This refers primarily to women, and echoes Genesis 49:25-26.

Two great poems have been inserted in the section that concludes not only Deuteronomy, but the Pentateuch as a whole. The Song of Moses is a historical psalm that ends with a catechetical admonition (Deut 32:44-47): all that has been said is to be handed on to the children, so that they may keep the laws and live by them. Catechesis is here understood as the duty of parents toward their children; it is not only fathers or sons who are addressed. The blessing of Moses in Deuteronomy 33 is a collection of sayings about the tribes from Genesis 49. The last chapter describes the death of Moses and the installation of his successor, Joshua, upon whom the spirit of wisdom descended when Moses laid hands on him.

Concluding Remarks

Deuteronomy is a fascinating book and offers a great deal of material for feminist inquiry. Probably because of its genre, it has until lately not been the object of very extensive feminist research, and this essay cannot fill the gap. What are lacking in particular are relevant studies comparing the biblical law codes with those outside Israel (the same point is made by Müller 1996), in order that we may get a clearer focus on the legal position of women in Israel against the ancient Near Eastern background, and also present a history of the roles of women from the beginnings of Israel to New Testament times. This task remains a challenge.

LITERATURE

Braulik, Georg. 1991. "Die Ablehnung der Göttin Aschera in Israel." In *Der eine Gott und die Göttin,* edited by Marie-Theres Wacker and Erich Zenger, 106-36. Freiburg.

——. 1992. "Haben in Israel auch Frauen geopfert? Beobachtungen am Deuteronomium." In *Zur Aktualität des Alten Testaments,* edited by Siegfried Kreuzer and Kurt Lüthi. Frankfurt am Main and New York.

Crüsemann, Frank. 1992. *Die Tora. Theologie und Sozialgeschichte des alttestamentlichen Gesetzes.* Munich.

——. 1995. "Fünf Sätze zum Dekalog." In *Kirchentag '95 gesehen-gehört-erlebt,* edited by Rüdiger Runge on behalf of the Deutscher Evangelischer Kirchentag. Gütersloh.

Crüsemann, Frank, and Hartwig Thyen. 1978. *Als Mann und Frau geschaffen.* Gelnhausen and Berlin.

Frevel, Christian. 1995. *Aschera und der Ausschließlichkeitsanspruch YHWHs.* Bonner biblische Beiträge, vol. 94, 1 and 2. Weinheim.

Frymer-Kensky, Tikva. 1992. "Deuteronomy." In *The Women's Bible Commentary,* edited by Carol A. Newsom and Sharon H. Ringe, 52-62. London and Louisville.

Goodman-Thau, Eveline. 1989. "Höre die Stimme." In *Feministisch gelesen,* edited by Eva-Renate Schmidt, Mieke Korenhof, and Renate Jost, 2:63-73. Stuttgart.

Levinson, Pnina Navè. 1992. *Eva und ihre Schwestern. Perspektiven einer jüdisch-feministischen Theologie.* Gütersloh.

Locher, Clemens. 1986. *Die Ehre einer Frau in Israel. Studien zum Dtn 22,13-21.* Orbis biblicus et orientalis, vol. 70. Fribourg and Göttingen.

Lohfink, Norbert. 1977. *Unsere großen Wörter. Das Alte Testament zu Themen dieser Jahre.* Freiburg.

——. 1990. *Studien zum Deuteronomium und zur deuteronomistischen Literatur I.* Stuttgarter biblische Aufsatzbände, vol. 8. Stuttgart.

——. 1992. *Die Väter Israels im Deuteronomium.* Orbis biblicus et orientalis, vol. 111. Freiburg.

Müller, Iris. 1996. *Stellung der Frau im Recht altorientalischer Kulturen und Altägyptens. Eine Bibliographie.* Weinheim.

Nielsen, Eduard. 1995. *Deuteronomium.* Handbuch zum Alten Testament, vol. 1, 6. Tübingen.

Pressler, Carolyn. 1993. *The View of Women Found in the Deuteronomic Family Laws.* Beihefte zur Zeitschrift für die alttestamentliche Wissenschaft, vol. 216. Berlin.

Pusch, Luise F. 1990. *Alle Menschen werden Schwestern: Feministische Sprachkritik.* Frankfurt.

Schroer, Silvia. 1994. "Die Aschera." *Schlangenbrut* 44:17-22.

Schüssler Fiorenza, Elisabeth. 1984. *Bread Not Stone: The Challenge of Feminist Biblical Interpretation.* Boston.

————. 1988. *Brot statt Steine.* Fribourg.

Sorge, Elga. 1987. *Frau und Religion.* 2nd ed. Stuttgart.

Van der Toorn, Karel. 1989. "Female Prostitution in Payment of Vows in Ancient Israel." *Journal of Biblical Literature* 108:193-205.

Wacker, Marie-Theres. 1991a. "Feministisch-theologische Blicke auf die neuere Monotheismus-Diskussion." In *Der eine Gott und die Göttin,* edited by Marie-Theres Wacker and Erich Zenger, 17-48. Freiburg.

————. 1991b. "Aschera oder die Ambivalenz des Weiblichen." In *Der eine Gott und die Göttin,* edited by Marie-Theres Wacker and Erich Zenger, 137-50. Freiburg.

————. 1991c. "Gott/Göttin II: AT." In *Wörterbuch der feministischen Theologie,* edited by Elisabeth Gössmann et al., 163-65. Gütersloh.

————. 1996. *Figurationen des Weiblichen im Hoseabuch.* Freiburg im Breisgau.

Wacker, Marie-Theres, and Erich Zenger, eds. 1991. *Der eine Gott und die Göttin.* Questiones disputatae, vol. 135. Freiburg.

Weiler, Gerda. 1989. *Das Matriarchat im Alten Israel.* Stuttgart.

Translated by Linda M. Maloney

Joshua: Tradition and Justice — Women's Share in the Inheritance

Kerstin Ulrich

State of the Problem

We can briefly and accurately summarize the content of the book of Joshua in the words "war" and "violence." The book depicts how a group of people, men and women, pushed their way by force into a land and tried to take possession of it as their own. YHWH helps these people reach their goal. Even though we are told that only men (8:3, etc.) took part in the campaigns of conquest, the women nevertheless had their part in the occupation of the conquered country. They even demanded their own property (Achsah and the daughters of Zelophehad). A feminist interpreter of the book of Joshua must therefore pose the question of complicity and not too quickly dismiss it as ahistorical literary fiction shaped by the Deuteronomistic-theological influence on what is depicted in the book.

Method

The classic commentaries on the book of Joshua in German (as representative, let me mention Fritz 1994; 1996) make an effort to distinguish the several redactional levels of the book and to relate these to the historical situation in the land at the times the respective levels originated. Using the results of archaeological research and the location of the texts in time, they attempt to present as comprehensive a picture of the historical events as possible. The composition of the book as a whole is illustrated by the figure of Joshua: there is a consensus among scholars that the individual Joshua cannot be pinned down; rather, his person is to be understood as a kind of red thread running through and connecting the parts of the book. Traditions with differing origins that need to be connected to the conquest and settlement of the land of Canaan and the common identity of the Israelite tribes that originated there are narratively related to him. The beginning of the book, which depicts the installation of Joshua as Moses' successor and thus the transfer of responsibility for the whole people to him, creates a unified perspective within which all the individual episodes that follow are to be read.

In my feminist interpretation of the whole book, I accept the results of historical-critical scholarship insofar as I presume that the military conquest of the land as presented in the book does not represent the historical processes by which the land was occupied. So it cannot be a question of studying the part played by women de facto in the conquest of the land; rather, we seek to investigate the book of Joshua's construction of history through a feminist theological lens. This construction of history is shaped by the Deuteronomistic perspective and reflects a particular politically and theologically influenced worldview. Thus the great themes of the book are the occupation of the land as a precondition for a political unity of the people projected into the future, as well as unconditional obedience to YHWH. The question I ask in my commentary is: How and to what degree are women seen in the book of Joshua as representatives of these ideas? I will then discuss how much women today can identify, politically and theologically, with all this.

First, in a brief overview of the book, I will present and interpret the female figures visible in the narrative within their historical situation, in order to determine the purpose for which they are mentioned within the overall composition of the book.

Overview

Construction of History

The book of Joshua is meant to tell its readers, retrospectively, how the (re)settlement of the land of Canaan took place. It links to the preceding history in the book of Deuteronomy. This is clear from Joshua's continuing actions: in Deuteronomy 34:9 he receives Moses' blessing and becomes his successor. With divine authorization, he leads the people Israel across the Jordan into the Promised Land. His name is thus tied to the conquest and distribution of the land. The name of Joshua combines past and future. The procession through the Jordan concludes the period of desert wandering. As once the Red Sea had divided (Exod 14), opening the way into the wilderness, so now the Jordan parts, and with the transit into the land of Canaan the future lies open. The wandering people become a settled people.

In the circumcision ceremony and the celebration of the Passover meal also (Josh 5:2-12), Joshua is depicted as a man who brings together past and future. Through circumcision of all the males born in the wilderness, and through the meal, a new, common identity is presented before all eyes, and at the same time this constitutes a link backward to the history begun by God. This history, too, has as its precondition the book of the law, the Torah (Josh 1:8).

Composition and Intent

That this book was not written by a single hand is undisputed among historical scholars. In the book of Joshua we encounter widely differing literary material that appears to come from a variety of traditions. Gilgal, Benjamin, and Shechem in particular should be mentioned as loci of traditions, but there are also material with cultic origins and a variety of lists of borderlines and places. We can also perceive a number of different literary genres within the traditions collected here.

This material was collected and revised by the Deuteronomistic redaction. In the "final version" of the book as we have it, we can see that the occupation and conquest of the land of Canaan are described from a particular theological angle. Differently from the previous period in the wilderness and the time of the judges that will follow, when Israel is presented as threatened in its very right to live, in the time of the occupation of the land we see sketched a picture of Israel that reflects strength, unity, and fidelity to YHWH: all the able men of the people take part in the military conquests of the Canaanite cities. To the evidently superior power of their kings and armies, as depicted, for example, in the conquest of the city of Hazor (Josh 11:1-5), is opposed the help of YHWH in achieving the conquest (11:8). Through this depiction the readers are given the impression that Israel is cleansing its future land for YHWH: the inhabitants and the king are slain; the ban is proclaimed, the city burned, and the cattle divided (11:10-12). We may assume, with Dietrich and Link (1995, 12-13), that the description of the conquest of Canaan as a whole represents "an ideologically shaped special case." "One has the feeling that this is not a description of real wars of annihilation against real peoples, but the emptying and cleansing of Israel's own economic and living space, given to it by its God. Thus it is not surprising that a scholarly investigation of the Bible's picture of a military conquest of the land has shown it to be largely fictional." The various theories of the occupation of the land developed in First Testament scholarship also confirm that the historical and archaeological picture we can reconstruct does not jibe with the military conquests depicted in the book of Joshua. This does not mean that the models of the occupation of the land exclude outbreaks of violence, but broad and well-planned military operations seem not to have taken place.

The book reveals an outline in which a particular course of events is narrated, and at the same time the narrative is shaped by different literary forms:

1. Conquest of the Land West of the Jordan (chapters 1–12)
   Primarily *narratives*, some with etiological character (chapters 2–9), ending with a *list* of the conquered kings (chapter 12).
2. Distribution of the Land (chapters 13–20)
   The distribution of the land constitutes the *framing narrative*, into which are inserted *boundaries* (e.g., 15:2-12) and *lists of places* (e.g., 15:21-62).

3. Designation of Cities of Refuge and Cities for the Levites (chapters 21–22)
   Some *cultic regulations* have been incorporated here.
4. Concluding Discourse and Renewal of the Covenant (chapters 23–24)
   Joshua's *speech* with *historical retrospective. Account* of Joshua's death.

Women within the Overall Composition

Within the book are three narratives in which a total of seven women are named and are themselves the subjects of the narrative (Rahab in 2; 6:22-25) or intervene actively in the events narrated (Achsah in 15:16-19; Mahlah, Noah, Hoglah, Milcah, and Tirzah in 17:3-6).

The rest of the women remain invisible. We cannot determine the part taken by women in the conquest, but we can say something about their share in the settlement of the land, as we shall show. The tribes of Reuben and Gad and the half-tribe of Manasseh are ordered to leave their women and children on the other side of the Jordan while the men help their brothers to conquer the land west of the river. Here it is clear that all the "warriors" of the male sex are called upon to cross the Jordan with the others (1:14).

This description is a reflection of a picture well known to us even today: men go to battle and women and children remain behind. In our case this is mentioned because the women and children remaining behind in the land east of the Jordan had already received their lands, where they could now stay.

The remaining tribes are said to have crossed the Jordan together. This description shows that, in the mind of the author of this history, women and children also entered the "hostile" land. So the whole people built a camp at Gilgal to carry out the campaigns of conquest from that base. As the story goes on, however, distinctions are drawn between the people actively involved in the war and those who "passively accompany it." This is especially clear in the legend of the conquest of Jericho. Not only the warriors but also the whole people marched around the city walls to intimidate the inhabitants (6:8-11, and elsewhere).

Nevertheless, it is nowhere said explicitly that women actively intervened in the events of the war; that is, there are no women warriors in the book of Joshua. In that book, active participation in war is a matter for men. The construction of history we encounter here, however, does not, in turn, explicitly exclude women from responsibility for what happens; that is, we also do not meet any woman in the book who rejects the violent entry into the land. Still, the attribution of roles does not permit the conclusion that women cannot be made responsible for what happened. The common responsibility is clearly brought before our eyes in the story of Achan's theft of the dedicated objects (chapter 7). Not only the thief but also his whole property and family are punished with destruction (7:25).

Focal Points of Feminist Scholarship

To this point, feminist research on the book of Joshua has concentrated essentially on the texts in which women are explicitly named. Here the focus of research has been historical location of the texts and their social-historical background. The value of this research lies in the illumination of the contexts in which women lived in prestate Israel (e.g., the prostitute Rahab in Jericho) and their position within the family (Achsah) or the tribe (Mahlah, Noah, Hoglah, Milcah, and Tirzah).

The significance of the "women texts" we have mentioned in the overall context of the book of Joshua, and so in the history of the conquest of the land of Canaan, is clarified, if at all, only in the margins. The feminist engagement with biblical traditions of violence that Silvia Schroer has called for in this context (Schroer 1995, 150ff; ET, 156-60) is something that, as far as the book of Joshua is concerned, we are still waiting for.

Rahab (Chapter 2 and 6:22-25)

The "prostitute" Rahab is the object of some individual feminist-theological studies, especially with respect to a practical application to congregational groups and in preaching (cf., e.g., the works of Bieberstein 1995 and Selzer-Breuninger 1990).

In studies of Rahab, the main object has been to shed light on the reality of her life in order to make it possible to locate the historical picture in its place in time. The text offers a number of clues for social-historical research: the word *zônâ* for Rahab, when read in comparison with other passages in the Hebrew Bible, gives us reason to say that the text here reflects "for the most part the conditions in pre-state Israel" (Jost 1994, 127). The word *zônâ* is not to be read as synonymous with Hebrew *qĕdēšâ*, which is derived from the word *qādôš* (holy) and evokes different connotations. Understood in this way, Rahab could be interpreted as the Canaanite priestess of a "moon sanctuary" in Jericho (Monheim-Geffert 1984). This variant does lend Rahab's confession of YHWH an additional edge, but Schulte's subsequent investigations lead us to reject it. Schulte concludes her comparison of the biblical passages using *zônâ* by asserting that the life of the *zônâ* reveals remnants of matrilineal family structures: "My thesis is thus that where we encounter the word *zônâ* in the narratives from Israel's early period, it does not mean 'prostitute,' but designates a woman living independently and able to make her own decisions about her relations with men. This was still true of the early royal period, whereas in texts from the ninth century B.C.E. onward a shift of meaning occurs and the *zônâ* becomes a 'whore' in the sense of 'prostitute'" (Schulte 1995, 75).

Rahab's residence, a house in the city wall of Jericho (2:15), has also occasioned speculation about Rahab's "business." Referring to paragraph 108 of the

Code of Hammurabi, which mentions a "woman tavern-keeper," Renate Jost (1994, 127) concludes that Rahab's house "was probably an inn as well." Schulte (1995, 72) comes to the same conclusion, but points to Flavius Josephus's history.

The conclusions of research contribute to the dating of a real situation suggested by the text to the extent that we can assume as regards the composition of the whole book of Joshua that Rahab's reputation had undergone a transformation, beginning with the time of the kings: her name, and her residence in the city wall, were supposed to demonstrate that she was an outsider, something that lends Rahab's "confession" (2:11b) a certain edge. Rahab here confesses herself an adherent of a different people and, as a woman, confesses YHWH, the God of Israel, by saying: "For YHWH, your God, is indeed God in heaven above and on earth below" (2:11). That Rahab's speech (2:9-13), with its confession in verse 11, is the core of the narrative is shown also by Bieberstein in her extensive literary-critical study of the Rahab story. She shows that there is a concentric structure to the story and concludes:

> The symmetrical form of the text shows clearly the central role played by the woman, Rahab. In the entire central section (C) [i.e., vv. 4-22] it is she from whom all the action originates and who moves the events forward: She reacts cleverly to the confrontation with the king's messengers, and she succeeds through a trick in sending away those who are threatening her guests, thus rescuing those under her protection. But she knows how to profit from this as well, and is able thus to make use of the situation for herself and her family and to bring them safely through this stormy time: In Joshua 6:22-23 . . . it is told how Rahab and her clan all escape the fall of Jericho. (Bieberstein 1995, 68)

Key to interpreting from a feminist perspective, it seems to me, is to link the two stories about Rahab (2; 6:22-25) with Achan (chapter 7). The Canaanite Rahab rescues her family and others by showing herself to be a God-fearing person and confessing the God of Israel as "God in heaven above and on earth below" (2:11). The spies thus recognize her as a woman who is on their side, and so her family is spared when Jericho is conquered.

Achan, of the tribe of Judah, whose story follows immediately after that of Rahab, brings death to his family because, in contrast to Rahab, he shows himself not to be God-fearing. He takes some of the dedicated goods from the city of Jericho, thus violating YHWH's command and arousing his wrath. He and his family have to die.

The conquest of Jericho constitutes, in some sense, the opening act of the occupation of the Promised Land, and both Rahab and Achan are parts of this first story of conquest. After Joshua, Rahab is the first actor named, followed by Achan. All other persons are described by their functions or positions: the spies and kings remain nameless. The story of the conquest of Jericho begins with Rahab's reception of the spies, and it ends with Achan's death. After Achan and, with him and his family, the dedicated objects have been destroyed, the conquest of Jericho is concluded, and the city of Ai can be seized.

It seems to me that, within the framework of the whole book, the naming and prominent positioning of these two persons are remarkable not only from a historical perspective, but also from a feminist point of view. Both people are used as examples to make clear how important it is, in this war, to be obedient to YHWH: life is possible for those who act out of their confession of YHWH, while death threatens those who do not keep YHWH's commandments. Confession, on the one hand, and falling short, on the other, have effects on the larger life context of individuals. What is presented here in detail can thus be transferred, programmatically, to all Israel: within the framework of their social contexts, men and women together bear the burden and the responsibility of war and the conquest of the land, just as they will be called to account, together, through their faith in YHWH. To attest to this, Joshua has an altar built after the conquest of Ai, and before it the whole congregation of Israel is gathered, women, children, and foreigners included (8:35).

Achsah (15:13-19)

The story of Achsah (→ Judges) is woven into the complex of narratives about the giving of land to the tribe of Judah (Josh 14:6–15:63). In the context of this distribution of land there is mention of Achsah, the daughter of Caleb. Since Caleb is, besides Joshua, the only one of the desert generation permitted to enter the land (Num 14:30), he has a special position within Israel: he *petitions* Joshua for his heritage (Josh 14:12-13) and is promised Hebron. The story of Caleb could easily end there. The episode concerning his daughter Achsah (15:13-19) is clearly a later addition.

Feminist research on Achsah has concentrated on two questions. The first is whether the figure of Achsah is a literary fiction intended to express the right of a father to dispose of his daughter.

In her study *Tochter und Vater im Alten Testament* (Daughter and father in the Old Testament, 1997), Elke Seifert has investigated the dependency relationship between daughter and father. However, she sees Caleb's attitude toward his property and the associated instrumentalizing of his daughter here as a contrast to the daughter with her independent request; in the text she appears as a mediator between her father and her husband. Seifert shows the uniqueness of this situation in the whole of the First Testament writings, and sees the reason for it in the fact that here, on the one hand, "one of the very few dialogues between a father and a daughter" occurs, and on the other hand there is "no other text in which a daughter approaches her father with such a far-reaching request" (1997, 75-76). So Seifert finds it remarkable "that the narrator can equip a daughter with so much influence, without giving the readers any explanation for it" (1997, 76). Seifert declines to decide whether there is any reality behind the narrative as constituted.

Unlike Seifert, whose primary interest is in the father-daughter relationship, Renate Jost inquires about the social conditions that speak to us from this text. In her feminist social-historical reflections on "Achsas Quellen" (Achsah's sources) (1997), her primary interest is in translating the story of Achsah in partisan fashion. She resolves text-critical problems and variant translations in favor of Achsah to uncover the androcentric viewpoint of the text, reflected for her also in the names chosen for the actors in the story. Thus she arrives at a translation of the text that shows a daughter making an independent request: "And it happened, when she came, that she persuaded him to ask a piece of land from her father, and she clapped her hands while seated on her donkey, and Caleb asked: 'What do you want?'" (1997, 111).

In making this translation, Jost presupposes that Achsah is asking her father for land and water as a dowry for her marriage to Othniel. Jost looks for biblical and extrabiblical parallels to establish her newly translated story of Achsah as historically possible. But both the biblical parallels (Gen 24:59, 61; 29:24, 29; 1 Kings 9:16) and the extrabiblical parallels from the Code of Hammurabi and the Assyrian laws (1997, 117) are unpersuasive. None of these is the case of a daughter's *request* for a dowry. Since, in addition, land is not a customary dowry, the comparisons are not helpful. This remains an exceptional situation, and so (contra Jost) we cannot derive a possible historical setting from the text. Neither of these interpreters, in her explication, takes into account the whole historical construction behind the text. In my opinion, neither the property relationship between father and daughter nor a request for a dowry can serve as a plausible aid to interpreting the text.

It is possible that 15:13-19 is an ancient, orally transmitted story that entered into the Caleb tradition to undergird the fulfillment of YHWH's promise that Caleb's posterity would take possession of the land: "But my servant Caleb . . . I will bring into the land into which he went, and his *descendants* shall possess it" (Num 14:24).

So if we interpret the episode in the framework of the Deuteronomistic view of history, the redactors may have seen in the person of Achsah a link between past and future: Achsah is not the price for the capture of the city of Debir. She will inherit land from her father. The land she receives is not a dowry, but her inheritance, given during her lifetime. It is possible that this passage, in contrast to Caleb's genealogy in 1 Chronicles 2, is based on a tradition according to which Caleb had no male heirs, leaving him only with a daughter through whom the promise made to his lineage could be fulfilled. He marries her to Othniel, the first righteous judge over Israel (cf. Judg 3:9-11). Achsah's request for her own land and springs of water articulates the desire for the continuance of life in the strange, uncongenial, arid land. Achsah's demand is thus directed to the future. In her person the promise is fulfilled and the future is open. There is a clear parallel with Joshua.

A look at daughters' right of inheritance, which must be considered in the case of Zelophehad's daughters, can strengthen this interpretation.

Mahlah, Noah, Hoglah, Milcah, and Tirzah (Joshua 17:3-6)

The story of the five sisters who are introduced as the daughters of Zelophehad should be interpreted in the context of the Deuteronomistic view of history and with reference to the mention of these sisters previously, in the Pentateuch (Num 26:33; 27:1-11; 36:1-13). The individual passages have not been clearly related to a single theological current by historical criticism, and thus the time of origin of a "right of inheritance for daughters" has not been clarified. The dominant exegetical opinion, as represented, for example, by Fritz (1994, 174), consequently dismisses the story of the sisters as "a genealogical construction without any background in tribal history." The occasion for this statement is the attempt at a retrospective interpretation that is not very persuasive: since three of the sisters have names that were known in the land west of the Jordan at the supposed time of the composition of the historical work (Noah in Zebulon, Hoglah in Judah, and Tirzah in Manasseh), the conclusion is drawn that the story was accommodated to reality. With this interpretation the situation described — the right of inheritance by daughters — is downgraded to a means to an end, and its theological and political content with regard to women is not honored. But even if we extract the story from its historical basis, we can still say that it was possible, in the mind of the author of the history, to think of a right of daughters to inherit their family's land. The central theme of the book of Joshua, the taking possession of the land, is thus not an exclusively male domain.

In the description of the situation in Numbers 27, of course, the patriarchal point of view is unmistakable: "Why should the name of our father be taken away from his clan because he had no son? Give to us a possession among our father's brothers" (v. 4; cf. Josh 17:4). Of this, Seifert observes: "The sisters here argue explicitly with the interest of their dead father; they do not speak of their own interest" (1997, 77).

The idea of history that underlies this sees the succession of inheritance as oriented to male descendants and also links the continuance of a line with the ownership of its own land. Here again, then, land acquires the dimension of life. Without landownership, a family dies out, and with it, its name. In Numbers 27:1-11 it is reported how the daughters of Zelophehad took this problem to the highest authority in the community (27:2). The issue gains importance because the sisters bring their case before the community's sanctuary, the Tent of Meeting, and appeal to Moses as YHWH's judge. And the sisters refer to his judgment when Joshua is distributing the land: "The daughters of Zelophehad are right in what they are saying; you shall indeed let them possess an inheritance among their father's brothers and pass the inheritance of their father on to them" (27:7).

The book of Joshua also describes how the sisters again come before the highest authorities in the community and remind them of the divine judgment (Josh 17:4). The five women speak independently on their own account and demand their right. It is clear in this story that ownership of the land is not tied to active cooperation in the conquest. The women receive their land even though they did not fight for it. Thus, it is not military strength that determines the ownership of land, but the justice the women asked of YHWH. Hence, having only daughters could no longer be seen as the loss of family identity. With their demand for land, women raise their claim to be able to maintain their family identity. The prescription from Numbers 36, which says that daughters who inherit may only marry within their own tribe, shows how much, all the same, Mahlah, Milcah, Hoglah, Noah, and Tirzah remained tied to the patriarchal structures.

Through the Dark Sides of History Shines the Desire for Life

"So Joshua defeated the whole land . . . he left no one remaining, but utterly destroyed all that breathed, as YHWH, the God of Israel, commanded. . . . Joshua took all these kings and their land at one time, because YHWH, the God of Israel, fought for Israel" (Josh 10:40, 42).

The "high point" of Israel's history — the occupation and settling of the land — is presented to us in the book of Joshua as a powerful tale of triumph. Men, women, children, and animals (6:21) had to die, because YHWH was fighting for Israel.

It is obvious that the book of Joshua is told from a male perspective. The people are described as a body of men trained for war. The conquest of the land is depicted as a grand, unified action by all the tribes. Power and military strength illustrate, through the book's imagery, men's ideals of how to wage war. The historian's theological program is the unanimity of the whole people under the leadership of a man authorized by YHWH. Through its faith in the one God, the people are strong. Such faith can bring down walls. It saves from destruction; the story of Rahab also illustrates this. She, too, recognizes YHWH's power, but she seeks protection in his name. Rahab fits the theological program of the Deuteronomistic historical writers insofar as she has a representative function. But from a feminist perspective, her story is not a sideshow en route to the conquest of the land; it represents the opening act. Rahab sets herself against YHWH's will to destroy and makes him the guarantor of her life, even though she is actually one of those he means to destroy. The story of Rahab reveals the ambivalence of the book of Joshua's image of YHWH. Death and life, destruction and preservation are all part of the nature of the one God. And here is a woman who, just before an impending war of destruction, makes YHWH the advocate for her own life and the lives of her family.

That responsibility for the military occupation of the land belongs to the whole people is expressed in the fact that Joshua summons all Israel, thus including women, children, and foreigners, to YHWH's altar on Mount Ebal to proclaim before them the law that commands the destruction of the others (Josh 8:30-35). The construction of history we find in the book of Joshua includes women in responsibility for the rooting out of what is foreign. They, just like the male descendants, claim land for themselves. The tradition does not depict them as military fighters; that is, they are not actively violent. But by their claims they become passive accomplices in this violent history.

Nevertheless, the stories of Achsah and of the sisters Mahlah, Noah, Hoglah, Milcah, and Tirzah show us that women were not merely subject to a craze for power and destruction; even in the dark phases of the story they were advocates for life, because they thought toward the future. In this sense they also offer us opportunities to identify with them. This does not, of course, justify the idea that one's own identity can be preserved only when the other, the foreigner, is brutally destroyed. But even today the ownership of land is for many people a precondition for the defense and preservation of their own identity. To that extent, the Deuteronomistic construction of history in the book of Joshua, which propounds an explicit exercise of violence in the sense of a "holy war" as the will of YHWH, is to be rejected from a feminist perspective, although the desire for a future in one's own place can well be understood. This is the sense in which the texts about women in the book of Joshua should be understood: through the dark sides of history there still shines the desire for life.

LITERATURE

Bieberstein, Sabine. 1995. "Gegen alte Gebundenheiten das tun, was Frau für richtig hält. Rahab (Josua 2 und 6)." In *Und sie tanzen aus der Reihe. Frauen im Alten Testament*, edited by Angelika Meissner, 61-77. Stuttgart.

Dietrich, Walter, and Christian Link. 1995. *Die dunklen Seiten Gottes. Willkür und Gewalt.* Neukirchen-Vluyn.

Fewell, Danna Nolan. 1992. "Joshua." In *The Women's Bible Commentary,* edited by Carol A. Newsom and Sharon H. Ringe, 63-66. London and Louisville.

———. 1995. "Deconstructive Criticism: Achsah and the (E)razed City of Writing." In *Judges and Method: New Approaches in Biblical Studies,* edited by Gale A. Yee, 119-45. Minneapolis.

Fritz, Volkmar. 1994. *Das Buch Josua.* Handbuch zum Alten Testament I/7. Tübingen.

———. 1996. "Die Entstehung Israels im 12. und 11. Jahrhundert v. Chr." In *Biblische Enzyklopädie* 2. Stuttgart.

Jost, Renate. 1994. "Von 'Huren und Heiligen.' Ein sozialgeschichtlicher Beitrag." In *Feministische Hermeneutik und Erstes Testament. Analysen und Interpretationen,* edited by Hedwig Jahnow et al., 126-37. Stuttgart.

———. 1997. "Achsas Quellen. Feministisch-sozialgeschichtliche Überlegungen zu Josua

15,15-20/Ri 1,12-15." In *"Ihr Völker alle, klatscht in die Hände!" FS für E. S. Gersten-berger zum 65. Geburtstag,* edited by Rainer Kessler and Kerstin Ulrich et al., 110-25. Münster.

Monheim-Geffert, Marga. 1984. "Die Er-Lösung der großen Mutter." *Schlangenbrut* 4:20-22.

Sakenfeld, Katherine Doob. 1988. "Zelophehad's Daughters." *Perspectives in Religious Studies* 15:37-47.

Schroer, Silvia. 1995. "Auf dem Weg zu einer feministischen Rekonstruktion der Geschichte Israels." In *Feministische Exegese. Forschungserträge zur Bibel aus der Perspektive von Frauen,* edited by Luise Schottroff, Marie-Theres Wacker, and Silvia Schroer, 83-172. Darmstadt. ET: *Feminist Interpretation* (Minneapolis: Fortress, 1998), 85-176.

Schulte, Hannelis. 1992. "Beobachtungen zum Begriff der *zônâ* im Alten Testament." *Zeitschrift für die alttestamentliche Wissenschaft* 102:255-62.

―――. 1995. *Dennoch gingen sie aufrecht. Frauengestalten im Alten Testament.* Neu-kirchen-Vluyn.

Seifert, Elke. 1997. *Tochter und Vater im Alten Testament. Eine ideologiekritische Unter-suchung zur Verfügungsgewalt von Vätern über ihre Töchter.* Neukirchener theo-logische Dissertationen und Habilitationen 9. Neukirchen-Vluyn.

Selzer-Breuninger, Ruth. 1990. "Josua 2,1-24: Rahab aus Jericho." In *Feministisch gelesen 2,* edited by Eva-Renate Schmidt et al., 74-79. 2nd ed. Stuttgart.

Sterring, Ankie. 1994. "The Will of the Daughters." In *A Feminist Companion to Exodus to Deuteronomy,* edited by Athalya Brenner, 88-99. Feminist Companion to the Bible, vol. 6. Sheffield.

Translated by Linda M. Maloney

Judges: Encoded Messages to Women

J. Cheryl Exum

Women in the book of Judges can be studied from a number of angles. Anthropological and sociological models are useful for reconstructing the daily lives of women in antiquity (cf., for example, Meyers 1988; Schulte 1995), or for examining the sources of power that were accessible to women and the factors that influenced the status of women in Israelite society, such as belonging to a certain class or living in a city (Hackett 1985; 1992). Examinations of women's roles in the family (Steinberg 1993) or specifically feminine forms of religious devotion (Bird 1987; 1991) furnish us with a better understanding of women's lives in biblical times. Historical investigations such as Lerner's (1986) that attempt to explain women's oppression as a historical process are especially revealing. Biblical texts can also be examined to discover and make heard traces of women's suppressed voices (Brenner and van Dijk-Hemmes 1993). Literary-critical methods are useful to reveal the strategies by which female subordination is inscribed in and justified by texts (Bal 1987; 1988a; Exum 1993). Clues most authors provide to alternative ways of reading the stories they narrate (even if unconsciously) can be starting points for a subversive or resistant reading of a text. A feminist literary-critical reading can focus on women characters, women as readers, or gender biases in interpretation, or on the way in which commentators read gender stereotypes into the biblical story (Exum 1996).

Here I will restrict myself to my own feminist literary-critical reading, which obviously is not the only one possible. To assert that there is a normative way of reading is, in my view, a means of controlling texts and their interpretation that feminist criticism can regard only with suspicion. Wacker's review of the hermeneutics and methods of feminist exegesis has shown how fundamentally pluralistic feminist exegesis is (Schottroff, Schroer, and Wacker 1995; ET: 1998).

In Search of the Woman in the Text

If they appear at all in biblical stories, women almost always play a subordinate role, as a rule that of someone's wife, mother, or daughter. Their stories are told in fragments and appear as parts of men's stories. If the Bible presents us with a male view of women, a feminist exegesis must ask how — if at all — a female perspective can be discovered in or read into this androcentric literature. As long as we remain within the androcentric ideology of the biblical text — that is, accept its male-centered worldview — we can do nothing more than describe men's views of women in antiquity. It is necessary therefore to step outside the ideology of the biblical text and ask not only what the text says about women but also what it does not say: What distribution of roles between the sexes does it presuppose? What is its purpose in depicting women in this particular way? What does the text conceal and what does it reveal — even unwittingly — about the oppression of women?

I regard female figures in the biblical literature as male constructs. That is, they are the creations of an androcentric (probably male) narrator. They reflect male ideas about women and they serve androcentric interests. In androcentric texts like the Bible, women often speak and act against their own interests. Therefore it is important to ask: Whose interests are being served? For example, is the text attempting to keep women in their place, under men's control? Does it present male control of women as necessary for the functioning of society — or even as something women themselves desire? What concealed and encoded messages does this text convey to women?

Consider an example from the realm of fairy tales: the story of Cinderella does not encourage women to take charge of their own lives. Instead it recommends passivity: wait patiently for the day when your Prince Charming will come and fill your life with happiness. He will fulfill your dreams and take care of you. You cannot do it yourself. Generations of women have internalized this hidden and encoded message. They wait for their heroes, with whom they will then live happily ever after. Such messages influence the decisions they make in their lives. Men are also given a subtextual message. They are expected to play the role of the hero who can offer his passive dream woman a new, better life. And of course, she should be beautiful and he should be rich.

The following analysis is limited to the stories in the book of Judges in which women play a principal role. We will ask: What androcentric interests do they serve? As in the case of Cinderella, we will look for the encoded messages these narratives convey about gender roles and expectations.

Achsah (Judges 1:11-15)

Achsah (→ Joshua) is, as usual with female figures in the Bible, defined in terms of men (here her father and her husband). She is the daughter of Caleb, who offers her as a prize to the man who will conquer the city of Kiriath-Sepher. The man who does so is Othniel, a younger kinsman of Caleb. The marriage to a close relative ensures that property remains in the family.

It is not clear in Judges 1:14 who asks whom for what. The Hebrew text seems to say that Achsah induces Othniel to ask her father for arable land, since in verse 15 her point seems to be that, since she must dwell in the Negev, the desert area in the south, she wants pools of water as well. But if Achsah has urged Othniel to ask for land, why does she, and not he, make the request in verse 15? According to the Septuagint and the Vulgate, on the other hand, Othniel incites her to ask her father for land. In that case, asking for pools of water to make the land arable would not be her idea but rather something her husband put her up to. A third possibility is that Achsah is the subject in verse 14, and her father Caleb, not Othniel, is the one "induced," "enticed," or "beguiled," thus: "When she arrived, she beguiled him (Caleb), asking from her father arable land" (Moska 1984). In this scenario both the idea of asking for arable land and the actual request originate with Achsah. Whatever the case in verse 14, it is Achsah herself who asks her father to give her a "blessing" or "present" *(bĕrākâ)* of springs of water.

Achsah's dismounting from her donkey before she makes the request of her father can be understood in two ways: as a sign of submission and as something she does in order to address her father face-to-face. The dual significance of her act presents Achsah both as a dutiful daughter and as a daughter who gets what she wants. The father has the right to marry his daughter to the man of his choice. Achsah does not challenge her father's authority, but accepts both the terms he sets for her marriage, which make her the prize for the victor, and the marriage itself. Because she behaves the way a daughter should, she is rewarded with the present she asks for: springs of water to make cultivation possible — a present that, not incidentally, demonstrates Caleb's generosity and his status as a powerful man. The message this story gives to women, then, is that cooperation in the patriarchal system has its compensations.

This story corresponds to what we know from anthropological studies about women's position and behavior in traditional patri-centered societies. In such societies, the subordinate position of women does not make them into helpless victims or mere objects. Here it is useful to distinguish between power and authority (Hackett 1985, 17-22; Meyers 1988, 40-44, 181-87). Power is the ability to gain compliance with one's wishes and to achieve one's ends. Authority is culturally legitimated power, power recognized by society and distributed according to a hierarchical chain of command and control. Achsah and the other women in the book of Judges are not powerless. But, with the exception of Deborah, they have no authority. Achsah had to ask her father for arable land (it was not, for example, hers by right of birth), and he could have refused. The stories about women in the book of Judges illustrate how cooperation with patriarchy enables women to better their lives whereas noncooperation has dire consequences.

Deborah and Jael (Judges 4–5)

This story in which a male warrior is eclipsed by a female (warrior) provides the opportunity to investigate constructions of masculinity and femininity (for maleness is just as much a construct as femaleness) and to see how the narrator uses a woman's voice to present a male ideology. Interpretations of this text that are influenced by its political worldview glorify the "heroes" — those on the "right" side: Deborah, Barak, the Israelite troops, and Jael (although they have difficulties in justifying the way in which Jael contributes to the Israelite victory) — and criticize those on the "wrong" side: the Canaanites, Sisera, and Sisera's mother. Since the gender code is independent of who is on what side or which side is the right one, we will not read the story against the background of the opposition between Israelites and Canaanites, but from the point of view of the gender positions represented by the characters. In this story, what do Israelite and Canaanite men, on the one hand, and Israelite and Canaanite women, on the other, have in common?

What is expected of a man? That he will be a warrior and a conqueror. This ideology is given expression at the beginning of the book of Judges in the paradigmatic story of the "model" judge Othniel (Judg 3:7-11). Othniel is inspired by God, judges Israel, goes to war, is victorious, and brings peace to the land. Like Othniel, Barak and Sisera are leaders of men, generals who rally their troops to battle. Sisera commands nine hundred iron chariots (4:13) and many soldiers, and Barak has ten thousand men who follow him (4:14). But in spite of all their military might, neither Barak nor Sisera achieves what is expected of a war hero. Barak is hesitant; he refuses to go to war unless Deborah goes with him. His holding back is implicitly criticized when Deborah replies that she will go with him, but he will not get the glory. A woman will snatch his glory from him (4:9). Sisera, too, fails to act heroically: he flees from the battle on foot.

What kind of picture lies behind the depiction of Barak? He seems almost childish in his dependence on Deborah. He is the little boy who still needs his mother — Deborah, "a mother in Israel" (5:7). Without her he will not fight: "If you will go with me, I will go; but if you will not go with me, I will not go" (4:8). Sisera also resembles a frightened little boy who seeks the security his mother gives him. Once the odds are against him, he stops fighting and runs away. He takes refuge with a woman who appears to be a nourishing mother but turns out to be a crafty murderer.

If the men in this story are in the symbolic position of little boys, the women are their mothers. Deborah is the good mother. She appears as "a mother in Israel," rescues her children from danger, and makes their lives secure (see Bechmann 1989). She is the life-giving mother. Jael, on the other hand, is the death-dealing mother. Her behavior is motherly: she offers Sisera refuge ("turn aside to me") and support ("have no fear"). The picture of Jael covering Sisera and giving him milk to drink recalls a mother putting her son to bed. She even watches over him while he sleeps in order to protect him from harm ("Stand at the entrance of the tent, and if any man comes and asks you, 'Is anyone here?,' say 'No'"). But the nourishing, protecting mother can, suddenly and unexpectedly, bring death. She can attack her son in his sleep, when he is absolutely defenseless (4:21). Or she may turn against him in the motherly act of feeding him (5:25-27).

The different versions of Jael's murder of the unsuspecting Sisera in Judges 4:21 and 5:25-27 are different expressions of the fear of the dangerous side of the mother. According to much psychoanalytic theory, the mother's body is the source of desire and fear, love and hate. The nourishing mother offers security and protection. But at the same time, the mother is the source of anxiety and frustration, because she can refuse the child her body. Or the child may feel smothered by her. Her presence can be experienced by the child as overpowering, threatening to its identity, and thus making the child's differentiation from the mother difficult. Anxiety over this duality of the mother leads to a fundamental ambivalence toward her. The text projects these fears onto the women, all of whom are mother figures.

At first glance the text seems to separate the two aspects of the mother by depicting Deborah as the good mother and Jael as the sinister one. But it is impossible to keep the two aspects separate. Jael is both nourishing and deadly. Deborah not only gives life to Israel, but also sends her "sons" to war, where many of them die. Moreover, one can never be sure, as in the case of Sisera, when the good mother might become the bad mother.

The child's desire for its mother's body has a sexual aspect that explains the interweaving of erotic and maternal imagery in the text's description of Sisera's encounter with Jael. She invites Sisera into her tent, as the "strange" woman in Proverbs invites the young man to come to her. While he is sleeping there, she "comes to him," a description that calls to mind the phrase "come to/unto her," used of a man having sexual intercourse with a woman. He bends over between her legs, falls, and lies there. The word used here for "lie" can also refer to sexual intercourse. Indeed, the entire scene can be read as a rape with the roles reversed (Bal 1988b, 134; Fewell and Gunn 1990, 394). The fact that erotic imagery does not extend to Deborah may reflect patriarchy's attempt to deny the mother's sexuality. The good mother is not a sexual mother (see below on Samson's mother).

There is another mother in this story, too: Sisera's mother (5:28-30). She is worried and anxious about the welfare of her son, but she cannot protect him. She longs so much for his success that she tries to persuade herself that his delay has been caused by the division of the spoils of war. "Are they not finding and dividing the spoil? — A female, two females for every hero; spoil of dyed stuffs for Sisera, spoil of dyed stuffs embroidered, two pieces of dyed work embroidered for my neck as spoil?" (Judg 5:30). This mother functions as the mouthpiece for the male ideology of war, in which plundering and rape go hand in hand. To the victor belong the spoils; the victorious men can rape the women of the defeated, and the women on the victors' side receive the finery of the conquered (this is how I understand this difficult Hebrew text). The androcentric narrator who puts these words in the mouth of Sisera's mother suggests thereby that men go to war in order to steal and plunder for their women, and that this is something women want. He has a mother endorse the rampant rape of other mothers and their daughters. Literally the Hebrew text says: "a womb or two for every hero."

Placing these words in the Canaanite women's mouths puts them in the position of approving their own imminent rape (Fewell and Gunn 1990). The narrator who puts words in the mouths of the Canaanite women puts their words in Deborah's mouth. The result is a victory song that Deborah, a woman and "mother in Israel," sings about another woman, Sisera's mother, who in turn sings about women being raped in war. By means of this song within a song not only is Sisera's mother's voice but also that of the good mother, Deborah, appropriated to advocate the male ideology of war in which rape is taken for granted as a weapon of terror and revenge. This is not Canaanite ideology; it is male ideology.

If one wished to argue that the narrator makes use of Sisera's mother to condemn rape, one would have to say at the same time that he also condemns plunder and war. But Israel's task is to dispossess and despoil the Canaanites, and that is what the song of Deborah expresses. There is no reason to expect that the Israelite victors would treat the women of the defeated enemy any better than their Canaanite counterparts are pictured as doing (cf. Deut 21:10-14; Judg 21:11-14, 20-23).

We lose sympathy with the Canaanite women when they callously imagine the rape of innocent women. Should we not, in the same way, lose sympathy with Deborah, who imagines Sisera's mother and her attendants imagining the rape of innocent women? Should we not, rather, hold the narrator responsible for using the voices of his female characters in the interests of his own ideology, causing them to accept rapists who exploit women's bodies?

Pelah, the Woman with the Millstone (Judges 9:50-54)

The woman with the millstone is one of the many anonymous women in the book of Judges. A way of restoring her to a subject position is to give her a name. Following Mieke Bal, I call this woman Pelah, which means "millstone." "Pelah" also calls to mind the verb *plh* (cleave, slice) and thus alludes to Pelah's smashing of Abimelech's skull with a millstone (Bal 1988b, 217).

Abimelech, who had previously slain his seventy brothers on a stone, has had himself declared king. When he and his followers besiege the city of Thebez, a woman throws a millstone from the tower, where the citizens had taken refuge, onto Abimelech below, crushing his skull. We do not need to look far for the message this story gives to women. Abimelech voices it for us in no uncertain terms: "Immediately he called to the young man who carried his armor and said to him,

'Draw your sword and kill me, so people will not say about me, "A woman killed him"'" (Judg 9:54). To be killed by a woman was a disgrace for a warrior (cf. Judg 4–5). To avoid that stigma, Abimelech asks his armor bearer to kill him so that his death will come at a man's hands.

A millstone is a domestic tool, associated with women's work, not a weapon of war. If a man had killed Abimelech from the wall, it would not have been with a millstone but with a man's weapon, perhaps with arrows (as in 2 Sam 11:20), or with rocks intended for military defense but certainly not for domestic use. In that case, Abimelech would not have needed to ask his armor bearer to kill him, but his death would still be shameful, for he was foolish in coming so close to the tower in the first place (cf. 2 Sam 11:20-21).

It appears that the narrator of the Judges story wants not only to punish Abimelech for his wickedness but also to shame him as much as possible. He therefore not only tells a story in which Abimelech is killed for committing the tactical blunder of coming too close to the tower in order to set fire to it (he could, after all, have sent one of his minions to do this), but adds insult to injury by having a woman drop the murder weapon right on his head. And he further shames Abimelech by telling us, the readers, precisely what Abimelech did not want us to know — that a woman killed him. The tactic is extremely successful, for this is reported about Abimelech not only in the book of Judges but also in 2 Samuel 11:20-21.

Is it skill or luck that enables Pelah to hit her mark with the millstone and thereby to save her city from destruction by its attacker? The fact that she uses a domestic tool as a weapon might suggest the chance nature of her accomplishment. The narrator is not telling this story to exalt Pelah but rather to shame Abimelech. Since God has ordained Abimelech's downfall (Judg 9:56), God can use even the most unlikely instrument — a woman — for the purpose. It could be argued that indirectly the account illustrates that a woman, acting on her own initiative, can perform a valuable service for her people. But significantly, Pelah receives no praise whatsoever for killing a tyrant and delivering her city (as happens, for example, in Jael's case). Perhaps, like the story of Deborah and Jael, where a woman also kills a warrior, this account also has a subtext about male fear of women's power.

If an unconscious fear of women lies behind this account, what does the story of Pelah try to conceal or suppress about male fear of women's power? If woman herself is a tower to be conquered, as Bal suggests in her analysis of the intertextual relationships between this story and that in 2 Samuel 11, Pelah demonstrates what happens when women resist. On a psychological level, the message this text gives to men about women is "one dies a shameful death as soon as one is so foolish as to fight woman when she is defending her wall/entrance from her mighty position as the feared other" (Bal 1987, 33). This message tells us more about men than about women. The message to women is that men are afraid of us. I suspect that the minimizing of Pelah's accomplishment, the absence of any praise for her, has something to do with concealing or suppressing this fear: the less said about women's power, the better. Men may well have reason to worry that women may take revenge when they, like Abimelech, are off their guard.

Bat-jiftah (Judges 11)

Jephthah's daughter is another of the unnamed women in the book of Judges. Mieke Bal calls her Bat — "daughter" in Hebrew — to remind us of her role (Bal 1988a, 43). Following Bal, I will call her by the fuller form of the name, Bat-jiftah.

Bat-jiftah is offered as a human sacrifice by her father in fulfillment of his vow. Incomprehensibly, she does not resist her fate, but accepts with alarming composure the fate determined for her by her father's vow. It is striking how the narrator has the young woman speak against her own interests in Judges 11:36: "My father, if you have opened your mouth to YHWH, do to me according to what has gone out of your mouth, now that YHWH has given you vengeance against your enemies, the Ammonites." She neither questions her father nor blames him for her misfortune. Like her father, she accepts the vow as irrevocable and unalterable (God likewise does nothing to prevent the sacrifice, as he did, for example, in the story of Abraham and Isaac). Bat-jiftah, in supporting her father in the fulfillment of his vow, subordinates her life to the interest of the community. She accepts her role as an innocent victim so that the sacrifice can be carried out. The seriousness of the vow is thus upheld, the sacrifice promised to the deity is performed, and paternal authority is not challenged.

Bearing children was, in the patriarchal society of ancient Israel, the principal role of a woman, through which she gained the greatest respect. Nevertheless, this unnamed daughter who left no children behind is not forgotten. Her memory is kept alive by women's ritual remembrance. Since Bat-jiftah does not protest her fate, she represents no threat to paternal authority. The narrator rewards her for her submission to the paternal word by keeping her memory alive through an annual ritual of remembrance: "So there arose an Israelite custom that for four days every year the daughters of Israel would go out to lament the daughter of Jephthah the Gileadite" (Judg 11:39-40). Patriarchal ideology here co-opts a women's ceremony in order to glorify the victim. The encoded message is: submit to paternal authority. You may have to sacrifice your autonomy; you may lose your life and even your name, but your sacrifice will be remembered, even celebrated, for generations to come. In my opinion we find here the main reason the name of Jephthah's daughter is not preserved: she is memorialized not for herself, but as a daughter.

If we allow the women's ceremonial remembrance to encourage the glorification of the victim, we repeat the crime done to Bat-jiftah. How can we reject the concept of honoring the victim without also sacrificing the woman? Recognizing that the narrator uses the women of Israel to elevate the willing victim to honored status allows us to expose the text's valorization of submission and glorification of the victim as serving androcentric interests. Acknowledging the victim's complicity in the crime enables us to move beyond a simplistic view that sees Bat-jiftah as an innocent victim (for a positive evaluation of her sacrificial act, see Trible 1984). She does not resist (that is, the narrator does not allow her to resist). She speaks on behalf of the sacrificial system and patriarchal authority, absolving it of responsibility.

Even as the narrator controls Bat-jiftah's words, however, her speech bears traces of her attempt to assert herself: "But she said: 'My father, if you have opened your mouth to YHWH, do to me according to what has gone out of your mouth, now that YHWH has given you vengeance against your enemies, the Ammonites.' And she said to her father, 'Let this thing be done for me: Grant me two months, so that I may go and wander on the mountains, and bewail my nubility, I and my companions'" (Judg 11:36-37, author's translation). Whereas Jephthah places the blame on his daughter by making her the cause of his trouble, she reminds him — and us — of his responsibility: "*You* have opened *your* mouth . . . do to me according to what has gone out of *your* mouth" (Judg 11:36). More important, although in the first part of her speech she surrenders her will, at the end she arrives at a point of solidarity with her friends. Her last word in the story is *ra'yotāy*, "my companions"; *'ābî*, "my father," was the first. Her speech transports her symbolically from the domain of the father who will destroy her life to that of her female friends, who will keep her memory alive. This image is too powerful to be fully controlled by the androcentric interests of the narrator.

Samson's Women (Judges 13–16)

According to this story, there are two kinds of women: good (safe) women and bad (dangerous) women. The good woman is normally put on a pedestal, as a mother (like Samson's mother) or a virgin (like Jephthah's daughter). She is idealized in her nonsexual role. The bad woman is defined by her sexuality. She is the sexually available and "wanton" woman (from the point of view of male ideology), who arouses in men both desire and animosity. We still encounter this stereotype today. Such a distinction is made only in the case of women; men are not judged on the basis of their sexual behavior. Delilah is often described as a "loose woman," but nobody calls Samson a "loose man."

Samson's mother belongs to the category of "good women." The story shows her in a favorable light and emphasizes her virtues. For example, she learns more from the heavenly messenger about what is planned for her child than her husband does. Only she is told that the boy's hair may not be cut, and only she learns that he will be the first to deliver Israel from the Philistines (cf. 13:3-5 with 13:7, 13-14). In addition, she is more perceptive than her husband Manoah: she senses something otherworldly about the visitor from the very beginning (13:6), whereas it takes a miracle for Manoah to recognize him as a divine messenger (13:21). In addition, she understands the divine intention better than Manoah does (13:22-23).

But if she is more favorably portrayed than her husband, that is because she represents no danger. She may be more perceptive than her husband, but she does not question his authority. We learn nothing about how she sees the situation (did she long for a child?) or about her circumstances (is her sterility a source of misery?). We do not even know her name. The situation here is much the same as that of Jephthah's daughter, whose name is not preserved because she is remembered as a daughter. Similarly, this woman's name is not preserved because she is remembered as a mother. She, too, needs to be given a name to restore her to her full subject position. A rabbinic text calls her Hazzelelponi, and I shall borrow this name (see Midrash Rabbah on Num 10:5). To understand how the positive portrayal of Hazzelelponi serves male interests, we must interrogate the ideology that motivates it.

Patriarchy could not exist without women's cooperation. Rewarding women for their complicity is one of patriarchy's most successful strategies. Motherhood is an important form of reward because it offers women one of the few roles in which they can achieve status. It is also in the interest of patriarchy that women *want* to be mothers, and thus motherhood is depicted as something women themselves greatly desire (e.g., in the many biblical stories about sterile women who desperately long for a child and finally give birth to the long-awaited son).

If motherhood confers honor and respect, what aspects of women's experience does it fail to address? Patriarchal literature severs the relationship between eroticism and procreation. It affirms motherhood but at the same time denies the mother's sexual pleasure. Judges 13 even goes so far as to dissociate Manoah's wife's pregnancy from the sex act, not even acknowledging in typical biblical fashion that "Manoah knew his wife, and she conceived." Instead, the story begins with the (male) messenger telling the woman that she is pregnant. The miraculous birth of a child to a sterile woman demonstrates that the deity controls her reproductive ability. Eroticism is not associated with the mother, but with another kind of woman — the disreputable, bad, foreign ("other") woman.

Samson becomes amorously involved with three women. Although the text specifically identifies only one of these as a Philistine (the woman from Timnah), most readers assume that all three are Philistines. Is the prostitute Samson visits in Gaza a Philistine just because she lives in a Philistine city? She could be a "foreign woman," perhaps even an Israelite, who happens to live in Philistia. Few interpreters consider that Delilah, who has a Hebrew name and lives on the border between Israel and Philistia, could be an Israelite. Most see her as a Philistine, just as they assume that the other women are Philistines, because an Israelite woman would surely not betray Samson to his enemies!

Although the text does not call Delilah a prostitute, it is often assumed that she is one (perhaps because Samson visits a prostitute in 16:1-3). Because Delilah seems to have her own house and Samson is her lover but not her husband, other possibilities for understanding her position in society are rarely entertained. Another assumption one frequently encounters about Delilah, and about the Timnite woman as well, is that they used their seductive arts to discover Samson's secrets. Are readers who make such assumptions and draw such conclusions about these women simply reading in accordance with the ideology of the text? Or do their own prejudices evoke such associations, which are then projected onto the text? I would argue that both processes are at work and that the story invites us to read in accordance with an ideology that classifies women according to negative and positive images, the mother and the foreign woman. Both the negative image of the foreign woman and the positive image of the mother are so common in the Bible that the narrator does not need to establish this contrast. He simply assumes it, builds on it, and counts on us to accept it and apply it when we read this story.

Why does Samson reveal his secrets to women? The key lies in the answer to his riddle: "What is sweeter than honey? What is stronger than a lion?" One answer is: "love." Love is Samson's weak point, his Achilles' heel. The story expresses the male's fear of surrendering to a woman. It also recognizes the temptation that a woman offers, the male's attraction to her. Samson sees women as desirable, but chooses to ignore their danger, even though he has three chances to learn. Delilah does not betray Samson so much as he betrays himself when he reveals the secret of his strength. She does not hide her intentions. By the fourth time she inquires about Samson's strength, it is clear what she will do with this information.

Like the book of Proverbs, this text teaches the Israelite man a lesson about the dangers of foreign women. Nationalism reinforces its gender ideology. Philistines are bad by definition. The reader who adopts the ideology of the text expects the worst of women associated with them. The women do not have to be explicitly identified as foreign women, they need only behave like foreign women to *be* foreign women and therefore dangerous, capable of robbing a man of his vitality. The text complicates the nature of the male-female relationship by casting it in terms of Israel's relationship to foreigners. The only good woman is an Israelite woman, though the text is uneasy about her as well, for she is good only insofar as her sexuality is controlled. Thus the only Israelite woman in the story appears in the role of mother. Beneath the apparent surface distinction between Israelite and foreigner lies the gender issue of nonsexual (and thereby nonthreatening) woman versus sexual (and threatening) woman.

In teaching its lesson about the danger of women, the text applies strategies that patriarchy has traditionally used to control women. One of these strategies is women's fear of male aggression: in other words, by intimidation, as in the case of the woman of Timnah, who tells her countrymen the answer to Samson's riddle because they threaten to set her on fire, along with her father's house (Judg 14:15). The threat of physical harm has long been an effective method by which men control women, but it is not always the most desirable. Often a better way is by reward, as Delilah's example shows. Of course, there are more subtle forms of reward than outright bribery. Samson's mother illustrates how patriarchy rewards women with honor and status in return for their willing subordination and cooperation.

Now we can see why Samson is not endangered by the prostitute at Gaza, as he is by his wife and Delilah. The prostitute represents no threat to the patriarchal system; she already appears in an inferior, subordinate, and carefully regulated role in society. The women to whom men are inclined to make a commitment are the ones they must beware of. Samson gave in because he loved.

Patriarchy uses the notion that women are not to be trusted to justify their subordination. Women, as the story of the woman of Timnah shows, are easily intimidated and manipulated, and, as Delilah shows, morally deficient. Not even Hazzelelponi is above suspicion. She does not tell Manoah everything about Samson's future, nor does Manoah fully trust her. He is not content with her account of the visitation, but prays for the messenger to come "to us" to "teach us" about the boy. Although Manoah never learns as much about his son's future as Hazzelelponi, he does receive confirmation of what Hazzelelponi says from the (male) messenger.

If the text teaches men a lesson about the dangers of women, its lesson to women depends upon women's accepting its distinction between "respectable" and "disreputable" women. The story encourages women to become lawful and loyal mothers. The only alternative this text presents is the figure of the disreputable woman.

In Judges 13–16, the Philistine oppressors are represented by women, and Samson stands for the oppressed Israelites. Whereas the narrator wants to see Israel's situation of oppression reversed, the oppression of women is taken for granted, and women's subordination is regarded as the natural state of things. But the recognition in the story that something is wrong with the structure of power relations between Israelites and Philistines opens the possibility that other power relations (such as those between men and women) may also be imbalanced. To deny that this is the case with the position of women and to justify patriarchy, the narrator portrays women as either esteemed in (Hazzelelponi) or deserving of (the three "foreign women") their inferior status. But the fact that Samson loses his life in attempting to establish his superior position over the threat posed by women's sexuality shows how costly the struggle for superiority is.

Bat-shever (Judges 19)

In Judges 19 we encounter another unnamed woman. On the analogy of the name Bat-jiftah, I call her Bat-shever (daughter of breaking), a name that brings to mind her treatment by the men of Gibeah and her subsequent dismemberment by her husband. In addition to the meaning "breaking" or "fracture," the Hebrew word *šeber* ("shever") also refers to interpretation in the phrase "breaking of a dream" (Judg 7:15). Thus the name also signifies the role feminist interpretation plays in breaking open the text's androcentric ideology and exposing the encoded messages it gives to women.

Verse 2 says: "She prostituted herself against him." But the text offers no evidence of sexual misconduct on the woman's part. What if the Hebrew term meant something entirely different (Schulte 1992)? Bat-shever leaves her husband and returns to her father's house. This sounds more like divorce than adultery, but Israelite law made no provision for a woman to initiate divorce. Let us assume therefore that Bat-shever's assertion of autonomy is tantamount in the narrator's eyes to an act of prostitution. The concept of "whore" or "prostitute" has meaning only within an ideology according to which women's bodies are the property of men. Only women are whores and prostitutes; the concepts are applied to men only in an extended and figurative sense. At issue in Judges 19, then, is male ownership of women's bodies, control over women's sexuality. A woman who asserts her sexual autonomy by leaving her husband (and whether she stays with him or not is a sexual issue) commits a sexual offense. In the end the woman is raped by a mob and dismembered by her husband. As narrative punishment for her sexual "misconduct," her sexual "freedom," she is sexually abused, after which her sexuality is symbolically mutilated.

At what point the woman died, or even that she was dead when her husband dismembered her, is not clear. The dismemberment is a superfluous act of violence. Why is it necessary? It conveys to women an implicit message about sexual behavior. Bat-shever, in leaving her husband, makes a gesture of sexual autonomy so threatening to patriarchal ideology that she must be punished sexually in the most extreme form. It is not enough that the woman who has offended sexually, by acting as if she and not the man owned her body, is abused sexually, by having her body possessed by many men. Because it has offended, the woman's sexuality must be destroyed and its threat diffused by scattering.

If one man, her husband, cannot possess her, then many men will. But ultimately no one can possess her. Her husband destroys the evidence of the rape in a way that symbolically repeats it, by sharing the woman's body among men, but that at the same time desexualizes the female body by dismantling it and scattering the parts. In addition, he destroys the evidence of the crime against the woman by making a false statement before the assembly of Israel (Judg 20:4-7).

The story presents the men of Gibeah as intending to rape the Levite: "Bring out the man who came into your house, that we may know him" (19:22). Rape is a crime of violence, not of passion. The men of Gibeah want to humiliate the Levite in the most degrading way by forcing him into a passive role, into a woman's position. But instead of the man, they get a woman. Moreover, they are offered two women, and get only one. Why are they satisfied with Bat-shever, since they could easily overpower the host and his guests? I suggest that two impulses are at work here: male-male rape is too threatening to narrate, and, in terms of the gender-motivated subtext, the woman would be left unpunished. The narrative possibility of the Levite's rape by the mob is therefore abandoned. But why is only Bat-shever thrown out when both she and the host's daughter are offered to the crowd? If Bat-shever's rape is understood to be her narrative punishment, then the sparing of the virgin daughter makes sense: she is not mistreated because she has not committed a sexual offense against male authority. The encoded message of the story to women is that any claim to sexual autonomy (depicted here as unfaithfulness or misconduct) has horrible consequences. Every woman fears male violence. The best defense is to stay out of the way; maybe you will not be noticed. The survival of the host's daughter illustrates that occasionally this strategy works.

In cases of rape, the question of the woman's responsibility is often asked. Why was she dressed like that? What was she doing alone at night in that neighborhood? Had Bat-shever stayed in her place where she belonged, under the authority of her husband, she would not have been in the wrong place (Gibeah of Benjamin) at the wrong time. By insinuating that women, by the way they behave, are responsible for male aggression, the narrator relies on one of patriarchy's principal strategies for exercising social control over women. Using women's fear of male violence as a means of regulating female behavior is one of patriarchy's most powerful weapons. And it remains effective. If the message to women encoded in the story of Jephthah's daughter is "yield to the paternal word and you will be remembered and celebrated for generations to come," and that of the story of Samson is "there are only two kinds of women, and you don't want to be the wrong kind," the message of Judges 19 is a cautionary one: if you do anything that even remotely suggests inappropriate sexual behavior, you invite male aggression.

Women and Violence

At the end of the book of Judges, Israel is in chaos. There is no conclusion to the book, only the implicit question: Should Israel have a king (cf. Judg 17:6; 18:1; 19:1; 21:25)? Violence against women is part of the social and moral decline in Israel with which the book of Judges ends. The breakdown of social and moral order is presented as if the gender of the victims of violence were irrelevant. Yet the fact that Israel's decline into lawlessness is illustrated in terms of the gang-rape and dismemberment of a woman calls attention to the role gender plays, on a deeper level, in the presentation (and as Müllner 1996 points out, we need to examine not only gender ideology but also other ideologies). The book of Judges ends with women who — again — are the victims of male violence: women of Benjamin (Judg 20:48), Jabesh-Gilead (21:11-14), and Shiloh (21:20-23).

What do the stories of women in the book of Judges examined here have in common? They are all aimed at limiting and controlling women's behavior. In biblical times, women were under the control of men: fathers, husbands, and brothers. These stories justify and inscribe women's subordination to male authority. Of course, the literary justification of patriarchy is no easy task, and traces of women's countervailing voices can be found in these stories. Achsah, Deborah, Jael, Pelah, Bat-jiftah, the women in the Samson story, and Bat-shever may be the literary constructs of androcentric narrators, but they betray the male interests they are meant to serve. The more patriarchy tries to present itself as the natural state of things, the less it is able to eradicate the traces of its fears and internal contradictions. The story of Deborah and Jael, for example, unsettles the ideal of the nourishing and self-sacrificing mother by acknowledging her threatening side. The mother cannot be controlled. The mother, whose role is so important for patriarchy, also presents it with a genuine problem.

LITERATURE

Bal, Mieke. 1987. *Lethal Love: Feminist Literary Readings of Biblical Love Stories.* Bloomington, Ind.

———. 1988a. *Death and Dissymmetry: The Politics of Coherence in the Book of Judges.* Chicago.

———. 1988b. *Murder and Difference: Gender, Genre, and Scholarship on Sisera's Death.* Bloomington, Ind.

Bal, Mieke, Fokkelien van Dijk-Hemmes, and Grietje van Ginneken. 1988. *Und Sara lachte . . . Patriarchat und Widerstand in biblischen Geschichten.* Münster.

Bechmann, Ulrike. 1989. *Das Deboralied zwischen Geschichte und Fiktion. Eine exegetische Untersuchung zu Richter 5.* St. Ottilien.

Bird, Phyllis. 1987. "The Place of Women in the Israelite Cultus." In *Ancient Israelite Religion,* edited by Patrick D. Miller et al., 397-419. Festschrift for Frank Moore Cross. Philadelphia.

———. 1991. "Israelite Religion and the Faith of Israel's Daughters: Reflections on Gender and Religious Definition." In *The Bible and the Politics of Exegesis,* edited by David Jobling et al., 97-108. Festschrift for Norman K. Gottwald. Cleveland.

Brenner, Athalya, and Fokkelien van Dijk-Hemmes. 1993. *On Gendering Texts: Female and Male Voices in the Hebrew Bible.* Leiden.

Exum, J. Cheryl. 1993. *Fragmented Women: Feminist (Sub)versions of Biblical Narratives.* Sheffield and Valley Forge, Pa.

———. 1996. *Plotted, Shot, and Painted: Cultural Representations of Biblical Women.* Sheffield.

———. 1997. *Was sagt das Richterbuch den Frauen?* Stuttgarter Bibelstudien, vol. 169. Stuttgart.

Fewell, Danna Nolan, and David M. Gunn. 1990. "Controlling Perspectives: Women, Men, and the Authority of Violence in Judges 4 and 5." *Journal of the American Academy of Religion* 58:389-411.

Hackett, Jo Ann. 1985. "In the Days of Jael: Reclaiming the History of Women in Ancient

Israel." In *Immaculate and Powerful: The Female in Sacred Image and Social Reality,* edited by Clarissa W. Atkinson et al., 15-38. Boston.

———. 1992. "1 and 2 Samuel." In *The Women's Bible Commentary,* edited by Carol A. Newsom and Sharon H. Ringe, 85-95. London and Louisville.

Lerner, Gerda. 1986. *The Creation of Patriarchy.* New York.

———. 1991. *Die Entstehung des Patriarchats.* Frankfurt am Main and New York.

Meyers, Carol. 1988. *Discovering Eve: Ancient Israelite Women in Context.* New York and Oxford.

Moska, Paul G. 1984. "Who Seduced Whom? A Note on Joshua 15:18//Judges 1:14." *Catholic Biblical Quarterly* 46:18-22.

Müllner, Ilse. 1996. "Tödliche Differenzen. Sexuelle Gewalt als Gewalt gegen Andere in Ri 19." In *Von der Wurzel getragen. Christlich-feministische Exegese in Auseinandersetzung mit Antijudaismus,* edited by Luise Schottroff and Marie-Theres Wacker, 81-100. Leiden, New York, and Cologne.

Schottroff, Luise, Silvia Schroer, and Marie-Theres Wacker. 1995. *Feministische Exegese. Forschungserträge zur Bibel aus der Perspektive von Frauen.* Darmstadt. ET: 1998.

Schulte, Hannelis. 1992. "Beobachtungen zum Begriff der Zônā im Alten Testament." *Zeitschrift für die alttestamentliche Wissenschaft* 102:255-62.

———. 1995. *Dennoch gingen sie aufrecht. Frauengestalten des Alten Israel.* Neukirchen-Vluyn.

Steinberg, Naomi. 1993. *Kinship and Marriage in Genesis: A Household Economics Approach.* Minneapolis.

Trible, Phyllis. 1984. *Texts of Terror: Literary-Feminist Readings of Biblical Narratives.* Philadelphia.

———. 1987. *Mein Gott, warum hast du mich vergessen? Frauenschicksale im Alten Testament.* Gütersloh.

Ulrich, Kerstin. 1994. "Evas Bestimmung. Studien zur Beurteilung von Schwangerschaft und Mutterschaft im Ersten Testament." In *Feministische Hermeneutik und Erstes Testament,* edited by Hedwig Jahnow et al., 149-63. Stuttgart.

FOR FURTHER READING

Ackerman, Susan. 1998. *Warrior, Dancer, Seductress, Queen: Women in Judges and Biblical Israel.* New York.

Jost, Renate. 2006. *Gender, Sexualität und Macht in der Anthropologie des Richterbuches.* Stuttgart.

Translated by Linda M. Maloney

Ruth: Border Crossings of
Two Women in Patriarchal Society

Ina Johanne Petermann (Batmartha)

Ruth: Between a Women's Book and a Men's Story

The intrepid Moabite Ruth declares she will share the life and fate of her mother-in-law Naomi and moves with her to Bethlehem in Judah. There the two women care for each other and win over Boaz, a wealthy landowner, as husband and lawyer, respectively. The fact that Ruth and Boaz manage to have a son and heir whose name ends up in the list of ancestors of David is just as unexpected as it is well planned. And so it is that the "story" of the women Ruth and Naomi enters into the "history" of the people of Israel and Judah. The narrative conveys a colorful picture of the reality of women's lives in biblical times. In its center are two women who do not fit into the norm of the patriarchal system. Both are childless widows; Ruth, moreover, is a penniless, but dangerously attractive, foreign woman, while Naomi is an old woman. Acting with unconventional independence, these women bring about their social reintegration — husband and son being the evidence of this fact. The women-centered perspective of the narrative is conspicuous; only in the framing of the narrative and the somewhat longer gate scene of the final chapter is the gaze devoted entirely to men. It is enticing to imagine that this book with its pointedly gender-distinctive perceptions has its origins in the circles of wise women (cf. Jost 1992, 9-10 and the articles in Brenner 1993).

The writer shows great skill in structuring the narrative: four dramatic scenes describe the existential struggle of Ruth and Naomi within the context of the survival narrative of a male patriarchal family line. Form and content constitute an inseparable unity within the circular composition of the narrative, its rhetorical structure and style, for example, in the repetition of leitmotifs, mirroring the poetic migration of the women between death and life, between feminine self-help and divine leading, between radical and traditional choices (cf. Trible 1987). The "speaking" names of the characters and locales fit programmatically into the action and point to a fictitious origin of the story's narrative material. There are many diverse methodological and hermeneutical approaches to probing this origin, including for purposes of feminist interpretation (cf. on this subject the continuation of Brenner's essay collection, for example). A possible key — one to be taken up below — to understanding the narrative form and meaning of the book of Ruth lies in its intertextuality, its many different resonances to other biblical narrative motifs and imaginative contexts. Next to Ruth, Naomi, and Boaz we see all kinds of prominent figures from the store of biblical literary material whose actions and behavior are theologically evaluated by loading seemingly unimportant words with meaning. For example, traditional patriarchal legal notions such as "ransom" or "levirate" (the duty of the brother-in-law to marry the widow of the deceased husband) are reinterpreted with a view to the self-interest of women (cf. Fischer 1995). Ruth reads like a "Commentary on the Torah," as a festival scroll for the Jewish Feast of Weeks, Shavuot (Bal, van Dijk-Hemmes, and van Ginneken 1988, 82). In the canon of the Greek (and Christian) Bible, the story comprises a counterpoint to the descriptions of the murder and kidnapping of women in the preceding chapters of Judges and at the same time anticipates Hannah's song about the reversal of power (1 Sam 2:1-10) and the coming of the kingdom with *the* king, David.

Now the association between the Ruth narrative and David offers a crucial key to feminist interpretation. Its genealogical ending arouses the suspicion that a "women's book" — perhaps even a matriarchal one (cf. Wild 1989) — may have been co-opted for this patriarchal "men's story." But presumably the book of Ruth is consciously modeled on the structural principle of Genesis in that the basic theme, "(female) ancestry and ethnic identity" — brought to focus in the issue of the "foreign woman" — is delivered here along with a genealogical perspective running down to David (on this as well, see Fischer 1997). If the Judah genealogy in 1 Chronicles 2:5-15, which generally corresponds with that in Ruth 4:18-22, was known already at the time Ruth was written down, it is possible to date it back to the third or second century. The vision of this book of a society in which *ḥesed* — unselfish solidarity — is the guiding principle (cf. 1:8; 2:20; 3:10) corresponds to the postexilic vision of a messianic-Davidic era of salvation characterized by *ḥesed*.

With or without David, Ruth can hardly be read as feminist propaganda. While the limits of patriarchy are tested in numerous instances, they are never really violated:

1. The partnership of women breaks open male-centered thinking and proves to be a lasting and productive model as the plot moves along. At the same time, because of Ruth's initial rejection of marriage, the family she later founds in Judah is marked as a miraculous gift from God.
2. Patriarchal self-interest is found here contrasted with the vital interests of women — yet in each case the narrative places the women's perspective without comment opposite the men's perspective, thereby providing gender-political "balance."

3. Male prejudice in terms of attitude toward the "foreign woman" seems to be cautiously questioned, yet in the end the Jewess Naomi is named in writing as the mother of the Moabite woman.
4. The basic principle of social solidarity *(ḥesed)* stands for just dealings of men and women with one another, yet it remains locked up in the patriarchal ideal of the family.

From a theological point of view, the autonomy of the female characters Ruth and Naomi is shown as an expression and motivating factor of the hidden salutary power of God. It is presumably a matter of individual judgment whether male authority over women is softened or stabilized in this process. Thus the feminist relevance of the book of Ruth remains strangely in suspense — woman thinks, man provides, but God's at the wheel ("Die Frau denkt, der Mann schenkt, Gott aber lenkt").

Ruth 1: Between Moab and Judah

The time of the judges when the action takes place is considered a terrible time, one without benefit of kings (cf. Judg 21:25), even if we can associate it with certain ideals (cf. Isa 1:26). The fact that hunger sets events in motion leaves the world of Judges behind and recalls the ancestral times when a famine forced Abraham into flight to Egypt. Along with the promise of land, the promise of descendants is also called into question when Abraham fearfully hands his wife Sarah over to the pharaoh (Gen 12:1-3, 10-15). If a famine is contradictory to the notion of the Promised Land, the news of the famine in Bethlehem ("house of bread") is equally nonsensical. The name Bethlehem promises not only nourishment, but it is inseparably associated with the name of David. Thus it is "Ephrathites from Bethlehem in Judah" who must flee to Moab — only Jesse, the father of David, is described in this way (1 Sam 17:12)! The period of the judges and the famine announce danger, but all's well that ends well with the abundance of the harvest and the Davidic kingdom.

The name Moab calls forth many different associations. There is the saga of the incestuous origins of the Moabite and Ammonite peoples (Gen 19:30-38 — Moab = "from the father"). Moabite women are seen as the epitome of the erotic, seductive power of alien cults (cf. Num 25:1-5). In the postexilic period, marriages even with Moabite women are considered incompatible with the self-image of the newly constituted temple congregation (cf. Ezra 9:1-2; Neh 13:23-27). Yet the exclusion of male Moabites and Ammonites from the YHWH congregation demanded in Deuteronomy 23:4 is explained on the basis of the Moabites' lack of hospitality and the Moabite king's hostility. These obstacles notwithstanding, David's parents enjoy protection as guests of the Moabite king for a time (cf. 1 Sam 22:3-4).

The book of Ruth reports without commentary the death of the patriarch

Elimelech (= "my God is king") and the marriage of his sons with daughters of Moabite countrymen. The two young husbands — Machlon (= "sickly"!) and Kiljon (= "weakling"!) — naturally languish their way to an early death without fathering any children.

For the first time a woman enters the scene. Naomi is alone, a social nobody without a husband or a son. Ten years have passed; Sarah, too, waited ten years in vain for progeny, then she hired her Egyptian maid Hagar as a surrogate mother (Gen 16:3). Naomi has no foreign maid to hire on with (new) sons. Yet amidst all this hardship, God has good intentions: there is bread again in Bethlehem. The time for setting out has come.

In her words of farewell Naomi admonishes her daughters-in-law, who are accompanying her, to turn back to their own "mother's house" — a striking concept. In other places (Gen 24:28; Song 3:4; 8:2) this term describes the place where man and woman meet; on the other hand, the term "father's house" describes, in the case of Tamar, the childless widow, the place of forced ascetic life without a sexual partner (Gen 38:11).

By calling upon YHWH, Naomi emphasizes her wish to bless her daughters-in-law. For the first time the concept of *hesed* occurs here: the *hesed* practiced in the family of the deceased husbands of the Moabite women is held up to the God of Israel (!) as exemplary. The best thing that YHWH can grant to them from Naomi's perspective is a peaceful life *(měnûḥâ)* in a man's house. This will take further work of persuasion — Naomi points to her age: she herself can no longer provide any sons who could assure her companions social security in a marriage. Even if she were still able to become pregnant, it would be too much to expect the women to wait for the sons to grow up and isolate themselves from all men. The legal custom of "levirate" (Deut 25:5-10) only loosely coincides with these ideas. To be sure, Naomi's plan provides that the brother of a deceased man posthumously fathers an heir for him and of course enters into the "levirate" marriage with the widow. But in the patriarchal tradition, it is a patrilineal system that is presupposed, and not — as in Naomi's explicit descriptions — a matrilineal one. Naomi must still assume herself to be rejected by YHWH after her social demise. Yet the events to come are already announced in her words: much like the aged Sarah (cf. Gen 17:17; 21), in the end she will have a son and heir on her lap. Much like Tamar, Ruth will use erotic means to bring a patriarch to perform his duty as a father.

While one of the daughters-in-law, Orpah (= "back"), finally makes an exit from the story (1:14), Naomi's admonishments go unheeded with Ruth (= "friend" or "refreshment"). She "cleaves" *(dbq)* to her Judaic mother-in-law and will not be deterred by her repeated request that she return to "her people and God." Even when not a malicious word is spoken against the god or the people of Moab (a similarly "tolerant" attitude is seen only in Mic 4:5), Ruth rejects the idea of staying in Moab as an obscene thing to expect of her: "Do not force me!" In a later passage (Ruth 2:22), the same expression will suggest a possible rape! In a unique vow of faithfulness Ruth makes known to her mother-in-law her limitless commitment. Naomi's way shall be Ruth's way, and where Naomi lays her head, Ruth shall lay her head; Naomi's people shall be Ruth's people and Naomi's God shall be Ruth's God. Indeed, neither death nor grave nor higher power shall separate Naomi and Ruth. Ruth's words have become a popular marriage vow — yet it is a woman who confides unconditionally here in another woman. Ruth's incredible break with all conventions voids Naomi's objections.

When the women of Bethlehem joyfully welcome their old neighbor (1:19), she resists. She does not want to hear the name Naomi (= "lovely"); Mara (= "the bitter one") suits her better. The divinity has meted out a bitter fate to her. Twice in Naomi's words to the women of Bethlehem, when she uses the name of God, YHWH, it is accompanied by the epithet "Shaddai" for God, which is continuously used in Job (cf. Job 5:17; 6:4 and passim). Naomi, a female Job! When she left home, she was still a "complete" person, having a husband and sons. Now she returns with nothing, inwardly and outwardly "empty," embittered and endangered in her faith. Naomi's words reflect her emotional state, but not her reality. After all, dire need drove her to Moab, and after all, Ruth now stands behind her and the barley harvest is ripe.

Ruth 2: Between Self-Sufficiency and Patronage

In a text heading, we are now introduced to a male figure in the narrative, Boaz, a wealthy relative of Elimelech, a man of power and prestige — hence a true patriarch. Already the "women's story" is reaching its turning point.

The narrative first describes how the two women begin their shared everyday routine. They agree that Ruth will try her luck in a field where harvesters are working — as a foreigner she is allowed, according to ancient Near Eastern custom, to reap from the corners of the fields and glean the remainder (cf. Lev 19:9-10; 23:22; Deut 24:19-22).

"By chance," the narrative roguishly assures us, Ruth chooses the field belonging to Boaz, who soon comes over from Bethlehem and catches sight of the foreigner among the laborers. He does not approach her right away; first he gathers information among his people. Whom does this young woman belong to? A woman must have a master; she must belong somewhere. A woman who does not belong to a man belongs to every man. But no one has anything to say about Ruth except that she is of Moabite origin and that she arrived with Naomi. Meanwhile she seems quite diligent, has been working since the early morning hours, and has not even taken a break yet. In fact, she does not leave a single corner of the field unworked, and even squats down to look for ears that may have been left under the sheaves that had been stacked upright. Boaz hears this and seems impressed. There's no way this Moabitess has any other intention than to bring home a lot of corn! Now the man turns to Ruth with a fatherly tone of voice ("Now listen, my daughter!") and makes her a generous offer: Why don't you remain in my field for the whole harvest time and glean close to the maids (2:8)? He tells her he has already ordered his boys not to bother her. But when she is thirsty, she should ask one of the servants who get water from the well. Boaz thinks of everything — work, safety, well-being. Nothing has changed yet about the life choice that Ruth made at the border between Moab and Judah; she remains committed to a female partnership *(dbq)* and the young men are kept at a distance from her. No sexual harassment at the workplace! However, when Ruth has the young workers draw water for her, the gender constellation of the bride-suitor stories (Gen 24:15-61 and Exod 2:16-22), where the man in each case has his future bride give him water, is reversed.

Following Oriental custom, Ruth throws herself to the ground before her patron. Whenever women behave this way in First Testament narratives, they have a concrete purpose with the man (cf. 1 Sam 25:23-24; 2 Sam 14:4; Esther 8:3). Ruth wants information from Boaz: Why is he behaving so graciously toward her? Why is he even taking notice of her as an alien woman? In an untranslatable play on words, two concepts that sound the same in Hebrew are used in association with one another here (Ruth 2:10: *nkr* = "to take notice, recognize, look kindly upon," and *nkr* = "to be foreign or alien"). The Hebrew phrase for "alien woman" or "foreign woman" in the sense of "loose woman," the fantasy image of a *femme fatale* who murders men, is found in Proverbs 2:16, 5:20, 6:24, 7:5, and 23:27. In the writings of Ezra and Nehemiah the "alien women" who have been married into the family must be driven into exile. Leah and Rachel describe themselves as "alien women" to emphasize their distance from their father Laban and their decision to emigrate to Canaan (Gen 31:15).

To "take notice of the alien woman," with a kind view to the concrete person — this statement has the character of an appeal! And in fact, Boaz does see Ruth more kindly: the Moabite woman has left father and mother and homeland behind and has moved to an unknown land with her mother-in-law. Boaz's words are pregnant with meaning and rich with allusions: leaving one's father and mother precedes a man's union with a woman (Gen 2:24); Abraham (Gen 12:1-4) and Rebekah (Gen 24), too, left their relatives and homeland. Ruth — a "(male equivalent) partner" for Naomi, a female partner for Boaz. The Moabite woman — a new Abraham, a new Rebekah. Of course, Ruth's self-interested decision to move to Judah stands in stark contrast to Abraham's obedient setting out to the promised land of Canaan, but it is similar to Rebekah's voluntary departure for the unknown new land.

Boaz promises the Moabite woman rich rewards from YHWH, the God of Israel, under whose wings *(kānāp)* she has sought refuge. Ruth will know how to cash in on this reward by asking Boaz to take her under his wings (cf. Ruth 3:9).

In her humble words of thanks, Ruth, in calling herself "slave," no longer emphasizes the ethnic-religious difference, but the social difference between herself and Boaz. Soon the two sit intimately at mealtime, husband serving wife, the man of Judah offering food to the woman of Moab. Ruth's frank wish to be allowed to join those gathering in the sheaves retroactively becomes Boaz's command; in addition to the sheaves, now ears of corn are to be pulled from the sheaves for her. In this way Ruth can bring in for her mother-in-law a shaken-down measure of barley in the evenings. The young woman takes care of the old woman; the Moabite woman feeds the woman of Judah. When Naomi learns whose field Ruth has been able to work so productively, she immediately realizes the favor of Providence and praises YHWH's *ḥesed* toward the living as well as the dead. This Boaz is the advocate in all matters pertaining to her; he is a redeeming kinsman *(gō'ēl)*, that is, one of those male relatives who is responsible, according to Israel's clan law, to see that spilled blood is avenged, social status and lost property restored (Lev 25:23-29; Num 5:8; 35:16-21). It remains unclear why Ruth now claims that Boaz has entrusted her to his harvest laborers. Does she want to point out the availability of young men who are of interest to her? Does she perhaps even want to accuse Boaz of irresponsibility? As if she knew better, Naomi expresses satisfaction about the fact that Ruth, working alongside Boaz's maids on another field, is protected from unpleasant "passes." And so this section of the narrative depicts a self-sufficient women's world: Ruth cleaves *(dbq)* to Boaz's female field workers and lives in her mother-in-law's house for the duration of the harvest period.

Ruth 3: Between Sacred Duty and Moral Guilt

Again, coming events are announced in a heading: Naomi now wants to create for her daughter-in-law the quiet life *(měnûḥâ)* in the care of a man alluded to at the beginning of the narrative (cf. Ruth 1:9). The following descriptions contain an explosive combination of sexual and religious allusions. Even the name Boaz, for example, who is being wooed, on the one hand means "the strong/potent one," and on the other is the name of a temple pillar (1 Kings 7:21 = 2 Chron 3:17). As the Promised Land is a place of "rest" (Deut 12:9; Ps 95:11) for the wandering people of God, and as the temple in Jerusalem is a "house of rest" for the ark of the covenant (1 Chron 28:2), so Ruth is to find "rest" in Bethlehem of Judah with a God-fearing, vital man. The threshing floor is of course known as a site of sexual orgies of the alien cults (Hos 9:1), yet the temple can be erected on a site where a threshing floor was previously located (2 Chron 3:1).

This time Naomi ignores convention and incites Ruth to become the sexual initiator toward Boaz. While Boaz had until now shown more of his fatherly side toward Ruth, now it is a matter of awakening his male drive. Whether Naomi's initiative is motivated in part by the observation that the men in this family are a little neglectful of their duty, or whether she thinks it is unlikely that someone will voluntarily woo the Moabite woman, is open to question. In any case, part of the harvest as well as the sheep-shearing ritual is always a sensual pleasure and a merry feast meal (cf. Gen 38:12; 2 Sam 13:23-27). Ruth is to prepare herself for the new situation with a bath, ointment, and a shawl and to go up to the threshing floor to Boaz during the night. Only when he sinks into sleep after enjoying a good meal and wine should she approach and pull the covers off the legs — hence also the genitals (cf. Exod 4:25; Deut 28:57; Isa 6:2; 7:20) — of the sleeping man and wait for his lead. Ruth obeys her mother-in-law. As expected, Boaz wakes up, feeling a strange bodily sensation. Whether the man shivers from cold, is terrified, or reacts sexually is left to the imagination. Scarcely has Boaz learned who is with him when Ruth demonstrates her desire to him without waiting for his direction. With her demand that he give her a corner of a blanket *(kānāp)*, Ruth alludes to Boaz's words to her in the field (cf. Ruth 2:12). Now she calls the man to account: what she is in fact demanding is sexual intercourse; what she formally requests is marriage (cf. Ezek 16:8). She tells Boaz he should follow his pious wishes for her with deeds. She reminds him of what Naomi had said already: he is a redeeming kinsman. Now fathering children is not really one of the duties of a redeeming kinsman. But the concept of redeeming kinsman is interpreted by the women of the Ruth narrative in their own self-interest, encompassing responsibility for (male) descendants in the family as well as the welfare of the (female) relatives. Thus the act of redeeming or avenging past losses and wrongs becomes the practical corollary of the ideal of *ḥesed* and comes very close to our concept of "redemption."

By addressing Ruth as "my daughter" (cf. Ruth 2:8), Boaz changes the level of interaction. His words of blessing indicate that he approves of Ruth's actions. Boaz views the fact that Ruth prefers him over the young men from all the various social classes as even greater evidence of Ruth's *ḥesed*. It remains unclear whether the man's exuberance can be explained by the fact that he himself is elderly and possibly unmarried or childless. Boaz's words clarify, moreover, that for Ruth, the taboo in the levirate provision of Jewish law, prohibiting a childless widow from marrying outside her family, is not valid. They also qualify her choice of partner as *ḥesed*, by means of which she provides for the future generation (1:8; 2:20 had always spoken of the dead as well).

Boaz expresses high esteem for Ruth when he points out her good reputation among those being honored by the elders at the city gates. While Boaz was introduced as a "man of power and respect" (*'îš gibbôr ḥayil*, 2:1), he now sees Ruth on an equal level with himself as a "respected woman" (*'ēšet ḥayil*). In Proverbs 31:10 this phrase signifies a female figure who embodies economic power and female wisdom. Ruth is like the figure embodying female wisdom in that her friendship brings others to life spiritually and materially. Thus in the Moabite woman the "alien woman" is rehabilitated, so to speak, as a countermodel to the woman called Wisdom (cf. Prov 1–9).

Surprisingly, Boaz now introduces formalities. There is another redeeming kinsman who has the right of first refusal and must be consulted; only if he should refuse the offer to serve as redeeming kinsman will Boaz be able to redeem Ruth. Here it becomes evident what risk Ruth has taken upon herself. Illegitimate sex can be cruelly prosecuted (e.g., Deut 22:13-21; Song 5:6-7). It remains unclear until the end of this section of the narrative whether Boaz perhaps did after all sleep with Ruth. She rests at Boaz's feet into the morning hours. So that no suspicion arises, Boaz presses her to get up and leave early. Before she leaves, Boaz pours six measures of barley into her scarf — a quantity difficult to determine, but certainly a huge amount.

Once back at Naomi's, Ruth is questioned about her condition: Is she the same person she was when she left, or has her status changed because of her visit to the threshing floor? Ruth gives her report and points to what she has brought along in her scarf: Boaz did not want her to "come home empty." The phrase points back to Naomi's arrival in Bethlehem (Ruth 1:21); the mention of being filled with food suggests that there will soon be fullness in the familial sense as well. Naomi is now full of calm reassurance; now things will be decided, the moment of redemption nears.

In terms of motifs, Ruth's visit to the threshing floor has several similarities to the stories of the daughters of Lot (Gen 19) and Tamar (Gen 38). In each case it is a father (Lot) or father-in-law (Judah) — in Ruth, to be sure, only the kinsman of the father-in-law! — who unsuspectingly, and in a more or less drunken stupor, becomes father to the descendants of the woman. To fulfill a sacred duty, namely, the concern for a son and heir, the women incur guilt in terms of patriarchal morality. Because the patriarchy failed in its duty to provide them protection and provide them husband and sons, the women's moral ends justify their means. Thus the foremothers of Moab and Ammon, the Canaanite Tamar and the Moabite Ruth, line up to become quite a unique female genealogy of ethnic-religious border-crossers.

Ruth 4: Between Male Law and Female Wisdom

Naomi and Ruth have set all the tracks so that their lives can run a normal course again. The "private" strivings of both women have now become a matter of "public" interest. A final word must be spoken by a powerful man to give blessing to their cause. The council of elders that holds court in the gate of the village has the last word and holds all power. Women must deliver their legal concerns to a middleman even if they appear in person. An example of this is found in 2 Kings 8:1-6. The woman who in the time of Elisha flees from a threatened famine with her family members into the land of the Philistines manages upon her return to resume ownership of her home and property, thanks to a male advocate. The possibility of a woman intervening, so to speak, on her own behalf in the legal process is provided for only in the ritual confirmation of a refused "levirate" in Deuteronomy 25:7.

The description of the procedure at the assembled council of elders at the gate is precise, as though taken directly from a textbook. The redeemer kinsman who appears rather incidentally is called merely "friend" by Boaz. Even the secondary figure of Orpah seems in the end more significant than this anonymous man who, in contrast to the Moabite woman, definitely does not practice *ḥesed*.

For the first time a parcel of land belonging to the inheritance of Elimelech is mentioned, over which Naomi possesses the rights of determination. Either the field, which has already been sold, is to be redeemed from ownership by others, or Naomi is to first present an offer of sale — the more likely option. The redeemer kinsman approves of this deal. The dice seem to have fallen and the issue settled. Now Boaz reveals to the redeemer kinsman that the acquisition of the field includes the acquisition of Ruth. In the original Hebrew text Boaz presumably describes himself as the "buyer" of the woman. However, the ancient translations offer another, more persuasive version of the passage. Boaz imposes on the redeemer kinsman the duty to acquire Ruth. This would preserve the fundamental concept of the law of redeemer kinsmanship, namely, to honor the memory and preserve the legacy of a deceased man. But for such a praxis of *ḥesed,* the nameless man is presumably lacking both inner motivation and material resources. Meanwhile he enters disruptively into the (sacred) course of events, much as the alien potentates in the Genesis narratives about the endangerment of the mother of women: it almost comes to pass that the wrong man takes possession of the mother of women and wreaks havoc on the divine plan for salvation. But the redeemer kinsman withdraws from the story; his name and the future belong to Boaz. Thus the sandal ritual that now follows seals the redemption and exchange deal between Boaz and the nameless man. One explanation points to the ancient roots of the custom; it is possible that it was intended to prevent confusion with the sandal ritual described in Deuteronomy 25:9. Boaz now declares before the assembled community of men in the gate that he is the rightful owner of the field and of Ruth. Once again he points to the intended purpose of both "properties," the nominal preservation of patriarchal rights of ownership. But Ruth is the pawn in the process of restoration of the old order in Bethlehem.

The men's assembly in the gate closes its gathering with a blessing of the couple wishing to be married. One after the other the (absent) woman and the man are remembered with blessings and good wishes and placed side by side with the central symbolic figures of the two parts of the kingdom, Israel and Judah. Ruth is compared with Leah and Rachel, the wives of Jacob who came from a foreign land to Canaan and together as one — like Ruth and Naomi — founded the "house of Israel." Boaz is compared to Perez, son of Tamar and Judah — as a reminder that only the risk taken by Tamar makes possible the creation of a "house of Perez" (and thus the continuation of the "house of Judah"). But the inner connection consists in the wish that Boaz might be blessed with success in Ephrathah/Bethlehem — the naming of names points back to the death of the "Ephrathites from Bethlehem-Judah" in the beginning of the narrative (cf. Ruth 1:2-5) and at the same time recalls the fact that "Bethlehem-Ephrathah" is David's and the messianic redeemer's place of origin (cf. Mic 5:1[2]).

Marriage, pregnancy, and the birth of a son are announced as formalities. Following the male negotiation of legal matters in the city gate, we now read the concluding female words of wisdom in the room of the women. If the concern of the male council of Bethlehem was the "preservation" of the name of the deceased, the newborn boy receives his name from the women's council of the neighborhood. Ruth is the only book of the Bible in which the right to give and interpret names is given to a community of women (cf. Ruth 1:19)! Finally Naomi's spiritual and social rehabilitation can be celebrated: YHWH has turned her fate; in the form of the newborn boy she has been given a *gō'ēl*, a redeemer from emotional distress and worry in old age, an advocate against the (self-)recrimination that she is being punished by God (cf. Job 19:25). Now Ruth's inestimable value to Naomi is manifest, her "love" — for the first time this word is used — has come to fruition. And even though it is the son who gives a woman social prestige, Ruth's significance for Naomi cannot be weighed in the balance against seven sons. The comparison recalls the fact that David exceeds the significance of all the seven sons of Jesse (cf. 1 Sam 16:10-12; 17:12-58). Ruth — another David. Naomi takes the child on her lap as if he were her own and becomes his foster mother. The concluding naming ceremony with the neighborhood women, reminiscent of the birth of the Redeemer in Isaiah 9:6, brings this full circle: a son has been born to Naomi! A woman has given the gift of a son to another woman, and in so doing has liberated her to new life! The name Obed (= "servant," "helper") demonstrates that the boy does a great service to the women. There is no devaluation contained in the name; serving is the essential characteristic, after all, of the messianic redeemer (Isa 42:1-4; 49:1-6; 50:4-9; 52:13-53 [v. 12]).

Thus it can hardly be surprising that the serviceable descendant is identified as the grandfather of David. To this fact is added a tenfold list of "begats" of Perez, at the end of which once again is David's name. But Ruth has received a memorial in the family tree of Jesus of Nazareth (Matt 1:5), the Messiah of the world of the Gentiles. And so the story of Ruth and Naomi announces to the Jewish as well as the Christian faith communities the universal salutary will of God.

LITERATURE

Bal, Mieke, Fokkelien van Dijk-Hemmes, and Grietje van Ginneken. 1988. "Kommentar des Kommentars oder: Das enge Tor im Buch Rut." In Bal, van Dijk-Hemmes, and van Ginneken, *Und Sara lachte . . . Patriarchat und Widerstand in biblischen Geschichten*, 77-97. Münster.

Brenner, Athalya, ed. 1993. *A Feminist Companion to Ruth.* Feminist Companion to the Bible, vol. 3. Sheffield.

Butting, Klara. 1994. *Die Buchstaben werden sich noch wundern. Innerbiblische Kritik als Wegweisung feministischer Hermeneutik.* Alektor Hochschulschriften. Berlin.

Fewell, Danna Nolan, and David Miller Gunn. 1990. *Compromising Redemption: Relating Characters in the Book of Ruth.* Literary Currents in Biblical Interpretation. Louisville.

Fischer, Irmtraud. 1991. "'Eine Schwiegertochter — mehr wert als sieben Söhne!' (Rut 4,15). Frauenbeziehungen im Buch Rut. Ein Lehrbeispiel des Affidamento." In *Mit allen Sinnen glauben. Feministische Theologie unterwegs,* edited by Herlinde Pissarek-Hudelist and Luise Schottroff, 30-44. Gütersloh.

————. 1995. *Gottesstreiterinnen. Biblische Erzählungen über die Anfänge Israels.* Stuttgart, Berlin, and Cologne.

————. 1997. "Der Männerstammbaum im Frauenbuch: Überlegungen zum Schluss des Rutbuches (4:18-22)." In *"Ihr Völker alle, klatscht in die Hände!"* edited by Rainer Kessler et al., 195-213. Festschrift for Erhard Gerstenberger. Münster.

Frevel, Christian. 1992. *Das Buch Rut.* Neuer Stuttgarter Kommentar Altes Testament, vol. 6. Stuttgart.

Gerleman, Gillis. 1981. *Ruth. Das Hohelied.* Biblischer Kommentar, vol. 12. 2nd ed. Neukirchen-Vluyn.

Jost, Renate. 1992. *Freundin in der Fremde. Rut und Naomi.* Stuttgart.

Trible, Phyllis. 1987. *God and the Rhetoric of Sexuality.* 3rd ed. Philadelphia.

————. 1993. *Gott und Sexualität im Alten Testament.* Gütersloh.

Wild, Ute. 1989. "Das Buch Rut: Denn wohin du gehst, will ich gehen." In *Feministisch gelesen. Ausgewählte Bibeltexte für Gruppen und Gemeinden, Gebete für den Gottesdienst,* vol. 2, edited by Eva Renate Schmidt, Mieke Korenhofand, and Renate Jost, 80-91. Zurich.

Zenger, Erich. 1986. *Das Buch Ruth.* Zürcher Bibelkommentare Altes Testament, vol. 8. Zurich.

FOR FURTHER READING

Dube, Musa W. 2001. "Divining Ruth for International Relations." In Dube, *Other Ways of Reading: African Women and the Bible,* 179-99. Global Perspectives on Biblical Scholarship, vol. 2. Geneva.

Fischer, Irmtraud. 2001. *Rut.* Herders theologischer Kommentar zum Alten Testament. Freiburg.

Kates, Judith A., and Gail Twersky Reimer, eds. 1994. *Reading Ruth: Contemporary Women Reclaim a Sacred Story.* New York.

Translated by Nancy Lukens

Books of Samuel: Women at the Center of Israel's History

Ilse Müllner

The Move to Monarchy

In the Christian canon, "David" is the last word before the beginning of the books of Samuel. The book of Ruth closes with a genealogy that ends with David and so points to the monarchy as the theme of the stories that follow. The end of the book of Ruth announces a profound political shift that will shake Israel's self-concept to its roots.[1] In the Tanakh, in the sequence of the Jewish canon, the books of Samuel are immediately preceded by the book of Judges. Judges 21:25 laments the lack of a king in Israel. Thus the book of Judges ends with an absence, a not-yet, and so also points toward the institution of the monarchy.

The narratives that follow are about the transition from the time of the judges to monarchical government, and about the threats to and the establishment of dynastic rule, the installation of the house of David as the royal house. No longer will charismatic judges be given the task of leading the people; men will be born to this duty through sonship.

The biographies of three men who embody three stages in the transition from the period of the judges to the period of the monarchy shape the books of Samuel: Samuel himself is the last judge in Israel (1 Sam 7:15), and he anoints the first king, Saul (1 Sam 9); Saul is the first king, but his kingship does not endure; ultimately David succeeds in establishing a dynasty and so in handing on the office of leadership as an inheritance.

The books of Samuel can be broadly divided along the lines of the biographies of these three men. A first major section (1 Sam 1–15) tells of the transition from the time of the judges, embodied by Samuel, the last judge, to the time of the

1. On the book of Ruth as a transitional narrative from the time of the judges to the monarchy, and for the links between the ending of the book of Ruth and the beginning of the books of Samuel, see David Jobling, "Ruth Finds a Home: Canon, Politics, Method," in *The New Literary Criticism and the Hebrew Bible,* ed. J. Cheryl Exum and David J. A. Clines, Journal for the Study of the Old Testament: Supplement Series, vol. 143 (Sheffield: JSOT Press, 1993), 125-39.

kings, embodied in Saul, the first king of Israel. His failure in war against the Amalekites (1 Sam 15) prepares the ground for the rise of his successor, David. The narrative of that process makes up the second major section (1 Sam 16 to 2 Sam 10). David's crime against Bathsheba and Uriah marks a turning point and opens the third major section, in 2 Samuel 11: the "story of the succession" to the throne of David, which ends in 1 Kings 2. This narrative structure, stretching over several books, recalls that, according to the witness of the Hebrew manuscripts, the books of Samuel were counted as a single book, and that the Greek and Latin tradition speaks of the books of Samuel and Kings as "1-4 Kingdoms."

Within the framework of an exegesis oriented toward literary criticism, our interest will be not so much in history as in the linking of past events, but more in the stories that narratively describe, present, and secure Israel's concept of itself. The exegetical position I have chosen concentrates on the biblical text in its final form. We must assume that the books of Samuel, as literary products, went through a process of growth, but that process is not the object of this investigation. Literary-critical work with biblical texts accords a high value to textual pragmatics. Therefore in what follows I will not only describe the content that is communicated, but also what the text does to its hearers and readers. Why and how are the stories in the books of Samuel told this way and not some other way? How are women presented, and how are men? What place does the text assign to women? A feminist interpretation of the books of Samuel is a balancing act between an analysis of the marginalization of women, as attempted by the text, and an appreciation of the female figures there presented. The acknowledgment of the female figures represented in the text will not lead, in the remarks that follow, to the reconstruction of a separate history of women, but will attempt to describe the place(s) of women within the narrated political world of Israel — that is, in a male-dominated system of coordinates.

Birth and Death: The Stories of Women Frame the Books of Samuel

Hannah's quest for a child (1 Sam 1–2) stands at the beginning of the books of Samuel, and Rizpah's action on behalf of her dead sons (2 Sam 21:1-14), almost at the end. Beginning and ending show women fighting for a life fulfilled and for an honorable death. In great detail, 1 Samuel 1–3 describes how the birth of Samuel and his special call to prophecy came about. Comparable to the birth narratives of other important men in Israel's history (Isaac in Gen 17; 18–21; Joseph in Gen 30:22-24; Samson in Judg 13; Jesus in Matt 1; Luke 1–2; and indirectly David also as the descendant of Ruth in Ruth 4:22), the birth of the prophet Samuel is traced to God's special intervention. The books of Samuel begin their treatment with a narrative imbalance. The same man has two wives, but one, Peninnah, has children, and the other, Hannah, has none. Childlessness is presented in the Bible as the harshest fate a woman can suffer. Peninnah personifies the social scorn that falls upon a childless woman (Brenner and van Dijk-Hemmes 1993, 95), and thus stands within a biblical tradition that associates motherhood with rivalry between women (Fuchs 1989, 161-62). Aware of YHWH's influence on barrenness (1 Sam 1:5) and pregnancy (1 Sam 1:19-20), something Hannah shares with the narrative community (cf., e.g., Gen 16:2; 21:1, 2; 29:31; 30:2, 17, 22), she becomes the first biblical female figure to turn, in the misery of her childlessness, to the Living One. She prays in the sanctuary with such intensity that the priest Eli thinks she is drunk and tries to expel her from the house of God.

Hannah's activity (see the extensive treatment in Habermann 1989, 97-98) stands in sharp contrast to the passivity of the men in this narrative. It is true that her husband first steps upon the story's stage and dominates the system of relationships, but he has neither direct contact with the divine nor any influence on the naming of Samuel or the plan for his life. Hannah has authority both to decide her child's career and to make and fulfill a vow (cf. Num 30:3-16). She chooses the child's name, decides how she will participate in worship, and presents her son for service in the sanctuary. Hannah's presence dominates that of the other people in the story; she is a partner in every narrated dialogue (Meyers 1994, 99). Hannah's vow can be interpreted against the background of the consecration of the firstborn (cf., e.g., Exod 13:2, 12-15). The associated hope for the gift of continued fertility is expressed in Eli's blessing and in Hannah's other five pregnancies (1 Sam 2:20-21) (Hackett 1992, 89-90).

Hannah's closeness to God is expressed in her threefold prayer, in which the third part has the form of a song of thanksgiving. Her song sets Hannah alongside the psalmist David (2 Sam 22:2–23:7). Hannah's and David's songs of thanksgiving stand at the beginning and end of the books of Samuel and are the only psalms in these narrative books. Hannah's song probably points to a women's tradition of songs of victory and thanksgiving on the occasion of a birth (Brenner and van Dijk-Hemmes 1993, 93-97). The text expands the individual experience of rescue and embeds it in the actions of the God who reverses unjust and oppressive social conditions. Hannah's song becomes a model for Mary's Magnificat in Luke 1:46-56. Motherhood is not individualized and understood as successful self-realization, but is grasped in its social dimension. The unexpected pregnancy is set alongside experiences of social and political liberation. In this the motif of competition between women, already visible in the story of Hannah and Peninnah, is taken up again. "The barren" is set in contrast to the one "who has many children" (1 Sam 2:5; cf. Isa 54:1); her pregnancy is a contribution to the reversal of the situation. The dualisms of mighty and feeble, full and hungry, barren and having many children, pious and wicked that run through this psalm are ambivalent. On the one hand they reduce enigmatic reality to black-white contrasts; the liberation of the barren woman requires the defeat of the one with many children. On the other hand, the possibility of a reversal of conditions releases a powerful potential for hope, as the reception accorded Hannah's and Mary's psalms in liberation theology reveals.

The story of Rizpah's vigil in 2 Samuel 21:1-14 shows that a woman's care for her children can extend beyond death. Rizpah, a concubine of Saul, is the mother of men who represent the continuation of the Saulide royal house. Her particular function in the course of the transfer of power from the house of Saul to the house of David is depicted in 2 Samuel 3:6-11 (see below). In 2 Samuel 21 it is her sons whose lives David extinguishes in order to put an end to a famine in Israel. The "blood-guilt" that, according to YHWH's decree, lies upon the house of Saul points back to Joshua 9; 1 Samuel 22:6-23, a covenant Joshua had made with the Gibeonites that was broken by Saul. The execution of seven of Saul's children is supposed to restore the balance. Like Saul and Jonathan (1 Sam 31), these dead are also denied burial. "To desecrate the corpses was to scorn the elementary right of the dead to be buried" (Schmidt and Ellmenreich 1990, 83). Rizpah cannot prevent her sons' murder, but she stands like an "Israelite Antigone"[2] against this disdain for the dead. The length of her vigil signals both the intensity of her protest and a positive link to the God who is so darkly depicted in this story. The beginning of the rains marks the end of Rizpah's vigil and also the beginning of the end of the famine, and it points forward to God's saving intervention (Exum 1992, 116). Rizpah's action is brought into causal relationship with David's (2 Sam 21:11); he causes Saul's and Jonathan's bones to be brought from Jabesh-gilead (1 Sam 31) and buried, together with the corpses of the executed Saulides, in the grave of Saul's father.

Women's concern for life and death brings them into conflict with representatives of the ruling order. Peninnah, Eli, and David personify attitudes of hatred for life and disdain for human beings. The position of women on the threshold between life and death brings dangers with it, dangers these women defy by their resistance to the powers of indifference and death.

Not Only Victims: Women in War

"Be men! . . . Be men and fight!" (1 Sam 4:9): in face of their own fears in battle against Israel, in whose camp God's power is embodied in the ark of the covenant, the Philistines shout this encouragement to one another. This challenge is probably the clearest indication of how masculinity is constructed in the books of Samuel. They are men who go to battle, and courage and warlike strength are elements of their masculinity. The power of such masculinity counters the power of the ark of the covenant — and wins (cf., in contrast, Jth 9:11). Showing themselves to be

---

2. Martin Buber, "Weisheit und Tat der Frauen," in Buber, *Kampf um Israel. Reden und Schriften (1921-1932)* (Berlin: Schocken, 1933), 104-14.

men ("Show yourselves to be men!" is another possible translation of the Hebrew text of 1 Sam 4:9) spurs the Philistines against their fear and on to victory. Masculinity is at stake in battle, and victory proves the masculinity of the victors.

Women do not participate in the wars as fighters. Fighting is men's business, and the perspective on the conquest is entirely male. In 1 Samuel 30, David and his men come into their city of exile, Ziklag, which has been captured by the Amalekites. "The women and all who were in it" or "wives and sons and daughters" (1 Sam 30:2, 3) have been taken captive. The mobility and activity of the fighting men contrast with the passivity of the women and other groups in the population who are incapable of fighting: "small and great" (NRSV) or "young and old" (vv. 2, 19), "sons and daughters" (vv. 3, 6, 19). Women are part of the spoils of war. A different perspective on war is presented when the destruction of Amalek is the subject. Here it is exactly the point that nothing that belongs to the Amalekites or constitutes them is to be left alive; the aim, in the destruction of the Amalekites, is comprehensiveness. Not by way of special mention, but in the same breath with men, children, and animals, women are spoken of as victims in the destruction of Amalek (1 Sam 15:3, 33; 22:19; 27:9). Saul and his troops cannot resist the temptation to take booty, a crime that causes the end of Saul's kingship. But women are also victims in war because they lose their husbands, fathers, and sons in battle. "As your sword has made women childless, so your mother shall be childless among women." So Samuel motivates the murder of the Amalekite king Agag in 1 Samuel 15:33. And the nameless daughter-in-law of Eli dies during the birth of her child when she hears of the loss of the ark of the covenant to the Philistines and the death of her husband and father-in-law (1 Sam 4:19-22). In the name given to her son (Ichabod, explained as the departure of glory — kābôd — from Israel) she holds this loss in memory.

Women participate actively in military operations, though differently from men. The wise woman of Abel of Beth-maacah negotiates with the commander Joab (see below). As singers of victory songs, women are not mere decorative elements; they influence the alteration of political situations (Brenner and van Dijk-Hemmes 1993, 32). It is their task to greet and celebrate the warriors on their return home. This is depicted as the custom not only in Israel, but also among the neighboring peoples (2 Sam 1:20). The women use this forum to make public their view of the political situation. "Saul has killed his thousands, and David his ten thousands!" That is the song the women sing, accompanied by instruments and dancing, when David returns from a victory over the Philistines (1 Sam 18:6-7). Current translations relate the preposition liqra't ("against" or "toward") in verse 6 to the verb "come out." Thus, for example, NRSV: "the women came out of all the towns of Israel, singing and dancing, to meet King Saul, with tambourines, with songs of joy, and with musical instruments." But the Hebrew text applies "against" to the verb "sing": "and the women came out of all the towns of Israel in order to sing in round dances against Saul." The first type of translation insinuates that this is a triumphal entry for Saul. In the Hebrew text, however, Saul is not among those who enter, returning from the victory. David's entry into the city is celebrated, and the women sing against Saul. Thus it is clearer in Hebrew than in the usual English translations that the women take David's part against Saul. The song has a high degree of resonance for both internal and external politics. Saul understands it as an attack on his kingship, a reaction that emphasizes the power of these women (Brenner and van Dijk-Hemmes 1993, 36). For the Philistines, this song defines David (1 Sam 21:12[Eng. 11]; 29:5); they cite it in giving expression to their fear of David.

Tu Felix David Nube![3] Wives and Daughters of Kings

The song of the women in 1 Samuel 18:7 is in the context of a whole series of demonstrations of love offered to David. Saul loves David (1 Sam 16:21; cf. 18:22). Jonathan loves David (1 Sam 18:1, 3; 20:17; 2 Sam 1:26; cf. 1 Sam 19:1). All of Saul's servants love David (1 Sam 18:22); all Israel and Judah love David (18:16); Saul's daughter Michal loves David (18:20, 28). Only David doesn't love anybody.[4] The love given to him from all sides is part of his political success. God's election of David (1 Sam 16) has its human echo in 1 Samuel 18 when Saul's children, his servants, and even the nation turn to David in love.

Saul attempts to channel this universal love for David in the form of a strategically beneficial marriage. Immediately after the assertion that "all Israel and Judah loved David" (1 Sam 18:16) follows Saul's offer to give David the oldest royal daughter, Merab, as his wife (18:17). This lays the foundation for a marriage policy that is intimately allied to David's governing policy. Saul's offer is no surprise to the readers of the books of Samuel; already in 1 Samuel 17:25 the Israelites had predicted that the king would give his daughter as wife to the man who would slay Goliath. Nevertheless, David reacts with surprise and, in his astonishment, puts the marriage offer in the correct light: "Who am I . . . that I should be son-in-law to the king?" (1 Sam 18:18). This is not about marriage to Merab, but about the status of the king's son-in-law. However, it is not Merab who will be David's first wife, but Michal.

Michal's story is so broadly distributed across the books of Samuel that, textu-

---

3. "You, fortunate David, marry!" — an allusion to the often-cited exclamation of Matthias Corvinus: "Bella gerant alii, tu felix Austria nube!" ("Let other countries wage war, you, fortunate Austria, marry!"). This is how at the end of the fifteenth century the Hungarian king portrayed the Hapsburgs' politics of marriage, in particular that of Frederick III. David's politics of governance does not rely on this alternative. His power is founded on sexual *and* military conquests.

4. 2 Sam 1:23, where David calls Saul and Jonathan "beloved," could indicate David's love, but he is not explicitly made the subject. In 2 Sam 19:7(6) Joab speaks of David's love, but does not say who the object of David's love is.

ally, she becomes one of the Bible's fragmented women (Exum 1993). Her history begins with an activity that is unusual for a woman. "Saul's daughter Michal loved David" (1 Sam 18:20). This makes her the only woman in the Hebrew Bible — with the exception of the female voice in the Song of Songs — who loves a man.[5] Her bride-price (so also the title of Grete Weil's novel about Michal)[6] is unusual. Saul asks for a hundred Philistine foreskins, in the hope that David will not survive the battle. But David murders not just 100, but 200 Philistines and becomes the king's son-in-law. In 1 Samuel 19:8-24, Michal helps David escape from Saul. In the conflict between her father, Saul, and her husband, David, she chooses David's side. She deceives Saul's messengers by putting an idol *těrāpîm* in the bed in David's place. (In Genesis 31, too, a woman, Rachel, chooses her husband, and here again the deception of the father in relation to an idol plays a role.) In 1 Samuel 25:44 a retrospective note mentions that Saul had given Michal to another man, Palti, as his wife. But he, weeping, loses her again to David, who, already by this time the king and the husband of six other wives, demands Michal back again (2 Sam 3:13-16). In 2 Samuel 6:16 Michal enters the stage of the narrative world for the last time. David roughly rejects her criticism of his dancing before the ark, and the narrator comments succinctly: "And Michal the daughter of Saul had no child to the day of her death" (2 Sam 6:23).

"Depriving her of children is a symbolic way of killing Michal. Denying her a reply to David kills her off as a narrative presence. By representing her as challenging the king from a position of weakness, the narrator has Michal essentially commit verbal suicide" (Exum 1993, 29).

The comment on Michal's childlessness writes this woman out of the story. As with the other female figures in the books of Samuel, and in sharp contrast to the important men in the story, there is no account of Michal's death. Her departure from the stage of the narrative world does not happen suddenly; she fades away. In a gruesome way, the Masoretic Text resurrects Michal in 2 Samuel 21:8, when Michal's sons are to be murdered by David as recompense to the Gibeonites. The text had denied her children; here it gives them to her only to take them away again (Exum 1993, 38). What is so horrible about this passage is that many textual variants read "Merab" instead of "Michal." The two sisters who were already interchangeable in Saulide marriage politics (1 Sam 18) are confused again here. Michal is in a position of danger, between the two houses of Saul and David, between her father and her husband. This corresponds to the deliberately varied designations of Michal as "daughter of Saul" or "David's wife." While, for example, in 1 Samuel 19:11 "David's wife Michal" acts against her father, in 2 Samuel 6 it is "Michal the daughter of Saul" who enters into conflict with David and ultimately remains

---

5. In Gen 25:28 Rebekah loves her son Jacob. Ezek 16:37 speaks of the love of the city, metaphorized as a woman. And finally it is Ruth (4:15) who loves Naomi.

6. *The Bride Price: A Novel*, trans. John Barrett (Boston: D. R. Godine, 1991).

childless. Thus in 2 Samuel 6:23 the continuation of the house of Saul through Michal is explicitly made impossible.

Chronologically, Ahinoam of Jezreel is the second wife David marries (1 Sam 25:43), but textually David's encounter with Abigail precedes the notice about this marriage. In 1 Samuel 25 this woman proves herself David's strategic equal. Her husband Nabal (his name means "idiot" or "criminal" and indicates that his behavior sets him outside Israel's ethics) takes David's measure quite incorrectly. He refuses to give material support to David, who, with his followers, is in flight from Saul. Abigail averts the impending catastrophe by addressing David in a "speech that can be regarded as a rhetorical masterpiece" (Schroer 1996, 90), pleading that he excuse her husband's action and giving him material support. When Nabal hears of it, he suffers a heart attack and dies within ten days. In the same verse in which David expresses his joy at Nabal's death, he sends messengers to Abigail to take her as his wife (1 Sam 25:39). Abigail's cleverness is in sharp contrast to the stupidity of her husband. The narrative shows this woman acting independently in the economic sphere and presents her as diplomatically skillful and politically astute. The style of her speech corresponds to the rhetorical conventions of biblical Hebrew. The frequent address "my lord," and formulations in which the conversation partner is spoken of in the third person, are not submissive gestures, but are elements of politeness. Abigail, through her intervention, averts the murderous rage of David and his troops on her household. She presents herself in verse 26 as a messenger of the Living One: "God sends this woman to make his will known, and in this moment Abigail is God's prophet. . . . God is against senseless shedding of blood, and it is altogether remarkable that here, in the tradition of the great prophets of Israel, a woman proclaims this message and successfully carries out God's mission" (Schroer 1996, 93).

After a summary note about other concubines, including some from Jerusalem, which David had captured, and who had borne him other sons and daughters (2 Sam 5:13-15), Bathsheba is cited as the next woman David takes to wife. At 2 Samuel 11–12, David is at the climax of his sexual and political-governing power. Bathsheba is the last woman he conquers sexually, and Rabbah is the last city he conquers militarily. From his rooftop, David sees Bathsheba bathing. He beholds, desires, and takes her. Nothing is said about Bathsheba's feelings and desires. The king wants her, and in view of the structural power relationships, it makes no sense to ask about Bathsheba's possible participation, much less strategic considerations, as has repeatedly been the case in traditional exegesis. While some women exegetes have described the sexual act described here as rape (e.g., Bal 1987, 11), Cheryl Exum above all has emphasized the textual side of this act of violence. This narrative, by offering no possible access to Bathsheba's feelings or her perspective, presenting her instead through the sexualized lenses of David, denies Bathsheba her subjectivity, an act of textual violence: "rape by the pen" (Exum 1993). "The narrator who disrobes Bathseba and depicts her as the object of David's lust is the real perpetrator of the crime against Bathseba, and commentators . . . , who imply that Bathsheba may have desired the king's attentions, perpetuate the crime" (Exum 1993, 174).

Bathsheba becomes pregnant. A note that her bathing was connected to her monthly indisposition makes it clear that the child she is expecting is David's, not her husband Uriah's; he was at the battle for Rabbah. David, in his interaction with Uriah, does everything possible to get around this textual clarity. He attempts to get Uriah to go to his house and sleep with his wife, so that Uriah could be fooled into thinking he was the child's father. But Uriah refuses, out of solidarity with the men who are camping on the field of battle.

David's whole sequence of actions — beginning with the fact that he has stayed in Jerusalem while "all Israel" (2 Sam 11:1) has gone to war, through adultery, to his dealing with Uriah and finally Uriah's murder — positions him as Israel's opposite, outside the ethics of the people whose king he is. 2 Samuel 11 is the turning point and crux of David's story. To this point David has built up his house; from now on his house is in danger: "Now therefore the sword shall never depart from your house" (2 Sam 12:10). This narrative is the beginning of a sequence of tragic events in which David's sons repeat his crime (Exum 1992, 129). In 2 Samuel 11 itself, David's dealings with Uriah already signal a crack in his power. Uriah is subordinate to David and nevertheless does not follow his commands. Uriah is not an Israelite, but a Hittite, and yet he shows himself, in contrast to Israel's king, to be solidly with "Israel and Judah" (2 Sam 11:11).

David has built up his house through his marriage policies (see below), and so has secured his dominance over all Israel by forging ties, by means of women as "representatives of the social environments connected with them" (Willi-Plein 1995, 355), with different social and geographical areas. Through Michal, David preserves continuity with the royal house that preceded him, in order at the same time to deny the house of Saul its continuance. Ahinoam and Abigail secure for David "good relationships with the highly regarded families of the southern highlands of Judea" (Schroer 1996, 92). Bathsheba and some nameless concubines anchor David's rule in Jerusalem. David's marriages are not primarily for the purpose of joining women to him emotionally, but rather to link areas of land and social classes to him politically.

Power and Sexuality in the House of David

David's house enjoys no period of stability or even of standing still. The phase of construction and expansion of power is followed, in the "narrative of the succession" (2 Sam 11 to 1 Kings 2), by a phase of conflicts over royal power. The protagonists in these confrontations are David's sons, especially Absalom and, in 2 Samuel 13, Amnon. Attacks also come from outside David's family (2 Sam 20), but the primary conflict over royal power takes place within the house of David. In these struggles, women are used and functionalized by the men in the narrative.

The story of David's adultery with Bathsheba, the murder of Uriah, and the consequences of those deeds (2 Sam 11–12) is followed immediately by the narrative of Tamar and Amnon. In 2 Samuel 13:1-22, Amnon rapes his sister Tamar. The first verses of the narrative spread the net of family relationships within which the deed of violence will be carried out. The frequency of terms referring to family relationships here and in the rest of the narrative indicates that the system of family connections is of the highest importance for understanding the narrative. With the exception of Tamar, all those concerned are described in terms of their family relationships to David. Tamar is introduced by way of her brother Absalom. Here it is already evident that her relationship with King David is not direct and does not have the same value as the sons' relationships with David. The king is at the center of the net of relationships; his lack of competence in the course of the narrative stands in sharp contrast to his narrative position at the central point and to his social position as king.

Amnon's lust initiates the action. He sees an obstacle to the fulfillment of his desire, namely, Tamar's status as a virgin. As such, she is part of the sphere that belongs to her father. There is some ambivalence in the Hebrew formulation of the obstacle. The verb *pl'* means both "impossible" and "wonderful." Tamar's belonging to David's sphere thus makes it both difficult and at the same time desirable to do something to Tamar (2 Sam 13:2).

Amnon's friend Jonadab functions, in correspondence to his designation as a "crafty man," as an adviser. Amnon is supposed to pretend to be sick, and the king is to come and, at Amnon's request, persuade Tamar to prepare some tasty food to strengthen him. Jonadab's plan works. The term "heart cakes" or "dear little cakes" for the sickbed food is from Amnon's perspective. It describes the form of the baked goods and also evokes the concept of the "heart." The latter, of course, does not represent romantic feeling in contrast to reason — that kind of thinking in contrasts is foreign to Hebrew. Rather, the heart is the seat of will and passion, and the place of decision. The concept makes it clear that more is at stake for Amnon than just being fed by Tamar. Amnon's desire is not merely a superficial wish for food. Amnon's point of view dominates the narrative. His eyes behold the preparation of the food (13:5-6). But in verse 5 the object of the verb "see" is missing, so that it remains open whether Amnon's interest is in the food or in Tamar herself. The voyeurism thus indicated (Schroer 1992, 171-72), and Amnon's wish to eat from Tamar's hand, make it clear that Amnon's desire is to be interpreted as sexual: "In this narrative, Amnon's eyes are an instrument of rule. Not only the sexual intercourse performed against Tamar's will, but already Amnon's look is an act of sexual violence" (Müllner 1997, 168).

Tamar resists Amnon (13:12-13). The rhetoric of her speech is brilliant. While Amnon had demanded that she sleep with him, thus making *Tamar* the subject of the sexual act (13:11), Tamar shows that *Amnon* would be the subject of a sexual act that would have different, but catastrophic, consequences for both participants. That act would be an act of violence. This is not just about physical superiority or the use of force. The emphasis lies on the social consequences. The community's opprobrium (that is the semantics of *ḥerpâ* in 13:13) would fall on the innocent Tamar. Amnon would become one of a series of criminals *(něbālîm)* in Israel (cf. the name of Abigail's first husband, Nabal, in 1 Sam 25). Tamar's speech shows clearly that the narrative community is on her side, for she is the one who formulates the common ethics of Israel in words that none of the hearers or readers can escape. Only Amnon, with his refusal to listen to Tamar (2 Sam 13:14: "But he would not listen *to her [voice]*"; 13:16: "But he would not listen *to her*"), dismisses her whole person.

Tamar's prophecies are fulfilled. Amnon rapes her. Tamar does turn to the public to accuse him of his crime and receive justice. But her brother Absalom orders her to keep quiet. This second act of violence (against Trible 1987, who interprets Absalom's role very positively) also takes Tamar's words away and sentences her to silent desolation. For Tamar, Absalom's house is not a place of security and restoration, but the place where she silently collapses. This story is told to counter Absalom's command to silence. That makes 2 Samuel 13 a contrast story to 2 Samuel 11. In 2 Samuel 11 the narrated sex act remains ambivalent as far as its violence is concerned, though the text acts violently. In 2 Samuel 13 the men within the narrative world are united in doing violence to Tamar. But the text breaks with the command to silence and reveals itself to be on the woman's side. As a consequence of Amnon's violent act against Tamar, Absalom murders his brother (2 Sam 13:23-37) and so eliminates a competitor for the succession to the throne. The resulting banishment of Absalom is ended through the intervention of a wise woman (see below). But Absalom's hunger for power is very great. In the course of his rebellion against his father David, Absalom amasses so much military and political strength that David has to flee Jerusalem. In his hasty flight, David leaves seven concubines in Jerusalem "to look after the house" (2 Sam 16:21). Absalom and his troops take Jerusalem. In Absalom's uncertainty about what he should do now, Ahithophel makes a suggestion about how Absalom could document his rule: "Go in to your father's concubines, the ones he has left to look after the house; and all Israel will hear that you have made yourself odious to your father, and the hands of all who are with you will be strengthened" (16:21).

Absalom follows this advice and sleeps with his father's concubines before the eyes of all Israel. The reference to 2 Samuel 11–12 is all too clear, since it suggests that one should interpret Nathan's prophecy in 2 Samuel 12:7-14 in terms of these events. The roof of the palace from which David had seen and desired Bathsheba is the place where Absalom "takes" his father's concubines. The direction of the look David had cast upon Bathsheba is reversed when now Absalom, "in the sight of all Israel," goes in to David's concubines (2 Sam 16:22). The roof that in 2 Samuel 11 marked the elevated and thus powerful position of the one looking is now the exposed location of an event at which the whole public looks. By his public sexual act with his father's concubines, Absalom demonstrates a claim to rule. The consequence of Absalom's deed is as gruesome for the women as was the consequence for Tamar of Amnon's violent act. David comes back to Jerusalem and provides for the women, but imprisons them; until they die they are "living as if in widowhood" (20:3).

These passages about David's ten concubines, so difficult to understand by themselves, must be read in the context of the whole corpus of the books of Samuel and the passage in 1 Kings 1–2 that is part of the "succession narrative." We may here say only this about the narrative in 1 Kings 1–2, in which Abishag the Shunammite plays a role: Abishag is supposed to care for the aged David, whose sexual impotence ("the king did not know her," 1 Kings 1:4) is a sign of his political powerlessness. Abishag is functionalized by David's sons when Solomon — who in the meantime has become king — interprets the desire of his brother Adonijah to marry Abishag as a claim to David's throne, and has Adonijah killed (1 Kings 2:13-25).

The thread that runs through all the sexual connections in the context of royal dynasties is the linking of sexual and political power. David's marriage policy falls within this context, as does a brief episode (2 Sam 3:6-11) in which Saul's son Ishbaal challenges the general, Abner, who had taken Rizpah, Saul's concubine, after the death of Saul. Ishbaal understands this sexual act by Abner with Rizpah as a claim to rule. David's sexual "conquest" of Bathsheba should be seen against that background, as also Amnon's violent act against Tamar and Absalom's sexual manifestation, on the palace roof, of his claim to rule.

The description of the task David assigns to his concubines during his flight from Jerusalem may furnish us with a key to understanding the relationship between sexuality and the politics of power. They are to "look after the house." This task is so important that it is repeated every time the women are mentioned (2 Sam 15:16; 16:21; 20:3). The concept of the house shifts back and forth, within the books of Samuel, among its quite concrete spatial, its familial, its dynastic, and its national meanings. Thus the "house" is both the specific place as well as the family, which in the narrated political situation is becoming a dynasty, and also the nation as the house of Israel and Judah. David's house especially is no "private" space, but represents public reality. When in 2 Samuel 15:16-17 David's "house" is paralleled with the "people" or "nation," it is clear that the Davidic house has national-political significance. David's concubines are not left behind in Jerusalem to watch over the palace (the "king's house"); rather, these women represent in this moment the (in)stability of the Davidic dynasty. Leaving them behind also means positioning them as a point of attack. That is precisely what the counselor Ahithophel recognizes, as does the rebellious Absalom, following his advice. These women embody the Davidic dynasty. If Absalom can take possession of them he will force his way, over the bodies of the women, into his father's sphere of power.

The women are a means by which to demonstrate a political claim to rule. The enormity of the functionalization of women, as presented in the stories of Rizpah, Bathsheba, Tamar, David's concubines, and finally Abishag, is related to the specific sexualization of the politics of power, as it takes place in the establishment of the dynastic kingship. Inasmuch as the family is made into an institution for the support of the state, the sexual relationships regulated by the family likewise acquire significance for the maintenance of the state. The "succession narrative" shows that the dynastic form of rule is vulnerable to the misuse of power within the family. These narratives are not simply ambivalent as regards David, or generally critical of royalty; they criticize the dynastic form of rule. In the context of the depiction of dynastic politics, then, women come particularly into focus as the objects of sexuality understood in terms of the dynamics of power.

Wise Women in Israel

The first woman from the "group of wise women counselors in Israel" (Schroer 1992, 119) who treads the stage of the narrative world of the books of Samuel is a nameless woman from Endor (1 Sam 28). It is true that this woman is not called "wise," but in view of her narrative function she can be counted as part of that group. After Samuel's death, King Saul is in terrible trouble. Samuel had been the prophet who anointed Saul as king and during his reign stood at his side as his adviser, albeit a critical one. Samuel dies, and so does Saul's access to God: "When Saul inquired of YHWH, YHWH did not answer him, not by dreams, or by Urim, or by prophets" (1 Sam 28:6).

Saul then bids his servants to look for a woman who is a medium, in command of a dead spirit. His servants react promptly by telling him there is such a woman at Endor (28:7). This brief dialogue shows not only that this one woman "was widely known for her services as a medium" (Schroer 1992, 119), but also that the narrative community was more inclined to associate the practice of invoking the dead with women than with men, since Saul asks specifically for a woman with this ability.

Saul brings himself, and the woman he then visits, into conflict with a law against mediums that he himself had promulgated (1 Sam 28:9; cf. Lev 19:31; 20:6, 27; Deut 18:11; Isa 8:19; 19:3; 29:4). The guest, who at this point in the story is not yet identified to the medium as Saul, allays her fear of punishment by promising that nothing will happen to her. And so the medium enables a last, weird encounter between Samuel and Saul. The narrative gives this meeting a character of "*fascinosum et tremendum* . . . that quakes throughout" (Dietrich and Naumann 1995, 108). Samuel confirms for Saul only what had already become clear during the prophet's lifetime: "YHWH has turned from you and become your enemy" (1 Sam 28:16). In the dialogue with the desperate king that follows, the medium shows herself to be the sovereign host and a self-possessed woman. She is on the same level as Saul when she says: "Your servant has listened to you; I have taken my life in my hand, and have listened to what you have said to me. Now therefore, you also listen to your servant!" (28:21-22).

The medium turns "listening to Saul's voice" around, and in so doing makes it clear that she is not acting in obedience to a command but has offered Saul her services. Her concern as a host shows that "here mercy [belongs] to the image of the wise woman" (Schroer 1992, 121).

Two other women are introduced into the narrative with the explicit title of "wise woman": the wise woman of Tekoa (2 Sam 14) and the wise woman of Abel of Beth-maacah (2 Sam 20). The fact that both women are known only by this designation and their belonging to their respective cities indicates that the narrative community must have had a picture of these women prior to the actual narrative (Camp 1981, 17). Both women exercise a normative influence on political events through their intervention.

The wise woman of Tekoa is summoned by Joab through a messenger, a sign of how well she was known. She is to induce King David to bring his son Absalom back from exile, after the latter's murder of Amnon. Similarly to the prophet Nathan in 2 Samuel 12:1-7 and a nameless prophet in 1 Kings 20:38-43, the woman of Tekoa also tells the king a story that turns out to be a parable. The rhetorical strategy is to induce the king to issue judgment in a case that purportedly has nothing to do with him, in order then to apply the judgment to the king's own situation. In 2 Samuel 14 the woman pretends to be the mother of two sons, one of whom has murdered the other. While her other relatives demand blood vengeance, the woman is concerned for the continuance of her family. David twice attempts to console the woman without making any promises. Only after her second response does the king issue the judgment that nothing should happen to the son who had struck down the other (2 Sam 14:11). Now the woman applies her own familial situation to David, although not by referring to his own family, but by asking him: "Why then have you planned such a thing against the people of God?" (14:13). The close connection, to the point of identity, between the house of David and the house of Israel enables this kind of transfer. David has decided in a fashion that he must now apply to his own son by bringing him back from exile.

The wise woman of Abel of Beth-maacah (2 Sam 20) intervenes in a siege situation. She seeks a parlay with David's general, Joab, and succeeds in saving her city, in which a man named Sheba, who has revolted against David, has hidden. At the request of the woman, Joab approaches the city wall. The very fact that Joab lets himself get so close to the wall points to the authority of this woman. Approaching a city wall has to be regarded as a dangerous business, since Joab himself, in 2 Samuel 11:20-21, had recalled that Abimelech, in Judges 9:50-54, had been killed by a millstone thrown by a woman from the city wall. Although he is the general, Joab at this point finds himself in the inferior and endangered situation, a danger that threatens not only his life but also his honor. For to be killed by a woman was a shameful end for a warrior (Judg 9:54). Against this background, Joab enters into negotiations with the woman. After a request to be heard and the assurance that her dialogue partner is really Joab the general, she begins her speech with a proverb that distinguishes her city as a counselor from of old. She also calls the city a "mother in Israel," a formulation that refers back to the characterization of Deborah in Judges 5:7. By emphasizing the city's function as a counselor and personifying it as a mother, the wise woman embeds herself in the context of a city personified as a wise mother. She thus evokes the tradition of the mother as wise teacher (Prov 1:8) whose authority is here expanded from the immediate family to a broader political context (Camp 1981, 24-26). The wise woman must also be assured of having the same authority toward her fellow citizens, since even before she has spoken with the people of the city, she assures Joab that they will meet his condition, namely, the killing and handing over of the rebel. Her going "to the people of the city with her wise plan" (2 Sam 20:22) can be compared, as to its influence, with the kind of counsel a court adviser would give to his king (Camp 1981, 18).

These wise women show that both counseling as a function and wisdom language were not restricted to men or to the court context. Both women include proverbs in their speeches (2 Sam 14:14; 20:18). The wise woman of Abel appeals to the value of traditional knowledge (2 Sam 20:18). Both women show their rhetorical skill in dealing with a social superior; both have "the ability to speak the right word at the right time" (Camp 1981, 21, referring to the wise woman of Tekoa).

The counseling function of wise women is so firmly anchored in Israel's tradition that wise women became models for personified Wisdom (Schroer 1996, 66, 72-73). The term "model" (German *Vorbild*) is used "in the sense of a shaping, effectual model" (Schroer 1996, 72).

Constructions of the Feminine and of Masculinity

The books of Samuel show women in the greatest variety of roles and functions. They do not present gender-neutral people, but women and men. They construct gender-specific images of how people are supposed to behave. In part, these images deviate from the ideas that are normative in the Western world at the end of the twentieth and beginning of the twenty-first century, but in part we can see some overlapping.

For example, when Tamar is depicted in 2 Samuel 13:1 as "beautiful" and Jonadab in verse 3 as "wise," we are inclined to interpret these two attributes as gender-specific clichés. But a search of the books of Samuel for these two attributes shows that such an interpretation is a projection. The depictions of wise women in the books of Samuel make it clear that wisdom is not a phenomenon restricted to men. And beauty is a quality belonging to men as well as women, though in different ways. Whereas women's beauty in the Hebrew Bible almost always arouses male desire, and often endangers the woman as well, male beauty is the attribute of the politically powerful and successful. Saul is a handsome man (1 Sam 10:23), and so are David (1 Sam 16:12, 18) and Absalom (2 Sam 14:25-26). Male beauty comes to the fore when the men in question begin their political ascent. And male beauty is always made concrete in comparative terms, being attributed to someone who is distinguished from others by some external characteristic. Saul is taller than others, while the color of David's hair and his eyes are emphasized, and Absalom's abundant hair is measured by its weight. Besides beauty and readiness for battle, rhetorical abilities, entering into close relationships with other men, emotional detachment toward women, and musical talent make up a construction of manliness that is developed in the books of Samuel above all in the example of King David (Clines 1995, 216-28).

Likewise, the contrast that is common in our society between public and private space, with the public space belonging to men and the private space to women, cannot be verified in the books of Samuel. In the "house" itself, with its varied connotations, the distinctions between "public" and "private" fall apart. Some narratives center on a woman. In other places women are mentioned only in passing. These seemingly offhand remarks about women that are tossed in are revealing in their very purposelessness (Hackett 1992, 85). They show that women have public duties. At the royal court, for example, we know of the professions of cook, baker, and perfumer (1 Sam 8:13; cf. Schottroff 1989). Women serve at the entrance to the Tent of Meeting (1 Sam 2:22), though it is not clear what the specific service was. The text reproaches Eli's sons for having had sexual intercourse with these women. We cannot conclude from this that the passage refers to a sexual service by the women in the sense of cultic prostitution. We should rather think of a cultic service different from that of the priests (Hackett 1992, 87). It is possible that these women were even bound by a vow of chastity. Eli's sons would then be accused "of having seduced the women into failing to keep separate their cult-related service and the exercise of sexuality" (Wacker 1995, 151). In 2 Samuel 4:6 a woman appears as a doorkeeper. Abigail has maidservants (1 Sam 25:42); young women draw water (1 Sam 9:11). In the context of the birth and upbringing of children, it is not only their own mothers who are present. Women are present when a child is born (1 Sam 4:19-22), and 2 Samuel 4:4 speaks of the function of the nurse.

The realms within which women and men are active are not strictly separated in the books of Samuel. With the exception of the battlefield, all spaces are accessible to women. The multiplicity of roles in which women act makes it impossible to sketch a single, unified picture of femininity.

Biographies of Men and Portraits of Women

Women are the victims of men's striving after power and of male violence; they take charge of their own history and exercise great influence on the political history of Israel; they are mothers, daughters, and wise women; they stand at the center and on the margins of the story that is told. A great deal that might have been told about the lives of women remains unsaid. Very seldom does the text permit access to women's perspective, their thoughts, their feelings, and the context of their daily lives. The androcentric perspective of the depiction presents men as the dominant subjects of the narrated events, and shows both men and women from men's point of view. This bars access to women's understanding of themselves. Their presence at the center of Israel's political history, however, remains not merely a challenge to methodology; it is already realized in the books of Samuel.

Of course, the depiction of women's presence is fundamentally different from the presentation of the men who became central to Israel's political history. The depiction of these men follows biographical lines, while the depiction of women is sporadic. Women enter the game when their actions or their status as objects are important for advancing "his-story." By the same criterion they disappear again from the stage of the narrative world. The fragmentariness of the female figures makes a reading whose interest centers on women awkward, jerky, and often unsatisfying. Such a reading brings together pieces of a puzzle entitled "her-story," in the knowledge that only the imagination can fill in the many empty spaces.

LITERATURE

Abraham, Dulcie. 1992. "Rizpa's Story." In *Women of Courage: Asian Women Reading the Bible,* edited by Lee Oo Chung et al., 17-33. Seoul.

Bal, Mieke. 1987. *Lethal Love: Feminist Literary Readings of Biblical Love Stories.* Bloomington, Ind.

Bal, Mieke, et al., eds. 1988. *Und Sara lachte . . . Patriarchat und Widerstand in biblischen Geschichten.* Münster.

Bechmann, Ulrike. 1988. "Michal. Retterin und Opfer Davids." In *Zwischen Ohnmacht und Befreiung. Biblische Frauengestalten,* edited by Karin Walter, 71-80. Freiburg im Breisgau.

Berlin, Adele. 1982. "Characterization in Biblical Narrative: David's Wives." *Journal for the Study of the Old Testament* 23:69-85.

Brenner, Athalya, ed. 1994. *A Feminist Companion to Samuel and Kings.* Feminist Companion to the Bible, vol. 6. Sheffield.

Brenner, Athalya, and Fokkelien van Dijk-Hemmes. 1993. *On Gendering Texts: Female and Male Voices in the Hebrew Bible.* Biblical Interpretation Series, vol. 1. Leiden.

Burrichter, Rita. 1987. "Die Klage der Leidenden wird stumm gemacht. Eine biblisch-literarische Reflexion zum Thema Vergewaltigung und Zerstörung der Identität." In *Weil wir nicht vergessen wollen . . . zu einer feministischen Theologie im deutschen*

Kontext. AnFragen, vol. 1, *Diskussion Feministischer Theologie,* edited by Christine Schaumberger, 11-46. Münster.

Camp, Claudia. 1981. "The Wise Women of 2 Samuel: A Role Model for Women in Early Israel?" *Catholic Biblical Quarterly* 48:14-29.

Clines, David J. A. 1995. "David the Man: The Construction of Masculinity in the Hebrew Bible." In Clines, *Interested Parties: The Ideology of Writers and Readers of the Hebrew Bible,* 212-43. Journal for the Study of the Old Testament: Supplement Series, vol. 205. Sheffield.

Clines, David J. A., and Tamara C. Eskenazi, eds. 1991. *Telling Queen Michal's Story: An Experiment in Comparative Interpretation.* Journal for the Study of the Old Testament: Supplement Series, vol. 119. Sheffield.

Dietrich, Walter, and Thomas Naumann. 1995. *Die Samuelbücher.* Erträge der Forschung, vol. 287. Darmstadt.

Engelmann, Angelika. 1989. "2. Samuel 13,1-22: Tamar — eine schöne und deshalb geschändete Frau." In *Feministisch gelesen. Ausgewählte Bibeltexte für Gruppen und Gemeinden, Gebete für den Gottesdienst,* edited by Eva Renate Schmidt et al., 2:120-26. Stuttgart.

Exum, J. Cheryl. 1992. *Tragedy and Biblical Narrative: Arrows of the Almighty.* Cambridge.

―――. 1993. *Fragmented Women: Feminist (Sub)Versions of Biblical Narratives.* Journal for the Study of the Old Testament: Supplement Series, vol. 163. Sheffield.

Fuchs, Esther. 1989. "The Literary Characterization of Mothers and Sexual Politics in the Hebrew Bible." *Semeia* 46:151-66.

Habermann, Hanna. 1989. "1. Samuel 1: Hanna steht auf." In *Feministisch gelesen. ✡ Ausgewählte Bibeltexte für Gruppen und Gemeinden,* edited by Eva Renate Schmidt et al., 1:92-100. Stuttgart.

Hackett, Jo Ann. 1992. "1 and 2 Samuel." In *The Women's Bible Commentary,* edited by Carol A. Newsom and Sharon H. Ringe, 85-95. London and Louisville.

Heilig, Petra. 1992. "'Und ich, wohin soll ich meine Schande tragen?' Tamar (2 Sam 13)." In *Und sie tanzen aus der Reihe. Frauen im Alten Testament,* edited by Angelika Meissner, 129-44. Stuttgarter Taschenbücher, vol. 10. Stuttgart.

Heym, Stefan. 1984. *Der König David Bericht.* (A novel.) Frankfurt am Main.

Kessler, Rainer. 1989. "2. Samuel 11: Batseba — durch Demütigung zur Macht." In *Feministisch gelesen. Ausgewählte Bibeltexte für Gruppen und Gemeinden, Gebete für den Gottesdienst,* edited by Eva Renate Schmidt et al., 2:114-19. Stuttgart.

Linafelt, Tod. 1992. "Taking Women in Samuel: Readers/Responses/Responsibility." In *Reading between Texts: Intertextuality and the Hebrew Bible,* edited by Danna Nolan Fewell, 99-113. Louisville.

Lindgren, Torgny. 1987. *Bathseba: A Novel.* Munich.

Meyers, Carol. 1994. "Hannah and Her Sacrifice: Reclaiming Female Agency." In *A Feminist Companion to Samuel and Kings,* edited by Athalya Brenner. Sheffield.

Müllner. Ilse. 1997. *Gewalt im Hause Davids. Die Erzählung von Tamar und Amnon (2 Sam 13,1-22).* Freiburg im Breisgau.

―――. 1998. "Blickwechsel. Batseba und David in Romanen des 20. Jahrhunderts." *Biblical Interpretation* 6:348-66.

Ohler, Annemarie. 1992. "Rizpa, die 'Witwe' Sauls tritt für ihre toten Söhne ein." In Ohler, *Mutterschaft in der Bibel,* 179-84. Würzburg.

Schmidt, Eva Renate, and Renate Ellmenreich. 1990. "2. Samuel 21,1-14. Rizpa — eine Frau protestiert." In *Feministisch gelesen. Ausgewählte Bibeltexte für Gruppen und Gemeinden, Gebete für den Gottesdienst,* edited by Eva Renate Schmidt et al., 1:81-90. 3rd ed. Stuttgart.

Schottroff, Willy. 1989. "Der Zugriff des Königs auf die Töchter. Zur Fronarbeit von Frauen im Alten Israel." *Evangelische Theologie* 49:268-85.

Schroer, Silvia. 1992. *Die Samuelbücher.* Neuer Stuttgarter Kommentar, Altes Testament, vol. 7. Stuttgart.

———. 1996. *Die Weisheit hat ihr Haus gebaut. Studien zur Gestalt der Sophia in den biblischen Schriften.* Mainz.

Schwartz, Regina M. 1991. "The Histories of David: Biblical Scholarship and Biblical Stories." In *"Not in Heaven": Coherence and Complexity in Biblical Narrative,* edited by Jason P. Rosenblatt and Joseph C. Sitterson Jr., 192-210. Bloomington, Ind.

Stone, Ken. 1996. *Sex, Honor, and Power in the Deuteronomistic History.* Journal for the Study of the Old Testament: Supplement Series, vol. 234. Sheffield.

Trible, Phyllis. 1984. *Texts of Terror: Literary-Feminist Readings of Biblical Narratives.* Philadelphia.

———. 1987. *Mein Gott, warum hast du mich vergessen! Frauenschicksale im Alten Testament.* Gütersloh. (German trans. of *Texts of Terror.*)

Wacker, Marie-Theres. 1995. "'Religionsgeschichte Israels' oder 'Theologie des Alten Testaments' — (k)eine Alternative? Anmerkungen aus feministisch-exegetischer Sicht." *Jahrbuch Biblische Theologie* 10:129-55.

Welzel, Petra. 1994. *Rembrandts Bathseba — Metapher des Begehrens oder Sinnbild zur Selbsterkenntnis? Eine Bildmonographie.* Europäische Hochschulschriften, ser. 28, Kunstgeschichte, vol. 204. Frankfurt am Main.

Willi-Plein, Ina. 1995. "Frauen um David: Beobachtungen zur Davidshausgeschichte." In *Meilenstein,* edited by Manfred Weippert and Stefan Timm, 349-61. Festschrift for Herbert Donner. Ägypten und Altes Testament, vol. 30. Wiesbaden.

Translated by Linda M. Maloney

Books of Kings: Images of Women without Women's Reality

Kyung Sook Lee

Preliminaries

Reading the books of Kings with feminist eyes immediately prompts some basic comments. The Deuteronomist redactors who gave the books their present form (Smend 1978, 111-25) have very little to say about women; the difference between what they do say about women and their narratives of the patriarchs (or "arch-parents") and David is crass. One will be disappointed if one wants to learn something from these books of the situation of women during the royal era. And when the redactors do speak of women — it is remote from objective presentation — they have chiefly two types in mind: women who are very poor and helpless or women who are extremely cruel and vengeful. Only the mothers of kings are highly respected and introduced by their name and origin. But this applies only to mothers of the kings of Judah; the mothers of the kings of Israel are ignored. This and the fact that the kings of the northern kingdom of Israel are judged negatively prove that the redactors represent the party line of the southern kingdom of Judah.

In terms of theology and cult, the Deuteronomists were believers in YHWH and Jerusalem-centered. Their primary interest was whether the respective occupant of the throne and his people revered YHWH or not. Whether the king was successful in economy or politics was of secondary significance to them. Faithfulness to YHWH and to the temple in Jerusalem was the yardstick of their judgment. Hence, it is not difficult for them to condemn the kings of the northern realm. They are all judged negatively because King Jeroboam had two official shrines built outside Jerusalem at the end of the tenth century B.C.E., one in Bethel and the other in Dan where he and the other kings of that kingdom subsequently offered their sacrifices. But one does not do justice historically to Jeroboam if one criticizes him with the anachronistic argument that he had set up altars outside Jerusalem. He had those places built for the worship of YHWH; both had sculptures of calves, most likely as pedestals for the deity. It is wrong therefore to assert that Jeroboam worshiped not YHWH but a golden calf, an idol. Still, the Deuteronomist redactors judged as if the whole royal era had been governed by the notion that Jerusalem was the place where worship was centered and by the prohibition of images, and then charged the northern kingdom with nefariously violating these truths from the outset (1 Kings 12:27-30).

Of all the kings of Israel, Ahab comes in for the harshest criticism. He was married to the Sidonian princess Jezebel, through whom the worship of Baal is supposed to have come to Israel. Accordingly, she is one of the worst figures in the First Testament: she plunged Israel into misery (1 Kings 18–21). The queen mother Athaliah, a granddaughter or daughter of Omri (2 Kings 8:26f.), is criticized for being an extremely cruel woman. She had her whole family killed so that she could rule herself (2 Kings 11:1f.). But here, too, precise analysis of the Deuteronomist redactors' tendentious historiography shows that the actual course of history was different from the reportage in the books of Kings. What we register here by way of introduction is that the redactors show little interest in an objective depiction of historical facts and that they are particularly ill-disposed toward women.

The redactors of the books of Kings drew on diverse sources, some of which they refer to by name: (1) the book of the history of Solomon, (2) the annals of the kings of Israel, (3) the annals of the kings of Judah, and (4) independent narratives of the prophets. It is not clear whether the book of the history of Solomon is a unified work. It could be a generally accessible work, but it is not identical with the annals recorded at the royal court, and while it is indeed based on official records, it also draws on other traditions. The annals of the kings of Israel and Judah were quite likely composed by officials at the courts. They registered only official activities such as military campaigns, enthronement ceremonies, how long kings ruled or the years of regency, etc. Accordingly, we expect few reports about women. Still, a few women do appear in the stories of the prophets Elijah and Elisha. The redactors combined these sources in a new way according to their theological criteria. That is why it is not easy on the whole to follow the books of Kings; the stories of the prophets especially are split into several pieces whose (original) chronological order can be discerned only with difficulty. That is particularly disadvantageous for feminist reading because those stories do allow for at least some insight into the situation of women.

In their present form, the books of Kings receive their character from the frame created by the Deuteronomist redactors to hold together their excerpted materials related to individual rulers. The frame consists of a five-part introduction and a four-part conclusion. The five elements of the introduction are as follows: (1) when each regency began (the dates from the two kingdoms are synchronized in each case), (2) the age of the ruler at his enthronement (only the kings of Judah are mentioned), (3) how long each reign lasted, (4) the name of the queen mother (only of the kings of Judah), and (5) a judgment concerning each king's religious devotion. The four elements of the conclusion are as follows: (1) a reference to more detailed sources, (2) a report of the king's death, (3) something about the king's burial among his fathers (only in relation to the kings of Judah), and (4) the name of the successor.

The Content of the Books of Kings

Bathsheba as Kingmaker?

The first book of Kings begins with a story that surely did not come from the official annals of King Solomon. It relates how complicated Solomon's accession to the throne was and why Adonijah, his brother and competitor, had to die. Given the story's anti-Solomon leaning, it would not be far-fetched to assume that it came from the pen of a redactor that had been influenced by the prophets (Würthwein 1977, 11f.). Presumably he took old reports and created an independent work that reflected his antipathy toward Solomon and his sympathizers. Many contemporary figures appear in that bundle of narratives; next to Solomon there are persons like Adonijah, Abishag, Bathsheba, and Nathan. On the surface, Bathsheba appears to be the story's main character, but the real protagonist is Nathan. He seeks out Bathsheba and explains to her that Adonijah's enthronement took place without David's knowledge and that as a result her life and that of her son Solomon are in great danger. What he does not say is that his life is also threatened, but it is clear that he is worried not only about Bathsheba and Solomon but also about himself. He wants Bathsheba to go to David and remind him of his promise to make her son Solomon his successor. Whether, historically speaking, there ever was such a promise by David to Bathsheba and, if there was, how Nathan could have known about it, are not known. Many commentators believe that such a promise lacks historical foundation. In any case, it is clear that Nathan is the real "kingmaker." It is illogical and false to stamp Bathsheba as a schemer (Kessler 1989, 118). It would be equally inappropriate to praise her as a woman who was very smart and made the best of her situation (Miller 1988, 81-91). She simply was not the driving force who orchestrated this process and deserved to be praised or criticized for it. It is very easy to understand why she accepted Nathan's suggestion and acted on it: for her it was a question of life and death. That David listened to and granted her request was her good fortune, perhaps even redounded to her merit, but that does not make her a hero or a witch.

Women at the Court of Solomon

Bathsheba was the first to hear the good news from David: "Your son Solomon shall succeed me as king, and he will sit on my throne in my place" (1 Kings 1:30). Solomon was anointed at the brook of Gihon. The balance between Adonijah's party — his mother Haggith, the priest Abiathar, and the commander Joab — had shifted in favor of Solomon's party — his mother Bathsheba, the prophet Nathan, the priest Zadok, and Benaiah, the leader of the palace guard. Fearing his brother, Adonijah fled to the altar in Jerusalem and clutched the horns of the altar for protection. Only after Solomon promised not to kill him did Adonijah return home. Still, the conflict between them ended in a death. As a man of honor, Adonijah did not want to do anything to Solomon; he asked that David's beautiful attendant Abishag the Shunammite be given him for his wife. Very little is known about her. When David was well advanced in years, she was given to him in the hope that she might give him a new lease on life. According to ancient Oriental belief, a young woman can give vitality to an old (male) body. Similar customs are still practiced today in many countries. But David was not helped by this therapeutic measure, he did not regain strength and could not love Abishag sexually (1:4). There is much debate about whether Abishag, described in the word *sōkenet,* was David's concubine or even the prefect of his harem (Schroer 1995, 116; ET, 118-19; Häusl 1993), or simply a servant. Be that as it may, she was young and beautiful and was supposed to remain at court for the rest of her life. If anyone could have her for his wife, it could only be Solomon, David's successor. But it seems that Adonijah was in love with her and tried, with the help of Bathsheba, to get Solomon to give her to him. Since he hardly had any further ambitions to the throne and accepted the course of events as a decree of YHWH, his marital plans could not have been an intrigue in disguise against Solomon (Würthwein 1977, 22). He no longer posed any danger to his brother, and Bathsheba would also have recognized that. But Solomon reacted differently. He took Adonijah's naïve wish to be a claim on the kingdom. (2 Samuel 12:8 and 16:21f. infer that possessing the royal harem established the right to lay claim to the royal throne.) Solomon panics and has Adonijah killed instantly (1 Kings 2:23-25).

The question remains why Bathsheba did not hesitate to present Adonijah's request to her son Solomon. Did she want to have Adonijah eliminated, after all, by presenting the request? We do not know what her motives were, but it goes too far to think of her as that cunning. As queen mother she perhaps saw nothing but a servant in Abishag and did not consider Adonijah's courting her to be a way to get to the throne. Perhaps she took pity on Abishag for being bound for life as a virgin to the king's court. The story mirrors the fate of a woman brought to the court to serve there. She was placed into the hands of lords (and ladies) she did not know, and no one asked about her feelings and wishes. She had to bear her lot in silence. We do not know whether she was glad that Adonijah, successor designate to the throne, wanted to take her as his wife, nor whether she was sad that he was murdered on her account. Many women at the royal court had to live lives like hers controlled by strangers. In the king's possession and as part of his harem, they had no right to an existence of their own. The narrator of the story is not interested in how Abishag's life continued; after Adonijah's death she is of no significance anymore.

On the other hand, Bathsheba enjoys an honored position as queen mother. She is received by King Solomon with pomp and great reverence. A throne is set up for her at his right hand — a symbol of her dignity and esteem (1 Kings 2:19). The queen mother *(gĕbîrâ)* held an influential position at the court (more on this below). She was an adviser to the king or represented him if he was too young or if something had happened to him. Apparently Bathsheba herself supervised the selection and assignment of the concubines. *Gĕbîrâ,* "sovereign lady," is the title of both the king's consort (1 Kings 11:19) and his mother — the highest title for women in the books of Kings.

Still, Bathsheba remains under androcentric control. Even though she enjoyed the highest rank and great fame at the end of her life, in the ancestral line of Jesus she is listed merely as the wife of Uriah (Matt 1:6).

Solomon's Wise Judgment

The story of Solomon's proverbial wisdom begins in 1 Kings 3. One example of it is the story of his wisdom in rendering judgment (1 Kings 3:16-28). Two sex-trade women come to Solomon, each claiming to have given birth to the same child. The king solves the issue easily and elegantly because he believes that a birth mother's compassion for her child outweighs the legal claim on it. We have known for a long time that this story had originally nothing to do with Solomon (Gressmann 1907); it became associated with him for the sole purpose of showing how wise he was. In the original story, there was a wise judge and not a king, and two married women and not two sex-trade women who fought over the child for the sake of their common husband's favor, their position in the family, or their eligibility to receive inheritance. Why did the redactors change the portrayal of the women? Did the redactors wish not to let such a less than pleasant process play itself out in an honorable Israelite family (Noth 1968, 47f.)? Or did they perhaps want to put cantankerous, irrational, or socially marginalized women into their narratives to heighten the dramatic effect and to show their disdain for women? In many of the stories they edited, there are poor widows, sex-trade workers, or humiliated childless women. The existence of "normal" wives is obscured by this tendency, and what emerges is an extremely negative image of women.

The Temple and the Queen of Sheba

The Deuteronomist redactors describe at great length what they consider to be Solomon's greatest achievement: the building of the temple of YHWH in Jerusalem (1 Kings 5–9). It took twenty years and enormous sums to complete the building of this spectacular edifice. Solomon even had to call upon his neighbor King

Hiram of Tyre to help out. When the building had been completed, the Queen of Sheba came for a visit (1 Kings 10:1-13). She was an extremely wise woman and came to test Solomon with hard questions. Of course, she was highly impressed by his wisdom and wealth. The story wants to show how far and wide his fame had spread and serves to glorify him. Whether the Queen of Sheba actually visited Solomon and what she sought to accomplish with this state visit is an open question historically. There is no transparent diplomatic reason for it, and it is hardly credible that all she wanted was to test the king with enigmatic questions. Either the story is a fabrication or else it has a complicated tradition the history of which is almost beyond our grasp. In any case, it is highly unlikely that there existed a queen in South Arabian Sheba in the days of Solomon, although we have evidence of queens in North Arabian states during the eighth century B.C.E. (Würthwein 1977, 121). From a feminist perspective, it is not irrelevant that the redactors depict the Queen of Sheba as a queen of wisdom and that at the end they let her pay homage to Solomon and praise him. According to verse 8, she is supposed to have said: "Happy are your wives" (as the old translations have it and not "your men" as in the Hebrew text). "Happy are these your servants who continually attend you and hear your wisdom." Coming from the mouth of a woman, this sounds rather erotic; probably this word of praise suggests that the queen had erotic feelings for Solomon (cf. 10:13). It is no surprise that this episode has given rise to countless tales around King Solomon and the Queen of Sheba in Jewish, Arabian, and African literature.

Foreign Women at the Royal Court

1 Kings 11 talks about Solomon's foreign women and does so in a highly negative manner. He is supposed to have had seven hundred main wives and three hundred concubines and to have built cultic sites for Chemosh, the god of Moab, and Molech, the god of Ammon. Originally traditions of such a large number of women and the building of cultic sites were meant most likely to demonstrate how wealthy and powerful Solomon and his capital city Jerusalem were (Würthwein 1977, 131). But the Deuteronomist redactors give it a different rendition: "his wives turned away his heart after other gods; and his heart was not true to the Lord his God, as was the heart of his father David" (1 Kings 11:4; cf. v. 2). This is the redactors' way of holding the foreign women responsible for Solomon's worship of foreign gods and laying the blame for the separation of the northern tribes from the Davidic dynasty on him (11:11, 32f.). But that charge against his wives is both anachronistic and highly exaggerated. When Solomon established his government in Israel and Judah, YHWH was the national deity. And yet foreign deities could be received as guests in the Jerusalem temple and have their statues and altars set up there (Lang 1981, 55). On a hill near Jerusalem there were sanctuaries for the

Moabite Chemosh and the Ammonite Molech (not "Moloch" as the Hebrew text puts it contemptuously). Foreign priests attended to those gods. In addition, Solomon gave his foreign wives the opportunity to offer smoke and other sacrifices to their gods at their holy places. All these phenomena would indicate that the syncretism of that time and its official advancement by Solomon were accepted in Israel without opposition. The redactors assess this ancient period in terms of the YHWH-centered conceptions. Holding foreign women responsible for the alleged errors of the past clearly shows their antipathy against women; as is often the case, women became scapegoats.

The Secession of the Northern Kingdom

The original reason why the northern kingdom seceded from the Davidic dynasty of Judah is recorded in 1 Kings 12:1-24. The oldest historical sources cite Rehoboam's recklessness during his meeting with the Israelites at Shechem for the breakup. Rehoboam, Solomon's son, did not heed the counsel of the older men but took that of the younger men who whispered the racy phrase into his ears: "My father made your yoke heavy but I will add to your yoke; my father disciplined you with whips, but I will discipline you with scorpions" (12:14 [the German text has *Geisseln* = "lashes" instead of "scorpions" — trans.]). It is not clear exactly who those "older" and "younger" men were. Presumably they were two groups of king's counselors differing in age. After Jeroboam the Ephraimite followed the people's will and accepted the crown, he brought about the secession from Judah and established centers of worship in Bethel and Dan (12:26-33). Since there had been a national temple only in Jerusalem until then, official sites of worship had to be established also in the northern kingdom. The concept of "the sin of Jeroboam" (cf. 12:30; 15:26; 16:2 and 31; etc.) is meaningful only in the light of the centralization of worship in Jerusalem that occurred at a later time (Debus 1967, 41). As mentioned earlier, the images of the calf in Bethel and Dan that the Deuteronomist redactors assailed with such vigor served as pedestals for the god YHWH who was believed to be present but not visible. They were cult objects like the cherubim and the ark in Jerusalem (Stolz 1996, 114-19). If looked at in this way, the temple in Jerusalem was no less syncretistic than the temples in Bethel and Dan.

Chapter 13 tells stories of two unnamed prophets and raises the question of who is and who is not a true prophet and what really constitutes the prophetic mission. Numerous narratives show how serious those questions were at that time. But no clear definition of prophecy is found in them. Still the term "a man of God" indicates that someone who speaks God's words and possesses supernatural powers with God's help is said to be a prophet.

The Queen Mother (Gĕbîrâ)

In 1 Kings 14:21-31 the redactor returns to the story of Rehoboam's enthronement (cf. 11:43) and mentions the name of Rehoboam's mother: Naamah the Ammonite. Apparently a queen mother did not have to be the same person as the chief wife of the king's father, even though that appears to have been the normal situation. Solomon's chief wife was a daughter of Pharaoh (1 Kings 3:1; 7:8; 9:16 and 24). According to 15:9-13, King Asa of Judah removed his mother Maacah from being queen mother. The fact that the gĕbîrâ of King Asa has the same name as that of King Abijam, Maacah (15:2), creates some difficulty: Was Asa a brother of Abijam or was his queen mother actually his grandmother? Perhaps gĕbîrâ does not refer every time to the biological mother of the king in question but to the possessor of a certain position. We can assume that she occupied an important and influential position with significant political and ceremonial rights at the court of Judah's dynasty (cf. Donner 1994). 1 Kings 15:13 also supports the view that gĕbîrâ signifies a position of dignity and official powers that could be withdrawn without affecting the continuing role of the mother of the king. Since the Deuteronomist redactors rarely speak more extensively of the gĕbîrâ and since the title was probably used only at the court of Judah, it is unfortunate that no detailed picture of this position can be developed (cf. Donner 1994; Andreasen 1983; and Ackerman 1993 on this topic). We cannot say with certainty whether the southern kingdom was more strongly structured by dynasty and therefore adopted the institution of the gĕbîrâ, or whether the Deuteronomist redactors, being hostile to the northern kingdom, deliberately suppressed reports concerning a corresponding position there. However, we do need to keep in mind that the northern kingdom harbored great reservations against the formation of a dynasty and the institutions associated with it, something the frequent bloody conspiracies tend to demonstrate. What we can state thus far is that the queen mother at the royal court of Judah had an essential function even when the redactors mention it only as an afterthought. For them the story of men ("his-story") was of greater weight.

Asherah and the Asherites

King Asa is said to have removed Maacah from her position of queen mother because "she had made an abominable image for Asherah" (1 Kings 15:13). The name Asherah seems to refer to a female deity; the Deuteronomist redactors faulted Maacah for having given glory to a deity other than YHWH alone. If this is a reworking of a historical reminiscence, we may assume that Maacah exercised her cultic obligations as a gĕbîrâ (cf. Ackerman 1993). Or else, she performed an act of personal piety that the redactors subsequently took to be a contravention of the exclusive worship of YHWH. 1 Kings 15:13 could then be taken as indirect proof that the goddess Asherah was worshiped in Jerusalem during the royal period. The word "Asherah" also has another meaning in the two books of Kings; it refers to wooden poles that could have been part of the cult of the goddess Asherah. Researchers disagree strongly about how extensive the worship of this goddess was in the Israel of the royal era (cf. Keel and Uehlinger 1992; Braulick 1991; Wacker 1991; Frevel 1994). The association of Asherah (or the Asherites) and Baal (or the followers of Baal) made in the Deuteronomists' construction of history represents their polemic perspective more than historical reality; the god Baal and the goddess Asherah are no divine couple (Olyan 1988). But it seems that for a time Asherah was venerated next to YHWH and the idea that she was the "partner" of YHWH is surely not to be restricted to "grassroots religion" (Albertz 1992, 131-35). Was the *gĕbîrâ* Maacah possibly someone who represented that idea? What is quite clear is that the redactors always speak of Asherah and Asherites when they want to criticize the kings of the northern and southern kingdoms for the idolatry and attribute the demise of both kingdoms to such worship. Their blatant misogyny notwithstanding, they did not one-sidedly taint only women with the cult of a goddess.

The Omrides (Ahab and Jezebel) and Elijah

1 Kings 15:16-32 recounts the rapid change of dynasties in the northern kingdom and provides several reasons for that development. The northern kingdom was theologically and ideologically opposed to kingship; for a long time geographical and external circumstances made the establishment of a dynasty difficult there. Only Omri (16:23-28) was able to establish a stable ruling family. It reigned over Israel for about forty years. Omri bought a hill from a man called Shemer and had a new, centrally located capital city built on it that he called Samaria after the previous owner's name. 1 Kings 16:29 launches into an interesting cycle of narratives around King Ahab, Omri's son, his "evil" wife Queen Jezebel, and the prophet Elijah. The Elijah stories are found in 1 Kings 17–19 and 2 Kings 1–2. Elijah ("my God is YHWH") came from Tishbe in Gilead. There he foretold the coming of a drought that would last for years (1 Kings 17:1). Later he lived as a hermit at the brook Cherith east of the Jordan; ravens brought him bread and meat. Some of his miracles are recorded in 1 Kings 17:2-6, 8-16, and 17-24; 2 Kings 1:9-17. He met a poor widow who was gathering firewood at Zarephath in the region of Sidon. When he asks her for a piece of bread, she tells him how desperately poor she is. He ends her distress as he utters these miracle-working words: "The jar of meal will not be emptied and the jar of oil will not fail" (1 Kings 17:14). Of course, it was YHWH who gave Elijah the power to do miracles. To demonstrate Elijah's identity as a miracle-worker, the redactor adds another miracle: Elijah brought the widow's deceased son back to life (17:17-24). With his powers he could bring rain and fire

and help poor people. But these poor folk are always women who have nothing to eat or have no sons who could support them. Old tales and legends often include many poor women who find help through miracles. Why is it that women play such a wretched role in such tales? Perhaps the storytellers wanted to heighten the curiosity of their hearers and increase the effect of their tale by including extremely poor protagonists. On the other hand, stories like that reflect more how bad the economic situation of women is. Perhaps the storytellers took precarious positions of women for granted. Almost always women suffer from poverty more quickly and to a greater extent than others in many parts of the world, even today. If anyone really needed God's help, it often was a woman — the stories of Elijah show that most clearly (Wacker 1989).

Jezebel emerges as Elijah's adversary (chapter 18). The name Jezebel has association with the Ugaritic word *zbl* (sovereign ruler), an epithet of the god Baal. But the redactors render its meaning as a combination of *zebel* ("shit" — German *Scheisse*) and *'î* (island), thereby turning her name into something like "a pile of shit" (Gray 1963, 332f.). The marriage of Ahab and Jezebel was of great benefit politically and economically for both Israel and Phoenicia. But that was irrelevant for the Deuteronomist redactors. According to 1 Kings 18:4 and 13, Jezebel is supposed to have killed all the prophets of YHWH; in an act of revenge Elijah killed all of Baal's prophets (18:40). Subsequently Jezebel persecuted Elijah. But the statements in 18:4 and 13 (cf. v. 19) are later additions and variations on the theme of prosecuting the prophets. At this stage of redaction Jezebel had been turned into a murderer of prophets to heighten the contrast between the queen who was hostile to YHWH and Obadiah, her minister, who greatly revered YHWH and is highly praised in the Deuteronomist history of the prophets (18:4, 13, and 16; cf. Würthwein 1984, 496-98). Nevertheless, we can presume why the redactors portrayed Jezebel as an evildoer, that is, as an enemy of God. She probably arrived in Israel accompanied with an entourage from Tyre who, like her, worshiped Baal. We already know that Solomon had built places of worship for his foreign wives. But the redactors, refusing to tolerate this, criticized Jezebel more severely than Solomon. That is why they, in what can only be called immoderate exaggeration, turned her into a hunter of the prophets of YHWH. If one reads 1 Kings 18–19 more closely, one gets the impression that the population was split at that time between one part that worshiped YHWH and another that worshiped Baal. Alt (1964) argues fairly persuasively that there are historical reasons for this division in the Mount Carmel region. Elijah wanted to make it absolutely clear in this situation that one cannot worship YHWH and Baal at the same time. Only YHWH is the god of Israel!

On Mount Carmel Elijah demonstrated that YHWH alone is God (1 Kings 18) and subsequently had a theophany of YHWH in the wilderness (chapter 19).

What is the significance of the overemphasized YHWH-Baal alternative? Was Elijah's attitude toward the faith in YHWH a fresh rediscovery of the monotheistic tradition of Moses that had been neglected after the people of Israel had taken possession of the land, or was it an innovation? In contrast to von Rad, for example (1969, 200), and many other exegetes of his generation, younger First Testament scholars such as Lang (1981) and, with modifications, Albertz (1992) consider the second possibility to be correct. When Ahab set up an altar for Baal, the god of Tyre, he only followed a well-established and uncontested practice of the day. In the middle of the ninth century B.C.E. the king of Damascus, Bar-Hadad, erected a stele for Melqart, the city god of Tyre, and called this foreign deity "his lord" (Lang 1981, 58). Presumably Baal had been worshiped in the territory of the Israelite kingdom for centuries. It is quite possible that as a result of Ahab's open politics in relation to Tyre, other earlier cults of Baal came to life again in the countryside, for example, on Mount Carmel. Nonetheless, it is improbable that the royal court initiated an aggressive religious policy against the religion of YHWH as the texts of 1 Kings allege. The court more likely consented to a coexistence of YHWH and Baal worship or even promoted it, and it certainly did not prevent the religion of Baal from being revitalized (Albertz 1992, 232). There is every appearance that Jezebel was an influential and popular queen in Israel who indirectly limited the influence of the priests of YHWH through the newly flourishing cult of Baal. The Deuteronomist redactors resented this and, in uncurbed exaggeration, portrayed her as one of the main figures in the persecution of YHWH's prophets. It escaped their attention, so it would seem, that the children of Jezebel and Ahab all have names containing elements of the name YHWH: Ahaziah, Jehoram, and Athalya. But then the redactors' falsification of historical facts corresponds to their tendency to demonize powerful women as godless evildoers.

Ahab and Jezebel quickly expanded their possessions, thereby solidifying their kingship. In this context, the Naboth novella (1 Kings 21) describes a probably quite typical event. It is quite likely that Queen Jezebel made questionable deals in order to have absolute royal sovereignty prevail over the ancient Israelite laws that protected individual citizens. This evoked sharp criticism of the northern kingdom's royalty, for the monarch's expansionism collided with the traditional rights of the clans according to which a family possessed an inalienable right on the land it owned. The traditional critique of kingship in the northern realm had always been virulent and had only grown stronger as a result of the offensive expansion of royal powers since Omri (Würthwein 1984, 249ff.). In connection with the violent dispossession described in the Naboth episode, it is important to remember that 1 Kings 21:1-16 is not a historical report but a novella in which the narrator develops the course of events as a means of characterizing the people involved and their time (Oeming 1986, 377ff.). The events are described all too accurately in some parts and all too vaguely in others to give them the air of authenticity. But for the Deuteronomists it was clear that Jezebel as a woman had to be guilty of all that happened. Yet they fail in making her the guilty party par excellence because her plans could not have worked without the complicity of the elders and King Ahab.

In 21:17-24 the redactors put a word of YHWH in Elijah's mouth, and it is not only Jezebel but also Ahab who is reproached for being the primary culprit.

Elijah fought against the politics of religion that the Omrides had introduced because it threatened to deform the religion of Israel through syncretism. A group of prophets that included Elijah and Elisha led an unmistakable protest that eventually led to the brutal collapse of the Omridic religious policies. At that time the kings began to give themselves names with elements of the name of YHWH. Jehoshaphat (that is: YHWH judges), king of Judah, and Jehoram (that is: YHWH is exalted), son of Ahab, were the first rulers of the two kingdoms who had such names. This pattern of naming possibly symbolizes the idea arising at that time of an exclusive relation between YHWH and the people of Israel.

The last chapter of 1 Kings describes at great length an alliance that Ahab and Jehoshaphat, king of Judah, entered into and a war they waged on Syria. The death of Ahab is reported in 1 Kings 22:29-37; despite Ahab's cunning, a Syrian soldier killed him with his bow and arrow. Ahab was buried in Samaria. Verse 38 adds a gloss that dogs licked up his blood and prostitutes washed themselves in it. In characteristic manner, the Deuteronomists put prostitutes and dogs on the same level.

Elisha, the Man of God, and Jehu, the Revolutionary

In the first chapter of the second book of Kings there is a brief notice of war between Israel and Moab (1:1; 3:1-27) and the last of Elijah's miracle stories (1:2-17). In the next chapter Elisha becomes Elijah's successor. His miracles are recorded in 4:1-5:27: an impoverished widow receives oil (4:1-7), a long-childless Shunammite woman's much-longed-for son falls deadly ill and dies but is raised up again by Elisha (4:8-37), a poisoned dish is made edible (4:38-41), bread is multiplied (4:42-44), and the Aramaic commander Naaman is healed from his leprosy (5:1-27). All these stories have a striking resemblance to the corresponding reports of Elijah's miracles; in terms of history of tradition, these stories belong together. Many exegetes believe that the Elisha stories predate those of Elijah (Smend 1978, 136). As a man of God, Elisha possessed the supernatural powers to perform miracles. Elijah, on the other hand, became characterized as a miracle-worker through the additions made by the redactors who wanted him to be seen as a second Moses (Kaiser 1984, 169).

The women we meet in the Elisha narratives are just as poor as those in Elijah's miracle stories. Either they have nothing to eat or their sons are deadly ill. Probably the narrators could picture only these two types of women who were in need of a miracle. In the story of Naaman's healing, the notion of the uniqueness of YHWH surfaces again: "There is no God in all the earth except in Israel" (5:15). Naaman had heard about Elisha's healing power from an Israelite slave woman; in a certain sense she is a missionary of her God and his prophets. This raises a different question: How can Naaman the foreigner worship YHWH as the one and only God at the royal court of Aram? Naaman inquires whether he can keep on practicing his Aramaic customs and usages and still serve YHWH. This was a highly important issue for proselytes. Elisha's reply is amazingly brief: "Go in peace" (5:19). This is the permission Naaman needed, and it shows the position the prophet of YHWH took toward other cultures. In this context it does not matter whether the story is true historically or not. Magnanimity in the required cultic practice corresponds to the belief in the universality of the God YHWH. This is regarded as a key text for the problems of inculturation and the hermeneutic of biblically based faith that occupy us today.

2 Kings 9–10 narrates the revolution of Jehu. On orders from Elisha, one of the prophet's disciples secretly anoints the Israelite commander Jehu king over Israel at Ramoth-gilead. Thereupon Jehu rose up in rebellion against the house of Omri, first killing Joram (9:16-24), then Joram's ally King Ahaziah of Judah (9:27), and finally Jezebel (9:30-35). In addition, he had all the priests of Baal killed and the places of Baal worship destroyed (10:18-27). It is quite likely that Jehu's brutal actions and his fervent devotion to YHWH had the support of the prophets of YHWH, especially that of Elisha and other groups faithful to YHWH (10:15-17). The revitalization of the cult of Baal and the royal claims of absoluteness in response to the stance faithful followers of YHWH had taken came to an abrupt end. But Jehu's revolution also destroyed the diplomatic relations the Omrides had created and completely changed the political situation of both kingdoms. His policies isolated the northern kingdom and exposed it without protection to the attacks by the Arameans. Jehu's politics of "YHWH alone" brought no fortune to Israel; even the Deuteronomists had to admit that.

Athaliah

2 Kings 11:1-20 is the story of Athaliah setting out to kill all the descendants of the royal house when she found out that her son Ahaziah had been murdered in Israel. The text adds that she also wanted to kill her grandson Joash so that she might rule supreme as queen. That gave Athaliah the reputation of being power-hungry and extremely cruel; she became the quintessential representative of a vile woman who does not shrink back when it serves her own advantage.

Who was Athaliah? Some say she was Ahab's daughter (8:18), others that she was Omri's (8:26). From the perspective of history, it is almost impossible to believe she was a daughter of Ahab. Presumably she was born Omri's daughter around 880 B.C.E. in the northern kingdom and was given in marriage to the Judean prince Joram, a symbolic gesture of peace between Israel and Judah, and lived in the southern kingdom. Her husband did become king of Judah but died early. Then her son Ahaziah became king, but he and forty-two other Judean princes were murdered by Jehu (9:27; 10:12-14). That left Athaliah alone in Jerusalem. In this situation she is said to have walked over the dead bodies of her own (already murdered) relatives and taken cruel revenge, and that is how she came to power — all this only to satisfy her ambition? Close reading of this report raises more questions. For what reason would she have killed her own grandson? How could he have presented a danger for her? Since her son Ahaziah was dead and all other legitimate successors to the throne murdered, Athaliah automatically had to come to power because she was queen mother.

The sister of Ahaziah, Jehoshabeath, is mentioned in the narrative of Joash. She is said to have taken Joash away from the royal palace and secretly raised him in the temple for six years. But how could she have abducted him in full view of Athaliah and hidden him for so long in the neighboring house of YHWH? 2 Chronicles 22:11 says Jehoshabeath was the wife of the priest Jehoiada. When Joash was seven years old, the priest led a successful conspiracy against Athaliah and had Joash proclaimed king. Jehoiada then assumed power himself until Joash could rule the land on his own.

According to Levin (1982, 46ff.), the account of 2 Kings 11 cannot correspond to the facts of history. The revolution of Jehu and King Ahaziah's death probably created political turmoil in Judah. Two factions likely claimed the leadership in that situation. One was the party of Athaliah; as queen mother she could be the legitimate representative of the king. The party opposing her wanted to take over David's dynasty and its power. Athaliah had come from the northern kingdom where her family, the Omrides, had been exterminated by Jehu. She was alone and could not count on support from her homeland. She probably also did not enjoy the support from the Jerusalem temple and the priestly circle because she was an Omride. Nevertheless, Athaliah succeeded in this difficult situation to seize the throne. Presumably she had friends at the royal court with whose help her adversaries there could be removed. But that she wanted to kill her own grandson sounds odd. It is more likely that she looked after him in a special way so that when he became king he could protect her. Thus, 2 Kings 11:1-2 appears to be an extremely distorted representation of one of Athaliah's political purges. Judged objectively, she was a competent politician who kept a cool head in difficult situations. That she held on to power for six years demonstrates her political adroitness. In the situation of those times it was a remarkable achievement for a woman from the northern kingdom to hold her ground for so long against the priestly group in Jerusalem. Her taking power was surely not welcomed in Judah with open arms; that a woman, and a foreigner at that, was the ruler would have caused exasperation.

Then came the coup d'état by Jehoiada and his followers. Joash was made king and Athaliah murdered. 2 Kings 11:20 reports that the people of the land, having been a major participant in the coup, rejoiced, whereas the city of Jerusalem and its courtiers, officials, and guards were quiet. The people probably wanted someone from David's line for their king. In Jerusalem, on the other hand, Athaliah would have been liked better.

If one considers the situation in Judah after Jehu's revolution, one cannot keep the picture of Athaliah as a cruel or power-hungry woman. Her account in 2 Kings 11 was written from Jehoiada's perspective. It alleges that the continuation of David's dynasty had been greatly endangered by Athaliah's rule but that with the help of God Jehoiada saved it. Whoever the narrator is, his intent is to give that troubled situation an air of high drama with that allegation (cf. Würthwein 1984, 346). To make the troubles even worse, he presents Athaliah the adversary as a kind of witch. It is closer to the truth that she was a capable and influential ruler. It was not she but Jehu who murdered the princes of Judah. True, she did eliminate some of her opponents. But the fact that the narrator describes her as such a wicked and cruel woman highlights the prejudices and antipathies that the narrator as well as the Deuteronomist redactors harbored against women, especially foreign women. It is sad and a pity that they did so. But it would be even worse if people reading the Bible today, influenced by such misogynist traditions, were themselves unknowingly to become antipathetic toward women in positions of leadership. A negative bias always spawns new biases. Feminists should begin to break free from this vicious circle.

Josiah's Cultic Reform and Huldah the Prophetess

2 Kings 12 and the chapters following it report on the wars between Israel and Aram and on the frequent change of rulers in the northern kingdom. In the end the Assyrian king conquers the land and Israel is carried away captive to Assyria. The demise of the northern kingdom is analyzed in 2 Kings 17:1-23 through the lens of the Deuteronomists' theology of history. The authors cite the erection of cairns and poles (ashers), the worship of stars and of Baal, that is, the trespasses against the exclusive worship of YHWH, as the reasons for that demise. The Assyrian armies conquered Samaria in the ninth year of King Hoshea's reign (722 B.C.E.). Israel's upper classes were taken off to Assyria and settled in Halah on Habor, the river of Gozan, and in the cities of the Medes (17:3-6).

Things were different in Judah. There kings Hezekiah, Manasseh, and Amon maintained limited independence of the land by payments of tolls to Assyria. Chapters 18–20 describe at length Hezekiah's politics in relation to Assyria, his so-called cultic reform, and the appearance of Isaiah the prophet. Eventually Hezekiah's son Manasseh comes to power and rules fifty-five years as a vassal of Assyria. He is accused of the same idolatry that brought down the northern kingdom (21:2-7) and is even said to have set up a statue of Asherah in the temple of Jerusalem. In his days the worship of the goddess apparently was part of the cult in the temple next to the worship of YHWH. In other words, Manasseh did everything YHWH had forbidden Israel. His rule of many years, itself pointing to a politician of competence, was in the eyes of the Deuteronomist redactors only a period of God's growing anger with his people. Manassch's son and successor Amon was murdered by his servants two years into his reign. "But the people of the land ('am hā'āreṣ) killed all those who had conspired against King Amon, and the people of the land made his son Josiah king in place of him" (21:24). Because Josiah was only eight years old when he succeeded to the throne, it seems reasonable to assume that the men of the 'am hā'āreṣ put someone of their own ranks on the throne. Würthwein (1984, 44) assumes that the clan of Amon's mother Jedediah of Bozkath stood behind the young king, and with her the population of Judah where the clan resided and had its roots. Obviously Josiah's descent from Jedediah sealed his being chosen. Because the queen mother must have held an important position as head of the house within the governmental structure, the influence of the free citizens of Judah over the royal court through her must have been significant.

In 2 Kings Josiah's rule is praised most highly. He is one of the three kings the Deuteronomists hold up as exemplary rulers (David, Hezekiah, Josiah). "He did what was right in the sight of the LORD, and walked in all the way of his father David; he did not turn aside to the right or the left" (22:2). The reason why he was so highly regarded lies in the cultic reform he implemented in the eighteenth year of his reign in Judah. Its process and substance are described extensively in 22:3–23:24. Ever since the introduction of historical criticism, this reform and what is said to have caused it (the discovery in the temple of a book of the law) has been one of the most discussed topics of First Testament scholarship (cf. the relevant contributions in Gross 1995). What is less known and discussed is that a woman prophet named Huldah played a major role in Josiah's reform. When that book was found and brought to the king, he sent a delegation to make inquiries of YHWH; they went to see Huldah. She pronounced an oracle. Then the king and the whole people made a covenant before YHWH in a great ceremony and launched the cultic reform. All the cultic paraphernalia of the male and female deities in the temple were removed and destroyed and the high places outside the city where Baal and Asherah and other gods had been worshiped were removed on Josiah's orders.

The person and significance of Huldah raise questions for feminists. She was the spouse of Shallum, keeper of the royal wardrobe. The king's delegation visited her in her home in a newer section of Jerusalem. Whether she was a "free" or a temple prophetess cannot be determined from that information. In any case, her name simply could not be left out of the account of the cultic reform. It is quite remarkable that in the thoroughly critical, even hostile, attitude toward women pervading the Deuteronomist tradition the oracle of YHWH was not associated exclusively with male mediators (Wacker 1989, 95). What Huldah pronounces according to 22:16-20 sums up the Deuteronomist theology of history, or more precisely the theology of the Deuteronomists' history of the prophets. And that means no less than that they let a woman sum up their theology! From that viewpoint, Huldah must have been a famous woman prophet; in fact, she is the only woman prophet of the royal era known by name.

Unfortunately, we know extremely little about women prophets of that era. Isaiah 8:3 mentions one of them but without name or what exactly her activities were (→ Isaiah). Ezekiel 13:17ff. speaks of women prophets during the Babylonian exile (→ Ezekiel). But in a tradition that on the whole is not interested in women, those are important indicators. In many cultures prophecy is a phenomenon that includes men and women. Therefore, we may assume that during the royal era there were other women prophets next to Huldah. For that reason she is for us a key figure who needs further research (cf. Camp 1992, 109).

In 23:29-30 we learn of Josiah's death in a battle against Egyptian Pharaoh Neco. In 23:31–25:30 we are given a summary of what led to the fall of Judah as a state: the conquests of Nebuchadnezzar, king of Babylon; the fall and destruction of Jerusalem (587 B.C.E.); and the deportation of the upper classes of Judah to Babylon. The books of Kings come to a close on the hopeful note of Jehoiachin's release from exile; he was the second-to-last king of Judah.

Concluding Remarks

From the books of Kings we cannot glean much objective information about women at that time; the Deuteronomist redactors' one-sided presentation of Israel's and Judah's history within their religious framework centered in YHWH and Jerusalem does not allow it. But what can be noted by way of concluding comments are the following three points. (1) The Deuteronomist redactors have little interest in women and seldom speak about them. If and when they do, their presentation is negative and hostile most of the time. Basically they know only two types of women: poor and helpless ones, and cruel, power-hungry, and vengeful ones. It should be obvious that such reduction of images of women does not correspond to historical reality. In fact, many women of the royal era were influential and active, for example, as a *gĕbîrâ*, a politician, and a woman prophet. (2) Jezebel and the foreign women at court must not be written off as schemers and adherents of an outlandish religion plotting to seduce the king and the population into idolatry. Such charges are anachronistic and excessive exaggerations. At that time foreign women at court were officially permitted to worship the gods and goddesses of their home countries. (3) There were also many underprivileged women at court, like Abishag the Shunammite, who had to live as concubines. They were treated as kings' property and subjected to the whims of their male and female superiors.

Women today should liberate themselves from the Deuteronomists' images of women and begin to construct new images. Otherwise, the negative, old images of women continue to work below the surface and prevent women from exercising and expanding their abilities and possibilities. The vengeful Athaliah and the cruel Jezebel are phantoms that have little to do with reality!

LITERATURE

Albertz, Rainer. 1992. *Religionsgeschichte Israels in alttestamentlicher Zeit.* 2 vols. Altes Testament Deutsch, Supplemental Volumes, vol. 8, 1 and 2. Göttingen.

Alt, Albrecht. 1964. "Das Gottesurteil auf dem Karmel (1935)." In Alt, *Kleine Schriften zur Geschichte Israels,* 2:135-49. 3rd ed. Munich.

Andreasen, Niels-E. 1983. "The Role of the Queen Mother in Israelite Society." *Catholic Biblical Quarterly* 45:179-94.

Braulik, Georg. 1991. "Die Ablehnung der Göttin Aschera in Israel." In *Der eine Gott und die Göttin,* edited by Marie-Theres Wacker and Erich Zenger, 106-36. Quaestiones disputatae, vol. 135. Freiburg im Breisgau.

Brenner, Athalya, ed. 1994. *A Feminist Companion to Samuel and Kings.* Sheffield.

Camp, Claudia V. 1992. "1 & 2 Kings." In *The Women's Bible Commentary,* edited by Carol A. Newsom and Sharon H. Ringe, 96-109. London and Louisville.

Debus, Jörg. 1967. *Die Sünde Jerobeams.* Forschungen zur Religion und Literatur des Alten und Neuen Testaments, vol. 93. Göttingen.

Dietrich, Walter. 1972. *Prophetie und Geschichte.* Forschungen zur Religion und Literatur des Alten und Neuen Testaments, vol. 108. Göttingen.

Donner, Herbert. 1994. "Art und Herkunft des Amtes der Königinmutter im Alten Testament (1959)." In Donner, *Aufsätze zum Alten Testament,* 1-33. Beihefte der Zeitschrift für die alttestamentliche Wissenschaft, vol. 224. Berlin.

Frevel, Christian. 1994. *Aschera und der Ausschließlichkeitsanspruch YHWHs.* Bonner biblische Beiträge, vol. 94, 1 and 2. Weinheim.

Gray, John. 1963. *I and II Kings.* Old Testament Library. Philadelphia.

Gressmann, Hugo. 1907. "Das salomonische Urteil." *Deutsche Rundschau* 130:212-28.

Gross, Walter, ed. 1995. *Jeremia und die "deuteronomistische Bewegung."* Bonner biblische Beiträge, vol. 98. Weinheim. (Cf. esp. the essays by Schreiner, Niehr, and Uehlinger on Josiah's reform.)

Häusl, Maria. 1993. *Abischag und Batscheba.* Arbeiten zu Text und Sprache im Alten Testament, vol. 41. St. Ottilien.

Kaiser, Otto. 1984. *Einleitung in das Alte Testament.* 5th ed. Gütersloh.

Keel, Othmar, and Christoph Uehlinger. 1992. *Göttinnen, Götter und Gottessymbole.* Quaestiones disputatae, vol. 134. Freiburg im Breisgau.

Kessler, Rainer. 1989. "Batseba — durch Demütigung zur Macht." In *Feministisch gelesen,* edited by Eva Renate Schmidt et al., 2:114-19. Stuttgart.

Lang, Bernhard. 1981. "Die Jahwe-allein Bewegung." In *Der einzige Gott,* edited by Bernhard Lang, 47-83. Munich.

Levin, Christoph. 1982. *Der Sturz der Königin Athalja.* Stuttgarter Bibelstudien, vol. 105. Stuttgart.

Miller, Gabriele. 1988. "Batseba. Eine Frau, die weiß, was sie will." In *Zwischen Ohnmacht und Befreiung,* edited by Karin Walter, 81-91. Freiburg im Breisgau.

Miller, J. Maxwell. 1967. "The Fall of the House of Ahab." *Vetus Testamentum* 17:307-24.

Montgomery, James M. 1976. *The Books of Kings.* International Critical Commentary. Edinburgh.

Noth, Martin. 1968. *1 Könige 1–16.* Biblischer Kommentar, vol. 9, 1. Neukirchen-Vluyn.

Oeming, Manfred. 1986. "Naboth, der Jesreeliter. Untersuchungen zu den theologischen Motiven der Überlieferungsgeschichte von I Reg 21." *Zeitschrift für die alttestamentliche Wissenschaft* 98:363-82.

Olyan, Saul M. 1988. *Asherah and the Cult of Yahweh in Israel.* Society of Biblical Literature Monograph Series, vol. 34. Atlanta.

Rad, Gerhard von. 1969. *Theologie des Alten Testaments.* Vol. 1. 6th ed. Munich.

Rofé, Alexander. 1988. "The Vineyard of Naboth: The Origin and Message of the Story." *Vetus Testamentum* 38:97-101.

Schroer, Silvia. 1995. "Auf dem Weg zu einer feministischen Rekonstruktion der Geschichte Israels." In *Feministische Exegese,* edited by Silvia Schroer, Luise Schottroff, and Marie-Theres Wacker, 83-172. Darmstadt. (Also found in *Feminist Interpretation: The Bible in Women's Perspective* [Minneapolis, 1998], 85-176.)

Smend, Rudolph. 1975. "Der biblische und der historische Elia." *Vetus Testamentum* 28:167-84.

———. 1978. *Die Entstehung des Alten Testaments.* Göttingen.

Stolz, Fritz. 1996. *Einführung in den biblischen Monotheismus.* Darmstadt.

Wacker, Marie-Theres. 1988. "Hulda — eine Prophetin vor dem Ende." In *Feministisch gelesen,* edited by Eva-Renate Schmidt et al., 1:91-99. Stuttgart.

———. 1989. "Eine Frau findet den Gott der Armen (1 Kön 17,2-24)." In *Feministisch gelesen,* edited by Eva-Renate Schmidt et al., 2:279-37. Stuttgart.

———. 1991. "Aschera oder die Ambivalenz des Weiblichen." In *Der eine Gott und die Göttin,* edited by Marie-Theres Wacker and Erich Zenger, 137-50. Quaestiones disputatae, vol. 134. Freiburg im Breisgau.

Würthwein, Ernst. 1977. *1 Kön 1–16.* Altes Testament Deutsch, vol. 11, 1. Göttingen.

———. 1984. *1 Kön 17–2 Kön 25.* Altes Testament Deutsch, vol. 11, 2. Göttingen.

For Further Reading

Ackerman, Susan. 1993. "The Queen Mother and the Cult in Israel." *Journal of Biblical Literature* 112:385-401.

Translated by Martin Rumscheidt

Books of Chronicles: In the Vestibule of Women

Marie-Theres Wacker

In recent decades the exegetical literature on 1 and 2 Chronicles has multiplied almost exponentially. In the process some coordinates previously considered firm have shifted. Thus the widespread historical-critical research consensus regarding a so-called Chronicler's history drawn from 1 and 2 Chronicles as well as Ezra and Nehemiah has disintegrated, making space for attempts to interpret Chronicles on its own, and on its own terms. New monographs were presented on topics like the "genealogical vestibule" of 1 Chronicles 1–9 (Oeming 1990), the theology of land in Chronicles, the significance of the figure of Moses, and the question of peace (Gabriel 1990). A series of Jewish exegetes have inserted themselves emphatically into the discussion of Chronicles (cf., e.g., Japhet 1989 and 1993; Kalimi 1995; Weinberg 1996), and from within their alternate traditions of interpretation have traced new contours of the historical and "ideological" perspectives of 1 and 2 Chronicles.

To date, however, no engagement with Chronicles focusing specifically on women has been written. This need not surprise us, as at first glance these books seem to present a world devoid of women. The broadly constructed genealogies at the outset of the book follow the lines of fathers and sons from Adam up through the twelve tribes of Israel (1 Chron 1–9/10); at the center of the book stands the figure of David, who meticulously plans the building of the temple not only architecturally but also with regard to its priestly Levitical institutions (1 Chron 11–20) and places its realization into the hands of his son Solomon (2 Chron 1–9). The rest is the history of the kings of Judah up through the destruction of Jerusalem (2 Chron 10–36). The concluding note of the book, according to which the Persian king ordains the rebuilding of the Jerusalem temple, once again underlines the centrality of the temple and its priestly Levitical — and thus androcentric — institutions as the theme of 1 and 2 Chronicles. On the other hand, of all the books of the Bible, these two contain by far the most names of women and notes about women. This paradoxical content spurs the feminist experiment of subjecting 1 and 2 Chronicles to an against-the-grain reading tracing the figures of women made visible there. In her woman-centered short commentary on 1 and 2 Chronicles, Alice L. Laffey (1992) has laid the groundwork for such an effort; in what follows, I will build upon Laffey's groundwork to provide better-differentiated observations on the material she presented and to open up several further dimensions. Above all, however, I will highlight open questions and points of research interest that even the present contribution cannot resolve but can only name as such.

Women in the "Genealogical Vestibule," 1 Chronicles 1–9 (10)

The majority of the women mentioned by name in 1 and 2 Chronicles appear in the genealogies of 1 Chronicles 1–9. Alice L. Laffey places the number at forty-two and enumerates Keturah (1 Chron 1:32), Timna (1:39), Mehetabel and Matred (1:50), Bath-shua (2:3), Tamar (2:4), Zeruiah (2:16) and Abigail (2:16f.), Azubah (2:18), Jerioth (2:18), Ephrath (2:19), Ephrathah (2:24), Atarah (2:26), Abihail (2:29), Ephah (2:46), Maacah (2:48), Achsah (2:49), Ahinoam and Abigail (3:1), Maacah and Haggith (3:2), Abital and Eglah (3:3), Bathsheba/Bath-shua (3:5), Tamar (3:9), Shelomith (3:19), Hazzelelponi (4:3), Helah and Naarah (4:5), Bithiah (4:17f.), Miriam (6:3),[1] Bilhah (7:13), Maacah (7:15), another Maacah (7:16), Hammolecheth (7:18), Sheerah (7:24), Serah (7:30), Shua (7:32), Hushim and Baara (8:8), Hodesh (8:9), and Maacah (8:29, 9:35). This list, however, conceals some problems.

Women in the Grip of the Textual Record

First, a number of text-critical decisions are concealed in this list, by means of which women are made visible — or invisible. These include the following: Azubah (2:18) is rightly to be restored through text-critical correction as the wife of Hezron; in the Hebrew text (Masoretic Text; hereafter MT) — here most probably mistakenly — she is not clearly identifiably female. In contrast, Matred (1:50) is recognizably female in the MT and in the NRSV; the German *Einheitsübersetzung* departed from MT and allowed Matred to "disappear" as a woman. On the other hand, in 2:31 this German translation provides an additional woman in Ahlai, daughter of Sheshan, once again contrary to the literal MT wording but in agreement with 2:34, where Sheshan is described as the father of daughters only.[2] Another woman's name not noted by Laffey is Abijah, who appears in the MT at 2:24. This woman appears to have been "invented" in the course of the text's development. The Zurich Bible translation and the Revised Standard Version (1952) reflect

---

1. Hebrew: 5:29
2. This is why the New King James Version speaks of a "child" here and the New Living Translation of a "descendant." See my comment in the following paragraph on the rendering of "son."

the presumably original text, according to which, after the death of Caleb's father Hezron, Caleb took Hezron's wife Ephrathah for himself and had a son with her. The NRSV follows the present MT in speaking of a wife of Hezron named Abijah who bore a son, and one can deduce that this son was born following the death of his father Hezron. The present MT has presumably eliminated, as being offensive, the original assertion that the son took the wife of his father (cf. Lev 18:8). It is also possible that a similarly structured problem stands behind the "double Maacah" of 7:15 and 16: the first-named Maacah is denoted as the sister of Machir; the second, as his wife. The text does not make entirely clear whether in fact two women are truly to be differentiated here. Alice L. Laffey opted for two, perhaps on the basis of Leviticus 18:9, 11. On both feminist social-historical and exegetical-historical grounds, it may well be worth investigating the disappearing or appearing of women (or women's names) in both ancient versions and new translations of Chronicles, and the reasons for these.

Names — of Significance for Gender?

The example of Miriam (5:29 MT; 6:3 NRSV), who appears in the list of the forty-two women, leads to a further and initially off-putting phenomenon: according to the Hebrew wording, Miriam is presented here as one of the "sons of Amram." The naming of Moses and Aaron alongside Miriam permits no doubt that the name Miriam points to the sister, named in the Pentateuch, of the two men. Some translations, including NRSV, take account of this by speaking here of "children" rather than of "sons." This inclusive rendering of the Hebrew word is not convincing, however, since in the text of Chronicles daughters are also explicitly mentioned in many cases alongside sons; thus apparently "sons" truly means "sons." Whoever then nevertheless opts for an inclusive reading for the "sons of Amram" should apply this throughout as well. By such means, the proportion of women mentioned can be proven to be considerably higher than has previously been assumed. For instance, "Gomer," who is mentioned as the first among the "sons of Japheth" (1:5), would be a new candidate; according to Hosea 1:3, Gomer is a woman's name.

The problem seems to be more complex, however. Whereas Shelomith is unambiguously identified in 1 Chronicles 3:19 as a sister alongside brothers, the same name Shelomith appears in the Hebrew text of 1 Chronicles 26:25 as a man's name. The same is true for the name Abihail, who according to 2 Chronicles 11:18 is the daughter of Eliab, but according to 1 Chronicles 5:14 is the son of Huri; it is also true for Athaliah, who according to 1 Chronicles 8:26 is son of Jeroham, yet according to 2 Chronicles 22:2-3, 10-12, and elsewhere is a queen mother, and for Timna, in 1 Chronicles 1:36 a man's name and three verses later a woman's. The assumption of great carelessness on the part of the Chroniclers as a general explanation for this is just as unconvincing as the suspicion (even if confirmed in particular cases) that in their new accounts these authors have intentionally caused the women to "disappear" from the given traditions of, above all, the Pentateuch and the Deuteronomistic histories. It is more likely that the assumptions current in our culture that given names are of significance for gender must be examined: in ancient Israel given names were presumably not assigned with such unambiguous gender specificity as contemporary German registry authorities demand from newly minted parents. That was also unnecessary since the personal name could always be amplified by adding "daughter of [name]" or "son of [name]." The numerous stories of naming in the Bible make clear that many children's names articulate others' thanks or desires, placing the child primarily into a web of relationships within its family, including the family's relationship to God (cf. Stamm 1980; for more recent literature on this topic, cf. Görg 1996).

In this context I must point to an observation with far-reaching implications for the history of religions. Rainer Kessler (1987) has proved that the giving of names in ancient Israel was de facto carried out by the mother, whereas stories of name giving that read differently "talk past" the social-historical reality. As a text-critical problem, this procedure is visible in 1 Chronicles 7:23. Some Hebrew manuscripts as well as ancient translations — and the Tanakh of the Jewish Publication Society — have the mother name her son here; in other American and the NRSV translations, following the majority of Hebrew manuscripts, it is the father (for more on this, cf. Bail 1997). Under the assumption that children receive their names from their mother, the Israelite personal names passed on biblically and textually would in every case need also — even if not solely — to be evaluated as testimonies to women's traditions not least in the realm of personal and familial piety.

The Woman and the City

Some of the names mentioned for women in the Chronicles genealogies, for instance, Timna, Maacah, and Ephrat/Ephrata, lead to a correlation that however makes gender specificity visible again: these women's names appear in other contexts of the Hebrew Bible as names of a city or region. In many biblical texts cities, above all Jerusalem, are portrayed using the image of a woman: as the mother of its inhabitants, as giver of nourishment and protector, or even as partner of the city god (on this cf. especially the prophetic writings). On the other side, however, the human realm of "city," already highly differentiated even in antiquity, explodes the image of woman conceived all too naturally; it portrays "the woman" as "bearer of culture."

From this background the mention, unique in the Bible, of a woman as the builder of a city gains significance: Sheerah (7:24), to whom the building or founding of three cities is ascribed, one of which, Uzzen-Sheerah, actually bears her name. Ulrike Bail and Silvia Schroer have pointed to the previously unexamined motif of city founding by women (Schroer 1995, 118-37; Bail 1997, 221). According to Joel P. Weinberg's analysis (1996, 139), we can assume a wave of urbanization in Judea and its neighboring provinces during the time 1 and 2 Chronicles were compiled, which historically situates the theme of "city building" in these texts. Then Sheerah, the city builder or city founder, could be evaluated in a similar fashion as an indicator for the factually social-historical, not "only" literary-fictitious, significance of women, as this is assumed by feminist exegetes with regard to the Wisdom figure of Proverbs 1–9 in its reference to wise women of Israel. To be sure, Sheerah's appearance in 1 Chronicles 7 remains as brief as it is ambiguous. She is noted as a postscript to the mention of her brothers: two of them were killed as cattle thieves; the name of the third, Beriah, is a remembrance of this event. Is the building of a city by a woman thus meant to be judged as a further negative element of this family descending from the ancestor Ephraim? This question suggests itself all the more in that the building of cities has by no means unambiguously positive connotations in the Bible: Cain, the builder of cities, is the murderer of his brother (Gen 4); it is even God who in a sense puts an end to the building of the city of Babel (Gen 11); and Hiel loses two sons in rebuilding Jericho (1 Kings 16:34).

Daughters without Brothers and Foremothers

In all, 1 and 2 Chronicles speak three times of daughters of a father who has no sons. The name Zelophehad (1 Chron 7:15) is known from the books of Numbers, Joshua, and Judges as that of a father with five daughters who demand their right to the land as its inheritors. The theme of land does not preoccupy Chronicles; the text does not divulge the names and fates of the daughters of Zelophehad. It is, however, interested in the continuation of a genealogical branch, as the example of Eleazar's daughters (1 Chron 23:22) shows: they are married to their cousins, and thereby remain within the extended family, but also contribute to its continuation.

In the third case of a family of solely daughters, the concern is similarly one of its continuation (2:34-35). Sheshan, the father, marries one of his daughters to his Egyptian slave, whose name, by the way — in contrast to that of his daughter — is mentioned. The son of these two is noted as the forefather of a genealogy of thirteen generations (2:36-41) and is manifestly seen as belonging to the lineage of Judah. The impression becomes unavoidable that it is here the mother, not the father, who defines belonging to the family. Nevertheless, we presumably cannot simply speak here of a "matrilineal principle" of descent but must follow the logic of a patriarchal household: to the extent the slave counts as part of the household, the daughter of the house is not marrying a "stranger."

The union of the nameless daughter of Sheshan and her Egyptian husband, however, points to the yet open question of the historical roots and significance of the matrilineal principle in ancient Israel and/or ancient Judaism (cf. simply the controversial works of S. Cohen on the one hand, particularly Cohen 1985, and of M. I. Gruber 1995 on the other). This question can also be approached by means of the figures of women mentioned by name who appear within the otherwise patrilineally conceived genealogies as foremothers of their own genealogy. The first to note here is Keturah (1:32-33), a concubine of Abraham, whose naming stands out all the more in that Sarah as the mother of Isaac is not named. There follow Bilhah (7:13), who is not even mentioned as a woman, according to which her high prominence as a foremother of Naphtali can clearly be assumed, and Zeruiah (2:16), who to be sure is genealogically part of the extended family of David, yet whose sons Abishai, Joab, and Asahel made history not as sons of their father but as "sons of Zeruiah" (2 Sam 2:18 and elsewhere). It is as if Joab in particular, David's general, cannot be spoken of in any other way than as "son of Zeruiah" (cf. in addition to the references in 2 Samuel, also 1 Chron 11:6, 39; 18:15; 26:28; 27:24).

Sisters of Brothers

A number of women's names are supplied with the qualifier "sister of." Some of these are presented as sisters of a brother also mentioned by name, others as sisters of men named as sons of their fathers — a somewhat surprisingly roundabout way of describing these women, since they could have been presented more simply as daughters of the father. In the case of Tamar, the sister of the sons of David (1 Chron 3:9), the Tamar tradition of 2 Samuel 13 could have played a role; according to it, Tamar is described as the sister of Amnon and Absalom. In any case, it is striking that Chronicles merely names Tamar but shows no interest in her story and fate. Are the "sisters" of the Chronicles genealogy merely ornamental confirmation of the blessing of God resting on the particular families multiplying so fruitfully, as is surely the case with the daughters often named in the Chronicler's royal histories (see below) alongside sons? Or does the mention of sisters by name have another meaning over against those sisters noted only summarily and namelessly after their brothers? The theme of "sister(s) of brothers" in the Hebrew Bible can be considered another promising area for further literary and social-historical research.

Figures of Women in the Royal Histories of 1 and 2 Chronicles

Beginning with 1 Chronicles 11, the depiction in Chronicles of the royal history up to the destruction of Jerusalem follows the narrative line of the books of Samuel and Kings; commentators generally assume that the Chronicler had these books available as literary sources. Comparing these narratives allows us to discern characteristic differences between them.

The Figures of Women in the Saul and David Tradition

According to the books of Samuel, the history of the "house of Saul," the first king of Israel, and the "house of David," his successor, is also and in not inconsiderable measure a history of women. In 1 and 2 Chronicles, however, most of the narratives in which women play a key role disappear. Alice L. Laffey suggests that everything that could detract from the honor and renown of the figure of David was purged from the depiction in 1 and 2 Chronicles. This would explain why in particular the figure of Bathsheba is reduced to a mere mentioning of the name, further modified to "Bath-shua" (1 Chron 3:5 MT), since the name Bathsheba is a reminder of David's adultery with her. Similarly, the story of the rape of Tamar by David's son Amnon (2 Sam 13) may have been omitted for this reason. However, in my opinion this explanatory approach is too narrowly focused on the figure of David. We do better to begin with the more fundamental assumption that the Chronicler's "historiosophy" (S. Japhet) is not the history of the accession or succession to the throne, as in the books of Samuel, and thus does not sketch the dramatic arc of the entanglements by which the "house of David" rose and the "house of Saul" fell. It appears rather to be oriented above all to the holiness of the "house of God" and all things and persons coming into contact with this and, for the sake of a clear differentiation of what is holy, places the accent not on entanglements, but quite the contrary on the drawing of boundaries. From this perspective, there is no need for a clever Abigail (1 Sam 25), who makes smooth David's path to the throne; there is no need for wise women who help to rehabilitate a son of David fallen into disgrace (2 Sam 14) or to save a city from David's commander (2 Sam 20:14-22); and rape and adultery are unmentionable transgressions of the boundaries.

The differing interests of 1 and 2 Chronicles can be clearly seen as well in their reception of the history of the "house of Saul" and the women of this first royal family of Israel. In the list of Saul's descendants (1 Chron 9:39), in contrast to 1 Samuel 14:49, the daughters are left out. Saul's elder daughter Merab, according to 1 and 2 Samuel a pawn of fatherly power politics also with regard to David, is not mentioned at all in Chronicles. Michal, the younger, who according to 1 Samuel 18–19 became David's wife, is elided from the Chronicler's enumeration of David's wives; the marital connection between David and Saul is never mentioned. Michal appears otherwise only in a single verse (1 Chron 15:29), which speaks of her disdain for David when he danced before the ark of the covenant. In the broad characteristics of the Chronicler's portrayal of David she stands, characterized as the daughter of Saul, thus outside the circle drawn around the king and the ark of God; in a sense she has placed herself outside this circle behind her window. Even the end of Saul and his family remains cut off from the fate of David: Saul dies and David becomes king (1 Chron 10:14); there is as little mention of any further pretensions to the throne from the side of Saul as there is of the lament of Rizpah, who moves David to make peace with at least the dead members of the house of Saul (2 Sam 21). While for the dramatic arc of the books of Samuel it is precisely the almost fated enmeshment of the houses of Saul and David that is essential, Chronicles is concerned with the clear drawing of boundaries, at least with regard to the inner space of the temple and with the king oriented to it.

The Royal History from Solomon to the Exile

In the history of Solomon (2 Chron 1–9), two shifts of accent in comparison to 1 and 2 Kings stand out. According to 1 Kings 11, the worship of idols comes (back) to Israel, already during the time of Solomon, when the old king embraces the gods of his foreign-born wives. This apologia for Solomon may well no longer have sufficed for the writing of a history that portrays him as the fulfiller of the building of the temple; the accusation of idol worship on the part of Solomon disappears from the Chronicler's narration. This too may make clear the Chronicler's striving to remove everything unbefitting of YHWH from the domain of the temple and from those oriented to it. The second shifting of accent has to do with the Egyptian spouse of Solomon. In 1 and 2 Kings, she is mentioned several times, corresponding to her particular significance within the marital politics of the king (1 Kings 3:1; 7:8; 9:16, 24; 11:1). The contextualization of these references suggests moreover that from the perspective of Kings, Pharaoh's daughter was of use to Solomon above all with regard to the more effective waging of war. In addition, she has value as an object of prestige: the palace of her own that he builds her corresponds, to be sure, to her rank but at the same time heightens the splendor of the royal estate. In contrast, in Chronicles the daughter of Pharaoh appears only once (2 Chron 8:11), and there as a "problem." The palace of her own that Solomon builds is motivated by the fact that her presence in the royal palace, in the precincts of the temple, affects the holiness of these locations. Behind this, as the reflection placed in Solomon's mouth makes clear, lie both her foreign provenance as the daughter of Pharaoh and her female gender as wife of the king — this is likely an instance of the problem of the "foreign wife/wives" whose presence fatally complicates the self-definition of the Chronicler's religious community (→ Ezra and Nehemiah). In contrast, the story of the Queen of Sheba is adopted unabridged (1 Kings 10:1-13; 2 Chron 9:1-12); as a visitor, she represents no lasting problem, and she further recognizes the honor of the God of Israel.

What stands out are the references to the kings' riches in wives and children (cf. for Rehoboam 2 Chron 11:21; for Abijah 13:21; for Joash 24:3; cf. for David 1 Chron 14:3), where in each case the daughters are named alongside the sons. Here women and children clearly matter — and more emphatically than in the Deuteronomistic history — as symbols of male-royal power and/or blessing by YHWH.

The kings' mothers are regularly named as individuals: Naamah, the mother of Rehoboam (2 Chron 12:13); Micaiah, the mother of Abijah (13:2); Maacah, the mother of Asa (15:16), who is here the only one to receive the title *gĕbîrâ*, or "queen mother"; Azubah, the mother of Jehoshaphat (20:31); Athaliah, the mother of Ahaziah (22:2); Zibiah, the mother of Joash (24:1); Jehoaddan, the mother of Amaziah (25:1); Jecoliah, the mother of Uzziah (26:3); Jerushah, the mother of Jotham (27:1); and Abijah, the mother of Hezekiah (29:1). But this too presents its own problems: Is Micaiah the same person as Maacah, who according to 1 Kings 15:2 and 2 Chronicles 11:18-22 is the mother of Abijah? Why, in contrast to the list in 2 Kings, are the names of the final seven kings' mothers absent, even of a reforming king as positively portrayed as Josiah? Why, in contrast, is the name of Queen Athaliah not suppressed even though, already in the Deuteronomistic tradition, she qualifies as a murderer and, even more, from the Chronicler's perspective, poses a danger for the purity of the temple (cf. 2 Chron 23:19)? Was she included as a contrasting figure over against another woman, Jehoshabeath, who not only has regular access to the temple as the wife of a priest (2 Chron 22:11-12) but uses it in the service of the Davidic dynasty by bringing the young ascendant to the throne, Joash, to safety from Athaliah?

Women in Prophecy and Cult

The consultation with Huldah, the female prophet (forgotten by Laffey?), appears in almost verbally identical form in both 2 Kings 22:14-20 and 2 Chronicles 34:22-28. Yet in the full context of the Chronicler's history of Josiah, Huldah's story takes on a somewhat different cast (cf. Micheel 1983, 30-34): Josiah has feared the Lord from the beginning of his reign and is already reforming the cult even before the book of the Law is found. Thus Huldah's prophetic word about the king and the city of Jerusalem gains above all the character of an irrevocable word of God's judgment. In the face of the "prophetic silence" of 1 and 2 Kings, which books mention none of the prophets of biblical writings beyond Isaiah, the narrative inclusion of the prophet Jeremiah into the Chronicler's history of Josiah stands out. It demonstrates that for the Chronicler's writing of history, Huldah and Jeremiah are considered contemporaries. All the more remarkable then is the division of their roles: Huldah speaks prophetic words of doom, and Jeremiah composes a lament for the dead king (2 Chron 35:25). In this way Huldah as a female prophet has taken over a task that even for the Chronicler is fulfilled in other circumstances by a male prophet (cf. Micaiah, son of Imlah, 2 Chron 18), and Jeremiah is placed into a tradition that even the Chronicler perceives as belonging to "singing men and singing women" (2 Chron 35:25). Huldah and Jeremiah represent arenas of public/

cult-related activity in which even at the time of Chronicles women as well as men can be depicted.

A great interest of the Chronicler's writing of history, noteworthy precisely in contrast to that of the Deuteronomistic portrayal, is the Levites. In this context, twice women are referred to specifically (though not named): the daughters of the singer Heman alongside his sons (1 Chron 25:5), and the daughters of the Levite Eleazar (23:22). The latter case has to do with the continuation of a family whose offspring consist solely of daughters; in the former, the three daughters are named alongside the fourteen sons surely in order to portray riches in children as an expression of the blessing resting on Heman's family (as in the lists in Genesis, the question arises in Chronicles as well whether the much lesser number of daughters in each case corresponds to the actual proportion of the offspring or whether the number of daughters has been narratively reduced to highlight the greater significance of the sons). On the other hand, the open formulation of the following verse, according to which "they were all under the direction of their father" in singing and making music in the house of YHWH, permits the interpretation that women from Levitical families also took part in the "professional" music of the temple. This reading finds further corroboration in that the singing activity of Heman's family in 1 Chronicles 25 is denoted using the verb "to prophesy" *(nb')*, and prophecy, as the figure of Huldah shows, could clearly also come from a woman.[3] The mention of singing women alongside singing men in the Josiah history (2 Chron 35:25) views women in the liturgies of lament similarly in "professional" roles. No particular emphasis accompanies either report; attention falls only incidentally on the women involved alongside the men. Yet this fact in particular may allow us to conclude that women were more fully involved in official functions in the cult also of the postexilic period than the transmitted biblical texts tend to imply.

From this follows an even more fundamental possibility to consider. The image that 1 and 2 Chronicles provide of the temple and its cult can be contrasted, on the one hand, with that of the books of Samuel and Kings, which at least with regard to the business of the temple during the period of the kings reveal different sorts of relationships throughout, albeit in general also already "processed" polemically (cf. in particular the mentions of the *qĕdēšôt*, or male temple prostitutes, in 1 and 2 Kings). The portrayal in Chronicles can be compared, on the other hand, with the priestly portions of the Pentateuch and its image of the furnishing of the tabernacle — here, for instance, women are made visible as donating to the appointments (Exod 25) and as those serving at the entrance of the tabernacle (Exod 38:8). Accordingly, all-too-glib negative historical inferences with regard to the extent of women's presence in the cult of the Second Temple are to be avoided. De-

---

3. At this point we can reach back to Miriam in 1 Chron 5:29 (Eng. 6:3) once more: Could it be that she, the singing and dancing prophet, was inserted by a later hand into the "sons of Amram" because it was simply not possible for her to be omitted?

spite the encompassing works of, for example, Urs Winter (1983) and Christian Frevel (1995) with many observations of detail, and Phyllis Bird's useful grid for systematizing the scattered material on women in cultic roles (1987), there still remains considerable need for research in this area (on the anti-Jewish tendencies of this research throughout its history and the contemporary feminist relevance of these questions, cf. Wacker 1995).

God and Goddess

The perspective presumed for the entire "historiosophy" of Chronicles, according to which the Chronicler placed value on a clear division of realms between sacred and profane, divine and nondivine spheres, and correspondingly eliminated everything that could cause such boundaries to collapse, is given a foundation by Joel Weinberg (1996, 247f.), specifically with regard to "boundary phenomena" involving quasi-divine beings. Thus, for example, of the fifteen instances of the term *rûaḥ* (spirit) in Chronicles, fourteen are said to manifest the tendency to depict here a life force emanating from God and not (any longer) to view *rûaḥ* as a quasi-divine and relatively autonomously active being. Beings that are considered to belong to the underworld have thus, according to Weinberg, almost completely disappeared. In corroboration of Weinberg, the story of Saul's encounter with the medium of Endor (1 Sam 28) can also be added, an account omitted from the narration of the downfall of Saul in Chronicles. According to 1 Chronicles 10:13, Saul's sin consists only in having consulted a spirit of someone dead rather than YHWH. Saul sought to cross the boundary to the realm of the dead and thereby brought about his own death. How this took place requires no further explanation; in fact, for the Chronicler's sensibilities this would concede too much weight to the reality and effective power of a spirit of the dead, whereas for the narrator of Samuel what matters is the tragedy of Saul's fate in which the woman from Endor is enmeshed.

Christian Frevel (1991) adds a further "case" of problematic blurring of boundaries not discussed by Weinberg: the *asherim,* the sacred wood poles that, according to the depiction and conception found in Kings, are inseparable from a being named Asherah, who is granted cultic devotion and is thus at least minimally quasi-divine. Frevel observes that the mention of the *asherim* in Chronicles is dramatically reduced in comparison with the Deuteronomistic works. Of the three instances in Kings in which Asherah appears unambiguously as the name of a goddess (1 Kings 15:13; 2 Kings 21:7; 23:4-7), Chronicles retains only one, the mention of the erection of a cultic image for Asherah by the king's mother Maacah (2 Chron 15:16). This leads Frevel to deduce a conscious elimination of the goddess from the worldview of the Chronicler. This would accord with the observation by Menachem Stern (1988) that in Persian-era Judea the female cultic figures so prevalent in the preexilic period are no longer archaeologically documented, and with the interpretation of the vision of Zechariah (Zech 5:5-11) held by Christoph Uehlinger (1994) of the woman in the basket as a "programmatic vision of the expulsion of the goddess figure" from Judea (cf. also Haggai and Zechariah). Proceeding from the observation that only two of the three references to Asherah have truly been eliminated, the thesis could be framed with a slightly different accent: Chronicles removes Asherah as goddess solely from the narrative traditions concerned with the Jerusalem temple and therefore eliminates her from both references having to do with the temple: 2 Kings 21:7 (2 Chron 33:7) and 2 Kings 23:4-7 (2 Chron 34:3-7). The mention of Maacah's cultic image, in contrast, and of the fate of this queen mother who is removed from her office by her son, the reigning king, could in a certain sense have been passed on as a cautionary example since Maacah's image of Asherah need not be presumed to be in the realm of the temple. The story has to do primarily not with the goddess but again with the purity and holiness of the temple.

In all these areas Chronicles is presenting not a real picture but an ideal image of the temple, and with its centering on the temple it also does not present the lived reality of the majority of the population of the much-reduced territory of Judea in the postexilic period. The margins of the text, above all the "vestibule" and the side comments tossed into the royal history here and there as if by accident, allow us to perceive that Chronicles is embedded in its daily reality in which the women of Judea assert for themselves traditional, expected, yet at times also surprising locations.

LITERATURE

Bail, Ulrike. 1997. "Mit schielendem Blick. Bemerkungen zu 1 Chronik 7:21B-24." In *"Ihr Völker alle, klatscht in die Hände!"* edited by Rainer Kessler et al., 214-25. Festschrift for Erhard Gerstenberger. Münster.

Bird, Phyllis. 1987. "The Place of Women in the Israelite Cultus." In *Ancient Israelite Religion,* edited by Patrick D. Miller et al., 397-419. Festschrift for Frank M. Cross. Philadelphia.

Cohen, Shaye. 1985. "The Matrilineal Principle in Historical Perspective." *Judaism* 34:5-13.

Eskenazi, Tamara C. 1992. "Out from the Shadows: Biblical Women in the Postexilic Era." *Journal for the Study of the Old Testament* 54:25-43.

Fischer, Irmtraud. 1997. "Der Männerstammbaum im Frauenbuch: Überlegungen zum Schluß des Rutbuches (4:18-22)." In *"Ihr Völker alle, klatscht in die Hände!"* edited by Rainer Kessler et al., 195-213. Festschrift for Erhard Gerstenberger. Münster.

Frevel, Christian. 1991. "Die Elimination der Göttin aus dem Weltbild des Chronisten." *Zeitschrift für die alttestamentliche Wissenschaft* 103:263-71.

————. 1995. *Aschera und der Ausschließlichkeitsanspruch YHWHs.* Bonner biblische Beiträge, vol. 94, 1 and 2. Weinheim.

Gabriel, Ingeborg. 1990. *Friede über Israel: Eine Untersuchung zur Friedenstheologie in Chronik I 10–II 36.* Klosterneuburg.

Görg, Manfred. 1996. "Name und Namengebung." In *Neues Bibel-Lexikon*, 2:898. Zurich.

Gruber, Mayer I. 1995. "Matrilineal Determination of Jewishness: Biblical and Near Eastern Roots." In *Pomegranates and Golden Bells*, edited by David P. Wright et al., 437-43. Festschrift for Jacob Milgrom. Winona Lake, Ind.

Japhet, Sarah. 1989. *The Ideology of the Book of Chronicles and Its Place in Biblical Thought*. Frankfurt.

————. 1993. *I and II Chronicles*. London.

Kalimi, Isaac. 1995. *Zur Geschichtsschreibung des Chronisten. Literarisch-historiographische Abweichungen der Chronik von ihren Parallelstellen in den Samuel- und Königsbüchern*. Beihefte zur Zeitschrift für die alttestamentliche Wissenschaft, vol. 226. Berlin.

Kessler, Rainer. 1987. "Benennung des Kindes durch die israelitische Mutter." *Wort und Dienst* 19:25-35.

Laffey, Alice L. 1992. "1 and 2 Chronicles." In *The Women's Bible Commentary*, edited by Carol A. Newsom and Sharon H. Ringe, 110-15. London and Louisville.

Micheel, Rosemarie. 1983. *Die Seher- und Prophetenüberlieferungen in der Chronik*. Beiträge zur biblischen Exegese und Theologie, vol. 18. Frankfurt.

Oeming, Manfred. 1990. *Das wahre Israel. Die 'genealogische Vorhalle' 1 Chronik 1–9*. Beiträge zur Wissenschaft vom Alten und Neuen Testament, vol. 128. Stuttgart.

Schroer, Silvia. 1995. "Auf dem Weg zu einer feministischen Rekonstruktion der Geschichte Israels." In *Feministische Exegese*, edited by Luise Schottroff, Silvia Schroer, and Marie-Theres Wacker, 83-174. Darmstadt. (Also in *Feminist Interpretation: The Bible in Women's Perspective* [1998], 85-176.)

Stamm, Johann Jakob. 1980. "Hebräische Frauennamen." In Stamm, *Beiträge zur hebräischen und altorientalischen Namenskunde*, 97-135. Orbis biblicus et orientalis, vol. 30. Fribourg and Göttingen.

Steins, Georg. 1995. *Die Chronik als kanonisches Abschlußphänomen: Studien zur Entstehung und Theologie von 1/2 Chronik*. Bonner biblische Beiträge, vol. 93. Bodenheim.

Stern, Menachem. 1998. "What Happened to the Cult Figurines? Israelite Religion Purified after the Exile." *Biblical Archaeological Review* 14:22-29, 53f.

Uehlinger, Christoph. 1994. "Die Frau im Efa (Sach 5:5-11): Eine Programmvision von der Abschiebung der Göttin." *Bibel und Kirche* 49:93-103.

Wacker, Marie-Theres. 1995. "'Religionsgeschichte Israels' oder 'Theologie des Alten Testaments' — (k)eine Alternative?" *Jahrbuch für Biblische Theologie* 10:129-155.

Weinberg, Joel P. 1996. *Der Chronist in seiner Mitwelt*. Beihefte zur Zeitschrift für die alttestamentliche Wissenschaft, vol. 239. Berlin.

Willi, Thomas. 1991. *Chronik*. Biblischer Kommentar, Altes Testament, vol. 24. Neukirchen-Vluyn.

Winter, Urs. 1983. *Frau und Göttin*. Orbis biblicus et orientalis, vol. 52. Fribourg and Göttingen.

FOR FURTHER READING

Gardner, Anne E. 2005. "The Identity of Bath-Sheba." *Revue biblique* 112, no. 4:521-35.

Ilan, Tal. 1999. *Integrating Women into Second Temple History*. Tübingen.

Labahn, Antje, and Ehud Ben Zvi. 2003. "Observations on Women in the Genealogies of 1 Chronicles 1–9." *Biblica* 84, no. 4:457-78.

Malamat, Avraham. 1999. "Naamah, the Ammonite Princess, King Solomon's Wife." *Revue biblique* 106, no. 1:35-40.

Steiner, Richard C. 1998. "Bitte-Ya, Daughter of Pharaoh (1 Chr 4,18), and Bint(i)-ʿAnat, Daughter of Ramesses II." *Biblica* 79, no. 3:394-408.

Translated by Lisa E. Dahill

Ezra and Nehemiah: The Return of the Others

Christiane Karrer-Grube

An attempt at a feminist-theological exegesis of the book of Ezra-Nehemiah (hereafter EN) is nearly always met with astonishment and bafflement: at first glance it seems that female figures and questions of gender difference play next to no role as regards the theme of this book. Hence there is almost no feminist literature on the subject. Only a closer analysis, and a questioning that gets below the surface of the text's intended statement, reveal a different picture. The attempt to make "the women" simply disappear from the concept of the book has not been successful. When we uncover the traces of their significance, we, at the same time, obtain a new insight into the book and its problems.

The Refounding of Judah: Theme of the Book

Ezra 1 begins programmatically with the order from the Persian king Cyrus permitting the Judeans in exile to return to Judah and rebuild their temple in Jerusalem. EN depicts the *reconstitution of the community of Judah/Jerusalem*. It can be roughly divided into three parts: a large group of exiles returns, and begins and completes the building of the temple under the direction of Zerubbabel and the high priest Joshua (Ezra 1–6); the scribe and priest Ezra, on the orders of King Artaxerxes, comes to Judah with a group of exiles to make sure that YHWH's law is promulgated and put into effect (Ezra 7–10; Neh 8); Nehemiah obtains from Artaxerxes the appointment to be governor of Judah and, through building the wall of Jerusalem, establishes a Judah independent of Samaria, with Jerusalem as its own capital (Neh 1–7; 9–13).

The description of these beginnings is not a historical account; it presents, in ideal fashion, some important elements of the *constitution of the postexilic community,* which had to be reconceived in this special crisis situation. The identity of preexilic Judah had been destroyed under Babylonian rule. It had become part of the province of Trans-Euphrates (Beyond the River), and no longer enjoyed any independent existence. Its lands belonged to others; they were occupied by a mixed population made up of the descendants of Judahites who had not gone into exile, together with members of other peoples. Rule by its own royal house had been brought to a violent end. The temple and the city wall had been destroyed. Jerusalem had lost its status as the capital city. Ultimately, had not its own God been defeated by the gods of the conquering peoples?

Once the Persians had incorporated Babylon and its realm into their own empire, they permitted the refoundation of a separate unit called "Judah/Jerusalem." In a kind of "zero hour," *concepts of leadership* had to be developed suitable to its shaping. Persian policy allowed the necessary freedom for this project, but at the same time established its limitations. This meant above all that there could not be an independent state of "Judah" again. It remained a tiny part of a great empire, in close contact with many other peoples in that empire. Its own laws and institutions were legitimated by a foreign ruler.

It was not possible to establish the identity of "Judah" through a seamless linkage with preexilic tradition. To forge its constitution, new concepts in accord with the new situation had to be found. For example: What would be the "core" of the new community — the temple with all its functions; the law, which shaped the common life; or the capital city Jerusalem, whose new wall showed its independence and defensive strength? How should the authority to make decisions be distributed within the community? What would political leadership be like, when there was no longer a kingship? Who belonged to the community? Should it separate itself strictly from others, or build contacts? Above all: What theological concept would permit the people to understand their situation and their identity in terms of their own faith?

EN reveals *traces of different ideas* about these problems, and these can be interpreted as *testimony to a conflict* over the desired way of constituting the community. Although, for example, throughout EN the Persian demand for loyal incorporation within its world empire is adhered to, and hope for an independent kingdom is rejected (cf. Neh 6:1-9), different models of political leadership are favored at different points: directly appointed by the Persian king, Nehemiah appears as a governor who — supported by his own armed forces — lays claim to sole decision-making authority in all important questions of internal and external policy. He always acts in the best interest of the people, but for the most part independently of them. Ezra, in contrast, receives authority for particular tasks through a letter from the Persian king. In carrying out those tasks he does, certainly, provide the impetus, but the authority to decide and to carry out the work remains that of the community as a whole.

Women and men formed part of the postexilic community, and they both, equally, made decisions about how it was constituted, yet women are scarcely mentioned in the texts. The cause and significance of their marginalization can be better understood against the background of the themes depicted. In conceiving

Judah's constitution, individual persons played a part only to the extent that they were in positions of political leadership. EN makes no provision for women in those roles! Family clans are pictured as the central structural units of society, but leading men are always named as their representatives. Obviously women were considered part of the collective "people," but since that is (almost) always implicit, we cannot perceive their significance in that area. *Hence in the concept of EN, women are almost invisible.* That makes the few passages in which they are mentioned all the more significant (see below).

In EN we can study a community's *process of self-constitution and discovery of identity in the tension between its own possibilities for formation and its dependence* on a given political and cultural system. Presupposed here is a *crisis situation* because of which a simple continuation of earlier traditions is impossible. New concepts must be discovered and discussed, such that what is "one's own" can be worked out and realized under the conditions imposed by the new situation.

This is all the more interesting to the extent that similar structural processes can be currently observed. Talk about a "regional Europe" throws light on the tension between the culturally and politically influential "empire" of Europe and the need of local and ethnic communities for identity and independence. In the territory of the former Yugoslavia and the Soviet Union, even the smallest ethnic groups are now making extreme efforts to achieve "autonomy." Their strivings were suppressed by highly repressive systems, it is true, but were not extinguished. They are now emerging more strongly than ever, despite — or precisely because of — an international political and economic web to which the "national states" are somewhat anachronistically attached.

Although the problems of EN are very close to us in some ways, they are almost completely absent from Christian perception, and even among First Testament scholars this is one of the "marginal fields" that are accorded scarcely any theological relevance. The situation is very different in Judaism, where the figure of Ezra in particular is highly regarded. Many of the most prominent scholars who study EN are Jews. It is seen as the foundational document for the Jewish state and religion. *The attitude of an author toward Judaism most often determines her or his evaluation of EN.* On the Christian side the book is often devalued when, for example, preexilic Israel is distinguished, in positive fashion, from postexilic Judah. Individual factors, such as the high importance of the Law or the tendency toward separation from the surrounding nations, are not understood in terms of the overall concept, but are labeled "typically Jewish" and made the dominant factors in interpretation. This view was given a dangerous emphasis in the period of National Socialism. Beyond a basic devaluing, the book's strategy of separation was adopted on behalf of a theory of racial separation. Especially the texts on "mixed marriages" (Ezra 9–10; Neh 13:23-27; see below) were imperiled in this context, being read as a Jewish affirmation of the National Socialists' own contempt for humanity.

This is not the place to attempt an adequate evaluation of the history of reception of EN (including, obviously, attempts to do justice to the book). A *feminist theological study* — necessarily — poses critical questions to the book's ideas. In posing these questions, it must remain aware of the problems described, so as not to fall into the *traps of common prejudices and positions.* It would be easy here to furnish new fodder to the charge of anti-Semitic tendencies in Christian feminist exegesis.

As important as was the process, when establishing the postexilic community, of setting directions for the further development of Judah and Judaism, in my opinion an engagement with the themes of EN touches on such an important general set of problems that it cannot be reduced to the question of "Jewish, Israelite, or Christian."

My Starting Point

I regard EN as a *literary text* in which certain *ideas* or *concepts* are formulated *within a historical setting.* An analysis of the text permits us to extract those concepts, on the basis of which we can obtain some understanding of the "beginning" of postexilic Judah and its foundational structures. These texts are, then, neither a direct account of historical reality nor seen as being completely detached from the historical situation. These concepts reflect a particular situation; they are supported by certain groups of people; and they attempt to influence reality. The traces of different concepts in EN can be read as testimony to a conflict over the desired form of the foundational structures that can be traced through the course of the history of reception of the text. (I will not further pursue here the relationship to a literary-historical origin in several stages.) These concepts also developed their influence independently of the historical situation in which they were formulated. Nevertheless, it is interesting to gather information from other sources about this latter development in order to compare it to the concepts themselves and thus to gain a more precise idea of their purpose and aims.

Against this background, two different sets of questions emerge for a *feminist theological exegesis.* First, we need to ask about the significance of women and their life contexts in the sense intended by these concepts. These can then be compared with social-historical information about the situation of women in Judah in the Persian era. Second, the texts can be read "against the grain" to find within them the hidden, unintended traces of women's experiences and ideas.

This latter inquiry presumes a reading of the text that supposes that the meaning of a text is not exhausted by *one* dominant primary meaning that we can derive from an analysis of its ideas. Rather, we can imagine a text to be like a many-layered weaving containing a spectrum of different and even contradictory meanings. For one meaning to emerge, others must be suppressed. Residual traces of this process always remain and lead us to the *suppressed dimensions of the text.*

The initiative of *"deconstructive reading"* (for a good description of which, see Fewell 1987 and 1995) concerns itself with uncovering such traces through questions that, from the point of view of the dominant concept, *may not* be asked of the text: first, meanings of words that are different from what appears to be established by the immediate context; second, the perspective and fate of persons who do not fulfill their (secondary) function in the text; third, notions of value that deviate from the system apparently represented by the text. The price of this way of proceeding, however, is a persistent absence of security: *the* meaning of a text can no longer be determined. Many questions that are asked cannot be answered, but "only" offer new ways of looking at the text. On the other hand, in this way the ambivalence of many biblical texts that has revealed itself in the course of their reception can be more adequately appreciated. A deconstructive approach to biblical texts corresponds in large measure to *a fundamental hermeneutical problem in feminist exegesis:* insofar as it is not content to restrict itself to demonstrating the androcentric conditions in which the texts of the First Testament originated and the equally androcentric intent of what they say, it poses questions that, for the most part, do not correspond to the dominant statement. Often female figures are auxiliary persons or are given a negative value, and "after all, it is really about. . . ." Or the "woman" serves only as a metaphor for the "real" subject. Feminist exegesis is frequently accused of avoiding *the* meaning of a text and offering arbitrary interpretations. An understanding of the text in the sense of a "deconstructive reading" can reveal traces of women's point of view, their experiences, and their way of life, without the need to deny the primary and intended statement of the text and its androcentric stamp. In my opinion, the varied dimensions of meaning in a text adequately reflect *a reality that is never absolutely unambiguous.* Since there is no complete separation of the lives and speech-worlds of men and women, texts, even when conditioned by an androcentric formation, can give us indications of the reality of the latter.

In what follows I will consider the dominant concepts in the texts from a feminist-theological point of view, but I will also attempt a deconstructive analysis of one passage by way of example. In my view, the spectrum of meaning in a text is best developed when both of these are considered and related to one another.

Who Is Israel?

According to the ideas of EN, *women are to be considered part of the collective "Israel,"* which represents the whole of those who belong to the new community. The text mentions their responsibilities while also establishing the criteria for membership and the boundaries separating the community from the outside.

This last is clearly expressed in the Nehemiah section through the appellation *"Judahites"* (or *"Jews"*). The term defines an *ethnos* characterized by a common language, law, religion, and history. All the Judahites/Jews who live in Jerusalem and Judah make up the community led by Nehemiah. As an *ethnos,* they are closely related to the Jews who live in other parts of the Persian Empire. The *differentiation from other* ethnoi is sharp; they are accused of having a hostile attitude toward the Jews and an interest in keeping them weak. Samaria and the region it controls play a special role in all this. As the capital of the former northern kingdom, Samaria had similar religious and cultural traditions and during the exile had achieved significant influence over Judah. Therefore a distinction was especially important politically. All attempts to acquire influence or establish closer contacts are branded by Nehemiah as hostile acts against Judah (cf. Neh 2:19-20; 4; 6:1-9, 15-19). It is thus unintentionally made clear how closely aligned Judah was with Samaria and the degree to which ethnic boundaries depended on ideological constructions. In contrast to the "enemies," Nehemiah often adopts the designation "Israel" for the Judahites, emphasizing his own community as the legitimate successor to preexilic Israel and placing it within Israel's religious tradition. The God of Nehemiah and the Judahites/Jews is the God of Israel; they alone represent "Israel." Here lie both the core of their religious self-concept and the legitimation for rejecting "the others" as "enemies."

In other parts of the book also, the community is understood to be the *"true Israel."* However, its borders are radically narrower than those drawn by Nehemiah, and they are differently defined: "Israel" is limited to the *"Gōlâ,"* the community of those who have returned from exile. *The others* are described as *"the people/peoples of the land/lands."* There is a demand not to mix with them, too, and to draw strict lines of division. Ezra 4 summarizes their hostile activities. One of the more difficult questions for scholars is: Whom exactly are we to understand as being included here? The descendants of the Judahites who were not exiled? Judahites with different religious practices? Members of other nations who had settled in the former Judah? Members of neighboring peoples? Behind this terminological murkiness is probably a variety of ideas within the exile community itself about the criteria for distinguishing "Israel." For example, Ezra 6:21 leaves open the possibility that others may separate themselves from the uncleanness of the nations and join the community of the returnees.

In the surrounding texts the boundaries are more tightly drawn. Here there is criticism of other returnees because they had married wives from the peoples of the lands (Ezra 9–10; see below). Did they reject such a strict delimitation, or did they count their wives as part of an "Israel" more broadly understood? At the same time, in the Ezra texts the collective of the assembled community has the ultimate authority to make decisions (see above). Moreover, this is the sole concept in which *women* are expressly named *as members.* They join in ordering the divorce of the "foreign women" (Ezra 10:1), and they are present when the Law is read aloud (Neh 8:2). They are even accorded *religious and political competency* (cf. also Neh 10:28-29). Does a concept that approves a high degree of influence for the community as a whole and really includes all its members have *a higher degree of need for delimitation and regulation of its membership?*

In all other parts of the text the collective appears, with a variety of assignments, without anything being explicitly said about the degree to which women are included. It makes sense to think of women as participants unless the contrary is proved. They are part of the people present at the building of the altar and rejoicing over the construction of the temple (Ezra 3). They celebrate the feast of Sukkoth (Ezra 3:4) and Passover after the temple is completed (Ezra 6:19-22). They certainly also support Nehemiah's building of the wall. In reading the book one should continually call this to mind whenever the text speaks in any way of the "people."

The presentation in EN creates a difficulty: no distinction is made to show whether a description of the people is intended to include only the men, or whether it refers to women as well. The impression is given that the people are only men. It would be interesting at various points to know the extent to which women shared in the rights and obligations of the people, but this can no longer be deduced from the text, so it is left to the interpretation of those who receive it. Ezra 2 (cf. Neh 7) is a good example. Verse 1 announces a census of the inhabitants of Judah who are returning from exile. In the first place one would obviously imagine that these are both men and women, just as in the description in Ezra 1. But then 2:2 introduces a listing of the number of men of the people Israel, and the list that follows gives the total number of men from various families and places. Does this mean that the returnees were only men? Surely not! But in this way women are entirely removed from the view of the readers. This is all the more striking since, in 2:64-65, slave women and singers are explicitly mentioned in the feminine. The total number of returnees given in 2:64 is different from the sum of the individual groups as given. Are the unnamed women concealed under this difference? If so, the number of them would be astonishingly small! In that case there would have been a substantial surplus of men among the returnees.

This process of *making women invisible* is supported by the purely masculine designations of all the groups in EN that have responsibilities (e.g., "the elders" in Ezra 5–6 or the "nobles" in the Nehemiah section, etc.). In the postexilic period family leagues, which had to have included women, played a significant role, and yet in EN they, too, are always represented only by their male leadership (cf. Ezra 8; Neh 3; Ezra 1:5; 2:68; and frequently). These are all called "heads of the families."

The complete marginalizing of women is — whether consciously or not — one of the fundamental ideas of the book. In reality their influence was probably not so minor. Unfortunately, we have very little information about the *lives of women* in Persian-era Judah. But what we do have are some private letters and contracts from the *Jewish military colony in Elephantine,* and from these we learn that women could marry more than once, that they had their own right to initiate divorce, and that they could inherit property, buy and sell, lend money, and make contracts. (See the detailed description in Eskenazi 1992, and *Women's Biblical Commentary*, 1992.) Undoubtedly there were some very well-to-do women there, with a corresponding degree of influence. We do not know the extent to which we can apply the same conditions to Judah; however, this does relativize the depiction in EN.

Women may also be concealed behind some of the book's specific formulations. The list of returnees in Ezra 2:55 uses a term that properly means "the woman scribe." Could this be a woman in an honored profession who was the leader of a family league? Likewise, a family in Ezra 2:61 traces itself back to Barzillai, the father *of a wife*. Tamara Eskenazi suggests that we should also interpret Shelomith in Ezra 8:10 as a female name (1992, 39). In that case, the family would trace its origins to a woman. Nehemiah 3:12 mentions the daughters of Shallum who took part in the building of the wall. We can here detect *the last traces of women of great significance,* which have everywhere else been eliminated from EN.

Nehemiah 5:1-13 shows how severely women were affected by economic and political conditions. Here women are spoken of as those who actively approach Nehemiah with their lament about the rising level of debt in large groups of the population and the threat of debt slavery that is affecting their own daughters in particular. The basis of the family's existence, and thus the community as a whole, is in danger. The text retains the memory of the initiative and responsibility women can assume in such situations.

Finally, let us mention the only woman in a position of leadership. Nehemiah 6:14 speaks of the prophet Noadiah, who evidently was so influential that she, together with her colleague Nehemiah, could be dangerous. She supported Nehemiah's enemies, and so, unfortunately, we learn nothing more about her duties. She is a witness to the great importance of women in the field of prophecy, even in the Persian era (Kessler 1996, who also offers a possible interpretation of the conflict).

Even these few references to women show that the overall impression EN gives at first glance must be nuanced.

The Return of the Others

In Nehemiah 13:23-29 and Ezra 9–10, women are twice made the principal theme of the texts. It is all about *one problem: there have been marriages between Judahites, or members of the exile community, and "foreign women."* This practice is regarded as a breach of YHWH's commandments and a danger to their own community, and is to be stopped as much as possible. A comparison of the two texts reveals a number of differences. In line with their different ideas about the political structure, Nehemiah's actions are described as being very different from Ezra's.

Nehemiah acts alone: he himself determines that things are awry, accuses those involved, and demands that they stop what they are doing. But, differently from the
other cases in which things are amiss (cf. Neh 13:4-22), he himself does not act
against these marriages. Ezra, in contrast, hears about this bad situation from the
leaders of the exile community. His lament and prayer are presented in detail, but
suggestions about how to proceed and the manner of carrying out the suggestions
remain the responsibility of the assembled community of returnees. The result of
the process is very much more radical than in the Nehemiah text: it is decided that
the men in question must divorce their foreign wives and send them away, together with the children they have begotten. A list of those affected follows.

On the level of dominant ideas, these descriptions are certainly not meant to
be regarded from the point of view of gender differences. The so-called mixed
marriages are seen as a *danger to the differentiation of their own group* from the
outsiders. However the boundaries were defined, they were apparently anything
but obvious, and first of all the identity of the group had to be discovered and established. These two texts show that this identity was endangered not only by "attempts at assimilation" of "others" from outside, but equally from inside by people
with other ideas and ways of life. The demand for a radical exclusion was probably
a reaction to a common practice of "mixed marriages." Even if today's readers —
at least in a Western context — will necessarily see this as problematic, still, setting
boundaries is an indispensable act in constructing one's own identity, and in crisis
situations it can take on forms that are difficult for outsiders to understand.

From the perspective of the ideas in Ezra/Nehemiah, precise boundaries had
to be found to make a clear definition of those who belonged to "our own." This is
made especially obvious by the following observation: the argumentation in both
texts rests on a commandment familiar to us from Deuteronomy, where it is formulated from two perspectives: "Do not intermarry with them, giving your
daughters to their sons or taking their daughters for your sons" (Deut 7:3). In
Nehemiah 13:25, Nehemiah quotes it in an expanded form: "You shall not give
your daughters to their sons, or take their daughters for your sons or for yourselves." It is thus made clear who the addressees are and where the accent of the argument lies. This is about Jewish men who have married foreign wives, and this is
not a future problem, but something acutely present. The depiction of the situation in Nehemiah 13:23 corresponds to this. Marrying their daughters to foreign
men is not in view as something actually practiced. Did this never happen? Probably it did, but when that occurred, and the woman, as usual, moved into the husband's family, it was not a question of foreigners penetrating their own society (cf.
Neh 5, where Nehemiah argues against the threatened sale of daughters into debt
slavery *not* with the danger of "mixing," but with the disparagement of "Jews").
This is still more pronounced in the Ezra text. He only mentions the twofold commandment in his prayer (Ezra 9:12); elsewhere he says the people have taken foreign wives for themselves and their sons. Both of these ideas are about the delimi-

tation of one's own community, not an abstract "commandment against mixing" with other peoples, as the text is frequently accused of saying.

However, the argumentation reveals the differences between these conceptions. Nehemiah's efforts to achieve a separated *ethnos* of "*Jews*" are visible in his lament about children's lack of knowledge of Jewish language (Neh 13:24). He explains his citation from the Law by using the example of Solomon (Neh 13:26), referring to a tradition related in 1 Kings 11:1-13, where "sin" is described as the worship of foreign gods and goddesses, something the foreign wives had brought with them and that Solomon not only permitted but himself supported. In this way the danger of *syncretistic religion* is associated with the "foreign wives." In 1 Kings 11:11-13 Solomon and his successors are told that the punishment for his behavior will be loss of his royal rule over a large part of his kingdom (see 1 Kings 12). Hence Nehemiah 13:26-27 suggests to the reader an association with the threatened loss of relative political autonomy, something that had just been achieved with great difficulty.

The text of Ezra also refers to the commandment from Deuteronomy 7:3, but places it in a different context. The accusation in Ezra 9:1 is at first very general: "The people of Israel, the priests, and the Levites have not separated themselves from the peoples of the lands with their abominations." According to Eskenazi and Judd (1994, 267-70), it is not clear from the Hebrew text whether the reference is to members of foreign nations or inhabitants of the land itself who have adopted the religious practices of other peoples. The Holiness Code contains expressions that may furnish the background for this charge: "I am YHWH, your God; I have separated you from the peoples"; "You shall be holy to me; for I, YHWH, am holy, and I have separated you from the other peoples to be mine" (Lev 20:24, 26). This is saying that God himself has separated his own people from the others so that they may belong to him (cf. also 1 Kings 8:53). This same *exclusive belonging* is what is meant by the term "holy," which is also applied to the people in Ezra 9:2: "holy seed (i.e., progeny)." Likewise, when the reason for the separation is named in Ezra's prayer: "The land . . . is a land unclean with the *pollutions of the peoples* of the lands, with *their abominations*" (9:11), there is reference to a text in Leviticus: "the inhabitants" have "defiled the land" by their "abominations," and therefore "the land vomited out its inhabitants" (Lev 18:24-30). Ezra 9:6-10, 13-14 is a vivid portrayal of anxiety about a complete loss of God's favor through the people's own fault, something that would cause their life in the land, restricted though it now is, to be utterly destroyed. They would be "vomited out" like the other inhabitants.

But while the "*casting out*" in the Leviticus text is clearly a *divine action* that Israel is to respond to by keeping a series of commandments so as not to fall into abominations as had the former inhabitants (Lev 20:25; 18:26, 30), the "*separating themselves*" in Ezra 9–10 is made a *duty for Israel*, something it is to bring about actively and that can be made the criterion for an accusation against it (Ezra 9:1-4). Its content is determined by the commandment in Deuteronomy 7:3 (Ezra 9:2, 12). This new combination creates, in turn, a new concept in the text of Ezra: when Israel's separation is interpreted as a prohibition against marriage with foreigners, "abominations" and the uncleanness of the land are no longer attributed to particular actions — according to Leviticus 18:26, the commandments are to be kept by the Israelites *and* the foreigners in the land — but are attached to persons, who are regarded as "peoples of abominations" (Ezra 9:14). Given that, a radical separation from them is indispensable.

Ezra's idea is also radicalized beyond that of Nehemiah by the incorporation of concepts and imagery from the realm of sacred law. This is not just about Israel's retaining its own language and tradition by keeping a divine commandment. The close adherence to God himself as a "holy seed" is called into question if the Israelites do not separate themselves from all foreigners. The basis for their very existence is at stake, as Ezra's prayer says. On that which belongs especially to him, God also lays a special claim. A consequence of this idea is that the cause of such a profound guilt and danger must be eliminated as quickly and thoroughly as possible. Therefore the assembled community decides to *carry out the divorce* of the foreign wives.

This is only possible because in Ezra's conception the authority to make political decisions lies with the whole people. In antiquity, marriage and divorce were entirely matters of private law, removed from the grasp of state institutions. So also Nehemiah the governor, despite his comprehensive authority, has to be content with the mere warning that, in future, marriages with foreigners should cease. The problem is not really solved. In Ezra's conception, on the other hand, the institution of the community-as-a-whole means that those affected are themselves involved in political decisions. Therefore the whole community can actually put into effect its decision for divorce through acceptance of this obligation by those involved. Hence Ezra's conception claims not only to comprehend the marriage problem more adequately than Nehemiah, but also, through *a different political structure,* to offer a *better proposal for a solution.*

The attempt at a strong ethnic separation corresponds to the *prescriptions of Persian policy,* which presumed an empire made up of clearly divided and distinguished *ethnoi* that — in full fidelity to their own traditions — supported the Persian throne. It was necessary to be able to say to what nation one belonged, even when living in a different part of the empire. And the reputation of one's people enhanced one's own! So also, the Persians kept themselves separate; the highest offices in the empire were reserved for Persians. The "success" of this concept was illustrated in themselves. Consequently, fears that, without one's own boundaries, a nation could "disappear" in this empire of so many nations were not altogether unfounded.

Ezra's and Nehemiah's ideas are formulated from an *androcentric perspective.* This is evident especially in the one-sided reference to the Deuteronomic marriage prohibition: the question of the "right kind" of marriage is asked from the perspective of Israel's own men. The corresponding female perspective is not in evidence. Women appear almost exclusively as objects of men's desire to marry. They are divided into *"right" and "wrong" women.* The criteria for the distinction are derived from the definition of "our own."

In the depiction in Ezra 9–10 the "right" women also appear actively; in 10:1 they support the decision for divorce. This is striking, since in Ezra's conception — except for Nehemiah 8 — only men appear as members of the self-determining community. So the "we" in Ezra 9:2 apparently applies to men, just as in Ezra 10:9 there is an assembly of the men of Jerusalem. The emphasis on a decision made by all the people together, men and women, in favor of a radical separation is part of the androcentric concept. From that point of view the "right" women are in complete agreement. But we must suppose that in fact women were also among the supporters of this idea. They could participate in the advantages of the separation and agree with its theological basis. The "foreign" women could easily appear as a danger to them, too (and as competition? cf. Mal 2:10-16).

The model of distinguishing "right" and "wrong" women and the temptation for the "right" ones to support that model are very common, even when the criteria for distinction are quite different. Undoubtedly it has negative consequences for women in the long term, and it needs to be critiqued. A well-known biblical example is the conflict between Sarah and Hagar in Genesis 16 and 21:1-21. But for those in a marginalized position all attempts to gain power and influence for oneself are only too easy to understand. It seems to me to make more sense to analyze the particular conflicts than to rush to disqualify the "victors." We find here traces of a conflict that, in many ways, has erupted in the modern feminist movement also. Women never define themselves simply as "women," but also — and often primarily — as belonging to another ethnic, religious, social, or otherwise defined group. Loyalty to that group conflicts with solidarity with "different" women. This is a conflict that women often find difficult to resolve, even when they are aware of its consequences. In many cases it is probably not even sensed, and women remain fully contained within their own group.

In contrast to their otherwise marginalized state, women are given a strikingly high significance in Nehemiah 13:23-29 and Ezra 9–10. Their great influence within the family is the basis for the whole issue. They are responsible for the children's acquisition of language and culture, and at least in the religious arena they influence their husbands as well. We need to consider that in the postexilic period the family was of the utmost importance for the continuation of the Jewish people, since all other institutions, in the public realm, were in flux or were not under their control. According to Ezra and Nehemiah, the *stability of the community as a whole* depended on family institutions in which both marital partners belonged to the same community. In Ezra 9–10 this is elevated to a question of fundamental significance for the community's *relationship to God.* Despite the patriarchal family structure, which, through the public dominance of leading men, had contributed to making women invisible, the influence of women had to be considered.

Unfortunately, EN itself does not yield any further information about the relationships between men and women within the family. Interestingly, the family narratives in Genesis 12–35, 38 reveal a similarly ambivalent structure: on the one hand we have the great significance of family clans, their clear patriarchal structure, and interest in a patrilineal sequence of generations. On the other hand, within the family stories we find the great significance and independence of female figures, who even dominate individual narratives. Moreover, at a strikingly large number of places in these stories marriage and begetting of progeny with the "right," that is, Israelite, woman plays an essential role (cf., among others, Gen 16; 17:15-22; 21:8-13; 24; 26:34-35; 27:46–28:9 — *perhaps we need to read Genesis if we want to know more about the structure of the "patriarchal households"*).

In the context of the concepts that can be understood as the deliberately intended statement of the texts, marriage with "foreign women" has proved to be where the problem of separation focused. To that end the concepts themselves had to relativize the marginal position they otherwise attribute to women. In the sense of "deconstructive reading," we can pose a whole series of further questions that open up a broader spectrum of meaning. What would it mean to look at the divorce policy from the point of view of those affected? What was the fate of the dismissed women and children? What were the conditions in the lives of the divorced women? What would it mean for the families as a whole if they were suddenly torn apart from outside? People had lived together for years, and close social ties had been created. Could the men really have agreed to the loss of their wives and children? Even the depiction in Ezra 10, which tries to assert that there was universal agreement with this idea, had to admit that there were countervailing voices (Ezra 10:15), though at first it seems that they were only raised against the proposed action. To what extent were women able to make use of all this for their own competitive situation? Did the "victorious women" really do themselves a favor in the long run?

It is entirely probable that the radical idea in Ezra was never really applied. Strikingly enough, the list in Ezra 10:18-44 only speaks of those who were "affected," not explicitly of "those who divorced." But even in that case such ideas have effects on the living conditions of "foreign" women, their children, and the "mixed" families. How much were they despised and disadvantaged if they really did not fit the concept?

The list of questions about the implications of the decision for those affected could be expanded. More important, it seems to me, is one fundamental observation: the setting of boundaries over against the "foreigners," the "others," was intended to secure the identity and existence of their own community, and yet the idea was not effective. *When "the others," the foreigners, appear in place of "the other," the woman, they reappear at the heart of what is "our own."* The families themselves are "mixed," made up of "our own" and "the others." The foreign comes threateningly close, and if it be removed, a part of one's own is lost. This is obvious in the case of the children from these unions: How, in those cases, can one distinguish one's own from the foreign? Ezra 10:3 says expressly that the foreign wives are to be sent away with their children. This is absolutely contrary to ancient divorce law and patriarchal family structures, in which children remain, as a matter of course, within the husband's family. It is apparent that the attempt to draw a hard-and-fast line excluding "others" leads to the sacrifice and destruction of families, precisely the institution that must guarantee the continued existence of the society.

Is it accidental that a strongly androcentric text focuses on the subject of "the others" in place of the women? *The foreign woman is "the other" in a twofold sense:* as woman, seen as the object of male interest, and as foreigner, regarded as a danger to her own group. The close association of "the woman" with the dangerous foreigner is made clear in a striking usage in Ezra 9:11. The uncleanness of the people and the land, from which the Israelites must separate themselves, is called *niddâ.* This Hebrew word is used primarily to indicate the uncleanness arising from menstruation and pregnancy (see, e.g., Lev 12:2; 15:19-23; Ezek 18:6; 22:10). It is clearly distinguished from the generalized *ṭāmē',* "unclean" (especially in Lev 15:24; in Ezra 9:11 *ṭum'â* is used in a subordinate function to describe the abomination). Ezra 9:11 cannot be read without the corresponding association. Land and people are not a "woman," but when they are described as *niddâ,* their uncleanness is imagined in terms of "woman." A focus on foreign women undoubtedly invited the use of this concept, which is not properly suited to the context. It may be that here we find a hint that *apprehending "the others"* in an androcentric society goes together with *apprehending women as other.*

Analysis of the ideas in EN clearly reveals a *fundamental problem in the construction of identity:* precisely in conditions in which foreign systems of norms and traditions are dominant, the construction of one's own identity requires the fencing off of "others," "foreigners." This requires a continually new decision about how much association and integration is possible and how much rejection and separation is necessary. In the course of a "deconstructive reading," we can see the price paid by "the others" in cases of radical separation, but also how much of one's own is unwillingly lost and destroyed, since human life is marked by ambivalences and always takes place in close relationship with "others." The fate of the women, men, and children in Ezra 9–10 is a prime example.

The process of the construction of feminine identity almost always takes place under the conditions imposed by a dominant androcentric culture. A high degree of separation is often indispensable. An engagement with EN can make clear for us the necessity and problematic nature of such a process. It also teaches us to take seriously the question of the price of such a separation, which is a painful reality for many women. The more we see how different the possible ideas are, the clearer it is that each must here seek her or his own way.

LITERATURE

Eskenazi, Tamara C. 1992. "Out from the Shadows: Biblical Women in the Post-exilic Era." *Journal for the Study of the Old Testament* 54:25-43.

Eskenazi, Tamara C., and Eleanore P. Judd. 1994. "Marriage to a Stranger in Ezra 9–10." In *Second Temple Studies 2: Temple Community,* edited by Tamara C. Eskenazi and Kent H. Richards, 266-85. Journal for the Study of the Old Testament: Supplement Series, vol. 175. Sheffield.

Fewell, Danna N. 1987. "Feminist Reading of the Hebrew Bible: Affirmation, Resistance and Transformation." *Journal for the Study of the Old Testament* 39:77-87.

———. 1995. "Deconstructive Criticism: Achsah and the (E)razed City of Writing." In *Judges and Method: New Approaches in Biblical Studies,* edited by Gale A. Yee, 119-45. Minneapolis.

Gunneweg, Antonius H. J. 1985. *Esra.* Kommentar zum Alten Testament, vol. 19, 1. Gütersloh.

———. 1987. *Nehemia.* Kommentar zum Alten Testament, vol. 19, 2. Gütersloh.

Kessler, Rainer. 1996. "Mirjam und die Prophetie der Perserzeit." In *Gott an den Rändern,* edited by Ulrike Bail and Renate Jost, 64-72. Festschrift for Willy Schottroff. Gütersloh.

FOR FURTHER READING

Boda, Mark J., and Paul L. Redditt, eds. 2008. *Unity and Disunity in Ezra-Nehemiah: Redaction, Rhetoric, and Reader.* Sheffield.

Karrer-Grube, Christiane. 2001. *Ringen um die Verfassung Judas. Eine Studie zu den theologisch-politischen Vorstellungen im Esra-Nehemia-Buch.* Beihefte zur Zeitschrift für die alttestamentliche Wissenschaft, vol. 308. Berlin.

———. 2008. "Scrutinizing the Conceptual Unity of Ezra and Nehemiah." In *Unity and Disunity in Ezra-Nehemiah: Redaction, Rhetoric, and Reader,* edited by Mark J. Boda and Paul L. Redditt, 136-59. Sheffield.

Translated by Linda M. Maloney

Esther: About Resistance against Anti-Semitism and Sexism

Klara Butting

The Social Context of the Narrative

Esther's world reveals itself to us in an overture. Before introducing Esther and her cousin Mordecai, the narrative's two Jewish main characters, chapter 1 describes the site of their interaction, the court of the Persian king in Susa. In all likelihood this place-name is not a historically precise indication of the *Sitz im Leben* of the Esther story, for in the book of Esther the Jewish people are threatened with pogroms, while no such excesses are known to have occurred during the era of Persian rule in the Mediterranean (ca. 550-331 B.C.E.). Rather, Esther reflects events under Hellenistic rule (ca. 332-142) (Berg 1979, 169-73). For example, we know that Antiochus IV Epiphanes tried to destroy the Jewish faith community toward the end of the Hellenistic rule in Palestine. But even though the time and place of origin of the Esther story remain unclear, its context is introduced to us in its essential features. Chapter 2 describes the web of power relationships in which Esther and Mordecai must act (cf. Beal 1995).

The story begins with a demonstration of power. The ruler of the Persian Empire, King Ahasuerus, sits on his throne — Achashwerosh is the Hebrew imitation of the Persian spelling of Xerxes, in this case Xerxes I. His rule is uncontested; the empire's order indestructible. The king demonstrates this by celebrating himself. In a gigantic 180-day festival he *displays* his wealth and greatness to the dignitaries of the empire (1:4). A second celebration is held for all the men of Susa. Queen Vashti is supposed to appear at the high point of the celebration, as part of the display of the king's wealth. The king wants to *display* Vashti the queen to his assembled male officials (1:11). The sight of this beautiful woman, whom the king calls his own, will give the men in attendance a feeling of the king's power and at the same time remind them of their own position of power as males in the hierarchy of the empire. The indestructible order of the kingdom is to be demonstrated once again in this way. "But Queen Vashti refused to come at the king's command" (1:12). In the moment of her refusal, the narrators place Vashti's title before her name, unlike in 1:9 and 1:11, emphasizing her refusal in her role as queen. Vashti defends her personal and political independence in defiance of the king.[1]

In the council of sages this refusal is seen as an attack on the whole system of patriarchal rule in the state. It is based on the widespread notion in antiquity that the power a man exercises in the state is no different from the power he exercises in the home (Foucault 1991, 195). On the basis of this conviction the sages conclude that resistance by women endangers the entire system of state power, since this one refusal will provoke other women to do likewise. They will have contempt for their husbands and start talking about Vashti's action (1:17-18). Thus the sages' counsel is to ban Vashti from the kingdom as a deterrent to such behavior. This will remind the women in the whole kingdom that they are obliged to obey their husbands. Finally a decree is proclaimed throughout the kingdom that describes and reinscribes the social status quo: "Every man shall be master over his house and shall speak in his people's tongue."

The man is to rule in the home and represent the social order there. And just as the government issues its decrees "to every people in its own language" (1:22), the men are to speak not the official Aramaic at home, but the *language of their people*. This measure is intended to address the danger of women finding their own language and learning to speak as they talk about a precursor (*Vorgängerin:* a woman who, at an earlier time, went before, leading the way). Male dominance is intended to penetrate the thinking of every man and woman through the self-image of all women and men.

The book of Esther names totalitarian sexist power structures as its narrative social context in this first chapter. An imperium that rules over many peoples and languages wants to gain power over the feelings and ideas of all by means of patriarchal rule. At the same time, Vashti's resistance and the panicked reaction of the sages reveal that patriarchy is not a natural order, but that it is established again and again by violence. Women's protest can shatter the system built upon male self-glorification.

Besides giving insights into the context of the story, this first chapter points to the book's authorship. The description of gender relations as one of violence points to women's participation in the creation of the book and allows us to speak of female and male narrators. The book of Esther reinforces this conclusion by representing Esther as a woman who writes (9:29). Additionally, the text refers to her words and says her commands were "recorded in writing" (9:32). The text itself gives signals that alert us to the written and oral participation of women in the authorship of the book of Esther.

---

1. The Luther Bible and NRSV use "Queen Vashti" from 1:9 on throughout the text.

A New Interpretation of the Joseph Story

To tell the story of Esther and Mordecai at the Persian court, the narrator takes up words and motifs from the Joseph story (Gen 37–50) (cf. Berg 1979, 123-65). Like Joseph in Egypt, Mordecai is honored publicly (Esther 6:11/Gen 41:42b-43), receives the king's signet ring (Esther 8:2/Gen 41:42), and becomes the second most powerful man in the nation (Esther 10:3/Gen 41:43). In the same way Esther's story is reminiscent of Joseph in Egypt. The beauty of both is described in nearly identical terms (Esther 2:17/Gen 39:6), and both are endangered by their beauty. Esther is gathered up by the king's bloodhounds and lands in the royal harem. Joseph is harassed by Potiphar's wife and lands in prison. In the king's harem Esther — much like Joseph in prison — experiences favor and mercy (Esther 2:9, 15/Gen 39:4; Esther 2:17/Gen 39:21). Finally, Esther is made queen of Persia, becoming second in command next to the king of a foreign land, much like Joseph in Egypt. And as Joseph uses his position to save his people from starvation, Esther succeeds as queen of Persia in saving her people from the threatened pogrom.

These similarities are best explained on the premise that the Joseph story served as a model for the book of Esther. In the process the book of Esther reinterprets the Joseph story. The decisive figure — Joseph himself — is re-created in two characters, a man and a woman (Butting 1994, 67-77). Several motives for this revision can be discerned already from the contextual sketch of the narrative (Esther 1): the declared will of the sages to remove resistant female precursors from their midst and to prevent conversation about the history of women's protests suggests how the authors of Esther interpreted the silence about the sufferings and struggles of women in large parts of the biblical tradition. Their book called Esther, by contrast, documents the protest against the fact that women's power is broken again and again; it demonstrates the insight that women need female precursors in order to find their own language.

Reexamining the Joseph story makes the book of Esther interesting for feminist hermeneutics (Butting 1994, 172-76). We become aware of precursors who read the Bible out of love for the God of Israel in the context of sexual violence. They take up the Joseph story to tell of God's faithfulness in alien lands and in oppressive contexts. But precisely this message of biblical tradition forces one to analyze the prevailing oppression of women in one's own tradition, to reject anthropocentric structures in Israel's writing of history, and to retell the old story as the story of a woman. In this way the authors of Esther testify to the fact that the Bible wants to be a partner in dialogue, not an authority. They recognize the divinity to whom the Bible testifies as one who challenges people to examine all traditional texts to see whether the way they speak of God legitimates and reinscribes the oppression of women and men. Feminists today can continue this intrabiblical reexamination as they reexamine the Bible. We are encouraged to listen carefully to the witness of the divinity who liberates, to listen carefully to the biblical text, and at the same time we ourselves are prodded to witness to this divinity by retelling its story through critical analysis of the tradition. I understand my own exegetical task in terms of this two-tracked movement.

Jewish Men and Women in the Diaspora

The totalitarian, sexist violence of the kingdom is shown again when the whole patriarchal apparatus is thrown into motion to register and gather up all the beautiful young women of the kingdom because the king needs a new queen (2:3). In this process Esther enters the king's harem. Now and then even feminist interpretations represent this process as a beauty competition in which Esther "was hired to enter — among a horde of beauties — as a possible replacement" (Altwegg 1988, 105). But the royal harem is the end of all hopes for the majority of women. Each candidate for twelve months is prepared for one night when she is to be at the king's disposal, only to disappear forever — unless the king should happen to desire her (2:12-14). Esther is also endangered in this setting by her ethnic identity. Mordecai's command that she keep her Jewish identity secret (2:10, 20) hints at the latent anti-Semitism that becomes visible later, when Mordecai's coworkers report him *because he is a Jew* (3:6)! This twice-repeated command has another important function in the narrative. Because Esther listens to Mordecai and keeps her Jewish identity secret, she remains — though a captive of the king — in a secret web of relationships that eludes the king's grasp. However, this continuing loyalty of Esther to Mordecai leads many interpreters to characterize Esther as an obedient woman. In her feminist-critical analysis of Esther 2:8-18, K. DeTroyer describes Esther's behavior toward Mordecai as obedience to a male norm. She sees in Mordecai another representative of the social norm besides the king; she also sees him as the king's guardian over women, who conveys hidden behavior norms for women (DeTroyer 1995, 51). In taking feminist criticism to this extreme, in my view, the author runs the risk of isolating the gender relations and oversimplifying the social conflicts represented in the book of Esther. What she leaves out are the anti-Semitism and the subversion present in the continuing relationship between Esther and Mordecai that serve to hide and protect the seed of Esther's future resistance to the king.

The coming conflict with the king smolders with the fear of underground anti-Semitism, while Esther and Mordecai represent, above all, an assimilated diaspora. Mordecai is a good king's official (cf. 2:21-23); Esther marries a non-Jewish man; food laws and prayers do not come into play at all (see Bronner 1995, 182ff. regarding the discussion in the Talmud and midrash). The double name Hadassah/Esther (2:7) also points to the custom of adopting an indigenous name along with one's Hebrew name when living in a foreign country. The Jewish people's journey into this alien existence is brought to mind by Esther's journey into the harem (cf. White

1992, 126). She realizes anew the fact that the Jews were deported by the king of Babylon (2:6). And her denial of her ethnicity confronts us with the issue of assimilation as a path chosen by victims as their only hope for survival. Perhaps this reflects the situation of those addressed by the text!

State-Sponsored Pogroms

The conflict over the Jewish population and the administration of the kingdom comes to a head when the king reorganizes his cadre of officials after an attempted coup (2:21-23) and Haman is appointed chief officer. The narrators describe his political frame of mind with the epithet "the Agagite." Agag was king of Amalel (1 Sam 15), which stood in the Bible for the fundamental hostility toward Israel and its story of liberation (Exod 17:8-16; Deut 25:17-19). Amalek embodies open anti-Semitism. For Mordecai, the political subjection to this ruler demanded here marks the limit of assimilation. He refuses to bow down before Haman. Because he is a Jew, his colleagues report his behavior (Esther 3:4). When Haman learns that Mordecai is a Jew, he plans to destroy the entire Jewish people (3:6). A day is designated when the Jewish population of the kingdom is to be murdered in pogroms organized by the state. Haman's speech of accusation before the king describes the danger he sees as arising from the Jewish people in words like those one can find in all his successors throughout the long history of the exile of the Jewish people: "There is a certain people, scattered and separated among all the peoples, in all provinces of your kingdom; their laws are different from those of every other people, and they do not keep the king's laws, so that it is not appropriate for the king to tolerate them" (3:8). With this speech by Haman, the book gives a theological explanation for the enmity of the nations against the Jewish people. It is an open or a blind revolt against Israel's divinity and that divinity's command to choose life. The Dutch Jew Abel Herzberg interprets the anti-Semitism of the National Socialists in a similar way. Their attack is directed against the insight "that there is something that is allowed and something that is not allowed. And for the sake of this first sentence that was once uttered by the Jewish people, or at least in part for this reason, Hitler hated and persecuted and murdered them" (Herzberg 1960, 45). Thus the modern concept of anti-Semitism can also provide a name for the ancient hatred of the Jewish people described in Esther. If anti-Semitism is engendered from the Torah, which God gave to Israel, then it is as old as Israel itself.

Anti-Semitism and Sexism

The way the Persian power elite treated Jewish men and women is described in Esther in a way that is reminiscent of the subjection of women by powers of state.

Twice in the narrative a man's injured vainglory and his resultant rage turn into a major affair of state (1:12; 3:5). One act of refusal to bow to absolute rule provides the occasion to organize the state response: first the subjection of women, then the extermination of the Jewish population. In each case the collective of an entire people is recognized in the individual person who resists. Because Vashti is a woman, her refusal — according to Memucan — does not violate the king *alone* (1:16). As a result, state violence is directed against *all women* (1:16, 20) and against *all Jews* (3:6). Those in power feel threatened by everyone who is different, threatened by the "other" sex and the "other" ethnic group. Both measures are in the end decreed as law over the entire kingdom (1:20; 3:13), in the script and language of each respective province and country (1:20; 3:12), giving form to the totalitarian spirit behind these decrees.

These observations are not intended to gloss over the difference between the two kinds of violent relationships. Women are to be degraded and broken, while the goal of the hatred toward the Jewish people is destruction. Yet it is precisely the uniqueness of the threat of destruction that makes it all the more astonishing that the authors of this book describe these plans for annihilation of the Jews as analogous to the plans for the subjection of women. They render visible the fact that one and the same spirit is at work in the subjection of women and the planned destruction of Jewry. Here we can recognize a radical confrontation by the authors with male complicity in totalitarian rule. The narrative uncovers structures of violence that must be resisted along with anti-Semitism. In the house of any man in which subjection and patriarchy are practiced, a totalitarian structure of thought and action will also be practiced that reveals its deadly dimensions in the form of hatred against the Jewish people. In this reflection we find a further motive for the authors to intercede in the writing of Israel's history and to tell the story of how Esther saves her people, following in the footsteps of Joseph. The revolt of women against patriarchal rule and oppression is necessary to prevent patterns of thought and action from arising anew from generation to generation, patterns that finally find their favorite outlet in anti-Semitism. Even if sexism and patriarchal violence are not broken in the course of the book, this textual connection of sexism and anti-Semitism indissolubly links the solution of the woman question with the salvation of the Jewish people from the threat of destruction. In this way the narrative prevents the Jewish struggle against anti-Semitism from becoming a national issue.

For women readers in the context of the feminist movement, the narrative is thus also a warning not to make the cause of women a "natural" cause affecting only women. The book speaks against the temptation to seek one's identity in one's own victimhood. For the sake of the liberation one hopes for, social contradictions must be considered in which the victims are themselves also perpetrators (cf. Siegele-Wenschkewitz 1988). We are reminded that liberation that does not want to be an exchange of one power elite for another has two faces: the end of our own subjection, and the end of our complicity in the subjection of others.

Liberation Theology

When the plans for the pogrom reach Mordecai's ears, he immediately thinks of Esther. If anyone at all can save her people, it is she and she alone. She should go to the king. But the king's harem is not really any place for hopes or perspectives for resistance. On the contrary! When Mordecai urges Esther to go to the king, she sees no chance of helping her people (4:10-11). She sees only the king's power. The king decides who is allowed to come before him and who is not. Approaching him without permission is punishable by death.

Yet Mordecai's reply makes these power relationships collapse (4:13-14). Over your life and death, he says to Esther, the Persian king and his officials have no power. Life and death are decided in the way one participates in the history of the Jewish people. If Esther leaves her people in the lurch in the midst of such danger, she will not survive, for her name and the name of her father's house will disappear from the annals of history. The power of political rulers over life and death is thus contested (cf. Mark 8:35-36). Israel's God is the one who gives life and takes life away. Mordecai formulates this certainty as the hope that the Jews will again see "relief and deliverance" (Esther 4:14), and it is in the light of this hope that he interprets Esther's journey of suffering up to her elevation to the status of queen as a sign that she is able to bring about the salvation of her people.

This conversation between Esther and Mordecai is an example of liberating theology. Without the external power relationships having changed, Esther becomes capable of action. Her perspective of the power relations changes. She herself becomes empowered. This becomes manifest immediately in the fact that it is Esther who tells Mordecai what must be done (4:17). She reestablishes community between herself and her people by means of a shared fast, and as a part of this community she confronts the possibility of death (4:16). At the same time, she gains a completely new analysis of her situation through the promise given to her that the masters who rule by death do not rule over life and death. Vashti's aborted resistance is no longer the possession of these male rulers.

Vashti and Esther

In many traditional interpretations, the point of the Vashti story is the duty of wives to obey their husbands, or the dominant position of the husband. Vashti's story is seen as having the sole function of providing a contrasting background to Esther's obedience toward her adoptive father and her respect for the king (e.g., Dommershausen 1968, 36). Protesting against such readings, some feminist scholars continue to contrast the two women but with the opposite emphasis: "My fascination was not primarily with Esther, whom I felt was rather pale, scheming and revengeful, but with Vashti, the wife of the almighty Xerxes, who refused to be paraded before the drunken buddies of His Majesty, her husband. . . . Esther accommodated herself, most obediently, as before with her adoptive father" (Altwegg 1988, 104f.). In women's discussion groups I have often encountered women who identified with Vashti as a precursor of the women's movement, at the same time showing a certain contempt for Esther. Actually, Esther is not suited for a heroine's role. Only after a long period of accommodation and humiliation does she rise up and act. It is through theological reflection that she is challenged to take this step, and then her resistance is more measured than Vashti's straightforward "no." Yet I am certain that the resistance of many women typically resembles Esther's more than Vashti's. Perhaps it is self-hatred that prevents one from seeing that even a fearful woman with her unspectacular deeds, when she does rise up and act, can carry on and revitalize the resistance of a silenced foremother.

Esther's Resistance

After it has become clear in Esther's conversation with Mordecai that the present is not determined by history's victors, but by the expectation of threatened and conquered women and men, Esther makes the desperate lot of the Jewish people her own (7:3) and learns to think of the story of a conquered woman as her own story. Vashti's story becomes a living source from which Esther draws schemes and plans for her own resistance. Esther breaks the king's law. She approaches his throne uninvited. As she does so, she wears a royal robe (5:1) to commemorate the fact that the king wanted to decorate himself with his royally decorated wife (1:11) — and she walks away with her life. She then chooses two banquets as the scene of action (5:4, 8) and stages the scenario that had served to demonstrate his greatness (1:3, 5). Learning from the experience of seeing Vashti made into a demonstration object of the king's power on such an occasion, Esther draws up her plan. She first prepares a banquet *for him,* the king, and invites the king and Haman to come to it (5:4). During this celebration she announces yet another one that she will hold *for them,* Haman and the king, and invites both men to come to it (5:8). Thus at the first banquet she bestows exactly the same measure of honor on Haman as on the king, sowing mistrust and fear in the king and beginning to play the two men off against one another.

The seeds of mistrust, once sown, grow unseen. Haman has himself celebrated with his friends and his wife (5:9-14). But the king, whose wife is celebrating someone else, has a sleepless night (cf. Magonet 1980). He leafs through the annals of the kingdom in search of a man who might measure up to Haman. And sure enough, he finds someone who had proven faithful once long ago during an attempted coup — Mordecai (6:1-14). Esther's second banquet turns into a celebration to parallel the king's second banquet, at which Ahasuerus destroyed Queen Vashti (7:1-10). Esther now exploits the violent relationship between the king and

Vashti that had been brought to light when he ordered her to come before him and his cronies, as a scheme to bring down Haman. Esther, who has still not told anyone that she is Jewish, accuses Haman of planning to attack her and her people (7:3-4). Esther calls Haman, who is otherwise called "oppressor of the Jews" (3:10; 8:1; 9:10, 24), "the man, the oppressor and enemy" (7:6). She generalizes the danger represented by Haman and suggests to the king that this danger is intended for her, the queen, and as such, for him, the king, and the kingdom. The plan works. The king feels threatened. Even when Haman falls to his knees before Esther begging for mercy, the king sees in him only the male rival. He misinterprets the scene as an attempted rape (7:8) and has Haman executed as a usurper. This plan and this struggle of Esther's would be unthinkable without Vashti's act of refusal. Vashti's resistance makes analysis possible and creates the necessary condition for Esther to envision being able to save her people by fighting within the existing structures (cf. Wallach-Faller 1993, 13). Only if we do not play off the dignity of the one woman against the scheming of the other, only if we do not play off the success of the second against the defeat of the first, can we begin to think about the history of women.

A Permit to Resist

After the fall of Haman, Ahasuerus turns over "the house of Haman, the oppressor of the Jews, to Queen Esther" (8:1). In this announcement we can see the light of the future, in which there is an end to anti-Semitism and women are liberated. Esther has gained independent wealth and a home of her own. Her struggle against Haman at the same time undermined the power of all those who want to see a man as master of every house (1:22). However, in terms of external social structure, the sexist gender roles remain. Esther appoints Mordecai as administrator of Haman's house and Mordecai becomes an official of the king.

Neither is anti-Semitism abolished with the fall of Haman. Although the king's signet ring gives Mordecai a position of power in the kingdom, Haman's orders for the destruction of the Jewish people remain in force. "An edict written in the name of the king . . . cannot be revoked" (8:8)! Esther and Mordecai are able to obtain a permit to resist in order to save the Jewish population alone. The Jews are granted a single day on which to fight to their last breath against "the armed force of any people or province that might attack them, with their children and women, and to plunder their goods" (8:11; on the translation of 8:11 see Gordis 1976, 49-53). It is wrong to assert — even if this verse is translated differently — that the Jews for their part wanted to instigate pogroms among the population of the kingdom. Their resistance is directed against those who, despite the political turn of events that began with the fall of Haman, are attacking the Jewish people on the day originally designated by Haman for their destruction.

The story seems surreal. The same king enacts two contradictory decrees, thus unleashing a civil war in his dominion. In fact, the book of Esther tells a story that seems almost unreal in view of the centuries-old history of exile and suffering of the Jewish people. This people, which is "scattered and separated among the nations" (3:8), is able to defend itself against the pogroms that threaten it.

The Resistance of Jewish Men and Women

The story continues with features reminiscent of fairy tales, telling how the Jews are able to conquer and kill their "enemies" and "foes" and "all who seek their ruin" (9:1-2). This ending has given Esther a bad reputation. Arndt Meinhold, for example, sees an "elitist segment of diaspora Jewry" at work here and thereby argues against the theological significance of the book (1976, 92-93). He does not recognize the overcoming of anti-Semitism as a theological issue. This blind spot reduces theology to a kind of ahistorical pursuit that finds its extreme expression in E. Haenchen, for example. Asked about the gospel message of Esther, he replies: "Yes, certainly — as long as you do not construct the story in romantic terms — only in the way that all human sin cries out for the One who takes away all sin. But in this way the Book of Esther is no different from Auschwitz and Maidanek, although there Haman triumphed" (Haenchen 1963, 128). If Christians criticize violent resistance in Esther, they must reexamine whether their criticism is based on a deadly understanding of sin and mercy, which is indifferent whether Jews are destroyed or the organizers of this destruction meet their own downfall. Scholars direct their criticism against Esther, who misses the chance "to go down in history as a heroine of reconciliation and peace" (Altwegg 1988, 107). Such questioning is important, for all too frequently violence has been justified in the name of God and the Bible. However, the following considerations must not be forgotten: (1) By repeating three times the phrase "but they did not touch the plunder" or "they laid no hands on the plunder" (9:10, 15, 16), the narrators remind the reader of the biblical law of renouncing war booty. Thus violence and warfare are rejected as means of achieving political ends. Violence may only serve to defend and save one's own people. (2) The texts are stories, not historical reports. Telling the story of the wish to kill people who are destroying you is not the same as writing a moral law that permits killing when persecuted people have the power to do so. Of course, words that allow oppressed people in a particular situation to breathe a sigh of relief are capable of legitimizing other power interests in a different situation. Nevertheless, there must be room in the faith community for hatred and rage against human beings who do not cease to torment others.

Purim

Haman had determined by casting lots (the *pûr*) the day on which the pogroms were to take place (3:7). The feast days celebrated from generation to generation in remembrance of the people being saved derive their name from this *pûr,* which thus indirectly also designated the day of escape. Purim does not celebrate violence or victory, but the peaceful, calm settlement that represented gaining relief from their enemies (9:17, 18, 22). Among the instructions for the celebration of Purim, the Talmud *Megillah* 4a reads: "Women are obligated to read the role of Esther, for they too were participants in the miracle." Thus the explosive power of this book, which attacks sexist power relations, continues down through the tradition until today (Levinson 1989, 83). Another instruction of the Talmud *Megillah* says: "On the Feast of Purim one must drink enough that one can no longer tell the difference between the curse of Haman and the praise of Mordecai" (7b). Hate is to be drowned, and in the moment of intoxication, hate becomes mockery. In a commentary on this instruction of the Talmud on the Feast of Purim 1951, Robert Raphael Geis tells about a Purim procession he experienced in Tel Aviv when he came directly from Buchenwald to Palestine before the beginning of World War II.

> In this Purim procession people were wearing caricatures of Hitler and his cronies — and the population laughed and laughed, although there must have been enough people among them who had just barely been able to escape from Hitler with their lives and had left their loved ones behind in the den of this beast. Back then we did not yet know what horrors were still to come to us. Crudeness? No. But according to the opinion of our teacher Raba, the Jews were conscious, given all the fear they had withstood, all the worry and suffering, that in the end the wicked, as the bearers of evil, must disappear and shall disappear, and that in the end all their power must prove to be a farce. We cannot yet laugh. Perhaps our generation will not be able to laugh that way again at all. Yet we know that the day of liberating laughter will be given, if not to us, then to our people, for Purim also tells the story of one of the many evils on our journey through history; Jewish custom reminds us of the necessary end of all so-called thousand-year empires of evil. (Geis 1984, 158-59)

One Exodus Has Yet to Occur

"Ahasuerus the King laid tribute on the land and on the islands of the sea" (10:1). With this comment at the end of Esther we are reminded of the beginning of Exodus. There, the oppression of Israel begins in Egypt with a tribute: "They set taskmasters over them to oppress them with forced labor" (Exod 1:11). This linkage reminds us that the exodus from oppression at the end of Esther has not yet occurred. This is true of the entire Jewish diaspora, and it is true for Esther, who remains in the king's harem and who is ignored by official history and historiography. The "Book of the Annals of the Kings of Media and Persia" notes only the special role of Mordecai (Esther 10:2). And within Israel as well, in 2 Maccabees, Purim is inscribed as the "Feast of Mordecai" (2 Macc 15:36). The book of Esther locates itself in the midst of imperialist politics and sexist violence. In this context the book bears the name of Esther, not that of Mordecai. Women's history is reconstructed and the story of the miracle is told, that the Jewish people can defend itself against the pogroms that threaten it. The narrative represents a breather in the history of alienation — and as such the history of the Feast of Purim!

The Greek Additions

In connection with the Greek translations of the book of Esther, we have additional portions that change the structure and content of the narrative (see the Unified Translation of 1980, for example). Religious elements are inserted into the narrative. Esther and Mordecai pray (Insert C at the end of Esther 4), and there is frequent mention of God. Revised are the secular theological language and reflection of the Hebrew book, which represents God's power as lying hidden deep in the compassionate solidarity of oppressed women and men who live at the brink of death.

We can gain some insight into the context of this revision process by looking at a letter of the king who orders the murder of the Jews (Insert B, Esther 3). It reads like a composite of various accusations of the anti-Semitism of antiquity. The danger seen as residing in Jewish men and women threatens not only the Persian Empire, but also the entire inhabited planet Earth. This people is hostile to all human beings and instigates unrest and uprisings (3:13d-3; cf. 1 Thess 2:15; Acts 17:6). In a second letter of the king, these accusations are discredited (Rest of Esther 8:12p-q), and we hear the classical formulation of state recognition of the Jewish faith: the Jews are allowed to live according to their own law (8:12s). In the background one can presumably hear the anti-Jewish propaganda and policy of the Seleucids, especially since Haman is described as a sympathizer of the Macedonians who wanted to bring the Persian Empire under the sway of the Greeks (8:12o).

While details of anti-Jewish propaganda are emphasized as well as contradicted in these translations, the connection between anti-Semitism and sexism is masked. A dream of Mordecai and its interpretation frame the book and emphasize Mordecai's significance (Insert A and F). Mordecai is introduced as an ally of the king against Haman, the secret instigator of the coup (Insert A, inserted before Esther 1). This introduction destroys the function of Esther 1 as an exposition of the narrative's context and makes it difficult as one reads on to connect Mordecai's refusal and Vashti's protest (Beal 1995, 109f.). In this same context of the deconstruction of antipatriarchal criticism, we should consider the revision of Esther's uninvited visit to the king (Insert D). Here, Esther falls unconscious at the sight of the king. The king turns to her with great concern and takes her in his arms. It is not Esther's clever scheme that overcomes the king, but the king's "protective instinct" that reacts to help her in her female weakness.

When we consider that in life-threatening times, even women have put off dealing with women's issues until better times, the Greek revision of the Esther text is not unusual. It underscores the extraordinary character of the Hebrew Esther book. The attempt to highlight two distinct relations of violence that at first glance appear unrelated, both in terms of social analysis and in terms of liberation strategies, poses a challenge even today.

LITERATURE

Altwegg, Leni. 1988. "Waschti und Ester. Eine verpaßte Chance." In *Zwischen Ohnmacht und Befreiung. Biblische Frauengestalten,* edited by Karin Walter, 100-108. Freiburg, Basel, and Vienna.

Beal, Timothy K. 1995. "Tracing Esther's Beginnings." In *A Feminist Companion to Esther, Judith, and Susanna,* edited by Athalya Brenner, 87-110. Sheffield.

Berg, Sandra B. 1979. *The Book of Esther: Motifs, Themes, and Structure.* Missoula.

Brenner, Athalya, ed. 1995. *A Feminist Companion to Esther, Judith, and Susanna.* Sheffield.

Bronner, Leila Leah. 1995. "Esther Revisited: An Aggadic Approach." In *A Feminist Companion to Esther, Judith, and Susanna,* edited by Athalya Brenner, 176-97. Sheffield.

Butting, Klara. 1994. *Die Buchstaben werden sich noch wundern. Innerbiblische Kritik als Wegweisung feministischer Hermeneutik.* Berlin.

DeTroyer, Kristin. 1995. "An Oriental Beauty Parlor: An Analysis of Esther 2:8-18 in the Hebrew, the Septuagint and the Second Greek Text." In *A Feminist Companion to Esther, Judith, and Susanna,* edited by Athalya Brenner, 47-70. Sheffield.

Dommershausen, Werner. 1968. *Die Esterrolle. Stil und Ziel einer alttestamentlichen Schrift.* Stuttgart.

Foucault, Michel. 1991. *Der Gebrauch der Lüste. Sexualität und Wahrheit.* Vol. 2. Frankfurt am Main.

Geis, Robert R. 1984. *Leiden an der Unerlöstheit der Welt. Briefe, Reden, Aufsätze.* Munich.

Gordis, Robert. 1976. "Studies in the Esther Narrative." *Journal of Biblical Literature* 95:43-58.

Haenchen, Ernst. 1963. "Hamans Galgen und Christi Kreuz." In *Wahrheit und Glaube,* edited by Hayo Gerdes, 113-33. Festschrift for Emanuel Hirsch. Itzehoe.

Herzberg, Abel J. 1960. *Amor fati.* Amsterdam.

Levinson, Pnina Navè. 1989. *Was wurde aus Saras Töchtern? Frauen im Judentum.* Gütersloh.

Levinson, Pnina Navè, and Martin Stöhr. 1988. "Das Buch Esther." In *Feministisch gelesen,* vol. 1, edited by Eva Renate Schmidt et al., 100-111. Stuttgart.

Loewenclau, Ilse von. 1994. "Apologie für Ester." In *Nachdenken über Israel, Bibel und Theologie,* edited by M. Michael Nieman, 251-77. Festschrift for Klaus-Dietrich Schunck. Frankfurt am Main.

Magonet, Jonathan. 1980. "The Liberal and the Lady: Esther Revisited." *Judaism* 29:167-76.

Meinhold, Arndt. 1976. "Die Gattung der Josephsgeschichte und des Esterbuches: Diasporanovelle II." *Zeitschrift für die alttestamentliche Wissenschaft* 88:72-93.

Siegele-Wenschkewitz, Leonore, ed. 1988. *Verdrängte Vergangenheit, die uns bedrängt. Feministische Theologie in der Verantwortung für die Geschichte.* Munich.

Wallach-Faller, Marianne. 1993. "Zwei Königinnen — zwei Studien feministischen Bewußtseins." *Israelitisches Wochenblatt* 8:13.

White, Sidnie Ann. 1989. "Esther: A Feminine Model for Jewish Diaspora." In *Gender and Difference in Ancient Israel,* edited by Peggy L. Day. Minneapolis.

———. 1992. "Esther." In *The Women's Bible Commentary,* edited by Carol A. Newsom and Sharon H. Ringe, 124-29. London and Louisville.

For Further Reading

Arzt, Silvia. 1999. *Frauenwiderstand macht Mädchen Mut. Die geschlechtsspezifische Rezeption einer biblischen Erzählung (Est 1).* Innsbruck and Vienna.

Breitmaier, Isa. 2006. "'Die ganze griechische Ester'. Ein Lehrstück in Sachen Textgerechtigkeit." *Schlangenbrut* 24, no. 95:9-12.

Butting, Klara, Gerard Minnaard, and Marie-Theres Wacker, eds. 2005. *Ester. Mit Beiträgen aus Judentum, Christentum, Islam, Literatur und Kunst.* Die Bibel erzählt, vol. 2. Wittingen.

Tkacz, Catherine Brown. 2008. "Esther, Jesus, and Psalm 22." *Catholic Biblical Quarterly* 70, no. 4:709-28.

Wacker, Marie-Theres. 2004. "Mit Toratreue und Todesmut dem einen Gott anhangen. Zum Esther-Bild der Septuaginta." In *Dem Tod nicht glauben. Sozialgeschichte der Bibel,* edited by Frank Crüsemann et al., 312-32. Festschrift for Luise Schottroff. Gütersloh.

———. 2005. "Das Buch Ester." In *Stuttgarter Altes Testament. Einheitsübersetzung mit Kommentar und Lexikon,* edited by Erich Zenger. Stuttgart.

Translated by Nancy Lukens

Job: Questioning the Book of the Righteous Sufferer

Christl Maier and Silvia Schroer

Fundamental Questions about the Book

The book of Job is the only biblical book that has been recognized as world litera-ture. Its history of interpretation is considerable, and up to this day the name of Job is associated with at least a vague knowledge of a man who experienced great misfortune and whose patience is proverbial. The patience of female readers, too, is severely tested: men speak and act in all forty-two chapters of the book, rich and educated men at that, as well as a God perceived to be male. Against those long speeches of the men there are a few verses where women are at least mentioned, and one single verse where a woman speaks (2:9). Most of these short remarks can be found in the frame story of the book (chapters 1–2; 42:7-17): in the actual dia-logue there are only marginal references to women, the life of women, or feminin-ity. Can a book that is so clearly and explicitly written from an androcentric point of view claim to deal with questions that are relevant for both men and women (cf. Clines 1995, 124)? Are we women touched by Job's suffering, his protest, and his righteousness? Skepticism is certainly in order here. Suffering has its own female face — this is true today as, most likely, it was in ancient Israel. How do we, in view of this knowledge, read this book about the righteous sufferer? Are we convinced by Job and are his problems ours? Do the images of God in this book open doors for us? Are the well-known speeches of God plausible answers to the questions of Job or to our questions?

It is difficult to find feminist readings of the book of Job. This is one reason why we are trying to approach it with various questions and methods that, never-theless, are based on historical-critical methods. We are linking our exegesis to a feminist option: it is not our concern to justify this biblical book but to show how far it silences or gives voice to women, their experiences or their world, and to what extent it represents suppression or liberation for women today (in accor-dance with the hermeneutics of Elisabeth Schüssler Fiorenza).

The Frame of Reference for a Feminist Exegesis of Job

In the context of the essay, we wish to discuss in thesis form some decisions we made in the course of our work. (See Ebach 1986 for a thorough overview of the current research about the book of Job.) We wish to define the frame of reference within which our feminist exegesis of Job will move.

The Tradition of the Righteous Sufferer in Ancient Near Eastern Wisdom Literature

The book of Job belongs to the wisdom literature of Israel that, to a great extent, was shaped by the literature and tradition of the surrounding great cultures and sought "international" contact with those cultures. Viewed from a literary-historical perspective, neither the figure of Job nor the theme of "unjust suffering" is a new idea. After the demise of the Old Kingdom in Egypt, at the end of the third millennium B.C.E., the first writings appear that describe the disintegration of all order (cf. "Complaints of Khakheperre-Sonb"; "The Eloquent Peasant," in Schmid 1966, 212f., or Lichtheim 1973-80, 1:145f. and 169f., respectively) in the form of a lament or sometimes also in a fictitious dialogue about injustice and chaos ("Dispute between a Man and His *Ba*," also called "Dispute over Suicide," in Schmid 1966, 213; Pritchard 1955, 405-7). In the "Admonitions of Ipuwer" (cf. Schmid 1966, 209f.; Lichtheim 1973-80, 1:149-150; and Pritchard 1955, 441-42), the speaker accuses God in no uncertain terms of not being a good shepherd, of hiding himself away and being insensitive to people's misery. In Mesopotamia the question of the righteous sufferer seems to have been discussed for centuries. In the Akkadian writing *ludlul bel nemeqi,* a desperate, sick man bewails his misery and testifies to his righteousness until the god Marduk comes to his rescue and heals him (twelfth century B.C.E.; see Lambert 1960, 32f.). In the so-called *Babylonian Theodicy,* a righteous sufferer pours out his misfortune to his friend, protesting his innocence in several cycles of speeches. But his friend does not share the view that the world is unjust (800-750 B.C.E.; Lambert 1960, 70f.). When we read the book of Job, we must therefore remember that behind it stands an old literary and theological tradition that influenced it. The discussion of suffering through the device of a fictitious male character to whom male friends are attached; the carrying out of theological discourse in the form of disputations; the presentation in the discussion of a certain repertoire of solutions to the problem; and, finally, the fact that a solution can come about through the direct intervention of the deity — all these features belong to the traditions of the ancient Near East.

Job as the Person Affected and Having a Problem

The reading of Job is usually strongly influenced by the frame narrative. In that story, Job is above all a man affected by concrete misfortune; thus, the book can be read as the examination by an individual of his situation as a suffering person. This dimension is important and indisputable, but also too narrow. The biblical figure of Job also carries a problem; that is, this fictitious character becomes the literary vehicle for fundamental ideological and theological questions of certain social groups. Job laments not only his misfortune but also, above all, reproaches his friends, circumstances, the world order, and the God behind all this. The dialogue is a wisdom discourse in which various ideological positions come under fire, including the divine speeches which — in the end — bring in a new, acceptable position.

The Concept That Actions Have Built-in Consequences

What, then, is the underlying problem of Job (and precursory ancient Near Eastern literature)? The experience of suffering was accepted in Israel, much more than today, as a basic constituent of frail human existence (cf. Job 14:1-4; Ps 103:15-16). The problem as such is due to the fact that, according to common Oriental thought, there is a connection between what a person does and how she or he fares. This connection is firmly anchored in the world order established and guaranteed by the deities, a world order that encompasses all domains of life and in which the individual is bound to her or his family and the successive generations. Therefore the just and god-fearing will experience happiness and blessing in their lives, while the godless will fail. Over forty years ago, Klaus Koch showed that this way of thinking is not couched in the categories of reward and punishment (Koch 1972; for further details, see Janowski 1994). Contrary to all experience, Israelites too clung to this postulated axiom. But during the time of the exile the prophets of Israel introduced a striking change in this theological connection between action and consequences. Since the catastrophe of the southern and northern kingdoms' fall was considered a generations-long punishment for the transgressions of the fathers (cf. the saying of the sour grapes in Ezek 18:2 and Jer 31:29), the basis for individual ethical behavior became fragile and fatalism took over. Thus Ezekiel's and Jeremiah's pupils pleaded for the abolition of the collective application of that connective scheme, stating that from now on each individual should be held responsible for her or his sins and no one else (Jer 31:29-30; Ezek 18:3-20). The book of Job presupposes those developments (Job 21:19-26). It revolves around the dramatically intensified question about the significance of Job's misfortune, namely, whether he really is a righteous man, as he claimed, and around what God has to say about this irresolvable contradiction.

In the prologue, the problem of this connective scheme is formulated somewhat differently from the (assumed) perspective of God. The question in 1:9, asked by Satan, and the cause of Job's misery, is: Does Job fear God *ḥinnām* — that is, for nothing, without reason, without compensation? Is Job's prosperity, therefore, the result of his piety? Or is it the other way around (cf. Ebach 1995, 15-31)? In the dialogue section of the book, Job complains to and against God who inflicts wounds on him "without cause" (9:17; cf. 2:3). But in his laments and disputes, does he hold on to God — *ḥinnām?*

The Relationship between the Dialogue and the Frame Narrative

The relationship between the larger dialogue section (chapters 3–42:6) and the frame narrative is a matter of controversy among scholars; there is no consensus on which is the older. Both parts are put together strikingly loosely. In the dialogue section there is no concrete reference to the story told in the prologue and the epilogue, there is only the presumption that Job has been afflicted with great misfortune. Mentioning the three friends in 2:11-13 and 42:7-10 has the purpose of linking the narrative and the dialogue. We assume that the whole book, in its final form, dates from the postexilic period, although older oral and also literary traditions may have been preserved in the speeches (cf. Brenner 1989, on the final form of the book). The dialogue uses ancient Near Eastern wisdom literature. This is one reason why it can be considered older than the frame story. In light of Ezekiel 14:14 it is, however, assumed that the frame narrative is old. But from the exilic text of Ezekiel 14:13-23 we only learn Job's name and that he was an exceedingly righteous man. Indeed, it is possible that there existed an ancient narrative about a man called Job who suffered misfortune, remained steadfast, and was restored. Still, in our opinion, both the prologue and the epilogue, as extant now, are literary creations with the aim of framing the dialogue and giving listeners or readers relevant interpretative context for reading it. In the dialogue, up to God's speeches, a complex and differentiated image of God and the world is developed dramatically, with no simple solutions. The frame story, on the other hand, tries to dissolve the tensions by comparatively simple theological means. Thus evil is excluded from the concept of God and wrapped up in the figure of Satan. In contrast to the sparkling, rebellious figure of Job as presented in the dialogue, the frame narrative only shows the pious sufferer who is completely vindicated at the end so that hardly a trace of his suffering is left. Also, the epilogue concludes the dispute about actions and their consequences with a simple solution, namely, with the reward of Job's hitherto uncompensated piety. A further reason for our assumption that the frame story is a later addition is the observation that, in other biblical writings, the beginning and the end were frequently added later on. That is certainly true of Proverbs 1–9; 31:10-31; Deuteronomy 1–3; 32–34, as well as in the Psalms; it is also possible that the first two chapters of the books of Samuel, or Esther, indicate a kind of "relecture" of the writings in question. A third reason for our thesis is that the epilogue mentions daughters who are entitled to inherit. This should be linked to the texts about Zelophehad's daughters in Numbers 27 and 36, which presuppose postexilic circumstances (→ Numbers and below for more).

An Attempt to Locate the Book Socially, Historically, and Religiously

The book of Job is part of the literature of the educated higher classes of Israel, as its elaborate and difficult language alone would indicate (cf. Clines 1995). The Job of the dialogue is depicted as an influential and affluent village potentate (chapter 29); the Job of the prologue and the epilogue, as a very wealthy farmer and owner of herds at the edge of the desert, somewhere in a fictitious northwest Arabia (cf. Knauf 1988). It is characteristic of the wisdom books to support the claim to universal validity of their teachings by avoiding precise references to the time and place of their compositions. Nevertheless, it is possible to find indications for contextualizing the book (viz., Crüsemann 1980; Albertz 1981; Schottroff 1982). It was probably written in the postexilic period by and for Judah's (formerly) affluent circles. Those circles, particularly in the fifth and fourth centuries B.C.E., were afflicted with social, economic, and religious troubles. The book of Job is "crisis literature," just as its ancient Near East precursors were. Under Persian domination, the population of Judah had to pay taxes in natural produce and above all in money. Years of drought and crop failure appear to have aggravated the already precarious economic situation (cf. Hag 1:11; 2:17; Mal 3:11). Personal righteousness no longer guarantees one's welfare; the connection between actions and well-being is invalidated; and more and more people fall into debt and poverty. Well-off Judeans are especially afflicted by showing their solidarity with the poorer people, providing loans, legal advice, and alms. Other Judeans, however, take part in the exploitation of their fellow citizens, since the blame for the desolate situation of the poorest — described in Job 24:2-14 and 30:2-8 (cf. also Isa 58) — is placed with the doings of godless people who would hardly be members of the Persian administration but rather were Judean compatriots (cf. the similar background in Neh 5). The accounts of the sinful rich and the suppressed poor in Job 22:6-9; 24:1-7 and 31 are a literary reference to the social legislation of Deuteronomy, especially Deuteronomy 19–25 and the Decalogue, but also to certain curses in Deuteronomy 28 (cf. Braulik 1996, 66-90). Job 24 bewails the inhuman effects of the pledge law, and formulates provisions for the poor that go much further than those prescribed by the law. In Job 31, Job composes a curse that is to fall upon him if he breaks the commandments of the Decalogue; in this act, he emphatically demonstrates his comprehensive concern for servants, male and female, and other fringe groups. The postexilic interpretation of the Deuteronomic Torah shows how relevant God's demand to express solidarity with the poor was, especially in times of economic distress. By showing himself to be a member of society's upper strata, in solidarity with the poor, Job intensifies his reproach to God, who obviously brings disaster upon those who live in accordance with the law.

Several religious or theological developments presupposed by the book of Job imply that the book belongs to the postexilic period. As already mentioned, the collective extension of the concept of actions with built-in consequences is no longer an issue, which suggests that the book was written after Ezekiel. Also, the author expects from the book's addressees a YHWH monotheism that is no longer questioned. On the one hand, the names for God in the dialogue — 'ĕlōhîm, 'ēl — and the poetic form 'ĕlôah, "deity," as well as šadday, "the almighty," are quite ambiguous. But the proper name YHWH appears in the heavenly council scenes in the prologue, in the introduction to the speeches by YHWH and in Job's replies, and in the epilogue (cf. 12:9). Thus, the book's deity, when seen in relation to another character, is naturally depicted as the God of Israel. Even though Job and his friends are not Israelites, they confront YHWH, who presents himself as Lord over the whole world. Although the cult of the moon practiced in Harran is hinted at in 31:26-28 (cf. Deut 4:19; 17:3), we know that the book's addressees tended to relate all areas of creation and human existence to the one God, with the exception of the netherworld, the abode of the dead. At the same time, it becomes clear that a huge religious effort is required to keep up this practice of monotheism. In his long laments Job wishes, in passing, for a witness in heaven (Job 16:18-21) or a redeemer (gō'ēl) who will release him (19:25-27). If both passages can be interpreted as inquiries from the one God (Kessler 1992, 153), then the only time when a messenger, a heavenly mediator, suddenly presents himself as a savior in mortal anguish is in Elihu's speech in 33:23. Now the only One has company. With the same outcome, the prologue explains the cause of suffering and evil by introducing a quasi-divine figure. As in the book of Chronicles (1 Chron 21:1; cf. Zech 3), this figure is called "adversary" (Satan) but is subordinated to the only One. This kind of phenomenon can quite definitely be assigned to the postexilic period (not so, according to Spieckermann 1994). Even before the exile, the whole symbolic, religious system in Palestine had undergone a process of strong "uranization" and "astralization," that is, removal of the divine powers to the sky and the attribution of increasing significance to the nocturnal stars. The late effects of this development are still tangible in Job. The God of Israel is remote, seems unapproachable and uninvolved. Job rebels against this concept of God and fights for a God "closer at hand." The disciples of Isaiah (the so-called Trito-Isaiah), who may have been contemporaries, did the same in their own way, since they proclaimed that YHWH sits enthroned high up but, at the same time, is close to the lowly and downtrodden (Isa 57:15).

Feminist Critique of and Approaches to the Book of Job

This essay cannot provide an analysis of the entire book. For this reason, we have selected thematic foci that seemed productive for feminist exegesis.

The Dialogue: A World without Women

With a clap of thunder, chapter 3 opens the long sequence of speeches and counterspeeches that constitutes the main part of the book. Job curses the day of his birth; he wants to wish the whole of creation back to chaos, and his only hope is the peace of the netherworld. His lament, however, is not just a complaint, but a targeted accusation against a God who has created a world where people, trapped in misery, have to go on living (Job 3:20). It is God who traps them there (3:23), with no route to escape. Thus Job not only speaks of his personal misery but also makes a general statement and directs his reproaches against God from this general, universal position. Generalizations of this kind can be found again and again in the dialogue section. A characteristic of this is the use of the Hebrew *'ādām* (Adam) or its equivalent *'ĕnôš*, which is used only in poetry. Both terms describe the human being, but only from a semantic point of view are they associated with the male (cf. 4:17; 10:5). Being male is seen as exemplary for being human. Whenever these terms are used, women are at best implied but do not appear as such. At this point the fundamental criticism of the book's androcentrism has to start. Women, their world and experiences, appear in patriarchal perspective only at the very margins and in very specific roles. Typically the mother's womb *(reḥem, beṭen)*, from which Job or the human being steps into the world, is mentioned (1:21; 3:10-11; 10:18-19; 19:17; 24:20; 31:15, 18). Lillian Klein (1995, esp. 198f.) even assumes that Job 19:17 speaks of Job's wife as the womb that belongs to him. Being woman is reduced noticeably often to the function of giving birth, even though Klein's interpretation is too narrow in our view. Also, the idea of humans being born of woman is associated with the fundamental sinful condition of human life several times (cf. 14:1; 15:14; 25:4).

Where else are women mentioned other than as birth givers? In Job 19:15, Job's maidservants are referred to as no longer recognizing their master in his suffering, and 19:17, two verses later, says Job's breath is repulsive to his own wife. In the dialogue his wife plays no part as a person in her own right. She is mentioned only one more time when, in 31:10, Job connects a kind of negative confession of his sins with a curse on himself: if he had committed the offenses mentioned, then his wife should "grind another man's grain," that is, serve him (possibly also in a sexual sense) and be handed over to strangers. Thus Job puts at stake the integrity of his wife, whom he considers his personal possession. Real relationships between

Job and women in the personal sphere are not perceptible here: the women remain shadows, be it the young wife of Job's neighbor whom — theoretically — he could cast his eyes on (31:1-9), the maidservant whose rights he respects (31:13), or the widow who represents a challenge to him to fulfill the law by helping her (31:16-17). The description of misery in the difficult chapter 24 mentions widows whose infants were used as pawns because their mothers were in debt, as well as infertile childless women. In the wider context Job's options seem clear: as a respectable patriarch it is his duty to help the poorest and, in Israel, this means (as it does today all over the world) women, amongst others.

In the dialogue section no woman speaks. It is Job, his three friends Eliphaz, Bildad, and Zophar, and later a young man called Elihu as well as the God of Israel (portrayed in male imagery) who do the talking. These are talks among men, motivated initially by Job's great suffering and the friends' desire to give comfort through explanations and deliberations. Then, in the divine speeches, it is a male God's decision to reply to Job's lamentations and accusations in order to correct the friends' words.

The different images of God in the book of Job on the whole do not contain any components that can be specifically allocated to women or to "the female." Divine care demonstrates itself in the careful handling of the human child (10:8-10) and in the womb (31:15; cf. Ps 139:13b, 15). More frequently, however, God is portrayed as a sovereign Creator God or else a God who treats Job with hostility, attacks and even persecutes him (Job 6:4; 16:7-17; 19:6-12). In the divine speeches, too, "male" characteristics dominate, such as "master of the animals" and "fighter against Behemoth and Leviathan." In 5:8-16, God is represented as a God of subversion, in the old tradition of the weather gods (12:13-25; 26; 34:20; 36:26–37:1; cf. also Ps 113:4-5, and Hannah's song, 1 Sam 2), a God who lifts up the humble and brings down the mighty. Yet, this concept of God is no consolation to Job since, for him, it is bound up with the experience of capriciousness.

Men's Suffering/Women's Suffering in Israel and the Book of Job

What is the cause of Job's suffering? Of what did women suffer at that time? Can this book claim to give voice to the problems of women?

Job loses his herds and his children, then his health and physical integrity. On this last point Job is afflicted worse than his wife. In his speeches he rebels against God because he is convinced that he has led an upright life; he cannot understand why so much suffering has come upon him. He suffers because he has been excluded from the community of the living, has lost his status and his standing on account of his impoverishment and disease, and has become a stranger to those closest to him. He suffers because of his friends' inflexibility; they do not believe in his uprightness.

Let us attempt a kind of corrective counterreading of the book of Job, with the help of other First Testament texts in which women's suffering is made apparent.

Women suffer at this time because of extremely dangerous, frequent pregnancies and births (cf. the programmatic verse Gen 3:16). Many women lose their lives in childbirth (e.g., Rachel in Gen 35). Quite likely numerous infants and children will also have died in front of their very eyes without their mothers being able to help them. Women suffer because of their childlessness, since the only really acceptable social standing they can have is due to being a mother (cf. Michal's fate in 2 Sam 6:23). Women suffer due to sexual violence (e.g., Gen 19 and 34; Judg 19), and when sexually assaulted they have to not only bear a man's violence but also be prepared for the social ostracism that such assault entails (2 Sam 13). Women suffer due to the machinations of male politics, as did Rizpah, whose several sons were eliminated in a political act of vengeance (2 Sam 21:8-14). Women suffer due to wars with all the attendant hunger, thirst, and expulsion (Lam 2:11-12). Furthermore, women have to live in fear of being sexually assaulted by foreign soldiers or abducted as prisoners of war (cf. Judg 5:30; Lam 5:11). Women suffer in particular when the population becomes impoverished. If they are widows, they fall very quickly through the social net and are exposed without protection to the corruption of more influential people. Somebody might move the boundary stone of their small field (cf. Prov 23:10), and the next harvest will not be enough to feed their children; a rich man may take their children as pawns because they are in debt (Job 24:2-3).

There are just as many references to specific women's suffering in Israel, great suffering that deserves to become the subject of a great book and the subject of a battle with the godhead, just as Job's material losses and disease did. However, the women who are mentioned only briefly in those texts only rarely turn directly to the God of Israel in their suffering. One fears that women's suffering was not important enough for the authors of the book of Job to write about as well. If women participated in writing this book — which we doubt — then they were not able to have their specific experiences of suffering included, or else they consciously decided to support their male coauthors' upper social class perspective.

God's Speeches as Answers to Job's Lament and Accusations

The two divine speeches (38:1–42:6) are also primarily introduced as disputations. God challenges Job to brace himself like a man and battle with God. Job had asked repeatedly in this debate for such a legal contest with God. God accepts the challenge, and now God and the man who has been wronged face each other. The imagery of war and battle seems offensive. But for Israelites faith was always connected with the firm conviction that the deity is great enough for people to rattle and struggle with. At the Jabbok, Jacob wrestles with a demon who turns out to be

YHWH (Gen 32). The sisters Leah and Rachel struggle with God over their fertility and their children, struggles that can be recognized in the names of their children (Gen 29–30). The women and men praying the Psalms ask YHWH in not at all squeamish ways to be partial and to intervene. Despite the battle imagery, such a concept of God seems to us worthy of attention.

The content of the divine speeches has to provide an answer to Job's lament and accusation. To claim that the very fact of God's answering at all is proof enough of the all-powerful God's grace, leads to a theology that is in danger of becoming cynical. Yet, it is not easy to recognize the plausibility of God's speeches at first glance, since they are imbued with images and ideas of the Israelite worldview that, in turn, is part of the ancient Near Eastern worldview. Othmar Keel (1978) presented a thorough exegesis of the divine speeches against this background that, in our view, is a workable basis for further detailed feminist study. According to Keel, the first of God's speeches replies to Job's charges, stated in condensed form in chapter 3, namely, that the world order is bad. Job has darkened, indeed blackened, God's plan for the world (Job 38:2). In chapter 38 God replies with extensive references to his cosmic creation that, according to ancient Near Eastern thought, establishes and daily upholds that order and within which human life is in fact possible at all. Then, in the second part of the divine speech (38:39–39:30) God presents himself as the shepherd of an initially mysterious flock of ten animals grouped in pairs. Keel has shown that the selection of animals is determined by a motif that is common in ancient Near Eastern and Israelite art, namely, the so-called master of animals. This numinous figure grasps on each side an animal or mythical creature, each allotted to the steppe or the desert, that is, from places that are inaccessible or even dangerous for human beings. In the iconography of seals, that "master of animals" is often depicted next to a symbol of the ordered world, a stylized tree above which the sky arches. The divine power that rules and simultaneously protects and defends the animals, is therefore probably responsible for the dynamic upholding of the world order. In responding to Job, the God of Israel is emphatically presented as the caring custodian of this animal world that, for humans, represents chaos, a threatening world. The role of a shepherd in the ancient Near East included both keeping and protecting as well as mastering and controlling (contrary to Oeming 1996).

God's second speech deals in more detail with the accusations made in chapter 9, especially verses 22–24. There Job had made the outrageous claim that God is utterly indifferent to what happens to humans, that God destroys the good and the wicked indiscriminately. The earth, Job concludes, is in the hands of a sadistic criminal. In chapters 40 and 41, God responds by presenting himself as the successful fighter against Behemoth (hippopotamus) and Leviathan (crocodile). They represent, also in well-documented iconography (Egyptian in this case), the chaos and evil forces that are overcome in Egypt by the king or the god Horus. Thus the God of Israel is engaged in the battle against injustice and the powers of evil. Chaos is given, as it were, its own space, its niches in the cosmos, but the God of Israel controls those powers and imposes limits on them. This reply would be disappointing only if Job expected God to be the controller of all this order. Obviously, such a concept of God would not be in accordance with feminist theology (cf. also Bechtel 1995).

Job accepts God's speeches as a genuine answer to his inquiries and accusations. Already in his first reaction (40:3-5) he promises to be quiet from now on. He acknowledges the greatness of creation, compared to which he himself feels slight and insignificant. "I put my hand over my mouth" (40:4). His final statement (42:1-6) makes it even clearer that Job was not just overcome or persuaded, but actually convinced.

The vision of God allows knowledge of God, and only a few are granted that knowledge. For Job this moment is a turning point; a change of heart has happened. But this is a change without an attitude of repentance, although the old translations and the majority of interpreters disagree on this count (e.g., Bechtel 1995, 250). Job wants to forget what he had said before because he had been persuaded and consoled (but not put off!). While still sitting in dust and ashes, Job becomes a different person (cf. Ebach 1996 on this passage and van Wolde 1995, 220). Is it possible to understand this development? Is God's answer an answer to questions about the meaning of the world order — an answer for Job as a "problem bearer"? Is it an answer in a situation of real suffering, to Job as someone afflicted by actual suffering? We would say: yes, it is. For within the various biblical models of creation, the divine speeches offer, together with Psalm 104, a concept that is not anthropocentric. Creation is not calculated for humans, as presented in different forms in Genesis 1 and 2. In the worldview of this wisdom literature, creation is a structure in which humans take the place allocated to them, next to animals and many other created beings and things. The creation of man and woman is not mentioned in chapter 38 — and that is no coincidence! Thus Job, who was brought into dire straits by suffering, is taken into the expanse of creation, an expanse that makes his relative importance plain but also unburdens him. He is not at the center of creation, something that he learns in a long and painful process of disillusionment but that also allows new beginnings. This concept of humanity should offer an opening for feminist exegesis, theology, and ethics, since it provides solutions to problems that our Western culture and its attendant androcentrism have not overcome to this very day. On the basis of the divine speeches, a new relationship between the human being and creation can be called for. But in those speeches there is no critique whatsoever of "man as the measure of all things," that is, the distancing from anthropocentrism is not coupled with a criticism of patriarchal orders. Even a worldview that presupposes a single divine power but that nevertheless allows the existence of "niches for chaos," is in our opinion worth discussing in terms of feminist theology since the separation of evil onto a devilish figure is out of the question.

The Undiscoverable Wisdom in Job 28

Just before Job begins his concluding speech, his speeches and those of his three friends are interrupted in chapter 28 by a self-contained poem on wisdom. Refrain-like, the verse "But where shall wisdom be found?" is repeated in verses 12 and 20 as a motto, "Where does understanding dwell?" Wisdom poems in which personified Wisdom appears or is taken up as a central theme can also be found in Proverbs 1–9, in Sirach 1 and 24, as well as in Wisdom of Solomon 6–10, in each case with a specific emphasis. In Job, wisdom is a hidden, incomprehensible entity to which God alone has access. For humans, wisdom is undiscoverable. She hardly ever appears in human shape; in the final verses of chapter 28 she looks like a secret plan that runs through everything. The personification is in keeping with the theme of the whole book: for Job the human being, it seems impossible to find ultimate wisdom and understanding; the paths to it are closed. Such feelings of deepest skepticism are to be found already in the older wisdom literature of Egypt and Mesopotamia. Job 28 is an important chapter for feminist reading not so much because a female divine figure is placed in proximity with God (personified *ḥokmâ* is altogether too pale a term here) but because in these verses thoughts critical of patriarchy are expressed implicitly, thoughts that could become a starting point for the reading of the entire book. Verses 1-11 use numerous images from mining, describing what *homo faber* is able to accomplish in his resourcefulness and how he manages to get access to the most inaccessible entrails of the earth. This seemingly technological approach has something almost offensive about it, as in all those actions people do things that are actually reserved for God's activity, such as raging like fire, toppling mountains, and splitting rocks (for a detailed discussion, see Zimmermann 1994). In spite of crossing the boundary in this area, the human being does not discover wisdom (28:13) and his abilities fail him. Verses 15-19 contain, in accordance with the traditional topos of wisdom theology, praise of the great, precious value of wisdom, the possession of which is greater than all the wealth and riches people knew at that time. This thought too contains a critical edge: wisdom cannot be bought; it is hidden from all, rich and poor alike. Only God, who has established it in creation, knows the way to it (28:23-27). In this sense chapter 28 prepares the need for the divine speeches.

Job's Wife and Daughters in the Frame Narrative

According to the prologue, Job, the rich man, has seven sons and three daughters. None of the children whom he loses all at once is mentioned by name. Job's relation to them is raised only insofar as he offers precautionary sacrifice for his sons to atone for any possible offenses on their part; he also mourns his children's death. Job's wife, too, has no name in the prologue. He does not lose her through his misfortune. In the epilogue she is not even mentioned again, since she is not one of the gifts Job receives anew. And yet, she bears him another ten children. In the prologue, she does not appear until chapter 2 when her critically ill husband is already sitting in the ashes. Traditionally her comment or question in verse 9 (which in Hebrew is open) has been interpreted as an expression of incomprehension and mockery. Her suggestion that Job bless/curse *(brk)* God and die has been related to Satan's prediction (2:5) that Job would bless/curse *(brk)* God to God's face. That is why Augustine called the wife a *diaboli adiutrix,* Satan's helper who was to tempt Job. This interpretation has to be countered on several counts (see Ebach 1995, 68-70). The woman does indeed use God's words at first (2:3). She states or asks if Job will hold on to his integrity. In the book of Job the term *brk* is used consistently in its ambivalent meaning of blessing and cursing. In this passage, as in others, the common interpretation of this term only as a euphemism for "cursing" would be too narrow. The text deliberately leaves the meaning undecided: as a curse in the sense of fending off disaster, or as a blessing in the sense of praising what is worthy of praise (Linafelt 1996). It is possible that the wife suggests that Job bless God once more as long as he holds on — or is able to hold on — to his integrity, and then die at peace with God after his farewell (as a midrash on Job 2:9 puts it; see Wertheimer 1968, 165). It is also possible that she points out to Job the absurdity of his holding on to God and proposes that he curse and turn away from his God who has forsaken him and then die, seeing that blasphemy always carries the death penalty (Lev 24:23; see Ebach 1996 on this passage). Both cases could involve compassion or, at any rate, healthy common sense instead of mockery or sarcasm. Job's wife wants a way out of this hopelessness even if it means death. But Job does not accept this and rejects her as "one of the foolish women" — the equivalent Hebrew masculine term represents, among other things, the socially inferior (cf. Job 30:8) but also the godless (cf. Ps 14:1). But Job does not want to escape through death; rather, he wants to bear his suffering. Together with his wife — as is suggested by the use of the plural — he wants to accept evil from God as much as good. This is the only place in the First Testament where the husband does not listen to his wife advising him, as was expected of Israelite wives (as can be found already in the midrash on Gen 3:12: Midrash Bereshit Rabbah 19). An important observation was made by Ellen van Wolde (1995): due to his wife, Job becomes someone who questions, and it is only through her that he, who in Job 1:20-22 is still highly loyal to his God and simply mourns his loss, reaches a point where he even considers the possibility of not accepting evil from God.

This brief confrontation between Job and his wife is ambiguous and, therefore, leaves the reader dissatisfied. It is not surprising then that the Greek text tradition has preserved a much longer version of this passage that is, however, dated even later than the Septuagint, as it represents an expanding interpretation.

After much time had passed, his wife said to him: "How long will you endure and keep saying, 'Behold, I shall wait a little longer and expect the hope of my salvation.' For behold, your memory is already blotted out from the earth, the sons and daughters, the travails and pangs of my womb, whom I brought up with toil in vain. And you, you sit in decay caused by worms, spending the nights outside, while I roam from town to town and from house to house like a tramp or day laborer, looking for the sun to set, so that I might find rest from my toils and pains which now oppress me. But speak one word against the Lord and die." (From the translation by Horst 1968, 22)

In this expanded passage the woman also remains nameless. But the suggestion that Job should speak out against God and then die is now put in a wider context. She speaks of herself as one involved in Job's suffering. It is her children who were snatched from her; her toil had been in vain. Trying to stay alive, she roams about restlessly, fleeing from pain. The Testament of Job, written in the first century B.C.E. or the first century C.E., probably bases its description of Job's wife on those verses above. There, at last, she has a name: Sitis. That name is reminiscent of *Ausitis,* the Greek translation of Uz, the homeland of Job, or *Sitidos,* an allusion to the Greek *sitizein,* "to give bread." Sitidos who, full of compassion, cares for her husband and feeds him, eventually dies and, in the end, Job has a second wife, called Dinah ($\rightarrow$ Testament of Job).

For a feminist reading of Job, the wife is a challenge in more ways than one. Through her, the patriarchal character of the book becomes dramatically apparent. Even though she is afflicted by the same disasters as Job, apart from the disease, her suffering is not mentioned. In fact, she herself is hardly mentioned. Contrary to all biblical role-conventions, her advice is not accepted by Job: she is called a foolish woman, is depicted as one without honor, and is excluded from the rest of the story. At the same time, however, the later narrative traditions show that this important gap had a stimulating effect on the readers' imagination and called for more details. It is no accident that the Testament of Job devotes much attention to this woman and to Job's daughters. A Job as devoid of relationships as the one in the Hebrew tradition could not be left like that. And it was seemingly also unbearable that the suffering and cosuffering of this woman were not mentioned at all.

Job's three daughters also provide a starting point for a feminist reading of the book. The first three daughters die without their names being given, whereas the three later ones are mentioned by name (42:13-15), a noticeable contrast to their seven brothers. The daughters' names are drawn from the domain of aesthetics and cosmetics; to our ears they sound cute. The daughters' beauty is emphasized and brings glory to Job everywhere in the land. Despite this renewed androcentrism, which forces the women into a specific role, it is worth noting that by naming the women their status is enhanced significantly as compared with the sons. It is similarly enhanced by the fact that Job gives his daughters an inheritance together with their brothers, quite an improper way of organizing one's will by Israelite standards. This short comment has to be related to Numbers 27 and 36, texts also written in the postexilic era when many of the properties in Judah had to be reorganized. Those texts speak of the daughters of Zelophehad, who are also mentioned by name. They call on Moses, because they consider it unjust that their father's inheritance *(naḥălâ)* should not go to them just because he had no sons. Their appeal is indeed granted: in such cases daughters shall be entitled to inherit from now on. The amendment to this legislation in Numbers 36 is a restriction of the law: it seeks to assure that the inheritance given to daughters is not lost to the tribe in the event of them marrying outside of it. Job's settlement exceeds these legal guidelines. His daughters are to be heirs just as their brothers are. What has caused the change in Job's relationships? Could it be that, as a result of his suffering and God's interventions, he has after all come to realize that his name will live on in his daughters, and that these women are also entitled to a self-sufficient, materially secure life, independent of men? If that were the case, the Job of the prologue, bereft of relationships, would have, at least, found a new role as a father through the course of the dialogues.

The daughters' status as subjects is also strongly emphasized in the Testament of Job. The entire third part of that book is devoted to them (cf. Lesses 1994). However, their share in their father's inheritance is no longer material but spiritual. Whether this is an advantage remains to be seen. What is interesting is that the three women are said to be eligible to inherit what pertains to piety and revelation. They are full religious subjects. The sparse verses about Job's wife and daughters in the book of Job literally call for a reinterpretation, possibly by women authors.

The Influence of This Book

Feminist exegesis cannot ignore the history of interpretation, since sometimes interpretation implies patriarchal constraints while, at other times, it offers keys to a diverse reading of the biblical texts. The book of Job has influenced an immense number of works of literature, art, and music (cf. Ebach 1986), which cannot be considered within the scope of this essay. But, at least, reference is to be made to the reception of this book in antiquity, in Jewish tradition (cf. Schreiner 1992; Wertheimer 1968; Gordis 1965), in Muslim tradition (cf. *Sura* 4:163; 6:84; 21:83f.; 38:41-44; cf. Paret 1980), and in Christian tradition. Byzantine history of art is interested consistently in Job as an individual and emphasizes his piety (cf. Huber 1986). In the Jewish tradition, especially since Auschwitz, and in liberation theology, there are collective interpretations of Job (cf. Schroer 1989a, esp. 57-62). One example for a Jewish collective interpretation is the 1946 book by the philosopher and essayist Margarete Susman; for her the fate of the Jewish people and, at the same time, how this people holds fast to God are mirrored in Job (Susman 1968). In the 1980s, Latin American liberation theologians presented collective interpretations of Job, discussing the book in the light of a "theology of the poor" (Dussel 1985 and Gutiérrez 1988).

Conclusion: Feminist Keys to the Book

For feminist reading of the book of Job, the presence and diversity of these interpretations are encouraging. Throughout history, interpretations have been presented that made Job topical and were triggered by specific groups and concrete situations. History is really only waiting for a feminist continuation of this practice. The feminist project can start from the gaps in the text, for example, with Job's wife (cf. Deninger-Polzer 1988, and the narrative exegesis by Chedid 1995), or with Job's daughters as his heiresses, not only beautiful but also equal to their brothers. It could start as well with the collective experience of the female people of God, with the unjust suffering of women. The latter approach is brought up in Käthe Kollwitz's images of women and children "in misery," since the art-historical tradition knows both "Job in misery" and "Christ in misery."

A key for an inclusive reading of the book could be a righteous female sufferer such as the poor widow in 24:3, 21, and 31:16 as a representative of marginalized people, above all, women. Their existence is comparable to that of desert animals (24:4), seen by other people as chaotic but who, according to the first divine speech, are nevertheless under God's loving care and protection. Job's wife is also a righteous female sufferer, deprived of her status as a religious subject and banned from the book. The search for her voice, the suppressed voices of women in the book, can be compared with the approach by Athalya Brenner and Fokkelien van Dijk-Hemmes that they call "gendering texts." Ulrike Bail relies on it in her interpretation of the Psalms (→ The Psalms). This approach looks for voices in the text that reflect the social gender of woman, in this case the experience of female suffering or the female struggle with God. Job's wife, who is not a subject but merely a nameless womb associated with finiteness and impurity; the violated Dinah; the Sidotos who demeans herself for bread; the woman who has been handed over to strangers (31:10) — texts such as 3:20, 7:2-8, 10:8-14, and 16:7-19 can be read as laments of such female figures. The "hymns of subversion," for example, 5:8-16 and 12:3-25, can be read as their songs of hope for a change in their circumstances. This way of reading is already part of the biblical tradition, as exemplified by Hannah's song (1 Sam 2) and Mary's praise (Luke 1). In this context the interpretations of the Deuteronomic Torah in Job 24 and 31 have to be seen as an ethical admonition to alleviate the suffering of women — beyond the customary measure. This is, however, a perspective that in the book itself appears only on the horizon; it becomes a reality only in the case of the righteous woman's daughters with their names and inheritance.

A further key for feminist reading could be the divine speeches in chapters 38–41, together with wisdom's description in chapter 28. From a theological point of view, chapter 28 offers several crucial delineations that can be filled with feminist critique: the critique of a male world and of an understanding of wisdom that almost sounds like that of the natural sciences, which subjects all areas of the world and leaves no secrets and yet does not manage to find the life-giving wisdom mysteriously woven into creation. It is a critique of a kind of wisdom that is open only to the rich and does not go hand in hand with the fear of God. Within the framework of this critique of androcentrism, the nonanthropocentric image of God and the world in chapters 38–41 opens up a perspective that is liberating for women. The divine speeches not only lead Job out of the confinement of his suffering, they also give readers a view of the wider context of creation. God turns out to be a power of life that is not focused on the male individual but provides space for everyone, male and female alike. At the same time, a worldview becomes apparent in which suffering and chaos have their place but are limited. After the change of heart, the hitherto isolated Job can rebuild his relationships with his friends, his relatives, and his daughters and treat them differently from the expectations of the patriarchal order. He can only continue to live once his point of view has changed. From this perspective, the book of Job stands for a theology that is experience-based and not androcentric; it offers its readers ethical standards not only in relation to their fellow human beings but also in relation to the world around them.

What we have shown is that feminist interpretations of Job start at the book's fringes or gaps. We believe that this approach should be reflected on and continued. For example, a comparative reading of the Masoretic and Septuagint texts does not exist as yet. It was important to us to put aside the interpretative context of the prologue and the epilogue and to fathom the depths of at least some of the texts in their contrariness and diversity.

LITERATURE

This list contains only selected contributions. Cf. the extensive bibliography in Jürgen Ebach's "Hiob/Hiobbuch," in *Theologische Realenzyklopädie* (Berlin and New York, 1986), 15:360-90.

Albertz, Rainer. 1981. "Der sozialgeschichtliche Hintergrund des Hiobbuches und der 'Babylonischen Theodizee.'" In *Die Botschaft und die Boten,* edited by Jörg Jeremias and Lothar Perlitt, 349-72. Festschrift for Hans Walter Wolff. Neukirchen-Vluyn.

Bechtel, Lynn M. 1995. "A Feminist Approach to the Book of Job." In *A Feminist Companion to Wisdom Literature,* edited by Athalya Brenner, 222-52. Sheffield.

Braulik, Georg. 1996. "Das Deuteronomium und die Bücher Ijob, Sprichwörter, Rut. Zur Frage früher Kanonizität des Deuteronomiums." In *Die Tora als Kanon für Juden und Christen,* edited by Erich Zenger, 61-138. Freiburg et al.

Brenner, Athalya. 1989. "Job the Pious? The Characterization of Job in the Narrative Framework of the Book." *Journal for the Study of the Old Testament* 43:37-52.

———, ed. 1995. *A Feminist Companion to Wisdom Literature.* Sheffield.

Chedid, Andrée. 1995. *Die Frau des Ijob. Erzählung, deutsch.* Limburg.

Clines, David J. A. 1995. "Why Is There a Book of Job, and What Does It Do to You If You Read It?" In Clines, *Interested Parties: The Ideology of Writers and Readers of the Hebrew Bible,* 122-44. Journal for the Study of the Old Testament: Supplement Series, vol. 205. Sheffield.

Crüsemann, Frank. 1980. "Hiob und Kohelet. Ein Beitrag zum Verständnis des Hiobbuches." In *Werden und Wirken des Alten Testaments,* edited by Rainer Albertz et al., 372-93. Festschrift for Claus Westermann. Göttingen and Neukirchen-Vluyn.

Deninger-Polzer, Gertrude. 1988. "Hiobs Frau. Leidtragende, nicht Randfigur." In *Zwischen Ohnmacht und Befreiung. Biblische Frauengestalten,* edited by Karin Walter, 109-21. Freiburg im Breisgau.

Dussel, Enrique. 1985. *Herrschaft und Befreiung. Ansatz, Stationen und Themen einer lateinamerikanischen Theologie der Befreiung.* Fribourg.

Ebach, Jürgen. 1986. "Hiob/Hiobbuch." In *Theologische Realenzyklopädie* 15:370-73.

———. 1995. *Hiobs Post. Gesammelte Aufsätze zum Hiobbuch, zu Themen biblischer Theologie und zur Methodik der Exegese.* Neukirchen-Vluyn.

———. 1996. *Streiten mit Gott. Hiob. Teil 1: Hiob 1–20. Teil 2: Hiob 21–42.* Kleine Biblische Bibliothek. Neukirchen-Vluyn.

———. n.d. "Feministische Aspekte des Hiobbuches." Unpublished.

Fuchs, Gisela. 1993. *Mythos und Hiobdichtung. Aufnahme und Umdeutung altorientalischer Vorstellungen.* Stuttgart et al.

Gordis, Robert. 1965. *The Book of God and Man: A Study of Job.* Chicago and London.

Gutiérrez, Gustavo. 1988. *Von Gott sprechen in Unrecht und Leid-Ijob.* Munich and Mainz.

Hainthaler, Theresia. 1988. *"Von der Ausdauer Ijobs habt ihr gehört" (Jak 5,11). Zur Bedeutung des Buches Ijob im Neuen Testament.* Frankfurt am Main et al.

Horst, Friedrich. 1968. *Hiob. 1. Teilband: Kap. 1–19.* Biblischer Kommentar, Altes Testament, vol. 16, 1. Neukirchen-Vluyn.

Huber, Paul. 1986. *Hiob — Dulder oder Rebell? Byzantinische Miniaturen zum Buch Hiob in Patmos, Rom, Venedig, Sinai, Jerusalem und Athos.* Düsseldorf.

Janowski, Bernd. 1994. "Die Tat kehrt zum Täter zurück. Offene Fragen im Umkreis des 'Tun-Ergehen-Zusammenhangs.'" *Zeitschrift für Theologie und Kirche* 91:247-71.

Keel, Othmar. 1978. *Jahwes Entgegnung an Ijob. Eine Deutung von Ijob 38–41 vor dem Hintergrund der zeitgenössischen Bildkunst.* Göttingen.

Kessler, Rainer. 1992. "'Ich weiß, daß mein Erlöser lebet.' Sozialgeschichtlicher Hintergrund und theologische Bedeutung der Löser-Vorstellung in Hiob 19,25." *Zeitschrift für Theologie und Kirche* 89:139-58.

Klein, Lillian R. 1995. "Job and the Womb: Text about Men, Subtext about Women." In *A Feminist Companion to Wisdom Literature,* edited by Athalya Brenner, 186-200. Sheffield.

Knauf, Ernst Axel. 1988. "Hiobs Heimat." *Die Welt des Orients* 19:65-83.

Koch, Klaus. 1972. "Gibt es ein Vergeltungsdogma im Alten Testament? (1955)." In *Um das Prinzip der Vergeltung in Religion und Recht des Alten Testaments,* edited by Klaus Koch, 130-80. Wege der Forschung, vol. 75. Darmstadt.

Lambert, Wilfred G. 1960. *Babylonian Wisdom Literature.* Oxford.

Lesses, Rebecca. 1994. "The Daughters of Job." In *Searching the Scriptures,* edited by Elisabeth Schüssler Fiorenza, 2:139-49. 2 vols. New York.

Lichtheim, Mirjam. 1973-80. *Ancient Egyptian Literature: A Book of Readings.* 3 vols. Berkeley.

Linafelt, Tod. 1996. "The Undecidability of *brk* in the Prologue of Job and Beyond." *Biblical Interpretation* 4:154-72.

Newsom, Carol A. 1992. "Job." In *The Women's Bible Commentary,* edited by Carol A. Newsom and Sharon H. Ringe, 130-36. London and Louisville.

Oeming, Manfred. 1996. "'Kannst du der Löwin ihren Raub zu jagen geben?' (Hi 38,39). Das Motiv des 'Herrn der Tiere' und seine Bedeutung für die Theologie der Gottesreden Hi 38-42." In *"Dort ziehen Schiffe dahin. . . ." Collected Communications to the XIVth Congress of the International Organization for the Study of the Old Testament,* edited by Matthias Augustin et al., 147-63. Beiträge zur Erforschung des Alten Testaments und des antiken Judentums, vol. 28. Frankfurt am Main.

Paret, Rudi. 1977. *Der Koran: Übersetzung.* 2nd ed. Stuttgart.

———. 1980. *Der Koran: Kommentar und Konkordanz.* 2nd ed. Stuttgart.

Pritchard, James B. 1955. *Ancient Near Eastern Texts Relating to the Old Testament.* Princeton.

Schmid, Hans Heinrich. 1966. *Wesen und Geschichte der Weisheit. Eine Untersuchung zur altorientalischen und israelitischen Weisheitsliteratur.* Beihefte zur Zeitschrift für die alttestamentliche Wissenschaft, vol. 101. Berlin.

Schottroff, Willy. 1982. "Zur Sozialgeschichte Israels in der Perserzeit." *Verkündigung und Forschung* 27:46-68.

Schreiner, Stefan. 1992. "Der gottesfürchtige Rebell oder Wie die Rabbinen die Frömmigkeit Hiobs deuteten." *Zeitschrift für Theologie und Kirche* 89:159-71.

Schroer, Silvia. 1989a. "Entstehungsgeschichtliche und gegenwärtige Situierungen des Hiob-Buches." In *Hiob. Bibelarbeit in der Gemeinde,* edited by Ökumenischer Arbeitskreis für Bibelarbeit, 35-62. Basel and Zurich.

———. 1989b. "In die Enge getrieben in die Weite geführt. Hiobs Klage und die erste Gottesrede (Hiob 3 und 38–39)." In *Hiob. Bibelarbeit in der Gemeinde,* edited by Ökumenischer Arbeitskreis für Bibelarbeit, 128-60. Basel and Zurich.

Sitzler, Dorothea. 1995. *Vorwurf gegen Gott. Ein religiöses Motiv im Alten Orient. Ägypten und Mesopotamien.* Studies in Oriental Religions, vol. 32. Wiesbaden.

Spieckermann, Hermann. 1994. "Die Satanisierung Gottes. Zur inneren Konkordanz von Novelle, Dialog und Gottesreden im Hiobbuch." In *"Wer ist wie du, HERR, unter den Göttern?" Studien zur Theologie und Religionsgeschichte Israels,* edited by Ingo Kottsieper et al., 431-44. Festschrift for Otto Kaiser. Göttingen.

Susman, Margarete. 1968. *Das Buch Hiob und das Schicksal des jüdischen Volkes.* Freiburg im Breisgau et al.

Van Wolde, Ellen. 1995. "The Development of Job: Mrs. Job as Catalyst." In *A Feminist Companion to Wisdom Literature,* edited by Athalya Brenner, 201-21. Sheffield.

Wertheimer, Solomon Aaron, ed. 1968. *Batei Midrashot.* Vol. 2. 2nd ed. Jerusalem.

Zimmermann, Ruben. 1994. "Homo Sapiens Ignorans. Hiob 28 als Bestandteil der ursprünglichen Hiobdichtung." *Biblische Notizen* 74:80-100.

For Further Reading

Engljähringer, Klaudia. 2003. *Theologie im Streitgespräch. Studien zur Dynamik der Dialoge des Buches Ijob.* Stuttgarter Bibelstudien, vol. 198. Stuttgart.

Maier, Christl, and Silvia Schroer. 1998. "What about Job? Questioning the Book of the 'Righteous Sufferer.'" In *Wisdom and Psalms: A Feminist Companion to the Bible,* edited by Athalya Brenner and Carole Fontaine, 175-204. 2nd series, vol. 2. Sheffield.

Translated by Martin Rumscheidt

The Psalms: "Who Is Speaking May Be *All* That Matters"

Ulrike Bail

Psalms are texts to be used. In their long history of reception that began already in the First Testament, they have been, and still are, spoken and sung by men and women in different sociocultural contexts. In the 150 psalms of the book of Psalms, people found, and still find, songs that mirror situations in their lives and with which they can enter into a conversation and sing or speak them as their own words. They are songs of hope and liberation, of lament and suffering, of joy and celebration, of looking at creation and of justice. These songs can be heard and spoken as voices of women. This article will present an exemplary reading in this way.

"Who Is Speaking May Be *All* That Matters"

In the interest of understanding the Psalms as affirmation, strengthening, and empowerment of women, Marchiene Vroon Rienstra presents her liturgically oriented book *Swallow's Nest: A Feminine Reading of the Psalms*. Readers are encouraged to understand the Psalms as prayers of individual women in various situations and conditions of life. Rienstra paraphrases psalms and imagines specific situations of women's experiences, which she then names in the new headings to the Psalms. For example, Psalm 6 has the caption: "This might be the prayer of a woman who was raped" (Rienstra 1992, 44). This creative feminist treatment of the Psalms points to the possibility of reading them from a woman's perspective.

   In the Hebrew text of the Psalms are several reading instructions that open up a way for a feminist rereading. One of these ways is to look at their headings. These headings were secondary additions to the text, and many of them mentioned men as psalms' authors (David, Sons of Korah, Asaph, Solomon, Ethan, and Moses). These notes are not historical references; the authors in these headings are fictional and literary characters. They are meant to anchor the individual psalm in a particular biblical narrative. This is particularly true for the captions that name

David as the author: they connect specific psalms with David's biography. For example, Psalm 51 and the narrative of David and Bathsheba in 2 Samuel 12 are brought together by the heading. As a result, Psalm 51 becomes the voice of David in a particular situation of his life.

One can also reread the Psalms by taking note of a psalm's context. For example, the psalm that Hannah prays in 1 Samuel 2:1-10 shows no particular "feminine language nor unequivocally female motifs" (Gerstenberger 1994, 352). Nonetheless, it gives voice to Hannah's experiences (Miller 1993, 237f.). By incorporating it into the Hannah narrative, the words of this psalm are spoken by Hannah's voice, giving a women-specific meaning. Hannah thanks God that he has delivered her from barrenness and acts in solidarity with all who are poor and humiliated (cf. Luke 2).

Psalms are also placed on the lips of other women, even though these are mostly shorter prayers (Hagar: Gen 16:13; Rebekah: Gen 25:22; Miriam: Exod 15:21; Deborah: Judg 5). "On the other hand, narratives of men are furnished more frequently with short, fervent prayers and detailed psalms" (Gerstenberger 1994, 352). In intertestamental literature many women speak psalms (Susannah: Dan 13:42-43; Jephthah's daughter: Liber antiquitatum biblicarum 40.5-8; Sarah: Tob 3:11-15; Judith: Jth 9:2-14; Esther: Rest of Esther C 12-30; Aseneth: Joseph and Aseneth 12).

In addition, there are references on the literary level of the Psalms to women singing psalms. Those instances have to be highlighted. For example, in Psalm 48:12(11) the daughters of Judah are encouraged to rejoice (cf. also 97:8), and in 148:12 virgins are to sing praises together with all humanity and the whole of creation (cf. also 45:16 [Eng. 15]).

The concept of the "voice in the text" enables the "gendering of texts" (Brenner and van Dijk-Hemmes 1993). Biblical texts are exclusively — or almost exclusively — written by men for men. Texts of women are only found embedded in these male narratives, formed and framed by the editorial activities of men (Brenner and van Dijk-Hemmes 1993, 2f.). Since the oral traditions of women are often written down by men due to their prominence and power in the literary terrain, the female voices are only hidden traces. Whether those traces are recovered depends on the interest of the readers and their willingness to search for those lost voices in biblical texts. Texts and readers are never gender-neutral, and often texts tell different stories if they are read as male voice or female voice. For example, one could think about which psalm could represent the voice of Bathsheba. Biblical texts should be understood as "dual gendered" (Brenner and van Dijk-Hemmes 1993, 9), which means that two parallel readings are possible. Psalms are open to both genders. It depends on the voice that reads or speaks the text: "Who is speaking may be *all* that matters" (Higgins and Silver 1991, 1).

Brenner and van Dijk-Hemmes's approach makes it possible to search for female voices in the Hebrew Bible without engaging the question of female authorship, which, at any rate, leads into the vexed terrain of speculative answers. Furthermore, one needs to remember that women in an androcentric-dominant culture always have to speak in a double voice anyway. They have to speak with the voice of the dominant discourses that drown out and overwrite their voices and, at the same time, with the voice of the repressed, secret discourses. The main focus of the search for female voices ("F voices") lies in the search for muted voices.

Linking the poetic psalm-text to the narrative-biographical text by means of a psalm's caption or embedding the psalm into a narrative context provides possibilities to read the Psalms from a feminist perspective. In addition, from the perspective of women, the web of intrabiblical connections can be employed in terms of intertextual reading to focus on the voices of women in the Psalms (Bail 1994 and 1998). The meaning of a text emerges only in the process of reading, as the text is related to other texts. No text exists in isolation from others, whether this is an overt connection or by implication only. Meaning is constituted by the relations of texts to which the text itself can hint. Moreover, exegesis can influence the interaction of texts in that readers decide themselves which kind of texts and how many comparable texts and points of contacts to choose. The specific partiality of feminist epistemological interest can readily be incorporated into the method of intertextual interpretation. Feminist-oriented intertextuality creates different connections and weaves different webs of texts that speak to each other.

Traces of Women in the Psalms

"According to young women. A Song" — this is the title of Psalm 46. This extraordinary mention of young women *('ălāmôt)* in the heading to the psalm points to other passages where young women are connected to music. In Psalm 68:26(25) young girls are playing the tambourine *(tôp)*. Other biblical passages narrate that women play drums and dance (Judg 11:34; 1 Sam 18:6; Jer 31:4; Exod 15:20; 1 Chron 25:21). Particularly noteworthy is the prophet Miriam, who, dancing together with all women, plays the tambourine and sings of the liberation from slavery in Egypt (Exod 15:20).

Behind these brief notes may be hidden a music tradition of women, perhaps even a genre of "drum-dance-song" (Meyers 1991). In any case, the tambourine was played as a solo instrument exclusively by women (Braun 1994, 1525f.). Whether these groups of women can be identified with the "female musicians of the court who, on special occasions, would perform in the procession of male musicians and singers" (Engelken 1990, 59) remains debatable. Similarly, whether the drum is to be seen as a gendered symbol because of its association with women is left open (Braun 1994, 1527).

Goitein regards women of First Testament times not as writers of particular texts but rather as "creators of biblical genres": "She sang in the days of love and during the days of mourning, expressed the joy of victory and the agony of defeat, words of wisdom and whispers of prayer" (Goitein 1988, 29). Goitein sees especially lyrical genres as expressions of women's creativity and initiative. For women whose emotional lives he characterizes as strong and empathetic, it is natural to be sensitive to religious lyric. But with this argument he equates women with emotionality, sensitivity, femininity, nature, and the poetic. Goitein's argument does support women's self-determined creativity, but it keeps women in a dualistic understanding of gender where they are reduced to nature and emotion.

There is another, almost invisible trace in the heading to Psalm 56: "According to the Dove of the Far-away Gods." This musical instruction might derive from an understanding in the ancient Orient that doves are messenger birds for the ancient Orient's love goddesses (Schroer 1996, 146ff.). Perhaps the heading of Psalm 22, "According to the Deer of the Dawn," also expresses this tradition. Like the dove, the deer inhabits the sphere that is marked by the power of the love goddesses (Keel 1984, 100). Moreover, some Jewish rites depict Psalm 22 as the voice of a woman, as a psalm of Esther, to be performed liturgically during the feast of Purim (Elbogen 1995, 131).

Despite great effort, the musical instructions in the psalm headings remain difficult to understand. Unfortunately, the concrete meaning cannot be reconstructed today. The traces point to a musical tradition of women but remain obscure. Whether there was a separate song-tradition also remains conjecture. However, it can neither be contested nor proven that women were part of the "formulation and use of holy texts" (Gerstenberger 1994, 359). Furthermore, the Psalms are poetic texts, and one cannot directly deduce from such texts the reality in which they originated. Psalms narrate lived reality in a metaphorical way as one that can be relived. They offer possibilities for identification, allowing the expression of one's own lived experience (Bail 1994, 71). Psalms are difficult to date, and considering their anonymity, it is nearly impossible to identify historically an author regardless of gender. The literary hints suggest that women prayed these psalms. Therefore I will speak in the following only of the woman who prays.

Psalm 6 — God, Liberate My Voice!

Psalm 6 does not contain any personal pronouns that point to the gender of the person who is praying. This already makes the psalm grammatically dual-gendered. What kind of meaning could this psalm provide for women who speak it? What kind of connections does it offer to women?

In verse 2, the woman expresses her need with the words "I am languishing" (*'umělal*). This verb can have women-specific connotations. In 1 Samuel 2:5 and Jeremiah 15:9 (cf. also Isa 33:9) the verb is used for a woman with many children who has become infertile. Without limiting Psalm 6 to this particular distress, it can be read as an expression of this painful experience. But because of its metaphorical language, the psalm is open for all experiences of violence and helplessness of those who pray it.

Psalm 6 shows that a seemingly inescapable situation of oppression can change: the perpetrators are recognized and named (v. 8). By facing the cause of her need directly, the woman who prays can give voice to it and thereby limit its influence (vv. 9-11[8-10]). At the same time, God is recognized as one who takes the side of the woman who prays and as one who hears her cry (vv. 8b, 9; Bail 1998, 114ff.).

Psalm 10 — to Speak in One's Own Voice

Language and power are closely connected; language represents power relations in that dominant societal discourses define what is significant, what meaning things have. That discourse regulates what is and what is not to be said, and who gets to speak and who is listened to — and ultimately it privileges a particular view of reality. In Psalm 10 the language of the powerful is rendered in four fictional quotations (vv. 4, 6, 11, 13). The woman who prays this psalm does not claim to render the voice of power accurately. Her intention is to expose the self-righteous intent of the powerful who hide their motivations behind their words. The fictional quotations allow a glimpse behind this deception in that she lets the powerful themselves tell the unvarnished truth. The fiction unmasks the ideology on which the construction of reality that legitimizes violence is based. The control of the powerful over language suffers a crack when the woman who prays claims her right to speak and puts the words of the powerful into her own words. In Psalm 10 the woman who prays is the one who determines who speaks and what they say and thus reverses power relations and defines them anew. She lifts up her own voice, thereby sketching on a literary level an alternative to the construction of reality of dominant discourse. The sociopolitical status quo, said to be unchangeable and natural, is found to be alterable. The oppressive reality loses its totalitarian character when the totalitarian domination of the here and now and of language is questioned and redefined (cf. Bail 1998, 33ff., 68ff.).

Psalm 12 — Opposition to the Violence of the Language of the Mighty

In Psalm 12 the dominance of certain social groups that threaten the praying woman is raised into language, for language seems to be the reason for their power. Language is "in the service of the ruling elite" (Butting 1996, 28). The asymmetrical and hierarchical structure of society is constructed by language. Power and powerlessness legitimate themselves through discourses; the group that has control over the dominant discourse also controls reality. Only its perception of things counts. It negates every other perception, renders it invisible and silences it.

This psalm is prayed in order to crack this particular construction of reality open. It does not end with praise but comes back to its opening (v. 1). The powerful "prowl" everywhere and oppress (v. 8). To translate the Hebrew verb in this instance *(sbb)* with "prowling about" is actually too mild if one takes into consideration its usage in militaristic contexts. The verb does not describe a leisurely strolling but more the action of encircling and cutting off with the goal to capture and secure the rule. Therefore the last verse of Psalm 12 realistically repeats the vicious circle of violence by referring back to and encouraging starting again at the beginning in verse 1. The text thus mirrors this circle of violence on the literary level. It seems impossible to imagine transformation on the level of the text. The woman praying remains enclosed within the discourse of power that is dominant and absolute. It encircles the woman who prays and besieges her destructively so that the psalm must begin again without offering words of liberation.

But God cuts off those self-appointed men who became powerful because of their control of language (v. 4) by having the poor and oppressed placed before them. The marginalized, imprisoned as they are by the violence of the language and violence of the powerful, are going to be liberated. They are placed at the heart of God's speech, and thus the wall of silence that surrounds them is broken down. The emphasis on *now* (v. 5) dissolves the totality of the present, because the present is positioned against the solidarity of God. The wish to "cut off all flattering lips" (v. 3) is related to the praying woman's liberation from the oppressors' hold over power of language and their violence. The psalm deals with liberation and solidarity that do not lose sight of the victim and push oppressors to the margin.

The psalms of lament spoken by individuals call for the disempowerment of the dominant social groups' control of language and violence. On the one hand, the victims are enabled — amidst the silence forced upon and suffered by them — to participate in a pattern of communication where they can speak, to pronounce words of opposition, to protest, and to accuse. On the other hand, God has the final word for speech, which becomes possible only in the communication with God. The discourse of liberation can emerge in the linguistic space of which it becomes possible for the praying woman truly to be a subject (cf. Bail 1998, 45ff., 72ff.).

Psalm 45 — between Reality and Utopia

Psalm 45 in its present version was probably written after the harrowing experience of the exile. It puts into words the yearning of Israel for a "renewed kingship as the 'divine' bearer of justice and righteousness" (Zenger 1993a, 279). Concretely, this is spelled out in the poetic imagery of the wedding between the "messianic" king and a princess. The imagery suggests the wedding between Zion/Jerusalem and the king as well as between Zion and God.

In her marriage to the king, the princess begins a completely new life. If we assume that this daughter is not a foreign princess but a daughter of Zion (cf. Ezek 16:3, 45; Gen 12:1), then "the Psalm in its final form celebrates the end of that catastrophe when the 'woman Zion' was despised, left behind and barren. Once despised and violated by the nations, now Zion even becomes the queen over those nations" (cf. Isa 49:21-23; 61:10-11; 62:3-5; Zeph 3:14-17) (Zenger 1993a, 279). However, the princess is commanded to obey the king completely:

> The king will desire your beauty.
> Since he is your lord, bow to him. (Ps 45:11)

This verse sketches a patriarchal marriage that is without doubt structured in a hierarchical way. The subordination of the princess ensures a new life to her, and she is instructed to leave her old life behind (45:10).

The "happy end" of a biography as celebrated in Psalm 45 is mentioned metaphorically in Ezekiel 16 (Maier 1994). The biography of the city-woman Jerusalem has the following stations: abandoned daughter, loved and cared-for wife, adulteress whose sexuality runs wild and who is raped as punishment. In Ezekiel 16:59-63, Jerusalem is addressed with words of deliverance reminiscent of the marriage covenant in Psalm 45:7 (Maier 1994, 91-101). Through this renewed, everlasting covenant the woman has regained a high status, but she is ashamed of her past deeds and thus remains silent (Ezek 16:62-63). Once again the husband is in control and determines what she does (Maier 1994, 101).

The vision of a new beginning is depicted in both Psalm 45 and Ezekiel 16 in terms of patriarchal marriage. This image can only be evaluated as androcentric and sexist. In the picture Psalm 45 paints, daughter Zion is rehabilitated and becomes the queen, but only by subordinating herself and wiping her past humiliations from memory (cf. Ezek 16). From a feminist perspective this image of womanhood has to be critiqued just as the vision that pictures the new beginning in an image of hierarchically structured marriage. The caption of Psalm 45 (cf. also Pss 60; 69; 80) provides a counterimage: "According to Lilies" (*'al-šōšannîm*). In the Song of Solomon lilies, or rather lotus flowers, are seen as "symbols and medium of the invigorating and intoxicating lust for life and life's abundance" (Zenger 1993a, 281; cf. Song 2:1, 16; 4:5; 5:13; 6:2; 7:3[2]). In the Song of Solomon, the female lover is not subordinate; instead an image of desire for a relationship of mutual love without hierarchies is developed. Even the name of the genre in Psalm 45, "a love song," provides an instruction of how to read and hear this psalm: a song of praise to the love that makes new beginnings possible (cf. Song 8:7; Isa 5:1). The caption stands in tension with the demand that the princess submit herself unreservedly. In patriarchal societies this tension is present in any love relationship. The psalm then reminds the reader of the utopian love that is equal and mutual while at the same time it speaks about the reality structured by a gender-specific hierarchy.

Psalm 46 — Peace Comes through God's Voice

Psalm 46, a hymn of trust, names God as one who protects his city (Jerusalem) in warring encounters and situations of siege. But he does not need arms to save his city; his voice alone suffices (v. 6). God takes away the power of the adversary with his loud voice and he creates worldwide peace by destroying all arms. Verses 5b and 9 are reminiscent of the exodus (Exod 14:27; 15:21). If one takes into account the caption, "According to [the manner] of (tambourine-playing) young women," then one can connect this to Miriam (Zenger 1993b, 287). After the liberation from Egypt, the prophetess Miriam takes the tambourine, dances and sings her song of God, who helps in hopeless situations, liberates, ends oppression, and destroys arms.

If psalms are sung by women's voices and if women can participate in the liberation tradition of these songs, then the God of Jacob (Ps 46:1, 7, 11) is also the refuge of Rachel and Leah (Farmer 1992, 138). Particularly in the face of the suffering wars bring to the lives of women (cf. Lam 5:11; 2 Chron 36:17; Jer 38:22-23; 6:11-12; 15:8-9; 22:26), women can lay hold of Psalm 46 and its God who is aligned with peace. God does not rejoice in the power and violence of warriors (Ps 147:10 and Jth 9:2-14). The longing that the sound of lament in the streets will cease is expressed in the language of the simile of young men as plants and young women as pillars (Ps 144:12).

Psalm 55 — the Lament of a Woman Raped

The woman who prays this psalm of lament expresses her experiences of terror and violence in the simile of a city under siege and where violence has advanced into the very core of the city, the marketplace (vv. 10-12). From the context of the whole psalm it becomes apparent that the city is not just the location but also the object of violence. There is a correlation between the persona of the psalm who verbalizes the experience of violence and the conquered and occupied city (cf. the connections in vv. 3 and 10 with the key word "trouble," and in vv. 5, 11, and 12 with "in its midst"). The city as well as the "I" of the psalm are objects of violence and powerless before it. If one links the verbs that describe the persona (vv. 3b-5) to the description of the city, it becomes apparent that violence totally dominates the whole space. While the threat of the city is expressed in terms of horizontal movements (encircle, not departing), the "trouble" visited upon the persona moves vertically (to bring upon, to fall on, to overwhelm). The topography of violence thus controls the space from which there is no escape.

In Hebrew, "city" has a feminine gender and is often personified as a woman. Daughter Zion, virgin Jerusalem, and whore Babylon are only some examples of this association. This linkage of the "I" with city, on the one hand, and city with woman, on the other, supports the supposition that the subject of Psalm 55 is a woman. The verb "to surround, to encircle" *(sbb)* also indicates this. In psalms of lament, the action of this word highlights the threat of violence, the terrible scale of violence, and the helplessness of the one who prays (cf., e.g., Ps 17:11). Often the verb implies immense terror (e.g., Jer 6:25; Ps 31:13). In the context of war and militarism, that is, in that of the siege and conquest of a city, the verb means "to be surrounded by enemies" (Jer 4:17; 50:14-15). The word used in the Hebrew Bible to describe the results of such a conquest of the city is *šmm*, "to be destroyed"; its purpose is to describe the strategy of war that leaves the enemy with nothing but scorched earth (Jer 51:43). Interestingly, this word can mean something else in connection to women (cf. Isa 54:1; 62:4; Jer 50:12-13; Ezek 23:33). It stands parallel to "being barren" and "abandoned"; its opposite is "being married." This word *šmm* expresses the condition of Tamar, the raped daughter of the king, in 2 Samuel 13:20: "So Tamar remained, a desolate *(šmm)* woman, in her brother Absalom's house." Given that this verb describes devastated land and destroyed cities, in relation to Tamar it means the destruction of integrity and identity through rape. The topography of violence creates an intertextual linkage between the narrative of the rape of Tamar and this psalm of lament. Furthermore, the perpetrator is described as someone known and trusted (Ps 55:14-15[13-14]). The violence takes place in a geographical and emotional space known to the victim. From a contemporary perspective, this also supports the reading of rape, because the topography of closeness can be found in most rape cases. In approximately half of all rape cases, the perpetrator is known to the woman before the deed. The greatest danger for women lies in known perpetrators and in familiar settings.

But the psalm does not only name the terror, it also portrays alternative spaces, spaces against violence. The very fact that the psalm allows the violent experience to be articulated and the perpetrator(s) to be identified removes the suffering from its subjective singularity and isolation. The lament allows the victims to name the terror and violence and thus breaks the wall of silence that the victors erect around their victims. The texts of lament are always on the side of the victims, also on the side of the victims of sexual violence. They reveal violence, name it, make it heard, unmask the perpetrators, and the structures of violence are laid bare.

Even the passages that call for the end of the perpetrator(s) (vv. 15, 19, and 23) mirror the attempt to end the violence. In a situation of absolute powerlessness, the death of the perpetrator(s) seems to be the only way to end violence. But the death of the perpetrator does not have the last word. Trust in God creates a counterdiscourse that allows the powerless object of violence to reclaim her position as a subject and her identity. This happens in the wilderness, which is contrasted with the space of the city (vv. 6-8). These verses portray liberation as an unrealizable reality, but they offer a strategy of survival, namely, that of disassociation. The image of the dove flying to the wilderness for refuge is not integrated through word association with the rest of the psalm; it stands isolated. The dove-desert image is to some extent disassociated. Disassociation means that feelings and the body are split from the "I" so that in situations of physical and psychological distress that have no chance of escape, a boundary between the "I" and the unbearable pain may be drawn. The imaginary flight of the dove to the desert also functions to prevent the destruction of the "I" to its uttermost depth. The image helps the "I" to survive the annihilating experience of violence without losing itself. The energy to articulate new images and to sketch new spaces in a situation of complete powerlessness corresponds to the "But I will trust in you" at the end of the psalm. What was only hinted at in verses 6-8, namely, finding a place of shelter, becomes more sure in this "But I will trust in you": God is on the side of the woman who prays. By claiming God as her advocate, the praying woman weaves God into the daily and nightly experience of violence against women. To refrain from the lament would mean to identify God with terror and violence. The loud and public lament could provide the dove a real refuge, a place where not only survival but also life without threat, every day and every night, becomes possible. The lament in the name of the dove could be the beginning of liberation. The heading to Psalm 55 could thus be rephrased: the lament of a woman. To be spoken against silence (cf. Bail 1994; 1998, 160ff.).

Psalm 131 — Image(s) of Women

In an essay published in 1967, Gottfried Quell presented Psalm 131 as having been written by a woman: "It is a woman . . . who prays and thanks God in powerful simplicity for her good fortune" (Quell 1967, 184; cf. Seybold 1978, 37f.; Miller 1993, 244ff.; Farmer 1992, 142f.). For evidence he points to the imagery of verse 2b, which talks about a mother with a (her?) child. Quell's argument thus works with a biologically oriented image of womanhood, in which motherhood, womanhood, emotion, humility, and simplicity become interlinked (cf. Quell 1967, especially 178). His interpretive rendition of the sentence "I do not occupy myself with things too great and too marvelous for me" (v. 1b) as "I am not drawn to theological and cultic reflection, I am completely uneducated" gives the psalm the air of a role model for women that seeks to keep them from intellectual reflection and sees their task in motherhood and child rearing (Quell 1967, 185).

Miller (1993, 244ff.) also thinks the author of Psalm 131 is a woman. The special experience of the relationship between mother and child can be seen as an image for the relationship between God and humans, a relationship characterized by security, dependence, and humility. At the same time, Miller explains that women at that time were forced by the sociopolitical circumstances to be subordinate and humble. In Psalm 131 the woman who prays speaks of having calmed and quieted the dynamics of her life and says that her heart is no longer haughty, her eyes are no longer raised up too high, and she no longer occupies herself with things too great and too marvelous for her. Behind this Miller sees a struggle against restrictive role models that want to keep women from engaging theological questions. But this expression of humility in the face of God's wonderful deeds comes from the same source that nourishes the intellectual traditions in the First Testament (cf. Prov 30:18; Job 42:1-6). It is a humble subordination before God and not before other people. Thus, Psalm 131 may be read as a prayer of hope and of trust in the God who accomplishes great and marvelous things (v. 1). Psalms are "songs of power and liberation but only as they praise the wonders of what God can do" (Miller 1993, 250).

But quite apart from the image of women reflected in this psalm — sketched as a mother with her child and as a potential pattern of behavior — one must ask: Can one take a literary piece of language and map it directly onto reality in order to deduce the gender of the author? Does it not rather depend precisely on what voice speaks the words of Psalm 131 and in what context?

In Genesis 18:14, what the messengers of God had to say to Sarah after she laughed in her tent about the promise of a son was: "Is anything too wonderful for the Lᴏʀᴅ?" God freed Sarah and Hannah (2 Sam 1–2) from their barrenness, which in the patriarchal family-oriented society implied that women were at the lowest end of the scale of values. In this context Psalm 131 could be read and interpreted analogously to Hannah's song of liberation and of a just social order. Another voice is suggested by Rienstra, who gives Psalm 131 a new heading: "This might be a prayer of a woman scholar and professor" (Rienstra 1992, 138). The image of women in this psalm changes according to the different ways of reading: it can be seen as limiting women or as liberation.

Images of the Womb and Birth

Noticeably often we find descriptions of women giving birth in the language of the Psalms in order to put into words experiences of pain, terror, and fear (e.g., Pss 48:6; 55:4; 77:16; 97:4). In Psalm 7:14 someone conceives evil and bears mischief; in Psalm 58:8 those who bring injustice into the country are compared to a miscarriage. At the same time, the metaphor of the mother's womb is used to express the wonder of human birth and of being human. God knits a human being in the womb (139:13), acts like a midwife (22:9 and perhaps 71:6). Human existence is considered "from the womb" onward (58:3; 71:6). Even creation is described as a birth (90:2), and with his voice God creates new life (29:7-8). God is responsible for conception, pregnancy, and birth; he opens and closes the womb (cf. 1 Sam 1:5-6; Gen 16:2; 29:31; 30:22; Isa 66:9).

Words like *raḥāmîm* ("mercy"; plural of *reḥem:* "womb") and *raḥûm* (merciful) are derived from the word *reḥem*, "womb." Both words speak of the ability to empathize and show pity, and are used to express God's mercy. The pithy confessional assertion given in Exodus 34:6 as a self-proclamation of God: "The Lᴏʀᴅ, the Lord, a God merciful *(raḥûm)* and gracious *(ḥannûn),*" is taken up in the Psalms (cf. Pss 86:15; 103:8; 111:4; 145:8; Schüngel-Straumann 1996, 64-65). For those who are threatened and marginalized by society (Pss 116:5-8; 106:46), the God of Israel is one of mercy and grace (6:5[4]; 116:5). That the word "mercy" has an echo of a women-specific experience in Hebrew is suggested by Psalm 77:9 (cf. also Ps 40:11), where the question is raised whether God has shut up his compassion *(rāḥamîm).* The phrase "to open/close the womb" *(reḥem)* describes birth and in-fertility (cf. 1 Sam 1:5-6; Gen 16:2; 29:31; 30:22; Isa 66:9). Similarly, Psalm 119:77, linking mercy and life, alludes to this.

Today, where pregnancy is available via technological means and a woman's womb is in a certain sense a public place, one has to ask critically whether the dis-course of birth and the womb, including the discourse about God, does not offer a liberation perspective for women.

God's Solidarity with the Poor and Widows

In Psalm 68:5 God is called the protector of widows, and in Psalm 146:9 he takes care of them. In both instances they are mentioned in the same breath as orphans; in the latter they are mentioned at the same time as strangers. This actualizes the social law of Exodus 22:20-23. Widows, orphans, strangers, and the wretched/poor are under God's protection, and he extends his solidarity to them. Their cry for help in oppressive situations (see Ps 94:6) is heard and answered by God. In the Psalms, those marginalized by society and pushed to the margins of life, or those threatened by the powerful and violent, are called needy or wretched *(ʿānî).* It is not probable that those would only be men. God's solidarity with the needy is ex-pressed in multiple ways in the First Testament (e.g., Pss 10:17; 12:5; 14:6; 22:24; and elsewhere; Jer 22:16; Isa 41:17; Gen 16:11; 29:32; Exod 2:23f.; 3:17; Deut 26:7; etc.). It is one of the fundamental experiences of the First Testament that God hears the cry out of the depth of misery and that he reassures the destitute of his presence and helps them out of their misery. We find many passages in the First Testament that speak of the distress of women (poverty, sexual violence, life in a foreign country, widowhood, difficult births, barrenness, being captured in wartime, etc.): to all these the word *ʿānî* can be applied.

In this sense the Psalms can readily function as prayers of hope for women, perhaps in the way that Flora Wanders initiates a dialogue between her own words and those of the psalm (see Kix 1996, 77):

> Hoping?
> My soul
> an abyss,
> deeper than deep . . .

There is nothing any more.
Life frozen,
dried up
dead?

Nothing but
emptiness,
solitude
ruins.

Hoping —
for what?!

"God,
you are my God, I search for you.
My soul thirsts for you,
my whole being
yearns for you
in a dry and weary land, where
there is no water.

My soul
clings to you;
Your right hand
holds me."
(Psalm 63:1 and 8)

LITERATURE

Bail, Ulrike. 1994. "'Vernimm, Gott, mein Gebet'. Ps 55 und Gewalt gegen Frauen." In *Feministische Hermeneutik und Erstes Testament. Analysen und Interpretationen,* edited by Hedwig Jahnow et al., 67-84. Stuttgart, Berlin, and Cologne.

———. 1996. "Die Klage einer Frau. Zu sprechen gegen das Schweigen. Sozialgeschichtliche Auslegung von Ps 55." *Junge Kirche* 3:154-57 and *Bibel und Kirche* 3:116-18.

———. 1998. *Gegen das Schweigen klagen. Eine intertextuelle Studie zu den Klagepsalmen Ps 6 und Ps 55 und der Erzählung von der Vergewaltigung Tamars.* Gütersloh.

Braun, Joachim. 1994. "Biblische Musikinstrumente." In *Die Musik in Geschichte und Gegenwart,* 1:1503-37. 2nd ed. Kassel.

Brenner, Athalya, and Fokkelien van Dijk-Hemmes. 1993. *On Gendering Texts: Female and Male Voices in the Hebrew Bible.* Leiden, New York, and Cologne.

Butting, Klara. 1996. "Das Ächzen wird zu Worten. Sozialgeschichtliche Bibelauslegung zu Psalm 12." *Junge Kirche* 1:27-30.

Elbogen, Ismar. 1995. *Der jüdische Gottesdienst in seiner geschichtlichen Entwicklung.* 2nd reprint of 3rd ed. Hildesheim, Zurich, and New York.

Engelken, Karen. 1990. *Frauen im Alten Israel. Eine begriffsgeschichtliche und sozialrechtliche Studie zur Stellung der Frau im Alten Testament.* Stuttgart et al.

Farmer, Kathleen A. 1992. "Psalms." In *The Women's Bible Commentary,* edited by Carol A. Newsom and Sharon H. Ringe, 137-44. London and Louisville.

Gerstenberger, Erhard S. 1994. "Weibliche Spiritualität in Psalmen und Hauskult." In *Ein Gott allein? JHWH-Verehrung und biblischer Monotheismus im Kontext der israelitischen und altorientalischen Religionsgeschichte,* edited by Walter Dietrich and Martin A. Klopfenstein, 349-63. Orbis biblicus et orientalis, vol. 139. Freiburg and Göttingen.

Goitein, Shelomo Dov. 1988. "Women as Creators of Biblical Genres." *Prooftexts* 8:1-33.

Higgins, Lynn A., and Brenda R. Silver. 1991. *Rape and Representation.* New York.

Keel, Othmar. 1984. *Deine Blicke sind Tauben. Zur Metaphorik des Hohen Liedes.* Stuttgarter Bibelstudien, vol. 114/115. Stuttgart.

Kix, Joachim, ed. 1996. *Ich hab' es niemand erzählt . . . Gedichte, Bilder und Texte zur Heilung sexuellen Mißbrauchs.* Kehl.

Maier, Christl. 1994. "Jerusalem als Ehebrecherin in Ezechiel 16. Zur Verwendung und Funktion einer biblischen Metapher." In *Feministische Hermeneutik und Erstes Testament. Analysen und Interpretationen,* edited by Hedwig Jahnow et al., 85-105. Stuttgart, Berlin, and Cologne.

Meyers, Carol. 1991. "Of Drums and Damsels: Women's Performance in Ancient Israel." *Biblical Archaeologist* 54:16-27.

Miller, Patrick D. 1993. "Things Too Wonderful: Prayer of Women in the Old Testament." In *Biblische Theologie und gesellschaftlicher Wandel,* edited by Georg Braulik, O.S.B., Walter Groß, and Sean McEvenue, 237-51. Festschrift for Norbert Lohfink, S.J. Freiburg, Basel, and Vienna.

Quell, Gottfried. 1967. "Struktur und Sinn des Psalms 131." In *Das ferne und das nahe Wort,* edited by Fritz Maass, 173-85. Festschrift for Leonhard Rost. Beihefte zur Zeitschrift für die alttestamentliche Wissenschaft, vol. 105. Berlin.

Rienstra, Marchiene Vroon. 1992. *Swallow's Nest: A Feminine Reading of the Psalms.* Grand Rapids.

Schroer, Silvia. 1996. *Die Weisheit hat ihr Haus gebaut. Studien zur Gestalt der Sophia in den biblischen Schriften.* Mainz.

Schüngel-Straumann, Helen. 1996. *Denn Gott bin ich und kein Mann. Gottesbilder im Ersten Testament — feministisch betrachtet,* especially 63-71. Mainz.

Seybold, Klaus. 1978. *Die Wallfahrtspsalmen. Studien zur Entstehungsgeschichte von Ps 120–134.* Neukirchen-Vluyn.

Zenger, Erich. 1993a. "Ps 45. Der Zionkönig und seine Braut." In Frank-Lothar Hossfeld and Erich Zenger, *Die Psalmen I. Psalm 1–50,* 278-84. Neue Echter Bibel, Altes Testament, vol. 29. Würzburg.

———. 1993b. "Ps 46. JHWH als Schützer der Seinen und als universaler Friedensstifter." In Frank-Lothar Hossfeld and Erich Zenger, *Die Psalmen I. Psalm 1–50,* 284-89. Neue Echter Bibel, Altes Testament, vol. 29. Würzburg.

Ulrike Bail

For Further Reading

Bester, Dörte. 2007. *Körperbilder in den Psalmen. Studien zu Psalm 22 und verwandten Texten.* Forschungen zum Alten Testament, series 2, vol. 24. Tübingen.

Gillmayr-Bucher, Susanne. 2004. "Body Images in the Psalms." *Journal for the Study of the Old Testament* 28, no. 3:301-26.

Grohmann, Marianne. 2007. *Fruchtbarkeit und Geburt in den Psalmen.* Forschungen zum Alten Testament, vol. 53. Tübingen.

Maier, Christl. 2001. "Body Imagery in Psalm 139 and Its Significance for a Biblical Anthropology." *lectio difficilior* 2. http://www.lectio.unibe.ch.

Translated by Tina Steiner

Proverbs: How Feminine Wisdom Comes into Being

Christl Maier

> *Wisdom has built her house,*
> *she has hewn her seven pillars. (Prov 9:1)*

Forms and Themes of This Book

The seven collections in the book of Proverbs, each identified by a heading, may be said to represent the seven pillars of the wisdom of Israel. With one exception (31:1), the headings name male authors. First is Solomon, also introduced as author of the book (1:1; 10:1; 25:1); next is a group called "the wise" (22:17; 24:23); and finally there is a foreign-born teacher of wisdom named Agur (30:1).

The book contains various kinds of texts that are also encountered in the wisdom traditions of Egypt and Mesopotamia: one- and two-line proverbs, numerical sayings, admonitions or instructions, and wisdom poems. Maxims about right speaking (12:6; 16:24; 25:11) appear together with others about appropriate behavior toward parents and fellow human beings (10:1; 17:21; 14:21; 17:17), with occasional references to the animal world for the sake of comparison (27:8; 30:24-31). The life of the peasant (10:4-5; 12:11; 20:4) is of just as much interest as that of the king (16:10-15; 25:2-3). The structure of the book suggests a distinction between the proverbial wisdom of chapters 10–30 and the didactic wisdom of the sayings and poems in chapters 1–9 and 31. Both are oriented toward practical experience, toward instructing the individual man or woman about sensible behavior. According to this code, that person is wise *(ḥākām)* who understands his or her profession or trade (Prov 22:29; cf. Exod 31:3), who knows good counsel (Prov 16:21; cf. 2 Sam 14:2); also wise are those who assert themselves with cunning (Prov 17:8; cf. 2 Sam 13:3). Many proverbs assign to particular actions a corresponding consequence to the person, for example:

> Whoever digs a pit will fall into it,
>> and a stone will come back on the one who starts it rolling. (Prov 26:27)

Early research saw a "doctrine of revenge" behind such proverbs, or an automatic causal relationship between action and consequence. However, as with similar sayings in Egyptian wisdom literature, the connection between action and consequence should be attributed to the principle of "connective justice" (Assmann 1990, 283): "Attributing the deed to the doer, whether good or evil, is . . . dependent on the understanding of justice prevalent in a society. One might say it depends on the 'communicative constitution' of the social world. Thus it is a matter of culture, not nature, and the human being is continually called upon to put it into action" (Assmann 1990, 178).

According to this principle, a society is thus based on justice if its members are not lethargic, deaf, and greedy, but act on one another's behalf, listen to and think of one another. Thus many proverbs that are formulated as statements should be understood as instruction in solidarity as a behavioral attitude. For example:

> Those who are generous are blessed,
>> for they share their bread with the poor. (Prov 22:9)[1]

The principle of remembering the good and evil deeds of an individual and acting accordingly toward that person presupposes social memory and the embedding of individuals in families and in the people as a whole. By contrast, not a single text of the proverbial wisdom speaks of YHWH as the highest guardian of the social order who would impose, or guarantee, a causal relationship between action and consequence to the person. Instead, God "is consciously introduced . . . in the concrete instance of conflict between two persons and named as a third party" (Hausmann 1995, 242).

The findings of previous research on Proverbs are as varied and diverse as the texts themselves. For example, the origin of the proverbial sayings collected in Proverbs is contested. Only Proverbs 22:17–23:11 has direct parallels in an Egyptian book of instruction. In view of the wisdom schools in Mesopotamia and Egypt, most scholars locate the source of proverbial wisdom in the royal court of Israel with its presumed training of officials and its diplomatic connections with neighboring peoples (Whybray 1995, 19-21). Other scholars see the majority of the proverbs in chapters 10–30 as derived from the experience of the clan elders because of their aphoristic character and the references to agrarian economy (Gerstenberger; cf. Whybray 1995, 27). A comparison with proverbs of African cultures supports this view (Westermann; Golka; cf. Whybray 1995, 30-32). The clans' experiences re-

---

1. NRSV departs here from the German cited by the author, which, literally translated, reads: "Whoever has a kind eye will be blessed, for he gave of his bread to the one who had less."

flected in the proverbs were likely transmitted orally and later recorded and collected at the royal court (cf. 25:1). Also of interest to scholars is the question whether Proverbs is "secular," an anomaly in the First Testament belief in salvation (Preuss; cf. Whybray 1995, 126-27), or whether it presupposes faith in YHWH as Creator of the world (cf. Camp 1985, 151-58). In view of the principle of connective justice, I find the theory of a later theologizing of originally secular wisdom obsolete, based as it is on a scant number of proverbs referring to YHWH.

It is hardly possible to establish exact dates for the texts, because they lack references to Israelite institutions and historical events. The majority of scholars now argue that although a few individual proverbs from chapters 10–30 may date back to the premonarchic period (1100-1000 B.C.E.), the proverbial wisdom largely originated over a longer period in the tenth to seventh centuries B.C.E., and the instruction in chapters 1–9 and 31 in the postexilic period from the fifth to third centuries B.C.E. (Schwienhorst-Schönberger 1995, 260). In my reading I attempt to show that the proverbs and teachings are not timeless and universally valid, but that at least some reflect the interests of historically and sociologically definable circles in the respective audience.

The Greek translators of the book clearly pursue different interests and lines of questioning. This is demonstrated by approximately 150 instances in which their translation differs from the text handed down in Hebrew, which they frequently paraphrase or add to. Additionally, the Greek translation, which should be dated in the second century B.C.E., establishes a different order after Proverbs 24:22 (30:1-14; 24:23-34; 30:15-33; 31:1-9 and 25-29; 31:10-31). It is unclear to date which order represents the original version (Whybray 1995, 161).

"Give Her a Share in the Fruit of Her Hands, and Let Her Works Praise Her in the City Gates" (Proverbs 31:31) — the Feminist Interpretation of Proverbs

Until now feminist research on Proverbs has focused primarily on individual women figures in the collections that form the frame of the book, Proverbs 1–9 and 31, or on particular themes. With the help of the category of gender, feminist interpretations study the representation and evaluation of women's and men's roles in the texts. Two distinct approaches are taken here. Feminist biblical scholars like Carol Newsom, whose interest is literary criticism, analyze the structure and message of the text and emphasize its literary references to other texts. In my view, a model study for the interpretation of Proverbs in this first context is the method of Athalya Brenner and Fokkelien van Dijk-Hemmes known as "gendering texts." In looking for traces of women's culture, they probe the texts for voices that represent the "female gender" (F-voice) or "the masculine gender" (M-voice). Using a critique of patriarchy to analyze opinions reflected in the texts, they uncover the voices of women that had often been silenced. Quite distinct from this approach is the historically and theologically oriented interpretation of texts, in particular those about Lady Wisdom, for example, in studies by Claudia Camp, Silvia Schroer, and Gerlinde Baumann. These scholars organize the texts by historical period and investigate the texts' contribution to the theology of their respective time period. The focus of their interest is the significance of female imagery for the image of God.

My interpretation attempts to combine major features of both of these approaches. It brings greater depth to the historical approach by asking social-historical questions, looking at the material objects and situations described in the texts as evidence for the economic and social conditions reflected in individual proverbs on the one hand, and longer instructions on the other. In my view, one cannot look for elements that liberate or oppress women before clarifying as far as possible the social-historical context in which the texts originated. My interpretation is based on the approach of Brenner and van Dijk-Hemmes, in that I seek to analyze how gender roles in the different layers of text are evaluated. I also follow their approach insofar as I understand these distinct voices as a discourse among different circles in which the texts were known, as an exchange of opinion on a literary level. Beginning with the older proverbs, I will trace a possible process by which this book may have emerged. In so doing I will treat the statements about women in the order they appear in the collections in chapters 10–30; 1–9; and 31. I will discuss the feminist "fruits" of this study after the last section, and finally in a summary.

"House and Wealth Are Inherited from Parents, but a Prudent Wife Is from YHWH" (Proverbs 19:14) — Women in Proverbs 10–30

In the maxims of proverbial wisdom (Prov 10–30) we find women portrayed as mothers, life partners, widows, and prostitutes, that is, in their relationships with men. The proverbs constantly speak about women, not to them, and primarily name problems that occur in the interactions of man and woman, with the woman not infrequently described as the instigator of arguments.

The mother of sons (daughters are mentioned only in 31:29) takes second place after the father in child raising and is to be honored like the father. Yet there is a striking division of labor. The father is assigned pride over the good son, while the mother is to fret about the one who has gone astray:

> A wise child makes a glad father,
>> but a foolish child is a mother's grief. (10:1; cf. 23:22, 25)

The married woman is viewed in relation to her usefulness to the family as a living unit:

A good wife is the crown of her husband,
  but she who brings shame is like rottenness in his bones. (12:4)

Like a gold ring in a pig's snout
  is a beautiful woman without good sense. (11:22)

The crown as a visible symbol of royal power (cf. 2 Sam 12:30) is used meta-phorically in Proverbs 12:4 to signify the high value of a diligent woman as life partner. To be sure, a woman's beauty is often praised (cf. Gen 12:11; 29:17; Job 42:15), but not sufficiently to characterize a "good" partner. She should be beauti-ful and clever at the same time, like Abigail, the wife of Nabal (1 Sam 25:3; cf. Prov 11:16). She knows the right thing to do at the right time. The man's "good" partner is thus beautiful, diligent, and clever.

These proverbs articulate experiential knowledge of an agricultural tribal cul-ture with households that are largely oriented toward raising their own food (cf. Meyers 1988), as it existed in Israel into the late monarchic period of the seventh century B.C.E. Women prepare the daily meals, spin, weave, and keep the house clean. As mothers of many children, they are responsible for the children's early education. The partnership of men and women is clearly characterized as eco-nomically based, according to Proverbs 10–29. There is not a single mention of love between the marriage partners. The fact that domestic partnership can also fail is a predominant theme. Thus five proverbs immediately name an argumenta-tive woman who makes life difficult for her male counterpart:

A continual dripping on a rainy day
  and a contentious wife are alike. (27:15)

It is better to live in a corner of the housetop
  than in a house shared with a contentious wife.
                                    (21:9; cf. also 19:13; 21:19; 25:24)

The concept *mādôn* (strife, contention) occurs almost exclusively in the pro-verbial wisdom, always in a negative connotation. It connotes the kind of conten-tiousness that destroys community or partnership, the kind that arises from rage (15:18; 29:22), greed (28:25), intrigue (16:28; cf. 6:14), or slander (26:20). The com-parison with continuously dripping water and the plural *mĕdônîm* or *midyānîm* characterize the woman as constantly arguing. Once rainwater has penetrated through the flat roof made of crossbeams of wood and straw plus a layer of mud, water, lime mortar, and chaff, a house quickly becomes uninhabitable. A con-stantly contentious woman is just as destructive to a family, so that several prov-erbs contend that living in the corner of the roof (21:9) or even in the desert (21:19) is more tolerable for the man. The judgment of the female life partner here occurs from the perspective of the male head of the family and the patriarch. Only women, who subject themselves to the lord of the household, are described as "good" (cf. Prov 13:24; 23:26), but so are sons who do so.

Since sexual relations of men with other women also endanger the cohesiveness of the home and the family, they are rejected in Proverbs. In this context the negative view of prostitutes and "alien" women[2] is taken over from the ancient Near Eastern wisdom tradition. "Whoever loves a street girl will have his purse slit open at the side" (Teaching of Anch-Scheschonki 22:1, cited by Brunner 1988, 286).

> For a prostitute *(zônâ)* is a deep pit;
>> an adulteress *(nokrîyâ)* is a narrow well.
> She lies in wait like a robber
>> and increases the number of the faithless. (Prov 23:27-28; cf. also 22:14)

The metaphors of well and pit connote oppression, even mortal danger. The comparison with the robber should be understood as a warning about loss of wealth (cf. 29:3).

With a view to the woman as widow, Proverbs 23:10 passes on the prohibition against violating the borders of a widow, well known from the Egyptian instruction of Amenemope (7:11ff.; cf. Brunner 1988, 241). That is, it prohibits taking possession of the land of a woman living without male support. Thus Proverbs, too, reinforces the idea of YHWH as protector of the weak that is widespread elsewhere in the First Testament. If Proverbs 15:25 describes YHWH as the one who sets the boundary for the widow, then any and every violation or movement of the boundary at the cost of the widow is considered a transgression against God's own boundaries.

Most of the proverbs in which a woman is named at all have conflict as their theme. Only two maxims speak almost without reservation of the woman as something good. And it is precisely these two that bring God into the formula: whoever finds a good life partner can be called blessed by God (Prov 18:22; 19:14; author's translation).[3] The life partnership of husband and wife is thus declared to be the lifestyle desired by God and the presupposed basis for the preservation of families, without any instruction for the husbands about their contribution to the success of such cooperative relationships.

So all in all, it is striking that in the proverbial wisdom, women are viewed exclusively from an androcentric perspective. The maxims discussed here can be characterized with Brenner as "M-voice," offering no reference to the self-understanding of women, and consciously judging the relationships between hus-

2. Where the NRSV and other English translations of passages discussed here have "adulteress," the Hebrew *nokrîyâ* is rendered in German as *fremde Frau* or *Fremde*, which can refer to any female stranger or foreigner, but in this context also traditionally carried the connotation of "loose woman." Cf. especially also note 5 below.

3. NRSV: "He who finds a wife finds a good thing and obtains favor from the LORD."

bands and wives one-sidedly (Brenner 1993, 197). At the same time, Brenner suggests a reading of these statements as F-texts. Based on what we can assume to be the historical and social background of the proverbial wisdom, this seems justified for some of the proverbs: the maxims about the life partner of the husband can be interpreted as an appreciation of the contribution of women to the preservation and propagation of extended families. The proverbs about prostitutes and "foreign" or "other" women, however, can hardly be understood, contrary to their message, as examples of the power of women. From a feminist point of view, the fact that women are blamed for broken relationships conceals the reality of power relationships in a patriarchal society.

"Hear, My Child, Your Father's Instruction and Do Not Reject Your Mother's Teaching" (Proverbs 1:8) — the Function and Dating of Proverbs 1–9 and 31

While the naming of women in Proverbs 10–30 threatens to get drowned out in a flood of themes, women do play the leading roles in Proverbs 1–9 and 31. The appeal cited in the heading "Hear, My Child" also occurs in Egyptian instructions that were written by officials or kings and addressed to biological sons or pupils (Brunner 1988, 72-73). What is unique, on the other hand, is that in 1:8, 6:20, and 3:1 the mother is expressly named as teacher.

I agree with Claudia V. Camp that Proverbs 1–9 is to be understood as an introduction to reading the rest of the book. Together with Proverbs 31, these chapters constitute a literary frame that integrates the heterogeneous collections into a new perspective of the whole. In this totality the metaphors of personified Wisdom and the "stranger" or "other" woman[4] serve as religious symbols intended to heal the devastations of the ethos and worldview of the postexilic period (Camp 1985, 282 and 290-91). With Gerlinde Baumann, I see the frame of Proverbs as an entity developed over time with quite diverse messages in terms of content. The foundational layer of the collection in Proverbs 1–9 is comprised of ten speeches of admonishment or instruction that are addressed to a limited circle of young men prior to their social interaction with socially marginalized people of the male sex (1:8-19; 4:10-19; 4:20-27; cf. 2:12-15), and especially of the female sex (5:1-23; 6:20-35; 7:1-27; cf. 2:16-20). The purpose of the speeches is to warn the audience about such contacts and recommend to them a certain relationship with God (3:1-2) as well as a way of behaving toward other people (3:21-35). Wisdom is only personified to some extent (cf. 3:13-18; 4:5-9) and urged upon the listeners as a source of help in life. Independent of these speeches are two first-person speeches of personified Wisdom (1:20-33; 8:1-36) that define the limits of the phenomenon of wisdom and system-

4. Cf. note 2 above.

atize the statements of the collections of proverbs in chapters 10–30 (Baumann 1996b, 144-45). Instructions and first-person speeches are connected by the parallel themes of the alien woman/folly and Wisdom. A later revision introduces two additional women figures in chapter 31 who combine aspects of the women from Proverbs 1–9. This revision corrects the juxtaposition of the two women figures of chapter 9. Finally, 1:1-7 is drafted as a heading for the entire book, and 9:7-12 as a transition to chapters 10 and following (cf. Baumann 1996b, 146 with a somewhat different sequencing of layers). The frame texts of Proverbs mirror a discourse among diverse circles of educated citizens of the Persian province of Yehud from the first decades of the fourth century B.C.E. The theme of the debate is how one should rightly understand wisdom, which is interpreted quite practically as right living before God and in the community. Implicitly, the texts before us offer diverse images of women and varied opinions about the role of women and men.

From a social-historical point of view, the significance of women increases in the postexilic period. Since Judah exists without a kingdom, but with limited self-governance under Persian rule, the extended family becomes the fundamental unit of social interaction, as it had been already in the premonarchic period (Albertz 1992, 474). This connects back to the norms of clan solidarity. In postexilic narrative texts, however, women are active not only in the realm of home and family. As members of the Jewish community, they participate in socially and politically important tasks such as the building of the Jerusalem wall (Neh 3:12), the discussion about debt relief (Neh 5:1-5), and the reading of the law (Neh 8:2-3). Individual women are called temple servants (Ezra 2:55) or prophets (Neh 6:14). Above and beyond these roles, late additions to laws (Num 36) and narrative texts (Job 42:15) recognize women as legal heirs. The temple, rebuilt in the midst of great economic difficulties, is the religious center of the postexilic community (cf. Haggai; Ezra 4–6). The discussion of mixed marriages that is described polemically in Ezra 9–10 and Nehemiah 13 points to mechanisms of marginalization between groups within the community. About the middle of the fifth century B.C.E. there was clearly an economic crisis in the province of Yehud that led to the indebtedness of a majority of the farmers (cf. Neh 5: Crüsemann 1985; Albertz 1992, 538-41). With the introduction of monetary taxes by the Persians, the agricultural products must first be sold. Thus they are subject to the principle of supply and demand, that is, their prices fall precisely when the harvest is good. Since the small Judean province of Yehud is located off the beaten track, it hardly benefits from the growth of international trade, and therefore loses in economic standing. Along with the economic crisis there arises a social crisis. Only a few groups in the upper class support the poorer population by offering them interest-free loans and legal support, as the social laws of the Torah command. The texts in Proverbs do not directly report such historical background information. However, the judgments forming the basis of their instruction in Proverbs 1–9 and Proverbs 31 are tangible if one keeps this social-historical situation in mind.

"Come, Let Us Take Our Fill of Love until Morning; Let Us Delight Ourselves with Love" (Proverbs 7:18) — the Warning about the "Other" Woman *(Fremde Frau)*[5]

Four instructions (Prov 2:16-20; 5:1-23; 6:20-35; 7:1-27) warn a young man of a mysterious woman who is described in ever more concrete terms as the texts progress, who is showered with negative epithets. According to 2:17, she is unfaithful to her human companion (cf. 7:19) and toward her God. Only the person who is inclined to Wisdom and thus knows righteousness and justice can, from the perspective of this teacher, resist this figure who destroys community (2:6, 9, 16). The teaching in Proverbs 5 warns the male listener against the smooth words of the "other" woman and threatens him with the loss of his possessions and his good reputation in the community (5:9-14). Instead the teacher recommends that he discover his own wife as the source of satisfying sexuality (5:15-19). According to 6:20-35, the "other" woman has the power to fan the flames of passion that lead to adultery with a single bat of an eyelash. This warning, with its connections between key words, is reminiscent of the prohibitions of the Decalogue against stealing, coveting one's neighbor's wife, and committing adultery. In Proverbs 6:32-35 the listener is threatened with wounds and dishonor or legal proceedings, for example, social death. In Proverbs 7 the teacher, looking out a window, describes a scene intended to unmask the real face of the "other" woman: while the man of the house is away (7:19), she wanders the streets under the protection of dusk to lurk in waiting for her victim (7:9, 12). She persuades a spineless man with flattery and deceptive words (7:14-20) and entices him into her house and onto her bed that has been arranged with fine quilts and perfumes — presumably a reference to Potiphar's wife (Gen 39:7-12). The warning is reinforced by drastic metaphors, representing the "other" woman's house as the antechambers to the underworld (Prov 7:26-27; cf. 2:18-19; 5:4-6; 9:18), and the woman herself as a murderous warrior (7:26). Although this imagery is reminiscent of the ancient Near Eastern love and war goddess Ishtar, the "other" woman in Proverbs 7 does not have the qualities of a deity, nor does she appear to worship a goddess. The association with foreign deities arises only implicitly. Thus the concept *nokrîyâ* is also applied to women who are accused of worshiping foreign gods (Ezra 9–10; Neh 13:26). Moreover, the description of the "other" woman in Proverbs 2:17 and 7:13 resonates with prophetic texts that use the metaphor of "adultery" to criticize the worship of foreign gods (Jer 3:3-5; 13:21, 25).

Thus the personification of the "other" woman unites several aspects of oth-

---

5. The connotation of the German term *fremde Frau* or *Fremde* is both "foreigner," "outsider," one from a different ethnic or social group, and "sexually promiscuous woman or prostitute," who violates the familiar norm (*fremd gehen* means sleeping with someone else's partner). We have translated it as "other" woman to suggest this double meaning. Cf. notes 2 and 4 above.

erness. She represents not only ethnically different women, as the word *nokrîyâ* implies. Since adultery is brought into view several times as a crime, the "other" woman, in the perspective of the teacher, potentially represents every woman who is positioned outside the family of the listener. Every woman who does not observe social conventions, who goes "abroad" and is not the sexual partner of just one man, can become an "other," a stranger. On a symbolic level, the figure at the same time connotes aggressive female sexuality and a fascination capable of sending one into ecstatic trances. "Other" as a *chiffre* connotes something mysterious and at the same time nonnormative.

In my opinion, the conservative perspective of the instructions, connecting back to the Torah commandments, represents the attempt in postexilic times to nurture traditional values of solidarity between extended families, to preserve inherited property and status, and at the same time to keep oversight over marriage and sexual relationships. The person delivering these instructions is defending the authority of the clan's elders. There is a warning against associating with foreign women, because this endangers an intact genealogy and bequests of property. There is also a warning against so-called crooked men from the upper class (Prov 1:8-19; 2:12-15) who ruthlessly enrich themselves and oppose the heads of families. The circle of those supporting the instructions can thus be assumed to be a group of educated laypeople of the urban upper class of Yehud who orient themselves to the values of the Torah, to righteousness and justice, and who instruct their sons accordingly. The teachings in Proverbs 1–9 mirror an affluent milieu in which property and privileged social status play an important role.

The portrait of the erotic and exotic woman who fans the flames of unbridled male desire, like that of the diligent wife and housekeeper from Proverbs 10–30, reveals a male perspective that is found in the novel and in encounters with other cultures down to the present time (Nützel 1994, 115-19). The literary and social-historical context of the teachings in Proverbs, however, shows that the portrait of the "other" woman definitely was not drawn only by men. The voice of the teacher in Proverbs 7 (cf. also Judg 5:28) includes that of the mother who is worried about her son. She assumes the androcentric perspective as the "female scolder" and in so doing supports the prevailing order (Brenner and van Dijk-Hemmes 1993, 57, 62). She is named as a teacher along with the father (Prov 1:8 and 6:20). Wisdom appears in Proverbs 7:4 as a sister of the listener, who is to protect him from association with the "other" woman. Thus both figures bring women into the patriarchal discourse and thus make them supporters of the prevailing order. This order aims for social control of the sexual behavior of women (Camp 1991, 26). Since the boundaries between the behavior of the "other" woman and her true nature are fluid, the instructions develop a defamatory and marginalizing effect. From a feminist point of view this cannot be accepted without objection, even if other female figures are represented positively. Moreover, the problematic image of women in the instructions is corrected by the figure of Wisdom and the later texts in Proverbs 31.

"I Have Good Advice and Sound Wisdom; I Have Insight, I Have Strength" (Proverbs 8:14) — Wisdom Introduces Herself

In contrast to the portrait of woman as seductress, a figure introduces herself in the first-person speeches of Proverbs 1:20-33 and 8:1-36; she combines diverse, positively valued women's roles and has features of ancient Near Eastern goddesses. Wisdom has great significance for the postexilic image of God, since she is associated with the Creator God. Through the stylistic device of personification, understood as a sub-category of metaphor (Camp 1985, 214-15; Schroer 1996, 38-39), the many different aspects of Wisdom are brought together into one entity. At the same time, the personification generalizes the diversity. She can only be understood when the abstract concept "wisdom" finds its correspondence in concrete "women."

Precursors of the figure of Wisdom (cf. Schroer 1996, 63-89) in the function of a wise woman or counselor (8:6-12) are the Israelite wives who advise their husbands, like Sarah (Gen 16), Rebekah (Gen 24), Michal (1 Sam 19), and Bathsheba (1 Kings 1). The wisdom of the wise woman from Tekoa (2 Sam 14) and the mother of the king (1 Kings 2:13-23) is comparable to the political adviser of kings. Wisdom appears with her instruction in the city gate and in public places in the city (Prov 1:20-21; 8:1-3), and in this way recalls the wise woman from Abel of Beth-maacah (2 Sam 20) who is able to prevent the destruction of the city by her persuasive speech. The prophetic function of wisdom manifests itself in her public reproofs of those who do not follow her instruction (Prov 1:20-33). Moreover, like the prophets, she advocates for righteousness and justice: the root *ṣdq* (to be just) occurs five times in Proverbs 8 (cf. 2:9). Wisdom's speech is straightforward and full of the knowledge of what is good (8:6-9). Her godlike authority is shown, too, in the fact that she promises wealth (8:19, 21) and security in life (1:33) to those who follow her instruction (regarding her audience, cf. Baumann 1996a, 75-78).

The contrast between the "other" woman and the figure of Wisdom is taken to its extreme in the poem in Proverbs 9:1-6, 13-18. To be sure, the negative figure is called "foolish woman" *(Frau Torheit),* but in both linguistic usage and characterization she is identical with the "other" woman. The words with which Lady Wisdom *(Frau Weisheit)* and Lady Folly *(Frau Torheit)* invite men into their houses sound almost identical: "You who are inexperienced [author's translation],[6] turn in here" (9:4, 16). Lady Wisdom is presented as an industrious homeowner and lady of high social standing who invites guests to a feast she has prepared. By instructing the inexperienced (9:6), she turns her house into a "house of instruction" *(Lehrhaus)* in the broader sense. This conception shows the beginning of a development that leads to the Jewish *Lehrhaus* as a place of religious teaching. By contrast, Lady Folly is described as a prostitute known all over town as one who destroys community. Her proverbial saying,

---

6. NRSV: "You who are simple . . ."

"Stolen water is sweet,
   and bread eaten in secret is pleasant" (9:17),

suggests that the reception she has prepared satisfies only sexual needs. Wisdom and Folly in Proverbs 9 stand for two directions one can follow on life's path. They give the male audience the choice between a meaningful life and one of social marginalization. Proverbs 9 thus provides images to illustrate individual sentences from the proverbial wisdom, such as Proverbs 14:1:

The wisdom of women has built their house,
   but folly tears it down with her hands. (author's translation; cf. 24:3)

The figure of Wisdom, besides recalling these characteristics of human antecedents, is also reminiscent of ancient Near Eastern goddesses. For instance, the poem about Wisdom in 3:13-26 that praises her as a tree of life belongs to the tradition of the life-giving and protective tree goddess. The self-laudatory first-person verses are structurally comparable to the Song of Praise of the Goddess Isis (Kayatz 1996, 89, 92). In Proverbs 8:30-31, Wisdom presents herself as a young woman acting playfully before the Creator God, a role also played by the Egyptian goddess Ma'at before the sun god Re, in which there is certainly also an erotic element (cf. Keel 1974, 63-70). But whereas Ma'at is seen as standing for the social and cosmic order, the figure of Wisdom in Proverbs 8 only knows and represents this order, without being identical with it (Baumann 1996a, 288). The primary evidence for this is Proverbs 8:22-31, which praises Wisdom as having been present at the creation, and as the mediating figure between God and human beings. In this section, unlike in Genesis 1–3, God and human beings are not at the center of creation. Wisdom is referred to as YHWH's first creature, who, as an "expert in world order" (Baumann 1996a, 151), of course knows about cosmic and human order. Above all, through her speech, she mediates a just social order by showing human beings a way of life pleasing to YHWH.

The figure of Wisdom is neither described as a goddess beside the God of Israel nor explicitly subordinated to YHWH. Yet YHWH is represented as one who acts gynecomorphically, bringing wisdom into the world amidst pains of childbirth (*ḥyl*, 8:24); YHWH weaves her (*nsk*, 8:23), practicing something attributed primarily to women (Baumann 1996a, 140-43). According to Proverbs 8:27-29, YHWH creates the world as a place for Wisdom to live, just as human parents prepare a home for their children. In the figure of the frolicking daughter, Wisdom represents God's intimacy with and care for human beings (Yee 1992, 95). In Proverbs 8:17, 21, Wisdom's love for those who seek her is described in words very similar to the way YHWH's love for human beings is described (cf. Baumann 1996a, 98-102). Although there are erotic connotations at play in the relationship of those seeking wisdom with Wisdom herself (1:28; 2:4; 3:13; 8:17), these do not take center stage. In texts that name Wisdom and Folly, or Wisdom and the "other" woman, in the same context, Wisdom is not eroticized; she is praised as a sister and kinswoman (7:4) or as a host of high social status (9:1-6).

If one understands the figure of Wisdom in Camp's sense as a way of systematizing the phenomenon of wisdom, two things are noteworthy. On the one hand, with her knowledge of the order of the world, wisdom represents the common sense of proverbial wisdom. On the other hand, wisdom-related phenomena such as magic and divination, as well as the kinds of counseling and lifestyles that exert a hurtful influence on others, are judged negatively. According to Proverbs 1–9, the only kinds of counsel and action counted as wisdom are those that take as their model the speech and actions of feminine wisdom.

The circle with a stake in these first-person speeches is aiming for insight, not intimidation of the audience. It is interculturally oriented, does not hesitate to refer positively to the goddess tradition, and does not share the proverbial saying's fears of foreign or foolish women or customs. It draws a female figure of almost supernatural dimensions who takes the place of YHWH in her attention to human beings (Baumann 1996a, 100). But in its personification, the ideal figure of Wisdom remains connected with human women. She is always an accessible mediator who advocates for righteousness and justice, and for a way of life oriented to the Torah.

Does the voice of the figure of Wisdom represent an F-voice that breaks through patriarchy? Does the future of women's spirituality lie with this figure? One must not overlook the fact that Wisdom, too, stands within a patriarchal framework (Newsom 1989, 157) and can thus be called a "poster child for the dominant male culture" (Brenner and van Dijk-Hemmes 1993, 54). However, with her diverse ways of speaking and acting, she is a living argument for recognizing the significance of women's roles for community. Synthesizing divine and human wisdom (cf. Baumann 1996b, 148), she simultaneously breaks open a strictly monotheistic image of God and links "the God of Israel with the experience and life of women in Israel especially . . . , and what is more, with the images and roles of the Ancient Near Eastern goddesses" (Schroer 1996, 42).

"A Strong Woman, Who Can Find Her?" (Proverbs 31:10 [Author's Translation])[7] — the "Other" Woman as a Mother Giving Wise Counsel and as a Mirror of the Figure of Wisdom in Proverbs 31

The seemingly clear distinction between Wisdom and the foreign, "other," or foolish woman, between the good and evil life companion, is invalidated in the concluding chapter of the book with the help of two other women figures. Proverbs 31 thus continues the discourse about true wisdom with a new accent.

7. NRSV has "A capable wife who can find?"

In Proverbs 31:1-9 we find the mother of Lemuel, the king of Massa, giving counsel to her son. As a personal and political adviser, the foreign queen mother warns her son about sexual contact and drinking bouts: "Do not give your strength *(hayil)* to women" (31:3). She assumes the role of the teacher from Proverbs 7, the position of the worried Israelite mother. At the same time, the mother of the king brings home to her son the importance of judging righteously and defending the rights of the destitute (31:8-9). She advocates for those of weak social status and thus makes tangible the ethical admonition of the figure of wisdom in Proverbs 1 and 8.

The poem in Proverbs 31:10-31, the twenty-two verses each of which begins with a letter of the Hebrew alphabet, also connects features of the "other" or foolish woman with the figure of Wisdom. The woman of strength *('ēšet hayil)* who is praised here stands out because of precisely the same perfection and power that the son of the king (31:3) is admonished not to give away to women. The concept of *hayil* expresses physical and mental strength and courage. The only woman in the First Testament who is assigned the title of respect "strong woman" is Ruth the Moabite (Ruth 3:11). The song of praise is intentionally multidimensional. On the one hand it names activities of a real woman; on the other hand it refers to the figure of Wisdom in Proverbs 1–9. There are strikingly frequent references to the figure of Wisdom from Proverbs 9:1-6 building a house and preparing a meal. Like her, the strong woman tends to feeding and educating the people for whom she is responsible (Schroer 1996, 34-37). Both women bring wealth and honor to the men around them; thus they are more worthy than corals (8:11; 31:10). With her wide range of activities, the strong woman acts like the head of a household and a farmstead from the premonarchical time, with male and female servants. Thus in the sense of the proverbial wisdom, she is a "wise" life partner (cf. 14:1; 18:22; 24:3), and one might ask what her husband actually contributes to earn his living.

Moreover, there are also aspects of the "other" woman in the way this woman is characterized: the comparison of the woman with merchant ships (31:14) and the fact that she possesses imported fabric and purple dye (31:22) make her appear as a Phoenician woman who has contacts with foreign dealers like the foreign woman in 5:9-10. The coverings she makes for herself (31:22) are conceptually identical to those in the house of the foreign woman (7:16). With perfumes and fine fabrics, both women have imported luxury goods that indicate the Persian era when trade in such wares was blossoming. That trade was carried on by Phoenicians, so that the mention of Tyrian fish traders in Jerusalem in Nehemiah 13:16 does not seem unusual. Additionally, the strong woman independently undertakes legal business, buying a field and a vineyard (Prov 31:16). This is not documented for women until the postexilic period, for example, in documents of the Jewish military colony on the Nile island of Elephantine from the fifth century B.C.E. (cf. Eskenazi 1992).

But does Proverbs 31:10-31 not represent an unattainable ideal (Camp 1985,

92)? What woman is active on so many fronts, and so inexhaustible? Is the question that introduces this section beginning in verse 10 not already a mere rhetorical question, intended to be answered in the negative (Hausmann 1992, 262, with cross-references to Job 38; Ps 88)? In my view, the text speaks here not about an individual woman, but of a generalized set of diverse characteristics, as with the personified figure of Wisdom. The surface structure of the text, which names activities of real women, does not contradict its deep structure, which refers to the figure of Wisdom. Instead, the very fact of listing women's *options* for action becomes in sum a manual for Wisdom action. After all, this text is claiming that wisdom can be experienced and lived by human beings, that it becomes real in strong women. When men and women inscribe aspects of the "other" woman into their portrait of the strong woman, they correct the juxtaposition of Wisdom and the "other" woman. The figure of the foreign queen as a scolding mother, too, contradicts the division into good and wicked in Proverbs 1–9. Of course, even the figures in Proverbs 31 remain ambivalent. For example, the oracle of the queen mother in 31:3 contains the prejudicial attitude that men's sexual relations with women rob them of physical and mental strength. Moreover, the strong woman's activities, no matter how self-sufficiently carried out, are all tied to her husband, her sons, and her daughters; she pays for "her praise in the gates" (31:31) with a considerable dose — from today's perspective — of self-exploitation.

How Feminine Wisdom Is to Be Honored — an Attempt

A major theme of the proverbial sayings, maxims, and poems in Proverbs is how women speak and act. Granted, the introductory chapters 1–9 affirm the juxtaposition between the good and the wicked life partner, but the distinction between the two lies in whether the instructions are heard and followed. The figure of the "other" or "foreign" woman represents various relationships between man and woman outside marriage and is judged as disruptive to the community. Personified Wisdom combines features and activities of real as well as literary figures and gives them the status of subjects. At the same time, Wisdom brings female imagery into the postexilic image of God. Not until the final chapter is the division between Wisdom and the "other" woman broken down, in that the foreign queen mother and the strong woman bring together traits of both figures.

A fascinating feature of these women figures from the diverse circles of educated laypeople in Yehud is that the older tradition is not erased, but preserved, and that models that contradict one another are passed on in creative ways. Only by discovering this can one begin to see the differences in women's lives on the one hand, and to see a feminine image of God on the other hand. In my opinion, the diverse roles of women shown here should not be obliterated by the objection that the overall image of women in Proverbs remains stuck within a male perspective.

Precisely against the background of a patriarchally structured and group-oriented society, this text contains liberating potential by introducing independent action by a strong woman, and the figure of Wisdom bringing unity between women's lives and the image of God. In this context, even the sexual life choices of the "other" woman can be positively interpreted, albeit against the intention of the text. The representation of the Wisdom of Israel by women continues, even if the tradition is ascribed to a man, King Solomon (1:1), and listed under the principle of the fear of YHWH (1:7; 9:10; 31:30) with its male connotation.

Within the given patriarchal framework, the figure of Wisdom is introduced as participating in divine knowledge of the order of creation and society, and as mediator of a way of life oriented toward YHWH. Thus she is represented as the side of God that is turned toward human beings. Proverbs 1:20-33 and 8 document the fact that the postexilic image of God was not strictly monotheistic, as was assumed by previous scholarship. Personified Wisdom opens the possibility of biblically documented God speech that resorts to feminine metaphor. I agree with Silvia Schroer that with the help of this Wisdom figure, contemporary discussion of images of God should bring to the foreground the dimension of justice in social relations among people from different geographical, cultural, or religious groups (Schroer 1994, 107). In the Song of Praise for the strong woman, contact with foreigners is positively valued. The portrait of the strong woman changes the category "foreign," first used to marginalize, to a positive epithet. To achieve a just order between the sexes on the one hand, and between different social groups on the other, there is a need for many wise women (and men) in the sense of the book of Proverbs who speak and act like the Mediator Wisdom.

LITERATURE

Albertz, Rainer. 1992. *Religionsgeschichte Israels in alttestamentlicher Zeit.* Grundrisse zum Alten Testament, vol. 8, 2. Göttingen.

Assmann, Jan. 1990. *Ma'at. Gerechtigkeit und Unsterblichkeit im Alten Ägypten.* Munich.

Baumann, Gerlinde. 1996a. *Die Weisheitsgestalt in Proverbien 1–9. Traditionsgeschichtliche und theologische Studien.* Forschungen zum Alten Testament, vol. 16. Tübingen.

———. 1996b. "'Zukunft feministischer Spiritualität' oder 'Werbefigur des Patriarchats'? Die Bedeutung der Weisheitsgestalt in Prov 1–9 für die feministisch-theologische Diskussion." In *Von der Wurzel getragen. Christlich-feministische Exegese in Auseinandersetzung mit Antijudaismus,* edited by Luise Schottroff and Marie-Theres Wacker, 135-52. Leiden et al.

Brenner, Athalya. 1993. "Some Observations on the Figurations of Woman in Wisdom Literature." In *Of Prophets' Visions and the Wisdom of Sages,* edited by Heather A. McKay and David J. A. Clines, 192-208. Festschrift for R. N. Whybray. Journal for the Study of the Old Testament: Supplement Series, vol. 162. Sheffield.

Brenner, Athalya, and Fokkelien van Dijk-Hemmes. 1993. *On Gendering Texts: Female and Male Voices in the Hebrew Bible.* Leiden et al.

Brunner, Hellmut. 1988. *Altägyptische Weisheit. Lehren für das Leben.* Darmstadt.

Camp, Claudia V. 1985. *Wisdom and the Feminine in the Book of Proverbs.* Bible and Literature Series, vol. 11. Sheffield.

———. 1987. "Woman Wisdom as a Root Metaphor: A Theological Consideration." In *The Listening Heart,* edited by Kenneth G. Hoglund et al., 45-76. Festschrift for R. E. Murphy. Journal for the Study of the Old Testament: Supplement Series, vol. 58. Sheffield.

———. 1991. "What's So Strange about the Strange Woman?" In *The Bible and the Politics of Exegesis,* edited by David Jobling, Peggy L. Day, and Gerald T. Sheppard, 17-31. Festschrift for Norman K. Gottwald. Cleveland.

Crüsemann, Frank. 1985. "Israel in der Perserzeit. Eine Skizze in Auseinandersetzung mit Max Weber." In *Max Webers Sicht des antiken Christentums. Interpretation und Kritik,* edited by Wolfgang Schluchter, 205-32. Frankfurt am Main.

Eskenazi, Tamara C. 1992. "Out from the Shadows: Biblical Women in the Postexilic Era." *Journal for the Study of the Old Testament* 54:25-43.

Fontaine, Carole R. 1992. "Proverbs." In *The Women's Bible Commentary,* edited by Carol A. Newsom and Sharon H. Ringe, 145-51. London and Louisville.

Hausmann, Jutta. 1992. "Beobachtungen zu Spr 31,10-31." In *Alttestamentlicher Glaube und Biblische Theologie,* edited by Jutta Hausmann and Hans-Jürgen Zobel, 261-66. Festschrift for Horst Dietrich Preuss. Stuttgart et al.

———. 1995. *Studien zum Menschenbild in der älteren Weisheit.* Forschungen zum Alten Testament, vol. 7. Tübingen.

Heijerman, Mieke. 1994. "Who Would Blame Her? The 'Strange' Woman of Proverbs 7." In *Reflections on Theology and Gender,* edited by Fokkelien van Dijk-Hemmes and Athalya Brenner, 21-31. Kampen.

Kayatz, Christa. 1996. *Studien zu Proverbien 1–9. Eine form- und motivgeschichtliche Untersuchung unter Einbeziehung ägyptischen Vergleichsmaterials.* Wissenschaftliche Monographien zum Alten und Neuen Testament, vol. 22. Neukirchen-Vluyn.

Keel, Othmar. 1974. *Die Weisheit spielt vor Gott. Ein ikonographischer Beitrag zur Deutung des meṣaḥäqät in Spr 8,30f.* Fribourg and Göttingen.

Maier, Christl. 1995. *Die 'fremde Frau' in Proverbien 1–9. Eine exegetische und sozialgeschichtliche Studie.* Orbis biblicus et orientalis, vol. 144. Fribourg and Göttingen.

Meinhold, Arndt. 1991. *Die Sprüche.* 2 vols. Zürcher Bibelkommentare Altes Testament, vol. 16, 1 and 2. Zurich.

Meyers, Carol. 1988. *Discovering Eve: Ancient Israelite Women in Context.* Oxford.

Newsom, Carol A. 1989. "Woman and the Discourse of Patriarchal Wisdom: A Study of Proverbs 1–9." In *Gender and Difference in Ancient Israel,* edited by Peggy L. Day, 142-60. Minneapolis.

Nützel, Gerdi. 1994. "Der befremdende Blick auf die 'fremde Frau' in Proverbien 7." In *(Anti-)Rassistische Irritationen. Biblische Texte und interkulturelle Zusammenarbeit,* edited by Silvia Wagner, Gerdi Nützel, and Martin Kick, 115-36. Berlin.

Schroer, Silvia. 1994. "Zeit für Grenzüberschreitungen. Die göttliche Weisheit im nachexilischen Monotheismus." *Bibel und Kirche* 49:103-7.

———. 1996. *Die Weisheit hat ihr Haus gebaut. Studien zur Gestalt der Sophia in den biblischen Schriften.* Mainz.

Schwienhorst-Schönberger, Ludger. 1995. "Das Buch der Sprichwörter." In Erich Zenger et al., *Einleitung in das Alte Testament,* 255-84. Stuttgart et al.

Whybray, Roger Norman. 1995. *The Book of Proverbs: A Survey of Modern Study.* Leiden et al.

Yee, Gale A. 1992. "The Theology of Creation in Proverbs 8:22-31." In *Creation in Biblical Traditions,* edited by Richard J. Clifford and John J. Collins, 85-96. Catholic Biblical Quarterly Monograph Series, vol. 24. Washington, D.C.

FOR FURTHER READING

Camp, Claudia V. 2000. *Wise, Strange, and Holy: The Strange Woman and the Making of the Bible.* Journal for the Study of the Old Testament: Supplement Series, vol. 230. Sheffield.

Fischer, Irmtraud. 2006. *Gotteslehrerinnen. Weise Frauen und Frau Weisheit im Alten Testament.* Stuttgart.

Gorges-Braunwarth, Susanne. 2002. *"Frauenbilder — Weisheitsbilder — Gottesbilder" in Spr 1–9. Die personifizierte Weisheit im Gottesbild der nachexilischen Zeit.* Münster, Hamburg, and London.

Maier, Christl M. 2003. "'Frau Weisheit hat ihr Haus gebaut': Sozialgeschichtliche und feministische Aspekte weisheitlicher Theologie." In *Theologie des Alten Testaments aus der Perspektive von Frauen,* edited by Manfred Oeming, 223-41. Münster.

————. n.d. "Weisheit (Personifikation) (AT)." At www.wibilex.de.

Yoder, Christine Roy. 2001. *Wisdom as a Woman of Substance: A Socio-Economic Reading of Proverbs 1–9 and 31:10-31.* Beihefte zur Zeitschrift für die alttestamentliche Wissenschaft, vol. 304. Berlin and New York.

Translated by Nancy Lukens

Qoheleth (Ecclesiastes): Man Alone, without Woman

Kumiko Kato

Apart from an editorial opening and ending (the title in 1:1 and the epilogue, or epilogues, in 12:9-14), the text of the book of Ecclesiastes reflects a man's speech. The whole text from 1:2 to 12:8 is framed by the formula-like phrase ". . . said Qoheleth" (1:2 and 12:8) and is given cohesion through the identity of the speaker Qoheleth (see below, about 1:3-11). At the core of this man's monologue is the question of what makes for the happiness *(ṭôb)* of human beings.

Some exegetes accept without comment the perspective of the speaker's presentation, believing that the book is about human beings in general. But for a feminist perspective, it is problematic when the speaker draws conclusions about human beings in general and the world as a whole on the basis of his own experiences and insights. For his concrete description of the social phenomena that he primarily focuses on reveals his androcentric perspective. The contexts of women's lives and experiences do not show up in what he sees. Women are rarely mentioned; when they are it is never as active subjects.

And yet, there is something of note for feminist readers in this book. "Human beings" are portrayed less in situations of success or joy than in those of failure or evil, and in the very passages where woman is explicitly spoken of, a self-critical outlook of a man appears (7:23-25, 27-29). There the speaker makes it known that discontent and evil are neither an essential nor an unavoidable feature of the "human" condition but the result of the history of men's — males' — failures.

The interpretation of the book presented here is based in an insight gained not only from impulses in recent literary critique but also from my engagement with this book itself. There are several voices in the text, irrespective of whether it is the work of one or more authors. But "prevailing exegesis" suppresses these voices in order to be able to present a systematic teaching of the book. To put it more concretely still: the text is being read on the assumption that basically two voices are heard there speaking about human beings, an impersonal voice claiming general validity and another, personal voice of a man who has failed. The prevailing interpretation of Ecclesiastes subordinates the personal voice to the impersonal one, what is historical to what is generally valid. And in this fashion the teaching or philosophy of this work is established. But such a procedure masks the androcentric perspective of the text even more than the text itself does. For in the text, the speaker's perspective is made explicit by giving the I who is teaching a (fictive) location in history that keeps the point of view of his experiences and opinions in focus. But what in prevailing exegesis is presented as the book's teaching has the air of a generally valid philosophy, that is, of something gender-neutral. It is the task in what follows to liberate the personal voice from the demand for general validity and to hold up the self-critical perspective of a lost man.

Two Forms of Presentation

Three Framed Compositions

The most notable literary characteristic of Ecclesiastes is the form of speech, the first-person singular. It is introduced in 1:12 and shapes the passages of 1:12–2:26, 3:10–6:9, and 7:1–11:8. But this form is preceded by another form of presentation. In 1:3-11 there is a poem without reference to the first-person singular; it follows upon a question that opens the passage: "What does man gain from all the toil at which he toils under the sun?" (1:3, author's translation). The issue is whether human labor achieves anything that lasts. This question presupposes a specific image of the human being, namely, as a being who toils to obtain possessions. This image is clearly shaped in accordance to the social role of men.[1] True, combining the question with a poem (1:4-11) shifts it from the social into the cosmic domain. Since the poem juxtaposes the transitoriness of human beings (1:4a) with the eternal cyclical course of the cosmos (1:5-7), and then also emphasizes their inability to comprehend cosmic events (1:8), the answer to the question in 1:3 appears to be negative. The introductory passage thereby sets up a cosmic horizon within which that question is to be answered.

The idea that transitoriness is a constitutive dimension of human existence appears not only in the opening poem of the book but also in the one that concludes it (11:9–12:7). Both poems share common motifs such as those that picture transitoriness and cyclical occurrence: "to go" (*hlk* — 1:4, 6, and 7; 12:5), "to return" (*šûb;* 1:6; 12:2 and 7), "to turn around" (*sbb;* 1:6; 12:5), and "the sun" *(haššemeš)* signifying the sphere of life of humans and of life itself (1:3 and 5; 12:2). The theme of transitoriness, touched upon several times in the book though not

---

1. The root *ʿml* is used in Ecclesiastes less in reference to toil in general being an elementary condition of human life than to the efforts human beings make in order to gain possessions. The noun *ʿāmāl* means not only "toil" but also "possessions gained through toil" (cf. 2:11 and 18-22; 4:6 and 8; 5:14-15).

its sole topic, receives a particular emphasis through being framed by these two poems.

The outer frame of the book's body (1:2 and 12:8) also seems to highlight the transitory aspect of human existence. Even though the word *hebel*, "vanity," often used in both verses and throughout the book, does not mean transitoriness in every instance (e.g., in 8:14 it probably means something irrational or incomprehensible), the context of both verses before the opening and then after the concluding poem lifts up this aspect.

We encounter a similar composition in 3:1-9 as in 1:3-11. The question in 1:3 is taken up again after the poem (3:2-8) in 3:9, albeit in a somewhat changed form. The idea stated at the beginning (3:1) that for every affair in the world there is a season is paraphrased in the poem in the form of fourteen pairs of contrasting actions or conditions of human beings. According to one current interpretation, this passage shows that for every human action there is a season determined by an external source and that is why what happens in history is beyond human disposition. Like 1:3-11, 3:1-9 appears to lay out an ontological and anthropological foundation for an answer to the question of what profit there is in what humans do.

It is at this point that feminist readers ask: On whose experiences is that allegedly ontological and anthropological foundation based? On experiences common to both genders? Most exegetes answer the latter question with a yes and refer to the first word pair (3:2a), which in their estimation is of great significance. According to them, that word pair refers to the inescapable fact that all human beings experience birth and death. Every other word pair is to be read in light of this first one. But this interpretation of the verse is based less on the rules of the Hebrew language than on a certain preunderstanding. The verb in this verse, *yld* (qal), translated as "to be born" in some Bible translations and commentaries, is used in the Hebrew Bible generally with a feminine subject and means "to give birth." But according to the exegetes, the reason for rendering the verb in its passive form is that "to give birth" is not an aspect of what each and every "human" does. But the active form of that verb, the action of giving birth, actually matches the other verbs of the poem better; they all depict active deeds (cf. Helm 1989, 159; Brenner 1993, 147).

Nonetheless, it is too early to read the poem as if it had been oriented by women's experiences despite the fact that the list of human activities begins with an action that is associated more with women than with men in Hebrew (the verb *yld* may also mean "to beget"). What stands out is that violent and aggressive actions prevail in more than a few of the word pairs, as a reader sympathizing with feminists, Lothar Helm, has pointed out (cf. Helm 1989, 156f.). And Athalya Brenner has proposed a way of reading this poem with its strong allusions to violence and love (Brenner 1993). She focuses on the stanza of 3:5; its placement in the structure of the poem alone gives it an emphatic and central position. She draws attention to its enigmatic expressions such as "to throw away stones" and "to gather stones." Analyzing different levels of meaning, she develops a basis on which those expressions can be related to male sexual behavior. Since the parallel word pair, "to embrace and to refrain from embracing" alludes to an intimate and possibly erotic relationship, it is possible to give the entire verse 5 a sexual interpretation: there is a time to enjoy sexuality and a time to refrain from being with a woman. On the basis of that verse, the whole text may be associated metonymically with sexual love. In the light of this, the poem may be read as a love poem that portrays heterosexual relations from a male perspective: love and sexual desire are not constant but arise in life's polar vicissitudes.

Brenner's reading highlights the androcentric character of the poem, which in the context of the book forms the universal basis of its anthropology.

The third passage, 6:10-12, which once again takes up the question of 1:3 in 6:11, is less poetic in form. Still, we can discern a similar function, namely, to provide what follows in the book with an interpretative frame through ontological and anthropological assertions. The idea of naming (6:10a) is used to state that all events are beyond human disposition (cf. 3:1-9). Formulated in the passive tense, the verse suggests that this human inability to have things at our disposition has to be understood in relation to God (cf. 7:13-14).

Speaking in the Terms and Perspective of the First-Person Singular

Two themes are present in the three frame-compositions: the transitoriness of human beings (1:3-11) and the inability to have all events at our disposition (3:1-9; 6:10). Both are givens of human existence. This gives the book an interpretative frame, creating the impression that Qoheleth is about problems pertaining to humankind in general. But if read on their own, the three framed units of 1:12–2:26, 3:10–6:9, and 7:1–11:8 present a quite different profile.

The First-Person Singular Form   Following the opening poem, the "I" introduces itself (1:12). Here we meet the first-person singular form found throughout the book and in which are embedded the addresses to a second-person singular as well as the proverb-like statements dispersed in the body of the work. The first-person singular form presents the text's facts and judgments as the personal experiences and valuations of the speaker.

In ancient Egyptian didactic literature as well as in First Testament wisdom writing, what is said in the form of an address is an elementary tool of "instruction" as a traditional genre. Instruction is located in a dialogical situation that presupposes a particular I-You relation; in most cases a father or a mother speaks to his or her son (cf. the mother teaching her son Lemuel, Prov 31:1-9). Locating statements in a fictive dialogue is a distinct literary characteristic of an earlier phase of writing that is still beholden to a conception peculiar to oral culture:

communicating by word of mouth is normal and normative for human beings. This feature distinguishes wisdom instruction from the catechetical manner of presenting doctrines in the form of data and also from modern scientific discourse and its claim to objectivity.

The book of Ecclesiastes shares the skeptical position of wisdom teaching toward written communication void of reference to the person who is speaking. That is why it presents its teaching and ideas in the first-person singular form. By introducing itself, the "I" that speaks is fictively located in history and the speaker's subjectivity is not concealed. But there is a difference in the first-person singular form between this book and traditional teaching in that the one spoken to is neither explicitly named nor addressed as "my son" so that the relation between the one who speaks and the one spoken to is not transparent.

Experience Orientation   A large part of the units conceived in the first-person singular form has the same argument structure. It is twofold: first, a concrete situation or a general condition of human life is introduced, most often by the formula "I saw/I have seen," and described thereafter. This is followed by conclusions as to what is good for human beings (e.g., Eccles 3:10-15; 3:16-22; 4:1-3; 4:4-6; 4:7-12; 5:12-19 [Eng. 13-20]; 6:1-9; 7:15-22; 8:9-15). This structure bases such conclusions on the experiences and reflections of the "I" who speaks.

Carole Fontaine finds a special relevance for feminist readers in Qoheleth's orientation in experience: "Ecclesiastes grounds his philosophy of life firmly in his personal experience. He contradicts some of the basic tenets of biblical faith. . . . Such revisioning of the basic givens of his tradition authorizes similar moves today" (Fontaine 1992, 154). The principle of making one's own experiences the standard for critically examining established worldviews and values is common to the speaker of this book and feminism. But it is advisable to differentiate as well. The experiences by which feminist movements and research orient themselves are those of women, those they have in common and that unite them. Because feminist orientation in experience strives for solidarity among women, one has to determine whether the experiences of Qoheleth unite him with someone and, if so, with whom.

Qoheleth's World of Experience   In his social-historical interpretation of Ecclesiastes, Frank Crüsemann endeavors to establish the connection between the book's central themes and Qoheleth's social class. (He does not distinguish between the author and the fictive speaker.) Crüsemann rightly points out that the problems addressed in the book are socially and historically conditioned (Crüsemann 1979, 100). But from a feminist perspective, those problems are not only socially conditioned but also gender-related. When it comes to depicting the concrete patterns of human life, the examples chosen are drawn from the world of men's experiences: a man who has no sons or brothers (4:8), a man of great possessions whose hoarded wealth was ruined when he fathered a son (5:12-14), etc. Never a woman as an example in the narrator's reflections on human beings![2]

The Designation Qoheleth In his self-introduction in 1:12, the "I" speaks of himself as "Qoheleth" (cf. also 1:2; 7:27; 12:8, 9, and 10). The Hebrew word *qōhelet* is the active feminine participle of the verb *qhl* in the singular: to gather. But the grammatically feminine form does not correspond to the gender of the person it designates and to whom the masculine form of the verb refers. (In my view, the feminine verb of the Masoretic Text of 7:27 is a scribal error; here I differ with Butting 1993, 110f.).

Some scholars maintain that the feminine participle form *qōhelet* was originally used to describe the function of a "gatherer" that was turned into a proper name in the book. Two participles were cited as examples of this kind of use of the feminine participle; one is *hassōperet* (Ezra 2:55; cf. Neh 7:59), and the other, *pōkeret hassĕbāyîm* (Ezra 2:57; Neh 7:59). But feminist scholarship argues that at least the former participle does not designate the function of a male professional group but refers rather to the "woman writer" to whom the clan mentioned in the verse goes back (cf. Newsom and Ringe 1992, 119; see Ezra, Nehemiah). If that is so, the assumption that the word *qōhelet* is a feminine participle designating a function is significantly less tenable. To this day the designation Qoheleth eludes clear definition.

The Wise, Rich King Qoheleth The "I" at the beginning of the address identifies the perspective from which human beings and the world are seen: "I, Qoheleth, when king over Israel in Jerusalem" (Eccles 1:12). Qoheleth prides himself in his wisdom and wealth; he surpasses everyone else in Jerusalem before him (1:16; 2:9). Jerusalem is the link binding the "I" and the history of Israel. Without mentioning Solomon's name, the "I" conjures up the image of that king who ruled over Israel in Jerusalem and who became known as a man of wisdom and wealth (cf. 1 Kings 5:9-14 and 26 [4:29-34 and 5:12]; 7; 10). But in the book of Qoheleth the role of the king differs in one aspect from the traditional pattern: the wise king who according to ethical tradition should be "the righteous judge" and "the defender of the weak" (cf. 1 Kings 3:16-28) emerges here as the richest man whose interest is in preserving his accumulated possessions — no thought being given to the king's social obligations.

In Ecclesiastes 1:12-16, the "king" tells of his own experience with wisdom and wealth and draws a conclusion from it. From chapter 3 onward, the first-person singular speaker talks less of what he experienced as a subject and more about

---

2. 2:8 is inconclusive: according to the New American Standard Bible, it is about "male and female singers and the pleasures of men — many concubines." Here "men" (literally: "all men," *kōl bĕnê-ha'ādām*) would be "every male." But the translation "many concubines" *(šiddâ wĕšiddôt)* is uncertain.

what he learned from his observations. Every sign of the speaker's royal status has disappeared in his report. And yet, there is some continuity. In 1:12–2:26 the king appears as a wise and wealthy person, and, correspondingly, in the chapters that follow, the speaker's primary attention is directed to the experience of those who toil for possessions (4:4-6 and 7-12; 5:12-19 [13-20]; 6:1-9) or who possess wisdom (4:13-16; 9:11-12 and 13-18). The interest of the "I" who speaks here, being concentrated on the fate of wealthy and wise men, reveals his point of view.

But the wise, wealthy king does not enter as a paradigm of the happy human being. He is portrayed not as someone happy and content but as a man of ill humor and disappointed (2:15-20). He discovers that there is nothing of endurance either in his wisdom or in his wealth (2:11). Just as "the King Qoheleth" could not attain happiness with all his wisdom and wealth, so the life of the wealthy or the wise men is replete with evil and failure (cf., e.g., 4:8; 5:12-15; 9:11 and 13-18). Such a description of the fate of wealthy and wise men undermines a conception found in an older written wisdom-tradition that had become fully developed and gained currency only in the time of the book of Ecclesiastes. It stated that wealth obtained through wisdom was something good (cf. Prov 21:20; 24:3-4) and that obtaining wisdom was a promise of prosperity (cf. Prov 3:16-18; 19:8). The book of Qoheleth puts this conception into the context of a contemporary social trend and subjects it to critical scrutiny.

At the time of the book's composition (between the middle of the third and the beginning of the second century B.C.E.), the land of Judea was under Hellenistic rule. There had not been a king in Jerusalem for a long time. With the introduction of the Greek system of lease-hold taxation, the indigenous upper class seized the opportunity to participate in the exploitation of their own population by purchasing with good money the privilege of collecting taxes and assessments of designated regions. Some of the Jewish aristocracy made use of that opportunity to increase their possessions. The book of Ecclesiastes goes against the grain of that period and the trend in the upper class: the wealthy do not reap happiness and contentment, the wise do not find success, and the memory of them fades away for there is no social interrelationship that would make those desired goals possible (Eccles 2:16 and 18-22; 4:8 and 13-16; 9:13-16). Not only is the traditional view that links wisdom and wealth put into question by the figure of the wise and wealthy albeit failed king, but also the widespread enthusiasm among the upper classes for the proliferation of wealth at the time of book's writing is contradicted and resisted in it.

Woman Is Not to Be Found (7:23-29)

- 23a: All this I have tested by wisdom;
- 23b: I said, "I will be wise," but it was far from me.

- 24a: That which is, is far off,
- 24b: and deep, very deep; who can find it out?
- 25a: I turned my mind to know and to search out and to seek wisdom and the sum of things,
- 25b: and to know that wickedness is folly and that foolishness is madness.
- 26a: I found
- 26b: more bitter than death the woman
- 26c: who is a trap, whose heart is snares and nets, whose hands are fetters;
- 26d: one who pleases God escapes her, but the sinner is taken by her.
- 27: See, this is what I found, says Qoheleth, adding one thing to another to find the sum,
- 28a: which my mind has sought repeatedly, but I have not found.
- 28b: One man among a thousand I found, but a woman among all these I have not found.
- 29: See, this alone I found, that God made human beings straightforward, but they have devised many schemes.

Two passages of the book explicitly mention woman (*'iššâ*): 7:26 and 28b. They are among those biblical texts that have been used in Christian traditions hostile to women as arguments against them. They were taken out of context for that purpose and recited like statements of dogma (e.g., Sprenger and Institoris 1987, 1:105; Schultze 1984, 130; cf. Schüngel-Straumann 1989, 19-21), even though the interpretation of them within the context of the book of Qoheleth is subject to much controversy. The widely held view that these passages manifest an outright misogynist stance on the part of Qoheleth has met with critical objection (cf. Butting 1991; 1993, 97-103; Krüger 1992; Riesener 1996).

Instead of discussing these different readings in detail, the following presents an interpretation stimulated to a large extent by Klara Butting but that also differs from hers in some points (as can be seen in my translation).

The Failure of the "I" in the Search for Wisdom

At first glance, the text of 7:23-29 appears to be divided into two units with different themes. The first addresses the "search for wisdom" (vv. 23-25); the second raises the topic of "woman" (vv. 26-29). But upon closer examination, it becomes apparent that both units are closely tied together by the leading motifs of "searching" (*bqš*, vv. 25, 28) and "finding" (*mṣ'*, vv. 24, 26, 27 [twice], 28 [thrice], and 29).

At the beginning of this text, the "I" concludes that his search for wisdom has failed: as far off as wisdom is for him (v. 23), so is that which is (v. 24a). His lament that what is cannot be found out may be understood in the light of the preceding section where he reflects on the breakdown of the connectedness of acts and their consequences (cf. 7:15-22). The experience of this breakdown of the just order obstructs Qoheleth's access to the world's happenings and, as a result, he cannot find wisdom (that is, the forms and rules of life together). And this does not affect Qoheleth only, but every human being (7:24b).

In terms of content and vocabulary, 8:16-17 is close to 7:23-24; the former also speaks of God's work as something that cannot be found out. This too can be related to the preceding passage, and the "I's" experience of the breakdown of the just order (8:10 and 14) and of the wickedness of human beings (8:9 and 11). Here, as in 7:15-24, the failure of the search for wisdom is traced back to the collapse of the acts-consequences connection.

The motif of not being able to find what is searched for is a core component of Qoheleth's anthropology and is located most of the time in a theological context (3:10-15; 7:13-14; 8:16-17): human beings "cannot find out what God has done from the beginning to the end" (3:11; cf. 8:17), and God acts in such a way that humans "may not find out what comes after them" (7:14). This idea is connected furthermore with that of the unchangeableness of God's work (3:14; 7:13). What kind of theology manifests itself when all these statements are combined? First, unsearchable happenings in the world are identified with God's action (8:17; cf. 3:11 and 14-15). Second, this is then said to be unchangeable (3:14; 7:13). Is this not a theology that declares the existing inscrutable world to be God's unchangeable work? And does such a theology not serve an ideological purpose, in that it legitimizes resigned acceptance of existing social injustice (cf. Crüsemann 1979, passim)? One cannot reject such critical questions as utterly untenable; still, the text of 7:23-29 may be drawn on to argue against that kind of theology. For it presents another view according to which the unsearchableness of God's action and of the world's happenings is not an unavoidable decree for human beings ordained by God. The very passage that ponders the problem from a personal perspective shows that not being able to find what is searched for is a historical condition the cause of which is to be found in humankind, to be precise, in its male component.

The Cause of the Breakdown of the Forms and Rules of Life Together (7:25-29)

The Purpose (7:25) The problematic of not being able to find what is searched for, while being addressed elsewhere in the book in rather abstract ways, is dealt with in this text concretely in the context of the relation of the sexes. The search for wisdom is defined by the "I" in two ways in verse 25. First, the word *ḥešbôn* (conclusion) is joined to the word "wisdom"; it signifies the human activity of planning (cf. Sir 9:15; 27:5-6) or the outcome, the result of it. Together with another noun with the same root, *ḥiššĕbōnôt* ("many devices," Eccles 7:29), it frames the reflection of 7:25-29. Second, the search for wisdom is summed up as the inquiry of injustice and folly (v. 25b). This characterization specifies that it is injustice and folly that cause wisdom not to be found, or, more concretely, that cause the forms and rules of life together to break down. The "I's" purpose is to put the cause into words ("*ḥešbôn*/to search for a conclusion"). His reflection proceeds in three steps (7:26, 27-28, and 29).

The Seductive Woman (7:26)   A participle of the verb "to find" in verse 26a introduces Qoheleth's preliminary conclusion of his examination. This distinguishes the verse from those that follow with the verb appearing in the perfect tense. The use of the participle in 7:26 indicates that the first-person speaker is quoting something he has come across again and again in his research on injustice and folly (cf. 8:12b, where a citation is similarly introduced by a participle). The cited opinion is a model for the interpretation of why wisdom's way of living has broken down.

Interpreters of these passages are not of one mind whether they are a judgment about women in general or a specific group of them; the particle *'ăšer* between verses 26b and 26c may be read in an explicative as well as a restrictive sense. The problem cannot be cleared up in terms of grammar alone; a tradition-historical study may help in seeing that Qoheleth is citing an opinion of his times. There are in fact some stylistic points in verse 26bc that are customary in the description of female figures in early Jewish wisdom literature: first, the metaphor of death (v. 26b); second, the comparisons from the world of hunting ("snares," "nets," v. 26c) and from war ("fetters," v. 26c). (The word *měṣôdîm* — in the Hebrew text it is in the plural — can be translated in two ways: "snare" and "mountain fortress." If the latter were meant, it would be another metaphor from the world of war. But I prefer the former because the image of woman as a snare is common in wisdom literature. See below.) The third stylistic point is the reference to parts of the body, which is part of the style of the "songs of description," a genre of love poetry that primarily lauds the beauty of the beloved (→ Song of Songs).

In Proverbs and Ecclesiasticus these notions are used above all in connection with warnings about the "foreign" woman (or "adulteress," NRSV); her way leads to the netherworld and death (Prov 2:18-19; 5:5-6; 7:27); the man seduced by her is like a deer bounding toward a trap or like a bird rushing into a snare (Prov 7:22-23; cf. Maier 1995, 179 on this text). The "foreign" woman sets out her traps (Sir 9:3; cf. Prov 6:26); she even is a catcher's net herself (Sir 26:22; this statement refers to a married woman).[3] She is a warrior who slays numerous men (Prov 7:26; cf. Prov 5:4; see Proverbs and Sirach).

This image of the "foreign" (or "other") woman is to alert young men to the dangers of associating with women who break the socially acknowledged norms

---

3. On this translation, cf. *Jüdische Schriften aus hellenistisch-römischer Zeit*, 3:570.

governing the relationships between the sexes and who liberate themselves from men's control over their sexuality. But this figure is portrayed in Proverbs 1–9 not only in terms of real-life aspects of women but also in terms of demonic features (e.g., her proximity to the netherworld and the spirits of the dead). She may therefore be regarded also as a metaphor for life-destroying forces. This metaphorical function is apparent especially in folly personified, a figure cast as the antagonist of wisdom. Lady Folly represents the way to death, Lady Wisdom that of life (Prov 9:13-18).

The warning against the "foreign" (or "other") woman views women as beings who are determined primarily by their sexuality; every woman except one's own wife is seen as a potential seducer (cf. Maier 1995, 269). And thus a negative judgment about the "foreign" woman extends to all other women whether as a suspicion or as an insinuation. (I agree with Butting 1993, 98 but not with Riesener 1996, 206). In this context, the earlier question whether Qoheleth 7:26 is a judgment about women in general or about a specific group of them seems no longer to matter. What is said in 7:26 about woman certainly belongs to the early Jewish discourse on wisdom in which woman is more and more associated with death, folly, and evil.

But what is said in that verse can also be read in two ways. On the one hand, it may be understood as an explanatory pattern where seductive women are held responsible for destroying the life of human beings. On the other, woman may be seen as "folly" *(siklut)* personified, which is given emphasis through the use of the definite article; then she is held responsible for the failure of the search for wisdom (Riesener 1996, 205).

Human Being Alone (7:27-28) In verse 26 Qoheleth tries to provide an explanation and then juxtaposes it in verses 27-28 with what he had discovered as he studied the broken-down relationships among human beings. Before divulging what he found, he once again declares that his untiring search has not reached its goal (7:28a; cf. 7:23). He found a human being *('ādām)* but no woman *('iššâ,* v. 28b). For ages the interpretation of this statement has been that Qoheleth found one "good," "reliable" man among a thousand human beings but had to confess that there is no "good," "reliable" woman. But this is a questionable rendition, chiefly for two reasons. First, this interpretation assumes that the phrase "one man among a thousand" is to be taken as a positive qualification of the one found; the text hardly supports this reading. The Hebrew phrase "one among a thousand" in Sirach 6:6 does, indeed, express the special value of a friend; in Job 33:23 it characterizes that of a heavenly mediator. But it is possible that it has another connotation in Ecclesiastes 7:28, especially because "*one* human being" (*'eḥād;* "the solitary individual" in NRSV) in 4:7-12 is portrayed negatively. Secondly, the interpretation silently accepts the use of a noun that is uncommon in the Hebrew Bible: in 7:28b the Hebrew word is *'ādām* (the generic term for the "human being") instead of *'îš* (man)

as over against *'iššâ* (woman). This peculiarity is made invisible in some translations by translating *'ādām* as "man."

Klara Butting connects this passage with the narrative in Genesis 2–3 where
'ādām (human being/Adam) is mentioned over against *'iššâ* (woman). The conditions Qoheleth found and described in 7:28b — the human being is alone and no
woman is to be found — are identified with the condition that God judges to be
"not good": "There was not found a helper as his partner" (Gen 2:20b; cf. Gen 2:18;
Butting 1993, 100f.). In his examination of injustice and folly, Qoheleth found the
human being whose God-given helper had disappeared. "A man, human being
and alone, represents a humanity without woman" (Butting 1993, 101).

Ecclesiastes 7:28b makes the case that it is not "the seductive woman" who is
responsible for the breakdown of the forms and rules of life together but the humanity from which women were driven out. In his assertion that woman could
not be found, Qoheleth also sounds his lament over his failed search for wisdom.
The unfulfilled longing for wisdom is expressed in words from love poetry: "my
soul," "searching" and "finding" (cf. Prov 3:1-5; 5:6; cf. Riesener 1996, 201f.).

God's Creation and the Seekers (Ecclesiastes 7:29)   The reflection concludes
with a reminiscence of creation, commenting on the condition of human beings
described in 7:27-29: "God made human beings straightforward." "The relation of
creation to the present is not that of a principle from which the present came
forth" (Butting 1993, 102). The breakdown of the forms and rules of life together is
not what God has decreed for human beings. The guilt of the seekers is now
named: "But they [third-person plural masculine] have devised many schemes."
The plural noun *ḥiššĕbōnôt* (many devices) that points to the root *ḥšb* (in the verbs
"to calculate" and "to plan") is used in wisdom literature to depict the attempt by
human beings to govern their lives by planning (cf. Prov 16:9a; 19:21a). In Genesis
it depicts the action of human beings that launched the formation of a world of
their own in opposition to God ("every inclination of the thoughts of their hearts,"
Gen 6:5). Drawing on that Genesis passage, Qoheleth asserts in 7:29 that the calculating scheming of human beings is the cause of the destruction of all humanity's
communal life. It is worth noting at this point that this noun, *ḥiššĕbōnôt*, occurs in
the Bible only in one other place: 2 Chronicles 26:15, where it refers to machines
that shoot arrows and rocks.

Like Genesis, Qoheleth tells the story of males as if it were the story of humankind by speaking of the man over against the woman as *(hā)'ādām:* human being
(7:28; cf. Gen 2:25; 3:12 and 20; 4:1). But Qoheleth's story has a critical self-critical
aspect: this kind of androcentric story about the creation of human beings goes
counter to creation. He speaks out against a misogynist interpretation of Genesis
that holds the woman, created second, responsible for the in-breaking of evil (cf.
Sir 25:24). Qoheleth does not search among women for reasons why they cannot
be found; rather, the reasons are to be found among the seekers. Here his self-

critique is apparent. He judges his own work negatively since he himself belongs to the *ḥiššĕbōnôt*, the device-seekers who attempt to find a conclusion — *ḥešbôn* — by means of rational, calculating thinking. (Both words, *ḥiššĕbōnôt/*"devices" and *ḥešbôn/*"result/conclusion," share the same root, *ḥšb*.)

Conclusion

Qoheleth has more in mind than to sketch the failures of "humankind's" history. He also tries to present an alternate form of life, calling on people to live by it: there is no happy life for people unless they eat and drink and find enjoyment in their toil (cf. Eccles 2:24; 3:12-13 and 22; 5:17-19; 8:15; 9:7-10; 11:9-10). This conception of happiness is part of a tradition celebrated in the culture of western Asian and eastern Mediterranean feasts. In ancient Egyptian, Babylonian, and Hellenistic-Roman literature there are close parallels to Qoheleth's calls for joyful feasting (cf. Assmann 1991, 221-23 on Eccles 9:7-10 in particular). Several differences notwithstanding, these texts share a common logical structure: since death is the fate of all human beings and since they cannot know what the future holds, let there be joyful feasts. In some texts, this is said to be one of the things the deities have destined for human beings (cf., e.g., the counsel of a goddess in the Old Babylonian version of the Gilgamesh Epic III, 1-15). The widespread presence of this topic is not the result of literary interdependence but of the spread of common festive customs and their underlying anthropology. It is likely that such songs were sung in those feasts that called to mind death as the fate of human beings and therefore exhorted people to enjoy themselves during the festive meal.

From a feminist perspective, it is especially noteworthy that next to bread, wine, scented oil, and fresh garments, "life with a woman you love" is mentioned (9:9; cf. the passage of the Gilgamesh Epic cited above and some of the Egyptian "Songs of the Harpers"; on these cf. Lichtheim 1945). People are called upon to enjoy life together with someone else, and, seeing that heterosexually loving men are presupposed here, that means life with a woman they love. In the context of the book of Ecclesiastes, the call to enjoy life with a woman serves to highlight the alternative to a life of the solitary "human being" (cf. 7:27-29). According to the biblical creation tradition, bread, wine, and oil (cf. Ps 104:15), as well as the life shared by woman and man, are a gift of God. The picture of the joyful feast filled with these gifts portrays the life Qoheleth has in mind, a life in which human beings accept creation with great joy.

But is this picture of the feast suitable from a woman's perspective for portraying forms of life in togetherness? What meaning did those feasts have for women at that time who took part in them as hostesses, servants, musicians, or dancers? Were those not occasions when women were exploited as objects of men's pleasure (cf. Esther 1:10-11) and where, on the other hand, women related to their lovers as active subjects (cf. Song 5:1)? To answer such questions would require a more differentiated study of the culture of the feasts of the western Asian and eastern Mediterranean world; it could perhaps bring us closer to the reality of the life of women at that time. That is why "the making of many books" (Eccles 12:12) must not yet come to an end in feminist study and research.[4]

LITERATURE

Assmann, Jan. 1991. "Der schöne Tag: Sinnlichkeit und Vergänglichkeit im altägyptischen Fest." In Assmann, *Stein und Zeit: Mensch und Gesellschaft im alten Ägypten*, 200-234. Munich.

Brenner, Athalya. 1993. "M Text Authority in Biblical Love Lyrics: The Case of Qoheleth 3,1-9 and Its Textual Relatives." In *On Gendering Texts: Female and Male Voices in the Hebrew Bible*, edited by Athalya Brenner and Fokkelien van Dijk-Hemmes, 133-63. Leiden.

Butting, Klara. 1991. "Weibsbilder bei Kafka und Kohelet. Eine Auslegung von Prediger 7,23-29." *Texte und Kontexte* 49:2-15.

———. 1993. *Die Buchstaben werden sich noch wundern. Innerbiblische Kritik als Wegweisung feministischer Hermeneutik*, 87-116. Berlin.

Crüsemann, Frank. 1979. "Die unveränderbare Welt. Überlegungen zur 'Krisis der Weisheit' beim Prediger (Kohelet)." In *Der Gott der kleinen Leute*, edited by Willy Schottroff and Wolfgang Stegemann, 80-104. Munich and Gelnhausen.

Fontaine, Carole R. 1992. "Ecclesiastes." In *The Women's Bible Commentary*, edited by Carol A. Newsom and Sharon H. Ringe, 153-55. London and Louisville.

Helm, Lothar. 1989. "Prediger 3,1-8. Alles hat seine Zeit." In *Feministisch gelesen*, edited by Eva Renate Schmidt, Mieke Korenhof, and Renate Jost, 157-63. 2nd ed. Stuttgart.

Krüger, Thomas. 1992. "'Frau Weisheit' in Koh 7,26?" *Biblica* 73:394-403.

Lichtheim, Miriam. 1945. "The Songs of the Harpers." *Journal of Near Eastern Studies* 4:178-212.

Maier, Christl. 1995. *Die 'fremde Frau' in Proverbien 1-9: eine exegetische und sozialgeschichtliche Studie*. Fribourg and Göttingen.

Newsom, Carol A., and Sharon H. Ringe, eds. 1992. *The Women's Bible Commentary*. London and Louisville.

Riesener, Ingrid. 1996. "Frauenfeindschaft im Alten Testament? Vom Verständnis von Qoh 7, 25-29." In *"Jedes Ding hat seine Zeit." Studien zur israelitischen und altorientalischen Weisheit*, edited by Anja A. Diesel et al., 193-207. Berlin and New York.

Schultze, Georg. 1984. "De blanda mulierum rhetorica." In *Das wohlgelehrte Frauenzimmer*, edited by Elisabeth Gössmann, 121-38. Munich.

Schüngel-Straumann, Helen. 1989. *Die Frau am Anfang. Eva und die Folgen*. Freiburg im Breisgau.

Schwienhorst-Schönberger, Ludger. 1994. *"Nicht im Menschen gründet das Glück" (Koh*

---

4. I thank Prof. Dr. Elisabeth Gössmann, Tokyo/Munich, profoundly for her great help with the German version of the text.

2,24). Kohelet im Spannungsfeld jüdischer Weisheit und hellenistischer Philosophie. Freiburg im Breisgau.

Sprenger, Jakob, and Heinrich Institoris. 1987. *Der Hexenhammer (Malleus maleficarum). Aus dem Lateinischen übertragen und eingeleitet von J. W. R. Schmidt.* Munich.

FOR FURTHER READING

Christianson, Eric S. 1998. "Qoheleth the 'Old Boy' and Qoheleth the 'New Man': Misogynism, the Womb and a Paradox in Ecclesiastes." In *Wisdom and Psalms*, edited by Athalya Brenner and Carole R. Fontaine, 109-36. Sheffield.

Fontaine, Carole R. 1998. "'Many Devices' (Qoheleth 7.23–8.1): Qoheleth, Misogyny and the Malleus Maleficarum." In *Wisdom and Psalms*, edited by Athalya Brenner and Carole R. Fontaine, 137-68. Sheffield.

Jost, Renate. 1999. "Frau und Adam, Feministische Überlegungen zur Auslegung von Kohelet 7,23-29." In *Hermeneutik sozialgeschichtlich*, edited by Erhard S. Gerstenberger and Ulrich Schoenborn, 59-67. Münster.

Schwienhorst-Schönberger, Ludger. 2004. *Kohelet.* Herders theologischer Kommentar Altes Testament. Freiburg im Breisgau.

Tamez, Elsa. 1998. *Cuando los horizontes se cierran. Relectura del libro de Eclesiastés o Qohélet.* San José (DEI).

————. 2000. *When the Horizons Close: Rereading Ecclesiastes.* Maryknoll, N.Y.

Translated by Martin Rumscheidt

Song of Songs — Polyphony of Love

Athalya Brenner

"The winter is past, the rain is over and gone. The flowers appear on the earth. . . . The voice of the turtledove . . . figs . . . vineyards." Every spring, from nursery school on, we sang songs containing these words. Later there were songs about a "shepherd" and a "shepherdess"; "I am yours and you are mine," "You are beautiful and your eyes are doves," "Many waters cannot quench love," and there were dances such as "I went down to the walnut orchard. . . ." One Passover night when I was a teenager it dawned on me that the biblical words my father was intoning in the Lithuanian style after the liturgical Passover meal were more than familiar to me. I knew the poems of the Song of Songs (hereafter Song) by heart because I had sung them for as long as I could remember. Its words were part of me before I knew they were in the Bible. And for me spring — even today — still means a stream of texts and melodies from this song of all songs, the *šîr haššîrîm.*

In the following, I will discuss various traditional ways of reading the Song and describe aspects of feminist literary critical reception of these songs. My purpose is not to stake out a particular feminist perspective. Instead, my approach — much more in line with my fundamental thesis that the Song is itself a collection of songs — is to allow the kind of diversity that enables the confluence of many voices. My understanding of literary criticism, to the extent that it confronts the cultural myths we live with, is as a means of working for social change. Feminist literary criticism directs much of its attention to identifying and criticizing unequal treatment of women and attempting to redefine the roles of women within literature and within the social context that is reflected in literature. Because every feminist method implies a whole worldview, the critique it develops tends toward

This article is based on the author's contribution in the Dutch journal *Schrift* 154 (1994): 111-39 (Birgit Springer assisted in her translation from Dutch into German); in the First Testament Guide, "The Song of Songs" (Sheffield, 1989); and in the *Feminist Companion to the Song of Songs* (Sheffield, 1993); it was edited for the *Kompendium* by Marie-Theres Wacker.

interdisciplinarity. It concentrates on, but is not limited to, their concerns, for its goal is to analyze all nuances of human behavior and its manifestations.

Types of Interpretation:

Allegory

At first glance the theme of the Song is the (heterosexual) relationship between man and woman. However, as early as antiquity, Judaism and, later, Christianity developed ways of reading the Song that relate its love theme allegorically to the love between God and the human being. This can be explained from the political context of the time, when this tendency to allegorical interpretation originated: worrisome times of military upheaval, conquest of the land by the Romans, destruction of the Second Temple in Jerusalem, the failure of anti-Roman uprisings, and the loss of all organizational structures for the Jewish community. In sum, these were times of crisis that also led to the development of Christianity in the first and second centuries. When it seemed as if God had left the people of the covenant completely in the lurch, the allegorical reading of the Song brought new affirmation of God's steadfast love and mercy toward Israel.

In the noncanonical Second Book of Esdras (Fourth Book of Ezra) 5:24 and 5:26, the community of Israel is called "dove," "lily," and "rainbow," symbolic attributes borrowed from the Song. These references to Israel as "dove" and "lily" are the first indications of symbolic interpretations of the Song, which became increasingly significant between the fall of the Second Temple and the Bar Kokhba uprising against the Romans in 132-135 C.E. In this period the Jewish sages began to read the Song as an allegory, as a love story between God, whom the Song calls "friend," "beloved," "shepherd," and "Solomon" — and the community of Israel, which the Song calls "bride," "dove," "sister," and "Shulamite woman." By the time of Rabbi Akiba (50-132 C.E.), the allegorical interpretation had supplanted the literal understanding. Rabbi Akiba warns people not to sing the Song in inns or taverns, for whoever did so would have no part in the world to come (Tosefta *Sanhedrin* 12:10; cf. Babylonian Talmud *Sanhedrin* 101a). The tradition of symbolic or allegorical interpretation was adopted by the medieval Jewish biblical scholars (Rashi; Ibn Ezra; Isaac and Judah Abrabanel). Jewish mysticism likewise made use of the Song and finally provided God with a female companion, called Shekhinah (Hebrew for "indwelling"), Matroni, and later even Shabbat. The association of two divine elements is described in explicitly sexual terms, and as such is likely dependent on an allegorical interpretation of the Song. This connection testifies to the psychological need to complete the divinity with a female element.

Christian interpreters of the Song generally followed the principles of allegorical exegesis established by Jewish biblical scholarship. In the third century the church fathers adopted the allegorical interpretation of the Song. Initially, Christ was emphasized as the central (masculine) figure of the Song, and the love the text describes was associated with the love of Christ for the human soul or for the church (e.g., Origen, Jerome, Augustine). Starting at certain places as early as the patristic period, a Mariological interpretation of the Song was developed in the Christian Middle Ages (especially by Rupert of Deutz); this made the female figure the center of attention. Christian mysticism, too, gratefully took up the Song and related it to the union of the (male or female) mystic with God.

Since the late eighteenth century, the allegorical interpretations of the Song have increasingly given way to understandings of the text that foreground their literal meaning. The influence of the allegorical model is still tangible, however, in that some of its assumptions continue to be considered valid in these modern readings, for example, that of a continuous plotline throughout the book and, accordingly, that of a sole male and a sole female protagonist of all the songs.

Modern Interpretations

Some of the Septuagint manuscripts from as early as the fourth and fifth centuries C.E. ascribe the poetic lines of the Song to specific male and female voices. These manuscripts are precursors of the perspective that gained dominance in the eighteenth century and was developed particularly in the nineteenth century, namely, that the Song is a drama. The plot relates the love story of a specific couple who are the male and female protagonists; in other variations there is a romantic triangle involving two men and a woman. The text is read as the script of a drama. But since the actual Song text does not correspond to such a form, it must be reconstructed in a certain way by adding "stage directions." Most of the interpretations in this category construct King Solomon as the figure of the male lover. The female beloved is of lower social status, a shepherdess from the countryside, a young girl from Shunem (= Shulam/a Shulamite), or a foreign princess. In texts that assume a love triangle, the third person is a shepherd to whom the young girl reluctantly returns after being seduced by the love of Solomon and the splendor of his court in Jerusalem.

However, the variously reconstructed plots with their formal divisions into dramatic subsections and freely created stage directions are not at all convincing. Moreover, it is doubtful whether in fact dramatic performances took place among the Hebrew people prior to the Hellenistic period.

In the twentieth century, it became popular among scholars to view large parts of the Bible as cultic material borrowed from neighboring cultures. Thus the Song, too, was read as the transposition of a liturgical composition (or as a religious-literary reflection on such a piece) that had been imported into Hebrew literature from an ancient Near Eastern source. These interpreters cite Egyptian (Isis/Osiris), Babylonian (Ishtar/Tammuz-Adonis), Sumerian (Inanna/Dumuzi), and Canaanite-Ugaritic (Anat/Baal) sources. All these suggested ways of reading the text share the basic premise that the Song has its origins in a narrative whose plot was influenced by the ritual presentation of the *hieros gamos* (sacred wedding) of a fertility god and a goddess as part of a recurring cycle of death and rebirth of the fertility god. Cultic interpretations thus assert that they are uncovering hidden historic and religious meaning that underlies the text. In this respect they represent continuations of the allegorical tradition and the drama theory. There are numerous critical objections to the cultic model of interpretation, and they also apply to the feminist development of this model (e.g., Weiler 1989). The reconstructions of the myth of death and resurrection of the divinity in the Mesopotamian and Ugaritic literature, for example, are anything but reliable. Moreover, the theme of the biblical poems is human love, not divine love. On the contrary! There is not a single unambiguous reference to God in the book. And is a text that honors foreign rites and feast days really supposed to have been accepted as part of the official scriptures of Judaism? The Jewish liturgical reading of the Song at Passover is documented too late (the oldest reference is in the eighth century [*Soferim* 14:18]) to prove a liturgical origin of the text. Finally, the cultic approach seems to be driven — consciously or unconsciously — by an association of ancient fertility gods with Jesus: their hypothetical resurrection myths are interpreted as foreshadowing that of Christ.

One further interpretive model should be mentioned that was widespread in the first half of the twentieth century and can be seen as a secular variant of the cultic combined with the dramatic interpretation. This model sees the Song as a collection of wedding songs whose sequence corresponds to the celebration of a "wedding week." Jewish sources do in fact show that at the time of the Second Temple a bride was celebrated in songs and the bridegroom was compared to a king. Both wore a crown (Song 3:11) and the bride sat in a litter (3:9). But there is no evidence that the Song was used as a comprehensive script for wedding celebrations. And the analogy to certain genres of nineteenth-century traditional Arabic poetry put forth by so many is too general to be convincing.

This leaves no option but to return to a "simple," literal, or literary reading. This means the Song is to be understood as a collection of secular love poetry whose individual poems were loosely — though often meaningfully — put into sequence. If we do not read the Song as a coherent and consistent "narrative" — as the drama theory does, for example — there is scarcely any pressing reason to continue to assume that the identity of the lovers, male and female, remains the same throughout the book. Of course, it is possible to attribute most of the various moods and descriptions to a single pair of lovers, but an equally attractive (and more plausible) option is to distribute them among several different couples. Such a reading, which I prefer, allows a large number of voices, sources, backgrounds, and previously borrowed ideas in the Song to be brought to modern ears.

Female Authorship and Women's Culture in the Song

Solomon as (Fictitious) Author

The title of the book can be understood to be "The Song of/for Solomon" (1:1). This title, added by an editor, was traditionally interpreted to mean Solomon was the author of the Song. According to biblical traditions (especially 1 Kings 3–11), many details of Solomon's life do make this superficially credible. The love of love and of women; literary skills; knowledge of nature and its "language," of architecture and construction, of international trade; glamorous city life, descriptions of the royal court, numerous references to Jerusalem — all this seems to provide indirect evidence for Solomon's authorship. Within the Song, aside from the title, Solomon is explicitly named in several more passages (cf. especially Song 3:7-11 and 8:11-12). Less explicit references to the "king," a royal harem, and an Egyptian foal (cf. Solomon's marital bond with an Egyptian princess in 1 Kings 7:8 and elsewhere, his chariot park and horses in 1 Kings 10) seem to reinforce the "Solomonic" aura of the Song. Furthermore, some commentators interpret the epithet "Shulamite," attributed to a dancing woman, as a feminine form of *šĕlōmōh*, Solomon.

This derivation is not at all persuasive or necessary, however. What is more, whenever the Song refers to Solomon, the name is in the third-person singular, whereas an author would be more likely to use the autobiographical "I." The word "king," where it occurs, can be an epithet or nickname for the bridegroom, as it is in many instances in Arabic wedding poetry. The same phenomenon could explain references to women as princesses or harem wives. But other Israelite and Jewish kings enjoyed international influence, carried on international trade, and had connections abroad, independent of Solomon. Other kings, too, owned horses and a chariot park and found pleasure in building projects. The specific references to Solomon and to the preexilic monarchy in general are ahistorical, since they offer no information about specific dates. The reports of luxury articles and geographical horizons would also be consistent with a postexilic chronology, when relatively open borders were the norm for the Persian Empire. In short, it can be assumed that a well-informed author/translator of the Persian period was able to collect diverse popular, even "Solomonic," love poems and edit them into the form of the Song we know today. Butting (1994) shows that the name "Solomon" can be interpreted quite differently in the Song. She hears the name as a code word for women's traditional hope for a "messianic" king who will create a just world for women in particular.

Female Authorship?

The Israeli scholar Shelomo Dov Goitein presented his theory of "women as creators of biblical genres" in 1957 (Goitein 1988). He begins by observing the literary activity of Yemenite Jewish women in the first years of the sovereignty of Israel, when ethnic, cultural, and literary traditions came into play there and were preserved and passed along by women in the oral tradition, even though these women were largely illiterate. Goitein then applied his findings to biblical literature and was able to show the probability of female authorship for certain Bible passages, including the Song — at least as far as an initial source of the songs is concerned, which does not exclude the possibility that men did the final editing.

It can in fact hardly be denied — to take up Goitein's thesis and expand upon it critically — that the female gender and feminine qualities are overwhelmingly dominant in this biblical collection of love poetry. This was noted by Christian David Ginsburg as early as the mid–nineteenth century. Ginsburg argues that womanhood and female characteristics appear free of all stigma in the Song, whereas in the rest of the Bible they are devalued and looked down upon (Ginsburg 1970). This insight was convincingly confirmed later on by feminist critics and generally recognized by modern biblical scholarship. Female figures are the dominant actors in the Song. They are strong, eloquent, open, and active; objectively, much more so than their male counterparts. This point must be especially emphasized. There is no equality of the sexes in the Song. On the contrary, surprisingly enough, female superiority prevails in the Song.

To point out some of the many details: military metaphors in the Song are associated with female ideas, although we expect male images in connection with warfare. Using war language for female characters is incomprehensible, except when it has the connotation of a superior position of the female being described. She is — or rather they, the women, are — both repulsive and beautiful, both threatening and bashful. This kind of description evokes the image of women who are completely different than what patriarchal stereotypes of women lead us to expect. They take initiative, and at least to a certain extent they are in control of their love and their life. Neither a father nor a patriarchal home appears anywhere in the book. Instead, the "mother's house" (3:4; 8:1) and "the mother's sons" (1:6), the woman's brothers, are very conspicuous. Furthermore, some of the fundamental customs associated with sexuality that are inherent to patriarchy are scarcely observed. A woman pursues her beloved at night (3:1-4; 5:2-8). Whether she does so in reality or in a dream is hardly relevant because she imagines that she does so — and her reward is that she finds him. When she is punished by the sentinels who watch over the city walls (and over social customs such as the woman's virginity), her punishment is not severe, unlike what one would expect from the legal material in the Bible. Her mantle is taken away, she is beaten (5:7), but she survives and is reunited with her beloved (6:2). And in the first song the dark-skinned beauty openly sings out that the sons of her mother (!) were angry with her for not guarding her own vineyard (1:6). In the Song, where vineyards and orchards as well as sweet-scented herb gardens serve as symbols of both female sexuality and the natural surroundings in which the lovers dwell, such a feminine explanation is in fact quite bold. To be sure, it assumes that the association of nature symbolism and female sexuality that was a cultural given is more or less a fact of nature, but it reinterprets it (van Dijk-Hemmes, in Brenner and van Dijk-Hemmes 1993, 80). Her explanation can mean only one thing: the female speaker boasts about the fact that she has not kept her virginity intact, in defiance of the explicit wish of her brothers. This defiance of sexual norms is unmistakably cunning — and gleeful.

The gynocentrism of the songs, moreover, is combined with the unmistakable absence of theocentrism, in fact with the unmistakable absence of God. It is a matter of speculation whether God plays any sort of role at all in the noun compound that is sometimes translated "the fire of Yah" (abbreviation for YHWH?; the Hebrew in 8:6 is cryptic). It is worth noting that the closing declaration of love, the final and definitive commentary on this theme in this god-less book, is spoken by a female figure:

> Set me as a seal upon your heart,
>   as a seal upon your arm;
> for love is strong as death,
>   passion fierce as the grave.
> Its flashes are flashes of fire,
>   the fire of God (or "a raging flame").
> Many waters cannot quench love,
>   neither can floods drown it. (8:6-7a)

Even if this passage were a reference to YHWH (from a linguistic point of view, the translation "a raging flame" would be closer), it would be an extremely indirect reference. Nowhere in the Song does God figure as one who acts; nowhere does God take initiative or supervise human activity. Nowhere is God affected by what happens. Interestingly, the same is true for other biblical texts such as the book of Esther, for example.

Women's Reality in the Song

The Song is a gold mine for facts about everyday life in ancient Israel: nature and the changes of the seasons, geography, wild and cultivated vegetation, wild and tamed animals, agriculture and cattle farming; urban and rural life; economics and trade, both local and international; social organizations; clothing and jewelry; architecture and defensive forts; military equipment; attitudes toward love and sexuality; aesthetic values. This is only a fragmentary list of the natural and cultural aspects of life that are referred to in passing. In the following discussion, I will highlight aspects that might have been relevant to the everyday life of women.

City life, specifically in Jerusalem, plays an important role in various poems.

Nighttime security is assured by guards patrolling the streets, who, coincidentally, also watch over the moral behavior of the inhabitants, especially of the women. The "daughters" of Jerusalem are probably girls of high birth and status whose lives offer sufficient leisure to allow them the luxury of love affairs. There are taverns for young people to go to. The city's definition of beauty seems to be that of a "peach skin" (cf. Lam 4:7), as opposed to the rural reality of a beautiful woman with dark, sunburned skin (Song 1:5-6; cf. Lam 4:8). Perhaps there is more going on here than the juxtaposition of urban and rural. Renita J. Weems (1992) hypothesizes that the dark-skinned woman in the first song is not (only) a sunburned field hand, but an ethnically different woman.

A conspicuous feature of the Song is the way the female lovers refer to their family and their homes. Again and again they refer to "my mother's house." Even contexts of a royal wedding or a royal harem are mentioned in connection with the approval of a mother. Brothers are a part of the family; they play their traditional role of protecting their sisters' virginity and they have authority within the family. The epithets "brother" and "sister," extended to lovers in this context, have clearly derived from the notion of sibling relationships. Father figures are totally absent from every scene. It is far from certain, however, whether this indicates that the social structures reflected in the Song are influenced by matrilineal or fratriarchal principles. The tension between the two perspectives, the personal and the social, is never resolved in the poems. We must nevertheless concede that the punishment experienced by the girl who violates the sexual code is not all that severe, that women in general enjoy the freedom of watching for their lovers, and that girlfriends and mothers offer help in their search. Moreover, the emphasis on the physical beauty of the lovers and on sexual attraction, as one would expect in love poetry, strongly contradicts another biblical view that states what is expected of a married woman — namely, the knowledge that attractiveness and beauty have no meaning for respectable women (Prov 31:30).

These and other details combine to form a certain picture of women's superiority within the Song. This is the context that should be assumed when asking about the social-historical significance of this literary image. In other words, it is indeed difficult to know whether female superiority in love — which becomes a tradition in the lyrics of the Song — is possible within the patriarchal biblical context. But this problem does not necessarily prevent us from acknowledging the fact of female superiority in the Song.

Intertextual Connections within and beyond the Bible

Egyptian and Tamil Love Poetry

Its love theme, its secular and ahistorical character, and its lack of emphasis on "nation" are characteristic of the Song. The book is unique within the literature of the Hebrew Bible by virtue of the cumulative weight these four features give it. Because of its unique character, it is especially important to consider the book against the background of other Bible passages and other literary genres.

We also find gynocentrism (the centrality of women and the feminine) in the vicinity of ancient Israel as it is reflected in ancient Egyptian love poetry. The Egyptian female voices are stronger, bolder, more open than their male counterparts. In the love poetry of the Tamils — geographically and historically distant from that of Israel and Egypt (cf. Mariaselvam 1988) — the same major features appear; the lover is virtually absent. The affinity of Egyptian and Tamil culture with the gynocentrism of the Song lends credence to the possibility that Near Eastern women were granted a freedom in love poetry, and perhaps in premarital love relationships in general, that was denied them in other life situations. In this respect Egyptian love poetry documents the textual and social validity of gynocentrism in the Song. The same is true of Tamil love poetry.

Female Wisdom

In the Hebrew Bible, wisdom is above all the worldly knowledge of practical skills. Intellectual knowledge, philosophical study, and religious thought are secondary with respect to the pragmatic purpose of wisdom. Wisdom means that one must acquire skill and dexterity at all levels of personal and social activity. Rhetoric, poetry, and music — along with other public and social skills — are then subcategories of "wisdom" because they are crafts learned and practiced like every other craft. This is so much the case that we can assume that guilds for poets and musicians existed among the Hebrew men and woman and their neighbors in biblical times.

Poetry comprised an integral part of Hebrew life in the context of joyous or sad occasions, whether accompanied by music or recited, with or without dance. Short and long poems, scattered throughout the books of the Bible, give evidence of this. Some passages define poetry explicitly as "wisdom" (the wisdom of Solomon in 1 Kings 5:10-12 [Eng. 4:30-32]). There is no reason to exclude the Song from this broad classification. Various passages of the Hebrew Bible attribute poetic and musical activity to women, whether these are spontaneous or professional (the song of Miriam, Exod 15:20-21; the hymn of praise of the women for David's victory in 1 Sam 18:7; 21:12[11]; 29:5; the song of Deborah in Judg 5). Jeremiah (chapter 9) explicitly explains that "wise" women serve as professional lamenters who write and perform their own texts. Given the prominence of women's voices and perspectives in the Song, it may be another text that is at least partially written by a woman. If this possibility proves tenable, it will provide more complete information regarding biblical wisdom traditions, since the majority of the teachings in the extant biblical texts reflect and are addressed to a man's world.

The Song of Songs and the Garden of Eden (Genesis 2:4b–3:24)

Genesis 2:4b–3:24 is, among other things, a narrative about relationships and a "garden" in which and out of which these relationships evolve. The image of the garden in Genesis as well as in the Song is symbolic of the female body, the true beginning of all human existence. Apart from this structural framework, however, the two texts are fundamentally different in attitude and message.

In the Garden of Eden the natural order of things is introduced in an unnatural way, in reverse: woman is born from the man (Gen 2:21-22) and the man cleaves to her (2:24). Then, through the initiative of the woman (3:1-7), the first two human beings acquire divine knowledge of "good and evil" as well as of human sexuality. The consequence of this act of disobedience corresponds to the violation of this order. It proves painful for female sexuality (childbearing) and for the social status of women (3:16). For the man it signifies difficulty in his predestined role as provider (3:17-19). The patriarchal order of things and the nature of relationships between the sexes are regulated before the couple is expelled from the (nonerotic) garden (3:22-24). The story of the garden speaks about the painful aspect of sexual love and about the lot of woman. Christianity has further developed the theme of guilt/sin/punishment as associated with sexuality. The story of the garden is the story of the "Fall," for which woman is blamed outright (→ Genesis 1–11).

By contrast, the Song is not sexist and generally not patriarchal. The poems show no sign of inferiority in women's judgment, intellectual capacity, or emotional nature. On the contrary, the women who populate these poems are allowed to speak and act openly. Love brings both pain and joy, but this pain has no far-reaching physical or social consequences. The pain of love is shared by both sexes (8:6-7). The couples in the Song live freely in their "gardens," both factually and metaphorically, without a divine or patriarchal power to drive them out. We can, if we will, interpret the development of the love relationship(s) in the Song as a return to a psychological (inner) Eden through the saving power of love. In the other "garden," sexuality is openly affirmed. In this garden, inequality pales at the same time as do the material and social conflicts between the sexes, and thus becomes meaningless (cf. also Trible 1993 on the intertextual reading of Gen 2–3 and the Song).

Love Texts in Prophetic Books: The Question of Men's Love and Women's Fickleness

Another field of feminist research undertakes to show the intertextual relationships between the Song and various prophetic passages of the Bible, especially from the books of Hosea, Jeremiah, and Ezekiel.

Hosea was the first prophet, as far as we know, who used the bold language of sexual love to describe the relationship between the Hebrew God and God's people (Hos 1–3). God is the devoted, loving "husband," bound by a marriage contract; the northern kingdom is the inconstant, adulterous "wife"; Baal or the Baals (in the plural!) is/are mentioned as the extramarital lover/s of the "wife." Because of the "wife's" heartless behavior, the relationship becomes dysfunctional. Divorce proceedings, punishment, isolation, and reeducation must be undertaken with the "wife" (2:7-16; 3) before a love relationship according to the law can be initiated again, this time without obstruction on the part of the converted "adulteress." This time everyone is to know that love and fertility come from the true God and not from extramarital "lovers."

According to a widely held scholarly opinion, this bold description was inspired by a dialectic that Hosea saw in the phenomena he wanted to oppose at the time, namely, the Canaanite fertility cult and its celebrations of sacred "wedding rituals" *(hieros gamos)*. The fateful love story is told by a male voice and from a male perspective; women are described as unfaithful and emotionally unstable. God, the husband, is a faithful, mature, and balanced lover. Hosea himself receives the command to take a "whore" as his wife, so that his personal life becomes a symbol for God's love, and by extension man's love (1:2); Hosea 3 contains a variant of this.

The prophecies of Hosea 1–3 certainly point to an unhappy love. The imagery alludes to an embittered, unrequited love by the man. On the surface, this does not suggest a connection between the texts of Hosea and the Song, except for the main theme (love). There is certainly not much agreement between Hosea's view of marital unhappiness and the reciprocal love that makes up the fabric of the Song. Nevertheless, connections can be found between the two texts. Both seem to originate in a common tradition of Hebrew love poetry, with a more substantial "survival" of this tradition in the literature of the Song. Some passages in the two texts even feel like two variations of the same text, seen from different vantage points. This is especially true of Hosea 2:4-25 (2-23) (van Dijk-Hemmes 1989). The text can be defined as a man's love poem that keeps the beloved locked up in the prison of patriarchal, even discriminatory and violent, structures. The comparison between Hosea and the Song becomes explosive when it comes to the question of God. The man's love poetry, represented by Hosea 2, is associated with the religion of YHWH, while the woman's poetry in the Song is associated with the worship of the (fertility) goddess. Numerous images in these texts point in this direction. Amulets and seals also found in Israel have shown that these images, such as the dove, the gazelles, and lotus blossoms (cf. Keel and Uehlinger 1992, passim), belong to the world of the goddess of love and fertility.

The love hyperbole used for the first time in Hosea was taken up by Jeremiah (chapter 2) in the seventh century B.C.E., not long before the destruction of Jerusalem and the First Temple. Jeremiah is dealing in a comparable manner with the same religious context of a heathen cult, which causes a breach in the covenant between God and God's people. Jeremiah extends the metaphor to that of implicit political arbitrariness and speaks of two "women" of equal sexual promiscuity, Judah and Israel (Jer 3). Again, God is the loving, patient husband, and the people a downright animalistic, lustful woman who must be threatened (→ Jeremiah) with divorce (expulsion from the country).

Ezekiel — his book was written about the same time as Jeremiah, but he lives and works in Babylon — uses even more energetic love imagery. In chapter 16, a different patriarchal feature completes the picture of marriage that was first sketched in Hosea. At first God is Jerusalem's adoptive father, then its loving husband. But Jerusalem lets God down. Following punishment and reeducation there is to be a new and lasting (marriage) covenant. Again there is reference to heathen cult practices in terms like "whoring" and "lewdness" of the "woman." In chapter 23, two sisters/women, Samaria and Jerusalem, are quoted and their "adultery" is just as religious as it is political: "Assyria" and "Babylon" are the "lovers" (cf. Jer 3). Here the language is explicitly sexual, vulgar, and openly sexist. God is a faithful lover. God's women are totally ordinary whores, adulteresses whose violations are punished with public scandal and death. Moreover, the same simile is found again, though in a different form and in kinder terms, in Deutero- and Trito-Isaiah (Isa 50:1; 54; 62) later on (in the sixth century B.C.E.). The people — or Zion/Jerusalem — are again a "woman" — wife, mother, beloved. The story begins with the husband-God leaving her in the lurch. This time he promises to turn the situation around and, after the exile, to reinstate the "wife" in her original status of beloved wife (and mother) (→ Ezekiel; Isaiah).

We see that the tradition of the love relationship between God and God's people remained alive for hundreds of years in this form of prophetic writing. We can read this form of expression as a bridge between the Song and the heathen fertility myths on the one hand, and on the other hand as early evidence of the development and, later on, the dominance of a Jewish allegorical interpretation of the Song. In the allegorical reading, too, as in the prophetic tradition, the main characters are God the lover and Israel the beloved. But their love relationship is represented very differently in the two traditions. This is even more true when we compare the prophetic tradition with the Song itself. If we read it with an eye toward the theme of the love relationship, a theme that is part of a coherent pattern in the biblical context, the poetry of the Song represents an appropriate and a salutary protest against the ruthless patriarchal view of heterosexual love as the prophets picture it. Such an intertextual reading does not necessarily imply any certain chronological order in the relevant texts. Some of the poems adopted in the Song — along with similar compositions — could date from an earlier time than at least some of the prophetic passages cited. The only thing one must assume is that the love relationship one text talks about illuminates and complements the love relationship in other texts as with any analogy or juxtaposition. It should be assumed that the theme, the literary origin, and the structures that form the basis of all the "love passages" belong in a fundamental way to the same poetic family, while the texts can vary a lot in their respective emotional content.

In Conclusion: A Way of Reading the Song of Songs Today

Today's readers, especially people of faith of any confession whatever, could say, "That is not very satisfying. If we are not supposed to read the Song primarily as a religious book, then what remains for us to do?" This book is, after all, part of canonical Scripture! What can we gain by holding on to its human character, while defining the spiritual, theological, God-oriented interpretation as secondary?

What remains for us is, first of all, a gloriously and richly woven tapestry of poetry. This poetry has aesthetic attraction, and, perhaps even more satisfying, it speaks immediately to the senses. If we read attentively, we can picture the lovers and the world they live in, or at least imagine ourselves in their places. We can hear them, for the Song consists of a series of monologues and dialogues. We can hear the turtledove cooing. We can taste the honey and the wine and the fresh fruits. We can smell the perfumes, spices, and aromas. We can reach out and touch body and soul.

The Song is a collection of love poetry. The love it celebrates is colorful and many-faceted. It is happy and sad, lonely and exuberant, easily fulfilled and easily frustrated, strong and uncomfortable, easygoing and serious, carefree and then again restricted. It is unconventional in the sense that it is essentially love between unmarried people. What remains for us is the power that we can derive from the knowledge that Scripture, that this part of the canon, does not gloss over this kind of love but affirms it in clear terms. One presupposition must, however, be stated emphatically. The love that is sanctioned throughout the Song comes with the responsibility to be socially engaged and live a stable life. Though it legitimizes relationships outside of marriage, it does not in any way legitimize so-called free love.

By recognizing the deeply human character of the Song and the human love that constitutes the book's theme, we humanize this poetry. When we do that, we are left with the feeling that love, erotic and bodily love, is in itself a positive value and does not exist merely for the purpose of reproduction, as the prevailing ideology of Scripture and of Judaism and Christianity alike would have us believe.

What remains for us is the knowledge that patriarchal behavior and patriarchal institutions typical for the Bible disappear in the Song. Women can be strong, women can take initiative in love without being called "whores." Women can and must be themselves, rather than adapting to any male fantasy in order to be somehow lovable. Women can and must assert their emotional purpose and do so by their actions. In a world in which human beings are still judged by their sex, this is a source of strength. The love that is welcomed at the beginning and at the end of the Song is not a Platonic love. It is erotic love, physical and unashamed. When we have read this collection of love poetry, we are left with the encouraging feeling that erotic love is completely permissible, completely desirable, that it keeps the world in motion, that it is life, stronger than death. That is more than small comfort in a hi-tech, technocratic, and exhausted world that is not free of moral and social prejudice.

One can find an allegorical intent in the Song. It has been seen there and doubtless will continue to be found. But in my view these interpretations — Jewish, Christian, or any other — represent a secondary level of interpretation. For this reason, and for the sake of love and life, such interpretations deserve to be challenged by readers.

Postscript

Reading, just as the discernment of beauty, occurs to a great extent through the eye of the beholder. When we read, we consciously or unconsciously use a certain method of reading. This is true whether we are reading religious or secular texts. What we want to read in a text will determine our understanding of it to a great extent. Recently one reading of the Song was brought forward for discussion, in which these songs are understood as male fantasies about women (cf. Clines 1995). The debate is open. Will women enter into it, and if so, how?

LITERATURE

Brenner, Athalya. 1989. *The Song of Songs.* Old Testament Guides. Sheffield.

———. 1994. "Het Hooglied." *Schrift, Special Issue* 154.

———, ed. 1993. *A Feminist Companion to the Song of Songs.* Sheffield.

Brenner, Athalya, and Fokkelien van Dijk-Hemmes. 1993. *On Gendering Texts: Female and Male Voices in the Hebrew Bible.* Leiden.

Butting, Klara. 1994. *Die Buchstaben werden sich noch wundern.* Berlin.

Clines, David J. A. 1995. "Why Is There a Song of Songs, and What Does It Do to You If You Read It?" In Clines, *Interested Parties: The Ideology of Writers and Readers of the Hebrew Bible,* 94-121. Journal for the Study of the Old Testament: Supplement Series, vol. 205. Sheffield.

Exum, J. Cheryl. 1973. "A Literary and Structural Analysis of the Song of Songs." *Zeitschrift für die alttestamentliche Wissenschaft* 85:47-79.

Falk, Marcia. 1990. *Love Lyrics from the Bible: The Song of Songs.* San Francisco.

Ginsburg, Christian David. 1970. *The Song of Songs and Cohelet* (1857). Edited by S. Blank. New York.

Goitein, Shelomo Dov. 1988. "Women as Creators of Biblical Genres." *Prooftexts* 8:1-33.

"Hohelied, Das." 1997. Special issue of *Bibel und Liturgie* 70, no. 2.

Keel, Othmar. 1992. *Das Hohelied.* 2nd ed. Zürcher Bibelkommentar. Zurich.

———. 1995. "Hoheslied." In *Neues Bibellexion,* 2:183-91. Zurich.

Keel, Othmar, and Christoph Uehlinger. 1992. *Göttinnen, Götter und Gottessymbole.* Questiones disputatae, vol. 134. Freiburg im Breisgau.

Mariaselvam, Abraham. 1988. *The Song of Songs and Ancient Tamil Love Poems.* Analecta biblica, vol. 118. Rome.

Müller, Hans Peter. 1991. *Das Hohelied.* Altes Testament Deutsch, vol. 16, 2. Göttingen.

Pope, Marvin H. 1977. *Song of Songs.* Anchor Bible. Garden City, N.Y.

Trible, Phyllis. 1978. *God and the Rhetoric of Sexuality.* Philadelphia.

————. 1993. *Gott und Sexualität im Alten Testament.* Gütersloh.

Van Dijk-Hemmes, Fokkelien. 1989. "The Imagination of Power and the Power of Imagination: An Intertextual Analysis of Two Biblical Love Songs." *Journal for the Study of the Old Testament,* 75-88.

————. 1993. "The Imagination of Power and the Power of Imagination: An Intertextual Analysis of Two Biblical Love Songs." In *A Feminist Companion to the Song of Songs,* edited by Athalya Brenner, 156-70. Sheffield.

Weems, Renita J. 1992. "Song of Songs." In *The Women's Bible Commentary,* edited by Carol A. Newsom and Sharon H. Ringe, 156-60. London and Louisville.

Weiler, Gerda. 1989. *Das Matriarchat im Alten Israel.* Stuttgart.

FOR FURTHER READING

Bergant, Dianne. 2001. *The Song of Songs.* Berit Olam. Collegeville, Minn.

Brenner, Athalya, ed. 2000. *A Feminist Companion to the Song of Songs.* 2nd ser. Sheffield.

Exum, Cheryl J. 1998. "Developing Strategies of Feminist Criticism/Developing Strategies for Commentating the Song of Songs." In *Auguries: The Jubilee Volume of the Sheffield Department of Biblical Studies,* edited by David J. A. Clines and Stephen D. Moore, 206-50. Journal for the Study of the Old Testament: Supplement Series, vol. 269. Sheffield.

Hagedorn, Anselm C., ed. 2005. *Perspectives on the Song of Songs. Perspektiven der Hoheliedauslegung.* Beihefte zur Zeitschrift für die alttestamentliche Wissenschaft, vol. 346. Berlin and New York.

Translated by Nancy Lukens

Isaiah: The Book of Female Metaphors

Irmtraud Fischer

Scholarship focused on Isaiah has for the last two decades undergone a similarly serious change as that on the Pentateuch. The book's classic three-part structure: chapters 1 to 39 (I, Proto-Isaiah), 40 to 55 (II, Deutero-Isaiah), and 56–66 (III, Trito-Isaiah) and the dating associated with it as preexilic, exilic, and (early) postexilic, are no longer tenable: there are texts in Isaiah 1–39 that are not older than those in chapters 56–66 and derive from particular redactions of the whole book of Isaiah. In terms of dating, a rough judgment is that early, preexilic texts are found in part one, that the second part certainly contains exilic texts, while part three consists exclusively of postexilic texts.

Hardly any other writing in the First Testament makes a claim similar to that of Isaiah, namely, that it be read as the work of a single source as a whole; even though this writing does not smooth out the diverse contexts of origin, it wants to be read as "Isaiah" from beginning to end. In this article, a commentary on the continuous text is not commendable because the relevant individual themes and motifs are taken up in various ways in the book that would result in continuous repetitions. The questions of feminist significance are thus presented in thematic order. The message of the book of the acts of "the Holy One of Israel" in the history of Judah and Jerusalem over half a millennium neither primarily speaks to nor talks about women. However, Isaiah makes remarkably extensive use of female metaphors to transmit God's message. They allow us to draw conclusions about the sociocultural conditions of the life of women and what ideas about the female gender existed in ancient Israel. When it comes to metaphorical language, one has to keep in mind that a certain basic image (e.g., "wife") can throughout have negative connotations (such as "whore") as well as positive ones (like "bride"). The two opposites have to be understood as the two sides of the same coin. The negative results of such imagery for women do not have to reside primarily in the intentions of the metaphorical choice of language, but they cannot be ignored in terms of their reception and of the history of interpretation.

Female Figures in Isaiah

"Historical" Personalities of Women

The few women mentioned in the book have no names and are wives of men who do (cf. Laffey 1988, 172). In the verse of the book Christians know best, Isaiah 7:14, the prophet announces a sign to King Ahaz that "the young woman" who is with child will bear a son. She will give him the name "Immanuel," "God with us." The name that this young woman chooses is an affirmation of trust in the God who protects the city (cf. Ps 46) and is an oppositional sign against the disbelief of the king (Isa 7:12). Apart from the reproductive function and the confession-like naming of the child, we know nothing of the woman (but then, there is also no explicit mention of who is the father of the child). It is likely that she was a young woman in the palace of King Ahaz. The definite article ("*the* young woman") suggests that she might have been present at the meeting between the prophet and the king (cf. Engelken 1990, 53). Typological exegesis, building on the Greek translation as "virgin," interpreted this heralded sign as a reference to Jesus' virgin birth (cf. Matt 1:23). This woman must be distinguished from the prophetess (Isa 8:3) whom Isaiah visits and who becomes pregnant and also gives birth to a son. But on God's commandment, Isaiah is to call the child "Maher-shalal-hash-baz," "the spoil speeds, the prey hastens." "The prophetess" cannot be read as a simple reference to Isaiah's wife because she would then be called the "wife of the prophet" and that would be rather unusual in the prophet's terminology. If "the prophetess" does refer to Isaiah's wife, then on the basis of this designation she must have been active as a prophet as well. However, there are no recorded words transmitted in her name. She is known in the tradition only in the classic gender role as mother, although she might also have been a cult-prophetess (cf. Fischer 2002, 189-220).

Neither the father nor the mother is known of the son who is born as savior in Isaiah 9:6. What we know is that on the throne of David he will bring justice and righteousness. The only thing said about the one who will bear the spirit (Isa 11:1-5) is his genealogical standing in the line of David. All the children mentioned in Isaiah 7–11 are boys; a girl with a sign-like name (cf. Hos 1:6), or more specifically, with temporary saving function, does not exist in Isaiah.

Recourse to the (Almost Exclusively) Male Traditions

Whenever the book of Isaiah mentions important personalities from the tradition and history of the people, they are exclusively male — with one single exception: in 51:2a the listeners are called to look to "Abraham your father and Sarah who bore you." But in 2b this promise is already concentrated solely on the patriarch. This makes clear that the grammatical form that describes the *parents* of Israel is male. But given the metaphor of the barren, childless woman (Zion) Deutero-Isaiah uses, Sarah, the arch-ancestress, who had been barren for so long, would have been a better example than the patriarch. All other passages referring to the arch-parents mention only the men: Abraham (29:22; 41:8; 63:16) and Israel (63:16)/Jacob (41:8). In the majority of passages that mention it, the name of Jacob the patriarch functions as a name for the people, similarly to how the name Israel functions. Referring to the time of the journey in the desert and the exodus, 63:11-14 recalls Moses but not Miriam (nor Aaron!). A (mythological) figure who gained more prominence in postbiblical times is mentioned in the First Testament only in Isaiah 34:14: Lilith finds rest in Edom, which YHWH has turned into desert land. Together with wild animals, she resides in barren land without people. She is seen as a demonic figure associated with the Mesopotamian deity *lilitu* (cf. Handy 1992, 324). According to later Jewish tradition, Lilith was Abraham's first wife who refused to renounce the equality between woman and man. Instead of submission to the man, she freely chose solitude in the desert (cf. Cantor 1983).

Constructions of the Female Gender in the Book of Isaiah

What the book Isaiah tells us about the context and experiences of the life of women does not mirror their reality pure and simple, but rather how men perceived it. When Isaiah uses female metaphors to bring a message of salvation or damnation, both the view of women and the aspect of women's lives built into the metaphor are shaped by the male author of that message.

Elemental Life-Processes and Female Biology

Metaphors that draw on the conditions or processes of female biology tend to illustrate primarily distressful and embarrassing processes as men see them: menstruation is regarded as unclean and serves in metaphorical language in the confession of sins to illustrate hopelessly guilty existence (64:6). The traumatic experiences of the cessation of contractions during birth (37:3) and of miscarriage that cannot give new life are, from a female perspective, images for the hopeful expectation that is tragically destroyed. Such events need to be met by consoling compassion, not by condemnation and humiliation. From an androcentric perspective ("male voice"; Brenner and van Dijk-Hemmes 1996) that judges female experience cliché-like and thus frequently misinterprets it, the pregnant woman in labor who does not give birth to a living baby becomes an image of failure and distress (26:18; 33:11; 59:4). Isaiah 59:1-8, a scolding delivered by the prophet, shows this in a particularly harsh form. The metaphorical language of being pregnant and begetting iniquity (v. 4) deteriorates into language of the animal world from verse 5 onward. But only the female part in the creation of new life, pregnancy and birthing, is animalized in the image of the poisonous snake hatching her eggs. The reproductive aspect of female sexuality is dehumanized with such metaphoric language (cf. Brenner and van Dijk-Hemmes 1996, 183 concerning the animalization of the female). The outsider perception of men takes note particularly of the inescapable agony of the contractions, the cramping pain and the screaming of the woman giving birth (13:8; 21:3; 26:17). The image of a woman in labor is used to illustrate the terror of the sudden, inescapable suffering of retribution for sinful behavior. Since such portrayal represents the process of giving birth as a consequence of guilt, the metaphor retroacts on women's life experiences: women have to interpret such androcentric prophecy differently than their male counterparts. According to van Dijk-Hemmes (Brenner and van Dijk-Hemmes 1996, 176), that kind of metaphorical language about the sins of the people gives the male public no other option but to retreat from the identification since it touches no reality of men's biology. But female listeners may well see their ability to bring life into the world as potentially harmful and caught in the wake of sin.

But when looking at the book as a whole, this gender-specific reception of metaphors of pregnancy and birth is substantially relativized: in God's speech in 42:14, YHWH compares his own acts of salvation with a woman giving birth (cf. also Num 11:12; Deut 32:18). The birthing process and the specific breathing techniques of puffing, panting, and crying-pushing-exhaling that make childbearing easier (Gruber 1983, 355) are not an image of distress but a liberating act of strength that looks toward bringing new life into the world. In female perspective, birth is evidence of female potency. While the prophetic speaker (in Isa 42:13 YHWH is spoken about!) chooses the image of the powerful warrior who defeats the enemy (Babylon) to paint the new thing that God's powerful activity has brought into being, the image of the woman in labor comes right at the beginning of God's speech. There is a similar transition in 66:6, 7-9: the prophet speaks first of the clamorous voice of God's retribution; beginning in verse 7 we hear about the woman giving birth, the last mention of her in the book of Isaiah. God's speech in verse 9 comments only on the image of the woman but not on that of the warrior. 66:7-8 reads like a cancellation of the verse against women in Genesis 3:16 that announces difficulty during pregnancy and pain in childbirth: now the child is to be born before the contractions even start. Birth without pain is obviously induced by the midwife YHWH and is quickly completed (Isa 66:9).

Even the painful experience of infant death, which affects the nursing mother more immediately than the father, is mentioned within the framework of God's speech in 65:20, 23. YHWH will see to it that life will be sustained for a long time, that the burdens of pregnancy and birth are also worthwhile. In the salvation oracle of 44:1-5, YHWH illustrates his help and support for his servant Jacob by pointing out that he created him and formed him in his mother's womb (v. 2). The creation statement is not linked to male participation in conception but to God, who causes the embryo to grow during pregnancy. Thus the servant (49:1, 5) knows that he is called to and equipped for his mission from his mother's womb. Those to whom Second Isaiah addresses his message from God are different from those of First Isaiah who closed their ears to God's message (48:8a with reference to 6:9-10) and therefore were called "rebels from birth" (48:8b).

Looking back at the metaphors around pregnancy and birth that are drawn exclusively from the life-context of women, one can state that, with the exception of 33:11, the image of women giving birth in the speeches of God is always seen from the female perspective and sense of inner self and therefore positions the woman in labor in a positive light.

Sociocultural Conditions of Women's Lives

Patriarchy does not just mean that men rule over women; it also has to be understood as a social-hierarchical system that structures the society (Schüssler Fiorenza 1983, 29). Women of the wealthy upper classes are represented in Isaiah as self-confident and self-assured (3:16; 32:9). They participate in the position of their husbands and fathers and thus in the "fruits" of the exploitation of socially weaker members of society, among whom women and their deprived children are the weakest. In this light, the passage 2:6–4:1 reads like a gender-specific accusation and threat: the triple refrain of 2:9, 11, 17 addresses the *men* directly. The high and mighty will all be brought low and humbled. 3:1-15 calls the whole ruling elite and their offspring to account. The corresponding accusation of *women*, the "daughters of Zion," follows in 3:16–4:1; they too are charged with haughtiness. The text reads like a fashion-magazine reporter might write watching from the edge of the runway: every item worn by the noble women is discussed in detail, as is their behavior, and the perversion of it all is named. YHWH will take away all the displayed wealth that shows off high-society status. 3:17, 26 threaten with sexual assault (Magdalene 1995, 332f.). 4:1 changes the obligation of marriage into its opposite: only to carry the name that authenticates the married status, seven women renounce the support that is due to them so that they can have a man. To be without a man obviously is a disgrace for women — especially if they had previously been sexually abused. Yet, the very late text of 4:2-6 appears to rescind the disgraceful situation of the daughters of Zion after the judgment (v. 4) when YHWH shall appear on Mount Zion as he did long ago on Mount Sinai (cf. Fischer 1995, 29ff.).

All social differentiations, including those between women, will be radically leveled when YHWH comes to judge. What happens between master and servant is exactly what will happen between mistress and maid (24:2). The economically well-off women, ruling over big households and throwing parties to celebrate the fruit harvest and the vintage season as feasts of overabundance, will have to wear the clothes of lament when the fruitful landscape becomes barren (32:9-14). The proverbial word pair "widows and orphans" registers the social reality of marginalization above all of women of lower status who are denied justice in the patriarchal system when they are without a male representative. Widows in this sense are not all women who have lost their husbands but only those who have remained without children or whose sons have not yet reached adulthood (cf. 47:8-9). There is no male relative who ensures the livelihood (cf. W. Schottroff 1992, 60). Whenever Isaiah scolds the socially powerful for denying widows and orphans their rights and depriving them of their livelihoods (1:17, 23; 10:2), he advocates for this disenfranchised group of women. But then, in the poem of the outstretched hand in 9:12-16, which is a radical charge against all sections of society, not even the widows and orphans are any longer under YHWH's mercy, for even they belong to the godless (9:17).

The catastrophic conditions in the political elite of the people are demonstrated in 3:12 by the fact that even women[1] rule. The (considerable) exclusion of women from public office is not understood in 3:12 as discrimination but is justified by an interpretive ideological framework that allocates gender roles within a patriarchal viewpoint: women are unfit to govern because of their gender. Isaiah 3:12 is thus not primarily an indication that sometimes women hold public office (according to Ackerman 1992, 164), but rather suggests the humiliation of the ruling elite who are degraded by being called "women" (*Weib* in Luther, which is a negative term for women; NRSV: "women"; NEB: "usurer"; NJB: "extortioners"). A similar emasculating humiliation of men (cf. also 60:16 in terms of servant of God and "Lady Zion") can be seen in the declaration of judgment on Egypt: "On that day the Egyptians will be like women, and tremble with fear . . ." (19:16). This verse shows the crass devaluing of the female, which therefore can be used to insult men. Men are humiliated not only through "discursive feminisation" (Müllner 1996, 96f.), but also through violence against their women. In the proclamation against Babel (13:16) one finds the threat that in the very presence of men their infants will be dashed to pieces, their houses plundered, their wives raped. Women in this instance are not even objects any longer to be victimized but means to an end to make victims of their men. Raping women and girls (cf. also 23:12) to humiliate the (male) enemy remains to this day the bitter reality of the extension of war with other weapons. When YHWH uses the same means for his judgment as hostile men do in their conduct of war, an image of God is developed that is fraught with problems, as is pointed out by Magdalene (1995) and Bowen (1995).

---

1. According to the Hebrew text (= MT); the German Einheits Übersetzung reads 3:12 according to the Septuagint (*Wucherer* — "usurer, profiteer").

Metaphors of Marriage and Women's Promise of Faithfulness

In Isaiah's metaphors of the relationship between the genders, the androcentric conceptions of those relations become apparent within the framework of patriarchal marriage. Since the relationship between husband and wife is applied to YHWH and his people, most texts talk about male love, devotion, and disappointment. If one reads the vineyard song in 5:1-7 as a love song, then the man is the only active party, tending his vineyard, the woman, with care and thus demanding in return behavior that matches his ideas. The potentially endangered position of wives can be seen in Isaiah 54: the husband can be wrathful toward his wife, can abandon her childless and without livelihood. This results in the decline of the wife's social status and leaves her to fight for her survival without any protection. But even the images of bride and bridegroom, taken from the sphere of love, see the gender roles in such a way that accords only the male part action and giving (cf. 61:10-11; 62:4-5; Sawyer 1996, 213).

The much more broadly developed metaphors of prostitutes and whores in the books of Jeremiah (→), Ezekiel (→), and Hosea (→), and used there to portray the faithlessness of the people pictured as a woman, are rarely drawn upon in Isaiah. In 1:21 the text bemoans the fact that the city where once justice and righteousness were at home has become a whore. This is not Zion's fault but the fault of her corrupt, incapable (male) ruling elite. When YHWH will give Israel judges and counselors as at the first, the city-whore will become the "city of righteousness, the faithful city" again (1:26). 57:3-13 obviously relates to this image. Even though in 57:3 the image of marriage cannot suggest the relationship of God and his people, because those addressed are called "offspring of an adulterer and a whore," the text speaks of the familiar image (in Jeremiah and Ezekiel) of the sexually insatiable woman (57:6-13). The people accused of whoring are apparently followers of foreign cults (57:5-10; cf. Jer 2:20-24). In my view, it is not likely that the prophets used the image of the whore because, in the male-dominated YHWH religion, women remained spiritually empty and thus turned primarily to foreign cults (Ackerman 1992, 164). The sexually insatiable and therefore unfaithful woman who — in the epitome of perversion of female "decorum" — buys her own lovers (Isa 57:8) is a logical image arising in the patriarchal idea of marriage that demands absolute faithfulness of the wife but not of the husband. When the people are compared to the wife of God, it follows that idol worship, being unfaithful to YHWH, is presented in the image of adultery.

Cities in the Image of Women

Prophetic writings frequently address countries and cities as women. This perception apparently comes from the Western Semitic cultural circle (the word "city" is grammatically female there) and is seen in connection to the city goddess (cf. Darr 1994, 126ff.; Maier 1994, 87-88). Israel borrows this metaphor but not the underlying belief in the goddess. The connotations of women metaphors for a city are a result of gendering: the city offers *shelter* through the protection within its walls; it *nurtures* its citizens who can make a living in her without owning land; its majestic buildings give *beauty* to a city; but the condition also arises in it of being *helplessly at the mercy* of an enemy who has entered the city.

Cities as Daughters — Daughter Zion

In Isaiah 1–39, the female figure of the daughter appears for foreign cities as well as for Zion. The "daughter" in this instance is seen less in the patriarchal relation to her father than as an independent young woman desirable to men. The foreign cities described as daughters are Dibon (15:2), who has to start the lament; Tarshish (23:10), whose port YHWH will take away; and Sidon, who as a raped virgin will find no rest (23:12). The third sea power in the Mediterranean, Tyre, will be forgotten for seventy years and can only get herself remembered by wandering through the streets at night like a whore with her harp so that people will take note of her (23:15-16). Isaiah quotes a prostitute's song in 23:16 (Brenner and van Dijk-Hemmes 1996, 82). When "business" is flourishing again because YHWH (!) takes care of her, her pay is not going to be hoarded but will be dedicated to YHWH and made available to those who live in his presence. YHWH as pimp — a daring image also in light of the prohibition in Deuteronomy 23:18 to bring the wages of a prostitute into the temple. This image has to be placed in the context of certain verses in Deutero- and Trito-Isaiah where YHWH also cares for his people in unconventional ways. Whether female interpreters of the message of the prophet can see such metaphors in the speech of God as expressions of care has to be left open.

Jerusalem is frequently addressed as "daughter Zion" in Proto-Isaiah but never as wife or woman. In Isaiah 1:8 the only city to be spared in Judah is referred to as "daughter Zion." She stands like an abandoned hut in the vineyard. Daughter Gallim is asked to yell with all her might, and the other suburbs of Jerusalem are to answer because the enemy is taking a position at the mount of daughter Zion (10:30-32). On the day chosen by YHWH, when Jerusalem will surrender, the city will be dismayed (22:1-8). The prophet, who has to announce the judgment, can only weep inconsolably about the violation done to the "daughter of my people" (22:4). But the text about Moab (daughters of Moab, 16:2) tells of a better time for the "mount of daughter Zion" (16:1).

In God's address to Hezekiah, who after the reception of the Assyrian delegation had looked for refuge with YHWH, the word against Sennacherib begins with the scorn of the "virgin daughter Zion," the "daughter Jerusalem" (37:22). She has nothing but scorn for the power-hungry ruler. With such mocking of the defeated enemy, daughter Zion joins the company of women in the ancient Orient who pour contempt on the (defeated) enemy and thereby celebrate the triumph that they have been spared the terrors of conquest, which always also included rape (Brenner and van Dijk-Hemmes 1996, 46ff.). In the text complex of Deutero- and Trito-Isaiah, the daughter Zion features only once in each. In the former, in 52:2, YHWH commands daughter Zion to loosen the chains around her neck so that she may enter upon a new exodus (52:11-12). In the latter, in 62:11, daughter Zion hears that her children will return to her. The statements associated with daughter Zion veer between the liberation and self-confident scorn of the independent woman (37:22) and the abandoned (1:8) and afflicted (10:32; 22:1-4). It is not "daughter Zion" who has to bear the responsibility for YHWH's disastrous retribution but her rulers, the mighty of the city (22:1-4; 1:10-15, 23). The consequence of violence and humiliation is never directly linked to her own behavior.

This perspective is qualified somewhat in Deutero-Isaiah in that the woman metaphor of First Isaiah is particularized because the woman Zion is now a wife. The relevant texts, beginning in Isaiah 49, can be read as a counterspeech to the most detailed text that presents a hostile power in the image of the daughter: Isaiah 47:1-4 announces the destruction of the "virgin daughter Babylon." "Daughter Chaldea" (47:1, 5) is presented as an egotistical woman who is secure in her life of luxury (47:8 and 10). In her hubris she thinks it impossible to become childless and a widow (47:8). YHWH, who will free his people from her domination, will also take revenge on her and make her work as a slave instead of being a ruler (47:2), humiliate her sexually by stripping her (47:3), and make her a childless widow (47:9). She will experience the typical consequences of war that women face and thus follow Jerusalem in her suffering. The prophet's announcement that God acts this way and how that metaphor has been received have given legitimacy to the continuous perpetration of violence against women in times of war and the excuse: "After all, YHWH does it too!"

Zion in Images of the Adult Woman

In contrast to the (still) carefree daughter Babylon, Zion sees herself as a childless, barren, abandoned, and rejected wife (49:21b; 54:1b, 4b, 6) of YHWH, her husband, who has divorced (50:1) and forgotten her (49:14). As defenseless woman, she has drunk the cup of wrath, but none of her many sons assisted her when she was staggering along. Helplessly she had to watch her children get killed in war (51:17-20) and saw the conquerors trample them underfoot (51:23). But the encouragement of Zion does not come in the image of the husband who takes his abandoned wife back but in the image of a mother who cannot forget her child (49:15). Even though Zion is never referred to as "daughter" in Isaiah 49 and, instead, the metaphor is widened by the images of bride (v. 18b) and mother with many children

(vv. 20-23), the impression that emerges as the book of Isaiah continues is that the relationship between YHWH and daughter Zion is that between mother and daughter (cf. Sawyer 1996, 212). In the context of Zion as a female figure, God never appears as father — only as mother!

God's Servant and "the Woman Zion"

While the male figure — God's servant — who (at least in the later literary layers of the text) symbolizes the people, has attracted massive interest in First Testament scholarship, its female pendant — "the Woman Zion" — has led a wallflower existence in exegetical literature until very recently. The manifold parallels between these two characters have been discussed in recent years (Wilshire 1975; Steck 1992 [1989]; Jeppesen 1993; Korpel 1996). Both have a task and a particular function to fulfill among the people and the nations. While the servant has the function of atonement, Zion's function as sheltering and nurturing city gives her "YHWH-like qualities" (Steck 1992, 132). Even though both metaphorical figures appear in a narrowly circumscribed area of the text, they are never connected to each other. The servant does not lead the people to Mount Zion, and Zion does not function as mother or partner to the servant. Her husband — like the master of the servant — is YHWH. Why does Deutero-Isaiah choose two figures of opposite gender to represent YHWH's actions with the people? Is it the same motivation that portrays God in chapters 40 to 66 not just as male but also as female, namely, the insight that maleness symbolizes only half — both in relation to the people and also in relation to God?

Zion's Sons and Daughters and Their Caregivers from the Nations

YHWH will bring back the children — sons and daughters alike — of the childless woman Zion (43:6; 49:22; 60:4). The foreign nations who in the service of YHWH take on the task of returning the children are also illustrated as people of both genders: they become Israel's male and female slaves (14:2); their kings are foster fathers and their princesses are nursing mothers (49:23). The most daring statement in 60:16 takes the image of 49:23 further: the children of Zion are nursed on the breasts of kings (!); they drink the milk of nations. The motherly care of YHWH for the children of Zion goes so far that he not only has the nations gather and returns them but he also enlists even the mightiest of the nations in his motherly care, even in suckling them. However, such inclusive language is not evident throughout the whole of Isaiah, and that has to be taken into account when interpreting the text. Those who are called "faithful servants of YHWH" above all in Trito-Isaiah are not only men. Isaiah's generic language with its exclusively male designations means to include women in it (e.g., the "man" and the foreigners who, according to 56:1-8, become proselytes; the "sons" as long as they are not contrasted with a female group).

Significant Feminist Aspects of the Image of God in Isaiah

YHWH, the Unconventional Husband

We indicated above (in "Cities as Daughters — Daughter Zion") that the prominent image of daughter Zion in First Isaiah changes, beginning in chapter 40, into the image of the "woman" Zion who is in a marital relationship with her God. In its metaphorical language Second and Third Isaiah use almost all possible status indicators for an adult woman: Zion is depicted as bride (49:18; 61:10; 62:4-5), wife (54:5), mother (49:20-23; 66:8-13), forsaken by her husband (49:14; 50:1; 54:6; 62:4), childless and barren (49:20-21; 54:1), even divorced (50:1) and widowed, without anyone caring for her (54:4). The last two images are explicitly negated because Zion's bridegroom and husband is the living God himself. That those images have been understood as the "life story" of the woman Jerusalem is mentioned in Baruch 4:5–5:9.

The image of the relationship between male and female as an expression of the relationship between YHWH and his people already appears in the prologue of Deutero-Isaiah, in 40:2. Jerusalem needs to be talked to "tenderly." This expression is also used for the attention of a man toward a woman who has suffered (Gen 34:3; Judg 19:3; Hos 2:15; Ruth 2:13; cf. Wacker 1996, 76f.). Even though Isaiah 40:2 mentions that the penalty for her sins has been paid and that she has atoned for her wrongs, she is not described (contrary to the marriage metaphors in Hosea) as unfaithful and as a whore but rather as a young man's cast-off early love (54:6). The husband is thus not cast as the disappointed partner who risks a new beginning, but as a husband who comes to his senses (Sawyer 1989, 94f.) and realizes the full extent of the tragic situation of his abandoned and uncared-for wife and tries to convince her patiently that his love for her is still there (54:6-8). The godly bridegroom and lover needs to speak tenderly to her heart, and it takes many attempts to convince her (49:14-18; 50:1; 51:17-23; 52:1-6; 54:1-8) to become his bride again (49:18; 62:1-5, 12). From a literary perspective, God's promise has to be seen each time as a reflex to the lament over the city. The miserable position of Jerusalem has changed too little for Zion to break into joyful celebration after the first promise.

Even though the image of marriage interprets the relationship between YHWH and Zion, Isaiah explicitly avoids the ultimate consequence of such an image: the many children that Zion is going to have are not conceived by the marriage partners themselves. Zion will get her children as the people are gathered and brought back from exile (cf. Steck 1992, 140). Zion can therefore not be understood as a city goddess who procreates with the male god YHWH and thus conceives her children, the inhabitants of the city. She is not an equal divine partner to YHWH (Winter 1983, 632-39). As wife, Zion is and remains a creature; YHWH as husband is her creator and spouse (54:5). As chosen bride she is and remains the built-up city whose walls are the royal diadem (62:3) and who wears beautiful robes (61:10, cf. also 52:1). But YHWH even as bridegroom is the one who builds her (62:5).

Female Images of YHWH

For those who strictly reject any incorporation of the female side in the symbolic dimension allegedly for reasons of faithfulness to the biblical image of God, the book of Isaiah is one of the best textbooks within the Bible to persuade them of the opposite. Those texts that describe God in female metaphors are all found in sections that are the earliest of late exilic or, even more likely, postexilic date; the "monotheistic" style of Deutero-Isaiah is already presupposed in them. Often feminist research maintains that by using female metaphors the (grammatically) male god YHWH usurps the symbols and functions of female goddesses (Schottroff, Schroer, and Wacker 1995, 161-64; 1998, 164-67). But the texts can be interpreted differently: the development of a monotheistic understanding of God makes it clearer than perhaps the previous preexilic "worship of the one alone" that it is impossible to speak of an exclusively male god. Because the female in the ancient Near East speaks to elemental needs and functions of humans, the one God has to speak to and incorporate those as well. YHWH can be imaged not only as man but also as woman. Even the images taken from the animal world use not only male animals (31:4, lion) to describe God but also female ones (31:5, mother bird; cf. also YHWH's special care for mother sheep in 40:11). Metaphorical language about God can and must include female *and* male images to insure that YHWH transcends every human experience and condition, even innermost realities, which can become points of comparison for metaphors of God. The rigorous prohibition of images (cf. Deut 4:15-20) finds correspondence in the metaphorical and its overabundance of linguistic images that simply does not allow fixation on and enforcement of one image alone. The polemic against idols in Isaiah 44:9-20 pokes fun at those who carve a male representation of God (44:13) so that they may worship it. The carving material even comes from the same wood that the women left over from making a fire to cook (44:15-16, 19; cf. also 27:11).

That YHWH uses the metaphor of birth to signify the new beginning of his act of salvation has been discussed under "Elemental Life-Processes and Female Biology." In addition, Zion's question in 49:21 about who has given her many children might point to God himself (Rupprecht 1989, 130). The twofold "woes" in 45:9-10 pronounce a warning to those who question the sovereignty of the creator

YHWH (45:11). The three parallel metaphors speak of the clay challenging the potter (45:9), of the child who asks his father why he begets and the mother why she has contractions (45:10). When one of these three comparisons equates the divine giver of life with a woman, then the speeches of God in 46:3-4 and 49:15 need no further clarification. The point of comparison in all these images is the never-ending love of the mother for her child to which she has given birth. Even if the unimaginable scenario of a human mother who stops loving her child should occur, God's motherly love never ceases (49:15). God will carry and bear his children as if they were still in the womb even when they have grown up or grown old (46:3-4):

> Listen to me, O house of Jacob,
>> all the remnant of the house of Israel,
> who have been borne by me from your birth,
>> carried from the womb. (v. 3)

In the Hebrew text it is not clear if the parallelism "borne by me from your birth" *(mny bṭn)* and "carried from the womb" *(mny rḥm)* is to be read as applying to YHWH (1QIsaᵃ: *mmny*). In the Vulgate this is much clearer: "qui portamini a meo utero qui gestamini a mea vulva" directly applies to the divine subject. Phyllis Trible (1993, 46-88), who has sketched the development of the "wandering metaphor" *rḥm* from "the womb of women to the mercy and compassion of God" (1993, 49), is supported in this by the Latin translation. In 66:7-13, the image of YHWH as the midwife who initiates the birthing process and brings it to a good end (v. 9) slips into the image of YHWH as mother:

> As a mother comforts her child,
>> so I will comfort you. (v. 13)

The preceding image of a woman who suckles her children and bounces them on her knees thus ends with the focus on YHWH. Obviously Isaiah 66 cancels the judgment of punishment against woman in Genesis 3:16 not only in terms of birth pains but also in terms of men's domination of women: in this final chapter, YHWH nowhere appears as husband of the woman Zion.

All statements that speak about God in the image of a woman are part of the speeches of God. According to Isaiah's testimony, he does not think it inappropriate or even impossible that YHWH should speak about himself in female terms. Femininity represents the holy just as well as masculinity! In the metaphors about pregnancy, birth, and breast-feeding, the association with the female element is inescapable. However, it would perpetuate gender-specific roles if only those metaphors that absolutely exclude the masculine were to be associated with femininity. It is therefore important to stress that all images that do not exclusively refer to men or deal with processes of the masculine areas of life (such as procreating, regular warfare, the sacrificial slaughter of animals by priests, or images of father and husband) are meant to refer to *humans* and not automatically to be associated with the male gender. This applies to all images in which the people are addressed as children or sons (cf. Darr 1994, 46-84). When God is not explicitly referred to as "father" of Israel, the image of those who bring up the people should be one of both parents. Gender stereotypes manifest their dichotomy also in metaphorical God language: YHWH in the image of a woman is never violent, whereas in the image of a man he is. The danger that God imaged as a man serves as a legitimating example to turn to violence — also against women, in their families, and during war — is latently present. Therefore, especially those texts that often are called the "Gospel of the Old Testament" offer in their images of God as a woman who gives life and sustains it a necessary and wholesome correction.

LITERATURE

Ackerman, Susan. 1992. "Isaiah." In *The Women's Bible Commentary,* edited by Carol A. Newsom and Sharon H. Ringe, 161-68. London and Louisville.

Bowen, Nancy R. 1995. "Can God Be Trusted? Confronting the Deceptive God." In *A Feminist Companion to the Latter Prophets,* edited by Athalya Brenner, 354-65. Feminist Companion to the Bible, vol. 8. Sheffield.

Brenner, Athalya, and Fokkelien van Dijk-Hemmes. 1996. *On Gendering Texts.* Biblical Interpretation Series, vol. 1. Leiden.

Cantor, Aviva. 1983. "The Lilith Question." In *On Being a Jewish Feminist,* edited by Susannah Heschel, 40-50. New York.

Darr, Katheryn Pfisterer. 1987. "Like Warrior, Like Woman: Destruction and Deliverance in Isaiah 42:10-17." *Catholic Biblical Quarterly* 49:560-71.

———. 1994. *Isaiah's Vision and the Family of God.* Literary Currents in Biblical Interpretation. Louisville.

Engelken, Karen. 1990. *Frauen im Alten Testament.* Beiträge zur Wissenschaft vom Alten und Neuen Testament, vol. 130. Stuttgart.

Fischer, Irmtraud. 1995. *Tora für Israel — Tora für die Völker. Das Konzept des Jesajabuches.* Stuttgarter Bibelstudien, vol. 164. Stuttgart.

———. 2002. *Gotteskünderinnen: Zu einer geschlechterfairen Deutung des Phänomens der Prophetie und der Prophetinnen in der Hebräischen Bibel.* Stuttgart.

Gerstenberger, Erhard S. 1988. *Jahwe — ein patriarchaler Gott?* Stuttgart.

Gruber, Mayer I. 1983. "The Motherhood of God in Second Isaiah." *Revue biblique* 90:351-59.

Handy, Lowell K. 1992. "Lilith." In *Anchor Bible Dictionary,* edited by David N. Freedman, 4:324-25. New York.

Jeppesen, Knud. 1993. "Mother Zion, Father Servant: A Reading of Isaiah 49–55." In *Of Prophets' Visions and the Wisdom of Sages,* edited by Heather A. McKay and David J. A. Clines, 109-25. Festschrift for R. Norman Whybray. Journal for the Study of the Old Testament: Supplement Series, vol. 162. Sheffield.

Korpel, Marjo C. A. 1996. "The Female Servant of the Lord in Isaiah 54." In *On Reading Prophetic Texts: Gender-Specific and Related Studies; In Memory of Fokkelien van Dijk-Hemmes,* edited by Bob Becking and Meindert Dijkstra, 153-67. Biblical Interpretation Series, vol. 18. Leiden.

Laffey, Alice L. 1988. *An Introduction to the Old Testament: A Feminist Perspective.* Philadelphia.

Magdalene, F. Rachel. 1995. "Ancient Near Eastern Treaty-Curses and the Ultimate Texts of Terror: A Study of the Language of Divine Sexual Abuse in the Prophetic Corpus." In *A Feminist Companion to the Latter Prophets,* edited by Athalya Brenner, 326-52. Feminist Companion to the Bible, vol. 8. Sheffield.

Maier, Christl. 1994. "Jerusalem als Ehebrecherin in Ezechiel 16." In *Feministische Hermeneutik und Erstes Testament,* edited by Hedwig Jahnow et al., 85-105. Stuttgart.

Mollenkott, Virginia R. 1984. *Gott eine Frau?* Munich.

Müllner, Ilse. 1996. "Tödliche Differenzen." In *Von der Wurzel getragen,* edited by Luise Schottroff and Marie-Theres Wacker, 81-100. Biblical Interpretation Series, vol. 17. Leiden.

Ohler, Annemarie. 1992. *Mutterschaft in der Bibel.* Würzburg.

Rupprecht, Friederike. 1989. "Jes 49,14-23: Leben für Zion — Leben für uns." In *Feministisch gelesen,* edited by Eva Renate Schmidt et al., 1:127-36. 2nd ed. Stuttgart.

Sawyer, John F. A. 1989. "Daughter of Zion and Servant of the Lord in Isaiah: A Comparison." *Journal for the Study of the Old Testament* 44:89-107.

———. 1996. *The Fifth Gospel,* 198-219. Cambridge.

Schmitt, John J. 1985. "The Motherhood of God and Zion as Mother." *Revue biblique* 92:557-69.

Schottroff, Luise, Silvia Schroer, and Marie-Theres Wacker. 1995. *Feministische Exegese.* Darmstadt.

———. 1998. *Feminist Interpretation: The Bible in Women's Perspective.* Louisville.

Schottroff, Willy. 1992. "Die Armut der Witwen." In *Schuld und Schulden,* edited by Marlene Crüsemann and Willy Schottroff, 54-89. Munich.

Schüngel-Straumann, Helen. 1993. "Mutter Zion im Alten Testament." In *Theologie zwischen Zeiten und Kontinenten,* edited by Theodor Schneider and Helen Schüngel-Straumann, 19-30. Festschrift for Elisabeth Gössmann. Freiburg.

———. 1996. *Denn Gott bin ich und kein Mann.* Mainz.

Schüssler Fiorenza, Elisabeth. 1983. *In Memory of Her: A Feminist Theological Reconstruction of Christian Origins.* New York.

———. 1988. *Zu ihrem Gedächtnis . . . Eine feministische Rekonstruktion der christlichen Ursprünge.* Munich.

Steck, Odil Hannes. 1992. "Zion als Gelände und Gestalt." In Steck, *Gottesknecht und Zion,* 126-45. Forschungen zum Alten Testament, vol. 4. Tübingen.

Trible, Phyllis. 1978. *God and the Rhetoric of Sexuality.* Philadelphia.

———. 1993. *Gott und Sexualität im Alten Testament.* Gütersloh.

Wacker, Marie-Theres. 1996. *Figurationen des Weiblichen im Hosea-Buch.* Herders Biblische Studien, vol. 8. Freiburg im Breisgau.

Wilshire, Leland Edward. 1975. "The Servant-City: A New Interpretation of the 'Servant of the Lord' in the Servant Songs of Deutero-Isaiah." *Journal of Biblical Literature* 94:356-67.

Winter, Urs. 1983. *Frau und Göttin*. Orbis biblicus et orientalis, vol. 53. Fribourg.

FOR FURTHER READING

Løland, Hanne. 2008. *Silent or Salient Gender? The Interpretation of Gendered God-Language in the Hebrew Bible Exemplified in Isaiah 42, 46, and 49*. Forschungen zum Alten Testament, 2nd ser., vol. 32. Tübingen.

Translated by Tina Steiner

Jeremiah: When Wise Wailing Women and Prophetic Pornography Show the Way into Exile

Angela Bauer-Levesque

The book of Jeremiah is a storehouse of literary metaphors of femininity with all its problematic and depth. At the same time, it offers a glimpse into the concrete reality of women in Israel shortly before the exile. Thus, literary as well as social-historical observations and corresponding feminist-theological questions form the scaffold of my brief commentary on the book of Jeremiah. My interpretation of the Bible is guided by feminist-liberation theological and epistemological interests and is housed methodologically in what is called literary criticism with particular attention to reader-response and social criticism. In this context it means that I intend to engage the book of Jeremiah in its final text form (in the Masoretic Text as well as in the Septuagint) in a feminist counterreading, that is, a reading that uncovers and deconstructs the narrator's rhetorical strategies. This is done especially with respect to power differences that become manifest in the use of gender-specific metaphors and in the traces of concrete women's reality. What characterizes the images of women in Jeremiah? Whom do they benefit? At whose expense? For what?

My choice of method is complex, as is my present interpretative stance. As a white, German, Protestant professor of Hebrew Bible at a small seminary of the Episcopal Church in the USA, I participate on different sides in the complicated webs of the structures of oppression of a racist, xenophobic, heteropatriarchal[1] society. My questions are sensitized by the bilinguality of complicity and oppression; it pushes me as I read First Testament texts to analyze critically the effects of power relations, to unmask mechanisms of oppression, and to name them, committing me openly to take sides.

The commentary is structured in two parts: first, a literary-theological diachronic reading that lifts up traces of feminine metaphors and concrete women's reality, naming their canonical connections; and second, a thematic

---

1. The term "heteropatriarchal" is meant to name the heterosexist aspects of patriarchal structures.

synchronic reading that critically probes the images and voices of women identified from a position of feminist liberation theology. This examination is undertaken from the perspectives of both history and the present.

Literary Metaphors of Femininity and Women's Concrete Reality in Jeremiah: A Diachronic Reading

Whether as brides, prostitutes, wives, or adulterous women; as women giving birth
or being sexually violated; as wise wailing-women, singers, or teachers; whether it
is Rachel weeping for her children or women who venerate the Queen of Heaven,
the images and voices of women in this book look complex and contradictory. Despite and yet precisely because of this, they embody the literary-theological movement of the canonical hither and yon that marks this prophetical composition
shortly before the exile. In the highs and lows of the history of Israel's inhabitants,
the book of Jeremiah is a document that reflects particularly from the perspective
of Jerusalem the experiences of the years just before the Babylonian exile, that is,
the final years of the seventh century B.C.E. and those leading up to the destruction of Jerusalem in 586. It also contains reactions to the experiences of exile in the
voices of the next generation. The book paints the discussions between the
prophet, the people, and God, between the man Jeremiah, the Israelites/Judeans,
and their God YHWH in their search for meaning, commonly and individually, in
this experience of chaos of war and resistance, defeat and everyday life shortly before the exile. Based in the traditions of the writing prophets (as distinguished
from the historiography of the royal court at that time), the fifty-two chapters of
Jeremiah consist of collections of poetic and narrative texts whose canonical order
lacks a clear chronology. In addition, repetition of specific historical associations
is found in poetic and narrative sections, themselves made yet once more complicated by different text versions of the Masoretic and Septuagint texts. As a result,
exegetes have been occupied long with the question of the book's composition and
proposed various answers. One of them suggests that Jeremiah has three different
sources and authors (Duhm 1901; Mowinckel 1914 et al.); another says it is a construction of different models of redaction (Carroll 1986; Rudolph 1958, among
others). Feminist exegetes, on the other hand, have thus far focused in particular
on the text's final literary form (cf. the literature section below). They have followed the traces of women's history (e.g., Jost 1995), uncovered gender dualisms
and stereotypes of women that had been left unattended (e.g., Bauer 1998; Weems
1995), exposed certain passages as being pornographic (e.g., Brenner 1993; 1995;
1996; Exum 1996), and examined functions of gender-specific metaphors in their
literary contexts (e.g., Bozak 1991; Bauer 1998; O'Connor 1992). In short, the focal
point of feminist exegesis of the book of Jeremiah is women's concrete reality and
the literary metaphors of femininity.

Jeremiah 1–6

For sheer quantity of women's images alone, the book's first part is a dense cluster of Jeremiah's metaphors of femininity: the prologue and the first two cycles of prophecies of calamity to come (1:1–6:30). Immediately following the introductory heading (1:1-3) that gives location to the prophet's words, history, and geography, the first words uttered by YHWH already revolve around such a metaphor. The womb, the uterus, the mother's body (in Hebrew *beṭen* and *reḥem*) are God's and refer to the place of Jeremiah's calling into prophecy: "Before I formed you in [my] womb *(beṭem)* I knew you, / and before you came forth from the womb *(reḥem)* I consecrated you" (1:5) (translation altered: "my" is inserted to clarify that it is the womb of God that is meant; the pronoun used here indicates this [from a communication with the translator]).

The Hebrew text is ambiguous whose body it actually speaks of, using as it does the definite article without a pronominal specification. That has prompted scholars to speak of motherly aspects in YHWH (Trible 1978 et al.). Several commentators, reacting to such openness in how the image of God is perceived in this verse, have brought Jeremiah's mother into this text (e.g., Carroll 1986 and others). But both the Masoretic Text and the Septuagint are ambiguous here. We can say, however, that the book of Jeremiah begins with the metaphor of birth (1:5) in which the divine "I" includes the prophetic "you" and calls upon it

> to pluck up and to pull down,
> to destroy and to overthrow,
> to build and to plant. (1:10)

The pregnancy motif that opens the book is quickly juxtaposed by very different metaphors in the prophecies of calamity (2:1–4:4) that follow directly upon the prologue of Jeremiah (1:1-19). The metaphor of birth/mother/parent is replaced by metaphors of wedding and marriage in order to depict YHWH's relation to the Israelites. Images of Israel as the bride of YHWH (2:2-3) in contrast to Israel as prostitute, unfaithful wife, and adulterous woman (2:20, 25-28 and 29-37; 3:1-5, 6-10 and 19-20) serve the prophet as examples in his threatening words that are meant to call the Israelites to turn back and return to YHWH as their God. The reminder of Israel as the loving bride of the covenant in days gone by, the bride holy to YHWH (2:2-3; cf. 2:32), forms the historical context and contrast to the image of Israel now as prostitute, a woman unfaithful and adulterous. The image of the bride symbolizes a woman whom this text represents as a desirable object for male hearers: "pure" and "innocent," properties of a holy woman (cf. Jost 1994). On this background, the prophet paints the picture of a male Israel that strays from its God (2:4-19), and then he condemns this Israel in another feminine image, that of a whore who prostitutes herself on the high hills and under the trees (2:20-22).

Finally, he even compares Israel (2:23-25) to a restive young camel and a wild she-ass who cannot control their sex drive. Here the prophet harshly critiques the cult of mountains and trees associated with goddess worship. This indicates on the one hand that in popular religion at that time there existed side by side with the "official" worship of YHWH the practice of venerating other deities, among them not least female ones (cf. 3:6, 13; 17:2; and others; cf. especially also the Queen of Heaven, 7:16-20 and 44:15-25; Jost 1995; Ackerman 1989; et al.). On the other hand, the language of the chosen images shows that the authors of the book do not shrink back from drawing offensive, indeed pornographic, images all the way to animalizing the "woman" allegedly to move their hearers to turn back and return to worshiping YHWH. Those images are not lacking in irony and consequently in brutality concerning the reality of women then and also now when women are accused of the same thing, whereas the reality of sexual aggressions between men and women moves chiefly in the opposite direction. But here in Jeremiah these accusations are meant to be reasons for justifying the judgments announced next. Israel, personified as a woman, is to be put to shame, to be disgraced and burdened with guilt and humiliation (2:29-37). The sentence imposed is divorce (3:1-5). Sexual activity, ironically described as an experience of sexual assault, is said to be responsible for the pollution of the land (3:2-3). Still, she (Israel) is urged to return to "her" marriage with YHWH.

In this chapter, images of sexual violence against Israel as a woman underscore the gravity of the threat and judgment. Here Jeremiah builds on corresponding metaphors in the book of Hosea (especially Hos 2:4-19; Wacker 1994; 1996) and paves the way for extremely objectionable image-language in the book of Ezekiel (chapters 16 and 23; cf. Galambush 1992). Athalya Brenner has exposed these texts as Jeremian pornography (Brenner 1993; 1995; 1996; cf. Exum 1996; Weems 1995 differs), as men's texts that do violence to metaphorized female sexuality. Alice Keefe shows how the violated body of a woman serves the function of a metonym for the body of a society destroyed by war (Keefe 1993). That may also apply to these texts in Jeremiah.

In the next cycle of prophecies of calamity to come (Jer 4:5-6:30), the admonition to turn back becomes a pronouncement of inescapable judgment; the placement of the metaphors of femininity has shifted slightly when the prophet addresses the Israelites facing the destruction to come as "Daughter that is My people" and "Daughter Zion." Yes, the prophet Jeremiah even identifies himself with Jerusalem and, in a way, assumes a feminine identity bemoaning her suffering (4:19-21) — a woman's voice with transgender undertones (Kaiser 1987): "My belly, my belly! I writhe in pain . . ." (4:19, translation altered).

The metaphor of a woman in labor here describes the highest distress of Jerusalem's inhabitants. Experiences of war become direct physical experiences. And the prophet Jeremiah claims this woman's experience for himself. Then in the next announcement the image of a woman suffering and struggling in the pains of labor is fused into the image of an adulterous woman all dressed up and made up who, instead of waiting for her lovers, awaits her death (4:29-31; cf. Bauer 1998). Israel is portrayed as a vulnerable and injured woman before the Babylonians' attack and the impending destruction. Women's voices palpably embody doom and condemnation; they are heard again in the next chapter where, in addition, children are accused of complicity (5:7-9). The judgment is all-encompassing. "Fair [Daughter] Zion" is threatened with total destruction; men as well as women will perish (6:2-3 and 11; cf. 6:21). Destruction is compared once again to women's experience of labor pains (6:23-24). And where public mourning is the only possible reaction left, "Daughter that is My people" is called upon to begin the lament for the dead (6:26) — a portent for what is to come (cf. 9:16-21).

Summing up, metaphors of femininity ranging from womb to labor pains, from bride to prostitute, mark the theological threads of these first chapters of Jeremiah (1:1–6:30); they simultaneously depict calling and discrediting, people being of age and being disenfranchised. We see images showing God being pregnant and giving birth; there are dualistic characterizations of Israel as "a holy one" (bride) and, at one and the same time, as a "whore" (adulterous woman); there is the phenomenon of a male prophet taking on a female personality. Metaphors of labor pains go hand in hand with those of sexualized violence. Far-reaching dissonances characterize this to-and-fro of life-giving and death-dealing language images.

Jeremiah 7–25

In the next part of the book (7:1–25:38), images of women and women's reality are employed in a variety of ways. The women of Judah who worship the Queen of Heaven (7:16-20) and the wise mourning-women and teachers are spoken of at the beginning of this section where impending disaster turns into actualized destruction. Jeremiah's speech in the temple (7:1-15) is followed immediately by a condemnation of the cult of the Queen of Heaven. Women who have leading roles in the worship of the goddess are not identified in this text by their patrilineal relations, that is, as "daughter of . . . ," "wife or mother of . . ."; they are referred to simply as *nāšîm* (women). They bake special cakes for the goddess (7:18) and, according to Jost (1995; cf. Ackerman 1989), are to be seen as employees of the cult performing their activities within the worship in the temple. The Queen of Heaven has been identified with diverse goddesses, particularly with the Assyrian goddess Ishtar and the Canaanite goddess Astarte. Presumably the Queen of Heaven incorporates traces of different local goddesses (cf. Ackerman 1989; Jost 1995). Other prophets of the time of the exile confirm the existence of religiosity unique to women, for example, in Ezekiel's reference to women who were weeping for the goddess Tammuz (Ezek 8:14; → Ezekiel). Prophets who are part of the "orthodox" cult of YHWH condemn this cultic activity of women as apostasy, naming it as the reason for the inescapable punishment said to come upon the whole of creation (Jer 7:20). The litany of the condemned cultic practices includes sacrifices of children (7:31), which the text — it is frightening! — deals with on the same level as what women do in their worship of the goddess. Other aspects of the announced all-encompassing doom named later (8:4-17) include more acts of violence, above all, the war crimes of sexual assault and the murder of women and children (8:10). Responding with mourning and lamenting is the only option (8:18-23).

In this situation YHWH calls upon the wise mourning-women through Jeremiah to raise their dirges (9:17-21). This "Jeremiad" contains the single, so-called prophetic formula in the First Testament that addresses women directly: "Hear, O women, the word of YHWH" (9:19 [Eng. 20]). The divine command calls upon women to teach their daughters a lament and their women friends, neighbors, and lovers *(rĕʿûtāh)* a dirge. Theirs is the task of mourning women: to sing, to teach, and to guide to wisdom (9:20). Jeremiah 9:17 employs the direct "job description" of mourning women *(mĕqônĕnôt),* and here the Hebrew root *ḥkm* characterizes the women as wise. But many translations of the Bible conceal this in contrast to the next verses that deal explicitly with wise men (9:23-24). To this day, the task of officially bewailing the dead belongs in most cultures essentially to women. Here, as in relation to the cult of the Queen of Heaven, women of Judah occupy leading roles in the ritual of wailing (Jahnow 1923; Bird 1987; et al.). This may be explained by the fact that men were absent in times of war. The song (fragment) cited in 9:21 is perhaps an old song women sung lamenting the approach of death from the perspective of those hiding at home.

The admonition to prepare for exile concludes this section of the book (10:17-25). What is remarkable within the framework of Jeremiah's composition is that women's voices are heard at this important juncture where the threat of death has actually turned into reality and evoked lamenting.

In the following chapters (11:1–20:18), when turning back is not a possible option (any more) to be offered to those the prophet is addressing, Jeremiah is deeply troubled about how or even whether he is to identify himself with the people of Israel. Images of women create thematic continuity in these texts that are structured around the so-called confessions of Jeremiah (11:18-23; 12:1-6; 15:10-21; 17:14-18; 18:18-23; 20:7-13 [18]). The prophet's voice is heard echoing the destruction that is depicted in female imagery: the metaphor of a woman, naked and sexually assaulted with the concurrence, yes, the participation, of YHWH (13:20-27) puts readers and hearers before the gruesome fate of the Israelites — porno-prophecy in the name of God. The metaphors of labor pain (13:21) and sexual assault (13:22 and 26) are the images of women's reality drawn upon in this passage. It aggravates the comparison of experiences of war with labor pains when it paints a female figure (Jerusalem) having her clothes torn off and being raped:

It is for the greatness of your iniquity
  that your skirts are lifted up
  and violence visited upon your genitals. (13:22, translation altered)

The Hebrew text uses the euphemistic *ʿăqēbāyik* (your heels), which, like *raglayim* (feet), has connotations of genitals (cf. Isa 7:20; Ezek 16:25). Sexual assault is presented here as punishment, and the figure of the woman (Jerusalem) is held responsible for the violence done to her — a phenomenon women today are also brutally familiar with. Her condition is deemed unchangeable in an image whose race ideology makes this passage even more problematic. Just as an Ethiopian cannot possibly change the color of her or his skin, a color looked upon with condescension, so the woman cannot possibly turn back (Jer 13:23). As the accusations mount, the brutality against the figure of the woman heightens — as if that were even possible any more — when YHWH himself threatens violence:

I myself will lift up your skirt over your face,
  and your shame will be seen. (13:26)

And this abuse is said to be deserved in the biblical text. I find it frightening and dangerous that most commentaries and interpretations of Jeremiah silence or explain away what is said in these verses. Verses like those are dangerous as long as biblical texts go on being functionalized in many circles to legitimate present behaviors. It is only recently that some feminist voices have raised objections and called violence against women, then and now, by its real name (e.g., Magdalene 1995; Exum 1996; cf. Bauer 1998).

The next chapters show how the pain of *bĕtûlat batʿ ʿammî* ("the maiden daughter, My people") evokes God's sorrow (14:17); the metaphor of a mother shamed and humiliated publicly describes the people of Israel during the destruction (15:8-9). In the "confession" following this, the image of mother undergoes further negative development in that Jeremiah curses his mother for having given birth to him (15:10; cf. 20:14-18).

In the final "confession" the prophet assumes a female identity for the second time (cf. 4:19-21) when he/she accuses YHWH of seduction and sexual violation (cf. Heschel 1962; Carroll 1986 and others differ on this point):

You have seduced me, YHWH,
  and I was seduced;
you have violated me,
  and you have prevailed. (20:7, translation altered)

Echoes of preceding chapters are heard in this personification of the prophet. Even though it is quite conceivable that the text has men's experiences of sexual assault in mind, it is more plausible to conclude that it is a woman's voice that is heard in that verse, given the context of Jeremiah's self-identification with Israel and Jerusalem and the multiplicity of contemporary women's experiences. To be sure, the prophet's voice very quickly generalizes the accusation in the succeeding verses. We are left with the question of what the purpose is of describing the YHWH-Jeremiah relationship in terms of the metaphor of rape and who benefits from it.

An explicit death wish follows the portrayal of sexualized violence; Jeremiah declares that the mother's womb who gave him birth should better have remained his grave (20:14-18). In terms of the literary structure of the first part of the book, this emphasis on the metaphor of the womb, functioning in terms of the literary structure of the book's first part as an *inclusio,* recalls the calling of the prophet (1:5) — creating highest ambivalence.

Metaphors of femininity appear one more time in the concluding chapters of the first half of Jeremiah (chapters 21–25); they depict and sum up the Israelites' fate. Their suffering in the exile (22:20-23) is painted in terms of sexualized violence against Israel personified as a woman in labor pains. Corresponding images of women in preceding chapters come to mind here. In retrospect, it is images of women and of women's reality in chapters 7–25 that characterize the women and men of Israel and the prophet himself. First, we see women as leaders in the worship of the Queen of Heaven and in rituals of mourning, then there are the sounds of harsh words about what is to befall the Israelites. Actual women of Judah and Israel, depicted metaphorically as a woman, are assailed for their activities and threatened with punishment imaged in terms of labor pains and sexual violence. The sexually assaulted body of the woman both experiences and symbolizes the brutality people suffer in times of war. The theological transition from turning back and returning to YHWH, an option that initially appeared still open, to the ultimately inescapable destruction is told in the voices of women.

Jeremiah 26–52

In the second half of Jeremiah (chapters 26–52), the third section of my arrangement of the text, the metaphors of femininity and the description of women's reality appear in new variations. This part is primarily narration; the images of women are concentrated above all in the poetic portions. After the destruction of Jerusalem had become reality and questions about the future were heard, women's voices are apparent throughout Jeremiah's "little book of consolation" (chapters 30–31). The widespread despair is compared to a woman's labor pains, which are then ascribed to a male warrior and depicted as the worst that can happen to a man (30:6). But in the next chapter the pain people felt in the actual situation of the Babylonian invasion is set over against the hopes for the future after the exile and is meant to help make the present bearable (Jer 31). The promise that "the virgin Israel" will dance and beat the tambourine (31:4 and 13) like her ancestor Miriam at the sea (cf. Exod 15:20-21) is contained in ruminations on the future. A new exodus is prophesied (Jer 31:2-6). Israel, in the figure of a woman, a musician, and a mourning woman (cf. 9:17-21), finds her mourning turned into joy. YHWH offers her consolation (31:13) and turns toward the matriarch Rachel (cf. Gen 29:31; 30:1-8 and 22-24; 35:16-20) weeping for her children and refusing to be comforted (Jer 31:15). In language reminiscent of Hosea 11:1-9, we see God showing motherly sympathy *(raḥēm ʾǎraḥǎmennû),* her womb *(hāmû mēʿay lô)* quaking with worries for Ephraim (Jer 31:20). Mother YHWH does what Rachel does (Trible 1978). Metaphors of femininity become more forceful so that an eschatological theology of sympathy will be heard. The whole poem (31:15-22) climaxes in a promise to Israel, who is addressed as "rebellious daughter" *(habbat haššôbēbâ).* One component of the vision of something quite new YHWH is creating is the male warrior being encompassed by femaleness (31:22b). Here the limits and role determinations of gender-specific images are transcended:

> For YHWH has created a new thing on the earth:
>> femaleness encompasses the man of war. (31:22b, translation altered)

The Hebrew text contains the three words *nĕqēbâ,* "female," the same word that in Genesis 1:27 expresses that creation is in the image of God; the verb form *tĕsôbēb,* "she encompasses"; and the object *gāber/geber,* "man, warrior." But the meaning of that verse has preoccupied interpreters for centuries. The Septuagint translates it as *en sōtēria perieleusontai anthrōpoi,* "people shall walk about in safety"; the Vulgate reads *femina circumdabit virum,* "the woman surrounds the man." The conceptions in translations of the Bible and commentaries fall into three categories: they either discern notions of protection against enemies that the woman accords the man and thereby the whole community in times of peace (e.g., Giesebrecht 1907; Holladay 1989), or they speak of procreation where the woman has a changed role (e.g., Weiser 1960; Carroll 1986). Still others believe that the woman is transformed into a man (e.g., Luther; Rudolph 1958). Interestingly, most traditional commentaries find the promise of a new creation troubling rather than hopeful. Feminist exegetes, on the other hand, propose different interpretations that have to do with new roles for women in a peaceable society, actively engaged in the planning of families and other imaginable relocations of roles (Bozak 1991; O'Connor 1992). Or else they search within the Bible for ways to understand the form of the poem that is reminiscent of the metaphor of the womb (Trible 1978).

The theological line from exile to eschatology, from the experience of the now to the expectation of the then, is outlined here. This new quality of the relations between women and men culminates in the promise of a new covenant (Jer 31:31-34) that will be concluded in the form of a marriage contract (31:33) but without the traditional stipulation of roles (Wacker 1994 differs slightly in emphasis). Images of women pervade the eschatological dimension, giving hearers and readers in the promise of a new exodus, a new creation, and a new covenant a foretaste of the end of the present experiences of history (story and history).

But Jeremiah does not come to its end with chapter 31. Rather, it returns from its look into the future to the reality of the present, from eschatology to the experiences of the exiles where words of doom are heard again that touch upon Israel and the nations. Once again the prophet Jeremiah condemns those who worship the Queen of Heaven (44:15-25; cf. 7:16-20). Women are directly referred to again in their role as leaders in the sacrificial rituals for the goddess. Women as well as men defend their practice in the light of the crisis created by the exile and the failure of YHWH to come and help. The voices of women are so powerful that no process of redaction could suppress them (cf. Jost 1995). In the texts of judgment on the nations (chapters 46–51), some of the same metaphors occur that had already described Israel as female; they are now used to express the fate of these nations. For example, Babylon is a mother, shamed and humiliated (50:12), and the land is personified as a woman stripped naked and put to shame (51:2 and 47). The image of a woman in labor pains is applied to Moab (48:41), to Damascus (49:24), and to Babylon (50:43). The imagery of judgment, painted in pictures of women put to shame, bearing suffering and violence, calls to mind how throughout the book of Jeremiah Israel's condemnation is spoken of in the image of a woman.

Just as in the book's first half (chapters 1–25), metaphors of femininity and of women's reality characterize the theological dynamics of the second half (26–52). Women's voices articulate promises of redemption and the condemnations repeated next to them; this is particularly so in the chapters focused on eschatology (30–31), in the second text about the Queen of Heaven (44:15-25), and, more diffuse, in the chapters on judgment over the nations. The pictures of women dancing and beating drums that symbolize a new exodus, the descriptions of God's motherly sympathy, the promise of a new creation where femaleness encompasses male war-prowess, and the prospect of qualitatively transformed relations between men and women in a new covenant: these images fit the ethically transformed side of Jeremiah's theology, whereas the images of sexual violence against women used as threats or as punishments fit a different side. It is the purpose of the following synchronic reading to submit these tensions to a feminist critique.

A Literary Synchronic Reading in the Context of Contemporary Questions in Feminist Liberation Theology

Voices

An analysis of the Hebrew word *qôl* (voice, sound, tone, noise, cry) in Jeremiah shows that this word occurs there in three different contexts: as *qôl YHWH*, the voice of God; as noise, cries, sounds of war (cries of pain and of mourning, the clamor of war, etc.); and as voices of women.

In relation to the last of these, there are some that intone and even embody war and the destruction echolike, as it were. Then there is the prophet's voice who laments as if in labor pains — *mē'ay mē'ay 'ōḥiwlâ*, "my belly, my belly, I writhe in pains of labor," unable to stay calm when hearing the *qôl šôpār*, the sound of the shofar (4:19). There is also the *qôl kĕḥôlâ*, the cry of a woman in labor (4:31), and the *qôl bat Ṣiyyôn tityapēah*, the noises of "daughter of Zion" gasping for breath (4:31), and tones that together make the noises of war heard (cf. 4:29).

And then there are women's voices that have the function of expressing contra-mindedness, voices that speak out against war, death, and destruction. There is the *qôl nehî*, the sound of lament that is heard coming from Jerusalem (9:18[19]) responding to the destruction of the city. And then the voices of the wise mourning-women who instruct their daughters in how to mourn and teach their friends and neighbors a dirge in the face of the death that surrounds them on all sides (9:19-21). Finally, there is the *qôl* that is heard on the hill (or in Ramah), Rachel's voice weeping for her children (31:15-16).

In relation to the conditions of war, those women's voices from the past have a frightening actuality in our days inasmuch as women voicing torture and sexual violence as well as sorrow and lament constitute an ever-present chorus in a discourse that takes place primarily in a context of men. The breaking of women's bodies is, symbolically and concretely, the breaking of social structures, and conversely, broken social structures manifest themselves in violence against the weaker members of society, but especially against women and children.

Hearers

When we endeavor to hear women's voices in the book of Jeremiah, whose voices do we, the readers and hearers, hear? Do we hear the voice of the prophet Jeremiah, of his scribe Baruch, of the narrator? Or do we hear the voices of the Deuteronomist redactors? As far as we can determine historically, most of these voices were quite likely those of men. And in the final form of the text, they cover up whatever other voices may have existed. But the voices of women or the echoes of such that we have identified here belong to actual women, women in pains of labor, mourning women, women lamenting, women hushed up, women sexually assaulted, women singing and dancing as something new is emerging around them, women worshiping the Queen of Heaven.

The polyphony of women's voices in Jeremiah resonates as these texts are read or heard together with the actual, present-day contexts of the readers and hearers. And it does not matter here whether we look to oral traditions of transmission as the place where the voices of women are to be found (cf. Brenner and van Dijk-

Hemmes 1993) or understand voices to be a construction emerging from the inter-action between texts and readers/hearers. The implied audience in Jeremiah is a collectivity of men. Jeremiah addresses his prophecies to the inhabitants of Jerusa-lem. What does it mean then that Israel and Jerusalem are personified in his image language as female and that his images of women are primarily negative ones? Is this a rhetorical device to shame men by what they associate with the images, their fear of female sexuality, their worry about losing control over their spouses, etc., and thereby to move them to turn back? What do such rhetorical tactics mean for the reality of women when mechanisms of oppression and sexualized violence against women are presented in this manner and become legitimated culturally and religiously thereby?

In connection with what women experience during war, one wonders whether the real voices of women, uttering pain and sorrow, are being used to advance men's discourse on war and destruction and to legitimate theologically what they have to say there. Or are these voices of women to be heard somehow as the whis-per of resistance? Might they be voices of hope in the midst of death? Might they be saying: "Live no matter what!"? Or is it both-and, in spite of, or precisely be-cause of? Moreover, do the voices of women from the past not need readers/hear-ers today who are women-identified or feminists so that those voices are not si-lenced yet again and again?

Present-Day Questions

If it takes present-day interpreters to make voices of women in the book of Jere-miah heard, then modern and postmodern constructions of reality and of gender and gender-specific voices function as an additional filter in this polyphony. The different feminist interpretations of texts in Jeremiah demonstrate this. Such present-day women's voices form their own polychromatic choir antiphonal to the choir in Jeremiah.

It is the voice of feminists and womanists today — not Jeremiah's — that cri-tiques the constrictions created by dualistic models. The Israel of the past is re-membered as the bride holy to YHWH (Jer 2:2-3); the Israel of the future is promised to be a young, dancing woman (31:4). On the other hand, the women and men of Israel in the days of Jeremiah are imaged as an adulterous woman with an uncontrollable sex drive (e.g., 2:20-22, 23-25 and 33-34; 3:1, 2-3, 6-10 and 19-20), who at the same time is sexually assaulted in a crime of rampant sexual vi-olence that is said to be "justified" (e.g., 13:22 and 26). This dualism of "holiness" and "harlotry" in Jeremiah denies women their full humanity and disregards the multiple experiences that make up women's reality (Jost 1994). In addition, read-ing and hearing such texts in places or situations where they are looked upon as authorities for defining reality codifies the dualistic positions of power of heteropatriarchal societies that have destructive consequences especially for marginalized groups of people.

Today it is women's voices — not Jeremiah's — that call for differences and ambiguities to be held in tension. The birth metaphor (e.g., 4:19-21 and 31; 13:21; 22:23 [30:5-7]) and the image of a woman in labor pain represent the suffering of Israelites. But, significantly, what is missing in the birth metaphor is the newborn child. And so, the boundary experience of giving birth becomes an image of death reduced to pain and that of death without the joy of new life. It is reminiscent of the depiction of birth pangs as "punishment" for "disobedience." The image of the womb as a symbol of death (20:14-18) emphasizes this polarized and exclusively negative use of the birth metaphor. In addition, it includes nuances relating to Jeremiah's birth (1:5). Labor pains are not spoken of as part of the birth experience of God and/or Jeremiah's physical mother. But here, too, the stress lies more on death than on life. Jeremiah curses his birth (15:10) and wishes that his mother's womb would have been his grave (20:14-18). Thus, in Jeremiah women's experiences are divided into polarized stereotypes of good and evil, life and death. The feminine is identified with judgment and punishment. Even the positive properties of caring, comforting, and sympathy that characterize YHWH in Jeremiah 31:20 are in danger of being appropriated by mother ideologies.

Motivated by current initiatives and experiences of breaking free of traditional gender roles and identifications, present-day voices search for flexibility in what determines gender, questioning limitations and role assignments. It is such voices — not Jeremiah — who hear this male prophet speaking with a woman's voice (4:19-21). If the voices in the biblical text become alive through the voices of readers who come from different social-cultural locations, then such variations come to be heard and experienced by some as liberating. While women readers discern women's voices in the text differently and even hear different voices of women, (male) readers may perhaps come to notice traces of very different audible, silent, or silenced voices.

In summary: in the book of Jeremiah voices of women contribute through metaphors of femininity and concrete women's reality to the literary-theological development of the book. These developments advance from the call to turn back in the face of imminent death and destruction, to mournful remembering, to the eschatological vision in the exile of redemption. The embodiment of women's voices, of their sexually violated bodies (and their occasional dances of joy), functions as a metonym for society as a whole. The ethical responsibility of readers/hearers is required for a sensitive interpretation of their depth and problematic. At the same time, political engagement for transforming unjust conditions of life could be stimulated — beyond the book of Jeremiah.

LITERATURE

Ackerman, Susan. 1989. "'And the Women Knead Dough': The Worship of the Queen of Heaven in Sixth-Century Judah." In *Gender and Difference in Ancient Israel,* edited by Peggy L. Day, 109-24. Minneapolis.

Bauer, Angela. 1998. *Gender in the Book of Jeremiah: A Feminist-Literary Reading.* New York and Frankfurt.

Bird, Phyllis. 1987. "The Place of Women in the Israelite Cultus." In *Ancient Israelite Religion: Essays in Honor of Frank Moore Cross,* edited by Patrick D. Miller Jr., Paul D. Hanson, and Sean D. McBride, 397-419. Philadelphia.

———. 1989. "'To Play the Harlot': An Inquiry into an Old Testament Metaphor." In *Gender and Difference in Ancient Israel,* edited by Peggy L. Day, 75-94. Minneapolis.

Bozak, Barbara A. 1991. "Life 'Anew': A Literary-Theological Study of Jer. 30–31." *Analecta biblica* 122.

Brenner, Athalya. 1993. "On 'Jeremiah' and the Poetics of (Prophetic?) Pornography." In Athalya Brenner and Fokkelien van Dijk-Hemmes, *On Gendering Texts: Female and Male Voices in the Hebrew Bible,* 178-93. Leiden.

———. 1995. "On Prophetic Propaganda and the Politics of 'Love': The Case of Jeremiah." In *A Feminist Companion to the Latter Prophets,* edited by Athalya Brenner, 256-74. Feminist Companion to the Bible, vol. 8. Sheffield.

———. 1996. "Pornoprophetics Revisited: Some Additional Reflections." *Journal for the Study of the Old Testament* 70:63-86.

———, ed. 1995. *A Feminist Companion to the Latter Prophets.* Feminist Companion to the Bible, vol. 8. Sheffield.

Brenner, Athalya, and Fokkelien van Dijk-Hemmes. 1993. *On Gendering Texts: Female and Male Voices in the Hebrew Bible.* Leiden.

Carroll, Robert P. 1986. *Jeremiah: A Commentary.* Old Testament Library. Philadelphia.

Day, Peggy L., ed. 1989. *Gender and Difference in Ancient Israel.* Minneapolis.

Diamond, A. R. Pete, and Kathleen M. O'Connor. 1996. "Unfaithful Passions: Coding Women Coding Men in Jeremiah 2–3 (4:2)." *Biblical Interpretation* 4, no. 3:288-310.

Duhm, Bernhard. 1901. *Das Buch Jeremia.* Tübingen.

Exum, J. Cheryl. 1996. "Prophetic Pornography." In *Plotted, Shot, and Painted: Cultural Representations of Biblical Women,* edited by J. Cheryl Exum, 101-28. Gender, Culture, Theory, vol. 3. Sheffield.

Frymer-Kensky, Tikva. 1992. *In the Wake of the Goddesses: Women, Culture, and the Biblical Transformation of Pagan Myth.* New York.

Galambush, Julie. 1992. *Jerusalem in the Book of Ezekiel: The City as Yahweh's Wife.* Atlanta.

Giesebrecht, Friedrich. 1907. *Das Buch Jeremia.* Göttingen.

Gordon, Pamela, and Harold Washington. 1995. "Rape as a Military Metaphor in the Hebrew Bible." In *A Feminist Companion to the Latter Prophets,* edited by Athalya Brenner, 308-25. Feminist Companion to the Bible, vol. 8. Sheffield.

Holladay, William L. 1986. *Jeremiah 1.* Hermeneia. Philadelphia.

———. 1989. *Jeremiah 2.* Hermeneia. Minneapolis.

Jahnow, Hedwig. 1923. *Das Hebräische Leichenlied im Rahmen der Völkerdichtung.* Beihefte zur Zeitschrift für die alttestamentliche Wissenschaft, vol. 36. Gießen.

Jost, Renate. 1994. "Von 'Huren und Heiligen': Ein sozialgeschichtlicher Beitrag." In *Feministische Hermeneutik und Erstes Testament: Analysen und Interpretationen,* edited by Hedwig Jahnow et al., 126-37. Stuttgart.

———. 1995. *Frauen, Männer und die Himmelskönigin: Exegetische Studien.* Gütersloh.

Kaiser, Barbara Bakke. 1987. "Poet as 'Female Impersonator': The Image of Daughter Zion as Speaker in Biblical Poems of Suffering." *Journal of Religion* 67:164-82.

Keefe, Alice. 1993. "Rapes of Women/Wars of Men." *Semeia* 61:79-97.

Magdalene, F. Rachel. 1995. "Ancient Near Eastern Treaty-Curses and the Ultimate Texts of Terror: A Study of the Language of Divine Sexual Abuse in the Prophetic Corpus." In *A Feminist Companion to the Latter Prophets,* edited by Athalya Brenner, 326-52. Feminist Companion to the Bible, vol. 8. Sheffield.

Meyers, Carol. 1991. "Of Drums and Damsels: Women's Performance in Ancient Israel." *Biblical Archaeologist* 54:16-27.

Mowinckel, Sigmund. 1914. *Zur Komposition des Buches Jeremia.* Oslo.

O'Connor, Kathleen M. 1992. "Jeremiah." In *The Women's Bible Commentary,* edited by Carol A. Newsom and Sharon H. Ringe, 169-77. London and Louisville.

Rudolph, Wilhelm. 1958. *Jeremia.* Tübingen.

———. 1996. *Figuren des Weiblichen im Hosea-Buch.* Freiburg.

Trible, Phyllis. 1978. *God and the Rhetoric of Sexuality.* Philadelphia.

Wacker, Marie-Theres. 1994. "Was ist neu am 'Neuen Bund'?" *Junge Kirche* 55:224-26.

———. 1996. *Figuren des Weiblichen im Hosea-Buch.* Freiburg.

Weems, Renita J. 1995. *Battered Love: Marriage, Sex, and Violence in the Hebrew Prophets.* Minneapolis.

Weiser, Artur. 1960. *Das Buch des Propheten Jeremia.* Göttingen.

For Further Reading

Bauer-Levesque, Angela. 2006. "Jeremiah." In *The Queer Bible Commentary,* edited by Deryn Guest et al., 386-93. London.

Baumann, Gerlinde. 2003. *Love and Violence: Marriage as Metaphor for the Relationship between YHWH and Israel in the Prophetic Books.* Collegeville, Minn.

Fischer, Irmtraud. 2002. *Gotteskünderinnen: Zu einer geschlechterfairen Deutung des Phänomens der Prophetie und der Prophetinnen in der hebräischen Bibel.* Stuttgart.

Heschel, Abraham. 1962. *The Prophets.* New York.

Maier, Christl. 2003. "Tochter Zion im Jeremiabuch. Eine literarische Personifikation mit altorientalischem Hintergrund." In *Prophetie in Israel. Beiträge des Symposiums "Das Alte Testament und die Kultur der Moderne" anlässlich des 100. Geburtstags Gerhard von Rads,* edited by Irmtraud Fischer et al., 157-67. Münster.

———. 2006. "Ist Versöhnung möglich? Jeremia 3,1-5 als Beispiel innerbiblischer Auslegung." In *"Gott bin ich, kein Mann,"* edited by Ilona Riedel-Spangenberger and Erich Zenger, 295-305. Festschrift for Helen Schüngel-Straumann. Beiträge zur Hermeneutik der biblischen Gottesrede. Paderborn.

———. 2008. "Jeremiah as Teacher of Torah." *Interpretation* 62, no. 1:22-32.

Sharp, Carolyn J. 2003. *Prophecy and Ideology in Jeremiah: Struggles for Authority in the Deutero-Jeremianic Prose.* Edinburgh.

Translated by Martin Rumscheidt

Lamentations: Zion's Cry in Affliction

Maria Häusl

Influence and Interpretation of Lamentations

Lamentations gives us insight into the situation of the city of Jerusalem and its people after the conquest in 586 B.C.E. The immediacy of the depiction of the crisis impresses us on the very first reading. These texts do not obscure women, mothers, and widows, and they give voice to Zion herself, embodied as female. But in spite of these insights into the "world of women," neither the naming of women's fates nor the voice of Woman Zion gives us immediate access to women's experiences. Rather, the texts present their own reality, which encompasses both the dramatic presentation of the crisis and the female voices.

Therefore an interpretation of the text must comprehend both the reality of the text and the ideas of the feminine it contains. We are interested in the content that is associated with the feminine, the aspects that are emphasized, what is *not* said, and the function assigned to the "feminine" as constructed by the texts. It is not sufficient for a feminist interpretation simply to name the feminine aspects. Rather, it must grasp the historical and social conditions that shape what is said about the feminine in order not to present its own one-sided construct of what the feminine may be.

Previous feminist exegeses have looked at Lamentations in their search for female voices in the First Testament (van Dijk-Hemmes 1993) or in examining the attribution of female roles to Zion/Jerusalem (Kaiser 1987; Frymer-Kensky 1992, 168-78). A complete feminist exegesis of Lamentations does not yet exist. Such an exegesis must engage a strand of Christian history of interpretation that acknowledges no "high theological" content in Lamentations, since long passages do not move beyond "lamenting." Such interpretations see the third song, with its statements about acknowledging God's judgment and one's own guilt, as central. But there are also interpretations that do not see the third song as central, but instead acknowledge the naming of the crisis situation as an element of the lamentation and consider it important in light of the catastrophe (Bail 1999).

The following interpretation is structurally oriented to the question of the construction of the feminine, and therefore will concern itself thematically with the depiction of Zion/Jerusalem in particular, against a background interpretation of all the texts. The consideration of the third song, which has very little relationship to the underlying question, will focus on the history of its interpretation.

Interpretation of the Songs

General Literary and Historical Considerations

I regard the five chapters of Lamentations as independent songs. Their content reveals no explicit references to one another, though the first, second, and fourth song are more similar in content and form, while the third and fifth go their own ways. The third song is usually said to be that of an individual (man) (v. 1), the fifth is called a community lament. In the other three songs, an affinity to the Hebrew memorial for the dead and to ancient Near Eastern city laments is posited.

The history of exegesis of the death-song genre contains an element of women's history. Hedwig Jahnow was the first to do a thorough study of "the song over the corpse in the context of popular poetry" in her 1923 monograph with the same title, for which she received an honorary doctorate in 1926 (see Wacker 1995, 13-14; 1998, 23). In treating the question of the locus of the lament for the dead, she examined the specific life-contexts of women and the institution of women mourners. Her work is still cited today in describing the genre of Lamentations.

All the songs reveal a strict poetic structure; with the exception of the fifth song, the verses are oriented to the Hebrew alphabet both in number and in the order of their initial letters. Therefore I consider these texts to be literary productions, not primarily derived from a liturgy.

The determination of the time of composition cannot depend on particular references in the texts. But in light of the themes and intentions of the songs we may perceive an immediate relationship to or greater distance from the destruction of the city, and so we can at least indicate a chronology for the songs. The first, second, and fourth song are shaped by the hopelessness of the situation; they contain no explicit petitions to the deity to turn aside the catastrophe. These three songs are probably the original cycle. The fifth song, while recalling the event of the destruction, speaks more of a long-enduring situation of misery, so that it was probably added to the other three songs at a later time. The third song refers only in verses 48-51 to the destruction of the city; it is primarily a disputation about a situation of suffering and should be regarded as the final addition. In what follows, the songs will be treated in this sequence, according to the history of their origin.

This collection of songs is located in different places in the Jewish and Christian canons. In the Hebrew Bible it belongs to the third part of the canon, the

Writings, more precisely to the five feast scrolls. Lamentations is part of the Jewish feast of remembrance of the destruction of the temple. Christian tradition, by contrast, has attributed Lamentations to the prophet Jeremiah (cf. 2 Chron 35:25), and therefore has inserted it after Jeremiah.

First Song

Verses 1-6 describe the situation of Jerusalem/Zion/Judah after its destruction. That catastrophe is depicted in contrast to the former well-being of the state by means of feminine images. The city formerly full of people is lonely, the great woman has become a widow and the princess a vassal, doing forced labor (v. 1). Her friends have become enemies (v. 2), and her inhabitants have been sent away as captives (vv. 3, 5, 6). The city and her inhabitants, priests and young women, little children and princes, lift up their laments and refuse to be silent. Such experiences awaken compassion.

The isolation and sense of being cut off in this crisis are especially evident in verses 8 and 9, where the city's situation is compared with that of a menstruating, sexually abused, and therefore unclean woman. The city withdraws and is alone. There is no one to console her (v. 9b). This statement is accented as key and is repeated a total of five times in the text (vv. 2, 9, 16, 17, 21).

Out of this misery and isolation, we hear the voice of Jerusalem twice calling to YHWH for help (vv. 9, 11). She affirms YHWH's justice (v. 18), but there is no plea for consolation or an easing of her misery. Her words are directed to passersby (vv. 12-16), telling of YHWH's wrath and his destroying deed and describing the horrible situation of her children. Over long passages in the text, misery is seen as a fate brought about by the deity's wrath. Only in a very few places is anything said about guilt (vv. 14, 18, 20). Guilt and sin are not further specified, and there is no attempt to detect a cause. Rather, in verses 21-22 the city turns to YHWH to plead that her enemies may suffer the same fate as she. There seems to be only an indirect hope for a change in her own condition.

Second Song

The second song begins with an extensive report of YHWH's hostile behavior toward the city of Jerusalem (vv. 1-10). The end of the rulers and the mourning of the elders and young girls in reaction, as well as the dreadful fate of the population in war, are brought before our eyes. The first-person speech of someone unnamed (vv. 11-19) is shaped by the dramatic situation after the collapse. How, in light of this suffering of starving children and helpless mothers, can there be any consolation? The only advice given to Zion is the challenge to turn to YHWH in the face of suffering. The gleeful speeches of the enemies stand in sharp contrast to all this.

In verses 20-22 we hear the voice of Zion, expressing the pain of her people. Those she bore and brought up healthy have fallen victims to the enemy: women and nurslings, priests and prophets, young and old, female and male youth. The second song also lacks any plea that this fate be turned aside.

Fourth Song

The fourth song, like the first and second, describes the situation after the destruction of the city, in contrast to its former flourishing and the well-being of the population (vv. 1-10, 14-16). Sorrow and lament as the people's reactions, however, are lacking, and YHWH is only briefly mentioned as the initiator of the catastrophe (vv. 11, 16). On the other hand, the song makes concrete the guilt of the people, still indeterminate at the beginning, as the fault of the priests and prophets (vv. 6, 12-13, 17-20). In view of the unexpected collapse, they acknowledge that they have wrongly interpreted reality. They believed the city was secure and did not see the danger. As a result of this self-recognition and insight, the city's guilt could be removed, since at the end it is said that Zion's guilt is at an end (v. 22).

If we read the first, second, and fourth songs as a unit, the cycle ends with the promise of an end to iniquity, achieved through the insight of the priests and prophets. However, in view of the horrible misery of the people, this insight comes rather late. Of course, the end of iniquity and guilt is still not the end of the suffering.

Fifth Song

The fifth song is spoken by a collectivity that turns to YHWH. The population has been subjected to foreign domination, is doing "slave labor," and suffers from hunger and thirst. The specific sufferings of individual groups are also listed: women and girls are being raped, rulers and elders are losing their honor and their lives, young men are being forced to do the most arduous labor, old and young are missing the loveliest aspects of life. Verses 15-18 describe the people's internal disposition: they are mourning, lamenting, and acknowledging their guilt. In verse 19 YHWH is addressed directly. The accusing question of why he has abandoned them is preceded by a confession of his eternity and followed by a plea that he will turn to them and improve their situation. Verse 22, however, lets doubt have the last word: Will you be angry forever?

The fifth song reveals similarities to and differences from the first, second, and fourth songs. They are comparable in viewing the misery of individual groups within the population, but only the fifth song implores YHWH to intervene and bring an end to the suffering. This petition, which is absent from the original cycle, might have been seen at a later time as a necessary addition, which would have led to its being inserted in the fifth song. The fifth song lacks a personification of Zion, which marks long stretches of the cycle made up of the first, second, and fourth songs; in 5:18 "Zion" is certainly nothing but an indication of the place. Why Zion as person is absent is something that the text itself does not reveal. Considerations regarding the tradition history of Daughter Zion (see below) may give us some indication.

Third Song

The third song is made up of very disparate parts that probably did not originally belong together. That makes all the more pressing the question why they were put together, especially since the alphabetical ordering presents the text as if it were a unit. A speaker who presents himself in verse 1 as "one who has seen affliction under the rod of his wrath" describes what suffering and misery the deity has brought upon him (vv. 1-20). Nevertheless, he clings to hope in YHWH (vv. 21-24). The wisdom text that follows then gives reasons for this hope. Here all are challenged to bear suffering with patience, since YHWH will not reject them forever and has no pleasure in suffering. Rather, YHWH is said to be the author of good and evil, while the human being is always guilty before God. In verses 40-47 a collective confession of guilt then follows, combined with lament and a description of misery. Verses 48-51 continue this description and depict the sorrowful reaction of an individual to the fall of the whole people. This section contains the sole reference to the destruction of the city. Another (?) speaker then reports, in verses 52-66, his individual situation of suffering, which YHWH has changed. This situation can be referred to the fall of the city.

Besides the aspects of the fatefulness of suffering and divine causality, in verses 39 and 42 the guiltiness of humanity is brought into the argument. Guilt and sin are, however, not made concrete. Rather, the thought here is that before God the human being is always guilty.

In addition to this, the text offers two contradictory answers to the question of what one ought to do in suffering: "Cry out, so that YHWH will intervene!" and "Bear suffering patiently!"

This second rule of behavior distinguishes the third song from the others and has frequently in the course of the history of interpretation led to an attitude that — emphasizing this idea of patience — accords a higher theological value to the third song. Therefore I will briefly sketch a comparison between the older cycle and the third song. In this, a feminist perspective also raises the question of how gender roles can be of service to the unquestionably different theologies present here.

The original cycle and the third song contain no petition for a change of fate; nevertheless, they treat the theme of guilt differently. The fourth song makes guilt concrete as a blinding of the priests and prophets, while the first and second songs contain only brief references to guilt as the cause of the suffering. The third song does not make guilt concrete, but it incorporates the idea of a general human guilt in its argumentation.

Whereas in the original cycle hope is only very subtly hinted at as an end of guilt (4:22), the third song makes the aspect of hope explicit. The speaker holds fast to God's unending care and reports on a rescue in a crisis situation. In addition, there are reflections on God's just mercy. The third song thus offers some points toward a cognitive means of overcoming suffering. Its aim is not so much to produce empathy with a situation of suffering as to achieve agreement with an interpretation of suffering. These aspects are absent from the rest of the cycle, which emphasizes the isolation caused by suffering and the lack of any consoler. In the first song the isolation is illustrated by the female bodily function of menstruation. In addition, a good deal of space is given to the attitude of a human being in crisis. The texts speak of fear and pain, weeping, groaning, and lamenting. In the third song the actions of the male speaker in his situation of suffering are instead presented with some restraint.

Although the texts do not establish explicit connections between the gender imagery they employ and the theologies they represent, we can observe that feminine imagery, especially that of Woman Zion, appears where there is a direct confrontation with crisis. In the third song, which is imbued more with reflective elements, the voice of the speaker is, through long passages, that of an individual man. If we are to conclude from these correlations that the texts see emotion as "feminine" and mental reflection as "masculine," we should not overlook the fact that this connection is only visible when the songs are compared, and may only exist through such a comparison. For neither the original cycle nor the third song explicitly speaks of a difference between feminine and masculine. Rather, Zion is the image for the whole population, and the mourner in the third song is an exemplary figure in suffering; both challenge us to identify with them. However, this makes evident a further difference in the use of the genders. Zion represents a collective and at the same time a (concrete and applied) place of hope for the people. Her identity oscillates between these two aspects. The mourning individual primarily lacks a collective identity, and only his exemplary character opens up this figure so that others may identify with him.

Important Individual Themes

Daughter Zion

Since cities in Hebrew have grammatically feminine gender, and since for persons we expect a gender assignment, it seems natural when personifying Zion to adopt the grammatical gender and describe Zion as a woman. But that does not explain the roles that are assigned to Zion. Beyond the morphology, the text shows that Zion is in fact the subject of a variety of female roles. We must also look into the tradition history of Daughter Zion.

The first song contains the broadest possible variety of statements about the personification of Zion. In the transition from person to city in the depiction of Zion, we find the many relationships her inhabitants have with her. The text speaks of her little children, her young women, and her priests. The people are called her people and the sanctuary her sanctuary. But when, at the same time, the text speaks of her gates and roads and of the great city, we recognize that Zion is a city. The identity of city and person is secured by the individual name Zion/Jerusalem.

How is the woman Zion described? When bodily functions or parts, such as menstruation or genitalia, are spoken of, then Zion is assigned a female body. But it is a sexist interpretation to say that this is why Zion has a female body: because menstruation signifies uncleanness and isolation, and because rape, indicated by nakedness and the uncovering of genitalia, serves as an image for the destroyed city.

Zion's femaleness is constructed still further by viewing the body in terms of its social roles. Princess and widow are explicitly mentioned; I would see in them the highest and lowest poles of a society as regards influence, power, and economic security.

When the text speaks of lovers and admirers, Zion appears indirectly as one who loves and is loved. Of course, the lover's role can be interpreted in two ways. A patriarchal evaluation would categorize these love relationships as illicit and, in the context of the city's fall, as Zion's sin. Such an assignment of guilt is not explicitly present (see below). Therefore I take it that the point of comparison is to be found in the lack of protection for a woman in such love relationships. She is subject to the whim of the lover, as Judah and Zion are helpless in the hands of the great powers.

Zion's screams of pain and mourning actions have their social-historical parallel in mourning women (cf. Jer 9:17, 18, 20, 21). Weeping and lamenting as reactions to the national catastrophe, however, do not appear to have been limited to mourning women. (Priests, too, sigh.)

The inhabitants of the city are called her children, suggesting the idea of Zion as mother.

In the second song the image of Zion as a city predominates; it mentions walls, gates, palaces, streets, and squares. The sanctuary and the altar belong to YHWH, and the people are inhabitants of a city. Zion is only a person when she is addressed, or herself speaks. One speaker challenges her to call to YHWH for the sake of her children, thus designating Zion as a mother. In Zion's own speech the image of a woman who bears and rears children is made explicit. Zion's trouble and danger in bearing and caring for children are contrasted with their destruction by her foes.

The fourth song contains only a few references to Zion as a person. Zion's duty to care for her offspring is compared and contrasted with the behavior of female animals. Femaleness is thus defined by reference to the nature and biology of the functions of the female body. The people are inhabitants of a city with walls and towers. Only verses 21 and 22 designate the contending cities of Edom and Zion to an extent in personal terms, calling them "Daughter Edom" and "Daughter Zion."

After this overview of the original cycle, we can summarize our observations as follows. The cycle reveals a quantitative decline in the personifications of Zion. While the first song is marked by descriptions of Zion as woman in a variety of female social roles, the second song contains only the maternal role, and the fourth song the care for offspring that is grounded in the nature of the female. At the same time, the descriptions of the city increase in the second and fourth songs.

Zion's identity shifts between personification as a woman and the idea of her as a city, so that on the one hand she represents the fate of the inhabitants and on the other hand she is a "place of hope" for people in both a concrete and a transferred sense. In the female roles of widow, menstruating woman, and shamed woman, she shares in the human fate. As mourning woman and as mother, she takes responsibility for the inhabitants and a mediating function with respect to the deity. Thus, for me, Zion contains aspects of emotional ties, responsibility, and care for human beings.

The lament of the personified city has a First Testament analogy in the work of mourning women and wise women (Jer 9:16-21), and a further ancient Near Eastern parallel in the goddess who laments the destruction of her city. (Ningal mourns over Ur.) Therefore in the history of exegesis the book of Lamentations, at least the original cycle, has repeatedly been located within the tradition of songs of the lamenting city. Since Judah or Zion is spoken of as "virgin" (1:15; 2:13), and since this title is closely parallel to the Ugaritic goddess Anat, an analogy of Zion to the lamenting goddess suggests itself. The titles of "great" and "princess" in Lamentations 1:1 attest to the city's royal character. The words "daughter" and "virgin" for Jerusalem and Zion are also often seen as the titles of a goddess. But there are no clear proofs for this. Rather, a survey of all combinations of "virgin" and/or "daughter" with the names of cities or states makes it seem more plausible that "daughter" and "virgin" are metaphors that compare a city with a daughter who has been raped, a young, marriageable woman who has thus been robbed of her future. In the case of "daughter" we should thus also think of a relationship with the (leading) group(s) in the population. Like a daughter, the city needs protection; care and responsibility are due her. She is the precious jewel whose destruction is inconceivable. This supposition is strengthened by the fact that the term "daughter" is found especially when the text speaks of the collapse and destruction of a city. Foreign cities are also portrayed in this light. "This image of the ruined-maiden victim enables the reader to empathize with the people, to forget the cause of the devastation and to join in the sorrow" (Frymer-Kensky 1992, 169).

As the texts show, we can scarcely see a goddess in Zion, but as we have shown above, she does have divine traits. Likewise, there are no indications in the text of a "marriage" between the city personified as female and a male deity. In summary, I posit that the mourning goddess in the songs of lamenting cities furnishes the tradition-historical background for the mourning city. This explains why Zion appears as an independent entity personified as female alongside the population, and that the city's acts of mourning reveal a relationship between the city and her population that is characterized by care and concern. In all this, the mourning acts both of the goddess and of the city are rooted in the experiences of women in war and in the acts of mourning women.

Women in War and Its Aftermath

Except in the third song, women are repeatedly mentioned as inhabitants of the city. First of all, war's fatal effects, which make no distinction of gender, fall on them: imprisonment, hunger, sickness, despair, death (1:18; 2:21; 5:14). The rituals of lament and sorrow are carried out by everyone — the king, the princes, prophets, priests, elders, and young women — with the young women apparently, like the other groups, having a duty to exercise the rituals on behalf of the community (1:4; 2:9-10). The naming of various groups also makes visible an aspect of the social structure.

The naming of the specific sufferings of individual groups (5:11-14) reveals that the social structures of a conquered people are also destroyed, and deliberately so. Sexual violence against women is an evident weapon of war. This violence is based in a twofold difference, that between the conquerors and the conquered, and that between men and women. The text is apparently interested in the first of these differences when it speaks of sexual violence in the framework of the ruined order of society. But to remain oblivious to the second difference is to run the risk of overlooking women's subjectivity and of regarding their fate as merely an illustration of the limitlessness of the misery and horror. In fact, the misery and destruction of the community should impress itself on us as especially drastic when we read reports of children who starve in their mothers' bosom (2:12) or mothers who engage in cannibalism (2:20; 4:10). It is contrast that makes these statements so vivid. Motherhood, understood as care for progeny and equated with a law of nature, is contrasted with the suffering of the children and perverted in the actions of mothers against their own children. The perversion consists in the violation of the law of nature, as is made clear in the comparison with the animal world (4:3). In the language itself, judgmental adjectives further indicate this perversion: "cruel, like the ostriches in the wilderness" (4:3); "compassionate mothers" (4:10).

"Because of Her Many Sins"

These texts thematize guilt and sin surprisingly seldom, and not very concretely. Only the fourth song recognizes sinful behavior in the false assurances of priests and prophets, and the third song speaks of a general sinfulness of humanity before God.

In view of this finding, I am unable to share two views of Lamentations that have been offered in the history of exegesis. I do not see the theological centrality of the third song; moreover, only in the middle section of that song is an answer offered, in terms of wisdom reflection, to the question of the role of guilt in the catastrophe, namely, that the human being is always guilty before God (see above). In the other songs I see no central function for the statements about consciousness of guilt and confession of sin. Rather, it seems to me that acknowledgment of guilt is part of the lament and the description of the suffering (Jer 50:14; 51:6 even speaks of Babylon's guilt).

Therefore I do not see Jerusalem depicted in Lamentations 1:2, 8-9 as an adulterous woman or a whore (unlike O'Connor 1992, 180). None of the concrete features are associated with such an interpretation, such as those we are familiar with from texts using marriage metaphors (e.g., Jer 2). It seems to me that Zion is primarily an image for the broken people and a voice of concern for them.

"Behold My Sorrow"

Zion herself is suffering, and she gives voice to human misery. This seems to me to be the only helpful action that is possible in such a situation: compassion and lament as the expression of pain. In analogy to the ancient Near Eastern goddess, we could see here a divine quality. But it is not a "female" quality, as the kinship of Daughter Zion and the Suffering Servant in Deutero-Isaiah demonstrates.

LITERATURE

Dobbs-Allsopp, Fred W. 1993. *Weep, O Daughter of Zion: A Study of the City-Lament Genre in the Hebrew Bible*. Biblica et orientalia, vol. 44. Rome.

Fitzgerald, Aloysius. 1975. "BTWLT and BT as Titles for Capital Cities." *Catholic Biblical Quarterly* 37:167-83.

Follis, Elaine R. 1987. "The Holy City as Daughter." In *Directions in Biblical Hebrew Poetry*, edited by Elaine R. Follis, 173-84. Journal for the Study of the Old Testament: Supplement Series, vol. 40. Sheffield.

Frymer-Kensky, Tikva. 1992. *In the Wake of the Goddesses,* 168-78. New York.

Jahnow, Hedwig. 1923. *Das hebräische Leichenlied im Rahmen der Völkerdichtung.* Beiheft zur Zeitschrift für die alttestamentliche Wissenschaft, vol. 36. Berlin.

Kaiser, Barbara B. 1987. "Poet as 'Female Impersonator': The Image of Daughter Zion as Speaker in Biblical Poems of Suffering." *Journal of Religion* 67:164-83.

Kramer, Samuel N. 1983. "The Weeping Goddess: Sumerian Prototypes of the *Mater Dolorosa.*" *Biblical Archaeologist* 46:69-80.

O'Conner, Kathleen M. 1992. "Lamentations." In *The Women's Bible Commentary,* edited by Carol A. Newsom and Sharon H. Ringe, 178-82. London and Louisville.

Van Dijk-Hemmes, Fokkelien. 1993. "Traces of Women's Texts in the Hebrew Bible." In Athalya Brenner and Fokkelien van Dijk-Hemmes, *On Gendering Texts: Female and Male Voices in the Hebrew Bible,* 17-109. Biblical Interpretation Series, vol. 1. Leiden.

Wacker, Marie-Theres. 1995. "Geschichtliche, hermeneutische und methodologische Grundlagen." In *Feministische Exegese. Forschungserträge zur Bibel aus der Perspektive von Frauen,* edited by Luise Schottroff, Silvia Schroer, and Marie-Theres Wacker, 3-79. Darmstadt.

———. 1998. "Part One: Historical, Hermeneutical, and Methodological Foundations." In *Feminist Interpretation: The Bible in Women's Perspective,* 3-82. Minneapolis.

Westermann, Claus. 1990. *Die Klagelieder. Forschungsgeschichte und Auslegung.* Neukirchen-Vluyn.

For Further Reading

Bail, Ulrike. 1998. *Gegen das Schweigen klagen. Eine Intertextuelle Studie zu den Klagepsalmen Ps 6 und Ps 55 und der Erzählung von der Vergewaltigung Tamars,* 177-94. Gütersloh.

———. 1999. "Wehe, kein Ort, nirgends . . . Überlegungen zum Sprachraum der Klagelieder Jeremias." In Charlotte Methuen, *Zeit, Utopie, Eschatologie. Jahrbuch der Europäischen Gesellschaft für theologische Forschung von Frauen/Yearbook of the European Society of Women in Theological Research,* vol. 7, 81-90. Leuven.

———. 2004. *"Die verzogene Sehnsucht hinkt an ihren Ort." Literarische Überlebensstrategien nach der Zerstörung Jerusalems im Alten Testament.* Gütersloh.

Berges, Ulrich. 2002. *Klagelieder.* Herders theologischer Kommentar, Altes Testament. Freiburg.

———. 2004. "Kann Zion männlich sein? — Klgl 3 als 'literarisches Drama' und 'nachexilische Problemdichtung'." In *"Basel und Bibel": Collected Communications to the XVIIth Congress of the International Organization for the Study of the Old Testament,* edited by Matthias Augustin, 235-46. Basel.

Häusl, Maria. 2003. *Bilder der Not. Weiblichkeits- und Geschlechtermetaphorik im Buch Jeremia.* Freiburg im Breisgau.

———. 2007. "Zion/Jerusalem — eine diakonische Gestalt?" In *Frauen gestalten Diakonie,* vol. 1, *Von der biblischen Zeit bis zum Pietismus,* edited by Adelheid v. Hauff, 43-53. Stuttgart.

Maier, Christl M. 2008. *Daughter Zion, Mother Zion: Gender, Space, and the Sacred in Ancient Israel.* Minneapolis.

Translated by Linda M. Maloney

Ezekiel: Male Prophecy with Female Imagery

Renate Jost and Elke Seifert

Introduction

The book of Ezekiel does not present easy access for a feminist interpretation. It uses violent imagery and voyeuristic speech about female sexuality. Ezekiel makes statements about ritual impurity that are discriminatory against women, and he polemicizes against women who do not correspond to his (prophetic) ideal image. Texts with that kind of content require critique from a feminist perspective. But the difficulties they present to readers should not lead us entirely to silence or forget this book. It is precisely an engagement with resistant and problematic statements that calls forth discussion and confrontation and sharpens our eyes for what exists in our own time.

The following reflections on the book of Ezekiel from a feminist point of view come from two different methodological perspectives. The first part (by Renate Jost) is in the tradition of social-historical biblical criticism. Fundamental to such an exegesis is a stance on behalf of the downtrodden in history. It uses the instruments of the historical-critical method, but pursues its interests further to the extent that it asks about the social content of historical situations. In the second part (by Elke Seifert) the texts will be examined on a literary level. Here our interest is in the way in which, in the prophetic book as we have it, the historical changes in Ezekiel's time are considered in the form of metaphorical discourse. We will indicate some patterns of argumentation and use ideological criticism to lay bare their misogynistic effects.

The Changed Situation of the Lives
of Women (and Men) in Ezekiel's Time

Ezekiel was among those who were deported to Babylon in 597 B.C.E. We know little about the lives of the exiles. A fairly large community settled in Tel-Abib, near the river Chebar (Ezek 3:15). Jeremiah's letter to the exiles suggests that they were permitted to build houses and plant gardens (Jer 29:5), but that freedom should not deceive us as to the suffering and anxieties of these women and men. They were not only insecure about their own future and that of those who had remained behind in the land; they had also endured the greatest crisis in the history of their country.

The clear social differentiation within the society at the end of the royal period, and the stated social position of women as still presented in the book of Jeremiah (cf. Jost 1995, 101-61), is no longer evident in Ezekiel. This is due, among other things, to the somewhat later origins of the book, in a period in which the old hierarchical structures of the Jewish state had collapsed.

In the description of the life situation of the women as victims of male misuse of power, we see a sharpening in comparison to the earlier prophets. In the framework of social criticism, the neglect of fathers and mothers is condemned (Ezek 22:7). There is frequent mention of adultery with a neighbor's wife in connection with the sacrificial meal (18:6, 11, 15; 33:25-26). In 22:10-11 the text speaks, moreover, of incest as adultery within the family. Sexual intercourse during menstruation is also denounced. The princes of Jerusalem are accused of having made widows of the women of the land — presumably by murdering their husbands (22:25).

Ezekiel as Priest/Prophet and Women

Ezekiel is said to have been a priest (1:3). For the female members of such a family, as for the priests themselves, special conditions applied as regards marriage and sexual activity (Ezek 44:22; cf. Lev 21:1-15). According to the text, Ezekiel's personal relationship to a woman — like those of Hosea (Hos 1–3) and Jeremiah — was determined by his prophetic significance and is described as a symbolic action referring to the fate of the people. Whereas Jeremiah was ordered to remain unmarried (Jer 16:1-4), Ezekiel was forbidden by God to mourn for his wife when she died (Ezek 24:15-18).

Overall Structure and Intention of the Book

For the book of Ezekiel, the status of God's temple and of the city of Jerusalem as the place that contains the temple is of central concern. This is reflected in the structure of the book itself. After a brief description of Ezekiel's call (Ezek 1–3), judgment and destruction are proclaimed for Jerusalem (Ezek 4–24). Then follow words of consolation that justify hope for the people of the city (Ezek 25–39); finally, there is a vision of the new city and the new temple (Ezek 40–48).

Ezekiel, in his prophecy, reflects on history and concerns himself with thematic complexes such as sin, God's wrath, judgment, repentance, salvation, restoration, divine mercy, and human responsibility. More than any other prophet, Ezekiel performs a great many symbolic acts and has ecstatic experiences (3:22-27; 4–5; 12; 21; 24; 37). It is striking that after the words of judgment in Ezekiel 4–24, the city is seldom mentioned again in the book. The prophetic words that speak of a new beginning and salvation are addressed to the "sheep" (34:11-31), the "mountain" (36:1-15), and the "house" of Israel, but never to Jerusalem. Even in the vision that describes God's return to his holy city, the name of the city is never mentioned. The people, the land, and the temple will be rebuilt, but Jerusalem itself seems to be excluded from the vision of a future reconciliation.

Social-Historical-Feminist Aspects

To examine the whole book of Ezekiel from a feminist perspective would be a rewarding task. Here it is only possible to describe the results of the investigation of texts and themes that have so far interested feminist exegetes (and those who examine women-specific questions).

The "Image of Jealousy" and the Women who Mourn for Tammuz (Ezekiel 8:1-16)

In a visionary experience the prophet is presented with four scenes portraying the religious situation in Jerusalem and the temple between 597 and 587 B.C.E. At the northern gate of the city, which leads to the interior of the temple, he sees "the image of jealousy that rouses jealousy." Then he sees seventy elders offering incense before images of unclean beasts, then women who are weeping for Tammuz, and finally twenty-five men worshiping the sun with their backs turned to God's temple. Dijkstra (1996, 113-14), beginning with the association of these places and rituals, shows their probable connection to an ancient festival of the fall equinox, celebrated in Israel, the source of the later Jewish feast of Sukkoth.

We cannot clearly determine what the "image of jealousy" was. Favoring its identification with a cultic image of the goddess Asherah is the fact that the Hebrew words for "image of jealousy" *(pesel hassemel)* appear in 2 Chronicles 33:7 for the cultic object designated in 2 Kings 21:7 as Asherah. If this is an accurate identification, the cultic image of Asherah, after having been — according to 2 Kings 23:6 — removed from the temple during Josiah's cultic reform, had been set up somewhere else, perhaps within another sanctuary at a different city gate (Ezek 8:5). The astral-religious background indicated in the text and the mention of Tammuz also suggest a connection with the Mesopotamian Ishtar, who at that time could have been identified in Judea with Asherah. Since it is improbable that two goddesses were worshiped in Jerusalem simultaneously, in this case we should also consider a connection with the queen of heaven mentioned in Jeremiah 7:18 and 44:17-19.

The actors are not precisely described, but the local context and its content (the events portrayed take place at the city gate, through which all who leave or enter the city must pass; the prophet's criticism, as it proceeds, is also directed against women's religious activities) make it probable that the masculine plurals here refer to women as well as men. The fact that they are not further described, while the other people spoken of in this chapter are more precisely specified, can be understood to mean that women and men of all classes are active here. The connection with an altar shows that sacrifices are being offered to the "image of jealousy." The subsequent context (Ezek 8:7-13), in which "laypersons" are accused of having carried out unauthorized priestly tasks, suggests that we should suppose that here women and men, with the tolerance of the priesthood, are offering sacrifices, which makes it seem superfluous to them to visit God's sanctuary.

The scene in which the women weep for Tammuz (8:14-15) is strikingly brief. Is this to be attributed to lack of interest in the religious lives of these women? The lapidary nature of the information leaves it particularly obscure whether there was such a ritual lament in Jerusalem in the autumn, that is, shortly before the coming of the rains (so Dijkstra 1996, 100-101), or whether we ought to think, following Mesopotamian sources, of high summer, the dry period. The event crowds close to the inner courts of the temple: the women who wept for Tammuz were sitting at the temple's North Gate. It is striking that the women have moved very close to the temple courts, still closer than the lay sector of the seventy elders. If we are correct in supposing that the men who follow (8:16) are priests (cf. Zimmerli 1969, 221), we may suppose that the women were also exercising a special function. The Hebrew article, which designates "the" women (and is eliminated by most interpreters), would point to this.

Could it also be that the word "sitting" *(yšb)*, besides its immediate significance of being seated and bending double in weeping, is also to be understood as an indication that this was a particular group of women assigned the duty of making ritual lament for the dead Tammuz, and that they were (regularly) to be found there? We have evidence of professional wailing women who mourned the dead, not as part of the regular cultic worship (Jer 9:16-20 [Eng. 17-21]). There can be no doubt that laments at the time of death were primarily sung by women. Since in Babylonian myth it is the goddess Ishtar who weeps for Tammuz, the women may have been seen as embodiments of the weeping Ishtar. As professional weeping women, they may have belonged to the class of male and female *qĕdēšôt* who, according to 2 Kings 23:7, had houses in the precincts of the Jerusalem temple (cf. Dijkstra 1996, 98).

We cannot deduce from the women's lament for Tammuz a ritual "sacred marriage" in Judea or at the Jerusalem temple. Such a ritual can be demonstrated only for the Sumerian centers at Uruk, Kullaba, and Badtibara (end of the third/ beginning of the second millennium B.C.E.). A priestess of the goddess Inanna had sexual intercourse with the reigning king in the role of the deified Dumuzi in a cultic context, and so conveyed to him political and religious authority and legitimation. In the Assyro-Babylonian period (second to first millennium) such a royal cult can no longer be shown to have existed, even though the worship songs that were probably associated with it were still handed down. To that extent there is no basis for supposing there was a tradition of "sacred marriage" in Mesopotamia at the time of ancient Israel, which might in turn have influenced such a cult in Israel/Judea.

When Ezekiel speaks of the sorrow of the women for "Tammuz," he is using a Babylonian god's name that echoes the ancient Sumerian name of Dumuzi. Ezekiel seems thus to be alluding to ritual mourning for the disappearance of Tammuz into the underworld, which was carried out every year in high summer in Mesopotamia, and which had now reached Jerusalem. However, we cannot exclude the possibility that Ezekiel is here using the Babylonian god's name polemically in order to brand a cult as "foreign worship" although in reality it already had a long tradition in Israel/Judea and celebrated a male deity who was there perhaps called not Tammuz, but Baal or Adon(is). The Ugaritic tradition from the end of the second millennium about the slain Baal who is mourned by his sister Anath, and the tradition found only in later sources about Adonis and Astarte, would then offer us comparative material closer in time. But there are too few secure points of contact in these sources for a "sacred marriage" in the sense intended by the Sumerian sources. On the other hand, both mythical complexes are not only about mourning rituals at the time of dying (desiccating) vegetation, but also about political contexts, however difficult it is to grasp their details. In view of the life situation of the women, as described above, and the crisis situation of the population as a whole, I think it is probable that the women at the temple who were weeping for "Tammuz," and who here may stand within a longer women's tradition in Judea as well, were lamenting not only for the vegetation, as is generally posited in scholarly literature, but also for the people killed in the war.

The Daughters of Your People Prophesy (Ezekiel 13:17-23)

The thirteenth chapter of Ezekiel is a major confrontation with prophecy in Ezekiel's time. The first section is aimed at male prophets (13:1-16), but the second section turns explicitly against prophetically active women (13:17-23).

A comparison of this second section with the preceding words against the male prophets reveals some differences that both point to the different activities of female and male prophets and also indicate the different evaluations the text presents of women and men who prophesy.

- The men are called "prophets" (13:2), just as Ezekiel says that he himself has been called to be a prophet (2:5; 33:33). The women, however, are called "daughters of your people who prophesy out of their own imagination." Is it possible that here the prophet is polemically denying them the title of prophet and at the same time accusing them of high-handed self-assertiveness?
- While the text speaks in metaphorical form of the prophets as doing something that goes beyond verbal prophecy, that is, rebuilding a wall for the house of Israel (13:5), the words against the women prophets reveal concrete activities that are to be seen as connected to their prophetic task.
- The women prophets are explicitly accused of making their talents available to all, without distinction, so long as they can pay.
- It is said of the prophets that they claim to speak in the name of God (13:6), while the women prophets are said to profane *(hll)* God (13:19).
- The critique of the male prophets consists of saying that they lie because they see good where there is evil. In contrast, the accusation directed at the women prophets is that they are supposedly able to determine whether individuals live or die.
- The women prophets are accused of using their activity to earn their bread, even if in modest amounts. But nothing is said about any possible earnings of the male prophets.

How can we assemble these different viewpoints into a coherent picture?

We learn that the women prophets "sew bands." The Hebrew word for "sewing" *(tpr)* is used elsewhere with the meaning "gather together/sew together" as a description of the work of women and men (Gen 3:7; Job 16:15; Eccles 3:7). The noun *kĕsātôt*, on the other hand, appears only here in the First Testament. Generally the Akkadian word for "bind/ban" *(kasū)* is taken as a reference point, and the noun is translated "bandages." Correspondingly, the head coverings *(mispāḥôt)* that women also made are related to the Akkadian word for "scatter, spread" *(sapāḥu)*, and thus mean a piece of clothing laid loosely over the head, hence a shawl, veil, or scarf. These women prophets, then, are first of all craftspeople who make the garments they need for their own work. They not only make them, but wear them in order to prophesy (Ezek 13:20-21). Apparently they receive foodstuffs in return for their activity, enough at least to keep them alive (Ezek 13:19). Whereas this was not regarded as offensive for prophets to do in Israel in prestate conditions and in the early monarchy (cf. 1 Sam 9:7; 1 Kings 14:3; we have no corresponding texts reflecting this period in Judah), the writing prophets vehemently reject any connection between prophecy and earning one's living (cf. Amos 7:10-12, and especially Mic 3:5). Ezekiel expresses the same criticism.

For an understanding of the women's use of the necessary accessory materials for their prophecy we are directed, among other things, to comparable phenomena from so-called traditional societies studied by ethnologists (cf. most recently

Wacker 1997, who discusses not only the "accessories" but also the appearance of these women as a whole against the background of the category of "shamanism"). Although the bands and head coverings are explained by reference to Akkadian concepts, Assyro-Babylonian parallels, which are also often adduced, are somewhat closer. Especially relevant in this context are the Akkadian collections of spells, Maqlu and Šurpu, which contain defensive spells against the negative effects of black magic. Before we follow this path any further, let me mention an alternative: Is it possible that the textiles in question were amulet-type bands bound on the wrists, similar to *tefillin,* the prayer bands that arose later from a literal interpretation of Deuteronomy 6:8 (cf. Deut 11:18; Exod 13:16)? In Matthew 23:5 these prayer bands are called phylacteries, which presumes that they are understood as defensive and protective materials. Correspondingly, then, the head coverings here could be an early stage of the later *tallit,* the prayer shawl. This is an exciting proposal, since in that case women at this time would have been wearing the prayer aids that were later reserved to men alone.

The aids that the prophetic women themselves produced are as a rule connected by interpreters — certainly influenced by their impressions from the Babylonian magical texts — with (black) magic, and therefore are judged negatively in the overall context (e.g., Bertholet and Galling 1936, 49; Zimmerli 1969, 299). Women's magical practices are also mentioned in the First Testament, in Exodus 4:24-26 without judgment and in 1 Samuel 28 from a more negative point of view. Exodus 22:17(18) speaks directly against the "witch/woman magician," but it is not only women who are accused of magic and witchcraft. Most of the texts of this nature are directed against both women and men (Lev 19:31; 20:6, 27; Deut 18:10, 11, 14). We should, however, note that magic rituals were incorporated into Israelite religion from an early period, if they were not, after all, a "genuine" part of the religion itself. Such include determining God's will by means of the lots Urim and Thummim (e.g., Deut 33:8; 1 Sam 14:41; Exod 28:30; Lev 8:8) and other practices that clearly belong to preventative or therapeutic magic. Add to this that Ezekiel is also portrayed as a prophet who makes use of magical practices: in Ezekiel 21:19 (English 21:14), for example, God's command to prophesy is associated with a magical clapping of hands. Moreover, his prophesying can have an immediate fatal (11:13) or life-giving effect (37:7-10). Thus Ezekiel, no less than the women, is involved in the connections between prophecy and magic, which slay or maintain human life; the only difference is that he denies that they have the right to act in the name of God. That here equally qualified "magicians" confront one another is evident from the fact that, different from the male prophets, Ezekiel directs his prophecy at the female prophets (Ezek 13:17; cf. also 4:7; 6:2; 21:2, 7 [English 20:46; 21:2]).

Something similar is true of Mesopotamia. In the major compendia of magical spells against sorcery, mentioned above, which were widely circulated in the first millennium, the same practices that were charged against the "witches" were being widely practiced. It is important to distinguish whether magical acts were done secretly, that is, by "witches," or by an appeal to and with the approval of the gods, that is, as a legitimate official defense measure. Magical practices, we may conclude, were probably also allowed in Israel/Judea when performed by priests and prophets, as long as they were members of the "official" cult. "Independent" women and men magicians, on the other hand, were prohibited.

In Ezekiel 13:17-23 the women are not criticized in the first place because of magical practices, which Ezekiel himself apparently carried out, though in a different form; they are attacked because their decisions about life and death contradict those of the prophet. Here we find two different and opposed positions, one of which — that of the women — is not permitted to be heard.

The Mother as Lioness (Ezekiel 19:1-9)

In Ezekiel 19 feminine word images are used against the kingship: the mother as lioness (19:2-9) and the mother as vine in the vineyard (19:10-14). Here we will examine only the image of the lioness.

The lioness is first sketched positively: her strength, power, and dignity are emphasized. Because of her motherly care, her young grow into strong lions that destroy other peoples (cf. Ezek 22:25; Zeph 3:3; Prov 28:15). This, and the cry "What a lioness was your mother!" could be read to mean that Ezekiel is lamenting more the loss of the mother than the evil deeds of her children. Some exegetes suggest that we should see the concept of "mother" as a corporate personality for Israel/Judah (Beentjes 1996, 29). Others suppose that this image could refer to actual women. In that case the lioness could be identified with Hamutal, the mother of Jehoahaz and Zedekiah, or with Nehushta.

Hamutal, whose name means "the little lizard," occupied the office of king's mother twice, with an interruption (→ Books of Kings). Her son Jehoahaz was crowned king before his older half-brother Jehoiakim, the legitimate successor to the title (2 Kings 23:31, 36). This can be explained by the fact that, for one thing, she was from a Judean family, in contrast to Jehoiakim's mother, who was from a Galilean family (2 Kings 23:36). If the sayings in Ezekiel 19:1-9 are applied to Hamutal, it would appear that the king's mother was the real person pulling the strings behind the event so briefly described in 2 Kings 23:31-35. In that case the context would be this: since Hamutal, in contrast to Jehoiakim's mother Zebidah, came from a Judean family (2 Kings 23:36), it was possible for her, by making use of the anti-Egyptian inclinations and support of the *'am hā'āreṣ*, to set her son Jehoahaz on the throne; he was subsequently deported to Egypt (2 Kings 23:33). When the political situation shifted in favor of the Babylonians, another of her sons, Zedekiah, became king.

Nehushta, the wife of Jehoiakim, was sent into exile along with her son

Jehoiachin. The name Nehushta, "the iron one," attributed to her by the tradition in 2 Kings 24:8, could be associated with the iron columns in the temple, which may have symbolized the sacred trees/Asherahs. It also evokes associations with the iron serpent Nehushtan (2 Kings 18:4), which may likewise be linked with Asherah (Olyan 1988, 70-71). Frank Moore Cross (Milik and Cross 1954, 8-9) considers it probable that the goddess Asherah was called "the lioness." He refers to a cultic stand from Taanach (tenth century), on the lower part of which a female figure, who may be understood to be a goddess, reaches for two lions. Since the king's mother had both political and religious influence (cf. Jost 1995, 141-45), and may possibly have represented the Asherah (cultically) as well, this text — if the lioness is identified with Nehushta — may be criticizing not only the god-representing royal mother, but also the goddess she personified.

Rûaḥ as Creative Power

The noun *rûaḥ* is one of a group of Hebrew nouns whose grammatical gender is not clearly defined, but can change (another such noun is *šemeš* [sun]). The concept of *rûaḥ* is more strongly in the foreground in Ezekiel than in the earlier writing prophets. Helen Schüngel-Straumann (1996) has pointed out that this noun is always used as feminine in Hebrew when it is in life-promoting, creative contexts, which may be traceable to an original connection between the concepts of "wideness" *(rewaḥ)* and "spirit" *(rûaḥ)*. She employs birth as an example to explain the connection:

> The audible panting when giving birth and the relieved intake of breath after a successful birth, which again "makes room" for the woman in the literal sense, is at the same time creative, life-giving. That it is always also dangerous, i.e., closely connected with the threat of death, makes the event all the more tension-laden, namely ambivalent. The repeated experience of such life-threatening, but — with a positive outcome — also life-continuing events could, because of their frequency and their existential significance, also furnish the background for the concept of *rûaḥ*. This may also be the primary reason why *rûaḥ* is always feminine when it is found in life-promoting, creative contexts. (Schüngel-Straumann 1996, 203)

Almost every passage in the book of Ezekiel in which *rûaḥ* appears uses the feminine. In Ezekiel's accounts of his visions (Ezek 1–3; 8–11), *rûaḥ* is used with various meanings. In 1:4 the *rûaḥ*/wind is the vehicle of the divine appearance. The concept is used most frequently in the sense of the power that sets the prophet on his feet (2:2; 3:12; 3:24) or brings him to a different place (3:14; 8:3; 11:1; 11:24). In the wheel visions in chapters 1 and 10 it is *rûaḥ* that moves the four living creatures and the four wheels. The *rûaḥ* that can be linked to spirit, but also to strength, is here a feminine life principle that binds together what is separated. In 37:1-14 *rûaḥ* is the power that creates wholeness, bringing the dead bones together. She puts things in motion, leads into the land, is the creative life force that first joins humanity with God and thus opens a future.

What is unclear, on the other hand, is the grammatically feminine relationship of *rûaḥ* in 1:4 and 1:20, two verses from the first vision of the wheels. In the second of these visions *rûaḥ* appears once in a clearly masculine gender (10:17). The shift could have occurred because here *rûaḥ* is identified with the cherubim, presented as masculine.

Although *rûaḥ* as creative feminine power usually moves or inspires male beings, she nevertheless, being only vaguely defined in distinction from God, reveals something so unpredictable and independent that she cannot be limited to male creativity (Schüngel-Straumann 1996, 215). This conception of *rûaḥ* offers a positive starting point for a feminist interpretation of the book of Ezekiel.

Ideological-Critical Assessment of the (Feminine) Metaphors in the Book of Ezekiel

The most powerfully feminine-shaped metaphor in the book of Ezekiel appears in reference to the city of Jerusalem. The basis of the metaphor is the ancient Near Eastern idea of a city as the woman rich in blessings, who shelters the inhabitants and is the partner of the (male) protective god of the city. A city could be identified with its city goddess who, as "mother" and "queen," cared for it. She was then spoken of in metaphorical imagery as "the woman-city." Old Testament prophecy linked with this tradition, but changed it from the ground up. For these prophets, while cities could be represented as metaphorical female persons, they were never divinities, but always mortal, vulnerable women, subject to seduction, and often standing on a low moral plane.

Ezekiel takes up the image of the city as God's female opposite in order to find language for the desecration of the temple and the ruin of the city. If God's city, on a symbolic level, is a female body, the temple, on the same symbolic level, is like a vagina and a womb. It is always in danger of being soiled by menstruation and illegitimate sexual intercourse. Ezekiel describes the relational encounter between the city and God in terms of a male-female relationship. In the image of "the city as woman," the cultic and political "false moves" of the city are defined as violations of her loyalty to God, her "husband." The metaphorical event illustrates how deeply God is dishonored by his city's "missteps." This dishonor can only be removed through revenge and punishment.

In Ezekiel 16 and 23, Jerusalem is explicitly described as a woman. Therefore we should look first and most thoroughly at those chapters.

Jerusalem as Daughter and Wife (Ezekiel 16)

In Ezekiel 16, Jerusalem is represented by a "female person" who is viewed negatively from the outset: her parents are from non-Israelite tribes, so that there is a blemish even on her origins (16:3). At her very birth this girl is so despised that she is thrown on the ground like garbage (16:4-5). But then God passes by, sees her flailing about in her blood, and says to her: "Live!" (16:6). This creative act opens a future for the girl; God assumes a paternal role in her regard. However, that role is not characterized by active care. The girl grows like a "plant of the field," and her growth is reduced to the development of sexual attributes: her breasts and pubic hair form and grow (16:7). Now God looks at her again and realizes that she is at "the age for love." He extends an act signifying marriage to her and takes her as his sexual possession (16:8). By this act, and by his gifts, he underscores her sexual attractiveness and makes her a partner fit for himself (16:9-14).

The expressive power of the imagery is in its presentation of the female figure's weakness, without God, and her lack of a future. She is completely dependent on him. From a feminist perspective, parallels with male behavior classified as "sexual abuse" are brought to mind, for there is a fundamental asymmetry in the relationship between God and the city/woman that is exploited by the stronger party for the satisfaction of his sexual needs. In the face of this crass imbalance of power, the female person has no chance to develop a will of her own with which to oppose the will of God. Respect for the human dignity of the girl is not a matter of course on the level of the text: the girl is here, in fact, nothing more than a piece of "dirt" or "trash," and every form of attention paid her is "undeserved kindness." Rights derive from the male act of graciousness, including his taking sexual possession of her. In this way what we must denounce as paternal abuse of power is depicted as honoring of the woman, something for which gratitude is demanded again and again in what follows.

Only after she has been taken sexual possession of is the "woman" allowed by the narrator to be active. She acts in a way that, according to his value system, could scarcely be more despicable: she does not behave as if she were God's property, but instead trusts in her beauty and "plays the whore." The descriptions of her actions are voyeuristic: her sexual activities are depicted in detail (16:15-21). She does not think of "the days of her youth, when she was naked and bare" (cf. 16:22), and thus proves herself to the utmost degree ungrateful. She is perverse, because she does not even take money for her sexual "services," but pays her lovers instead (16:34).

What the text calls "whoring" we, from a feminist perspective, must call a woman's self-determined sexual behavior. But for the prophets of the First Testament, it seems that sexual self-determination is an anachronistic category. Here a woman's sexuality is regarded as the property of a man, something not at her own disposal. If one follows this logic, it is all the more despicable that the actions of the "woman" in Ezekiel's metaphor are motivated by "sheer insatiable lust" (cf. 16:25, 28, 29, 30) and she seeks satisfaction from strangers instead of from her husband (16:32). Female sexuality is thus distorted, being depicted as a lust-driven evil that disdains and flouts all relationships.

God reacts to the serious injury done him by "Jerusalem" through her behavior by committing sexual violence on her before the eyes of her lovers and destroying her body with gruesome finality (16:36-40). This "woman" is made an example, so that all women will be warned not to disrupt the patriarchal order and be unfaithful to their husbands (16:41). The brutality practiced on the city/woman appears in the narrative as justified because her moral depravity is excessive. Ezekiel, in his prophecy, makes the woman a kind of negative template as an aid to illuminating all the more clearly God's greatness and justice. The more helpless the woman, the more superior is God. The more depraved she is, the more righteous does he appear.

The form of the divine discourse draws the reader directly into the course of events depicted in Ezekiel 16. Women are scarcely able to distance themselves from the description of the "depraved" female figure representing Jerusalem. They do have the opportunity to adopt the androcentric, defamatory image of the female depravity of this "city/woman" and to agree with the patriarchal system of values according to which a woman is the property of a man. But every woman also knows that she herself is not protected from being treated and punished like "adulterous Jerusalem" — quite independent of whether she is a faithful wife or has sexual relationships with different men. Especially in war zones, women must expect that, simply because of their gender, they will be treated by military opponents as if they were nothing more than "despicable whores." When cities are conquered and captured, women are the primary victims of (sexual) violence; they and their children are especially affected by the burning and destruction.

Sexual Abuse and Its Consequences (Ezekiel 23)

The historical retrospective in Ezekiel 23 contains images and models of argumentation similar to those in Ezekiel 16. Here the history of the cities of Samaria and Jerusalem is told as the story of the sisters Oholah and Oholibah. Oholah and Oholibah are depicted as women who went in search of sexual satisfaction even as children. "They played the whore in Egypt; they played the whore in their youth; their breasts were caressed there, and their virgin bosoms were fondled" (23:3). This description of the sisters' childhood represents what Fokkelien van Dijk-Hemmes called "misnaming of female experience": the picture of a reality in which girls may be seductresses and "little whores" rests on male fantasies that veil male desires and legitimate them. Girls see a different reality from that described in Ezekiel 23: it is not they who seek sexual pleasure with adults; rather, they are frequently made use of for adults' sexual gratification. The adults — usually men — initiate sexual contact. The assertion that children themselves desire this kind of contact and enjoy it is "blaming the victim." Taking this fact into account, it would be more appropriate to describe the events in the sisters' childhood in these words: "They were sexually mistreated in Egypt; in their youth they were sexually abused" (van Dijk-Hemmes 1993, 166).

God espouses Oholah and Oholibah (23:4). But in the text's depiction, the girls' initial sexual contacts with the Egyptians contain in themselves a kind of "fundamental depravity" that repeatedly erupts even after marriage. Both women "whore" and thus reveal, according to the text, an unlimited and perverse sexual appetite. The women's lust for strange men has something compulsive about it (23:20, 21, 43). The description of their behavior calls for emphasis on the fact that their sexuality is and must be an object of male possession and control.

While it is true that, from a feminist perspective as well, compulsive sexual behavior by women can be linked with their having been sexually abused as children, that connection is not what the text suggests. Sexual abuse does not lead to a "fundamental depravity," but can evoke (among other things) serious disturbances in sexual experience and behavior. That is, as a result of having been exploited, many of those affected "learn" that sexuality is a product they can or must exchange to gain attention, affection, recognition, and the like. In extreme cases, exploited women are socialized into the prostitute's role. When a sexually abused woman becomes a prostitute or frequently changes sexual partners, it is often falsely seen as evidence that, even as a child, she was already "depraved" and a "nymphomaniac." This fatal reversal of cause and effect makes it possible to maintain an androcentric interpretation of reality in which the man appears as the victim and the guilt for sexual "bad behavior" is laid exclusively at the doors of girls or women. Ezekiel 23 hands on a cliché about "lewd women" that was not yet in Ezekiel 16: the story of the eternally enticing woman, "Lolita."

In addition, the consequence of the women's behavior in Ezekiel 23 is, again, the most brutal sort of punishment. In the metaphorical depiction the violence against Oholah and Oholibah, in the carrying out of the sentence, is at least as broadly drawn as their preceding "whorish" behavior (23:9, 10, 22-26, 29). The intention is to issue a warning to all women: they should not even think of engaging in lewd behavior (23:48). Male readers can distance themselves from the city/woman thus described; they see themselves in the betrayed and vengeance-filled husband, on the side of the justice-dealing man who imposes an appropriate punishment on the degenerate woman subject. While women can attempt to set themselves alongside these "justice-dealing men" and to join them in destroying the "whore," it is still true that this cannot protect women from discovering that in certain circumstances they themselves can become the victims of sexual violence and be confronted with the accusation that they wanted that kind of sex and would enjoy it.

The Role of the Female Figure of Jerusalem in the Book of Ezekiel

Nowhere, outside Ezekiel 16 and 23, is Jerusalem explicitly called a woman. Nevertheless, such personification is apparently not restricted to these chapters because, on the one hand, feminine Jerusalem is implicitly spoken of throughout the condemnations in chapters 1–24 (cf., e.g., Ezek 5:7-17; 7:22; 22:1-5; 24:7), and the same vocabulary as in chapters 16 and 23 (e.g., "whoring") is applied repeatedly to the city in Ezekiel 1–24. In addition, the statements about the city adopt words that, in the Old Testament context, reveal a specific link to women, though these do not appear in chapters 16 and 23 (such as "uncleanness"). Remarkably enough, the final action at the end of the words of judgment — the death of Ezekiel's own wife as a sign of the fall of the city (24:15-27) — completes the idea of the status of the city as "God's symbolic wife." In turn, it can be assumed that the death of Ezekiel's wife reflects and seals the "death" of the "city/woman" Jerusalem.

In contrast to this, after Ezekiel 24 there is no more talk of female pollution and shame. Only in 36:18 does God recall that the people of Israel are like "a menstruating woman." The rebuilt temple-city in chapters 40–48 is not personified as a female figure, and no explicitly female imagery is applied to the city. It is true that, on a symbolic level, the new city fulfills female roles, since it is a home, God's exclusive possession, and a life-giving place, but it is always described as a collection of buildings and not as a woman. The city's fidelity is thus guaranteed: a congeries of buildings is unable to be unfaithful. The "city/woman" has become an object on the literary level and thus incapable of further disobedience. When God has built the city anew and entered into it, the punished and humiliated city/woman "Jerusalem" will be missing from the scene. While the people receive from God a heart "of flesh" in place of their stony heart (36:26-27), the new city consists of lifeless stones. So is fulfilled the prophecy that Jerusalem will never again open her mouth (16:63): she can no longer open her mouth, because she is no longer depicted as a woman. The rebuilt city is faithful, but only because every feature of femaleness has been removed from it.

Julie Galambush (1992) points out that in describing the temple, Ezekiel uses the technique of focusing. In light of Jerusalem's sexual depravity, voyeuristically displayed in Ezekiel 16 and 23, it seems significant that in Ezekiel 8–11 and 40–48 — the two inspections of the temple — the prophet makes people and objects the focus of interest: in the ancient temple Ezekiel spies in order to discover the elders who, in turn, are looking at idols. In Ezekiel 40–48, in the demystified and objectified (female) temple, voyeurism as such is abandoned, but the temple itself has now become a kind of fetish. It is an object of extraordinary external beauty, pointing to its Creator. Focusing is a strategy for maintaining control. The transformation of the city/woman into a lifeless object has removed every reason for unease, since perfect control is now possible.

LITERATURE

Becking, Bob, and Meindert Dijkstra, eds. 1996. *On Reading Prophetic Texts: Gender-Specific and Related Studies.* Festschrift for Fokkelien van Dijk-Hemmes. Leiden, New York, and Cologne.

Beentjes, Panc C. 1996. "What a Lioness Was Your Mother: Reflections on Ezekiel 19." In *On Reading Prophetic Texts: Gender-Specific and Related Studies,* edited by Bob Becking and Meindert Dijkstra, 21-36. Festschrift for Fokkelien van Dijk-Hemmes. Leiden, New York, and Cologne.

Bertholet, Alfred, and Kurt Galling. 1936. *Hesekiel.* Handbuch zum Alten Testament. Tübingen.

Darr, Katheryn Pfisterer. 1992. "Ezekiel." In *The Women's Bible Commentary,* edited by Carol A. Newsom and Sharon H. Ringe, 183-90. London and Louisville.

Dijkstra, Meindert. 1996. "Goddess, Gods, Men and Woman in Ezekiel 8." In *On Reading Prophetic Texts: Gender-Specific and Related Studies,* edited by Bob Becking and Meindert Dijkstra, 83-114. Festschrift for Fokkelien van Dijk-Hemmes. Leiden, New York, and Cologne.

Galambush, Julie. 1992. *Jerusalem in the Book of Ezekiel: The City as Yahweh's Wife.* Society of Biblical Literature Dissertation Series, vol. 130. Atlanta.

Jost, Renate. 1995. *Frauen, Männer und die Himmelskönigin. Exegetische Studien.* Gütersloh.

Milik, Jozef T., and Frank M. Cross. 1954. "Inscribed Arrowheads from the Period of the Judges." *Bulletin of the American Schools of Oriental Research* 134.

Olyan, Saul. 1988. *Asherah and the Cult of Yahweh in Israel.* Atlanta.

Schüngel-Straumann, Helen. 1992. *Rûah bewegt die Welt. Gottes schöpferische Lebenskraft in der Krisenzeit des Exils.* Stuttgarter Bibelstudien, vol. 151. Stuttgart.

———. 1996. "Rûah und Gender-Fragen am Beispiel der Visionen des Propheten Ezechiel." In *On Reading Prophetic Texts: Gender-Specific and Related Studies,* edited by Bob Becking and Meindert Dijkstra, 201-16. Festschrift for Fokkelien van Dijk-Hemmes. Leiden, New York, and Cologne.

Seifert, Elke. 1997. *Tochter und Vater im Alten Testament: Eine ideologiekritische Untersuchung zur Verfügungsgewalt von Vätern über ihre Töchter.* Neukirchen-Vluyn.

Van Dijk-Hemmes, Fokkelien. 1993. "The Metaphorization of Woman in Prophetic Speech: An Analysis of Ezekiel XXIII." *Vetus Testamentum* 43:162-70.

Van Dijk-Hemmes, Fokkelien, and Athalya Brenner. 1993. *On Gendering Texts: Female and Male Voices in the Hebrew Bible.* Biblical Interpretation Series, vol. 1. Leiden, New York, and Cologne.

Wacker, Marie-Theres. 1997. "SchamanInnen in der Welt der Bibel? Ein kulturvergleichendes Experiment." *Schlangenbrut* 57:17-21.

Zimmerli, Walther. 1969. *Ezechiel 1–24.* Biblischer Kommentar, Altes Testament, vol. 13, 1. Neukirchen-Vluyn.

FOR FURTHER READING

Cook, Stephen L., and Corrine L. Patton, eds. 2004. *Ezekiel's Hierarchical World: Wrestling with a Tiered Reality.* Society of Biblical Literature Symposium Series, vol. 31. Atlanta.

Fischer, Irmtraud, et al., eds. 2003. *Prophetie in Israel.* Münster, Hamburg, and London.

Greenberg, Moshe. 2001. *Ezechiel 1–20.* Herders theologischer Kommentar, Altes Testament. Freiburg, Basel, and Vienna.

———. 2005. *Ezechiel 21–37.* Herders theologischer Kommentar, Altes Testament. Freiburg, Basel, and Vienna.

Kamionkowski, S. Tamar. 2003. *Gender Reversal and Cosmic Chaos: A Study in the Book of Ezekiel.* Journal for the Study of the Old Testament: Supplement Series, vol. 368. Sheffield.

Odell, Margaret S., and John T. Strong, eds. 2000. *The Book of Ezekiel: Theological and Anthropological Perspectives.* Society of Biblical Literature Symposium Series, vol. 9. Atlanta.

Translated by Linda M. Maloney

Daniel: Not Counting Women and Children

Ilse von Loewenclau

Introduction

Daniel is one of the latest books in the Hebrew Bible. It is no accident that within that corpus it is placed nearly at the end, among the Writings. This may be connected with the fact that the canon of the Prophets was already closed and permitted no further additions. In German and English Bibles, Daniel is placed according to the Septuagint (LXX) order, after Ezekiel. Since our book brings its readers to Babylon, where Daniel and his friends, after their deportation, live and are educated at the royal court, the LXX is applying chronological considerations (as in the rearrangement of Ruth after Judges!).

It may now be regarded as established that the Babylonian setting is fictional, and that Daniel is not a historical figure from that period. He owes his name to an earlier sage who is seen in the book of Ezekiel, with Job and Noah, as an example of righteousness (Ezek 14:14; 28:3). That Daniel is probably identical to the legendary *dn'il* who, in Ugaritic tradition, supported widows and orphans. The fictional name is matched by incorrect historical information (Dan 1:1-2: Jehoiachin, and not Jehoiakim, was deported, and the inhabitants of Jerusalem not until the time of Zedekiah; 5:1, 11: Belshazzar was actually the son of Nabonidus and never had the title of "king"; 6:1: Babylon was conquered by Cyrus, not by Darius, and Darius was a Persian, not a Mede; 9:1: he was also not the son of Xerxes, but his father). Either the author did not know better, which is questionable, or he wanted to give his readers to understand that what followed was about something else altogether (cf. the collection of historically contradictory information in Jth 1:1-12, for the purpose of proclaiming, in the book of Judith, the victory of the people of God over all the hostile attacking powers).

The book of Daniel divides clearly into two halves containing narratives and visions. The narratives in chapters 1–6 are about Daniel and his friends. They are intended, on the one hand, to present vivid examples of fidelity to the Law in a foreign environment (chapters 1; 3; and 6), and on the other hand to demonstrate

Daniel's wisdom, since he knows how to interpret troubling dreams and signs (chapters 2; 4; and 5). These dreams and visions also link the first half of the book to the second half in chapters 7–12. These chapters are dominated by visions that are significantly different from the visions of earlier prophets (e.g., Amos 7:1-9; Jer 1:12-15). Not only is their symbolic world strange; even the wisdom of Daniel, previously so highly praised, fails before it. Daniel, who before this was always his king's interpreter, is here a disturbed recipient. In his dismay at what he has seen, he then receives the promise of the angel Gabriel, sent to him for this purpose (Dan 8:15-26). Gabriel continues to function as an interpreting angel (9:21-27; 10:11-14; earlier, in 7:16, 23, the interpreter is unnamed).

With these chapters we have entered the world of apocalyptic, a movement that prophesied the end of this age with its dissolving and rapidly collapsing empires (chapter 2). It will be replaced by an eschatological reign of God in which the "saints of the Most High" rule, originally God's heavenly realm but in a later reinterpretation possibly Israel. Equally disputed in this regard is the figure of the Son of Man (7:13-14). Regarded by some interpreters, in view of 7:27, as a collective representation of the Jewish people, it is more probably an angelic figure; some think it is Michael, Israel's guardian angel (first appearing in Dan 10:13, 21 and 12:1).

Although it is a branch of First Testament prophecy, apocalyptic is clearly different from it. The prophet speaks; the apocalypticist writes (12:4!). Apocalypses are literature, "underground literature" for people in times of persecution; they impart comfort, instruction, and hope. Their authors are anonymous, concealing themselves behind major figures of an earlier time like Daniel, and they project events that reflect the present into times long past, such as the time of the exile in Babylon. The present is to be deduced from the coded images, and in the book of Daniel it points to the Maccabean period. The visionary prospect on the course of history from the point of view of Daniel in Babylon (made possible by interpreting Jeremiah's seventy years of exile as seventy weeks of years, i.e., 490 years: 9:24-27) mentions no names; these must be deduced. All the information beyond the Hellenistic period is very vague. Our author is specific only about his own time, which is marked by the appearance of Antiochus IV Epiphanes, his prohibition of Jewish worship, and the desecration of the temple through the setting up of a statue of Zeus ("an abomination that desolates"; cf. 9:27, and also 8:12-13 and 11:31-32). These actions (169-167 B.C.E.) set off the Maccabean revolt, about which the author of our book is not especially confident (11:34: "a little help"). It may be that he is close to those who, awaiting God's help, retreated to the mountains (1 Macc 2:29-30). Probably he is part of the group of the wise (Dan 12:3) who, ready to accept martyrdom, remained faithful to their God (11:33; for their attitude, cf. 3:17-18). Since Antiochus IV died in different circumstances from those described in 11:44-45, and there is no awareness of the rededication of the temple by Judas Maccabeus in December 164, the redaction of our book must have taken place before that date. We may doubt that it was originally planned as a complete whole.

The striking and never fully explained shift in language, at 2:4b, from Hebrew to Aramaic, and the return to Hebrew in 8:1, speaks against literary unity.

Likewise contrary to the idea of the book as a literary whole is the growth of the book of Daniel in its Greek translation. It exists in two versions: the older LXX from the first century B.C.E. (G) and Theodotion's version (Th) from the second century C.E. It remains unclear, however, whether the latter is a revision of the older text. In the ancient church, which knew the First Testament only in its Greek form, these "additions to Daniel" were just as canonical as the Hebrew-Aramaic basic text. The church read the book in Theodotion's version, which also underlies our biblical translations. In what follows we must also include G in our interpretation in order to get a clearer view of our theme. Rahlfs's edition of the LXX (1935) contains both versions of the text. Engel (1985) includes in his monograph on the Susanna narrative a synopsis that I have gratefully adopted, including its translation.

In the Catholic tradition the additions, though "deuterocanonical," appear together with the canonical text (in the New American Bible as well as in the New Jerusalem Bible). They are inserted into the text (in chapter 3 as the Prayer of Azariah and the Song of the Three Young Men in the Fiery Furnace) or added as chapters 13 (Susanna) and 14 (Bel and the Dragon). In the Lutheran tradition all the additions (if included) are printed as "apocrypha" between the Old and New Testaments; they are not "to be regarded as equal to Sacred Scripture" since they are absent from the Hebrew Bible and Luther regarded only the *Hebraica veritas* as binding. Correspondingly, Protestant scholars treat the additions to the biblical books in special commentaries (Moore 1977), while Catholic exegetes include them in their commentaries on the respective biblical books (Collins 1993). The *Bibel im heutigen Deutsch*, indebted to both Catholic and Protestant contributors, presents a compromise solution: it prints the disputed texts between OT and NT as "the late writings of the Old Testament," a terminology that has probably remained undisputed for some time. It could be questioned particularly as regards the book of Daniel, since the book itself in its canonical form (note the location in the *Biblia Hebraica*!) should already be regarded as a late writing. At any rate, as regards our particular theme, the Greek parts of the text are in the same line as the Hebrew-Aramaic texts (very much in contrast, for example, to the additions to Esther!).

Women in the Book of Daniel

Not one woman is mentioned by name in the entire book of Daniel, not even the queen who makes the crucial identification of Daniel in 5:10-12. Susanna is the only exception; since she is the principal figure in the narrative about her, she must have a name, and thus an identity. The few women other than Susanna who appear in the book of Daniel have no name, and so they have no identity of their own. If the cultural history of woman is essentially one of silencing, exclusion, and absence, the book of Daniel is one of the foremost witnesses to that fact. Our book loves to group women and children together (6:25 [Eng. 24]; 14:10, 15, 20-21). That would not be noteworthy in itself and has parallels in other ancient authors. When there was warfare, women and children were put in places of safety if possible (Herodotus 1.164); when a city was conquered, they were treated differently from the men: the latter were killed, the former sold into slavery (Herodotus 6.19). Even today women and children remain the weaker groups in society, entitled to expect special protection. If it is not given them (in case of defeat or other deficiencies on the part of the responsible authorities), they become victims of the society — perhaps in very humiliating ways (slavery). They can scarcely be said to deserve their fate, since that presumes individual freedom of decision, which from the point of view of those in power should be denied to women and children inasmuch as they are immature beings. They must bear the consequences of society's actions. Therefore the wives and children of the men who accused Daniel were thrown into the lions' den along with the men and died with them (Dan 6:25[24]). According to Th, the same punishment also befell the wives and children of the priests of Bel (14:22). They had participated in the treachery of their husbands and fathers (14:20) and enjoyed its benefits. G, however, is silent about a punishment of the wives and children; only the (guilty!) priests are handed over to Daniel, and their further fate goes unmentioned. In contrast to this differentiated portrayal in G, Theodotion's version recurs to the general rule, as enunciated in 6:25[24] (which, given the "lions' den" in 14:31, is a natural association). In other cases also, Theodotion is careful to draw connections with the canonical book of Daniel.

While the number of the priests of Bel is said to be seventy, the number of wives and children is not given; it must certainly be a multiple of seventy. G and Th both write — with a slight variation in wording — "not counting their wives and children" (14:10). The same expression recurs in Matthew 14:21: five thousand men are satisfied by the miraculous meal, "not counting women and children." If we counted them we would arrive, here again, at a multiple of five thousand (McKenna 1994). Since Matthew 14:21 certainly did not have our Daniel chapter in mind, it seems to me that this can only be a fixed formula of words. It announces that women and children are statistically of no importance. The texts that attest to this formula extend over a relatively short period from the second century B.C.E. to the first century C.E. They must certainly reflect a social reality of that time, against which Jesus acted in his own way — a way that was offensive even to his own disciples (Mark 10:13-16; 14:3-9).

In the ancient Near East a banquet — unlike in Greece — was unthinkable without women (Esther 1). We can perceive in Herodotus (5.18-19) that more was expected of them than their mere presence. It is said of Belshazzar's feast that his wives — queens, that is! — were present, along with his concubines (the number is not given, but it could be estimated as rather high if we consider Song of Solomon

6:8 — which again shows that women and children were not counted!). G eliminates this information, which would have been offensive to Greek readers, in Daniel 5:2-3, 23; Th removes only the queens throughout and qualifies "concubines" as
"women who slept with him." Probably he thinks there was only one queen ("the"
queen), who appears in 5:10 (Th) or is summoned by the king (G, 5:9). She makes
the crucial identification of Daniel, who was able to interpret the secret message
on the wall, which appeared — as if written by a human hand — at the moment
when the feasting company was drinking from the vessels stolen from the temple
while singing hymns of praise to their own gods. This "queen," however, is actually
the mother of the reigning king (hence: "your father, King Nebuchadnezzar")
who, as the queen mother, enjoyed high station at the ancient Near Eastern court.
Her only function here is to point out Daniel. Her name — despite her high standing — is unimportant.

In the apocalyptic sections proper there is no mention at all of women. Mark
13:17 shows that it is especially they who are affected when the end-time breaks in:
"Woe to those who are pregnant and to those who are nursing infants in those
days!" Such a thought is foreign to the book of Daniel. It seems to be true throughout that women and children do not count. But what about the chapter in the
Greek translation entitled "Susanna"?

Susanna

Some manuscripts place the title "Susanna" over this narrative, and that title was
adopted by Rahlfs in his edition of the Septuagint (cf. Rahlfs 1935, 864-70). It may
point to an originally independent tradition (according to Baumgartner 1959, 64-
65, it was in itself a "purely secular popular tale" that was secondarily "made the
instrument of an instructional and edifying purpose"). Only toward the end
(v. 45) is Daniel introduced. In accordance with the motifs, he has to be still a child
(cf. Baumgartner 1926), but in G he is a "youth" in contrast to the "elders" who
condemn Susanna. When Th adds "young," he intends — in contrast to G — to
minimize Daniel's age: "a young boy" (Engel 1985, 165), or "a very young lad"
(Engel 1985, *9). That is why the ancient church, which read this narrative in
Theodotion's version (the introductory words from Th in vv. 1-5a were deliberately inserted before G's introduction in v. 5b!), linked the young Daniel
typologically with the twelve-year-old Jesus! So it is altogether appropriate for Th
to set Susanna at the front of the book of Daniel, as its first chapter. Daniel's proving himself even in childhood is an impressive introduction to the narratives that
follow, which are prepared for by the words "and from that day onward Daniel had
a great reputation among the people" (13:64). So Susanna and the humiliating injustice perpetrated on her are ultimately included *ad maiorem gloriam* of Daniel.

It is different in the G tradition, for which Daniel is a young adult whose clever questioning reveals the "elders," who are also judges, as G repeatedly emphasizes, to be lawless. (This is summarized at the outset in v. 5b: "Wickedness came forth . . . from elders who were judges.") There was a great demand for young people like Daniel, marked by wisdom, genuineness, and directness. The closing verses state this clearly: "We must take care (that the) young (people become) wise and virtuous sons; for (if) the young (people) are Godfearing, they will have a spirit of knowledge and wisdom at all times."

When the narrative is aligned in this way, the case of Susanna becomes a peg on which to hang the proving of an exemplary young man in contrast to a corrupt leadership. The representatives of that leadership wrongly claim an authority that the crowd follows without complaint, while the victims — Susanna is nothing more than one example — are in danger of falling by the wayside. One may ask whether the narrative in the G version may have reflected the Hasmonean dynasty (cf. Engel 1985, 180). The last verses do seem to suggest a contemporary application, while, in contrast to Th, no link to the book of Daniel itself is established beyond the significant name "Daniel" (which rather recalls the legendary *dn' il*).

In contrast to the book itself (and the other Greek additions!), we have left behind the pagan environment and its worship of idols. We find ourselves entirely within the sphere of the Jewish community, which maintained its own system of justice in Babylon; some of their families had achieved a considerable degree of comfort and wealth, enabling them to follow the Law within their own households. The community is not threatened by some kind of idol worship imposed by outsiders, but by "lawlessness" emanating from the appointed leaders of their own people, the "elders who were judges," who were thus really "Babylon" (13:5; cf. Engel 1985, 90). Both G and Th presume the same situation (note how they are interwoven in 13:1-5!), although they shape it quite differently in detail. G sticks with a story about judges and says only the minimum necessary to the theme about Susanna as a person. Th, from the outset, includes information about her family, describes her beauty and piety, her instruction in the law of Moses, the wealth and respected position of her husband Joakim, in whose house legal judgments are given — the precondition for the bathing scene in the garden, which is absent from G. (Here Susanna is ambushed during her morning walk: "They approached her together and tried to rape her.") The bathing scene, which is supposed to take place at noon because of the midday heat, and naturally in Joakim's garden, is found only in Th. Perhaps inspired by 2 Samuel 11:2, and in contrast to it (Bathsheba surrenders to King David!), Th may be in accord here with contemporary taste, which was attracted by such erotically titillating scenes (cf. also Testament of Reuben 3:11-14 and Jubilees 33:2ff.). The frequent artistic depictions of the bathing scene only serve to confirm this function (according to Moore 1977, there are thirty-three versions of the bathing scene from the Old Masters, but only one of the boy Daniel's questioning; cf. the illustrations in *Bible Review* 8, no. 3 [1992] and Bail 1996 on this subject). It is readily apparent that it is much more effective as a narrative than the short account in G.

Susanna's crucial words are the same in both versions: "if I do this, it will mean death for me; if I do not, I cannot escape your hands. It is better for me to fall into your hands without having it done, rather than sin in the sight of YHWH" (13:22-23). The next words in G confirm that Susanna has rightly estimated the danger threatening her from these elders: "but the criminal men turned away, threatened within them and planned maliciously to bring about her death." In this context of Susanna's refusal, it is striking that in G her name is not given; she is called "the Jewess." The decision of the woman who follows Torah (here Th has rightly interpreted it: in 13:3!) represents the people of YHWH, shamed by their official representatives. In this she turns into the true heroine, and not only for "modern readers" (Baumgartner 1959, 43-44)! As soon as they return home (in G; in Th the next day), the rejected elders have Susanna brought to judgment, stripping her even before an accusation has been made, like an adulteress (Th softens this to unveiling), in order to satisfy themselves by looking at her beauty.

G gives a full account of the false testimony and its effect on the congregation in the synagogue (G has the judgment take place in the synagogue):

> We were walking in the park belonging to the husband of this woman (here), and as we were strolling around the grounds we saw this one lying with a man, and we stopped and watched them having intercourse with each other, and they did not know that we were standing there. Then we consulted with each other and said: Let us find out who these people are. And we went close and recognized her, but the young man covered himself and escaped. But we grabbed her and asked her: Who (was) that person? And she did not tell us who it was. This is our witness. And the whole synagogue believed them, since they were elders and judges of the people.

Joakim, Susanna's husband, does not even appear to be present; her parents are silent, and so are her four children (the number is given by G) and the servants (not present according to Th, since they had been mentioned before, in 13:27). Everyone gulps, but no one dares to raise any doubt, and certainly not to object. Susanna herself, who so bravely withstood the calumny of the lustful elders, is also silent. She knows that her words have no chance of being heard before this forum. In the same situation, a man by himself could not have raised a defense against the twofold witness of the elder-judges — how much less a woman! She knew this when she refused the suggestion of her rapists (13:22, where G = Th). Nothing remains for her but prayer to the "One who knows what is secret" (13:42) — in G, weeping within, under the hands of the false witnesses pressing down upon her; in Th crying in a loud voice on the way to her execution.

The answer to this prayer is Daniel's appearance. This unmistakably expresses the fact that, until Susanna was condemned, he had been as silent as everyone else — that as a young person or even a child he could do nothing but keep silent. Without God's miraculous intervention — it has to be put this way in the context of the book of Daniel as a whole — even a Daniel would have been witness to the execution of an innocent person. The divine intervention is differently described in the two versions. In G, an angel equips Daniel with the "spirit of understanding," by means of which he, facing the crowd, reopens the case in which no hearing had been held thus far. The elders who are accusing Susanna are questioned separately, and their statements are contradictory. Thus they are revealed as liars and receive their rightful punishment — the same one they had intended for Susanna.

At the same time, Daniel's questioning presents their present conduct as the end point of a whole series of unjust judgments, as well as sexual crimes. "The daughters of Israel had intercourse with you because they were afraid. But a daughter of Judah was unwilling to endure your passion in lawlessness." The attempted rape is thus not an isolated case, according to G; it is symptomatic of the lawlessness lamented in verse 5b, and symptomatic of Babylon in Israel. In this, G and Th agree. (Incidentally, we also get a glimpse of how fear can promote lawlessness: "because they were afraid. . . .")

One might take offense at the fact that Daniel — very irregularly, in juridical terms — in G and Th brings this accusation before the two elders have been arraigned. Apparently he at first exercises a prophetic function, in order then to effect a skillful resolution of the case, in good criminal-process style, through separate interrogations. Since the two contradict each other in what they say, they are convicted of lying and false witness.

Differently from G, in Th God intervenes in person, so to speak, by awakening "the Holy Spirit of a young lad named Daniel." The phrase presumes that Daniel already has the Holy Spirit, which needs only to be activated by God. We may recall that in 5:12 and 6:4 (G) also Daniel has "holy spirit." This makes me think it is likely that Th — intending to build a bridge to the book of Daniel with his version of the Susanna story — has such an idea in mind. The "holy spirit," however one may interpret it (for the problem cf. Engel 1985, 165-66), is for Th a gift the child Daniel already possesses! Through the power of this spirit he can declare in a loud voice: "I am innocent of this woman's blood!" and with his declaration draw attention to himself, show the people their own failure, and demand a reopening of the case. Before that even happens he — a child — is already acclaimed: "God has given you the standing of an elder" (13:50).

The social reality incorporated in the formula "not counting women and children" can be broken up. This happens here with Daniel, when he in Th (in essentially the same way as in G) takes over the interrogation of the two false witnesses and hands them over to judgment. But that all happens — even though Th puts the accent on Daniel — for Susanna's sake. She is the one who counts in this chapter! The God of Israel takes the part of a woman who, in her obedience and faithfulness, represents his people, who know that he knows her, though she has become unknowable to all others, even her own family. The community praises God, who exalts those who hope in him (13:60). Susanna's family, in turn, praises God because "she was found innocent of a shameful deed" (13:63). For me, these words of her relatives fall short of the community's praise. Did they, too — impressed by the false authorities in their little world — doubt Susanna's integrity? One could almost think so. None of her own takes Susanna's part, none of her own has a good word for her, even afterward. How differently are the three men in the fiery furnace thanked for their fidelity to YHWH (3:30)! A world in which women and children do not count does not know how to thank, in a personal way, even a Susanna for her faithfulness to the Law.

LITERATURE

Bail, Ulrike. 1996. "Susanna verläßt Hollywood. Eine feministische Auslegung von Dan 13." In *Gott an den Rändern. Sozialgeschichtliche Perspektiven auf die Bibel,* edited by Ulrike Bail and Renate Jost, 91-98. Festschrift for Willy Schottroff. Gütersloh.

Bal, Mieke. 1993. "The Elders and Susanna." *Biblical Interpretation* 1, no. 1:1-19.

Baumgartner, Walter. 1926. "Susanna — Die Geschichte einer Legende." *Archiv für Religionswissenschaft* 24:259-80.

———. 1929. "Der weise Knabe und die des Ehebruchs beschuldigte Frau." *Archiv für Religionswissenschaft* 27:187-88.

———. 1959. "Susanna — Die Geschichte einer Legende." In Baumgartner, *Zum Alten Testament und seiner Umwelt,* 42-65. Leiden.

Brenner, Athalya, ed. 1995. *A Feminist Companion to Esther, Judith, and Susanna.* Feminist Companion to the Bible, vol. 7. Sheffield.

Collins, John J. 1993. *Daniel.* Minneapolis.

Craven, Toni. 1992. "Daniel and Its Additions." In *The Women's Bible Commentary,* edited by Carol A. Newsom and Sharon H. Ringe, 191-94. London and Louisville.

Engel, Helmut. 1985. *Die Susanna-Erzählung. Einleitung, Übersetzung und Kommentar zum Septuagintatext und zur Theodotion-Bearbeitung.* Orbis biblicus et orientalis, vol. 61. Fribourg and Göttingen.

Glancy, Jennifer A. 1995. "The Accused: Susanna and Her Readers." In *A Feminist Companion to Esther, Judith, and Susanna,* edited by Athalya Brenner, 288-302. Feminist Companion to the Bible, vol. 7. Sheffield.

Levine, Amy-Jill. 1995. "'Hemmed In on Every Side': Jews and Women in the Book of Susanna." In *A Feminist Companion to Esther, Judith, and Susanna,* edited by Athalya Brenner, 303-23. Feminist Companion to the Bible, vol. 7. Sheffield.

McKenna, Megan. 1994. *Not Counting Women and Children.* Maryknoll, N.Y.

Moore, Carey A. 1977. *Daniel, Esther, and Jeremiah: The Additions; A New Translation with Introduction and Commentary.* Anchor Bible, vol. 44. Garden City, N.Y.

———. 1992. "Susanna: A Case of Sexual Harassment in Ancient Babylon." *Bible Review* 8, no. 3:20-29, 52.

Rahlfs, Alfred, ed. 1935. *Septuaginta. Id est vetus Testamentum graece iuxta LXX interpretes.* Vol. 2. Libri poetici et prophetici. Stuttgart.

FOR FURTHER READING

Brenner, Athalya, ed. 2001. *Prophets and Daniel.* Feminist Companion to the Bible. 2nd ser., vol. 8. Sheffield.

Leisering, Christina. 2008. *Susanna und der Sündenfall der Ältesten. Eine vergleichende Studie zu den Geschlechterkonstruktionen der Septuaginta- und Theodotionfassung von Dan 13 und ihren intertextuellen Bezügen.* Exegese in unserer Zeit, vol. 19. Münster.

Translated by Linda M. Maloney

Hosea: The God-Identified Man
and the Woman/Women of Israel

Marie-Theres Wacker

The book of Hosea is one of the prophetic writings the first words of which declare that they deliver "the word of YHWH" (cf. 1:1). The book presents a prophetical "I" that in many passages fuses nearly indistinguishably with the "I" of God. At the same time, it is a biblical work that in essential sections is determined by the dynamics of the relationship between the sexes. Right at the beginning the prophet is to confront a woman who represents Israel unfaithful to its God. The drama of this disturbed relationship between man and woman, between YHWH and Israel, is developed throughout the book exclusively from the perspective of the divine-prophetic, that is, the male "I" — an androcentric theology or theological androcentrism in pure form. Feminist readings of the book of Hosea, many of which have appeared in the last few years, seek each in its own way to undermine the power of that perspective that the history of interpretation has delineated ever since its Jewish and Christian origins. The following reflections set out from different methodological points of departure but converge with the shared feminist-hermeneutical agenda to hear the book of Hosea as a literary deposit of an unfinished feud about the "word of God" and to make a beginning of rearticulating it.

The names of several kings are mentioned in what we may call the book's heading (1:1); they are frequently taken to be a historical reference to Hosea's appearance in the eighth century B.C.E., particularly in the northern kingdom of Israel (of Jeroboam II and successors). But this heading already intones the book's theological program according to which idolatry leads to political decline (as in the days of Jeroboam) and returning to YHWH leads to salvation (as in the days of Hezekiah). Less than a deposit of a particular prophet's concrete preaching, the book of Hosea is a reflection of several generations reaching far into postexilic times. For that reason, concrete historical references are hardly to be expected and are generally avoided in our discussion. But the text manifests problematic structures that have evidently made their presence felt again and again and to which we can make connections (in a variety of ways).

Who Is Gomer? — Hosea 1

"Go, take for your wife one driven by lust and children like her, for like one driven by lust the land turns away from YHWH" (1:2, author's translation). If the first words God addressed to the prophet are rendered this way, a decision has been made about how to present Gomer, the woman who according to the text marries the prophet (1:3). Described in 1:2 as *'ēšet zĕnûnîm,* she is neither a whore nor simply an adulterous woman but one who enters into relations with men from "pure lust." The basis for this interpretation is given in the intensifying abstract plural word *zĕnûnîm,* whose root form in the verb *znh* certainly does not primarily depict the profession of prostitution but, more generally, forms of sexual relations outside of marriage (Bird 1989).

If Gomer and her relation to Hosea stand for the "land" and its relation to YHWH, then the issue becomes what the root form *znh* means in relation to the significance of worship. Here lies one of the fundamental problems for the understanding of the religious-historical contexts of the book of Hosea. Are we dealing with "profane" sexuality as a metaphor in a cult polemic the targets of which in themselves have nothing to do with sexuality? Or does Gomer's "lust" refer to specific sexual rites in Israel's cult and, if so, to which ones? This discussion cannot proceed without reference to Hosea 4:12-14 (see below).

The nature of the relation — or nonrelation — described in Hosea 1 catches the attention of feminists: God is in an intensive verbal communication with the prophet about the children Gomer bears, two sons and a daughter (1:3-9). Gomer herself remains voiceless whereas her biological relation to the three children is pointedly described: she is pregnant, gives birth, and weans them. Hosea's relation to them is left open in the text — a jumping-off place for two thousand years of men's exegetical fantasies about the cheated husband and Gomer, who has shown what she really is (cf. Bitter 1975). But the feud in the text is really between Gomer and YHWH: Do the children belong to the side of Gomer, the *'ēšet zĕnûnîm,* who brings them into the world and nourishes them, or to the side of God, who gives them calamitous names and declares them to be living metaphors of the wicked Israel? The "children" appear rehabilitated in 2:1-3 (Eng. 1:10–2:1), a passage according to the context of which it is YHWH himself who speaks or, alternatively, another voice that is not specifically introduced. In particular, the daughter's calamitous name, "Lo-ruhamah," announcing the withdrawal of God's mercy *(raḥămîm),* appears transformed into a renewed promise of mercy (a feminine-motherly term). But the physical mother of the children has disappeared from view. Something like that applies also to the "historical Gomer": even her name is transmitted in stunted form and her alleged "lust" is more likely the product of andro-logical projection of the history of Israel's guilt into the human counterpart of the God-identified prophet. What we have, perhaps, is a woman from the northern kingdom who bears the name "Perfected" — a name expressing gratitude — and is the daughter of a man whose own name, *dblym*, lauds the sea god Jam as a ruler.

"The Imagination of Power and the Power of Imagination" (F. van Dijk-Hemmes) — Hosea 2

Recent exegesis most often speaks of the opening chapters 1–3 as an independent composition in contrast to the oracle units following in chapters 4–14. The preferred assessment is that those three chapters are structured as a circle: the more narrative chapters 1 and 3 frame the poetic second chapter in which YHWH as a jealous husband accuses his "wife" of going after "lovers" instead of attending only to him as her provider. The key term "Baal/Baals" (2:8, 16, and 17) identifies the basic problem as one of worship (but that can hardly be situated historically any more with precision). The name "Baal" obviously refers to the dispute about the true lord of the land and its produce. The personification of YHWH's opponent as a woman is highly significant in terms of the history of religion: it is least likely that Israel was thought of here as a (feminine) "community" (however, cf. 2:16-17). But the understanding of the earth as "mother land," a perception alive and well also in Israel, certainly played a role here (1:2! cf. below on Hos 13–14). Finally, one may also associate this with the motif of the city as a woman and as the partner of the deity who is the protector of the city (→ Ezekiel; Zechariah).

According to the supposed circle structure, chapter 1 develops the drama of the troubled relationship of Israel to its God in terms of the family conflict in the house of Hosea (the "object level"). 2:4-25 (2-23) develops the drama in terms of the "metaphorical level" (YHWH-Israel) but not without itself touching on the "object level" of the marital conflict between Hosea and Gomer: the marriage partners will get divorced, as one would assume on the basis of 2:4-6. Chapter 3 then would narrate YHWH's demand of the prophet to buy back his wife from the relationship with the men she had after the divorce, which represents an unambiguous return to the "object level," which itself is transparent to God's mercy toward Israel. Such a concentric structure can easily accommodate a theology of a prophetic man who represents the actions of God, a man who leaves his wife (2:4-13) but subsequently condescends and graciously reconciles with her (2:16-20) but not without subjecting her to "withdrawal therapy" (3:3) (cf. Deissler 1985). Mercy and guilt seem to be gender-specific since the "aberration" of the woman is depicted in categories of deviant female sexuality. In contrast to this, Mary Joan Winn Leith (1989) points out that men were the primary hearers of this text and were expected to see themselves in this mirror image of the "lust-driven" woman. Only when they are prepared to enter into such self-alienation and leave behind their entrenched position can men enter as if in a rite of passage into the new relationship with God that is painted in images of paradise-like bliss in 2:16 (2:14). But they still must recognize themselves in the image of a woman, a woman reconciled with her husband/God. Here Leith does indeed remind us that the image of a nymphomaniac does not govern the text of Hosea 1–3 exclusively, but she has nonetheless shoved aside too easily the power of the feminine caricature. Womanist theologian Renita Weems (1989), looking at 2:4-13, insists on acknowledging the violence done by the speaker to his counterpart, the "wife/mother." Deprivation of freedom (2:6) and sexual humiliation (esp. 2:10) are for the divine ego legitimate expressions of husbands' marital violence; they facilitate the development of an image of God who is ready to use violence that then is misused to legitimate male and especially marital violence against women (and children). The devastating power of an image like that has to be broken, according to Weems, by recalling and drawing upon different forms of God talk. She judges the final part of that chapter (2:16-23) unusable for that purpose: that section smacks too much of an overly hasty reconciliation. For Fokkelien van Dijk-Hemmes (1989), that part is mired in the perspective of the divine ego in monologue, for it does not allow the woman herself to speak even where she is allegedly cited (2:7, 9, and 18[5, 7, and 16]). To make that woman's voice heard as that of an independent counterpart, van Dijk-Hemmes makes an intertextual link between Hosea 2 and the Song of Songs. The parallels to texts in the Song of Songs (especially to 3:1-5), which are found only in Hosea 2 (and 14), could indicate that genuine utterances of women are made use of in Hosea 2 but in a polemically distorted form. If one places particularly the song of the woman in Hosea 2:7 into the context of songs in the Song of Songs that center on women and the erotic, then that verse clearly no longer rings of nymphomania but expresses the wish that the world of love poetry become part of the worship of God.

A Reading of Hosea's Book in Feminist Perspective

Instead of making an interpretative break between Hosea 1–3 and Hosea 4 and the chapters following, the narrative in the first-person singular in chapter 3 may be read as the upbeat for the speeches beginning in chapter 4. This creates a narrative frame for the entire book. First the prophet "experiences" failure and new beginnings in the domain of his family, in and from his own wife and her children (Hos 1–2). Those experiences serve as a symbol of the relationship of God to the people. Then the prophet makes what he experienced privately public through a symbolic action with (another?) woman (Hos 3) before he himself turns outward (Hos 4–14), to the "children of Israel" (4:1). But from a feminist perspective there is a problem with this way of reading: the image of the woman who sits and waits (Hos 3), herself the image of the "children of Israel," is not resolved positively. On the contrary: in the vision of healing that brings the book to its conclusion (14:2-9), Israel appears as a masculine "You." The book's last female image is the brutally destroyed city of Samaria (13:16 in the NRSV, 14:1 in the original Hebrew). That is why a third way of reading the entire structure of the book is proposed: the opening verse (1:2) is taken as a "mirror text" that the book lays out in four units. Hosea 1:3–2:3 (2:1) develops the motif of the children "driven by lust" introduced in 1:2 but which at the same time looks like an eloquent attack on the "mother." Hosea 2:4-25 (2-23) is essentially about the conflict between husband and wife but into which the children are drawn. Hosea 3:1-5 paints the drama of two people's relationship, which is transparent to God's relationship with the "children of Israel." Hosea 4 and following is once again about the "children," the "inhabitants of the land" that, according to 1:2, is represented by Hosea's wife. This way of reading has two advantages: first, it shows that the principal theme, announced in 1:2, is not unidimensional but is dealt with in several different discourses that can hardly be harmonized one with another in terms of their content, signaling thereby that the reflection on that theme is incomplete. Second, what becomes apparent is that chapters 4–14 speak about women, children, and men in a different manner than the three opening ones.

The Problem of Priests and Patriarchs — Hosea 4

In an introductory passage (4:1-3) this chapter announces the basic note of the "polemic" *(rîb)* with Israel and, in two large sections, hammers away at Israel's failed relationship to God. If according to the present construction of the text, the focal point of 4:4-10 is the guilt of the priests who keep the people in ignorance, then 4:11-14 talks about the consequences of that ignorance: the priests tolerate, indeed support, cults that the prophet judges to be ruinous, that lead into nothingness. 4:15-19 follows the overall direction in that the cultic aberration of Ephraim, the northern kingdom, is once again presented in strong language as a warning to the neighboring people of Judah.

In the opening verse of the book, 1:2, the "land" had been depicted as an erotomaniacal woman and mother who was abandoning YHWH; however, in 4:1-3, the "land" is said to have taken YHWH's side and not that of its "children/inhabitants." The land distances itself, so to speak, from the deeds of those who live in it; it "mourns" by letting things "dry up" (4:3; *'bl* means both "to mourn" and "to dry up"). Feminine connotations reverberate here as well: in the Hebrew Bible and the manner it uses language, "to dry up/to wither" applies to fields and plants, in other words, to what constitutes the earth, the land (both feminine words!) or what it brings forth. But those verbs are also used in relation to women who can no longer give birth to children and, finally, to crumbling stone masonry and cities without protection. The land on which Israel lives withholds its life-giving, motherly functions; YHWH, the spokesperson in the (family) feud, and the land, the "mother," stand together against the "sons/inhabitants."

4:11-14 laments a desolate condition in the "people" of YHWH: there is no understanding, no insight. This is blamed concretely on the cultic situation. 4:12a and

4:12b seem to refer to practices of divination; in three couplets, arranged ring-like one into the other, 4:12c-13c describe a cult on mountaintops that includes communal sacrifices and smoke offerings, a cult that leads away from God and is conducted under trees; it can only be understood as something altogether inspired by the "spirit of erotic mania" *(rûaḥ zĕnûnîm)*. Lines 13d-14e form a third unit; the attention is turned to the activities of the people's young women described like the woman in 2:4-5, that is, in terms of their sexual activity within and outside of marriage. The young women are called "daughters" or "daughters-in-law/brides," in other words, set in relation to men. Since men are spoken to directly, the women's dependency is made the more obvious. But the young women are explicitly excluded from any punishment for their activities. Instead, a group of men is mentioned, introduced emphatically by the pronoun *hēm*/"they," who themselves display behavior that causes the "people without understanding" to come to ruin (4:14) and that encourages the young women in their activities in the first place. Given the context, those men are quite likely the priests present during the cult. The behavior they are accused of relates to their sexuality ("they go aside with whores") but also to an act of the cult itself ("they sacrifice with sacred women"). "Whores" and "sacred women" are not spoken of as independent or even guilty agents but, rather, are mentioned to highlight the greater responsibility of the men and what they do.

Tree Goddesses and Sacred Women *(qedeshot)*

As I see it, Hosea 4:11-14 gives relatively clear indications that the veneration of a female deity must have had a not small significance in Israel. If the structural opposition in 4:12 is taken seriously in our interpretation, the "trees" are perceived as the power that in fact opposes YHWH and draws the people of Israel to itself. The striking feminine pronoun "her" (shade) has a direct feminine correlative in the previous line, the last-named tree ("terebinth"). Its designation with *'ēlâh* is homonymous with the feminine form of *'ēl* — God — and can therefore (also) be interpreted as *'ēlâh* — Goddess. Even though this word occurs nowhere in the Hebrew Bible in the sense of "goddess," nonetheless, this homonymy needs to be heard since another consequential argument comes up in addition to this linguistic consonance. On a jar from Lachish, dated from the Late Bronze Age, there is a drawing of a stylized tree flanked by goats, animals frequently associated with a goddess who herself is often portrayed as a woman standing on a lion. In Egyptian images, she is given the Semitic name of *qĕdešet/qudšu*. On the aforementioned jar, the word *'ēlat* — "goddess" — appears above the tree, which leaves no doubt how the constellation of "tree with goats" was understood. One can substantiate through iconography alone the connection between female deity and tree symbolism in the ancient Orient, particularly in Israel. Silvia Schroer and her rich pictorial material show this clearly (Schroer 1987; cf. now also Keel 1998). Images of this kind from Israel's monarchical period are rather scarce, but in light of Jesus Ben Sirach's second century B.C.E. comparison of the feminine Wisdom to a tree that showers its fruit on the adept (Sir 24), we may presuppose a continuing tradition of the tree goddess also in Israel. This warrants the assumption that the trees cited in Hosea 4:13 are transparent in a certain sense to a female deity present and venerated in them, and that this belief is precisely what the polemics attacks.

The prophet's complaint and charge in 4:12-14 appear to be that in the domain of that tree goddess worship and sexuality are intertwined and that women have a central role in all this. In explaining the religious beliefs apparent here, older studies readily drew on the basic category of the "sacrifice of virginity" demanded by the goddess of love irrespective of whether the sacrifice was a onetime act of a young woman before marriage or the regular service of consecrated women who offer their sexuality. Since the 1930s, interpreters of Hosea have increasingly worked with the theory that in the days of Hosea the union of goddess and god in heaven was ritually reenacted within cultic celebrations particularly in the northern kingdom. This was done to assure — quasi-magically — the fertility of the land, of livestock and human beings. In addition, it was the task of the sacred women, the *qedeshot*, understood as the "sacred" or "cultic prostitutes," to represent the goddess. It may have been customary in Hosea's day that "brides" in Israel had their first sexual intercourse with a priest within such cultic celebrations in order that, under the protection of the goddess, this form of opening a bride's womb progeny would be assured. Helgard Balz-Cochois (1982a) has provided a synthesis of these theories. For her, behind Hosea's polemics are cultic feasts that include animal sacrifices, cider, wine, raisin cakes, incense offerings, and consultations of an oracle. In feasts like those, the rite of initiation of young women was meant to call for and receive the blessing of Asherah, the maternal goddess. At the same time, these feasts were also sacrifices and orgies in honor of Astarte, the erotic goddess, where the men present had sex with sacred women and women with "strangers."

If one examines the literary form of Hosea 4:11-14 from the point of view of history of religion, one has to be fundamentally prepared that the perspective on the cult suggested by verses 11 and 14 framing it may not necessarily match the historical situation and that the charge of "whoredom" may well include a range of diverse factors. Are the references to "brides" and "daughters" perhaps much more about "domestic" problems that are blamed on worship gone awry? The sacred women in particular ought not to be defined a priori in terms of alleged sexual functions in the cult. If the charge in 4:14 is directed at the priests, the role of these sacred women as servants of the god becomes quite clear: with the priests they are part of the context of the cult, apparently sharing with them their functions in the sacrificial procedure, but they are now utterly disqualified with their male colleagues by being named with whores in the same breath. Their inclusion in the administration of sacrifice is flatly put on the same level as the prostitution of which the priests are culpable. This way of disqualifying them, the intent of which is to delegitimize their acting as cult officials, is initially no more than rhetoric but may perhaps also be more than that. In light of the story of Tamar (Gen 38), who is called both a whore *(zônâ)* and a sacred woman *(qĕdēšâ)* without any polemical undertones, one may surmise that sacred women lived outside of patriarchal marriage and family unions. The exact circumstances of their life are a matter of guesswork. Were they a profitable component of the temple economy, possibly given to the temple by their parents as a result of vows? Are they to be compared to the *devadasis* of southern and eastern India, the highly respected temple dancers, said to be the brides of God and who as such — as well as in their own understanding — bestow on men divine blessing by their sexuality (cf. Wacker 1992)? Were the sacred women, like the *devadasis,* consecrated; did they belong permanently to a sacred shrine or did they move (alone or in groups) across the countryside instead? Did their designation call to mind also in biblical Israel the Syriac-Canaanite goddess Qedeshet/Qudshu of the Late Bronze Age? How did they view themselves? Who gave them a bad name in Israel, and when? As is often the case in historical research on women, none of these questions can (yet) be answered because of the deficient situation of our sources.

Israel among the Nations — Hosea 5–8 and 10

In the controversy in Hosea 1–3, as well as in Hosea 4 against the cults, the verb *znh* is used frequently. That polemic also marks 5:1-7 (and appears once again in 6:10) but not specifically in reference to female sexuality; the verb occurs here in a masculine form. Here its meaning is connected with "soiling" or "defiling" *(ṭm'),* which includes the reproach of someone having conceived/given birth to "illegitimate children." Are the problems discussed in Ezra/Nehemiah foreshadowed here?

Hosea 5:8–7:16 is one continuous unit held together by its rigorous theocentric perspective. War will come upon Ephraim because social injustice reigns (5:8-11), which Judah, the neighboring state, sees itself involved in (more accurately, a redaction of the book of Hosea in Judah has inserted that perception into this text). The policy of entering into an alliance with Assyria is contrary to returning to the true God (5:12-15), and even though Ephraim/Israel (Judah) do return to God (6:1-3), YHWH does not accept that act (6:4-5). The dawn's early light of YHWH, who is pictured as a sun god, changes into the noon's harsh light of judgment the heralds of which are the prophets. The reason for the judgment is that there is no knowledge of God and no "solidarity" (6:6); the sacrificial cult is measured against conditions of social justice. That knowledge of God and solidarity are absent is shown in the following verses 6:7-10: even the priesthood is banded together with robbers and murderers; chaos reigns even at the royal court (7:2-7). In a variety of ways, the conclusion of the chapter (7:8-9, 10, 11-12, 13-16)

shows how indistinguishable Ephraim is from other nations; its lack of understanding is lamented but followed by a reproach for letting the politics of alliance
with Assyria and Egypt fuse with false worship.

The leitmotif of chapter 8 is the breach of covenant, the rebellion against God's
Torah. In the first part of the chapter, it is developed as a problem of the idolatrous
monarchy; it allows that idols are manufactured and has itself all the features of idol
worship inasmuch as it does not submit to God's will (the prophets' instructions?).
The second part takes up "Ephraim and the nations" again. The approach to Assyria is censured paradigmatically as Israel's self-destruction: Israel will get lost
among the nations and, because of the multitude of cult sites in Ephraim, it will be
exiled to Egypt. The picture of Ephraim as a luxuriant vine (10:1-2) forms the
bridge from chapter 9 into 10:3-15 and the vision of the demise of the northern
kingdom, and connects that to the end of the cult in Samaria. The verse on the calf-
god image (10:5) may well contain an older word of mourning turned here into a
biting mockery that once again ties the idol and the monarchy together (10:5-7). Every call to return by the one who speaks (God/prophet) falls on deaf ears (chapters
11–12); enthusiasm for war will reap destruction by war (13).

The Harvest That Failed — Hosea 9

Chapter 9 may be read as a diptych with two sections: 9:1-6 and 9:10-17. Verses 7-9
act as a hinge between the two pictures; the passage looks at the prophet who is persecuted on account of his God, but it is textually difficult to understand on its own.

The chapter also deals with Israel and the nations in a variety of ways; the first
section (9:1-6) looks at this theme in relation to the harvest. When the harvest itself is turned into an idol, when grain is venerated instead of God, then Israel has
become just like any other nation and shall indeed be made like them and will
have to live in an unclean land and without appropriate worship of God. The reproach that Israel has walked away from God talks of a "harlot's fee" using the root
form of the verb *znh* (9:1-2), which calls to mind the woman in Hosea 2 who runs
after her "lovers" in order to get grain, new wine, and oil. However, the context
makes this association problematic in that this section uses the masculine form of
the verb throughout and the feminine form only once.

In the second section (9:10-17), the theme of the "nations" is spoken of in relation to Baal-Peor, the adversary of the true God. But, unlike in Numbers 25:1-5,
Baal-Peor is not introduced as the problem of the alien woman and their seductive
powers but as the problem of an alien god into whose hands the "fathers" (patriarchs!) of Israel have delivered themselves (Hos 9:10). The destructive powers of
that deity are now at work and will destroy the future of the people. This is portrayed in an image of a flock of birds in disarray, on the one hand, and in a reversed sequence of birth, pregnancy, and conception, the feminine component of

progeny, on the other. This is the first instance where women of Ephraim make an appearance, but they are reduced to their organs of reproduction, objectified in the truest sense of the word. Within the context, this is the result of the "fathers" having gone astray; their arbitrary decision to turn away from the benevolent gaze of YHWH (cf. "I looked" in v. 10) resulted in their own patriarchal-deforming gaze at their own women. (From a woman's perspective, one might say that the women rebelled with their bodies against the manner in which the military and religion directed society that disdained what women do to provide subsistence and their ability to give life; cf. Sampaio 1993.) On the whole, this section may be interpreted as a prophet's critical scenario of the actions of Israel/Ephraim's "fathers" who become ever more deeply entangled in their own patriarchal paradoxes, thereby preparing their own and their families' demise in a spiral of violence and separation from God. The precious harvest that they represented in the eyes of YHWH (9:10) now reveals itself as having failed: Ephraim, the plentiful tree, will be bare; Ephraim, the mighty flock of birds, will flutter aimlessly in all directions. (That is how verse 17 is to be literally understood, contrary to the image of the "eternal Jew" occasionally evoked by interpreters.)

In the eyes of feminist theology, such a critique of patriarchy that comes from within patriarchy is remarkable, particularly in the form found in Hosea 9:10-17, since it provides a hermeneutical key that delivers to critical-feminist exegesis possibilities for making new connections. But, given the biblical text as we have it, it will primarily not be so much developing a positivistic "teaching" as — at least initially — critically questioning what dominates theology, church, and society.

God as Mother — Hosea 11

Chapter 11 pictures the love God has had for the little son Israel ever since his sojourn in Egypt (11:1). But he goes his own way and meets with misfortune, which is concretized once again in terms of the concept "Egypt" (11:5). But God cannot and will not leave the son to his fate; God has a change of heart (11:8-9) that allows for Israel itself to turn back (= return) from Egypt (11:10-11).

Helen Schüngel-Straumann (1986) revived the discussion about this text, which had previously been consistently related to God's "father love." In her view, Hosea 11 is an internally coherent (except for v. 10) and gynocentric speech of God in every detail. The most important aspect of her argument is the observation that in 11:1-7 Israel is presented not only generally as a boy but also quite specifically as an infant or very small child: he is "nursed," "taken up in arms" (11:3), lifted to the "breast," and by "bending down" is fed (11:4). And, finally, the people are once again said "to be summoned upward" (11:7). The core metaphor of feeding is utterly maternal, and it seems right to Schüngel-Straumann to interpret 11:8-9 in terms of "the womb" and, as many authors before her, read that word as the Old

Syriac translation has it: "compassion" (*raḥămîm;* cf. *reḥem/*womb) instead of "repentance" *(niḥûmîm).* But then one could understand Hosea 11:9 and its statement: "I am *'ēl* (God), not *'îš* (human being/man)," only as a renunciation of male behavior, driven by anger and the desire to punish. Instead, it would have to be seen as an affirmation of God's incomparable divinity revealing itself, according to 11:8, in motherly compassion. With this image of YHWH as mother, Hosea would have sought to bring hope to his crisis-ridden time.

Schüngel-Straumann raises from this chapter the icon of a mother-goddess and says that here the God of Israel appears in her figure. Yet the text of Hosea 11 is not quite as unambiguous as it appears in this integrating perspective; she acknowledged that it was her hermeneutical position by which she oriented her decisions relating to text criticism and semantics of a text that in places is quite difficult. It is therefore remarkable that another author, Nissinen (1991), using other methods, arrived at the conclusion that the actions of a female, motherly divinity are apparent in this chapter. Next to Hosea's deity, he sees the royal goddess Ishtar or Mulittu of the Neo-Assyrian royal oracles. According to the texts concerning these two, they labor for the king's realm claiming to be wet nurses. It is quite consistent that Nissinen puts the God-as-mother simile in Hosea 11:1-4, which he also affirms, into a political context.

As far as Hosea 11:8-9 is concerned, it is not necessary to change "repentance" to "compassion." The text is an altogether strong play with sounds and, for the sake of assonance, speaks of *niḥûmîm* but may be understood in the sense of *raḥămîm.* The noun *'îš* in 11:9 may indeed mean "human being" in general, but it often does refer to a man (as *homme* in French). The general concept of *'îš* is constructed from what is seen to be maleness. But biblically based anthropology should not just pass on such androcentrism in the formation of concepts; it should break it down instead. As early as 1973, Phyllis Trible presented a literary-theological interpretation of Hosea 11:9; she takes the statement "I am God and not a man" and its opposition of *'ēl* and *'îš* "literally" and interprets it as a renunciation of theologies that seek to understand God in terms of male images: God is not a man. Within the overall scope of the book of Hosea, 11:9 may also be read as a critical negation of 2:18 (16): if the "woman" there is to address YHWH as *'îšî,* "my man" (= husband), 11:9 revokes it. Furthermore, an interpretation that pays attention to history could call attention to the fact that the contextual specification of *'îš* in Hosea 11 is one of "anger" that discharges itself by destroying towns and human beings (cf. 11:9 and 11:6 and 8) by waging war, an activity that in Hosea highlights the specifically male connotations of the word *'îš.* The opposition "*'ēl* and not *'îš*" negates not least those warlike male features that are contrasted in 11:1-4 with the motherly demeanor of YHWH.

Even though the text gives the divine mother the last word, it also speaks of a struggle within God in that the motherly side fights against the bellicose-destructive side. Therefore, the text does not present YHWH unalloyed in a feminine-motherly form; rather, it shows a divine figure with the two dimensions of anger, ready to destroy, and compassion. The asymmetry of the contrast between "warrior" and "mother" may be read as a warning against constructing a gender ontology that has women to be more motherly and men more anger-prone by nature. But Hosea 11 is a suitable text for the demand that in reference to the Bible the language of God's motherly face be incorporated into theology and liturgy.

The Womb as Tomb and as Place of Life — Hosea 12–14

Israel is depicted symbolically in chapter 11 as a small or growing child whose upbringing is the labor of both father- and mother-god; this rehearses the motif of the sons of Israel found at the beginning of chapter 4. The entire middle section of Hosea is recapitulated in chapter 11 and brought to a good conclusion. The book could end there. But a new polemic *(rîb)* is introduced in chapter 12; it is not directed against a mother or the children of Israel but against Jacob, who, according to the Genesis saga, became the "ancestral father" of Israel, receiving his new name "Israel" after a fight with God. And so Hosea 12 once again explores another dimension of the metaphor of family that marks the entire book profoundly. As I see it, this section, surrounded by much controversy in research and interpretation, presents Jacob as a deeply ambiguous figure from his mother's womb onward (12:3). In his first encounter with YHWH at Bethel, he was given the chance to turn back to God again and again (12:6) but he consistently turned down the offer (12:7-9). Against this background one may understand the reference to Jacob's wife (wives) (12:12) as a negative contrast to the guidance given to Israel by one of YHWH's prophets and possible hint that when Jacob was in Aram, among the "nations," he had a relationship with an "alien" woman (cf. Wacker 1996a, 310ff. for more details).

The last two chapters of Hosea are a coherent composition in three pictures (13:1-11; 13:12–14:1; 14:2-9; for more details, cf. Wacker 1996b). On the surface, the first picture is about the men of the northern kingdom of Ephraim who did not follow YHWH but followed his adversary Baal, thereby bringing about their ruin. Idols (13:2-3) or, alternatively, the king (13:10-11) seems to represent Baal. YHWH is depicted as a raging mother bear (13:8) going after human beings: an image that deflates overly romantic-bourgeois images of mothers (Sampaio 1993). But many allusions to Hosea 2 reintroduce the image of the unfaithful woman as a substructure; at the end of the book the metaphors at the beginning are taken up anew. This is also true for the second picture; it appears to be a variation of the mother-child motif in chapter 1. Initially, Ephraim is compared to the unborn child that drags itself and its mother into death because, even though she is experiencing birth pangs, the unborn child cannot present itself at the mouth of the womb (13:13). From another angle, this image projects the perception, indeed the reality, of the womb as a tomb from which the child cannot escape. And that connects the picture with another: that of the underworld as the womb of mother earth into which the dead enter (13:14). Finally, following the scenario of a drought caused by a dry, hot wind (13:15), the third picture: the city of Samaria, spoken of as female, cannot protect her children any more; grown-ups and little ones, men, women, and even the unborn in her are cut down (14:1[13:16]).

Hosea does not end with the terrifying picture of 13:1–14:1 but with a call to turn back (14:2-4) and a promise of healing (14:5-9). In light of this and as we look back on the whole book, we may give meaning to the juxtaposition of unconditional promises of healing, according to which YHWH brings about a change of heart in himself (Hos 1 and 11), and promises of healing that are tied to the demand that people turn back (Hos 3 and 14:2). God's own "turning back" that precedes the demand that the people turn back stands for God's decision not to punish them for their transgressions; because the evil deeds are so vile, Israel would be in ruins were God to insist on punishment. What is depicted in Hosea 2 and 11 is the demolition of the image of a God who demands satisfaction. But in response to this prophetic promise Israel is now itself called upon to turn back again to God. The book of Hosea follows this line of thought twice: once in Hosea 1–2 and 3, in the juxtaposition of God/prophet and "woman," and again in Hosea 4–11 and 12–14, in the juxtaposition of YHWH and "the children of Israel."

The vision of healing that brings the book to its close (14:5-9), as it were, transposes Israel (presumably the northern kingdom of Ephraim and Judah, the southern kingdom) into the garden of Eden. Here, as in chapter 2, we find images reminiscent of the Song of Songs, in particular that of the lover as a tree in whose "shade" the woman-friend reclines and in whose "fruit" she delights (Song 2:3; cf. Hos 14:7-8). This observation helps in interpreting the marked structural differences between Hosea 2:4-15/16-25 (2:2-13/14-23) and Hosea 13/14. While there is wide continuity of imagery in the former — the "woman," her children, and her "husband" — there is discontinuity in the latter between the vision of healing in Hosea 14:5-7 and Hosea 13:1–14:1. In Hosea 13:1–14:1 images of the world of animals and human beings dominate, while Hosea 14:5-7 draws on "nature," on plant life: Ephraim is compared to a lily, an olive tree, a vine, and YHWH to the dew that comes from on high; it speaks of God as the God of heaven who is present and now cooperating with the earth who brings forth plants from her womb (cf. Gen 1:11-12). The images of drought and drying up (Hos 13:15; cf. 2:5, 11, and 14[2:3, 9, and 12]) are withdrawn, and the female body indirectly receives back its dignity. But above all, instead of the death-dealing power of the female earth (Sheol), her life-giving power is acknowledged and celebrated: the new Israel/Ephraim sprouts like a plant from her.

In the penultimate verse, YHWH is compared to a greening tree the fruits of which benefit Ephraim-Israel. Given the unmistakable critique of the fascination with the tree goddess in chapter 4, it is natural to assume that this metaphor was placed into language about God with deliberate purpose. Used in comparison, her symbol is related to the God of Israel with great care. YHWH assumes the features of the tree goddess: her numinous presence in the shade (14:7) and, above all, the nourishing aspect of her fruit. As Helgard Balz-Cochois in particular has pointed out, Hosea 14:5-9 in contrast to Hosea 4 shows how the God of Israel can take the fascination emanating from the goddess into him/herself positively. Nonetheless, this last image of the book of Hosea is strictly monotheistic; after all, it relates the figure of the goddess to YHWH himself.

This utopian picture, reminiscent of Hosea 2:16-25 (2:14-23) in some of its individual features, is less dominated by patriarchal characteristics; it may serve as a counterimage to the images of mourning and destruction that abound in the book of Hosea. And yet, women today can appropriate this only as a "resistant-reader": as a gesture of the search for what has not been destroyed, as a prefiguration of another reality, mindful of the prevalent trend to define women in terms of nature/harmony and with an eye toward today's ecological devastation that threatens to make it impossible for "nature" to provide refuge.

LITERATURE

Andersen, Francis I., and David N. Freedman. 1980. *Hosea*. Anchor Bible, vol. 24. Garden City, N.Y.

Balz-Cochois, Helgard. 1982a. *Gomer. Der Höhenkult Israels im Selbstverständnis der Volksfrömmigkeit. Untersuchungen zu Hosea 4,1–5,7*. Frankfurt.

———. 1982b. "Gomer oder die Macht der Astarte. Versuch einer feministischen Interpretation von Hos 1–4." *Evangelische Theologie* 42:38-65.

Bird, Phyllis. 1989. "'To Play the Harlot': An Inquiry into an Old Testament Metaphor." In *Gender and Difference in Ancient Israel*, edited by Peggy Day, 75-94. Minneapolis.

Bitter, Stefan. 1975. *Die Ehe des Hosea*. Göttingen.

Brenner, Athalya, ed. 1995. *A Feminist Companion to the Latter Prophets*. Sheffield.

Day, Peggy, ed. 1989. *Gender and Difference in Ancient Israel*. Minneapolis.

Deissler, Alfons. 1985. *Zwölf Propheten: Hosea — Joel — Amos*. 2nd ed. Neue Echter Bibel. Würzburg.

Jeremias, Jörg. 1983. *Das Buch Hosea*. Altes Testament Deutsch, vol. 24, 1. Göttingen.

———. 1986. "Hosea — Hoseabuch." In *Theologische Realenzyklopädie*, 15:586-98. Berlin.

Keel, Othmar. 1998. *Goddesses and Trees — New Moon and Yahweh: Two Natural Phenomena in Ancient Near Eastern Art and in the Hebrew Bible*. Sheffield.

Leith, Mary Joan Winn. 1989. "Verse and Reverse: The Transformation of the Woman in Hosea 1–3." In *Gender and Difference in Ancient Israel*, edited by Peggy Day, 95-108. Minneapolis.

Nissinen, Martti. 1991. *Prophetie, Redaktion und Fortschreibung im Hoseabuch*. Alter Orient und Altes Testament, vol. 231. Neukirchen-Vluyn, Kevelaer.

Sampaio, Tania Maria Vieira. 1993. "El cuerpo excluido de su dignidad. Una propuesta de lectura feminista de Oseas 4." *Revista de interpretación Latino Americana* 15:83-96.

Schroer, Silvia. 1987. "Die Zweiggöttin in Palästina/Israel." In *Jerusalem. Texte — Bilder — Steine*, edited by Max Küchler et al., 201-25. Novum Testamentum et Orbis Antiquus, vol. 6. Fribourg and Göttingen.

Schüngel-Straumann, Helen. 1986. "Gott als Mutter in Hos 11." *Theologische Quartalschrift* 166:119-34.

Seifert, Brigitte. 1996. *Metaphorisches Reden von Gott im Hoseabuch.* Göttingen.

Sherwood, Yvonne. 1996. *The Prostitute and the Prophet.* Sheffield.

Simian-Yofré, Horacio. 1993. *El desierto de los Dioses. Teologia e Historia en el Libro de Oseas.* Cordoba.

Törnqvist, Ruth. 1994. "The Use and Abuse of Female Sexual Imagery in the Book of Hosea: A Feminist Critical Approach to Hosea 1–3." Ph.D. diss., Uppsala.

Trible, Phyllis. 1973. "Depatriarchalizing in Biblical Interpretation." *Journal of the American Academy of Religion* 41:30-48.

Van Dijk-Hemmes, Fokkelien. 1989. "The Imagination of Power and the Power of Imagination." *Journal for the Study of the Old Testament* 44:75-88.

Wacker, Marie-Theres. 1992. "Kosmisches Sakrament oder Verpfändung des Körpers? 'Kultprostitution' im biblischen Israel und im hinduistischen Indien." In *Auf Israel hören. Sozialgeschichtliche Bibelauslegung,* edited by Renate Jost et al., 47-84. Lucerne.

———. 1996a. *Figurationen des Weiblichen im Hoseabuch.* Herders biblische Studien, vol. 8. Freiburg.

———. 1996b. "Gendering Hosea 13." In *On Reading Prophetic Texts,* edited by Bob Becking and Meindert Dijkstra, 265-82. Leiden.

Weems, Renita. 1989. "Gomer: Victim of Violence or Victim of Metaphor?" *Semeia* 47:87-104.

Wolff, Hans Walter. 1976. *Dodekapropheton I. Hosea.* Biblischer Kommentar, vol. 14, 1. 3rd ed. Neukirchen-Vluyn.

Yee, Gale A. 1992. "Hosea." In *The Women's Bible Commentary,* edited by Carol A. Newsom and Sharon H. Ringe, 195-202. London and Louisville.

FOR FURTHER READING

Baumann, Gerlinde. 2003. *Love and Violence: The Imagery of Marriage for YHWH and Israel in the Prophetic Books.* Collegeville, Minn.

Ebach, Jürgen. 2004. "Gott ist kein Mann. — Aber warum? Hosea 11,9 und Numeri 23,19 im Diskurs." In *Dem Tod nicht glauben,* edited by Frank Crüsemann et al., 214-32. Festschrift for Luise Schottroff. Gütersloh.

Goldingay, John. 1995. "Hosea 1–3, Genesis 1–4, and Masculist Interpretation." *Horizons in Biblical Theology* 17, no. 1:37-44.

Keefe, Alice A. 2001. *Woman's Body and the Social Body in Hosea.* Journal for the Study of the Old Testament: Supplement Series, vol. 338. Sheffield.

Nutt, Aurica. 1998. "Die lebensfördernde Macht der Göttin und ihre Vitalität im Hintergrund von Hos 2? Ikonographische Untersuchungen." *Biblische Notizen* 91:47-63.

Sampaio, Tânia Maria Vieira. 1999. *Movimentos do corpo prostituído da mulher. Aprocimações da profecia atribuída a Oséias.* São Paulo.

Wacker, Marie-Theres. 2011. "Gott Vater, Gott Mutter — und weiter? Exegese und Genderforschung im Disput über biblische Gottes-Bilder am Beispiel von Hosea 11." In *Geschlechter bilden. Perspektiven für einen genderbewussten Religionsunterricht,* edited by Andres Qualbrink et al., 136-57. Gütersloh.

Translated by Martin Rumscheidt

Joel: God's Self-Justification

Marie-Theres Wacker

"Then afterward I will pour out my spirit on all flesh" — this verse from the book of Joel (2:28; in the Hebrew text, 3:1) is known to Christians as the prophecy of Pentecost (Acts 2). But apart from this promise, this second work in the "Book of the Twelve Prophets" is probably among the lesser-known biblical books, and with its images of giant locusts, rattling war-machines, and blood-dripping heavenly bodies that look like precursors of the work of painter Hieronymus Bosch, it really does not appear to be an open book at first glance. The following approaches, oriented by feminist interests, set out from the position that Joel — that is, the book in its present form[1] — focuses on the question of how God's wrath, goodness, and righteousness are related one to the other. Such a question does indeed impose itself in a context (the era of the Second Temple in Judea or Jerusalem) where threats of natural disaster and war are the order of the day. In that situation, the book seeks to initiate a tradition of storytelling for the coming generations (cf. Joel 1:2-3). By recalling a catastrophe of enormous dimension in which YHWH's wrath gave way to his goodness, hope is kindled that in the future the justice of YHWH will have the final say. Inasmuch as the book of Joel presents itself in toto as "the word of YHWH" (1:1), it is YHWH himself who gives rise to this narrating memory and who justifies himself before his congregation. A literary historical-theological question presents itself immediately to the feminist perspective: What opportunities does the text create for its female actors; that is, what does it foresee in terms of symbolic spaces for the feminine or for women, in what way does it take note at all of women as "hearers of the Word"? Once this has been addressed, what has to be explored, to the degree it is possible at all on the basis of the given text, is what social-historical realities Joel refers to. And finally, what needs to be discussed within the more specifically feminist-theological outlook and in the face

---

1. For reasons of space, questions concerning the history of the book's origin have been set aside. But in light of the text as we have it, such questions beg for attention far beyond the degree both Wolff (1969) and Prinsloo (1992) deem necessary.

of current conditions is the theological claim the book makes and presents: it is God who justifies himself.

A Community in Accord with "Nature"

Joel 1

We are given to understand in 1:4 that the impetus and cause for the tradition of storytelling to be started now are the devastating plague of locusts the likes of which did not exist in anyone's memory. The "elders" (1:2a), the presbyters of the community as it were, are addressed and called upon to keep on telling the story. They are placed between their "fathers" and "sons" and their male descendants (1:3); the community is introduced exclusively in terms of its male members. On the other hand, the address "all [you] inhabitants of the land" (1:2b) goes much beyond that group and pictures the totality of human beings in relation to their foundation, namely, the land on or in which they live; it may well also include the animal world (cf. a similar use of language in Hos 4:1-3).

In the following verses of this chapter, direct address framed in the imperative and passages of reporting and description alternate, offering as it were to those who are to tell the stories a script prepared in dramatic (or liturgical) form. Its framework is the call to lament and weep, and it is again addressed to individual groups (of men): wine-drinkers, most likely celebrating something, merry from sweet wine but whose merriness is nipped in the bud (Joel 1:5); peasants and wine-growers whose harvest is ruined; priests in the house of God who are to call the people to attend the rites of lamentation (1:13-14). In between a call is addressed to a female subject who is compared to a young woman mourning for her partner (1:8). In this context, it is quite likely the community as a whole is visualized in this "woman" (as the Targum on this text and the medieval Jewish commentary of David Qimchi-Radaq specify; cf. Widmer 1945, 30). There is the soil of the fields (*'ădāmâ;* fem.) "mourning" or "withering" (the verb *'ābāl* has both meanings). The image of the plague of locusts merges into one of drought. The "inhabitants of the land" (1:2) live on the land (conceived of as feminine) that, mourning and withering, can no longer nourish those who live on her (cf. Hos 4:1-3). The lament, the mourning, is the female component of this drama, and even the men of the community in particular are subordinated to it both metaphorically and in actual practice.

Joel provides the community with two laments for their use in the rituals of mourning (Joel 1:15-18 and 19-20). Each hymn has an "inclusive" perspective, each in its own way. The second, phrased in I-language (vv. 19-20), offers a lament in empathy with the "suffering creature," the trees and animals. Refrain-like, it speaks of fire that even dries up the watercourses, thereby adding a threatening and frightening dimension to the drought. The first hymn (vv. 15-18) names the cattle and sheep individually as pasturing animals that lack nourishment. This gives visibility to the work areas of cattle-herders and shepherdesses. In that hymn, the motif of the "day of YHWH" is sounded for the first time; it occurs throughout the book of Joel. The devastation (*šdd*, 1:10) described here is seen as a harbinger of that "day" that will bring (even more) devastation (*šōd*, 1:15). The sign that this "day of YHWH" must be close at hand is, above all, the absence of food and drink offerings in the temple of Jerusalem (1:16; but see already in 1:9).

Joel 2

The second chapter begins a new note: a call is given that connotes war (blow the shofar and trumpet). A hostile people is invading the land, destroying everything in its wake and once again causing all "the inhabitants of the land" (v. 1) to be frightened. The words describing the hordes entering through windows (v. 9) echo the experiences of old people, women, and children who had remained behind in the house (cf. Jer 9:20 [Eng. 21]). The first call for lamentation had depicted the swarm of locusts as a "huge nation" with teeth like lions (Joel 1:6); now the description of the invading enemy army turns almost unnoticeably into images that would be just as suitable for the invading locusts (2:3-10). The images of the army and the locusts overlap and interpret one another. At the same time, they amplify the catastrophe mentioned in chapter 1: now the cosmos is drawn in, sun, moon, and stars (2:2 and 10), and the motif of "the day of YHWH" that frames this scene (2:1 and 11) is related directly to YHWH; he is said to be the author; none other than he leads the army of destruction.

Verse 12 creates the impression that the bellicose YHWH and his hordes are right at the gates but not yet *inside* them. The speaker exhorts the community to try everything in its power to avert the disaster, and once again everyone is called upon to do so. The urgency of the situation is painted in the example of a bride-groom and bride having to stop their lovemaking and retreat from their room (v. 16). And another lament is prescribed to be addressed to YHWH (v. 17).

The text goes on to say that this lament causes YHWH to spare his people (v. 18). The passage of verses 19-27 is crafted as YHWH's response and speaks of the new prosperity in paradisiac tones. In reverse order, it speaks first of the destruction of the enemy army (v. 20; cf. 2:1-11), then extensively of the end of the drought brought about by abundant rain (v. 23; cf. 2:10-12 and 17-19), and finally, of the plague of locusts and how all they had devastated was to be restored again (v. 25; cf. 1:4). The sense of having enough and some to spare surrounds this vision (vv. 19 and 26); clearly, the theme of the catastrophic drought in the first chapter is back at center stage. The suffering herds (1:18 and 20) are mentioned specifically: they will be comforted (2:22); the soil is spoken to (1:10) in language using the feminine form of the imperative and urged to break forth into (harvest) jubilation (2:21). Only then are human beings addressed and called "sons of Zion," a reference to Jerusalem, the city of Zion also thought of as feminine.

Thus, we see a community in mourning and filled with happiness. On the one hand, it is patriarchal in its structures of public life, political self-administration, and worship; on the other, it defines itself in the perspective of its God in "ecological" terms (cf. Simkins 1993). The community is conscious of its bond with and dependence on "mother earth" and the creatures that live on her. Even the political threat from the hostile army and the new life in the prosperous city are taken into and viewed in this perspective.

An image of such a community guards against feminist critique viewing its subject of study in too narrow a fashion. Surely, a community structured along patriarchal lines and that is aware at the same time of the earth and animal and plant life in distress is different from modern forms of the subjugation of nature such as that of Francis Bacon, who wanted to put nature on the rack and torture its secrets out of it. The specifically modern escalation of contempt for nature — and concomitantly for women — can hardly be overestimated. In the face of this, the picture the book of Joel paints in its first two chapters prompts us to translate it into practical visions of spaces where human beings live and plan, who "do not build towers with tops in the heavens and do not test animals to death."[2]

The Coming "Day of YHWH"

Joel 3 [Heb. 4]

Joel 2:27 concludes with the formula "You shall know that I am YHWH"; the book could well have ended there. But the next section, beginning at verse 28, returns to the setting and continues the narration in that it projects it into a far-distant and indeterminate future and thereby gives a new, unexpected interpretation to the decisive themes of 1:1–2:27.

The threatening day of YHWH, signaled by the catastrophic locust "people" (1:15) and the hostile enemy "people" whose army was about to invade the land (2:11) but was held back by the whole community's lament, is mentioned again as the day that is to come (2:31; 3:14-15). But no longer will it merely come upon "the" land and its inhabitants; it will come with decisions and divisions. It is the day when YHWH will judge those "nations" that violated YHWH's "heritage people" (*naḥălâ*; 2:17; 3:2). Here we come face-to-face once again with actual human beings: girls and boys of Judea are used by the victorious powers as a cheap means of

2. Cf. Dorothee Sölle, "Und ist noch nicht erschienen. Ein Gebet nach 1. Johannesbrief 3,2," in Sölle 1987, 7f.

paying for their pleasures, girls used to pay for abundantly available wine and boys as payment for a prostitute (3:3). Men and women of the winners profit from the enslavement of the losers; neither victims nor accomplices are specifically identified by gender. And references to the "sons" of Judah sold into slavery (3:6) have to be understood to include the "daughters" unless they specifically have captured soldiers in mind. 3:8 wishes the same cruel fate upon the sons and daughters of those who perpetrated these acts.

The passage of 3:4-8 in particular may presuppose the actual experiences of war; what is depicted may well be "typical" despite the concrete identification of the nations involved. (The conglomerates of nations named there were present in the history of Judea most likely during the fourth century B.C.E.) Verses 9-15 are even further removed from historical experience in that they envision a final, great military campaign of the "nations" against Judah and Jerusalem, the outcome of which YHWH himself will decide in favor of his people. The final image of the book pictures YHWH on Mount Zion, his abode and locality (vv. 17 and 21), the center of three concentric circles. The first is formed by the city of Jerusalem; no one who does not belong to it will be able to enter it any longer (v. 17 speaks of "strangers" in that sense). It is surrounded by the land of Judah, the second circle, paradise-like and rich in water (v. 18). Outside the land of Judah live those who shed blood in Judah or shed the blood of Judah's inhabitants, the third circle; Egypt and Edom are cited specifically (v. 19). They shall become desolate places; the blood they spilled will spread over and glue up the fertile land.

Joel 2:28-32 [Heb. 3:1-5]

The promise of the spirit to be poured on "all flesh" (vv. 28-32) is taken up in the story of Pentecost (Acts 2); it is said to be the spirit that filled the community gathered in Jerusalem of those who believed in Jesus. Their spirit-filled speech was understood by the God-fearing people assembled in the city from all nations in the *oikumene*. Given how Christian tradition has narrowed Joel's prophecy to the community of believers in Christ, we need to make note of the following. The Jewish Easter pilgrimage at that time from all parts of the then known world presupposed as a matter of course and without fanfare that "everyone who calls upon the name of the Lord shall be saved" (Joel 2:32), that YHWH will not turn away anyone from among the nations, and that they who turn to him do not belong to the "strangers" (3:17). We must also note that when looked at more closely, verses 28-32 have an orientation that does not readily match the *oikoumenē* of the Pentecost story. The book of Joel explicitly mentions daughters next to sons, female servants next to male servants. Like the rain falling upon the earth, the spirit of God knows no gender and class distinction but brings them into awareness thereby. In the face of present class and gender distinctions, Joel's words in verses 28-29 may therefore be read critically: here the wish of Moses in Numbers 11:29, that God's spirit would come upon all, has been taken up and, at the same time, Miriam's claim that she too is a prophet (Num 12:2) has been confirmed, albeit belatedly. To be sure, the "signs" mentioned directly thereafter: blood, fire, columns of smoke (Joel 2:30), place the outpouring of the spirit hard between the preceding picture of paradise (2:21-27) and the ominous pictures that follow in chapter 3 and give it an air of something confusing, even chaotic. Looked at in this way, the short interlude of Joel 2:28-29 serves to unsettle the sense of calm and safety of the preceding blissful scene and to prepare for the coming revolutions of the "day of YHWH." Here, Joel speaks for the first time of the female members of the community explicitly as a group; together with the "male and female slaves," they are depicted there primarily as aspects of the confusing conditions that upset old orders.[3] The perspective of what Joel says here, that women and female slaves are perceived as "mischief-makers" who interfere in "sacred orders," took root right away, as is well known, in the earliest Christian communities (cf. Gal 3:28 and its "consequences"), and flourishes to this day.

The decidedly inclusive, albeit androcentric, perspective of Joel 1:1–2:27 carries over into 2:28-32 and into chapter 3. New there is the explicit recourse to class distinctions that show up in the distresses of war and, according to Joel, also in the confusion that precedes the establishment of God's justice in the "outer world" of the nations. The revolution he said would come (in 2:28-32) is not profiled further in this prophet's writing; it does leave a "subversive" trail that feminist theologians today can follow and develop.[4]

"Theodicy" in the Book of Joel

Shame and "Turning Back"

"Turn back!" the prophet urges the community in the face of the catastrophe and its cosmic dimensions (2:12-13). Commentaries generally link the catastrophe to a previous transgression of the people (cf. Glazier-McDonald 1992) and see it as a punishment for the transgression. "Turning back" is the only means to avoid or at least minimize the catastrophe. This perception of "turning back" would be supported by the fact that "Joel," a prophet well versed in Scripture (cf. esp. Bergler 1988), quotes the call to turn back and would understand it in the traditional sense as a call to penitence.

3. This feature of the presentation goes against the otherwise stimulating thesis of Redditt (1986) that Joel gives utterance to a "peripheral prophecy" (opposed to the Jerusalem priesthood) wherein particularly women also have a voice.

4. Ruth Ahl (1990) gave her introduction to feminist theology the insightful title "Your Daughters Shall Be Prophets" (German: *Eure Töchter werden Prophetinnen sein*). That not only gives visibility to the women in the feast of Pentecost described in Acts 2 but also houses feminist theology in the center of the messianic community oriented in Christ.

Since the book of Joel follows directly on that of Hosea where there is clear, unmistakable talk of the people's transgression and of their God waiting for them to turn back, it might well follow that Joel has a corresponding understanding of "turn back!"

But the concepts of sin and guilt are not found in Joel, nor are there unambiguous statements pointing to a specific wrongdoing of the people or to the awareness that they have sinned.[5] "Sin" and "guilt" as such are not an explicit topic in this book. If one reads this text without that presupposition (cf. Crenshaw 1995), a quite different picture emerges, namely, a view of God whose motives, impulses, and reasons for acting are not tied to "good" or "bad" human actions but in the end remain hidden. It is a God who sends calamities and is unpredictable but on whose favor one can count for that very reason to the very end. And so "Joel's" references to "turning back" take on new meaning. When he recalls God's forbearance and mercy (2:13b), he does not think of God's readiness to grant amnesty to evildoers (cf. Exod 34:6-7 and elsewhere) but instead thinks that this God never lingers long in his anger. The call to "turn back" is not about repentant turning away from sin but about "concentration" on God, a God who does good things and creates bad ones (cf. Isa 45:7). Given the lack of grain and wine for sacrificial giving, this concentration has to take place in the "heart" and be made visible in rites of mourning. Moreover, the relations between God and the community presupposed here should be interpreted in terms of the conceptual patterns of honor/shame and humiliation/exposure/disgrace (cf. Malina 1993, 40-66 and Simkins 1996; the commentary by David Qimchi already deals well with the question of honor/disgrace; cf. Widmer 1945, passim). In Joel 1:10-12, there is a play on similar-sounding verbs: *yābēš* (to dry up) and *bôš* (to be ashamed). On the basis of it, that interpretation of the relations between God and the community can be substantiated and elucidated. Fruit trees and vines dry up *(hôbîš)*, all trees of the fields suffer drought *(yābēš)*; vinedressers are put to shame/exposed by the drought *(hôbîš)*, joy "withers away"/is turned into shame *(hôbîš)*. In a sense, "drought" in the land is equivalent to the land being "put to shame," "exposed" together with all who live on it. In response the people who suffer it perform rites in which they deprive themselves of necessities of life and enact self-diminishing and self-shaming rituals (1:13-14). This includes abstaining from food (fasting), from everyday clothing (wearing the garment of penitence instead), from sleep (keeping awake at night), and from rejoicing (mourning instead). In such self-shaming the people react to the shame they experience as something that has come from and was brought upon them by YHWH. Here too, the language of sin and punishment is out of place (other than in Malachi!), for it is not a matter such as God being insulted by

5. In her text-semiotic sketch, Danielle Ellul (1979, 429) points merely to the statement in 1:18 that even the herds of animals "groan for atonement" in support of her view that there is divine "punishment." But this statement is an isolated one in Joel. Her reading is also not supported by the versions of the text, and the verse itself can hardly bear the weight of such an interpretation.

evil human actions and demanding satisfaction. YHWH's motives remain hidden; those in high social places can shame those in low places even without an identifiable reason and not suffer loss of honor in so doing. Faced with a life-threatening catastrophe that is traced back to divine initiative, an entire community ritually diminishes itself "with its heart" (2:13a) and hopes that by this affirmation of the immense distance between itself and God and this demonstration of reverence, God will "turn back," "relent," and — "who knows?" (2:14) — give a blessing. But there is still another way to appeal to God's honor, namely, by asserting that since the honor of YHWH's people is tied up with his honor, the disgrace and ridicule heaped upon his people revert back to him. YHWH reacts to the lament: "Do you want the nations to make a mockery of us?" (cf. 2:17); according to 2:17-18, in the end this causes God to be "jealous" for his people. The divine response (2:19-27) confirms the hope that the goodness and mercy of YHWH have the final say.

Mourning Like the Goddess Anat?

Close study of 1:8 adds yet another dimension to the text of Joel 1–2. The verse begins with an address to someone; it is formed in the feminine singular. We do not know who is spoken to, only that it is someone compared to a young woman in mourning. The comparison assimilated the addressed other to the image of the young woman. It is the community itself that is the young woman (*bĕtûlâ*) making lament for the man of her life (*ba'al nĕ'ûrêhā*). Recent German-language commentaries, such as those by Wolff (1969) and Deissler (1985), take the word *bĕtûlâ* to mean "virgin" and, concomitantly, do not regard the man she weeps for as a husband. That would correspond to the usual meaning of *ba'al*. Instead, they see him as her fiancé whom she lost shortly before their marriage. An extraordinary situation such as that then would require an extraordinarily vehement lament. But this reference to *bĕtûlâ* and *ba'al* may well go back to a phrase still in vogue in Joel's time, a phrase that itself goes back to the Western Semitic, mythical picture of the lamenting "virgin" (*btlt*) Anat, who weeps for her dead lover and brother Baal. The literature of Ugarit (fourteenth to twelfth century B.C.E.) makes rich use of this image that could be associated with the heat and drought of summer and the return of autumn rain. This is not to infer that Joel's text — nearly one millennium younger — refers directly to this myth of the goddess and god. (Loretz 1986, 121 and elsewhere, rightly warns against all too hasty a conclusion such as that.) Even the origin of that phrase need not have been known in Joel's time. Yet what should be considered is the possibility that the absence of guilt-and-punishment language in Joel 1–2 is based in a specific historical tradition of interpreting this catastrophic drought. In this interpretation, the necessity to recognize God's honor through actions of self-diminishing merged into rites whose elements of tears and laments were analogous to the end of the drought and the coming of rain that everyone hoped for. Such rites may have had their origin in an ancient "rain ritual" (Loretz 1986) that was associated with the goddess lamenting the dead god. That would give the conspicuous presence of this lamenting woman (and her voice) in Joel 1 an even stronger profile.

"Justice"

Joel 3 puts a new twist on the character of its preceding chapters. The lament's affirmation that YHWH "regrets evil" (2:13) (author's translation; "relents from punishing," NRSV) is now concretized in the fight against the nations and their "wickedness." This matches the traditional prophetic promise of God's victorious justice and its underlying belief that what humans do is connected to how they fare. An assault of other nations on the body and life of YHWH's people, especially on their children, falls back on those nations themselves; the blood they shed will be exacted from them and turn their land into a desert. YHWH does not forget when human beings are enslaved and murdered. But this is asserted not so much as an experience of the present but more as a hope for a time yet to come. The reversal of ecological-political hardships in days gone by serves in Joel's narrative as a guarantor that also future-oriented hope is not in vain.

How the book of Joel depicts God's presentations of himself seems strange at first sight. Does not a God whose disposition can be mellowed when everything diminishes itself before him to the utmost resemble the picture, reinforced all too often in reality, of an unpredictable man before whom wife and children have to cower in order not to be victims of his rage? What difference does it make if this same God, in a moment of "holy anger," strikes out to protect and help "his" people? The book of Joel has the audacity to consider the possibility that suffering and misfortune in the world are not the fault of sinful human beings but may come from God for no reason. It keeps the question of evil in the world and the question of God together but refuses to establish their interconnection through the moral failure of humans. Here it resembles the book of Job. But whereas in Job a suffering person rises up and hurls, as it were, his accusations in God's face — thereby defrocking God at least rhetorically of his superior power, forcing him down to the person's level of discourse — Joel shows the way of self-diminishment. With its presupposition that we come face-to-face with an other of overwhelming power, that way seems to correspond altogether too much to traditional socialization of women. It could be said — with a degree of bitterness — that it is not for naught that the very protagonist of that position is the community portrayed as a lamenting woman.

But what if one could extract from this lament dimensions that are not subsumed under self-diminishment? What if that lament could also be understood as an act of resistance that does not fizzle out in humble surrender to the inevitable but in its own way brings charges and keeps awake the memory of injustice and demands justice? Or, conversely, what if horror has reached such overwhelming degrees that in fact only diminishing oneself almost to the level of self-extinction offers any hope of survival? The book of Joel leads us to questions like that and keeps them alive. Whatever objections it elicits notwithstanding, as one voice in the discussion of theodicy, this book, next to the book of Job, is an indispensable intervention.

LITERATURE

Ahl, Ruth. 1990. *Eure Töchter werden Prophetinnen sein . . . Kleine Einführung in die feministische Theologie.* Freiburg.

Ammicht-Quinn, Regina. 1992. *Von Lissabon bis Auschwitz. Zum Paradigmenwechsel in der Theodizeefrage.* Fribourg and Freiburg im Breisgau.

Bergler, Siegfried. 1988. *Joel als Schriftinterpret.* Frankfurt am Main.

Crenshaw, James L. 1995. "Who Knows What YHWH Will Do? The Character of God in the Book of Joel." In *Fortunate the Eyes That See: Essays in Honor of David Noel Freedman in Celebration of His Seventieth Birthday,* edited by Astrid B. Beck, Andrew H. Bartelt, Paul R. Raabe, and Chris A. Franke, 185-96. Grand Rapids.

Deissler, Alfons. 1985. *Zwölf Propheten. Hosea — Joël — Amos,* 65-87. 2nd ed. Neue Echter Bibel. Würzburg.

Ellul, Danielle. 1979. "Introduction au livre de Joël." *Etudes théologiques et religieuses* 54:426-37.

Glazier-McDonald, Beth. 1992. "Joel." In *The Women's Bible Commentary,* edited by Carol A. Newsom and Sharon H. Ringe, 203-4. London and Louisville.

Gross, Walter, and Karl-Josef Kuschel. 1992. *"Ich schaffe Finsternis und Unheil." Ist Gott verantwortlich für das Übel?* Mainz.

Jeremias, Jörg. 1988. "Joel/Joelbuch." In *Theologische Realenzyklopädie,* 17:91-97. Berlin.

Loretz, Oswald. 1986. *Regenritual und Jahwetag im Joelbuch.* Altenberge.

Malina, Bruce J. 1981. *The New Testament World: Insights from Cultural Anthropology.* Atlanta.

―――. 1993. *Die Welt des Neuen Testaments. Kulturanthropologische Einsichten.* Stuttgart.

Prinsloo, Willem S. 1992. "The Unity of the Book of Joel." *Zeitschrift für die alttestamentliche Wissenschaft* 104:66-81.

Redditt, Paul L. 1986. "The Book of Joel and Peripheral Prophecy." *Catholic Biblical Quarterly* 48:225-40.

Simkins, Ronald. 1993. "God, History, and the Natural World in the Book of Joel." *Catholic Biblical Quarterly* 55:435-52.

―――. 1996. "'Return to Yahweh': Honor and Shame in Joel." *Semeia* 68:41-54.

Sölle, Dorothee. 1987. *Und ist noch nicht erschienen, was wir sein werden. Stationen feministischer Theologie.* Munich.

Widmer, Gottfried. 1945. *Die Kommentare von Raschi, Ibn Esra, Radaq zu Joel.* Basel.

Wolff, Hans Walter. 1969. *Dodekapropheton 2. Joel und Amos.* Biblischer Kommentar, vol. 14, 2. Neukirchen-Vluyn.

FOR FURTHER READING

Jeremias, Jörg. 2007. *Die Propheten Joel, Obadja, Jona, Micha.* Altes Testament Deutsch, vol. 24, 3. Göttingen.

Wacker, Marie-Theres. 2000. "Gottes Groll, Gottes Güte und Gottes Gerechtigkeit nach dem Joel-Buch." In *Das Drama der Barmherzigkeit Gottes. Studien zur biblischen Gottesrede und ihrer Wirkungsgeschichte in Judentum und Christentum,* edited by Ruth Scoralick, 107-12. Stuttgarter Bibelstudien, vol. 183. Stuttgart.

Translated by Martin Rumscheidt

Amos: The Truth Is Concrete

Marie-Theres Wacker

Reading Amos with a Feminist Lens — but How?

Like virtually no other figure of biblical Israel, the prophet Amos stands for God's solidarity with the poor, the disenfranchised, the disadvantaged. His social criticism is aimed at a society that is split into "haves" and the desperately poor, and he unmasks it as self-destructive. Like virtually no one else, therefore, Amos was and is the model for Scripture-based intervention in solidarity with society's disadvantaged people in concrete political circumstances.

Until now, however, feminist theologians and feminist biblical scholars have made little or no reference to this figure, and when they have, it has been linked to the objection that no matter how concrete Amos's critique is, he is incapable of taking notice of the real extent of miserable poverty of women in particular, while in his derisive poem to the rich Samaritan women, the "cows of Bashan" (4:1-5), he vulgarly exaggerates the complicity of women (Sanderson 1992; Bird 1996). From a feminist perspective, even when it takes a decidedly political or liberation theological direction, this seems to suggest that a certain "hermeneutical suspicion" is called for with respect to Amos.

Added to this is another complicating factor. In recent German exegesis there has been increasing support for the view that the book of Amos as we know it, with its compositional structure and the numerous layers of textual expansion, is much further removed from the historical Amos, the prophet of the eighth century B.C.E., than has been previously assumed even in form-critical or redaction-critical interpretations of the book of Amos (cf. Fritz 1989; Jeremias 1995; and Loretz 1992, each with a different model). This makes the conventional practice

---

The title of this chapter is also the sentence with which Willy Schottroff begins the introduction to his small volume of social-historical exegesis of First Testament texts (Schottroff and Stegemann 1979), to which he also contributed an exegesis of Amos. The present essay is an attempt to continue in the direction of his interpretation.

more difficult, if not impossible, especially if attempting to connect the social-critical passages of the book to historical circumstances that can be precisely reconstructed and thus interpret Amos in terms of social history or liberation theology (cf. Schottroff 1979; Schwantes 1991; Reimer 1992).

In view of this situation, one research option is to concentrate on the Amos texts in their current form (without implicitly or openly attributing them to the historical Amos as did Andersen and Freedman in 1989, and — with obvious scorn for the "German approach" — Paul in 1991). But even in focusing on the analysis of texts, one must do justice to the great significance of social criticism in this prophetic writing, not only quantitatively but qualitatively. A textually oriented feminist exegesis that aims to incorporate explicitly and critically the voices of social history and liberation theology can do so by adopting a method of literary research that reflects on its frame of reference and the contextual system in which one is reading (cf. García-Treto 1993 on this subject). Such an exegesis will consciously emphasize the political, social, and economic context in which the reading of the text is taking place. The situation of late-twentieth-century German readers is quite different from that of previous social-historical interpreters of the book of Amos. The long-standing affluence of relatively broad social classes, the costs of which remained mostly invisible because they were paid for far away on other continents or left to future generations to pay, is now giving way to the impoverishment of increasingly large sectors of people. Here we see a force that has meanwhile become global and pervasive striking back — a force that governs states and international alliances by its laws, where economic growth is considered a cure-all, human beings are seen merely as cost factors, and, in sum, capital and markets seem to be removed from any concrete political or personal responsibility. Women have more occasion and reason than ever to bring into focus such global contexts that threaten to constrict their possibilities for action in new and different ways. In such a frame of reference it makes sense, and is in fact essential for a feminist reading, to accentuate precisely the "global" perspectives of the book, which are directed toward the world of peoples, cultures, and nations, on the one hand, and on the other, toward the cosmos, "nature," and creation.

International Law and the Voice of the Lion (Amos 1–2)

The first major part of the three-part book of Amos (1:3–2:16) consists of six similarly structured units, which are addressed to neighboring peoples of Israel/Judah, plus a verse directed against Judah itself, and a longer one against the northern kingdom of Israel. It is clear from this compositional scheme that Amos conceives of YHWH as Lord of the Nations, who judges the peoples according to a basic standard of humaneness that must be applied even in war — which is not, however, called into question as such. Pregnant women are also expressly included in this context (1:13). There is no sign of sensitivity in Amos, however, for the fact that the women of conquered peoples are always threatened with rape by the conquerors, although this is frequently documented in the prophetic writings in particular. The partly masculine and partly feminine personification of the peoples correspond to their political organization; the cities/city-states of Gaza and Tyre appear in the traditional image of a city as a woman, while the others are masculine entities. The feminine images in connection with Moab (2:3) could refer back to the city of Kerioth (2:2), unless they are read as a case of rhetorical disqualification by means of feminization (→ Obadiah; Malachi et al.).

Rhetorically speaking, the fact that Judah and Israel are listed among the neighboring peoples places them in the same category; by their actions they have become like their neighbors. Although they had special knowledge of God's will (cf. 2:4) and were privileged to experience God's intervention (cf. 2:9), they acted contrary to their knowledge and experience. While the complaints against Judah are kept rather general and amount to "idolatry," Israel is accused of a series of concrete offenses against the poor and disenfranchised. Included here is the charge that "a man and his father go to the young girl to defile my holy name" (2:7). We can assume that this means that a young woman who is working as a servant on the estate of large landowners (perhaps to help repay the debt her family has incurred) is sexually exploited (for discussion of this, cf. Fleischer 1989, 61-65). The fact that the next verse (2:8) mentions the altar and the house of God has led some to ask whether the young woman of 2:7 is to be seen in the same cultic context, perhaps even as employed in service of the cult (outlined by Barstad 1984, 17ff.) and thus less a victim of men's misdeeds than their "instrument" of false cultic practices. This hypothesis is insufficiently supported by the text. "Cultic thinking" in the broader sense of this concept does likely come into play here. The reference to "defiling my holy name," which profiles the sexual assault against the young woman as an offense against God's very name, points to Levitical tradition and its sexual laws (Lev 18:20), where the men are also instructed to consider certain women in their family as taboo for the sake of the "sanctity" of their community (cf. Leviticus).

The introductory verses of the book (Amos 1:1-2) present a complex picture as a backdrop to the scenario of offenses against human dignity in Amos 1-2. The voice of YHWH, on Mount Zion, is heard roaring like a lion (1:2). It is as if sound waves from this voice bring about a drought on the distant summit of Mount Carmel in the north and in the pastureland between Zion and Carmel, foreshadowing the earthquake that it states occurred two years later (1:1). This reaction of the land, a reality that is both anticipated and already present, is understood as the earth's "grief" (1:2) (cf. also Hos 4:1-3 and Joel 1:10-12), which in turn interprets the voice of the lion YHWH as a voice of rage and accusation, as the following words of the peoples express very concretely. "Nature" is on the side of God in the struggle against the inhumanity of human beings.

Cows of Bashan and the "Maiden Israel" (Amos 3–6)

The first "Shema" ("Hear!") of Amos (3:1) marks the beginning of the second part of the book (chapters 3–6). It is consistently addressed to the northern kingdom of Israel, but includes the mountain of Zion, the cultic center of the southern kingdom, in its scope (6:1). Already in the Israel verses of part 1 (2:6-16) the text had shifted from speaking about Israel to addressing Israel directly (2:10), sounding the same theme that here opens the new unit addressed to the "whole family of Israel": remembering the exodus from Egypt. This call to remember is connected with the statement of YHWH's special intervention corresponding to the fact that Israel is also especially called to account for its misdeeds (3:2). Introduced in this way, the second unit has in effect already pronounced judgment on Israel/Zion. As if Amos could not bear the severity of this judgment, he again hides behind the "voice of the lion" (1:2) of his God, which is forcing him to speak, as it were (3:8).

The three units of text (3:9-12; 3:13-15; and 4:1-3) focus on the luxurious lifestyle of the upper class who occupy the palaces, mentioning sofas, ivory, and summer and winter homes. But all this exists only as a result of violence, of human beings literally being crushed to death (4:1). The third unit (4:1-3) looks particularly at the upper-class women. Scholars have enjoyed the comparison of these women with "cows of Bashan" as a reference to their corpulence (male exegesis sometimes stoops to tavern language here). Nothing in the text necessarily leads to this particular reading. More likely it is an allusion to the well-fed cows of Bashan on their abundant pasture as a metaphor for the life of luxury. There is also too little support in the text or in iconography for the claim that the term "cows of Bashan" ironically distances the upper-class women's own self-description in the cultic context as servants of the bull/calf of Bethel (on the other hand, see the reading of these images from a "farmer's perspective" by Weippert 1985, 10f.). The shifts between feminine and masculine pronouns and verbs that can be observed in the Hebrew text of 4:1-3 can be taken as evidence that it is not only the rich women who are targeted here for accusation; they are seen together with their masters (husbands?). Conversely, the text also speaks of the "sons of Israel" (3:1; 3:12) in the sense of the *entire* family (3:1) of Israel.

Amos now counters the positive reminder of the exodus from Egypt with a depressing series of catastrophes in which Israel could have recognized God's hand (4:6-12). He concludes with a hymnlike sentence that suggests a hymn of praise to God will follow, but instead it contains a threat: God's creative power, theme of many hymns of the Bible, will turn against Israel in the form of a "dawn" that precedes the divine judgment, and a "striding over the mountains" that signifies God's coming to judge (cf. Mic 1:3; cf. also Gillingham's thorough discussion, 1993). And so now all that remains is a funeral lament to be sung over Israel (Amos 5:1-2) in which this people is visualized as a young woman (unless the phrase "maiden Israel" is to be understood in the sense of "maiden of Israel," i.e., the city of Samaria). Her end is all the more painful because her life has been cut off much too early and she — as "young woman" or "maiden" — has no children. Either reading stands in contrast to the previous representation of Samaria, its power and fullness of life, so that the funeral lament at this point in the text — and the lament after 5:16-17 — should be read as ironically distancing the status quo, but at the same time anticipating the end that has been announced.

This image of Israel's/Samaria's end is followed (unexpectedly) by a call to "life" (5:4-6): "Seek me and you shall live." "To seek YHWH" means first of all to go to the cultic site, but Amos warns the people about the land's great holy sites like Bethel and Gilgal, as well as Beer-sheba farther south (5:5; cf. 4:4 and also Hos 4:15), which by now he can only describe as embroiled in the sin of the people. YHWH can no longer be found in these places under the present circumstances (which does not mean, however, that the book of Amos rejects cultic practice in general!). But where, or how? The repetition of the words "seek" and then "live" in Amos 5:14 provides the key: "Seek good and not evil, that you shall live." But this "good" is quite concrete: "establish justice in the gate" (5:15). Thus a system of justice in the cities and towns that does not "turn justice to wormwood" (5:7) includes the mandate not to "afflict the righteous" or "push aside the needy," that is, oppress the poor, of all people (5:12). The context shows that we are not talking about individual conflicts here. The concept of "perversion of justice" illuminates the meaning of "treading upon the poor" and vice versa. "Perversion of justice" is thus nothing other than the practice of multiplying one's own wealth on the backs of the poor, which has been consistently attacked throughout the book. The crucial point of chapter 5 is the right of these members of the "family" of Israel, too, to have life. Wherever a society orients itself around justice for the poor, there "may be" (5:15) sustainable life. The middle part of the book of Amos concludes, however, with the renewed complaint that the people of Israel have turned justice to bitterness (6:12) and with the recurring motif of a people pressing in on Israel in hostile action (6:14). And following the call to seek YHWH, there is another short hymnlike unit about YHWH's creative power, dominated by images of chaos and of the order of creation being taken back (5:8-9).

Visions of the End and Traces of Hope (Amos 7–9)

The third part of Amos is characterized by five scenes depicting visions, the first three of which form a direct sequence (7:1-3, 4-6, 7-9). The third and fourth are separated by Amos's encounter with the high priest of Bethel, Amaziah (7:10-17), and the fifth and longest stands alone (9:1-4). The first two visions sketch the picture of a natural catastrophe in the form of locusts that devour the harvest and a fire that threatens to destroy the fertile homeland (see Joel 1 in this context). The seer Amos appears as an advocate for the threatened people and is able once more to avert the disaster. Both visions give concrete meaning to the power of YHWH to "darken day into night" (Amos 5:8); they also state concretely what is about to happen to Israel, brought about by its crimes against humanity (Amos 2).

The third vision follows the scene of ruin back to the house of the king (7:9). The dramatic construction of the text then has the high priest Amaziah from Bethel appear on the scene. He has Amos's words against the royal house delivered to the king, adding the dire warning of disaster to befall all of Israel, thus summarizing to a certain extent the book's previous points. The leitmotif of his message is the "land" (this key word appears three times in 7:10-11); Amaziah claims that the "land" is on his side and against Amos. In the words he addresses to Amos, the priest, accordingly banishes the seer from the land; he is executing the judgment of the land against him. At the same time, he claims the king's authority, which stands behind the sacred site at Bethel. Amos replies with recourse to a different authority, none other than YHWH's. He confirms the prophecy spoken over Israel that Amaziah had reported as coming from him: the people will in fact have to leave their land. It is clear to hearers/readers of the entire book of Amos that this announcement is "true," since it corresponds to the words of YHWH, whose lion's voice had called the land to come to his side (1:2).

The prophetic message against Amaziah minutely dissects the meaning of resistance to God's word. The priest's own actions backfire on him, and the consequences affect his wife, his children, his acreage, and his life's end. That Amaziah's wife will become a whore is spoken not to arouse empathy with her but is significant instead in causing Amaziah's disqualification to continue serving as a priest (cf. Lev 21:7, 13). The death of his children — both daughters and sons are mentioned — means the end of his house and his name. It is pronounced against him as is the threat that he will lose his land and property and will find no proper burial place. This focus on the person of the high priest may confirm Amos's androcentrism on the one hand. On the other hand, it reflects precisely the situation the book of Amos describes. The objectification of Amaziah's family in the words of the prophet corresponds to the view that this priest, by his actions, takes his people down with him. His removal from the land of Israel mirrors the entire people's loss of land; it is to a certain extent a metaphor for the fate of Israel.

Once the power of the king and the priest has met head-on in the cultic center of the northern kingdom, seemingly irreconcilably, with the power of God, represented in the word of the exiled prophet, there is no stopping the end of Israel according to the fourth vision. As its context suggests, this end is located at the royal palace, but it is by no means defined in the figure of the king. Instead, it involves a group of his servants; the singing of the women musicians in the palace is transformed into weeping and wailing (Amos 8:3). Among the upper classes, too, there are "people of low estate" who are pulled into the maelstrom by the misdeeds of their masters. There follows a unit that once again weaves together the dominant themes of the book. The disenfranchisement of the poor all across the land (8:4-6) brings about the enraged and aggrieved reaction of the earth (8:8); even the stars react (8:9). Young people — women and men are both named here — lose their vital powers (8:13). The last vision (9:1-4) and the following two short units (9:5-6, 7-8) once again raise the cry to a crescendo. There is no escaping it: the whole cosmos is against Israel and even the special case of Israel's being led out of Egypt now appears superseded; Israel has become like one of the many peoples.

Within the larger perspective of this scene of the end is the remarkable formulation in Amos 8:14 that has been weakened in most translations:

> They who swear by the "guilt" of Samaria,
>> who say "As your god lives, O Dan,"
> and "As the way of Beer-sheba lives" —
>> they shall fall, and never rise again.

Here, again, what is at stake is the alternative of "life" or "death." The extant Hebrew text speaks of empty oaths to figures who are corrupt in any case. In all of Amos, Samaria and Beer-sheba are seen as sites of Israel's sin. The fact that the "god" of Dan is mentioned, however, gives rise to the hypothesis that the nouns "guilt" (*'ašmâ*) and "way" (*derek*) might possibly be conscious distortions of names of divinities and that the original text spoke of oaths by Ashima (or Aschera?) of Samaria and by "Dod(?)" ("darling") of Beer-sheba.[1] Amos in general makes no effort to discredit idols, unlike Hosea, for example. Few references (cf. 2:4 and 5:26) touch upon this theme. A text that speaks rather uninhibitedly about people who swear by other gods but who will not benefit from doing so would make sense if it came from an older version of the book that is no longer documented. The god or goddess worshiped in Samaria would be mentioned as a divinity only to affirm his or her impotence or that of other divinities. Later scholars would have erased this trace of goddess worship (along with the worship of the god of Beer-sheba), as is the case with the "queen of heaven" (Jer 44).

After all these images of the end there follows in 9:8b-9 a surprising qualification: no longer shall everyone without exception fall to ruin, but only the "sinners" (based on this, Reimer 1992 reread Amos from the end forward, so to speak). Accordingly, there is no more mention of "natural disasters," but of the "sword." The last image of the book builds upon this small ray of hope (9:11-15). The reconstructed "tabernacle" likely refers to the postexilic temple in Jerusalem. Thus the circle is cast back to the beginning of the book where YHWH begins to act threateningly from Zion/Jerusalem, and at the same time a new beginning is heralded. Yet another transformation can be seen here: the decrepit state of the tabernacle is the equivalent of the "fallen" virgin of Israel/Israel itself (5:2), which will be lifted

1. Translator's note: The NSRV has "Those who swear by Ashima of Samaria," thus not translating the extant Hebrew text but the supposed original text.

up again. And the "tabernacle" evokes the festival at harvest time; the grieving, drought-stricken land (1:2) has been transformed into a fertile land, sown with new seed, in which Israel itself, like a plant, can grow and thrive in safety.

The book of Amos delivers no formulas for current political analysis or strategies for action. This prophetic book, however, is and will remain a source of the kind of semantic potential that can spell out basic choices for a humane life of compassion, and/or hold them up to be remembered. Amos stands for the longing and the demand for truly universal justice that encompasses "nature" and the cosmos.

LITERATURE

Andersen, Francis I., and David N. Freedman. 1989. *Amos.* New York.

Barstad, Hans. 1984. *The Religious Polemics of Amos.* Supplements to Vetus Testamentum, vol. 34. Leiden.

Bird, Phyllis. 1996. "Poor Man or Poor Woman? Gendering the Poor in Prophetic Texts." In *On Reading Prophetic Texts,* edited by Bob Becking and Meindert Dijkstra, 37-52. Leiden.

Carroll R., Marc Daniel. 1992. *Contexts for Amos: Prophetic Poetics in Latin American Perspective.* Journal for the Study of the Old Testament: Supplement Series, vol. 132. Sheffield.

Ebach, Jürgen. 1989. "Schöpfung in der hebräischen Bibel." In *Ökologische Theologie,* edited by Günter Altner, 98-129. Stuttgart.

Fleischer, Günther. 1989. *Von Menschenverkäufern, Baschankühen und Rechtsverkehren.* Bonner biblische Beiträge, vol. 74. Frankfurt.

Fritz, Volkmar. 1989. "Amosbuch, Amos-Schule und historischer Amos." In *Prophet und Prophetenbuch,* edited by Volkmar Fritz, 29-43. Festschrift for Otto Kaiser. Berlin.

García-Treto, Francisco O. 1993. "A Reader-Response Approach to Prophetic Conflict: The Case of Amos 7.10-17." In *The New Literary Criticism and the Hebrew Bible,* edited by J. Cheryl Exum and David A. Clines, 114-24. Journal for the Study of the Old Testament: Supplement Series, vol. 143. Sheffield.

Gillingham, Susan. 1993. "'Der die Morgenröte zur Finsternis macht'. Gott und Schöpfung im Amosbuch." *Evangelische Theologie* 53:109-23.

Jeremias, Jörg. 1995. *Der Prophet Amos.* Altes Testament Deutsch, vol. 24, 2. Göttingen.

Loretz, Oswald. 1992. "Die Entstehung des Amos-Buches im Licht der Prophetien aus Mari, Assur, Ishchali und der Ugarit-Texte." *Ugarit-Forschung* 24:179-215.

Paul, Shalom M. 1991. *Amos.* Minneapolis.

Reimer, Haroldo. 1992. *Richtet auf das Recht! Studien zur Botschaft des Amos.* Stuttgarter Bibelstudien, vol. 149. Stuttgart.

Sanderson, Judith E. 1992. "Amos." In *The Women's Bible Commentary,* edited by Carol A. Newsom and Sharon H. Ringe, 205-9. London and Louisville.

Schottroff, Willy. 1979. "Der Prophet Amos. Versuch der Würdigung seines Auftretens unter sozialgeschichtlichem Aspekt." In *Der Gott der kleinen Leute,* vol. 1, edited by Willy Schottroff and Wolfgang Stegemann, 39-66. Munich and Gelnhausen.

Schottroff, Willy, and Wolfgang Stegemann, eds. 1979. *Der Gott der kleinen Leute.* Vol. 1. Munich and Gelnhausen.

Schwantes, Milton. 1991. *Das Land kann seine Worte nicht ertragen. Meditationen zu Amos.* Munich.

Weippert, Helga. 1985. "Amos: seine Bilder und ihr Milieu." In Helga Weippert, Klaus Seybold, and Manfred Weippert, *Beiträge zur prophetischen Bildsprache in Israel und Assyrien,* 1-29. Orbis biblicus et orientalis, vol. 64. Fribourg and Göttingen.

Zenger, Erich. 1988. "Die eigentliche Botschaft des Amos." In *Mystik und Politik. Zu Ehren von J. B. Metz,* edited by Edward Schillebeeckx, 394-406. Mainz.

FOR FURTHER READING

Carroll R., M. Daniel. 2002. "Reading Amos from the Margins: The Impact of Context of Interpretation Since 1990." In M. Daniel Carroll R., *Amos — the Prophet and His Oracles,* 53-72. Louisville.

Clines, David J. 2002. "He-Prophets: Masculinity as a Problem for the Hebrew Prophets and Their Interpreters." In *Sense and Sensitivity,* edited by Alistair G. Hunter and Philip R. Davies, 311-28. Journal for the Study of the Old Testament: Supplement Series, vol. 348. Sheffield.

Steins, Georg. 2005. "Amos 7–9 — das Geburtsprotokoll der alttestamentlichen Gerichtsprophetie?" In *Das Manna fällt auch heute noch,* edited by Frank-Lothar Hossfeld et al., 585-608. Festschrift for Erich Zenger. Herders biblische Studien, vol. 44. Freiburg.

Strydom, Johannes G. 1995. "Redistribution of Land: The Eighth Century in Israel, the Twentieth Century in South Africa." *Old Testament Essays* 8, no. 3:398-413.

Translated by Nancy Lukens

Obadiah: Brother Edom

Marie-Theres Wacker

War against Lady Edom, the Brother

> The Vision of Obadiah.
> Thus says the Lord GOD concerning Edom:
> We have heard a report from the LORD,
>   and a messenger has been sent among the nations:
> "Rise up! Let us rise against her [author's translation] for battle!"
> I will surely make you [masculine] least among the nations.

The book of Obadiah, with its mere twenty-one verses the shortest book of the First Testament, appears not so much as a direct "Word of God" comparable to books such as the preceding ones, Hosea and Joel. Instead, with its heading it presents itself as a "vision" of a "servant of YHWH" (ʿōbadyâ). To be sure, this is immediately followed by the messenger formula "thus says YHWH," which customarily introduces a passage of God's words. But the expected word of God to be delivered by the prophet still does not appear; instead there appears a collective ("we") that in turn claims they have heard God's word, whereupon a messenger was sent to the neighboring peoples to call them to war against Edom. This change of perspective between the divine "I" and the addressed "we" — presumably added only by later editors — pervades the entire book of Obadiah.

With verse 2 the divine "I" begins speaking. While it addresses Edom as a masculine "you," Edom appears in the preceding messenger's call as a feminine counterpart — a rhetorical discrediting device frequently found especially in the prophetic literature. It seems to have been strengthened in the course of the handing down of the Hebrew text. Thus it does not appear to belong to the oldest known form of the text, and for this reason it is most often "corrected" in exegesis (→ Malachi; Hosea). However, in accordance with the Hebrew text available to us, the word of God is to be heard as addressed both against Edom the masculine "you" and Edom the woman.

406

In an initial rhetorical round (vv. 2-4), this word speaks of humiliation, of a mighty people being "brought down" after being "deceived" by their "proud heart" into thinking they were great. On the one hand, the comparison of Edom with an eagle that builds its nest among the stars may mean the cities of Edom that literally lay in high rocky areas. On the other, it evokes the fate of Babel, the "arrogant" city and the center of a world power (Jer 50:29-31) whose king reaches for the stars (cf. Isa 14:13), who wants to penetrate what is God's sphere (just as in the story of building the "Tower of Babel" in Gen 11!). Like Babel, the city (depicted as a woman) and its king, YHWH will also bring down Edom, which stormed heaven. In this section it can already be seen that the book of Obadiah is not (merely) about the Edom of history, but about power that thinks of itself as godlike — though the relationship of this power to Israel is not yet brought into view.

In a second section (Obad 5-7) the fate of Edom/Esau is formulated in a different way: Edom is plundered and driven out of its territory. Its wealth and its political and economic power are finished. The reference to "searching out" the treasures of Edom may be aimed at the copper resources of that land. The image of the vintners *(bōṣĕrîm)*, who leave no gleanings, representing the extensive pillage, at the same time plays with the name of the capital of Edom, Bozra. She, the "invincible" *(boṣrâ)*, will be laid open to thievery. It is the former allies of Esau/Edom who now turn against it. YHWH is not an actor here as in the previous section. Thus in these verses apparently it is the voice of Obadiah again, or the collective that already sees the peoples who have been called to join forces in war against Edom (v. 1).

In the third section (vv. 8-11), a further famous cultural achievement of Edom comes into consideration: its wisdom, mentioned here together with its military strength. Both of these strong points, we hear again explicitly in a word of YHWH, will be brought down. The reason this time is not Edom's "reaching for the stars," but its behavior during the takeover and destruction of Jerusalem, namely, having become complicit with the conquerors. This is not seen as mere opportunism; rather, this is fratricide; it is the violence of Esau toward his brother Jacob (vv. 9-10). Thus, as it becomes clear here, this is about an especially acute conflict, not merely about the destruction of Jerusalem by foreign peoples, but about the brother who becomes the mortal enemy (cf. the story of "Cain and Abel," Gen 4!) and takes sides with the other (peoples).

The fourth section (vv. 12-14) walks through this conflict once again in the form of eight warnings or prohibitions that in each case juxtapose Judah/Jerusalem's day of dire need and the behavior of the brother Edom who showed no solidarity in the respective situation. His action will fall back onto him. The reference to the "day of the LORD . . . against all the nations" (v. 15) must be understood in the sense that this "day" will catch up with Edom, too, as "brother," not a people like the others but one that, through its actions, has become like the others (v. 11). At the same time, the phrase "day of YHWH" rather than "my day" might suggest that the writer again is thinking not of YHWH himself as speaking, but of "Obadiah"/"we."

If until now the focus has been on Edom, who for his part views his brother Jacob/Judah/Jerusalem without compassion (cf. vv. 12-13), the perspective shifts beginning with verse 16. From now on the action concerning the fate of Edom takes place beginning from Zion, the holy mountain of God in Jerusalem, and once again in such a way that God's voice can be heard ("on my holy mountain," v. 16), though by verse 19 at the latest this voice of God is continued by a different voice. Edom's fate will be like that of the other peoples who participated in the downfall of Jerusalem, who will disappear from the face of the earth (v. 16). In a great conflagration, "Jacob" is in a certain sense transformed and becomes himself the force who destroys Edom (vv. 17-18), and now, in a reversal, starting from "Mount Zion," the land around "Mount Esau" is taken over (vv. 19-20). The final sentence of the book (v. 21) returns again to "Mount Zion," leaving the human agents clearly in the background, however. Judgment shall take place over "Mount Esau"/Edom — but who the "rescuers" will be who will carry this out, according to the Hebrew text before us, remains open, and the (sole) sovereign in this kingdom is declared to be YHWH.

Does Obadiah Need Female Readers?

If we are to accept the reflections of Ehud Ben Zvi (1996, 260ff.) about the first audience to whom the book of Obadiah was addressed, we should think in terms of urban circles in Judah of the Achaemenid (Persian) era (fifth-fourth century B.C.E.) who were literate and familiar with the tradition. According to feminist studies of women's history in the postexilic period (Proverbs; Ezra; Nehemiah), it is hard to say whether women belonged to these audiences, and if so, how many. Even more uncertain remains the question whether or to what extent women supported the perspectives of "Obadiah." But what if women in the latter part of the twentieth century or later, women readers interested as feminists, set about to take this biblical text seriously?

Beth Glazier-McDonald has developed the motif of fraternal feuding as central to the book of Obadiah in her short commentary (1992). But then the starting point and message of this text become not the historic hatred of Judah for Edom, but the theme of feuding brothers who compete with one another for dominance and for the love and recognition of their (genealogical as well as divine) father (Mal 1!) and who in the process do not shrink from fratricide (cf. Gen 4 as well as the Joseph story, Gen 37 and following). It is precisely in Genesis that this theme takes up a not inconsiderable space with its stories of Jacob and Esau. In Obadiah this conflict is fought rhetorically in such a way that the brother "Edom/Esau" is represented as one who belongs among the "other" (peoples/*gôyim*), whereas "Jacob," through the repetition of synonymous or associated names — besides Jacob (vv. 17-18), there is Jerusalem (11, 20), Zion (17, 21), Judah (12), Joseph (18), and Israel (20) — appears as the true Israel (Ben Zvi 1996), which, furthermore, has God himself in its midst and on its side.

Today's female readers of Obadiah may be inclined to skip over this text about feuding brothers and the co-opting of God with a shrug. However, female Christian readers find themselves located within a long history of the reception of this conflict. This reception has identified "Mount Zion" with the church and has declared "Mount Esau"/Edom, merging it with "Mount Sinai," to be a symbol of Judaism as a religion that has been superseded. As if that were not bad enough, this interpretation is supported with references to the female figures Sarah and Hagar (Gal 4). This historically and theologically disastrous reception history cannot be overcome by ignoring it, but must be recognized for what it is and taken to task. Moreover, the theme "fraternal feuding" can stimulate further questions challenging to feminist and feminist-theological thinking. "Sisters," too, feud, must feud. They fight over and about the dependence from various fathers that they have freely chosen, or accepted against their will, or had forced upon them. They fight among themselves for recognition or rank; thus they can recognize themselves in the mirror of the brothers fighting before and over God. The placement of the book of Obadiah between the books of Amos and Jonah also opens further possibilities for viewing this text. Is it possible to sustain the tension between the cry for justice in the face of wrongs that peoples do to one another (cf. the word of Edom in Amos 1:11-12 in the context of the "Sayings of the Peoples" of Amos 1–2), and the recognition of God's mercy that is not limited to the "favorite child" Israel, but as Jonah must learn, reaches to the ends of the earth?

LITERATURE

Ben Zvi, Ehud. 1996. *A Historical Critical Study of the Book of Obadiah.* Beihefte zur Zeitschrift für die alttestamentliche Wissenschaft, vol. 242. Berlin.

Dicou, Bert. 1994. *Edom, Israel's Brother and Antagonist.* Journal for the Study of the Old Testament: Supplement Series, vol. 169. Sheffield.

Dietrich, Walter. 1994. "Obadja/Obadjabuch." In *Theologische Realenzyklopädie,* 24:715-20. Berlin.

Glazier-McDonald, Beth. 1992. "Obadiah." In *The Women's Bible Commentary,* edited by Carol A. Newsom and Sharon H. Ringe, 210-11. London and Louisville.

Knauf, Ernst Axel. 1991. "Edomiter." In *Neues Bibellexikon,* edited by Manfred Görg and Bernhard Lang, 1:468-71. Zurich.

Schüssler-Fiorenza, Elisabeth. 1994. "Der 'Athenakomplex' in der theologischen Frauenforschung." In *Für Gerechtigkeit streiten. Theologie im Alltag einer bedrohten Welt,* edited by Dorothee Sölle, 103-11. Festschrift for Luise Schottroff. Gütersloh.

Sölle, Dorothee. 1994. "Schwesternstreit." In *Für Gerechtigkeit streiten. Theologie im Alltag einer bedrohten Welt,* edited by Dorothee Sölle, 112-16. Festschrift for Luise Schottroff. Gütersloh.

Struppe, Ursula. 1997. *Die Bücher Obadja und Jona.* Neuer Stuttgarter Kommentar, Altes Testament, vol. 24, 1. Stuttgart.

Translated by Nancy Lukens

Jonah: The Jonah Experience — for Women Too?

Maria Kassel

Exegetical Approach

Does the book of Jonah have *feminist* relevance? It would seem difficult to respond positively to this query, since the drama of the Jonah story evolves only among men, and God, who initiates the drama, has a good role in that story. What deserves a closer look, however, is whether the real issue the story deals with is a purely androcentric one. It is easy to approach the book from the perspective of *depth psychology,* since even a cursory look shows that the protagonist is faced with an inner struggle of the soul, that his life enters a crisis period that can bring him through developmental stages of progress, stagnation, or regression. From the point of view of depth psychology and *theology,* what is interesting about the book of Jonah is, above all, how God's call to Jonah and the image of God that becomes visible in that call are intricately interwoven with the internal process that evolves within the human protagonist of the story.

The interpretation of a biblical text from a depth psychology perspective, as I would like to introduce it here, includes a feminist perspective, for such an analysis uncovers spoken as well as suppressed and split-off realities of one's life — including those of women — and especially those of their background experience. The study of a female world and female life experience might well fail to produce any results; that would then be an indication that we are dealing with a thoroughly patriarchal text of the Bible.

As part of a *religious* tradition, Jonah requires that its symbolism be understood if it is to be appropriately interpreted. An interpretation from a merely historical perspective cannot do full justice to a text with a religious message. In the case of Jonah, this requirement literally jumps out at the reader, in that the scene with the fish that swallows Jonah and spits him out again whole (chapter 2) has no historical perspective whatsoever, as is in fact the case with the entire book. The scene is of a mythical genre, represented exclusively in symbolic language. Thus it makes no sense to reject this scene as of no importance to the biblical message, as fairy-tale-like or even as historically irrelevant. Like the Gospel scenes of mythic-symbolic significance, such as Jesus' walking across the water (Mark 6:45-52), Jesus' transfiguration (Mark 9:3-8), or the encounters with the resurrected Christ (Matt 28:16-20; Luke 24:13-35, 36-49; et al.), this scene of Jonah and the fish mirrors processes of human beings coming from a state of unconsciousness into consciousness that can find no other form of expression than in symbolic language, that is, in a language related to that of dreams. To make this symbolism more accessible, this interpretation will be based on dream analysis, in this case with the help of the psychoanalytic theory of C. G. Jung. Such symbolic tales in the Bible transmit a view of the inner development of human beings, into which faith in God is integrated. Thus traditional images of God are always tied to the status of the psychic development of those who are in relationship with these particular images of God. For Jonah, then, one must ask what image of God is at work in him — not in his insight or understanding, but at the level where unconscious energies drive his action.

The questions relevant to the fish scene are also key to understanding the entire book of Jonah from a depth-psychological point of view — though the language and imagery of chapters 1, 3, and 4 are not as obviously symbolic as in chapter 2. Although it tells the story of a single person, Jonah — and this is true of all religious texts that have been handed down to us — offers not only the individual psychology of one person, but also a pattern of events and life constellations that have grown through the telling of the story and that are significant from a depth-psychological perspective, influenced by the experiences of many people, usually over several generations. This is the case even though the book is said to have been written by an individual author; Jonah is a *collective person* in whom are mirrored psycho-theological processes and conflicts over the period during which the book took shape (fourth to third century B.C.E., postexilic), and in whom lies the potential for the patterns of experience and the solutions to problems narrated in the book to be reactivated later on. The depth-psychological method of interpretation uncovers the deeper levels of such a complex configuration of storytelling; it is not to be confused with the therapy conducted with a single real person. A therapeutic approach to depth-psychological interpretation such as that of Eugen Drewermann is thus questionable, because it reduces the significance of religious tradition to its therapeutic effect and narrows religious experience to psychic healing (cf. Kassel 1993a).

Depth-Psychological Interpretation

If depth-psychological exegesis consisted exclusively in the *interpretation* of biblical texts, it would be one of many new exegetical approaches. It is that, too. However, in this regard one must ask whether other exegeses are necessary that, while quite different, nevertheless share the basic quality of interpreting the texts on a verbal-discursive level. As a result, they only speak *about* the biblical experiences, but cannot reactivate these experiences. A depth-psychological exegesis that seriously deserves this name, on the other hand, must in my opinion begin with transposing the biblical experience into experience possible in the present, must work out a systematic depth-psychological approach and a set of methods. A second step would then be the interpretation in the context of a depth-psychological hermeneutic. The order in which these steps are followed is not simply interchangeable in this work. The first step is difficult to write about, however, because in the moment one describes a current experience with a biblical text, in this case a Jonah experience, one has spoken *about* it and it enters — not without undergoing change — into the state of representation. Nevertheless, to explain a main characteristic of depth-psychological exegesis, I will here sketch by means of an example the first step: a hands-on depth-psychological exegesis, as distinct from the second step: depth-psychological interpretation.

Reactivating the Jonah Experience Today

In a group of young women, an experiential exercise on Jonah is carried out using a nonverbal medium: they paint pictures. To be sure, such exercises have no rules, but there is a certain framework of interpretation. Since every experience, including in a group, can only be individual experience, the text is related to each person's respective "I." Thus in the group, the theme for the painting exercise is "The Jonah in myself." The theme is formulated after the book of Jonah has been read aloud; then each participant paints her picture of Jonah. Out of the meditative silence that arises in the group come images with strong symbolic expression. They are hung on the wall, and the participants can express how they respond to the images. They do not interpret the images. By enriching (amplifying) the images with many diverse experiences of Jonah, a rich potential is created that is able to expand and deepen individual experience.

Here I shall describe two of the pictures produced in the groups, rather than describing the next step in the group process, where the groups compare their own experiences with Jonah. The first image relates to Jonah in the belly of the fish, represented as a deep, black chasm, narrowing toward the bottom, at the bottom of which stands a tiny human being, connected with the world above only by a thin sunbeam. Here the depth of Jonah's crisis has been grasped; the constriction, anxiety, and limited state of the person's emotional situation are expressed, but not without hope for the brightness and openness of a new phase of life. Another picture shows people in different walking positions in loose formation lined up one behind the other. Some are touching each other's hands, forming a chain that reaches across a river. This image expresses experiences of Jonah transformations, where instead of the stormy sea that swallows one up, there is a river that appears as a symbol of a transition from one life-form that is left behind to a new life.

Each of these pictures, like the rest, takes up one aspect of the book of Jonah, apparently the one that touched upon the particular issue about Jonah that the person had chosen to work on. From this one can conclude that it is not through a complete interpretation that it becomes possible to experience Jonah today, but rather that such experience is called forth through the convergence of fundamental human situations that cut across history and culture (i.e., archetypal situations) in biblical times and in the present. A striking feature of the pictures drawn by the group was that none of the women translated into their Jonah experience anything about Jonah's hopeless situation at sea or under the sea, or about his death wish, or about his resistance to following God's direction, or about God as a relational figure. This raises the question whether these aspects of the Jonah story are less significant in the experience of the women participants, and also whether God is experienced more as an inner dynamic than as a personal force influencing their lives from beyond themselves.

Moving on to depth-psychological interpretation, we will now consider the entire Jonah story, unlike the preceding step of immediate experience.

Depth-Psychological Interpretation as a Framework for Understanding the Jonah Experience

It is possible, despite the very diverse text genres within Jonah (the calling of the prophet, historicizing narrative, myth, prayer psalm, prophetic preaching, repentance story, God's words), to line them up according to a common theme. To be sure, the way they are combined is puzzling to logical thinking, for example, Jonah's prayer of thanksgiving in the moment of greatest danger; his only half-hearted execution of God's command even the second time around; the abrupt ending, inconclusive in its meaning. But the story of Jonah follows the logic of the course of a crisis in a person's development in which, as in a dream, sequences emerge that appear to be disparate. The crisis is of interest to depth psychology not in its outward course, but as an inward experience of the particular person that masks itself as an — allegedly — objective representation.

Jonah the human being falls apart when he experiences fundamental change in his life. In fact, he himself is required to bring about that change. The fact that he experiences this as a call from God points to the inevitability of the change. The fact that he refuses to follow the call plunges him into crisis. That he understands this inner call as a prophetic task points to a particular consciousness of himself as set apart from ordinary humanity. In striking contrast to this consciousness is Jonah's behavior, which resembles that of a boy in the midst of puberty. Throughout the book he appears recalcitrant, stubborn, egotistical, uncommunicative and lazy with words, narrow-minded, and persisting for no good reason in his lack of insight. He is so identified with his image of God — that God must punish, even destroy, sinners — that to change his image of God would utterly destroy the world he inhabits. The strength of his ego, or his human identity, as well as his faith, stands or falls with his merciless God, who is his only stronghold in life. A change in Jonah's image of God — which has long since begun with the experience of having a task he must fulfill — therefore drives him to despair. His despair is manifested in his repeated death wish (1:12; 4:3; 4:8), which at the same time proves his prophetic sense of self to be quite exaggerated.

This Jonah — is this not a fundamentalist whose faith is not (any longer) integrated with his rational abilities, whose personality is threatening to split? To be sure, he does offer a valid answer to the sailors' questions (1:9); he also knows that he himself is at fault because he is not following the inner call (1:12). In fact, he even knows very well the kindness of God, which he rejects (4:2) and yet claims for himself (2:3, 7b, 10b [Eng. 2:12, 6b, 9b]). But all this knowledge of God is merely in Jonah's head; it has not reached the level of his psychic energy, so it cannot be a motivating force of his faith. Thus Jonah in all his trials gives the impression of one who is emotionally deprived — in contrast to the ship's crew and the Ninevites. Cut off from his consciousness, his emotions — strangers to him — make him into a man driven, running away without presence of mind or understanding, who takes offense when things don't go his way (chapters 1 and 4). He is full of suppressed aggression, which he acts out only in his fantasy of the imagined destruction of Nineveh (chapters 3 and 4) and wants to have carried out violently by others (sailors: 1:12; God: chapter 4; i.e., projection). Jonah is fixated on a single view of the world; he denies the diversity and nontransparency of life and tries to avoid adulthood and its responsibilities. The walls he is running against are thus walls that he himself constructs.

Jonah's downward tendency, psychically speaking (regression) — not only to Joppa (1:3), to the bottom-most hold of the ship (1:5), to the depths of the sea (1:12, 15), but also toward his own ruin — ends in the belly of the fish (2:1), the most hopeless place of those Jonah strives to reach. But this is one place he reaches not by an act of his own will, but because of God (2:1[1:17]), who is the greater power within him, who ultimately motivates him. The story of Jonah and the fish, an echo of the ancient myth of the hero's nocturnal sea voyage, lifts up the stubborn and narrow-minded prophet into a universal and cosmic dimension. The complex symbolism of the myth — from the sun's nocturnal journey through the dark sea below the horizons, the disappearance of the moon for three days in the darkness, the hero's (God's or human's) journey across the waters of death into the netherworld — while it does point toward new life, toward rebirth, nevertheless leaves open whether it might also end in death. In the book of Jonah the myth speaks of the transformation of the "hero" in the eye of the storm at the point where the pressure of unconscious energies comes to a standstill. There is nowhere else to flee from this underworld, that is, from himself. Here Jonah is caught, and the one who had resisted his own calling suffers a fearful and lonely (emotional/psychic) death. At the same time, his transformation takes place through a rebirth. Artistic iconography has preserved this understanding of the story through the centuries in representing Jonah as emerging from the belly of the fish naked and hairless like a newborn infant.

The prayer (chapter 2) of Jonah in the fish is like a commentary on his inner death and renewal. From a depth-psychological point of view it is properly placed, though historical criticism has stated that it was added later and wrongly placed. It expresses the paradoxical experience of confidence in redemption precisely in the most extremely threatening moment. If I transpose the psalm from the past tense into the present, which is semantically possible, then Jonah expresses in the psalm his horrific plunge into the depths: into the underworld, into the heart of the sea, into the waves of the sea that roll over him, into the abyss, to the very base of the mountains, into a world bolted shut, the grave. Yet *at the same time* he expresses the redemption he has experienced: rejected by God and yet gazing upon God's presence in the temple; turning to God, from whom he had wanted to run away to the end of the world (Tarshish); freed by this God and brought to life from the grave. Present time and simultaneity of past and sequential events, such as one's downfall and rescue or redemption, are factual elements of dream time, in which the rules of historical temporality do not apply. Jonah's experience is constructed according to an imaginative logic that reflects the contradictoriness of his life. By bringing this into the discourse of his prayer, he brings it to consciousness and engages with a process of transformation. This process cannot happen in retrospect, but must occur at the lowest point of his life. In this respect the prayer occurs at the appropriate point in the narrative from a depth-psychological point of view.

Jonah's prayer consists largely of indirect references to other biblical traditions. This reflects a certain understanding of tradition, namely, that in the belly of the fish, the intractable prophet is able to regenerate his image of God, which had become narrowed by fundamentalism, through the accumulated collective experience of his people with God. The way the story proceeds confirms this. Only after Jonah has experienced for himself the saving, merciful God, who protects all living things, can he go about his task, which is to share the experience of this God in the world (Nineveh).

The Jonah we meet after the experience in the belly of the fish is different from the Jonah we saw before that experience — and at the same time he is not (chapters 3 and 4). He gives up trying to flee and fulfills his mission; however, it is reluctantly and minimally that he does so. He walks for only one day into a city so big it would take three days to cover; he calls out only five words, and says nothing about the possibility of repentance for Nineveh. He is so cocksure that he is right — "Didn't I know . . ." (4:2). He has no pity on the people of Nineveh, but plenty of self-pity — a withered bush and a sultry east wind (4:7-8). He is furious (4:1, 9) and retreats in silence (cf. the ending). Did Jonah really change at all in the belly of the fish? He has made a beginning at translating his inner experience into everyday life, but has not yet gone beyond that. Yet things are stirring in him, as evidenced by the activities of the Ninevites and God, so contrary to Jonah's behavior. Jonah is given object lessons in turning around. Both Nineveh and God may be understood as powers that are at work within Jonah; his "I" observes and registers.

The repentance of Nineveh is drastic, but genuine and profound (3:5-9), as drastic as Nineveh's/Assyria's earlier reputation as a brutally violent regime and presumably also as a liberal and libertine cosmopolitan city, as a prototype of the "modern" world. Nineveh's conversion makes its inhabitants democratic; they are all equal participants, from the "man on the street" to the king. Merits and favoritism do not count any more. They radically reduce their consumption, including the cattle they eat, and thereby protect the earth's resources that had been exploited by such a large city. They pray; that is, they shift the priority of their life to the spiritual in order to escape the destruction that is the consequence of a life too focused on outward things. The Ninevites work hard on themselves — a path that Jonah only now, after all he has experienced, begins to see.

God's conversion is different. Like human action, it is directed by feelings. But in contrast to Jonah, God's feelings are connected with reality and are integrated with God's whole being. God's anger is directed only at Nineveh's evil ways (1:2; 3:9); it is not the arbitrary rage of a powerful ruler or the jealous rage of Jonah (4:9-10); rather, it is directed at the redemption of creation, humans and animals (4:11). God's conversion means that his anger is transformed, in view of the changed situation in Nineveh, into sympathy and pity for the people living in stupid ignorance "who do not know their right hand from their left" (4:11). Thus God remains the same throughout the entire book of Jonah and yet is one who changes, and Jonah knows that (4:2). He experienced it himself in the belly of the fish, for there he implored the God of mercy.

The ending of the book is an open question, even more as a challenge to Jonah to make room in his life not only for the angry God but also for the kind God, and in so doing to move forward in his development toward more complete personhood and toward becoming a more convincing prophet. There will be much more for Jonah to do toward this goal. Jonah presents its protagonist's issues with life and with God in fragmentary form as a variation on a heroic myth, in which the male hero fails at his task. However, its uncertain ending leaves a way open for him. The question remains whether this rather negative version of the heroic myth can offer women guides for their development as well.

New Insights for Feminism

The book of Jonah speaks of human experience that is neither historically nor individually unique; indeed, it can be repeated again and again. But is this the case in view of women's experience? A religion-historical comparison of symbols provides important discoveries for a feminist perspective regarding biblical structures of experience. In view of Jonah's inner development, the turning point of which is his experience of the underworld, the Sumerian myth of the goddess Inanna's descent into the underworld offers an analogous symbolic tale (first half of second millennium B.C.E.; cf. Kramer 1974; Wolkstein and Kramer 1983). As the oldest known form of the motif of rebirth in the netherworld, this myth presents its origin in a female-oriented religion. This goddess myth symbolizes female patterns of experience at a time when patriarchy had not yet become as dominant a force in the religions of the ancient Near East as it was in the monotheism of Israel or in Christianity. Thus this myth is more informative than the Jonah story in terms of what it tells about women's experience.

The goddess's journey of her own volition into the underworld, including preparations for her return, her death, and her three-day sojourn in the realm of her sister, the goddess of the underworld, who lies in childbirth, and the resurrection or rebirth of Inanna, indicate marked differences in the Inanna myth from the patriarchal book of Jonah. Differences include her freely willed descent into the netherworld in full responsibility for whatever happens, her resurrection, which is associated with female creative power (the sister in the underworld giving birth): the understanding of death not as a last refuge from one's own life calling, but as a conscious passage through the painful transformation of life. Instead of being driven by unrecognized emotionality, there is a conscious shaping of the course of the journey to the psychic underworld, with the goal of greater consciousness for human beings and the world in the goddess's sphere of influence.

Inanna's myth shows that on the feminine search for self-determination and for fulfillment of one's life purpose, the experience of the underworld manifests itself in other images and patterns where the patriarchal influence is not yet fully felt — or in the case of the present, no longer fully felt. Although the book of Jonah can stimulate women, too, to represent their own experiences authentically through symbolic expression, there should be a new *Jonah story for women* created that is based on nonpatriarchal experiences and patterns of living. Emancipation alone, however, will not suffice to create a feminine Jonah myth as a mirror for women's experience. Based on the model of the goddess myth, such a new Jonah story would require women's conscious passage into and through the underworld, since the imaginative powers out of which symbols arise are not generated in rational thought or the will, but in the unconscious.

A feminine Jonah-story would produce different symbols than the First Testament Jonah book, not only for historical reasons related to the dominance of patriarchy in the Bible, but also for reasons of the realities of creation, or, in secular terms, of nature. For *women* not only undergo transformation by journeying through the underworld — as do men! — but at the same time they themselves are *part of the transformative power*. The goddess myth points to this when the death goddess in the underworld gives birth and when Inanna rises from the dead. Even in Jonah there is still a weak echo of the heroic myth of the nocturnal sea journey where the "hero" emerges from the belly of the fish to his renewed chance in life, from the heart of the seas and from the innermost core of the earth onto solid land. The metaphors of Jonah's prayer all relate to the structures of the female body. They render symbolic expression to women's capacity — not only their bodily but also their psychic and spiritual capacity — to regenerate life to a more conscious, and thus to a more complete, humanity. In the framework of a patriarchal-theistic belief system like Christianity, the question arises for women whether they also want to look to the fruits of nonpatriarchal imagination and nonpatriarchal images of divinity to find inspiration for their transformative potential, which transcends the biblical Jonah book. To the extent that a comparative critical study of Jonah shows its deficits with regard to the reality of women's lives, it can also — or even — produce new insights for feminism.

LITERATURE

Feminist Readings

Balz-Cochois, Helgard. 1992. *Inanna. Wesensbild und Kult einer unmütterlichen Göttin.* Gütersloh.

Kramer, Samuel Noah. 1974. "Innana's Descent to the Nether World." In *Ancient Near Eastern Texts,* edited by James Bennett Pritchard, 52-57. 4th ed. Princeton.

Langer, Heidemarie, et al. 1984. *Wir Frauen in Ninive. Gespräche mit Jona.* Stuttgart. Also in Erika Godel, *Gegenreden. Bibelarbeit von Frauen auf Deutschen Evangelischen Kirchentagen. Mosaiksteine zur verborgenen Kirchengeschichte der Frauen* (Munich, 1992), 55-69, 195-98.

White, Marsha C. 1992. "Jonah." In *The Women's Bible Commentary,* edited by Carol A. Newsom and Sharon H. Ringe, 212-14. London and Louisville.

Wolkstein, Diane, and Samuel Noah Kramer. 1983. *Inanna — Queen of Heaven and Earth: Her Stories and Hymns from Sumer,* 51-73. New York.

Depth-Psychological Readings

Drewermann, Eugen. 1984-85. *Tiefenpsychologie und Exegese,* 1:291, 292, 422; 2:259f., 363, 372, 388, 389. Olten.

Goldbrunner, Josef. 1982. "Der Walfisch des Jona als Modell seelischer Krise." In Josef Goldbrunner, *Not und Hilfe.* Regensburg.

Kassel, Maria. 1991. *Traum, Symbol, Religion. Tiefenpsychologie und feministische Analyse.* Freiburg, Basel, and Vienna. Esp. "Tiefenpsychologie und feministische Theologie," 166-79.

―――. 1993a. "Durchgeisternde Angst. Eugen Drewermanns tiefenpsychologische Exegese." *Lutherische Monatshefte* 32:7-9.

―――. 1993b. *Sei, die du werden sollst. Tiefenpsychologische Impulse aus der Bibel,* esp. 110-23. Freiburg.

Steffen, Uwe. 1982. *Jona und der Fisch. Der Mythos von Tod und Wiedergeburt. Buchreihe Symbole.* Stuttgart.
———. 1994. *Die Jona-Geschichte. Ihre Auslegung und Darstellung im Judentum, Christentum und Islam.* Neukirchen-Vluyn.

Historical Critical Readings
Litzenburger, Roland Peter, and Rainer Russ. n.d. *Jona. Bilder und Texte.* Stuttgart.
Schüngel-Straumann, Helen. 1975. *Israel — und die anderen? Zefania-Nahum-Habakuk-Obadja-Jona.* Stuttgarter Kleiner Kommentar, Altes Testament, vol. 15. Stuttgart.
Struppe, Ursula. 1996. *Die Bücher Obadja, Jona.* Neuer Stuttgarter Kommentar, Altes Testament, vol. 24, 1. Stuttgart.
Wolff, Hans Walter. 1975. *Studien zum Jonabuch.* 2nd ed. Neukirchen-Vluyn.

Jewish Perspectives
Simon, Uriel. 1994. *Jona. Ein jüdischer Kommentar. Mit einem Geleitwort von Erich Zenger.* Stuttgarter Bibelstudien, vol. 157. Stuttgart.
Wiesel, Elie. 1986. "Jona oder die Chancen des Menschen." In Wiesel, *Von Gott gepackt. Prophetische Gestalten,* 119-43. 2nd ed. Freiburg, Basel, and Vienna.

FOR FURTHER READING
Drewermann, Eugen. 2001. *Und der Fisch spie Jona an Land. Das Buch Jona tiefenpsychologisch gedeutet.* Düsseldorf and Zurich.

Translated by Nancy Lukens

Micah: Call for Justice — Hope for All

Sophia Bietenhard

Celebrated Message

The book of Micah speaks out of the fullness of human experience. It demands compensation for violated rights, hopes for a new beginning, attacks abuse and destruction, and outlines visions for life. It is striking in its this-worldliness, its sense of what needs to be done here and now and what opens doors to the future of the world. The substance and measure of its proclamation is God's justice. This is the prophet Micah's starting point. He represents this cause with confidence; the purveyors of his tradition take up the task left to them and spread the message in the celebration of worship. Thus the key phrase in the following commentary is "celebrated memory" (Schüssler-Fiorenza 1988, 49ff.).

The book moves between accusation and assurance of comfort, between sharp criticism, even signaling impending judgment, and visions of a salutary world. This polarity constitutes a basic pattern that gives the book its structure and form. The concluding chapter (7:8-20), recapitulating the alternation of threatened judgment and promise of the preceding sections, summarizes in the form of a prayer the book's recurrent themes of guilt and punishment, hope and renewal, Jerusalem/Zion — the city as friend and foe — and Israel and the peoples. The book ends not with judgment but with the confident assurance of God's forgiveness and mercy. In the worship celebration the community experiences remembrance and encouragement. Its identity can be inferred from the final prayer, which contains wishes for the destructive punishment of enemy forces. Such utterances, not easily accessible to us contemporary readers, should be read against the background of Israel's experience in the sixth century B.C.E. Under oppressive foreign rule, struggling for their survival and identity after exile, the returned and current residents of the destroyed Jerusalem are trying to build a new life. However, it is not only by excluding others that this nation seeks its own identity in a threatening situation. On the contrary, in ruthless self-criticism they interpret their own fate in the affairs of the world as a consequence of mistakes they have made. The people's prayers give witness to their guilt and their welfare and make it clear that God's forgiveness makes new beginnings possible. The arc that extends backward from 7:20 to the first call in 1:2 includes everyone in this divine invitation: "Hear, all ye peoples!"

The Work — a Process

The book of Micah grew over a long period of developing prophetic and worship practice. It is in this context that people again and again remembered, updated, and reformulated their faith traditions (Beck 1972, 75 and passim; Childs 1987, 436ff.). The traditions that go back to the prophet Micah constitute the smaller portion of the book. In terms of its redaction history, we can assume three stages (Willi-Plein 1971; Renaud 1977; Wolff 1982).

The book is assumed to have received its final form in postexilic Jerusalem in the Nehemaic period under Persian rule around the mid–fourth century B.C.E. This redaction process affects chapters 4–7 in particular, but it can also be seen in the previous chapters. It posits an overarching theological plan for the book, the basic message of which, according to Willi-Plein (1971, 111ff.), is found primarily in the middle section (3:9–5:14). The themes influenced by early eschatology such as "catastrophe" or "Zion's future glory," "Israel's new existence," and "threat and promise for the nations" give rise to the concluding chapter (7:5-20). In it the editors take up again the prophet's lament (7:1-6), and with it introduce the turnaround (7:7) and the adoration of God. The prayers in 7:8-10 and 14-20 once again take up the conflict with the nations and the visions for Jerusalem's future (3:12; 4:1-4; 5:6-7 [Eng. 7-8]; 7:11-13). The final revision creates contrast with the received tradition, adding new material to constitute a dialogue of utterances that appear both to give rise to and to contradict one another. Thus the assurance of salvation (4:1-4) contrasts with the announcement of judgment over the nations (5:10-15); the victorious daughter (4:8) is followed by the suffering daughter of Zion (4:9); the humbled judge (4:14[5:1]) is juxtaposed with a messianic savior figure (5:2-4).

In the exilic period, the destruction of Jerusalem is interpreted theologically, preparing the way for the later theme of Zion by using the Jerusalem polemics of the older Micah. The present version, however, created in the midst of catastrophe, accents the aspect of punishment. The exilic redaction process sees the old announcement of impending judgment in 3:12 as fulfilled in the events of 587 B.C.E., and uses it as an organizing principle for the presentation of both the traditional and their own new material: threat (chapters 1–3), promise (4:1-8; 5:1-3[2-4]), and prophetic dialogue in the time of waiting (6:1–7:4).

A first collection and reworking of traditional Micah material is written down either shortly before or shortly after the collapse of the southern kingdom in Deuteronomic/Deuteronomistic tradition (Renaud 1977, 399ff.; Willi-Plein 1971,

110-11). Willi-Plein organizes it into four parts, each of which is introduced by the call to hear (Part I: 1:2–2:11; Part II: 3:1-3, 8; Part III: 3:9–5:12; Part IV: 6:2-15). The heading in 1:1 and the conclusion in 6:16 frame the entire text. The themes of this collection are the social message, the threat of catastrophes for Samaria and Jerusalem, conflict with the enemies, the false prophets, and the instruments of unbelief. All this culminates in the controversy of YHWH with Israel.

The passages that point back to the prophet Micah or at least to his immediate interpreters essentially constitute the first three chapters after 1:6. Moreover, 6:9-15 is assumed to contain a basic core of Micah material. The mention of the prophet Micah of Moresheth by the elders of the land in Jeremiah 26:18 scarcely allows us to conclude that there was a Micah school of prophets (Willi-Plein 1971, 110). Rather, we can assume that Micah's oracle was passed along in a living tradition in his community, the neighboring countryside with its families, villages, and cities (Renaud 1977, 386).

Micah is at work in the last third of the eighth century B.C.E. in the midst of the Assyrian campaigns of destruction against Samaria and large parts of Judah. He is a Judean from Moresheth, located southwest of Jerusalem. His confident presentation and his defense of the rights of farmers and country residents lead one to assume he held a responsible position, for example, as a village elder (Wolff 1982, xiiiff.).

Feminine Imagery

The City as a Woman

The city in the ancient Near East and the Mediterranean is feminine in language and in the imagination. The reasons for this may lie in the evolution from the agricultural and rather matriarchally defined Neolithic age to the city-states of the Bronze Age, which were formed through a politics of war making, conquering, and security in a culture dominated by patriarchy (Schmitt 1985, 567; Schroer 1995b, 104). The city becomes the real sociocultural and economic center of the life of a region. As an employer, the city takes on the function of the earth as giver of life; above all, it is also the power that defends and protects people in times of war (Uehlinger 1987, 153ff.). This is not the least of reasons why changes of regime through violent means are decided by taking control of a city. The city becomes the focal point of radical political change and the object of violence and war. The suffering of women as victims of the violence of war metaphorically describes the destruction of an ancient Near Eastern city and with it of an entire nation. The talk of the pangs of childbirth (Isa 26:17-18; Jer 4:31; 6:24; 50:43; see Eltrop 1996, 168-69 on Mic 4:9-11) and of rape (Schroer 1995b, 122; see Bail 1996, 116-18 on Ps 55:10-12) personifies the violence of war and is symbolic of its reality. In the ancient Near East and in the ancient Mediterranean area, the city is represented in the bodily form of a goddess, the female equivalent of the male god of the state (Maier 1994, 87). The city of Jerusalem, however, is never a female-divine equivalent of YHWH (Steck 1989, 275).

In the oldest parts of Micah, the cities are often the objects of prophetic speech. For Micah the prophet, who lived in a rural area, the cities reflect the political situation at the time of the Assyrian threat, showing them to be responsible for the calamitous situation. No other prophet opposes Jerusalem as vehemently as Micah when he associates the city's buildings, including the temple and its cult, with exploitation and compulsory labor on the backs of the rural population (3:9-12). As centers of responsibility the cities are obliged to implement the policies decided in Jerusalem by the city fathers and administrative officials as well as the courts and tax collectors. Micah learns that the upper classes of these religious-political centers of power are sucking the countryside dry by every economic means possible: corruption (3:11), deception (6:10-12), abuse of the law (2:10b; 3:1-3; 6:12), and — especially bitter for Micah — through the complicity of prophets and cult officials (2:11; 3:5–6:11). If religion becomes the instrument of exploitation in the hands of the powerful, then the buildings that represent the institution, the temple and the city of Zion, are nothing other than the expression of the abuse of religion (Vincent 1986, 170). Thus the destruction of the temple and the city of Zion is, like that of Samaria, a programmed consequence of the behavior of those in power. It is difficult to imagine a harsher criticism of religious institutions than Micah expresses in 3:9-12.

Although Micah's accusations articulate a conflict between city and rural areas (Beck 1972, 90, 92), the cities themselves do not only embody evil. The rural resident Micah perceives in the threatened destruction of the cities and their inhabitants the fate of his people and breaks out in a loud lament (1:10-15). His grief over the fallen cities of the rural district is like that of a mother over her lost children (v. 16; presumably the lamenting woman here is the countryside of Judah [Wolff 1982, 13-14, 34]).

The destruction threatened for Zion provides the fertile literary soil in which to develop the later images of its downfall and its rebuilding (4:6-12). In the Deuteronomic polemic, the city becomes the figure with which to identify the transgressions of the nation (1:5a, 13b), and in the image of the house of Jacob is seen the godlessness of Israel in general (2:7; 3:1). Samaria and Jerusalem are synonymous with the transgression that leads to ruin (1:5a). The association of city, prostitution, and sin leads to the identification of woman and sin, as does the image of the city as an adulterous spouse of God.

A well-developed language of metaphors for the city is found in late and postexilic texts (→ Isaiah; → Jeremiah; → Lamentations; → Psalms; Schmitt 1985; Steck 1989; Schüngel-Straumann 1993; Hanford 1996). They reflect upon the fate of the city of Jerusalem, its destruction in 587 B.C.E. and its reconstruction, and they interpret the past, present, and future of Israel. Jerusalem/Zion is a personal figure — a daughter, childbearer, mother, partner in marriage; a grieving widow, a humiliated and imprisoned woman, and a suffering as well as a rejoicing woman. She gains her character in her relationships, including with the men and women with whom she lives, and with Israel (1:9b; 2:13; 6). The early eschatological visions begin with the reconstruction of Jerusalem, and with the metaphor of the mother of Zion they construct the future world (Schüngel-Straumann 1993).

We do not find in the book of Micah the troubling patriarchal image of the adulterous wife of YHWH (Ezek 16; Lam 1:2-19; Maier 1994) or the imagery of the whore introduced by the Hosea traditions (→ Hosea; Wacker 1996, 323-24). Here the postexilic imagery of the city is based on the utterances of judgment over Samaria and Jerusalem that announced their end over a hundred years earlier. The experience of destruction takes on an end-time dimension, thanks to the image of the woman writhing in the pangs of childbirth (Mic 4:9).[1] Later, in association with the return from exile and the reconstruction in the Persian period, the notion of Zion as a substitute for the Davidic kingdom comes to the fore (4:8), symbolizing the end-time. The images of passive victims suffering violence give way to those of an active force that anticipates and helps to give shape to happy fulfillment.[2] The coming of a new time brings with it what it requires: trust, prayer, listening to God. The image of childbearing, earlier a symbol for the pain and depravity of death, now becomes an expression for new life (5:2; Lescow 1967, 202). However, this resurrection of Zion from victim to one who gives shape to things also signifies the turn from victim to perpetrator. For YHWH is to bring about the time of happiness at the expense of those who had been victorious before, the foreign nations and their capital cities (4:6-13; 5:10-13; 7:8-10). In accordance with the bipolar structure of Micah, these statements are juxtaposed with those that speak of a comprehensive salvation for all (7:11-13) and include mutual acceptance (4:5-6). Jerusalem, as capital city and temple site, symbolizes Israel and its faith, and in the visions of peace it is the center of a new world (4:1-4; 7:11-12).

The language of Micah about the city develops in a kind of imagery that begins with women's experiences of life, integrates them into its theological reflection, and eventually becomes the creative, formative energy that enables one to manage the present and hope for the future.

---

1. Until our time, birth and the period of early life were of exceeding danger for both mother and child. This real experience of women must under no circumstances be romanticized out of the perspective on modern times and their achievements; Meyers 1988, 112; cf. Eltrop 1996, 168f. on Mic 4:9-11.

2. Steck 1989, 265 makes a mistake to limit the character of the ancient city to its quality as a "giver." It is precisely the sharp prophetic criticisms the prophets deliver to the cities that show that they also demand and devour life, especially in times of great need and war.

Right and Justice as the Center of the Prophetic Message

For Wolff (1982, 80), Micah is "one of the great early defenders of justice." The harsh criticism of the responsible religious and state authorities is based on a highly developed sense of justice (chapters 2–3). Otherwise not prone to self-representation, Micah now legitimizes himself as a mouthpiece for the victims of abuse of power, claiming to be filled with strength, courage, and a sense of right. The key word in his utterances against Jerusalem in 3:1-12 is "right" *(mišpāṭ)*. By claiming for himself the role of the politicians, that of administering justice, he directly confronts the authorities (3:8). The right is "the same legal order, which provides us orientation, for which the chiefs and leaders are supposed to be responsible (1b), the fundamental order that teaches the difference between good and evil (2a), between right and wrong (9b)" (Wolff 1982, 80, 75). Micah is rooted in the tradition that says God's justice takes sides with the meek and the vulnerable. A high point in the older Micah material is certainly the powerful argument between YHWH and those who twist justice (6:1-8). Still, Micah lives within his time's patriarchal understanding of justice. Those who deliver justice are the free, landowning men. The other members of his people and the foreigners are objects of this righteous action. If they cannot fight for their established rights or if the authorities responsible for enforcing the law do not represent them, then they are literally without rights and become subject to the whims of those who define or possess the "right" and therefore are "right." Micah, in fact, makes tangible his accusation against those who pervert justice, their corruption, greed, and gluttony, through the image of cannibalism (3:2-3). He names those concretely affected by injustice: farmers and landowners (2:2),[3] peaceable and unsuspecting nomads (2:8), women and children (2:9). The affected are "his people" (2:4b-9; 3:3-5). Micah does not undertake to determine a priority order of rights by class or gender; he feels responsible for everyone. Is his approach patronizing? Today it would likely be seen as such. In his time, the prophet was a radical. With his option for the disenfranchised, he prepared the way for the rights that can be claimed and administered by all people.

Those who passed along the Mican tradition further developed Micah's central concern, that of seeking justice and criticizing injustice (6:9-12). Thus the Deuteronomically influenced "didactic lesson" about the love of justice in 6:8 summarizes the ethical will of Israel (Deut 10:12-22; Hos 12:7 [Eng. 6]; Mark 12:28-31; Wolff 1982, 158).

---

3. In his translation of the second part of Mic 2:2b ("a man *('îš)* and his house"), Wolff 1982, 37 heightens the masculine formulation of the first part ("They oppress a householder and his house"; NRSV: "householder and house") so that it becomes a general statement including the women named in 2:9.

Lament and Grieving: The Prophet in a Woman's Role

The critical opposition of the prophet fills him with great grief. Micah sees no future for his country and people any more. He laments their end with a loud voice (1:9; 2:4; 3:12; Hentschel 1996, 155). It is left to later generations to find such hope in carrying on Micah's tradition. Micah goes back to the tradition of the lament for the dead to express the gravity of the situation. The lament for the dead at burials and in situations of catastrophe is primarily the task of women *(Klagefrauen)* (2 Sam 1:24; Ezek 32:16; Jer 9:17-22; Keel and Uehlinger 1992, 141), although there are also indications of grieving rituals involving both women and men (2 Chron 35:25; Zech 12:11-14; Winter 1987, 50, 254; Brenner and van Dijk-Hemmes 1993, 83ff.). The female custom of lamenting the dead merges with the image of the city when it is represented as grieving on behalf of its inhabitants (Mic 1:10-16). Clearly it is part and parcel of the prophets' role to adopt the practice of lamentation of the dead (1 Kings 13:30; Jer 9:9[10]; 22:18; 34:5). The prophets slip into the role of lamenting women, as it were, when they weep over the state of their country. Micah describes in detail the lament that he puts on display (1:8). This drastic demonstration must have brought him a good deal of criticism and mockery, even from those whose vocation was prophecy (2:6-11). Micah is a radically political and radically religious person. Incorporating the feminine in a patriarchal culture makes him a person at the boundary and a transgressor of boundaries.

Treading Softly with Micah's Message — a Summary View[4]

Micah 1:2–2:13: "Hear, You Peoples, All of You!"

The beginning widens the horizon against which Micah and those who follow in his footsteps proclaim their message. What happens in Israel and Judea, insignificant in terms of international affairs, nevertheless affects the whole earth because the prophetic tradition interprets it in the context of human behavior and God's intervention. Heaven and earth touch one another when YHWH, an awe-inspiring God, comes down and causes everything and everyone to tremble (1:2-4).

After the threatening of Samaria, which first provokes the warnings of Micah (1:6), comes the lament about the threat to the rural towns of Judah (1:9-16). One can assume a political subtext behind the sharp polemics against Samaria in 1:7b. The prophet describes as "whore's wages" the "gifts" of the superpower Assyria to the vassal city of Samaria, which funded the construction of its buildings, in re-

---

4. For those wishing to study this in greater depth I recommend the commentary by Eleonore Beck 1972.

turn for which high taxes were paid to Assyria on the backs of the rural population (Wolff 1982, 27). In this context prostitution is unmasked as an act of violence by the stronger party, who takes advantage of the victim, the city of Samaria, and drives her to ruin with dubious gifts. It is only the later Deuteronomic critics who associate the "whore's wages," and in turn prostitution itself, with the cults devoted to the images of gods and goddesses (1:7a).

The powerful appearance of YHWH finds its feminine counterweight in the form of Micah's loud outcry (1:8, 16). It is striking how verse 16 connects feminine grieving with the practice of head shaving in the grieving ritual. With this, Micah underscores the deathly finality of his lament. To bring this home he uses the image of the bald eagle, an ancient symbol in the Near East for regeneration and motherliness, for the female divinity, who ruled over life and death (Schroer 1995).

Micah sees the reasons for the catastrophe in the concrete social-political dysfunction at hand (2:1-11). The accused are the rich; the victims are the exploited inhabitants of the land. The prophet describes their suffering by giving evidence of the violation of property rights of the simple population. They move him to deep compassion (2:8-10). Whoever cannot pay their debts must, according to the law of the time, turn over their warm clothes (Exod 22:25; Crüsemann 1992, 95). Men are willfully drafted into forced labor, presumably to build the fortress walls of Hezekiah in Jerusalem (Mic 2:8; Hentschel 1996, 156). The wives of the men who have been driven into forced labor or into debtors' servitude (3:2-3, 10) are vulnerable to the invasion and stealing of the land of their inheritance. Driven out and homeless, they are exposed to misery, and their children will have no future (2:9-10). Unlike Amos and Isaiah, Micah does not directly refer to the fate of the poor. Rather, he describes the process of becoming poor as it affects women and children in particular (Bird 1996).

Micah 3:1–5:6: Out of Fields of Death Arises New Life

Micah continues his ruthless criticism of those in positions of responsibility and names them according to their actions, titles, and functions: greedy, rich people (2:1-2), corrupt officials and judges (3:1), opportunistic prophets and priests (3:5, 11). To be sure, they are Judeans like Micah himself, but as city dwellers they are cut from the same cloth as those in power (3:9-11). They are responsible for the inevitable and final ruin. Zion, built "with blood" (3:10; Wolff 1982, 79), is no place for YHWH; its buildings embody the justice built with blood money. Micah is radical when he finally applies to the city of Jerusalem (3:12) what is happening to the women of his country. Jerusalem will become a plowed field; no city will grow on its land any more. It is possible that Micah is alluding here to grieving rites that were familiar in Jerusalem when it had belonged to the land of Canaan: plowing and turning over the (masculine) fields symbolize grieving over the death of Baal (cf. 4:13-14; Vincent 1986). The city is transformed into dead ground. Whoever robs the city/the woman of her means of existence destroys life itself.

The next section, too, illustrates a comprehensive vision of a peaceful world using images from agriculture (4:1-5). Its center is the newly created mountain of Zion. The dream comes from Israel's experience of living as a cultural and religious minority among many nations. This leads not to exclusivity but to peaceful coexistence. Jerusalem in the figure of the powerful, royal, and protective daughter of Zion is the destination point of the future greatness of Israel (4:6-8). By contrast, softening the abrupt change from the uncultivated field in 3:12 to the re-created Jerusalem in 4:1-4, 4:9-10 refers to the actual destruction of the city and the expulsion of the people into exile in Babylonia in 587 B.C.E. In these images of a powerful woman in the pangs of childbirth, the postexilic community can imagine the end and the rebuilding of Jerusalem and their own fate. The contrast between the excessive power and the powerlessness of Jerusalem is repeated in 4:13-14 (4:13–5:1). The image of the city as childbearer and giver of life is extended to Bethlehem of Ephrathah as the birthplace of the expected Messiah (5:1-5). The exiled and decimated people of Israel project their struggle for identity longingly onto YHWH's powerful intervention (5:6-14).

Micah 6:1–7:20: For the Sake of Justice

The great theme of the book of Micah, the struggle for justice, reaches its climax in the controversy between YHWH and YHWH's people. But the text, staged as a court case (6:2), turns the cliché of the punitive, judgmental God on its head. YHWH expresses self-doubt, imploring the people to explain why they have turned away from their YHWH. This questioning opens up room for dialogue between God and human beings as partners. YHWH recalls in the opening argument that YHWH's liberating actions in history have never demanded the sacrifice of human life. The rejection of the worship of images likely also includes women's religiosity, at home mostly in the domestic sphere. The cult of YHWH alone, on the other hand, is managed entirely by men (Schroer 1995b, 126-27; ET, 128-29). Still, the historical summary also names Miriam as a leader sent by God in the struggle for freedom (6:4). This rare biblical reference to a female prophet documents the existence of female prophets in ancient Israel and up until the Jerusalem of Nehemiah's time (Sanderson 1992, 216; Schroer 1995b, 92; ET, 94-95), as well as the great significance of the Miriam literature (Wacker 1995, 66; ET, 68). Yet the text mirrors the conflict for dominance between the Torah (Moses), the priests (Aaron), and the prophets (Miriam). The book of Micah follows the prophetic tradition and thus opposes Persian rule (cf. Num 12; cf. Wacker 1988; Kessler 1996).

The debate over justice culminates in the ethical imperative of Micah 6:8. It is directed at the human being *('ādām)* in general, following the inclusive tone of the

entire book. The traditional translation of *wĕhaṣnēaʿ* with "walk humbly before
your God" only inadequately addresses the claim of biblical justice as the encounter between God and human beings. Suggested wordings such as "live with devotion before your God" (Beck 1972, 91) or "walk thoughtfully alongside your God"
(Wolff 1982, 137, 157) or "walk carefully with your God" (Ebach 1996) place Micah's
message into a liberating, breathing space in which God and human beings set out
in relationship to one another on the path of justice. Here, future is possible. Yet
justice must be won again and again and in the midst of difficult conflicts (6:9-16).
The crises escalate to the point of the beginning of the end-time; every kind of social coherence, even that of families, falls apart (7:1-6). The final section of the
book almost allows retreat into inwardness, into the I-Thou relationship between
praying human being and God as a solution (7:7-10). The power struggle between
the two woman-cities of Jerusalem and Babel (Jer 50:14-16) flows into justice and
righteousness for the world. The maternal compassion (Mic 7:19) of the incomparable God moves God to reconciliation (7:18-20). In the celebration of their hope
the people in prayer experience his/her help (7:8-17).

LITERATURE

Bail, Ulrike. 1996. "Die Klage einer Frau. Zu sprechen gegen das Schweigen. Eine
    feministisch-sozialgeschichtliche Auslegung von Psalm 55." *Bibel und Kirche* 51:116-
    18.
Beck, Eleonore. 1972. *Gottes Traum: eine menschliche Welt. Hosea — Amos — Micha.*
    Stuttgarter Kleiner Kommentar, Altes Testament, vol. 14. Stuttgart.
Bird, Phyllis A. 1996. "Poor Man or Poor Woman: Gendering the Poor in Prophetic
    Texts." In *On Reading Prophetic Texts: Gender-Specific and Related Studies,* edited by
    Bob Becking and Meindert Dijkstra, 37-57. Festschrift for Fokkelien van Dijk-
    Hemmes. Leiden et al.
Brenner, Athalya, and Fokkelien van Dijk-Hemmes. 1993. *On Gendering Texts: Female
    and Male Voices in the Hebrew Bible.* Leiden et al.
Childs, Brevard S. 1987. *Introduction to the Old Testament as Scripture.* 3rd ed. Philadel-
    phia.
Crüsemann, Frank. 1992. "'. . . wie wir vergeben unseren Schuldigern'. Schulden und
    Schuld in der biblischen Tradition." In *Schuld und Schulden: biblische Traditionen in
    gegenwärtigen Konflikten,* edited by Marlene Crüsemann and Willy Schottroff, 90-
    103. Munich.
Ebach, Jürgen. 1996. "Was bei Micha 'gut sein' heißt." *Bibel und Kirche* 51:172-81.
Eltrop, Bettina. 1996. "Du aber, Betlehem Efrata . . . aus Dir soll mir einer hervorgehen."
    Bibel und Kirche 51:168-70.
Hanford, Sally Greig. 1996. "From Harlot to Widow to Wife to Mother: The Transforma-
    tion of Zion in the Book of Isaiah." Typescript, Mémoire of the Ecole biblique et
    Archéologique Française, Jerusalem.
Hentschel, Georg. 1996. "Enteignung. Die soziale Frage in Micha 2." *Bibel und Kirche*
    51:155-58.

Keel, Othmar, and Christoph Uehlinger. 1992. *Göttinnen, Götter und Gottessymbole. Neue Erkenntnisse zur Religionsgeschichte Kanaans und Israels aufgrund bislang unerschlossener ikonographischer Quellen*. Freiburg.

Kessler, Rainer. 1996. "Mirjam und die Prophetie der Perserzeit." In *Gott an den Rändern: sozialgeschichtliche Perspektiven auf die Bibel*, edited by Ulrike Bail and Renate Jost, 64-72. Festschrift for Willy Schottroff. Gütersloh.

Lescow, Theodor. 1967. "Das Geburtsmotiv in den messianischen Weissagungen bei Jesaja und Micha." *Zeitschrift für die alttestamentliche Wissenschaft* 79:172-207.

Maier, Christl. 1994. "Jerusalem als Ehebrecherin in Ezechiel 16. Zur Verwendung und Funktion einer biblischen Metapher." In *Feministische Hermeneutik und Erstes Testament. Analysen und Interpretationen*, edited by Hedwig Jahnow et al., 85-105. Stuttgart et al.

Meyers, Carol. 1988. *Discovering Eve: Ancient Israelite Women in Context*. New York et al.

Renaud, Bernard. 1977. *La formation du livre de Michée. Tradition et actualisation*. Etudes bibliques. Paris.

Sanderson, Judith E. 1992. "Micah." In *The Women's Bible Commentary*, edited by Carol A. Newsom and Sharon H. Ringe, 215-16. London and Louisville.

Schmitt, John J. 1985. "The Motherhood of God and Zion as Mother." *Revue biblique* 92:557-69.

Schroer, Silvia. 1995a. "Die Göttin und der Geier." *Zeitschrift des Deutschen Palästina Vereins* 111:60-80.

———. 1995b. *Feministiche Exegese. Forschungserträge zur Bibel aus der Perspektive von Frauen*. By Luise Schottroff, Silvia Schroer, and Marie-Theres Wacker, 81-172. ET, 1998, 83-176.

Schüngel-Straumann, Helen. 1993. "Mutter Zion im Alten Testament." In *Theologie zwischen Zeiten und Kontinenten*, edited by Theodor Schneider and Helen Schüngel-Straumann, 19-30. Festschrift for Elisabeth Gössmann. Freiburg et al.

Schüssler Fiorenza, Elisabeth. 1984. *Bread Not Stone: The Challenge of Feminist Biblical Interpretation*. Boston.

———. 1988. *Brot statt Steine. Die Herausforderung einer feministischen Interpretation der Bibel*. Fribourg.

Steck, Odil H. 1989. "Zion als Gelände und Gestalt. Überlegungen zur Wahrnehmung Jerusalems als Stadt und Frau im Alten Testament." *Zeitschrift für Theologie und Kirche* 86:261-81.

Uehlinger, Christoph. 1987. "'Zeichne eine Stadt . . . und belagere sie!' Bild und Wort in einer Zeichenhandlung Ezechiels gegen Jerusalem (Ez 4f)." In *Jerusalem. Texte — Bilder — Steine*, edited by Max Küchler and Christoph Uehlinger, 111-200. Festschrift for Hildi and Othmar Keel-Leu. Fribourg et al.

Vincent, Jean M. 1986. "Michas Gerichtswort gegen Zion (3:12) in seinem Kontext." *Zeitschrift für Theologie und Kirche* 83:167-87.

Wacker, Marie-Theres. 1988. "Mirjam. Kritischer Mut einer Prophetin." In *Zwischen Ohnmacht und Befreiung. Biblische Frauengestalten*, edited by Karin Walter, 44-52. Freiburg im Breisgau et al.

———. 1995. *Feministiche Exegese. Forschungserträge zur Bibel aus der Perspektive von*

Frauen. By Luise Schottroff, Silvia Schroer, and Marie-Theres Wacker. Darmstadt. ET, 1998.

————. 1996. *Figurationen des Weiblichen im Hosea-Buch*. Herdes biblische Studien, vol. 8. Freiburg im Breisgau et al.

Willi-Plein, Ina. 1971. *Vorformen der Schriftexegese innerhalb des Alten Testaments. Untersuchungen zum literarischen Werden der auf Amos, Hosea und Micha zurückgehenden Bücher im hebräischen Zwölfprophetenbuch*. Beihefte zur Zeitschrift für die alttestamentliche Wissenschaft, vol. 123. Berlin et al.

Winter, Urs. 1987. *Frau und Göttin. Exegetische und ikonographische Studien zum weiblichen Gottesbild im Alten Israel und in dessen Umwelt*. Orbis biblicus et orientalis, vol. 53. 2nd ed. Fribourg.

Wolff, Hans W. 1982. *Dodekapropheton 4. Micha*. Biblischer Kommentar, Altes Testament, vol. 14, 4. Neukirchen-Vluyn.

FOR FURTHER READING

Bail, Ulrike. 2004. *"Die verzogene Sehnsucht hinkt an ihren Ort". Literarische Überlebensstrategien nach der Zerstörung Jerusalems im Alten Testament*. Gütersloh.

Baumann, Gerlinde. 2003. *Love and Violence: Marriage as Metaphor for the Relationship between YHWH and Israel in the Prophetic Books*. Translated by Linda M. Maloney. Collegeville, Minn.

Ben Zvi, Ehud. 2000. *Micah*. Grand Rapids.

Gruber, Mayer I. 2007. "Women's Voices in the Book of Micah." Lectio difficilior 1. http://www.lectio.unibe.ch/07_1/mayer_gruber_womens_voices.htm.

Kessler, Rainer. 1999. *Micha*. Herders theologischer Kommentar, Altes Testament. Freiburg im Breisgau, Basel, Vienna.

Maier, Christl M. 2008. *Daughter Zion, Mother Zion: Gender, Space, and the Sacred in Ancient Israel*, esp. 55-59. Minneapolis.

Waltke, Bruce K. 2007. *A Commentary on Micah*. Grand Rapids.

Translated by Nancy Lukens

Nahum: The Just God as Sexual Predator

Gerlinde Baumann

Theme and Historical Context of the Book

The book of Nahum places images before the eyes of the reader — images of war, images of desolation and horror, images of violence, destruction, and ruin — of the men and women of Judah and their land, and of the personified city of Nineveh. Armies fight battles, lions tear prey, Nineveh lays Judah to waste, YHWH avenges Nineveh, and swarms of grasshoppers lay Assyria to waste. However, this horror scenario is depicted in poetic language.

The general consensus of researchers is that the core material of the book originated in the mid–seventh century B.C.E. Parts of it contain "genuine" prophecy, in that it predicts the fall of Nineveh prior to its historic fall (612 B.C.E.). "Nineveh," in its characterization as a female personification of the capital city, stands for the entire Neo-Assyrian Empire. Nothing is known about the prophet Nahum (from *nḥm*, "to comfort") other than his place of origin, Elkosh (Nah 1:1; cf. Dietrich 1994, 739), the exact location of which is unknown. Nahum raises his voice in the midst of Judah's oppression by Assyria. The book can be understood as the impotent cry of a prophet who longingly wishes for the draconian punishment of the oppressors in view of the excessive suffering of his people.

My examination of Nahum will include current historical-critical scholarship, particularly of the book in its final textual form. I shall engage in a conversation with the text as a document of its time and context. In particular I shall pay attention to the feminine metaphors around the personified city of Nineveh. My hermeneutical perspective is one of feminist liberation theology, and in the case of Nahum in particular, ideology criticism.

Structure and Content of the Book

After the heading (1:1), the book is introduced in its final textual form with the "acrostic" psalm of Nahum 1:2-8. Thus, the beginning of each line consists of a consonant, following the order of the Hebrew alphabet. With the help of older Israelite traditions and motifs, the text describes YHWH's power and glory, strength and victorious justice. Scholars regard Nahum 1:2-8 as an addition to the book from the exilic or postexilic period, especially because of its style. As a result of this thinking, it has also been assumed that the tension between the YHWH of the beginning of the book, who is expressly praised as just, and the violent YHWH of the visions that follow was added in the exilic to postexilic period.

The acrostic psalm breaks off after the letter kaph (2:8). Is this break intended to indicate what awaits the readers in the further course of the book — the description of similarly "cutoff" lives, lives ended too early and by violence? Does the praise of God become stuck in the throats of those uttering it when they consider the horrors that then follow? The text does not expressly answer these questions. But since Nahum is a book conceived in poetic language, it can be assumed that the structure of the text is intended to convey such a message.

The psalm is followed first by six verses the contextual reference of which is not utterly clear: Nahum 1:9-14. In 1:10 the text is scarcely logically translatable in its mixed metaphors of "thorns" *(sîrîm)* and drunkenness (from the root *sb'*). Nineveh is presumably being addressed in 1:11, though this is not explicit; likewise in 1:14, where great devastation is predicted. The lines in between, 1:12-13, make sense only if they refer to Judah, which is promised an end to its suffering.

There follows in 2:1, 3 a promise of salvation to Judah. The joy to be awaited here is not unbroken; the verses alternate with a prediction of devastation, the Nineveh poem in 2:2, 4-11 with its graphic, bloody vision of conquering the enemy's capital city. Feminine metaphors for Nineveh are found already in 2:7-11. Sanderson (1992, 217) sees in this figure a representation of the city goddess of Nineveh, Ishtar. This feminine personification is depicted here as one who sees herself as unprotected, vulnerable to violence. The imagery here already suggests that the "woman" Nineveh experiences sexual violence (Magdalene 1995, 333): the "gates" of Nineveh are "opened" (2:7). She is "bared" (*glh*, 2:8;[1] see the discussion of 3:5 below), while only her slave women can still sigh (2:7). But no one pays attention any longer to her cry for help (2:8). After the violence and the plunder (2:9), the state of Nineveh is described in a string of superlatives that breaks forth like stammering: "devastation, desolation, destruction" (2:10a).

Once again the text turns its interest toward Assyria's past. Like a lion, the great empire has robbed (*ṭrp/ṭerep;* 2:13-14; 3:1) and devoured everything it could hunt down (2:12). Another word of judgment over Nineveh in 2:13 begins with the

---

1. The root *glh* is often translated as "exiled" but can also mean "exposed."

same words as the description of the act of sexual violence toward Nineveh in 3:5-7: "See, I will come over you[2] — says the LORD of hosts." "Over you" (*'ēlayik; 'el* in the sense of "against"), when used together with "see" *(hinĕnî)*, always has YHWH as subject (Jer 50:31; 51:25; Ezek 13:8; 21:8 [Eng. 3]; 34:10), who takes revenge for injustice mostly with warlike actions.

Once again in Nahum 3:1-3, the taking of Nineveh, the "city of bloodshed" (3:1), is lamented in descriptive litany. Again (as in 2:10) the description ends by stammering in the face of the sheer scale of devastation of war:

> many pierced-through,[3]
>> heaps of corpses,
> dead bodies without end —
>> they stumble over the bodies! (3:3)

In 3:4-7 the book's imagery of sexual violence becomes more dense; the next section will look more closely at these verses. First, Nineveh is typified (3:4) as a "beautiful whore."[4] She is sexually violated (3:5-6) until she is "devastated" and no comforters can be found to bemoan her (3:7).

Nahum 3:8-19 then returns to a more argumentative style. The text reminds us of the fate of the city of No-Amon, the Egyptian Thebes, which was conquered by the Assyrians in 663 B.C.E. Thus Nineveh — already in ruins — is mocked by comparison with the fallen city of Thebes. Once again the writer resorts to a similar set of metaphors to those at the beginning of the book, to "drunkenness" (3:11; cf. 1:10) as a sign of helplessness and "gates of your land wide open" (3:13; cf. 2:7[6]). The land is unprotected (3:15-17) and being laid waste by swarms of grasshoppers eating it bare. Powerless rulers and a disparate people that no one gathers together any more (3:18): those who had been enslaved before by the powerful and much-feared king of Assyria are now clapping their hands over his destruction (3:19). This ironic lament of the dead (3:18-19) even outdoes the utter lack of redemption in 3:7b; for Assyria/Nineveh all that remains in the end are mockery and derision.

Nahum 3:4-7: Sexual Violence by YHWH against the Personified City of Nineveh

The clearest instance of sexual violence against the personified city of Nineveh is described in 3:4-7. These verses are likely part of the original prophecy of Nahum.

2. German: "Siehe, ich will über dich (kommen)" (2:14 and 3:5). NRSV has "See, I am against you" (2:13 and 3:5).

3. NSRV translates "piles of dead."

4. The author's argument builds on a translation of the Hebrew text that uses much stronger wording than the NRSV.

Here YHWH is characterized in the image of a man who perpetrates sexual violence against the personified woman Nineveh. While traditional exegesis has not seen this as a problem, here feminist criticism sets to work with its particular tools. How is this violence described?

> 4 Because of the countless debaucheries of the prostitute,
>   gracefully alluring, mistress of sorcery,
> who enslaves nations through her debaucheries,
>   and peoples through her sorcery;
> 5 See, I will come over you,
>   says YHWH of hosts,
>   and will lift up your skirts over your face;
>   and will let the nations look on your nakedness
>   and the kingdoms on your shame.
> 6 I will throw filth at you
>   and violate you [NRSV: treat you with contempt]
>   and make you a spectacle.
> 7 Then all who see you will shrink [in disgust] from you and say:
> "Nineveh is devastated; who will nod [show sympathy] toward her
>   [NRSV: bemoan her]?"
> Where shall I seek comforters for her?

The first thing that occurs in 3:4 is the shift to sexual metaphors, which then function to interpret the punishment inflicted on Nineveh. Nineveh is given the title of prostitute, whore *(zônâ)*. This naming is frequently used in the First Testament in the context of metaphors of sexual violence, for example, in Isaiah 47, Jeremiah 13, Ezekiel 16 and 23, and Hosea 2 (cf. Gordon and Washington 1995, 319-21 as well as the relevant essays in this volume). In addition, there are ancient Near Eastern parallels in curse formulas from treaties that characterize the city found deserving of punishment for disloyalty as a prostitute (Magdalene 1995, 343-46). Nahum 3:4 raises the additional charge of "sorcery" *(kešep)*. It is also found in Isaiah 47:10-15, for example, in the context of the punishment of the "daughter Babylon" through the use of sexual violence. The charge is furthermore intended to discredit the female figure being punished as a religious misfit and thus to reinforce the legitimacy of the act of violence.

Nahum 3:5aα again takes up the phrase "See, I will come over you" from 2:14(13). Then follows the description of the scene of sexual violence. In 3:5aβ Nineveh is "bared" *(glh);* the verb was used in 2:8 already in a different form. In the context of sexual violence, *glh* occurs in the First Testament much more frequently: Isaiah 47:2-3; Jeremiah 13:22; Ezekiel 16:36-37; 23:10, 29; and Hosea 2:12(10). In Nahum 3:5ab *glh* occurs together with *šûlayik,* "your skirts/hems." The same expression is used also in Jeremiah 13:22 in relation to Jerusalem. In this context it becomes crystal clear what is happening: the personified city of Jerusalem is being raped by "her" suitors. Thus one can assume a similar action for Nahum 3:5aβ.

With the motif of uncovering one's "shame, or private parts," Nahum 3:5bα repeats a word that occurs in other texts as well as in situations of rape. The word *'erwâ* (also meaning "shame, or private parts") is from the same root as *ma'ar;* it is used together with *glh* in Leviticus 18:20 and Ezekiel 22 in connection with coitus, and in Isaiah 47:3; Ezekiel 16:37; 23:10, 29 in the context of humiliation. Its connection with Nahum 3:5a points to an act of sexual violence. Nahum 3:5bβ, with the word "defamation" *(qālôn),* emphasizes that the purpose of the action is primarily a matter of degradation and devaluing. Sexuality is merely the means to that end.

In 3:6 the word *nbl II* is chosen; it means "to disgrace, reject, or consider worthless." The comparable occurrences of the verb in Deuteronomy 32:15, Jeremiah 14:21, and Micah 7:6 have no explicit sexual connotation. The verb emphasizes the degree of degradation and destruction that Nineveh experiences through the sexual violence of YHWH. However, the noun *nablût**, derived from *nbl II* and not unambiguously translatable, occurs only once in the First Testament in Hosea 2:12(10) in the context of sexual violence.

In Nahum 3:7aβ the verb *šdd* must be especially noted. It means "to experience military defeat, to be raped" and implies a complete destruction of the person in question or his or her being.

Finally, in 3:7b the consequence of sexual violence is spelled out: no one can be found any more to comfort Nineveh. Possibly the use of the participle of the verb *nḥm* (comforting) constitutes an allusion to the prophet's name Nahum *(naḥûm):* whereas YHWH appears as (avenging) God of Israel through the "comforting" Nahum, there is by contrast no comfort left for the raped city of Nineveh.

Feminist Theological Analysis

The description of the act of sexual violence against Nineveh in Nahum 3:4-7 avails itself of certain typologies frequently used in the First Testament. We cannot understand the contemporary historical implications of these typologies without understanding their contemporary-historical context. However, this representation of violence has an equally powerful effect in today's understanding. There are at least two levels of meaning on which one can interpret the text, which must be differentiated.

Nahum's metaphorical language should first be considered in the framework of the time in which it was written. Here YHWH and Assyria/Nineveh are personified and represented as man and woman within patriarchal gender roles. According to these patterns, the "woman" as a city is also always subject to the "man" as God, or, as his wife, she is considered his property. In the ancient Near East there was no such thing as protection for women comparable to the contemporary right to bodily freedom from harm or sexual self-determination. This is all the more the case for prostitutes, whose sexuality would not be controlled by a man.

In the context of that time, rape was not considered a violation of the raped woman, but "theft of sexual property" (Thistlethwaite 1993, 62-63), a crime of theft against the man as owner of the woman. In this respect, rape was also a means of humiliating other men (Magdalene 1995, 336-41). Sexual violence against a prostitute was not a crime, since a prostitute was not the property of any man (Magdalene 1995, 341). A further legitimization of sexual violence occurs in Nahum 3:4 with the typology of the woman victim as "beautiful" whore: the "desire" that is the basis for the rape in this way of thinking is caused by the beauty of the woman. The man acting violently in this case is merely "reacting" more or less "naturally," with uncontrollable desire that expresses itself through violence. From a contemporary feminist perspective, all these objectifications and degradations of women are just as worthy of rejection and condemnation as the assumption that rape is a matter of a predominantly sexual act that serves to satisfy the male. Sexual violence and rape are genuinely misogynous acts of violence whose purpose is to injure or destroy the body and soul, the dignity and integrity of a woman.

The Problem of the Image of God in Nahum

In the prophetic vision, YHWH is seen as the victor who demonstrates his superiority over his Assyrian opponents, among other things by acts of sexual violence against the enemy city, the metaphorical "woman." In so doing, he humiliates the king of Assyria and demonstrates to him his weakness. The kingdom is no longer capable of protecting its capital, its "woman," from attacks. In the context of wars in the ancient Near East, the punishment of the conquered people by raping their women was more the rule than the exception. In that context, the YHWH characterized by Nahum as a man within a patriarchal way of thinking acts violently, but consistently within this pattern. Furthermore, YHWH behaves within a framework of legality, since he does violence to a "prostitute." In favor of such an interpretation is the fact that the psalm added to 1:2-9 in the exilic-postexilic period praises YHWH as a good and just God; this allows no voicing of doubts in the justice of God's actions.

Today the role of YHWH as a perpetrator of sexual violence takes on a different dynamic. Under today's legal conditions, YHWH's action in 3:4-7 would have to be condemned as a rape or a war crime. The text can be used as a divine legitimization or even as an encouragement for male sexual violence against women (cf. Sanderson 1992, 221), especially in view of still patriarchal contemporary male socialization that encourages boys to violate sexual boundaries (Heiliger 1996,

208-17). The thought pattern in Nahum agrees to a horrifying degree with the attempts of contemporary rapists to legitimate their actions: a woman who arouses the rage of a man must be punished by sexual violence (cf. Seifert 1997, 487-88).

How Can the Book of Nahum Be Read?

The prophet Nahum speaks from the perspective of a male Judean, that of a tortured man who lives amidst the violence of war. He wishes his inability to protect himself and his family from the Assyrians' violence would be turned into the opposite and that, instead, God would be capable now of inflicting the violence that they have suffered on the personified city of Nineveh.

In my view, it is this perspective of those who were once victims, and are now perpetrators, that the text wants its readers to assume. It is the way from powerlessness to (male) superpower. However, as a woman who is always potentially threatened with sexual violence on the basis of my gender, I cannot count on the solidarity of this God who himself commits sexual violence. A "woman" is broken in Nahum 3:4-7 by means of a kind of violence that is perpetrated especially on women. The primary possibility for identification for women today in the text is with the former perpetrator Nineveh, not with the rehabilitated Judah. Thus "perverted," the text is distorted for women readers (Sanderson 1992, 219). It cannot be understood as comforting by contemporary (potential) female victims of war or violence, but only as an affront toward God in the face of their suffering. Male readers will experience the text differently if they assume the role, for example, of soldiers and therefore perpetrators, so that they can play out wishful revenge fantasies in reading the sexual violence scene. The book has in fact been read in such a gender-specific way, as shown by Seifert (1997, 296), who cites the example of Karl Elliger's commentary (1982, 19), which expresses admiration for Nahum's description of violence.

Feminist researchers suggest that one should "resist the metaphors" of such texts as Nahum (Gordon and Washington 1995, 323-25; Magdalene 1995, 352). Phyllis Trible prepared the way for such an approach to violent texts of the First Testament. "To resist the metaphors" means, when applied to Nahum, not to understand the passage about the sexual act of violence against the personified city of Nineveh or the Assyrian kingdom as a description of a "metaphorical" sexual act of violence, but as a representation of sexual violence against a particular woman. This way the metaphor that is so disastrous for women in our context, the metaphor that gives divine sanction to the violence perpetrated against them, is brought back into the social context in which it arose, so to speak, namely, into the concrete life of women. By bringing the text back into its social context, we can regain the memory of the suffering of real women. After all, there were cases of sexual violence in the lives of real women behind the texts that reference sexual violence, such as Nahum 3:4-7. The frequency of such texts in the First Testament points to this fact. This suffering can be allowed to stand on its own as factual suffering without trivializing it by using it as a metaphor, at least in certain contexts. In Ezekiel 16 the raped sister of Judah is later "restored," which could create the illusion that this is possible with women of flesh and blood. Through such a reading, what had been a text of revenge becomes one of lament, lament over the lives of women in past and present damaged by sexual violence. Now readers can take up an appropriate attitude toward the victims of sexual violence, that of mourning, of compassion, and of empathetic silence.

Beyond these points for discussion, there are other possible interpretations of the text I would like to point out. They begin with the scope and complexity of the violence of Nahum, of this book that simply rocks with violence. Violence is described in drastic colors and in diverse contexts: the violence of oppression, the corresponding violent reaction in the conquering of a city by burning; sexual violence against the hated enemy Nineveh; violence in the form of images of the lions and swarms of grasshoppers that were feared by people at that time. Through these images Nahum can lead us to two further ideas.

First, the Nahum narrative weaves together the diverse forms of violence. Like a net, they drape themselves over a perspective on life so that it becomes so narrow that it sees nothing but violence, oppression, and revenge. Sexual violence against women, Nahum demonstrates, is woven into other contexts of violence. From a feminist and liberation-theological perspective, Schüssler Fiorenza (1994, 95-96), for example, points out that violence against women seldom occurs in isolation. Violence is encouraged, or even made possible in the first place, by oppressive social structures that can manifest themselves in various ways. In the book of Nahum the oppression of patriarchy is closely tied to the tyranny of a despotically ruled state. This observation can, if applied to current situations, lead to an analysis of violence against women and children that more forcefully insists on considering its social context. Structural or systemic violence privileges individual violence; it creates the climate in which individual violence thrives and can be lived out (Brown 1994, 109-10). To work more effectively against individual acts of violence, more far-reaching structures of violence must be taken into consideration.

Secondly, violence always brings forth a violent reaction — at least among those who can defend themselves. Nahum shows no way out of violence. If one takes Nahum's way of dealing with violence through to its logical conclusion, one arrives at nothing but more and more new violence, more brutal and more horrible than what went before. Violence escalates if it is answered with violence. In this respect, Nahum rides the violence horse to death, so to speak. The book goes no further than this point. We ourselves, the readers, must go further and seek ways beyond violence. Without these, without our search, there will be no end to violence.

LITERATURE

Brown, Joanne Carlson. 1994. "'Mit Rücksicht auf die Engel.' Sexuelle Gewalt und sexueller Mißbrauch." *Concilium* 30:108-14.

Dietrich, Walter. 1994. "Nahum." In *Theologische Realenzyklopädie*, 737-42.

Elliger, Karl. 1982. *Das Buch der Zwölf Kleinen Propheten. II. Die Propheten Nahum, Habakuk, Zephanja, Haggai, Sacharja, Maleachi.* Altes Testament Deutsch, vol. 25, 2. 8th ed. Göttingen.

Gordon, Pamela, and Harold C. Washington. 1995. "Rape as a Military Metaphor in the Hebrew Bible." In *A Feminist Companion to the Latter Prophets*, edited by Athalya Brenner, 308-25. Feminist Companion to the Bible, vol. 8. Sheffield.

Heiliger, Anita. 1996. "Jeder Mann ein potentieller Täter? Männliche Sozialisation und sexuelle Übergriffe auf Mädchen und Frauen." In *Skandal und Alltag: Sexueller Mißbrauch und Gegenstrategien*, edited by Gitti Hentschel, 203-19. Berlin.

Magdalene, F. Rachel. 1995. "Ancient Near Eastern Treaty-Curses and the Ultimate Texts of Terror: A Study of the Language of Divine Sexual Abuse in the Prophetic Corpus." In *A Feminist Companion to the Latter Prophets*, edited by Athalya Brenner, 326-52. Feminist Companion to the Bible, vol. 8. Sheffield.

Sanderson, Judith E. 1992. "Nahum." In *The Women's Bible Commentary*, edited by Carol A. Newsom and Sharon H. Ringe, 217-21. London and Louisville.

Schüngel-Straumann, Helen. 1975. *Israel — und die anderen? Zefanja. Die Propheten Nahum, Habakuk und Obadja. Jona.* Stuttgarter Kleiner Kommentar Altes Testament, vol. 15. Stuttgart.

Schüssler Fiorenza, Elisabeth. 1994. "Gewalt gegen Frauen." *Concilium* 30:95-107.

Seifert, Elke. 1997. *Die Verfügungsgewalt der Väter über ihre Töchter im Alten Testament. Eine ideologiekritische Untersuchung zur Tochter-Vater-Beziehung und zur Vater-Tochter-Beziehung in Erzählungen, Rechtstexten und Metaphern des Ersten Testaments.* Neukirchen-Vluyn.

Seybold, Klaus. 1989. *Profane Prophetie. Studien zum Buch Nahum. Stuttgarter.* Stuttgarter Bibelstudien, vol. 135. Stuttgart.

Thistlethwaite, Susan Brooks. 1993. "'You May Enjoy the Spoil of Your Enemies': Rape as a Biblical Metaphor for War." *Semeia* 61:59-75.

Trible, Phyllis. 1984. *Texts of Terror: Literary-Feminist Readings of Biblical Narratives.* Overtures to Biblical Theology, vol. 13. Philadelphia.

————. 1990. *Mein Gott, warum hast du mich vergessen! Frauenschicksale im Alten Testament.* 2nd ed. Gütersloh and Munich.

FOR FURTHER READING

Baumann, Gerlinde. 2003. *Love and Violence: The Imagery of Marriage for YHWH and Israel in the Prophetic Books.* Collegeville, Minn.

————. 2005. *Gottes Gewalt im Wandel. Motivik und Theologie von Nahum 1,2-8 — eine intertextuelle Studie.* Wissenschaftliche Monographien zum Alten und Neuen Testament, vol. 108. Neukirchen-Vluyn.

Chapman, Cynthia R. 2004. *The Gendered Language of Warfare in the Israelite-Assyrian Encounter.* Harvard Semitic Monographs, vol. 62. Winona Lake, Ind.

Fabry, Heinz-Josef. 2006. *Nahum*. Herders theologischer Kommentar zum Alten Testament. Freiburg im Breisgau.

O'Brien, Julia Myers. 2002. *Nahum, Readings: A New Biblical Commentary.* London and New York.

Translated by Nancy Lukens

Habakkuk: A Political Night-Prayer

Ulrike Bail

In July 1940 the ecclesiastical journal of the city of Basel is censored by the Swiss military censor. The reason is a passage from Habakkuk printed under the heading "Word on the (Current) Situation," which the censors found could no longer be read as "neutral" (Vischer 1958, 40). Thus the military censors read the Habakkuk passage as current resistance literature against the National Socialist terror regime.

The book of the prophet Habakkuk has as its theme various dimensions of violence and the rule of violence. It names not only societal and social ills, lack of justice, and exploitation, but also terror, war, and violence in the international sphere. As clearly as Habakkuk points to the scope of violence on the one hand, he leaves the historic subjects of this violence equally unclear on the other. To be sure, the *kaśdîm* (Chaldeans), that is, the Babylonians, appear in Habakkuk 1:6, but they can also be understood as symbolic of the aggressive expansionist policies of other superpowers. Already in antiquity the book of Habakkuk was read as commentary on the current time. The commentators of Habakkuk in Qumran (*Pesher Habakkuk* 4.5) recognize the Chaldeans as the Kitteans (Cypriots), that is, Greeks or Romans (Lohse 1964, 230-31). The Septuagint locates Habakkuk as a contemporary of Daniel in the Babylonian exile (Septuagint: Bel and the Dragon). Discussions in the literature about the historical context of Habakkuk assign it to various historical locations, which one can also interpret as giving it a contemporary meaning, albeit after the fact. Attempts to date the text range from the late reign of King Manasseh, to the time of Kings Josiah, Jehoiakim, and Zedekiah, down to the exilic and late exilic period, in each respective case naming the corresponding ag-

---

Translator's Note: "Political Night Prayer" *(Politisches Nachtgebet)* was the name of a late-night liturgy introduced in September 1968 at the general assembly of German Catholics in Essen by an ecumenical group around Dorothee Sölle. The group's intention was to bring the Vietnam War into reflection in light of biblical texts and meditation. Beginning in October 1968, similar sessions were held monthly in Cologne, and the themes expanded to include other concerns. The meditations are published; thus the name and the model have become widely known since the 1970s.

gressor superpowers such as the Scythians, Medes, Babylonians, Persians, Greeks, and Romans (cf. Jöcken 1977).

There are as many hypotheses about the book's literary cohesion as there are about where to locate the book historically (cf. Mason 1994, 66ff.). One hears different voices in the book, but their entry is hardly ever clearly marked in a certain place. "The scribes and editors responsible for preparing the canonized version of traditional text saw in 'Habakkuk' something like the written by-product of a dialogue in which several voices from different times took part" (Seybold 1991, 51). In my opinion, the individual voices are not strengthened by literary-critical attempts to separate them into individual passages or by text-critical corrections, but rather by listening for associations between themes, motives, and key words within the book and between this book and other texts of the First Testament. For example, just as God's words are differentiated from those of the prophet (cf. 1:5, 12), it is very striking how the individual voices flow into one another as if they were composed into, over, and against one another. One hears not only voices of accusation and complaint, but also voices of wisdom, hymnlike, liturgical and prophetic voices that are connected by a fine net of key words and connecting motifs. In a wider context one also hears among these voices those from Qumran and the voice of Paul (Rom 1:17; Gal 3:11).

This chapter attempts to read Habakkuk as an open score of a conversation with God that demands a reply, a conversation in which other voices are heard beside, with, and against that of Habakkuk. Because it offers only vague information about its historic time and place, Habakkuk practically begs to be read against the background of whatever the current situation might be. Its structure and language open it for the participation of other voices — including contemporary voices — in the conversation with God.

But who is this prophet Habakkuk who speaks with these different voices? The heading calls the book a vision[1] that the prophet Habakkuk saw. The meaning of the name Habakkuk is uncertain. It could be derived from the verb "to embrace" *(ḥbq)*. Széles (1987, 5) takes this etymology a step further by saying the name could be understood to mean that Habakkuk shares the suffering of his people, taking it in his arms, but also that he struggles with God in his complaints and accusations against God (cf. Gen 32:23-31). A different etymology derives the name from an Assyrian garden plant *(hambaûku)*, which was possibly used as a herbal curative plant (Széles 1987, 5).

If one makes the connection between Habakkuk's name and his message, one could say that in a certain way Habakkuk is embraced by the pain of what he sees and that he desperately seeks healing. He cannot turn his eyes away from the wrongdoing in the national and international sphere. The sense of sight plays an

---

1. NRSV: "oracle"; Bail: "Lastspruch" — "an utterance laying a charge"; Luther translated the term similarly: "Klage" — a charge. [Translator's note.]

important role in his prophecy. Words having to do with seeing occur with far greater frequency than words for hearing. God is for Habakkuk also "not a God who listens but one who sees" (Keller 1973, 159; cf. especially Hab 1:3; 1:13; also the light phenomena that occur with God's appearance in chapter 3). Habakkuk is not a neutral observer, but one who, while standing at his observation post, is imprisoned by his perspective (2:1). As a victim of violence, his gaze is fixed on catastrophe. He sees reality with eyes that suffer from violence and injustice, and he brings this in a complaint before God. At the same time he accuses God because he must see injustice:

> Why do you make me see wrongdoing
>> and look at trouble?
> Destruction and violence are before me. (1:3)

With this question Habakkuk puts into words his vision of the reality of violence. But at the same time he contradicts the totality of this reality by expressing his vision before the God who cannot look on wrongdoing, whose eyes are too pure to behold evil (1:13). Here we also hear Hagar's voice, who likewise calls God a God who sees (Gen 16) — a God who sees misery and intervenes in a liberating way.

From a feminist perspective, violence is always gender-specific and must be differentiated, since women are affected by violence differently than men. In patriarchal social systems, women are subject to the violence of male power over their bodies, their freedom of movement, and their social status.

Habakkuk's visual description of social relationships of violence culminates in this statement:

> So the law becomes perverted [NRSV: slack]
>> and justice never prevails. (Hab 1:4)

The instructions of the Torah have no power any more, the law is manipulated, and violence is the order of the day. As applied to women, this could mean that a commandment such as the protection of widows (Exod 22:21 [Eng. 22]; Deut 10:18; 24:17-22; Ps 146:9) is perverted to bring about its opposite.

The aggressive superpower, too, which brutally invades and conquers the land, is characterized by injustice. It defines justice by its own power (Hab 1:7). Its might is its god and compassion is a foreign concept (1:17). The transition from seeing social violence to seeing the violence of war, which also marks a shift from the words of the prophet to those of God (1:4-5), strikes one as very muted. Without any clear signals we go from the prophet's vision to God's words, from the description of social violence in the land to that of war making by an aggressive superpower. Both relationships of violence are characterized by the fact that the justice that makes peace possible has become perverted.

Seen superficially, Habakkuk contains no notable gender-specific analysis of violence. The totality of terror and brutality (cf. the animal images in 1:8) is in the foreground of the views of violence. It is as if the victims of this violence are imprisoned in a net and cannot escape (1:14-17). Their dwellings and cities are being occupied, their land conquered (1:6), and they themselves are taken captive. These effects of war on the population affect both sexes and are clearly expressed. This must not necessarily be seen as a defect of the text; one can fill in the gaps with experiences of war specific to women as they are formulated in other texts. In the process of the violent conflicts of war, women are kidnapped and enslaved (Judg 5:30; Jer 8:10-12), and torn away from their children (Mic 2:9; Jer 18:21). "Sexual assault and brutal murder of pregnant women were very likely part of how armies in the ancient Near East fought their wars" (Schroer 1995, 122; ET, 1998, 124; cf. 2 Kings 8:12; 15:16; Hos 14:1 [Eng. 13:16]; Isa 13:16; Jer 8:10; Lam 5:11). Compared to other prophetic writings, Habakkuk strikingly does not use the metaphor of the faithless city as a woman, Jerusalem, who is therefore conquered and raped, language that must be considered sexist and pornographic (cf., for example, Jer 13:26; Ezek 16:36-42; Hos 2:5-15[3-13]; Nah 3:5 in reference to Nineveh). Habakkuk's vision of violence does not exclude the experiences of women, but gives them space through his open language.

Habakkuk does not dismiss God from these experiences of social violence and the violence of war. He interprets the catastrophe as God's working in history (Hab 2:13). But rather than taking the role of a passive victim or turning his eyes away from the terror, Habakkuk demands an answer from God to his accusation: "Why do you look on the treacherous, / and are silent?" (1:13).

I will keep watch to see what he will say against/through me,[2]
and what he will answer concerning my complaint. (2:1)

To a certain extent Habakkuk struggles with God about the appropriateness of the means of punishment. "[I]f violence within Judah is bad, it should not be punished by worse violence from people who worship their own might" (Sanderson 1992, 223). God's justice stands in contradiction to what Habakkuk envisions.

The hope that a word from God will oppose this reality does not allow Habakkuk to close his eyes to violence and leave his "observation post." Yet God's answer redirects Habakkuk's gaze by telling him to write the vision of hope on tablets so that it can be read or called out (the Hebrew verb *qr'* has both meanings). Recording the vision in writing ensures that an end to the terror will in fact come. Hope only becomes possible when people's ability to see, which has been bound up by the catastrophe, is restored by the vision of the possibility of an end to violence. Even if the promised end to violence and terror brings hope to the edge of

---

2. NRSV: to me.

despair because it cannot yet be seen, but only read (or called out) as a promise, life is possible by holding fast to this hope (2:4). It is only the written vision that seems to free the people's perspective on violence, and thereby allow the expression of hope for an end to violence, hope for liberation.

The five cries of woe that follow (2:6-20), against greed for goods and for power, against brutality in carrying out large construction projects, against boundless violence against people and animals, and against idolatry, may refer to internal and external political structures of violence and oppression. The voices of these cries raise a lamentation for the dead, a "pre-emptive lamentation over someone still alive" (Seybold 1991, 69). These lamentations bring attention to actions destructive to community by characterizing the perpetrators of violence as fictive dead people. In this way the evildoing is dramatically brought into the present, and grief is expressed over asocial behavior.

In the First Testament, the lamentation is primarily the task of women (cf. Jer 38:22; 49:3; Ezek 8:14; 32:16; Amos 8:3; 2 Sam 1:24; Lam 1:18-22; Judg 11:40; cf. Jahnow 1923, 59; Jost 1995, 145-53), and it is passed on by women from generation to generation (Jer 9:19[20]). Jost argues, in view of the frequency of "lamentation and in association with it the naming of women as the ones lamenting in the context of prophetic proclamation, that women play a more powerful role within the prophetic movement than is visible from the texts that explicitly name women prophets" (Jost 1995, 135 n. 165). Thus it would be conceivable that women's voices, too, are heard in the chorus of voices of Habakkuk, through the medium of its lamentations for the dead.

Chapter 3 gives voice to Habakkuk's imaginative vision of liberation from terror and oppression. This chapter is a prayer of Habakkuk in which he challenges God "in wrath [to] remember mercy" (3:2) and to come forth to save his people (3:13). What is being described is a theophany or epiphany of God on a cosmological scale. God has the power to set creation into chaos, and he has the power to break the might of the evildoers. His horses and chariots (3:8) prove superior to the brutal Chaldean cavalry of 1:8. But by means of the clear reference to the exodus events, God is not characterized in completely militaristic terms: "With your horses you prepare the way through the sea" (3:15; cf. 3:13).[3] God's cosmological victory over the "chaotic enemy power of the mighty waters" (Seybold 1991, 81) relates to the liberation from slavery in Egypt. As God acted at the Sea of Reeds (Red Sea) to liberate Israel, so God now acts anew to lead Israel into freedom and peace. It is a matter of the rescue of a brutally conquered and oppressed people.

Many women reject violence as a means of conflict resolution and seek other models that avoid violence and oppression. On these grounds many reject biblical traditions that speak of violence. But "[I]t is all too easy for those who are in the luxurious position of not having to defend themselves and their very existence

---

3. NRSV: "You trampled the sea with your horses, / churning the mighty waters."

against violence to take strong positions" (Schroer 1994, 685). In biblical tradition it is often women who celebrate the military victories with drumming, singing, and dancing (Exod 15:19-21; Judg 11:34; 1 Sam 18:7). The relief of having escaped violence may be a factor in this. But another factor is that women do the work of grieving for the dead (Jer 9:17-21; 2 Sam 21). Their lamentation performs the function of ensuring "that people will remember those who have disappeared and died, and will not be at rest until the guilty parties are held accountable" (Schroer 1994, 681).

Habakkuk voices his hope for an end to the terror and violence in a prayer. He speaks out of a situation of fear and powerlessness. In situations of suffering, such texts can be the last thing that people who fear for life and limb "have left — as protest, accusation and cry for help. It follows as a matter of course that these texts are legitimate as they arise in this context from the lips of the victims, but spoken by the perpetrators are blasphemous" (Zenger 1994, 693). In situations in which even the stones cry out from the wall and the wooden beam joins in (Hab 2:11),[4] everything is invested in the hope that someday joy and jubilation will again be possible because God will come to their rescue. The book of Habakkuk gives witness to the fact that this hope must again and again be expressed liturgically in contemporary terms as a lamenting-accusing conversation with God (cf. the liturgical instructions in 3:1; 3:3; 3:9; 3:13; 3:19). Thus the book can be called a "political night-prayer" that lives in the tension between lamentation, accusatory outcry, and liberating hope:

> Why do you make me see wrongdoing
>   and look at trouble?
> Destruction and violence are before me. . . .
> Why do you look on the oppressor,[5]
>   and are silent? (1:3, 13)

> Yet I will rejoice in God
>   and exult in the God of my salvation.
> GOD, the Lord, is my strength;
>   he makes my feet like the feet of a deer
>   and makes me tread upon my heights. (3:18-19)

LITERATURE

Jahnow, Hedwig. 1923. *Das hebräische Leichenlied im Rahmen der Völkerdichtung.* Gießen.

Jöcken, Peter. 1977. *Das Buch Habakuk. Darstellung der Geschichte seiner kritischen*

---

4. NRSV: "and the plaster will respond from the woodwork."
5. NRSV: "the treacherous."

Erforschung mit eigener Beurteilung. Bonner biblische Beiträge, vol. 48. Cologne and Bonn.

Jost, Renate. 1995. *Frauen, Männer und die Himmelskönigin. Exegetische Studien.* Gütersloh.

Keller, Carl-A. 1973. "Die Eigenart der Prophetie Habakuks." *Zeitschrift für die alttestamentliche Wissenschaft* 85:156-67.

Lohse, Eduard, ed. 1964. *Die Texte aus Qumran. Hebräisch und deutsch.* Munich.

Mason, Rex. 1994. *Zephaniah, Habakkuk, Joel.* Sheffield.

Sanderson, Judith E. 1992. "Habakkuk." In *The Women's Bible Commentary,* edited by Carol A. Newsom and Sharon H. Ringe, 222-24. London and Louisville.

Schroer, Silvia. 1994. "Gott — gewalttätig? Frauen und die Gewaltfrage im Ersten Testament." *Katechetische Blätter* 119:676-86.

———. 1995. "Auf dem Weg zu einer feministischen Rekonstruktion der Geschichte Israels." In Luise Schottroff, Silvia Schroer, and Marie-Theres Wacker, *Feministische Exegese. Forschungserträge zur Bibel aus der Perspektive von Frauen,* 83-172. Darmstadt. ET, 1998.

Seybold, Klaus. 1991. *Nahum. Habakkuk.* Zürcher Bibelkommentar Altes Testament, vol. 24, 2. Zurich.

Széles, Mária Eszenyei. 1987. *Wrath and Mercy: A Commentary on the Books of Habakkuk and Zephaniah.* International Theological Commentary. Grand Rapids and Edinburgh.

Vischer, Wilhelm. 1958. *Der Prophet Habakuk.* Biblische Studien, vol. 19. Neukirchen.

Zenger, Erich. 1994. "Der Gott der Bibel — ein gewalttätiger Gott?" *Katechetische Blätter* 119:686-96.

Translated by Nancy Lukens

Zephaniah; or, The Threefold Jerusalem

Ulrike Bail

Zephaniah — the prophet with the lantern in the streets of Jerusalem. This is how the prophet Zephaniah is portrayed in medieval Christian iconography (Zeph 1:12). The medieval line *dies irae, dies illa* from the *Requiem for the Dead* of the Roman Missal can be traced back to him. It is a text full of rage and judgment. Both reminiscences, taken together, allow the dark image to emerge of a person crying out in the streets and houses of Jerusalem to announce a martial razzia of God on the day of wrath. Does this image match the content of the prophetic book of Zephaniah? Is Zephaniah 1:12 the key verse for the whole book? Who is the prophet whose name can be translated "YHWH hid/protected"?

The medieval Christian reception of the book reduces its message to the pronouncement of judgment and punishment. But a close reading of the prophetic book shows a wealth of theological statements that cannot be reduced to the *dies irae* message. Zephaniah accuses the Jerusalem upper class of injustice and of oppressing and exploiting the poor. He criticizes accommodation to "alien" customs in the cult practices and everyday life. He speaks in military images of God's judgment against his own people and against foreign peoples; he demands a humane and just social order in the hope that destruction might perhaps be averted. He speaks of the remnant of Israel that will survive the judgment, of the conversion of the peoples, worldwide peace, and the end of poverty, and he outlines the "project of a society without social distinctions or domination" (Gorgulho 1991, 85).

The message of the prophet is not linear; the threefold prophetic scheme of announcement of doom for Israel, doom for the foreign peoples, and salvation for Israel does not occur in such clear form. The individual parts of the book are constructed concentrically. A long process in the tradition of the text formed the prophetic book, reworked its production and reception, and updated it (Lohfink 1984; Weigl 1994; Zenger 1995). Its origins date presumably from before the exile into the time of the exile. This is reflected in the shifts of emphasis within the book. Threatening words are followed by promising words; future times are a central theme and then — read from the point of view of the book's conclusion (3:16-20)

— are understood as past times. God speaks alternatively in the first-person singular and then as a prophetic voice from the perspective of an observer. Threatening, satirical (Seybold 1985), comforting, and rejoicing voices can be heard. The prophetic voices speak within differing discourses in order to react to the failure of the Jerusalem elite and the threat of Assyria. These discourses are woven together in the motif of the "day of God" (NRSV 1:14: "The great day of the LORD"), which is expressed in cosmic, topographic, and military as well as sociological terms. At the same time, the day of God cannot be clearly fixed in any particular time frame. Instead, it is a time in which places and groups of people are reevaluated and brought into different relationships with one another; a time in which — metaphorically speaking — the margins move to the center. Jerusalem as center, and the center of Jerusalem, is the main theme of the book. Both in terms of content and topography, this is the focus of the whole book. But the quality of the center can only be determined by defining the relationship between the center and the spaces surrounding it. One must look at how the center relates both to the margins that are closer in and those more distant; how the center relates to the people who act in certain ways at the margins and in the center. Jerusalem as center holds within itself the potential for both violence and justice.

Zephaniah, a Prophet of Ethiopian Origin?

The heading of the book locates Zephaniah's origin four generations back, which is unusual for a prophet. Accordingly, the prophet would have been speaking during the rule of Josiah (641-609 B.C.E.). There is controversy about any more precise dating of his activity (Zenger 1995, 421; Mason 1994, 35ff.; Seybold 1991, 87-88). Mason argues against the attempts to locate the book in a specific historic period by asserting that the principal interest of the prophetic message is theological, not historical, and that there are too few historical references (Mason 1994, 41-42). "It is probably a mistake to attempt to isolate a prophet, and certainly a prophetic book, in a single historical context. Whoever he was and whenever he lived, tradition saw him as a much more universal figure who went on speaking to each successive generation; and the book reflects this belief. The force of his message for their own day was the readers' concern, not his personal biography of the history of the times in which he lived" (Mason 1994, 43).

Nevertheless, there remains a tension between the first and the last name of the genealogy of the prophet, between his father Cushi, possibly a black Ethiopian, and his great-great-grandfather Hezekiah, possibly king of Judah. The research resolves this tension by assigning the name Cushi to a Bedouin tribe, by attributing no ethnic relevance to it at all (cf. Rudolph 1975, 258-59), or by not identifying Hezekiah as a king. However, some have considered whether the name Cushi is not significant after all. Sanderson sees Cushi as a black slave in Jerusalem (Sanderson

1992, 225). Rice sees Zephaniah as a prophet of Israel with Ethiopian and royal ancestry (Rice 1979/80). Feminist exegesis emphasizes that the categories of gender, social position, and ethnic origin of an author relate to his or her literary work. Thus the social and ethnic location of the prophet Zephaniah in Jerusalem society would be of crucial importance. But aside from the observation that Zephaniah is well informed about the topography of Jerusalem and the dominant elite (royal court, officials, priests, prophets, merchants) and has a certain interest in Ethiopia (Zeph 1:1; 2:12; 3:10), nothing can be said about his person.

Whether his Ethiopian origins possibly indicate a marginalized position in society and whether this can be connected substantively with a reevaluation of the poor as a historic force for liberation from imperialistic domination (see Gorgulho 1991) must remain an open question.

"I Will Cut Off from This Place . . ." (1:4)

> I will gather up everything, yes, everything,
>> and remove it from the face of the earth![1]

Thus begins Zephaniah. While in this opening line we hear an association with "harvest," reading further leads us to understand God's action in reality as destruction, as a taking back of creation (1:2-3). The totality of the animal world (animals on the land, in the air, and in the water), the earth *('ădāmâ)*, and human beings *('ādām)* is affected. Also mentioned are those (third-person feminine plural) who "cause the wicked to stumble" (1:3). To avoid the irritation of this feminine ending, editors frequently attempt to conjecture the following reading: "I will make the wicked stumble," or omit it entirely as an act of textual criticism (see examples in Rudolph 1975, 259-60; Weigl 1994, 5-6). Does the participle refer to the animals, "in which case the writer is thinking of images of gods in the form of animals and with heads of animals (as in Egypt)" (Rudolph 1975, 262; Seybold 1991, 92; Weigl 1994, 8), or is the writer thinking of female human beings? If so, which ones, and what are they doing, exactly? It seems that no answer is possible; what remains is the question, the irritation.

Into this cosmic dimension comes the threat to Judah and Jerusalem that begins with verse 4:

> I will stretch out my hand against Judah,
>> and against all the inhabitants of Jerusalem;
> and I will cut off from this place

---

1. NRSV: "I will utterly sweep away everything / from the face of the earth, says the LORD." Our more literal translation includes the reference to the harvest metaphor.

the priests who change the religious practice (1:4-5), and those who carry on this practice and who, according to the prophet, "have turned back from following the LORD" (1:6); the court society that has taken on alien ways and whose behavior is characterized by fraud and violence (1:9); rich men who misuse God to legitimate uninhibited amassing of capital (1:13), and wealthy homeowners. The list of figures among the political and religious leadership in Jerusalem is continued in chapter 3. There, too, their asocial behavior is criticized. The princes, the judges, the prophets, and the priests are all criticized and their downfall is foretold. They are to be removed from the city of Jerusalem: "For then I will remove the arrogant braggarts from your midst" (3:11).[2]

The day of God is not a generalized day on which the world will come to an end; instead its criterion is justice. Zephaniah does not separate religious and societal behavior; social status and the relationship to God belong together. Recognizing this makes it impossible to avoid seeing that the social and religious elite is characterized by injustice, dishonesty, and violence, and uses an alleged silence of God to legitimize their actions (1:12). The prophet does not find trust in God or observance of his community-building ordinances among the elite of society. Thus he sees a connection between social status and the relationship to God.

On the day of God, justice will enter into the middle of Jerusalem (3:5).[3] The lanterns God uses to search out the exploitative and unjust political and religious elite to call them to account have their counterpart in the light that is associated with God's justice, which he brings every morning (3:5). The day of the Lord does not bring the same thing for every man and woman; it has different outcomes for those who stomp on social justice and community and for those who live at the margins of society, poor and powerless (cf. Ebach 1985).

"I Will Leave in the Midst of You a People, Lowly and Impoverished"[4] (3:12)

While the rich and powerful are told they will be driven out of the midst of Jerusalem, the poor and lowly remain in the center of Jerusalem (3:12). The words *'ānî* and *dal* indicate an economic situation rather than referring to a mental attitude.

> The context does not allow the widespread view that the text refers only to humble people, the "poor in spirit" or those "poor in the eyes of God," rather than to truly impoverished people. Such ideas do exist throughout the ancient oriental world, but this context does not indicate their presence here. The narra-

2. NRSV: "for then I will remove from your midst / your proudly exultant ones."
3. NRSV: "The LORD within it [Jerusalem] is righteous; / he does no wrong."
4. NRSV: "humble and lowly."

tive speaks of real rich people and thus also of real poor people, and it is only on condition that this is understood that the connection can be made to the attitudes of pride and humility. This applies to all parts of the book. (Lohfink 1984, 107 n. 6; cf. Gorgulho 1991, 83-84; Weigl 1994, 258ff.; on the other hand see Neef 1996, 154)

The beginning of the section about the poor (2:1) provides further evidence for understanding the poor as socially marginalized groups. The verb *qšš* signifies the "activity of people existing at the margins of society" (Weigl 1994, 269). In Exodus 5:7, 12 as well as in 1 Kings 17:10, 12 *qšš*, meaning "the gathering of stubble and straw," refers to forced labor by exploited people. In Exodus 5, Pharaoh increases the repression and exploitation of the laborers by no longer delivering straw to the Israelites, so that they must gather it themselves in laborious effort. In 1 Kings 17, the verb refers to utmost physical distress and poverty of the widow of Zarephath. The Israelite slaves in Egypt and the poor widow of Zarephath provide concrete examples to illustrate who the poor are in Zephaniah: women and men at the margins of society and surviving at a marginal level (cf. Bird 1996, who, in contrast, believes the prophetic reference to the poor always means the poor man). The place of the poor and those at the margins is juxtaposed to the "midst" of Jerusalem. A life in the midst of excess and power is contrasted with a life at the margins of survival; Jerusalem as a traditional place of the presence of God is juxtaposed with a place outside, in the country, where God is present in the form of his just order.

But it must also be said that being at the margins does not in itself bring salvation. To be sure, the prophet sees God's justice *(mišpāṭ)* being realized there (Zeph 2:3), but the oppressed people in this place are challenged to turn to God:

> Seek the LORD, all you humble of the land,
>   who do his commands;
> seek righteousness, seek humility;
>   perhaps you may be hidden
>   on the day of the LORD's wrath.

Salvation is preceded by a "perhaps," and the "perhaps" is preceded by the seeking of God. But this means recognizing God's presence "as source of justice on all levels of economic, political and ideological life. . . . Seeking justice means changing the entire social structure of domination" (Gorgulho 1991, 84-85).

The process of transformation that allows the center of the city to become a place of peace and truth (3:13) begins at the margins, where no silversmiths are at work but where, on the contrary, straw is gathered for survival. No longer will the rich and the violent inhabit the center of the city, but justice (3:5), God as king (3:15), and the lowly and humble (3:12). Jerusalem will become the place where there will finally be no more oppression or exploitation, no deceit or lying, no act of violence or poverty. Even if the prophet hopes for God's presence solely among the poor and lowly, this does not imply a legitimization of poverty. Poverty and closeness to God are not automatically connected with one another. "God does not want the end of his ways with his people to be misery, but wealth and blessing" (Lohfink 1984, 108) — but this orients us toward God's justice and law — "which can be described in the image of a herd of sheep moving across the meadow and lying down in the evening without having to be afraid of being startled out of their sleep (3:13b)" (Lohfink 1984, 108). A radical social and political shift precedes this peace — a change of conditions that Hannah sings about in 1 Samuel 2.

"And to Him Shall Bow Down, Each in Its Place, All the Coasts and Islands of the Nations" (Zephaniah 2:11)

It is not only nationally defined spaces that Zephaniah organizes around Jerusalem as center; he also includes the neighboring peoples of Israel in his view (2:4-15). He names the peoples in all four directions of the compass, and threatens them with destruction: the Philistines to the west, the Moabites and Ammonites to the east, the Cushites to the south, and Assyria and Nineveh to the north. They will all be laid waste and become uninhabitable, steppe-like landscapes. While the geographical focal point of this listing of place-names is Jerusalem, in terms of textual structure, the actual midpoint of the text is 2:11c. Where the east-west axis and the north-south axis meet, the text mentions the islands of the peoples:

> And to him shall bow down,
>   each in its place,
>   all the coasts and islands of the nations. (2:11)

This creates a tension between the nearby regions, on one hand, and the islands, the "coastal margins of the earth" (Seybold 1991, 107; cf. Lohfink 1984, 104; Weigl 1994, 127ff.), on the other, between the threat of destruction close by and the turning to God in distant places. And these faraway marginal zones are brought to the center of the text, as it were, right next to Jerusalem.

In the midst of the destruction, Zephaniah names places where there is hope for salvation and preservation: "Not in the center, in the metropolis of Jerusalem, and not among the peoples surrounding Judah, but precisely in those places where one would least expect it: among the 'poor of the land'[5] (Zeph 2:1-3) and — literally — at the end of the world (Zeph 2:11)" (Weigl 1994, 134). Both marginal groups become "allies" who have a positive relationship with God. Chapter 3 clearly says these marginal groups will move to the center (3:10, 12). Beginning with the peo-

---

5. NRSV: "humble of the land."

ples at the greatest distances, the peoples of the world will call upon the name of God, will honor God with one voice (Hebrew: shoulder to shoulder) (3:9), and will bring offerings to God from afar (3:10).

As the margins become the center, the center is changed. Jerusalem is no longer the city characterized by violence, oppression, deceit, and exploitation, but a city in which God and his justice dwell. It is only with the orthopraxis of the marginalized that Jerusalem becomes a place where God's presence is realized as justice and peace.

Desolate Cities and a Threefold Jerusalem

The threat of destruction of the Philistine cities in the west (2:4) is described with the words:

> For Gaza shall be deserted,
>   and Ashkelon shall become a desolation;
> Ashdod's people will be driven out at noon,
>   and Ekron shall be infertile.[6]

Through literal translation of the text, it becomes clear that the fate of the cities is being described as women's fate (Seybold 1991, 104-5; 1985, 43ff.). The cities are compared to an abandoned (*'zb*), and therefore vulnerable, woman, a desolate woman who has been raped (*šmm*) (cf. Bail 1998, 196ff.), one who has been driven out or deported (*grš*), and finally to an infertile (*'qr*) woman who has no future any more. In several places in the Hebrew Bible, a conquered and destroyed city is brought into the picture personified as a woman who suffers (sexual) violence (e.g., Lamentations; Nahum; cf. Seifert 1997, 237ff.; Bail 1998, 175ff.). Is this a way of calling attention to the fate of real women when cities are conquered, or is the suffering of these women rendered invisible precisely by the female personification of the city as an abstraction of real women?

Jerusalem, too, is characterized as a city personified as a woman. In Zephaniah 3:14 she is addressed as "daughter" and called upon to rejoice and be glad about her salvation. Seifert (1997, 292) points out that these words of the prophet nevertheless presuppose the androcentric idea that without God, the daughter Jerusalem/Zion remains without protection. The city as woman "appears as a daughter who is completely dependent on the satisfaction and care of her father: She was ashamed of her deeds when YHWH was angered about her behavior and punished

---

6. The German text has gender-specific feminine forms and images for all three cities where the NRSV uses adjectives: Gaza is *eine Verlassene,* a deserted woman; Ashdod is referred to as *sie* (she); and Ekron is "infertile," where the NRSV has "uprooted."

her. After her successfully completed punishment, she no longer needs to be afraid. Because YHWH is again pleased with her and is once again by her side, all distress has ended (cf. Zeph 3:17)." It is striking, however, that the book of Zephaniah only begins to speak of the personified daughter Jerusalem/Zion when Jerusalem has become a city of justice (3:14). Violence, oppression, and the unlawful amassing of capital and real estate are attributed solely to concrete male groups of the population. Jerusalem "seems to be more than the sum of its evildoers for the prophet" (Weigl 1994, 262). Only when these have been removed from the city can Jerusalem become a city of social justice with open gates. The men and women living there can be compared with the Israelite slave men and women in Egypt and with the widow of Zarephath. They are the marginalized people of that time, the women, men, and children driven to the margins. Zephaniah's speaking about Jerusalem is not one-dimensional; he seems to speak in several discourses. Jerusalem is not only a daughter, but it is more than the sum of its male evildoers, being described in both urban and rural *topoi*.

The series of cities and peoples listed in Zephaniah 2 finds its culmination in the description of the destroyed and desolate *(šmm!)* city of Nineveh. It has become a desert, a city of ruins uninhabited by human beings. Here, too, there is a hint of personification of Nineveh as a woman when we read in Zephaniah 2:15:

> Is this the joyous city
> > that sat secure on her throne,
> who said in her heart:
> "I and no one else!"[7]

But she, too, is desolate and abandoned, and calls forth terrified horror. Zephaniah 3:1 then introduces a lamentation over a dead city. Only in reading further does it become clear that the text no longer refers to Nineveh, but to Jerusalem. Between the lines, Jerusalem is put on an equal footing with Nineveh, with radical clarity, rendered even stronger by the cry of lament "Woe" *(hôy)*. The narrative creates an "associative bridge" (Lohfink 1984, 104) between Nineveh and a city that is still alive, but full of violence, whose death is being lamented. In this subtle, underhanded way, Jerusalem's alternatives are announced in drastic terms.

Yet still another image is added. Jerusalem is introduced in Zephaniah 3:1 in a cry of lament for the dead containing three participles. This linguistic usage opens up several semantic possibilities: "Woe! Soiled/glittering and defiled/redeemed, the city of violence/a dove!"[8] "Depending on how they are pronounced, the words used here change their meaning. . . . In this way the saying becomes transparent,

---

7. NRSV: "Is this the exultant city / that lived secure, / that said to itself, / 'I am, and there is no one else'?"

8. NRSV: "Ah, soiled, defiled, / oppressing city!"

and two images of the city become visible. One in the foreground is of a dirty, guilt-ridden, violent city in the present; another in the background is a glorious, redeemed and beloved ('dove' as term of affection) city of the past. A third image is suggested in the cry of lament: a dead city of the future. That is the history of Jerusalem in images" (Seybold 1991, 110; cf. Seybold 1985, 55-56; Weigl 1994, 135ff.).

Jerusalem in itself does not possess the qualities of salvation or the presence of God. The city's territory is open in three directions. It will become an uninhabitable desert if it continues to harbor violence and oppression within its walls, or it can become a peaceful and nonthreatening place of grazing if it allows justice and lawfulness to dwell in its midst. A third dimension announces itself between the lines: Zephaniah holds fast to the vision of Jerusalem as the city of God, a vision nourished by his past experiences and pointing to the future. The physical space of the city itself, however, bears no character. It depends on the human beings and what they fill it with — the religious and political elite with violence, exploitation, and wealth on the one hand, or the impoverished at the margins of society with lawfulness, integrity, and social justice on the other. Zephaniah hopes for the presence of God in the city, contrary to all experience; he desperately hopes that God will turn the fate of humankind (Zeph 2:7; 3:20). Reading from the perspective of the beginning of the book, the prophet's writing makes every hope appear unfounded, and the day of God would seem to be the end of life on earth. Reading with the end of the book in mind, however, the day of God proves to be a new beginning that transforms Jerusalem into a city to which it is said:

> As king of Israel God is in your midst;
>   you need fear/see no more evil.[9] (3:15)

Zephaniah sketches three Jerusalems: a city filled with deeds of violence and injustice whose circles of leadership he radically criticizes; a city in which a universal peace is realized and whose margins — the impoverished women and men bent with shame and the distant islands — become its center; and a Jerusalem where through the interplay of memory and hope is created a place of God's presence and the presence of human beings who make this presence concrete in the form of lawfulness and justice.

LITERATURE

Bail, Ulrike. 1998. *Gegen das Schweigen klagen. Eine intertextuelle Studie zu den Klagepsalmen Ps 6 und Ps 55 und der Erzählung von der Vergewaltigung Tamars.* Gütersloh.

Bird, Phyllis A. 1996. "Poor Man or Poor Woman? Gendering the Poor in Prophetic Texts." In *On Reading Prophetic Texts: Gender-Specific and Related Studies,* edited by

---

9. NRSV: "The king of Israel, the LORD, is in your midst; / you shall fear disaster no more."

Bob Becking and Meindert Dijkstra, 37-51. Festschrift for Fokkelien van Dijk-Hemmes. Leiden, New York, and Cologne.

Dietrich, Walter, and Milton Schwantes, eds. 1996. *Der Tag wird kommen. Ein intertextuelles Gespräch über das Buch des Propheten Zefanja.* Stuttgarter Bibelstudien, vol. 170. Stuttgart.

Ebach, Jürgen. 1985. "Apokalypse. Zum Ursprung einer Stimmung." *Einwürfe* 2:5-61.

Gorgulho, Gilberto. 1991. "Zefanja und die historische Bedeutung der Armen." *Evangelische Theologie* 51:81-92.

Lohfink, Norbert. 1984. "Zefanja und das Israel der Armen." *Bibel und Kirche* 39:100-108.

Mason, Rex. 1994. *Zephaniah, Habakkuk, Joel.* Old Testament Guides. Sheffield.

Neef, Heinz-Dieter. 1996. "Glaube als Demut. Zur Theologie des Propheten Zephanja." *Theologische Beiträge* 27:145-58.

Rice, Gene. 1979/80. "The African Roots of the Prophet Zephaniah." *Journal of Religious Thought* 36:21-31.

Rudolph, Wilhelm. 1975. *Micha. Nahum. Habakuk. Zephanja.* Kommentar zum Alten Testament, vol. 13, 3. Neukirchen-Vluyn.

Sanderson, Judith E. 1992. "Zephaniah." In *The Women's Bible Commentary,* edited by Carol A. Newsom and Sharon H. Ringe, 225-27. London and Louisville.

Seifert, Elke. 1997. *Tochter und Vater im Alten Testament. Eine ideologiekritische Untersuchung zur Verfügungsgewalt von Vätern über ihre Töchter.* Neukirchener Theologische Dissertationen und Habilitationen, vol. 9. Neukirchen-Vluyn.

Seybold, Klaus. 1985. *Satirische Prophetie. Studien zum Buch Zefanja.* Stuttgarter Bibelstudien, vol. 120. Stuttgart.

————. 1991. *Nahum. Habakuk. Zefanja.* Zürcher Bibelkommentar, Altes Testament, vol. 24, 2. Zurich.

Weigl, Michael. 1994. *Zefanja und das "Israel der Armen". Eine Untersuchung zur Theologie des Buches Zefanja.* Österreichische biblische Studien, vol. 13. Klosterneuburg.

Zenger, Erich, et al. 1995. *Einleitung in das Alte Testament.* Kohlhammer Studienbücher, vol. 1, 1, 418-22. Stuttgart, Berlin, and Cologne.

Translated by Nancy Lukens

Haggai and Zechariah: A New Temple — New Life for All

Beate Schmidtgen

At first glance the books of Haggai and Zechariah do not deliver much for feminist exegesis. Women do not appear at all in Haggai and only barely in Zechariah; in standard commentaries they are altogether passed over. Hence, there is hardly any feminist literature on these two books. As is the case for other biblical writings, one has to work here with the "hermeneutics of suspicion," that is, to search for traces of women's history by reading these books against the text.

The Books

The book of Haggai is the first in a group of three writings: Haggai, Zechariah, and Malachi. They all share the same theme: the new ordering of political, social, and religious life in Judah (Jerusalem) after the Babylonian exile. The symbol for the new beginning is the rebuilding of the temple.

The postexilic texts of the Hebrew Bible reflect the religious-cultic and political conflict between the *gôlâ*, the people returning from the exile, and the population that had remained in Judah. This thesis is fundamental for the reflections about the origin of Haggai and Zechariah. But there are also problems between a group that leans more strongly toward the priests and another, more politically oriented group; both originate in the *gôlâ*, but perhaps from two different waves of returnees.

Haggai is a very short prophetic book: it has only two chapters. It is structured formally by its precise dating in the reign of the Persian king Darius. Both chapters begin with a specific date, each introducing a complex of prophetic speeches about the rebuilding of the temple that had been delayed on account of the grave economic situation of Judah and Jerusalem.

The first part of Zechariah is also about the building of the temple (Zech 1–8). The so-called night visions (1:7–6:8), eight in number, describe the divine preparations for the return of YHWH to Jerusalem. Chapters 7 and 8 are in the form of prophetic speech; as commentary on the visions, they interpret history: the exile and the new future of the people.

Zechariah 9–14 was composed in view of Haggai and Zechariah 1–8 and is closely related to other prophetic traditions. In this part of the book, the building of the temple no longer plays a role, but the era of well-being to come is tied as ever to the universal significance of Jerusalem. Even though some of Haggai's and Zechariah's expectations did not come true, the eventual victory of YHWH is sure. This hope shapes the final six chapters of the book.

Zechariah also has some formal elements that allow for an arrangement of it in two or three larger sections. The structures of Haggai, such as dating in terms of the reign of Darius, are found in Zechariah 1–8, while the structures of Zechariah 9–14, namely, the arrangement according to the "sayings," are found again in Malachi. The break between chapters 8 and 9 notwithstanding, there are thematic conformities between the two parts of Zechariah as well as references to Haggai and Malachi. Both books address the theme of cultic feasts, but only Zechariah makes use of the metaphor of the city as a woman. All three books contain the promise that the land will be blessed and fruitful after the temple has been rebuilt.

Historical Background

Haggai describes the economic situation circa 520 b.c.e.; it is desolate. Poor harvests, caused by droughts, have led to high prices for food and clothing. Income can barely cover daily necessities. The situation is aggravated by the groups of returnees who, according to Ezra 2 (→ Ezra and Nehemiah), are said to have numbered almost 50,000 people. It is not clear whether that figure includes women and children. In Haggai these groups are referred to as "all the remnants of the people" (e.g., Hag 1:12). Whenever they are mentioned, it is always together with their political and religious representatives, Governor Zerubbabel and High Priest Joshua. It is plain in the texts that the returnees are thought to be superior to the people who had remained in Jerusalem as far as politics and religion are concerned. The book of Haggai is shaped by that conflict; it can be seen also in Zechariah.

But the situation in Zechariah has changed in comparison to that in Haggai. Now the temple is being rebuilt; Zerubbabel has laid the cornerstone, and the completion of the building is expected within his term of office. Beginning with chapter 9, references to actual persons disappear, the historical background cannot be determined to the same extent as in the first two parts, and both the language and content of those six chapters are shaped increasingly by eschatological images.

Composition

It is unlikely that in their present form the two books go back to individual prophetic figures as authors or redactors. It is more likely that the text emerged from the theological and political activities of several persons.

At least two literary layers can be discerned in Haggai. The younger layer — the one that produced the present version — strongly emphasizes the chronological fixation of tradition. To it we owe the dates and the audience of the older prophetic activities and speeches that are framed by the younger layer of redaction.

It is generally assumed that these dates are historically valid and were already contained in an older version of the texts. In my view, they are more likely "theological" dates meant to relate the prophetic sayings to specific feasts such as Succoth and the consecration of the temple.

The difference in how people are named is also important. In the younger layer, Zerubbabel, Joshua, and Haggai are addressed curiously by their full titles. But within the older prophetic sayings, Zerubbabel alone is named and never addressed by his title (Hag 2:4 and 23). Besides the whole people, he is the only one addressed and is accorded an inclusive divine legitimation through the address "my servant" (2:23). In the younger layer, his political function is important. The new figure of Joshua the high priest is placed next to him. And both are associated only with one part of the population: "All the remnant of the people."

One suspects that this redaction is meant to give prophetic legitimation to the claim of one of the groups of returnees that they are the political and religious leaders. It is clothed in the argument that some prophetic figure had recognized this even before the temple rebuilding had begun.

Zechariah 1–8 reinforces this thesis. The sayings and visions of the prophets are framed by dates that correspond to those in Haggai. But in Zechariah it becomes clearer that those sayings and visions were collections gathered and unified later under one date. Thus, one has to think of them as a number of reworkings particularly in relation to the "night visions" (Zech 1:7–6:8).

The vision in Zechariah 3 that deals with the installation of the high priest Joshua next to the servant of YHWH into the functions of priest and judge is clearly secondary. In contrast, Zerubbabel is spoken of repeatedly in his function as the master builder of the temple without any mention of Joshua whatsoever (4:5-10). An attempt to mediate between the two parties is found in 6:9-15 (especially in v. 13). One may conclude from this that chapters 1–8 were also reworked by a group strongly interested in a settlement between the followers of Zerubbabel and those of the high priest. The texts show that the redactors sought to achieve this by working the figure of the high priest into the existing material. A comparison of it with the redaction of Haggai is in place here. It was most likely the work of priestly circles. And it is possible that their redactors' activity was connected with a failed political action of Zerubbabel.

Not a trace of something like this can be found in the texts beginning in chapter 9. Instead, they refer back to Haggai and Zechariah 1–8, thereby connecting all three parts.

Eschatology

The expectation of imminent salvation characterizes Haggai and Zechariah 1–8. These texts are written for people suffering under the desolate situation where elementary necessities of life are no longer being met (Hag 1:6; 2:16; Zech 8:10). Parallel to the economic situation is the political one, which, despite relative improvements, is still marked by oppression, the danger of war, and experiences of violence (Hag 2:21-22; Zech 2:1-4, 12, and 14). The texts address that situation with the pledge of YHWH that he stands by his people and, as their king, stands up against the nations (Zech 2:4-5; 9:9-13). That may take the form of war or it may be that the nations will make the "pilgrimage to Zion" (Zech 8:20). When YHWH shall reign, it is expected that finally there will be peace and prosperity for his own people, but that will also have repercussions the world over. But the precondition for God taking the reign is that the temple's rebuilding has begun.

Zechariah 9–14 has fewer concrete things to say about the future but makes use of more general eschatological imagery and sayings. The night visions in particular depict the rebuilding of Jerusalem as an event being prepared and supported by the domain of the divine. The activities of humans correspond to those of God. This shows that divine action takes place on earth, that is, within history and not in some new aeon yet to come, as some apocalyptic writings maintain.

The peace that will come to Jerusalem is painted not only in dramatic scenes but also in calm pictures that mirror day-to-day life in the city: children playing in the streets, old people in doorways and town squares (Zech 8:4-5). The presence of girls and old women, of boys and aged men in public life outside the home is perfectly normal and a sign of peace. There is no danger in the streets, and their families need not rely on them for support. The future is visible in the young women and men (Zech 9:17). In verses where concrete expectations are expressed, both sexes are spoken of — true well-being exists only when both share in it in common. As long as there is any inequality, this future has not yet arrived.

Over against this vision of well-being stands the depiction of the conquest of Jerusalem (Zech 14:2). What awaits women and their families in times of war is painted in shrill realism: "The city shall be taken and the houses looted and the women raped; half the city shall go into exile."

What we read here is what effect war and peace have on the civilian population, but especially on women and children.

The Significance of the Temple

Why is rebuilding the temple so important? In the first instance, the temple is the symbol of the new situation in Jerusalem and Judah. Politically dependent on the supreme ruler of Persia, national identity is transferred from the palace to the temple. The liberal politics of religion exercised by the Persian government not only makes this shift easier but actually advances it. At the same time, political-historical expectations are transferred to the domain of cult and religion that, combined with older elements of the tradition about Zion, fuels the anticipation that Jerusalem will have a central cultic position for the whole world. Secondly, the specific function of the temple is as important as its symbolic function. The temple's administrative body can contribute decisively to how pressing problems are dealt with. This body has to see to it not only that all cultic activities and the worship of God are properly carried out but also that the oversight of the property and income of the temple are attended to, as these two are important aspects of the temple economy. The temple priesthood can thereby intervene in the entire economic domain and regulate it. But all these obligations can be met only when the religious administration functions and is located in a place recognized beyond ambiguity: the temple. Thus, the references to the economic problems "now" and the hopes for their solution after the rebuilding of the temple have throughout a real economic background. But this should not be overemphasized at the expense of the specifically religious aspects, for, in the perception of the world held by those who composed and heard these two books, the blessing and curse of YHWH encompass everything, including the economy.

The Book of Haggai

Haggai 1: Time

The concept of time has two different meanings in this book: "real" and "eschatological." Because "the times" are bad and the economic situation difficult, people believe that "the time" to rebuild the temple has not yet come. The prophet stands this argument on its head: "the times" are bad because "the time" to rebuild it has not been seized.

In the older version of chapter 1 (without vv. 1, 3, 12a, and 14), God appears in the prophet's speech as the plaintiff who lays this charge against those the prophet addresses. An analysis of the situation is appended to the charge; YHWH interprets the drought and economical hardship as punishment for neglecting to rebuild the temple. Haggai 1:11 uses "drought" in a variety of ways; here it means unsuccessful human labor and infertility. The Hebrew text does not distinguish here between men and women. For example, the intention is not to elucidate the action of YHWH in terms of the particular fate of a barren woman; the point is to differentiate in general between "human being" *(hā'ādām)* and animal. The sanctions of YHWH jeopardize the future of the people in every aspect differently than in war but just as pervasively. In accordance with older liturgical formularies, such as the so-called psalms of lament, when the people confess their transgression the promise of God's help is renewed. The redaction and its priestly orientation extend this liturgical answer in its own sense, for the acting subjects are limited to Zerubbabel, Joshua, and "the remnants of the people."

Haggai 2:10-14: Who Is Unclean?

There is much dispute among exegetes about the meaning of these five verses. Haggai asks the priests whether cleanness or uncleanness can be communicated by touch. They answer in the affirmative in relation to uncleanness. Haggai interprets this answer as follows: "So it is with this people, and with this nation before me, says the LORD; and so with every work of their hands; and what they offer there is unclean" (2:14).

Against the background of chapter 2, these verses may also be applied to the rebuilding of the temple. That chapter deals with the past and future glory of the temple. God causes the nations to come to the temple with their riches in order to adorn it appropriately, for it is at the center of the world. Like the first chapter, this one similarly describes the changed economic situation as promising: once the cornerstone has been laid, things will no longer be what they are now, for God will send blessings.

Many interpreters identify the people named in verse 14 as the Samaritans and base this on the request by the Samaritans to help rebuild the temple. Their request is turned down because they are unclean (2:10-14). The interpretation of Ezra 4 plays an important role here. However, Haggai makes no reference to Samaritans. There is no reason to think of the people here as other than those the rest of the book speaks to. The judgment of "unclean" applies to the population of Jerusalem and Judah.

The text clearly indicates two groups, which are described differently: the "(whole) people" and "(all) the remnant of the people." Both groups lay claim to being the people of God as indicated by their Hebrew designation *'am.* The "remnant group" may be counted among the *gôlâ.* The term "remnant" makes a link to Isaiah and other prophetic writings. The returnees understand themselves as those whom YHWH chose to be the new Israel and whom the exile purged of the guilt of their parents. Religious elitism stamps the self-consciousness of this group: it thinks of itself as the real people of God and debases others. In contrast, the "whole people" refers to those who had remained in the land; they too think of themselves as the Israel made new but are not perceived by the *gôlâ* as coequals. This conflict is mirrored in the book of Haggai.

Only once is "the whole people" spoken of in tandem with the synonymous

465

concept otherwise used for alien nations: "this people and this nation" (2:14). Uncleanness has made the people like an alien nation without direct access to God. There are various forms of uncleanness; the one found in this text is not gender-specific. Contact with the dead has made the people unclean. This implies that the whole people is to be understood as unclean.

What is at issue here is not how the people became unclean but, rather, the obvious fact (in the eyes of those who want the temple rebuilt) that the people and everything they do are unclean. The context of the accusation in chapter 1 suggests that as far as the prophet is concerned, the people are unclean because they have neglected their common obligations.

The Book of Zechariah

One of the special features of Zechariah is the long series of visions and sayings (1:7–6:8) known by their classic designation as "night visions." They comprise the largest connected complex of the first part of this book. The theme of the visions is the end of the exile and the conditions for "new" life in Judea. A section follows (6:9–8:23) that elaborates that theme in terms of a collection of sayings by YHWH (the so-called fasting discourse).

Zechariah 9–14 is divided into two blocks of sayings (9–11 and 12–14), although certain themes appear in both parts. The metaphor of the bad shepherd shapes one part of these texts, while the other focuses on the fate of Jerusalem and the cities of her enemies.

The Woman in the Ephah (Zechariah 5:5-11)

The vision of the woman in the basket, as told in this chapter, is commonly counted as the seventh night vision.

An angel calls the seer's attention to a flying vessel; as the cover of it is lifted, the figure of a seated woman emerges. The angel violently pushes her back into the vessel and seals it with a heavy cover. Two winged women carry the vessel away. Upon inquiring where they are taking her, the seer is told that she is being taken to the land of Shinar where a temple is to be built for her.

The interpretation of this narrative in the course of history is misogynist and anti-Jewish. The figures of the three women also created problems for exegetes. They gave rise to wild speculations such as Luther's (in his interpretation of the prophet Zechariah [Luther 1995]) or Rudolph's (1976, 119f.) where femaleness becomes identified with sin. Schöttler (1987, 134-40) sought to solve the problem of the woman; in her literary criticism she is removed from the vessel. But this only robs the story of its dynamism and intention.

In terms of the history of tradition in the Hebrew Bible, this text is difficult to place. It indeed gives rise to a wide range of associations, but its pictorial language is completely distinct. The concept of *rišʿâ* (godlessness) is characteristic of Ezekiel, and Zechariah's use of it in this text — the only place it occurs in the book — links him with that prophet.

The vision has different pictorial elements, but not all of them are interpreted in the text itself. In this passage, the envoy of YHWH who accompanies the prophet in all visions has a special function. He introduces the vision with the question that is otherwise raised by the one who has the vision: "What is it?" What the vision shows is clearly not obvious right away, so that the envoy's question has to point to it.

The first of these elements is an ephah (Zech 5:6), a vessel for measuring wheat; it has a capacity of about forty liters. It is to represent the "iniquity in all the land" (Uehlinger 1994, 95 differs). Most likely this picture expresses the people's fundamental failure to do God's will and not individual sinful acts. The ephah itself should not be seen as a sanctuary, since that would create an unnecessary duplication of sanctuaries in the text (contra Meyers and Meyers 1987, 296 and elsewhere; Glazier-McDonald 1992, 231).

The second element the text interprets is a woman (5:7). She sits in the vessel, and as its cover is lifted she becomes visible. Her name is *rišʿâ*, translated as "godlessness" in the Luther Bible; the word also means "wickedness" or "iniquity" in contrast to the derivatives of *ṣdq:* "righteous" (van Leeuwen, 1993, 813). The concept of *rišʿâ* has a religious but also a legal and moral dimension.

The next element is the two women who come and carry the vessel away. The interpretation provided is not about their action but about where they are taking the ephah. The destination is the land of Shinar, Babylon, the symbol of godlessness and iniquity. A house is to be built for her there and is to be her fixed abode.

Hanhart (1990-95) vigorously challenges the interpretation that the woman in the basket is a goddess. Yet he cannot put that view aside altogether. She is a caricature of a goddess who opposes the exclusive veneration of YHWH as was demanded vehemently in postexilic circles. In a grotesque representation, some material of Ezekiel's visions (Ezek 1; 10; 11; cf. Jeremias 1977, 195ff.) is adopted and alienated. The woman is taken by the winged women to the place where YHWH was in exile with his people. Contrary to the favorable treatment given goddesses and gods in processions, her voyage lacks every comfort and is almost unaccompanied. Uehlinger names this scene "deportation of the goddess."

There are vestiges of the woman's original divine status such as her "godlessness," her being transported by winged women, and the building of a house where she is to be set up. But in the eyes of the observer the woman in the basket is deprived of all divine dignity. She is so powerless that she can be pushed back into the vessel by the envoy and has no chance of liberating herself from her prison. In light of this and the fact that the woman is said to be immobile, Uehlinger sur-

467

mises that the vision is about an image of a goddess. That she is to be set up and secured in a newly built temple would also support this view (Uehlinger 1994, 96).

The designation *ris̆ʿâ* indicates that she personifies and is the cause of the sin in the land. In the Hebrew Bible, that sin is defined as forsaking YHWH and worshiping other male and female deities who bring social disorder and political chaos along with them. And so, the woman in the ephah may be said to exemplify the worship of other divine figures. The reason the figure is female may be that in Israel and Judah YHWH united in himself the veneration and attributes above all of male deities with the goddess being alive and well in popular piety as his "competitor."

The two carrier-women (Zech 5:9) belong to the tradition of other winged figures whose function as hybrid beings mediates between the divine and human spheres. But this is the single place in the Hebrew Bible that they are explicitly said to be women. Here they are portrayed as helpers of YHWH, but it is possible that their female gestalt is modeled on the goddess's female priests who go with her into exile.

The construction of a temple for the woman in Shinar (5:11) is the counter-image to the construction of the temple for YHWH in Jerusalem that preoccupies the book of Zechariah. The fact that the concept *bayit* is used in connection with both buildings supports that assumption. There is to be no more iniquity where YHWH reigns, and that is why her place is to be in Shinar where *ris̆ʿâ* reigns. But here too we see the effort not to ascribe divinity whatsoever to the former goddess. Nothing is said about venerating her; rather, she is to be firmly secured.

The vision, marked on the whole by a strong dynamic, comes to a rest only at the end. Her immobility and quasi imprisonment in a place designed for her stand as a stark contrast to the activity and mobility of those who engage themselves on the side of YHWH.

If this text is understood in the sense of the "deportation of the goddess," then it is indeed mockery of the goddess. Zechariah 5:5-11 portrays the process of her expulsion and thereby testifies to the fact that she was worshiped.

Rejoice Greatly, Daughter of Zion! (Zechariah 9:9-17)

The most widely known passage in Zechariah speaks to a woman (9:9-16). Verses 9 and 10 are applied in the Gospels to Jesus (Matt 21:1ff.; John 12:14) and are the direct source for the Christmas carol "Tochter Zion."

It is a matter of course that the book personifies the city as a woman; she appears as such in quite diverse contexts. And so we are now looking less at individual verses than at the book as a whole, for the contours of the text in question cannot be unambiguously demarcated. The theme of the personified city can be described as a complex of metaphors and is found predominantly in the Hebrew

Bible's prophetic and poetic texts. The purpose of Lady Zion/Jerusalem is above all to represent and evaluate the relation between YHWH and Israel/Judah. But the city/woman is not to be identified with the people; she is a distinct entity who acts independently and whose fate is clearly determined by conditions of women's life.

In biblical texts different aspects of the metaphor are used as needed so that the figure of the city/woman enters in the role now as daughter or wife, mother or widow and others. Every experience of a woman's life is reflected here, providing an abundance of potential identifications. But this is also exactly where the problem arises that readers today have with this metaphor: the male perspective on women's lives in a patriarchal society. Individual aspects are tied up in patriarchal criteria of judgment. When city/woman shows womanly behavior deemed to be bad, she is punished; she is rewarded when it is deemed to be good. And so normative elements are also embedded in the interpretation of history that inform readers of the texts how to behave and what sanctions they can expect when they disregard social norms. And, as a contrast, readers are offered, for purposes of identification, the role of sons or children of the city/woman, on the one hand, and the different roles attributed to YHWH such as father, husband, soldier, on the other. But it is also possible that, as in Hosea, attentive men pushed into the role of the woman, thus alienating the situation at issue.

In his choice of aspects, Zechariah aligns himself with the tradition associated with Isaiah, but there are also references to Ezekiel. This shows that the texts are rooted in different prophetic traditions.

The title "daughter" in conjunction with the name of the city signals the use of the metaphor. This key concept raises the question to what extent the metaphor figures in places that speak about a city but where it is not explicitly used. This is indeed not the case in every instance. The grammatical use of the feminine verbal and adjectival forms must be distinguished from the use of the metaphor. Still, the conception of the city as a woman is so strong that it reverberates even when the city is understood as a building (cf. Zech 2:4: "Jerusalem shall inhabit" instead of "Jerusalem shall be inhabited").

The negative side of the metaphor relating to who is responsible for the exile (→ Ezekiel) remains in the background among the numerous aspects in Zechariah. For what matters to him now is the proclamation of a new time of well-being that begins with the impending return of YHWH. For that reason, conceptions like daughter and mother are chosen because they may have positive meaning. The message of new well-being is addressed to Daughter Zion. She is to rejoice (9:9). She is to receive great compensation for all the suffering she had to bear. Lady Zion is a mother whose children, the *gôlâ,* return from an alien land (9:12). But she is to rejoice above all for the coming of YHWH her king. His impending arrival sets these events in motion.

Zechariah 9

By its very form, the whole of the ninth chapter sticks out from the rest of the book. It is a poetic text whereas all other chapters are in prose form. In its substance, chapter 9 represents something unique in the context of Zechariah of which thus far exegetes have not taken note. 9:1-8 contrasts the fate of different cities with that of Zion/Jerusalem. Even though none of the foreign cities are accorded the title of "daughter" or "virgin," they are all thought of as female persons. For example, Gaza's fears are described in terms of a concept that is often used in relation to labor pains (v. 5). The cities referred to stand in for the enemies of Israel but without any discernible connection to actual times. Every group has a particular fate. Damascus will pass without war into the domain of YHWH's reign. The cities of Phoenicia face losing their political autonomy while the cities of Philistia will have a status equal to that of Israel.

Where there was fear of the once enemy cities, there now is the joy and jubilation of Zion/Jerusalem (from 9:9 onward). In the context of the Daughter Zion metaphor, it is quite likely that the king who comes to Daughter Zion is YHWH himself. It is not Messiah who is spoken of here! The presentation of YHWH's arrival (vv. 9-10): that he comes in humility and promises to bring peace, contradicts the bellicose language of the next verses. There are also formally strong differences between the two parts such that the adoption of an older poetic text may be assumed here. Verses 11-17 continue to be marked by the image of Lady Zion, as the address in the form of the feminine singular indicates. Therefore, it is not Israel that is addressed in the passage beginning at verse 11. Verses 9-17 have to be understood as a unit.

The reason the *gôlâ* returned is said to be "the blood of my covenant" (v. 11). Israel is not the only (male) covenant partner of YHWH; Zion/Jerusalem in the figure of a woman is also a partner. The meaning of that phrase is uncertain; most exegetes refer to the covenant of Sinai. But it is plausible that it may mean the marital covenant given the context of the metaphor of the woman/city. Isaiah (from chapter 49 onward) and Ezekiel take the idea of marriage between Lady Zion and YHWH for granted. Since the entire section resembles in content statements in those two books, such an understanding of the covenant may also apply to Zechariah 9:9-17.

The conjunction of blood, covenant, and marriage is found also in Ezekiel 16, although blood is not valued positively there as a sign of the covenant but negatively as a sign of the uncleanness of the woman Jerusalem, which YHWH then removes (Ezek 16:9). Zechariah 9:12 adopts a phrase from Isaiah but gives it its opposite meaning. The woman Zion has paid doubly for her iniquities (Isa 40:2). What Zechariah wants to say is that the woman Zion will receive double in restoration for her suffering. The promise of Isaiah 61:7 is here made to the whole people.

Beginning at Zechariah 9:13, YHWH is pictured as a king of war who whips up the sons of Zion for war. Presumably the "sons of Greece" is a later addition that presupposes an actual enemy. In this war Zion is to be deployed as a sword. There is not a trace in verse 10 of the announcement of peace. Only when all the enemies have been destroyed is the well-being spoken of in verse 17 to be a reality. The new well-being will be reflected in the strength of young men and women, a picture of the blessing that has come upon the land.

Summing Up

Haggai and Zechariah document how Judah's postexilic society sought to integrate the diverse groups and to develop a positive outlook on the future. In addition to its own efforts, there is hope in the intervention of YHWH on behalf of the oppressed. This hope is not only focused on the events of world politics, such as the destruction of weapons, but also has the everyday existence of "the lowly" in view. God's blessing is seen when men and women live without fear of violence and hunger. The Daughter of Zion, rejoicing, welcomes YHWH as the king who assures this blessing on the land and the whole world. Despite the universal orientation of well-being, this vision is not without limits: with the "deportation of the goddess," the domain of sin is excluded from where the reign of YHWH exists.

LITERATURE

Bauer, Lutz. 1992. *Zeit des Zweiten Tempels — Zeit der Gerechtigkeit.* Beiträge zur Erforschung des Alten Testaments und des antiken Judentums, vol. 31. Frankfurt am Main.

Glazier-McDonald, Beth. 1992. "Haggai and Zechariah." In *The Women's Bible Commentary,* edited by Carol A. Newsom and Sharon H. Ringe, 228-31. London and Louisville.

Hanhart, Robert. 1990-95. *Sacharja.* Biblischer Kommentar, vol. 14, 7, 1-5. Neukirchen.

Japhet, Sarah. 1982. "Sheshbazzar and Zerubbabel — against the Background of the Historical and Religious Tendencies of Ezra-Nehemia." *Zeitschrift für die alttestamentliche Wissenschaft* 94:66-98.

Jeremias, Christian. 1977. *Die Nachtgesichte des Sacharja. Untersuchungen zu ihrer Stellung im Zusammenhang der Visionsberichte im Alten Testament und zu ihrem Bildmaterial.* Göttingen.

Larkin, Katrina J. A. 1994. *The Eschatology of Second Zechariah: A Study of the Formation of a Mantological Wisdom Anthology.* Kampen.

Leeuwen, C. van. 1993. "רשׁע." In *Theologisches Wörterbuch zum Alten Testament,* 2:813-18. 4th ed. Gütersloh.

Luther, Martin. 1995. *Luther's Works.* Vol. 20, *Commentary on Minor Prophets III.* St. Louis.

Meyers, Carol L., and Eric M. Meyers. 1987. *Haggai, Zechariah 1–8.* Anchor Bible, vol. 25b. Garden City, N.Y.

————. 1993. *Zechariah 9–14*. Anchor Bible, vol. 25c. Garden City, N.Y.

Reventlow, Henning Graf. 1993. *Die Propheten Haggai, Sacharja und Maleachi*. Altes Testament Deutsch, vol. 25, 2. Göttingen.

Rudolph, Wilhelm. 1976. *Haggai, Sacharja 1–8, Sacharja 9–14, Maleachi*. Kommentar zum Alten Testament, vol. 13, 4. Gütersloh.

Schöttler, Heinz-Günther. 1987. *Gott inmitten seines Volkes. Die Neuordnung des Gottesvolkes nach Sacharja 1–6*. Trierer theologische Studien, vol. 43. Trier.

Tollington, Janet E. 1993. *Tradition and Innovation in Haggai and Zechariah 1–8*. Journal for the Study of the Old Testament: Supplement Series, vol. 150. Sheffield.

Uehlinger, Christoph. 1994. "Die Frau im Efa (Sach 5,5-11). Eine Programmvision von der Abschiebung der Göttin." *Bibel und Kirche* 49:93-103.

Wolff, Hans W. 1986. *Dodekapropheton 6 Haggai*. Biblischer Kommentar, vol. 14, 6. Neukirchen.

Translated by Martin Rumscheidt

Malachi: To the Glory of God, the Father?

Marie-Theres Wacker

The book of Malachi is the last writing in the Christian First Testament and the last writing of the prophets. In the Hebrew Bible, the Prophets encompasses the complete Deuteronomistic history from Joshua to Kings and the prophets from Isaiah to Malachi. The last verses in Malachi (4:4-6) can be read as a summary of the Torah and the prophets. These verses place the law of Moses (4:4) and the (returning) prophet Elijah (4:5-6) next to each other: the Torah of Moses to follow in the present and the prophet Elijah as the carrier of hope for the future. Thus these verses constitute the final words of a book that, after a title (1:1), consists of six parts of differing length but with a similar structure (often described as words of disputation) that was written in the Persian time of Israel (mid–fifth century?). The very frequent references to the Torah and the prophets suggest it is a document of the (early) tradition of scribehood.

To meet expectations of a Christian-feminist exegesis (so far only available for individual aspects) of Malachi, the following elaborations seek to explore the women-specific themes of the text in their textual immanence (this includes intertextual references but not the meanings suggested by a supposed textual development). Furthermore, this article seeks to establish connections between the text and (Jewish) female reality at the time of origin of this book, and lastly — following the style of disputations suggested by the different sections of the text — will end in suggestions to reread the complete book from a critical feminist perspective.

Arguing God's Honor

Quarrel among Brothers

The first section of the book (1:2-5) affirms YHWH's affection ("love") for not specified addressees, an attachment the opposite of which is given as rejection

473

("hate"). This is argued with reference to the inexplicable and never explained motif of Jacob's favor over his brother Esau, as attributed to YHWH's self. YHWH has "loved" Jacob, just as he "loves" the addressees — implicit here is that they can see themselves in line with the favorite son. In contrast to this, the visualization of a postwar situation for the neighboring country Edom, resting on ruins, is hyperbolically compared to Esau's position in relation to Jacob's elevation. Rhetorically this emphasizes again that the addressees are positioned on the side of Jacob.

Intertwined with this line of argument is another, which emphasizes the disparagement of Edom through the use of "discursive feminization." In 1:4 the name Edom is connected to a female verb form ("when she, Edom, says . . ."), and its land is described as the "country of wickedness" *(rišʿâ)*, the same description used in the preceding book of Zechariah (5:8) for the exiled "woman in the ephah." Read in this way, the "woman of Edom" is an area where the "woman of wickedness" resides. This area is given to jackals (Mal 1:3), which appear only here in the Hebrew Bible in the feminine plural (instead of the usual masculine plural).[1] God intervenes destructively in this area (1:4) and thus proves that his might reaches beyond Israel/Jacob (1:5). We find here Judeo-postexilic hostility toward neighbor Edom. However, one needs (self-)critically to distinguish between this and the later Christian reception of the Jacob-Esau typology that served as the foundation for anti-Judaism and led to the structural hatred of Jews in Christian theology (see Lescow 1993, 43-60, particularly 59f.).

Alongside the motif of the rivalry between brothers one can position the motif of rivalry between the sisters Rachel and Leah (→ Genesis 12–50). In this instance one is loved and the other rejected — by Jacob the husband. Also here we find scenes of triumph of one over the other (cf. Gen 30). The conflict between these two sisters has "political" consequences in the rivalry of their sons, where favor does not fall on Jacob's favorite wife Rachel's sons, Joseph and Benjamin, but on the two sons of the rejected wife, Leah, namely, Judah and Levi. Their story plays a significant role in the book of Malachi and in the history of Israel, or rather, in the history of Judaism.

Priests Jeopardize God's Honor

The second unit (Mal 1:6–2:9) singles out one group, the priests *(kōhănîm)*, from the collective "Jacob" and addresses them specifically. This group of the postexilic temple cult in Jerusalem is an all-male institution. The text tackles one problem of the praxis concerning sacrifices. The presentation of sick, malformed, or even stolen animals to YHWH is severely criticized by comparing God the receiver with a

---

1. This is even more noteworthy, as in Lam 4:3 the text speaks of jackals who nourish their young. Those jackals are however given in the plural, masculine *tannîn* and *tannîm*.

governor (a reference to the Persian presence in the area), who might get offended by a wrongly chosen gift (1:8). This comparison draws attention to the fact that the sacrifice in the cult of the temple is seen as an expression of honor given to God, the sovereign (king: 1:14; Lord: 1:6) in and of Israel. The offering of bad sacrifices is a direct attack on God's honor. On this background the book of Malachi introduces a name for God that appears seldom in the complete Hebrew Bible, and those few times more frequently in postexilic scriptures (cf. Strotmann 1991). Of these, the term can be found most frequently in Malachi — it is the name "father" (1:6). In this verse the term means foremost that the addressees — like a son, a father — have to show honor to God worthy of him. In this the father-son relationship is similar to that of the relationship between the master and his servant; God's "fatherhood" is in this instance inseparable from his rule. The connection between God's sovereign fatherhood and the honor he demands has been ignored by the priests and offended by their malpractice.

In contrast, the text points to the regard with which the God of Israel is held by other nations: there exists fear of God (1:14), their sacrifices are acceptable to God (1:11). The reference to the "others," the *gôyîm,* may serve the purpose of embarrassing the addressees. In light of this interpretation, the first section can be read differently: although the addressees are especially loved by the God who is held in awe by other nations, they may forfeit their privilege by their disrespectful manner. Besides the effect of blame, this second unit may contain an element of warning.

The judgment of the priests (2:1-9) explicitly mentions the motif of "honor" *(kābôd)* and explicates it with the announcement that those who dishonor God's name (*bzh,* 1:6-7, 12) will be degraded (*bzh,* 2:9) themselves. In other words, their honor will be turned to shame in front of "all the people." The cause and justification for this do not refer back to imperfect sacrifices but establish a new causal link. The name Levi is introduced (2:4), clearly pointing to the forefather of the presently acting priests. In this text Levi's task is less the cult of sacrifices than the teaching of the people (compare to Hos 4:6!). He is even called the "messenger of the LORD of hosts" (Mal 2:7) in analogy to the one called the messenger in the title of this book, *mal'ākî* — my messenger, the one who has to spread the word of YHWH. Levi's task of being the messenger was constituted and regulated by a covenant with YHWH, who granted life and salvation to the one who was willing to give YHWH the honor, which is now threatened by the behavior of the priests. It almost seems as if "Malachi" sees himself as the substitute for the priests who have failed.

The name Levi also addresses an all-male group. It is possible, though, that the task of the women waiting at the entrance of the Tent of Meeting with the bronze mirrors (Exod 38:8) was regarded as a Levitic activity. This is substantiated by the mysterious name for these women, *ṣōbě'ôt* (from the stem *ṣb'*), which is also used in the labeling of the work by male Levites, *ṣb'* (compare Num 4:23; 8:24).

These kinds of activities cannot be compared to the role of Levi as the messenger described in Malachi. On the other hand, the text assumes that the Levites have wives and children — this is the associative bridge from the second section to the third section of the text.

Women as Touchstone

The third section begins like the second section with the metaphor of the father. Here it appears as a parallel image to the term of God the creator; thus it focuses mainly on the one origin, which the addressees as well as the narrator can claim as their own. The metaphor of the father does not necessarily point to God; it can also be read as pointing to a common human ancestor. There are some indications that support the former, though: the parallel sentence construction of one father/one creator, the fairly frequent use of this connection in other biblical texts (see, for example, Deut 32:6; Isa 64:7 [Eng. 8]), and the used name for God, "El," which in its West Semitic–Ugaritic tradition carries connotations of fatherhood. To have a common origin in a creator god, a father god, as Malachi 2:10 can be read, results in solidarity toward each other. Here again a community of men is envisioned, who are supposed to show brotherly solidarity to each other, because their "fathers" stand in a covenant with God, the father. The text questions the existence of such solidarity; 2:10 speaks of "faithlessness" (verb stem *bgd*) and "desecration" (*ḥll*).

The Hebrew text of verses 11-16, which concretizes the problem, is quite difficult and thus results in different reconstructions and interpretations. Exegetes have often maintained that this verse speaks about the marriage of a Jewish man to a woman who does not worship YHWH. The description of this woman as "daughter of a foreign god" together with the accusation that the holy place of YHWH is desecrated, evokes the image of the woman as the point of invasion of foreign cults that are against YHWH. This image can be found in the legal texts (Exod 34:15-16; Deut 7:3-4) and the narrative texts (Num 25:1-3) of the Torah as well as in the Deuteronomistic history, the so-called Former Prophets (1 Kings 11:1ff.).[2] The following verse, Malachi 2:12, threatens that the affected male will be cut off from the "tents of Jacob," the community of Judah/Israel, and from the circle of those who bring sacrifices to YHWH.[3]

According to the Hebrew text, the first sentence in 2:11 links the name Judah, which in preexilic times already described the southern part of the country, to a

2. The early Jewish translations have separated those two themes: while the LXX at this point speaks in very general terms of "idolatry," the *Targum of the Prophets (Targum Jonathan)* speaks specifically of women as "the daughters of nations."

3. The enigmatic Hebrew phrase ʿēr wěʿōneh, which the *Targum of the Prophets* uses in terms of the descendants of the man, might include the end of male fertility; see discussion of Glazier-McDonald 1986.

feminine verb form of the stem *bgd* ("faithless was she, Judah"). The sentence following after that in 2:11 switches to a passive verb form ("abominable things are done in Israel and Jerusalem"); the third sentence with this verb changes to a masculine form. This is necessary, because the text speaks of the man Judah, who takes the "daughter of a foreign god" as his wife. In the exegesis of Malachi this sentence results in the change of the feminine verb form at the beginning of the verse. It makes sense to regard this as a move to reconstruct the "original text"; the current text, however, invites a reading of considerable difference. In the relationship of the sons of the father, that is, among the "brothers" (2:10), and in the relationship to the wife, "Judah" appears male, but in the relationship to YHWH Judah appears as an unfaithful woman, as seen in similar polemic in Hosea, Jeremiah (3:8, 11, 20 with the stem *bgd*), and Ezekiel (chapters 16 and 23). Perhaps this punctual discursive feminization of Judah, including the feminization of Edom in Malachi 1:3-4, shows, as in Hosea, that the work of scribes on the Hebrew text highlights more gender-specific roles than the older translations (Wacker 1996, 5, 162, 266, 273).

The verses 2:13-16 develop the theme "woman" and "unfaithfulness" from a different angle. They speak of the men of Judah who have been "unfaithful" to the "wife of their youth" (2:14, 16). The term "wife" in this instance *('ēšet nĕ'ûrêkā)* has been chosen to sound similar in tone to the term "daughter of a foreign god" (*bat 'ēl-nēkār*, 2:11). There is another term to describe the wife, "wife of your covenant," which relates directly to the "covenant of our forefathers" (2:10) and thus signifies that the wife, in contrast to the "foreign woman," is a suitable life-partner *(hăberet)* for a Judaic man. The following verses 2:15-16 are linguistically very complex and have become obscure in their present form, because they are based on a seemingly incomprehensible template, which has been reinterpreted to attempt to make some more sense. The *Targum of the Prophets,* the base for the traditional Jewish exegesis of that passage, links verse 15 to Abraham, whose relationship with the Egyptian Hagar does not compromise his faithfulness to Sarah because it is based solely on the wish for progeny. Verse 16 is interpreted to advocate divorce if there is "hate" between the marriage partners,[4] whereas in Christian tradition this verse supports the notion that divorce is forbidden (see widely used Bible translations).

In scholarship on the historical background of Malachi 2:10-16, it is often assumed that men from Judea, after their return from exile, tried to marry wealthy (non-Judean) women of a higher class. For this they would have had to first divorce their wives of Judean origin. However, since the passage combines two different trains of thought, it is questionable whether it is possible to see the two as describing one historical problem: Can the "breaking of the covenant" be read as a combination of the motif of marriage to foreign women who worship "foreign" gods and the motif of "faithlessness" toward one's own wife?

---

4. The LXX also offers in this section a more interpretative rather than a translated text (see Utzschneider 1992, 385f.).

Julia O'Brien (1996) further wonders whether the portrayal of Judah as a husband of a "daughter of a foreign god" does not also influence the portrayal of YHWH. The close relationship between Judah and YHWH could suggest that the image of Judah as husband positions YHWH as his (lawful) bride. The description in 2:13-16 supports this reading as it pits the daughter of a "foreign god" (El) against the sons of the one god (El) in 2:11. The foreign woman personifies idolatry — without suggesting that this hints at a cult of goddesses. But at the same time, one cannot exclude the possibility that women are to be denigrated by this polemical and rhetorical reference to traditions of goddess worship (cf. discussion in Glazier-McDonald 1987b). In a reversal, the "wife of his youth" becomes a living metaphor for worship that pleases YHWH, so that the relationship of the Judaic man with YHWH positions YHWH indeed in the role of such a woman. The main explicit representations of YHWH in the text as father, Lord, and King are counteracted by this tiny trace of an implied metaphor that positions YHWH in the role of "bride/woman" of "his" people.

The Messenger of Judgment

The fourth section, Malachi 2:17–3:5, asks the question, which is reminiscent of wisdom tradition, about God's justice in the face of unhindered evil by wrongdoers. The answer points to God's imminent intervention, after the appearance of a "messenger." Perhaps it can be deduced that the text talks about a historical figure of a prophet, who saw himself in the role of "messenger" of the coming of God to judge. The current version of the book of Malachi refers to the motif of the messenger again right at the end and reinterprets it anew: while 3:2 focuses on and describes the threat of God's coming on the day of judgment, 3:23-24 (4:5-6) talks about Elijah as a messenger, who before that day of YHWH restores forgiveness between fathers and sons in the whole country and thus prevents the day of judgment from becoming a day of terror for the land. The book of Malachi thus presents a chain of "messengers": from the Levites who fail, to the voice of "Malachi," who warns and threatens, to the last prophetic messenger Elijah (and this is what the Gospels of the New Testament have adopted).

The day of judgment, which is announced and prepared by the "messenger," is directed foremost at the accused priests. The dominant image of their being called to account for their misdeeds is that of the melting of fine metals in very high temperatures. God is compared to that great heat. This "process" culminates in the re-establishment of sacrificial offerings in Judah and Jerusalem. Alongside this, the text draws attention to "sorcerers, adulterers, those who swear falsely, and those who oppress hired workers, the widow and the orphan and reject strangers" (3:5). The focus thus rests on those who in one way or another openly damage society. "Widows and orphans" is a traditional pair of words pointing to a group of human beings who need specific protection. "Sorcery and adultery" are mentioned in similar accusatory terms in 2 Kings 9:22 against Queen Jezebel and in Nahum 3:4 against the city of Nineveh, which is personified as a woman. Here in Malachi 3:5 these words are not gender-specific.

Tithing and the Honor of God

The fifth section (Mal 3:6-12) begins with the accusation that the addressees as "sons of Jacob" have not changed since the time of their fathers. The name "sons of Jacob" is used in this context, in contrast to the use in section one (1:2-5), to critique and point to a history of sin. This passage plays with the name Jacob insofar as the sons of Jacob *(ya'ăqōb)* are accused of fraud (*'qb*; see similar puns on the name Jacob in Hos 12:4 and 8[3 and 7]). The passage is concerned with the question of tithing, which is the offering to the temple. This question is connected to the hope for a positive course of the harvest cycle (rain, no locusts, rich grape harvest, Mal 3:11-12; one can detect thematic similarities to the book of Joel). The attention on the nations that praise the people of YHWH appeals to the sense of "honor" of the addressees, who are urged to act so that they are praised by others.

Sun of Righteousness

The sixth and last section (Mal 3:13-21[3:13–4:3]) comes back to the topic of God's righteousness in the face of the seemingly successful wrongdoers. In section four (2:17–3:5) the argument speaks to those who are guilty and expect judgment. Here in section six it addresses those who pose the question about God's righteousness. At first, they are comforted that God will spare them, as parents spare their children. The essential decision is compared to the image of a hot summer's day, in which the heat burns the wicked, while the faithful remain unharmed. This motif evokes the image of the oven in 3:1-5. The combination of words in "sun of righteousness" (3:20[4:2]) functions as a metaphor for God's righteousness: like the sun, God's righteousness will have burning consequences for the wicked while for the faithful it shines benevolently. The combination can also be interpreted as an image of God himself: God, the sun, corresponds in her righteousness to the good deeds of the righteous; for those who fear God, this God-sun-light means the brightness of a rising day. This mythological-sounding talk of God, the sun, has the advantage that the metaphors express one coherent set of imagery. This talk makes clear that both "faces" of the sun(-god) are equally important: what was singeing, ovenlike heat for wrongdoers is bright sunshine for the faithful. This interpretation connects well to the further development of the text, which introduces the "wings" of the sun. Mainly through Egyptian art this image of the sun with wings as a symbol for God is familiar to us. Also in ancient Israel, during the time of the Kings as well as in postexilic time, this symbol would have been used to signify power and protection; for example, there is an imprint of a bull from En-Gedi (southern Dead Sea) that has been dated from the sixth century and depicts a sun with wings and a feathered tail (Keel and Uehlinger 1994, 297a with plate no. 8d). Biblical texts and such imagery converge in the assumption that the perception of the God of Israel as having such solar traits has a long and unassailable "orthodox" tradition (see Keel and Uehlinger 1994). This is particularly interesting from a feminist perspective because the grammatical genus of the sun (like that of *rûaḥ*) can be masculine *or* feminine (in Ugarit and the empire of the Hethites the sun deity was worshiped as a goddess whereas in Egypt and Assyria it was worshiped as a god).

Verse 19 (4:1) directs the attention to the wicked, verse 20 (4:2) focuses on the righteous, and verse 21 (4:3) brings the two together. The righteous leap like playful calves out of the stall and trample the ash of the wicked underfoot. The imagery rests on wordplay here: "calf" (*ʿēgel*) and "foot" (*regel*) correspond, and "healing" *(marpēʾ)* through the wings of the sun corresponds to "stall" *(marbēq)*. The image expresses zest and vitality for life but leaves no doubt that the evildoers will be robbed of any future and will be quite literally thrown into the dust.

Yield for Feminist Interpretation

The book of Malachi presents itself as a reflection of a threatened and frightened community. The main image of God is that of a ruler: governor, lord, king, and father. Likewise, the central relationship between father and son is one where the son has to honor the father and the father also intervenes for the son in a paternalistic and protective way. Within this patriarchal or kyriarchal system, the "foreign" women represent a potential threat to the (cult) community whereas their "own" women are either in need of protection (widows) or have an important significance (as wives) for the collective as well as for the individual male. At this point one has to address the underlying problem of a feminist exegesis of such kinds of texts and the structures evolving from them. Interpreted in terms of its application, many Christian and Jewish exegetes have solved the "women question" by focusing on the valued role of women as partners in the covenant with their husbands, or rather, as being part of the covenant of the fathers. Indeed, for individual (Christian or Jewish) women, this might be a treasured and sufficient position to occupy with self-esteem. However, this positioning comes at the price of dichotomizing between "good" women and "bad" women, between women worth protecting (wives and widows) and those one wants to keep outside ("daughters of a foreign god"). Further, the discursive feminization as a rhetorical strategy is either unquestioned (perhaps even affirmed) or relegated to a marginal problem. From a feminist perspective — be it Jewish or Christian — it is therefore perceived as necessary to draw a broader critique, which locates the symbolic place of the woman/female in the larger system, which is then contextualized historically to show its own ambivalence.

The book of Malachi shows signs of harsh self-criticism also: even though the promise of YHWH's love to his people stands at the beginning, this does not mean that deplorable states of affairs are ignored; rather, they are included within the framing promise. Moreover, the father-god does not signify authority and power alone but urges solidarity between those who define themselves through him. There are some, even if few, traces of a way of talking about YHWH that unhinges the "kyriarchal" metaphoric language. Further, the book also includes other nations that praise YHWH's name and thus, while rhetorically focused on Judah, it allows for a wider inclusive conception of the worship of God.[5] To employ a feminist critical outlook, the reader must find a framework in which women can occupy new symbolic places and highlight the moments that are critical of patriarchy within this patriarchal book.

LITERATURE

Glazier-McDonald, Beth. 1986. "Malachi 2:12: ʾēr weʿōneh — Another Look." *Journal of Biblical Literature* 105:295-98.

———. 1987a. *Maleachi: The Divine Messenger.* Society of Biblical Literature Dissertation Series, vol. 98. Atlanta.

———. 1987b. "Intermarriage, Divorce, and the Bat-ʾEl Nekar: Insights into Mal 2:10-16." *Journal of Biblical Literature* 106:603-11.

———. 1992. "Malachi." In *The Women's Bible Commentary,* edited by Carol A. Newsom and Sharon H. Ringe, 232-34. London and Louisville.

Keel, Othmar, and Christoph Uehlinger. 1994. "Jahwe und die Sonnengottheit von Jerusalem." In *Ein Gott allein?* edited by Walter Dietrich and Martin A. Klopfenstein, 269-306. Orbis biblicus et orientalis, vol. 139. Fribourg and Göttingen.

Lescow, Theodor. 1993. *Das Buch Maleachi. Texttheorie — Auslegung — Kanontheorie.* Stuttgart.

O'Brien, Julia. 1990. *Priest and Levite in Malachi.* Society of Biblical Literature Dissertation Series, vol. 121. Atlanta.

———. 1995. "Malachi: Currents in Research." *Biblical Studies* 3:81-94.

———. 1996. "Judah as Wife and Husband: Deconstructing Gender in Malachi." *Journal of Biblical Literature* 115:241-50.

Reventlow, Henning Graf v. 1993. *Die Propheten Haggai, Sacharja und Maleachi.* Altes Testament Deutsch, vol. 25, 2. Göttingen.

Sölle, Dorothee. 1989. "Bilder machen Bilder stürzen. Eine feministisch-theologische Kritik am Vaterbild." In *Sturz der Götter? Vaterbilder im 20. Jahrhundert,* edited by Werner Faulstich and Gunter E. Grimm, 17-30. Frankfurt am Main.

---

5. Mal 1:11 has been taken up enthusiastically by Christians and turned against a supposed Jewish legalism. A feminist rereading of Malachi from a Christian feminist perspective has to distance itself from this history of interpretation.

Strotmann, Angelika. 1991. *'Mein Vater bist Du!' (Sir 51,10). Zur Bedeutung der Vaterschaft Gottes in kanonischen und nichtkanonischen frühjüdischen Schriften.* Frankfurter theologische Studien, vol. 39. Frankfurt am Main.

Utzschneider, Helmut. 1989. *Künder oder Schreiber? Eine These zum Problem der Schriftprophetie auf Grund von Maleachi 1,6–2,9.* Beiträge zur Erforschung des Alten Testaments und des antiken Judentum, vol. 19. Frankfurt am Main.

———. 1992. "Die Schriftprophetie und die Frage nach dem Ende der Prophetie. Überlegungen anhand von Mal 1,6–2,16." *Zeitschrift für die alttestamentliche Wissenschaft* 104:377-94.

Wacker, Marie-Theres. 1996. *Figurationen des Weiblichen im Hoseabuch.* Herders Biblische Studien, vol. 8. Freiburg im Breisgau.

Translated by Tina Steiner

1 Maccabees: Women's Existence at the Edges of the Text

Claudia Rakel

Thus far, feminist exegesis has approached the First Book of Maccabees with noticeable restraint; after all, both it and the Second Book of Maccabees describe a male-dominated world. Men are the acting subjects; they engage themselves in the liberation of Israel from totalitarian regimes such as that of Antiochus IV Epiphanes. His brutal enforcement of a uniform religion and culture threatened to destroy Jewish faith and tradition. So that this does not happen, men wage war, sign treaties, and make peace; in the end they succeed in bringing about the political independence of Israel, eventually securing the offices of high priest and governor for the clan of the Maccabees. The first book describes events in Israel between 175 and 135 B.C.E. (cf. Schunk 1991, 737), beginning with the first uprising of the Israelites under the priest Mattathias against the Seleucids (1 Macc 1–2). Then follow the battles led by his son Judas Maccabeus (1 Macc 3–9:22) and, after his death, by his brothers Jonathan (9:23–12:53) and Simon (13–16). The book concludes with the period when, under Simon's son John Hyrcanus, the administrative, cultic, and military authority over Israel rests in the hands of the Maccabees. The entirely positive portrayal of the Maccabean revolt and the Hasmonean dynasty that came to power as a result has apologetic features (cf. Mittmann-Richert 2000, 31). For example, when the book draws on specifically selected material from biblical books, like the books of Samuel, and with it molds the Maccabeans in the image of David (cf. Dobbeler 1997, 44-46), it seeks to give stability to the Hasmonean dynasty and present it as the legitimate heirs of the royal house of David.

Few exceptions notwithstanding, women are not present in 1 Maccabees. Their presence is acknowledged only occasionally in moments of grave crisis (cf. Schuller 1992, 238). However, feminist exegesis that claims to be feminist critique and revision of the entire biblical tradition will not limit itself in its interpretation of biblical texts to those where women are at the center of the narrative or when readers with a feminist perspective can discern their presence in a text. Such exegesis seeks to overcome the androcentric perspective in texts like 1 Maccabees, where women can be found only with difficulty and then only at the edges, so that the re-

483

ality of women's lives may be portrayed, for example, in terms of social history (cf. Sakenfeld 1989, 71-72).

It is not only the marginal status of women that makes a feminist exegesis of this book so difficult. Its topics make it hard for women reading this text today to unlock it since, as a historical report, it deals almost exclusively with war, the various battles, victories, and defeats of the Maccabean brothers Judas, Jonathan, and Simon. For some time now the First Testament has "often been the focal point of criticism because it does not distance itself fundamentally and consistently from violence but, rather, readily documents and legitimates its use and often has no problem with uniting faith in God with violence" (Schroer 1998, 153).

When it addresses the subject of war and violence in biblical texts, feminist exegesis should, for one, reappraise women's specific experiences of violence in war that biblical texts often cover up and that are similarly invisible in traditional exegetical interpretations. This is needed for two reasons: first, the sacrificial status of women must not yet again be reinforced retrospectively in the reception of biblical texts, and second, women need to be raised out of oblivion and silencing through critical revision. And then feminist exegesis should address the subject of violence and war in the Bible as a brutal expression of a *multidimensional* system of oppression the victims of which were not only women and the perpetrators of which were not only men. We seek to express this matter linguistically in what follows through the consistent use of male and female Maccabees, male and female Israelites, male and female Seleucids, etc.[1]

Women in War

We hear something about women in this book above all when it describes affliction in Israel. The laments about Israel's situation repeatedly contain references to the whole people, most likely to indicate how great were the danger and oppression facing the faithful men and women of Israel.

There was deep mourning in Israel throughout the country.

Rulers and elders groaned;
girls and young men wasted away;
the women's beauty suffered a change;
every bridegroom took up a dirge,

1. The German text speaks of *MakkabäerInnen, IsraelitInnen, SeleukidInnen*, etc. As there is no adequate English equivalent to this German terminology, the translator, finding a repetitive use of "male and female . . ." awkward, assumes that Maccabeans, Israelites, and Seleucids will be understood to mean both women and men except when the text makes it clear that it does not. [Translator's note.]

the bride sat grief-stricken
  on her marriage-bed.
The earth quaked
  because of its inhabitants
and the whole House of Jacob
  was clothed with shame. (1:25-28 NJB)

1 Maccabees speaks of women primarily as victims of the conditions prevailing at the time. That is the depressing conclusion when one reads this book with the intent of knowing what it says about women's history. Since the text seeks chiefly to describe the oppression the people of Israel suffered under the Seleucids' occupation, we learn especially of the violence inflicted upon Israelite women. They are the victims of the politics of cultural imperialism of Antiochus Epiphanes; he desecrated the temple by forcibly establishing the worship of pagan deities in it and sought by his decrees to impose a uniform culture and religion in his territories. Because the people of Israel resisted this, Jerusalem was conquered and subdued with force. Israelite women faced and experienced violence not because of their gender but because they offered resistance by clinging to their religion and tradition. Their fate was death or slavery (1:29-64). Again and again we read of the abduction of women into slavery. "[Antiochus] pillaged the city and set it on fire, tore down its houses and encircling wall, took the women and children captive and commandeered the cattle" (1:31-32 NJB).

The same happens to women in the Jewish diaspora. As Judas Maccabeus grew more and more successful in Israel, the pressure on the Jewish population outside Israel increased further and further. Messengers told Judas Maccabeus that Jews in cities like Gilead and Tubias were being killed, their women and children taken into captivity and their property seized (cf. 5:9-13). Upon hearing this, Judas marched with his army to the places where Jews were persecuted and succeeded in bringing them to Israel. "Judas assembled all the Israelites living in Gilead, from the least to the greatest, with their wives, children and belongings, an enormous muster, to take them to Judaea" (5:45 NJB).

It may safely be assumed that such descriptions also intend to legitimate the resistance and the Maccabean movement with its military interventions. Under the conditions described, it appears that the spiral of violence and counterviolence cannot be halted. It would be false to conclude from this that biblical texts celebrate violence or that Israel was disposed to and obsessed with violence. Such wholesale reproach is untenable because the passages cited already show how menacing violence is and that it is an injustice to be opposed. The Maccabean liberation movement sought to gain freedom from such structures of violence and not their renewal. Still, 1 Maccabees is not a document critical of war as other writings of the time are (such as the book of Judith). The narrative is presented from the perspective of the military leadership, and not from that of victims.

When one looks at all the texts that mention women together, it is clear that almost without exception their status is that of victims either because Judas and his men rescue them (in the diaspora) or because the enemy takes them as spoils of war and enslaves them. Nowhere are women the subjects of action; even in their suffering the text does not give them a voice of their own, thereby textually multiplying their status as objects in the violence perpetrated on them by the enemy. One cannot reject offhand the suspicion that the women's and children's fate is mentioned not for their sake but simply because the people of Israel had been attacked and it is ever so easy to evoke "moral outrage" around them.

The few texts about women in this book let us see what fate awaited women during war in the ancient world and when their people were defeated. Israelite women were not the only ones affected; women and children of every party waging war became victims in antiquity of the imperialist and colonial politics of the superpowers (and not only then). What the Seleucids do to the women of Israel, the Romans do to the women of Greece. We know this from documents cited in the book of Maccabees that are meant to give warrant to the alliances between the Maccabeans and Rome: "[The Romans] carried their [the Greeks'] women and children away into captivity, pillaged their goods, subdued their country, tore down their fortresses and reduced them to slavery lasting to the present day" (8:10 NJB).

In the ancient world, women and children were regarded as the spoil of the winner of war. One aspect of the violence women experienced during war was being raped by the victors — a phenomenon not restricted just to antiquity. As the war in the former Yugoslavia has shown, it is still possible in our own time. According to the laws of ancient days, the population of a conquered city was either killed or sold into slavery (cf. Hengel 1969, 512). This demonstrates that women's experiences of violence in the wars of antiquity were embedded in a multifaceted system of oppression. We are not dealing here simply with a one-dimensional patriarchal form of oppression where women are held down by men or fathers. This is not to say that this did not happen in the ancient world. When 1 Maccabees relates that the daughter of the king of Egypt, Cleopatra Thea (the only woman mentioned by name in this book), is given in marriage as part of a political alliance arrangement first to Alexander Epiphanes (10:57) and later, after Alexander's influence had waned, to King Demetrius (11:12), we get to see a patriarchal form of oppression in which daughters are "used" through the instrumentality of marriage for the solidification of their fathers' power. The oppression and persecution of Israelite women occur by a multilayered system of domination and suppression (cf. Schüssler Fiorenza 1992, 114-20) that targets women not because they are women but on account of their religion and their status as noncitizens. We hear of merchants who come to the camp of the Seleucid army of Nicanor with much gold and silver to buy Israelites for slaves (3:41; cf. Hengel 1976, 121). It surely is not farfetched to assume that the Israelite women and children mentioned here were bought by the merchants to be sold again for profit. The lament of Mattathias, the father of Judas Maccabeus and his brothers, speaks of the people of Israel as a female slave.

> Is there a nation that has not claimed
> a share of her royal prerogatives,
> that has not taken some of her spoils?
> All her ornaments
>   have been snatched from her,
> her former freedom has become slavery. (2:10-11 NJB)

Israel, Judea, and Jerusalem also are frequently compared to a woman in biblical texts, especially in the tradition of the prophets. Mattathias does not do what Hosea and Ezekiel do: compare Israel that has become disloyal to the covenant with YHWH to an unfaithful and sexually promiscuous woman, leaving us with a misogynist image (cf. Hos 1–3 and Ezek 16 and 23; → Hosea; Ezekiel). The contrast between "freedom" and "slavery" characterizes the metaphor for Israel in Mattathias's lament. Female slaves were utterly without rights, on the lowermost level in the ancient world's hierarchy of patriarchy or, as Elisabeth Schüssler Fiorenza puts it with an eye on the interconnectedness of the numerous and widely differing systems of oppression, hierarchy of kyriarchy (cf. Schüssler Fiorenza 1992, 117). The very use of this metaphor in the lament indicates how actual the experience of slavery must have been in Israel. The image of Israel as a female slave bundles together concrete experiences of women and men who at that time were carried off into slavery.

Women in the Maccabean Movement

Did women participate in the Maccabean movement and the resistance against the ruling house of the Seleucids? The Maccabean movement was certainly not restricted to men, even though 1 Maccabees says very little about any women belonging to it. One reference is found in 2:29-30: "Many people who were concerned for virtue and justice went down to the desert and stayed there, taking with them their sons, their wives and their cattle, so oppressive had their suffering become" (NJB). Except for the occasional mention of women as in this text, there are no indications that women took part in the Maccabean movement. And even this text relegates them to a passive state: they were taken along.

In dealing with the androcentric language of the Bible, I shall follow Elisabeth Schüssler Fiorenza. She regards the male grammatical forms as the Bible's conventional way of speaking about women and men unless the context of a specific text clearly indicates that its language is unambiguously gender-specific (cf. Schüssler Fiorenza 1992, 43). Thus, when 1 Maccabees uses only male grammatical forms in its language, it is to be assumed that "Israelites" also signifies Israelite women. That means that women supported the Israelites' resistance more strongly than the sparse references to them in the text suggest. True, we do not know much explicitly about how they were involved in the movement. For example, what role did the mother of the Maccabees brothers play in it? She is mentioned for the first time at the end of the book. Simon, the last of the brothers, has a pyramid built for every member of his family, his father, his mother, and his four brothers (13:28). Why does this woman receive her own pyramid for a tomb? Is this an expression of how she was revered as the mother of her sons, or did she play a role in the liberation movement, such as supporting her sons' activities with her counsel? Even though the family of Mattathias and his sons is of central importance to the book and its author, we hear of the mother's existence only as she is laid to rest. Does this reference to her once again serve just to legitimate the sovereignty of the Hasmoneans in that reciting what surrounds her burial and the place of it locates her in the tradition of the ancestral women?

Another passage shows that women were more actively involved in the resistance against the Seleucids' domination than 2:29 seems to indicate. In 1:60-64 we learn that women opposed the occupiers' edicts by continuing to honor the religious traditions of their people and having to pay for it with their lives. "In accordance with the royal decree, they put to death women who had had their children circumcised. Their babies, their families, and those who had circumcised them, they hanged by the neck. Yet many in Israel found strength to resist, taking a determined stand against eating any unclean food. They welcomed death rather than defile themselves and profane the holy covenant, and so they died. Israel lived under a reign of terror" (NEB). This text reports that women did not let themselves be driven to renounce their allegiance to the covenant. (For the author of the book, only the Israelite women who were part of the Maccabean resistance movement kept the covenant.) Women continued the religious traditions such as circumcision. According to this, women did participate in the resistance against the imperialist regime that was intent on establishing a uniform rule and a uniform culture, that of Hellenism, and doing so in brutal fashion. Women were part of the group of pious Jews that "obeyed the law" and would rather suffer martyrdom than submit to the demands of Antiochus (cf. Schuller 1992, 238). In their active resistance they risked their lives. The Second Book of Maccabees assigns considerably more space and a more significant role to the martyrdom of the mothers as well as to the narrative of the murder of the mother and her seven sons (2 Macc 6–7) than the first book. According to the narrative in the second book, these women cause YHWH to show mercy once again to the people of Israel (cf. Engel 2008, 328).

That women supported the Maccabean movement is indicated also in 1 Maccabees 1:60-61. That text describes a central domain of life that Israelite women organized. Persecution affected the whole house *(oikos)* (1:61). The project of Hellenization penetrated even individual house-communities. There is no boundary here between private and public life. The goal of Seleucid politics was the total Hellenization of even the smallest social structures. In safeguarding religious traditions within the household, women obviously played a highly valued role. They made sure that food regulations were honored (1:63). In addition, according to 1:60-61, mothers were assigned the task of their sons' religious initiation: circumcision (cf. Goldstein 1976, 139). Even if they did not administer circumcision themselves, the decision to circumcise, and when to circumcise, was theirs. If we can accept that Israelite women participated in the resistance against the Seleucid rulers, we would naturally want to know also whether Israelite women supported or belonged to those groups in Israel that approved of the Hellenization of their land and culture. There is no evidence of this in First Maccabees. Even though the book speaks of many men who made common cause with the Hellenists, offered sacrifices to the new idols, and profaned the Sabbath (1:43), that does not mean the movement of Jews for the Hellenist reforms consisted exclusively of men. The same would have to be said about the Israelites who observed the law, thereby bringing brutal persecution at the hands of the Seleucids, yet responded with resistance: they were not only men. We can assume that the split in the population of Israel at that time did not bypass women. As there were women who sided with the Maccabean uprising, there would have been those who supported the Hellenistic reforms. First Maccabees provides no information about the latter. The reason is not only that women were not accorded the status of equal subjects. The men and women in Israel who favored the reforms are described on the whole in a rather summary manner; the book is not interested in profiling that group. We know only that they renounced the covenant with YHWH, plotted with the Seleucids against the Maccabean movement, and joined them in the war.

The Story of War — a Story of Success?

Many passages in the book confirm that the Maccabees showed the same behavior in war that they had experienced at the hands of their enemies. The reports of the war often list how many enemies had been killed. The fact that Israel had prevailed against much, much more powerful foes is particularly stressed. Another episode narrates how Jonathan took revenge on the sons of Jambri who had captured and killed Jonathan's brother John when he and his baggage train that quite likely included women, children, and herds (cf. Dommershausen 1985, 65) wanted to cross the Jambrites' territory. Jonathan had heard that Jambri's sons were celebrating an important wedding. The daughter of one of the great nobles of Canaan was to be escorted home from Nadabath with a large retinue. The bridegroom, his friends, and his brothers came out to meet her with tambourines and songs; they were also well armed. Not even a wedding is free of danger. At that moment Jonathan emerged from his ambush and attacked the procession; he and his Maccabeans created a bloodbath and captured the whole baggage train. "So the wedding was turned into mourning, and the sound of music to lamentation" (9:41 NEB).

But next to such reports are others, such as that of Simon, who, upon being implored by the citizens to have mercy, spares the city of Gezer, which also had joined the Hellenists (cf. 13:43-48). Still, the overall structure and flow of the book accept the violence of war manifested by the Maccabees. The author of this book is faithfully devoted to the family of Judas Maccabeus (cf. Schunk 1980, 292), inasmuch as he tells the history of the beginnings of the Hasmonean high-priestly and royal dynasty "with undisguised sympathy" (Engel 2008, 319). His aim is "to remove any and all misgivings about the legitimacy of the Hasmoneans as the highest administrative, cultic and military leaders (14:41-42)" (Engel 2008, 319). Accordingly, the story of the war is told broadly as one of heroes and their successes. The war is presented in the book as a necessity. Again and again the text speaks of Seleucid attacks that had been instigated by the Hellenistic party against which the Maccabean movement had to defend itself. It is therefore not far-fetched to assume that this was a "civil war" (Bickermann 1937, 137) between those in Israel who supported the Hellenistic party and the Maccabeans, who, in the eyes of the author, fought for the preservation of Jewish religion, tradition, and culture. But the chief enemy and oppressor remains the Seleucid king Antiochus IV Epiphanes; his desecration of the temple and massive religious persecution represent the apex of the Seleucid occupation. First Maccabees does not reject violence and war but justifies them *within* the movement for liberation and in connection with self-defense against oppression. It is not for naught that the need to respond to the attacks by the Seleucid party is stressed repeatedly. The Maccabean movement is given approval not because it resorts to violence but because it fights for the preservation of its religious tradition and the liberation from the Hellenistic control of every aspect of life.

If we read the First Book of Maccabees as the story of a people attempting within a given historical context to resist the forceful imposition of a unitary culture and religion, we can look upon the aim of this liberation movement positively without consenting to the violence associated with it. (The Jewish feast of Hanukkah, recalling the rededication of the temple, relates *exclusively* to this liberation tradition; cf. Bickermann 1937, 137.) "After the event, nothing coerces us women particularly to justify violence in this history" (Schroer 1998, 154). The biblical tradition concurrent to the writing of this book of Maccabees also manifests quite diverse views on violence and war. Books such as Judith ($\rightarrow$ Judith), Daniel ($\rightarrow$ Daniel), and the Second Book of Maccabees ($\rightarrow$ 2 Maccabees) clearly show that next to the positive attitude to the Hasmonean dynasty, there are voices in the Bible critical of this ruling clan and the events related to the time in question. For example, the book of Judith not only contrasts Judas Maccabeus with the figure of a woman called Judith who succeeds in averting a threat to Israel by not resorting to the instrument of war; it also develops a theology in which YHWH is the one who *makes wars to cease* (cf. Jth 16:3). The First Book of Maccabees wants to present the wars and successes of the Maccabees. If we read between the lines, we find there a tale of a tragic conflict that reappears also today in many ethnic and religious conflicts. Cultural vulnerability (cf. Young 1998, 320) and fear of losing one's cultural identity in times of turbulent change or when facing an intolerant superior power can turn into violence when the world is unable to accept cultural, ethnic, and religious differences.

LITERATURE

Bickermann, Elias J. 1937. *Der Gott der Makkabäer.* Berlin.

Dobbeler, Stephanie von. 1997. *Die Bücher 1, 2 Makkabäer.* Neuer Stuttgarter Kommentar, Altes Testament, vol. 11. Stuttgart.

Dommershausen, Werner. 1985. *1. und 2. Makkabäer.* Neue Echter Bibel, vol. 12. Würzburg.

Engel, Helmut. 2008. "Die Bücher der Makkabäer." In *Einleitung in das Alte Testament,* edited by Erich Zenger et al., 312-28. Stuttgart, Berlin, and Cologne.

Goldstein, Jonathan A. 1976. *1 Maccabees.* Anchor Yale Bible, vol. 41. Garden City, N.Y.

Hengel, Martin. 1969. *Judentum und Hellenismus. Studien zu ihrer Begegnung unter besonderer Berücksichtigung Palästinas bis zur Mitte des 2. Jh v. Chr.* Tübingen.

———. 1976. *Juden, Griechen und Barbaren. Aspekte der Hellenisierung des Judentums in vorchristlicher Zeit.* Stuttgarter Bibelstudien, vol. 76. Stuttgart.

Sakenfeld, Katharine Doob. 1989. "Feministische Verfahrensweisen im Umgang mit der Bibel." In *Befreien wir das Wort. Feministische Bibelauslegung,* edited by Letty M. Russell, 63-74. Gütersloh.

Schroer, Silvia. 1998. "Toward a Feminist Reconstruction of the History of Israel." In *Feminist Interpretation: The Bible in Women's Perspective,* by Luise Schottroff, Silvia Schroer, and Marie-Theres Wacker, 83-176, Minneapolis.

Schuller, Eileen M. 1992. "The Apocrypha." In *The Women's Bible Commentary,* edited by Carol A. Newsom and Sharon H. Ringe, 235-43. London and Louisville.

Schunk, Klaus-Dietrich. 1980. *1. Makkabäerbuch. Jüdische Schriften aus hellenistisch-römischer Zeit,* vol. 1, 4. Gütersloh.

———. 1991. "Makkabäer/Makkabäerbücher." In *Theologische Realenzyklopädie,* 21:736-45. Berlin.

Schüssler Fiorenza, Elisabeth. 1992. *But She Said: Feminist Practices of Biblical Interpretation.* Boston.

FOR FURTHER READING

Mittmann-Richert, Ulrike. 2000. *Einführung zu den historischen und legendarischen Erzählungen. Jüdische Schriften aus hellenistisch-römischer Zeit,* vol. 4, 1, 1. Gütersloh.

Young, Robin Darling. 1998. "1 Maccabees." In *The Women's Bible Commentary,* 318-21. London and Louisville.

Translated by Martin Rumscheidt

2 Maccabees: The Teaching of History

Christine Gerber

Introduction

Content and Structure of Second Maccabees

Like the First Book of Maccabees (→ 1 Maccabees), the second book also deals with the life of the Jewish people during the rule of the Seleucids, the attacks on the freedom of religion, and the struggle against them under the leadership of the so-called Maccabeans. The second book presents more extensively a briefer period and in part an earlier time than the first book, namely, the events of the years 175-161 B.C.E., and deals only with activities of the first brother of the Maccabees, Judas.

At the core of the first chapters are the temple and the assault on its holiness by the Seleucid chancellor Heliodorus (chapter 3). These chapters also tell of the Hellenizing moves of High Priests Jason and Menelaus and their followers (chapters 4–5) and the Seleucid king Antiochus IV Epiphanes (5–6). Antiochus plunders and profanes the temple, occupies the city later on, prohibits the observance of the law, and has observant Jews executed (chapters 6f.). After that martyrdom, Judas starts a movement of resistance (8:1-4), and while Antiochus comes to a horrible end (chapter 9), Judas restores the cult of YHWH (chapter 10) and defends the temple, the city of Jerusalem, and the people against further attacks by the Seleucid potentates (10:9-15), in particular Nicanor. His violent death in war and the return of self-government conclude the book (15:37).

Two letters precede (1:1-10a; 1:10b–2:18) but are unrelated to this narrative; each calls for the celebration of temple feasts.

Corresponding to the threefold threat to the temple, there is a three-part structuring of chapters 3–15, namely, chapter 3, chapters 4–10:8, and 10:9-15 (cf. Doran 1981, 47ff., who supports this linguistically; Goldstein 1983, 12; Schunk 1991, 739; and Dommershausen 1985, 8 all propose a two-part structure placing the division at 10:8; Mittmann-Richert 2000, 43 sees a five-part ring composition around 6:18–10:8). Chapter 3 stands alone as an introductory narrative; parts two and three report parallel events that respectively recall particular events: the torments experienced by Jewish men and women at the hands of the enemy, the attack on the temple, the death of martyrs and the victory of the Jews over their foes and their punishment by death, and, finally, the institution of the temple feast commemorating these events.

Literary Layers and Their Dating

It is clear even at first glance that 2 Maccabees did not come into being as a unified work, and there is no consensus on the history of its origins. As its preamble states (2:19-32), the main part of the book is an abridgment *(epitome)* of a five-volume history by Jason of Cyrene. We know nothing else about this man. Attempts to draw conclusions from this abridgment from Jason's work (such as Goldstein 1983) or to determine a later redaction of the *epitome* (cf. esp. Habicht 1976, 174-77) lack sufficient grounding (cf. Doran 1981, 12ff., 83f.). This also applies especially to the assumption that the seventh chapter — which will be dealt with more extensively later — is a later addition. It is quite probable that the story of the martyrdom of the seven brothers and their mother developed independently, as the absence of the otherwise ever so important temple would indicate, yet it now makes up an integral part of the *epitome* (Doran 1981, 22f.). There are good reasons for dating the *epitome* in the final third of the second century B.C.E. (Doran 1981, 111f.; Habicht 1976, 175, who dates it similarly but for other reasons; Goldstein 1983, 71-83 dates it later).

When the letters were placed at the head of the work is uncertain; the first is presumably a genuine letter from 164 B.C.E., the second, quite likely, is a fake from the first century B.C.E. (cf. Habicht 1976, 199ff.).

The Literary Character of 2 Maccabees 3–15

However rigorously Jewish in its moral concepts, the main part of this book (chapters 3–15) is Greek in its literary form. As a work of historiography, it shares style, rhetorical usages, and *topoi* with other Greek and Roman history writings of the epoch (Doran 1981, 84ff.). It would be more precise still to categorize the book as "rhetorical" or "tragic" or "pathetic" historiography (cf. Habicht 1976, 189f.; Goldstein 1983, 19-21; an opposing view is Doran 1981, 86-97) so as to express how much 2 Maccabees incorporates emotions in its narrative formation and presentation to enable the hearers/readers to experience the story themselves. In this it differs from pragmatic historiography, which seeks to provide objective information and an objective foundation for judgment, as well as from what today's historiography claims to be for itself: the "objective" presentation of "what really happened" (Goldstein 1983, 84). This has to be kept in mind if 2 Maccabees is to be used as a source for reconstructing historical events. In terms of (post)modern insight into the rhetorical and interest-conditioned character of every presentation of history, this book is a consciously partial work (see below) with an explicit learning goal (cf. the following reflections).

The Reception of the Book in the History of Theology and Research

Until recently the stirring tales of martyrdom were of primary interest. The story of the death of the seven brothers and their mother above all seems to have been the archetypal tale of martyrdom (Kellermann 1979, 35ff.); the effect of it has its own rich history (Cohen 1971; Schatkin 1974; Doran 1980). Because of these stirring tales, 2 Maccabees was incorporated into the Greek canon of the First Testament and, consequently, into that of the Catholic Church; chapter 7 was taken into the Roman Catholic lectionary. As a work written in Greek, it is not part of the Hebrew Bible and is counted in the churches of the Reformation at most among the apocryphal writings (Schunk 1991, 742).

Three aspects draw the interest of current study of this book. First, its depiction of historical events differs from and is more detailed than that of 1 Maccabees and shows that it was not only the Greek occupiers who imposed Hellenistic ways of life and culture. Within the Jewish people there were those who favored acceptance of Hellenistic customs even though they contradicted Jewish law (Bickermann 1937). Second, the work contains very early evidence of resurrection hope. Third, chapters 6 and 7 play a role in the modern discussion about Jewish and Hellenistic traditions behind the Second Testament's conceptions of the vicarious assumption of guilt and atoning death (cf. de Jonge 1991; also below).

Since 2 Maccabees manifests no interest in women (cf. the next section), feminist exegesis of the Bible has also no interest in it. I am not aware of any explicitly feminist interpretation of the book.

The Interest and Subject of This Presentation

To make the silence about women in this historiography audible, it is worthwhile to look first at the references to women and what purpose they serve and then focus more extensively on the presentation of the only woman cited in the book, the mother of the seven brothers (chapter 7). The tales of martyrdom are remarkable illustrations of the resistance against oppressors; they can be assessed appropriately only when the wider theological horizon of the *epitome* is known. The subject of *my* interpretation is chapters 3–15 as a unified text (even though a longer period of development may lie behind), as we have received it from a final but otherwise unknown writer. The premise is that 2 Maccabees does not reveal what "really" happened but constructs a history while pursuing a specific interest.

Women's History and Historiography in 2 Maccabees

Historical Events and Their Picture in 2 Maccabees

Only one woman is mentioned by name in this book, and that in a half-sentence: Antiochis, a concubine to the Ptolemaic king (4:30). Otherwise and without exception, only men have names and are characterized; they determine the course of history whether as leaders or soldiers, winners or sinners. Women play only minor supporting roles; the sole exception is to be discussed further on. What 2 Maccabees presents is an androcentric view of history. To ask when and how women enter the picture at all exposes an interest of the presentation. Women are often identified in reference to family status: wives, mothers, widows, "virgins." The stereotypical conjunction of "women and children" is preponderant (5:13; 12:3; 15:18; cf. also 12:21: "women and children with all the baggage," or 3:10; 8:28 and 30: "widows and orphans"). Only twice are women not referred to in this fashion or as mothers: in 3:19 women and unmarried women are depicted as a "choir of lamenters"; in 6:4 prostitutes and married women are spoken of as objects of (men's) lust. Women have no role to play in public life, which, incidentally, is true also of the mother of the seven brothers.

Women and children, widows and orphans are more objects of welfare (8:28 and 30), in need of protection (12:21), although they are not worthy of the kind of protection the temple requires (15:18). Women have no role in war and are worth mentioning only as its victims (5:13 and 24). The men "make themselves manly" for their tasks in war (15:17). And what do they do in peacetime? "[Nicanor] urged [Judas] to marry and start a family. So Judas married and settled down to the quiet life of an ordinary citizen" (14:25 NEB).

Women are not named either from the camp of the "bad Jews," lawbreakers and collaborators; however, they are mentioned specifically as active subjects among those who pay with their lives for their fidelity to the law (6:10; cf. chapter 7). But here, too, as soon as they are active subjects, their role is that of victims. Women are spoken of hardly for their own sake: their lamenting (3:19-20) serves to depict the magnitude of the calamity, the share of the spoils given them is meant to show the justice of Judas's regime. When the martyrdom of women is narrated, we are to see primarily the uncompromising fidelity of the righteous to the law and the brutality of the enemy.

War is men's business, and women are only its victims: this is what 2 Maccabees teaches. Women are not worth identifying by name; they are defined in terms of family relationships and belong to the private sphere, to children, and, when unmarried, they should be secluded indoors. What does deserve mentioning is their commitment to the law.

In Aid of Reconstructing Women's History

We are not able to unearth more than a few details from this book that are of use in reconstructing a history of women given how its historiography hides women; in the opinion of Habicht (1976, 211), 3:10 is "significant for the emancipation of women." There we read that contributions given by widows and orphans were held in trust at the temple; therefore, according to 2 Maccabees, widows could have their own property.

Later in the chapter we hear of unmarried women who had been kept in seclusion running to the gateways and walls of their houses and lamenting (3:19). There are references to women under "house arrest" elsewhere (Archer 1990, 120), but that formulation does not signal that this was a general practice, nor does such idealized depiction allow conclusions about reality at that time.

That women were among those who paid with their lives on account of their obedience to the law (6:10) can be assumed not only because 6:10 mentions women specifically. 1 Maccabees 1:61 also reports that two mothers were thrown down from the city walls because their sons had been circumcised. Given the stylized and idealized presentation, the idea that the story of the mother and her seven sons also contains historical recollection (Young 1991, 68) cannot be substantiated.

It is not quite clear in 2 Maccabees 6:10 whether the women circumcised their children themselves; in later rabbinical practice that was prohibited (e.g., *Qiddushin* 29a; cf. Archer 1990, 223). The active form of the verb, present also in the parallel texts of 1 Maccabees 1:60-61 and 4 Maccabees 4:25, may signify a causative meaning so that this action had only been arranged by the women (contrary to Schuller 1992, 238). In any case, according to the narrative, the women were responsible for their children's circumcision.

The Main Theological Features of 2 Maccabees

God, the Powerful Ruler of History, and His People

God is omnipotent and "visibly" determines the course of history: this is the fundamental theological conviction of the book (as indicated by the many epithets for God, in particular *despotēs* and Pantocrator). The events of history are presented in such a way that they become transparent to the action of God; this applies not only to the successes of Jewish fighters and the defeats of their enemies but also to the suffering of the Jewish people. The people, the city, and the temple are threatened (cf. 2 Macc 2:22; 3:1-7; 8:2-3). Here the temple is not of higher importance than the people (5:19), even though the fate of the former is occasionally asserted to be the real theme of the book (cf. Doran's title "Temple Propaganda"), marking the concern about and struggle for the temple as the dramatic high points of events and stressing the feasts of the temple in the introductory letters.

The narration takes it for granted that God has a special relationship with his own, the Jewish people (cf. 14:15). It manifests itself in that God is present in the one temple in the "holy city" (3:38-39; 5:20), as well as in that God defends and saves his people. The first episode of the narration speaks about this: when Heliodorus comes to plunder the temple's treasury and the whole city cries out for help, God saves the temple in a powerful epiphany (chapter 3, esp. 3:24-28; cf. also 8:16-20; contrary to Attridge 1984, 181, who states that God's help is the reward for piety so that the people showed piety in order to receive God's help).

Another dimension of the special relationship is strict observance of the laws of God. The book is not concerned with whether it is possible to keep the law and to what extent. Rather, it is taken for granted that God's law is good and therefore to be obeyed at all times; for example, the Sabbath rest has to be kept even in extreme danger of war (15:1-5). (A judgment such as Habicht's — 1976, 187 — that "[i]n matters of cult, Second Maccabees is narrowly and unrealistically severe," derives from a failure to grasp the Jewish understanding of law.)

God's Action in History: Acts and Their Effects

According to 2 Maccabees, history teaches that what happens to human beings corresponds to what they do. That God punishes the wicked becomes particularly obvious when the punishment matches deeds of injustice (cf., e.g., 4:38; 9:5-6 and 28). But punishment comes not only upon the foes of the Jewish people; it also comes upon the people themselves because the initially untroubled relationship between God and his people is disturbed when Jews break the law, especially when the high priests emulate the Greek lifestyle. "The very men whose way of life they strove after . . . turned out to be their vindictive enemies" (4:16 NEB). The historical narrative is particularly concerned to show that not only the negative elements among the Jewish people will receive punishment in accordance with their trespasses (cf. 4:26; 5:9-10; 13:8) but that the people as a whole must suffer punishment by their enemies but are nonetheless not abandoned by God. In the punishment that is soon to come upon the people, God teaches his people, whereas he lets other nations bring their misfortune to its completion themselves (6:12-16; 7:33).

The close connection between guilt and suffering is demonstrated even in the reverse judgment that someone who suffers must have become guilty beforehand. During the war, some of the fallen Jews were found with amulets on them; this subsequently convinced Judas and his men that even though those warriors had fought on the Jewish side, it was just that they lost their lives (12:39-40). Even martyrs die on account of guilt; they do not die because of personal offenses but because of those of the people (7:18 and 32).

Martyrdom and Reconciliation

The narratives of the martyrdom of Jewish men *and Jewish women* who would rather die at the hands of the enemy or take their own lives than break the law (6:18-28; 7; 14:37-46; cf. also 6:10-11) are of special significance in the account of history of 2 Maccabees.

In the struggle for an uncompromising observance of God's law, the martyrs are the ideals who not only call upon others to be faithful to the law (cf. 6:27-28) but also illustrate how the potentates of this world lose power. Setting themselves up as the antagonists of God (7:9 and 30; 9:8; 15:4-5; cf. 2:20-21), the latter have their power diminished by those Jews who fear death at the hands of those sinners less than they fear God's law. Antiochus's fit of rage (7:39) shows that he saw this quite clearly. And so the dying testify that the power behind them is greater (7:9, 16 and 35) — something confirmed later by Antiochus's punishment by death (chapter 9).

As the story moves on, the several incidents of martyrdom it reports in chapters 6–7 take on even greater significance: they reverse the fate of the people. When they have come to an end (8:1-7), Judas — like the martyrs, he too is an ideal of the Jewish people (van Henten 1989, 145f.) — finally appears, gathers a throng of observant Jews, and enters the struggle victoriously. The reversal of defeat into victory is possible because "the Lord's anger had changed to mercy" (8:5 NEB; cf. 7:33 and 37-38). In the face of the death of such faithful for the sake of the observance of the law, God shows compassion and intervenes in the liberation struggle (5:20; 8:27). (In my interpretation of this passage I leave aside the customary reference to "atoning" or "vicarious death" because these conceptions are not explicitly present here. Cf. the discussion in de Jonge 1991.)

All's Well That Ends Well

Judas succeeds in defeating the enemies of the Jewish people; he reinstates the temple cult and reestablishes the Jewish people's self-determination. Before they come to their deserved end, the enemies, and Antiochus in particular, have to acknowledge God's power (8:36; 9:8 and 12-17; 11:13-14; cf. already 3:28 and 36-39).

The suffering of the righteous also is redressed, for after their death they shall receive back in the resurrection what they lost. This assurance of faith is repeated several times (7:9, 11, and 14; 14:46; cf. 12:43-45; 15:12-16) and is expressed especially by the mother of the seven brothers, for which reason she will be mentioned here particularly.

"Women's Knowledge and Men's Courage": The Mother's Wisdom about Resurrection — 2 Maccabees 7

Moved by the dignified bearing of the mother of the seven brothers, later ages sang her praises (4 Maccabees), gave her names (above all, "Hannah"; cf. Cohen 1971), and wrote about her death (Kellermann 1979, 17ff.). And yet, 2 Maccabees knows rather little about her. Nonetheless, according to this book, her role and her words deserve "to be remembered with special honour" (7:20 NEB). After six of her sons had courageously gone to their deaths because they had refused to eat pork, the mother enters center stage; until then she had been left so much at the margins of the narrative that it looks as if her appearance was written in later (cf. especially Nickelsburg 1972, 106). Her courageous bearing is particularly highlighted in contrast to that of her sons because in one single day she endures the experience of witnessing the loss of her seven sons (7:20), that is, the promise of a large progeny (cf. 4 Macc 16:9-11). While Antiochus is determined to instrumentalize her so that he can demonstrate his power at least with the last son and thereby save face (2 Macc 7:25-26), it never occurs to her for a moment not to exhort all her sons to go to their deaths (7:21). She can bear the loss of her children because she is convinced of the godliness of their conduct and because her hope is in God (7:20). For she hopes that God will give them back to her in the day of his mercy (7:29). And it is precisely as *mother* that this woman becomes a prime witness to the faith in the martyrs' bodily resurrection; she does so in two ways.

First, her exhortation to the sons to go to their deaths is a special testimony to the resurrection faith since one would expect that the earthly life of her children — the very ones she carried in her body, gave birth to, nurtured, and raised up — matters more to her than anything else. Her second speech makes that plain (7:27-29) where references to her motherly care and attachment to her sons frame the argument for resurrection. (This aspect is central in 4 Maccabees 14:11ff. and, especially, in 15:5ff. where she is portrayed as the greatest example of reason conquering passions, that is, mother love.)

Second, it is no coincidence at all that the substantiation of resurrection faith comes from the mouth of a mother despite the utter neglect of women that characterizes 2 Maccabees. The author himself signals this in the introduction to the mother's speech: "she reinforced her womanly argument *(logismos)* with manly courage" (2 Macc 7:21 NJB). This does not have to mean what some commentators think it does, namely, that the mother compensated for womanly weakness ("womanly sentiment" — as Dommershausen puts it, 1985, 183; or Habicht 1976, 236: "women's way of thinking") with "manly courage" or thought in a womanly way of her role as mother (Goldstein 1983, 107). If *logismos* (reckoning, argument) is related to the mother's subsequent argument for resurrection, then her logic cannot be "typically womanly"; after all, she has to convince her sons and male readers. What is "womanly" is the knowledge, the experience with which she presents the proof of resurrection. In her speeches (7:22-23 and 27-29) she grounds her conviction of the power of resurrection in God's power to create "out of what did not exist" (7:28 NJB; cf. Goldstein 1983, 307 on the original meaning of this expression known as *creatio ex nihilo*) and in the creation of humankind in miraculous fashion. Both demonstrate God's power to give back life even to those who had been killed, their bodies mutilated and burned. Her second reason is of particular note because the reference to the mysterious, divine origin of every human being's life in the mother's body takes up the experience of a mother (7:22). While this idea occurs frequently in Jewish First Testament wisdom and other writings of antiquity (cf. references in Kellermann 1979, 29 and 69), it presents itself here in the perspective of a mother, of someone who knows best what is involved because she experiences life coming to be in her body. Her words manifest how well acquainted she is with the Bible (Kellermann 1979, 28f.); they also show much philosophical knowledge (Goldstein 1983, 311ff.).

Still, this mother does have a "womanly role" in this narrative. She is defined through her sons (who are only called "brothers" and never "sons"); she stays in the family domain and appears not to be listened to by her youngest son at all (7:30-38). Even when she stands before the king and is addressed by him, she herself talks only to her sons, using their "father tongue" (7:21 and 27, that is, Hebrew or Aramaic in contrast to the Greek the king speaks). She speaks of her role during pregnancy as passive, and that is even what she bases her argument for resurrection on: *God alone is creative.* And while the death of the brothers is described at great length, *her death* is mentioned only briefly (7:41), and it is not clear whether she also died at the hands of others.

On the other hand, the self-assurance she manifests should not be overlooked. When she speaks of her pregnancies and concern for her children, she does so without reference to a progenitor or father. (4 Maccabees took offense at that; in an appendix it put words in the mother's mouth that recall the sons' deceased father and what he taught them. Cf. 4 Maccabees 18:6-19 and Klauck 1989, 657f. on that passage.) Finally, she is sure that she is as worthy of the resurrection promised to the martyrs as her sons are (2 Macc 7:29).

Moving, Strange, and Annoying: A Feminist View of 2 Maccabees

The narrative of Second Maccabees is full of deep faith in God's omnipotence and his superiority over earthly potentates. It is convinced that perfect observance of the law is right and that it is wrong to compromise the restrictions given in traditional religion. Those holding such convictions deserve respect regardless of how strange their understanding of God's law may appear to others. In my view, the idealization of the martyrs' self-sacrifice and the mother's denial of her feelings must also be respected within the scope of these Jewish values.

The tales of martyrdom are moving. As they were for Jewish and Christian women and men of past centuries — the seven brothers and their mother are the only martyrs honored equally by Jews and Christians — they can be an impressive example even now of resistance against a superpower's unbearable demands. The tales want to arouse and strengthen the courage to resist, to accept physical pain, even destruction and the loss of loved ones. Those who suffer are strengthened and empowered by their hope in a higher justice, in a future where the injustice of the present age is rectified. On the one hand, this is the hope of the resurrection of the body, the reconstitution of present relationships; it is a hope that especially the mother of the seven brothers expresses impressively. This woman "deserves to be remembered with special honour" (7:20 NEB): her words of the experience of transcendence she had as a pregnant woman, her testimony to God's life-giving care for individual women and men.

But 2 Maccabees also gives courage to those who suffer with its theological assurance that, in the end, God punishes the wicked and that his anger is assuaged through the suffering of the righteous. This (not specifically Jewish) theology, and particularly its solution of the question of theodicy — the wicked will meet their just punishment and all suffering is just punishment for iniquity — was met with criticism already in the Hebrew Bible. Today, that view lacks plausibility and is even perceived as cynical. It could be upheld even in the historiography of the Maccabean era only because the narrative of 2 Maccabees came to a close before subsequent changes in history.

The one-sidedness of the book in leaving aside the experience and suffering of women unless they conform to the ideal of the "house- and self-sacrificing wife" must be criticized. But if we want to correct it, all we can do — since the sources are mute — is use our imagination and invent what has been forgotten: write women back into the narrative (cf. Plaskow 1991, 25-60).

That way there was handed down to us — in a "paragon" of men's war historiography — the remembrance of a wise woman and courageous mother and of the power of resistance against oppression. And we have an example of how offensive an undialectical theology of God's omnipotence can be.

LITERATURE

Archer, Léonie. 1990. *Her Price Is Beyond Rubies: The Jewish Women in Greco-Roman Palestine.* Journal for the Study of the Old Testament: Supplement Series, vol. 60. Sheffield.

Attridge, Harold W. 1984. "2 Maccabees." In *Jewish Writings in the Second Temple Period,* edited by Michael E. Stone, 176-83. Compendia rerum iudaicarum ad Novum Testamentum, Section 2. Assen.

Bickermann, Elias. 1937. *Der Gott der Makkabäer.* Berlin.

Cohen, Gerson D. 1971. "Hannah and Her Seven Sons." In *Encyclopedia Judaica,* 1270-72. Jerusalem.

De Jonge, Marinus. 1991. "Jesus' Death for Others and the Death of the Maccabean Martyrs (1988)." In *Jewish Eschatology,* edited by Marinus de Jonge, 125-34. Supplements to Novum Testamentum, vol. 63. Leiden.

Dommershausen, Werner. 1985. *1 Makkabäer. 2 Makkabäer.* Neue Echter Bibel Altes Testament, vol. 12. Würzburg.

Doran, Robert. 1980. "The Martyr: A Synoptic View of the Mother and Her Seven Sons." In *Ideal Figures in Ancient Judaism: Profiles and Paradigms,* edited by John J. Collins et al., 189-211. Septuagint and Cognate Studies, vol. 12. Chico, Calif.

————. 1981. *Temple Propaganda: The Purpose and Character of 2 Maccabees.* Catholic Biblical Quarterly Monograph Series, vol. 12. Washington, D.C.

Goldstein, Jonathan A. 1983. *II Maccabees.* Anchor Bible, vol. 41A. New York.

Habicht, Christian. 1976. *2. Makkabäerbuch. Jüdische Schriften aus hellenistisch-römischer Zeit,* vol. 3, 1. Gütersloh.

Kellermann, Ulrich. 1979. *Auferstanden in den Himmeln. 2 Makkabäer und die Auferstehung des Märtyrers.* Stuttgarter Bibelstudien, vol. 95. Stuttgart.

Klauck, Hans-Joseph. 1989. *4. Makkabäerbuch. Jüdische Schriften aus hellenistisch-römischer Zeit,* vol. 3, 6. Gütersloh.

Nickelsburg, George. 1972. *Resurrection, Immortality, and Eternal Life in Intertestamental Judaism.* Harvard Theological Studies, vol. 26. Cambridge.

Plaskow, Judith. 1991. *Standing Again at Sinai: Judaism from a Feminist Perspective.* San Francisco.

————. 1992. *Und wieder stehen wir am Sinai. Eine jüdisch-feministische Theologie.* Luzern.

Schatkin, Margret. 1974. "The Maccabean Martyrs." *Vigiliae christianae* 28:97-113.

Schuller, Eileen M. 1992. "The Apocrypha." In *The Women's Bible Commentary,* edited by Carol A. Newsom and Sharon H. Ringe, 235-43. London and Louisville.

Schunk, Klaus-Dietrich. 1991. "Makkabäer/Makkabäerbücher." In *Theologische Realenzyklopädie,* 736-45. Berlin.

Van Henten, Jan W. 1989. "Das jüdische Selbstverständnis in den ältesten Martyrien." In *Die Entstehung der jüdischen Martyrologie,* edited by Jan W. van Henten, 127-61. Studia post-biblica, vol. 38. Leiden et al.

Young, Robin Darling. 1991. "The 'Woman with the Soul of Abraham': Traditions about the Mother of the Maccabean Martyrs." In *"Women Like This": New Perspectives on Jewish Women in the Greco-Roman World,* edited by Amy-Jill Levine, 67-81. Early Judaism and Its Literature, no. 1. Atlanta.

FOR FURTHER READING

Mittmann-Richert, Ulrike. 2000. *Einführung zu den historischen und legendarischen Erzählungen. Jüdische Schriften aus hellenistisch-römischer Zeit,* vol. 4, 1, 1. Gütersloh.

Wacker, Marie-Theres. 2006. "Theologie einer Mutter — Eine Mutter als Theologin. Feministisch-exegetische Anmerkungen zu 2 Makk 7." In *Gott bin ich, kein Mann. Beiträge zur Hermeneutik der biblischen Gottesrede,* edited by Ilona Riedel-Spangenberger and Erich Zenger, 259-70. Festschrift for Helen Schüngel-Straumann. Paderborn.

Translated by Martin Rumscheidt

Tobit: A Lesson on Marriage and Family in the Diaspora

Helen Schüngel-Straumann

Overview

The book of Tobit was not included in the canon of the Hebrew Bible. Its original Semitic version has been lost, and the book has come down to us only in Greek, in three divergent versions (Hanhart 1984). In Catholic tradition it is regarded as a deuterocanonical writing, that is, one belonging to the LXX but not to the Hebrew Bible; for Jewish and therefore for Reformed traditions it is an apocryphal book. The consequence of this is that there have been scarcely any recent commentaries on Tobit in German. It is not treated in any of the current Protestant commentary series, and has not yet appeared in the series Jüdische Schriften aus hellenistisch-römischer Zeit (Jewish writings from the Hellenistic-Roman period). It is, however, included in the brief and relatively recent commentary in Neue Echter Bibel (1987), and that translation is the basis for the present essay. It is identical to the *Einheitsübersetzung,* which is used in churches of the Catholic tradition in both liturgical and instructional contexts.

Time, Structure, and Genre

When the book originated is important for certain woman-specific issues, for example, the extent to which misogynistic or woman-friendly tendencies, as well as which customs and usages, play a role in marriage and the wooing of a bride. It is certain that the book does not belong to the period in which it pretends to be located (the end of the eighth century B.C.E.); it is, rather, a historicizing fiction. The narrative is dated back to a time before the Babylonian exile, but it originated in the Hellenistic era. The most common opinion today is that it was written around 200 B.C.E. (before the Maccabean revolts).

As to its genre, the narrative is similar to a novel, but it contains some elements of the fairy tale. Since it also has some strongly didactic elements responding to the question "how can a pious Jew, male or female, live a faithful life in the diaspora?" it is likewise possible to call Tobit a midrash. That this is an *artistic* narrative is evident from the clearly dual structure: the same event happens in different places simultaneously. While Tobit is lamenting his suffering and presenting to God his desire to die, Sarah is praying in faraway Ecbatana, also lamenting her misery before God; she leaves her chamber just as Tobit leaves his: "At the same time that Tobit returned from the courtyard into his house, Sarah daughter of Raguel came down from her upper room" (3:17).

The two distant stages on which the story plays itself out are joined together by a long journey taken by Tobias, the son of the ancient Tobit, to obtain a wife from his own kindred. The two families are linked in a number of ways. The repeated back-and-forth, geographically impossible if the narrative were understood as purely historical, is to be read in a transferred sense on the narrative level: life is a way, a journey; the Greek *hodos* is one of the key concepts in the book.

The different places where the action takes place, and the stages of the journey, are each introduced or left behind with a prayer. These numerous prayers are like hinges in the narrative; men and women alike turn directly to God and beg him for help.

Besides the key word "way," other major concepts run through the narrative and allow us to discern the content of its theological teaching; these are justice, mercy, and the desire to praise God. All these things characterize a pious Jew in the pagan world, who attempts to keep Israel's Torah in contemporary terms and to do justice to the tradition of the fathers (and mothers).

Content

No feminist interpretation of the book of Tobit has yet appeared. Therefore, in what follows I will lift up the themes relevant to such an interpretation. Since this is a *family* narrative, a whole series of women appear, as a matter of course, at significant moments. These female roles must be examined. In addition, we will examine the two main themes of the book: the desire to keep the commandments — here we will pay special attention to the commandment of respect for parents — and the marriage of a Jewish man to a woman from his own people and tribe. Both themes are developed in relation to traditions from the Hebrew Bible, those regarding both the commandments (the Decalogue) and the narrative literature (especially Gen 24: the courtship of Rebekah).

Women's Roles

The narrative juxtaposes two married couples: Tobit and Hannah, the parents of Tobias, and Raguel and Edna, the parents of Sarah. At the end we find a new family, Sarah and Tobias (and their children), the goal of the narrative.

In his introductory presentation (Tob 1:3-9), Tobit, in the first person, describes his origins. It appears that he married a wife from within his father's family, but also that his father apparently died young and he was raised by his father's mother, Deborah — that is, his grandmother (nothing is said about his own mother). He learned from her the tradition of the commandments to which he adheres. Thus in Tobit's family it is not the father but the grandmother who has handed on the tradition of the faith. However, this woman does not appear in the narrative proper; she is mentioned only in retrospect. The narrative begins, then, with the impoverished Tobit, who is being persecuted because of his acts of mercy, namely, burying the dead. Tobit secretly buries his fellow believers, and in doing so he thwarts the intention of the pagan opponents to humiliate his people. The theme of "burial" is central to the whole book (cf. the ending!) and also serves to demonstrate Tobit's fidelity to the Law. Ultimately, he has nothing but his wife and his son Tobias. After he has become blind in the aftermath of carrying out another burial, Tobit is entirely dependent on his wife: she is now responsible also for feeding the family.

Hannah's role is described in very ambivalent terms. She weaves cloth to support the family and on one occasion receives a young goat as a gift in addition to what she is paid. Tobit does not believe her; in his fidelity to the Law he suspects that she has stolen the animal, and he becomes angry at her. The trust between the married couple is destroyed. Tobit's wife, in turn, gets her revenge by mocking her husband: "Where are your [rewards for your] acts of charity? Where are your [wages for] righteous deeds? Everyone knows [what they have brought you]" (2:14). This statement strongly recalls the reaction of Job's wife to his suffering: "Do you still persist in your integrity? Curse God, and die!" (Job 2:9).

The commentaries seize on this mockery, which apparently represents a model in the postexilic period: the suffering of the righteous is magnified by the lack of understanding he receives from his wife! One example of commentary on Tobit 2:14 can serve as representative: "It is altogether a repetition of the scene in Job (2:9-10): the agitated woman, whom the devil loves to lead astray and uses to tempt the righteous, but in doing so only increases his virtue and fame, in contrast to the calm and objectively-judging righteous man" (Miller 1940/41, 48).

The misogynistic history of reception, particularly with regard to Job's wife, has been very powerful. It is noteworthy also that the Neue Echter Bibel puts a heading on this paragraph: "Tobit Is Mocked by His Wife" (Gross 1987, 20), without considering that Tobit had previously accused his wife falsely of theft, thus distrusting his own wife, who supports him through her work. There is scarcely any commentary on this fact.

Apart from this passage at the beginning, Hannah has an active role only once more, namely, when her son Tobias returns. She is the one who shows concern and who looks down the road every day, to see if he is coming home. So she is the first one to see him, and she tells her husband. At the end of the story she survives her husband: Tobias first has to bury his father decently, and then his mother, before he returns to his in-laws in the East.

At every point where the subject is the son's journey to fulfill his duty to recover his father's money, and whenever there is instruction about orders and recommendations for the journey, the father alone is the subject: he sends Tobias on his journey; he alone gives commands and advice. The mother is depicted solely as one who mourns and laments because she is afraid for her son's life, while Tobit apparently knows from the beginning that the affair will have a good outcome: "'Do not worry; our child will leave in good health and return to us in good health. Your eyes will see him on the day when he returns to you in good health. . . . For a good angel will accompany him; his journey will be successful, and he will come back in good health.' So she stopped weeping" (5:21-23).

How does he know all that? Tobit is depicted in the role of one who, despite sickness and poverty, retains the long view, who knows everything with certainty and has the function of leadership in every respect, while his wife Hannah leaves rather a pitiful impression. An active figure she is not.

The division of roles is similar for the other married couple, Raguel and Edna. The active person is always the father. Sarah is Raguel's only child, as is repeatedly emphasized. She wanted to hang herself to escape her troubles, but she did not because "she thought it over and said: 'Never shall they reproach my father, saying to him, "You had only one beloved daughter but she hanged herself because of her distress." And I shall bring my father in his old age down in sorrow to Hades'" (3:10).

The house to which Tobias and his traveling companion come is Raguel's (7:1). Sarah is given to Tobias as his wife, but the only one active in the business is Raguel. His wife Edna's sole task is to decorate the bridal chamber. Even the marriage feast made for the couple is arranged by Raguel alone (8:19-20).

When the son returns, again Tobit alone has an active role. Although it is Hannah who first sees Tobias, since she had gone to meet him, Tobias goes into the house with his father alone and tells him all the miraculous things he has experienced on the journey (11:15); nothing at all is said about his mother. Likewise, the new daughter-in-law is greeted only by Tobit and received by him into the house; Hannah is not mentioned.

Thus the relationships in both families are described in altogether patriarchal and patrilineal terms. What matters is the house of the father; the father decides, gives in marriage, and receives; he distributes property. The mother — although she must be thought of as present — is scarcely more than a statistic. Again, the great hymn of praise in chapter 13 is placed on the lips of Tobit alone; he prays in the first person and does not mention his wife at any point.

The division of roles between the young couple, Sarah and Tobias, is somewhat different. Here the personal relationship of the bridal pair is emphasized several times. When the travelers arrive in Ecbatana, Sarah comes to greet them and leads them into the house (7:1). The scene recalls Jacob's arrival at the house of Laban (Gen 29), when it was also the future wife, Rachel, who greeted the guests. But as regards the marriage itself, Sarah is not asked; in Tobit 7:13-14 the bride is given by her father to the young Tobias. Differently from Rebekah (Gen 24), she is also not asked whether she wants to go with her relative (cf. Gen 24:57-58). Whether this can be traced to the fact that the matter was settled previously by the angel's words is a question we need not ask. The rest of the story, as with the two older couples, speaks only of Tobias or his children; his wife, we suppose, is silently included. Only when they return to Ecbatana (Tob 14:12) is there express mention of Sarah again.

Honoring Parents

While the patriarchal structure of the marriages as depicted causes the women almost never to be explicitly named, the strong emphasis on the honor due to parents makes for a different usage. There is no word for "parents" in the Hebrew Bible; the reference must always be to father and mother. In the instructions Tobit gives to his son Tobias before his journey, the first thing he says is: "My son, when I die, give me a proper burial. Honor your mother and do not abandon her all the days of her life. Do whatever pleases her, and do not grieve her in anything. Remember her, my son, because she faced many dangers for you while you were in her womb. And when she dies, bury her beside me in the same grave" (4:2-5).

The first commandment his father emphasizes to him is thus the honoring of father and mother. Apparently Tobit expects that his wife will survive him. What is interesting here is not only the strong emphasis on the mother, but also the grounding of the instruction in the difficulties of pregnancy. Tobias is to show himself grateful for what his mother suffered for him. We have here strong echoes of older biblical traditions, not only the commandment in the Decalogue (Exod 20/Deut 5), but probably also Genesis 3, where there is explicit mention of the difficulties of pregnancy and birth. Since Tobit also contains strong echoes of Genesis 2 (see below), this is probably a recollection of the narratives of the creation of man and woman (→ Genesis 1–11).

As in the Decalogue, the father comes before the mother, but all the commandments regarding parents mention *both*; in Leviticus 19:3 the mother even comes before the father. The emphasis on a decent burial, which is a central interest of the whole book of Tobit, is here applied also to the parents. It is only through a proper burial that the dead person comes to his or her well-earned rest. Hope for a resurrection of the dead is not yet a presumption in the book of Tobit; human life is fulfilled here on earth. The grown son is responsible for seeing that life finds its worthy end. That is his final service to his parents. The fact that this obligation is emphasized here before any other reveals the significance of the family. Those who have no son — a daughter cannot assume this responsibility — are deprived of the most important honors and cannot die in quiet and peace.

Consequently, Tobias must also assume this obligation toward his in-laws in faraway Media, for they have no son (Tob 14:12-13). So, after the death of his parents, Tobias must return with his whole family to Ecbatana; with this, the little book ends. Tobias has thus fulfilled all his family obligations, and the whole solidarity of the generations has been assured through his actions.

The Marriage Arrangements for Sarah and Tobias

The chief problem for the whole book is the maintenance of endogamy, that is, finding a wife for Tobias from his own people, as his father had done. Tobit's family seems to be quite isolated, living within a pagan environment. This is evident also from the difficulties he encounters in burying other members of his nation, which he sees as an important service. But for his own family there is a problem in continuing the Jewish tradition: if that tradition and the faith itself are not to be abandoned within a few generations, it is of the utmost importance that a marriage partner be taken from within the Jewish people. Tobit goes still further: the partner must come from within the family itself. Hence a pious Jew in the diaspora must do everything to preserve his Jewish identity. For this, no journey is too long, as the little book of Tobit demonstrates. In the postexilic period this fundamental law of endogamy sometimes was carried so far that marriages with non-Israelites were forbidden. In fact, in Ezra 9–10 the men of Israel are commanded to expel all their non-Jewish wives (and their children!) and send them back to their own people. Tobit here again points to the example of the ancestors, who also married endogamously.

Besides the problem of endogamy, which seems to be solved in Tobit when a relative in distant Ecbatana is chosen as a wife for Tobias, some special difficulties, traceable to a demon, face the wedding itself. Sarah, it turns out, has already been married seven times, and all those men died; that is, they were killed by the demon Asmodeus before they had slept with Sarah (Tob 3:8). This last note is important, since Sarah must enter her marriage with her (future) husband Tobias as a virgin.

Parallel to the fate of old Tobit, Sarah is also ridiculed; that is, she too is accused of being responsible for her fate: "So the maid said to her, 'You are the one who kills your husbands! See, you have already been married to seven husbands and have not borne the name of a single one of them. Why do you beat us? Because your husbands are dead? Go with them! May we never see a son or daughter of yours!' On that day [Sarah] was grieved in spirit and wept" (3:8-10).

The hope for a future — here meaning a continuation of the family and thus necessarily also the blessing of children — is very slight for both families. By their desire to die, both Tobit and Sarah have as good as given up what little hope there was. Their prayers are parallel. But now, by God's intervention through the angel Raphael, things take a turn for the better: 3:16-17 is the hinge in the book of Tobit, already anticipating the happy ending: "At that very moment, the prayers of both of them were heard in the glorious presence of God. So Raphael was sent to heal both of them: Tobit, by removing the white films from his eyes, so that he might see God's light with his eyes; and Sarah, daughter of Raguel, by giving her in marriage to Tobias son of Tobit, and by setting her free from the wicked demon Asmodeus. For Tobias was entitled to have her before all others who had desired to marry her."

Now Tobit can send his son on his journey, and he gives him orders to take a wife only from his own tribe (4:12-13). During the journey the angel Raphael takes command. Under his instruction Tobias finds a fish in the Tigris; its heart, liver, and gall will be used later as medicine, both for Sarah's healing and for that of his father, Tobit. The angel's name expresses what he does: Rapha-el means "God heals."

Tobias had heard about the dangers threatening every man who approached Sarah. Therefore he says to Raphael: "[A demon loves her and] kills anyone who desires to approach her. . . . I am afraid that I may die and bring my father's and mother's life down to their grave, grieving for me — and they have no other son to bury them" (6:14).

The death of Sarah's seven husbands is here attributed to the "love" of a demon. That a demon, or the woman herself, kills all the men who approach her sexually is a common motif appearing in many fairy tales. Raphael, whom Tobias still thinks of as a traveling companion — he knows nothing of his status as an angel — calms Tobias and predicts a good outcome: "'[This young woman] was set apart for you before the world was made. You will save her, and she will go with you. I presume that you will have children by her, and they will be as brothers to you. . . .' When Tobias heard the words of Raphael . . . he loved her very much, and his heart was drawn to her" (6:18-19). When the two enter Raguel's house, Raphael becomes the bridegroom's friend, the one who negotiates for the bride. In Israel, marriages were arranged between the parents; the children need not be asked, neither the son nor the daughter. At a later time negotiators were used; they took care of all the negotiations until the marriage contract was concluded in the bride's house.

The marriage became legal when the bride's father handed her over to the bridegroom: "Then Raguel summoned his daughter Sarah. When she came to him he took her by the hand and gave her to Tobias, saying, 'Take her to be your wife in accordance with the law and decree written in the book of Moses. Take her and bring her safely to your father.' And he blessed them" (7:12).

The first evidence of a written marriage contract in the corpus of the First Testament is given in the book of Tobit. For that purpose Raguel also summons his wife: "Then he called her mother and told her to bring writing material; and he wrote out a copy of a marriage contract, to the effect that he gave her to him as wife according to the decree of the law of Moses. Then they began to eat and drink" (7:13-14). Although the marriage was now complete in its valid legal form, the tension here rises to its climax because the consummation of the marriage is yet to come and everyone is wondering whether this time the bridegroom will escape alive. Sarah's father, at any rate, is skeptical; the next morning he has already dug a grave in which to bury this marital candidate in secrecy before daylight. When he learns the next morning that both the children are still alive, he has the grave filled in again.

Although the readers know from the outset that there will be a happy ending to the story, it remains an open question how the demon will be rendered harmless. This is accomplished through a ritual prescribed by Raphael. What kind of background, especially what kinds of fears, underlies this story? We know that the whole Hellenistic-Roman period was marked by strong belief in demons. Even in Jesus' time unknown illnesses and other hard-to-explain phenomena were attributed to demons. The fact that the demon in Tobit was expelled by medical means shows that it was regarded as a sickness from which one could be healed.

It is an intercultural phenomenon that the transition from one state of life to another, in this case the wedding night, bore strong taboos and was beset with fears. This transition was fear-laden and required particular rituals or precautions. The fact that in Sarah's previous marriages the men always died while Sarah remained alive, shows that the primary problem was male sexual fears, especially the man's anxiety in the face of female sexuality.

We have a comparable narrative in the First Testament in which a number of men die while the woman remains alive: the story of Judah and Tamar (Gen 38). The patriarch Judah gave his eldest son to Tamar as her husband. He died, and it is said that he was not pleasing to God. So, according to levirate law, Judah gave Tamar his second son, Onan. The latter spilled his seed on the ground instead of begetting a son for his dead brother. Therefore this second husband also had to die. Now Judah was reluctant to give his third son to his daughter-in-law, Tamar, because he feared that he might die also. This is the same fear that is the subject here in the Tobit story. Apparently Judah saw Tamar as a man-murdering being who was guilty of the deaths of his two sons. But the biblical text has a different view: it says explicitly, in both cases, that *God* was the cause of the deaths of the two men, not the woman, Tamar (on this cf. Schüngel-Straumann 1984).

In the book of Tobit as well, guilt does not belong to the woman, Sarah, but to the demon Asmodeus. Apparently there was a popular belief that survives in many myths and fairy tales, including the later Jewish story of Lilith, that woman, or certain women, is/are fatal to men. Therefore special protective measures are required for the wedding night. This reflects the ancient awareness of the superiority of women in matters of life and love, and especially men's primeval fear of women's sexuality, which brings with it life and death. The awareness that the woman creates new life — and in doing so, in earlier times, often lost her own — was surrounded by anxiety and apparently made the man aware that his own power and role are limited, that for him, too, the time will come when he must withdraw from the scene. At the latest with the birth of a son, he enters the second phase of life. It is therefore no accident that Judah's two sons had to die because they did not want to beget a son. For marriage and birth are closely linked and are seen as parts of a whole. Tobit takes a clear position toward such ideas: contrary to a common misogynistic popular belief, which assigned the danger of sexual activity to the woman alone, both the book of Tobit and Genesis 38 step back from such notions. It is not the woman, her sexuality, or her desire that is the origin of evil. A popular view — we can also call it superstition — is here corrected. Sexuality, rather, is something positive when carried out with the right attitude and the right partner. It is not explicitly said why Sarah's previous suitors had to die. Later interpretations have frequently attributed to them a warped attitude, for example, pure lust and improper purposes, unlike those the young Tobias expresses in his prayer. The prayer Tobias prays with Sarah, and to which she explicitly says her "Amen," expresses the attitude of the couple:

> "Sister, get up, and let us pray and implore our Lord that he grant us mercy and safety. . . ." Tobias began by saying, "Blessed are you, O God of our ancestors, and blessed is your name in all generations forever. Let the heavens and the whole creation bless you forever. You made Adam, and for him you made his wife Eve as a helper and support. From the two of them the human race has sprung. You said, 'It is not good that the man should be alone; let us make a helper for him like himself.' I now am taking this kinswoman of mine, not because of lust, but with sincerity. Grant that she and I may find mercy and that we may grow old together." And they both said, "Amen, Amen." Then they went to sleep for the night. (8:4-9)

The right attitude includes — once again — reference to the biblical tradition. This is a unique reference in the First Testament, in such complete clarity, to the creation of man and woman in Genesis 2, with the statements about the purposes of their common life made central. The first human beings are here regarded as individuals and given the personal names Adam and Eve (on this cf. Schüngel-Straumann 1989). This shows that Tobias knows the history and tradition of his people and intends to carry them on (→ Genesis 1–11).

However, a certain narrowing appears here. For one thing, there is the androcentric view, with the *man* as the standard, whereas in Genesis 2 *'ādām* originally referred to the human being as such. We can observe a further restriction to marriage and family, while in contrast, in Genesis 2, the relationship between man and woman is described *as fundamental* (and without any reference to future progeny). In addition, in Tobit 8 everything is set in a clear order that must be maintained. True partnership exists for the sake of mutual support, so that the burden of loneliness may be avoided and the couple may reach an advanced age together. As in the angel's statement to Tobias (6:17) that Sarah had been chosen for him from the beginning, here also the androcentric point of view is as drastic as it gets: the woman is regarded exclusively in terms of her value for the man.

This description, suggestive almost of an idyllic situation by male standards, is the goal of the Tobit narrative, which, as a story of guidance, shows how all difficulties are overcome when one trusts in God, whose greatness appears even more brilliantly the larger the dangers surmounted. Only through a marriage like that between Tobias and Sarah can the Jewish people's existence and their tradition be preserved in the diaspora; only thus can Jewish identity be maintained.

LITERATURE

Bow, Beverly, and George W. E. Nickelsburg. 1991. "Patriarchy with a Twist: Men and Women in Tobit." In *"Women Like This": New Perspectives on Jewish Women in the Greco-Roman World,* edited by Amy-Jill Levine, 127-43. Atlanta.

Deselaers, Paul. 1982. *Das Buch Tobit. Studien zu seiner Entstehung, Komposition und Theologie.* Orbis biblicus et orientalis, vol. 43. Fribourg and Göttingen.

Eskenazi, Tamara C. 1992. "Out from the Shadows: Biblical Women in the Post-exilic Era." *Journal for the Study of the Old Testament* 54:25-43.

Gross, Heinrich. 1987. *Tobit, Judit.* Neue Echter Bibel. Würzburg.

Hanhart, Robert. 1984. *Text und Textgeschichte des Buches Tobit.* Göttingen.

Ilan, Tal. 1995. *Jewish Women in Greco-Roman Palestine: An Inquiry into Image and Status.* Texte und Studien zum antiken Judentum, vol. 44. Tübingen.

Küchler, Max. 1979. *Frühjüdische Weisheitstraditionen. Zum Fortgang weisheitlichen Denkens im Bereich des frühjüdischen Jahweglaubens.* Orbis biblicus et orientalis, vol. 26. Fribourg and Göttingen.

Levine, Amy-Jill. 1992. "Tobit: Teaching Jews How to Live in the Diaspora." *Bible Review* 8:42-51.

Mayer, Günter. 1987. *Die jüdische Frau in der hellenistisch-römischen Antike.* Stuttgart.

Mayer-Schärtel, Bärbel. 1995. *Das Frauenbild des Josephus. Eine sozialgeschichtliche und kulturanthropologische Untersuchung.* Stuttgart.

Miller, Athanasius. 1940/41. *Das Buch Tobias übersetzt und erklärt.* Die Heilige Schrift des Alten Testaments, vol. 4, 3. Bonn.

Moore, Carey A. 1996. *Tobit: A New Translation with Introduction and Commentary.* Anchor Bible, vol. 40a. New York.

Nowell, Irene. 1983. *The Book of Tobit: Narrative Technique and Theology.* Washington, D.C.

Rabenau, Merten. 1994. *Studien zum Buch Tobit.* Beihefte zur Zeitschrift für die alttestamentliche Wissenschaft, vol. 220. Berlin.

Schüngel-Straumann, Helen. 1984. "Tamar. Eine Frau verschafft sich ihr Recht." *Bibel und Kirche* 39:148-57.

———. 1989. *Die Frau am Anfang. Eva und die Folgen.* Freiburg. 2nd ed. Münster, 1997.

Standhartinger, Angela. 1995. *Das Frauenbild im Judentum der hellenistischen Zeit. Ein Beitrag anhand von "Joseph & Aseneth."* Leiden.

Talmon, Shemaryahu, ed. 1991. *Jewish Civilization in the Hellenistic-Roman Period.* Sheffield.

Weskott, Hanne. 1974. "Die Darstellung der Tobiasgeschichte in der bildenden Kunst Westeuropas. Von den Anfängen bis zum 19. Jh." Ph.D. diss., Munich.

Zimmermann, Frank. 1958. *The Book of Tobit: An English Translation with Introduction and Commentary.* Jewish Apocryphal Literature Series. New York.

For Further Reading

Schüngel-Straumann, Helen. 2000. *Tobit. Übersetzt und ausgelegt von Helen Schüngel-Straumann.* Herders theologischer Kommentar zum Alten Testament. Freiburg im Breisgau.

Translated by Linda M. Maloney

Judith: About a Beauty Who Is Not What She Pretends to Be

Claudia Rakel

Named for its female protagonist Judith — the Hebrew name Jehudit means "Jewess" (cf. Levinson 1992, 124) — the book of Judith tells of the salvation of the people of Israel from being conquered by a huge Assyrian army. The intelligent, God-fearing, and beautiful widow Judith gives her life as she averts war by entering the enemy camp and killing their general, Holofernes. The story does not report historic events. Instead, in this book various historic events from different periods are woven together as in a collage. Thus Nebuchadnezzar is not the king of Babylon in this text, which would correspond to historical fact, but the king of Assyria. This is a well-chosen anachronism, to be sure, since Nebuchadnezzar represents the Babylonian exile (586 B.C.E.), the destruction of the temple, and the end of the sovereignty of Judah as a separate state, whereas, by contrast, Assyria is associated with the destruction of the northern kingdom (722 B.C.E.) and the threatening of Jerusalem (701 B.C.E.) by Sennacherib. So it is not just anybody that is attacking the people of Israel here, and it is not just any history of the people of Israel that is being told. Rather, what we have here is a retrospective narrative of *the* history of Israel with all the threats by great powers to its people as well as to its city of Jerusalem. In novel-like form the narrative, which took shape about 100 B.C.E., processes above all the events of the Maccabean period (→ 1 Maccabees; 2 Maccabees), since it recounts how this threat was averted and the temple at Jerusalem was saved from desecration by the enemies of Israel (cf. Jth 4:3).

Although the Judith narrative is not contained in the Hebrew Bible, for many Jewish women it is connected with the tradition of the Festival of Hanukkah, the Feast of Lights, which reminds people of the rededication of the temple of Jerusalem, since it is close to the books of the Maccabees. Some Jewish congregations today still sing a Judith hymn (cf. Levinson 1989, 89). Hanukkah lamps, especially medieval examples, that integrate representations of the figure of Judith demonstrate the close connection between the events described in the books of the Maccabees and in Judith for Jewish tradition. The question why Judith found acceptance in the Greek canon but not in the Hebrew one is difficult to answer. Possible reasons include the fact that the book was written late, and the original was in all likelihood written in Greek (all texts found to date have proven to be derived from the Greek text). On the other hand, the assumption that the book was not included in the Hebrew canon because it conveyed too autonomous and powerful an image of women (cf., among others, Craven 1983, 117) seems excessively speculative (cf. Hopkins 1998, 281) and in my view relies on a problematic understanding of early Judaism.

Scarcely another book of the Bible has experienced such an ambivalent reception history. Judith has seen intensive treatment especially in the visual arts, dominated by the motif of the beheading of Holofernes (cf. Stone 1992; Stocker 1998). In the exegetical interpretations, the characterizations of the protagonist Judith range from heroine, as embodiment of true piety, as mother of Israel, as wise woman and widow, as savior of Israel, to deceptive *femme fatale,* as a phallic woman and warrior who makes use of the "weapons of a woman" (cf. Elder 1991, 4). How can such different and contradictory interpretations of the figure of Judith and her history exist side by side? Mieke Bal calls the book the classic case of an "ideo-story" (Bal 1995, 264). By this term she means a narrative whose structure offers a foil onto which different, often contradictory, ideologies and messages can be projected. Ideo-stories have an extremely open structure, which requires that they be filled with a statement, a cohesive message (cf. Bal 1995, 264). Thus, here, the narrative itself provides the foil for the androcentric reception. Does it also offer the foil for a feminist reception that is liberating? A feminist interpretation of an ideo-story will always move between the pole of suspicion toward the androcentric structures of the text and the pole of trust in the potential of the text to critique dominance. The following interpretation of Judith uses primarily the tools of literary criticism to analyze the final text. It attempts to explain central points of Judith on the basis of the fundamental themes in the text. It does not intend to, and cannot, cancel out the tension between suspension and trust, but instead will attempt to allow both impulses to have a voice.

Putting an End to Wars

War and the God Question

The theological center of Judith is the question of God. To be sure, a female figure plays the central role in the narrative, yet the story's primary emphasis is on the greatness and might of YHWH (*dynamis* is a key word in the text). The book provides an answer to the question, Who is the true God, YHWH or Nebuchadnezzar? At the beginning of the book King Nebuchadnezzar formulates a destructive policy for his regime, threatening the brutal annihilation of all the western nations that would not fulfill their duties as vassals in Nebuchadnezzar's war against King Arphaxad. Nebuchadnezzar not only presumes to order the world by means of war, but also does so with the claim of being the true god, for Holofernes, his general and the instrument with which his policy is executed, not only destroys the places of worship and sanctuaries of the peoples he conquers, so that all the nations will worship Nebuchadnezzar (cf. Jth 3:8), but he also questions the God of Israel when he is warned by Achior about the power of this God (cf. 6:2). The book rejects this claim, which alludes to the Hellenizing policies of Antiochus IV Epiphanes (175-164 B.C.E.), as pseudoreligious, and counters the claim with "YHWH's way of ruling," which consists of putting an end to wars. This essential message is given to Judith to utter in two central places in the text. In her prayer before she enters the enemy camp to preserve Israel from destruction and downfall, Judith asks YHWH to look at the Assyrians, flaunting their military might and refusing to see that he is the God who puts an end to wars (cf. 9:7). After Judith has returned from the enemy camp with the head of Holofernes, thereby putting Israel in the position of sending the enemy army into flight, she begins a hymn to the glory of God with the words: "Glorify him, and sing his praise, exalt his name and call upon him! For YHWH is a God who puts an end to wars" (16:1-3);[1] [Goodspeed: "who crushes wars" (9:8) and "shatters wars" (16:3)]. The true being of God is shown in putting an end to wars. In Judith YHWH is not described as a warrior who measures his might against other lords of war. Thus the book does not at all glorify war or violence, but criticizes war.

Pamela J. Milne has attempted through her analysis of the narrative to show that the figure of Judith, because of the central role of the God question, does not have the role of heroine, but merely plays a supporting role to a male hero, YHWH. With this interpretation, Judith serves the interests of men, making her into the "antithesis of a woman-identified woman" (Milne 1993, 54). However, the mere fact that YHWH only appears one single time as an active subject in the entire book (4:1) speaks against such an analysis. This is incompatible with the narrative role of the hero, since traditionally most components of the plot are associated with that role. The central function of the God question does not mean that the role of Judith is not that of heroine in the narrative sense. Yet, to be presented with a female biblical heroine also does not mean that Judith must represent a figure whom women can receive positively. Female hero figures, too, can have androcentric characteristics.

1. Textual references by the author to the book of Judith often do not concur with English versions of the Apocrypha. Cf. "Judith," trans. Edgar J. Goodspeed, in *The Apocrypha* (New York: Modern Library, 1959), 133-64. Where we depart from Goodspeed's wording to follow the author's argument, this is indicated in a note. [Translator's note.]

Androcentrically Occupied Femininity

The question arises whether the critical potential of the book, that is, the critique of war and dominance, also includes the problem of gender. YHWH's option for the weak and oppressed is tied to the rejection of war. In it Judith finds affirmation for her action: "Break their pride[2] by a woman's hand! For your might is not in great numbers, your rule needs no strong men; on the contrary, you are the God of the weak and the helper of the lowly; you are the champion of the weak, the protector of the despised and the savior of the hopeless" (9:10-11). YHWH ends the war in a different way than the generals, and in so doing makes use of the weak and oppressed. In the context of this kind of rule, there is no place for men who represent military might, aggression, and hegemony: "YHWH, the almighty, outwitted them by the hand of a woman. Their war hero fell not at the hands of young men, it was not the sons of Titans that slew him, nor did giants come to meet him. No, Judith, daughter of Merari, dazed him with the beauty of her countenance" (16:6).[3] It is not by male and military dominance that YHWH unfolds his power, but through female beauty that can paralyze men. Thus the form of rule of the God of Israel becomes a program that takes up the issue of gender. The book of Judith opts against a male form of conflict resolution and for a female form. The might of male war making and paralyzing female beauty are antithetically juxtaposed here. Thus both male and female stereotypes are reinforced. The action of the narrative has a gendered binary structure. The book brings into focus a very specific form of femininity. Beauty, wit, and seduction are attributed to women as a sex; violence and war are attributed to men. Here we also see an androcentric perspective of the text, namely, that beauty is constructed in terms of its effect on men, and femininity in relation to them. Yet within this androcentric and binarily structured framework, the construction of femininity has a positive value, while male forms of rule and behavior (strength, use of violence in war) are rejected. At this point there is a glimpse of a critical perspective toward patriarchal forms of rule and forms of rule that are understood as male, such as war and imperialism. The problematic construction of femininity remains, even though Judith represents femininity positively. For the text of Judith, it is clear that men and women are determined to be and act differently on the basis of their sex. What seems on the surface "misogynist" and critical of men comes down to a stereotypical reinforcement and shortchanging of femininity. Femininity in the book of Judith remains a femininity occupied by androcentrism. Perhaps it is therefore not surprising

2. Goodspeed: "Break down their state with a woman's hand. For your strength is not in numbers, nor your might in the strong, but you are the God of the lowly, the helper of the inferior, the champion of the weak, the protector of the neglected, the savior of the despairing."

3. Goodspeed: "The Lord Almighty brought them to naught / By the hand of a woman. For their champion did not fall at the hands of young men, / The sons of the Titans did not strike him down, / Nor the tall giants set upon him, / But Judith, the daughter of Merari, / Made him faint with the beauty of her face."

that it is primarily male exegesis that claims that Judith is "the feminist's kind of person" (Moore 1985, 65).

The gender question thus plays an explicit role in the text, but it is contained within an androcentric frame that holds fast to the binary structure of "male" and "female" that reinforces gender attributes and thus participates in the patriarchal construction of "femininity." This is one of the profound contradictions of Judith, which conceives of a female as a "counter-figure to the bellicose world of violence" (Zenger 1996, 31) within the liberating conception of an image of a God who ends wars on the one hand, yet on the other hand holds fast to patriarchal constructions in this very figure.

The binary structure of the text has contributed to Judith being stylized as a female warrior who makes use of female weapons: "In Judith the sexual element is so pronounced because it is *the* military weapon" (Craghan 1982, 16). But it is precisely according to androcentric logic that feminine beauty, seduction, and wit are weapons. It must not be overlooked that Judith slays Holofernes with his own weapons. She beheads him with his sword, not with her beauty. The murderous sword is pointed at its owner and destroys the one who intended to destroy.

Rape in War

The book of Judith is characterized by two closely related threads of narrative running parallel to one another. In the first thread, two collective entities face each other: Israel and the mighty army of Holofernes. The book describes the power relationship most impressively. The Assyrian war machinery, wherever it turns up, leaves total ruin and devastation in its wake. Israel, which is threatened by this army, is militarily completely inferior. This power relationship exists within the second thread of the narrative as well, where two individuals face each other: Holofernes, general of this war-making power, and Judith, widow and resident of Betulia. The fight between YHWH and Nebuchadnezzar is decided in the individual fates of Judith and Holofernes. On this level, too, strength and weakness seem to be able to be clearly assigned — strength to the man, weakness to the woman. When Judith calls upon YHWH in her prayer for help with her plans, because he is the God of the humiliated and the weak (cf. Jth 9:11), she as a widow is counting herself as belonging among these weak people.

Person or Personification?

Israel's weakness is thus represented on the individual level of the plot by the figure of Judith, the strength of the army by the figure of Holofernes. The events that take place between Judith and Holofernes are parallel to the events between the threatened people of Israel and the threatening army. By means of this structure, the text creates a relationship between sexist and imperialist oppression. Both imperialism and sexism are described as structures in which the stronger party attempts to exploit the weaker one by brutal means, ignoring its dignity and integrity. This does not mean that the "battle of the sexes" as a human theme is the central theme of the book (cf. Gierlinger-Czerny 2000, 171-72). In biblical tradition, the body of a woman often provides the image for a city or a country, her raped body the image for the conquered city (cf. Ezek 16; Nah 3; et al.). What Holofernes' army intends is to take violent and illegal possession of the land and people of Israel. What Holofernes himself intends to do with Judith is to take violent and illegal possession of her as a woman. Thus the book clearly demonstrates that different forms of violence and oppression are interrelated, without one canceling out the other or being subsumed within the other. For this reason the idea of a "vicarious battle" is not appropriate. What Holofernes' army plans to do to Israel is commit violence toward, exploit, and oppress the people; what Holofernes intends to do to Judith is rape.

The relationship between the threatened conquest of Israel and Holofernes' planned rape of Judith has been understood by various interpreters in reference to the female body as a metaphor for the land, so that the figure of Judith was in the last analysis a personification or embodiment of Israel (cf. Schuller 1992, 242). Linda Bennett Elder objected to interpreting the Judith figure as a metaphor or personification of Israel. She claimed that allegorizing or identifying Judith with the people of Israel erases the independence of Judith's role in the narrative and criticizes it as an androcentric attempt to turn the biblical figure of this woman into an object and rob her of her existence as an acting subject (cf. Elder 1994, 457). The plot threads that weave between Holofernes and Judith, as well as those connecting the army and Israel, are narratively interwoven; because Judith kills Holofernes, Israel can be saved. But they are also symbolically interwoven. Judith also represents Israel in the sense of acting the part, not only in the sense of advocating for them. This symbolic level does not rob the figure of its narrative independence.

Rape — "It Must Not Be Done" (Judith 9:2)

Just as Holofernes is unable to rape Judith, Israel is not conquered by Nebuchadnezzar's army. The fact that Holofernes has the intention of possessing Judith is made clear at several points in the text: "And the heart of Holofernes was out of control, he burned with passion for her and desired to be with her. He had been watching for the chance to seduce her ever since the day he had first seen her" (12:16).[4]

---

4. Goodspeed (12:16): "Holofernes' mind was amazed at her and his heart was stirred, and he was exceedingly desirous of intimacy with her for he had been watching for an opportunity to deceive her ever since he had seen her."

As dominance over a people is to be won by violence, by the same logic, a woman, too, can be "'conquered' by violence" (Müllner 1993, 403). When Judith remembers her ancestor Dinah (Gen 34) in prayer before she goes into the enemy camp (→ Genesis 12–50), we are looking at a central motif of the narrative. As a memory of danger it brings into clear focus the fact that Judith here is Dinah, threatened by rape. She prays to YHWH: "Lord, God of my father Simeon, in whose hand you put a sword to take vengeance on the aliens who had loosened a maiden's belt[5] to defile her and stripped her thigh to shame her and profaned her womb to disgrace her. For you said: 'It must not be done,' yet they did it" (Jth 9:2). Judith addresses YHWH as the one who rejects rape. She remembers Dinah because the crime committed against Dinah was a wrong done before the God who Judith now trusts will not allow it to happen again.

The connection between war and the rape of the women of the conquered people is recorded in biblical texts such as Numbers 31, Genesis 34, and Judges 5:30.[6] When Judith speaks about the enemy army planning to drag off the women of Israel as war booty, it is implied that rape would have been the fate of the Israelite women from the Assyrian conquest. Rape in war is not an act of violence for many biblical texts, but is considered a legitimate way to deal with war booty (cf. Thistlethwaite 1993, 59). It is not understood as a crime against women, as injury to her body and her dignity, but merely as theft of a man's property. The book of Judith clearly rejects this treatment of women as illegitimate and criminal. Just as war and imperialism are condemned, so is this form of sexism that is linked with these mechanisms of domination, namely, rape in war.[7] "It is striking in the text of 'Judith' that the rape of a woman is compared, contrary to expectation, perhaps, not with other sexual acts, but with the violence of war. Thus one can begin to see the possibility of speaking of rape in terms of violence rather than in terms of sexuality" (Müllner 1992, 130). The parallel structure of the destructive mechanisms of dominance sheds light on the text's perspective that rape is fed not by sexual passion, but by hate and lust for power. The suffering of a people in wartime and also the specific experiences of women suffering in war become a theme told from the perspective of those suffering (cf. Jth 16:5). The threat of rape of the Israelite women and of Judith was averted because YHWH was able to prevent the war through Judith's intervention.

5. Goodspeed (9:2): "loosened a maiden's headdress."
6. "Are they not finding and dividing the spoil? — A girl or two for every man."
7. The book of Judith does not present rape as more than "a symptom of war or as a proof of its excesses of violence" (Susan Brownmiller, *Against Our Will: Men, Women, and Rape* [New York, 1975]).

Beauty and Power

Feminist exegesis of Judith has dealt intensively with the figure of Judith and her (deceptive) beauty. Assessments of the figure vary greatly. Some discover in her a positive female figure with feminine qualities, a feminist heroine. Others find the book not only not feminist, but extremely patriarchal, and the figure of Judith a classic *femme fatale*. In the following I intend to take a closer look at the related motifs of "beauty and power" and "beauty and seduction," which form the basis for the divergent interpretations of the text.

A Beauty Who Is Not What She Pretends to Be

Beauty and seduction are central to the way Judith's character is drawn. Both are decisive to her success in killing Holofernes, thereby saving Judith from being raped and Israel from being subjected to war and conquest. This does not mean, however, that only beauty and seduction make the salvation of Israel possible. In addition to Judith's beauty there are her intelligence and her gift with words. The conversation she has with Holofernes in the camp is a "masterpiece of irony and double-entendre" (Schuller 1992, 242) when she assures him: "Yes, God sent me to perform the things with you at which the whole earth, when they shall hear of them, shall be astonished" (Jth 11:16).

It is not merely that Judith is beautiful (8:7); rather, she made herself beautiful. The text makes it abundantly clear that Judith's self-ornamentation is not an end in itself, but for a specific purpose: "she made herself beautiful to beguile the eyes of the men who would see her" (10:4). The fact that the text measures the beauty of a woman by how attractive she is in the eyes of men, shows the androcentric background of the narrative (cf. Müllner 1992, 129). Other female biblical figures, too, like Ruth (cf. Ruth 3:3, 7) and Esther (cf. Esther 5:1) follow this pattern, but in so doing pursue specific purposes (cf. Hellmann 1992, 109). This text, however, creates an unambiguous connection between beauty and seduction. Judith does not make herself beautiful for the enemy soldiers or for Holofernes. On the contrary, she makes herself beautiful in order to seduce and to blind the enemies and the general. The beauty that saves Israel and brings death to Holofernes is therefore an erotic act and a strategy. Judith is described in the narrative as a woman who is conscious of the power of her beauty, and who uses it with clever intelligence for her purposes. By taking possession of the male-defined beauty and with it an androcentrically defined femininity, she carries out a mimesis, an act of representation.

The concept of mimesis is discussed and favored in the feminist philosophy of Luce Irigaray as a female that allows women within patriarchy to define themselves against the role assigned to women by men. This concept also allows Judith's action to be understood. According to Irigaray, women in patriarchal society do not have the opportunity to be themselves; they are always only the Other of the One (of the man). Their only possibility is to play with full consciousness the role that is forced on them by male society. "In conscious play, in *mimesis,* there arises an awareness that this is a game and not one's actual and chosen way of being" (Schlör 1996, 31). The woman becomes a successful actress; she imitates reality in order to be able to distance herself from it: "if women are that good at mimicking, it is because they do not simply disappear into this function" (Irigaray 1979, 78).

The mimesis concept applies precisely to the actions ascribed to Judith by the text. She plays a beauty whose reality is not consistent with her own, but rather with that of men. Judith fulfills male expectations of a beautiful woman; she performs the imitation of beauty as an aesthetic and erotic experience for the male gaze. By imitating beauty with its erotic impulses without allowing them to become her own reality, she makes these into a form of resistance, which she uses to create a different reality: the liberation of Israel (cf. Sawyer 2001, who likewise interprets Judith using this approach).

The Unmasking of the Masculine

The power of "mimetic beauty" consists in the fact that Judith is not recognized in the enemy camp as an enemy. She is perceived by the men as a beautiful woman, not as an Israelite woman, and therefore turns beauty against those who want to reduce her to an erotic beauty. Judith 10 describes very impressively and without irony that the male gaze is incapable of perceiving beauty other than as erotically stimulating to the male. On the way from Betulia to the Assyrian camp, Judith is seen a total of four times by men (cf. 10:7, 13, 14, 18). The structure of the text is the same each time, repeating itself to the point of monotony and thus exposing the male gaze to ridicule. The Judith narrative thus also becomes a "story of vision" (Bal 1995, 277). However, whereas the Israelite men praise God after viewing Judith, since they recognize in her an Israelite woman and thereby recognize her beauty as a strategy, the reaction of the enemy troops is different. For them Judith's attractiveness is an additional argument in favor of conquering Israel: "It would not be good, given so many beautiful women, to let even a single Israelite live" (10:19). These men see only the beauty of Judith and of Israelite women they want to possess. In their blindness they do not see Judith's religious and national identity (cf. Schüssler Fiorenza 1988, 160; 1983, 117), which is her strength. "[S]oldiers and victim (Holofernes) misinterpret Judith's attractive appearance as harmless, just because, blinded by lust, they could only see what they already knew — about women" (Bal 1995, 277). If mimesis criticizes the dominance of the universally valid, of the all-too-unambiguous (cf. Schlör 1996, 27), Judith's "mimetic beauty" opposes the myth, above all else, that female beauty gives license to male-imperial gazes upon the body of the woman and to free male disposal over women.

Dangerous Beauty?

Betsy Merideth compares the story of Samson and Delilah in Judges 16:4-22 with the book of Judith, showing structural similarities between the way Delilah deceives Samson and the way Judith deceives Holofernes. Both texts, according to her thesis, contributed to the deeply rooted cultural ideology that women's sexuality is dangerous for men (cf. Merideth 1989, 63). In both texts women make use of their sexual attractiveness and their feminine skills at seduction in order to deceive a man (68). Delilah entices the secret of Samson's strength out of him and cuts his seven locks of hair off as he sleeps so that the enemy Philistines can overpower him. Delilah is a dubious character; she is not pure and chaste, as is repeatedly emphasized with Judith (75). The fact that Judith acts with the "weapons of a woman" (her beauty, her body, and her sexuality) and yet remains pure, makes her simultaneously desirable and dangerous for men. This shows that even women depicted by the text as "positive" can be vehicles of an anti-woman ideology. For the Judith figure, this comes in the form of a warning to men: female beauty and sexuality are dangerous for men, for women use their attractiveness to deceive men, to do them harm, to kill them (76). This message is more subversive in this book because Judith, the deceiver, kills with the permission of men, and because she as a female Israelite represents a figure with whom readers are to identify. By contrast, in the Samson and Delilah story, it is Samson, the victim of the deception, who as a male Israelite will draw greater sympathy from readers (69).

Carole Fontaine, on the other hand, chooses a different approach to the biblical narratives about cunning and deceitful women. Without denying that patriarchy privileges such stereotyping of women in order to reinforce androcentric ideology, Fontaine sees in such narratives a certain "truth" about the conditions of women in patriarchy: as long as women, on the basis of their status, are kept from achieving their goals directly without fear of reprisal, they will resort to indirect strategies such as deception that are available to people of lower status (cf. Fontaine 1988, 85). The concept of mimesis should also be reconsidered in this direction: mimesis can function only in the context of patriarchal society for it relies on patriarchal gender role assignations that it then seeks to overcome by imitation. A question for further discussion would be whether mimesis is in fact always sufficient to overcome its role, or whether imitation does not threaten to remain stuck in affirmation of the role and thus become counterproductive.

The sentence "Feminine beauty is dangerous for men" must not be read without its opposite — "Feminine beauty endangers women in patriarchal culture." For after all, the book also clearly shows that Judith is threatened with rape. The criticism that must be leveled against the concrete mimesis that the text allows the Judith figure to perform is the following: the fact that Judith must expose herself to the danger of rape in order to destabilize patriarchal and imperialist rule represents too great a risk — even if this danger may not exist for Judith within the logic of the text because she is protected by YHWH.

A frequently raised point of critical feminist exegesis is that the power of "mimetic beauty" remains a mere episode in Judith. Judith is allowed to use her beauty to liberate herself and Israel from the threat of the enemy army, but her mimetic beauty is allowed to become dangerous only to the enemy men and to Holofernes. To be sure, the text is directed against hegemony and oppression. In the way it portrays the situation of violence, it recognizes the structural relationship between individual violence against a woman and collective violence against a people. However, when Judith returns to her community, the text has her give back the power of "mimetic beauty" that she was allowed to have beyond Betulia, that was given to her to liberate Israel, just as she took off the dress she had put on to save Israel with the power of "mimetic beauty." "Judith liberates neither herself nor her countrywomen from the status quo of the biblical gender ideology" (Milne 1993, 55).

At the end of the book, Judith returns to her isolated, ascetic existence as a widow, stylized in the end from childless woman into the mother of Israel (cf. Craven 1990, 39), and is thus assigned a role that fits neatly into patriarchal ideology. There is, however, another possible interpretation for Judith's retreat in the end back into her widow's existence. If Judith remains a widow, she remains in the only space in ancient Near Eastern societies where women have the right to speak for themselves without a male guardian (cf. Fischer 1999, 13).

Numerous Allusions

It has been asserted again and again that Judith refers to many different biblical texts and traditions. "[The] modeling technique is a good example of the use of earlier biblical literature in the literature of the Second Temple period" (White 1992, 14). Sidnie Ann White pointed out that the story of Jael and Deborah (→ Judges) was a model for the figure of Judith (5). The connections between Judith and Jael are obvious since in both cases a woman kills a sleeping general, the deadly attack in both cases being directed at the warrior's head (9). Judith beheads Holofernes; Jael drives a tent peg into Sisera's head. Both women are praised in a hymn later on in the text for their decisive action that leads to Israel's liberation (Judg 5 and Jth 16). In fact, to some degree motifs and word choice even agree among the hymn texts (cf. White 1992, 11).

Aside from this story, though, it is primarily Exodus that belongs to the central text that provides decisive background and a foil for Judith, especially with regard to its theology: the theology of the book of Judith "is consciously modeled after the Exodus narrative where 'by the hand of Moses' Israel is liberated (Ex 9 and 14)" (Schüssler Fiorenza 1988, 158; 1983, 115).

A New Exodus

Again and again the text emphasizes that Israel was saved by Judith. It expresses this with the phrase "by the hand of a woman" (Jth 8:33; 9:10; 12:4; 13:14 and 15; 16:6). While the people of Israel in Exodus are led by YHWH with a strong hand out of Egypt (Exod 13:3), and Moses stretches out his hand to divide the sea (Exod 14:26), in Judith YHWH saves the people by the hand of a woman.

Jan Willem van Henten pointed out the intertextual connections between Judith 7–13 and Exodus 17:1-7. Both stories are about drought (van Henten 1995, 235). While the people in Exodus turn to Moses to give them water, saying it would be better to be slaves in Egypt than to die of thirst, the inhabitants of Betulia in Judith turn to their male leaders and demand capitulation to the enemy, which they see as better than dying. The city elders prove to be poor leaders for they present YHWH with an ultimatum: if the situation does not change within five days, the city would hand itself over to the enemy (Exod 17:2-3; Jth 7:26-27). Judith, by contrast, criticizes the elders' reaction as lacking trust in YHWH. She acts like Moses in that she, like him, calls upon YHWH for help for her plans (Exod 17:4 and Jth 9) and then sets out, like Moses (Exod 17:4-6), to engage herself for Israel's liberation (Jth 10:21–13:2). The parallel to this Exodus narrative shows that Judith advances to an alternative leadership figure of the Israelite community (van Henten 1995, 238). She is an alternative to men, even to Moses, in a new historical context (247).

The hymn in Judith (16:1-17) also refers to the book of Exodus and uses Exodus 15:1-18 in its Greek version as a basis for its theology. "For the Lord is a God who puts an end to wars" (Jth 16:3) is a direct citation of Exodus 15:3. Thus a central assertion of Judith 16:1-17 is that the exodus is not a historic event of the past, but ongoing present reality for the Israelites. YHWH leads the people out from under the burden of war and oppression. In this context Judith becomes "the leader of a new exodus from Egypt, a new Moses, but also a new Miriam (Ex 15), when she, like Miriam, sings the victory hymn in ch. 16" (Schroer 1992, 126). Judith can thus be read as a retelling of the exodus. By having a woman participate in the biblical story, it constitutes the story of YHWH with his people Israel as a history in which women like Judith play a decisive role (cf. Rakel 1999, 47).

Judith, who is also praised for her wisdom (Jth 8:28), at the same time represents "the working of personified Wisdom, who delivered and guided the Exodus people from oppression (cf. Wisdom of Solomon 10:15-21 and 11)" (Schroer 1992, 126). As a wise woman, she stands in the tradition of women like Abigail and the wise woman of Abel-Beth-Maacah, who as givers of counsel contributed to the formation of the image of personified Wisdom, and in so doing "integrated an essential element of the image of woman, but also authentic experience and identity of the women of Israel, into the feminine image of God in the post-exilic period" (Schroer 1991, 19). As the beautiful (Wis 7:29) liberating Lady Wisdom, Judith takes on characteristics of a "female epiphany of the savior God" (Zenger 1996, 33).

Epithets are attributed to her (Jth 15:9f.) that are otherwise only appropriate in relation to YHWH (Zenger 1996, 33).

A Celebration of Women

In chapter 16 Judith raises a hymn together with the women of Israel. On the way to Jerusalem, a victory procession forms. All the women in Israel come to join in, praising Judith and performing a dance in her honor. Judith takes palm branches, which she hands out to the women, and they adorn themselves with them (Jth 15:12-13). Here Judith places herself in a women-centered tradition that is documented several places in the First Testament. The text has Judith show solidarity with the other Israelite women. The tradition that women celebrate the end of a war in song has a solid *Sitz im Leben* in Israel (Exod 15:20-21; Judg 5; 1 Sam 18:6-7). But here it is not only one woman who begins a song. The very theme of the song is this woman; it does not praise some king or other who is returning victorious from battle, but a woman as savior of Israel (cf. van Henten 1995, 250) who has averted a war.

The tradition of victory hymns represents women as active agents in both religious and social spheres (Poethig 1985, 250). Women in Israel expressed their liberation in victory hymns; in their songs they expressed public opinion on political and religious themes (van Dijk-Hemmes 1993, 33). Fokkelien van Dijk-Hemmes discusses this tradition as a possible source of women's literature in which women's voices become audible in the otherwise androcentric discourse of the Bible. For her, one can detect indicators of women's voices when the text contains traces of a less androcentric intention and when it deals with a (re)definition of reality from a feminist perspective, so that the text demonstrates differences between the male perspective and that of female figures (106).

A primary characteristic of this women's tradition is its theological concentration on the liberation from oppression. It delivers a refusal to the claim of worldly dominance and celebrates YHWH as liberator from oppression (Poethig 1985, 253). When Judith praises YHWH at the end of the book for ending the war, reasoning that "he tore me out of the hands of my persecutors" (Jth 16:3), the hymn expresses thanks not only for Israel's salvation, but also for the fact that YHWH did not allow rape as the most aggressive and brutal form of sexism. The fact that the hymn not only celebrates the end of war but also takes into consideration the relationship between war and the rape of women by praising YHWH for protecting Judith from being raped, shows traces of female voices. At the same time, it cannot be denied that the narrative on the whole remains androcentric, for in the end the Israelite women who are so present during the victory procession are once again given over to silence and consistently inscribed back into the male order of things (Levine 1992). Judith and the Israelite women are only granted presence and power in the public sphere for a brief moment. The questioning of traditional gender relationships in Judith remained by necessity a temporary shift, just as saving the temple and saving Jerusalem also remained temporary historically.

LITERATURE

Bal, Mieke. 1995. "Head Hunting: 'Judith' on the Cutting Edge of Knowledge." In *A Feminist Companion to Esther, Judith, and Susanna,* edited by Athalya Brenner, 252-85. Feminist Companion to the Bible, vol. 7. Sheffield.

Craven, Toni. 1983. *Artistry and Faith in the Book of Judith.* Society of Biblical Literature Dissertation Series, vol. 70. Chico, Calif.

———. 1990. "Tradition and Convention in the Book of Judith." In *Feminist Theology: A Reader,* edited by Ann Loades, 29-41. London and Louisville.

Elder, Linda Bennett. 1991. "Transformations in the Judith Mythos: A Feminist Critical Analysis." Ph.D. diss., Florida State University.

———. 1994. "Judith." In *Searching the Scriptures,* edited by Elisabeth Schüssler Fiorenza, 2:455-69. 2 vols. New York.

Fontaine, Carole. 1988. "The Deceptive Goddess in Ancient Near Eastern Myth: Inanna and Inara." *Semitic* 42:84-102.

Friedman, Mira. 1987. "The Metamorphoses of Judith." *Jewish Art* 12/13:225-46.

Hellmann, Monika. 1992. *Judit — eine Frau im Spannungsfeld von Autonomie und göttlicher Führung. Studie über eine Frauengestalt des Alten Testaments.* Frankfurt am Main et al.

Irigaray, Luce. 1979. "Macht des Diskurses/Unterordnung des Weiblichen." In Luce Irigaray, *Das Geschlecht, das nicht eins ist,* esp. 70-88. Berlin.

Levine, Amy-Jill. 1992. "Sacrifice and Salvation: Otherness and Domestication in the Book of Judith." In *No One Spoke Ill of Her: Essays on Judith,* edited by James C. VanderKam, 17-30. Atlanta.

Levinson, Pnina Navè. 1989. *Was wurde aus Saras Töchtern? Frauen im Judentum.* Gütersloh.

———. 1992. "Judith und wir Juden." *Bibel heute* 110:124-25.

Merideth, Betsy. 1989. "Desire and Danger: The Drama of Betrayal in Judges and Judith." In *Anti-Covenant: Counter-Reading Women's Lives in the Hebrew Bible,* edited by Mieke Bal, 63-78. Sheffield.

Milne, Pamela J. 1993. "What Shall We Do with Judith? A Feminist Reassessment of a Biblical 'Heroine.'" *Semeia* 62:37-58.

Müllner, Ilse. 1992. "Der Gott Israels verwandelt Schwäche in Stärke. Das Gebet der Judit in Kapitel 9." *Bibel heute* 110:128-31.

———. 1993. "Mit den Waffen einer Frau? Stärke und Schönheit im Buch Judit." *Katechetische Blätter* 6:399-406.

Poethig, Eunice B. 1985. "The Victory Song Tradition of the Women of Israel." Ph.D. diss., New York.

Schlör, Veronika. 1996. "Mimesis, das Erhabene und der verrückte Diskurs des Weiblichen." In *Feministische Theologie und postmodernes Denken. Zur theologischen Relevanz der Geschlechterdifferenz,* edited by Andrea Günter, 27-38. Stuttgart et al.

Schroer, Silvia. 1991. "Weise Frauen und Ratgeberinnen in Israel — Vorbilder der personifizierten Chokmah." In *Auf den Spuren der Weisheit. Sophia — Wegweiserin für ein neues Gottesbild,* edited by Verena Wodtke, 9-23. Freiburg im Breisgau.

————. 1992. "Zerschlage ihren Stolz durch die Hand einer Frau!" *Bibel heute* 110:126-27.

Schuller, Eileen M. 1992. "The Apocrypha." In *The Women's Bible Commentary,* edited by Carol A. Newsom and Sharon H. Ringe, 235-43. London and Louisville.

Schüssler Fiorenza, Elisabeth. 1983. *In Memory of Her: A Feminist Theological Reconstruction of Early Christian Origins.* New York.

————. 1988. *Zu ihrem Gedächtnis. Eine feministisch-theologische Rekonstruktion der christlichen Ursprünge.* Munich.

Stone, Mira. 1992. "Judith and Holofernes: Some Observations on the Development of the Scene in Art." In *No One Spoke Ill of Her: Essays on Judith,* edited by James C. VanderKam, 73-84. Atlanta.

Thistlethwaite, Susan Brooks. 1993. "'You May Enjoy the Spoil of Your Enemies': Rape as a Biblical Metaphor for War." *Semeia* 61:59-75.

Van Dijk-Hemmes, Fokkelien. 1993. "Traces of Women's Texts in the Hebrew Bible." In Athalya Brenner and Fokkelien van Dijk-Hemmes, *On Gendering Texts: Female and Male Voices in the Hebrew Bible,* 17-109. Leiden.

Van Henten, Jan Willem. 1995. "Judith as Alternative Leader: A Rereading of Judith 7-13." In *A Feminist Companion to Esther, Judith, and Susanna,* edited by Athalya Brenner, 224-49. Feminist Companion to the Bible, vol. 7. Sheffield.

White, Sidnie Ann. 1992. "In the Steps of Jael and Deborah: Judith as Heroine." In *No One Spoke Ill of Her: Essays on Judith,* edited by James C. VanderKam, 5-16. Atlanta.

Zenger, Erich. 1996. "'Wir erkennen keinen anderen als Gott an . . .' (Judit 8:20). Programm und Relevanz des Buches Judit." *Religionsunterricht an höheren Schulen* 1:23-36.

For Further Reading

Craghan, John F. 1982. "Esther, Judith and Ruth: Paradigms for Human Liberation." *Biblical Theological Bulletin* 12:11-19.

Fischer, Irmtraud. 1999. "Judit. Die alttestamentliche Frauengestalt und ihre Wirkungsgeschichte in der abendländlischen Kunst." In *Minna Antova. Revolte im Ornament — Bilder zu Judit,* edited by Irmtraud Fischer, 9-16. Vienna.

Gierlinger-Czerny, Elisabeth. 2000. *Judits Tat. Die Aufkündigung des Geschlechtervertrages.* Vienna.

Hopkins, Denise Dombkowski. 1998. "Judith." In *The Women's Bible Commentary,* 279-85. Expanded ed. Louisville.

Kobelt-Groch, Marion. 2005. *Judith macht Geschichte. Zur Rezeption einer mythischen Gestalt vom 16. bis 19. Jahrhundert.* Munich.

Moore, Carey A. 1985. *Judith.* Anchor Bible, vol. 40. Garden City, N.Y.

Motté, Magda. 2003. *"Esthers Tränen, Judiths Tapferkeit". Biblische Frauen in der Literatur des 20. Jahrhunderts.* Darmstadt.

Rakel, Claudia. 1999. "'I Will Sing a New Song to My God': Some Remarks on the Intertextuality of Judith 16:1-17." In *Judges,* edited by Athalya Brenner, 27-47. Feminist Companion to the Bible, 2nd ser., vol. 4. Sheffield.

———. 2003. *Judit. Über Schönheit, Macht und Widerstand im Krieg: Eine feministisch-intertextuelle Lektüre.* Beihefte zur Zeitschrift für die alttestamentliche Wissenschaft, vol. 334. Berlin.

Sawyer, Deborah F. 2001. "Dressing Up/Dressing Down; Power, Performance and Identity in the Book of Judith." *Theology and Sexuality* 15:23-31.

Schmitz, Barbara. 2004. *Gedeutete Geschichte. Die Funktion der Reden und Gebete im Buch Judit.* Herders Biblische Studien, vol. 40. Freiburg.

Stocker, Margarita. 1998. *Judith: Sexual Warrior; Women and Power in Western Culture.* New Haven.

Translated by Nancy Lukens

Baruch: Mail from Distant Shores

Marie-Theres Wacker

Terra Incognita

The book of Baruch is part of the Jewish writings Martin Luther called "the Apocrypha," and which he added as a mere appendix to his edition of the First Testament. Catholic editions of the Bible, on the other hand, consider them to be "deuterocanonical" books, parts of the First Testament written in Greek. Baruch is placed there after Lamentations, whose author tradition identifies as the prophet Jeremiah, because the book of Jeremiah names Baruch as "Jeremiah's scribe" (36:4). Critical editions and commentaries of the Bible occasionally treat the "Letter of Jeremiah" (Bar 6) as a separate composition.

As far as I know, the book of Baruch has thus far not been studied at all from a feminist-exegetical perspective. For that reason, only preliminary steps can be taken in what follows. They proceed along the lines of the new, exegetical orientations proposed by O. H. Steck in his monograph on Baruch (1993): all recognizable indicators that this book belongs to the tradition of scribal literature notwithstanding, the book has not been "understood" (and, possibly, been set aside as a piece of "epigonic" writing) when its sources have been laid out. Only when its overall structure has been made plain and situated in the time of its composition (in the second or perhaps even the first century B.C.E.) will it be understood. The following reflections — to state Steck's point yet more sharply — are methodologically oriented toward a literary-narrative analytical reading of the book as a whole on the one hand, and, on the other, toward a historical retrospective on women's history at the time of the book's composition. Here and there feminist-hermeneutical questions will be inserted into the reflection.

Proclamation as Correspondence — the Overall Structure of the Book

In its present literary form, the book of Baruch has a clearly discernible structure; an eloquent narrative structure corresponds to it. The book's title, "This is the book of Baruch," shapes the whole text as words of Baruch (1:1) written in Babylon at the time Jerusalem was being destroyed (1:2). A group of exiled Judeans lives in Babylon, by the river Soud (1:4). "All the people" come to hear Baruch; among those present, representatives of Jerusalem's royal house and "elders" are named specifically, creating the picture of a well-organized community. Initially, no trace of its women is visible. Baruch reads his book to this assembled congregation with the result that all begin to weep and lament, and raise an offering of money to be sent to Jerusalem. Baruch's book accompanies the offering there as well as a letter asking the congregation in Jerusalem to hold a service of prayer and sacrifice during which the book is to be read aloud and a long confession of sin to be offered (in the first-person plural), the wording of which then follows (1:15–3:8). The new section, beginning in 3:9 with the words "Listen, Israel" (author's translation; cf. Deut 6:4!), is not so much a continuation of the letter from the exiles as the beginning of the book accompanying it. The book is about God's wisdom (Bar 3:9–4:4): Israel has disregarded it and therefore "grown old" far away from its home. Formulations like that indicate that Baruch as it now exists clearly looks back over a longer period of the Babylonian exile. The situation of the "zero hour," the destruction of Jerusalem, is imagined and made up in the form of a fiction for a later time, when a Babylonian Judaism had already become a structured reality. This is followed by words of encouragement to the city of Jerusalem (4:5–5:9); the city is made present through a lament worded in first-person-singular language. This section is most likely also part of the book sent to Jerusalem from Babylon. Chapter 6 pretends to be a copy of a letter Jeremiah had sent to the Judean deportees in Babylon, admonishing the community to be wary of idols and of the fascination they elicit even though they are empty of any reality. This letter functions like a response of Jeremiah to the exiles, namely, to let their own prayer of repentance and Baruch's words persuade them to remain faithful to God in Babylon, the land of idols.

Thus, "Baruch's book" is part of the narrative that begins at 1:3 and is to be placed within it in the passages of 3:9–5:9. But the title in 1:1 makes the story of the book's journey from its first reading at the river Soud to Jerusalem part of the book itself, thereby already emphasizing the linkage between east and west, between the Babylonian diaspora and the homeland. "Baruch's book," as we have it today, accepts that linkage when it even adds in chapter 6 what is made to look like a "reply by return mail" from Jeremiah to Babylon. Inasmuch as the book in its present form was written or compiled to be passed on or read again and again, we are dealing with a complex communication process that leads far beyond the fictive original situation, apparently seeking to clarify and influence the relationship between Palestinian and Babylonian Judaism (cf. Steck 1993, 60ff.). We highlight only the written component of that communication process: a book is to be passed on which consists of an exchange of letters at the core of which is once again a book. What would need more precise clarification from a woman's perspective is how this process of committing the (prophetic) "word" to writing and the beginnings of a "book religion" touched Jewish women (those in Babylon and those living in and around Jerusalem). Were there "women writers," as Tamara Eskenazi (1992, 36f.) assumes, referring to Ezra 2:55/Nehemiah 7:57 (→ Ezra and Nehemiah), and (to what extent) were they involved in the growing postexilic scholarship of the scribes?

The Confession of Guilt

The confession in Baruch 1:15–3:8 begins with the justice of God: God gave the people instructions for living (commandments/regulations), but they did not heed them. The people are reminded repeatedly that God's voice was present in Israel, mediated not least through the prophets. But guilt is also confessed in ever new phrases, the guilt of the "fathers" and "kings" that comes upon the people as a whole but which they also take upon themselves as a whole. Since early Judaism at the time of "Baruch" (the fictive author of the book) had already developed the awareness of individual responsibility, it is possible to regard this collective acceptance of guilt and its consequences as a manifestation of the understanding that we are embroiled in our own history and cannot extricate ourselves from it through appeals to "the grace of late birth." Yet women continue to be invisible: we see them neither among those making their confession nor as potential accomplices; once or twice, and only briefly, we do see them as victims (2:3 and 23). "Baruch's" perception is cut in half androcentrically; what is needed is a women-specific memory, a retrospective examination of and discussion about the actual forms of how we are embroiled in the past.

The Wisdom of the Almighty

The "admonition" (Steck) of 3:9–4:4, now in the form of poetic couplets, takes up the theme of ignoring the commandments, the cause of Israel being in exile. But, contrary to the preceding confession of guilt, it develops the theme in relation to a different area of tradition, that of wisdom. In describing the particular quality of the book of Baruch, it is instructive to compare it to the relevant texts of the books of Job (→), Proverbs (→), Ecclesiasticus (or Sirach; →), and Wisdom (→).

As in Job 28, wisdom in Baruch is also an entity that ultimately remains hidden in God; as in Ecclesiasticus 24, wisdom is made concrete for Israel in the commandments, in God's Torah. But other than in those wisdom texts and in Proverbs 1–9, wisdom does not have a profile and a "gestalt" of its own in the book of Baruch, and is not conceptualized as a feminine counterfigure to God. Instead wisdom remains in terms of syntax and semantics the object of God.

(Here we can only make passing reference to the scholarly discussion of the heterogeneous Baruch 3:28 and the anti-Jewish clichés that pervade it.) An additional charge is brought against Israel here, namely, that it has forsaken the "fountain of wisdom" (3:12 NJB). If taken literally, that formulation makes God himself that "fountain." While wisdom literature throughout leaves a certain "free space" between God and wisdom (cf. Prov 8:30!), in Baruch wisdom is taken back into God's omnipotence.

Another point of difference is that whereas the Bible generally recognizes other people's wisdom with admiration, the book of Baruch asserts that no other people have found the way to wisdom. The neighboring cultures that are known for their acclaimed wisdom traditions are named explicitly, among them the "children of Hagar" (3:23 NJB), but only to make it clear that their search for knowledge was unsuccessful. Wisdom is unattainable if it has not been given by God, who alone has access to it. But God has given it as a gift to his people Jacob/Israel. In the light of the identification of wisdom with Israel's commandments, this assertion means that Israel alone has received the Torah. To that extent, Baruch's view corresponds to that expressed also in such texts as Ecclesiasticus 24. But whereas Sirach places the Torah into the context of a comprehensive divine wisdom, Baruch seems not to allow for any other wisdom than the Torah, which, in his view, is reserved for Israel alone (cf. Bar 4:3). Would this be the voice of a community that, feeling its identity under threat, can no longer perceive the "ecumenical" commonalities shared with the world around it and is able to define itself only by setting itself apart?

The Roles of Jerusalem

The "admonition" of 3:9–4:4 concludes with the reminder that with wisdom/Torah Israel has been shown a way in which to find life. And that is why Israel may take heart for a better future (4:5). But before such words of encouragement can be uttered, it is necessary to hearken back to the past. The voice of the city of Jerusalem is heard here (4:9-29). Appearing as a woman in mourning, a lamenting Jerusalem addresses herself to other "women," the neighboring cities, calling on them to behold with her the fate of her deported children (4:9, 14; cf. 4:24). She appeals to her neighbors' solidarity and, at the same time, locates herself in the tradition of the "mourning women" of Israel (cf., e.g., Jer 9:17-22). It is true, she does indicate that her children brought their fate upon themselves because they had left the "ways of his commandments," the "paths of discipline as his justice directed" (Bar 4:13 NJB). But overall, the elements of mourning and pain, caused by the "imprisonment" of her children, prevail in this lament. This is the first instance where women come into sight in Baruch; the children of the woman Jerusalem are "sons and daughters" (4:10, 14). Even an especially close relationship of the mother to her daughters seems to be indicated when "Jerusalem" laments that "they carried off the widow's cherished ones; they left her quite alone, bereft of her daughters" (4:16, author's translation). Small indicators like that in the text may alert us to the possibility that something like female voices resonates in Jerusalem's lament as Baruch expresses it.

Here Jerusalem is cast in the role of "mother" of her children, the mother also and in particular of the Judeans in Babylon. The wide-ranging preoccupation of the Hebrew Bible with Jerusalem is here applied to novel conditions. One understands why, on the "narrative stage" of the book, the congregation, gathered at the river Soud in Babylon and having heard the reading of Baruch's book, breaks out in tears and collects an offering for Jerusalem and sends the book there. On the historical plane, a further element of the linkage the book creates between the diaspora and the "motherland," between Babylonian and Palestinian Judaism, can be seen.

Jerusalem's "motherhood" is depicted throughout implicitly by means of references to her children. The introduction to her lament (4:8) goes a step beyond: God himself, the "Eternal," is said to be the one who "reared" Israel and is spoken of, as it were, in the same breath with Jerusalem who "nurtured you" (NEB). God and Jerusalem appear as parents who perform similar tasks for the child Israel (but without linking any of them explicitly with gender-specific roles). On one hand, this quasi-mythological perception of Jerusalem is based on the great significance of the city and the rich imagery applied to it already in the Hebrew Bible. On the other, given that at the time Hellenistic cities around Jerusalem appeared personified for example on minted coins in images of their tutelary goddesses, this perception of Jerusalem may be seen as a specifically Jewish way of appropriating and integrating the powerful mythology of the city goddess. Perhaps we may even say: Jerusalem, the mother and city-woman, has in the book of Baruch taken the place that in wisdom literature is occupied by the figure of Wisdom who, on her part, may be understood as an attempt to integrate traditions of different goddesses. Still, in Baruch, as in the numerous prophetic texts it refers to, especially those from the book of Isaiah, Jerusalem, the mother of her children, clearly remains subject to the instructions and the power of God, the "Eternal One": it is God who can bring back her children; it is God who changes her mourning into joy.

Idols and Women

The "Letter of Jeremiah" (chapter 6), the reply from Jerusalem to the congregation in Babylon, revolves around the question of idols. They and the cults associated with them had undoubtedly left a strong impression on the exiles and their descendants. Without much ado, "Jeremiah" begins with that fact and sets out right away to offer a small "countermagic": a short and fervent prayer imploring the one God of Israel (6:5). But then the text musters up all its rhetorical power to pour scorn on the idols, thereby undermining their fascination. This is done in nine sections, each of which concludes in refrain-like manner with a call not to be afraid of the images (6:7-15a, 15b-22, 23-28) or with the question whether such monsters are in fact worthy of veneration (6:29-39, 40-44, 45-51, 52-56, 57-68). At the end, as in a sigh of relief, there is the assertion: "Better, then, is an upright man who has no idols" (6:73 NEB).

Occasionally women also come into view in those passages. But reference to them also serves throughout to discredit the veneration of idols. Idols are comparable to girls fond of finery (6:8), and since that already is ill-befitting for a "proper girl," it is so much more for an idol. Priests have been known on occasion to filch some gold and silver used in the production of idols and to give it to prostitutes (6:10): how awful that those precious metals are not strictly reserved for their higher purpose (this charge is also behind 6:32) and that priests carry on with prostitutes! And then the priests' wives take portions of the meat set aside for sacrifices and preserve them for use of their families but are greedy and unwilling to share the meat with the poor (6:27). In addition, they do not observe the times of their indisposition when they handle the meat for sacrifices (6:28). These charges presuppose the validity and acknowledgment of the Levitical code in relation to the priesthood (→ Leviticus) and demonstrate to the readers or hearers how unworthy the Babylonian priesthood is.

Another argument, one that cannot be directly derived from the Levitical code of the First Testament, presupposes the knowledge that there obviously were female cult officials in Babylon: "Why should they be called gods? These gods of silver, gold, and wood have food served to them by women" (Bar 6:30 NEB). The charge does not envisage the offering of food sacrifices, a customary element also in the worship of the God of Israel; it must refer instead to women in the sacrificial cults. What this suggests conversely is that "Jeremiah" (the pseudepigraphic author of the letter) could not imagine women officiating in the sacrificial cult of the true God. There may be two reasons for this: he took the Levitical code a step further in this direction, or he may have had in mind the polemic of the Hebrew Bible against female sacred persons (cf. Deut 23:18; → Hosea).

Another reason why veneration should be withheld from idols is that these supposed gods are quite unable to act on behalf of those who worship them (Bar 6:33-40). If one judges them in relation to their commitment to the powerless, these "gods" have nothing to offer: "they do not pity the widow or befriend the orphan" (6:38 NEB). They are also unable to make the dumb speak since they themselves lack the capacity of sense perception (6:40-41). This may well be a form of mocking the rituals of "opening the mouth of idols" known in Mesopotamia, which, it is true, distinguish between an idol that has just been manufactured and one that has subsequently been possessed by a deity.

Baruch 6:42-43 is a much-discussed passage and has been interpreted in greatly diverse ways even in the exegetical traditions of antiquity. "The women too sit in the street with cords round them, burning bran for incense. And whenever one of them was taken by one of the passers-by and has lain with him, she taunts her neighbor, because she has not been thought as worthy as herself and her cord has not been broken" (author's translation). "Jeremiah" has in mind a practice related to gods and idols and uses it both as a paradigm for how the Babylonians bring their own gods into disrepute (6:40) and as an example of mendacity (6:44). In relation to this context, exegetical literature frequently cites Herodotus's note in his *History* (1.199) and talks of "cultic prostitution." Behind that note may well be the practice of (a woman's onetime or repeated) "unfettering" of female sexuality for which, as the burning of bran for incense suggests, women invoke the protection of a deity, most likely a goddess. It is interesting that "Jeremiah" does not so much mock this custom as such (for which scholars have not found a convincing explanation as yet) as he highlights the humiliations the women perpetrate on one another.

The "Letter of Jeremiah" strengthens the Babylonian congregation in its faithfulness to the one God who is to be worshiped without images, although it does so in terms of a rhetoric that paints the different social and cultic roles of women in the Babylonian context as strange, "other," and, for that reason, repulsive. All the same, when read against their intention, these polemical passages yield valuable clues for a women's history that perhaps was marked in the course of everyday life by far fewer boundaries between the Babylonian and Jewish female "neighbors" than "Jeremiah" and "Baruch" would have preferred to see.

LITERATURE

Eskenazi, Tamara C. 1992. "Out from the Shadows: Biblical Women in the Postexilic Era." *Journal for the Study of the Old Testament* 54:25-43.

Kellermann, Dieter. 1979. "Apokryphes Obst. Bemerkungen zur Epistula Jeremiae (Baruch Kap. 6) insbesondere zu Vers 42." *Zeitschrift der Deutschen Morgenländischen Gesellschaft* 129:23-42.

Moore, Carey A. 1977. *Daniel, Esther, and Jeremiah: The Additions.* Anchor Bible, vol. 44. Garden City, N.Y. Baruch, 255-316; Epistle of Jeremiah, 317-58.

Schökel, Luis Alonso. 1986. "Jerusalén inocente intercede: Baruc 4:9-19." In *Salvación en la Palabra,* edited by Domingo Muñoz León, 39-51. Festschrift for A. Diez Macho. Madrid.

Schreiner, Josef. 1986. "Baruch." In Josef Schreiner, *Baruch — Klagelieder,* 45-84. Neue Echter Bibel. Würzburg.

Steck, Odil Hannes. 1993. *Das apokryphe Baruchbuch. Studien zur Rezeption und Konzentration 'kanonischer' Überlieferung.* Forschungen zur Religion und Literatur des Alten und Neuen Testaments 160. Göttingen.

FOR FURTHER READING

Assan-Dhôte, Isabelle, and Jacqueline Moatti-Fine. 2005. *Baruch, Lamentations, Lettre de Jérémie.* La Bible d'Alexandrie, vol. 25, 2. Paris.

Mukenge, André Kabasele. 1998. *L'unité littéraire du Livre de Baruch.* Etudes bibliques, n.s., vol. 38. Louvain.

Steck, Odil Hannes, and Reinhard Gregor Kratz. 1998. *Das Buch Baruch. Der Brief des Jeremia.* Altes Testament Deutsch Apokryphen, vol. 5. Göttingen.

Translated by Martin Rumscheidt

Sirach (Ecclesiasticus): On the Difficult Relation between Divine Wisdom and Real Women in an Androcentric Document

Angelika Strotmann

Introduction

The book of Jesus Sirach is one of those First Testament scriptures that were not accepted into the Hebrew Bible and therefore are classified in Christian tradition — depending on denomination — as deuterocanonical or apocryphal writings. In Judaism Sirach was quite popular up to the Middle Ages as texts found in Qumran and Masada as well as recovered medieval Hebrew manuscripts of Sirach indicate. The Reformers of the sixteenth and seventeenth centuries often willingly made use of this book even though they denied its canonical status.

The Basis of the Text

To this day the basis of the text is uncertain, which is a major problem for the interpretation of the book of Jesus Sirach; this is connected with the complicated history of the text. Its Hebrew text was lost between the twelfth and the nineteenth century, and the book was accessible only in ancient translations (Greek, Syriac, Latin). Fragments of an eleventh- or twelfth-century manuscript were found in the Karaea Synagogue in Cairo in 1896, followed by discoveries of manuscripts in Qumran and Masada about fifty years later. Today about three-fifths of the Hebrew text is available to us. The full text of the Wisdom of Ben Sira, however, still exists only in its Greek translation.

Reconstructing the original Hebrew text is difficult because the different Hebrew manuscripts of the same text often differ from one another and also diverge significantly from the ancient translations. When doubt arises — which occurs quite frequently — one has to clarify first which version of the text an interpretation of a specific passage is based on.

Occasionally, there is also confusion on account of the mix-up of sheets in the Greek text of Sirach 30:25–36:16. Today modern translations, however, follow the sequence found in the Latin and Syriac translations and the Hebrew manuscript E, which exists only in fragmentary form. Furthermore, in modern translations and in corresponding secondary literature the numbering of verses also varies sometimes. All these difficulties are visible even for nonspecialists when they just read two different translations of the book. The differences often affect the contents of the text.

Author and Time of Composition

Sirach is the only sapiential writing in the ancient Orient whose author we know by name. The Greek translation refers to him in different forms only as "Jesus"; the Hebrew text gives his name as "Simon Ben Jesus (Ben Eleazar) Ben Sira" (50:27; 51:30). This wisdom teacher, whom we will refer to as Ben Sira, wrote his book between 190 and 175 B.C.E., probably in Jerusalem. This was before the Maccabean uprising, which began in 167 B.C.E., a time in Palestine already marked by increasing tensions between Hellenism and Judaism.

Scholars disagree about how Ben Sira and his sapiential writing fit into that situation. Some see him as a representative of the Hellenistic spirit, others as a guardian of Jewish tradition fighting against precisely that spirit. I find the middle position of Marböck (1995) and others persuasive; according to this, Ben Sira tries to combine what he had learned in his many travels with a strong positive presentation of Jewish tradition. He appears to be influenced particularly by Egyptian wisdom. Moreover, his preference for the priestly tradition of his people leads to the assumption that he was a priest himself. But this must ultimately be left open. He certainly belonged to the Jerusalemite bourgeoisie and therefore seems to have been a man of means.

Structure and Content

With its fifty-one chapters, the book of Jesus Sirach is the most extensive work of wisdom literature in the ancient world. Its overall structure is clearly close to that of Proverbs, but it differs considerably from it as its material is often presented in thoroughly structured larger units.

The beginning, end, and middle of Sirach are dominated, not unlike Proverbs (→ Proverbs), by the theme of the personified divine Wisdom. Sirach 1–2 introduces us to the book by linking wisdom and the fear of God. The themes Ben Sira addresses in the next chapters are repeatedly interrupted by reflections on Wisdom personified (4:11-19; 6:18-37; 14:20–15:10). Those chapters move single-mindedly toward the middle of the book: Wisdom's first-person speech in chapter 24. This chapter functions as a kind of hinge; it concludes the first part of the book and launches the second part at its close by identifying wisdom and Torah. In this part, personified divine Wisdom barely plays a role any longer. Instead, several reflections are shaped by the order of creation and lead into a great, two-part hymnic composition: the praise of God's glory in creation (42:15–43:33) and in Israel's history (44:1–50:29). Only at the end of the book, the so-called appendix (51:13-30), does Wisdom personified appear once again but is now presented by the Wisdom Teacher, who urges all his students to take the search for Wisdom to heart.

Even though the theological reflections in Sirach are much more expansive in comparison to the book of Proverbs, they alone do not provide an adequate idea about the character of this sapiential writing. As a wisdom teacher, at home not only in the wisdom tradition of Israel but also in that of the ancient Orient in general, Ben Sira is basically interested in showing how human action can be shaped by wisdom in all areas of life. The perspective of this instruction, however, is unmistakably that of a well-educated upper-middle-class male, enjoying relatively secure conditions and some influence in public life. And so he does not teach concretely how *human beings* but how *men* should arrange their lives with wisdom. Accordingly, the topics of his sapiential sayings derive from the experience of men of his social class, his time, and his culture.

The topics of family and home play an important role here by sheer quantity alone; they often precede sections of concrete instruction. Next to units dealing with various persons in the house, (e.g., Sir 7:18-28 or 33:19-32), there are others about individual groups of persons: parents (e.g., 3:1-16), wives (e.g., chapters 25–26), sons (e.g., 30:1-13), daughters (e.g., 42:9-14), slaves (e.g., 33:25-32). Part of the sayings about friends also belongs here (e.g., 6:6-16). Other units that touch on life outside the home, in the public sphere, are concerned with providing bail for someone (29:14-20) or with dealing with the rich and powerful (8:10-19 and elsewhere); they equally address sacrifice and justice (34:21–35:12) and how to behave properly at a banquet (31:12–32:13).

According to Claudia V. Camp (1991), the hermeneutical key to understanding many of the concrete instructions is the (male) value system with its two poles of honor/shame and disgrace that is prevalent to some extent still today in the Mediterranean world. To gain honor and to keep away shame, one must show great prudence in dealing with others but also in relation to oneself and one's passions. Here the text often uses the nominal and verbal form of "to be ashamed." And so, for Ben Sira, proper shame, in addition to prudence, is the best means a man has to ward off disgrace and to gain honor. Camp points out that there is a particular correspondence between this value system of honor and disgrace on the one hand, and how women are expected to behave on the other. This is true also for Ben Sira, so that for him women in the household of the wise are among the greatest risk factors for the life of honor the paterfamilias desires.

Ben Sira on Real Women

Overview

No other work of wisdom literature in the Bible devotes as many verses to women as the book of Jesus Sirach. Even within the book itself, no other group receives the Wisdom Teacher's attention as often as women. Only what he says about good and bad friends compares quantitatively to his words about women. With a few exceptions, Ben Sira speaks about women only when behavior toward them in specific situations is at issue. Thus, he does not address women directly. Instead, corresponding to his addressees (see above), he seeks to induce Jewish men of his social milieu to embrace what in his view is wise behavior toward diverse groups of women. He does so not only in terms of warnings or admonitions, prohibitions, and commandments, but also in terms of maxims and phrases that reflect men's experiences with different women.

Ben Sira mentions the following women or groups of women: one's own mother, the widow, the mistress of the household, the wife and, by extension, the adulterous woman, the daughter, and various strange women, that is, women who do not belong to the household of the wise. For Ben Sira, the house is the preferred place for women to stay and work. He therefore hardly takes note of women in public life, including the women who have to make a living outside the household.

The roles Ben Sira ascribes to women basically fall into four groups. First, there are the women who may lead the wise man off his road to wisdom; he ought to avoid them. "Foreign women"[1] above all belong to this group. Secondly, there are those who may become dangerous yet also helpful to him as he journeys toward the fear of God and wisdom. Particularly wives belong to this group. The third group are women to whom the man has God-given commitments such as widows and his own mother. A special group is the fourth: daughters who continuously cause the wise man worries. It is clear that with the exception of the third group all women are judged from the perspective of whether they are harmful or useful to the wise man. If they are harmful, he has to avoid or control them; if they are useful, he has to seek them. Thus, women appear almost only "in their connection with or in the perspective of men, never independently" (Schroer 1996, 98). But it is better not to draw sweeping conclusions, for Ben Sira views nearly all social groups, including various groups of men, from his perspective (such as

---

1. The German expression *fremde Frau* cannot be translated as "strange woman" in this context. The meaning of "strange" as "someone I do not know" or "have never met" is not intended here. It is much more "someone who is not of us, of our morality, ethos, community-spirit, religion" but is "other" in a possibly dangerous yet seductive, undermining manner. The translation "foreign" was chosen over "alien" to exclude the notion of someone being "from another place or country" even though a "foreign woman" may well be from such a location. The word "foreign" signals a warning: "be aware of her!" [Translator's note.]

friends, advisers, medical doctors, the powerful, laborers, merchants, etc.) and judges them as well according to the harm or usefulness, the honor or disgrace they can bring to the wise man.

Mothers and Widows

The introductory chapters in Sirach about Wisdom and the fear of God are followed by the first concrete instruction in 3:1-16, a didactic poem that gives a new interpretation of the Decalogue's commandment to honor one's parents and makes use of the concept of honor and disgrace. Ben Sira here demands that the son has to honor both father and mother. If he honors his parents up to their old age, he himself will have favor with God; if he curses or disrespects them, he will be in disgrace.

However, the obligation to honor the father in 3:1-16 predominates by its sheer quantity, and where honoring both parents is called for in parallel fashion the father is always mentioned first. The same is true for all other passages where Ben Sira speaks of the mother (7:27-28; 23:14; 41:17).

Next to mothers, the wise man is unambiguously obliged to behave exclusively in favor of the well-being of only one other group of women. These are widows, women who, next to orphans, had the fewest rights in ancient society, that is, the smallest chance to demand their rights. Indeed, the wise man can expect to be rewarded for correct behavior (4:10) and to be punished if he disregards a widow's rights (35:17-22), but this form of motivation is in line with that of wisdom literature in general. In both places, reward and punishment are up to God, which suggests that such supportive acts toward widows and orphans can hardly count on receiving recognition from human beings.

"Foreign" Women and Men's Sexuality

Whereas the wise man is to care for his own mother and for widows, he had better get as far away as possible from "foreign" women because they will not bring him honor. On the contrary, they will prove to be his undoing and steer him off the road to wisdom. The *topos* of the "foreign woman" together with that of the "loose woman" is typical of wisdom literature. The most extensive text about the "foreign woman" is Proverbs 7. According to Christl Maier (1996, 189ff.), that text already uses this *topos* to refer not only to a woman from a foreign country — as Nehemiah still does — but quite generally to a woman who is a stranger, foreign to the man. Ben Sira is interested in "foreign women" in the latter sense only. For him all women are foreign who do not belong to one's household and to whom one has no commitments whatsoever. The wise man needs to be wary of them.

It is to this rather heterogeneous group of women that Ben Sira devotes the longest passage (9:1-9). He begins it — surprisingly — by admonishing the husband not to be jealous over his wife so that she does not learn anything from his jealousy to do evil against him. The next verse warns generally against selling oneself to a woman; only then begin the actual admonitions about the foreign women. Verse 3 and its reference to the "foreign woman" could be a kind of heading for the categories of women in the following verses: women who play stringed instruments (v. 4), virgins (v. 5), prostitutes (v. 6), graceful or shapely women (v. 8), and another man's wife (v. 9).[2] For Ben Sira and Proverbs 7, to be wary of these women means to avoid sexual contact with them. But unlike Proverbs 7, where the woman is portrayed as a seductress and the man as the naïve victim, Ben Sira knows that a man is responsible for his action himself. But he does not think of himself as someone who would seduce a woman; rather, he is highly afraid that he might lose control over himself and his body (cf. Camp 1991, 20). Passages such as Sirach 23:16-21 (cf. also 23:2-6) show that the blame for a man losing control over his desires is not put on women or on the foreign women alone; they describe the behavior of an unchaste and adulterous man and how he justifies himself. Nowhere is a woman held responsible for this.

But how does the wife come to be at the opening of this poem about the foreign women? Very different answers have been proposed. One has to consider that the catchword "wife" in verses 1 and 9 frames the poem. In addition, these two verses do not really fit into the rest of the poem. After the concluding words about the dangers of female beauty in verse 8cd, verse 9 looks like an afterthought. Therefore I assume that Ben Sira added those two verses to an already existing poem in order to alert men who go after "foreign women" to a further consequence: by their behavior they will evoke their wife's jealousy, who will do the same wicked thing their husband did and get involved with a strange man at a banquet.

Daughters

There is no hint anywhere in Sirach that a father derives an advantage or use from the existence of a daughter. What is said in 22:3b applies to all daughters, including the wise and judicious ones: "A daughter means loss" to the father. In fact, the father gets nothing back from what he has invested in her. If she is sensible (22:4a), she finds herself a man and makes him the heir of her dowry (*klēronomēsei* is subject to different interpretations), but for the family of origin her sensibility and money are lost. If, however, in contrast her behavior is shameful and sulky (22:4b

---

2. I follow the Greek text of Ben Sira. The Hebrew manuscripts add two lines about prostitutes between verses 3 and 4 and differ from the Greek version in verse 7.

and 5), her father is responsible for her even after she is married because if her husband sends her away on account of her behavior her father has to take her back into his home and care for her.

Sirach 42:9-12 goes yet one step further. Here Ben Sira tersely describes a daughter basically as a problem. A father has continuously to worry about her (vv. 9-10):[3] "in her youth, for fear she may remain unmarried (literally 'wither'), and having married, for fear she may be hated; in virginity, for fear that she may be seduced and become pregnant in her father's house, being with a husband, for fear that she may be unfaithful, and having married, for fear she may be barren" (author's translation).

All these paternal fears are concerned with the possibility of his daughter disgracing him in the eyes of the public and burdening his wallet for the rest of his life. Verses 11-12 make radical suggestions about how in his own house a father can reduce the risk of his daughter giving him a bad name. In a nutshell: keep her under lock and key so that she will not come into contact with men and foreign women.

Given such an outlook — surely it was not Ben Sira's alone — it is almost understandable that fathers preferred sons. Of course, sons could also cause headaches, but a good son always benefited the father; he could be proud of him (30:1-6) since the son remained in the household, continued his father's profession, and cared for him in his old age. Indeed, a father needs to discipline his son physically to prevent him from going astray (30:1, 2, 6-13), but he also teaches him his ways. The son is usually aware of his father's love. A daughter, however, is of no benefit to her father; therefore he keeps her at a distance. She is spared physical chastisement, but the father has no vital positive interest in her.

The texts concerning daughters discussed above clearly show their androcentric or patriarchal perspective but are still free of misogyny. It is in the following two verses (42:13-14) that Ben Sira appears to let go of his restraint and shows his true position on women: "13 For out of clothes comes the moth, and out of woman comes woman's wickedness. 14a Better a man's wickedness than a well-doing woman 14b and a daughter." Verse 14a is the absolute epitome of misogyny in Sirach. Unfortunately the Hebrew text of 14b is corrupt, so that scholars argue about its meaning. Sauer (1981) confirms the presence of misogyny in 14a when he translates it as follows: "and a daughter causes more dismay than any and all disgrace." Trenchard (1982) makes the same point in his translation: "And a daughter causes fear regarding disgrace more than a son." Slightly different, the New American Bible writes: "and (better) a frightened daughter than any disgrace." The translation of Skehan and DiLella (1987) moves in the same direction, but with a stronger positive focus: "but better a religious daughter than a shameless son." Of

---

3. I essentially stay with the Greek text of verses 9 and 10 because the Hebrew manuscripts B and M provide only an incomplete or corrupted text.

course, were these last two translations to correspond to the original meaning, they would put the misogynist epitome of 14a into perspective, perhaps even ironically abolish it. Can we confidently believe that this is what Ben Sira meant? Still, we have to consider that verse 14a directly contradicts much of what he has to say about the good wife.

The Good and the Bad Wife

Ben Sira has more to say about wives than about anything else. He basically divides them into good and bad wives. A good wife is wise, graceful, of help and support to her husband; a bad one is morally wicked and spiteful, and causes her husband grief and suffering. Ben Sira talks about no other category of women in such polar opposite words as he does wives. This becomes apparent in how he uses the Hebrew and Greek noun for "evil, wickedness," which comes close to being the key word of chapters 25–26. Neither mother and widow nor — amazingly — the foreign woman is represented by that noun. At most, daughters are associated with the wickedness of women (42:13-14), but Ben Sira draws back from characterizing them as "bad, wicked" (cf. 22:3-5).

What Ben Sira has to say about wives is found especially in chapters 25–26. Unlike previous studies, I view 25:1–26:18 as a formal and material unit that Ben Sira carefully composed by borrowing from older materials.[4] He introduces the unit with three groups of numerical proverbs, of which the first and last speak positively of wives. The main part (25:13–26:18) begins quite unexpectedly with a tirade against the bad wife and does not abate until 25:26. Verses 13-15 and their sweeping judgment of women's spitefulness serve as a heading, followed by four verses (16-19) that describe the effects of a wife's spitefulness on the husband but do not spell out concretely what this spitefulness amounts to. In verses 20-22 we learn something about the garrulous wife, the wife whose beauty is desirable, and the rich wife who supports her husband (cf. Camp 1991). Finally, verse 23 summarizes the negative effects wives such as those mentioned in verses 16-22 have on their husbands.

Even though formally quite disparate, all these statements seek to persuade young men to be careful when choosing a wife. To reinforce that being careless in this important matter can have serious consequences, verse 24 recalls the narrative of man's fall. This is the first instance in Scripture where the first woman (Eve) is blamed for the Fall and, consequently, for the death of the human being. However, the allusion does not serve as a warning against women in general, but — as the context shows — as a warning against evil wives (cf. Levison 1985).

---

4. The following section, 26:19-27, however, is clearly a secondary elaboration found only in two Greek manuscripts.

Without transition, Ben Sira contrasts the bad wife with the good one in 26:1. If the bad wife does nothing but harm, the good and strong ("manly" in Greek) wife brings only fortune. She doubles her husband's lifetime (v. 1); she "fattens his bones," that is to say, she causes him to prosper (vv. 2a, 3a), and is his joy (vv. 2b, 4); and "she is one of YHWH's gifts to those who fear him" (v. 3b). This verse surprises for it says, contrary to the impression created by the context, that it is the man who through his life and actions determines in large measure himself whether he gets a good or a bad wife. If he fears YHWH he can be sure that he will be given a good wife. Verse 3 is not accidentally in this position, nor does it say something about wives that can safely be ignored. The verse is set at the very center of the main part (25:13–26:18)[5] and takes up the second theme in Sirach next to that of wisdom, namely, "the fear of YHWH."

In 26:5-12 Ben Sira once again collects diverse sayings about women who make their husbands unhappy, wives who are jealous, wicked, drunken, and unchaste. Those verses warn particularly forcefully against the unchaste and shameless woman. (Here I follow the Syriac version, which, unlike the Greek version, speaks of "woman" rather than of "daughter" in verse 13; the Hebrew version is missing.) The warning's truly obscene climax is in verse 12. It is hardly surprising that Ben Sira changes topics one more time and concludes his tract about wives with praise of the good wife: she is graceful, lovable, wise, taciturn, well bred, modest, and beautiful. According to Ben Sira, all these characteristics also apply to the wise man. Controlling one's tongue is of special value to him, so much so that he can even beg for a seal to close his lips (22:27). Only beauty appears to be reserved for the wife. In the final three verses (16-18) she not only is compared to objects in the temple — the light on the sacred lampstand and the golden pillar on its silver base — but the real beauty of a woman is made manifest only in "the holiest of holies of the temple" — a daring metaphor in verse 16 for the innermost chamber of the house.

As we have seen, Sirach 25–26 begins and ends with statements about the good wife. Two large blocks gather statements about the bad wife, interrupted by four verses on the good wife, of which 26:3 is not only the formal but also the material center in the main part. It can hardly be disputed that Ben Sira himself shared at least some of what is said about the bad wife. But the composition of chapters 25–26, as we have just described it, and the conception of the "good wife–bad wife" antithesis might suggest that Ben Sira had more in mind than simply gathering positive and negative presuppositions about wives. Analogous to the book of Proverbs, he also ties the good wife very closely to Wisdom personified as well as to YHWH. The bad wife, in contrast, he ties closely to foolishness and to the road that leads to perdition (on Proverbs, cf. Camp 1985 and Schroer 1991). According to this scheme, the good wife would be concretely experienced wisdom and the bad wife concretely experienced foolishness.

---

5. I count seventeen distichs before and seventeen after this verse.

Ben Sira and the Personified Divine Wisdom

Ben Sira refers to Proverbs regarding the construction of his sapiential writing and also adopts the Wisdom figure as well as her conceptualization. Both writings represent Wisdom personified as a woman inviting guests to a meal, serving everyone who seeks her out with food and drink of insight and wisdom (Prov 9:1-6; Sir 15:2-3; 24:19-21), but Ben Sira also ascribes to Wisdom prophetic features when she warns in harsh words against rejecting or abandoning her (Prov 1:22-33; Sir 4:19). In addition to many of these similarities, however, there are also several differences between the two books. First, there is a noticeable increase in the number of texts concerning personified divine Wisdom. Whereas Proverbs has only two sections dealing with wisdom, Sirach has six. Furthermore, Sirach relates wisdom not only to God and to human beings but also to other entities: to the fear of YHWH, to the Torah and the commandments, to the temple and therefore especially to Israel. Many exegetes believe that the universalism of wisdom in Proverbs seems to have given way to a particularism in Sirach. In the following, I shall address all sections dealing with personified divine Wisdom (except Sir 51:13-30).

Wisdom and the Fear of God

The wisdom of Ben Sira starts with a poem about wisdom and the fear of God (1:1-27). It gives an initial clue of how Ben Sira understands wisdom and who receives it. "All wisdom comes from the Lord," he says (1:1), and then develops and substantiates this thesis in the poem's first part (1:1-10). This way he immediately distances himself from all those who reject Jewish wisdom and Jewish religious tradition and turn to Greek-Hellenistic wisdom teachings instead. But that does not mean that he himself rejects non-Jewish wisdom teachings. YHWH has given wisdom to all living creatures (1:9c-10a); all wisdom, and therefore also Greek-Hellenistic wisdom teachings, comes from YHWH. However, according to verse 10b, that is true only to a certain extent, for God gives full wisdom only to those who fear him. This leads into the poem's second part (vv. 11-13), which focuses, rather than on wisdom, on "the fear of the Lord" and the goods it offers. Part III (vv. 14-20) connects and almost identifies "wisdom" and "the fear of the Lord" with one another: the fear of the Lord is the beginning, fullness, crown, and root of wisdom. In this part Ben Sira joins a wide range of motifs with wisdom that he takes up again in subsequent chapters. Among these motifs are "dwelling," "house" and "nest," "tree," and "provider of nourishment" together with the associated metaphors: "fruits," "roots," "crown," "branches," and "to flourish." Part IV (vv. 21-25) reflects briefly on the sin-resisting power of the fear of the Lord, after which Ben Sira concludes the poem in verses 26-27. Once again he joins wisdom with the fear of the Lord (v. 27), but in verse 26 also with keeping the commandments:

> If you desire wisdom, keep the commandments,
>> and the Lord will furnish her abundantly to you.

This formulation literally restates verse 10b; there wisdom is given to those who fear YHWH, here to those who keep the commandments. We can only draw the conclusion that YHWH gives the fullness of wisdom only to those who fear him — who are the ones who keep the commandments.

Wisdom Who, Like God, Acts and Teaches

The next poem (4:11-19) paints a quite different picture of Wisdom. From the outset Wisdom is clearly personified as a self-assured woman teacher in the tradition of Proverbs 8:4-21, 32-36, and Proverbs 1:22-33. In Sirach 4:15-19 Wisdom even speaks to her disciples herself; this occurs only one more time in Sirach (chapter 24). Wisdom's speech not only describes the promises that await the seekers of Wisdom but also for the first time names her rough sides. According to verses 16-17, Wisdom disguises herself and tests the seekers of wisdom with temptations, a most unusual conception, given that only God puts people to the test (e.g., Gen 22). In Sirach 4:19 she threatens those who stray away from her with harsh punishments, a behavior the First Testament generally ascribes also only to God. Even apart from Wisdom's first-person speech, the closeness of Wisdom and YHWH is striking, such as in verse 14: "Those who serve her minister to the Holy One." Thus, the liturgical service in the temple is to be seen as equivalent to the liturgical service of Wisdom. In contrast to the first poem, wisdom is neither subordinate to YHWH nor brought into relation with the fear of the Lord and keeping the commandments.

The third Wisdom poem (6:18-37) stresses the initial effort demanded of those who seek Wisdom. As in 4:11-19, Ben Sira again calls attention to the rough side of Wisdom. Those who seek her should willingly put their feet into Wisdom's fetters and their necks into her collar. In the end they will rest and the fetters, the yoke, the collar, and the bonds will turn into costly robes. In this poem once again the closeness of YHWH and Wisdom is apparent: according to Deuteronomy 6:5, humans are to love God with all their soul and all their might; in Sirach 6:26 they are to approach Wisdom in the same way and heed her ways. Also, the peaceful rest that Wisdom eventually grants to those who seek her with all their might is said to be a special gift from God in Deuteronomy 12:9-10. Unlike the second poem (Sir 4:11-19), this one reverts back to the first poem by affirming in the last verse (6:37) that wisdom is given only to those who direct their mind to the fear of God and constantly meditate upon God's commandments.

The fourth Wisdom poem (14:20–15:10) resembles the third in how it structures the movement from "searching for Wisdom" to "Wisdom coming to meet the searcher" but has a different character otherwise. It consists of three parts: part

I (14:20–15:1) describes the active search for Wisdom, part II (15:2-6) shows how in reaction to this search Wisdom comes to meet the searcher, and part III (15:7-10) asserts that Wisdom will avoid the sinful. Right at its beginning in 14:20, this poem clearly alludes to Psalm 1, except that the place of the Torah is now taken by Wisdom, on which human beings/men are to meditate. In Sirach 14:22 this rather contemplative approach to Wisdom already begins to change. Now the man has to stalk her, lie in wait for her, and spy on her through door and window so that he may derive profit from her. At the same time, the image of Wisdom also changes. Not until now is she personified, namely, as a woman the man must court. The man's spying at her window, however, should not be pushed too far. According to Proverbs 8:34, Wisdom herself invites people to watch daily at her gates and wait beside her doors. Of course, that is possible only if the seekers of Wisdom settle in her direct vicinity. Yet again the picture changes in Sirach 14:26-27. As he already did in 1:1-27, Ben Sira now depicts Wisdom as a shady tree. The first part of the poem then surprisingly concludes with a reference to the fear of YHWH and — for the first time — to the Torah and not only to the commandments: they who fear YHWH (and that means nothing else but to follow the Torah) will conduct themselves like the blessed man in the preceding verses, and in doing so they will enter upon the road to wisdom.

The second part of this Wisdom poem (15:2-6) describes in detail how Wisdom comes to the seeker. She comes like a mother or a young bride; she feeds him with the bread of learning and gives him the water of understanding to drink; she supports him and will exalt him, open his mouth so that finally he will find joy and exultation and receive everlasting honor from her. Strikingly, this explicit comparison of Wisdom with two female figures, a mother and a young bride, occurs only here in Sirach, confirming his generally positive view of mothers and wives. The image of Wisdom as the hostess of a banquet (v. 3) is borrowed from Proverbs 9:1-6 and does not displace the images of mother and wife. Even Sirach 15:4a still alludes to the wife's action, but is now fused with YHWH's. According to Sirach 36:24, the wife is not only a helper to her husband — possibly an allusion to Genesis 2:20 — but also a safe stronghold and a supporting pillar. These are metaphors that otherwise describe YHWH's support (e.g., Ps 18:1-3 and 19; Ps 23). What appears to be implied in Sirach 15:2-4a, namely, the identification of Wisdom and YHWH, becomes quite apparent beginning with verse 4b. Only they who trust in YHWH will not be put to shame (e.g., Ps 22:5); only YHWH can exalt and open lips in the midst of the congregation (e.g., Ps 51:17 [Eng. 15]); only YHWH can give an everlasting name (e.g., Isa 56:5). Wisdom seems to be YHWH himself.

Personified Divine Wisdom and Her Relation to the Temple, to Israel, and to the Torah

The first part of Sirach reaches its climax and completion in Sirach 24:1-22 and the following verses 23-34. Like Proverbs 8, this poem is a hymn in which — as had been announced in Sirach 24:1-2 — Wisdom praises and recommends herself (Sir 24:3-22). Wisdom's speech can be divided into four sections. In part I (vv. 3-7), Wisdom tells of her divine origin, cosmic activity, and search for a place where she can come to rest. In part II (vv. 8-12) she finally finds that place in Israel, in the temple on Mount Zion. In part III (vv. 13-17), employing beautiful tree-metaphors, she describes how she spreads out from the temple all over Israel in order to invite, in part IV (vv. 19-22), all who like to eat of her fruits. Verses 18 and 24 are later additions.

Despite her impressive cosmic activity (vv. 3-7), Wisdom is clearly subordinated to YHWH in this poem. As in 1:1-27, she is YHWH's creature; she obeys his commands (vv. 8-9) and serves him in the temple (v. 10). In verses 13-22, Ben Sira again takes up the motif of "the tree that provides nourishment and shade" from 1:1-27. As Silvia Schroer has shown (1987, 218-21), this motif — which probably also is behind Sirach 14:20–15:10 — can be traced back to Egyptian traditions of tree goddesses. The tree goddess provides shade and thereby protects against the scorching sun but, above all, gives food and drink and sometimes even offers her breast to the thirsty. An atmosphere of fullness, life, and love surrounds Wisdom. It is probably no coincidence that these images are reminiscent of the imagery of love in the Song of Songs (4:12–5:1 and elsewhere). This is also where the comparison of Wisdom with sweet-smelling and costly fragrances (Sir 24:15) belongs, which Ben Sira connects in verse 15b with the fragrances used in the liturgical service in the temple. This way, he refers back to Wisdom's place of rest in the temple and her liturgical service there (vv. 8-11). In her speech Wisdom therefore commends herself not only as a nourishing mother and a great lover, but also as a liturgist and priest.

According to 24:3-22, Wisdom is present in its fullness only in Israel and in the temple; it is not surprising then that in verse 23 the Torah of Moses is mentioned, which regulates the life of pious Jews as well as the temple service. What is new is the explicit identification of Wisdom and Torah: "All this [what has thus far been said about Wisdom] is the book of the covenant, of the Most High God, the law [i.e., Torah] that Moses commanded us as a heritage for the gatherings of Jacob."

What at first looks like a restriction of the universal wisdom that is given to all — a move manifest already in verses 3-22 — broadens out again in the next verses (vv. 25-27) where the Torah is compared to the four rivers of Paradise: Pishon, Tigris, Euphrates, and Gihon, as well as to the Jordan and the Nile. I interpret the relation between Wisdom and Torah in Ben Sira similarly to Johannes Marböck, who follows Gerhard von Rad (von Rad, quoted in Marböck 1995, 57; Schroer 1996 differs in her interpretation): "Wisdom is not overshadowed by the Torah; the reverse is true: Ben Sira seeks to legitimate and interpret the Torah from the perspective of Wisdom. Thus, the Torah becomes part of God's universal wisdom which he founded in creation. Ben Sira's further reflections on the Torah and the commandments also suggest such a broad and in no way exclusive understanding of the Torah as Wisdom. For example, such typically Israelite commandments concerning Sabbath, food, and purity are missing in his book, as is any form of polemics against idolatry" (Marböck 1995, 16).

Summary and Conclusion

Personified Divine Wisdom and Wives

Numerous references in the book of Jesus Sirach suggest a special connection between divine Wisdom, which is represented as a woman, and wives, especially good wives. Chapters 24–26 and the end of chapter 23 are particularly significant: Wisdom's high praise of herself in chapter 24 is thereby surrounded by texts on wives. That cannot be coincidental. In 23:22-27 the bad, adulterous wife — whose counterpart in the previous section, by the way, is the adulterous man — is threatened that her children, offspring of an illegitimate liaison (v. 22), will not put down roots and their branches will bring forth no fruit. The very same arguments reappear in 24:12-19 where they are applied to Wisdom herself; here they are developed in a positive way. The adulterous woman becomes the counterimage to Wisdom. Chapters 25–26 enlarge on that image, but Sirach 26 breaks it by the presentation of the good wife. She is given to a man who fears YHWH in verse 3, just as Wisdom is given to the one who fears YHWH in 1:10. The good and strong ("manly" in Greek) wife brings her husband good fortune so that he can live his years in peace (i.e., only in Greek manuscripts). Wisdom rewards her disciples in similar fashion (cf. esp. 1:17-20). The objects in the "temple" that Ben Sira compares to the body of the good wife (26:16-18) clearly bring to mind what he has said about Wisdom as a liturgist in the temple (24:10 and 15). Another commonality between Wisdom and the good wife is the supportive and helping function for the man (15:4 wisdom, 36:24 wife), both offering him a protective nest (14:26 wisdom, 36:25 wife).

Of course, Ben Sira does not say that divine Wisdom and the good wife are identical, but it does seem that the good wife, as well as the temple and the Torah, represents divine Wisdom in a special way. On the other hand, the bad wife represents the very negation of wisdom; she represents the way of perdition that Ben Sira, unlike the book of Proverbs, no longer calls folly. Sirach 26:3 offers an inverse argument: the bad wife will be given to the man who does not fear YHWH. However, Ben Sira is less concerned than his sources with warning men against "taking" a bad wife or, if they are burdened with one, taking them in hand appropriately.

Instead, with his attractive images of women and of wisdom, he seeks above all to make the way of the fear of the Lord attractive and desirable to the young men of his society. At the same time, he knows that positive motivation alone is not enough. Consequently, he paints a horror picture of the bad wife who awaits all who do not walk the way of the fear of God.

In my view, Ben Sira can no longer generally be judged a "woman-hater," because his misogynist statements should not be looked at in isolation but should be set into the wider context of his sapiential writing. The perception that he generally rejects and denounces women cannot be sustained persuasively (contra Trenchard 1982). The text of 42:14b, which thus far has not been reliably reconstructed, should rather be read as an ironic crack at the blanket judgment of 42:14a.

Nevertheless, what Ben Sira has to say about women, whether good or bad, is shaped by the patriarchal, respectively androcentric, perspective that perceives women essentially as beings meant for men or, in our context, as those who impede or advance men's motivation to seek Wisdom. It would require clarification how my hypothesis of the antithetical conception of the bad and the good wife and their relation to Wisdom fits into Ben Sira's obviously important honor-shame scheme (cf. Camp 1991), for instance. But since we have made only a beginning in the interpretation of Ben Sira's pericopes on women, he might well hold more surprises.

Personified Wisdom and Her Relation to YHWH

Contrary to what might be expected, divine Wisdom represented as a woman is burdened with remarkably few gender-role clichés. She has her rough and soft sides, and is active and passive; she nourishes and protects, on the one hand, but she is also a prophet who warns and is a teacher of hard lessons. Even though the book is addressed to men, divine Wisdom is attractive not only for them but in the same way also for women. The relation of Wisdom to YHWH, however, is difficult. On the one hand, she is clearly subordinate to him (1:1-27; 24); on the other, she cannot be differentiated from him and his actions (4:11-19; 6:19-37; 14:20–15:10). Her position is made more complicated when Ben Sira connects her with "the fear of God or YHWH" and "Torah." In any case, the statement that Wisdom is identified with the Torah and is consequently restricted to Israel cuts down the problem disproportionately. More attention than before has to be paid to her relation to concrete women.

I suspect that the ambivalence in how Ben Sira sees the relation between personified Wisdom and YHWH has to do with his understanding of God. On the one hand, he has recognized the deficits of a monotheism that is determined by a male YHWH and has tried to solve them with the introduction of the figure of

Wisdom as the book of Proverbs had done before. On the other hand, he was not able to let go of the monotheism but was not yet in a position to see Wisdom as an aspect within God instead of as a second deity next to him whenever she acts as a woman. To avoid this impression, Ben Sira had to subordinate Wisdom clearly as one of God's creatures. But ultimately, for Ben Sira as for the book of Proverbs too, God is "the God of Israel in the image of a woman" (Schroer 1991, 167). Whoever finds her finds life to the full and thus finds God himself.

LITERATURE

Camp, Claudia V. 1985. *Wisdom and the Feminine in the Book of Proverbs.* Sheffield.

———. 1991. "Understanding a Patriarchy: Women in Second Century Jerusalem through the Eyes of Ben Sira." In *"Women Like This": New Perspectives on Jewish Women in the Graeco-Roman World,* edited by Amy-Jill Levine, 1-40. Atlanta.

Levison, Jack. 1985. "Is Eve to Blame? A Contextual Analysis of Sirach 25:24." *Catholic Biblical Quarterly* 47:617-23.

Maier, Christl. 1996. "Im Vorzimmer der Unterwelt. Die Warnung vor der 'fremden Frau' in Prov 7 in ihrem historischen Kontext." In *Von der Wurzel getragen. Christlich-feministische Exegese in Auseinandersetzung mit Antijudaismus,* edited by Luise Schottroff and Marie-Theres Wacker, 179-98. Leiden et al.

Marböck, Johannes. 1995. *Gottes Weisheit unter uns. Zur Theologie des Buches Sirach,* edited by Irmtraud Fischer. Freiburg im Breisgau.

Sauer, Georg. 1981. *Jesus Sirach. Jüdische Schriften aus hellenistisch-römischer Zeit,* 3:483-644. Gütersloh.

Schroer, Silvia. 1987. "Die Zweiggöttin in Palästina/Israel. Von der Mittelbronze II B-Zeit bis zu Jesus Sirach." In *Jerusalem. Texte-Bilder-Steine,* edited by Max Küchler and Christoph Uehlinger, 201-25. Fribourg.

———. 1991. "Die göttliche Weisheit und der nachexilische Monotheismus." In *Der eine Gott und die Göttin. Gottesvorstellungen des biblischen Israel im Horizont feministischer Theologie,* edited by Marie-Theres Wacker and Erich Zenger, 151-82. Questiones disputatae, vol. 135. Freiburg im Breisgau.

———. 1996. "Der eine Herr und die Männerherrschaft im Buch Jesus Sirach. Frauenbild und Weisheitsbild in einer misogynen Schrift." In Silvia Schroer, *Die Weisheit hat ihr Haus gebaut. Studien zur Gestalt der Sophia,* 96-106. Mainz.

Skehan, Patrick W., and Alexander A. DiLella. 1987. *The Wisdom of Ben Sira.* Anchor Bible, vol. 39. Garden City, N.Y.

Trenchard, Warren C. 1982. *Ben Sira's View of Women: A Literary Analysis.* Chico, Calif.

Translated by Martin Rumscheidt

Wisdom: An Example of Jewish Intercultural Theology

Silvia Schroer

A Feminist Approach to the Figure and the Book of Wisdom

The book of Wisdom, written in Greek, is probably the latest Jewish writing accepted as part of the Greek canon of the First Testament. It is interesting for a feminist exegesis because here, as in other postexilic writings (Prov 1–9; Job 28; Sirach), the text speaks of personified Wisdom (Hebrew *ḥokmâ;* Greek *sophia*), a female figure who is immediately associated with Israel's God and who advances a divine claim. Thus far traditional exegesis has not succeeded in reaching a consensus about the meaning of Sophia in these writings or in the religious symbol system of postexilic Israel, because the figure of Wisdom is difficult to reconcile with the patriarchal concepts of a monotheistic religion. Although studies in the history of religions have repeatedly emphasized the influence of Egyptian and Hellenistic goddesses on the figure of Sophia, as soon as the discussion turned to her importance within Israel and her theological meaning, very little attention was paid to her femaleness. Claudia Camp in particular (1985), through her feminist-exegetical investigation of the framing of the book of Proverbs, has pointed the way out of the old blind alleys by tracing the relationships between the literary and historical roles of women in Israel and the image of God in the wisdom literature, and by making the function of personification as a stylistic means the starting point for her reflections. Camp's work (cf. Schroer 1996, chapters II and III) shows how important it is for a feminist exegesis of the wisdom writings, methodologically speaking, to move

This essay is a very much shortened version of a feminist-critical commentary on the book of Wisdom that appeared in English under the title "The Book of Sophia," in *Searching the Scriptures: A Feminist-Ecumenical Commentary,* ed. Elisabeth Schüssler Fiorenza (New York: Crossroad, 1994), 17-35; it has also appeared in German in Walter Dietrich and Martin A. Klopfenstein, eds., *Ein Gott allein? JHWH-Verehrung und biblischer Monotheismus im Kontext der israelitischen und altorientalischen Religionsgeschichte,* Orbis biblicus et orientalis 139 (Fribourg: Universitätsverlag; Göttingen: Vandenhoeck & Ruprecht, 1994), 543-58.

from texts to their community, social, political, cultural, and religious contexts. It also becomes clear that personified Wisdom cannot be separated from the context of the particular wisdom writing: that in each of these documents she has a different function and meaning. Therefore the following essay is not restricted to the goal of a new discovery of a female image of God in Israel. Rather, my purpose is to reconstruct, in feminist theological terms, a bit of theological history as a part of the history of Jewish women at the end of the first century B.C.E.

However, at the outset this book seeks to thwart interest in that kind of knowledge, for it seeks anonymity by, for example, clothing biblical traditions in disguises of Greek and Hellenistic language and forms. It avoids concretizations and seeks to present the appearance of a timeless, universal validity. There is, as yet, no consensus about the authorship of the book (is it from a single hand, or is it a collective product?). On the other hand, there is increasing agreement about the place of origin and dating (Kloppenborg 1982; Engel 1991), according to which it may have been written by Greek-educated authors in Alexandria in Egypt, where many wealthy Jews lived. According to Larcher (1983), the three principal parts could have been composed in succession during the last three decades before the common era. The historical background is formed by the destabilized political situation after the naval battle of Actium (31 B.C.E.), which may have worsened the situation for Jewish communities in Egypt. There were many apostates, and apparently there were also denunciations and persecutions within the communities. In 30 B.C.E. Egypt became a Roman province under the emperor's control. In light of these important events in secular history, the book of Wisdom seeks with the utmost seriousness to stabilize Jewish identity by aiming its barbs outward against apostates and at the same time securing, within the communities, those who had remained true to Judaism in their faith. As the Pax Romana began to be felt in Egypt, the author or authors raised the voice of reason, issued reminders about the mortality of rulers, and presented, in the images of Wisdom and of the ideal wise king (Solomon), the indispensable preconditions for an enduring rulership, which simultaneously satisfied the highest demands of intelligence and ethics. In a sweeping projection, the Jewish tradition was newly translated and made contemporary to the demands of the time, and also explained for the benefit of non-Jews.

The Manifestations and Attributes of Sophia in Wisdom 6–10

Three major structural sections can be distinguished within the book of Wisdom (for basic questions see Schroer 1995). Part I (1:1–6:21) is dedicated to a traditional theme of Israel's wisdom literature, namely, the relationship of cause and effect. It begins with an admonition in wisdom style to love justice and seek God, and to give no place to death in one's life. In what follows, the attitude of the godless is revealed to be a deep-seated skepticism in the face of the ephemeral nature of life. Resignation and cynicism are characteristic of these reckless profiteers and practitioners of violence, for whom the righteous, with their pious attitudes, are only objects of ridicule. The book of Wisdom, however, says emphatically that the righteous will receive the "wages" of their righteousness from God. But in contrast to the older wisdom tradition, the outcome of cause and effect is here awaited in a world beyond time, after a final judgment. The idea of survival of individual souls, so atypical of the traditions of Israelite faith, is evidence of the strong Greek influence on the communities in Egypt. Part II (6:22–11:1) is an encomium, a speech in praise of Wisdom, although chapter 10 is formally connected to the third section of the book. In part III (11:2–19:22) there is a hymnic reminiscence of the exodus. In this part the themes include the signs of God's power, false notions of God or forms of worship, and hope for God's support against the xenophobia experienced in Egypt.

The first chapters of the book refer only marginally to Wisdom. It is primarily the middle section that is devoted to personified Sophia (for chapters 6–8 see Engel 1991). In the introduction to his speech to the kings and tyrants of the earth (6:1-2, 9), Solomon, the teacher of wisdom, proclaims that he will teach Wisdom (6:9, 11, 25). When, in what follows, the text speaks of Sophia as a female figure, the nonpersonified meaning of wisdom (i.e., study, knowledge, experience, cleverness) is always implied, even when these aspects recede into the background.

In the descriptive song in 6:12-15 Sophia is first described, in line with sayings in Proverbs 1 and 8 and Sirach 4, 6, 15, and 51, as a woman whom the students of wisdom seek and love. The wisdom teacher who speaks in Wisdom 6:22-25 emphasizes expressly that Wisdom has nothing to do with "mysteries" (secrets). He will openly proclaim her nature and her origin; he will bring knowledge of her before the public and will not (selfishly) keep it to himself. According to 7:15-21, wisdom and knowledge come from God. Insight into all the scientific disciplines of Hellenism is ultimately the gift of God, but it is Wisdom who, as architect or builder of all things, undertakes the instruction of the wise. Sophia's nature is described hymnically in 7:22–8:1 in twenty-one epithets. Many of the things said about Sophia in this hymn contain references drawn from the corpus of Stoic philosophy and its descriptions of the divine (see Engel 1991, 72-80). Here Sophia is a veil of mist, an emanation, a reflection, mirror, or image of divine reality, in a sense the dynamic-active, self-expressive side of the divine being.

Chapter 8, with its biography of the "ideal" sage, takes up the idea already expressed in 7:28 that God cannot love any human being who does not live with wisdom (i.e., sleep with her, have intercourse with her). The love relationship between Solomon and Sophia is described in strongly erotic language. The erotic language of these images is nothing new (cf. Sir 51:13-17, and the Qumran *Psalms Scroll*[a] 21.11-17), but what is astonishing is that it is applied to the relationship between God and Wisdom, when, in Wisdom 8:3, Sophia is called the beloved and the companion of God. Sophia's marital communion with God explains pictorially why she is *the* mystic of divine knowledge pure and simple. Her omniscience, not her beauty, is the motive for the sage to marry her. For only Wisdom, because of her knowledge of the divine and of all things, can be a perfect counselor to a wise king (cf. Prov 8:12-16). Only the well-qualified advice of Wisdom guarantees the young king renown, the ability to judge rightly, an immortal name, governance over nations, and success in war. The middle section of the book of Wisdom reaches its climax in the prayer of the wise king in chapter 9. The sage asks God (9:4) for the *paredros* of the divine throne. Both the concept of the *paredros* (the one-who-sits-beside) and the image of the enthroned couple are, in the history of religions, very closely connected with the divine couples in polytheistic religions. The authors of the book of Wisdom, however, have no hesitation about employing daring images when it is a question of describing divine reality in its various aspects.

Only with Sophia's help can anyone recognize and carry out the divine will (9:17); her instruction is indispensable for the salvation of human beings. In chapter 10, biblical stories and characters are cited as examples of people who have been saved by Wisdom; their names, however, are omitted in order to avoid a narrowing of that salvation to the biblical and Jewish tradition. It is likewise Sophia who saves "a holy people and a blameless race" (Israel) from the nation of oppressors (Egypt) (10:15-21). Thus God's saving deeds in and for Israel are retold, with the name of Sophia taking the place of the traditional name of God. It is she who rescues the ancestors of Israel and leads the exodus. The key words used here to allude to the biblical traditions are unusual. They offer us clues about the tribulations of those to whom the writing was addressed (10:9, 17). In the midst of all these trials (lapses, apostasy, fraternal murders, the wickedness of the nations, alienation between the generations, greed, enemies, temptations, life in foreign lands, imprisonment), Sophia brings security, wealth, and success, and even shows the righteous the realm of God (10:10). The recollection of the exodus assures those in travail that, with the help of Wisdom, they can once again resist ferocious rulers and escape from their oppression in Egypt.

An initial conclusion we may draw is that the femaleness of Sophia in the book of Wisdom is by no means only eroticism; it is also and primarily bound up with knowledge, rule, teaching, counsel, the most exalted origins, the power to form and create, trustworthiness, salvation, guidance, and virtue, especially justice. Most of these characteristics are not ordinarily associated with the roles assigned to women in a patriarchal society (cf. Georgi 1988, 252-53). That makes it all the more important to ask whether we can find clues to the reason why, toward the end of the first century B.C.E., Sophia was able to become a persuasive religious symbol within these female roles. Is there a connection between this female image of God and the image of women, or the reality of women, at the same period? What influences impelled Jewish women and men in Egypt to develop such an image of God?

From Text to Context

At an initial level the book of Wisdom contains little direct information about women. In the fiction employed, a male sage directs his teaching to male kings. Women are mentioned explicitly only in 3:12, 13, and 9:7. According to 3:13-15, the childlessness of a woman (and of a man), contrary to the older Israelite tradition, is no longer regarded as the greatest misfortune that can befall a person. The childless woman, so long as she has had no premarital or extramarital sexual relations, is promised fruit at the end of the ages. This is the first place in the First Testament tradition where a fundamental preference is expressed for virtuous, voluntary sexual abstinence over a less virtuous manner of life accompanied by the bearing of many children. Concretely, this means that women who could not (or did not wish to) bear children and who voluntarily lived as virgins, single women, or widows were accorded the same status in the religious congregation as married mothers. We encounter this unusual image of the childless and "virginal" woman in a similar fashion in a short writing by Philo of Alexandria, *De vita contemplativa*.

The Therapeutrides: Jewish Women in Contemplative Communities

Philo of Alexandria (25 B.C.E. to about 40 C.E.) reports in *De vita contemplativa* (abbreviated *Comtempl*) on the community of the Therapeutae and Therapeutrides, who, in rural isolation primarily in the vicinity of Alexandria, devoted themselves entirely to prayer, the study of the scriptures, and an ascetic style of life. The Therapeutae or Therapeutrides are "dropouts." Out of a longing for eternal blessedness they leave earthly life behind them. Sheltered in small settlements, they lead a strongly regimented common life. During the week the members spend most of their time in individual cells, engaging in philosophical and theological studies and composing hymns. But on the Sabbath the men and women come together to listen to a lecture (*Contempl* 32). Women are also fully integrated in the principal festival of the Therapeutae and Therapeutrides, a simple but festive meal followed by a liturgy. In this connection, Philo adds that the female members are mainly "aged virgins" who voluntarily live in a state of sexual abstinence (*Contempl* 68). Ross S. Kraemer (1989) posits that the "aged virgins" may not have been only unmarried, childless women or real virgins, but also older women who had already passed through menopause. Interestingly, Philo gives as a reason for these women's choice of sexual abstinence that they desire to live with Sophia and are striving for an immortal posterity. The teaching of Sophia is a kind of heavenly food to the ascetic Therapeutae and Therapeutrides, from which they seek to live in the most literal sense of the word (*Contempl* 35). Still, jubilant singing and festivals are also part of this life with Wisdom. In the community's evening celebration after the agape meal, a choir of women and men makes present in song the rescue of Israel at the exodus from Egypt. The presentation closes with a common choral song, in which the men are led by the prophet Moses and the women by the prophetess Miriam (*Contempl* 83-84). Thus in shaping their liturgical practices the Therapeutae and Therapeutrides had a regard for traditions of particular importance to women and included them alongside the dominant patriarchal traditions.

We can conclude from *De vita contemplativa* that in Greco-Roman Egypt there were monastic Jewish groups to which certain women were admitted. The members of these communities, probably for the most part well-to-do, educated people, withdrew from their family ties in order to live together in a new, spiritual family (much like the Jesus movement). They considered childlessness an admirable form of life, while despising material wealth and every kind of luxury. They rejected slavery as contrary to nature and a consequence of greed and violence (*Contempl* 70). The women living in the community are depicted by Philo as religious subjects of full maturity who not only brought to the community the consciousness of their history as women (Miriam was, in Hellenistic-Roman times, by far the most common name for Jewish women, in Egypt as well; see Mayer 1987, 33-42), but perceived themselves also as life companions of divine Wisdom.

Research on the book of Wisdom has repeatedly postulated connections with the Therapeutrides. In fact, there are points of contact in the structure and content of both writings that cannot be peripheral or accidental (cf., for example, *Contempl* 3-9 with Wis 12–15). Personified Sophia plays a central role in the spirituality both of the Therapeutae and Therapeutrides and of the authors of the book of Wisdom. Both groups combine recollection of the exodus (Wis 10:15-21; 11–19) with songs of praise. In each case, this exodus is led by female figures, namely, the prophetess Miriam or Sophia. Both in the circles of the Therapeutae and Therapeutrides and in those of sapiential thought it appears that the consciousness of a special kind of friendship with God was cultivated (Wis 7:27; *Contempl* 90). Also common to both writings are an internal posture of distance toward current attitudes to life in their cultural environment (cf., e.g., Wis 3–4) and a strong orientation toward a divine or heavenly world and order of things that could be experienced in the past and present and was accepted as a certainty for the future. For the Therapeutae and Therapeutrides, however, this worldview effected a very drastic turning away from the world that cannot be demonstrated in the book of Wisdom. Nevertheless, the connections between the two writings are so marked that we must suppose that they originated in a similar milieu and that there was a spiritual kinship between the two groups. Comparable examples of connections between radical "dropout" groups and a broader circle of sympathizers who did not share their extreme style of life but did participate in their ideas include Qumran and the Essenes, and also the itinerant charismatics of the Jesus movement and their (resident) associates.

The Power of the Goddess: Isis and Sophia

Even in the older wisdom literature the figure of personified Wisdom is strongly inspired by the images and mythology of the ancient Oriental and Egyptian goddess cults. Maat, Hathor, the tree goddesses of Egypt, and even the Syrian goddess gave Sophia her image and power of fascination. The observation that Sophia in the book of Wisdom is essentially shaped by the figure of Isis and the theology of Isis in late Ptolemaic or early Roman Egypt was expressed in individual studies as early as the first half of the twentieth century. Major publications by James M. Reese, Burton L. Mack, and John S. Kloppenborg contributed to a more precise development of the connections between Isis and Sophia.

In the late period of Egyptian autonomy, the cult of the goddess Isis, who according to mythology was the sister-spouse of Osiris and mother of Horus, spread throughout the Aegean region and the western Mediterranean, through Greece and into Italy. The popularity of the Isis cult was attributable to the unlimited variety of the "universal goddess." As described in the mythology, her functions of creating and protecting life as wife and mother made her ruler over the mystery of life. To her was attributed rule over cosmic and earthly powers and over destiny, for she was not subject to Heimarmene, the Greek goddess of unavoidable fate. The Hellenistic Isis aretalogies praise the goddess as one who gives to the nations languages, alphabets, and the sciences. She is the patron of sea voyages and commerce; she gives rule to kings and makes laws valid; she helps those who implore her to achieve prosperity and the blessing of children. Isis was worshiped across almost all groups of the population (with the exception of the military), by men and women; nevertheless, her cult exercised a special attraction for women and probably had a positive influence on women's position in society. It is said of Isis in the hymns of praise to the goddess that she made the power of women equal to that of men, or that she invented marriage contracts.

Whole lists can be made of similarities between the attributes of Isis and those of Sophia in the book of Wisdom, but simple motif-comparisons are of little value insofar as some of these epithets are also to be found in hymns to other divinities (e.g., Zeus), so that no specific link to the Isis cult can be demonstrated. Hence Kloppenborg (1982) has attempted to isolate certain general theological concepts that are perceptible in the epithets and to relate this theology to that of Sophia. He distinguishes three types of Isis worship in the first century B.C.E.: the Isis worship of the simple people, that of the Ptolemaic and Roman royal theology, and that of the Greeks as found in the aretalogies or the writings of Plutarch or Diodorus Siculus. While the first type had scarcely any influence on Alexandrian Judaism, the authors of the book of Wisdom deliberately entered into dialogue with the royal theology, and even more so with the strongly missionary Isis worship of the Greeks.

The relationship between Solomon and Wisdom, extensively described in the middle section of the book, acquires a special mythological dimension against the background of the royal Isis theology. As Solomon attains immortality through Wisdom, so Osiris and Horus achieve immortality through Isis. As Sophia is at the same time "goddess" and (desired) spouse of the king, so Isis is goddess and royal spouse, counselor and guarantor of the ruling house. She puts an end to injustice, tyranny, and wars.

Isis is honored in many dedicatory inscriptions as the (universal) savior, because she has power over fate and all the cosmic forces. She is the patron of farmers, seafarers, prisoners, those seeking justice, married couples, and mothers, but also of scientists. She is said to be able to rescue those who are in distress at sea, in prison, and in other disasters and to bring her worshipers prosperity, knowledge in all fields, professional success, and long life. She is responsible for law and custom, giving laws and taking care that they are obeyed, so that all human beings may live in peace as equals. The saving power of Sophia is described in like terms, especially in Wisdom 10, but also in many other passages. She knows how to steer a ship (10:4 and 14:1-6); she comes to prisoners in their dungeons (10:14); she brings riches to the just (3:3-6); and so on.

The statements about Sophia in the book of Wisdom are imbued to the highest degree with features from Isis mythology; in fact, they apparently quote and allude to the language of the Isis mission quite deliberately when sketching the portrait of Sophia. Sophia is the Jewish response to the challenge of Isis and mystery cult piety in Egypt before the end of the era. This response consists not of negative rejection but of constructive integration. The book of Wisdom is addressed to Jews, and perhaps also to Jewish sympathizers, who came into immediate contact with Isis religion in Alexandria and for whom the Isis cult quite possibly furnished a very real religious alternative. Rather than demonizing Isis religion, the book of Wisdom attempts to set up an equal figure over against Isis. This attempt reflects, on the one hand, the readiness of the Jews in Alexandria — despite their skeptical attitude toward their Hellenistic environment — to get involved with Greek culture, education, and religious observance and to orient themselves accordingly. On the other hand, this theological project profiles a fragment of women's history. Both Egyptian and Greek women in Egypt possessed a notable degree of legal and economic freedom. In the philosophical schools there was discussion of the traditional roles of women (for the history of women in Hellenism, see Pomeroy 1984). The Hellenistic emancipation of the individual had the additional consequence that the practice of religion was partly transferred to the charge of private cultic associations and became a matter of individual choice.

These changes did not wash over the Jewish groups living in Alexandria without leaving a trace. Jewish women (at least the upper class) may have formulated to an increasing degree their own self-concept, as well as their demand to take an active part in the shaping of religious life and to formulate "modern" approaches to faith that were capable of offering contemporary and attractive images of God.

Feminist-Theological Evaluation

The Function of the Personification of Sophia in the Book of Wisdom

Sophia in the book of Wisdom, as a personification, serves less to combine the various teachings in the Jewish tradition (as in Prov 1–9) than to unite the whole Jewish wisdom tradition with that of Greece and Hellenism. Thus she mediates between the strongly ethical dimensions of biblical wisdom teaching, with their interest in a just order of things, and the intellectual concept of wisdom of Greek antiquity. What the Hellenists call *philo-sophia,* the striving for wisdom, exists also in the Jewish tradition: that is the message of this writing. The effort to achieve knowledge and education is seen as a weighty common interest of both cultural groups and a basis for intercultural dialogue. The religious and national identity of educated Jewish circles in Alexandria revealed itself, even in times of crisis, as strong enough to react to the challenges of the Hellenistic world by maintaining a dialogue.

Nationalism and the independence of Israel are combined in Sophia with universalism and a considered and deliberate theological inculturation. This dialogue is not uncritical. Wisdom, as Jews understand it, is not a private matter and is not reserved to a few initiates in the mysteries. It is the sole guarantee of the continuance of any kind of rule or governance, since education is indispensable for just rule. Against the background of the expanding Pax Romana, Sophia is a symbol critical of the governing power, directed against arbitrariness and tyranny.

She appears in the image of a wise, omniscient, just, and saving woman whose autonomy is transparent both to the God of Israel and to the goddess Isis. Isis herself, though originally an Egyptian goddess, had entered the Hellenistic-Roman world as a religious symbol with an unusual capacity to create unity. By incorporating the mythology and theology of Isis in the figure of Sophia, Egyptian Judaism sought to lend power to its own integrating forces through the use of a female symbol of the divine.

The importance of personified Sophia as a creator of unity is also manifest in the theological structure of the book of Wisdom. The first section begins with the programmatic appeal: "love righteousness, you rulers of the earth." The purpose of the first section of the book is to demonstrate that the righteous, contrary to appearances, are on the better and more productive way — in fact, that God's rules of governance will ultimately triumph. The real world, with its unjust order of things and its striving for riches, is contrasted with a just world, a contrast world, whose symbolism already strongly resembles the Christian Testament ideas about a "reign of God" (cf. Wis 10:10, 14). This contrast world really exists, since it is possible to live according to its laws, but it is also utopian, because complete justice will only be established by God in a "then." Nevertheless, Wisdom is the teacher of righteousness who is accessible to all. Righteousness and wisdom are like the outer and inner sides of a life pleasing to God. Without wisdom there can be no just "reign of God."

Sophia: Symbol of Unity in Diversity and Teacher of Righteousness

Sophia in the book of Wisdom is the symbol of an interreligious and intercultural dialogue in a multicultural society of the first century B.C.E. She attempts a positive interaction with the existing religious and cultural pluralism by reinterpreting her own tradition, readily opening herself to foreign influences and taking inspiration from them. The "contextual theology" of the work is not averse to speaking about the God of Israel in new language and in images similar to those of the goddess. This process of reformulation, however, does not lead to a surrender of accepted tradition, to a leveling of the independence of Jewish thought and belief, or to eso-teric indifference. The common history affords identity "at all times and in all places" (cf. 19:22). The irreplaceable measure that endures through all changes is the justice of God. Not without reason does the book of Wisdom engage itself inten-sively against idol worship and the blasphemous worship of rulers (Wis 11–19).

Sophia shows the way to a just Jewish life amid a pluralistic world. The opti-mistic attitude of the time toward the transforming power of knowledge, educa-tion, and consciousness is worthy of consideration even and especially for our own time. In an attempt to work toward a just world order at the end of the twen-tieth century and the beginning of the twenty-first, one that could offer resistance to the "new" world orders of existing systems of power, the experience and knowl-edge, and especially the wisdom, of women will stand in the forefront. Wisdom can save women; she could even lead a worldwide exodus from the complicated and tangled nets of patriarchal oppression. As an integrative religious symbol, Sophia is well suited to create community between religions; as a cosmopolitan symbol she can contribute to the struggle against nationalism through a national identity that is open to the world.

Sophia, as an authentic biblical image of God, offers remarkable possibilities for breaking up the petrifactions and ontologizations of androcentric God lan-guage, and for doing so on the basis of a Jewish tradition. (For the further develop-ment of wisdom theology in Christian writings, cf. Schroer 1996, chapter VIII.) Her attributes are the attributes of God; when she speaks, God speaks; what she proclaims and does is God's will. She is the "wholly other," yet she makes herself known. The authors of the work dared to think of Sophia within the horizons of the imagery of the goddess Isis, who promises salvation because she stands above the powers of destiny. Sophia in the book of Wisdom is Israel's God imaged as woman and goddess.

LITERATURE

Bergman, Jan. 1968. *Ich bin Isis. Studien zum memphitischen Hintergrund der griechischen Isisaretalogien.* Uppsala.

Camp, Claudia V. 1985. *Wisdom and the Feminine in the Book of Proverbs.* Sheffield.

Engel, Helmut. 1991. "'Was Weisheit ist und wie sie entstand, will ich verkünden.'" In *Lehrerin der Gerechtigkeit,* edited by Georg Hentschel and Erich Zenger, 67-102. Erfurter theologische Schriften, vol. 19. Leipzig.

――――. 1998. *Das Buch der Weisheit.* Neuer Stuttgarter Kommentar Altes Testament, vol. 16. Stuttgart.

Georgi, Dieter. 1980. *Weisheit Salomos. Jüdische Schriften aus hellenistisch-römischer Zeit,* vol. 3, 4. Gütersloh.

――――. 1988. "Frau Weisheit oder das Recht auf Freiheit als schöpferische Kraft." In *Verdrängte Vergangenheit, die uns bedrängt. Feministische Theologie in der Verantwortung für die Geschichte,* edited by Leonore Siegele-Wenschkewitz, 243-76. Munich.

Kloppenborg, John S. 1982. "Isis and Sophia in the Book of Wisdom." *Harvard Theological Review* 75:57-84.

Kraemer, Ross S. 1989. "Monastic Jewish Women in Greco-Roman Egypt: Philo Judaeus on the Therapeutrides." *Signs: Journal of Women in Culture and Society* 14:342-70.

Larcher, Chrysostome. 1983/84/85. *Le Livre de la Sagesse ou la Sagesse de Salomon.* 3 vols. Paris.

Mack, Burton L. 1973. *Logos und Sophia. Untersuchungen zur Weisheitstheologie im hellenistischen Judentum.* Göttingen.

Mayer, Günter. 1987. *Die jüdische Frau in der hellenistisch-römischen Antike.* Stuttgart.

Pomeroy, Sarah B. 1984. *Goddesses, Whores, Wives, and Slaves: Women in Classical Antiquity.* New York.

――――. 1995. *Frauenleben im klassischen Altertum.* Stuttgart.

Reese, James M. 1970. *Hellenistic Influence on the Book of Wisdom and Its Consequences.* Analecta biblica, vol. 41. Rome.

Schroer, Silvia. 1995. "Das Buch der Weisheit." In *Einleitung in das Alte Testament,* edited by Erich Zenger et al., 277-84. Stuttgart. (7th ed. Stuttgart, 2008, pp. 396-407.)

――――. 1996. *Die Weisheit hat ihr Haus gebaut.* Mainz.

――――. 1997. "Vom Text zum Kontext. Versuche der Situierung des Buches der Weisheit in der religiösen Zeitgeschichte und ihre feministische Relevanz." *Bibel und Kirche* 52:174-78.

Winston, James. 1979. *The Wisdom of Solomon.* Anchor Bible, vol. 43. Garden City, N.Y.

FOR FURTHER READING

Blischke, Mareike Verena. 2007. *Die Eschatologie in der Sapientia Salomonis.* Forschungen zum Alten Testament, 2nd ser., vol. 26. Tübingen.

Keppler, Martina. 1999. *Hellenistische Bildung im Buch der Weisheit: Studien zur Sprachgestalt und Theologie der Sapientia Salomonis.* Beihefte zur Zeitschrift für die alttestamentliche Wissenschaft, vol. 280. Berlin.

Neher, Martin. 2004. *Wesen und Wirken der Weisheit in der Sapientia Salomonis.* Berlin and New York.

Translated by Linda M. Maloney

4 Ezra: On the Struggle for New Life, the Time That Is Being Fulfilled, and the Transformation of the Earth (2 Esdras 3–14)

Luzia Sutter Rehmann

Introduction

Chapters 3 to 14 of the Second Book of Esdras are regarded by some scholars (e.g., Collins 1984, 156) as one of the most important of the apocalypses. In spite of this, this work has remained for the most part uncommented on by feminist scholars.

This rather extensive book is found in the "apocrypha" section of some Bibles. Since there are a number of "Ezra" or "Esdras" books, numbered according to various criteria, let me say for clarification that 2 Esdras contains chapters 3–14 of a Latin apocalypse. The beginning and end of 2 Esdras, chapters 1–2 and 15–16 of that apocalypse, are a Christian frame and are counted as 2 and 5 Esdras or 5 and 6 Ezra. 4 Ezra, or the Ezra Apocalypse, is a Jewish apocryphal apocalypse in a broad Ezra tradition (for the whole complex, see Charlesworth 1983). This chapter is interested in 4 Ezra, chapters 3–14 of 2 Esdras. The contexts revealed by these many different books of "Ezra" have scarcely been investigated. Why were works repeatedly named after Ezra through several centuries? It could be interesting for feminist theology to look at the self-transforming "Ezras" and to consider their different attitudes toward women.

In addition, the placement of 2 Esdras in the Vulgate is worth thinking about. In the old edition of the Vulgate prepared by the church father Jerome, 2 Esdras was placed among the apocrypha of the First Testament. In the Clementine edition of the Vulgate, published at the time of the Counter-Reformation, we find 2 Esdras after Revelation, in an appendix to the New Testament. In the ancient church 4 Ezra was highly regarded, which is why it quite naturally found a place in Jerome's edition of the Vulgate. But we can also understand, historically, why the fourth book of Ezra was shifted to a place following the New Testament writings: 4 Ezra was written around 100 C.E. ("In the thirtieth year after the destruction of the city . . ." [3:1] is usually interpreted to mean thirty years after the destruction of Jerusalem in 70 C.E.) — thus about the same time as Revelation. These two exciting apocalypses can well be read together, since both deal theologically with the traumatic event of the destruction of Jerusalem and the crushing of Jewish resistance to the Roman colonial power in Palestine (→ Revelation).

Overview

4 Ezra is usually divided into seven visions, the first three of which are written in dialogue form. The seer Ezra engages with the divine messenger Uriel, who attempts to answer his questions.

In Vision 1 (3:1-5, 19) Ezra mourns the fate of his people and asks questions about the origins of the world, about sin and suffering. In Vision 2 (5:21–6:34) he again laments that so many are dying before the present evil age has passed away. Signs of the end are given. In Vision 3 (6:35–9:25) he suffers for the lost and longs for the final judgment. Again he receives signs that portend the end.

The next visions are very different in style. Now it is not so much Ezra's questions that drive the text forward as the visions he receives. For this reason the unity of the book is often called into question. But the content of the visions is anchored and prepared for in the preceding dialogues: Vision 4 (9:26–10:59) is the description of a sorrowing mother who is transformed into a city, the rebuilt Zion. In Vision 5 (11:1–12:39) an eagle rises out of the sea and a lion proclaims to it that the end is at hand. In Vision 6 (13:1-58) a man arises out of the sea and destroys his enemies with a great army, by means of a storm of fire issuing from his mouth. In Vision 7 (14:1-48) Ezra is given the task of writing books for forty days with five men. They write ninety-four books (twenty-four of them canonical and seventy that are secret).

Searching for Hope

4 Ezra is a Jewish, apocalyptic, pseudepigraphical book. This is seen by the prevailing trend in exegesis as a threefold difficulty. The three attributes often lead to a devaluation of the book, as is evident, for example, in Gunkel's commentary: "Where does this peculiar compassion of the author for sinners come from? Certainly it is in part because he sees his own sinful people as themselves sinners (8:15-19, 45); but for the most part it is the whole of sinful humanity he has in mind. This sympathy for sinners . . . foreign to strongly ethical religions and thus also to the Gospel, is a sign of the effeminate temper of broken Judaism" (Gunkel 1900, 338; cf. also Bousset 1926; Knibb 1979). The anti-Jewish designation of the Judaism of the period as "late Judaism," which was supposed to be shattered — a thoroughgoing historical inaccuracy — also generally presumes that there were *a* normative Judaism and a number of splinter groups as well. This prejudice reveals itself in the evaluation of pseudepigraphical writings. Thus, for example, Leonhard Rost

can still explain that pseudepigrapha are "Jewish writings that were accorded validity only within particular groups, although they arose in more or less the same period as the apocrypha" (Rost 1971, 22).

But pseudepigrapha were important not only in special groups; they were accepted in a great many communities in the greatest variety of localities. As diverse as Jewish groups of the period were, they all considered themselves true "Israelites" with the correct belief, and not sectarian marginal bodies or subgroups. This view of the colorful and lively phenomena of early Judaism (200 B.C.E. to 200 C.E.), resting as it does on a historical misunderstanding, influences the understanding of the pseudepigraphical writings as sources that could help us to understand early Jewish theology and practice. In addition, it neglects the opportunity to reflect on lines of tradition (such as, for example, the rich Ezra traditions). Instead, the label "pseudepigraphical" (writings that give false information about their authorship) suggests that these writings are somehow "pseudo," that is, ungenuine. (For an examination of the apocalyptic literature, see my essay on the book of Revelation.)

Therefore, in reading 4 Ezra I want to pay respect to this book that has suffered from such threefold discrimination. When we read about Ezra's struggle with God, I join him in his search for hope: How can we do justice to this marginalized book that was held in high regard for centuries and, at the same time, read it critically in relation to all forms of androcentrism and be attentive to discrimination of women?

The theology of relation in 4 Ezra offers us some help. Reading the dialogues between Ezra and Uriel only on a literal, content-focused level can leave us confused and dissatisfied. But as soon as we understand Ezra's questions as an insistent, untiring struggle for God, we have access to this desperate, critical, loving human being. For Ezra, the spokesperson for his people, perceives the suffering of the people and allows his theology to be moved by it. He provokes God; he calls him to account much as Job does. Whereas Job complains: "[The wicked and the pious] lie down alike in the dust" (Job 21:26), Ezra asks: "Are the deeds of those who inhabit Babylon any better? . . . Or what nation has kept your commandments so well?" (2 Esd 3:28, 36). In the first three visions Ezra laments and questions again and again. The divine messenger who has been sent to give answers has no easy task. Ezra is not impressed by the angel's wisdom teachings, sometimes elegant, sometimes overly subtle: "I did not wish to inquire about the ways above, but about those things that we daily experience: why Israel has been given over to the Gentiles in disgrace; why the people whom you loved has been given over to godless tribes" (4:23). Ezra represents the Jewish tradition that seeks help in dialogue with God. The position of the divine messenger, on the other hand, is oscillating. He often points Ezra toward the unexpected (e.g., "go and ask a pregnant woman . . . ," 4:40). The image of God is also shaped by him. In part God remains hidden behind the angel, and in part God is identical with him. Ezra also experiences him as an internal voice (5:15). Ezra does not discover an almighty God who corrects and impresses him. But he finds a patient interlocutor in the angel, who invites him to reflect and dig deeper — yet does not silence him. Ezra is alert to hope for his dishonored people and for humanity as a whole, which does not fulfill God's will and therefore cannot endure to the end. Ezra hopes for the judgment that will bring justice, but he is afraid that it will be too long before it finally arrives. We do not find in 4 Ezra any speculations about the end; here are no calculations about "how long?" The angel does not pay any attention to Ezra's impatience. He repeatedly turns him back upon himself: he himself must know how it is with the world. He cannot be relieved of this painful process of coming to knowledge.

In the last vision (14:1-2) Ezra turns to his people, who, in their sorrowful state, are depending on him. His struggle with God leads Ezra to the place where the prince of the people, Phaltiel, has long wanted him to be: Ezra may not forget his people for the sake of fasting and praying (5:16-18). Ezra can finally accept the wish to put his house in order, to console the poor, to empower his people. He begins to write, and he gives the people anew the writings that had been burned (the twenty-four books of the First Testament), and he presents seventy additional books to the sages. So in the course of his struggle Ezra allowed himself to be transformed from a critical questioner to a creative theologian, from a man alone to a shepherd for his people. In the midst of Ezra's pain we can detect an unbroken relationship with God, whom Ezra believes to be endlessly patient and ready to listen to sorrowful questioning.

The Fourth Vision: Mother Zion

Ezra is changed. But exactly when and how does this transformation occur? Recent studies of 4 Ezra agree that the fourth vision (9:26–10:59) answers these questions and is the turning point of the entire book. Edith McEwan Humphrey (1995) has described the significance of the fourth vision in this process of Ezra's transformation. She has also compared the transformation of the sorrowing mother into a city with similar transformations of female figures in other writings (Joseph and Aseneth, the Shepherd of Hermas, and the Revelation of John; see also the Testament of Job).

But first let me briefly describe this impressive fourth vision. Ezra is sent into a green field. He enters a field of flowers and nourishes himself with the plants of the field. Then his heart is moved, and he begins to speak with God. Suddenly, when he turns around, he sees, on his right, a woman mourning and weeping. Her garments are torn and there are ashes on her head (9:38). Ezra turns aside from his theological brooding and toward the sorrowful woman. She tells him of her long barrenness, how she begged for a son and finally was given one. But after she had raised him and found a wife for him, he died (10:1). After that the woman fled to this open field, and now she will no longer eat or drink, but lament and fast until she dies (10:4). Ezra becomes angry; he cannot endure her pain. He associates her suffering with what he sees as the still greater sufferings of Mother Zion. "For Zion, the mother of us all, is in deep grief and great distress. It is most appropriate to mourn now, because we are all mourning, and to be sorrowful, because we are all sorrowing. . . . Now go, ask the earth, and she will tell you that it is she who ought to mourn over so many who have come into being upon her" (10:7-9). She should restrain her sorrow and accept God's will; then she will receive her son back in due time. But the mourning woman by no means submits to this consolation. Only after Ezra has painted a picture of the misery of the Jewish people is there the beginning of a transformation. "While I was talking to her, her face suddenly began to shine exceedingly; her countenance flashed like lightning" (10:25). Ezra is frightened; the woman cries out, the earth quakes, and Ezra sees, in place of the sorrowing woman, a city on huge foundations (10:27).

God himself has announced that he will talk with Ezra (9:25). Ezra sees an old, weeping woman, despairing and alienated from her own identity. Is this old woman God? Ezra does not recognize God in this figure. He acts in a traditional manner at first: he tries to instruct the woman. He even belittles her and calls her foolish. He applies what he has just learned from his conversation partner, Uriel, to this woman. But it is only when he joins her in her lament that something happens. Ezra weeps over the suffering of the war-tested people, the woman over the loss of her son. Ezra does not recognize that the private is political, that his weeping and that of the woman meet in God's weeping. The sorrowing mother is not God per se, but in the way she embodies the painful absence of God, the participative, passionate love of God for his people gleams through the mists of her sorrow.

Luise Schottroff, who has studied this vision from a social-historical perspective in terms of the meaning of the barrenness of the old woman (1994, 273-74; 1995, 187-88), sees a connection between Ezra's lament over the absence of God, his lament over the destruction of his people, and the mother's lament over her dead son. She regards these three laments as three sides of the same disaster: that of Mother Zion (→ Isaiah). She arranges these visions within a metaphorical interpretation of Israel's history in which the fate of the suffering woman is that of the people, which has been forced to the margins of existence by war and its consequences. This personification creates a link between the experiences of women and the suffering of the whole people (cf. Testament of Job 39:1–40:6). The vision is transformed in Ezra's lament. He does not abandon this inconsolable woman, even though he cannot easily console her. He stands by her and, in all his helplessness, he becomes an eschatological support. But the woman is transformed, filled with light; she cries out — the earth quakes — and a city becomes visible.

Crying out and quaking are part of the dramatic moment of giving birth; they announce the end of the opening phase of the birth pangs and lead to the active part, the expelling of the baby (Sutter Rehmann 1995, 210). If we try to remain within the image language of 4 Ezra, we can say: the sorrowing mother gives birth to the city. This is strange only if we deny the sorrowing mother her collective symbolism (cf. Stählin 1974). The angel Uriel points us toward the idea that this mother is Mother Zion. In her sorrow she is the destroyed, razed city mourning for her children and having no future (2 Esd 10:18). But she brings forth the new city; she gives birth to the new earth, which is here concretely the rebuilt city (10:27). Now she again has honor among women (10:26): in the end she will again emerge as a livable, sheltering city that can be a home for her children. Now, since Ezra has seen the birth of the new city/earth, he can also understand the previous time as "birth pangs," as work toward the new world. So this vision helps Ezra to see his present time as a crisis that will continue to intensify until the moment of birth. In this sense Ezra can now undertake an eschatological dating of the present (Schottroff 1990, 73-95): the suffering that he and his people must presently bear is not simply the absence of God, but is also work that must be done so that the new city can be born. I see this work as both the tasks of mourning and the work of support: Ezra must learn not only to question, but also to render support, to endure the pain of others and search actively for hope. To stay within the image of giving birth, we can say: Ezra becomes a birthing assistant who supports the woman in her difficult hour.

The Passion Stories of the Mother and Her Sisters

In the humiliation of the mourning mother who has been barren for thirty years, we can recognize passion stories of other women: for example, that of Hannah (1 Sam 1:2; see Schottroff 1994; 1995). Her joy over the end of her humiliation — due to childlessness — echoes 1 Samuel 1:11, as do the words of Elizabeth: "This is what the Lord has done for me when he looked favorably on me and took away the disgrace I have endured among my people" (Luke 1:25). But the mourning mother in 2 Esdras tells her whole story, which did not end with her joyful conception or the birth of the long-desired son: after she had raised her son and found a wife for him, he died. The mother is inconsolable, for so late in life she will not conceive again. There is no more hope for the childless old woman. Schottroff sees in this the theme of barren women who, from a patriarchal point of view, have failed to fulfill their social and God-given purpose. The perspective of the text is that of a woman who endures social death and has fallen to the lowest level of the patriarchal order.

The motif of the inconsolable mother is widely used in the Bible. Ezra's attitude toward her, his sharp rebuke, is therefore incomprehensible. The "daughter of my people" girds her garment of weeping, rolls in the ashes, and mourns "as for an only child, / most bitter lamentation" (Jer 6:26).

> A voice is heard in Ramah,
>> lamentation and bitter weeping.
> Rachel is weeping for her children;
>> she refuses to be comforted for her children,
>> because they are no more. (Jer 31:15; Matt 2:18)

In Genesis 29:31, Rachel is the barren wife, who therefore is wearied unto death. She thus shares the twofold humiliation of Zion, or the reverse: the author is drawing on the Rachel traditions in Genesis and Jeremiah. The hope of 4 Ezra lies in the same God as Rachel's, who has mercy on the hard fate of women and gives them life in a twofold sense (as living children and in their own lives). The mother's mourning is described with precision: "And on my right I saw a woman; she was mourning and weeping with a loud voice, and was deeply grieved at heart; her clothes were torn, and there were ashes on her head" (2 Esd 9:38).

So also Tamar mourned after having been ravished (2 Sam 13:19). The cries of the miserable woman have no words in this story. That is why the sorrowful story of Mother Zion, which seems to reflect Tamar's mourning and to link her humiliation with that of Tamar, moves me. Judith's fasting also expresses such a link: "Then Judith prostrated herself, put ashes on her head, and uncovered the sack-cloth she was wearing" (Jth 9:1). Then she cries aloud to the God who revenged the rape of her ancestress Dinah (Gen 34). She, the widow, lays claim to the God of the ravished. With her prayer of lament, Judith also gives a voice to silent Dinah (Jth 9:2). She parallels the sad fate of Leah's only daughter with the military conquest of a city. The suffering of a woman is identified, here too, with the people tested by war.

Thus, other humiliated women become visible in the mourning gestures of the mother deprived of her child — women like Tamar and Dinah. Judith, in her song of thanksgiving, becomes a mother of the people, even though she herself never bore children:

> He boasted that he would burn up my territory,
>> and kill my young men with the sword,
> and dash my infants to the ground,
>> and seize my children as booty,
>> and take my virgins as spoil. (Jth 16:5)

Mother Zion's sorrow makes visible a chain of suffering by many other women. Besides the legends of Hannah, Sarah, and Rachel, there is the story of Manoah's wife (Judg 13:2), who ultimately bore Samson. The story of Naomi (and Ruth) takes place "in the days when the judges ruled." Rich, with two sons and her husband, Naomi goes forth, and poor she returns, as Mara, the bitter one, a widow without progeny. As an old woman she has no prospect of children or a husband.

But in the end, thanks to her daughter-in-law Ruth, she is praised by the women: "A son has been born to Naomi" (Ruth 4:17). Her neighbors join their praise of God with the fate of old Naomi; she again has a name and honor among women. This, then, is the only consolation Ezra can hold out to the sorrowing mother (2 Esd 10:16).

Ruth is placed within the sequence of those who built up the house of Israel, along with Rachel and Leah (Ruth 4:11). We have encountered them both previously in our examination of this text: Rachel, twice humiliated, will nevertheless have a future (cf. also Jer 31:38). Leah we have mentioned as the mother of the ravished Dinah. The theme of barrenness always leads, sooner or later, to Sarah (Gen 18:13).

All that is lacking now, among the proto-mothers and builders of the house of Israel, is a link to Rebekah. Hopefully we are not stretching things too far if we do in fact find her in 4 Ezra. In the second vision Ezra asks about the sequence of the worlds. When will the present, unjust world vanish, and when will God's new world begin? When will be the end of the first and the beginning of the second? The angel answers: "From Abraham to Abraham, for Jacob and Esau were his descendants, and Jacob's hand held Esau's heel from the beginning" (2 Esd 6:8). Ezra is by no means satisfied by these wisdom riddles, but they rouse him to reflection and point the way. It is much the same for me. I see the underlying direction in the birth of the two brothers (Gen 25:26). Rebekah is not only one of the builders of the house of Israel, but also the tribal mother of the Edomites. Her labor of birthing links the two houses. This birth underlies the angel's speech. Rebekah is the mother of both. One world will follow the other as children of the same mother.

Hannah, Elizabeth, Judith, Dinah, Tamar, Ruth and Naomi, the wife of Manoah, Sarah, Rebekah, Leah, and Rachel — in the sorrowing mother they all link hands. I hear their stories echoing like overtones. They make Mother Zion an icon, rich and transparent for the sufferings and hopes of women, the builders of the nation.

A Theological Gynecology

Ezra's struggle is ultimately the object of the book's eschatological statements. (For what follows, see Sutter Rehmann 1995.) The future will not be served on a silver plate. Ezra's struggle stands for the struggle for new life, even though he does not realize this. Therefore the angel has to remind Ezra of the womb, which is necessary to give birth to new life. The strength of the womb is a source of energy that Ezra appears to forget and to which the angel frequently calls his attention: Ezra must inquire of those who give birth in order to learn more about the eschatological events.

Ezra says:

"It is perhaps on account of us that the time of threshing is delayed for the righteous — on account of the sins of those who inhabit the earth." He answered me and said: "Go and ask a pregnant woman whether, when her nine months have been completed, her womb can keep the fetus within her any longer." And I said, "No, lord, it cannot." He said to me, "In Hades the chambers of the souls are like the womb. For just as a woman who is in labor makes haste to escape the pangs of birth, so also do these places hasten to give back those things that were committed to them from the beginning." (2 Esd 4:39-42)

We see here the notion that at the given time the earth's uterus will give back the dead who have been entrusted to it; that is, it will give birth. This is an adequate reflection of the gynecological ideas of the time: the physicians distinguished a strength in the uterus to hold back, which was effective during the time of gestation, and a strength for pushing the child out, which was in effect during birth. Here the womb cannot hold back the child once the out-forcing power has taken hold. Likewise, the length of pregnancy, fulfilled in nine months (4:40), corresponds to the average length as experienced, even though it could not be accurately determined how long a pregnancy lasted. We cannot say exactly when the birth of the new world will take place. In any case, it will only happen when the time is completed. This birth is also equivalent to a resurrection of the dead, for the earth gives back those who rest in her (7:32).

This talk about the fulfilling time of ripening makes it clear that we are dealing here with something other than a linear notion of eschatology. In the pregnant body the new life is already active, present, and can be felt by the mother as well as those close to her. Its presence is gradually made known, even though it has not yet been born. So the presence of God and his justice, which makes new life possible, are already effective for those who, like Ezra, long for them. A longing for fulfillment causes us to sense that fulfillment in the present, and this changes our lives already now — not only in the future. The term of the birth will come, certainly, at some time — as the day of the great struggle, and the delivery, which brings relief. It is, so to speak, something one can anticipate but not determine for certain.

The work of earth's labor is repeatedly accompanied by quaking (3:18; 6:16; 6:23; 10:26). This is a phenomenon also known to midwives and mothers: when the birth process is well advanced and the pelvic floor and musculature are softened, it can happen that the bearing woman's limbs quiver and shake, so that they have to be supported by other people. For midwives, that is the sign that the expulsive contractions are about to begin, and the child can be pushed out. Many apocalyptic texts transpose this experience (Isa 13:8–14:1; Ps 18:5, 8, 20 [Eng. 18:4, 7, 19]; Jer 4:31; 13:21; Hos 13:13). The earth quakes because it senses that the good life is near.

God demands that it open its womb and give back the dead. For God's new world begins with the demand for justice for all those who have been violently put to death (cf. Revelation) — and so the dead will stand up for justice, against what they experienced as injustice.

The *hope for resurrection* stems essentially from apocalyptic theology (Dan 12:1-2). It is not individualistic in its orientation, proposing the personal survival of the individual or separate moral reward for good behavior in life. Rather, it has to do with the changing of the age, the coming of God and God's justice. It is not some place beyond and outside of this earth that is the scene of resurrection, but this blue planet of ours, the little earth, is the place of transformation — the transformation of injustice into justice, lovelessness into love. But hope reaches out beyond this violent history: that one day it will be different for everyone, that there will be no more oppression and exploitation, since God will be all in all (1 Cor 15:28).

The principal eschatological themes in 2 Esdras are the struggle for the new life, the time that is being fulfilled, and the transformation of the earth. Out of these concepts it develops a *theological gynecology* and effects a fundamental transformation not only of the seer Ezra, but also of our own ideas of eschatology. The basic features of this eschatology can be derived from the following motifs:

- references to the womb of the earth (2 Esd 4:39-43; 5:46-49; 5:50-53);
- the earth's quaking, which precedes the birth of the new world;
- frequent references to sowing, seed, and fields;
- the earth's bringing forth: it brings forth people (3:4-5), animals (6:53), treasures (7:49-61), the dead (7:32), and reason (7:62);
- the motif of the barren woman who becomes pregnant, and of the old, childless mother, who becomes a city;
- the discourse about the time that is ripening, being fulfilled; and
- the signs of the approaching end, in which pregnant women appear twice (5:8; 6:21).

In this context, 5:8 presents us with an interesting passage: "There shall be chaos also in many places, fire shall often break out, the wild animals shall roam beyond their haunts, and menstruous women shall bring forth monsters." Here we find no women quaking in labor, but rather bleeding women. The earth behaves analogously: it, too, opens its abyss, its womb — but beasts come forth from it. This horrifying idea is carried further:

"Blood shall drip from wood,
    and the stone shall utter its voice;
the peoples shall be troubled,
    and the stars shall fall.

And one shall reign whom those who inhabit the earth do not expect, and the birds shall fly away together." (5:5-6)

The trees bleed like the women. The stones cry out, but the women remain silent. The stars are confused like the peoples, who become disoriented by the suffering they must bear. For now we learn who is responsible for this disaster: a horrible ruler robs the inhabitants of the earth of all hope. Therefore birth is no longer successful, and those who can flee do so.

The whole land is experiencing what the miscarrying women experience: its work bears no fruit. The people strive, they hope, they try to gain insight — but their efforts are fruitless (5:12). This commonality of earth and people (constantly called inhabitants of the earth here) is something I find very impressive. The earth reveals the corrupt condition of affairs. As long as the unjust ruler is in power, nothing can succeed. As long as God does not come, the inhabitants of the earth strive and yet achieve nothing.

In 6:18-19, God promises to come when Zion's humiliation is at an end. For the defeat of the Jewish revolt against the Roman reign of terror in Palestine had brought Zion into destruction and childlessness. But now an end to this time of suffering is prophesied; God's coming will turn the page. God is approaching fast and will begin with questioning like that of a midwife hastily summoned. Here we find knowledge of the necessity of having a helper present for a birth. It is applied eschatologically; that is, the turning of the age and the transformation of the unjust world into a world of blooming life are compared to the work of birthing, because this eschatological transformation requires the cooperation of earth and its inhabitants. But for the earth's cooperative work, its giving birth, to succeed requires the support of the most experienced of all midwives: God. Thus a thrilling cooperation between the earth, its inhabitants, and God is made manifest. This eschatological gynecology makes it possible to express a human-divine cooperation that wakens energy without demanding too much. For I cannot do it alone; it requires God and ourselves, it needs cooperation. New life needs me, us, quite existentially. That is something every pregnant woman knows.

The cosmic depth of this hope for the transformation of the earth is impressive. The claim to redemption encompasses all people, all nations, and the whole earth. The longing for justice excludes not a blade of grass. So we have here also a starting point for a broader effort, an ecologically engaged theology. The experiences of giving birth that are fundamental to this image of hope are made evident by a view of the text that is not obscured by androcentrism. Women's experiences of giving birth, and thus women's experiences of their bodies, need not be interpreted in ways that are inimical to the body, to work, or to women; here they are made fundamentally fruitful for theology.

LITERATURE

Bousset, Wilhelm. 1926. *Die Religion des Judentums im späthellenistischen Zeitalter.* 3rd ed. Tübingen.

Charlesworth, James H. 1983/85. *The Old Testament Pseudepigrapha.* 2 vols. Garden City, N.Y.

Collins, John J. 1984. *The Apocalyptic Imagination: An Introduction to the Jewish Matrix of Christianity.* New York.

Gunkel, Hermann. 1900. "Das vierte Buch Esra." In *Die Apokryphen und Pseudepigraphen des Alten Testaments,* edited by Emil Kautzsch, 2:331-401. Tübingen.

Humphrey, Edith McEwan. 1995. *The Ladies and the Cities: Transformation and Apocalyptic Identity in Joseph and Aseneth, 4 Ezra, the Apocalypse, and the Shepherd of Hermas.* Sheffield.

Knibb, A. Michael. 1979. *The First and Second Books of Esdras.* Commentary on 1 Esdras by R. J. Coggins and commentary on 2 Esdras by M. A. Knibb. Cambridge.

Metzger, Bruce M. 1983. "The Fourth Book of Ezra." In *The Old Testament Pseudepigrapha,* edited by James H. Charlesworth, 1:517-59. 2 vols. London.

Myers, Jacob M. 1974. "I and II Esdras." In Anchor Bible, vol. 42, 107-39. New York.

Rost, Leonhard. 1971. *Einleitung in die alttestamentlichen Apokryphen und Pseudepigraphen.* Heidelberg.

Schottroff, Luise. 1990. "Die Gegenwart in der Apokalyptik der synoptischen Evangelien." In Luise Schottroff, *Befreiungserfahrungen,* 73-95. Munich.

———. 1994. *Lydias ungeduldige Schwestern. Feministische Sozialgeschichte des frühen Christentums.* Gütersloh.

———. 1995. *Lydia's Impatient Sisters: A Feminist Social History of Early Christianity.* Louisville.

Schreiner, Josef. 1981. *Das 4. Buch Esra. Jüdische Schriften aus hellenistisch-römischer Zeit,* vol. 5, 4. Gütersloh.

Stählin, Gustav. 1974. "Das Bild der Witwe." *Jahrbuch für Antike und Christentum* 17:5-20.

Sutter Rehmann, Luzia. 1995. *Geh, frage die Gebärerin. Feministisch-befreiungstheologische Untersuchungen zum Gebärmotiv in der Apokalyptik.* Gütersloh.

Translated by Linda M. Maloney

Joseph and Aseneth: Perfect Bride or Heavenly Prophetess

Angela Standhartinger

Joseph and Aseneth (hereafter Jos Asen) tells the story of Aseneth, the daughter of Pentephres (Potiphar) of Heliopolis (On), who, according to Genesis 41:45, is given to Joseph as wife by Pharaoh. In Genesis Aseneth is only mentioned in passing. The ancient novel *Joseph and Aseneth,* on the other hand, tells a long story about their marriage and their life. Today this is one of the Jewish intertestamental writings. It was written in Greek, presumably shortly before or after the start of the common era, possibly in Egypt. Although it could be found in some Armenian Bibles in the Middle Ages, it belongs today neither to the Jewish nor to the Christian canon.

Feminist investigation of the text began late and with hesitation, because the text is the subject of controversy. In contrast to other intertestamental writings, it has been transmitted in a large number of manuscripts. Christoph Burchard (cf. Fink 2008) and Marc Philonenko (1968) reconstructed two archetypal texts, which differ markedly in length. Philonenko's short text contains only 8,256 words, while Burchard's long text contains 13,403. Which of the two texts is older has not yet been clarified (Kraemer 1994, 860).

A further problem is the fictitious character of the story. The text offers hardly any clues for a reconstruction of the story's origin and thus for a sociohistorical investigation. In feminist research, interpretations and evaluations of the work differ, depending on the surmised intention for its composition. While some see in it a legitimation of patriarchal role models and views about a woman's place in marriage (Wire 1988; Lefkowitz 1991; Langford 1992), others emphasize themes relating to gender relationships that give central roles to women and to female divine images (Doty 1989; Kraemer 1989; 1991; 1992; Standhartinger 1995). The evaluation also depends in each case on the edition of the text that is being evaluated.

In my opinion, the two versions of the text are part of the ancient discussion about the way in which female characters are presented (cf. also Kraemer 1988). Through the way in which the story is told and the characters described, two different images of Aseneth arise in the two versions of the text, each of which finds its place in the ancient discussion about the role of women and women figures in the biblical tradition. In this way each version of the text takes a specific standpoint in this controversy.

Aseneth in the Short Text

At the beginning of the narrative Aseneth lives in a tower beside the home of her parents. She avoids contact with all men (2:1/1).[1] Her parents suggest that she marry Joseph, wise and endowed "with the Spirit of God" (4:7/9). But Aseneth rejects being handed over "like a captive to a man (who is) an alien" (4:9/12). But as Joseph comes into the house of her parents, she sees him as a shining light and recognizes her mistake (6:1-8/1-8). Joseph is not prepared to greet her until he is assured that she is a "virgin who hates all men" (7:7/8). Even then he rejects her attempt to greet him with a kiss, because she is an alien woman (→ Proverbs) who worships idols. Nevertheless, he blesses her. After his departure, Aseneth rejects her idols during a seven-day period of lamentation. On the seventh day she prays a psalm that is reminiscent of creation psalms and psalms of individual lament (12; Strotmann 1991, 257-71) and confesses her wrongs (idol worship and her error with respect to Joseph; 13).

After her prayer a HUMAN FIGURE appears from heaven. Joseph and Aseneth 14–17 takes up motifs from biblical and intertestamental epiphany stories (Dan 10:5-12, for example). Aseneth is instructed to lay aside her mourning clothes and to put on a new shining garment (Jos Asen 14:12-16 [Ph]; cf. 2 Enoch 22:8-10). The Aseneth of the short text keeps this shining form all the way to the end of the story, and her appearance is like that of her heavenly visitor (cf. Jos Asen 14:1, 9 [Ph] with 18:7 [Ph]). She is told that she is renewed and made alive again, and she receives the new name "City of Refuge" (15:2-6 [Ph]). Moreover, it is revealed that God has given her to Joseph as a wife (15:5 [Ph]). She thanks God in 15:13 (Ph) that she has been saved from darkness and brought into the light. In chapter 16, together with the HUMAN FIGURE, she eats a honeycomb. The significance of the various symbolic actions in chapters 16 and 17 has never been fully clarified. In my view, however, some of it calls to mind the stories of the calls of the prophets. Aseneth is called blessed, because God's ineffable mysteries have been revealed to her (16:14/8). The honey motif is reminiscent of Ezekiel 3:1-3. Like Jeremiah and Isaiah, Aseneth's mouth was touched by the bees coming out of the comb (Jos Asen 16:14 [Ph]; Jer 1:9; Isa 6:6-7). Finally Aseneth, in the role of Elisha, sees how

---

1. Unfortunately, Philonenko has changed the verse numbering in his edition. The citations will be given as follows: (Ph) designates the text and verse numbers of Philonenko = the short text. (B) designates the text and verse numbers of Burchard = the long text. References to the parallels first give the long text and then the short text: 1:1/1 = 1:1 (B) /1 (Ph).

the HUMAN FIGURE, or Elijah, is taken up into heaven in a fiery chariot (Jos Asen 17:6 [Ph]; cf. 2 Kings 2:11). The message of the heavenly prophetess Aseneth is given in the second part of the story (Jos Asen 22–29 [Ph]; see below).

After the HUMAN FIGURE has returned to heaven, Aseneth is told that Joseph is standing at the door. Like her father in 3:4/5, Aseneth gives instructions that the house is to be prepared. She brings Joseph into the house (20:1 [Ph]) and sets him on her father's throne, in order to wash his feet. She meets his protest with the words, "My hands are your hands, and your feet are my feet" (20:3 [Ph]). As her parents see the two of them sitting in such splendor, they want them to get married right away. But Joseph insists on being "married" by Pharaoh, who, on the occasion of the wedding, gives a seven-day feast, to which he invites the whole country (21:8/6-7).

Aseneth in the Long Text

The long text, apart from some differences in the choice of words, contains the entire text of the short text. But a different characterization of the woman character Aseneth emerges through some passages that occur only in the long text. For example, the long text characterizes Aseneth's rejection of all men as "boastful" and "arrogant," thus adopting a not infrequently uttered critique of independent women in antiquity (2:1 [B]; Plutarch, *Moralia* 140C-D and more frequently). In Joseph and Aseneth 11 (B), Aseneth carries on a silent conversation with herself before she ventures to pray her psalm in chapter 12. Remaining silent is an ideal for women not unknown in the ancient world (cf., for example, Sir 26:14). To the errors listed in the short text, "hatred of men" is added here (Jos Asen 11:6 [B]; 21:18-19 [B]). "Arrogance" is also listed as an additional sin (12:5 [B]; 21:12 [B]). The repetitious summary in 21:11-21 (B) confirms the great attention that the long text devotes to Aseneth's errors.

Significant differences between the two forms of the text can be seen during and after Aseneth's heavenly vision. Aseneth appears intimidated and timorous toward the HUMAN FIGURE. The narrator frequently interrupts the action to report on Aseneth's momentary state of mind (16:2, 9, 13 [B]; cf. also 18:7 [B]). She is unable to understand what is happening. Only after the departure of the HUMAN FIGURE (17:8 [B]), who in this text calls to mind not so much 2 Kings 2:11 as Joseph and Aseneth 5:4/5, does she recognize the identity of the visitor (17:9 [B]). Like Manoah in Judges 13:17-18, Aseneth asks the name of the HUMAN FIGURE, which she, however, like Manoah, is unable to learn (Jos Asen 15:12x [B]). The allusions to the calls of the prophets are, by comparison to the short text, unclear. The bees do not touch Aseneth's mouth but build on it a honeycomb (16:19 [B]). A person whose mouth is covered with a honeycomb cannot, of course, speak. This has consequences as the text continues.

It is not God but the HUMAN FIGURE who gives Aseneth to Joseph as his wife. The Aseneth of the long text does not receive her splendor through the heavenly encounter, but she gains her beauty only after she calls to mind the commands of the HUMAN FIGURE (18 [B]). Moreover, she does not give thanks because she now stands in the light but because of her rescue from the abyss (15:12 [B]). The description of Aseneth's beauty is more extensive (18:9-11 [B]). Her cheeks, lips, teeth, hair, neck, and breasts are compared with God's paradise. The description corresponds not only to the beauty ideals of antiquity but also to a bust without hands and feet and, thus, without any possibility of moving and expressing itself in the world. The gender-specific logic behind all this is especially striking in comparison to the description of Jacob (22:7 [B]). With the beauty she has gained, Aseneth is able, contrary to her fears (18:7 [B]), to impress Joseph (19:4 [B]). The new Aseneth in the long text now behaves according to the standards for a demure woman, in keeping with antiquity's conservative ideology. There were no foreign men, like Joseph's messengers, for example, in her presence (18:1 [B]; 22:12 [B]; cf. Xenophon, *Oeconomicus* 7.35). She is not in charge of a household (*oikos;* Jos Asen 18:2 [B]; 20:2 [B]), as is the Aseneth of the short text (16:5-6 [Ph]; 20:1 [Ph]), and remains within the confines of her chambers (16:4 [B]; 19:2 [B]; cf., for example, Philo, *De specialibus legibus* 3.169). Finally, she is definitely occupied with household chores (Jos Asen 16:4 [B]; 20:1 [B]) and puts her body at Joseph's disposal (20:4 [B]; cf. Plutarch, *Moralia* 138B-146A, for example).

A Retelling of the Joseph Story

Already in chapters 1–21 Joseph and Aseneth takes up a series of biblical motifs and traditions and retells them interpretively. Ross S. Kraemer (1994) has assembled further allusions to Genesis 1–3, Proverbs, and Song of Songs. In chapter 22 of Joseph and Aseneth, the work is linked to the biblical story of Joseph by the account of the move of Jacob's family to Egypt. The two versions of the text actually begin in different places. The short text says that the reencounter between Jacob and his son (Gen 46) is initiated by Aseneth. Consequently Jacob blesses them both in like measure (Jos Asen 22:5 [Ph]). In the long text Joseph takes the initiative in order to introduce his bride to his father. Consequently Jacob blesses Aseneth alone (22:9 [B]) and adopts her into his family (Gen 48).

Joseph and Aseneth 23–29 tell how the son of Pharaoh attempts to overthrow his father and Joseph and abduct Aseneth. The short text calls the motivation "madness" *(mania/emmanēs)* over Aseneth (23:3 [Ph]). In the context of numerous contemporary interpretations of the Joseph story, the word "madness" actually belongs to the story of Potiphar's wife (Gen 39). This woman is the epitome of the "madness of love" (Testament of Joseph 8.3; Philo, *De Iosepho* 40 and more frequently). Genesis 39 is taken up into Joseph and Aseneth only in a quite summarizing manner (Jos Asen 4:10/14; 7:3-4/3-5). The short text tells a story that is the polar opposite of Genesis 39, in which a woman renowned for her chastity is set upon by a "love-stricken" man but saved by God. The long text has, it's true, the same story structure, but since Aseneth's chastity or hatred of men is condemned and the parallel between the son of Pharaoh and Potiphar's wife is avoided, a critique of the interpretive history of Genesis 39 is less clear.

A Retelling of Genesis 34

Joseph and Aseneth 23–29 is also a retelling of the story about Dinah. Thereby this writing joins a broad discussion of Genesis 34 (→ Judith; Standhartinger 1994). To carry out his plan, Pharaoh's son seeks allies, whom he finds in the sons of the maidens Leah and Rachel. This succeeds primarily through the use of two arguments. For one thing, he calls it to their attention that as the sons of slaves they have no inheritance rights according to ancient law (Jos Asen 26:8-9/8-9). Secondly, he appeals to their manly pride: "I know that you are strong men and do not wish to die like women, but act like men and take vengeance on your enemies" (24:7/7). But his overthrow attempt fails because of his father's headache (chapter 25). The attempt to ambush Aseneth also goes awry, because God battles for her (chapters 26–27). The swords stretched out against Aseneth fall to the ground like ashes (27:8/11). Aseneth, who, like Dinah, left her house (26:4/4; cf. Gen 34:1), is spared from being raped (Jos Asen 27).

The bias in favor of women is stressed in the short text by an additional feature in the story. The maidens' sons now seek refuge with (of all people) Aseneth (28:1-4/1-3). In the short text Aseneth consoles the brothers with the assurance that it "is not fitting for a God-fearing person to repay anyone evil for evil" (28:14 [Ph]). This statement (cf. also 1 Thess 5:15; Rom 12:17; 1 Pet 3:9; 1QS 10:17-18; and more frequently) is expanded in its application from "neighbor" to "every person" (Jos Asen 23:9 [Ph]). In this way Aseneth in the short text is able to avoid a bloodbath (28:16 [Ph]). Aseneth's change of heart causes her to leave the restrictive imprisonment of her tower and act for reconciliation in the world (Doty 1989). This is the message of the heavenly prophetess Aseneth. She becomes a "city of refuge" for the sons of Zilpah and Bilhah.

The Aseneth of the long text is also saved from her tormentors. But it is the sons of the maidens rather than Aseneth who here make the statement forbidding retaliation (28:5 [B]). Not Aseneth but Levi saves his brothers in the long text (28.15-17 [B]), and Aseneth remains in the role of an intercessor (24:14 [B]). As a perfect bride, she behaves like a demure wife, in keeping with ancient conservative views of morality, and she stands under the protection of her new family.

Images of God in Joseph and Aseneth

The differing depiction of male and female characters in the two textual versions of Joseph and Aseneth also has an effect on the images of God. While the long text describes the relationship between God and Aseneth as that of an underage child and her loving father (12:8 [B]), the short text calls God "father and mother" (12:7 [Ph]). In 15:7-8/7-8, the heavenly figure *Metanoia* (change of mind, conversion) is described; at God's side, she is interceding on behalf of all who "change their thinking." *Metanoia* is clothed with the attributes of wisdom/*sophia* (cf. Prov 8:22-23, 30; Sir 15.2; Wis 7.12; 9.4; and more frequently; Kraemer 1994, 878-79). In the short text she prepares a heavenly nuptial chamber for the wise, God's sons and daughters, who marry (her) (cf. also Wis 7:28; 8:9-18). In the long text *Metanoia* prepares a place of rest for the virgins. At her side, as her brother, the HUMAN FIGURE appears as Aseneth's male bridal attendant. In this text Joseph receives the wisdom attribute "firstborn" (Jos Asen 18:11 [B] and more frequently; cf. Prov 8:22-31; Sir 24:9). He imparts the spirit of wisdom to Aseneth (Jos Asen 19:11 [B]) and takes the place of God for her (cf. 12:8 [B] with 19:10 [B]; cf. also 22:9 [B]).

On the Question of the Authors

Joseph and Aseneth chooses the ancient romance novel as its genre (Pervo 1991; Hezser 1997; Standhartinger 2009a). But, in contrast to the ancient romance novels that have come down to us, Joseph and Aseneth does not end with the joyous reunion of the lovers. In addition, the short text develops an image of women different from that in many ancient novels. It depicts an independent woman who is out in the world intervening in what is happening and thinking and acting theologically (Standhartinger 1995, 225-37). The awareness of gender roles and their frequently ironic depiction lets us suppose that women participated in the production of this text (Kraemer 1989; 1991). Both versions of the text mirror a lively discussion about the interpretation of various biblical texts. They thereby testify to an important controversy in ancient Judaism about women characters in the Bible, which points to the fact that women have not remained silent.

LITERATURE

The Long Text
Burchard, Christoph. 1983. *Jüdische Schriften aus hellenistisch-römischer Zeit*, vol. 2, 4, 631-720. Gütersloh.
Denis, Albert-Marie. 1987. *Concordance Grecque des Pseudépigraphes d'Ancien Testament*, 851-59. Leiden.

The Short Text

Chesnutt, Randall D. 1991. "Revelatory Experiences Attributed to Biblical Women in Early Jewish Literature." In *"Women Like This": New Perspectives on Jewish Women in the Greco-Roman World, Early Judaism, and Its Literature,* edited by Amy-Jill Levine, 1:107-25. Atlanta.

Cook, David. 1984. "Joseph and Aseneth." In *The Apocryphal Old Testament,* edited by Hedley F. D. Sparks, 465-503. Oxford.

Doty, Susan E. H. 1989. "From Ivory Tower to City of Refuge: The Role and Function of the Protagonist in 'Joseph and Aseneth' and Related Narratives." Ph.D. diss., Denver.

Hezser, Catharine. 1997. "'Joseph and Aseneth' in the Context of Ancient Greek Erotic Novels," *Frankfurter Judaistische Beiträge.* 24:1-40.

Kraemer, Ross S. 1988. *Maenads, Martyrs, Matrons, Monastics: A Sourcebook on Women's Religions in the Greco-Roman World.* Philadelphia.

———. 1989. "Monastic Jewish Women's Religions among Pagans, Jews, and Christians in the Greco-Roman World." *Signs* 14:324-70.

———. 1991. "Women's Authorship of Jewish and Christian Literature in the Greco-Roman Period." In *"Women Like This": New Perspectives on Jewish Women in the Greco-Roman World, Early Judaism, and Its Literature,* edited by Amy-Jill Levine, 221-42. Atlanta.

———. 1992. *Her Share of the Blessings: Women's Religions among Pagans, Jews, and Christians in the Greco-Roman World.* New York and Oxford.

———. 1994. "The Book of Aseneth." In *Searching the Scriptures,* edited by Elisabeth Schüssler Fiorenza, 2:859-88. 2 vols. New York.

Langford, Sally O. 1992. "On Being a Religious Woman: Women Proselytes in the Greco-Roman World." In Peter J. Haas, *Recovering the Role of Women: Power and Authority in Rabbinic Jewish Society,* 61-83. Atlanta.

Lefkowitz, Mary R. 1991. "Did Ancient Women Write Novels?" In *"Women Like This": New Perspectives on Jewish Women in the Greco-Roman World, Early Judaism, and Its Literature,* edited by Amy-Jill Levine, 17-30. Atlanta.

Pervo, Richard I. 1991. "Aseneth and Her Sisters: Women in Jewish Narrative and in the Greek Novels." In *"Women Like This": New Perspectives on Jewish Women in the Greco-Roman World, Early Judaism, and Its Literature,* edited by Amy-Jill Levine, 145-60. Atlanta.

Philonenko, Marc. 1968. *Joseph et Aséneth. Introduction, texte critique, traduction et notes.* Studia post-biblica, vol. 13. Leiden.

Standhartinger, Angela. 1994. "'Um zu sehen die Töchter des Landes': Die Perspektive Dinas in der jüdischhellenistischen Diskussion um Gen 34." In *Religious Propaganda and Missionary Competition in the New Testament World,* edited by Lukas Bormann et al., 89-116. Festschrift for Dieter Georgi. Supplements to Novum Testamentum, vol. 74. Leiden.

———. 1995. *Das Frauenbild im Judentum der Hellenistischen Zeit. Ein Beitrag anhand von Joseph und Aseneth* (with partial translations of both the short and long texts). Arbeiten zur Geschichte des antiken Judentums und des Urchristentums, vol. 26. Leiden.

———. 1996. "From Fictional Text to Socio-Historical Context: Some Considerations from a Textcritical Perspective on Joseph and Aseneth." In *Society of Biblical Literature, Seminar Papers* 35:303-18.

Strotmann, Angelika. 1991. *"Mein Vater bist Du!" Zur Bedeutung der Vaterschaft Gottes in kanonischen und nicht-kanonischen frühjüdischen Schriften.* Frankfurter theologische Studien, vol. 39. Frankfurt am Main.

Wire, Antoinette C. 1988. "The Social Functions of Women's Asceticism in the Roman East." In *Images of the Feminine in Gnosticism,* edited by Karen L. King, 308-23. Philadelphia.

FOR FURTHER READING

Brooke, George John. 2005. "Men and Women as Angels in Joseph and Aseneth." *Journal for the Study of the Pseudepigrapha* 14, no. 2:159-77.

Fink, Uta Barbara. 2008. *Joseph and Aseneth, Revision des griechischen Textes und Edition der zweiten lateinischen Übersetzung.* Fontes et Subsidia ad Bibliam pertinentes, vol. 5. Berlin and New York. Cf. the review of this book by Angela Standhartinger in *Catholic Biblical Quarterly* 71 (2009): 644-45.

Reinmuth, Eckart, ed. 2009. *Joseph und Aseneth.* Scripta Antiquitatis Posterioris ad Ethicam Religionemque pertinentia, vol. 15. Tübingen.

Standhartinger, Angela. 2009a. "'Nicht wenige der vornehmen griechischen Frauen' (Apg 17,12). Aspekte zum Religionswechsel von Frauen im Spiegel der jüdischen und christlichen Adaptionen des antiken Liebesromans in Joseph und Aseneth und den Theklaakten." In *Ehrenmord und Emanzipation. Die Geschlechterfrage in Ritualen von Parallelgesellschaften,* edited by Bernhard Heininger, 145-69. Geschlecht — Symbol — Religion, vol. 6. Berlin.

―――. 2009b. "Zur Wirkungsgeschichte von Joseph und Aseneth." In *Joseph und Aseneth,* edited by Eckart Reinmuth, 219-34. Scripta Antiquitatis Posterioris ad Ethicam Religionemque pertinentia, vol. 15. Tübingen.

Stenström, Hanna. 2008. "Masculine or Feminine? Male Virgins in Joseph and Aseneth and the Book of Revelation." In *Identity Formation in the New Testament,* edited by Bengt Holmberg, 199-222. Wissenschaftliche Untersuchungen zum Neuen Testament, vol. 227. Tübingen.

Translated by Everett R. Kalin

Testament of Job: Job, Dinah, and Their Daughters

Luzia Sutter Rehmann

Introduction

The Testament of Job (hereafter T Job) is a down-to-earth, humorous narrative full of details, psychological dynamics, and theologically provocative phrases — for those who can hear them. (The text of this writing can be found in Riessler 1928 or Schaller 1979.) We should not let ourselves be deterred by the androcentric narrative-perspective of Job nor by his willingness to believe in the devil. Job learns a lot during his suffering, and as readers we are encouraged to make this journey with him. Especially his fellow traveler Sitidos/Dinah can open his (and our) eyes and mouth; she becomes the driving force of the narrative. It is she who positions her husband in the Job tradition and thus encourages him to speak out against the suffering that is silencing him.

The Testament of Job has not often been investigated by feminist scholars, even though it is very suitable for a reconstruction of historical memory in a feminist Jewish perspective. Rebecca Lesses hopes that the scholarly engagement with the Testament of Job, which allows for the contact of women with heaven, will lead to further discoveries of early Jewish life. This reading could destabilize and challenge the conception of Judaism as being patriarchal that results from an uncritical reading of androcentric texts (such as the Mishnah) (Lesses 1994, 147).

She bases her argument mainly on chapters 45–53 of the Testament of Job, the narrative of Job's three daughters, which she characterizes as a sort of midrash on Job 42:15. Perhaps we could read the figure of Sitidos/Dinah and her story as a midrash on Job 2:9 as well.

Prevalent scholarship accords only a very marginal position to this writing and is primarily concerned with whether it is a Jewish or Christian document, that is, in which group or groups it circulated, and whether it is a unit.

The circulation and production of the book are difficult to determine. It has been suggested that it is pre-Christian but not Essene (Spitta 1907), that it is a Jewish scripture of Egyptian-Therapeutic origin (Philonenko 1968), an example of

Jewish martyr literature (Jacobs 1970), or a product of Egyptian Jews (Collins 1974). Spittler reconstructs a history of origins that links the Testament of Job to the Montanists (Spittler 1983, 834). These attempts are based on the fact that the daughters of Job become ecstatic prophetesses and that there is one geographic reference (Job is called the king of Egypt, T Job 28:7). Dating the text is difficult because there are no temporal references. It is suggested that it was written between the first century B.C.E. and the second century C.E.

Even though rabbis and the church fathers rejected the text as apocryphal, it was read in many churches on the day of Saint Job (May 6) as a life story. As early as the tenth century, it was translated into Coptic and Slavic. The Testament of Job exists still today in three Greek manuscripts from the eleventh, twelfth, and thirteenth centuries. This suggests that the text held meaning in a time when the critique of church hierarchy became more pronounced and the search for a more Christian life was a priority. These centuries also saw the rise of heretic movements, mendicant orders, women orders, mysticism, and, sadly, witch hunts.

The Story of Jobab and Sitidos

Jobab's Fall (1–12)

This narrative is framed as a wistful and humorous speech of old Job, who gathers his children around him to tell them his life story with God and of his great suffering. This story resembles the one in the biblical book of Job and is structured similarly to its Septuagint version but extends it by thematic questions that the book of Job does not entertain.

Jobab — Job's name for a long time (2:1) — lived next to a well-frequented and revered temple. Because it was well frequented, he asked himself: "Is this the God who created heaven and earth and sea and us? How can I find out?" (2:4).

Job presents himself to his children as a seeker of God. His theological questions serve as a starting point to his life narrative of suffering. Job desires knowledge of God but hears a voice at night that tells him the much-revered temple is a location of the devil. But we never find out if the voice is really God's voice. The further development of the narrative suggests there is room for interpretation. Jobab wants to heroically "cleanse" the temple of the devil. Rather reluctantly the voice gives him the permission but with a warning: Satan is going to fight him and take everything but his life from him. If he perseveres, his name will become famous and he will regain double his wealth. Moreover, he will be raised to life and will gain the knowledge of God's righteousness and faithfulness (4:2-11). The double meaning of Jobab's question now becomes apparent. Jobab asked whether the much-frequented site is a location of God. The answer draws him toward the next step already: if the site is of the devil, then Jobab wants to fight the devil, and on this path eventually he will gain knowledge of God. Knowledge in this context is closely associated with praxis, with living life in a certain way. The naïve question quickly becomes an existential dynamic that undergirds Jobab's path of suffering. Jobab was not asked by the voice for anything, but he quickly stumbles into the task with heroic determination. Just now he was promised his life — but he assumes the hero and declares: "until death shall I persevere and I will not give up" (5:1). Eagerly he surpasses the expected capacity for suffering: he is willing to die, even though the voice assured him life.

That night Jobab destroys the temple with the help of fifty servants (5:3). But from then on he expects the devil to attack him. Is that strange beggar who comes to his house begging for a piece of bread already the expected Satan (6:4)? Jobab gives him a piece of burnt bread. This offends the pride of the beggar and he swears revenge: "Like this completely burnt bread, so I will make your body" (7:12).

How do we understand the narrative at this point? What causes Jobab's passion: the destruction of the temple or the rejection of the strange beggar? These two reasons converge in one thing: his fear of the devil's power. Jobab was a big landowner, king of Egypt (28:7), and the owner of huge herds of livestock. He praises himself in front of his children for being generous to the poor and for using his riches for their benefit (9:1–15:9). These passages of self-praise are of interest because they tell of the social history at the time, mentioning bread ovens, tables for the poor, and clothes for widows. However, these lists also leave an ambivalent feeling. His generosity is seen retrospectively through the knowledge of his riches being doubled seven years after this momentous night. What did he do before? Is it possible that in the realization that he cannot hold on to his possessions he becomes openhanded? The narrative concentrates in such a way on his generosity that the irony oozes from every line. For example, Jobab signs loan documents liberally and lends money in huge amounts and, if necessary, waives the repayment in a friendly manner (11:1-12). Jobab sings to widows so that they gain new hope and plays the harp to disgruntled servant girls.

But Jobab is not portrayed as an uncritical man. He is not simply the victim of a deal between God and the devil. At the moment Jobab wants to gain knowledge about God, he is willing to "sacrifice" the life of his children and his wife Sitidos, that is, he risks their lives to gain his own truth. He was warned that he would lose everything, and nobody asked him to destroy that temple. He acted out of his passion for truth. Jobab: a fundamentalist in the pursuit of truth? Does Satan appear as a logical result of such destructive thinking that divides the world into right and wrong and wants to gain truth whatever the price may be? The devil is mentioned as the source of suffering. But even the erstwhile friendly neighbors are drawn into pogrom-lust and complete the devilish task: they plunder the palace and steal Jobab's herds (16:5). Jobab reacts with apathy: "Like a woman who is exhausted in her hips from many contractions I was silent" (18:2).

Jobab sits on a garbage dump outside of the town. He becomes ill, his skin burns: "Highly disturbed and upset I left the city to sit on the garbage dump outside of town. My body was eaten by worms and the puss that flowed wet the earth, so many worms were in my body. Whenever a worm crawled out of my body, I took it and put it back on my body, saying: 'Stay in this place where you hatched until you are given a different place by the one who commands you'" (20:7-9). This passage also demonstrates the humor of the text, which almost caricatures the sufferer. His patience is so great that he places the worms back on himself! He does not harm the worms; his destructive energy and meanness have dissolved. He talks to the worms and checks that they get enough nourishment. Is this a loving and admirable stance, or is Jobab as excessive in his suffering as he was in the pursuit of the truth?

The Passion of Sitidos

Now a second interesting narrative begins. In 21:2 the old Job mentions his wife Sitidos for the first time by name. She also lost everything. Yet up to this point Job only spoke of *his* story, in the singular. *He* lived in Egypt, *he* lost his children, and *he* had to live outside of the town. Now we hear that his wife shared in everything, that she stayed by his side. But only in 21:2 does the narrative perspective fall on her: Jobab sees that his wife has become a water-carrier slave in order to raise money for bread. Only now we are told of her fate. Her masters reduced her rations because they did not want her to feed her husband as well. From then on she shared her own ration with her sick husband. She even started begging for his sake, and when the people refused to help her any more, a horrible bread seller asked for her long hair in return for three breads. She said to herself: "'What use is my hair when my husband goes hungry?' And so she pushed aside all considerations and told him: 'Take it then.' He took the scissors, cut her hair off and gave her three loaves of bread in front of everybody watching" (23:8-10).

Sitidos's loyalty seems to know no boundaries. Humble, like Jobab's shadow, she endures the misery. Yet, when his patience becomes excessive, she becomes impatient with him: "Job, Job, how long do you want to sit on the garbage dump thinking that it will soon be over and waiting for the hope of your deliverance? I roam homeless from place to place and serve. . . . But you sit in the rot of the worms and spend your nights uncovered under the sky" (24:1-3). Sitidos gives Jobab his new name. From now on he is called Job. After a moving lament she charges him to take action: "Stand up, take the bread and eat until you are satisfied, tell God about this matter and stop. Then I will be free from the burdensome worry about the misery of your body" (25:10).

Most translators read this passage as a parallel to Job 2:9: "Curse God, and die" (Schaller 1979). I believe that this negative interpretation is misleading and misogynist. Sitidos chooses different words: *kai eipon ti rhēma pros kyrion kai teleuta* (T Job 25:10). "Tell God what is the matter." Sitidos calls on God as the advocate. God needs to finally intervene — here we see the apocalyptic impatience of suffering humans coming to the fore. This is following in the tradition of the book of Job. But our long-suffering Job forgot until now to talk to God. His silence (12:4) is unmasked as problematical by Sitidos's intervention. Why does he not start crying out (cf. Rev 12:2; Exod 6:5)? Why do we not hear him praying, arguing, lamenting? Does he not have faith in God's power to save? Here Sitidos bears the tradition of the biblical Job. It is she who reminds him of God's role as defender of the sufferers, and, at the same time, she gives her husband the new name: Job.

Thanks to her intervention, Job confronts his belief in Satan. He still thinks his wife is led astray by Satan and sees him behind her actions. But in Testament of Job 27:1-7 he confronts him face-to-face and does not evade him any more. Satan tells of his wrestling with Job. Job endured until Satan could not bear it any longer. Sorrowful, he lets go of Job, so the narrative tells us. Is Satan sorrowful because he did not win? Or does he feel human emotions in himself, such as mercy? Or is it Job who can recognize mercy in his adversary? Is this the first step toward Job's healing, that he reassesses the images of his enemies?

Sitidos also receives a new name. Sitidos was always mentioned in association with bread. Her name is connected to a legend about bread. *Sitidos* means nourishment through grain products (*sitizein* means "to give bread"). She is the provider, the bread-giver and a source of strength. Her mouth speaks the life-saving formula of the angels, "Arise and eat!" (1 Kings 19:5). As the exhausted Elijah is urged by an angel to get up and eat, so she exhorts her suffering husband to rise, eat, and take action. We do not hear blasphemy here but the admonition to embrace life.

But when her hair is shorn in public, Sitidos's passion reaches its lowest point. The shearing is like a denuding that humiliates Sitidos. Her indignation and lament are depicted in full detail. Sitidos has lost everything now, her honor, her status as wife, her identity. In this sense, we can speak of the "rape" of Sitidos.

Job mentions her new name at the beginning of his speech to his children (T Job 1:6). The Aramaic translation of the Hebrew Bible (the Targum) identifies his wife with Leah's daughter Dinah of Genesis 34. Unfortunately, Job's androcentric narrative-perspective does not sufficiently explain the connection of the names Sitidos and Dinah. That is why some exegetes suggest that Sitidos had died and Job had married a new wife. I cannot follow this interpretation. The narrative development makes the connection clearer. Thus, the new name establishes a sisterhood between the suffering woman and the rape of the daughter of Leah (Gen 34:1-2). On the level of the narrative, her humiliation is condemned as public rape. Moreover, the name Dinah etymologically comes from *'ădônâ* (ruler). The change of name then functions as a promise of release into an autonomous existence, an eschatological turnaround for the abused water slave and forsaken wife. At the same time, other meanings are evoked, *dîn, dayyān,* that is, "judgment, lawsuit" and "judge, advocate." Dinah calls on the God of Job as an advocate for the sufferers when she tells her husband to arise and speak up to God.

It is really amazing to see what interpreters have made of Sitidos in this story! They interpret her name via *śṭh* — "to lose one's way" or even "Satan" (Schaller 1979, 345). That Sitidos is renamed like Job is not noticed. Sitidos is seen as Satan's victim, unable to see the devil at work. With this interpretation the readers unquestioningly accept the androcentric perspective of the sick Job. Job sees Satan behind everything, even behind his faithful wife. Only when he starts to confront his belief in Satan does Job become communicative again.

The Transformation

With the cry of lament in Testament of Job 25:1, "Is this Sitidos?" her transformation begins. Her humiliation and her protest change her into Dinah. Her husband admits to himself his belief in the devil, and subsequently the devil leaves him (27:6). Only now do more characters begin to appear in the narrative, as Job has regained his ability to perceive and to communicate.

Three men come to visit their sick friend (28:2). They cannot believe that this wretched man on the garbage dump is their former friend. When they deplore the loss of his possessions, he loses patience with them: "Be quiet! Now I will show you my throne and the glory of its might in the temple" (33:2). Job does not want pity. He insists on the promise that he will regain everything and that he will rise again. "My throne is in the heavens and its glory and splendour are on the right hand of the Father" (33:3). Finally he speaks of God as father! With this he follows the direction Dinah had indicated. He was moved by her plea. He rejects pity and points to a different solution: God will comfort him as a father comforts his son. He thus provokes God to hurry to help his son. But his royal friends declare him mad.

Sitidos/Dinah appears for the last time. She throws herself at the feet of the kings and begs: "I ask you to tell your people to remove the rubble of the house that fell on my children so that their remains can be buried properly. We were not able to do this because of the costs involved. To visit at least their remains! Am I a wild beast, or do I have an animal's womb that ten of my children died and I have buried none of them?" (39:8-10). The kings want to act immediately. But Job stops them, because he knows that his children are with God already and not underneath the rubble. Oh, if only he had spoken earlier! Sitidos would not have been so distraught, for she lets herself be comforted right away by Job: "Now I know that God thinks of me!" she exclaims, relieved. She also sees her children with God (40:4).

This narrative of Sitidos's passion echoes the story of the suffering of Mother

Zion (cf. 2 Esdras). To understand the theological importance, it is helpful to compare both women's narratives, because the moving scenes have a parallel structure:

1. The suffering woman appears: 39:1 / 2 Esdras 9:38
2. She weeps and is dressed in torn clothes: 39:2-3 / 2 Esdras 9:38
3. She narrates her own story of humiliation: 39:8-9 / 2 Esdras 9:41–10:1
4. Her ability to bear children is discussed: 39:10 / 2 Esdras 10:14
5. Her grief is rebuffed: 39:12 / 2 Esdras 10:15
6. Reminders of resurrection or transformation: 40:3-6 / 2 Esdras 10:16-27

In these six steps we find a theology of resistance in tight narrative space. The women put up resistance against suffering that imposes silence. They contradict their interlocutors who want to put them off. They resist the pressure of suffering by lamenting, telling their stories, remembering their will to life — until they rise up and are made new, until they are transformed. Yes, both women have difficult interlocutors (Job and Ezra, respectively), but they develop their ability to resist within a relationship. They need the partner who notices, hears, and reacts to them. Both women were childless and are likened to an infertile woman. Both are transformed in analogy to a city. On this level, the individual fate of the woman tried in suffering metaphorically embodies the suffering of the people who wrestle with their God for new life.

The translators struggle with the following verses (T Job 40:4-14). The narrative tells of Sitidos/Dinah's walk to the city, to her cows that had been stolen from her. At a manger she takes a rest and dies. Commentators are at a loss to explain this. It seems irrelevant to them that, after her declaration of faith, there follows this walk to the city and the animals and her death.

But in these verses are hidden the transformation and resurrection of Sitidos. I translate *teleuta* (40:6) not as "she dies" but as "she finishes/completes" her passion (see above, 25:10). In an androcentric interpretative discussion the resurrection of a woman has no place. Sitidos simply dies, and that is all there is to it.

But the following evidence speaks for a transformation and resurrection of Sitidos/Dinah: Dinah prophesies her own resurrection: *anastēsomai*. She will rise (40:4). This echoes the end of the book of Daniel: "But you, you go your way, and rest; you shall rise for your reward at the end of the days" (Dan 12:13). Finally, oppressed Dinah finds rest and shalom. Her resurrection stands in the context of a holy city. We find the same motif also in 2 Esdras 10:27: "I looked up and saw no longer a woman but a complete city, built on massive foundations" (NEB; cf. also Rev 21:10–22:5).

Dinah herself speaks of her entry into the city and her reward: "I will be raised up and enter into the city and rest there a little; then I will take my reward for my service as a slave" (T Job 40:4).

Her reward consists of her new name that inserts her into the Jacob and Leah tradition, into the house of Israel, and transforms her from a slave into a woman of status. I read the animals around her ("the animals lament for her around her," 40:11) as an image of her finding her children again, because in 39:10 she exclaimed: "Do I have an animal's womb?"

This short glance at related motifs shows the connection of the holy city of God where justice and tranquility reign with the transformation of a woman (cf. Humphrey 1995). In the book of Revelation the bride is the city; in 2 Esdras the weeping woman becomes Zion, the rebuilt city, while in the Testament of Job the humiliated Sitidos is transformed into Dinah in the holy city. Receiving a new name as a consequence of an experience of God is a widespread tradition (cf. Jacob-Israel in Gen 32:28; Sarai-Sarah in Gen 17:15; Abram-Abraham in Gen 17:5). In Revelation, those who have persevered are given a stone with a new name (Rev 2:17). This new name is clearly linked to the city of God (Rev 3:12).

The transformation of Sitidos can be reconstructed as a resurrection. However, the extant text causes some difficulty. It remains peculiarly ambivalent in relation to Sitidos. It is much more interested in Job's fate than in that of Sitidos or her daughters. The songs about Sitidos that were sung by the poor, the *ptōchoi*, have not been found, and thus any suggestion about her resurrection in the songs is lost. Neither have the songbooks of the three daughters survived.

Precisely because of these androcentric difficulties in the text, it is invaluable to compare and read similar texts next to the passion of Sitidos (2 Esdras and Revelation). Revelation 2:10 mirrors the suffering of Job and Dinah: "Do not fear what you are about to suffer. Beware, the devil is about to throw some of you into prison so that you may be tested, and for ten days you will have affliction. Be faithful until death, and I will give you the crown of life." Even the throne of Satan is mentioned in Revelation 2:13, the very throne that in the Testament of Job stands at the center of the venerated temple and thus functions as the trigger of the suffering. To overcome, *hypomenein*, a central verb in the Testament of Job, is also found in other martyr writings (such as 4 Maccabees) as well as in the book of Revelation.

The Daughters of Job and Dinah

From Testament of Job 46 onward we do not hear Job's direct speech any more. The narrative tells of the division of goods between his seven sons. Then the three daughters insist on their part of the inheritance as well (46:2). This insistence on their right is similar to Job 42:15. Job concedes their claim: "Do not grumble, my daughters. I have not forgotten you. For you I have thought of a better inheritance than that for your seven brothers" (T Job 46:3-4). In the following section it is shown what they will inherit and what effect this inheritance brings.

Rebecca Lesses sees this narrative of the heirs as a separate unit from the rest of the book. She substantiates this on the basis of a change in the image of women: while Sitidos is good but insensitive to the presence of the devil (an image of women that accords little spiritual depth), the three daughters are better than their father (Lesses 1994, 141). Susan Garrett disagrees and maintains that the women in the Testament of Job are all concerned with earthly matters. The three daughters have to get new hearts to be able to embrace what is spiritual (Garrett 1993, 57-58).

I discern a yet different image of womanhood in the Testament of Job; it derives from a new appraisal of the passion of Sitidos/Dinah. Perhaps we have here two midrashim (corresponding to Job 2:9 and 42:15) that are coherent and not dependent on each other. But I agree that the rebellious nature of the three daughters indeed presupposes a mother with religious competence. The three daughters show that they are true daughters of Sitidos/Dinah when they demand justice for themselves: they approach Job as father (T Job 46:2) and thus link him to the image of the just and righteous father, the advocate of the weak, the same image with which Sitidos provoked Job. Even in the holy city where Job and Sitidos and their friends finally find themselves, justice still needs to be claimed by women. This time Job is willing to support these claims of the females in his family. After his bidding, the daughter Hemera brings a golden chest that contains three belts. These golden belts shine like the sun. Yet the three daughters remain critical: "Of what use are these belts? Will they bring us some good for our life?" (47:2). Now Job tells them that God gave him these belts on the day he was healed (47:4). The daughters gird themselves and immediately are given new hearts and speak in the language of angels (48:3), of powers (49:2), and of the cherubim (50:2). There are supposed to be books written by all three of them with their songs and prayers. Job gives Hemera his harp, Kasia his censer, and Amaltheia Keras his drum, so that they can praise those who have come to fetch him. Job's soul departs on a carriage while his body is buried. The daughters are the only ones who see the fatherly God sitting on the big carriage and taking Job into his arms (52:9). They also sing the songs of the father (52:12).

Open Questions

Have they become father-daughters? Have they kept their mother's request for justice or have they forgotten about it? Is the transformation of the daughters not a devaluing of real women? Or can we recognize them as ecstatic prophets, women who see God, theologians and priests? Where are their traces, their books, their traditions? Where is Dinah? How are we to read her transformation/resurrection? What happens with the seven worldly and rich sons? Why did Job not divide his wealth and his spiritual inheritance equally among his sons and daughters? The daughters wanted equality but got spiritual power. Job insisted that that was the better part of the inheritance. Can we trust him?

The golden belts never feature in the narrative of Job's healing but only when it comes to the inheritance for the daughters. Golden belts belong in apocalyptic contexts, such as Daniel 10:4-14, Apocalypse of Zephaniah 6:11-12, and Revelation 1:13 and 15:6.

The messengers with the golden belts in Revelation carry priestly vessels, move freely in and out of the temple, appear in visions and interpret them. They are even similar to a son of man. They work with God to achieve his justice by singing, praying, interpreting, and transmitting messages from God. Yet, women are very rarely seen as messengers. In this text we see the birth of three female messengers who receive not only Job's inheritance but also that of their mother Dinah (T Job 25:10).

If the books of these four women are not found, we have to search more intensively. And what if they were never written? Then we have to write them today as late descendants of Dinah.

LITERATURE

Collins, John J. 1974. "Structure and Meaning in the Testament of Job." *SBL Seminar Papers* 1.

Garrett, Susan. 1993. "The 'Weaker Sex' in the Testament of Job." *Journal of Biblical Literature* 112:55-70.

Horst, Pieter W. van der. 1989. "Images of Women in the Testament of Job." In *Studies on the Testament of Job,* edited by Michael A. Knibb and Pieter W. van der Horst, 93-116. Cambridge.

Humphrey, Edith McEwan. 1995. *The Ladies and the Cities.* Sheffield.

Jacobs, Irving. 1970. "Literary Motifs in the Testament of Job." *Journal of Jewish Studies* 21:1-10.

Kraft, Robert A., ed. 1974. *The Testament of Job according to the SV Text.* Missoula.

Lesses, Rebecca. 1994. "The Daughters of Job." In *Searching the Scriptures,* edited by Elisabeth Schüssler Fiorenza, 2:139-49. 2 vols. New York.

Philonenko, Marc. 1968. "Le Testament de Job, Introduction, traduction et notes." *Semitica* 18:1-75.

Riessler, Paul. 1928. *Altjüdisches Schrifttum ausserhalb der Bibel.* Augsburg.

Schaller, Berndt. 1979. *Testament des Job. Jüdische Schriften aus hellenistisch-römischer Zeit,* vol. 3, 3. Gütersloh.

Spitta, Friedrich. 1907. *Das Testament des Hiob und das Neue Testament.* Göttingen.

Spittler, Russell P. 1983/85. "Testament of Job." In *The Old Testament Pseudepigrapha,* edited by James H. Charlesworth, 1:829-68. 2 vols. London.

Translated by Tina Steiner

Testaments of the Twelve Patriarchs: How Men Use Power

Renate Kirchhoff

Introductory Remarks

In the Testaments of the Twelve Patriarchs (German text: Becker 1974), women are viewed exclusively as sexual partners. If sexual immorality plays a large role in my interpretation, this androcentric perspective of the Testaments of the Twelve Patriarchs is reflected in the thematic emphasis. I consider this to be unavoidable, since at the end I would like to pass judgment and show analogies to androcentric ways of thinking and arguing still in use today.

After a general introduction I present the themes of the individual books. The third section explains what *porneia* is and in what sense it is a cardinal sin. Its particular effect on men and the function of women is described in the fourth section; the fifth introduces Leah and Rachel as the good alternatives to dangerous women. How the Testaments of the Twelve Patriarchs gives increased importance to the sphere of sexuality and its passions can be explained on the basis of Joseph's struggle with the Egyptian woman. The conclusions show what the addressees gain from this revaluation and the disadvantages it gives women.

The hermeneutic of Elisabeth Schüssler Fiorenza provides the basis for my interpretation. My exegetical observations are based on the findings of historical criticism. I rely on sociopsychological categories for the evaluation of the findings and for the conclusions.

I hesitate to make suggestions about the way women conduct their lives. It appears to me to be more methodically honest, at the end, to infer what the consequences of the Testaments of the Twelve Patriarchs are for women.

It is striking that, as far as I know, no woman has made a detailed analysis of the Testaments of the Twelve Patriarchs. This is all the more remarkable since the document not only contains interesting midrashim on texts in the First Testament, but connections (tradition-historical, among others) could also be drawn to Jubilees, 1 Enoch, the Wisdom of Solomon, and Pauline texts, for example.

Introduction to the Testaments of the Twelve Patriarchs

"Listen, my brothers and my sons; give heed to the things which I, Reuben, your father, command you." This is how the dying Reuben begins his farewell address to the men of his tribe; those of his brothers begin similarly. The testaments pick up from Jacob's farewell address to his sons in Genesis 49–50 and let his sons proclaim, one after the other, what will happen "at the end of days." On the basis of their own experiences — as they relate them, we are reminded especially of stories from Genesis 29–47 — the twelve sons, each in a particular way, warn of dangers and call for behavior in accord with the law. And what the law calls for, in this document's interpretation, is brotherly love. On the basis of *vaticinia ex eventu*, the fate announced for the sons of the patriarch also becomes an example that teaches by warning or encouragement. The hour of death not only imparts special importance to what is taught but also offers the best possibility to assess the past and to pass on one's own experience. The imparting of tradition in the testament genre, on the basis of its patriarchal interests, happens as a rule from man to man, ideally from father to son, as in the Testaments of the Twelve Patriarchs (on the Testament of Eve, the only testament by a woman in the Jewish-Christian tradition, cf. de Groot van Houten 1994b). Thus the one doing the teaching is, at the same time, the model for what is being taught.

The Jewish text shows traces of several reworkings. The basis for the following interpretation is the most recent Jewish version, which I take to be a composition of considerable significance. In the exclusion of Christian additions, I am following Jürgen Becker. Becker dates the foundational stage of the Testaments of the Twelve Patriarchs in the first half of the second century B.C.E. It probably arose in the Hellenistic-Jewish diaspora in Egypt. The idealization of farming and of the simple life (in the Testament of Issachar, for example), the wisdom character of the document, its stoic ideas as well as the themes of the testaments make locating the Testaments of the Twelve Patriarchs in the underclass quite unlikely.

Themes

Each testament is devoted to a particular complex of themes. The Testament of Reuben deals with sexual immorality (*porneia*, e.g., 1:6; 3:3; see below): Reuben tells how it happened that he succumbed to the beauty and the sight of women, and became sick (1:7) and brought grief to his father (3:15), and that it was only thanks to his father's intercession that God ended the hopeless dynamic of his actions (4:4).

The Testament of Simeon deals with jealousy/anger and envy (*zēlos, phthonos*; 2:6-7, for example), for Simeon was jealous of Joseph and angry with Judah. That is the reason that his hand was paralyzed for seven days. The only thing that helps is the fear of God (3:4) and simplicity of heart (4:5).

Issachar is a model of integrity *(haplotēs),* which God rewards with blessing (T Iss 3:1, 8, for example). As a simple farmer, he resists every desire: neither the sight of women nor riches can lead him astray (4:4; 6:1).

Zebulon is typified by the compassion *(eusplanchnia,* e.g., T Zeb 2:2, 4) he shows. God blesses him because he has compassion on Joseph and does not participate in his brothers' plans.

The Testament of Dan deals with lying and anger *(thymos,* e.g., 1:3, 8), which can dominate a man's body completely (3:1-2).

Naphtali explains that the correct measure for one's actions is their accord with the order *(taxis,* e.g., T Naph 2:8-9) God has established in creation, and thus with the law (3:2). The Watchers (3:5) and Sodom (4:1) are offered as examples of the violation of God's order.

Gad wanted to kill Joseph many times and imparts knowledge and experience about the spirit of hatred *(misos,* e.g., T Gad 1:9; 3:1). The one who hates, first of all, violates the command to love one's neighbor (4:2) and is inclined to lying and envy (5:1).

The Testament of Asher is about people who combine virtues and vices within themselves. For example, the person who steals and has mercy on the poor is two-faced *(dysprosōpos,* e.g., 2:1-2, 5). These actions are as a whole evil, and those who act this way do not belong to God (2:5; 3:2).

Joseph is a model of endurance *(hypomonē,* e.g., T Jos 2:7) and self-control, which become apparent, first of all, in his chastity *(sōphrosynē,* e.g., 4:1; 6:7). He wages a true martyr's battle against the temptation offered by the Egyptian woman. Yet he resists her through prayer and fasting (3:3-5). Joseph's love for his brothers is also exemplary (17:3-8).

Benjamin reminds us to set our minds on what is good *(dianoia agathē,* e.g., T Benj 3:2; 5:1), enabling us to see everything clearly and to lead a God-fearing life. Those who do this combine several virtues spoken of in the previous testaments, for they are immune to Beliar's machinations.

The Testament of Levi and the Testament of Judah, because of their significance for all Israel, are conceived differently. They do not urge the avoidance of certain kinds of behavior but teach that their violations of the law have consequences for all Israel. Thus it is disregard for the purity laws, mixing with other nations, and sexual immorality that lead to the destruction of the temple and to exile (T Levi 9; 14–16; T Jud 12–15; 23).

Some testaments take up common themes (sexual immorality, for example; see below), but aside from the admonition to be obedient to the law, no thematic red thread ties all twelve testaments together. Above all, obedience to the law is understood to mean the obligation to show brotherly love and abstention from sexual sins. In this regard, sexual desire is used to exemplify other emotions that lead to sin. The patriarchs teach nothing else, and the Testament of Joseph shows this by way of conclusion.

Sexual Immorality as a Cardinal Sin
in the Testaments of the Twelve Patriarchs

The admonition to avoid *porneia* has special importance in the Testaments of the Twelve Patriarchs. Thus it is the principal theme already in the First Testament, and most of the twelve brothers report about their own experience with sexual immorality and/or take it for granted that their sons are exposed to the temptation to commit *porneia* (e.g., Testament of Reuben, see below; T Sim 5:3-6; T Levi 9:9; T Jud 12; 13:2-3; T Iss 7:2-7; T Dan 5:5; T Ash 2:1-10; T Jos 3:6-10; T Benj 8:2).

The Testament of Simeon states the priority of *porneia* over the other vices because it is from it that the others stem: *porneia* is the mother of all other vices. It gives birth to all misfortune — here political injustice is named — and it is therefore the greatest danger for the sons. In the Testament of Levi it is *porneia* that leads to the desecration of the temple, and it is the cause of the destruction of the temple and the exile (on the Testament of Levi, see below). According to the Testament of Judah, the *porneia* committed by Judah is the cause of the loss of the kingdom (on the Testament of Judah, see below). The Testament of Issachar and the Testament of Asher illustrate exemplary behavior *(haplotēs)* with abstinence from sexual pleasure and from sexual intercourse (e.g., T Iss 2:1; 3:5; T Ash 2:8). With his resistance to the Egyptian woman, Joseph shows himself to be resistant to particularly severe temptation (T Jos 18:1). Correspondingly, a man shows his good and pure understanding in the Testament of Benjamin 6:1-3 and 8:2 by not looking at a woman with the intention of having sexual relations with her. And *porneia* is the first to be named among the wicked deeds at the end (T Benj 9:1).

Porneia occupies this special place, first of all, because it pulls other offenses into its wake and leads to falling away from God (see also Plutarch, *De placita philosophorum* 4.21; Aëtius 4.4.1; see also Philo, *De Abrahamo* 236-244), and secondly, because the temptation to engage in *porneia* is stronger than temptations to commit other offenses (cf. T Reu 4:6; 6:4; T Sim 5:3; and more frequently). Whoever resists this temptation will also withstand all others (T Reu 4:11). *Porneia* is a generic term for various sexual transgressions:

a. The sexual intercourse between Judah and Tamar in Testament of Judah 12 is *porneia,* as is the sexual intercourse that Testament of Levi 14:5 announces that the Levites will commit with prostitutes at the end of time.
b. Adultery, that is, intercourse a man has with a woman who belongs to another man, is *porneia* (cf. T Reu 1:6; T Jud 13:3a).
c. Sexual intercourse that an Israelite has with a non-Israelite is *porneia,* even if a lifelong relationship has been established (T Jud 13:3b; T Dan 5:5; T Jos 3:8).

Sodom's *porneia* is not viewed in Testament of Benjamin 9:1 as intercourse with males (nor as the desire to commit rape), but instead as a foundational story that shows that every sexual offense is a violation of the order established by God and revealed in creation and in the law (see below).

The Testaments of the Twelve Patriarchs treats the theme of *porneia* exclusively from the perspective of men and to their advantage. Thus it is also the men who through the given examples are to be kept from *porneia* and its consequences.

"Do Not Devote Your Attention to a Woman's Looks" (Testament of Reuben 3:10)

The greatest danger for a man is sexual immorality. There are four principal reasons.

a. Men are prone to *porneia*.

Testament of Reuben 2:3–3:7 counts, in two rows of seven each, the spirits with which men have been created by God. The text uses noninclusive language because it is dealing exclusively with the inclination and destiny of males. *Ho neōteros* ("the young[er] man," 2:2) and *pneuma tēs sporas* ("the spirit of procreation," 2:8) have males exclusively in view, and the example of Reuben as well as the admonitions that follow are directed to males.

The seven spirits of the first row (2:3–3:2) are assets that have specific purposes in the life of a man: the spirit of life creates what holds the body together; seeing creates desire; through the spirit of hearing instruction is enabled; the spirit of smell is there for breathing and smelling, with the spirit of speech knowledge is set in place, with taste, the enjoyment of food and drink and a man's strength. The seventh spirit is the spirit of procreation and of intercourse, with which sin arises. The list is shaped by the Stoic subdivision of the soul into eight parts: the five senses; the capacities of reproduction and of speech, as well as the part that has control of everything *(Hēgemonikon);* the natural ability of a man to make rational, that is, virtuous, use of the seven abilities mentioned first. In distinction from Stoic lists, in Testament of Reuben 3:1, 7 the *Hēgemonikon* is not created as the eighth spirit. Rather, standing over the enumerated seven abilities, the organs assigned to them, and their (except for reproduction) positive accomplishments, is the spirit of sleep, which is responsible for the decay and eventual death of the organism (3:1).

If the spirits of the first row designate a man's abilities, then the spirits of the second row (3:3-7) designate the excessive dynamic of the respective ability, which leads to sin. It is true that there is no symmetry between the two rows, yet the second row reads like a continuation of the first, since it shows that every positive ability is perverted if it is used ignorantly and carelessly. A dynamic arises that can only be halted by prayer (cf. 1:7; 4:4).

The ability to procreate garners the most attention: this is the only one that the first row says leads to sin. Not only is ignorance mixed in with it, as with the other abilities, but it is filled with ignorance (2:9). As the first ability of youth, it completely determines a young man's behavior. The spirit of prostitution is the first one named in the second row, and the temptation to sexual immorality (3:9-15) characterizes every deception that obstructs knowledge of the law and prevents a son's obedience to his father. Every ability can be perverted, but the ability under the greatest danger of misuse is procreation. For it has special power in a man's youth, when he still lacks experience, is easy to lead astray, and is not yet schooled in the law and paternal instruction. The danger exists for every man who underestimates the power of sexual immorality and is not careful. The two rows teach men that because of their nature they have a propensity for misusing their procreative ability and for committing sexual immorality and that they therefore need the commandments as well as paternal instruction.

b. All it takes is looking at a women to awaken the impulse to sexual immorality (Testament of Reuben 3:10–4:11; Testament of Judah 12–14).
The two rows about men's nature culminate in the demand to listen to Reuben. What follows is the warning not to look at women at all, which is argued on the basis of the example of Balla (Bilhah) and Reuben (T Reu 3:11-15; in calling Bilhah Balla, the Testament of Reuben is following the Septuagint). The Testament of Reuben combines the story of Reuben's intercourse with Bilhah (cf. Gen 35:22) with the motif of seeing a woman bathing, which we encounter in the stories of David and Bathsheba (2 Sam 11:1-5) and Susanna and the elders (Dan 13). According to the example used here, the sight of the naked Balla (Bilhah) is sufficient to unleash an urge to commit sexual immorality in Reuben (T Reu 3:12). This happens in that Reuben receives this sight in his heart *(dianoia)*, just as a women receives the seed of a man when she becomes pregnant (cf. *syllabein*), and with a necessity similar to that with which a woman gives birth, after men receive the sight, to carry out the deed. For this reason, the Testaments of the Twelve Patriarchs speaks about the spirit of sexual immorality as an independent entity that influences a man the way Beliar does. The underlying concept is that of a sphere of activity under the control of fate (see below).

Aside from looking away and avoiding being in the presence of women, what helps is simplicity of heart and concentration on fulfilling the law (4:1; cf. the Testament of Joseph). But basically no one is immune to the danger, neither rich nor poor, neither young nor old men (T Reu 4:7).

c. Women are determined to seduce men into *porneia*.
The role women play when men engage in sexual immorality is depicted most clearly in the Testament of Reuben. In the Testament of Joseph, because of Joseph's virtue, the act was not committed.

"Women are evil, my children . . ." is the way Testament of Reuben 5 begins its expositions, which consists of judgments about women (they are evil, more prone to *porneia* than men, and only by duplicity able to gain the upper hand over a man) and of a description *(ekphrasis)* of women's behavior, which documents the judgments (they guilefully make use of their beauty, concoct plans against men, use jewelry to beguile, sow poison by their glances, and then take men captive). The judgments and descriptions are given further verification in that an angel reveals or confirms them (5:3). Next Reuben instructs his sons about their behavior, telling them to protect themselves and to forbid the women in their familial sphere of influence to beguile with their looks. The necessity of this prohibition is illustrated by the example of the watchers (cf. Gen 6:1-4). The way in which the Testament of Reuben describes the episode confirms the preceding descriptions and explains that cunning women (a) were always a danger for men and for all of humanity; that the danger that comes from them is so great that (b) even the sons of God succumb to them and that (c) their aggressively employed beauty is an attack on the order that is and is intended to be part of God's creation (see below). But in contrast to Genesis 6, in Testament of Reuben 5:6-7 sexual intercourse with the sons of God does not happen. But seeing and desiring the women have the same effect, namely, the birth of the giants, which were not envisioned in God's order. Thus, (d) it is shown that the desire is just as reprehensible as the act itself, because it can have the same effect. Why are women so aggressive and filled with lust? For one thing, they are evil (5:1), and, in the second place, this is their only chance to exercise power over a man (5:1, 4). Their inferiority is given by nature (5:4), and they therefore need guile to control a man, for in a fair fight they would be defeated.

d. Women bear responsibility for the actions of men.

A man has a propensity for sexual immorality, but it is within his power to guard against giving in by following the admonitions of the fathers. In this way his accountability and the scope of his actions are clearly delineated. Nevertheless, a man is under constant threat from sexual immorality and from women. The admonition to "flee sexual immorality" (T Reu 5:5) personifies sexual immorality. Since sexual immorality (like other offenses as well) involves the emotions, the dynamic forces in which a man is caught up — so that in the end he commits the deed — are designated as the activity of the spirit of sexual immorality (T Levi 9:9; T Jud 13:3). Here we are not dealing with a mythological way of speaking (as is the way of speaking about the spirits in the eschatological passages; cf., for example, T Sim 6:6; T Levi 3:3; 18:12) but instead with a metaphorical way of speaking that is connected with thinking about one's actions: through his desire and the consummation of the deed, a man creates a sphere that unleashes the urge within himself to do the deed or to keep on sinning (on this way of speaking and on the concept of the sphere of action that affects the man and woman committing the act, see Kirchhoff 1994, 145ff.). The metaphorical way of speaking shows how strong the emotion is and how disastrous its effect. Nevertheless, the man is responsible.

It is a different matter when the role of a woman or of women is discussed with reference to the consummation of the act. For they are determined to lead men astray, so that it comes to a battle that the man wages not just with his emotions but also with the woman (cf. T Reu 5; the Testament of Joseph). Because women, in the view of the Testaments of the Twelve Patriarchs, are dangerous, want to lead men astray, and influence the strength of men's emotions, they bear the responsibility for men's actions.

Leah Wanted to Sleep with Jacob for the Sake of Children, "but Not for Sexual Gratification" (Testament of Issachar 2:3)

Leah and Rachel are alternatives to women who pose a threat. Thus Issachar serves as evidence that not only bad but also proper sexual behavior puts its mark on the children. Issachar is the model of a virtuous farmer who leads a simple life (T Iss 4:2). His way of life immunizes him against the spirits of error and the lure of feminine beauty (4:4). Until his thirtieth year the desire for women doesn't enter his head. He is immune to their deceptive power (3:5; 4:5), knows only his own wife, and desires no other (7:2).

How good women deal with sexuality is shown by a midrash on Genesis 30:14-25 LXX in Testament of Issachar 1 and 2. Like Genesis 30, the midrash tells that Leah let Rachel have two May apples for two nights with Jacob. But the midrash tells the story in a way that explains why the eight sons are divided six and two between the two women. The reason lies in the differing, but exemplary, behavior of the women. Rachel is exemplary because she chooses abstinence and doesn't even yield to the desire to eat the apples, but uses them for an offering. She is rewarded with two sons. Leah is exemplary because it was not for sexual gratification but for the sake of having children that she sought to lie with Jacob. She receives six instead of eight sons. An angel reveals to Jacob the logic of the division of sons between the two women. The train of thought that turns on the number of apples and sons is understandable if one takes into account not only the relationship between the women's behavior and the number of children they have — if only that were considered, the number of children Leah has would have to be interpreted as a punishment (de Jonge 1978, 298) — but also that the number and division of the children were a given and also that according to the Testament of Issachar both women behaved in an exemplary manner. In any case, Rachel's abstinence is fundamentally superior to being with a man. When, however, a woman sought to be with a man, then this should happen, as in Leah's case, not for sexual gratification but solely for having children.

By means of an etiology the midrash connects the number of the patriarchs with the exemplary behavior of their mothers with respect to sexuality. They stand for the two possible ways in which married women can deal with sexual (and other kinds of) desire: either rejecting sexual intercourse (Rachel, 2:1) or seeking it in order to have children. For wanting to have children is obviously an alternative to desire (Leah, 2:3).

"I Struggled against a Shameless Woman" (Testament of Joseph 2:2)

Joseph is the virtuous wise man who resists all temptations to violate the law and remains committed to brotherly love. Therefore God rescues and exalts him (1:7) completely, as the wise man deserves (cf. 1 Macc 2:53; Wis 10:13; Philo, *In Flaccum* 48). What is exceptional about this case is that Joseph's enemy is not a tyrant but the Egyptian woman who is the wife of Pentephres. Because she is a slave to lust (T Jos 7:8), she tries to seduce Joseph into having sex with her. To accomplish this she resorts to several tricks. Moreover, she threatens him with death (3:1; 6:1) and promises him power and riches. Like the pious who face threats to life and limb, however, he resists her through endurance *(hypomonē)* and steadfastness *(makrothymia)* and does not violate the law (cf., e.g., Wis 16:3; 4 Macc 1:11; 5:23). Like the three men in the fiery furnace (Dan 3:88 LXX), Joseph is saved by God from the threatening flames unleashed by the Egyptian women (T Jos 2:2). As Nebuchadnezzar hears the song of praise sung by the men in the fiery furnace, the Egyptian woman hears Joseph's praise in prison (8:5) — with the difference that the Egyptian woman is not converted to Joseph's God and to a life of virtue. Joseph's patient endurance in the face of sexual temptation happened because of his love for his brothers (17:1, 8). Because of this same love, he does not shame his brothers and is neither arrogant nor proud (10:5-6; 17:8). Even if the addressees are not threatened in the same way Joseph was (as is also true in other acts of martyrs), the accounts about Joseph move them to identify with him and thus to obey the law, that is, to battle against sexual immorality and to show brotherly love.

The Benefits of the Testaments of the Twelve Patriarchs for Those Addressed and What That Means for Women around Them

Every text, to gain acceptance, must promise to benefit its addressees. The Testaments of the Twelve Patriarchs, first of all, naturally offers the prosperity promised the one who is faithful to the commandments and precepts. Secondly, it makes the recipients sure about their norms and objectives, strengthens their feeling of oneness, and defines what makes them, or can make them, one group.

Sexual sins are in the testaments one of the principal causes of disaster. Therefore, it is specifically the sphere of sexuality that stands at the center of the text's interest rather than, for example, the relationship to those outside the group, external threat, or the loss of religious self-determination. Rather, it is all of a man's conduct in this sphere that affects his relationship to God and other people. Therefore reward and punishment, the necessary consequences of sexual behavior, have full communal relevance (cf., e.g., impotence [T Reu 1:7] or having many children [T Iss 1:2]; loss of a kingdom [T Jud 15:2]; brotherly love [T Jos 17:1-3]; premature death [T Reu 1:7; 4:6] or eternal life [T Ash 6:6]; ridicule [T Reu 4:7] or admiration in the eyes of outsiders [in T Levi 13:3]; behavior in conformity with the law brings admiration by and friendship with strangers; and the desecration of the temple through sexual [and other] misbehavior that leads to exile [T Levi 14–16]). The individual knows that his sexual behavior affects his position within the group and also how the group as a whole is viewed by outsiders. For behavior in everyday situations and especially for the correct structuring of contacts with women, social reward is to be expected. The depiction of Joseph's steadfastness in the face of the deceptive power of the Egyptian woman shows how much importance the Testaments of the Twelve Patriarchs ascribes to the decisions made in these everyday realms: this high import has a stabilizing effect on an individual man and the group to which he belongs, if the individual or the community knows itself to be capable of handling the situations. The fatherly admonition teaches how the sons can behave in conformity with the law and makes possible by means of identifying with the fathers the anticipation not only of defeats and punishments but also of victory and reward. Beyond that, the Testaments of the Twelve Patriarchs offers models of interpretation and behavior that assure the addressees of their moral and material superiority and solidify the patriarchal ways of regulating the relationships between men and women. Thereby, the avoidance of sexual immorality is both a central theme of the text and a *modus vivendi* that promises enhanced prestige and a shining image.

It accords with this conclusion that the Egyptian diaspora experienced comparatively little harassment. For the characterization of emotions as the greatest danger permits the conclusion that the group does not see itself under external threat and, in addition, does not seek its identity by means of a clearly defined separation from others but by means of a hierarchicalization of its inner structure and by exemplary virtue. The hierarchicalization occurs at the expense of women, because control over one's own emotions is completely tied up with control of and superiority over women.

Women are not, it's true, direct addressees, but as mothers, daughters, sisters, potential or actual wives or sexual partners or sacrifices to sexual force, they live with men's images of ideal or evil women. According to these images, an ideal woman has no sexual desire, nor does she evoke any. A married woman seeks sexual relations solely for the sake of having children. The Testament of Issachar offers criteria for the choice of a wife, and in so doing provides women with models of behavior.

On the other hand, a woman who arouses and has emotions bears responsibility for the man's sins, the sight of her already triggering the misconduct. That women are made to share responsibility for men's misconduct does not, it's true, let men escape the consequences of their own deeds. Yet Joseph's exemplariness shows not only what is to be gained for men when they are unyielding, but also that they can reckon with understanding when they succumb. For the stories of his brothers' failures also invite identification with them.

The assertion that women are responsible for men's actions and the emphasis on the power of emotions and of women's attractiveness are still met today in arguments aimed at trivializing violence used against women. Then, as now, it is clear that on this issue what matters is the relationship between the sexes and that the perspective of the perpetrator legitimates the status quo (see above). Thus the expositions on the sexual attractiveness of women denigrate their initiative and self-determination not only in the sexual sphere but also in every sphere in which they compete with men (cf. T Reu 5).

LITERATURE

Becker, Jürgen. 1974. *Unterweisung in lehrhafter Form. Die Testamente der zwölf Patriarchen. Jüdische Schriften aus hellenistisch-römischer Zeit,* vol. 3/1. Gütersloh.

De Groot van Houten, Christiana. 1994a. "Rachel's Virtuous Behavior in the Testament of Issachar." In *Greeks, Romans, and Christians,* edited by David L. Balch et al., 340-52. Festschrift for Abraham J. Malherbe. Minneapolis.

———. 1994b. "Will the Real Eve Please Stand?" *Society of Biblical Literature Seminar Papers* 33:301-11.

De Jonge, Marinus. 1978. *The Testaments of the Twelve Patriarchs: A Critical Edition of the Greek Text.* Pseudepigrapha Veteris Testamenti Graece, vol. 1.2. Leiden.

Hollander, Harm W., and Marinus de Jonge. 1981. *Joseph as an Ethical Model in the Testaments of the Twelve Patriarchs.* Studia in Veteris Testamenti pseudepigraphica, vol. 6. Leiden.

———. 1985. *The Text of the Testaments of the Twelve Patriarchs: A Commentary.* Studia in Veteris Testamenti pseudepigraphica, vol. 8. Leiden.

Ilan, Tal. 1995. *Jewish Women in Greco-Roman Palestine: An Inquiry into Image and Status.* Texte und Studien zum antiken Judentum, vol. 44. Tübingen.

Kirchhoff, Renate. 1994. *Die Sünde gegen den eigenen Leib. Studien zu pórne und porneia in 1 Kor 6,12-20 und dem soziokulturellen Kontext der paulinischen Adressaten.* Studien zur Umwelt des Neuen Testaments, vol. 18. Göttingen.

Translated by Everett R. Kalin

Gospel of Matthew: Jewish-Christian Churches in Opposition to the Pax Romana

Martina S. Gnadt

The question about the origin of the Gospel of Matthew is pivotal and crucial for its interpretation. This issue is decisive for understanding not only individual texts but also the Gospel as a whole. I take the Gospel of Matthew to be Jewish-Christian; that is, my assumption is that it arose in Jewish-Christian churches of the Jewish diaspora, probably in Syria. The Matthean churches, seeing themselves as Jewish men and women who believe in Jesus, the Messiah and Son of God (cf. Matt 1:1), are a part of the Judaism that struggles for the future of Jewish faith and life after the destruction of Jerusalem and of the temple by the Roman forces of occupation in 70 C.E.

In the first century and beyond, Judaism is not yet unified (Saldarini 1994, 11ff.). Rather, it consists of a number of local congregations significantly different from one another. At this time rabbinic Judaism is not yet normative. The rabbinic leaders compete with other prominent groups for influence in the congregations and can only gradually gain the upper hand. And the influence of the prominent groups on what actually happens in the congregations is frequently overestimated, if their positions are simply equated with congregational reality and practice. The reality in Judaism in the first and second centuries C.E. is so varied that quite a few scholars (Levine, for example, in Brenner 1996, 307) choose the plural "Judaisms" to describe the Judaism of this period. Standing over against the local Jewish congregations, early Christianity also has a great variety of churches of diverse character; it is not a single monolithic entity. Simply to distinguish Jewish-Christian from Gentile-Christian does not accurately characterize this diversity. Like many Jewish congregations, many Jewish-Christian congregations were open to non-Jews (Godfearers, proselytes) and integrated them as full members. Even so-called Gentile-Christian congregations did not establish themselves outside of Judaism in the first two centuries. Men and women from the nations who see themselves as fol-

---

I would like to thank Bettina Eltrop for her helpful references and stimulating suggestions.

lowers of Jesus the Messiah count themselves, as well as Jewish Christians, as part of Judaism. In what follows, when I speak of "early Christianity" or of "early Christian churches," what I mean are groups that are fully and completely part of Judaism — which does not exclude intense *inner-Jewish* disputes. The early Christian churches, including those the Gospel of Matthew has in view, actively participated in the struggle for the Jewish way of life *(halakah)* in the face of the Roman superpower. The Gospel of Matthew offers a "snapshot" both of inner-Jewish disputes among the various Jewish and Jewish-Christian congregations and of disputes within Jewish-Christian congregations over burning questions about the Jewish way of life, and thus it belongs in the context of Judaism in the first century C.E.

Serving God in Daily Life

The Jewish identity of the Matthean churches is clearly shown in numerous ways. Of primary significance are the naming of God as Father (Greek: *patēr;* Aramaic: *'abbā'*), which is of great importance in the Gospel of Matthew, and the Lord's Prayer (6:9-13) as the prayer of the Matthean churches. I understand this prayer, which is put in a prominent place in the Sermon on the Mount (5–7), in the context of the practice and piety of Jewish prayer in the first three centuries. Numerous prayers in Greek and Hebrew indicate that in this period persecution, repentance, conversion, and forgiveness are burning themes in prayer to God the Father, both by individuals and congregations (D'Angelo 1992, 617ff.). The increasing importance of using the name Father for God in this period is striking, as we can establish in various ways, including the clear increase of its use in Matthew in comparison with Mark and Q. Without doubt, one of the factors in this development is the increasing importance of the concept that Jesus was the Son of God, with which the concept of God as Father corresponds. But that does not explain everything. "Matthew" stresses that God is "our" and "your" Father, referring to the Matthean churches, for whom Jesus is the only master and teacher (23:8, 10), just as he is for the disciples and the people (23:1). "Matthew" states emphatically that they also have only one Father, whom they have the right to address with this name and who — as the one "who is in the heavens" — is set in opposition to fathers "on earth" (23:9). This strict directive to accord a father's authority to no one but the heavenly Father has an antipatriarchal function (according to Schüssler Fiorenza 1988, 199ff.). The churches have only one master and teacher, Christ, and only one Father, God. Ultimate authority is ascribed to Jesus, as the conclusion to the Sermon on the Mount states programmatically (7:28-29).

The sociohistorical context of the churches within the Roman Empire suggests applying the commanded refusal to confer the title of father also to claims imposed on the churches from the outside. With the titles *pater patriae* and *parens patriae,* the Roman rulers, starting with Augustus, claimed supreme authority not only over the Roman people but also over the nations forced into the so-called Pax Romana. Against this background, the confession of the Matthean churches to God as the sole Father — located, on top of that, in the heavens — is an expression of their refusal to comply with, and an act of resistance against, the demands for loyalty put forward by the earthly Roman "fathers," and, most likely, also against the local representatives who in their own areas pressed Rome's claims to power, at times with unbounded aggressiveness. The destruction of the temple and the devastation that Rome brought upon the Jewish congregations in response to the two Jewish uprisings will have contributed to the growing importance of calling God Father. A number of rabbinic prayers connect calling God Father with these catastrophes or ascribe this usage particularly to rabbis who are associated with the Jewish uprisings. Thus an early version of the prayer *'abînû malkênû*, "Our Father, our King, we have no king but you; our Father, our King, for your name's sake, have mercy on us" (Babylonian Talmud *Ta'anit* 25b), is ascribed to Rabbi Akiba, who, as a messianic pretender, suffered a martyr's death in 135 C.E. Even though this prayer received a fixed written form only after the Gospel of Matthew had been written, it still can be used as a possible analogy to the naming of God as Father in Matthew and, especially, also to the Lord's Prayer, since the Roman imperial use of the title of father can be assumed as a background for both prayers. Against this background of daily disputes with the Roman rulers, the prayer to the *heavenly* Father and King, asking that *his* kingdom come and that *his* will be done on earth as in heaven (Matt 6:10), is to be understood as an act of resistance, as a refusal to acknowledge the claims to power by the Roman "fathers" and their local representatives. I make the assumption that the Jewish resistance against the Roman rulers was carried out not only in spectacular, at times armed, actions, such as the revolts of 66-70 and 132-135 C.E., but also, as numerous archaeological finds suggest, in day-to-day life, for example, through tenaciously holding on to traditions and practices they had received (Kuhnen 1996, 10ff.) and through the people's battle to maintain ritual purity (Deines, in Kuhnen 1996, 70ff.; cf. Matt. 15:1-20). It is here that the prayer to God, the Father in heaven, has its original liturgical setting, imbedded in the everyday life of the disciples of Jesus in the Matthean churches, part of their daily resistance.

The heavenly Father's most important characteristic is that one can depend on his care for all his creatures. Building on this, the Gospel of Matthew calls for freedom from anxiety (6:24-34): for day-by-day resistance to submitting to mammon, that is, to a life defined primarily by concern about food, drink, and clothing, a life in which a real dependency on these goods has the last word, enslaving those who live in this way (v. 24). For the Matthean churches such a life is pagan and lacking in faith (vv. 30, 32). By appealing to their heavenly Father's dependable care, these churches reject such a life and, instead of depending on priorities determined by someone or something else, they establish their own priorities: the kingdom and righteousness of God, their king (v. 33). In this passage it is not a matter of renouncing possessions in the sense of a radical ethic for itinerants (cf. the feminist critique of the concept of "radical itinerancy" in Schüssler Fiorenza 1988, 109ff.; 1983, 72ff., and see the more detailed critique in Schottroff 1994, 15ff.; 1995, 3ff.); rather, the issue deals with power relationships. The churches see the possibility of resisting the power of mammon and everything it represents. Later, I will treat their understanding of the righteousness that contrasts with the reign of mammon. Here I show to what degree the churches' life of resistance, their attempt to maintain their identity in the face of the numerous difficulties that are a consequence of Roman rule, is controlled by their concept of God as the caring heavenly Father. The one who feeds (6:26) and clothes (6:30) his creatures can be counted on to care for his human family all the more, knowing full well their need for food, drink, and clothing. Confidence in this Father and King, that is, in his kingdom and his righteousness, sets people free from the slavery mammon imposes. Not the least of the burdens we are thinking about are the great sums the people are forced to pay, the diverse taxes and duties that weigh them down until what they owe makes them slaves, who worry every day about getting what it takes to survive (Unruh, in Kuhnen 1996, 35ff.). The Matthean churches counter this rule with the rule of God, the caring Father. For them, serving God (6:24) means freedom from the power of anxiety, a freedom that comes from the resistance they put into practice every single day.

The heavenly Father's dependable care is also the basis for their hope of being heard, which in the Gospel of Matthew motivates, indeed impels, them to pray (7:7-11). The thrice-repeated summons to pray — the verbs "ask," "seek," and "knock" (7:7) have religious connotations — corresponds to a threefold justification, which must be understood to be all-inclusive. The promise of being heard applies to all, regardless of who is praying: everyone who asks receives; everyone who seeks finds; and the door is opened to whoever knocks (7:8). The men, women, and children addressed in this way are included in the parable that follows: "Is there a person among you who . . . ?" (7:9-10). It is about what they experience every day, an arena wide open for the activity of God. To be sure, the inclusive tendency of the encouragement to pray that is provided by the parable seeking to show a solid basis for that encouragement, is broken by the androcentricity of the language and of the image of God. The word *Mensch* (Greek *anthrōpos*, "person, man"), a favorite term of Matthew's, suggests, based on its use elsewhere in Matthew, that the person in view is a man whose son asks him for food. The argument from the lesser to the greater, culminating in the caring activity of God the *Father* (7:11), supports this androcentric view. However, the fully inclusive tone set at the beginning (7:7-8) won't allow us to see in the parable a story only about men. Finally, the scene — a hungry child asks for food — more readily describes the everyday reality of women, who are responsible for making the bread (13:33) and caring for the children. It is the children who feel most strongly the blows of need and want. As a rule sons are given preference, but even they cannot always count on getting bread (Eltrop 1996, 58). Thus the theme of want and care in the parable takes up the everyday life of women and children in particular. With the granting of the request, the parable pictures an ideal case and uses it to demonstrate God's care. In my interpretation I am not generalizing from the deprivation and hunger that children in particular experience on a daily basis. Rather, I see addressed in them the actual reality of concrete women, men, and children, the reality that evokes the urgent asking, seeking, and knocking. As with the petition for bread in the Lord's Prayer (6:11), here also the plea is for what is needed to stay alive, with no guarantee that it is going to be available. The good gifts that parents can give their children in an ideal situation (7:11) stay the hunger of the children and keep them alive; how much greater is the good that God the Father bestows on all those who ask. In the plea for what is needed to stay alive, freedom from anxiety (itself an act of resistance) assumes its authentic form: it is the expression of confidence that one can depend on God the Father's care — experiences of want to the contrary notwithstanding.

The place in which the Matthean churches serve God, as the Sermon on the Mount portrays it, is everyday life in the patriarchal world, with its claims and power relationships, its demands and tribulations. The concept of God as Father does not spring the bounds of this context, but at a decisive point breaks it open: set in opposition to the imperial fathers' power claim, which reaches right into people's daily lives, is the claim of the heavenly Father. His power is expressed in his knowledge and in his active care for the needs of his "children" (6:8, 32). Care and forgiveness are his gifts, gifts that they desperately need and that they are able to expect and request confidently from their heavenly Father.

On Doing Righteousness

The Gospel of Matthew emphasizes the connection between prayer piety and how one lives. Thus our forgiving others is the presupposition for God's forgiving us (6:12, 14-15; cf. 18:21-35), and the offering of a gift at the altar, to which this Gospel holds firm although it is no longer practiced, cannot happen until reconciliation takes place first (5:23-24). At a central place in the Sermon on the Mount, the instruction on prayer (6:5-15; 7:7-11) is framed by instructions on doing righteousness. At the conclusion, the parable of the wise house-builder (7:24-25) sums up what Jesus' whole sermon is pointing toward: the hearing and doing of what has been heard. Jesus' instructions are firmly anchored in the Torah of Israel. That is made clear by the prologue (5:17-20) to the antitheses (5:21-47). The key word used in this context (Greek: *nomos;* Hebrew: *tôrâ*) is normally translated "law," and the emphasis with which the Gospel stresses the validity of the whole law and the binding nature of the individual commandments is understood as an expression of Jewish legalism, often as a tradition that "Matthew" brought along without really standing behind it. In contrast to this interpretation, which tears apart law and gospel and defames the doing of righteousness as Jewish work righteousness, I consider 5:17-20 as authentically Matthean *and* Jewish. In the name of Jesus, the Matthean churches emphasize the validity of the *tôrâ*, that is, the gift that God entrusted to Israel as a "pledge of liberation, a space for the relationship to God and a foundation for shaping a righteous life" (Crüsemann 1997, 37; cf. also Plaskow 1992, 51ff.). These churches' fidelity to the *tôrâ* applies to all the individual commandments, even the least of them. In this connection the Matthean churches make a distinction between large and small commandments (23:23, 26) and proclaim the double love-command (Deut 6:5; Lev 19:18) the highest and greatest commandment (Matt 22:34-40). This ranking of or giving emphasis to individual commandments would be misunderstood if one wanted to make a distinction in principle between laws about ceremonies and customs or rituals and the commands to love. As 5:17-20 shows, what is important in Matthew is God's good will, affirmed by Jesus (cf. 7:12, 21), which finds expression even in the smallest commandment of the *tôrâ*. This attention to the individual commandments and their validity, which is often smeared with the pejorative concept of "Jewish casuistry," is found in the so-called antitheses in the Sermon on the Mount (5:21-48). In them is expressed Jesus' authority as the churches' teacher, who with authority (7:28) explains the will of God the Father and insists that what matters above all is the *doing* of this will (7:21). Through the antitheses, which are to be understood as contemporary interpretations of the *tôrâ*, the striving for God's kingdom and righteousness (6:33) is shown to consist in the righteous person doing what is required in the context of a particular situation. In this way the authority of the *tôrâ* is not contested but confirmed.

I would first like to explain that by using the example of the last "interpretation" (5:43-48; for a fuller explanation see Gnadt 1997, 65ff.). There is no commandment in the First Testament explicitly calling for love of the enemy; but a command to hate the enemy is missing as well. In its antithetical fleshing out of the command to love your enemy (5:43-44a), the Gospel of Matthew quotes the command to love your neighbor from Leviticus 19:18b. It is precisely this commandment that Jesus validates as the "greatest commandment" (Matt 22:34-40). For this reason the command to love your enemy cannot simply be set in opposition to it. Thus "Matthew" adds "and hate your enemy," and in this way gives the love command in the First Testament a particular interpretation, to which he contrasts Jesus' command to love your enemy. In this antithetical construct an inner-Jewish controversy finds expression — not over the interpretation of the command to love your neighbor (cf. 22:34-40) but over the question of the proper way to relate to enemies. The command to love your enemy is not an expansion or heightening of the love command to include enemies, but it is about something else entirely: How shall the churches treat those who treat them with hostility and persecute them? Jesus' command (5:44) has reference to the unequal relationship between persecuted and persecutors. The difference in power is made to crumble: the hated become those who do good, the mistreated and persecuted become intercessors. Those under attack act with freedom and incorporate their enemies into their fellowship. *Love* for the enemy is understood to be a concrete act whose object is to overcome the enemies' enmity (cf. Rom 12:20b) and in this way finally to bring about a change in the enemies themselves (thus Schottroff 1990, 28ff.). The action Jesus summons the righteous to undertake when his churches are persecuted, namely, countering hate and persecution with intercession and kindness, shows them to be children of their heavenly Father. Here it is not a question of a childish and naïve trust in the power of love, but rather an audacious demand to the mature, who are aware of the risk in the action required of them. At the same time, they are ready, because they are disciples (Matt 5:48), to renounce the use of force, and even to be wronged without resisting (5:38-42; for a feminist critique on the androcentrism of the Sermon on the Mount, cf. Schottroff 1994, 170ff.; 1995, 112ff.).

Inner-Jewish Controversies about Power and Authority

The woes are the culmination of Jesus' controversies with the Jerusalem leadership, beginning with the cleansing of the temple (21:12-17) and continuing in chapters 21–23 with disputes, parables, and woes. Jesus' entry into Jerusalem (21:1-11) reveals a distinction that is of fundamental importance: the people receive Jesus with all kinds of tributes to him as the messianic king. The crowd calls him "Son of David" and the "prophet from Nazareth in Galilee." The children in the temple take up the people's "Hosannas" (21:15). While the people keep on following him as a prophet and teacher (21:46; 22:33), the controversies between Jesus and the chief priests, scribes, and Pharisees intensify. As it turns out, Jesus' superiority has the last word (22:46). That Jesus in his biting criticism opposes various groups of Jewish leaders but not the Jewish people as a whole becomes clear in the disputes, which illumine the burning issues within Judaism at that time. The chief priests and elders ask Jesus about his authority (21:23-27) — an appropriate question in the light of his influence on the people and his messianic actions at the entry and when he cleanses the temple. The Pharisees get their disciples and the Herodians to question him about his attitude toward Roman taxes (22:15-22). The political context of the inner-Jewish controversies becomes clear here. Not only the question about taxes but also the Sadducees' question about the resurrection has sociopolitical connotations. To whom is loyalty owed, the emperor (22:21) or God, who is not a God of the dead but of the living (22:32)? The Pharisees' question about the greatest commandment (22:34-40) finally makes clear God's claim on one's whole life. What is under discussion is the *tôrâ*, which is God's will for God's people. The question Jesus asks the Pharisees about the "Anointed One" (22:41-46) returns to the beginning of the issues under discussion, to the issue of Jesus' authority. If the Christ is not David's son, then he is the Son of God, and his power and authority are from God. What he does and says has divine authorization; God's will is encountered in his interpretation of the Torah.

Embedded in these discussions are parables of Jesus (21:33-44; 22:1-14) in which his criticism of the Pharisees is sharpened. Especially the parable of the wicked winegrowers (21:33-44) is often understood as Jesus' renunciation of Judaism, as his rejection of the Jewish people. This is said to mirror the Matthean community's break with Judaism, their conviction that God had rejected Israel and replaced it with the Christian church. The statement in 21:45 all by itself is enough to refute this interpretation, since it says that the chief priests and Pharisees understand that Jesus is speaking about them and not the people as a whole. In this way "Matthew" gives the reader an important clue to understanding the parable, making it possible to understand it as part of the conflict with the Jerusalem leaders. The parable itself also makes a distinction between the vineyard — Israel — that brings fruit (21:34, 43) and the tenants working in the vineyard, who deny the owner a rightful share of the harvest, mistreat and kill the slaves, and finally even kill the owner's son (21:39). The owner of the vineyard does not punish the vineyard but the evil tenants, by preparing for them an evil end and replacing them with other, reliable tenants. The "replacement theory," according to which Israel or Judaism is replaced by the Christian church because the Jewish people had killed Jesus, the Son of God, is based primarily on verse 43: God took the kingdom away from Israel and gave it to another "people" *(Volk)*, the Christians, the church. The rendition of *ethnos* by *Volk* at this place, however, is to be questioned. Indeed, verse 45 makes it clear from whom the vineyard will be taken, the chief priests and Pharisees. "Matthew" applies the parable to them, as those who are working in the vineyard. They have forfeited their right to do that. In their place, this task will be given to others. One *Volk* is not replaced by another, but the leadership of the people will be placed in other hands. *Ethnei* is used to designate these other, reliable tenants. They will bring the owner of the vineyard, God, the fruits that the vineyard will produce under their care. *Ethnos* is here an eschatological concept that leaves open who on judgment day will finally be shown to be reliable tenants (cf. 13:24-30; 25:31-44).

The parable about the royal wedding (22:1-14) is also to be understood as a conflict over the leadership of the people. In distinction from the parallel account, "Matthew" speaks of a king who sends out invitations to his son's wedding. The parable makes the previously mentioned chief priests and Pharisees, and probably also the Sadducees and scribes, responsible not only for rejecting the invitation to the kingdom of God (22:2) but also for the military violence and destruction that Jerusalem had suffered. It is they, according to "Matthew," who are to blame for the death of the son (21:39). The reference to the destruction of Jerusalem in 70 C.E., which is also found in Jesus' lament over the city (23:37-39) that follows the woes, and to the death of Jesus, sharpens to an immense degree the criticism of the Jerusalem leadership, it is true, but it is not to be mistaken for anti-Judaism. The Matthean churches continue to be convinced that Israel can bring fruit to its God, if only it has good "tenants," and that God is finding in the streets of God's own city guests for the royal banquet.

The reproach addressed to the leaders in Jerusalem — for being responsible for the death of Jesus, for being to blame for the destruction of Jerusalem and for flogging and persecuting Jesus' messengers, thus incurring responsibility for all the innocent blood shed on earth (23:34) — sets the stage for the narrative about Jesus' passion (chapters 26–28). The intention of the chief priests and elders of the people to kill Jesus is explicitly mentioned right at the start, as is their intention to proceed stealthily, so as to avert a riot among the people (26:3-5). Once again the difference between the people and their leaders is emphasized here. At the same time, the fear of a riot at the Passover indicates the political reality that provides the context for the inner-Jewish conflicts: an uprising of the people in Jerusalem, caused by a messianic uprising, could bring about the military intervention of the Romans (cf. Kuhnen 1996, 10ff.). At this time the leaders fear the influence Jesus and his followers have on the people (21:46). Their concern about their own positions of leadership intermixes with their fear of the Romans. The inner-Jewish conflicts over power and authority have to be understood in the context of the Pax Romana, that is, in the context of the ongoing conflicts the Jewish people have with the tyrannical control exercised by their foreign rulers, the Romans. At no time — as Jesus' crucifixion shows to a special degree — are there purely religious, purely inner-Jewish conflicts. The ongoing pressure on the Jewish people to show loyalty in the face of Rome's claims, which encompass every sphere of life, every word one says, makes understandable the intensity of the inner-Jewish conflicts in Jesus' time as well as at the time of the Matthean churches.

The Matthean passion narrative tells how Jesus falls into the hands of the Jewish leaders in Jerusalem. With the help of Judas they can take him captive (26:47-56). They try to incriminate him through false witnesses (26:59-68); they hand him over to Pilate (27:1-2, 11-26) and persuade the people to choose Barabbas instead of Jesus, thereby bringing about his death (27:20). This enables us to understand what caused the people, who up to this point had followed Jesus, to turn against him. The dream of Pilate's wife about Jesus' innocence, which "Matthew" alone reports (27:19), and Pilate's hand washing in front of the people (27:24) emphasize that, in the end, the chief priests and elders are responsible for the death of Jesus. The people are exonerated, yet not relieved of responsibility. The curse called down on themselves by the people *(laos)* remains a problematic statement of great importance in the Gospel of Matthew. The people's cry, which is often understood as a confession of guilt for the death of Jesus, is an expression of their willingness to take responsibility for their own actions. It documents the people's conviction that this death does not make them guilty in the sight of God (Limbeck 1988, 295).

The Gospel of Matthew does not explicitly declare the people to be guilty, but neither does it excuse them, as Luke does in Acts 3:17.

On Entering the Kingdom of Heaven

Jesus' final discourse in Galilee, before he departs for Judea and Jerusalem (19:1), is about the "disciples." Matthew 18:1-35 is a programmatic discourse that reveals a great deal about the Matthean churches. The discourse opens with the "controversy among the disciples about greatness" (18:1-5) as they ask, "Who is the greatest in the kingdom of heaven?" (v. 1). This question's prominence at the beginning of the discourse suggests that the issue of hierarchy is of fundamental importance for the Matthean churches. As I see it, although the *basileia tōn ouranōn* is not identical with the churches in the Gospel of Matthew, it does include them as the "place" in which the kingdom of God can begin to be experienced. Jesus answers the question about greatness with a symbolic action: in the sight of all, he places a child in the midst of the disciples. For "Matthew," in a far more decisive way than for Mark and Luke, this child is the "linchpin" of the church. Jesus gives a child preference over those who ask about hierarchy *within* the kingdom of heaven. Then he calls on them to become like children in order to be able to *enter* the kingdom of heaven. He elaborates on this requirement with the demand that they humble themselves and *become* like this child. The instructions to the churches found among the woes (23:8-12) help us to understand the concept of humbling oneself found in 18:4. What is envisioned is a specific action, renouncing titles of honor and the positions of honor that accompany them for the sake of a community of equals: "But you are all brothers and sisters" (23:8). *Adelphoi* is inclusive and refers to the whole church (cf. 23:1), whose master and teacher is Jesus. His leading enables and requires life together as brothers and sisters instead of hierarchy (23:6-7). This life together as brothers and sisters is also the issue in the call to humble oneself in 18:4 (cf. 23:12). It is not an end in itself, a universal "Christian" attitude, but an action required of the great ones in the church for the sake of the well-being of the little ones, with whom Jesus identifies himself (18:5). How fully their well-being is at issue, but also how fully their well-being is threatened, is indicated by how the discourse continues. It is the great ones who continue to be addressed. They are warned neither to cause the little ones to fall (18:6-9) nor to despise them (18:10-14). The parable inserted here about the sheep that has gone astray (18:12-13) emphasizes how much God is concerned about every one of these little ones. It would be contrary to God's will if even a single one of these little ones was lost from the church. Those responsible for such a thing should harm themselves rather than causing one of these little ones to leave the church (18:8-9; cf. 5:29-30). In these admonitions is expressed the concept of a church as a place of life together as brothers and sisters "from the bottom up." The well-being and dignity of the little ones are the basis for evaluating the church's life. This is the criterion by which the great ones must evaluate themselves. The sharpness of the admonitions about life within the church suggests that there were conflicts within the churches in "Matthew's" time. Standing up for the children and the other little ones in such a decisive way shows that the life together as brothers and sisters that Jesus, the churches' leader and teacher, brings is endangered (Schottroff 1990, 51ff.). One person's well-being and dignity must be defended against the claims of another. Conflicts within the churches are also discussed in what follows. Ways of resolving conflicts between members of the church are introduced: through correction (18:15-17) and forgiveness (18:21-22). The parable of the unmerciful debtor (18:23-35) once again lays the whole weight of the matter on unlimited mutual forgiveness. Conflicts are there, but they are to be resolved.

That the great and small are to live together as brothers and sisters in the church is also the subject of the parable of the laborers in the vineyard (20:1-16) and the denial of the request that the mother of the sons of Zebedee brings on their behalf (20:20-28). That "Matthew" puts the request for preferential positions in the mouth of this woman has to do less with the desire to emphasize a mother's false ambition — the mother of the sons of Zebedee is among the women who follow Jesus and stand before his cross (27:55-56) — than with exonerating the two disciples, who do not come to Jesus themselves with this request. In the final analysis, Jesus' programmatic answer is addressed to the disciples in the Matthean churches: neither domination nor force should shape their relationships with one another. "Discipleship" means, negatively, rejecting dominance and force; positively, it means becoming servants of all, following Jesus' example (20:25-28). From the perspective of the kingdom of heaven, the life of the Matthean churches should be shaped by rejecting titles and positions of honor, and by relinquishing domination, force, and privileges, and by concern for the children, the little ones, the ones who are last, and, above all, by serving. The picture of the judgment of the world in Matthew 25:31-46 shows that the concern for and service to the lowly cannot stop at the boundaries of the church. The *elachistoi* (25:40) were unknown to the righteous as they served them with food and drink, gave them clothing, and cared for and welcomed and assisted them. Thus their surprise. At the same time, the enumeration of the good things they did shows how concrete and ordinary their service was thought to be, their service to those with whom Jesus identifies himself, as he does with the children. Discipleship means service to those who are last, the littlest ones inside and outside of the church, and includes comprehensive concern for their well-being. These instructions suggest that there are social distinctions in the Matthean churches, as well as tensions or conflicts that emerge from these distinctions. It appears that the lowly were being pushed to the margins or even led to leave the churches. But, for God's sake, that dare not be.

Also about entering the kingdom of heaven is the short dialogue between Jesus and the Jerusalem authorities that follows the first parable Jesus uses to begin the controversy that culminates in the woes. The point of the parable of the two sons (21:28-32) is the importance of living in accord with the *tôrâ*, in accord with the will of God: only the first son, who actually goes to work in the vineyard, does the will of his father. On this point, the chief priests and elders agree with Jesus. It is possible that the Matthean churches have to defend themselves against the accusation of holding community meals in which low-level henchmen of the Romans (cf. also 9:9-13) and prostitutes participate and at which men and women eat together (cf. Corley 1993, 152ff.). Matthew is the only Gospel to mention *pornai*, prostitutes, who enter the kingdom of God (21:31-32). It is conceivable that prostitutes were also among the sinners with whom Jesus has table fellowship in 9:10 and 11:19. But "sinners" and "prostitutes" are not moral categories. The feminist discussion of Luke 7:36-50 takes up the issue of whether or not the sinful woman who anoints Jesus is a prostitute. If, using sociohistorical methods, the life situation of prostitutes is made the starting point of the interpretation of this story (as with Schottroff 1990, 317ff.; 1991, 148ff.; with reference to Matt 21:31, cf. Lamb and Janssen 1995), then we gain illustrative material that helps us to get a better understanding of Matthew 21:31-32, 9:10, and 11:19. From a sociohistorical perspective, the prostitution of (Jewish) women is a social, not a moral, problem. As a rule, the women became prostitutes for economic reasons, some of them as young girls, to contribute to the family's survival in this way. The Roman army also plays a big role, as the brothels in Sebaste and Caesarea attest (Josephus, *Antiquitates judaicae* 19.357). Jewish prostitutes offend — by force of circumstances — against the will of God. Thus they are sinners, but God forgives them and rejoices in those who avert their need (Babylonian Talmud *Ta'anit* 1.64b.41). I understand Matthew 21:31-32 against this background. Women and girls who have to provide the (supplementary) income to support themselves and their family as prostitutes are becoming connected to the Matthean churches. They are numbered among the little ones to whom the great ones are summoned to give care and attention. It is not only the chief priests and elders to whom they are introduced as those who go before them into the kingdom of God. Verse 32 stresses that the tax collectors and prostitutes believe John. If one considers the significance that the Matthean churches ascribe to faith (cf. 8:13; 15:28), then the reference to the faith of the tax collectors and prostitutes also acquires a significance within the church. They, who on the basis of their faith enter the kingdom of heaven, are among those to whom the churches are to pay particular attention. Matthew 26:6-13 tells of a woman who anoints Jesus. I consider it possible that this woman, whose remembrance the Matthean churches are interested in preserving (v. 13), is a prostitute, who earned the money for the very costly ointment with her own body. That would be a plausible sociohistorical explanation that does not operate with the hypothesis about the "rich women associated with Jesus," but starts with the assumption that many women associated with Jesus and in the Matthean churches need to work hard and under degrading circumstances to earn their living. That Matthew 26:7 speaks not about a *pornē* but about a *gynē* does not invalidate my sociohistorical hypothesis.

That table fellowship in the Matthean churches brought together men, women, and children is shown by the examples the feeding stories provide (14:13-21; 15:32-39). In 14:21 and 15:38 "women and children" are explicitly mentioned. This creates the impression of two enormous family meals, especially since the Matthean tradition does not have them sit down "in groups" (Mark 6:39) or "in groups of about fifty each" (Luke 9:14). Men, women, and children sit down to eat — a large, colorful group all eating together, just as the guests do at a large wedding banquet at which men, women, and children are present (cf. Matt 22:1-14; 25:1-13). But in contrast to a large wedding banquet with plenty of food (22:4), the feeding stories are about alleviating hunger and need (14:15, 17; 15:32, 34). These common meals, like the acts of healing, are an expression of Jesus' compassion for the people (14:14; 15:32; cf. 9:35-36). This is reminiscent of the interpretation of Jesus' table fellowship with tax collectors and sinners (9:13; cf. 12:7). Jesus heals the sick (14:14; 15:30-31) and feeds the hungry (cf. 6:25-34). Both belong together here. The detailed way in which Jesus' actions are described reminds the churches of their own meals, both in the family and in the church, and also of Jesus' last meal with his followers (26:17-30; this is the view of Luz 1985, 401). They envision what they are themselves experiencing again and again: the fellowship Jesus established at common meals. Jesus, the teacher and leader of the churches, is at the same time the "father in their homes," who takes the bread, blesses and breaks it, and distributes it to those who are in the family. The circle of those who come to enjoy this healing and satisfying fellowship is large (14:21; 15:38) and could become even larger, as the bread that is left over attests (14:20; 15:37). The astonishing abundance is a kind of open invitation. Even more men, women, and children can share in this meal. This abundance points beyond the community meals. It is an indication of the churches' eschatological hope, which has found expression at the end of the Gospel in the so-called missionary command (28:18-20). What this presents as a charge to the Eleven, the feeding stories set before our eyes in the baskets full of bread: the hope that all people, *panta ta ethnē*, both men and women, become disciples, that all people may enter the kingdom of heaven. The feeding stories illustrate the inclusiveness of this hope — men, women, and children — which is also the case with the "missionary charge": "Make disciples, both men and women, of *panta ta ethnē*" (28:19).

That the kingdom of heaven has something to do with the smell of fresh bread and with the abundance of loaves too numerous to count becomes clear in the short parable of the woman and the yeast (13:33). The feminist discussion stresses the contribution of the woman to the success of the whole endeavor (cf. Schottroff 1994, 120ff.; 1995, 79ff.; Ringe 1988, 159): she takes the yeast and mixes it in with the flour. Only then can it do its work. There is a large amount of flour, three measures, that is, about a bushel. It is possible that the parable is picturing how the woman prepares the initial mix for the dough. She kneads the yeast, along with some water, under the bushel of flour, covers the mix, "hiding" the yeast, and letting it sit over night. Then, the next morning, she kneads into the mix two additional bushels of flour and the appropriate amount of water. Strenuous work. This dough also has to sit for a while before, finally, about a hundred loaves can be made. Bread in abundance. The woman's strenuous work, together with the powerful working of the yeast that leavens the batches of flour the woman labored over, throws light on the kingdom of heaven. It concerns a woman's hands, laboring mightily, and with her waiting while the dough is rising. Working on behalf of life and trusting in the mysterious and effective growth that is a gift of God belong together. The kingdom of heaven smells like dough and also like fresh-baked bread. It signifies food in abundance for a multitude of people. The abundance, here as with the feeding stories, is an expression of hope for the fullness of the kingdom of heaven, of which the women and men disciples receive a foretaste at their common meals: women, men, children, tax collectors, sinners, prostitutes, the great and the small. It is an inclusive community, for whose preservation battles must always be waged anew, but over which stands the promise of the "God with us."

On Great and Little Faith

Framed by the two feeding stories, by the vision of many men, women, and children who are healed and satisfied and even have bread left over, is the story of an unnamed woman, a Canaanite, who pleads for the healing of her possessed daughter (15:21-28). The frame is important for the understanding of this story. Both healing and feeding stories tell of the efficacious working of Jesus on his people. The Gospel of Matthew does not distinguish between a feeding for Jews and a feeding for Gentiles (so also Luz 1985, 442). The so-called healing summaries in 14:14 and 15:30-31, which bind the feedings with the healings, are to be seen in the context of the other summaries (4:23-25; 9:35-36; 11:5; 12:15; 14:35-36; cf. 21:14), which refer to the healing of the sick and possessed of the people of Israel. The fullness of salvation that Jesus, as the Messiah of Israel, brings is also emphasized. The people respond to the experience of healing by praising their God, the God of Israel (15:31).

The story of the Canaanite woman recorded in Matthew is unique in the Gospels. The woman remains nameless, like the woman with the flow of blood in 9:20-22, and, like her, she is not described further by incorporation into the structure of a patriarchal family (in contrast to Peter's mother-in-law in 8:14-15 and the mother of the sons of Zebedee in 20:20-23). Nor is any information given about her social standing (cf., by contrast, the centurion in 8:5-13, who pleads on behalf of his son, and the leader of the synagogue who, in 9:18-19, 23-26, pleads on his daughter's behalf). The mother is introduced as the mother of a sick daughter, for whom she is responsible and on whose behalf she intervenes assertively. The category of a "single mother" suggests itself, if this modern expression gives voice to the burden to which a woman is exposed when she needs to support herself and her daughter all by herself. A difficult task, especially since her daughter is gravely ill. The woman's trouble is great, and she is facing it alone. To say that she is discriminated against on the basis of her gender, her ethnicity, or her or her daughter's uncleanness is a problematic way of reading the story. The feminist discussion, especially that between Jewish and Christian women, sensitizes us to the Christian anti-Judaism that is also present in feminist interpretation (on this issue, cf. Plaskow 1994). It is problematic to assume that women in ancient Judaism experienced special discrimination and that by turning to them Jesus crossed boundaries in a unique way. The assumption that Judaism had erected discriminatory boundaries of this kind against Gentiles, which Jesus had the audacity to tear down, goes in the same direction and is also in need of critical revision (cf. Schottroff 1994, 27ff.; 1995, 11ff.). And, finally, the assumption that the sick and the possessed face special discrimination because of their impurity and that in touching and healing them Jesus acts in opposition to the prevailing Jewish thinking about impurity is part of this anti-Judaistic way of interpretation that deserves to be criticized (on this see Janssen 1997, 98ff.). Viewing this woman as an outsider, which is common to all three assumptions, works with the untenable assumption that a normative, prevailing Judaism sets up certain boundaries in order to discriminate against those who do not meet the norm: boundaries of gender, of ethnic origin, and of belonging to the cultic-religious group. In interpreting 15:21-28, consider that the woman's problem is stated. It involves the sickness of her daughter and the attendant concrete social and economic problems, recoverable through social history, that she as a single mother faces in the patriarchal Roman-Jewish society. In the Matthean tradition she is identified as a *gynē Chananaia* (v. 22). This is not to be equated with "Gentile" in the sense of the interpretive category "Gentile Christianity," if this category anachronistically projects back into the first century the strict distinctions between Judaism and paganism and Judaism and Christianity. The Canaanite woman is well acquainted with the language of Israel's psalms and implores Jesus' help with the same words used by other Jewish suppliants (v. 22; cf. 9:27; 17:15; 20:30). She calls Jesus "Son of David" and with this confesses him as the Messiah of Israel, the one who brings healing. Her language and the confidence she has in Jesus allow us to see her as one of the many proselytes and Godfearers who ally themselves with Judaism and its God. She is well acquainted with Jewish tradition and shares the Jewish hope that the whole people will experience the wholeness God has promised. She claims for herself what the healing summaries and healing stories in the Gospel of Matthew deliver: the God of Israel desires the well-being of the people and God's Messiah Jesus brings it to all who need it. Really to all? Or are there limits? *Must* there be — for heaven's sake

— limits? Matthew 15:21-28 is an expression of the struggle over this issue in the Matthean churches. We are accustomed to connecting the setting of limits with discrimination: the insiders determine who the outsiders are, declare them to be inferior, exclude them. With regard to the Matthean churches in their sociohistorical identity as Jewish messianic groups under pressure from the Pax Romana, I would like to propose another paradigm, which understands the struggle about boundaries mirrored in this story as a struggle about the Jewish identity of the people of God. The woman sees more than Jesus does. She sees the bread crumbs that the dogs get when they fall from their master's table. Even the dogs get some of the bread. In contrast to Jesus, the woman has an inclusive vision of the wholeness God offers, and she holds it fast in the face of persistent attempts to get rid of her — and in the end she is proven right. Jesus makes a fundamental change in his attitude. He has been shown the better way. He acknowledges the woman's "great faith" and heals her daughter (v. 28; cf. 9:22). What is so striking about this story is that here Jesus is espousing a position that in the course of the discussion is shown to be "short on faith" and is overcome. That confers authority on the woman's point of view. It cannot be set aside without further ado. On the contrary, it has such an inner weight that it must be wrestled with. The inclusive position that in the end is shown to be correct must first win the day through persistence and superior insight. Through the conflict it gains in contour and persuasive power.

In the course of the passion narrative, which, like the Gospel of Matthew as a whole, is male-dominated, additional women align themselves with Jesus — in contrast to his male betrayers, deniers, and persecutors. His disciples all flee (26:56). Peter's betrayal during Jesus' hearing before the high priest is told as an example (26:69-75). Two maids recognize Peter as one who was with Jesus (26:69, 71). Before them and the bystanders Peter denies Jesus, saying that he does not know him (26:70, 72, 74; cf. 26:33-35). The two women, however, know Jesus, as what they say to Peter shows. Thus, at least symbolically, they are on Jesus' side. While Jesus is being questioned by the Roman prefect Pilate, with the choice between Jesus and Barabbas on the agenda, a woman injects herself into affairs of state: Pilate's wife, who, like Joseph (1:20-23), had a dream about Jesus. Her words, by which she designates Jesus as an "innocent man," are in sharp contrast with the many accusations against him. But her words have no effect. The chief priests and elders persuade the people (27:20), and Pilate, her husband, turns Jesus over to the crowd and washes his hands to signify his own innocence (27:24).

Women are at the cross and at the empty tomb, the two high points of the narrative that follows. They are witnesses to God's demonstrations of power at the crucifixion (27:51-53) and the resurrection (28:2-3). They are present as Jesus dies on the cross (27:55) and when he is buried (27:61), and they are the first to encounter the risen one (28:9). "Many women" were looking on at the crucifixion. They are further characterized as those who "followed" Jesus from Galilee and "served" him (27:55). *Akolouthein* is constitutive of discipleship in the Gospel of Matthew, and *diakonein* signifies the activity to which Jesus accords central significance for living together from the perspective of the *basileia*.

In the story of Peter's mother-in-law (8:14-15), we can clearly see a tension that pervades the entire Gospel (on this, cf. Anderson 1983, 6ff.). On the one hand, there is the fixed group of twelve male "disciples," who are all named (10:2-4), who appear throughout, travel about with Jesus and have a special status in the Gospel, as is shown, for example, by the mission discourse (10:1-15) and other special teaching they receive on numerous occasions, such as the passion predictions (16:21-23; 17:22-23; 20:17-19) and the so-called Great Commission (28:16-20). Even if the Gospel of Matthew modifies the Markan motif about the disciples' lack of understanding (cf. 13:16), the "disciples" do not always appear exemplary. On the contrary, they ask about who is greatest in the kingdom of heaven and must be taught about humbling themselves and serving (18:1, 4; 23:11-12). They turn aside those who are bringing children to Jesus and need to learn that the kingdom of heaven belongs to the children (19:13-15). They count on positions of honor and need to be taught that suffering and serving are a part of discipleship (20:21-22, 26-27). They do not understand the anointing of Jesus for his burial (26:8-9); one of them betrays Jesus for the sake of money (26:14-16); they sleep while Jesus wrestles with the fear of death (26:36-46); they all forsake Jesus and flee (26:56); and, finally, Peter explicitly denies Jesus (26:69-75).

Standing in contrast to this fixed group of "disciples" are individual, usually unnamed women, who fulfill the ideal for "discipleship." Peter's mother-in-law serves Jesus (8:14-15); the "faith" of the woman with the flow of blood helps her to receive healing (9:20-22); the Canaanite woman overcomes Jesus' resistance through her "great faith" (15:21-28); a woman anoints Jesus the Messiah for his burial (26:6-13); two maids know Jesus, the one condemned to death (26:69, 71); in her dream Pilate's wife recognizes that Jesus is an innocent man (27:19). And, finally, many women are present at the crucifixion. They have followed Jesus and served him (27:55-56); the mother of the sons of Zebedee is also among them; two women are present at the burial of Jesus' body (27:61) and are the first to meet the risen one (28:9) and proclaim the resurrection to the "disciples" and, in accord with Jesus' command, instruct them to go to Galilee (28:10). Although these women in Matthew are of central importance for understanding what the discipleship called for by Jesus entails, they go for the most part unnamed and are not included in the group of "disciples." Only Mary Magdalene, at the cross and at the tomb, is referred to by her own name. All the others have no name at all or are designated by reference to their sons(-in-law). These tensions between the group of disciples and the individual women as representatives of "discipleship" and between the high and the low regard for these women can, in the final analysis, be explained only by tensions in the Matthean churches, to which I have already made reference. The different groups, whose interests in part conflict with one another, have a share in the formation, reworking, and transmission of the traditions in the Gospel of Matthew (cf. on this Wainwright 1994, 668ff.; in more detail, Wainwright 1991), as is shown even at the very beginning of the Gospel with the genealogy (1:1-17) and the birth narrative (1:18-25; cf. Schaberg, in Brenner 1996, 149ff.; in more detail, Schaberg 1987). Here the Matthean churches reflect on the origins of Jesus, the Davidic Messiah, through Joseph, his adoptive father (1:25), and on the origins of the Son of God through his physical mother, Mary (1:16, 18). In this passage, in my view, they are also reflecting on the story of their own origins. The five women ancestors who break the genealogy's androcentric, patriarchal line are also the ancestral mothers of the churches, who commemorate at the beginning of their Gospel the presence and vitality of these women. Tamar, Rahab, Ruth, Bathsheba, and Mary throw light on the other women who appear in the course of the Gospel and who, each in her own way, make clear how present, vital, and resisting women in the Matthean churches have been.

LITERATURE

Anderson, Janice Capel. 1983. "Matthew: Gender and Reading." *Semeia* 28:3-27.

Brenner, Athalya, ed. 1996. *A Feminist Companion to the Hebrew Bible in the New Testament.* Feminist Companion to the Bible, vol. 10. Sheffield.

Corley, Kathleen E. 1993. *Private Women, Public Meals: Social Conflict in the Synoptic Tradition.* Peabody, Mass.

Crüsemann, Marlene. 1997. "Tora." In Dagmar Henze, Claudia Janssen, Stefanie Müller, and Beate Wehn, *Antijudaismus im Neuen Testament? Grundlagen für die Arbeit mit biblischen Texten,* 36-38. Gütersloh.

D'Angelo, Mary Rose. 1992. "*Abba* and 'Father': Imperial Theology and the Jesus Traditions." *Journal of Biblical Literature* 111, no. 4:611-30.

Eltrop, Bettina. 1996. *. . . denn solchen gehört das Himmelreich! (Mt 19,14). Kinder im Matthäusevangelium. Eine feministisch-sozialgeschichtliche Untersuchung.* Stuttgart.

Gnadt, Martina S. 1996. "'Abba Isn't Daddy.' Aspekte einer feministisch-befreiungstheologischen Revision des Abba Jesu." In *Von der Wurzel getragen. Christlich-feministische Exegese in Auseinandersetzung mit Antijudaismus,* edited by Luise Schottroff and Marie-Theres Wacker, 115-31. Leiden.

———. 1997. "Die Rache ist mein, spricht der Herr! Zum biblischen Gottesverständnis (Mt 5,43-48)." In Dagmar Henze, Claudia Janssen, Stefanie Müller, and Beate Wehn, *Antijudaismus im Neuen Testament? Grundlagen für die Arbeit mit biblischen Texten,* 59-69. Gütersloh.

Henze, Dagmar, Claudia Janssen, Stefanie Müller, and Beate Wehn. 1997. *Antijudaismus im Neuen Testament? Grundlagen für die Arbeit mit biblischen Texten.* Gütersloh.

Janssen, Claudia. 1997. "Verachtet und ausgegrenzt? Menstruation und jüdisches Frauenleben (Mk 5,25-34)." In Dagmar Henze, Claudia Janssen, Stefanie Müller, and Beate Wehn, *Antijudaismus im Neuen Testament? Grundlagen für die Arbeit mit biblischen Texten,* 98-106. Gütersloh.

Kuhnen, Hans-Peter, ed. 1996. *Mit Thora und Todesmut. Judäa im Widerstand gegen die Römer von Herodes bis Bar-Kochba.* 2nd ed. Stuttgart.

Lamb, Regene, and Claudia Janssen. 1995. "'ZöllnerInnen und Prostituierte gelangen eher in das Reich Gottes als ihr' (Matt. 21:31)." In . . . *so lernen die Völker des Erdkreises Gerechtigkeit,* edited by Kuno Füssel, 275-84. Salzburg.

Levine, Amy-Jill. 1992. "Matthew." In *The Women's Bible Commentary,* edited by Carol A. Newsom and Sharon H. Ringe, 252-62. London and Louisville.

Limbeck, Meinrad. 1988. *Matthäus-Evangelium.* Stuttgart Kleiner Kommentar Neues Testament, 2nd ser., vol. 1. Stuttgart.

Luz, Ulrich. 1985/90. *Das Evangelium nach Matthäus.* Evangelisch-katholischer Kommentar zum Neuen Testament, vol. 1, 1 and 1, 2. Neukirchen-Vluyn.

Plaskow, Judith. 1990. *Standing Again at Sinai: Judaism from a Feminist Perspective.* San Francisco.

———. 1992. *Und wieder stehen wir am Sinai. Eine jüdisch-feministische Theologie.* Lucerne.

———. 1994. "Anti-Judaism in Feminist Christian Interpretation." In *Searching the Scriptures,* edited by Elisabeth Schüssler Fiorenza, 1:117-29. 2 vols. New York.

Ringe, Sharon H. 1988. "Matthäus 13,33: Das Brot geht auf." In Eva Renate Schmidt et al., *Feministisch gelesen,* vol. 1. Stuttgart.

Saldarini, Anthony J. 1994. *Matthew's Christian-Jewish Community.* Chicago.

Schaberg, Jane. 1987. *The Illegitimacy of Jesus: A Feminist Theological Interpretation of the Infancy Narratives.* San Francisco.

———. 1989. "Die Stammütter Jesu." *Concilium* 25:528-33.

Schottroff, Luise. 1990. *Befreiungserfahrungen. Studien zur Sozialgeschichte des Neuen Testaments.* Munich.

———. 1991. *Let the Oppressed Go Free.* Feminist Perspectives on the New Testament. Louisville.

———. 1994. *Lydias ungeduldige Schwestern. Feministische Sozialgeschichte des frühen Christentums.* Gütersloh.

———. 1995. *Lydia's Impatient Sisters: A Feminist Social History of Early Christianity.* Louisville.

Schüssler Fiorenza, Elisabeth. 1983. *In Memory of Her: A Feminist Theological Reconstruction of Christian Origins.* New York.

———. 1988. *Zu ihrem Gedächtnis. Eine feministisch-theologische Rekonstruktion der christlichen Ursprünge.* Munich and Mainz.

Wainwright, Elaine Mary. 1991. *Towards a Feminist Critical Reading of the Gospel according to Matthew.* Beihefte zur Zeitschrift für die neutestamentliche Wissenschaft, vol. 60. Berlin and New York.

———. 1994. "The Gospel of Matthew." In *Searching the Scriptures,* edited by Elisabeth Schüssler Fiorenza, 2:635-77. 2 vols. New York.

Translated by Everett R. Kalin

Gospel of Mark: Women as True Disciples of Jesus

Monika Fander

Feminist evaluations of Mark are quite diverse. Fander (1993), Tolbert (1992), and Kinukawa (1995), for example, stress the liberating aspects of Mark's stories about women, above all, putting positive emphasis on the fact that only women are reported to have followed Jesus during his passion and engaged in a discipleship of service, while the Twelve denied Jesus, betrayed him, and, after his arrest, fled. The authors see in the concept of the *familia dei* (Mark 3:34-35) and in the discipleship of service (10:42-45) an egalitarian concept of the church, which Mark defended against contrary tendencies in his church.

Dewey (1994) ascribes the strong stories about women to oral tradition, Mark himself subordinating them to an androcentric tendency. In her view Mark did not use these accounts to give encouragement to women. Rather they served the didactic purpose of calling a predominately male audience to discipleship. Schüssler Fiorenza (1983) does not see actualized in Mark the paradigm of a discipleship community of equals she has proposed; women are not visible from the start as female disciples. Anderson (1992), in her treatment of the daughter of Herodias (6:14-29), and also the daughter of Jairus, sees dependence on the father, and sees Peter's mother-in-law exclusively in the context of the household. She ascribes the negative presentation of Herodias and her daughter to the fact that they are the only women with power in Mark. She asserts that their negative depiction makes the patriarchal tendencies of Mark clear. Dannemann (1996) makes it clear that Mark depicts women in positive terms not because of their gender, but, as with Herodias, for example, their social status plays a role in the way they are evaluated. Dannemann finds in Mark aspects that both criticize and support patriarchal views. By going unnamed in the accounts, women were often made invisible, and their interests and points of view often unmentioned. It is true that women were shown to be disciples and followers of Jesus, but the presentation of men and women is not evenhanded. Again and again, the failure to mention the women by name is an object of feminist critique.

In my investigation I am referring to the final edition of the Gospel of Mark and not taking the oral tradition into account. A purely numerical comparison of accounts about women and men doesn't seem to me to go far enough. I am trying to show the context in which the accounts about women appear in Mark and what importance they have for Markan theology. The analysis focuses on the role the accounts play, how they are utilized in the context of Markan Christology and ecclesiology and of the Markan concept of discipleship. It asks about androcentric tendencies and attempts with care to say something about the historical role of women in the Markan church.

The Prologue

The prologue introduces Jesus, the central figure. Despite a programmatic announcement of Jesus as Messiah (1:1), his "installation" as the Son of God occurs only at his baptism. Silvia Schroer (1986, 198-225) puts forward the thesis that the dove as a symbol for the Holy Spirit has its origin in the messenger birds of Oriental goddesses of love. She sees the bridge between the pagan symbol and Christology and pneumatology in Philo, who also called the divine wisdom turtledove.

We know that in Philo Sophia, in her function as revealer, is identical with the Spirit. According to Schroer, the wisdom hypostasis is not derived from a particular goddess myth but, as Schüssler Fiorenza also says (1975, 32-33), from reflection on the process of mythologization. In the pericope on the baptism of Jesus in Mark, it becomes clear how the wisdom-symbolical event combines with prophetic tradition. The voice from heaven ("You are my beloved Son; with you I am well pleased"; 1:11) cites Isaiah 42:1 with relative freedom:

> Here is my servant, whom I uphold,
>   my chosen, in whom my soul delights;
> I have put my spirit upon him;
>   he will bring forth justice to the nations.

As the fulfillment of the First Testament promise, Jesus appears as God's servant, elect one and son, on whom the Holy Spirit rests.

> Thus in all the gospels the baptism pericope hands on a Sophia theology in which Jesus is understood as wisdom's prophet and emissary, but by this time also as an incarnation of Sophia, as wisdom, who stands in a most intimate relationship with God. . . . In the earliest Jesus tradition, Sophia Christology is closely tied to a wisdom theology that understands God in feminine form as divine Sophia. The boundless loving-kindness of God is the divine Sophia, whose yoke is easy, who desires to open up the future for the heavy-laden, the outcasts and oppressed, and who requires no sacrifices. The loving-kindness and favor of

(the emissary of) Sophia, however, are rejected, and her prophets must die. (Schroer 1986, 214-15)

The prologue grants the hearers of the Gospel of Mark a knowledge that the persons spoken about do not (yet) possess.

Crossing Boundaries: Jesus' Way through Galilee and the Surrounding Regions (1:14–8:26)

The first main section of Mark tells about the public proclamation of the kingdom of God by Jesus. Galilee is the primary scene. The inbreaking of God's kingdom becomes evident in exorcisms, healings, nature and feeding miracles, in the integration of the socially and religiously disabled. With an increasing rejection of Jesus by family, hometown, and people, we are told of the crossing of boundaries, both of geography and message content. The first section of Mark is about who Jesus is and who belongs to him.

Jesus Makes His First Public Appearances (1:14-39)

The first day Jesus appears he calls four men whose names are given. The concept of "disciple" does not yet appear. The first step to discipleship demands leaving old connections behind, in this case leaving job and family.

The first day in Capernaum (1:21-39) has a programmatic character for Mark and introduces his major themes. The healing of a man with an unclean spirit (1:21-28) displays the first characteristics of Mark's Christology and of his understanding of miracles. This is followed by the healing of Simon's mother-in-law (1:29-31), an event that at first glance does not appear all that significant. It is told in three verses and is reduced to the essential elements of a miracle story. Precisely because of its brevity, it is striking that the woman is indirectly named and that the conclusion states that "she began to serve them" (1:31). At the end of a healing story one expects — if anything at all is said — that the one who is healed, to demonstrate her recovery, eats something, but not that the healer is served. Here it is not simply a woman's activity that is meant — even if that note is also sounded — for *diakonein* is in the imperfect and describes continuing action. In Mark serving is a facet of discipleship for men as well as for women and not a form of discipleship specific to women, as several exegetes believe. What is being told is how the mother-in-law of Simon begins serving Jesus. The story stands in contrast to the exorcism that precedes it. The people who are present in that case react with shock and then with enthusiasm and eagerly broadcast the sensational occurrence — a hunger for sensation shows up here and not discipleship. The reaction of Simon's mother-in-law is different. Her reaction is quiet and sober. She enters into service to Jesus through what she does every day. This description shows what Mark understands discipleship to be. In Mark's Gospel, therefore, Jesus instructs the lame and the blind, or the Gerasene possessed by a demon, to go home after the healing (2:11; 5:19; 8:26).

In the tradition available to Mark, the healing of Simon's mother-in-law, along with 1:32-34, served as a legend about the founding of the church in Capernaum (Fander 1993, 17-30). The beginnings of the Palestinian churches were not associated with the Twelve, who were missionaries and itinerant preachers, but with resident groups, the first disciples in a community, often relatives of the missionaries. Such legends about the founding of the churches frequently tell of the healing of one of the first people in the church. This tradition presupposes a house as location and, possibly, an allusion to serving. How the discipleship of service by women is to be evaluated can only be determined at the end, in the context of the Markan Gospel.

Disciples and Opponents (2:1–3:35)

Mark depicts varied responses and reactions to Jesus. While the crowd — including the sick — enthusiastically presses up to him, Mark at the same time presents various controversy discourses with Pharisees and scribes in 2:1–3:6, at the end of which in 3:6 the decision to kill Jesus already appears. The Markan polemic against the religious leaders is at the same time a polemic against the powerful. The growing throng of an enthusiastic crowd from all over Palestine (3:7-8) is contrasted to the people of Israel as a religious and national entity. From this crowd a people emerges that carries on the tradition of the twelve tribes of Israel, as the call of the Twelve (3:13-19) makes clear. By analogy to the twelve tribes of Israel, Jesus designates and names twelve men as a narrow circle who are sent out, as he is, to preach and cast out demons. It cannot be decided with certainty in Mark whether the term "disciples" refers only to the Twelve or to a wider circle as well. Mark 2:15 and 10:32 suggest the latter. In any case, Mark presupposes a wider circle of followers, to which women also belong (for example, 1:31; 3:35; 15:41).

Even Jesus' family, including his mother (3:20-21), is portrayed negatively. They want to bring Jesus back home, for they think he is insane. The family of Jesus is equated with the scribes, who put Jesus in league with the devil (3:22-30). Traditional ties and relationships are shattered and replaced by a new one: "Whoever does the will of God is my brother and sister and mother" (3:35). Mark adopts the model of the *oikos* (house) for the church, but in altered form. In Jesus' time, the head of the family was the father, under whom the wife, children, and slaves were set in a hierarchical relationship. The Pastoral Epistles, for example, adopt this model (1 Tim 3:2-13; Titus 1:6-9) for a hierarchical and patriarchal ordering of the church. It is different in Mark: the community of disciples consists of brothers, sisters, and mothers. In this picture the father is missing. The name "father" is reserved for God and does not serve to structure the church. This raises the question of the relationship between this picture and the fact that the Twelve are exclusively men.

Crossing Other Boundaries (4:1–8:26)

The collection of parables in Mark 4:1-34 has as a central theme the success or failure of Jesus' mission. Accordingly, the quality of the different soils on which the word of God falls is also the key to evaluating the people in the narratives. The section 4:35–8:26 picks up this theme: opponents and followers are clearly portrayed. The many journeys to the other side of the Sea of Galilee, the healing of a Gentile, and the geographic expansion of Jesus' route (the Decapolis, Tyre, etc.) indicate that the topic is crossing boundaries, both of geography and subject matter. In earlier material, with the exception of its programmatic beginning, all those healed were men. Now, parallel to the theme of crossing boundaries, the healings of three women are reported in close proximity (5:21-43; 7:24-30).

The healing of the woman suffering from hemorrhages (5:25-34) and the raising of Jairus's daughter are connected in a kind of sandwich. Moreover, the number twelve connects them (twelve years of hemorrhaging, twelve-year-old daughter of Jairus). Both stories are animated by the polarities house (synagogue)/not in the house and daughter/not a daughter.[1] Jairus embodies the established side of society: he is a leader of the synagogue, leader of a household with wife and children, within an intact social sphere. The woman suffering from hemorrhages is alone, without a family, physically and financially bled dry. The difference in status and life situation is also visible in where they are to be found. As the story begins we find Jairus next to Jesus, surrounded by the disciples and the crowd; he belongs to the inner circle. The woman, on the other hand, is standing on the outside and has to sneak up on Jesus from behind (5:27). The woman has heard about Jesus. Emboldened by the report, she begins to take changing her circumstances into her own hands. In the sense of 4:20, her hearing of the message may be understood to be the kind Jesus is looking for. To get to Jesus, the woman suffering from hemorrhages shoves her way through the crowd "from behind" and then, as she speaks with Jesus, she is all at once in the inner circle, like Jairus. In the moment in which she gives up her isolation and touches Jesus' cloak, her situation changes and she is immediately healed. It is unusual that no healing word or gesture from Jesus is reported.

---

1. My interpretation of 5:21-43 is dependent, at times heavily, on that of Brigitte Kahl (1996, 61-78).

It is disputed whether or not the Jewish purity laws are to be used as background for reading the account of the healing of the woman suffering from hemorrhages. Speaking in favor: the vocabulary of 5:25-34 is identical with concepts in the LXX version of Leviticus 12 and 15, while ancient non-Jewish authors speak of this illness using different concepts.[2] Against such a reading: the terms "clean"/ "unclean" are not explicitly used here. If one reads the healing of the woman suffering from hemorrhages with the purity laws as background, the woman would be violating the laws in Leviticus 15. She, the impure one, dares to touch the one who is holy. And yet the story does not follow the logic of the thinking about purity. Jesus does not become unclean; instead, the woman is healed. Thus, indirectly, the story would tell about a rejection of this way of thinking. These laws were controversial not only among Christians but also within Judaism at the time of Jesus.

Independent of this controversial issue, the story is to be read as a story about social integration. When Jesus turned around to look at the woman, she, like Jairus, stood in the center, next to Jesus. Jesus acknowledges the woman's norm-defying behavior and calls it faith (Mark 5:34). He addresses her as "Daughter" and in this way grants her a new status. She is a daughter within a new *familia dei*. The healing of the woman suffering from hemorrhages means (for the moment) the death of Jairus's daughter and puts them both in deadly competition with one another.

In contrast with the healing of the woman suffering from hemorrhages, the story of the daughter of Jairus is a story of disintegration. The scene in Jairus's house once again makes his social status clear. The statements "Do not fear, only believe" (5:36) and "The child is not dead but sleeping" (5:39) bring Jesus nothing but mockery from the mourners. The house of Jairus is not standing on the side of faith, and thus of life. Only after Jesus sends away those gathered in the house (5:40), thus separating Jairus and his wife from their social surroundings, is new life also possible for Jairus's daughter. Here we see reintegration of the marginalized into a new *familia dei*. Membership therein is also possible for those who are part of the social establishment, if they break with their surroundings. It is possible that the number twelve in both stories points to the twelve-tribed people as a fundamental socioreligious integrative entity.

As is already the case in Mark 1–3, the person of Jesus demands a decision. Those who are healed in chapter 5 find their place in the *familia dei* and, at the same time, the opposition is formed. Jesus' hometown (6:1-6) and Herod appear as opponents. In 6:16 Herod takes responsibility for the beheading of John the Baptist. His death makes clear what happens to those who fall into Herod's hands,

---

2. For the details, cf. Thea Vogt (1993, 113). The following women exegetes see the Jewish laws as background for 5:24-34: Vogt (1993, 182-99); Hisako Kinukawa (1995, 51-76); Joanna Dewey (1994, 481), and Marla J. Selvidge (1990). Brigitte Kahl (1996, 61-78) does not use this background to interpret the account.

even when, as with John, Herod is sympathetic to the prisoner. For supporters of Herod are also among those who in 3:6 already decided that Jesus must die. The vocabulary with which Mark describes the imprisonment of John is identical with that used for the imprisonment of Jesus (*krateō*, 6:17/14:44-49; *deō*, 6:17/15:1). The role of Herod corresponds to that of Pilate; both are sympathetic to the prisoner. The pressure from Herodias corresponds to that from the chief priests. The daughter is brought in as the instrument in 6:14-29, the crowd in 15:3-11. The behavior of Herodias and her daughter is countered by the story of the unknown woman from Bethany (14:3-9). In 6:14-29 John the Baptist is beheaded, in 14:3-9 the head of Jesus is anointed. Neither John nor Herod stands at the center of the story — instead, two women play that role. And yet the responsibility of Herodias or her daughter for the death of John the Baptist finds no historical confirmation. Rather, we have here a legend with mythic details (the promise of half the kingdom, for example, and the designation of Herod the tetrarch as a king). The daughter's dance, the behind-the-scenes intrigues of Herodias, the serving of the head as a kind of second course on a platter like those used to serve freshly slaughtered meats — all this turns the story into a scandalous, legendary tale that's hard to forget. The daughter's dance, which stimulated many men to erotic (horror-) fantasies as the story was commented on down through the centuries, receives no commentary by Mark. Thus he allies himself with the evaluation that prevailed at that time: such a dance was morally reprehensible. It is also possible that the notion of the immorality found in the houses of Roman rulers, specifically including women rulers, is transferred here to the house of the ruler in Galilee (cf. Dannemann 1996, 125-94).

The daughter attracts attention not as an autonomous individual but through her body. It's quite different with Herodias: she is active and goal-oriented and she bears the primary guilt in the story. According to Mark, John the Baptist's criticism is directed against the marriage between Herodias and Herod Antipas, the half-brother of her first husband. Josephus (*Antiquitates judaicae* 18.5.4) reports that Herodias left her first husband. Josephus considers the divorces of Herodian woman as a violation of Jewish law. New studies of Jewish divorce laws (Brooten 1982, 65-80; Fander 1989, 200-257) raise doubts about Josephus's comments. Herodias was probably able to secure a divorce even according to Jewish, though not rabbinic, law.

Mark 6:14-29 places the principal responsibility for the event on the women. While Herod's feelings are described, Herodias's are not, thus making her appear cold and calculating. What she does behind the scenes makes her appear to be a malicious schemer. The criticism directed at Herodias's behavior is not a criticism of everything women do. It has a component critical of rulers insofar as it is evaluated as an abuse of power. It is part of this critique of rulers that Herodias is one of the very few women mentioned by name. In Mark, it is above all men of prestige or status who are named. Nevertheless, the criticism of rulers in this account has androcentric interests. On the one hand, all that is visible of the daughter is her body, and she is introduced to the public in an almost voyeuristic way. And so much blame is put on Herodias's shoulders that Herod almost appears to be a victim, although, in the final analysis, he is responsible for the beheading. In this way of stating the events, the story is hostile to women.

The portrayal of the women in 6:14-29 is different from the way things are usually framed in Mark, for in the very next story about women the activity of a woman is once again stressed in a positive way. Once more we encounter the clever resourcefulness of a woman "who has no right to make a claim" in the story of the Syrophoenician woman (7:24-30). The parallel to the healing of the woman suffering from hemorrhages lies in the fact that it is a woman who is the predominant actor and in the issue about the daughter. In both instances it is about the healing of a daughter from the perspective of belonging/not belonging or being a child/ not being a child. Once again the issue is crossing boundaries, in geography and subject matter.

Not only locating the story in Tyre but also the way the woman is characterized emphasizes the fact that she is not Jewish. She is a Hellenistic woman, a Syrophoenician by birth. From a Jewish perspective, "Hellenistic" characterizes the difference between Jewish and Greco-Roman religion. "Syrophoenician" distinguishes the woman from Carthaginian and Libyan residents of Phoenicia. Since Jesus has already healed a non-Jew, the demon-possessed man in Gerasa, and, right after the story of the Syrophoenician woman will heal another (the deaf man with a speech impediment in the Decapolis), the question arises why, in 7:27, he is so dismissive, indeed almost racist, in his response to the request for healing. The controversy between Jesus and the Syrophoenician woman is part of a growing line of argument and on principle settles in the affirmative the issue of membership of non-Jews in the Markan church. The debate about the purity laws in Mark 7:1-23 settles the issue on the theological level by understanding the purity laws in ethical terms, as Philo did, making their observance possible for all.

In no other controversy story is Jesus the one who loses or the one who changes his point of view. Here, through her quick-witted reply, the Syrophoenician woman changes Jesus' perspective. She agrees with Jesus, but points to the fact that at the table the children leave crumbs for the dogs. In this way she is acknowledging the priority of Jews over non-Jews. The narration of two feeding miracles in Mark (6:30-44 and 8:1-9) also makes this clear. In 6:43 twelve baskets of bread are left over. Twelve points to the twelve tribes of Israel and, through the term "twelve apostles," it is a symbol for the new *familia dei*. At the end of the story of the second feeding miracle, seven baskets are left (8:7). Seven is the number of perfection; after the meeting with the Syrophoenician woman the table is now also set for non-Jews. It is the Syrophoenician who establishes the connection between the house in which Jesus is staying and her house. It is possible that the establishment of a local congregation is alluded to by means of the healing story, as is the case in a similar manner with Simon's mother-in-law. The setting of the house and of eating could be an indication of that. In this context it is interesting that the Syrophoenician woman owns her own home and, as with several stories about women in Mark, that no male relative is named.

In the *familia dei*, it is by means of eating (bread) that membership (Simon's mother-in-law, Zacchaeus, the daughter of Jairus, the feeding miracles, the Last Supper) or nonmembership (plucking grain, anger over table fellowship with tax collectors and sinners, the beheading of John the Baptist during a meal) is established. It is striking that only four accounts about women are part of stories about this kind of integration or, in the case of Herodias, disintegration.

By virtue of its context, the story of the Syrophoenician woman occupies a key position in the unfolding of Markan theology. The Syrophoenician woman's *Kyrie* is not a polite address but a christological title. The first section of Mark's Gospel deals with the question of who Jesus is and who belongs to him. At the same time, it is shown that the traditional entities, such as family, people, and hometown, reject Jesus and do not understand who he is. Herod's conjectures — that Jesus is John the Baptist risen from the dead, Elijah, or another prophet — are, on the basis of the miracle stories that follow (6:30–8:26), rejected as insufficient. These miracle stories take up First Testament motifs but go beyond them to make clear that Jesus is more than Elijah or another prophet. In this context, the Syrophoenician woman is the first person who makes a proper christological confession, and, as a non-Jew, she points to the Gentile centurion under the cross. It is interesting that even after the account of the second feeding miracle the disciples are still puzzled about who Jesus is, and even regarded as those beset by hardness of heart (8:17). In 8:27-29 Peter does, of course, give the proper messianic confession, but he has a false understanding of it.

The Way to Jerusalem or the Time for Instructions (8:27–10:52)

After Peter's messianic confession, there is no longer a question about who Jesus is but, instead, what the consequences of this are. The new travel destination — Jerusalem — brings into play the theme of the passion. The second main section of Mark (8:27–10:52) consists above all of instructions for the disciples. The three passion predictions give the section its structure, and they are built according to the same pattern: a passion prediction is followed by conflict with some of the Twelve and instruction on discipleship. The second theme to receive emphasis in this section is ethics (dealing with riches, divorce, and life in the Markan church). With reference to the discipleship of suffering and the discipleship of serving, the fact that only women are spoken about in positive terms (15:41) is evaluated diversely in the feminist literature. Therefore, I would like to look at the two concepts of discipleship more closely.

The Discipleship of Suffering

The discipleship of suffering is explained after the first passion prediction:

- 8:31: First passion prediction: the Son of Man must undergo great suffering; he will be rejected by the elders, chief priests, and scribes; he will be killed and on the third day will rise again.
- 8:32-33: Peter refuses to accept the passion prediction and is sharply rebuked by Jesus.
- 8:34-38: Instruction about the discipleship of suffering.

Renate Kirchhoff[3] interprets Markan Christology against the background of Jewish martyr theology, which acquires its characteristic form in the Maccabean period (Daniel and 2 Maccabees). "By their deaths the martyrs secure for themselves a place in heaven, and for their murderers condemnation on judgment day. Through death they atone for the sins of their comrades, whose firmness of faith they strengthen anew, and they bewilder their opponents through the price they are willing to pay for their witness" (Kirchhoff 1982, 3).

Thus Jewish martyr theology, like Markan Christology, has the following elements: an announcement of judgment on your enemies, conversion at the death of the martyr, a prediction of your own suffering and death as a righteous person. Martyrs know about their own imminent death by means of a dream, a vision, a messenger, or a revelation. The *dei* in 8:31 ("the Son of Man *must* die") points to the revelatory character of Jesus' passion predictions. The *dei* does not point to a bloodthirsty God, even though God actually does impose the suffering on the Son of Man (8:33). The *dei* is derived from the context of martyr theology. Since the chief priests and scribes have resolved to kill Jesus if he continues in the way he is going, being true to himself and to God can even mean taking upon himself a violent death. In the final analysis, for the martyr, to take death upon yourself means victory. To draw back means to show that your own message is a lie (= false prophets). The martyr's willingness and the depiction of a decision are always stressed. In Mark, this is the decision on the Mount of Olives. As in 4 Maccabees 10:5, obedience to the will of God is understood as "the freedom of the righteous in the face of the fate that awaits them." Its opposite is the fearfulness that enables violent rulers to enslave others, here Peter's fear. The fact that Jesus here castigates Peter as "Satan" also sets the aversion to suffering in the larger context of the battle between God's power and all that opposes it. The temptation consists in pointing out that it is possible to avoid suffering and in the demand to follow such a course. Moreover, this possibility — that the divine *dei* is not an unavoidable fate —

---

3. I express my thanks to Renate Kirchhoff for providing me with copies of her two as-yet-unpublished manuscripts, as well as for the permission to incorporate them into what I am writing.

shows much more clearly that taking suffering upon yourself is an "act of obedience" (Kirchhoff 1982, 16-17).

The instruction on the discipleship of suffering parallels the fate of Jesus and his disciples. "To take up your cross" is more than a metaphor for "enduring your fate," as the detailed instructions in Mark 13 show. In 13:9-23 trials, betrayal, persecution, and flight threaten Jesus' disciples. The beginning of 8:34 is commonly translated "Let those who wish to follow me deny themselves." It can also be translated "Let them renounce themselves." Self-denial here is not the opposite of self-development and selfishness; rather, the point is the contrast between renouncing yourself or renouncing Jesus. Concretely, for those who are commanded, before a judge or under threat of persecution, to renounce Jesus, discipleship means renouncing themselves and confessing Jesus. The discussion about an earlier dating of Mark offers further arguments for concrete threats facing members of the Markan church.

The reaction of the disciples to this announcement is fear, the opposite of faith for Mark (9:6, 32; 10:26, 32). Fear leads the disciples to avoid the discipleship of suffering: Peter denies Jesus, the Twelve flee after Jesus' capture. It is only (!) the women's discipleship of suffering that is reported in positive terms (15:41). People who at the place of execution allow themselves to be seen as followers of the victim of a crucifixion are also in danger of arrest, torture, perhaps even execution. There is historical evidence for the execution also of women in this context (Schottroff 1990a, 136-37; 1993, 171-72). That the discipleship of suffering is not synonymous with masochistic behavior is shown by the conflict with the sons of Zebedee following the third passion prediction and by the instruction about the discipleship of serving.

The Discipleship of Serving[4]

The sons of Zebedee ask Jesus to let them sit at his right and left hand in the glory to come (10:37). "But Jesus said to them, 'You do not know what you are asking. Are you able to drink the cup that I drink, or be baptized with the baptism that I am baptized with?'" (10:38). Both say that they are. Evidently the Markan church knows about the martyrdom of James (41 c.e.) and possibly also of John. The discussion among the disciples concerns the question of whether a special place in heaven can be earned by death as a martyr. The notion of sitting at the right and left hand takes up images from Jewish martyr theology. God grants satisfaction to those who have experienced injustice on earth by granting them a seat at the judgment of their enemies. *Doxa* not only means glory but also has associations with participation in power and rule. With this pericope Mark is fighting a false understanding of the

---

4. This interpretation is based principally on a lecture by Renate Kirchhoff (1995).

discipleship of suffering. The discipleship of suffering means faithfully standing with Jesus in the hour of distress and, perhaps, taking upon yourself the consequences that go with that. But the discipleship of suffering does not mean masochistically looking for suffering in the hope of gaining in heaven a corresponding reward. Jesus decisively opposes this conception (10:40). Instead, he points to a second aspect of discipleship, which establishes criteria for relationships in the church: "You know that among the Gentiles those whom they recognize as their rulers lord it over them, and their great ones are tyrants over them. But it is not so among you; but whoever wishes to become great among you must be your servant, and whoever wishes to be first among you must be slave of all" (10:42-44).

It is particularly the dispute over rank among the representatives of the Twelve that makes it clear that the decision about a person's rank and standing is God's alone. With the reference to power relationships out in the world, it becomes clear that what is at issue is not simply an altruistic way of doing things among Christians. Rather, specific statements about the structuring of the Markan community are being made that, in accord with Mark's tendency to oppose power-based relationships, consciously distance that structuring from the structures based on power and hierarchy that prevail out in the world. Already in 3:35 Mark favors a strikingly antipatriarchal ecclesiastical model, which knows only of mothers, brothers, and sisters and uses the concept of father only for God, not as a picture of how things are structured in the church. Mark 10:35-40 clearly reacts against disputes over rank in the church, and in 10:42-44 a nonhierarchical model for the church is favored. It is interesting that the disputes about rank among the Twelve are reported, while serving is spoken of positively only with respect to women. As has already been shown, the story about Simon's mother-in-law has relevance for understanding the church's origins, and, with the use of *diakonein* in that story, functions and tasks in the church are also discernible.

Final Confrontations with the Opponents (11:1–13:2)

Jerusalem is reached. The final days before the passion are marked by a last test of strength with the opponents: the cleansing of the temple and the controversies that accompany it (11:12-33), the parable of the murderous winegrowers (12:1-12), and controversies over various themes (12:13-40). It is striking that many of these pericopes have something to do with money. As a conclusion to this section, the sacrifice of a widow is held up as exemplary (12:41-44). What she does is spoken of positively, setting her apart from the rich young man, the temple establishment, and the scribes, who are said even to devour widows' houses (12:40). Jesus indirectly calls for imitating the widow. Let it be briefly noted that in the apocalyptic discourse that follows, the suffering of women who are pregnant and nursing infants (13:17) is highly esteemed.

The Passion (14:1–16:8)

The Anointing in Bethany (14:3-9)

Between the depiction of the plans of the chief priests and scribes (14:1-2) and the betrayal by Judas, the story of the anointing in Bethany is told. Its significance becomes clear when closer attention is given to its structure:

- The anointing (v. 3). On the evening before the passion an unnamed woman breaks into a closed gathering of men and anoints Jesus' head (not his feet) with nard, a very costly ointment.
- Opposition from those who are watching (vv. 4-5).

The anointing evokes strong opposition. Two reasons are given for the opposition to the anointing:

- an economic argument (v. 4): the anointing with the costly nard is a complete waste of money. Three hundred denarii is what a day laborer earns in a year.
- an ethical perspective (v. 5): it would have been better to give the money to the poor.

Justification of the anointing by Jesus (vv. 6-8):

- a rejection of the reproach (v. 6) and counterargumentation by moving from the ethical to the christological level ("you will not always have me" — v. 7).
- the interpretation of the anointing as a symbolic anticipation of a future event, as an anointing for burial (v. 8).

On the basis of this structure, the text is to be assigned to the '*ôt* genre, that is, prophetic actions of a symbolic nature (e.g., 1 Kings 11:29-33; 2 Kings 13:14-19; Isa 20:1-6). Possible elements of such a narrative genre are the order to do something (not spelled out here), the execution of the prophetic sign, and its interpretation. Often the strong opposition of the onlookers is also reported. Prophetic acts symbolically anticipate a future action by God.

The costliness of the ointment and the anointing of the head call to mind the anointing of kings (e.g., 1 Sam 9:16; 16:12-13; 2 Sam 12:7; Ps 89:21 [Eng. 20]; 2 Kings 9:3; among others). By means of Christology the motif of the anointing of kings is connected in Mark 14:3-8 with that of anointing for burial. The woman anoints the suffering Messiah and in this way gives a prophetic sign that points to the death of Jesus and the confession of the centurion and also anticipates the anointing for burial, which is no longer carried out in the scene at the grave. The more provocative the sign, the stronger the opposition: the break with traditional concepts immediately occurs twice. It is not a well-known prophet but a nameless woman who anoints Jesus. Jesus is not a political messiah but one who suffers. The disciples' protest is economic or ethical in nature, which already indicates their lack of understanding.

In Mark 14:3-8 the woman is contrasted to Judas. Holding nothing back, the woman gives away all she has, while Judas, by contrast, sells Jesus for money. Economic thinking comes into play here in an ironic way. As already mentioned, she also exhibits a marked contrast to the daughter of Herodias, who has the head of John the Baptist cut off, thereby making any kind of fellowship impossible. The saying in 14:9, "Truly I tell you, wherever the good news is proclaimed in the whole world, what she has done will be told in remembrance of her," emphasizes the ecclesiastical significance of the woman's act.

Women and Men in the Passion Narrative

The story of the Twelve in the passion narrative is a story of failure. They betray (Judas) and deny (Peter) Jesus and flee at his arrest. The denial scene in the courtyard of the high priest parallels Jesus' interrogation before the Sanhedrin. The servant girl takes the role of the high priest. While Jesus reveals that he is the Son of God (14:61-62) and is condemned to death, Peter denies him in order to save himself. According to Dannemann (1996, 269, 278), the servant girl is not presented in completely negative terms, for she does not become an informer.

The Twelve refuse to practice the discipleship of the cross. They are no longer present during the passion, and, according to Mark's account, they are not eyewitnesses to Jesus' death and resurrection. It is totally different with the women: they observe the crucifixion from a distance (15:40). Contrary to the opinion of many exegetes, it was not less dangerous for women than for men to become known as relatives or adherents of someone being crucified. In this context, Josephus also reports about the arrest and crucifixion of women (*Bellum judaicum* 2.305). Mark 15:41 explicitly says a group of women used to follow Jesus and provide for him when he was in Galilee. That women belonged to the circle of disciples was up to this point not explicitly mentioned. The impression that only men followed Jesus is the result of a clearly androcentric presentation, and here it is corrected. The concept of disciple in Mark is to be read inclusively. Something else stands out: in contrast to the Twelve, women have up to this point appeared only as individuals; in 15:40-41 women are for the first time spoken of as a group. Paralleling the group of three spokesmen for the Twelve (Peter, James, and John), there is now an inner circle of three women, who are mentioned by name (!) — Salome and two Marys.

According to Mark, it is not men but women who are eyewitnesses to Jesus' death and resurrection. And yet, they are not presented in wholly positive terms.

The further the narrative moves away from the execution, the more the faithfulness of the women diminishes. Only two of the three are present at the burial. The behavior of the women at the tomb is thoroughly vexing: within the framework of the passion predictions Jesus stressed several times that he would rise on the third day. Here for the first time something is said about the women that is quite frequently reported about representatives of the Twelve: they listen and yet do not hear. Their interest is directed to the dead, not to the living Jesus. The conclusion (16:8) evokes even greater shock. Although they are expressly instructed by the messenger to tell the Twelve everything, now the women flee, just like the men, and say nothing. With the first application to the women of the disciples' misunderstanding, the Gospel of Mark ends. The conclusion of the Gospel is anything but satisfying for the readers. The narrative reports neither that the Twelve were healed of their blindness nor that the women broke their silence, nor even that Jesus actually appeared. The readers know about the resurrection and about Jesus' true identity only through the narrator. The narrator is the guarantor of continuity. If the readers read the book correctly, they are no longer blind but seeing. The Gospel of Mark's open-ended conclusion is a summons. Jesus' way goes further only when it becomes a model for action in one's own life.

Evaluation

The lack of a name is not something unique to narratives about women in Mark, but is true of most of Mark's stories (the deaf-mute, the rich young man, the lame man, the Pharisees). Including those named indirectly, the following are mentioned by name: the Twelve, especially those who were the first to be called, Peter, James, and John, Zebedee, and, in addition, Judas, Simon's mother-in-law, Jesus' mother, Jairus, Herod, Herodias and her daughter, Bartimaeus, Pilate, Barabbas, Simon of Cyrene, Salome, Mary Magdalene, Mary the mother of James and of Joses, and Joseph of Arimathea. To be sure, those mentioned by name are, for the most part, men. And yet it is striking that almost all the people mentioned by name are depicted either negatively or with ambivalence and often have high social or political status. This observation also applies to the people who are known in the church. By means of the motif of the disciples' lack of understanding and their failure during the passion, the Twelve are depicted very negatively. Salome and the two Marys are also presented ambivalently. It's true that they are the only group whose discipleship of suffering and discipleship of service are reported in positive terms, but in the narrative about the tomb the motif of the disciples' misunderstanding is applied also to them.

Those who are depicted in wholly positive terms are Simon's mother-in-law, Bartimaeus, Jairus, Simon of Cyrene, and Joseph of Arimathea. The last two appear only briefly. The acceptance of Jairus into the *familia dei* is not possible until his social standing falls apart. It is precisely very important narratives like that about the Syrophoenician woman and the centurion under the cross that are handed on with no mention of their names. The omission of names is a part of Mark's theology and his critique of those with authority. It is not a sign of animosity toward women. It is true that this omission of names rendered many of Mark's accounts less well-known to the broad masses than those in the other Gospels.

It is striking how dominant a role is played by the actions of many women: the woman suffering from hemorrhages, Herodias, the Syrophoenician woman, the woman who anointed Jesus, the servant girl, Salome, and the two Marys. A husband is never mentioned, the woman's family context with relative infrequency. Simon's mother-in-law is, of course, defined by her relationship to Simon, but Simon plays no role in Mark 1:29-31. Her work in the house does not restrict women to this context; rather, it is part of the setting for a legend about the founding of a church. Jesus' mother is also defined with respect to her family context, but it is precisely in this role that she acts in a negative way. The restriction of women to a particular stereotype is nowhere to be seen in Mark, with the exception of Herodias and her daughter. With respect to two Markan themes, Christology and discipleship, the narratives about women play a special role. In 1:14–8:26 the issue is who Jesus is. The disciples' lack of understanding in the first main section of Mark has a christological focus. Although the miracles surpass First Testament parallels, the disciples see and yet fail to see, hear and yet fail to hear. Their position is unchanged in the entire main section. They exhibit the same uncomprehending point of view, for example, after the stilling of the storm (4:35-41), the walking on the water (6:45-53), and the two feeding miracles. Even after the second feeding miracle they are worried about their failure to bring bread (8:14). Jesus says to them, "Do you still not perceive or understand? Are your hearts hardened?" (8:17). The disciples' point of view is twice described, like that of Jesus' opponents, as obduracy and hardness of heart (6:52; 8:17). In this context the Syrophoenician woman's *kyrie* is of critical importance. She does what Israel and the disciples have up to this point not done: she is the first person to make a christological confession. As a Gentile woman she builds the bridge to the Son-of-God confession by the Gentile centurion under the cross. The discipleship of suffering and the discipleship of serving are spoken of in positive terms only with reference to women. In the light of the persecutions to which the Markan church was exposed, the discipleship of suffering is to be understood literally. It is the women who are courageous. The discipleship of serving corrects a false understanding of the discipleship of suffering. The concept is critical of hierarchy and authority and makes statements about the way Mark wants to see the church structured. Mark 10:35-40 already presupposes a conflict in the Markan church, with the Twelve appearing as its representatives.

The Twelve as a sociocultural entity, by allusion to the twelve tribes of Israel, is comprised of twelve men. At the same time, Mark operates with the disciples' lack of understanding. Set over against the model of the Twelve is the model of the *familia dei*, which is strikingly antihierarchal and antipatriarchal.

Despite this basically positive perspective, the portrayal of women as disciples is androcentric, for their role only becomes visible in 15:41. It is interesting that in 16:1-8 the disciples' lack of understanding is applied to the women for the first time. The reader is given assurance about the message of the resurrection only through what the author says. The Markan church found itself in a desperate situation, which led it to doubt everything it had taken for granted and to waver in its faith. The open ending suggests the possibility that everything could end in failure and takes the form of an appeal to the reader.

LITERATURE

Anderson, Janice Capel. 1992. "Feminist Criticism: The Dancing Daughter." In *Mark and Method: New Approaches in Biblical Studies,* edited by Janice Capel Anderson and Stephen D. Moore, 115-33. Minneapolis.

Brooten, Bernadette. 1982. "Konnten Frauen im alten Judentum die Scheidung betreiben? Überlegungen zu Mk 10,11-12 und 1 Kor 7,10-11." *Evangelische Theologie* 42:65-80.

Dannemann, Irene. 1996. *Aus dem Rahmen fallen. Frauen im Markusevangelium. Eine feministische Re-Vision.* Berlin.

Dewey, Joanna. 1994. "The Gospel of Mark." In *Searching the Scriptures,* edited by Elisabeth Schüssler Fiorenza, 2:470-509. 2 vols. New York.

Fabella, Virginia, and Mercy Amba Oduyoye, eds. 1992. *Leidenschaft und Solidarität. Theologinnen der Dritten Welt ergreifen das Wort.* Lucerne.

Fander, Monika. 1992. "Frauen in der Nachfolge Jesu. Die Rolle der Frau im Markusevangelium." *Evangelische Theologie* 5:413-32.

———. 1993. *Die Stellung der Frau im Markusevangelium. Unter besonderer Berücksichtigung kultur- und religionsgeschichtlicher Hintergründe.* Münsteraner theologische Abhandlungen, vol. 8. 3rd ed. Altenberge. 1st ed. 1989.

Kahl, Brigitte. 1996. "Jairus und die verlorenen Töchter Israels. Sozioliterarische Überlegungen zum Problem der Grenzüberschreitung in Mk 5,21-43." In *Von der Wurzel getragen. Christlich-feministische Exegese in Auseinandersetzung mit Antijudaismus,* edited by Luise Schottroff and Marie-Theres Wacker, 61-78. Leiden, New York, and Cologne.

Kinukawa, Hisako. 1994. *Women and Jesus in Mark: A Japanese Feminist Perspective.* Lucerne.

———. 1995. *Frauen im Markusevangelium. Eine japanische Lektüre.* Lucerne.

Kirchhoff, Renate. 1982. "Jesus als Märtyrer bei Markus. Studien zum Leidensweg Jesu als dem Märtyrergeschick des Messias." Unpublished manuscript, Heidelberg.

———. 1995. "'Um sein Leben zu geben als Lösegeld für viele' (Mk 10,45). Feministische Rezeption neutestamentlicher Deutungen des Lebens und des Todes Jesu." Lecture on feminist theology at the Evangelical Academy in Tutzing, September 9, 1995.

Schottroff, Luise. 1990a. "Frauen in der Nachfolge Jesu in neutestamentlicher Zeit." In Luise Schottroff, *Befreiungserfahrungen. Studien zur Sozialgeschichte des Neuen Testaments*, 96-133. Munich.

———. 1990b. "Maria Magdalena und die Frauen am Grabe Jesu." In Luise Schottroff, *Befreiungserfahrungen. Studien zur Sozialgeschichte des Neuen Testaments*, 134-59. Munich.

———. 1993. *Let the Oppressed Go Free: Feminist Perspectives on the New Testament.* Louisville.

———. 1994. *Lydias ungeduldige Schwestern. Feministische Sozialgeschichte des frühen Christentums*, 297-325. Gütersloh.

———. 1995. *Lydia's Impatient Sisters: A Feminist Social History of Early Christianity.* Louisville.

Schroer, Silvia. 1986. "Der Geist, die Weisheit und die Taube." *Freiburger Zeitschrift für Philosophie und Theologie* 33:198-225.

Schüssler Fiorenza, Elisabeth. 1975. "Wisdom Mythology and the Christological Hymns of the New Testament." In *Aspects of Wisdom in Judaism and Early Christianity*, edited by Robert L. Wilken. Notre Dame, Ind., and London.

———. 1983. *In Memory of Her: A Feminist Theological Reconstruction of Early Christian Origins*, esp. 316-23. New York.

———. 1988. *Zu ihrem Gedächtnis . . . Eine feministisch-theologische Rekonstruktion der christlichen Ursprünge*, esp. 385-93. Munich.

Selvidge, Marla J. 1990. *Woman, Cult, and Miracle Recital: A Redactional Critical Investigation of Mark 5:24-34.* Lewisburg, Pa.

Tolbert, Mary Ann. 1992. "Mark." In *The Women's Bible Commentary*, edited by Carol A. Newsom and Sharon H. Ringe, 263-74. London and Louisville.

Vogt, Thea. 1993. *Angst und Identität im Markusevangelium. Ein textpsychologischer und sozialgeschichtlicher Beitrag.* Novum Testamentum et Orbis Antiquus, vol. 26. Fribourg and Göttingen.

FOR FURTHER READING

Dewey, Joanna. 2006. "Women in the Gospel of Mark." *Word and World* 26, no. 1:22-29.

Diebold-Scheuermann, Carola. 2008. "Frauen in Panik? Überlegungen zur Osterbotschaft des Markusevangeliums." *Christlich pädagogische Blätter* 121, no. 1:48-53.

Kraemer, Ross Shepard, and Mary Rose D'Angelo, eds. 1999. *Women and Christian Origins.* New York.

Melzer-Keller, Helga. 1997. *Jesus und die Frauen: eine Verhältnisbestimmung nach der synoptischen Überlieferung.* Freiburg im Breisgau.

Metternich, Ulrike. 2000. *"Sie sagte ihm die ganze Wahrheit". Die Erzählung von der "Blutflüssigen" feministisch gedeutet.* Mainz.

Miller, Susan. 2004. *Women in Mark's Gospel.* Journal for the Study of the New Testament: Supplement Series, vol. 259. London and New York.

Strube, Angelika Sonja. 2000. *"Wegen dieses Wortes . . ." — Feministische und nicht-feministische Exegese im Vergleich am Beispiel der Auslegungen zu MK 7.24-30.* Münster, Hamburg, et al.

Swartley, Willard M. 1997. "The Role of Women in Mark's Gospel: A Narrative Analysis." *Biblical Theology Bulletin: A Journal of Bible and Theology* 27, no. 1:16-22.

Translated by Everett R. Kalin

Gospel of Luke: The Humbled Will Be Lifted Up

Claudia Janssen and Regene Lamb

The Gospel of Luke follows the structure of Mark's Gospel (except for the omission of Mark 6:45–8:26); it presents parts of the Q source, which is also the basis for Matthew's Gospel, and it reworks parts that are found exclusively here (special material). In the following discussion we will focus especially on these parts, because they contain many narratives in which women play a central role. However, this does not mean that we are limiting ourselves in terms of content, since themes central to the entire book are addressed in the special material. In the history of the interpretation of Luke, it was often assumed that the special material could be based on a female source. Many called Luke the "women's evangelist." An analysis of these texts is intended to show whether the community reality reflected in Luke's Gospel becomes transparent by revealing the actions of women, or whether it does not instead intentionally circumcise women's activity. This latter view is taken particularly in recent feminist discussion. Our purpose here is to make women's practice, their hopes and longings for change, their visions and their actions visible through the texts and to uncover the conflicts that arise in this connection. We see our research as a contribution to the development of a feminist social history of early Christianity.

Many speculative hypotheses have been proposed regarding the origin of these texts and their place in the Gospel. Luke 1:2 especially has been assumed to come from Jewish-Christian circles, and many authors assume this is true for the rest of the special material as well. But even if one presupposes Jewish or Jewish-Christian authorship of these texts, the question remains how Luke relates to these sources. It is often hypothesized that he incorporated the sources available to him into his own presentation of the *Heilsgeschichte* (redemptive history), and edited accordingly. We assume, however, that the texts of the special material represent ideas and theological foundations of Lukan communities and originated in their circles. They were incorporated into the Gospel not merely for historical reasons, but instead represent core texts of Lukan theology. Furthermore, we assume that the Lukan writings are to be located in Jewish-Christian circles, based on their reworking of First Testament traditions and their creative interaction with them. Many elements locate the community within the Jewish diaspora: their eschatological expectations and the descriptions of the kingdom of God as "near at hand," their belief in the Jewish Messiah Jesus, and their confession of faith in the hope of Israel, to which they hold fast despite the missionary activity practiced among them by Gentile peoples. We see the Lukan churches as a part of the Jewish-prophetic-messianic liberation movement within the Pax Romana.

The *Heilsgeschichte* (Redemptive History)

Scholarly representations of Luke's redemptive history have been especially influenced by the conceptual framework posed by Hans Conzelmann, who sees a tripartite structure to the narrative: (1) the period of the law and the prophets, in which Israel is the bearer of the promise (from the creation to John the Baptist); (2) the time of Jesus, which is characterized by the realization of salvation; (3) the time of the church, which henceforth is the bearer of salvation (from Jesus' ascension to heaven until the parousia, the second coming). According to Conzelmann's scheme, Luke is making clear in his work that the beginnings of Christianity are closely tied to the synagogue and the temple, but that "the Jews" hardened their hearts and did not fulfill their responsibility as a chosen people. Therefore the church as bearer of salvation is becoming "Israel." In this view, Christians fulfilled the law at the beginning but were freed from it in the course of history.

We wish to critique this presupposition in its very foundations. The concept of a Gentile Christianity free of the law in Second Testament times must be fundamentally disputed (see Schottroff 1994, 27-30; 1996; 1995a, 11-14). The discriminatory view of the "law," that is, the Torah, does not yet exist in biblical times; it cannot be considered a stereotype used to marginalize Judaism until the postbiblical era. There is no longer any basis for dividing the history of redemption in Lukan writing into three parts. Instead it should be considered against the background of Jewish history in the first century. The experiences of devastation and the destruction of Jerusalem in 70 C.E. are of central importance here. They necessitated a correction to the messianic expectations. The community saw itself confronted with the question whether their expectation of an end to all oppression and all suffering (cf. 1:46-55; 2:38) had not been totally annihilated by the victory of the Romans and the destruction of the temple. Was Jesus really the promised Messiah? Luke's Gospel makes it clear that Jesus' suffering and the suffering of the people are part of the story of salvation (cf. 24:21, 44-49). With Jesus' coming, the kingdom of God was not yet fully at hand; God's reign would only be fully realized with the parousia. The eschatological coming of the Messiah will bring liberation; the destruction of Jerusalem and the occupation by the Romans are limited (cf. 21:24, 28). In the Lukan writings that are universally directed toward mission among the peoples, too, salvation remains linked with Israel (cf. Acts 1:6; 26:6). With Jesus, the Jewish Messiah has come into the world. His presence signals the beginning of the messianic era of salvation in which the nations, too, will participate if they confess faith in him (cf. Luke 2:32).

Thus Luke's Gospel does not speak of Israel being superseded in the course of redemptive history (Stegemann 1993). Luke is to be seen as a Jewish book. This is no Gentile Christian speaking who must promote his own tradition at the expense of Judaism. All the conflicts described in the book should be seen primarily as internal disputes among the Jews. One must also bear in mind that every statement in the book occurs in the context of the Roman occupation. The texts of the Second Testament can only be understood in the context of the Roman Empire. The Gospel according to Luke points to this especially by narrating all events in the context of the respective periods of political rule (cf. 1:5; 2:1; 3:1; 9:7).

Gospel of Women or Testimony to Their Subordination?

Even in the feminist discussion of Luke's Gospel the emphasis has been on its tendency to impose limits on women. While it concedes that Luke shows remnants of traditions that reflect gender-equal practices and signs of women serving in leadership positions, it finds that the patriarchal context in which these traditions were located robbed them of their expressive voice and their liberating force. Feminist exegetes have found women in Luke limited to passive, maternally nurturing, and silent roles. They assert that traditional gender roles within the worshiping communities were not eliminated, but only modified. The subordination and service of women to their husbands in patriarchal marriages are seen by some as shifting now to the disciples (Seim 1994). The women's role in the church communities is at home, while the men proclaim the gospel in the public sphere, it is argued. This image of women in the early church, feminists claim, was projected back to the beginnings (Kahl 1987, 145). Thus feminist scholarship on Luke fundamentally questions the widespread acceptance of Luke as "women's evangelist," which is often based only on the number of women mentioned in the Gospel (e.g., Schaberg 1992). Most studies of Luke's Gospel are based on the concept of "patriarchalism of love" that is claimed to have been practiced in the church communities. According to this view, the so-called delayed parousia necessarily resulted in accommodation to the Hellenistic-Roman world. Thus the Christian communities adopted the patriarchal social order that was based on the rule of the paterfamilias over women, children, and slaves (e.g., Schaberg 1992; Stegemann and Stegemann 1995). However, the argument continues, this hierarchy is superseded "in Christ," with the practical consequence that the father as head of the family ruled over his subordinates and was honored and respected by them. "Luke" is seen as the Gentile Christian who sought harmony with the Roman-Hellenistic society and therefore vehemently insisted that women be relegated to the domestic sphere.

Such a consistent practice of "patriarchalism of love" is never explicitly mentioned in Luke. Furthermore, the "delayed parousia" thesis must be regarded as a theological construct of the modern era; it does not correspond to the concepts of time inherent in Jewish-Christian eschatological expectations. Eschatological thinking is not linear. It describes the hope of people struggling for liberation that God stands with them in the present, in their struggle for just social relations (Sutter Rehmann 1995; Schottroff 1995b; 1998). These hopes are still alive in Luke's Gospel; they become powerfully tangible through the testimony of women in the Magnificat (1:46-55), for example.

Could gender relationships in Luke be read differently if one assumes that it arises out of the Jewish tradition, which is not relinquished in favor of accommodating to Roman-Hellenistic culture? A review of the texts shows no grounds for a monolithic view of gender relations in the Lukan writings. The results of our study are contradictory. (1) Important women who are known by name appear in Luke alongside women who are not known by name and are rendered invisible. More men than women are named (the twelve disciples are especially highlighted), but many also remain nameless. (2) In many cases the matter at hand is demonstrated with parallel examples of women and men, whatever the context (cf., e.g., 7:12 and 8:42; 13:10-17 and 14:1-6; 15:4-7 and vv. 8-10). (3) Besides traditions that reveal actions and preaching by women, some narratives deny their activities (e.g., 14:26; 8:21), as contrasted with source material in Mark. Consequently, every statement must be studied on its own; hasty generalizations are to be avoided. When analyzing texts about women, therefore, one should always ask how they are represented, whether they are named, what roles they play in the context of the narrative and compared with men, and whether they speak or are silent. One should always ask who could have what interest in how the narrative is constructed and what conceptual framework of gender relations the narrative bias reflects. Luke as a whole should be understood as a document testifying to a dynamic process of working out differences over questions of equal rights; it shows evidence of conflicts that had to be worked through in everyday life. The women working and living in the church communities do not allow others to silence them; they bring their theological views into the texts. They clearly show what the coming of the realm of God means concretely for them and their sisters. Their story is not silenced even when in many cases they remain nameless. Many texts keep their memory alive despite numerous attempts to dim it. (On the women disciples in the Gospel of Luke, see Bieberstein 1998.)

On the Question of Authorship

The existence of contradictory traditions passed down through parallel narratives raises the fundamental question whether the prevalent concept of "author" can apply to Second Testament texts. In general, "Luke" is described as a Hellenistic Gentile Christian. His linguistic skills are considered notable, pointing to his upper-class origins and his good education, which must have included Greek rhetoric as well as methods of interpretation of Jewish scripture. Luke is described as a Greek who turned early on to the Jewish religion. Though scholars always point out in the course of their exegeses that the Gospels reflect diverse oral, and to some extent written, sources, the history of these sources takes a back seat to the figure, the influence, and the presumed theology of the author. In the last analysis, a Gospel appears as the work of a single, significant person.

However, there was no such person as one male author "Luke" who alone organized and added to the received source material. Indeed, we should assume as given a process by which texts arise out of community life in the churches, where men and women together composed them, documenting their hopes, expectations, visions, and conflicts. Individual contributions by a single author are few and should be regarded as minimal (Schottroff 1995b, 206-9; 1998, 212-14).

Many have argued that the Lukan writings, because of their tendency to curry favor with Rome, are to be read as having the apologetic intent of presenting Christianity as politically harmless. However, we do not find this interpretation consistent with all the message of this text. The majority of narratives are stories of liberation from unjust oppressive structures. The hope for salvation (cf. 21:24, 28) is a concrete historical-political hope for an anticipated end to the Roman occupation (Cassidy 1978). Presumably the men and women authors as well as the intended audience are Jewish-Christian communities who already have many Gentile Christian members. The language, which picks up on the Septuagint, contains numerous diverse allusions to First Testament traditions. The fact that they cling to Jewish expectations of the coming time of salvation clearly demonstrates this (Busse 1991). The Magnificat especially characterizes the Lukan material as a document of a prophetic-messianic liberation movement within the Pax Romana (cf. 1:71; 4:18ff.). Stories of encouragement from the Bible, the First Testament, were told here and brought into the present context. In these communities people reached out to one another with help and support. These worshiping communities are also the place where traditions of resistance reside; they expect the liberation of Israel and are contributing through their actions and prayers as a community to the realization of the realm of God. Luise Schottroff calls the Gospels a "hymnbook of the poor" to emphasize their community character and origin (1995b, 207; 1998, 213).

Dating the Text

One can assume that Luke was written down after the destruction of the temple in 70 C.E. This experience of catastrophe raised existential questions about Jewish identity and the validity of messianic expectations. The Gospel represents a theological reflection about this experience. In spite of many conflicts and theological differences of opinion, the Lukan worshiping communities still considered themselves Jewish. In Luke, one cannot yet assume a division that would have led to separate organizational structures. The date of the Lukan writings is therefore prior to the Bar Kokhba uprising (133-135 C.E.), which can be seen as the decisive date for the separation of Judaism and Christianity (Schottroff 1996).

Luke 1–2 as Key to the Understanding of the Gospel

Luke 1–2 should be understood as the introduction to the entire body of writings; these two chapters raise almost all the theological themes that are then picked up and further developed. The description of the larger community of people and their actions found at the beginning of the Gospel sets the overall standards for the values and principles of the churches for discipleship as followers of Jesus. Elizabeth, Mary, Zechariah, Joseph, Simeon, and Anna prefigure the path of John and Jesus, and that of the other men and women disciples. Their stories provide a key to understanding the events that follow. They personally attest to the continuity with the First Testament traditions; as righteous Jews they see in Jesus' birth the sign of the coming of the messianic era of God's salvation.

Elizabeth — the Exaltation of a Humiliated, Old, Barren Woman (Luke 1)

Elizabeth is the central figure of Luke 1. Her pregnancy structures the chronology of the narrative (cf. 1:24, 26, 36, 56). Her autonomy is emphasized. As one of the few women in the Gospel, she utters a powerful prophecy. Elizabeth is described as a righteous Jewish woman — an extraordinary assessment of the life of a woman who has remained childless into old age (1:6). It is made very clear here that her infertility is not associated with sins or offenses. In the beginning of the narrative, however, she is not the actual subject; she is introduced only as the wife of Zechariah, who is the subject (1:13, 18, 24). From the moment she raises her song of praise (1:25), she appears as an autonomous person, as Elizabeth (cf. 1:36, 40-45, 57). The story of her suffering as a barren, old woman is made visible and serves as a key to understanding the message of the entire chapter. God stands with women and will liberate the people from oppression and humiliation. In her hymn of praise Elizabeth articulates her experience of liberation and her special relationship with God. Here she anticipates the central messages of the Magnificat: God "looked favorably on me and took away the disgrace I have endured among my people" (1:25). At the same time, her words accuse this society that assigned her to one of the lowest rungs of the hierarchical ladder and denied her true womanhood because of her failure to produce a child. She has preserved a sense of her dignity in spite of the insults and humiliations she likely experienced, and she has lived "blamelessly before God" (1:6). She is a believing Jew who is firmly rooted in her traditions, names her son (1:60), and in addition enables Zechariah to find his faith again.

In spite of this, Elizabeth has remained one of the "unknown" women in the tradition of interpretations of Luke. Presumably because of her age and her female gender, many interpreters have seen her merely as an extra, as mother of John the Baptist. Elizabeth is a postmenopausal elderly woman, likely about sixty years old. In gynecological studies of antiquity, older women are rarely encountered because they are past childbearing age and therefore not of interest to the patriarchal mind. The fact that she becomes pregnant in old age flies in the face of all previous experience and the medical science of the time. The motif of the barren woman that is given new relevance in Luke 1 clearly establishes the close link between this text and First Testament traditions and texts. This motif serves to articulate the fears and despair of the men and women authors, but at the same time also their hope for an end to their suffering and for God's intervention. The experience of an old, childless woman who conceives and bears a child through God's help signifies the connection between life and death. At the same time, it describes the experiences that men and women disciples had of the resurrection after the death of Jesus. It connects the beginning of the Gospel with its ending, the women of the First Testament with those of the Jesus movement, Zechariah with Abraham and the doubting disciples, Jesus with the sons of the matriarchs.

Through the emphasis placed on the pregnancies of Elizabeth and Mary, the reader's attention is focused on the body, the pregnant mother-to-be, which characterizes the two women in a particular way. They seem defined and limited to their role as pregnant women, mothers, and nurturers (Schaberg 1992). In Luke 11:27 we see a similar understanding when Mary, the mother of Jesus, is identified solely in her childbearing function. She is blessed by a woman for only one reason — that she bore and raised her child. She herself, her identity, her capacity for action and independence remain invisible. In Luke 11:28 this narrow view of women is explicitly criticized. Jesus' reply in this context should be taken as a critique of the reduction of women to their capacity as childbearers and mothers. Women can have an autonomous existence; mothers can become disciples too. Elizabeth and Mary are not defined by their role as mothers. Elizabeth praises Mary in 1:45 not for her motherhood, but for her faith. Frequent pregnancies characterize the everyday life of women of antiquity in a significant way. Given this background, to describe the "mother-to-be" as a locus of God's redemptive action means to recognize women's capacity to bear children as a special fact of everyday life that can serve as a springboard for women's activity. This activity is not related solely to nurturing and raising their children, but extends to other areas of social and religious life. God's activity is very closely connected with the creaturely world, with the way human beings come into being and grow, and with their bodily nature. Luke's narrative does not devalue the body, but describes it as fundamental to human being in relationship to God and other human beings.

The Magnificat — Gospel of the Poor (Luke 1:46-55)

Mary sets out on her way to see Elizabeth. Her autonomous decision to enter as a slave of God *(doulē kyriou)*, an acting subject, into God's redemptive activity, and as a disciple into discipleship, foregrounds her actions and her active character in the narrative. Elizabeth and Mary have often been described as in competition with one another. Mary, as mother of God, is held in higher esteem than Elizabeth, as if the miracle of Mary's pregnancy makes that of Elizabeth even more miraculous. What Luke 1:39-56 describes, however, is quite different: the two women's solidarity with one another binds them into a community of mutual support and assistance. Elizabeth welcomes Mary *en gynaixin,* into the community of women. This signals the creation of a vision of women as able to survive and exist autonomously outside of patriarchal marriage. This community offers a model for a structure of life in which an ethic of mutuality and brotherly and sisterly relationships can become everyday reality. Together they celebrate their liberation and the liberation of the entire people. Their descriptions evoke associations of Zion and its traditions (Janssen 1998, 133). As prophets and disciples who stand firmly rooted in the traditions of the First Testament, as old and new Zion, they praise God. The Magnificat should be seen as their common song — not because the extant manuscripts attribute it sometimes to one, sometimes to the other, but because the Magnificat is embedded in the relationship of the two women (1:39-56). It makes manifest the fact that the encounter of the two women is not merely about individual experiences. The Magnificat describes the signposts of the kingdom of God in objective detail: the reversal of social, economic, and political conditions, the uplifting of those who have been downtrodden or devalued, the option for the poor, the decisive measure of which is the degree to which it is applied to women (Schottroff 1994, 282; 1995a, 193).

In Mary and Elizabeth we meet two Jewish women who live in Palestine in the first century C.E. The country is occupied and living under Roman control. The security of the occupying authority is achieved through the use of military force. Numerous archaeological artifacts from the various Roman fortresses in Palestine bear witness to this fact. Taxes and tributes were very high and every form of resistance was defeated. In a context such as this, the language of the Magnificat must be seen as a language of resistance. It is a song in which what may not be spoken is sung out loud. It expresses what is not allowed in political discourse because explicit criticism of authority was not tolerated. There are precedents for this song in the Hebrew Bible. Mary and Elizabeth recall these traditions and bring them into their present reality. They praise God for intervening in history through them. They confess their faith in God, who stands on the side of those who are laid low, who are hungry, who have no access to power. They themselves belong to this group, and in their song they work through experiences of how alien rule, oppression, and military occupation specifically affect women. In 1:48 Mary describes her situation as "humiliation," *tapeinōsis*. This concept is often translated as "lowliness" or "humble stature," that is, of the speaker before God. In biblical usage, however, this concept occurs not in religious contexts, but instead frequently in contexts calling attention to sexual violence against women; it is often used to describe rape (Schaberg 1990, 97ff.). It cannot be clearly ascertained whether the historical Mary actually became pregnant in this way, but because the word used suggests this, one must consider the possibility. Present-day reports of mass rapes in war situations make the realities of a country under alien rule and military occupation horrifyingly real.

According to the narrative of Luke, Mary is not immediately enthusiastic in the moment she receives the news of Jesus' impending birth. She asks thoughtful and critical questions about how this is supposed to happen, but then declares her willingness and seeks out Elizabeth, an older woman whose faith and whose hopes she shares, for understanding support. This meeting signals a radical change in existing sociopolitical and economic conditions. In Jesus' practice and preaching these promises become reality: in his sermon in the synagogue in Nazareth he summarizes his mission, based on Isaiah 61, as a message for the sick and oppressed and as a gospel for the poor (Luke 4:18-19). In the Beatitudes, God's reign is described as both present and future (cf. 6:20-23).

Jesus is described as Messiah, who makes miracles happen in the present: weeping, starvation, and marginalization are brought to an end, the last shall be first and the first shall be last (cf. 13:30). Last and first are understood as social categories; the fact that this saying is recorded in numerous places (Mark 10:31; Matt 19:30; 20:16) suggests that it belongs among the oldest tradition of narratives about Jesus of Nazareth (Schottroff and Stegemann 1978). In many texts the hope of poor people in a just God is spelled out. In Luke 16:19-30 the poor man is even given a name, Lazarus, while the rich man remains nameless. This text contrasts the organizational form and the way responsibility is practiced in the disciples' community with that of well-known forms of dominance and hierarchy: not those who sit at table will be greatest, but those who serve (cf. 22:24-27).

Anna — the Aged Prophet in the Temple (Luke 2:36-38)

The title of prophet signifies special distinction and contains a value judgment that its bearer proclaims the Word of God. As an old woman, Anna stands in the tradition of wise old women of the First Testament who were held in high esteem as matriarchs and advisers. Anna is found in the temple, not tied down by family commitments; that is, she acts in the public sphere. Her title points to religious and political activity. Her speech shows what God's action through Jesus, the expected Messiah, will mean concretely: she proclaims the liberation of Jerusalem. She prophesies to the people of Israel the fulfillment of God's promises, which become concrete in the actions of Jesus and his disciples. With her service in the temple she gives expression to her hope for the fulfillment of these promises; she expects liberation by God. This hope must not be misunderstood as a passive hope for divine salvation. True worship, true divine service means living by the Torah and actively working for justice. In this sense Anna's service to God is a form of action that must be characterized as resistance, aimed toward liberation and an end to the suffering of the oppressed people. Moreover, the occurrences described in Luke 2 can be understood as a manifestation of Jewish temple piety, which ties its eschatological expectations to this site. Anna's praxis of prayer and worship serves to describe her participation in the Jewish worship practices at the temple and to affirm the validity and significance of these practices for the worship of God (cf. also 19:45-48; 24:53). Anna becomes the iconic opposite of the high priests and the rest of the temple hierarchy who enrich themselves in collaboration with the Romans. Her description implicitly says: "In the temple, it is God who shall be served, not the Romans!" On another level, the insistence on the central significance of the temple even after its destruction — which has of course already occurred at the time the Gospel was written down — means that the Jesus movement must clearly be understood in relation to the other Jewish messianic liberation movements that cling to the temple as a central symbol of Jewish identity.

In the communities of disciples many different women and men came together and found support and resources for mutual caregiving. Elizabeth, Zechariah, Simeon, and Anna are representative of a group of elderly people who are certainly not insignificant. The respect and reverence rendered to the elderly people in Luke 1–2 clearly indicate that they were not regarded as mere recipients of alms. Instead, they signify the continuity from received traditions; surely they had many stories to tell. Together with the other, younger members of the worshiping communities, they were participants in the process that led to the written works in the Lukan corpus.

Women's Work — Women's Poverty: The Realm of God Breaks through in Everyday Life (Luke 8:1-3)

Many interpretations of the Gospel of Luke assume that it is addressed primarily to wealthy women. Evidence for this assumption is seen in the remark in Luke 8:1-3 that many read as meaning that the women disciples supported Jesus financially. Luise Schottroff offers a different translation: "(They served them) according to what was possible for them in their circumstances" (1994, 307; 1995a, 210). Their resources included not only money, but also their capacity for work, for providing accommodations, their solidarity, faith, imagination, vision, and hopes. Ivoni Richter Reimer's study of Acts (1992) demonstrates that many poor women who had to work to support themselves were active in the Lukan worshiping communities. Compared to Acts, Luke offers even clearer traces of single working poor women. In Luke 15:8-10, for example, one woman's struggle for survival becomes the image for God's action as she searches for a single *drachmē* — the amount of money needed for her daily bread (Schottroff 1994, 139-51; 1995a, 91-100; Lamb 1995). The bleak financial situation of single women provides the backdrop for the story of the persistent widow who insists on her right to receive support (18:1-8). Even more strikingly emphasized is the miserable poverty of the widow who, in offering two small coins, is sacrificing her entire means of subsistence (21:1-4). Further evidence of women's poverty is the fact that prostitutes are mentioned as present in the worshiping communities. The story of the woman who anoints Jesus refers to their existence (Schottroff 1990, 310-23; 1993, 138-57). For many poor women, their body was the only commodity of value they had to offer to earn a living (Kirchhoff 1994; Lamb and Janssen 1995). Alongside their work as a weaver, trader, or laborer, they would work as a prostitute to earn enough to survive, since their wages would be at most half that of a man's. Even a man's wage was often insufficient to support a family. We must assume women's presence among almost all the vocational groups named in the Second Testament texts, though they remain invisible because of the masculine plural noun usage. Women were employed in fishing, tax collecting, arts and crafts, agriculture (cf. 17:35), slave labor (cf. 12:45; 22:56), and in all other areas of life (Schottroff 1994, 122-30; 1995a, 80-85). The everyday life of these women lies behind many of these narratives and becomes transparent for the coming reign of God.

Mary and Martha — Two Servant Women (Luke 10:38-42)

In the Gospel of Luke different texts have been handed down that describe the activities of women as serving *(diakoneō)* (cf., e.g., 4:38-40; 8:1-3; 10:38-42; 23:49). Should this service be interpreted as a model for discipleship or as the relegation of women to the position prescribed to them by patriarchal society? Mary and Martha in particular have been the subjects of thorough feminist discussion. One line of interpretation has emphasized the restrictive view of women. This view is seen as discounting Martha's role as mere serving at table as contrasted with Mary's passive listening while seated at the feet of Jesus (Schüssler Fiorenza 1988a; Seim 1994). Others see this text as foregrounding a way of viewing service in general. They see the sisters as modeling discipleship for women as well as men, and Jesus as defending women's discipleship as opposed to their being relegated to the role of mother and housewife (Schottroff 1990, 132; 1993, 116; Reinhartz 1991). Luke 9:10-17, too, shows that serving at table is not viewed exclusively as a woman's job. It is assumed here that the male disciples, too, feel responsible for shopping, distributing the food, and collecting the leftovers (cf. also Acts 6:1-7). In Luke 10:38-42 Mary remains a passive listener. This does not mean it is written in stone, however, that women are limited to this role.

It becomes clear from many texts that hearing the gospel is always associated with action. In Luke 1 Mary and Elizabeth speak prophetically; the women mentioned in 8:1-3 accompany Jesus as disciples and show their courage as they observe the crucifixion from afar (cf. 23:49). Martha expresses her annoyance and argues with Jesus (10:40). A woman sets out to search for what she has lost, and joyously celebrates with her women neighbors and friends who are showing solidarity with her (15:8-10). A widow defends her rights (18:1-8); the women at the tomb proclaim what they have experienced (24:1-11). The male disciples do not believe the women when they announce that Jesus is alive, because the men are looking at the tomb and at his death (24:11). In this context, this experience of women says a lot about their struggles in a patriarchal society, but it by no means testifies to women's incompetence to serve as witnesses. Such an interpretation narrows the concept to a juridical level that is not relevant here. In Luke's Gospel we see traces of the struggles of women who made themselves heard within patriarchal structures. They are capable of encouraging us and can set women into motion even today. They describe everyday conflicts without whose solution changes on a large scale are impossible.

Daughters of Abraham (Luke 13:10-17)

The story of the healing of a woman who had been crippled for eighteen years shows especially poignantly how closely such narratives are connected to Jewish traditions and ideas. In the history of exegesis of this text, the separation of the Lukan Christian community from Judaism prior to the writing of the narrative has been consistently assumed as historical fact. Interpreters see the process of separation reflected in the conflict between Jesus and the representative of Judaism, the leader of the synagogue. As a result, exegesis emphasizes this aspect and regards the healing of the woman as merely providing an opportunity for a basic theological dispute between two opposing parties. In this conflict, so the argument goes, Jesus breaks through the barriers of the Jewish social order and the limits of cultic religious practice. He is seen as using his act of healing to demonstrate to the leader of the synagogue the true character of the Sabbath as a day when healing can be experienced, thus exposing the keepers of the law who want to cling to rigid norms and frown upon any disturbance to this order. It is frequently assumed that women were allowed to attend worship in the synagogue only as passive listeners in separate galleries. Thus the very fact of Jesus' attention to the woman is seen as breaking with the misogynist patriarchal character of Judaism. Bernadette J. Brooten's re-search (1982) has shown these arguments to be based on an anti-Judaistic pattern of interpretation. Starting from historical sources, she shows that women were active participants in synagogue worship and served in leadership functions. She shows that it is not possible to assume the existence of galleries for women at this time. In the feminist discussion of this text, the focus is on the woman who has previously remained almost entirely invisible. But here, too, Jesus appears as the one who by his actions distances himself from the Judaism of his time (Bauer 1988). According to such readings, he turns his attention to marginalized women (Seim 1994) and re-scinds notions of purity and impurity (Seibert-Cuadra 1993).

However, the healing Jesus performs on the Sabbath does not represent a re-jection of Jewish Sabbath practice. Luke 13:10 mentions that he participates in worship at the synagogue and reads and interprets the Torah like a rabbi. The con-flict with the leader of the synagogue is to be understood as a lively and controver-sial discussion about the Sabbath that was ongoing within the framework of Juda-ism and that is extensively documented in the Mishnah and the Talmud. The question at hand in this text is which activities are allowed on the Sabbath and which are not. Jesus' criteria correspond to the First Testament concepts of mercy and preservation of life, which include restoring a person to health. By healing the woman he is thus not breaking the law, but expressing his understanding of the Torah, which he seeks to fulfill. The core of his argumentation is the fact that the woman is a descendant of Abraham, which makes her an heir to the promise of healing and liberation. And it is with this argument that he convinces his oppo-nents in the debate, who show by their reaction that they have to admit to the merit of his interpretation of the Sabbath law.

In the story, the woman who is healed by Jesus remains without a name and without a voice. Her song of praise is not among the received texts. She is not pas-sive, however. She dares to enter the public sphere with her suffering, takes part in worship, and thereby puts herself in a place where she meets Jesus. She creates the condition for her healing by not accepting her illness as fate and remaining in isola-tion. At the end of the story all the gathered people rejoice with her. She must be seen as representing the people as a whole, embodying the social and economic conditions of the dregs of society. Her body bears the signs of hard labor, the traces of oppressive conditions of work and life, which bend and cripple human beings.

By calling the woman "daughter of Abraham," Jesus emphasizes her Jewish-ness, her belonging to the Jewish people. In the Gospel of Luke, Abraham is the bearer of the promise that God gave his people. He will liberate his children out of the hands of their enemies and create a sacred and holy life for them (Luke 1:55, 72-75). Through Jesus' action the promise given to people as children of Abraham is fulfilled. The sick, crippled woman who experiences the healing of her body praises God. She proclaims what she has experienced, the good news that affects all the people: the people's salvation is at hand and can already be felt. The rejoicing over the healing of the woman should be understood as an eschatological joy like that of Mary and Elizabeth in Luke 1. The healings of individuals are signs for the coming of the reign of God, for the acts of God of which the Magnificat sings: God lifts up the lowly and helps his people Israel (1:46-55). The fact that the woman in the story remains nameless can be attributed to a discriminatory attitude against women on the part of the storytellers, but in the overall context it can also be read differently. She and all she stands for represents many women and men from among the people who suffer from oppressive circumstances as she does. Like other people whose healing is reported, she herself does not speak. Jesus takes the initiative in the act of healing. This corresponds to the pattern of all stories of Sabbath healings, including those when the person healed is a man (cf. 4:31-37; 14:1-6). The blind man healed in Luke 18:35-43 is also nameless, unlike his counterpart in Mark 10:46-52, Bartimaeus. The people who tell of their healing or that of their sisters and brothers surely did not have perfect bodies. Their intention in telling their stories is not to propagate an ideal of health against which all humankind should be measured. Rather, they tell about themselves and their daily life and thereby make visible their suffering and the markings of their life stories that they bear on their bodies. The narratives of healing are stories of encouragement that bring their hopes to life.

Women as Witnesses to the Resurrection (Luke 24)

In Luke 1 and Luke 24, the beginning and the conclusion of the Gospel, we see a number of parallels. Women play an important role in both chapters. They set out on a journey, and begin to act out of a situation of suffering. They do not remain resigned and helpless, but believe in God's message, which they pass along. The men are skeptical at first; they do not believe that change and salvation can begin with women. Zechariah bases his doubts about the annunciation of the angel on his wife's age (1:18); the disciples do not believe what the women returning from the empty tomb tell them (24:11, see above). Chapters 1 and 24 also have similar characteristics in terms of the settings of the action. The temple in Jerusalem is where the Gospel begins (1:8-23; 2:25-35, 36-38, 41-51). The disciples return there at the end to praise God (24:53). Additionally there are important references to Galilee. This is where Mary lives and where she meets the angel; the women at the tomb are reminded of what Jesus told them in Galilee (1:26; 24:6). At the core of both texts is the reference to the words and deeds of God or Jesus, in whom Mary trusts and whom the women at the tomb remember. Angels recall these deeds; they proclaim the good news and speak to the women (1:19, 30; 24:5, 23). Mary, Elizabeth, and the women at the tomb believe in it and spread it further, while Zechariah and the male disciples doubt them (1:20; 24:11, 25, 41). Those who recognize God's signs and can interpret them, like Mary, Elizabeth, and her unborn child, and those who "see" the fulfillment of the promise like the relatives after

Elizabeth has given birth, and the women disciples who in the end believe in the resurrection, react with great joy. Eschatological joy and jubilation describe the basic tone of the texts that began with the description of suffering and (social) death (1:41, 44, 47, 58; 24:41, 52). The Gospel begins and ends with a blessing: Elizabeth blesses Mary and the resurrected Christ blesses the women disciples. These parallels clearly demonstrate the conceptual structure of the Gospel. Luke 1 and 2 must not, therefore, be considered merely "background" material. Here, in the form of stories of births, we have the description of how the movement is carried forward through the initiative of women who proclaim the "Living One" (cf. 24:23) after the horror and shock over the death of Jesus. Beginning and ending belong together; the good news can be heard anew again and again. It must not be seen as a closed chapter but as a present that is ever being made new.

LITERATURE

Albrecht, Ruth. 1988. "Anna. Symbol weiblicher Integrität." In *Zwischen Ohnmacht und Befreiung. Biblische Frauengestalten*, edited by Karin Walter, 132-38. Freiburg im Breisgau, Basel, and Vienna.

Bauer, Andrea. 1988. "Lukas 13:10-17. Die Heilung einer gekrümmten Frau." In *Feministisch gelesen*, edited by Eva Renate Schmidt, 1:210-16. Stuttgart.

Brooten, Bernadette J. 1982. *Women Leaders in the Ancient Synagogue: Inscriptional Evidence and Background Issues*. Brown Judaic Studies, vol. 36. Atlanta.

Busse, Ulrich. 1991. "Das 'Evangelium' des Lukas. Die Funktion der Vorgeschichte im lukanischen Doppelwerk." In *Der Treue Gottes trauen. Beiträge zum Werk des Lukas*, edited by Claus Bussmann et al., 161-79. Freiburg, Basel, and Vienna.

Cardoso Pereira, Nancy. 1990. "Vem Espirito Santo . . . renova toda a criacao!" In *Mosaicos da Biblia*, 2:14-18. Rio de Janeiro.

Cassidy, Richard J. 1978. *Jesus, Politics, and Society: A Study of Luke's Gospel*. New York.

Conzelmann, Hans. 1977. *Die Mitte der Zeit. Studien zur Theologie des Lukas*. 6th ed. Tübingen.

Gebara, Ivone, and Maria C. Lucchhetti Bingemer. 1988. *Maria, Mutter Gottes und Mutter der Armen*. Düsseldorf.

Janssen, Claudia. 1996a. "Hanna — Prophetin der Befreiung. Lk 2,25-38." *Junge Kirche* 12:686-89.

———. 1996b. "Maria und Elisabet singen. Lk 1,39-56." *Junge Kirche* 11:620-24.

———. 1998. *Elisabet und Hanna — zwei widerständige alte Frauen in neutestamentlicher Zeit. Eine sozialgeschichtliche Untersuchung*. Mainz.

Kahl, Brigitte. 1987. *Armenevangelium und Heidenevangelium. "Sola scriptura" und die ökumenische Traditionsproblematik im Lichte von Väterkonflikt und Väterkonsens bei Lukas*. Berlin.

———. 1993. "Toward a Materialist-Feminist Reading." In *Searching the Scriptures*, edited by Elisabeth Schüssler Fiorenza, 1:225-40. 2 vols. New York.

———. 1995. "Lukas gegen Lukas lesen. Feministisch-kritische Hermeneutik des Verdachts und des Einverständnisses." *Bibel und Kirche* 4:222-29.

Kirchhoff, Renate. 1994. *Die Sünde gegen den eigenen Leib. Studien zu pornē und porneia in 1 Kor 6,12-20 und dem sozio-kulturellen Kontext der paulinischen Adressaten.* Göttingen.

Lamb, Regene. 1994. "Wenn ich meinen Rücken beugen würde! Der alltägliche Kampf gegen Herrschaftsstrukturen. Eine Auslegung zu Lukas 13,10-17." In *Für Gerechtigkeit streiten. Theologie im Alltag einer bedrohten Welt,* edited by Dorothee Sölle, 71-75. Gütersloh.

―――. 1995. "Ein Licht ist angezündet." *Bibel und Kirche* 4:230-34.

Lamb, Regene, and Claudia Janssen. 1995. "'ZöllnerInnen und Prostituierte gelangen eher in das Reich Gottes als ihr' (Mt 21,31). Frauenarmut und Prostitution." In *". . . so lernen die Völker des Erdkreises Gerechtigkeit." Arbeitsbuch zu Bibel und Ökonomie,* edited by Franz Segbers and Kuno Füssel, 275-84. Lucerne.

Reid, Barbara E. 1996. *Choosing the Better Part? Women in the Gospel of Luke.* Collegeville, Minn.

Reinhartz, Adele. 1991. "From Narrative to History: The Resurrection of Mary and Martha." In *"Women Like This": New Perspectives on Jewish Women in the Greco-Roman World,* edited by Amy-Jill Levine, 161-84. Atlanta.

Richter Reimer, Ivoni. 1992. *Frauen in der Apostelgeschichte des Lukas: eine feministisch-theologische Exegese.* Gütersloh.

Schaberg, Jane. 1990. *The Illegitimacy of Jesus: A Feminist Theological Interpretation of the Infancy Narratives.* 2nd ed. San Francisco.

―――. 1992. "Luke." In *The Women's Bible Commentary,* edited by Carol A. Newsom and Sharon H. Ringe, 275-92. London and Louisville.

Schottroff, Luise. 1978. "Das Magnificat und die älteste Tradition über Jesus von Nazareth." *Evangelische Theologie* 38:298-313.

―――. 1990. *Befreiungserfahrungen. Studien zur Sozialgeschichte des Neuen Testaments.* Munich.

―――. 1993. *Let the Oppressed Go Free: Feminist Perspectives on the New Testament.* Louisville.

―――. 1994. *Lydias ungeduldige Schwestern. Feministische Sozialgeschichte des frühen Christentums.* Gütersloh.

―――. 1995a. *Lydia's Impatient Sisters: A Feminist Social History of Early Christianity.* Louisville.

―――. 1995b. "Auf dem Weg zu einer feministischen Rekonstruktion der Geschichte des frühen Christentums." In Luise Schottroff, Silvia Schroer, and Marie-Theres Wacker, *Feministische Exegese. Forschungserträge zur Bibel aus der Perspektive von Frauen,* 175-248. Darmstadt.

―――. 1996. "'Gesetzesfreies Heidenchristentum' — und die Frauen? Feministische Analysen und Alternativen." In *Von der Wurzel getragen. Christlich-feministische Exegese in Auseinandersetzung mit Antijudaismus,* edited by Luise Schottroff and Marie-Theres Wacker, 227-45. Leiden, New York, and Cologne.

―――. 1998. *Feminist Interpretation: The Bible in Women's Perspective,* 179-254. Minneapolis.

Schottroff, Luise, and Wolfgang Stegemann. 1986. *Jesus and the Hope of the Poor.* Maryknoll, N.Y.

————. 1990. *Jesus von Nazareth — Hoffnung der Armen.* 3rd ed. Stuttgart, Berlin, and Cologne. 1st ed. 1978.

Schüssler Fiorenza, Elisabeth. 1983. *In Memory of Her: A Feminist Theological Reconstruction of Early Christian Beginnings.* New York.

————. 1988a. "Biblische Grundlegung." In *Feministische Theologie. Perspektiven zur Orientierung,* edited by Maria Kassel. 13-44. Stuttgart.

————. 1988b. *Zu ihrem Gedächtnis . . . Eine feministisch-theologische Rekonstruktion der christlichen Ursprünge.* Munich.

Seibert-Cuadra, Ute. 1993. "A mulher nos evangelhos sinóticos." *Revista de Interpretação Bíblica Latino-Americana* 15, no. 2:68-84.

Seim, Turid Karlsen. 1994. "The Gospel of Luke." In *Searching the Scriptures,* edited by Elisabeth Schüssler Fiorenza, 2:728-62. 2 vols. New York.

Stegemann, Ekkehard W., and Wolfgang Stegemann. 1995. *Urchristliche Sozialgeschichte. Die Anfänge im Judentum und Christusgemeinden in der mediterranen Welt.* Stuttgart, Berlin, and Cologne.

Stegemann, Wolfgang. 1993. "Jesus als Messias in der Theologie des Lukas." In *Messiasvorstellungen bei Juden und Christen,* edited by Ekkehard W. Stegemann, 21-40. Stuttgart et al.

Sutter Rehmann, Luzia. 1995. *Geh — frage die Gebärerin. Feministisch-befreiungstheologische Untersuchungen zum Gebärmotiv in der Apokalyptik.* Gütersloh.

Ulrich, Beise Claudete. 1991. "Marta e Maria: as mulheres dao sinais da vivencia de una nova espiritualidade." *Estudios bíblicos* 30:52-58.

Wind, Renate. 1996. *Maria aus Nazareth, aus Bethanien, aus Magdala. Drei Frauengeschichten.* Gütersloh.

FOR FURTHER READING

Beavis, Mary Ann, ed. 2002. *The Lost Coin: Parables of Women, Work, and Wisdom.* Biblical Seminar, vol. 86. London and New York.

Bieberstein, Sabine. 1998. *Verschwiegene Jüngerinnen — vergessene Zeuginnen. Gebrochene Konzepte im Lukasevangelium.* Novum Testamentum et Orbis Antiquus, vol. 38. Göttingen.

Kurth, Christina. 2000. *"Die Stimmen der Propheten erfüllt." Jesu Geschick und "die" Juden nach der Darstellung des Lukas.* Stuttgart.

Löning, Karl. 1997. *Das Geschichtswerk des Lukas.* Vol. 1, *Israels Hoffnung und Gottes Geheimnisse.* Stuttgart et al.

Schiffner, Kerstin. 2008. *Lukas liest Exodus. Eine Untersuchung zur Aufnahme ersttestamentlicher Befreiungsgeschichte im lukanischen Werk als Schrift-Lektüre.* Beiträge zur Wissenschaft vom Alten und Neuen Testament, vol. 172. Stuttgart.

Schottroff, Luise. 2005. *Die Gleichnisse Jesu.* Gütersloh.

————. 2006. *Parables of Jesus.* Minneapolis.

Wasserberg, Günter. 1998. *Aus Israels Mitte — Heil für die Welt.* Beihefte zur Zeitschrift für die neutestamentliche Wissenschaft, vol. 92. Berlin and New York.

Translated by Nancy Lukens

Gospel of John: Spaces for Women

Ruth Habermann

Inquisitive Approaches

The Gospel of John discloses a world quite distinct within the New Testament. Upon close feminist reading, some things initially appear oddly detached, others disconcertingly foreign: for instance, portrayal of "the Jews" in almost exclusively negative terms. Yet at the same time, there are images of liberation and comfort, texts that literally nourish us because they speak so intensely of fear and break-through, of love and community.

In my experience, when women dare to approach the Gospel of John, to take what is foreign as their signpost opening to them the heart and perspectives of times long past, then the calling forth and retrieval of women's realities long for-gotten become possible. Moreover, they receive an incomparable gift: a *counter-force* to the rituals of capitalism, breaking the spell of the fear and doubt we have internalized so deeply. For these are the themes of John's Gospel: anxiety, distress, and the transformation of fear and doubt in the small communities of women and men setting out to build up the reign of God in their relationships, everyday life, communal structures, and political praxis. And then, over and over, this fourth Gospel ceases to be off-putting and enigmatic and becomes approachable particu-larly for women, for whom reflection on the means by which our world can truly be changed is a necessity.

Here, on the one hand, is the Johannine conception of mutuality and its prac-tice in the unparalleled, sensual sacrament of foot washing. The conception of mutuality means believing not only in God but also in one another and in oneself: God is with them and they are with one another. At the same time, it means insist-ing on being able to accomplish something and not allowing oneself to be victim-ized by any situation. In the passion narrative itself we encounter a Jesus who is decisive and does not allow his life to be taken away from him. And here, on the other hand, is the nonpatriarchal language with which Jesus and his followers are depicted in this Gospel. Christ is described as Light, as Door/Gate, and as Way;

faith, as a powerful and empowering love relationship. The following aspects of the Gospel of John seem particularly important to me for a feminist reading and exposition:

1. What is the background of those texts that could be read as anti-Jewish?
2. What relation exists in John's Gospel between the powerful stories of women and the tradition of political resistance?
3. What did the conception of mutuality mean for the faith and action of Johannine women and men?
4. Did Johannine messianism mean empowerment or escapism for the believers?

Fear and Distress: The Background of the Johannine Discourse about "Jews"

Like all the Gospels, John has a complex oral and written prehistory. The period between 80 and 90 C.E. is the probable time of the composition of this Gospel. Through its texts we can discern a situation in which the Johannine Christians were experiencing distress and exclusion.

In 70 C.E. rabbinic Judaism succeeded in the establishment of rabbinic orthodoxy, attempting to preserve the meaning of the inheritance. If before this point there were still various intra-Jewish groups, now, following the catastrophic experience of the destruction of the temple, rabbinic Judaism became the reigning power. At stake was an internal unanimity so that something indestructible might be created to prevent a new catastrophe. At the same time, however, other groups that did not prove themselves capable or desirous of being integrated were excluded. The gravest means of exclusion was expulsion from the synagogue. Three times the Gospel of John speaks of such expulsion, and in each case it is clear that the text is describing not an event at the time of Jesus but an urgent problem in the present time of those writing the Gospel (John 9:22; 12:42; and 16:2).

The Greek word *aposynagōgos* is used in all three passages and is found in the New Testament only here. This demonstrates that this term brings to expression a very specific experience of the Johannine Christian community: the experience of being regarded as heretics, as troublemakers, and of being excluded from the synagogue community. For those affected, this exclusion was linked with dire consequences, above all in the social and economic realms, for exclusion from the synagogue was by no means an isolated religious measure; rather, it cut into all human relationships. Economic boycotts were imposed and social, personal, and business connections severed.

In the Gospel of John we learn that the Pharisees, acting as the continuation

of the abolished Sanhedrin, and their exegesis of the Torah played a dominant role
(7:48-49) in the leadership of the Jewish people, and that their actions were determined by their fear of the Romans. They authorize the death sentence against Jesus because above all they feared that the Romans might intervene cruelly if the Jesus movement became a mass movement (*pantes*, 11:48; *ho kosmos*, 12:19). Into this
situation of distress and extraordinary uncertainty, which led within the small
congregations to a movement toward defection, the Gospel of John was written.
Its authors wanted to exhort their readers and hearers to "abide" and to place before their eyes what Jesus meant for them.

The Johannine congregations consisted for the most part of people from Jewish backgrounds. They also contained women and men of non-Jewish heritage,
however. The living situation of these Johannine women and men was powerfully
determined by conflicts with other Jewish people and with societal institutions in
the face of which the Christian congregations were in the minority. They felt
themselves excluded and threatened by the Jewish majority. At the same time,
however, they had a clear sense that the Jewish majority of the population for its
own part stood threatened under the control and pressure of the Roman Empire.
All this is tangibly present in the Gospel of John: the leadership of the people in
which the Pharisees play a decisive role; the fear of this leadership by the male and
female disciples and also the secret disciples; the messianism occupying and dominating the people's attention; the restless and turbulent mood of the people. For
an outsider reading this, the bitter conflict between the Jewish majority and
Jewish-Christian minority is striking because it makes sense and at the same time
makes no sense. For between the two Jewish-Roman wars, *all* people were living in
a situation of uninterrupted threat; the struggle for the Torah as the center of Jewish life, and for mutual solidarity with one another over against Rome, was a matter of survival for all. The Johannine anti-Judaism is not yet the later Christian
anti-Judaism that declares the Jewish people as useless and evil from a perspective
on the outside and from above.

Johannine Congregations as Places for Women

Mary Knows the Hour Better — John 2:1-11

Jesus' public activity begins at a small family celebration: in John 1:35-51 he finds
his first disciples, and in John 2:2 he appears with them at a wedding. For the time
being Jesus is a guest like everyone else. Mary is the first one mentioned, before Jesus. The self-evident sovereignty with which she is portrayed, in conjunction with
the simplicity of her introduction — her name and her marital status are not
mentioned — permits the conclusion that women were not defined according to
patriarchal norms in the Johannine communities. What mattered was her action.

In a textual sense Mary is the main figure. *She* discovers that the wine has run out (v. 3). *She* takes the initiative and alerts Jesus to the situation. *She* awaits his help and has no doubt it will take place (v. 5). *She* is the one who urges the miracle and thus helps to bring it about. Her clear authority communicates itself to the servants (v. 5).

Prevailing exegesis finds two ways of coming to terms with Mary's striking authority: one track of interpretation privatizes and blunts her powerful appearance in the story; Mary is said to have a personal, private relationship with the bridal family, helping them behind the scenes, and this is why she feels so responsible. The second predominant track of interpretation sees Mary as merely a symbol of a particular Jewish-Christian group. With this move she herself is made quite invisible.

Neither interpretation, however, does justice to the text. The story emphasizes that Mary becomes the advocate of the festival community. A feast cannot take place without wine. The wine running out is a genuine emergency in which Mary takes the floor. The dominant exegesis speaks not of "emergency" but rather of the "predicament" of the host, the "embarrassment" of the situation. For us, to whom practically anything is readily available, and for whom running out of wine represents at most a minor mishap, the actual crisis here can be difficult to perceive.

Jesus' response (v. 4), "Woman, what concern is that to you and to me? My hour has not yet come," bears no connection to a stereotypical mother-son relationship. Traditional exegeses differ here; some take a harmonizing interpretation of outrage at the roughness with which Jesus here addresses his mother, whereas others are gratified that Mary is put in her place. Jesus' use of the term *gynai* in addressing his mother is striking. This term shows that no particular value is attributed to physical motherhood.

Jesus uses the same term, *gynai,* to address the Samaritan woman (4:21) and Mary Magdalene (20:15). Both women have prominent significance within the Gospel of John; both texts have to do with the women's apostolic status. Within this context, Mary too could be seen as an apostolic figure: she knows about Jesus' powers and passes this trust along.

In the Hebrew Bible the phrase *ti emoi kai soi* (2:4) denotes the irreconcilability of two viewpoints, a staking out of boundaries between two personal domains (e.g., 2 Kings 3:13). This rhetorical question creates distance and sets up an unbridgeable opposition, indeed a demarcation of spheres of power. But such dissociation is formulaic, and Mary is not deterred. "My hour has not yet come." Jesus' *hōra* is the hour of his passion and death. From the beginning of his hour on, Jesus works no more miracles but walks the path to the cross. Alongside the coming of this hour, its present reality is also simultaneously emphasized in John's Gospel (4:23; 5:25). Whereas here Jesus thus denies that his hour has come (v. 4), Mary appears to know the hour better than he does. In verse 5 she says to the servants, "Do whatever he tells you." She trusts that Jesus will act and at the same time leaves open how that action is to look.

Thus her faith opens the period of Jesus' becoming visible. Her faith means seeing Jesus' power, claiming it, and thereby making God incarnate. In this story a Jesus is shown who, despite ritualistic distancing, is dependent on other human beings and needs a push to use the power (God) dwelling in him.

Mary sees her hope in Jesus' amazing power fulfilled beyond all measure. He makes the new wine gush forth in abundant excess, making it taste better than the old wine ever did. In this first sign the reign of God is already present among them: women and men drink wine and celebrate a feast.

Herald of Living Water — John 4:1-42

The Samaritan woman lives in Sychar and regularly draws water from this well (John 4:7, 11, 15, 28). The narrative presupposes that it is a lengthy walk from Sychar to the well. When the men and women traveling with Jesus go to buy food, that takes an extended period. Drawing water was difficult physical labor associated with considerable expenditure of time; it even affected women's physical posture.

The text does not say why she is drawing water in the heat of noon, of all times. The explanation given by some exegetes — that, as a known sinner, she chose this time to avoid meeting other women drawing water — is implausible. Even a large village by the standards of the day would still have been small enough to make such evasion impossible. The depiction given in John 4 suggests rather that the woman was obliged to draw more water than was typical for a housewife, such as perhaps for laundering, which was similarly women's work. At the end she leaves her bucket behind, leaves what had been her labor to that point; she cuts the connection to her old life. The water bearer has become a disciple. In the history of exegesis, the tendency at all costs to overlook this call narrative has been powerful and conspicuous.

The prevailing exegesis reads the life history of the Samaritan woman as a story of sexual voracity and instability. This interpretation rests on verse 18: "You have had five husbands, and the one you have now is not your husband." In his epoch-making commentary on this verse, Rudolf Bultmann (1956 [trans. 1971], 188) wrote, "This unrest is portrayed by the woman's disturbed past and her unsatisfied present state. Perhaps one may go so far as to say that the married life of the woman 'who reels from desire to pleasure' portrays not only the unrest, but the aberrations of the desire for life."

The overwhelming mainstream within the dominant exegesis sees in the Samaritan woman a sexually depraved woman. According to it, Jesus is the one who "convicts" the woman, who exposes her "way of life." A tributary of this misogynist exegesis interprets the woman's life symbolically, relating it to the pagan polytheism of the Samaritan people. This interpretation rests in part on 2 Kings 17:30-31, 41, and on the metaphor of adultery for unfaithfulness toward God in Hosea and Jeremiah. But the woman did not commit adultery. The narrative gives no support for this interpretation that unites misogyny with discrimination against the Samaritan religion.

A pure inversion of these interpretive types — the woman's five husbands are merely incidental to the story, or the woman was in fact a sinner but Jesus is not concerned about that (e.g., Schneiders 1982 and others) — is unsatisfactory because it does not inquire after the reality of the Samaritan woman's life, and she is thereby made invisible all over again. In this way this feminist inversion merely reinforces the dominant interpretation.

In the biblical context, serial marriages of women are mentioned repeatedly, not as immoral but as legitimate within the framework of the Torah. The New Testament reports a woman's sevenfold levirate marriage (i.e., marriage to one's brother-in-law in Mark 12:18-27 and parallels; cf. Deut 25:5). If a woman loses her husband before a son has been produced from the marriage, then she and the husband's next brother are obliged to marry in order to produce a son for the deceased husband. Mark 12:18-27 presupposes that seven brothers die in turn, and that therefore the woman is widowed seven times.

The book of Tobit reports on a young woman, the only child of her parents, who is under great pressure to bring an heir for her father into the world. One after another, seven men die on their wedding night with the young woman because an evil demon is killing them. She is derided: "You have had seven husbands, but not one of them remains to you" (Tob 3:8, author's translation). Serial marriages were widespread both in the upper class and among economically poor people. For women, marriage was not merely the social norm but also an economic necessity. The reasons for this are readily understandable if we make use of data about the economic, legal, and social situation of widows and single women. The possibilities for women to survive by wage labor were exceedingly meager. Thus we must conclude that the Samaritan woman was obliged to marry repeatedly for economic and social reasons. Her situation was so grave that she was forced to enter a nonmarital working and sexual relationship with a man who did not even bother to give her the relative security of a marriage contract. In Jesus' speaking with the woman about her serial marriages there is no trace of disparagement of her conduct. Twice he affirms her description of her present bad situation (John 4:17, 18). Through his behavior toward her she perceives him to be a prophet (v. 19) and the Messiah (v. 29), because he helped her to liberate herself from her painful situation. The Johannine Jesus does not, to be sure, criticize marriage in general here but does criticize its use by society for the exploitation and dependence of women.

In contrast to the predominant tradition of exegesis that classifies the Samaritan woman as limited, superficial, or at the very least failing to understand in the conversation, the narrative itself reproduces a focused conversation. They are not talking past one another but to one another. Here we see the double inversion of roles: a Jew wants to receive water from a Samaritan; a man wants to serve a woman.

Is Jesus acting unusually in speaking with a woman? Many exegetes draw this conclusion from verse 27. For a rabbi it would have been unthinkable to speak with a woman, they argue, appealing to *Pirqe Aboth* 1:5. Yet Jesus' conversation with the Samaritan woman is obviously modeled on the scene in Genesis 24. The conceptual imagination of the hearers of John 4 therefore is more likely the remembrance of Rebekah than of one of the more misogynist rabbis who does not speak with women. First, a recommendation like *Pirqe Aboth* 1:5 does not present the view of all rabbis, and second, it is to be seen within the context of instruction regarding sexual discipline. Men are to scrupulously avoid situations that could make adultery or sexual overtures possible. *Pirqe Aboth* 1:5 is not to be interpreted as a general ban on speaking with women but more likely as a directive on dealing consciously with one's own situations of sexual temptation.

When Jesus' companions left him, he was weary and exhausted (John 4:6). Thus when they return (v. 27), they are amazed to find him now *speaking* with a woman. They are amazed that he is conducting a conversation at all, not that he is speaking with *a woman*.

Jesus' request for water, with its clear reminder for Jewish people of the encounter between Abraham's servant and Rebekah, shows already that Jesus as herald of God is addressing a Samaritan woman as a future herald of God. The conversation is driven forward across broad terrain by the Samaritan woman's initiative. Twice, however, Jesus takes the initiative: in verses 7 and 16 he begins the conversation with his request for water. He does not seem to answer her request for his living water (v. 15); he fulfills it by taking a new initiative: "Go, call your husband, and come back." This new impulse is his response to her request.

The story does not say that the Samaritan woman gave Jesus water, but it presupposes that he drank from her bucket (vv. 11, 28). For this is the reason the Samaritan woman asks Jesus who he actually is in that he, a Jew, violates Jewish purity regulations forbidding the use of drinking vessels belonging to pagan people. Jesus answers her that he can give her God's gift of living water. He invites her to ask him for this water. The conditional sentence in which his answer appears is meant to express that she should perceive him as revelatory of God in asking him for water. Thus both of them ask for water and both give one another water; both are changed by this encounter led by God: Jesus becomes the Messiah of the Samaritan people, and the woman becomes a messenger of God who tells her Samaritan neighbors that Jesus is the Savior of the world (v. 42). In verse 11 the woman asks about the divine nature of the water, not comparable to normal drinking water. Jesus' response says that he is the Savior of the world by whose water all thirst will be quenched and who can transform human beings into a spring of water. In verse 14, then, the image of living water is expanded. The living water of God that quenches all thirst is transformed within a person into a spring whose water gushes up to eternal life. A thirsty woman becomes a woman who passes on living water to others. She will not thirst, and she will no longer work as a hauler of water but be a spring of living water.

Jesus gives her the living water in that he intervenes in her living conditions and wants to help change them. She cannot become a spring of living water if she continues to live in her dependence on a man who exploits her. Now the woman answers with a sentence by which she herself steps free of her situation: "I have no husband" (v. 17). In this moment she makes the decision to become independent of this man. The story presupposes that Jesus knows her life story on the basis of his divine gifts, but not for the purpose of manifesting himself as all-knowing. He confirms her statement, "I have no husband," twice, because she has had the courage to renounce this humiliating relationship.

The Samaritan woman leaves her jar behind and leaves her nonhusband. The story, like many other liberation stories in the Second Testament, presupposes the reality of small Christian communities in which the woman finds a new community and in which she can survive economically even as a single woman.

In verses 19-26, the woman who is about to set out as messenger of living water for her people asks how the Samaritan religion will look concretely for those who follow Jesus. Jesus presents himself as a new way for the Samaritan religion. The Samaritans give up their Samaritan cult and the sacred place Gerizim, but they do not become Jews. They will worship God without any sacred place; in contrast, Jewish people will worship God in Jerusalem even as followers of Jesus. Here a Jewish perspective is given on a non-Jewish religion. According to the Gospel of John, salvation comes from the Jews even for Samaritans and for followers of Jesus from non-Jewish peoples. John 4:20-26 was interpreted in the prevailing Christian exegesis as follows: God is worshiped in Christian churches, not in Jerusalem and not on Mount Gerizim. But in verse 21 Jesus addresses the Samaritan woman and her people; this anti-Jewish exegesis thus reads right past this text.

For the women in the Johannine congregations, the Samaritan woman was a courageous example in two instances: she dared to break out of the situation of patriarchal oppression once and for all, and she placed herself in solidarity with a Jewish Messiah in a time when even the smallest suspicion of Jewish messianism was punished with the death sentence by Roman authorities. Both temples, the Samaritan one on Mount Gerizim and the Jewish one in Jerusalem, were destroyed both by Titus and by Hadrian.

Reprieve and Release of the Adulterer — John 8:1-11

The narrative of the rescue of a woman who was to be stoned as an adulterer has had an eventful history. Pushed back and forth like a tiresome piece of furniture, it was included in the canonical Gospels only in the third century, and even then was repeatedly omitted in the transmittal of texts. These great difficulties point to the fact that this story was not well suited for a large church geared toward domination. Nevertheless, the first noncanonical witness to its existence is ancient (Papias, ca. 125 C.E.).

In the early church this story was suspected of emboldening women to sin. It was fought and suppressed because Jesus' forgiving of an adulterer seemed irreconcilable with the church's discipline of penitence. In language and style of narrative, the story fits better in the Synoptic Gospels than in the Gospel of John.

In verse 11 we realize that in the narrative the nameless woman really is an adulterer, and also that her adultery is called "sin." The woman had been "caught in adultery" (8:3) — scribes and Pharisees assert that she was "caught in the very act" (8:4). Such an assertion had to be based on at least two witnesses (Deut 19:15; Num 5:13). It is reasonable to assume that the woman was caught in a trap prepared for her. Her partner in adultery is not present, although according to the law he was to have been arrested and punished along with her. Here the text is reflecting a societal praxis in which patriarchal law, contrary to its original intent, is enforced unilaterally against women. The narrative itself describes this situation. It also presupposes the acquisition of witnesses and the isolating of the woman as the sole perpetrator, yet manifests no awareness of injustice or the misuse of law. This too points to a practice of the time. We can assume that individual women were regularly disposed of with the help of patriarchal marital law, for example, to advance a husband's economic interests. In the process, lethal acts considered unjust even within the framework of patriarchal law were committed. The description of the stoning of an Iranian woman, albeit from within a different historical context, makes clear how the awareness of injustice among those participating actively in the stoning was fought and repressed by means of an inflamed mood and peer pressure (Sahebjam 1992).

For patriarchal marital legislation in the Jewish tradition, adultery signified the violation of the husband's right to possess the sexuality of his wife. Thus the punishment was directed against the woman and the adulterous man. Even the tiniest suspicion posed a deadly threat. The *śôṭâ* proceedings of Jewish law allowed a husband who suspected his wife of adultery to subject her to a "judgment of God" in which she was forced to ingest publicly a certain drink. For the woman affected, this procedure meant — assuming she survived at all — an excruciating, humiliating experience that marked her for the rest of her life.

Stoning was a collectively executed death sentence. The order in which the stones were to be thrown at the victim was of significance, for example, according to the degree of supposed injury (cf. Deut 17:2-7). In the stoning in John 8, this rank is reflected in the order by which the men leave the area, one by one (v. 9).

The ancient world was thoroughly aware of the atrocity of this form of execution. At the time of the Mishnah, therefore, an adulteress was instead to be strangled (*Sanhedrin* XI 1:6). John 8 shows that collective stonings punishing female adultery were definitely still practiced, despite awareness of their problematic nature. From the collective character of judgment and capital punishment, it is reasonable to assume that in verse 5 Jesus is being challenged to condemn the woman and thereby also to have a role in the stoning. He is to participate first as a judge and then as a thrower of stones in the male collective. Whatever the gesture of writing in the sand means, he chooses it instead of the sentence of condemnation demanded of him. Despite the pressure the men place upon him (8:7), Jesus refuses the role of the Jewish man who restores the honor of the people violated by adultery. In the process he prevents a woman's execution. Thus the patriarchal order is called into question at the crucial point of its control of female sexuality.

We can take for granted that the acquitted adulterer was unable to return either to the husband who set a trap for her to get rid of her, or to her earlier parental home. Here as well the reality of small communities in which she was able to find a new home is assumed.

Martha and Mary — John 11:1-46

The context in which Martha and Mary appear in the Gospel of John is completely different from that in Luke. Mary, Martha, and Lazarus are introduced as Jesus' friends whom he loved (John 11:5). Lazarus's role is passive. Martha is the dominant figure in the story. She is described as the householder. She goes out to meet Jesus and takes the initiative in their conversation. In John 12:2 Martha serves at dinner *(diēkonei)*; Mary is the woman who anoints Jesus' feet (11:2 and 12:3).

According to Elisabeth Schüssler Fiorenza, both sisters are described as having ministry offices. Mary Rose D'Angelo concretizes this observation and sees Mary and Martha as a missionary pair like Paul and Sosthenes.

Just as Paul calls himself an "apostle" and Sosthenes his "brother" *(adelphos,* 1 Cor 1:1), thus, according to her interpretation, Martha is described as *diakonos* and Mary as her "sister" *(adelphē)*. D'Angelo concludes from the significance of the house in the story and the fact that the house belonged to Martha and Mary that both women were the leaders of a house church, comparable to Prisca and Aquila. Thus, behind the story of Mary and Martha lies the tradition of a missionary pair well known in the early Christian movement. The history of exegesis, with its powerful gaze focused on the person of Lazarus, has obscured this tradition, and two missionaries have been made into supporting roles. Martha's confession, "I believe that you are the Messiah, the Son of God, the one coming into the world" (John 11:27), is the counterpart to Peter's confession in the Synoptic Gospels.

Lazarus is raised not into paradise but back into the oppressive political situation. John 12:10 and 11 describe how the leading authorities waste no time in attempting to kill Lazarus in order to get rid of him because so many people were believing in Jesus through him and because of him. In the text there remains no doubt that his resuscitation is only temporarily a victory over death and that Lazarus will one day die again. But the raising of Lazarus is a sign that points to Jesus. The story is framed by the deadly threats against Jesus (10:31-41 and 11:8-16). Jesus' death is the key to eternal life. For the women and men of the Johannine communities, the sign Jesus became for them and to which Martha gave voice in her confession was more significant than the sign he performed.

The Foot Washing: The Sacrament of Resistance — John 13:1-35

In this story the women in the Johannine communities are not mentioned even once, but nevertheless — from another perspective — we can learn something of them here.

We perceive right away that this is a story about power, power on three levels: the power of Jesus in his connection with God, the power of Jesus in connection with those who belong to him, and the power of Satan, which stands in complete opposition to the two spheres of love's power. These three levels appear in close proximity to one another; indeed, in part they overlap. Verse 1 speaks of the power of Jesus in his relationship with God and with his own; verse 2 speaks already of the power of Satan.

Here a community is articulating its experience with power, its experience with the possibility of accomplishing good, experiencing and suffering evil, and perceiving in its gathering the power of God. I will explore the following questions: Does the text reveal hints of leadership and guidance structures in the Johannine congregations? What power did women have in those communities? Are there indications of conflict? How did the women experience God's presence? To what experiences does the sacrament of foot washing correspond?

Along with everyone else, the women and men in the Johannine communities were raised knowing that their feet represented their connection with the earth and that uncovering one's feet demonstrated total openness and receptivity to the Holy.

An everyday action can simultaneously be used as the bearer of social and religious order. In the washing of feet the hierarchical pattern of the patriarchal society was reflected. At the lowest level of the hierarchy were the female slaves; they were obliged to wash the feet of their masters and their male guests. The next rung was occupied by the male slaves. In Israel, however, male Jewish slaves represented an exception: because they had to stay away from anything causing personal defilement, they were not obliged to perform these sorts of services. We see an allusion to this very lowest form of service in Psalm 60:8 where God wants to make Moab a washbasin for God's feet.

One of the imperative duties of a wife was to wash her husband's feet. She was not allowed to delegate this duty, unlike others, to female slaves. The Talmud argues that this task is an expression of particular marital intimacy and love. Nevertheless, it was also an instance of a power gradient, in that the husband was not obliged to perform similar duties of love. In the discussion in the Talmud it becomes clear that foot washing had a thoroughly erotic flavor. A tight linkage between service, dependence, and sexuality emerges. Foot washing in the ancient world was an act of hospitality, of honor, and of love, and at the same time an unequivocal signal of hierarchical power relationships. A free man would never wash another's feet. Yet this is precisely what the text reports.

For the Gospel of John, Judas is a particularly significant figure. In him numerous unbelievers who also existed in the Johannine community are incorporated. Betrayal from within their own ranks was a difficult and oppressive reality for the little congregations. The Gospel of John depicts how suspicions were cast on people close to Jesus as well as those sympathizing from a distance (cf. John 3:1-15). There were attempts to silence his followers religiously and politically; they were ostracized and led before a Pharisaic investigative commission. Testimonies of unswerving, courageous confession appear; but so does the opposite sort of behavior. That is what Judas stands for. The strong pressure and fear of reprisals are understandable. It was a problem for the community that someone from within its midst had handed Jesus over. So in the depiction of Judas' role the community accomplished a transformation: now it was predetermined by God that Judas must become Jesus' opponent. From the juridical role of the betrayer — still recognizable in John's Gospel — a theological role emerges. This reinterpretation is not so much repression as it is the attempt to come to terms with an extremely difficult situation.

The Gospel describes Jesus' preparations for the foot washing and its implementation almost contemplatively, liturgically, solemnly. I sense how the disciples, women and men, sat mute in amazement. What took place there is something unheard of, revolutionary. Jesus girds himself with a linen towel, the uniform of a slave. Something offensive is occurring: a free Jewish man washes the feet of women; a rabbi washes the feet of his female and male pupils.

Numerous exegetes are of the opinion that verses 12-17 represent a second, independent interpretation of the foot washing. While the first interpretation (vv. 6-10) is christologically oriented, they say, the second one refers to the necessity of imitating Jesus; thus it argues in ethical terms. This separation of Christology and ethics is not convincing. Jesus sees that his action requires reflection and explanation. He speaks to the scandal and the paradox: the power of Jesus deriving from his relationship with God allows him to emphasize his sovereignty. He is "Teacher" and "Lord." His adherents must follow after him and live as he does — but precisely in his renunciation of sovereignty. *This* is how they are to live, and *this* is how they are to practice foot washing. The text is unequivocal. The sacrament of foot washing will be practiced in the Johannine communities, indeed as a sacrament on its own terms. Comparison with the Synoptics at least opens the question whether perhaps foot washing was of comparable significance for the Johannine communities as the Lord's Supper was for other Christian communities.

Jesus' commandment that we love one another is expressly grounded in the love of Jesus for these communities. I cannot hear in this command any sense of limitation in comparison with, for instance, Jesus' command in the Synoptics to love our enemies. This is so because those who obeyed the command to reveal themselves as members of the Christian community placed themselves in danger. That is why there were so many secret sympathizers. Verses 34 and 35 are to be understood in such a way that for the Johannine Christians love could be manifested only in a particular social configuration: in small groups living counterculturally and thus representing a radical challenge.

From the outside the Johannine communities were vulnerable to the most difficult afflictions of a hostile environment; as a result, many did not stand up to such anxiety and fell away. Into this situation the Gospel of John has the departing Jesus give voice to his legacy — the command of love — intentionally between Judas's betrayal and Peter's denial.

The entire context is a reflection on dealing with conflicts and profound crises within and outside the community. To follow the command of love is by no means a withdrawal into a pious conventicle. What power these communities had — to insist on mutuality in a context in which every embrace represents, in the eyes of the occupying forces, a threat that must be fought and nipped in the bud! To serve one another and love one another: the agenda of the Johannine communities can be summed up in these two phrases, an agenda that promised temptation and danger.

Women as Leaders — John 20:1-2, 11-18

Mary from Magdala is named by the designation of her birthplace. This indicates that she had no husband and no family. She lived without family members among/in the groups of those who followed Jesus.

Early, while it is still dark, she comes to the tomb. These few words reveal the danger of this undertaking. Crucifixion was the Romans' form of capital punishment of political insurgents. For friends and relatives it had dangerous consequences: burial and mourning were forbidden. In many cases it is reported that persons who wept at the death of someone executed in this way were themselves crucified.

Mary of Magdala runs to Peter and the Beloved Disciple to tell them that Jesus' body is no longer lying in the tomb. Then she returns. The following verses give expression to a very close relationship with Jesus: she weeps and searches desperately for him. The climax of the scene is reached at the point when the dialogue between Mary and Jesus is most spare. But then Jesus seems to withdraw: "Do not touch me." In the language of the New Testament, "touch" means a transfer of power and participation in the person touched. When Jesus refuses Mary's touch, he is saying, "You cannot partake of what I now am," as if Jesus were now of a different world than Mary. We find this motif of untouchability in other passages of the Bible as well (e.g., Exod 33:20; 3:5). Mary receives a mission from the risen Jesus: "But go to my sisters and brothers and say to them, 'I am ascending to my Father and your Father, to my God and your God.'"

The first part of the message gives Mary the mission to witness to Jesus' resurrection. The second part is similarly decisive: Jesus' God is now also the God of the disciples. That which Jesus had previously lived and modeled alone is now entrusted also to the women and men who followed him (cf. John 7:37-39). The love and strength deriving from the intimate relationship between Jesus and God are now to be in them as well (cf. 17:26). Mary goes at once, without hesitation. In distinction from the accounts of Matthew (28:17), Mark (16:11), and Luke (24:10ff.), here the disciples accept Mary's testimony.

The information the Gospel of John gives us about Mary Magdalene belongs among the most important references regarding women in the early Christian communities. It makes clear that women were regarded as eyewitnesses of the Easter event and as proclaimers of this testimony. Mary is the apostle to the apostles.

Love and Mutuality as Lived Counterstrategies

On every page of the Gospel of John we experience something of the labor of the Johannine communities to practice just and respectful interaction with one another, to build communities that in the face of societal fear and injustice present something completely different. For the feminist search for traditions offering a new, liberating conception of sexuality and the relationships of our bodies and souls to other human beings, to the world, and to God, the Gospel of John is an inspiring wellspring. In John's Gospel alone the formula "love one another" occurs fifteen times. Here this mutual love is related to extremely varied dimensions of life. All women and men proceed downward within the socially established structures of rank. Higher rank or superiority is permitted for no one. Against the backdrop of the fundamental meaning of the foot washing and of mutuality in the Gospel of John, we can be sure that free men served slaves and free women; that is, they shopped for and prepared meals, served at table, and cleaned up again afterward. The mutuality of men and women is inherent within their relationship with Jesus.

In contrast to the Synoptics, John extensively portrays Jesus' relationship with God as his heavenly Father as a consummate relationship of mutual love. The Father loves him (5:20; 3:35 and passim; *philein* and *agapan* are used interchangeably and are thus not to be interpreted over against one another). Jesus loves the Father (14:31). Jesus is called the only Son (1:18). This love relationship encompasses the

675

intimate touch of bodies. The only Son rests on the Father's breast (1:18); in the same way, the Beloved Disciple rests on Jesus' breast (13:23). The expression "to lie at the breast/*kolpos*" depicts the most intimate physical communion. Nursing infants lie at their mothers' breasts (Num 11:12; Ruth 4:16). In a similar way, the intimate physical communion of parents and children and of a man and his wife is called resting "at the breast" (Deut 13:6; 28:54). *Kolpos* can refer to either the breast or the lap. The love and mutuality of Jesus' relationship to God, his Father, culminate in expressions of their being one: "I and the Father are one" (John 10:30; cf. 14:9-11; 17:11, 21, 26). The image comes from mystical traditions that understand sexual fusion as the primal image of union.

Jesus' body is the site of his relationship with believers. From Jesus' *koilia* ("belly" or "womb") flows living water that believers drink (7:38-39; cf. 19:34). Believers themselves similarly become a spring of living water (4:14). In 7:37-39 the expression *ek tēs koilias* means that believers drink the water of life from the *koilia* of Jesus, and also that the believers who have drunk from Jesus themselves become wellsprings. Another striking assertion about Jesus' body that in its directness has always been somewhat offensive to the dominant interpretations is that Jesus' flesh is eaten as the bread of life (6:54-56) and his blood drunk. This leads to consummate communion between Jesus and believers (6:56). This consummate communion and faith in the women and men recapitulate Jesus' union with God. The result of that union is that believers too are united among themselves (17:26). All these images and assertions about union strain toward unceasing mutuality. Believing women and men love one another with the love of God.

Jesus' body is the door. The way into life leads through his body. Jesus' body (*sōma*) is called a temple (2:21). Jesus gives his life for his friends (15:13). His body is raised in three days (2:21). The body of Jesus and the bodies of believers are sites of God's new creation and of a loving, just union.

A Feminist-Theological Reading of Johannine Messianism

Is the Gospel of John a document of withdrawal from reality? Did the women and men in the Johannine communities feel bound "more to heaven than to earth" (Käsemann 1966, 17)?

In fact, the Gospel of John does think in a dualism very close to that of Gnostic groups. Over and over two realities stand juxtaposed. For instance, the Samaritan woman gives Jesus water to drink, and he gives her the water of life (4:9-16). The ancestors ate manna in the wilderness; Jesus is the Bread of Life (6:48-51). On the one hand, here is the world in which people are born, eat, drink, get hungry, know fear, are healed, die. Jesus too lives in this world and performs miracles that belong in this reality. But on the other hand this world is only the surface. For the eyes of faith it is transparent. The statement "My kingdom is not from this world"

(18:36) encapsulates in one sentence the entire faith content of the Gospel of John. How are we to understand this step "into the beyond," into another world? The predominant interpretation was widely promulgated through Rudolf Bultmann's fascinating commentary on John. He explains Johannine dualism in such a way that bodily reality, including the political and practical dimensions of human life, is inauthentic, superficial, and thus unimportant. The other interpretation asks from the perspective of the women and men in Johannine communities: What did it mean for them when they spoke of a Jesus whose kingdom was not from this world? Why did they believe in him as Messiah and thereby move in a different direction from the messianic faith of the Synoptic Gospels? Within the context of the Gospel of John, it is clear that 18:36 represents neither a declaration of loyalty to Caesar nor a silent enduring of the reigning power. Instead of these it contains a political claim. This becomes clear when Jesus, even before Pilate, remains true to his claim to be king, and when he allows himself to be acclaimed as a politically revolutionary king at his entrance into Jerusalem.

In other ways as well, the assessment that the Johannine communities lived as conventicle groups locked away from the external world, cultivating a religion of escape within, does not stand up. In 12:42-43, persons who do not publicly declare themselves for Jesus as the Messiah are sharply criticized. "My kingdom is not from this world" thus means in this second interpretation that this kingdom has its origin and its goal in God, not in this world, yet that it takes place *in this* world.

The background of the Johannine dualism is the situation of double threat: exclusion from their own people and oppression by Rome along with their people. Johannine dualism is the attempt to live on in Jesus' manner within a world of fear. Instead of what is "dangerous" (Käsemann), I can more readily see in this theology what is creative, resistant, and liberating. With enormous depth, the Gospel of John conveys experiences of constriction, anxiety, exclusion, and real, deadly threat, as well as how, despite this constriction, human beings can open a space to act and to breathe.

This does not mean to flee, to run away. It means to have sufficient strength to be able to meet the difficulties and conflicts effectively. In that the women and men of the Johannine communities juxtaposed two realities, this helped them to live their experiences differently: as if they were free to accept them or not. Thus for a few moments they are subjects and not objects of history. They make something of what others have made of them. Perhaps this appears to have been an illusion. And yet it was more than that. It was something that played out in their consciousness, something we call faith, moments of respite, of identity. It was something that expanded beyond these moments (though for some this was not the case; see 12:42-43). Only in this way did that which had never been seen before become possible. A springboard was there without which things crashed to a halt, but from which a space for decision could be launched. This changed people like the Samaritan woman, who exited her harsh life of labor and exploitative relationship with a man; like the adulteress who found a new home though all signs pointed to her death; like Mary, who let no one stop her when the time came for action on behalf of those in need; like Mary Magdalene, who came to mourn the dead but was then made a prophetic herald. And like the women and men in the Johannine communities themselves, who in a situation of real and encompassing threat regularly celebrated a sacrament of mutuality and love. They are beyond the reach of death even when they die. And they continue to make Jesus' proclamation available.

LITERATURE

Bechtel, Lynn M. 1996. "A Symbolic Level of Meaning: John 2:1-11; The Marriage in Cana." In *A Feminist Companion to the Hebrew Bible in the New Testament,* edited by Athalya Brenner, 241-55. Sheffield.

Brown, Raymond E. 1970. *The Gospel according to John.* Anchor Bible, vol. 29/29a. New York.

Bultmann, Rudolf. 1956. *Das Evangelium des Johannes.* Göttingen.

———. 1971. *The Gospel of John: A Commentary.* Philadelphia.

D'Angelo, Mary Rose. 1990. "Women Partners in the New Testament." *Journal of Feminist Studies in Religion* 1:65-87.

Kahl, Brigitte. 1994. "Die Frau am Väterbrunnen." In *Für Gerechtigkeit streiten: Theologie im Alltag einer bedrohten Welt,* edited by Dorothee Sölle, 53-58. Gütersloh.

Käsemann, Ernst. 1966. *Jesu letzter Wille nach Johannes 17.* Tübingen.

Kitzberger, Ingrid Rosa. 1994. "Love and Footwashing: John 13:1-20 and Luke 7:36-50 Read Intertextually." *Biblical Interpretation* 2, no. 2.

Lieu, Judith. 1996. "Scripture and the Feminine in John." In *A Feminist Companion to the Hebrew Bible in the New Testament,* edited by Athalya Brenner, 225-40. Sheffield.

O'Day, Gail R. 1987. *The Word Disclosed: John's Story and Narrative Preaching.* St. Louis.

———. 1992. "John." In *The Women's Bible Commentary,* edited by Carol A. Newsom and Sharon H. Ringe, 293-304. London and Louisville.

Reinhartz, Adele. 1994. "The Gospel of John." In *Searching the Scriptures,* edited by Elisabeth Schüssler Fiorenza, 2:561-600. 2 vols. New York.

Ringe, Sharon. 1986. "Homiletical Resources on the Gospel of John: The Gospel as Healing Word." *Quarterly Review* 6:75-103.

Sahebjam, Freidoune. 1992. *Die gesteinigte Frau.* Hamburg.

Schneiders, Sandra. 1982. "Women in the Fourth Gospel and the Role of Woman in the Contemporary Church." *Biblical Theology Bulletin* 12.

Schottroff, Luise. 1990. "'Mein Reich ist nicht von dieser Welt': Der johanneische Messianismus." In Luise Schottroff, *Befreiungserfahrungen: Studien zur Sozialgeschichtliche des NT,* 170-83. Munich.

———. 1992. "Die Samaritanerin am Brunnen (Joh 4)." In *Auf Israel hören: Sozialgeschichtliche Bibelauslegung,* edited by Renate Jost, Rainer Kessler, and Christoph M. Raisig, 105-32. Lucerne.

————. 1994. *Lydias ungeduldige Schwestern. Feministische Sozialgeschichte des frühen Christentums.* Gütersloh.

————. 1996. "Important Aspects of the Gospel for the Future." In *"What Is John?"* vol. 1, *Readers and Readings of the Fourth Gospel,* edited by Fernando F. Segovia, 205-13. Society of Biblical Literature Symposium Series, vol. 3, 7. Atlanta.

————. 1997. "Sexualität im Neuen Testament." *Evangelische Theologie* 5:437-44.

Schüssler Fiorenza, Elisabeth. 1985. *In Memory of Her: A Feminist Theological Reconstruction of Christian Origins.* New York.

————. 1988. *Zu ihrem Gedächtnis . . . Eine feministisch-theologische Rekonstruktion der christlichen Ursprünge.* Munich and Mainz.

Wengst, Klaus. 1990. *Bedrängte Gemeinde und verherrlichter Christus: Ein Versuch über das Johannesevangelium.* Munich.

Translated by Lisa E. Dahill

Acts of the Apostles: Looking Forward and Looking Back

Ivoni Richter Reimer

Introduction

The Acts of the Apostles is an important book; it is read often and intensively in the Christian base communities in Brazil. At this time, two particular aspects or lines of inquiry are of special interest in these circles: the structure of Christian community and notions of utopia. Both originate in the reality of our own experience, which is more and more defined by the effects of the massively practiced neoliberal, globalizing system of exclusion.

People recount past events so that these events can have a positive effect on the present. What does Acts have to say to women? Can it contribute something toward nonpatriarchal lifestyles based on solidarity in home, church, and society? These are questions we ask in approaching Acts. We do not merely want to read and understand. We want what we read to have a liberating effect in our lives. We try to read Acts from a feminist liberationist perspective. We consider the whole as well as the smallest elements of the text. Thus I begin with an overview of Acts and then go into each story that describes women in their social-historical context. These stories, because they are treated as examples, assume paradigmatic function in relation to the rest.

The Text of Acts

Luke's Acts of the Apostles is a theological book about Christian beginnings and mission. Embedded in it is the description of the spreading of the Jewish-Christian faith, especially through the evangelism of Peter and Paul. Women, children, and men who came into contact with them are also named here and there, depending on whether they were important to Peter's and Paul's journeys.

A book like Acts is not the work of a single man. Stories that are told are not "Lukan" stories in the individual sense. They belong to larger groups or worshiping communities that lived them, and also to those people who passed them on orally or in writing. We must assume there are children, women, and men behind and in the process of the creation of Acts, who contributed to the fact that the "Lukan double oeuvre" — the Gospel of Luke and Acts — was consciously or unconsciously created and that we today can be heirs of its history. So many hands helped to create the "Lukan double oeuvre." At a certain point someone, or perhaps even a team, put all the material together and wrote the text down. In the tradition of the early church, "Luke" is named as the author and identified with the physician Luke who worked for a time in Paul's mission team (Philem 24; Col 4:14; 2 Tim 4:11; Acts 16:10-17; et al.). Acts says he also wrote the Gospel of Luke (Acts 1:1-2). Since then, this view has found widespread acceptance in Second Testament research.

But there are also reasons to question this assumption. For example, there is a lack of historical or theological agreement between what is reported about Paul in Acts and what Paul writes in his letters. Thus it is claimed that the writer of Acts was unfamiliar with Paul's letters. Despite this, Paul seems to have served as his model for mission as he learned about him through word of mouth (see Comblin 1987, 1:59-62; Martin 1994, 763-64; Pesch 1986, 1:25-28).

We cannot know for certain who the author was. The two books, however, bear the mark of a writer with a Greek-Hellenistic education who had extensive knowledge of history and theology and put these to use in his writing. He is very familiar with the Septuagint, identifies with Judaism, and is likely one of the "Godfearing ones." His name is not mentioned in either book. Not until the end of the second century c.e. are both books attributed to Luke. They are both, in fact, anonymous books that belong to the worshiping communities — children, women, and men — from the moment they were conceived. In this sense, then, with due respect to the tradition of the text, I can continue to call the author/writer "Luke."

There is consensus among researchers that Acts can be dated to the last two decades of the first century c.e. Acts was written later than the Gospel of Luke. That Gospel seems to know nothing about the persecutions that Domitian perpetrated against Christians in Rome and Asia Minor at the end of his reign (81-96). But Jerusalem and the temple are already spoken about in the past tense (Luke 21:20-24). Thus we can assume that Acts was written about 90 c.e. The place where Acts was written is uncertain. There are different hypotheses. The early church tradition suggests Rome. Others assume Antioch, Ephesus, or Corinth (Pesch 1986, 1:28). In composing Acts as a literary work, "Luke" writes the Greek-Hellenistic language of his time, *koinē*. Acts is a literary work of high quality both in terms of word choice and in terms of grammatical usage. "Luke" creates a unity out of various elements of Greek literature and the Septuagint. "He has Peter preach in Jerusalem in a simple, awkwardly semiticizing style, whereas Paul speaks before the Areopagus in Athens in the artful style of elegant Greek rhetorical phrases" (Pesch 1986, 1:35).

The style of Acts is never boring. To achieve this, "Luke" uses various devices such as long speeches, short commentaries, dialogues, inserted letters, resolutions, prayers, and the "we" sections, which he organizes into a nicely readable work of art. These are basically an "expansive and versicolored mosaic of Christian beginnings" (Martin 1994, 765). The shifting scenes and rhythms of the narrative are major formal literary characteristics that serve a certain purpose. Acts wants to encourage children, women, and men whose lives are rooted in suffering to bear witness, and to build hope along with them against all loss of perspective.

Purpose and Theological Intention

"Luke" dedicates Acts, as he did his Gospel, to a certain Theophilus (Luke 1:1-4; Acts 1:1-2). The prologue (Luke 1:1-4) introduces the entire double oeuvre and actually announces its purpose. "Luke" intends to describe the life and work of Jesus and the beginnings of the church. For Acts, this means that the purpose of writing it down consists especially in "assuring the dependability of its witness to Christ by demonstrating the continuity and identity of the one story whose author is God, the exalted Lord and the Spirit, for the generation following after the Apostles" (Pesch 1986, 1:29).

"Luke" writes to church communities of various origins, to children, women, and men who want to live their faithfulness to God on a daily basis as a response and a testimony to the love of God. Countless are the situations that might lead them away from the Jewish-Christian faith: the number and the attractiveness of other religions, the pressures of political authorities, the lack of perseverance in view of the long and difficult journey, or even the regression into patriarchal lifestyles in families and church communities. Persecution for religious and political reasons is present and is increasing. What should be done now, and how? What is our story and our identity?

"Luke" writes about the past partly to show answers and guidelines for "today." The two books are intended to help in the process of building viable structures for Christian life on the personal and the social level.

According to the prologue (Luke 1:1-4), which also introduces Acts (1:1-2), Acts can be understood as proclamation *(kerygma)* of what has been hoped for and fulfilled. Thus it also has a catechetic purpose, namely, for training people in the Christian faith and for information about the beginnings of Christianity, to strengthen the foundations of the faith of Theophilus and the readers.

"Luke" writes to demonstrate that the promised good news has been fulfilled in Jesus and that it continues to be at work in the churches through the transforming and liberating power of the Holy Spirit. It is this dynamic that creates community, which becomes fruitful in everyday life and which spreads abroad in the form of mission, as confession and as a sign of the kind of good and just life that God intends for all people.

The "events that have been fulfilled among us" (Luke 1:1) are a part of God's redemptive history, which continues to be at work among the communities of disciples through the power of the Holy Spirit. The time of fulfillment is also the time of the church, which gives expression to the apostolic commission of the resurrected One through fellowship and solidarity (Acts 1:2) and thus concretely realizes the presence of the resurrected Christ.

In my view, Acts is not a "political apology" for Christianity over against oppressive political power structures, nor does it intend to trivialize the Christian faith. Core guidelines for conflict situations with those in power can be found in Acts 4:19, 5:29: It is better to obey God than human beings, in 10:34-35: anyone who loves God and does what is right is acceptable to God, and in 24:25: justice, self-control and the coming divine judgment are signs that are brought before the rulers of the day. Obedience to God and the everyday practice of justice define and characterize Christian everyday life in the world. Thus "Luke" is certainly not inclined to be friendly toward any oppressive ruler. His only friendly disposition is toward the reign of God, which is defined by and brings about peace and justice, and which invites, calls upon, and empowers people to participate in it in freedom and solidarity.

Acts testifies to and thus awakens one again and again to utopias that come into being with unquestionable certainty. God's good news is a transforming and liberating power that has inclusive character in diverse times and cultures. It can therefore solidify faith and love and build up hope in the midst of oppressive situations, and those where liberation is occurring, whether past or present.

Numerous suggestions have been made as to how to approach the structure of Acts. Typically there are two different levels on which the structure of Acts has been ascertained. First, if the analysis is oriented around the two main figures of Peter and Paul, then the book appears to be divided into two parts (chapters 1–12 and 13–28). Otherwise, if the analysis is geographically oriented and dependent on Acts 1:8, then we have a three-part construction: 1:1–8:3 (Jerusalem); 8:4–11:18 (Judea and Samaria); 11:19–28:31 (to the end of the earth as we know it).[1]

With both suggested structurings of the book, the boundaries between the sections are not that clear; Peter still appears in the "Paul cycle" and vice versa; Jerusalem plays an important and central role throughout Acts, which makes it impossible to restrict oneself solely to Acts 1–8.

Whichever structural division is preferred, one should always take note of how and in what contexts and in what functions women and children occur in the text.

---

1. Cf. the informative commentary and suggestion as to how to structure the book by Pesch 1986, 1:36-41. In my view it is difficult to support a chronological division (basic structure: Israel period, Jesus period, church period) as does Martin 1994, 765, who repeats a commonly held view.

What Are These Women Doing in Acts?

Women do not appear in isolation in Acts. When they do appear, it is always in relationship to others. Thus our task is also to understand "women passages" in a larger context of relationships. Women as well as men and children should be understood in their sociocultural and literary context. Such a relational approach brings to light how a story functions as well as what an author intends in the context of the reception history of biblical texts. It is often impossible, however, to find a common denominator between the actual story and the author's intention. I am thinking, for example, of the role of women as eyewitnesses and the apostolic office of men, a question to which I shall return.

I shall attempt to analyze in which contexts women occur. In the first and most important part, I shall analyze the groups in which women participate. In a second step I shall address the coupling structure used in Acts to convey equal status of men and women. I shall conclude with a summary of Acts with respect to the activity and influence of women, and the history of the effect of androcentric and patriarchal historiography and interpretation.

Women's Groups

Women can be found in groups. This is indicative of the fact that women are everywhere, whether in homes, synagogues, or on the streets. They are religiously and professionally active, and often participate in such groups independently. They are leaders. And debaters. Even where both the patriarchal view of history and androcentric language are at work to suppress women's voices, they emerge in the moment that they are being denounced, and announce, from then till now: this would be a great time and place for a liberating new beginning!

Mary and the Other Women in Jerusalem

This can be seen already in the first group we shall discuss. It consists of Mary, the mother of Jesus, the other women, and the brothers of Jesus, who were together with the Eleven in Jerusalem (1:12-14). These people together constitute the community who are united in anticipating Pentecost. Now they find themselves in the "Upper Room," a room that for Jewish people serves as a living and prayer space and is also used for studying the Torah. It is precisely in this sense that the "Upper Room" can here be understood as the regular gathering place of this united community.[2]

---

2. See Richter Reimer 1992, 235-37. Concerning women and men as members of the community, Codex Bezae also speaks of children, and some Vulgate manuscripts allude to infants. This could be an attempt by patriarchal editors to read "women" as "wives" and/or "mothers."

So here we have a gathering of women and men who have followed Jesus from Galilee to Jerusalem — women who were eyewitnesses not only of the crucifixion and resurrection of Jesus, but also of his entire life and ministry. They are apostles who were never officially named to this office. They are bearers of the good news, but they have no official status. The criterion for the office of apostle was clearly formulated by men: it must be a man (1:21)! Women were excluded here because they were women! By the way: Who was this Matthias who was chosen by casting of lots, anyway?

Right at the beginning of Acts a part of women's history is hidden behind a veil, in that the women themselves — except for Mary, the mother of Jesus — remain nameless after the names of the men have been mentioned. This is slightly different than in the Gospels, where they are named (e.g., Luke 24:10).

The mention of Mary, the mother of Jesus, indicates that she and her children had entered into discipleship with Jesus and wanted to live as disciples after his death and resurrection (see Luke 8:19-21; Matt 12:46-50). Thus Mary took an active part in the reign of God.

To be sure, the text could not leave women out completely since it places them as equals in the community (all are persistently of one heart and mind in prayer), yet at the same time it textually suppresses and makes impossible their apostolic office — though not their apostolic work! — and relegates them to the sidelines of historical power.

After 1:14, women "disappear" in the text. The androcentric language creates the impression that there are no women present in the development of the story as described so far. This language is deceptive; it distorts the image of, and the reader's perspective on, reality. After this, women are expressly mentioned, namely, in conflict situations and when they are known leaders in the churches who cannot be left out of the narrative. To omit mentioning them would contradict the author's stated intent of giving "precise and reliable" (NRSV: "careful" and "orderly") testimony (Luke 1:1-4). And then, only in Acts 5:1-11, a woman appears with her husband in a narrative that is rather detailed for Acts, after a long silence about the presence and participation of women at the Pentecost events, and at the beginning of the building of the new church community.

Ananias and Sapphira

Ananias and Sapphira constitute the second group in which a woman explicitly takes part in a significant event in the church community (see Richter Reimer 1992, 29-54 on this subject).

A private life story unfolds within the community. Private and community matters become intermingled in the process. The narrative describes and addresses conflicts and questions of identity. It becomes clear that private matters are indeed embedded in community contexts; personal decisions become political in their effects, and vice versa. The story of the married couple Ananias and Sapphira is embedded in the literary context of the "community of goods." It follows the account about the community's policies regarding solidarity and survivor rights and about the example of Joseph Barnabas's actions in this regard (4:32-37). The couple is thus mentioned in this concrete context of solidarity, shared material goods, and community *(koinōnia)*. Thus it is in this context in Acts that we find the first, and in this particular form the only, reflection about violation of boundaries, transgression, and sin. This happens not in some moral realm or sense, but quite concretely in everyday life, and that is where its consequences are felt.

For a feminist hermeneutic of liberation and feminist exegesis, it is important and necessary to pay attention to the social-historical details in the text that can also bring to light the whole web of relationships. If there is potential for liberation that can be realized for the lives of women as well as men, both in reading the text and in using it as a springboard for insight, it should first be that we understand both the negative and the positive actions of Sapphira within her social-historical context, and then second, that we also learn to read the text from the point of view of its negation, namely, the death of both husband and wife. For the saving factor, the liberation is found precisely on the other side of this negation.

This potential for liberation not only makes it possible and opens the way for us women to be willing to help and to share, but also challenges us to assume a critical view of what others do with our willingness to help and even with our solidarity and our initiatives.

The text should be read with an eye critical of patriarchy. In the first part (5:1-4), Ananias is the subject of the actions. In the second part, however, in Peter's speech, Sapphira is included as cosubject. Ananias makes the decision, plans and carries out the plan to embezzle a portion of the funds. Sapphira plays along. She is complicit by knowing what is happening *(synoida, 5:2)*. Thus she is an active participant in the embezzlement. Here we can see the structure and dynamic of the patriarchal household as it was common both in Judaism and in the Roman-Hellenistic world (cf. Schottroff 1994, 34-70; 1995, 17-42). The text reveals both an action it judges positively and one it condemns. Sapphira is showing solidarity when she agrees to selling the field. By giving her consent, she is renouncing the security of the *kethuba,* the contractually secured estate in the event of divorce, which Jewish law guarantees to her. Sapphira sacrifices her marital rights for the sake of the community. She takes an active legal position in the process of the sale. What happens next, however, reflects her traditional, passive role within a patriarchal system. She plays the role of the complicit partner who then also becomes an active coperpetrator in certain concrete circumstances. This negative side of her participation is related to patriarchy, in which this couple, too, was caught. Such complicity can only exist where there continue to be structures characterized by injustice and subordination, as, for example, in patriarchal marriages. The problem is, after all, not that they carried out the sale together, but that Ananias planned and carried out the embezzlement and that Sapphira knew of this. Here she is entangled in a marriage of subordination.

The text shows how difficult and nearly impossible it is to live the good news of God's reign in a world and in a church community (the word *ekklēsia* appears here for the first time in Acts) that is characterized by a model of equality and at the same time by the reality of patriarchy. The voice of the man, and the silence of the woman, constitute their "unity" (5:9), to tempt the Spirit by deceiving the community. To lie to God, to tempt the Spirit of God, is equated with depriving the community of what it needs to live and survive. This is also related to the attempt to destroy utopian models and utopian experiences. This whole spectrum of action creates the "sin" that leads the couple to their death. Complicity is no excuse for anyone. It participates in the creation and maintenance of injustice (and structures of injustice) by an attitude of omission. Death functions here to uncover the structure of sin that is patriarchy,[3] to reveal lies that again and again had become necessary to cover up the truth, and to unmask structures that make it impossible for women and men to translate the freedom given to them by Christ into a liberated life.

Ananias and Sapphira, too, stood under the power of sin. But there is an important difference between the sin of the one and the sin of the other. Ananias sinned by asserting himself, while Sapphira sinned by failing to assert herself. In so doing, Sapphira actually even missed the chance to distance herself from her husband when Peter took her to task (5:8). Her immediate death is the negation of such an attitude and action. And yet the couple is then buried by the church community. That is the last service the community provides even to people who have hurt it. This shows that the church leaves judgment and punishment to God alone.

The traditional function of this text is that it creates, or is used to create, great fear in the congregation and with everyone who hears or reads the story (5:11)! But for us today, it can also take on a new function. If we read the story from the perspective of reversing its negation, we might have an antenna for the liberating aspects of it. Unlike Sapphira, women should not fail to resist the power of sin. They should disassociate themselves from the corrupt and death-bringing decisions of their husbands and of other men such as those encountered in the story. Take a position and keep your distance! Here, active disobedience is called for so that women will not be sentenced along with their husbands and the other men, and so that such choices that lead to death can be reversed. Not subordination and silence are required, but resistance.

So that women can take them, they must receive support for such liberating steps in their concrete life circumstances as well. Not only self-respect and self-determination are necessary, but effective and supportive solidarity as well. There

3. This goes against the traditional interpretation of the death of the couple as based on a "punishment invoked upon them by a word" from Peter. Cf. the extensive discussion in Richter Reimer 1992, 45-53.

must be a "community of saints" that actually receives women, children, and men, and strengthens them through action and prayer when they become disobedient in the sense of the story. If we do not manage such support, then our world will continue to be full of Sapphiras who join their silence with the corrupt and planned actions of many Ananiases the world over. And death will continue to win out over good and achievable utopias of life liberated for justice.

The Widows in the Church at Jerusalem

The Hellenistic widows in the church community at Jerusalem (6:1-7) appear in the literary context of the news of the growth of the congregation (6:1 and 7: *plēthynō*). The apostles had been given an order by their superiors not to speak in public, but had violated the order. Their preaching leads to the growth of the community of disciples. At the same time, the text addresses the second internal conflict within the church, which concerns the "everyday ministry" *(diakonia)*, in that the Hellenistic widows were being neglected. This happened not just once, but frequently (imperfect tense: *paretheōrounto*). "Luke" understands and interprets the conflict between "Hebrews" and "Hellenists" as the consequence of neglect in the area of the diaconate or caregiving to needy members of the church community. Against this background, "Luke" wants to explain why the number of chosen workers is increasing, and why there is now a distinction between various forms of service.

Traditional exegesis has understood "everyday ministry" *(diakonia)* to mean "care for the poor" in the sense of "meal service," as an arrangement involving preparation of meals for strangers and poor people in Judaism. It is possible that this is what it means, but it is not necessarily limited to this. The "everyday ministry" is also mentioned in the summaries (2:42-47; 4:32-37), and there it signifies participation in the eucharistic meal gathering as well. So this conflict could also have to do with "the role and participation of [Hellenistic] women at the eucharistic meal" (Schüssler Fiorenza 1983, 166). "Everyday ministry" is not necessarily limited either to feeding the hungry or to the eucharistic meal gathering. In my opinion, this text, as others, deals with a more comprehensive kind of service (Matt 25:35-40) in which everyone who is involved in ministry actively participates. Thus the neglect of the Hellenistic widows might relate to their daily welfare as well as to their religious work, which could take forms such as prayer, preaching, solidarity with others, and presence at meal gatherings. The very fact that the conflict described here resulted in the concept of ministry being split into "ministry of the table" and "ministry of the Word" is in itself evidence that until that moment, the concept of "ministry" always signified a unified ministry. The criterion for this "ministry" is androcentric: seven men were chosen (Acts 6:3 and 5). But this division of labor did not continue in such limited fashion, especially after the persecution (8:1-4) when the women and men scattered afar also proclaimed the Word.

Tabitha and the Widows in the Church at Joppa

The disciple Tabitha and the widows in the congregation at Joppa (9:36-43) present themselves as a group who live an everyday life of holistic ministry, that is, who celebrate worshipful service to God in the everyday life of the world. In this congregation Tabitha is described as a "disciple" *(mathētria)*. In this feminine form the word "disciple" occurs only this one time in the entire Second Testament; otherwise women are understood to be included in the masculine plural form. Tabitha is thus lifted up as leader of the congregation. As such she is praised and loved. Her ministry is so important that the text characterizes her with other attributes that are also part of her function: "She was devoted to good works and acts of charity" (9:36). The Greek expressions *ergōn agathōn* and *eleēmosynēn poiein* cannot be restricted to giving alms as is customary in the commentaries (cf. Richter Reimer 1992, 240f.). On the contrary, they describe a Jewish practice of solidarity that is utterly rooted in religious faith. They are the expression of a spirituality that expresses gratitude and signifies justice. They include ministries such as visiting the sick, offering strangers a place to stay, participating in burials, supporting widows and widowers, and also giving alms to the poor. This Jewish spirituality is affirmed in the church community, for it presents no barrier to belief in Christ, and therefore it is also not dissolved.

Tabitha dies. At her burial, an example of her own ministry is highlighted by the presence there of the widows and their pain. When Tabitha lived with them, she made clothing — outer garments and undergarments — for them, hand-sewn clothing in a cooperative. Making goods needed by a community in a community is also faith witness. And now the widows and the clothing they had made with Tabitha give testimony to her presence among them. Tabitha's life resides in this work and this group. Everyday solidarity and lived spirituality endure forever and conquer death. The literary form of miracle story connects Peter both with First Testament prophetic tradition (Elijah and Elisha) and with the Jesus tradition (Luke 7:11-17; 8:41-56), where through relationships of solidarity God's power proves itself as liberating. Wherever God is present in life, there death is also conquered, and resurrection makes possible new and renewed perspectives on life. This occurred in Joppa as well. The life and death of Tabitha set many things and many people into motion. Processes of reawakening can set new energies in motion in churches today as well, for the benefit of the socially weaker members.

In the Jewish-Christian community at Joppa, women and men are together. Together they comprise the communion of saints in which the widows are not neglected, in which women take leadership roles and in which men, too, run for help.

One of the important functions of this story is the affirmation of a woman disciple's life lived in solidarity, which is intended to continue to be an effective paradigm. Such a paradigm can win other women, children, and men over to this Jewish-Christian faith (Acts 9:42). They can now serve the one God, too, by doing life-giving works of justice and mercy in word and deed.

Mary and Rhoda

Mary and Rhoda, living and working in a house church in Jerusalem (12:12-17), open the door for us to the third church community in Jerusalem, but one that is led by a woman. The literary context provides an overview of the situation of persecution of the emerging Christian church and the dangers to which Christians are exposed. Therefore it is crucial that Peter goes not just anywhere after his release from prison, but that he becomes conscious of this whole situation and goes straight to the home of Mary, the mother of John Mark, who later works with Paul (13:5-13; 15:37; Philem 24; Col 4:10; et al.). Mary is identified with her son because she was not dependent on a husband, and because mother and son are very important to the life of the community and for preaching the gospel. Her house constitutes an antipatriarchal center within a patriarchal system.

There are "many" assembled in the house. This could mean women, children, and men. They gather there for worship *(synathroizomai)* in the night of Passover. They celebrate and remember events of liberation in the history of Israel, certainly also their liberation through Christ. And they pray, including in their prayers all who are suffering from oppression and pleading for liberation. Surely also Peter.

Peter stood on the street in front of the house and knocked on the outer gate. A slave woman named Rhoda went to open the door. The text does not say that she was Mary's slave whose job it was to answer the door (Acts 12:12-17). The only important detail for the story, pure and simple, is that there is no reference whatever to the power relationship between the woman slave and the woman of the house. The slave acts with autonomy, as though she were not a slave. She is part of the community of equals. Hence she recognized Peter's voice. She knew him and is now glad that he has been set free. She is so overjoyed that instead of opening the gate, she runs inside to proclaim the good news *(apangellō)* to the others. "You are out of your mind!" The response of the gathered friends shows that they do not believe that Peter has been freed, although they had prayed for just that. This news was hoped for, but now seems less than credible to them. What they say to the slave woman is exactly what the male apostles said to the women apostles who proclaimed Jesus' resurrection (Luke 24:11, 22-23). They call them crazy, not because they are women, but because what they are proclaiming is enough to make you crazy; it is something incredible. But the slave woman persists. She fights for the right to recognize the truth before everyone else. Rhoda asserts herself in Mary's house because she, too, has been given the space and the ability to do so. Mary's house constitutes an antipatriarchal center because here the barriers between masters and slaves have also been eliminated (Gal 3:28). Peter then also asks the friends to proclaim his liberation to the "brothers," which certainly testifies to the relevance of this house church to the organizational work and preaching of the larger church in Jerusalem. Is this a sign that only the Hellenists count in this house church? Possibly (Schüssler Fiorenza 1983, 166). But this is not a persuasive argument.

The main reason that Mary's house should be considered an antipatriarchal center, in the end, is that she does not work with the political power that is persecuting the people. The political-military regime under Herod Agrippa I is unmerciful; it has the soldiers responsible for the escaped prisoners executed (Acts 12:18-19). Peter is a refugee who is being sought by the authorities, but who is not betrayed by the house church community. And the Word could continue to be spread after Herod's death.

Lydia and the Women in Philippi

Lydia and the women in the church in Philippi (16:11-15 and 16:40), as an organized women's group in the Roman colony of Philippi in Macedonia (present-day eastern Europe), are unique in the Second Testament. They had gathered on the Sabbath in the synagogue building *(proseuchē)* at the river's edge outside the city. The Greek-speaking diaspora used the word *proseuchē* to refer to synagogue buildings that served other social and community purposes besides worship, such as housing the community water supply (see the thorough discussion of this by Richter Reimer 1992, 98-122). The association of concepts and terms like *synerchesthai* (to gather), *kathizein* (to sit down), and *lalein* (to speak) in the context of the synagogue indicates that the text is about a worship service on the Sabbath in which the missionaries took part, as was the custom elsewhere as well. The great difficulty this text presents to interpreters is that it deals only with women. For this reason they conclude that there is no synagogue and no worship service in this case.[4]

However, it has been established through informative literary and archaeological research (Brooten 1982, 35ff. and 90ff.; Schottroff 1990, 302ff.; 1993, 73-75; cf. Tosefta *Megillah* 4:11; Babylonian Talmud *Megillah* 23a) that women, too, had leadership functions in the Jewish synagogue and that women and minors also belonged to the *minyan*, the minimum number needed to constitute a synagogue worship service.

The missionaries seek to join the synagogue congregation, as elsewhere. According to Luke, a group of women are leading the Jewish worship service on the Sabbath in Philippi. One of the women in particular is mentioned by name. She is characterized with a few brief attributes: Lydia, a worker in purple dye, from the city of Thyatira (in present-day Turkey), a God-fearing woman. Among the God-fearing people in Philippi were women and men who had assumed a Jewish way of life and practiced the Jewish religion. These included both rich and poor people,

---

4. Pesch (1986, 2:104f.) also considers *proseuchē* as referring to a synagogue building, but one in which no women were present: "One may likewise imagine that Paul and his co-workers sat down with the women gathered in front of the Synagogue and that their interest, especially that of Lydia, did not allow them a chance to visit the worship in the Synagogue."

but more women than men. This is explained not by circumcision, in my opinion, but because the Jewish religion "has to have offered women a possibility to express their identity collectively, something that did not exist before" (Schottroff 1990, 300; 1993, 70; cf. Richter Reimer 1992, 114-22), and because they were able to enter actively into religious practice and worship as subjects.

The geographical description "from the city of Thyatira" together with the vocational designation *porphyropōlis* allows insight into the social and vocational reality of Lydia's life, which also can be projected to the other women. The Lydia region of Asia Minor and especially the city of Thyatira was known for the production of clothing of purple fabric. The purple dye was created from plants grown in this region. The work involved in the production of this dye was not only hard, but also dirty, since the workers also used urine to give the dye greater shine and endurance.

In the Roman-Hellenistic world, such people were discriminated against and marginalized. They practiced vocations that were unworthy of a "free man." Working in the production of purple dye and textile products was for slaves or freed slaves. It is documented by inscriptions that production and sales were carried out in groups. Normally they were mixed groups of women and men who moved around, probably in order to sell the products. These people constituted *collegia* (clubs) in which they could pursue both their vocational and their social interests and could express their religious faith or spirituality. This organization was also frequently called a "house."

This background throws some light on the women's group in Philippi. They formed such a house, in which they organized and could give expression to both their vocational and their religious life. Lydia appears as their leader; thus the text speaks of her "house."

It is theologically significant in this story that women lead worship services and that God chooses a woman and "opens her heart" so that she understands what Paul is now preaching here, too: the expected Christ. And when God opens people's hearts, then women, too, can live according to what they have come to understand. They do not need a man to tell them what to do! Because God opens Lydia's heart in this way, Lydia and her house accept the Jewish-Christian faith and are baptized.

Of ecclesiological significance, I find, is not only that a women's church is founded, but also what happens there. Lydia is able to proclaim it herself. Christian life consists in being true to the "Lord," who liberates, which translates into acting in solidarity with others. The "pressures" felt by the missionaries (Acts 16:19-24) are based on the anticipated and imminent danger to which they are exposed in the Roman colony, which is hostile to Jews. Lydia's house offers protection; she bases her theological argument with the missionaries on the maxim of being true to Christ. That is faith. That is the expression of the choice to serve only one "Lord."

Lydia's house, too, appears as an antipatriarchal center in its social context. This is shown both in the realm of work and in religious life. It remains the case when men enter into the house community, since Lydia remains the leader of the congregation. This is emphasized by Luke in 16:40. This solidarity, the ecclesiology of this house community that breaks through the status quo, would be worth further study, for example, in the story of the slave girl who had a "spirit of divination" (16:16-18; see Richter Reimer 1992, 162-201). The religious-political conflict arises because Paul drove out the spirit of divination from the slave girl, which had been the source of a secure, good income for her masters. It is a complex story. Even if this spirit guaranteed the slave girl a better position with her masters (good food and no abuse), it keeps her bound in slavery to her masters; it is not in a position to free her. On the other hand, one must ask whether Paul's action of driving out the spirit of divination, which began with the fact that the slave girl's divination activity was in competition with his own, in fact signified liberation for the slave girl. It is not "Luke's" interest to inform his readers about this. But we must include the question in our creative reconstruction of the text. What happens with her, now that she no longer has any special skill to secure the economic well-being of her masters? What value does the injured slave woman now have for her masters, who have also suffered damages? In my opinion, this story becomes important ecclesiologically for the history of liberation only if we can consider the historical possibility that this woman, who has lost her economic value, was taken into the community of saints in Lydia's house (16:40). This is the only way she would have had a chance to free herself and give new shape to her life. According to Luke, women were the beginning point of the Jewish-Christian congregation at Philippi. Paul, too, knows the leadership role of women in this congregation (Phil 4:2), although he does not name Lydia, for reasons unknown to us. The participation of women has been remembered differently, but the fact that they were protagonists cannot be erased. Upon this fact we can build engaged congregations.

The missionary work of Paul, Silas, and Timothy with various groups brings them into contact again and again with women, children, and men in various cities of the Roman Empire (Thessalonica, Berea, Athens) that accept the Jewish-Christian faith, but not only with these. In their work they also meet other missionary men and women who preach the gospel like them. Acts gives us an example when it tells about Paul in Corinth.

Priscilla and Aquila

Priscilla and Aquila appear for the first time in Acts doing missionary work in Corinth (Acts 18). The working couple had been expelled from Rome by the edict of Claudius, which ordered all Jews to leave Rome. Aquila, a Jew from Pontus, and his wife Priscilla were likely already Christians when they were in Rome. It can be assumed, on the one hand, that at that time no sharp distinction was made between Jewish and Christian believers (see Acts 16:20 in this context). On the other hand, this also means that Priscilla and Aquila were already active as missionaries in Rome long before Paul's epistolary message. Priscilla and Aquila serve as an example for women and men from the class of small business people and artisans who had accepted the Jewish-Christian faith and who furthered this liberating message as they traveled and in their work life.

All three, Priscilla, Aquila, and Paul, worked as tentmakers *(skēnopoioi,* 18:3). Priscilla and Aquila probably produced tents made of leather that they then also sold (Richter Reimer 1992, 206-18). They made their living from this hard work. Their house was their workplace and a worship space at the same time (cf. Lampe 1989, 159ff.). There they could always take in other travelers who were passing through. Their mission was also one that they lived every day in the midst of their work life. Their house was one of the many house churches in which women like Priscilla, Lydia, Mary, Tabitha, and many others worked together as equals and nonmarginalized people, translating mission and teaching into reality, just as Paul, Barnabas, and Apollos were doing.

Priscilla's teaching activity is directly described in Acts 18:24-28. There, in the context of the synagogue, we hear that the scribe Apollos is talking in detail about Jesus, but that he knew only about baptism by John. Afterward, Priscilla and Aquila took him aside and taught him "in more detail" *(akribesteron)* by describing God's way to him. This concept implies that this occurred without any sense of competition or arrogance as a supportive act, to enlighten and edify Apollos. Thus a scribe is taught by a working missionary couple.

The important missionary activity of Priscilla is a part of church history that was suppressed only much later. Paul mentions Priscilla and Aquila in his letters together with their house church community (1 Cor 16:19; Rom 16:3; in the Pastoral Letters, see 2 Tim 4:19). Priscilla and Aquila stand beside Paul as missionaries of equal status. Their preaching was praised in much of the tradition of the church of antiquity. John Chrysostom kept their memory alive by recalling both of their areas of work: their tentmaking, carried out in poverty, and the mission work they were doing at the same time. Priscilla is remembered as "the excellent missionary" (John Chrysostom, *Salutate Priscillam* 2.1), who was known throughout the *oikoumenē* of the time.

The marriage of Priscilla and Aquila was not defined in such a way that the wife was to be subordinated to the husband or to live in his shadow. Their relationship was of decisive importance in allowing the two to realize a kind of teamwork carried out at a local level in a community of people of equal status where their ministry was lived out as service in the unity of Word and deed (cf. Schüssler Fiorenza 1983, 178-79).

Women and Men

Women appear in Acts named in couples with men. This is a special way to express in literary terms the equal importance of women and men.

a. Thus there are, on the one hand, many passages that simply say "men and women," for example, 1:14, 2:18, 5:14, 8:12, 17:4, and 17:14, passages that describe the growth of the churches or report about baptism. The only individuals named here are Dionysius and Damaris, who were working as philosophers in Athens (17:34; Richter Reimer 1992, 253-54). Other passages, such as 8:3-4, 9:1-2, and 13:50, report about the persecution of Christians, where women are persecuted as well as persecuting others. From this one can conclude that in all situations where there is a crowd of people, women and children are part of that crowd. But they are only mentioned when the author wants to emphasize something.

b. On the other hand, Acts represents women and men by name as couples in certain contexts, relationships, and actions. On some occasions there are also a combination of three: men, women, and children (one time only, in 21:5); Philip, his four daughters or female prophets, and Agabus (21:8-9). These are women and men who were very important in the beginning stages, who were considered protagonists and therefore served as models. They could not be left out of the narrative, for their memory was still alive in the various church communities: Priscilla and Aquila (18:1-4) and Sapphira and Ananias (5:1-11) are couple figures of equal status in a single story. But there are other women and men whose stories should also be understood as narrated about couples. I am thinking here of two examples: Tabitha and Cornelius, and Lydia and the jail-master who, though they do not appear in the same story, have much in common and can thus be evaluated on an equal basis. The story of Tabitha is part of the mission that involves providing single and socially disadvantaged women a nonpatriarchal home. This story cannot simply be reduced to a kind of "prelude" or "opener" for the story of Cornelius (Pesch 1986, 1:320; Roloff 1981, 158), since this would shift readers' attention directly to Cornelius. The same is true of Lydia and the jailer at Philippi. Each story has its own unique meaning and significance within the Jewish-Christian mission and history. If one story crosses boundaries in the sense of "reaching out to other peoples" (Cornelius and the jailer), the other crosses boundaries in the sense of reaching out to the "other" in overcoming discrimination in sex roles (Tabitha and Lydia). Women and men who come from different cultural traditions have a characteristic in common that is important for their participation in the Jewish-Christian community and history, namely, honoring God and practicing justice (10:34-35). All these did that: Tabitha, Cornelius, Lydia, and the jailer. Therefore they should be remembered as equals, for a multicultural church can be built on this basis.

In conclusion, a summary view is to remind us again both of the work of women and of the history of the influence of an androcentric and patriarchal historiography and its interpretation. There is no doubt, given the passages and contexts we have analyzed here, that women were of equal rank with men in mission work, that they were active in preaching, and that they had leadership and teaching roles both in the context of the synagogue and in the house churches. Beyond this, however, one must also raise the question about the silence of women and/or the silencing of women and women's stories.

In Acts, "Luke" suppresses the role of the women as witnesses from the very beginning, resulting in their exclusion from the office of apostle. He also suppresses the fact of women's preaching ministry, for nowhere does he expressly state that women preached. As we have seen, it is only in carefully reconstructing a text linguistically and historically that this comes to light. Even where women hold key offices in a community, they are hardly mentioned. So there are two tendencies that can be traced to the very beginnings of the Christian tradition: one liberating and one oppressive, and the two exist simultaneously and side by side.

One reason for this is androcentric historiography, which "normally" hides women and thus includes or subsumes them within masculine concepts (e.g., 2:41; 4:4; 4:32; et al.). Thus it is always appropriate to read texts with this silencing in mind, or, in addition, to bring a critical perspective to reading the entire text from the perspective of the women and their stories that are mentioned in it. The few texts that do recount women's voices (Sapphira in 5:8; the slave women Rhoda in 12:12-17; Lydia in 16:15; and the slave woman diviner in 16:17) must be taken as a basis from which to read other texts as well. Context and vocabulary are decisive in this process; they provide key information about the content of women's life praxis.

"Luke" is neither a great feminist nor a great misogynist. He writes his history of the church and theology, choosing and ordering the tradition available to him according to his primary interest, which is to present the history of the beginnings through the work of Peter and Paul. In so doing, he does allow us to reconstruct a portion of the history of women in that society and in the church, and to have a renewed sense of courage as utopian models emerge. In his work it also becomes clear that in spite of his complicity as an agent in the formation of a hierarchical culture, he was not a supporter of the prevalent tendency in his time, namely, the patriarchal subordination of women in the home and the church.

Thus Acts can be read critically as part of the history of women, which is constructed not in isolation but within sociocultural contexts rich with conflict. This history, too, is part of our inheritance, intended to empower us in our engagement for justice, and able to encourage us to live in solidarity with others. And herein also lies the joy of the experience of resurrection.

LITERATURE

Brooten, Bernadette J. 1982. *Women Leaders in the Ancient Synagogue: Inscriptional Evidence and Background Issues.* Brown Judaic Studies, vol. 36. Atlanta.

Comblin, José. 1987. *Atos dos Apóstolos. Comentário Bíblico NT.* 2 vols. Petrópolis, Vozes.

Lampe, Peter. 1989. *Die stadtrömischen Christen in den ersten beiden Jahrhunderten. Untersuchungen zur Sozialgeschichte.* Wissenschaftliche Untersuchungen zum Neuen Testament, 2nd ser., vol. 18. Tübingen.

Martin, Clarice. 1994. "The Acts of the Apostles." In *Searching the Scriptures,* edited by Elisabeth Schüssler Fiorenza, 2:763-99. 2 vols. New York.

Pesch, Rudolf. 1986. *Die Apostelgeschichte.* Evangelisch-katholischer Kommentar zum Neuen Testament, vol. 5, 1 and 2. Zurich, Einsiedeln, and Cologne.

Richter Reimer, Ivoni. 1992. *Frauen in der Apostelgeschichte des Lukas. Eine feministisch-theologische Exegese.* Gütersloh.

Roloff, Jürgen. 1981. *Die Apostelgeschichte.* Das Neue Testament Deutsch, vol. 5. Göttingen.

Schottroff, Luise. 1990. "'Anführerinnen der Gläubigkeit' oder 'einige andächtige Weiber'? Frauengruppen als Trägerinnen jüdischer und christlicher Religion im ersten Jahrhundert n. Chr." In Luise Schottroff, *Befreiungserfahrungen. Studien zur Sozialgeschichte des Neuen Testaments,* 281-304. Munich.

————. 1993. *Let the Oppressed Go Free: Feminist Perspectives on the New Testament,* 60-79. Louisville.

————. 1994. *Lydias ungeduldige Schwestern. Feministische Sozialgeschichte des frühen Christentums.* Gütersloh.

————. 1995. *Lydia's Impatient Sisters: A Feminist Social History of Early Christianity.* Louisville.

Schüssler Fiorenza, Elisabeth. 1983. *In Memory of Her: A Feminist Theological Reconstruction of Christian Origins.* New York.

————. 1988. *Zu ihrem Gedächtnis. Eine feministisch-theologische Rekonstruktion der christlichen Ursprünge.* Gütersloh.

For Further Reading

Baumgart, Norbert C. 1999. *Die Umkehr des Schöpfergottes. Zu Komposition und religionsgeschichtlichem Hintergrund von Gen 5–9.* Herders biblische Studien, vol. 22. Freiburg.

Feministische Auslegung ausgewählter Beispiele aus der Urgeschichte. Rückblick auf ein Vierteljahrhundert feministischer Auslegung von Gen 2 und 3. Conference Proceedings, IOSOT Basel August 5-10, 2001. 2002. Leiden.

Gössmann, Elisabeth, ed. 2000. *Eva — Gottes Meisterwerk.* 2nd ed. Archiv für philosophie- und theologiegeschichtliche Frauenforschung, vol. 2. Munich.

Kvam, Kirsten E., Linda S. Schearing, and Valerie H. Ziegler, eds. 1999. *Eve and Adam: Jewish, Christian, and Muslim Readings on Genesis and Gender.* Bloomington, Ind.

Schüngel-Straumann, Helen. 1999. *Die Frau am Anfang. Eva und die Folgen.* 3rd ed. Münster.

————. 2002. *Anfänge feministischer Exegese. Gesammelte Beiträge.* Münster.

Translated by Nancy Lukens

Romans: A Feminist Reading

Elsa Tamez

The Sender of the Letter and Its Context

A feminist reading will interpret Romans as the product of a particular context that changes and challenges the reader, rather than as an abstract dogmatic treatise. For feminist theology, the concrete experience of reality is an integral component in the development of an argument. The everyday life of the author is extremely dynamic. In 56 or 57 C.E. Paul writes to the church in Rome from Corinth. A short time before that he had been imprisoned in Asia and later released. He traveled to Macedonia, returned, wrote the so-called letter of reconciliation to the Corinthians, and afterward returned again to Corinth. He intended to go to Spain, but before he could travel to that country he had to go to Jerusalem to turn in the offering he had collected in Macedonia and Achaia for the poor among the saints of Jerusalem (Rom 15:24-26). He wanted to travel from Jerusalem to Spain and visit Rome on the way (1:12; 15:28). Although his relationship with some members of the church in Jerusalem was strained (15:30-31), it probably never occurred to him that they would arrest him when he arrived in Jerusalem and that he would arrive in Rome as a prisoner facing trial. Naturally he knew the risks of those who proclaimed a messiah who had been crucified by the Romans and who had been resurrected by his God. But he probably never thought that he himself would be sentenced to death just a few years later, ironically enough right in the capital of the empire.

The situation in Rome was not unknown to Paul, even though he himself had never been there. He had been together with Aquila and Prisca, members of the church in Rome (16:3) who had been banned from Rome together with the other Jews on the grounds of Emperor Claudius's decree (Acts 18:2) in the year 46. On the other hand, he had already traveled a great deal and had been an eyewitness to Roman domination in economic, political, and military affairs, which proclaimed "peace and security" in the occupied areas in opposition to unconditional subjugation.

In reading the letter to the Romans, the context of subjugation by the Roman Empire is as conspicuous as the internal theological conflict within Judaism resulting from the event of the Messiah, who was crucified by Roman justice but raised by the justice of God. Finally, one can also not fail to hear the voice of the author: a Jewish craftsman with the "marks of an apostle," such as imprisonment and torture (2 Cor 6:5), that grant him a certain degree of authority to make theological statements of an eschatological nature based on his everyday experience. Also not to be overlooked is his everyday relationship with women who are church leaders, and the way in which he valued and respected them (chapter 16). Unfortunately the language of his theological arguments is often so androcentric that it masks the nature of his everyday relations with his companions in missionary work.

Thus, on the one hand, we have the practice of an apostle who does not marginalize women and a treatise about the righteousness/justice of God, who takes sides with the outcast, if we read it with a view to the political and economic practices in the Roman Empire. On the other hand, we have some statements about the state (Rom 13:1-7) or cultural ideas (1:26-27) that not only contradict the two previous points, but also work to the disadvantage of the outcasts, despite the fact that they may be based on formulaic sacrificial rituals (3:24-25). Among these three positions, the first two carry more weight than the last. Strangely, although the sacrificial formulas are pre-Pauline and 13:1-7 is possibly post-Pauline, the tradition has increasingly emphasized these statements of marginal importance. In this commentary we intend to remain faithful to the logical direction in which the text points, and therefore we adopt the first two positions and give the third a more relative weight.

The Woman Who Delivered the Letter

A woman is assigned the task of personally delivering the letter to Rome. It is Phoebe, a person of high rank with important leadership functions. Paul calls her "sister," servant or deacon and protector (NRSV: benefactor). She is a deacon (*diakonos,* a masculine word in Greek pointing to an official usage in this context) of the whole church of Cenchreae, so she is not merely assigned to some helping function; the word does not occur in Acts 6, which speaks of service at table. The title *diakonos* is also held by Paul, Apollos, Epaphras, and others. According to the usage in other writings of Paul and in extrabiblical sources, the term applies to men and women missionaries who are preaching and teaching (Schüssler Fiorenza 1983, 170). Moreover, the very inclusion in a letter of that time of a recommendation of the person delivering it serves as a signal that he or she knows its contents and can explain it if necessary. Paul recommends Phoebe by mentioning her titles. She is also a *protectora,* a *patrona (prostatis).* That is a term with legal meaning signifying someone who vouched for foreigners who had no security guarantee. It is a title of honor and authority in antiquity and applies to persons to whom others are subject. Paul acknowledged the status of those who were subject to him. The fact that translators rendered the word *diakonos* with "servant" and *prostatis* with "helper" merely reflects the prevalent sexist perspective of the translators. To be called "sister," as also with "brother," means one is part of a group of missionaries working together.

Thus, Paul entrusts to the hands of Phoebe, servant of the church of Cenchreae, his coworker and "sovereign lady" *(Herrin)*, the letter that was intended to be read in a loud voice to the Christian churches of Rome. Phoebe will be present to clarify any doubts or questions about its contents.

The Churches of Rome, the Addressees

Rome was an overpopulated city, full of contrasts and social problems. For some reason or other there was a need for 20,000 armed men at the beginning of the empire "to maintain order." The Christians (Gentiles and Jews) lived and met for the most part — not all of them — in the Trastevere district and in the Via Appia. These were the unhealthiest places in the city, very densely populated and with heavy traffic passing through. This is where traders from the Orient and sailors arrived and found lodging. The Christian churches presumably consisted of poor people, but there was no lack of those of higher rank as well who were able to help those living in great need. These were likely businesspeople who had to pay a tax (*telos;* 13:7). It is possible that the church was composed chiefly of foreigners; as foreigners they were forced to pay tax (*phorous;* 13:6) from which the citizens of the city were exempt. The equal treatment Paul admonishes them to practice (12:10; 15:7) and the greeting to the nine women of twenty-six people mentioned (16:1-15) allow us to recognize the author's vision of a church in which there is not supposed to be discrimination of any kind. The letter is addressed in particular to the Gentile Christians (1:5-6). However, it appears that the churches of Rome maintained a very close relationship to the church of Jerusalem. Paul wants to make his position on the law and on circumcision clear. Certainly the church in Rome had already heard something about Paul's radical theology. On the other hand, 14:1–15:13 describes a particular situation of discrimination by Christians — Gentile or Jewish — toward those who continued to adhere to certain religious norms.

In chapter 16 Paul sends greetings to a good number of church members he had come to know in other places. If we take into account the context of patriarchal forms of social relationships, the greeting sent to rather numerous women is striking. From the manner in which Paul relates to them, we can conclude that in this period there was no difference at all between his own missionary work and that of the women. Likewise, the same risk of persecution and imprisonment existed for both men and women. It is interesting that Prisca is mentioned before Aquila. Surely she was the more active of the two. The couple had risked their lives for the apostle. This heroic act must have been well known in the whole church community, since the whole church is grateful to the couple and since Paul devotes two verses (16:3-4) within the greetings section to them. Now, back in Rome, Prisca and Aquila offer their house for the church's gatherings (16:5). Among the women, Junia is also singled out as an apostle (16:7). As women interpreters have long realized, the translators robbed Junia of the function of apostle for many years because she was a woman. Junia was an apostle together with Andronicus, her companion, many years prior to Paul, and they were in prison together with him. The other women, tireless in their work, are Maria, Tryphaena, Tryphosa, and Persis. The author also does not forget to greet three other women whom he knew: Julia, the mother of Rufus, and the sister of Nereus.

The Letter

My feminist reading of the text itself will not go into a critique of the language, which is already well known. I know that the language is androcentric and that the production of the text took place in a patriarchal culture. Instead I shall attempt to formulate several theological statements in a new way, from a feminist perspective, namely, following the logical direction taken by the content of the text.

The tradition has taken up aspects of the epistle, such as sin, grace, faith, election, and others, and has developed doctrinal opinions on each based on an abstract view. This has contributed to the fact that the message has lost its power. The feminist method, oriented toward a liberating reading, frees the letter from this prison. It begins with the concrete situation. In so doing it supports not only the women, but both sexes, and all of society. Thus the letter must be read within the socioeconomic, cultural, and religious context of the first century, and that is the place from which one must try to understand its theological perspective.

A useful key for entering into the text is to read it beginning with the theme of exclusion. In this way we can work out a new feminist reading without any great difficulties. Whether one looks at the meritocracy of the class-oriented Roman society or any religious experience whatever, Christian or Jewish, there is the tendency to exclude and to discriminate. Paul would like Jews and Gentiles to be able to participate in the promises of God. The creation is a house in which there must be room for everyone, with equal rights as sons and daughters of God. Paul takes up the words from the baptismal formula in Galatians 3:28 precisely in order to include the outcasts, among them the women. A reading that applies this method builds a bridge to an actualization of the text.

I will analyze two sections of the text: Romans 1–8 about God's justice and Romans 9–11 about election. I will conclude briefly with Romans 12–15 with the invitation to discernment in everyday life and to mutual acceptance.

Romans 1–8: God's Justice and Justification as Good News for Women

Traditionally, justification by faith or God's justice has been understood as forgiveness for the sinner and liberation from guilt. If this statement is not located in a concrete historical context, it makes no sense; in fact, it can even be irresponsible if the necessary clarification does not follow. The sin that kills today is quite a tangible fact, just as the victims of sin can be named. Above all, what we expect is that God's justice should manifest itself, not that the guilty be forgiven. If we read this false understanding of justification from a feminist perspective, the result is even worse.

In speaking of being freed from guilt, one assumes that the guilt corresponds to a real, criminal act. But this definition cannot be applied to woman in this way. If we proclaim justification to woman as liberation from guilt, we must ask: Which guilt are we attributing to woman? That she does not want to be the woman that society defines her to be? That she wants to be a person with an identity of her own?

As we know, woman was damned by society for no reason. It was not her deeds, that is, unjust actions, that were the basis of her damnation but simply the fact that she was born in a patriarchal world. The great injustice of society is making a guilty person out of an innocent one.

If we read justification and forgiveness from the perspective of salvation from guilt, we reinforce that woman is guilty of the offense of overstepping the boundaries of her role as woman. She committed the offense of wanting to be herself. Even if woman is a "sinner" like every human being, her sin does not consist in overstepping the boundaries of her identity as second-class being that society has ascribed to her.

Thus one cannot speak of liberation from guilt or forgiveness of the sinner without analyzing this concrete reality. Justification by faith must go deeper and analyze the sinful relationships within society.

Injustice and Sin

In Paul's theology of sin *(hamartia)* and God's justice *(dikaiosynē theou)* (Rom 1–3), the empire is not explicitly mentioned. He speaks of the ungodliness and wickedness of the people who suppressed the truth in injustice *(adikia)* (1:18), and of the fact that no one is capable of practicing justice. But if we study the situation in Rome from the perspective of those who were excluded, we immediately discover the connection between the power of sin and the socioeconomic situation, between God's justice and the justice of the empire, between God's mercy, in which justice is given as a gift (in view of the practical inability of human beings to realize it on our own), and persons earning it through status, wealth, and power, which is at the root of the law of the empire.

I believe that Paul sees in the Roman Empire an economic, political, and military power that it is impossible to oppose. That is why it assumes the dimension of a structural sin that leads to death. He sees it as a system that gives the appearance of being a protector and liberator of the provinces, but that behind that appearance hides its inner injustice. For Paul the absence or the nonrecognition of God is pure idolatry.

Paul uses the term "sin" *(hamartia)* in the third chapter, not before. In chapters 1 and 2 he speaks only of injustice. The practice of injustice by everyone has turned the true knowledge of God into its opposite. This led to truth being imprisoned in injustice (1:18). Sin is the society turned into its opposite, in which everyone is an accomplice, even though they may not intend to be. In 1:18-32 Paul describes in three steps the process through which society turns into its opposite. First, God reveals who God is (1:19, 20), then people distort this knowledge (1:21, 23, 25), and finally, people do what is not healthy (1:21c, 22, 24, 26, 27, 29-31). Unfortunately Paul uses homosexuality — a common critique directed at Gentiles — as an example to demonstrate the obfuscation of society. In so doing he allows himself to be led by the patriarchal, heterosexual perspective.

This absence of justice, or the absence of the true God, leads Paul to theologize about sin since Adam. The Roman Empire was not the first, and not the only, experience of domination of entire peoples, so there must be something deeper within human beings that allows them to practice injustice and become entangled in it. For at some point the injustices take on a life of their own and lead to sinful social structures that cannot be controlled and that enslave all people (cf. Schottroff 1979, 496).

Paul finds no justice in his time that bears the seal of truth. Paul proves the contrary to be the case: people want to practice justice according to the law, but the result is injustice (2:21-23). Sin took advantage of the good God-given law and absorbed it (7:7-13).

Structural Sin in Patriarchal Society

Violence against women is the dark blemish of the perverse structure of a patriarchal, racist society such as that of the Roman Empire of the first century. Violence against women is one of the most shameful facts of today's civilization. There is no country, rich or poor, in which charges are not brought daily for physical, emotional, and sexual assaults against women of all ages, races, and social classes; the poor are particularly targeted. Violence is systematic and occurs in the workplace, at school, on the street, and in the home. All women are afraid of being attacked physically and sexually in one of these places. The deceptive separation between the private and the public spheres hides this reality or trivializes it.

On the basis of sworn statements by women, it is known that physical, emotional, and sexual aggression distorts the self-image of the woman and brings about changes in the depth of her being, diminishes her human quality and her self-respect. Systemic violence against women often leads to a powerless rage that can only be discharged against children, the beings who are even more fragile than the women themselves. This spiral of violence that is carried on from the strongest to the weakest demonstrates the monstrousness of the patriarchal system.

Structural sin permeates the entire society and the cosmos. The list presented in 1:29-31 shows that the weight of wickedness consists in "violations of relationships to other people" (Ruether 1994, 130). If violence is a manifestation of relations of dominance, this becomes visible in the manner in which men and women behave toward one another, and in the violent way in which human beings behave toward nature. Systemic violence is manifested in international and economic militarism. A detailed analysis of each of these areas shows clearly that women and girls are the first victims. In the current situation of the feminization of poverty, in this culture of survival, consumerism, and competition, violence gains in strength, beginning with a refined, subtle form and ending in the murder of women and girls.

In this situation, neither men who are aggressors nor women who are victims, nor the society as a whole, can mirror a complete humanity, for the attackers are themselves victims of their own violence and the society as a whole is complicit in the sin, because it fails to name it as such.

We need a radical transformation of this patriarchal, racist, and sexist society in order to be freed from this sin. Salvation does not come from judicial laws, though these perhaps help. We know what progress societies have made with regard to laws, and at the same time we register an increase in violence. Moreover, we know about the manipulation of the laws to benefit those with power and money. We need a radical conversion that makes us conscious of this sinful situation and our personal structural complicity with sin. We need faith in a different logic in relationships between men and women, and the concrete commitment, with the renewing power of the Holy Spirit, to live by it. The pre-Pauline baptismal words in Galatians 3:28 are a fundamental commitment of faith to live in a new creation. "For one believes with the heart and so is justified, and one confesses with the mouth that Jesus is Lord" (NRSV: "confesses with the mouth and so is saved") (Rom 10:10). To utter these words means for men and women to confess from the heart that in Christ there is neither man nor woman, neither master nor slave, neither Greek nor Jew nor foreigner. Violence against young girls and against women reveals a sick society that needs divine healing, for "There is no one who is righteous, not even one" (3:10) who would be capable of dealing with this structural sin.

The Justice of God is Diametrically Opposed to the Justice of Patriarchal Society

The term "God's justice" *(dikaiosynē theou)* has various connotations. It relates to a legal understanding of justice, the just manner in which God has always acted in history, and to a justice that human beings should practice. Despite these different connotations, all point to the difference between this justice and that which the first-century Christians experienced, whether as the justice of the legal system or as social justice. One was discriminatory (punishments were different for the poor and the rich), and the other represented its own negation: injustice.

So there was, according to Paul, neither an objective nor a subjective possibility to practice justice with one's own resources in an unjust world dominated by sin (3:9-18). The proclamation of God's justice appears as significant news (3:21).

Paul comes to the conclusion that in view of the endangerment of life and the human incapacity to oppose injustice, while being its victim and at the same time responsible for it, only God's justice gives human beings dignity and enables them to be doers of true justice. Jesus was the first just person. Because of him all have access to this grace, even those who victimize others, if they can believe in the God who brings the dead back to life (4:24-25). This faith in the impossible (4:19) strengthens Paul in his everyday struggles and dangers (cf. 1 Cor 15:31-32).

Thus, God's justice is realized in patriarchal society out of the principle of equality of justification by faith, and not by fulfillment of the requirements of a patriarchal tradition and culture. It is a matter of a gift given by grace in a society that knows no grace, but that judges by merits in order to evaluate persons.

Through sworn statements of women, we know that they constantly observe themselves in order to be loved, in order not to leave any obligation that society places on them unmet. Nevertheless, they do not reach this goal, no matter how hard they try. The expectations that women are supposed to meet cannot possibly be met: overburdening domestic responsibilities; excessive demands in bed; overexploitation in the workplace; excessive demands regarding the physical care of their bodies in order to make a good impression on others; overwhelming media expectations to consume more and more in order to become a real woman or to be a good and modern housewife. Punishment and judgment to the point of physical and emotional violence threaten women if they don't achieve all this. This is why we say that woman is not free and does not feel free. Our patriarchal, hierarchical society functions according to this logic based on merit. This is the way it makes its judgments; this is how its justice looks.

God's justice is diametrically opposed to this justice. Above all, it is based on the logic of grace. Women do not need to bargain for human dignity, by piling up economic, cultural, or social achievements in order to gain recognition. By grace all are recognized as equals with the right to be respected in their difference. Women are loved by God "just as they are," without a fuss; it is a gift given to every woman and every man. There is no exclusion with God's justice. God's justice manifests itself out of compassion for the crucified one, as one can see in the passion of Jesus Christ, and in the overcoming of the crucifixion through the resurrection. In God's justice there is no demand for useless sacrifices by women. The good news is that the crucified one was raised again. The justice of God is demonstrated in the fact of resurrection.

When women recognize the structural sin of patriarchal society, they liberate themselves from false feelings of guilt. They feel challenged to take everyday reality and the life of the society upon themselves in accordance with the wisdom of grace rather than in accordance with the identity of slave women that society ascribes to them.

From the perspective of the Christian canon, we Christian women see God's justice in the Jew Jesus-Messiah, as historically revealed, as the one who lived a life of faith according to the logic of grace, always benefiting those discriminated against. The freedom attained through Jesus Christ is the freedom to live in accordance with grace, as an antipode to slavery, whose victim on the basis of the laws of patriarchal society is woman.

When a woman accepts herself as a free person because God's justice accepts her as woman, she has the capacity to judge for herself and can violate every law that diminishes her life, for she is justified by her position of faith. It follows the position of Jesus and not the standards of patriarchal society.

Since God's justice exists for everyone, not only for women, men can internalize this justice and be led by the logic that is diametrically opposed to the violence of patriarchy. The fact that justification is a gift for everyone, not only for women, is a dependable basis for breaking with the logic of structural sin, which is directed against women.

Traditionally it was thought that one is justified by faith in Jesus Christ *(dia pisteōs Iēsou Christou)* (Rom 3:22) on the basis of his death on the cross. A possible translation is that one is justified by the faith of Jesus Christ, that is, through his lived faith, that revealed itself in his works of justice in Palestine, in his faithfulness to the Torah of God.

God justified Jesus because of his service of justice. The fact that he was resurrected shows that he was justified by God, whose judgment stood in opposition to the damnation by the Roman masters and the Jewish leadership that was subject to them.

Paul juxtaposes Adam and Jesus Christ in Romans 5:12-21 as the dual pioneer icons who introduce two different aeons. They are icons of the old and new humanity. Though both represent a masculine identity, at least Paul gives no reason to reinforce the general thinking of patriarchal society that blames Eve for the entry of sin into the world because she seduced Adam into tasting the forbidden fruit. Paul's interest in these texts relates to the superiority of the new aeon that has begun through Jesus Christ, the new Adam. While the first Adam, in whom all of humanity participates, leads to death, damnation, and sin, the second Adam, in whom, likewise, all of humanity participates through grace, leads to life, grace, justice. For women who fight against the ideology of patriarchal culture, with its roots in societies since antiquity, it is fundamentally necessary to point to the newness of this era (Russell 1987, 18), in which human relationships take place in a framework of justice and grace.

From a Theology of Sacrifice to a Theology of Praxis and Gratuitousness

In recent years, feminist theology and the theology of liberation have fought against the theology of sacrifice. The values that tradition emphasizes in this theology are similar to those that patriarchy demands of women: sacrifice, suffering, self-denial, and voluntary submission. Moreover, the language about God as one who sends an innocent son to his death on the cross finds a parallel in the misuse of the authority of the fathers in the way they deal with their sons and daughters. It is clear that the metaphor of sacrifice as demanded by God the Father, and the sacrifice of the son, were worked out according to the patterns of a patriarchal society.

An understanding of grace according to Romans automatically excludes the theory of satisfaction by punishment (Anselm of Canterbury), which suggests that God had to offer his son as a blood sacrifice in order to satisfy divine justice and to bring about the forgiveness of sins as a necessary work of salvation, in order to compensate for the guilt of humans before God, brought about by insulting God through sin. In Romans, justification has its roots in God's freewill act of solidarity with the outcasts of history. Thus God cannot at the same time demand the shedding of blood by the outcast par excellence: "the stone that the builders rejected has become the very head of the corner" (1 Pet 2:7), in order to reconcile the world unto himself and at the same time to reconcile himself unto himself. Tradition has overemphasized the aspect of the sacrifice of Christ, his shedding of blood on the cross, and allowed us to forget the whole story of his conflict-ridden life that lies behind this later reading of the historical event of the condemnation of Jesus by the Roman Empire to die by crucifixion.

When Christ's bloody death is mentioned in the epistle, pre-Pauline formulae are used. But Paul does not consistently use them; on the contrary, he associates the discussion of justification with the resurrection. In Romans 4:25 we read: "[He] was handed over to death for our trespasses [pre-Pauline formula] and was raised for our justification." Romans 3:24-26 is a pre-Pauline cultic fragment that was possibly already known in the earliest church communities and that calls attention to the liberating function of Christ and the forgiveness of sins.

Paul uses *hilastērion* simply as an image for sacrifice that brings the life and work of Jesus-Messiah into clear focus for us. It serves as a simile.

The world and humanity are described as a dead end, for which the good news of God's justice is not that God forgives sinners on the basis of his son's blood. Rather, the great news is that God offers the opportunity to transform this upside-down, inside-out world that discriminates against and excludes people because of their sex, their race, or their class. The one who was condemned because of his practice of justice is raised from the dead. The real intention of God's justice is not to forgive, but to create God's creatures anew as people of dignity and worth who are capable of transforming the world turned upside down by sin. That is why God's justice does not take account of sins. This is also good news, for "the wages of sin is death" (6:23). In this sense God shows compassion and pity. Using the sacrificial cult as a key to reading the letter to the church in Rome is not a path feminist theology can follow.

Women reject the idea of sacrificial love and self-denial because these values were forced upon them by the ideology of the dominant culture. Such duties are like laws from which women seek to liberate themselves, namely, without guilt feelings. That is why it is a liberating message for women to speak of the grace of God.

Grace stands primarily against the norms that demand meritorious service in order to be considered a human being with worth of one's own. For those who have been transformed by God's justice, doing justice is neither a burden nor something forced upon them. The practice of doing justice is oriented toward the logic of grace, and that originates spontaneously, not from duty, but from insight and from the heart, which wants to show "the love of God, poured into our hearts through the Holy Spirit" (5:5). In the end, grace opens up spaces in which it is possible to live together and celebrate concrete everyday life along with its feasts. The pressure to be efficient or to be a "superwoman" is not what rules the realm of grace. There is the knowledge of the limits of humankind as the heirs of the fallen nature of Adam, but there is also the certainty of faith that wherever sin is powerful, there grace is even more powerful.

Women stand in the context of exclusion between the logic of death and the logic of faith.

The Epistle to the Romans, like that to the Galatians, elaborates on the fact that God justifies human beings by faith and not by their works. Paul offers a radical critique of Mosaic law and circumcision. This criticism, like other hard sayings about the Jews in the Gospels have brought about and legitimized an anti-Judaistic way of thinking that was totally irrational at times. For this reason and also because of progress in recent years in research on the rhetoric of antiquity and on Judaism, interpretations of the Second Testament have become very cautious in their statements about the Jews.

We cannot overlook Paul's critique of the law and of those who want to obligate people to observe it because they attribute saving character to the law. Paul is a Jew, and he is practicing self-criticism toward a blind obedience to the law. He does not reject the law; on the contrary, he relativizes the real possibility of changing the sinful world, in which "the truth is imprisoned in injustice." He sees no other option but to seek and to demonstrate a greater power that is capable of making justice possible on earth. This power is the grace, the faith, made manifest in Jesus, the Messiah, and present in the human beings that have been created anew. Thus they weave new relationships, relationships with other human beings, with the cosmos, and with God. Paul as a Jew seeks reconciliation between the Jewish and the non-Jewish world. He puts them on an equal level: both are sinners and both have access to grace. All are sons and daughters of Abraham and Sarah, not only their descendants according to the flesh. Faith makes it possible to put an end to the inequalities.

This statement also applies to relationships between men and women. An interpretation of the Torah with its focus on circumcision and the law emphasizes their differences. This is the case in Roman law as well, as it applies to women and to different social classes. The regulations of these two worlds allow the exclusive structure of patriarchal culture to become effective. The area of faith, by contrast, makes it possible to include the outcasts in every way in the church community (Gal 3:28). Peculiar to faith is a perception of the world and a capacity for judging people with a benevolence toward life, a capacity that stands above social and political norms. The baptismal ritual (Rom 6:11) that was taken up as a symbol for the new creation contains no obligation to be circumcised (an exclusively male bodily marker). In the new creation everyone — men and women, communities and cultures — has the same rights. Baptism symbolizes the death of sin of patriarchal society and the new life that manifests itself in new relationships between people. This all occurs according to the will of God, the Friend who reconciles us with herself and with her creation. She is the one who has made us into brothers and sisters by making herself known as mother of all. The terms "mother" and "friend" understood as "she" correspond to the terms "father" and "friend" understood as "he" used by Paul.

Discrimination has no place in the realm of faith. When Paul is critical toward those who want to impose the law and Jewish circumcision on other cultures, he is also very critical toward the Gentile Christians who discriminate against everyone who has different cultural customs, as is the case with the Jews (Rom 11:16-24; see 14:1–15:13).

Up to this point one can understand very well the problem of an interpretation of the Torah that excludes other cultures and other people. However, Paul goes further. By juxtaposing the law to faith and grace, he discovers in different types of law, whether it be legalistic law or "invisible" law — such as the law or logic of tradition, of institutions, of culture or dogma — an ominous rule, because it allows no intervention on the basis of new personal insights. It has immovable rules and determines people's lives with no room for grace. Paul criticizes this law and contrasts it with the law of the Spirit, a different logic, which is also called grace and faith.

Paul does not reject Mosaic law; he considers its intentions just, good, and sacred (7:12). He criticizes the dynamic every law takes on, including Mosaic law, leading to just such a law becoming a law unto itself. Put in more contemporary terms, we are talking about the so-called dominion of the law *(Gesetzesherrschaft)*. Mosaic law can, like any other law, be made to serve structural sin because it can be easily manipulated (7:8). The problem is not the law itself but the sin that prevails with the dominion of the law, leading to death, since it leaves no room for changes on the basis of human insight.

Sin leads to death, and grace or faith leads to life (8:6). An interpretation of the Torah can be influenced by sin or by grace. If it subjects itself to grace, it will become the law of God or of the Spirit. Faith, says Paul, does not make the law invalid but confirms it. But if the law is put in the service of sin, it becomes a structure that prepares the ground for sin and leads to death.

For feminist theology, a structure that "only makes the power of sin visible" (3:20) and prepares the ground for the living effectiveness of sin (7:8-9) is played out within the patriarchal paradigm, or more precisely in the fulfillment of male-oriented tradition and culture, in which every institution is permeated with patriarchal and hierarchical ideology. To accept the gift of justification by faith means to entrust oneself to a different paradigm than the "patriarchal" structure of sin and death. The good news of those justified who accept faith as a new way of life, to live by faith like Jesus, consists in becoming conscious of being free women, and in having the faith that it is possible to change the society in which the dominion of sin manifests itself in the misogynist structure described. Out of faith we affirm that, although we live in the world in which sin prevails and which is permeated with sin, this world nevertheless does not have those in its grip who are led by a logic of grace. "You are no longer under the law, but under grace" (6:14).

Believing in the Resurrection of the Body

Abraham made himself the friend of God because he believed that God gives life to the dead and calls into existence the things that do not exist (4:3, 17). The ancestors of the faith, Abraham and also Sarah, believed that from their bodies, Abraham's weak body and Sarah's infertile and exhausted womb, new life could arise. Abraham and Sarah were justified because they had faith in that which was impossible according to human logic, but not according to God's logic. To have faith means to trust that God raises the body of the innocently crucified victim who was condemned by deadly structures that patriarchal society brings into play. The body of the Crucified One is brought into the present by the bodies of beaten, raped, and tortured women. This is not done to legitimize the sacrifice, but to be in solidarity with the victim and to raise the victim from the dead. For feminist theology it is of fundamental importance to emphasize the resurrection of the body in order to break with the ominous patriarchal dualism that treats with contempt the qualities of matter and emotion that are associated with women, and values the soul and the intellect as associated with men.

Paul juxtaposes spirit and flesh; in this he is possibly influenced by the dualistic anthropology of the Platonic tradition (cf. Bautista 1993, 138), but with a completely different meaning than the dualism that disrespects the body. Spirit *(pneuma)* is the realm and the energy that lead to life and to peace; men and women can live in this dynamic realm. Flesh *(sarx)* is the realm and the energy that lead to sin and to death, which is what God rejects. Men and women can also behave according to the logic of the flesh. The bodies of women and men are clothed anew and brought to life by the *pneuma* that lives in them. When women and men allow themselves to be guided by the spirit, they become brothers and sisters through this divine ancestry (8:14-17). In this way new human interrelationships are founded that are characterized by solidarity. In this new humanity there is no human gender that is considered inferior.

Very well, for Paul this new experience is only lived in faith at first, since the new creation, too, though it has begun already in Jesus Christ, has yet to come into fullness. The dimension of grace is present, but the dominion of sin that manifests itself in patriarchal society remains. Thus there continue to be systemic violence and discrimination. The difference consists in the fact that we now trust with faith and hope in the real possibility of a new creation that includes all of humanity and the cosmos. This faith in the resurrection of the body is the power that helps to resist our present sufferings and to struggle for the "revelation of the sons and daughters of God" (8:18). All of creation, says Paul, groans like a woman in the pangs of childbirth and longingly hopes for liberation. In Galatians 4:19 Paul also uses the image of a woman in the pain of childbirth in reference to himself. Our groaning *(stenazomen)* unites with the groaning *(systenazei)* of creation and the groaning *(stenagmois)* of the spirit in a concert of prayer to God for the resurrection of the body.

In this way, new human interrelationships make themselves known between men and women, women and women, men and men, if we appropriate for ourselves the gift of faith as our own faith and our own practice. We must know that violence against the bodies of adult women, girls, and adolescent women will come to an end, not because we vehemently assert that it will, but because we announce the good news of the liberation of women, because in our everyday life we practice new human interrelationships oriented toward grace, and because we already give witness in faith to the coming back to life of the suffering bodies of women. This means that we present "our members to God as instruments of righteousness, as those who have been brought from death to life" (Rom 6:13). We women rebel against every kind of condemnation.

Romans 9–11: Election, the Wisdom of Mercy

Romans 9–11 are discussed in view of their position within the letter, although there is a fundamental relationship between these chapters and the entire epistle. The central issue is the mercy and justice of God for all people, which, however, are interpreted from a new perspective in light of the question of election.

In Romans 1–8 Paul discusses how life becomes new through the revelation of God's justice, and he explains the event of justification by faith as it concerns Jews and non-Jews. The immediate theological question arising from Paul's context is the question of the role of Israel, the chosen people, and its place in the salvation story — the question of who sets the realm of faith or of the Spirit into motion. Paul attempts to answer this question in chapters 9–11. This section allows the role of Israel to be reevaluated and seeks to decrease the anti-Jewish sentiment that has accompanied the history of Christianity and that has feminist theology today worried.

However, the text allows a reading that goes beyond the question of the relationship of Jews and Christians. It is possible to read chapters 9–11 beginning with the exclusion to which the women, as well as many other discriminated groups, were subjected who could not demonstrate any meritorious deeds that would make them worthy of human recognition and acceptance. In the logic of the present system of patriarchal society, it is a valid practice for a minority sector (economic, social, cultural, or religious) to be treated as the "elect." By privileging the privileged, who have earnings based on their sex, race, and class, and who continue to accumulate wealth, the system excludes the great majority. Romans 9–11 puts into our hands biblical-theological criteria with which we can rethink God's practice of election, or privileging, of the outcast.

Marginalized people, like women of all races, reject the theology of election. It was used de facto to legitimize the attack on entire populations and the exclusion of groups with different religious convictions. For persons who find themselves in positions of privilege, it is dangerous to feel elected by God. An analysis of the argumentation of the text shows us that God's action of election happens out of mercy, so that there will be no one excluded in the history of humankind.

Election Comes from God's Mercy

For Paul it is clear that God's intention in the election *(eklegomai)* of a people does not follow the pattern "elect versus exclude." More important than election is God's mercy. Since the creation of the world, God's intention has been that all God's creatures become daughters and sons. God's mercy *(eleos)* is the foundation for chapters 9–11. The words "show mercy" and "mercy" occur frequently (nine times). God's goal, according to Paul, is that everyone, men and women, Jews and Gentiles, attain God's mercy.

Paul wants to shore up this argument in chapters 9–11. On the basis of particular features of the letter, we can reconstruct a scenario in which the Gentile Christians of Rome had no respect for the converted Jews who had not yet managed to free themselves from their tradition of ritual prescriptions, the so-called weaknesses mentioned in chapters 14–15. Paul would like these Jews and their tradition to be respected. They must be accepted as they are. This is why Paul reminds his audience of the special place of the people of Israel. It is striking how positively Paul represents the people of Israel before God, as well as his great hope that they will be saved and "accepted" (11:14-15). God elects in order that no person, no religious community, and no ethnic group should be excluded.

In this section we note a movement of inclusiveness the intention of which is to leave no one out of God's plans for liberation. To inscribe this inclusiveness into his letter, Paul alludes to election by mercy and grace. God elects those who have been excluded. On the basis of the chosen remnant (11:5, 7), he begins by invoking Israel as the chosen people, which, however, is currently in a state of rejection *(apobolē)* (11:15), because they insist on their own righteousness (10:3). Their election has been suspended but not canceled. God's mercy also includes the non-Jews, the noncircumcised, and those without the law. It is based on God's righteousness and the faith of Jesus Christ (3:22), and the faith that God raised him from the dead (10:9). Nevertheless, it seems that the non-Jewish Christians in the church in Rome began to discriminate against the Jews. The parable of the olive tree is a warning against excluding them (11:16-24).

Paul is faced with two audiences: Jewish Christians with their traditions, and non-Jews who have converted to Christianity. The Jews (both non-Christian and Christian) had the tendency to exclude those who were without the law and circumcision. And the Gentile Christians tended to treat the Jews with contempt because of their conservative traditions and their following of certain prescriptions of the law. Paul's intention is for all these people to come to enjoy the mercy of God. Here he repeats the pre-Pauline baptismal formula of Galatians 3:28, though omitting naming the binary pairs male-female and master-slave, since here he wants to emphasize the theme of all the peoples (10:12).

Thus Paul expects that all the peoples *(plērōma tōn ethnōn)* as well as all of Israel *(pas Israēl)* (11:26) participate in the grace of God (11:25).

To emphasize that all shall participate in God's grace, Paul resorts to somewhat strange and unpersuasive arguments, yet he manages to set in motion the circular movement that makes inclusion possible. His arguments are as follows: (1) Israel's failure or fall *(paraptōma)* had the purpose of bringing salvation *(sōteria)* to the Gentiles (11:11). But "the fall" is not forever. (2) The "hardening" *(pōrōsis)* of Israel (11:25) makes possible the inclusion of the non-Jews, but their hardening is only partial *(apo merous)* and will last until the full number of the Gentiles has come in. (3) The rejection *(apobolē)* of Israel by God served to reconcile the others *(katallagē)* (11:15). Their "being readmitted" *(proslēmpsis)* will be much more, namely, "a resurrection from the dead." (4) The gospel and the election are the guarantee of inclusivity, for inclusion of all into the design of God's mercy; the gospel because of Jesus Christ's faith, and the election because of God's gifts *(charismata)* (11:29) to the ancestors of Israel. In Paul's view, the Israelites are enemies of God with respect to the gospel, but on the basis of election they are beloved because of God's faithfulness to Israel's ancestors. The non-Jews are children of God, primarily because of the gospel, and they are chosen of God because the election happens not according to the flesh, but according to the promise (9:8), according to faith. Israel, the chosen people, will also come into God's righteousness, will renew their friendship with God through the gospel because of the remnant *(leimma)* (11:5), chosen *(eklogē)* by grace. (5) Disobedience *(apeitheia)* and mercy *(eleos)* also join in the movement of inclusion. God elects Israel out of mercy; Israel, on the contrary, becomes disobedient or rebellious; because of its disobedience God shows mercy to the non-Jews who were disobedient; now the Jews rebel, in order to obtain God's mercy (vv. 30-32). This is clarified in 11:32: "God has imprisoned all in disobedience so that God may be merciful to all." (6) Israel's jealousy. Paul confesses that with his mission among the non-Jews he wants to arouse the Jews to jealousy *(parazēlōsai)* when they see that the others have been accepted. The purpose is for some of them to be saved (11:9, 15). "Some of them" contradicts Paul's position that all should obtain God's mercy. Perhaps this can be explained by the fact that there is an eschatological undertone to Paul's reflections about God's plan for the salvation of all. In any case, for Paul this, too, is a mystery (11:25). (7) The image of the olive tree throws light on the movement of inclusion (11:16-24). The root is election by grace and mercy. The branches, which can be natural or grafted onto the tree, share in the root and the sap. All can be torn off or replaced by others in the very moment that they become "proud" toward others (the Gentiles) or because of their "unbelief" (the Jews). But God can graft on wild branches, or graft back onto the tree originally grafted branches that had been torn off. The mercy of God's election by grace stands above all else; this root remains. Here Paul favors Israel as the archetype of God's election in faithfulness to its ancestors.

God chooses by grace. Nothing about one's meritorious achievements or privileged status counts. That is why Paul writes: "So it depends not on human will or exertion, but on God who shows mercy" (9:16). If achievements and privilege are important, competition enters in, the human "rat race" arises, and with it a situation of exclusion. For this reason, grace stands above achievements.

God rejects exclusion and out of sheer mercy chooses precisely those who are excluded (women and people marginalized for reasons of race or economics), in order to prevent every kind of exclusion. He chose Israel as his people because it was small and oppressed by foreign empires (cf. Deut 7:7-8).

In Romans 9:13 Paul repeats the tradition of God's option for those pushed to the margins. Unfortunately, because of his androcentric culture, he only mentions men. "The elder shall serve the younger" refers to the free decision of God to favor Isaac and Jacob. They were the younger brothers (with no right to inheritance), and for that reason alone God favors them, not because they had a record of good or bad deeds (9:11). By taking this position, God does not reject the elder or exclude him. (In Hebrew thought, "I have loved Jacob, but I have hated Esau" [9:13] means simply that he has favored the one over the other.) What we discover anew is that God shows solidarity with the younger, disinherited one. This is how God acts. Naturally the younger one is no longer the one favored by God when he becomes arrogant and excludes others. Israel experienced this many times, and Christians, too, always face this danger (11:20).

Why must God choose at all? Would it not be better if God treated all people alike without having to favor anyone? In a society full of divisions, God favors excluded men and women so that God's decision to show mercy can be realized in all its fullness. This means that no one stands outside God's plan for salvation. In patriarchal society, it is women who most need God's solidarity. Only by being accepted as they are by God in a way that privileges them do they witness to God's love, which is valid regardless of a person's status. The excluded, both men and women, will always be God's chosen people. This is the guarantee that God's mercy is available to everyone and that God's plan for liberation is being carried out.

Election is visible in everyday life. Israel was chosen so that it would be a light among the nations and would bear witness to God's righteousness by its deeds of justice. Paul finds fault with Israel. He makes use of a very harsh self-criticism from the Scriptures: "The name of God is blasphemed among the Gentiles because of you" (2:24).

In this sense election becomes manifest in the behavior of the elect. This privilege is maintained as long as the chosen remain true to this witness of God. If the chosen people do not act in harmony with God's righteousness, election is suspended until they return to these ways of righteousness and God's mercy becomes visible. Paul mentions the circular binary of participation and exclusion in the parable of the olive tree when he says: "Do not boast over the branches [that were broken off]. . . . For if God did not spare the natural branches, perhaps he will not spare you" (11:18-21).

Election as God's act of solidarity results in the excluded person feeling like a human being with dignity of her own and included in God's plan of liberation. By becoming conscious of being chosen by God, excluded persons gain new energy to resist the forces of animosity and enmity they face, and their hope in the face of an uncertain future is strengthened.

Romans 12–15: Everyday Wisdom

This part of the letter serves as the exhortation. It contains general admonitions and focuses especially on one particular problem faced by the church in Rome

(14:1–15:13), namely, the challenge of accepting one another with respect and behaving wisely in everyday life, both within and outside the believers' community. No one is to put him/herself in charge of another. Mutual tolerance — if it has not fallen by the wayside — is important for mutual encouragement. 13:1-7 interrupts the unity of the section; for this reason it is thought to be a post-Pauline commentary.

The theological statements spoken of in Romans 1–11 give one's everyday actions an orientation, and based on these concrete activities in everyday life, the dominant patriarchal culture is subverted, having already lost its legitimacy through the theological statements. A praxis of mutual respect is an alternative way of life in patriarchal society, which is characterized by asymmetrical relationships. In 12:1-2 Paul demands a constant renewal of the mind and body in order to recognize *(dokimazein)* God's will in every moment. In inviting the people of the community to present themselves as a living sacrifice *(thysian zōsan),* Paul's language is drawn from cultic usage. Feminist theology rejects this analogy with sacrifice because of the way the theology of sacrifice was applied to women. However, 12:1-2 draws attention to the importance of human beings being transformed (in the imperative form: *metamorphousthe)* and opposes their taking on the way of life of the contemporary culture. In verse 2ab, with its analogy to the act of sacrifice, it is life itself that should be seen as sacrificial gift, as authentic service to God *(logikē latreia).* There were no sacrificial rituals in the Christian churches as there were in other religious communities. The people themselves were the sacrificial gift, dedicated to God as they made God's justice real in the community by the way they lived.

Conducting oneself according to the logic of the Spirit or of mercy requires the skill of discernment. Sometimes it means subjecting oneself to social structures in order to survive (even if we know that 13:1-7 is a doubtful and contradictory text of Paul's in view of his other clear and liberating statements, and that it is a momentary statement, not a fundamental one). At other times it means limiting one's freedom for the sake of others and their cultural practices, but only as long as the dignity of the human being and the coming of the new creation are not put at risk (15:17). Rejection of the current perverse world order (patriarchal society), continual renewal, wise discernment, doing justice, and the daily experience of grace are the guarantors of the fact that we are living in the logic of the spirit and of faith, whose promise is life, justice, and peace.

LITERATURE

Bautista, Esperanza. 1993. *La mujer en la iglesia primitiva.* Estella.
Käsemann, Ernst. 1980. *An die Römer.* Handbuch zum Neuen Testament, vol. 8a. Tübingen.

Roberts, Beverly Gaventa. 1992. "Romans." In *The Women's Bible Commentary,* edited by Carol A. Newsom and Sharon H. Ringe, 313-20. Louisville and London.

Ruether, Rosemary Radford. 1994a. *Gaia and God: An Ecofeminist Theology of Earth Healing.* San Francisco.

―――. 1994b. *Gaia und Gott. Eine ökofeministische Theologie der Heilung der Erde.* Lucerne.

Russell, Letty M. 1987. *Household of Freedom: Authority in Feminist Theology.* Philadelphia.

Schottroff, Luise. 1979. "Die Schreckensherrschaft der Sünde und die Befreiung durch Christus nach dem Römerbrief des Paulus." *Evangelische Theologie* 39.

―――. 1995. *Mulheres no novo testamento.* São Paolo.

Schüssler Fiorenza, Elisabeth. 1983. *In Memory of Her: A Feminist Theological Reconstruction of Christian Origins.* New York.

―――. 1994. *Jesus: Miriam's Child, Sophia's Prophet; Critical Issues in Feminist Christology.* New York.

―――. 1997. *Jesus — Miriams Kind, Sophias Prophet. Eine feministische Christologie.* Gütersloh.

Stuhlmacher, Peter. 1989. *Der Brief an die Römer.* Neues Testament Deutsch. Göttingen.

Suchocki, Marjorie Hewitt. 1996. "Sin." In *Dictionary of Feminist Theologies,* edited by Letty M. Russell and L. Shannon Clarkson. Louisville.

Tamez, Elsa. 1998. *Gegen die Verurteilung zum Tod. Paulus oder die Rechtfertigung durch den Glauben aus der Perspektive der Unterdrückten und Ausgestoßenen.* Lucerne.

Williams, Delores S. 1996. "Atonement." In *Dictionary of Feminist Theologies,* edited by Letty M. Russell and L. Shannon Clarkson. Louisville.

Translated by Nancy Lukens

1 Corinthians: How Freedom Comes to Be

Luise Schottroff

The Church in Corinth (1 Corinthians 1:1-9)

In the first three verses of chapter 1, the congregation in Corinth is addressed and assessed theologically. The androcentric language conceals that there are more women than men in that Corinthian congregation (cf. in particular 7:1-39).

One may conclude from 1:26-31 that the majority of Christians in the congregation in Corinth are drawn from that city's lower class. Corinth was a significant port and trading center. In addition, commercial and industrial production played a notable role. Earthenware (vessels, roofing tiles), metal products (containers, mirrors, weapons), rugs, and other merchandise were manufactured and exported. In the two ports of Lechaion and Cenchreae (cf. Rom 16:1) there was a significant turnover of goods, especially those from the east en route to the west and to Rome. In spite of this, the majority of the population had no part of the city's prosperity, an indication of how low wages were. Since as a rule women's wages did not allow them to survive independently, single women in the congregation were dependent on additional means of support, such as prostitution or the organization of women's groups in the congregation. Such groups have been shown to exist in other Christian and Jewish congregations. Their care for one another included economic support (cf. 1 Tim 5:16; Acts 6:1; 9:36-43; Mark 15:40-41; reference is made in Acts 20:34 to a corresponding group, presumably of men for whom Paul counts himself responsible).

In Corinth at that time there were a significant number of Jews and several synagogues. The Christian congregation consisted of Jewish Christians and Christians from the Gentile nations.

In 1 Corinthians 1:4-9, the thanksgiving, Paul names the common foundation on which he sees himself and the congregation resting. On this theologically crucial foundation it is both possible and necessary to debate matters of detail. In verses 4-7 Paul speaks of the richness of spiritual gifts present in the congregation, and in verses 7-8 he proclaims the eschatological hope in the day of divine judgment. That hope brings about in the present time a life-praxis oriented by the To-rah (v. 8) and an intimate relationship *(koinōnia)* with Jesus (v. 9).

The Wisdom of God (1 Corinthians 1:10–4:21)

The Aim of Paul's Exhortation (1 Corinthians 1:10–4:21)

Paul understood this part of the epistle to be a fatherly exhortation (4:14-16; 1:10). What did he seek to achieve with this exhortation, and how did he perceive his "exhorting"? His own understanding of his relation to the congregation in Corinth is decisive for answering these two questions.

In 3:10 Paul says that "like a skilled master builder I laid the foundation" of the congregation. In contrast, exegetical tradition ascribes a lesser significance to the one who carried on with building it up further. Many hold this person to be Apollos. The following verse makes a highly authoritative statement: "For no one can lay any foundation other than the one that has been laid; that foundation is Jesus Christ." This verse has been read as the assertion of *Paul's* absolute authority. Yet, it has always been noted that Paul does not say in 3:11 "the foundation that *I* laid" but the foundation "that has been laid" already. This relativization of his own founding labors can be explained in terms of the context. Paul understands himself and other preachers of the gospel to be "servants" *(diakonoi,* 3:5; cf. other corresponding images in 3:6, 8; 4:1-2). They have been commissioned by God, equal in rank (3:5-9) and *sub*ordinate to the congregation (3:21-23). The congregation is seen to be the temple of God (3:16-17; see 3:9, "God's building"). "Temple" of God is a metaphor rooted in Jewish tradition (Kirchhoff 1994, 183-85) and not a new anti-Judaistic interpretation of the temple in Jerusalem where the Christian congregation as the temple of God replaces the Jerusalem temple. Through God's calling humans have been collectively transformed. Together they are God's residence, the place of God's holiness and presence. The "servants" of God, too, are part of the community. All have the same divine spirit (12:4-11). The actions of the individual members, including the preachers like Paul, are subject to the same criterion: the judgment of God on "the day of our Lord Jesus Christ" (1:8). This eschatological judgment of God is the decisive authority, the court where all shall have to render account, including Paul himself. All relations between human beings and between them and God are seen here and lived out eschatologically. God calls the human being and grants the Spirit; in this way every member of the community receives divine dignity. But the Spirit may also be lost, namely, through false action. "If anyone destroys God's temple, God will destroy that person" (3:17).

The foundation has been laid by Paul inasmuch as he understands himself to have been one of the first to proclaim Christ in Corinth; others continue to build. But the actual foundation has been laid by God, and it is not this or that *proclama-*

tion of Christ, such as Paul's, but Christ himself. For Paul the formulation "that which has been laid" derives from the holiness of the congregation that Christ's and God's presence bestows and not from an authoritarian self-assessment on Paul's part.

The aim of Paul's "fatherly" admonition is to create the awareness that to destroy the holy temple is a grave danger. The congregation is to recognize the structures of competition within its own ranks as something dangerous (e.g., 3:18 next to 3:17). What Paul wants is to promote both recognition of and resistance against *structures* of competition rather than competitors and rivals themselves. Nowhere does Paul deny that Apollos, who is often said to be his rival, has the same authority as one who, like Paul, is commissioned by God. Rather, it is precisely the egalitarian relation between them that he wants to promote as a model (4:6). The competitive struggles in the congregation had made it necessary for Paul to address them in harsh language and feed them milk like infants rather than adult food (3:1-4). Within that qualification, such language continues to mark his relation to the congregation. Paul employs sharp criticism, but in doing so he does not claim special authority for himself. The Holy Spirit endows everyone with the power of critique (2:15) and with the power to refute critique (4:3) in order to submit to what alone is decisive: *God's* judgment.

If God alone is judge, then those who have faith in God are unburdened of the need to assert themselves, to achieve success, and to earn praise: "then each one will receive commendation from God" (4:5).

Paul's Perception of the Competitive Struggles in Corinth

What Paul knew of the competitive struggles was not the result of his own experience. Chloe's people — that is, her followers (1:11) — had informed him, and in this admonishing letter he takes sides based on that information (Wire 1990, 41). The presence of such women's groups within the congregation would substantiate the assumption that Chloe's people are a women's group in the Corinthian congregation and that they had asked Paul's support against having hierarchical structures imposed by some of the congregation. It is probably no coincidence that, in this instance, the woman's name stands in juxtaposition to the names of the men around whom the "parties" had formed.

Astonishingly, the name of Priscilla does not appear in 1:10-17, where people are named who were significant for the Corinthian congregation's history. But those seven verses are to be read together with Acts 18:1-3 and 18:24–19:7. Paul says he founded the congregation (1 Cor 3:6; 4:15), presumably in the house of Priscilla and Aquila (Acts 18:1-3). As may be concluded from Acts 18:25-26, and the right of all believers to baptize, Priscilla had baptized people in Corinth in the name of Jesus. The baptizers must have played a role in the competition among Corinthian groups to be more important than the others. In Tertullian's *De baptismo* 17, one still sees the conflict between the right of all Christian women and men to baptize and an ecclesiastical hierarchy that concedes baptizing solely to the bishop and those he authorizes. The so-called parties in the Corinthian congregations had granted individual baptizers *special* authority to baptize, as baptizers, but obviously they had not granted that authority to all who baptized. In 1 Corinthians 1:10-17, the absence of Priscilla as someone who baptized and had founded a congregation indicates that the understanding of baptism played a role in the Corinthian conflict. Like Tertullian, some Christians in Corinth assigned a particular authority to baptizers in spite of the awareness that baptizing in the name of Jesus actually is the task of *all* believers. On the contrary, Paul, Priscilla, Chloe, Chloe's group, and many others insist on the egalitarian structure of the congregation, where all have one spirit and the baptizers do not enjoy any privileges over other baptized persons.

The Pauline Wisdom Theology

As he often does, Paul makes use of antitheses in this text. Positive is set against negative: the wisdom of God (1:21, 24; 2:7; cf. also 1:30 and 2:5) stands over and against the wisdom of the world (1:20; 3:19) and the wisdom of the word (1:17; 2:1, 4, 13). In paradoxes he plays with the word "foolishness": for those who are to perish (1:18) the crucified Christ is "foolishness," while on the positive side "foolishness" is God's action in Christ (1:25), in proclamation (1:21), and in the election of the believers (1:26-31). Paul's antitheses tempt one to link what he regards as the negative side with the people of the Corinthian congregation against whom he argues. And thus the picture is developed of a Pauline theology of the cross that is set against a Corinthian theology of wisdom that combines rhetorical competence with an unbroken revelation of God's wisdom in the believers. But such a religion-historical classification of the negative side of the Pauline antitheses is based on a misinterpretation. Those antitheses are a stylistic device and not descriptive of how he sees the theology of the "opponents." The significance of the cross was much debated in early Christianity; 1 Corinthians 1:10–4:21 is part of that debate. The issue of Paul's intensification of his wisdom theology is differences within Christianity, verse 1:23b notwithstanding. In terms of social history, this text is part of the ever recurring discussion within early Christianity as to whether believers should seek or avoid martyrdom. "[T]he unsophisticated souls know not what is written, and what meaning it bears, where and when and before whom we must confess, or *ought*, save that this, to die for God, is, since He preserves me, not even artlessness, but folly, nay madness." Tertullian, 150 years later, put these words on the lips of Christians who refused martyrdom and provided a theological rationale for doing so (*Scorpiace* 1; cf. Pagels 1979, 70-101 for additional material on

Christians refusing martyrdom). In early Christianity discussion about the cross of Christ was always related to people's own reality of life. Even at this early time, when 1 Corinthians was composed, agents of Rome viewed Christian congregations with suspicion. "The rulers of this world" crucified Jesus (2:8). To venerate the crucified as God's revelation was, as such, tantamount to political resistance and resulted in dangerous persecutions. Even if Tertullian's words are not an exact repetition of what people refusing martyrdom said of themselves, the basic theological idea is apparent: Why should I risk my life in resisting Rome for the sake of God when it is my salvation that God desires? That is why resisting Rome and the danger of martyrdom is "folly to [non-Jewish people]" (1:23). The critique of the cross that Jews present (1:23) has a completely different basis, presumably the refusal to look upon Jesus as the Messiah. That Christ is the wisdom of God (1:24, 30) is not at issue for Paul. His issue is that resistance against Rome is a genuine task of the followers of Christ, the crucified and resurrected wisdom of God. The debate is about the necessity of holding cross and wisdom together.

In the Corinthian congregation, the discussion about what Christ's crucifixion means existentially for believers merges with the conflict around how that congregation is to organize itself. 1 Corinthians 1:17 and 1:18 are not an opening to an excursus on the matter of competition, as is often proposed, but show how those two issues are related in substance. God's election of the degraded, which is apparent in the crucifixion and in the social composition of the congregation, has consequences for how it organizes itself. As far as Paul is concerned, no one ought to claim from the bestowal of God's Spirit and wisdom particular qualities that other baptized people do not have and that result in social privilege. The election of the degraded is also the theological measure by which Paul interprets his own existence as a Christian itinerant preacher (2:1-5; 4:6-13). The so-called *peristasis* catalogue of 4:11-13 depicts the real threat that hangs over the itinerant preacher but does so in the certainty that God does not forsake but is present to those society degrades.

Paul's mythical dualism, wherein God and world are in hostile confrontation, is integrated into his understanding of God's eschatological judgment that exalts the degraded. The way Paul deals with the dualism of world and God is in tension with many texts of Christian gnosticism. Salvation in those texts means to be distanced from the body, from matter, and from the cosmos — the location of powers hostile to God. The realized eschatology that, in Paul's opinion, has in some Corinthian groups become combined with hierarchy in the congregation, and the refusal to offer resistance against Rome, is not to be read as some superficial "wanting it all." "Already you have become rich! Quite apart from us you have become kings!" (4:8). That verse and its context point rather to a Christian-gnostic conception of redemption that distances the divine and the worldly spheres, salvation and perdition, in terms of both practical life and theology (Schottroff 1970, 180-83).

This Christian soteriology should not automatically be labeled heretical.

Christian gnosticism is a variety of early Christian religion that shares much with Paul and the Gospel of John.

The Election of the Degraded (1 Corinthians 1:26-31)

1 Corinthians 1:26-31 interprets God's election of the uneducated poor as a "shaming" (1:27) and a "bringing to nothing" (1:28) of the wise, as the end of their boasting. Being shamed and brought to nothing is what takes place in the last judgment of God. For congregations here and now this means that boasting and insistence on dominating others and on privileges are now already over and done with. God's judgment on individual human beings is not anticipated but does have structural consequences for the congregation. In addition, the eschatological exaltation of the degraded signals even now a new structure of relationship: women and men slaves, free women, the poor, and manual laborers are partakers in the divine spirit and power. Women are prophets of the judgment of God that will elevate what the world puts down low.

Antoinette Wire interprets Paul's statement, especially in 1:26-29, as an attempt to persuade the Corinthians to *remain* foolish and weak, not to translate any changes in their lives into practice (Wire 1994, 162; cf. also Wire 1990, 61, and Schüssler Fiorenza 1987 and 1994, 150). Wire sees Paul as a representative of the affluent few, of the men of privilege, who, having embraced the Christian faith, voluntarily renounce their privileges. The basic hermeneutical decision behind Wire's interpretation is her reading of *klēsis* in 7:17-24 as "state, condition" ("In whatever condition you were called . . . , there remain . . .") and of Paul's position as seeking to solidify social hierarchies (Wire 1994, 170; on this issue, cf. Schottroff 1994a, 203 n. 78; 1995, 258 n. 78). I read 1:26-29 differently. God takes sides with the degraded. As the foolish, the foolish have become God's daughters and sons through God's calling. Their election by God is for them not a solidification of the social status quo. Their whole life becomes transformed in the common shaping of the new "way of living" in the congregation. This means indeed a gain for women and slaves and a loss of privileges for free men. But in no way is it a social advance in the sense of the very rare social careers in Roman-Hellenistic society. Rather, the overall special perspective is that of God's reign, of the new earth and the new heaven. In 7:17-24 as well, *klēsis* means God's calling and does not suggest that Paul seeks to solidify the status quo. Instead, it means shaping life in accordance with the Torah (7:19) and in peace (7:15).

Holiness and Sexuality (1 Corinthians 5–7)

In chapters 5 to 7, Paul addresses questions of *porneia* and marriage or marriage liberated from patriarchal structures of domination. *Porneia* refers to unlawful sexual relationships. The legitimacy or illegitimacy of such relationships is determined by the Torah and its halakhic interpretation. In these chapters Paul moves within the framework of Jewish halakha (Tomson 1990). Before interpreting this text, I need to address two hermeneutical considerations. (1) Paul does not orient himself by just any code of morality or customs but by the Torah as the will of God. Unlawful sexual relationships can endanger the holiness of the people of God and, hence, also that of the congregation. Paul conceives of holiness in the cultic sense: the relationship with God presupposes purity and creates holiness. This thinking must not be confused with moral judgment of just any sort (cf. Brooten 1996, 291). (2) It is obvious in this text that it is the relationship with Christ that renders the bodies *(sōmata)* holy, making them and their sexual ability important and of value. *Enkrateia* — most often translated as "abstinence" or "continence" — is understood in patriarchal hermeneutics as renunciation of genital sexuality. A feminist hermeneutic, on the other hand, understands *enkrateia* first of all as liberation from the structures of domination of patriarchal marriage, as being "marriage-free" (Sutter Rehmann 1994).[1] It is another matter how those living freely, exempt from such structural obligations, deal with their sexuality. *Enkrateia* encompasses the liberation of one's entire life, not only the renunciation of sexuality. It means to leave the world *(kosmos)* behind, that is, to turn away from social structures that do not correspond to God's will (5:10; 6:10-11; 7:29-35; Acts of Thecla 23; see also below). *Enkrateia*, freedom from the structures of patriarchal marriage, can be lived even in an existing marriage as a departure from worldly structures.

The Woman Who Lives Together with Her Stepson (1 Corinthians 5:1-13)

A man, a member of the Christian congregation, lives together permanently with the wife of his father; she is not his birth mother. For Paul this is a particularly difficult case of *porneia* (cf. Lev 18:8; 20:11; Mishnah *Sanhedrin* 7:4; and the extensive

---

1. Luzia Sutter Rehmann coined the German noun *Ehefreiheit* and its adjective *ehefrei*. No unambiguous single term is at hand in English. What the words intend to communicate is the following. "Marriage-freedom" does not imply the abolition of marriage. But it does take up the intense critique to which marriage was subjected in early Christianity. The "freedom" sought and lived was part of the understanding of being a follower of Jesus. To be "in Christ" meant that, having been given the Spirit of God, the human body was holy, was the temple of God. This was true for women and men, irrespective of their "marital status." Jesus has liberated human beings, so the argument went, from the structures of death that seek to subject humans to their yoke and in so doing separate people from God as well as from their God-given, creaturely identity. "Marriage-freedom" is, therefore, freedom from the ideological and other social structures that patriarchy imposes on (heterosexual) marriage. It is freedom *from* the structures of the powers of death and freedom *for* the holiness of the body and the life promised in relation to that by being a follower of Jesus. In the following, quotation marks before and after "marriage-freedom" and "marriage-free" indicate that the meaning as just described is intended. [Translators' note.]

collection of material in Billerbeck; on Billerbeck's anti-Judaistic tendencies, see Tomson 1990). For Paul, this man is subject to Jewish law. According to Roman law, marriage with one's stepmother is not permitted (Kaser 1962, sec. 58 IIIc). But it appears that no sanctions were to be expected when a man lived together with his stepmother. Jewish law, however, originally called for the death penalty for both (Lev 20:11). In postbiblical times, excommunication replaced execution; it is also what Paul calls for. One may assume that Paul thinks in terms of the Jewish practice of his day in relation to the sanctions he considers to be important (Tomson 1990). Excommunication is seen to be a social death that, under certain circumstances, is actually followed by physical death. We have to assume that this man is not Jewish by birth and therefore thinks it possible to live with his stepmother "in marriage." That the Christian congregation in Corinth tolerates this relationship also indicates that such an unlawful relationship was socially acceptable. But here Paul wants a full application of Jewish law. In his eyes, the man is wholly subject to the prohibitions of Leviticus 18. In this Paul shows that he is concerned not with a law-free Christianity but with a Christianity that is faithful to the law also for people of non-Jewish origin. He mentions the woman only once (5:1). According to Leviticus 20:11 and many postbiblical texts, she would have to be punished like the man. Presumably she is a widow or a divorcée and now lives without financial rights or the opportunity of having any possible children with her stepson legitimized. There is nothing unusual about Paul's androcentric depiction of this case (cf. only Mishnah *Sanhedrin* 7:4), and it should not be understood to indicate that the woman was not Christian. At that time the discussion about rights centered on the man. Should the woman be Christian, then the question is whether she will be excommunicated together with the man (cf. Sapphira in Acts 5:7-11). If she is not Christian, she may possibly lose her (unlawful) husband and presumably with him part of her economic means of existence. Whatever the case, she is the one to bear the major burden of suffering from this unlawful marriage because she must forgo significant rights as long as they live together. She faces the threat of death both for herself and for her husband as a result of the congregation's decision to tolerate this relationship. I believe it probable that she was a Christian. Paul regards her as an accomplice who is also to be excommunicated, but she is so unimportant to him that he does not once mention this aspect of his faithfulness to the Torah.

The Holiness of the Body Has Implications for Men
(1 Corinthians 6:12-20)

Many men (including husbands) of non-Jewish origin belonging to the Corinthian Christian congregation are having sexual intercourse with women sex-trade workers. As is usual, they do not consider this to be a moral or religious problem; it is simply taken for granted. In the everyday life of the city, sex-trade workers are omnipresent and integrated into society. They frequently work in jobs that involve public contact: hostessing, waitressing, or selling (Kirchhoff 1994). Paul considers relationships with sex-trade workers to be *porneia* and not adultery since a man cannot break his own marriage, only that of another man. Here Paul functions within the framework of Jewish sexual ethics (cf. Sir 26:12 = 26:9 in LXX). In his view, intercourse with a sex-trade worker does injury to the holiness of the baptized and, concomitantly, the holiness of Christ with which they are connected.

The Variety of Ways of Living (1 Corinthians 7:1-40)

The issue here is *porneia* of men and marriage and both women and men's "marriage-freedom." The text is not conceived as a normative sexual ethic or as comprehensively descriptive of Christian ways of living. Rather, the ways of living and the decisions mentioned here are actual cases chosen selectively. Paul says nothing about Christian marriages like that of Priscilla and Aquila. Such Christian marriages are quietly presupposed. 1 Corinthians 16:19 and Acts 18:1-3 show that in those Christian marriages the home is made open for the congregation and that the patriarchal structures of the family change fundamentally. To clarify the reality of Christian marriages like Priscilla and Aquila's, I refer to the Acts of Thecla. There Paul, "marriage-free," is guest of Onesiphoros and Lectra and their children, Simmias and Zeno (2-5). After having been driven out of town, Paul lives with this family in a cemetery outside the city. As a family, they have "left the world" (23), thus actualizing a bond to Christ that the historical Paul describes in 1 Corinthians 7:29-35 for those living free of the structures of patriarchal marriage. They celebrate the Christian meal in love and gladness (Acts of Thecla 25; cf. Acts 2:46-47). In the Acts of Thecla, this Christian couple is an unmistakable, Christian counterdesign to the patriarchal marriage into which the pagan men Thamyris and Alexander want to force Thecla. Thamyris's house is depicted as a place of excessive carousing (13).

On the one hand, Paul's description of ways of living is highly androcentric, yet, on the other, women are mentioned conspicuously often. The rhetoric of equality in 1 Corinthians 7 is not the result of Paul regarding women and men as equal, nor does such rhetoric signify a breach of androcentric perspective. Rather, Paul refers to the many married women who want to live free of the oppression that is part of patriarchal marriage and demands of these married women that they not seek "marriage-freedom" for themselves (cf. Wire 1994, who makes this case persuasively). The following ways of living by women are addressed:

- Christian women live as if free from marital obligation while married to a Christian husband for whom intercourse with a sex-trade worker is no religious problem (7:1-7).
- Christian women want to be divorced (from a Christian husband?) (7:10-11).

- Christian women want to be divorced from non-Christian husbands (7:13-15). They become Christians after marrying, but independently of their husbands. They now want to actualize the implications of the difference between their Christian way of living and that of their non-Christian husbands. Paul's decision to make divorce dependent on whether or not the non-Christian partner wants the divorce is not in line with what the women concerned have in mind. They obviously seek divorce even against the non-Christian partner's will. (Such a case is also described in the *Apology* of Justin Martyr, 2.2.)
- 1 Corinthians 7:15 presupposes that in the Christian congregation pressure is exerted on Christian women to preserve a marriage that the non-Christian partner wants to end. In this case Paul supports the woman's desire for a divorce. Tertullian vividly describes the conflicts between a Christian woman and a non-Christian husband in the everyday life of marriage (*Ad uxorem* 2.4).
- A virgin engaged to a Christian man is not asked for her consent when the man wants to marry her even though originally both may have decided in favor of "marriage-freedom." In such a case, it is to be assumed that virgins fear that they will sin if they consent to marriage (1 Cor 7:28b). It would appear that virgins *(parthenos)* decline marriage more often than their fiancés. That is why marriage demanded by a man (with Paul's approval) is tantamount to sexual assault, legitimized within marriage. It means the destruction of the relationship with Christ of the virgin who chose "marriage-freedom" (7:25-28, 36-37). The following situation is depicted in verses 36-37: the fiancé claims that he cannot control his sex drive. In order not to coerce his fiancée sexually *(aschēmonein)* while they are engaged, he wants to get married. Paul and the man (or men) concerned consider sexual coercion during that time unlawful. That is why the men want to marry.
- Widows want to decide whether or not to enter into a second marriage (7:39-40; 7:8). The young widows in 1 Timothy 5:11-12 also wanted both options open to them.
- Virgins and mature unmarried women, living "marriage-free," are mentioned in 1 Corinthians 7:34. As the placement of "virgins" next to "unmarried women" shows, "virgin" refers, in the sense of the Hebrew word *bĕtûlâ*, to marriageable girls who still live in their parents' home. They have decided on "marriage-freedom." The word "virgin" as such does not yet have the meaning of "a woman not living in marriage": that came about in later Christianity when all unmarried women came to be called "virgins."

Summation: Sexuality and Holiness

An understanding of *sexuality* similar to that on which 1 Corinthians 5–7 is based is to be found in Ecclesiasticus or in the Testaments of the Twelve Patriarchs.

There, as in Paul, the distinction is made between lawful and unlawful sexuality. Paul does not describe but simply presupposes lawful sexuality. When compared to the other texts referred to, what is new in his text is a critical perspective on patriarchal marriage.

Sexual relations that, measured against the Torah, are unlawful *(porneia)* compromise Christian men (1 Cor 7:9, 36-37) who have actually decided in favor of *enkrateia.* They lose control of their drive (v. 37; cf. v. 5); they are aflame (v. 9) and "too strong" in their passions *(hyperakmos,* v. 36). The imagery of fire applied to sexuality is imbued with negative connotations in both Paul and the texts in Ecclesiasticus and the Testaments. The beautiful female stranger and sex-trade workers set a man aflame (Ecclus 9:8; Testament of Joseph 2). Masturbation (Ecclus 23:16) and homosexuality (Rom 1:27) also inflame men. The alternative to the flame of unlawful desire is the sexual relationship legitimized within marriage, according to the extrabiblical texts cited. Paul discusses the connection between sexuality and holiness primarily in terms of negative aspects. Unlawful sexual relations contaminate or destroy the holiness of the body (1 Cor 6:16 and its context) and the holiness of the congregation (5:1-13). Chapter 7, too, is governed chiefly by the problems that arise from the sexuality of men that had chosen *enkrateia* but could not persist in it (7:1-7, 25-38). Yet these three chapters may also be read against this negative grain and be explored for what they may have to say positively about the *connection of sexuality and holiness.*

The congregation is a community of saints in the cultic sense (6:2, 11; 5:6-8). "Purity" is a key term that occurs twice (5:7; 7:14). A cultic argument is presented in 5:9, 11: do not mingle with the impure and do not eat together with them. Cultic purity, discussed in detail in the halakha, serves the preservation of holiness and of God's presence. The bodies of the saints are united with Christ (6:17); they are even now the site of the experience of resurrection (6:14). This bodily holiness may be connected with the renunciation of genital sexual relations (7:34) but is not tied to it. The holiness of the body may be lived even in marriage with genital sexual relations (6:12–7:7 shows this). And this holiness can include even a non-Christian marriage partner and the children of a "mixed" marriage (7:14). In all ways of life, bodies are sanctified through the presence of the Holy Spirit. They are part of the holiness of the congregation, irrespective of whether a Christian woman lives in a marriage with sexual relations, is married but lives in "marriage-freedom," or is "marriage-free" without relation to a man. The sanctified body *(sōma;* see in particular Kirchhoff 1994 on this subject) is the site of the experience of God *also* in its (genital) sexual relations (6:16 implicitly presupposes this for lawful sexuality). In a variety of ways Paul endeavors not to make holiness depend on a specific way of living. Marriage and "marriage-freedom" are possible ways of living, and under specific circumstances divorce is a right decision to take (7:16). What matter are God's calling and keeping the commandments (7:17-24). Remaining in one's state (circumcised or uncircumcised; slave or free) — like the changing of one's status through divorce (7:10-16) or through release from slavery (7:21) or marriage (7:25-39) — is a relative matter. The main thing is to live in accordance with God's calling as holy bodies. (On the misreading of *klēsis* as *"remain in the state in which you are called"* in 7:17-24, see above in relation to 1:26 and Schottroff 1995.) What becomes plain in 7:34 is that the praxis of women living "marriage-free" in the congregation is the decisive motivating force to express and give form to the holiness of the body and of the congregation. Even though Paul regards women as second-class citizens (11:7), it becomes clear even in him that the Christian women in Corinth are creating many new and diverse ways of living that make it possible to live as "the temple of the Holy Spirit" (6:19). The situations of conflict he addresses in 1 Corinthians 7 were brought about chiefly by women giving new shape to their lives. Many Christian men responded to this with sexual demands. The way of living "marriage-freedom" has antecedents in isolated Jewish groups such as the Therapeutics. "The women, too, take part in the feast; most of them are aged virgins who have maintained their purity . . . voluntarily through their zealous desire for wisdom" (Philo, *De vita contemplativa* 63; cf. Wis 3:13). Here an alternative to patriarchal marriage and family with its hierarchies is intentionally developed. The extent to which those in early Christianity lived free of structured marital obligations requires a social-historical explanation that the parallel in Philo does not supply. The majority of Christian women in Corinth were not of the educated upper class like the Therapeutics. The possibility of the Christian *enkrateia* way of living, of departure from the "world" and patriarchal marriage, seemed particularly attractive to women. This picture has been made known especially by the so-called Apocryphal Acts of the Apostles and is confirmed here in 1 Corinthians 7. The economic basis for freedom from the patriarchal structures of marriage is to be found in the communal responsibility the Christian congregation assumed for its members. In addition, as I see it, "marriage-freedom" appears to be based also in what Jewish women had already evolved in a tradition for "marriage-free" life or phases in their marriages free from patriarchal norms by taking a vow (cf. Babylonian Talmud *Nedarim* 81b and 15b; Tertullian, *De oratione* 22 on "virgins devoted to God" and their pledges; Mishnah *Nedarim* 10 on the cancellation of the pledges of young women engaged to be married would seem to fit into this context).

Idolatry and Liberation from the Powers of Alien Gods (1 Corinthians 8–10)

Peter Tomson's (1990) persuasive interpretation of chapters 8–10 based in Jewish halakha opens up a new understanding of the text. There are several versions of how the Corinthian congregation addresses the question about meat offered to idols. The majority of Christians regard themselves as enlightened; the alien gods are nothings: they have no more power over the members of the Christian congregation. Hence, Christians of non-Jewish origin are free to eat what is or could be regarded as sacrificial food. Paul shares this position only to a certain degree. One fundamental tenet of rabbinic discussion pervades the whole of his argumentation. The power of the alien gods is not associated with food but with people's consciousness *(syneidēsis)* (cf. Mishnah *Avodah Zarah* 4:1-2). The consciousness of fellow humans from the non-Jewish nations, including those who do not follow Jesus Christ, limits freedom. What is contentious between Paul and the Gentile Christian majority of the congregation is not the renunciation of idolatry. Rather, it is whether one's *own* consciousness and its conviction that other gods are nothing suffice to invalidate the assurance that eating food offered in sacrifice to the gods is not idolatry. Paul's argument begins with the consciousness of other people for whom such eating represents participation in the powers of those gods. In Jewish perspective it was simply outrageous that anyone worshiping the God of Israel (1 Cor 8:4-6) would eat food offered in sacrifice to idols or even take part in a cultic meal in a temple. But this is not so astonishing when one considers that such practice was quite thinkable in the stages of becoming Jewish (Cohen 1989). In 10:1-22 Paul basically impresses upon the congregation the necessity for those who worship the God of Israel to renounce idolatry. In chapter 9 he uses himself as an example of how voluntary renunciation of freedom can be a necessity.

In the context of the Pauline excursus on voluntary renunciation (chapter 9), a comment is relevant for the history of women in early Christianity (9:4-5). Paul describes his right as an apostle to food and drink at the congregation's expense and to claim that right also for a "sister" or "wife" traveling with him, just like "the other apostles and the brothers of the Lord and Cephas." What is at issue for him is obviously not that a missionary's wife traveling along has that same right. The issue for Paul is that she is a "sister." Couples traveling about as missionaries (two men, Acts 16:1-2; two women, Rom 16:12; see D'Angelo 1990; a married couple, 1 Cor 16:19 and elsewhere) play a conspicuous role. It is difficult to determine whether Paul is thinking here only of married women as "sisters." In the Thecla legend, Paul travels with Thecla through cities of Asia Minor (Acts of Thecla 25:26). Both live "marriage-free." Paul's androcentric perspective in 1 Corinthians 9:4-5 is in tension with the designation "sister." On the one hand, this creates the idea of a married woman who is taken along as an appendage to the apostle. On the other, such missionary couples are shown to be acting as equals (see Luke 10:2). The word "sister" signals just such equality, the same as the early Christian concept of sisterly-brotherliness in general (Leutzsch 1994; Ehrensperger 2007). Married women or not, 1 Corinthians 9:5 opens the view to how very significant women were as itinerant apostles and prophets in the mission of early Christianity.

The Community and Differences (1 Corinthians 11–14)

In chapters 11 to 14, Paul addresses different aspects of what happens when the Corinthian congregation gathers. In those gatherings women offer prayer and prophesy with their heads uncovered (11:5). Some people come to the gathering place
and eat a private meal that is more lavish than the common meal shared by the
majority of the congregation (11:21). This is done by people who want to flaunt
their status and affluence (11:19, 22). The presence of hierarchy within the congregation also affects how people's individual gifts or charisms are viewed (chapters
12–14). Glossolalia or spirit-induced but incomprehensible speaking to God is seen
by some Christians as the preeminent charism.

In this context, 14:34-35 indicates that in Paul's opinion women are excluded
from any charism that is related to speaking publicly in the congregation's gatherings. Such a demand contradicts 11:5 and the tenor of chapters 12 to 14. However
androcentric this text is, nowhere does it show that women are not touched by the
gift of speaking in tongues. For this reason I leave 14:34-35 aside in my interpretation of 11–14:33.

In terms of egalitarian notions, Paul always critiques the attempts to establish
hierarchies in the congregation. Those who possess less ought not to be made to
feel embarrassed by those who have more (11:22). All have the same spirit (11:4-11).
The parable of the body and its members is also used in this sense. An absurdity
has to be noticed here: in 11:2-6 Paul attacks a practice of women that is oriented
toward the equality of the sexes within a context where he decidedly argues for the
preservation of equality within the congregation. For him the ranking of the female gender as second-class humanity (11:7) is not an order of domination made
by humans and hence changeable, even though women (and possibly men, too) in
Corinth could have sensitized Paul to gender asymmetry by their very praxis.
However, he responds to the egalitarian praxis of the women (11:5) in the same way
he does to the lack of solidarity shown by the affluent (11:22). The absurdity of
Paul's conduct in relation to differences is not to be mitigated by apologetic arguments such as that in his time this injustice was not recognizable. There were
women in Corinth that openly fought against it; there were also other traditions to
interpret the story of creation, traditions that differed from Paul's.

Theological Constructions of Femaleness as a Weapon against the Liberation of Women (1 Corinthians 11:2-16)

In 11:2-16 Paul draws upon every argument he can find against the public practice
of women's liberation in the congregation; he does so rigorously and in a noticeably biased manner. His argumentation suggests that praying and prophesying by
women with their heads uncovered is an act of liberation. So it is not just that

731

women carry out a religious custom of acting in worship with their hair loose, or that they simply exercise an ordinary everyday practice. Their action in the worship of God is directed rather at the eradication of the gender hierarchy that Paul defends against them with all possible means. What he is about *basically* is the second-class order of women. He quite obviously understands Galatians 3:28 differently than many women and men in Corinth and elsewhere. It is no coincidence that in 1 Corinthians 12:13, his allusion to that verse in Galatians, he makes no mention of gender difference.

His arguments for the subordination of women are intended to get women (not only married women [Fatum 1989] but all women, including those who live "marriage-free") to cover their heads while praying and prophesying as a way of demonstrating the subordination to men that God wills for them (11:10; cf. Schottroff 1990, 123-27; 1993, 108-12). In the same vein, he finds that men have short hair while women have long hair (v. 14). As Bernadette Brooten has shown (1987), Paul attributes basic theological significance to gender polarity being made visible in dress and hairstyle.

His main arguments for women covering the head are drawn from his interpretation of the story of creation: in accordance with Genesis 3:16, the man is the head of the woman, her lord (1 Cor 11:3; see Rom 7:2, *hypandros*). The head covering expresses a relation of dominance (*exousia* as metonymy for the head covering, 1 Cor 11:10; McGinn 1996 sees this differently). When women pray and prophesy without their heads covered (11:5), the God-ordained dominance of men is publicly put to shame. The public humiliation and punishment of women by having their heads shaved (Tacitus, *Germania* 19), or the short haircut of women who want to look like men (which eventually became an expression of lesbian existence; cf. Brooten 1987, 133), is a disgrace to women (vv. 5b, 6). For Paul that disgrace is on the same level as the Corinthian women's doing away with covering their heads.

There are other arguments derived from the interpretation of the story of creation. Paul declares that the man alone is God's image and reflection. He means this to be an interpretation of Genesis 1:27, but, in fact, it is contrary to that text and how the rabbis interpreted it (cf. Boyarin 1995). The woman reflects the man, that is to say, the man receives his dignity and power from God, while the woman does not, receiving her dignity and power from the man (1 Cor 11:7). She was derived from the rib of the man (11:8; Gen. 2:22) and was created to be a "helpmate" (1 Cor 11:9; Gen. 2:18).

The comment that women should cover their heads "out of regard for the angels" (1 Cor 11:10) is in reference to Genesis 6:1-4. According to this interpretation, women without a head covering are in danger of being sexually attacked by angels. Therefore, for Paul the female gender means a God-willed subordination to the male gender; the boundaries of the latter are not to be questioned. Masculinity is defined in terms of God's image and domination of women, and femininity in terms of subordination and sexuality that need to be kept under control through men's dominance.

1 Corinthians 11:11-12 are clearly intended to be a positive assertion about women, but it remains within the framework of men's domination of women and is not meant as such to break it open. This is how Paul understands the equality of the sexes "in the Lord" in Galatians 3:28: heterosexual marriage is a structural norm for men and women and relates them one to the other (1 Cor 11:11; his own "marriage-freedom" and that of many Christians do not trouble him in this argument). All men are born of women (11:12). Even though verses 11-12 do not change the construction of femaleness of the entire section, one has to take seriously that Paul tries to create a positive counterweight against 11:3-10 by means of positive theological determinations of femaleness ("in the Lord," "all things are from God"). Still, it remains within the patriarchal frame of reference. But it is clear that Paul is caught up in a process of discussion that challenges him.

Verses 13-16 leave behind the theological argumentation and endeavor to draw on arguments from nature (11:14, 15; on the "natural" law of the gender boundaries, cf. especially Brooten 1996), on generally held customs and the sense of what is proper and decent (11:13, 16). Paul knows well that in this matter he does not have the last word. The one "disposed to be contentious" (11:16) refuses to be silenced by Paul; it is above all women who are meant here, women who pray and prophesy in public without their heads covered and who obviously are not at a loss for arguments. Presumably, their arguments are different interpretations of the Genesis narratives in Jewish tradition (cf. Boyarin 1995 and Jervell 1960, 112); they would also have different understandings of Galatians 3:28 and the equality of spiritual giftedness in Christ. Their conclusion is that according to the will of God, women are precisely not second-rate human beings subject to men.

Togetherness in Eating and in Memory (1 Corinthians 11:17-34; cf. 10:16-21)

It is because of the presence of a concrete conflict that Paul talks about the shared meal in the congregational assembly. Yet the Corinthian praxis is illumined far beyond the conflict.

The "Lord's Supper" (11:20; cf. 11:23) is a celebratory time around the evening meal (11:25: *deipnēsai*). It presupposes the holiness of the gathered congregation, expressing communion with the murdered (11:26) and risen Christ, and of the gathered people one with another as the body *(sōma)* of Christ. The holiness of the congregation and its common meal presupposes of course that Jewish dietary laws are kept, at least as far as they apply to Noachites/Gentiles. This applies in particular to food offered to the gods and the consumption of meat and blood. In addition, holiness is dependent on the inviolability of the community *(koinōnia)*: idolatry excludes communion with Christ (10:21), and communion of all, one with another, excludes a private meal *(idion deipnon)* in the place of gathering. Every participant is obliged to distinguish between holy and profane *(diakrinein,* 11:29, 31; *dokimazein,* 11:28). Whoever violates holiness falls ill or dies (11:30; cf. Acts 5:1-11). Participation is completely voluntary and whoever cannot fulfill the demands of holiness should eat at home (1 Cor 11:22, 34; the issue here is not the separation of private and public but the holiness of the congregation; Wire [1990; 1994] sees it differently). The holiness of the congregation also manifests and presupposes social justice among themselves (11:22). That is why a private meal in a small circle in the place where the eucharistic community comes together is a violation of holiness. The presence of women in these meals is taken for granted (cf. Luke 22:13-20; Quesnell 1983). It is even imaginable that groups of women celebrated the Eucharist without men being present, as Jewish women celebrated the Passover meal and proselyte women the Sabbath worship (Acts 16:13; cf. Schottroff 1990; Richter Reimer 1992). What is not to be assumed is that at this early period of Christianity there was a special role for women in the Lord's Supper that assigned them to kitchen duties (Schottroff 1994b; Wire 1990 and 1994 provide a different interpretation).

I understand what Paul notes in 1 Corinthians 11:18-19 in connection with 1:11. The group around Chloe had informed Paul and hoped for his support against those who sought to demonstrate publicly during the community meal that there were status differences in the congregation by showing off their economic superiority and affluence.

Like a festive Jewish meal, the community meal is built around a liturgy. It receives its own proper form as a commemoration of the martyr's death of Jesus Christ. The blessing of bread and wine makes present the participation in the body and blood of the martyr whose death is to bring liberation from oppression to the people and all human beings. Christian feminist women do have good reason to critique sharply the theology of the atoning death (11:24-25) that is found in the history of Christian dogma and the interpretation of the Second Testament texts, especially in connection with the sacrament of the Lord's Supper (cf. above, Tamez on Rom 3:21-26).

The common meal of the community is part of the Lord's Supper liturgy. In later Christian tradition, the meal and the Lord's Supper became separated. This separation of eating and liturgy, of eating and sacrament, is an expression of a hostility that arose subsequently; a hostility toward the body and also, in that respect, toward women. What was also lost through that separation was the awareness that the communion liturgy grows out of the liturgy of festive Jewish meals.

The Diverse Gifts of the Divine Spirit to Women and Men (1 Corinthians 12–14)

The opinions Paul expresses in this section are also a rich source for the practices of early Christian congregations. All those who acknowledge Jesus to be the Messiah and *kyrios,* and are baptized, are endowed by God with the Spirit of God (12:13). Undreamt-of powers and abilities arose in the women and men. They were able openly to sing and pray, interpret Scripture, critique others' interpretations, discuss, and speak out against something. The dynamic power of the Spirit enabled them to heal sick people, go to court without fear, and see God's future before them. These gifts were diverse, wild, inexhaustible, driven by the breaking-in of the communion and nearness of God. What Paul deals with in these chapters is the question of how to prevent the diversity of gifts from leading to the development of hierarchies.

Paul lists charismatic gifts more than once (12:4-11, 28-30; 14:26; Rom 12:3-8; in 1 Cor 13:1-3, 8, other listings are apparent). Arranged differently every time, these gifts are not ordered. The numbering in 12:28 (first, second, third) leads into an unordered list and does not express priority, for the congregation or for Paul himself. Nevertheless, there is in the congregation a pursuit for "weightier" charisms (12:31, where I read *zēloute* in the indicative).

There is a plethora of spiritual gifts in the Corinthian congregation. Depending on interest and situation, one person may claim to have several such gifts. Particularly treasured is the gift of glossolalia, speaking in tongues, a worship-happening like that in the story of Pentecost (Acts 2:1-13; 10:44-48).

Paul regards the preference for speaking in tongues as dangerous because the diversity of gifts is lost thereby and a hierarchical ordering of gifts may come about.

No depiction of gender asymmetry can be discerned in how these gifts are evaluated or distributed. Neither is the domestic work associated with house and feeding excluded from the service to the community or held to be a lesser charism, nor are there areas that are not open to women. Paul's highly favored gift of prophecy is freely granted to women as well (1 Cor 11:5; cf. Eisen 1996 on prophecy and other "offices" of women) as is speaking in tongues, which I see to be an aspect of women's praying (cf. 14:14). Women are apostles (cf. Rom 16:7 in relation to 1 Cor 12:29) and teachers (cf. 1 Tim 2:12, which implicitly refers to common early Christian practice, in relation to 1 Cor 12:29). I see no Pauline conception in 12:23 of "love patriarchalism," the maintaining of social asymmetries — including that of gender (cf. Wire 1994, 182 where she refers to her own and to the traditional interpretation of 7:17-24, which I critique fundamentally; see above). *Timē*/honor has material/financial connotations. Honoring parents (Exod 20:12; Deut 5:16) is understood in Judaism and early Christianity to mean, among other things, to look after aged parents also financially (see Mark 7:10-12). In other words, honoring does not consist only in well-pleasing words and friendliness in the interaction with people who provide "menial" services in society. Rather, everyone in the congregation has the same right to material survival. Social hierarchy is effectively broken down by the fact that all participate in being "slaves" (Mark 10:42-45 and par.) and in hard physical labor (*kopian;* cf. Rom 16 for the use of that word).

In 1 Corinthians 13 Paul praises *agapē* as the comprehensive praxis of every gift of the Spirit. He wants to put the valuation of this gift in place of the pursuit of glossolalia (13:1; 12:31). There are numerous references in chapter 13 to the literary context, making it possible to discern concrete manifestations of love from the context (or from a comparison with Rom 12:9-21). Traditional interpretation understands *agapē*/love to be sacrificing the self and voluntary suffering with others that have thereby evoked feminist critique (Wire 1990; 1994). I restrict myself to examining only those phrases that tend to support the traditional interpretation as sacrificing the self. Love "does not insist on its own way" (1 Cor 13:5), "bears all things" (13:7). There is a concrete example in 10:24, 33 of a demeanor that is oriented by self-interest: eating meat sacrificed to the gods when one's monotheistic consciousness asserts that those gods are nothing. For Paul love that "does not insist on its own ways" means being oriented toward another for whom the gods still have power (see above on those verses). Love that "bears all things" refers back to 9:12: Paul turns down financial support from the congregation, earning his keep with manual labor because in the congregations the right of itinerant missionaries to such support is sharply disputed and readily regarded as an easy way to enrich oneself at others' expense. Both contextual examples do not support the interpretation of love as sacrificing the self in the sense of patriarchal education of women.

For an overall interpretation of 1 Corinthians 13, it is important not to leave those phrases to a general praise of love, which in the text itself they are not. They need to be filled from the literary and social context.

Falsifying for the Benefit of Politics of Women's Oppression (1 Corinthians 14:34-35)

Marlene Crüsemann has formulated what I regard as the decisive argument that 1 Corinthians 14:34-35 was not written by Paul but was inserted later into the text (Crüsemann 1996, 211). Prohibiting women from speaking in public has no Jewish parallel but is to be found in Greco-Roman writers. "A text from Tosefta *Megillah* 4:11 is frequently cited as Rabbinic evidence, but most often the second half of the verse only: 'One does not let a woman come forward to read [from the Torah] in public.' The sentence preceding this, stating the overall principle, declares: 'All are counted among the seven [that read the Torah on the Sabbath], even a boy under age, even a woman.' This highlights that the active participation of women in the synagogue worship cannot be categorically rejected, and that their participation is subject, both in theory and in practice, to dispute" (Crüsemann 1996, 211). There is an example in Luke 13:13 of a woman speaking in the synagogue. Crüsemann's argument against the Pauline authorship of this text persuades me because throughout 1 Corinthians Paul moves within the framework of contemporary Jewish discussion and practice. His conception of the worship of God is shaped by the service of worship in the synagogue in which women's participation also takes the form of speaking. To this can be added these long-known arguments: the contradiction between 11:5 and the command to be silent is quite apparent (Vander Stichele 1995 sees it differently), and 14:34-35 is placed elsewhere in the text (after 14:40) in part of the manuscript tradition. Marlene Crüsemann's argument also refutes the widespread anti-Judaistic usage of the interpolation thesis: that it is not by Paul but is typically Jewish in the repression of women.

The text ties together the subordination of women (by the reference to "the law," presumably Gen 3:16), the absolute prohibition to speak in public, the enthronement of the man (husband) as woman's sole teacher, and the incarceration of women's activity in the home. In terms of content, it is to be seen as of equal substance with 1 Timothy 2:9-15. Like the Pastoral Epistles, it was inserted into the Pauline corpus most likely in the mid–second century c.e. Those additions wholly change Paul's hermeneutic of the politics of women. In the concrete case of 1 Corinthians 12–14, it means that all the Spirit's gifts to women associated with speaking are to be prohibited. The question is whether the designation of the Pastoral Epistles as "pseudepigraphs" and of 1 Corinthians 14:34-35 as an "interpolation" does not conceal that what we have here is a conscious manipulation of the text grounded in a specific politics of women. That is why I speak of "falsification."

Women and Resurrection (1 Corinthians 15)

Little of the praxis and thinking of the Corinthian congregation becomes visible in 1 Corinthians 15. The key verse, 15:12, tersely names a critique of the hope in the resurrection of the dead that is not simultaneously a critique of the significance of Christ's resurrection (cf. 15:3). The many attempts to identify the position of this group in the congregation in terms of history of religion have not yielded a conclusive result. In addition to this, these attempts are burdened by the hermeneutical conception that sees Paul in dispute with "opponents." Therefore, the chapter has to be read as an expression of Paul's opinion, that is, of Paul the apocalypticist, a link in the chain of Jewish apocalypticists (Sutter Rehmann 1995).

The text is utterly androcentric. Nonetheless, it is to be probed for its significance for the women of Corinth. To help with this task I draw on two statements from the ancient church on women and resurrection. In *The Dress of Virgins* 22, Cyprian cites Luke 20:34-36 with reference to "virgins," that is, Christian women of his time living "marriage-free." The passage cited from Luke ends with the words "children (sons) of the resurrection." Then Cyprian continues: "What we shall be, already you have begun to be. The glory of the resurrection you already have in this world; you pass through the world without the pollution of the world." I do not take this citation as an isolated opinion of a church "father," but as a summation of the early Christian view of "marriage-freedom," being mindful of the difference in the interpretation of *enkrateia* as sexual continence or as "marriage-freedom" and liberation from the "world's" structures of violence (cf. above on chapter 7). Next to the words of Cyprian I place some notes from the Acts of Thecla. Paul's preaching is spoken of there as "the word of God concerning autonomy [this is how I translate *enkrateia* here] and resurrection" (5). Resurrection is promise for the future and at the same time possibility and mystery of existence in the world now. Those whose body is the temple of God (cf. above, on 6:19; this applies to women and men and not only to those living "marriage-free") already know what it means to become angels of God (Cyprian, *The Dress of Virgins* 22; cf. Acts of Thecla 5; further references in the Apocryphal Acts of the Apostles; cf. 1 Cor 6:14, noting that some manuscripts have the verb in the present tense). Since *enkrateia* was lived out more by women than by men, there is a specific connection between women's lives and the experience of resurrection. The mythical scenario of the apocalyptic hope in resurrection ought not to be read in a rigorous dualism of now and then. This hope now transforms the bodies and lets them have experiences now of resurrection (see Rom 6:13). The experiences of resurrection in the present time are experiences of the body. The apocalyptic hope in resurrection, seen in the perspective of social history, is the hope of oppressed and threatened women, men, and children who rely on God's judging justice in the world that seeks to separate them inwardly and outwardly from God and to destroy them. Resurrection — like apocalyptic hope as a whole — means a qualification of the present: the present in relation to God who is creator and judge.

In 1 Corinthians 15:35-49 and 20-22, Paul shows the connection between creation and resurrection, between old and new creation. (Even though he does not use the words "old" and "new," they assist in understanding his meaning.) The (old) creation contains the future within itself like a seed (15:36-37). In its extravagant abundance of variety, creation can help our eyes to see resurrection bodies, the bodies wrought by the Spirit (*sōma pneumatikon*, 15:44) "in a mirror dimly" (13:12). In their variety, creation bodies are transparent to resurrection bodies. The present is marked by death (15:42-49, 53-57). This death is not primarily physical death but the pervasive antigodly power of destruction (cf. especially 15:26, "the last enemy"). Resurrection is victory over that death and its slave hustling (15:55; the *kentron* is a goad, studded with iron barbs used to drive slaves). The end-times battle has already begun. At its conclusion, death will be conquered (15:23-28) and all dominance will be at an end because "God will be all in all" (15:28; cf. especially Sutter Rehmann 1995 on 15:23-29). Understanding the "old" creation as a place of transitory vainglory obscures the power of hope in this text. The "old" creation is the very place of hope, of struggle (cf. only 15:32), and of the taste of God's future. The decision on how to interpret the resurrection chapter is made, in other words, on the level of hermeneutics: How do I understand apocalypticism? My interpretation of this chapter is based in a social-historical approach to apocalypticism. I ask about the significance of apocalyptic mythology for people and about the situation of their lives.

In a short statement (15:56) Paul addresses the problematic that he develops in the span of many chapters in Romans (→ Romans). The idea that the "law" gives power to sin has traditionally been given an anti-Judaistic meaning: Christ is the end of the law because the law, seeing that Jews want to fulfill it, leads to people wanting to earn salvation on their own and, in so doing, rebelling against God. Today an alternative reading can be given, for historical reasons, against that anti-Judaistic tradition of interpretation. The Torah is given by God as a means to life, while in the structures of death people become incapable of living according to the Torah's instructions. The Torah gives power to sin *because it is not being done* (Schottroff 1990).

Chapter 15 is thoroughly androcentric. Presumably, the women who were the first witnesses of the resurrection (Mark 16:1-8 par.) and the remembrance of them fell victim to androcentrism (1 Cor 15:3-8; how many women are among the five hundred "brethren," 15:6?) or, worse, to a patriarchal construction of history in which women have no importance. But I see Paul the apocalyptic on a level with many women and men to whom apocalyptic myths brought hope, strength, and experiences of resurrection now in the everyday existence of their lives. Therefore, since women emphatically related themselves to the resurrection tradition, I hear in Paul's words the voices of many women.

LITERATURE

Bassler, Jouette M. 1992. "1 Corinthians." In *The Women's Bible Commentary*, edited by Carol A. Newsom and Sharon H. Ringe, 321-29. London and Louisville.

Billerbeck, Paul, and Leberecht Strack. 1922-61. *Kommentar zum Neuen Testament aus Talmud und Midrasch.* 6 vols. Munich.

Boyarin, Daniel. 1995. "Paul, the Law, and Jewish Women." Paper delivered at Society for Biblical Literature meeting on November 19, 1995, at Philadelphia.

Brooten, Bernadette J. 1987. "Darum lieferte Gott sie entehrenden Leidenschaften aus. Die weibliche Homoerotik bei Paulus." In *Hättest du gedacht, dass wir so viele sind? Lesbische Frauen in der Kirche*, edited by Monika Barz et al., 113-38. Stuttgart.

————. 1996. *Love between Women: Early Christian Responses to Female Homoeroticism.* Chicago and London.

Cohen, Shaye J. D. 1989. "Crossing the Boundary and Becoming a Jew." *Harvard Theological Review* 82:13-33.

Crüsemann, Marlene. 1996. "Unrettbar frauenfeindlich: Der Kampf um das Wort von Frauen in 1 Kor 14 (33b) 34-35 im Spiegel antijudaistischer Elemente der Auslegung." In *Von der Wurzel getragen. Christlich-feministische Exegese in Auseinandersetzung mit Antijudaismus*, edited by Luise Schottroff and Marie-Theres Wacker, 199-223. Leiden.

Cyprian. 1975. *The Ante-Nicene Fathers.* Vol. 5. Grand Rapids.

D'Angelo, Mary Rose. 1990. "Women Partners in the New Testament." *Journal of Feminist Studies in Religion* 6:65-86.

Eisen, Ute. 1996. *Amtsträgerinnen im frühen Christentum. Epigraphische und literarische Studien.* Göttingen.

Fatum, Lone. 1989. "Women, Symbolic Universe and Structures of Silence: Challenges and Possibilities in Androcentric Texts." *Studia theologica* 43:61-80.

Foulkes, Irene. 1996. *Problemas pastorales en Corinto. Commentario exegetico-pastoral a 1 Corintos.* San José, Costa Rica.

Jervell, Jacob. 1960. *Imago Dei. Gen 1,26f im Spätjudentum, in der Gnosis und in den paulinischen Briefen.* Göttingen.

Kirchhoff, Renate. 1994. *Die Sünde gegen den eigenen Leib. Studien zu* porne *und* porneia *in 1 Kor 6,12-20 und dem sozio-kulturellen Kontext der paulinischen Adressaten.* Studien zur Umwelt des Neuen Testaments, vol. 18. Göttingen.

Leutzsch, Martin. 1994. "Apphia, Schwester!" In *Für Gerechtigkeit streiten. Theologie im Alltag einer bedrohten Welt,* edited by Dorothee Sölle, 76-82. Gütersloh.

McGinn, Sheila. 1996. "*Exousian Echein epi tēs Kephalēs:* I Cor 11:10 and the Ecclesial Authority of Women." *Listening: Journal of Religion and Culture* 31, no. 2:91-104.

Pagels, Elaine. 1979. *The Gnostic Gospels.* New York.

———. 1981. *Versuchung durch Erkenntnis. Die gnostischen Evangelien.* Frankfurt am Main.

Quesnell, Quentin. 1983. "The Women at Luke's Supper." In *Political Issues in Luke-Acts,* edited by Richard J. Cassidy et al., 59-79. New York.

Richter Reimer, Ivoni. 1992. *Frauen in der Apostelgeschichte des Lukas. Eine feministisch-theologische Exegese.* Gütersloh.

Schottroff, Luise. 1970. *Der Glaubende und die feindliche Welt. Beobachtungen zum gnostischen Dualismus und seiner Bedeutung für Paulus und das Johannesevangelium.* Wissenschaftliche Monographien zum Alten und Neuen Testament, vol. 37. Neukirchen.

———. 1990. *Befreiungserfahrungen. Studien zur Sozialgeschichte des Neuen Testaments.* Munich.

———. 1993. *Let the Oppressed Go Free: Feminist Perspectives on the New Testament.* Louisville.

———. 1994a. *Lydias ungeduldige Schwestern. Feministische Sozialgeschichte des frühen Christentums.* Gütersloh.

———. 1994b. "DienerInnen der Heiligen. Der Diakonat der Frauen im Neuen Testament." In *Diakonie — biblische Grundlagen und Orientierungen,* edited by Gerhard K. Schäfer and Theodor Strom, 222-42. 2nd ed. Heidelberg.

———. 1995. *Lydia's Impatient Sisters: A Feminist Social History of Early Christianity.* Louisville.

———. 1996. "Kreuz, Opfer und Auferstehung Christi. Geerdete Christologie im Neuen Testament und in feministischer Spiritualität." In *Ihr aber, für wen haltet ihr mich? Auf dem Weg zu einer feministisch-befreiungstheologischen Revision von Christologie,* edited by Renate Jost and Eveline Valtink, 102-23. Gütersloh.

Schüssler Fiorenza, Elisabeth. 1987. "Rhetorical Situation and Historical Reconstruction in 1 Corinthians." *New Testament Studies* 33:386-403.

———. 1994. *Jesus, Miriam's Child: Sophia's Prophet; Critical Issues in Feminist Christology.* New York.

Stach, Ilse von. 1928. "Die Frauen in Korinth." *Hochland* 26, no. 2:141-63.

Sutter Rehmann, Luzia. 1994. "'Und ihr werdet ohne Sorge sein . . .' Gedanken zum Phänomen der Ehefreiheit im frühen Christentum." In *Für Gerechtigkeit streiten. Theologie im Alltag einer bedrohten Welt,* edited by Dorothee Sölle, 88-95. Gütersloh.

———. 1995. *'Geh, frage die Gebärerin . . .' Feministisch-befreiungstheologische Untersuchungen zum Gebärmotiv in der Apokalyptik.* Gütersloh.

Theissen, Gerd. 1983. *Studien zur Soziologie des Urchristentums.* 2nd ed. Wissenschaftliche Untersuchungen zum Neuen Testament, vol. 19. Tübingen.

Thompson, Cynthia L. 1988. "Hairstyles, Head-coverings, and St. Paul: Portraits from Roman Corinth." *Biblical Archaeologist* 51:99-115.

Tomson, Peter J. 1990. *Paul and the Jewish Law: Halakha in the Letters of the Apostle to the Gentiles.* Assen, Maastricht, and Minneapolis.

Vander Stichele, Caroline. 1995. "Is Silence Golden? Paul and Women's Speech in Corinth." *Louvain Studies* 20:241-53.

Wire, Antoinette Clark. 1990. *The Corinthian Women Prophets: A Reconstruction through Paul's Rhetoric.* Minneapolis.

———. 1994. "1 Corinthians." In *Searching the Scriptures,* edited by Elisabeth Schüssler Fiorenza, 2:153-95. 2 vols. New York.

FOR FURTHER READING

Bieler, Andrea, and Luise Schottroff. 2007a. *Das Abendmahl. Essen, um zu leben.* Gütersloh.

———. 2007b. *The Eucharist: Bodies, Bread, and Resurrection.* Minneapolis.

Butting, Klara. 2000. "Pauline Variations on Genesis 2:24: Speaking of the Body of Christ in the Context of the Discussion of Lifestyles." *Journal for the Study of the New Testament* 79:79-90.

Crüsemann, Marlene. 2000. "Irredeemably Hostile to Women: Anti-Jewish Elements in the Exegesis of the Dispute about Women's Right to Speak (I Cor 14:34-35)." *Journal for the Study of the New Testament* 79:19-36.

Crüsemann, Marlene, and Carsten Jochum-Bortfeldt, eds. 2009. *Christus und seine Geschwister. Christologie im Umfeld der Bibel in gerechter Sprache.* Gütersloh.

Ehrensperger, Kathy. 2007. *Paul and the Dynamics of Power: Communication and Interaction in the Early Christ-Movement.* London and New York.

Horsley, Richard A., ed. 2004. *Paul and the Roman Imperial Order.* Harrisburg, Pa.

Janssen, Claudia. 2000. "Bodily Resurrection (I Cor 15)? The Discussion of the Resurrection in Karl Barth, Rudolf Bultmann, Dorothee Soelle and Contemporary Feminist Theology." *Journal for the Study of the New Testament* 79:61-78.

———. 2005. *Anders ist die Schönheit der Körper. Paulus und die Auferstehung in 1 Kor 15.* Gütersloh.

Kaser, Max. 1962. *Römisches Privatrecht,* sec. 58 IIIc. Munich and Berlin.

Martin, Dale B. 1995. *The Corinthian Body.* New Haven and London.

Richter Reimer, Ivoni. 1995. *Women in the Acts of the Apostles: A Feminist Liberation Perspective.* Minneapolis.

Schottroff, Luise. 2000. "Holiness and Justice: Exegetical Comments on I Corinthians 11:17-24." *Journal for the Study of the New Testament* 79:37-49.

Schowalter, Daniel N., and Steven J. Friesen, eds. 2005. *Urban Religion in Roman Corinth: Interdisciplinary Approaches.* Cambridge.

Schroer, Silvia. 2000. *Wisdom Has Built Her House: Studies on the Figure of Sophia in the Bible.* Collegeville, Minn.

Wehn, Beate. 2000. "'Blessed Are the Bodies of Those Who Are Virgins': Reflections on the Image of Paul in *The Acts of Thecla.*" *Journal for the Study of the New Testament* 79:149-64.

Translated by Barbara and Martin Rumscheidt

2 Corinthians: Sacrificing Difference for Unity

Caroline Vander Stichele

This is probably Paul's fourth letter to the Corinthian church. Before 1 Corinthians there was another letter, which has not been preserved (→ 1 Corinthians), and the so-called "tearful letter" or "intermediate letter" is to be located between 1 and 2 Corinthians (2 Cor 2:4). Some exegetes believe this letter is to be found in 2 Corinthians 10–13. In these chapters, which have the character of a self-defense, Paul reacts to people who have come into Corinth in apparent opposition to his mission and his apostleship. But that there are tensions between Paul and the church is clear not just from these chapters. For the prior chapters show that Paul wants to resolve a conflict. His second visit to Corinth had apparently created serious tensions (2:1; 13:2). Paul had probably written his "tearful letter" following this visit. In 2 Corinthians 12:14 and 13:1 Paul announces his third visit. The following events can be located in the interval between 1 and 2 Corinthians: Paul's second visit to Corinth and return to Ephesus, the tearful letter, the sending of Titus to Corinth, and Paul's meeting with him. According to 2 Corinthians 9:2-4, Paul is in Macedonia when he writes this letter. He went there following great difficulties in the province of Asia (1:8-9; 2:12-13; 7:5).

Both 1 and 2 Corinthians show that the relationship between Paul and the church was not without its problems and that there were differences between them. And yet, because we have insufficient information, and since we have only Paul's version of the facts, we can no longer reconstruct precisely what happened. It is likely that the relationship between Paul and the church moves to the foreground in 2 Corinthians, since it has become problematic (Bieringer 1996, 34).

While the authenticity of the letter, seen as a whole, is established, there is, however, doubt about its original integrity. Chapters 10–13 belonged, it is suspected, to a letter different from the one containing chapters 1–9, since the tone of

---

This chapter was written in Dutch and was translated for the German edition by Gabriele Merks-Leinen, MA.

both parts differs so markedly. But other parts of the letter also make a less than coherent impression. Paul's report about his journey in search of Titus is abruptly interrupted in 2:13 and resumed in 7:5. The intervening material doesn't appear to fit the context and is often seen as an interpolation. There is similar uncertainty about 6:14–7:1, since this section appears to interrupt the context. Moreover, many exegetes consider chapters 8 and 9 to be two originally separate documents about the collection for Jerusalem. Some authors explain the letter's lack of coherence by assuming that 2 Corinthians is a compilation of two or more letters or text fragments. Other authors defend the letter's original unity. In what follows, I proceed from the "objective" unity of the letter, that is, of the letter as we have it today.

My Standpoint as Reader and the Reading Strategy Adopted Here

I would gladly describe the standpoint from which I as reader wish to view the letter as feminist cultural criticism. By a "culture-critical" reading of the Bible I mean a reading that incorporates into the reading process the reader's own cultural background and perspective (Boyarin 1994, 1-4). More specifically, the culture to which I am attempting to relate is that of Europe. I am attempting this as a citizen of a country whose capital, Brussels, is practically equated with the "new Europe." But it is also as a feminist theologian that I am attempting to have a relationship to this Europe. And as such my place is marginal in this culture that continues to be androcentric and patriarchal. This is also the case with regard to my place in one of the oldest Christian churches, namely, the Catholic Church, which helped to give shape to the contemporary European, so-called Christian culture, including its colonial and imperialistic past. The Bible is part of the Christian heritage and thus it has authority over and influence on the Western canon and on Western culture. It is through this that my personal and collective identity is determined.

It is from this culture-critical position that I would like to read 2 Corinthians. The reading strategy I have chosen is inspired by feminist criticism, post-structuralism, especially deconstructionism, and rhetorical criticism. Here I understand "deconstructionism" to mean the dismantling of the structure of a text in order to identify what has been marginalized and suppressed within the text. By rhetorical criticism I mean the investigation of the text's power of persuasion in the rhetorical situation of text and reader, including the reader of today (Bible and Culture Collective 1995, III and IV).

To choose a particular reading strategy has the advantage of bringing into sharper focus particular possibilities for interpreting the text, but it also means that other possibilities are not used. However, this problem arises with every interpretation and is thus not peculiar to the way of looking at things described here. Moreover, I shall restrict myself in what follows to particular parts of the letter that are relevant for the standpoint I have chosen. Thus my intention is not to reconstruct Paul's original intention or the text's original meaning. My questions rather concern what (rhetorical) effect the texts have in the cultural context outlined above. Since references to women seldom occur in 2 Corinthians, this letter has not received so much attention from feminist exegesis as 1 Corinthians. 2 Corinthians 11:3 is without exception regarded as the most important text in this context. And yet I believe that 2 Corinthians can be an interesting document for feminist exegesis. Against the background of 2 Corinthians 10–12, I shall give attention, one after the other, to 3:1–4:6, 4:16–5:10, and 11:3.

The Difference between Old and New: 2 Corinthians 3:1–4:6

In 2 Corinthians 3:1–4:6 Paul defends his apostleship and defines it with concepts like serving the church. My discussion of this part of the letter concentrates on two aspects of Paul's argument: first, the comparison between Paul's ministry and that of Moses, and second, the interpretation of verse 17.

Paul begins his discussion in 3:1 with two rhetorical questions, to which he himself then gives negative answers. He has no need for letters of recommendation "as some do," since the members of the church themselves are his letter of recommendation, "written on our hearts" (v. 2). According to verse 3, this writing has four characteristics: it is "a letter from Christ"; it is delivered through Paul's ministry; it is "written not with ink but with the Spirit of the living God"; and it is written "not on tablets of stone but on tablets of human hearts." On closer examination, the images used in verses 2-3 constitute a combination formed from Scripture quotations. The expression "written on our hearts" (v. 2) is an allusion to Jeremiah 31:31-34, where God says that a new covenant will be made with the people, with the law written "on their hearts" (v. 33). In 2 Corinthians 3:3, moreover, various references appear, on the one hand, to the stone tablets that Moses had received on Mount Sinai, "on which the finger of God had written" (Exod 31:18), and, on the other hand, to the contrast between stone and flesh in Ezekiel 36:26, where God says the people will be given a heart of flesh instead of a heart of stone.

In this way Paul is implicitly comparing himself with Moses, the mediator of the covenant at Sinai. The comparison moves into the foreground in 2 Corinthians 3:6, where Paul explicitly calls himself a "minister of the new covenant." He describes the content of the new covenant by using an antithesis: "not of letter but of spirit; for the letter kills, but the Spirit gives life" (v. 6). In the verses that follow, this contrast is developed further in the form of an a fortiori argument, known in Judaism as *qal wāḥōmer* and in ancient rhetoric as a line of reasoning *a minore ad maius* (Witherington 1995, 380): if the one ministry is already glorious, then how much more the other. The glory of the one that is permanent shall outshine that of the transitory (v. 11). In verses 6-11, by means of four antitheses, the contrast between ministry in the old and in the new covenant is set forth in detail: the old operates through the letter, the new through the Spirit; the old kills, the new makes alive; the old leads to condemnation, the new to justification; the old is transitory, the new permanent. The comparison between old and new thus leads to a series of contrasts, with concepts like letter, death, condemnation, and transitoriness at the negative pole, and concepts like Spirit, life, justification, and permanence at the positive pole. The rhetorical effect of this way of looking at things is that the glory of the mediation of Moses is both confirmed and undermined. Paul assumes that ministry in the new covenant has even greater glory than that in the old, and for that reason he extols the glory of Moses, while at the same time, to emphasize the difference between the two, he characterizes the old covenant negatively (Hays 1989, 132).

The idea that in Christ the old covenant had reached its ultimate goal (vv. 13-14) was very soon interpreted by Christians to mean the supersession of the old covenant by the new covenant. The text's Christocentrism even makes such an interpretation possible. Moreover, the term *diathēkē* (covenant) was understood to mean "testament," and this then led to the designations Old and New Testaments for the Jewish and Christian scriptures, respectively. We already find this way of looking at things in Clement of Alexandria (about 215) and Origen (about 250) (Belleville 1996, 94). Moreover, since the time of Origen the contrast between letter and spirit was understood as a contrast between the literal and the allegorical interpretation of Scripture. Even if such a perspective is not necessarily anti-Jewish or anti-Semitic (Boyarin 1994, 104-5), and even if such an interpretation is not intended by Paul (Matthews 1994, 205; Schottroff 1996, 328), the history of the text's impact clearly shows that such an interpretation is and remains possible.

At a time in which neo-Nazism is finding new life, we must be on our guard against this kind of misuse. A text such as this still exerts a certain legitimizing and canonizing force, meant to give support to a Christian ideology that exalts itself as universal by contrast to Judaism's alleged particularity. This leads to the question whether the designations Old and New Testament, which are still in constant use, can be used any longer, precisely because of what the terms presuppose. To this day, Jewish criticism of this terminology is often not taken seriously enough by Christians.

Beyond this, we are struck by the dualistic character of the Pauline deliberations. This has consequences for his view of humanity, as will become clear in our discussion of the next chapter of 2 Corinthians. Finally, as far as chapter 3 is concerned, we look at verse 17: "Now the Lord is the Spirit, and where the Spirit of the Lord is, there is freedom." Paul could have intended this verse to be a commentary on the Scripture quote from Exodus 34:34 in the prior verse (Thrall 1994, 278-82). In that case, Paul makes clear in 2 Corinthians 3:17 that he understands "the Lord" in verse 16 as (a reference to) the Spirit. In this manner he applies the words of the text from Scripture to the present, giving them a new meaning. The interpretation of this verse in the past has led to all kinds of theological discussions, since two members of the Trinity are here identified with one another, either the Father and the Spirit or Christ and the Spirit, depending on how "Lord" is understood. These interpretations, however, are far from exhausting the interpretive potential of this verse. Within feminist exegesis this text can be employed subversively. To be sure, this possibility is largely lost in German, since there *Geist* (Spirit) is grammatically masculine. However, the Greek term behind this word is neuter. This means that the masculine Lord in verse 17a is identified with the neuter *pneuma*. In current interpretations there is a systematic suppression and thereby marginalization of the fact that through this identification in verse 17a the masculinity of the term "Lord" is neutralized and thus radically relativized. This interpretation of the text is iconoclastic, it's true — and also thoroughly biblical — but not impossible. For if verse 17 is understood to be a radical reinterpretation of the citation from Exodus 34:34 in 2 Corinthians 3:16, then this at the same time provides room for reinterpretations. As Hooker (1981, 308) observes, it is one of the ironies of history that Paul's own writings have been set in stone and followed to the letter, while his own use of scripture reveals how absurd this is. For him the Word of God is a living rather than a static reality.

Corporeality and Temporality: 2 Corinthians 4:16–5:10

Paul tries to make clear in 4:16–5:10 that despite all the difficulties with which he sees himself confronted (4:7-15), he does not lose heart. To show that, he distinguishes between the nature of the outer and inner person. The former is wasting away while the latter is being renewed day by day (4:16). This antithesis is further clarified in the verses that follow. It is not what is visible that is important, for this is temporary, but what is invisible, which is eternal (v. 18). In 5:1-10 the contrast shifts from outer and inner to present and future. Paul compares human existence now and in the future by references to our dwelling place and our clothing. A person's present, earthly condition can be compared to living in a tent. This picture is also used in Wisdom of Solomon 9:15, for example:

> "for a perishable body weighs down the soul,
>   and this earthly tent burdens the anxious mind."
>
> (NRSV, alternate reading)

Totally different from this temporal dwelling place, according to Paul, is the eternal dwelling place, which is in heaven, prepared by God. This image is expanded in 2 Corinthians 5:2 with a second metaphor, that of clothing. The ideal in Paul's eyes is not to be naked or unclothed (v. 3), but rather to be fully clothed, "so that what is mortal may be swallowed up by life" (v. 4). In this way he shows that he would prefer to exchange his present status "in the body" for being "with the Lord" (vv. 6-8). Naturally, this raises the question of what Paul intended to say with this metaphor and, consequently, to what the contrasts he employed refer. In this context I would primarily like to discuss two interpretive assertions, the first that Paul is dealing here with the resurrection and the second that the metaphors he uses presuppose a dualistic view of humanity.

The idea that Paul is speaking about the resurrection here is strongly influenced by the fact that this problem is already under discussion in 1 Corinthians 15 (Thrall 1994, 363; Gundry 1976, 150). It is true that both texts speak of the modes of human existence: now and in the future, after death. However, the way they are spoken about is different. First of all, in 4:16–5:10 the resurrection as such is not explicitly discussed. That only happens, in quite general terms, in the context (4:14; 5:15), in each case with a reference to Christ's resurrection. Secondly, the term "body" *(sōma)* is used only with respect to a person's earthly state. There is no discussion here of a spiritual body *(sōma pneumatikon)*, as in 1 Corinthians 15:44-46. Rather, Paul appears to be comparing quite generally a person's present earthly state with the future, heavenly state. He appears to want to make clear how viewing the future can be a basis for hope in one's present situation. The two situations are contrasted, the present described in negative terms, the future in positive terms. The resurrection of the body plays no role in this comparison, as it does in 1 Corinthians 15. Paul treats the transition from the one state to the other in 5:3, where he assumes that "we will not be found naked." Perhaps he is here alluding to the view that after death all that remains is the naked soul without a body (Thrall 1994, 374-75). Paul himself desires to be fully clothed rather than unclothed, by which he seems to be expressing his preference to go directly from this life to the next, without having to die first (v. 4). As prey is swallowed up by its captor, the present perishable state will be taken up into the new life (Belleville 1996, 136).

Paul's train of thought in this text, as well as in 2 Corinthians 3, is characterized by the use of antitheses that can be described as dualistic insofar as the inner stands in opposition to the outer and is accorded a higher value (4:16). The same is true of a person's future state as compared to the present one (5:1-10). Although the dualism of these metaphors is universally acknowledged, there is a diversity of views about its extent and content. In my opinion, it is going too far to assume that Paul's concept of humanity borders here on a radical dualism (Matthews 1994, 206). Instead, what we have here is a restrained anthropological dualism (Witherington 1995, 389; Boyarin 1994, 59-64). This difference in evaluation is connected with what these contrasts are referring to. Views differ on this. First of all, the difference between the nature of the inner and the nature of the outer person in 4:16 can be understood as a reference to the difference between the body and the soul. However, Paul does not use the terms "body" *(sōma)* and "soul" *(psychē)* here. Thus it is more natural to think of the "I" or the self being thought about from two different points of view (Belleville 1996, 126).

748

The distinction made in 5:1-10 between a person's present and future state is often perceived to be a reference to the mortal body and the resurrection body (Witherington 1995, 391; Thrall 1994, 367). But, as already stated, it is unlikely that Paul is referring specifically to the resurrection. Also, the term "body" *(sōma)* is only used with reference to the earthly, perishable body (cf. also 4:10-11). The metaphors of dwelling place and clothing that Paul employs show that he is actually thinking about a form of material existence after death (Belleville 1996, 137), which, however, he does not describe in addition as bodily but only as "being with the Lord." Even if this way of speaking makes it natural to see a connection with 1 Corinthians 15, in my view the two do not coincide. There is actually agreement insofar as in both texts a form of material continuity is affirmed. This is evidence for the fact that for Paul the contrast between now and later is not a radical one. It becomes clear in 4:16-18 that a person cannot be reduced to his or her outer form of appearance, while in 5:1-10 materiality is actually also ascribed to one's future existence. That a person today finds this quite "unthinkable" has more to do with modern than with ancient dualism. It was not until René Descartes (1596-1650) that the difference between body and soul was specifically expressed by means of the concepts physical or spiritual, material or immaterial. But this involves an alteration and limitation over against ancient dualism (Martin 1995, 4-6). The interpretation of 4:16–5:10 in these modern categories also thereby reduces the text's potential significance and its ability to render an ideological critique.

For what Paul's anthropology does is to unmask modern dualism and expose its simplicity. The kind of thinking that uses concepts of body and spirit is thus seen to be only one mode of observation, one, moreover, that is unable to grasp the whole of reality. But this does not make Paul's more restrained dualism an ideal alternative, for his anthropology is also trapped in a dualistic value system in which corporeality and temporality are evaluated negatively. In the Christian tradition this value system was expanded: body and spirit, temporality and eternity, natural and supernatural, woman and man, humanity and God entered into a hierarchical relationship to one another. Ascetic movements hostile to the body found fertile soil here. But the preference for celibacy over marriage that persists to this day in the Roman Catholic Church also has its roots in this way of thinking.

Acknowledging the dualism in Paul's thought is an important aspect of feminism's ideological critique. Within a dualistic system of thought, women are in the last analysis associated with nature, corporeality, and sexuality. Thus it is no accident that forms of misogyny are easily associated with hostility to the body and with sexual asceticism. At the same time, such a critique also shows that discrimination against women cannot be viewed in isolation from other forms of injustice. Therefore the struggle for greater justice and wholeness must also be understood inclusively. For our Western culture this means the inclusion of the body and of the earth, or, in other terms, of the economy and ecology.

Points of contact for a Christian feminist theology can be found, on the one hand, in a faith grounded in creation and, on the other, in an incarnational faith. It is precisely these elements that also play a central role in Paul's theology and that have softened his dualism, since the essential goodness of creation and also that of bodily existence are in both cases acknowledged.

How Utterly Female! 2 Corinthians 11:3

The final chapters of 2 Corinthians, especially 10–13, are without doubt the ones in which Paul defends himself most vigorously. On the one hand, he launches an all-out attack against unidentified people whom interpreters of these chapters usually call his "opponents." On the other hand, he defends his behavior toward the Corinthians and tries to win them over. The rhetorical nature of what he says shows itself not only by comparison to ancient rhetoric (Sampley 1988, 174-75) but also in its power to persuade, which is reflected in the fact that interpreters of these chapters, usually without further ado, assume Paul is in the right and uncritically support the normative character of his view.

However, if we analyze what Paul is saying with the help of concepts about power, then we see the matter in a different light (Castelli 1992, 198). Paul's self-defense can then be viewed from the perspective of his interest in defending his position and his interpretation over against others, his so-called opponents and the Corinthians. Paul's line of argument is silent about his opponents' arguments. What they are saying can be detected and reconstructed only on the basis of his reply. As in the texts we have already discussed, Paul delights in using contrasts to portray in the brightest colors his difference from "the others." A masterful rhetorical move is evident in the turnabout in which he knows how to exploit to his own advantage the charge that he is weak (10:10), by boasting in his own human weakness (11:30) and at the same time connecting this with divine power (12:10). For this, he appeals to the example of Christ, who was "crucified in weakness, but lives by the power of God" (13:4).

Paul strengthens his claims on the congregation even more by defining his relationship to them as one who is their father (11:2) or parent (12:14; 6:13). The patriarchal character of his language and its consequences becomes particularly clear in 11:2-3, in which is found the only reference to a women the letter can "boast about": "I feel a divine jealousy for you, for I promised you in marriage to one husband, to present you as a chaste virgin to Christ. But I am afraid that as the serpent deceived Eve by its cunning, your thoughts will be led astray from a sincere and pure devotion to Christ." From the context of this passage it becomes clear that Paul fears the influence of "certain people" (10:12), of "someone" who brings the Christians in Corinth a different Jesus, a different spirit, and a different gospel (11:4).

Paul introduces himself as a father who is presenting the believers in Corinth to Christ as a chaste virgin. Accordingly, the Corinthians are compared with Eve, while the serpent represents those who are proclaiming a gospel different from Paul's own. He thereby suggests that what these people are doing amounts to seduction. Paul appears to be referring to the Fall story, in which both Eve and the serpent are mentioned. Eve alone explicitly says there that she was led astray, even though the man as well as the woman violated the command that had been issued. In response to God's question about what they had done, Eve answers in Genesis 3:13: "The serpent led me astray, and so I ate" (→ Genesis 1–11). It is especially Eve's assertion that plays a central role in Paul's interpretation of this text. The verb "deceive" *(exapataō)* used in 2 Corinthians 11:3 also has the connotation of sexual "seduction." Contributing to this thought is the fact that the words for serpent both in Greek *(ophis)* and Hebrew *(nāḥāš)* are grammatically masculine. The same verb is also used in 1 Timothy 2:14, where Eve (v. 13) is also said to have allowed herself to be led astray (→ Pastoral Epistles). We don't actually find in the Bible the allegation that the serpent also seduced Eve sexually, but we do find it outside of the Bible (Schottroff 1988, 37-55). We find an important parallel to these texts in 4 Maccabees 18:7-9, where the Maccabean mother asserts her innocence by saying, "nor did the destroyer, the deceitful serpent, defile the purity of my virginity" (v. 8b) (Küchler 1986, 42-44).

Even if the comparison with Eve in 2 Corinthians 11 is used first of all with reference to the Corinthians, who, like Eve, allow themselves to be led astray to other ways of thinking (Belleville 1996, 271), the image of the virgin who needs to be watched over until the day she is wed does indeed evoke the suggestion of a potential for sexual seduction (Matthews 1994, 212). If we look at the way Eve is portrayed in 2 Corinthians, we discover that her sexual identity as a woman stands in the foreground, and moreover, that she is seen to be in a passive role. She herself does not take the initiative; she is simply led astray.

Although the creation account is also used in other passages in Paul's letters (especially in 1 Corinthians and Romans), this is the only passage with an explicit reference to Eve. The figure of Adam, on the other hand, plays a quite significant role in the other letters. The way in which the two figures are portrayed is strikingly different. Adam appears as the prototype of humanity universally, also in its fallen state. Thus it is striking that Eve is not portrayed as the one responsible for the Fall. Her relationship to Adam is rather that of the particular to the universal. She appears as a sexual, physical being while Adam doesn't. He is portrayed as the prototype of the old humanity, while Christ appears as the prototype of the new humanity. Through the former, sin entered the world, through the second, redemption (Schüngel-Straumann 1989, 151). In both cases humanity is portrayed as a unity that is asserted to be all-inclusive. This unity presupposes a universal subject, which is also male, and, with respect to the new humanity, also Christian. That women and Jews are essentially different is thereby for all intents and purposes denied. The depiction of unity apparently occurs at the expense of the difference and thus degenerates into uniformity.

Finally, the same conceptions are reflected in 2 Corinthians 11:2-3. The comparison of the Corinthians, the men as well as the women, with Eve as the prototype of someone who can be led astray, clearly has a rhetorical function. It can only "work" if the audience shares Paul's presuppositions. His argument is built on the contrast between the images of two different types of women, the positive image of the virgin (v. 2, *parthenos*), on the one hand, and the negative image of Eve as one capable of being led astray, on the other. In this way, of course, existing sexual stereotypes are also confirmed (Bassler 1992, 331).

So even if at first glance this text does not make an extremely negative impression with respect to women, things are different as far as the presuppositions are concerned. We also find these in 1 Timothy 2:9-15 and in other texts in the Christian tradition that are hostile to women. If we put 2 Corinthians 11:2-3 in the framework of this tradition, then the cultural significance of this text is doubtless greater than the one originally intended. It is also connected with the myth of Eve's primal sin, which makes the woman responsible for the evil in the world. The spread of Hellenistic dualism, which evaluates both life in the body and women in negative terms, gave continuing force to this way of thinking (Schottroff 1988, 49). These value judgments continue to live in our present cultural context, even if we are no longer aware of the precise traditions that underlie them. In the course of history the demonizing of women assumed horrendous forms, as evidenced by the phenomenon of witch hunts, among others. In reality, these mechanisms are not completely restricted to the past. For women are still identified with their sexuality and on this basis discriminated against. The nonacceptance of women into the priesthood within the Roman Catholic tradition is a flagrant example of this.

Concluding Reflections

Paul has his chance to speak in 2 Corinthians and seeks to justify and defend his conduct and his message. As especially the final chapters show, he often tries to convince his readers with the force of his rhetoric. But the harmony to which he wants to lead them tolerates no dissidents. The unity he has in mind assumes the form of uniformity, and he reserves to himself the right to determine its content. As he himself says, his unique position with respect to the church in Corinth gives him that right. They owe him childlike obedience. Thus he can also admonish them and call them to order.

This way of thinking about unity and hierarchy is also reflected in Paul's line of argumentation. Unity in Christ comes at the expense of difference. The universal subject Paul has in mind here is Christian and male. So Jews and women, in their particularity, appear as "the others" (Castelli 1991, 124-25; Boyarin 1994, 7-8). As a consequence of Paul's train of thought in 3:1–4:6 and 11:2-3, the particular ends up as the lesser in a hierarchical relationship to the universal, which is seen as the greater. A value system with the same structure also reveals itself in Paul's anthropology insofar as the perishable and the temporal are treated as inferior to imperishability and eternity (4:16–5:10).

Of course, Paul wasn't the only one to advocate these ways of thinking. But through the authority ascribed to his letters, his way of working out these ideas has had a considerable impact. The inclusion of his letters in the Bible ensured their dissemination and canonization to this day. Even if the significance of his thinking cannot be reduced to these structural components, in view of their inclusion and their consequences for the situation faced by women, a feminist critique is actually not only desirable but necessary.

LITERATURE

Bassler, Jouette M. 1992. "2 Corinthians." In *The Women's Bible Commentary*, edited by Carol A. Newsom and Sharon H. Ringe, 330-32. London and Louisville.

Belleville, Linda L. 1996. *2 Corinthians*. Downers Grove, Ill.

Bible and Culture Collective. 1995. *The Postmodern Bible*. New Haven and London.

Bieringer, Reimund. 1996. "Zwischen Kontinuität und Diskontinuität. Die beiden Korintherbriefe in ihrer Beziehung zueinander nach der neueren Forschung." In *The Corinthian Correspondence*, edited by Reimund Bieringer, 3-38. Leuven.

Boyarin, Daniel. 1994. *A Radical Jew: Paul and the Politics of Identity*. Berkeley, Calif.

Castelli, Elizabeth A. 1991. *Imitating Paul: A Discourse of Power*. Louisville.

———. 1992. "Interpretations of Power in 1 Corinthians." *Semeia* 54:197-222.

Gundry, Robert H. 1976. *SŌMA in Biblical Theology, with Emphasis on Pauline Anthropology*. Cambridge.

Hays, Robert. 1989. *Echoes of Scripture in the Letters of Paul*. New Haven.

Hooker, Morna D. 1981. "Beyond the Things That Are Written? St. Paul's Use of Scripture." *New Testament Studies* 27:295-309.

Küchler, Max. 1986. *Schweigen, Schmuck und Schleier*. Freiburg and Göttingen.

Martin, Dale B. 1995. *The Corinthian Body*. New Haven and London.

Matthews, Shelly. 1994. "2 Corinthians." In *Searching the Scriptures*, edited by Elisabeth Schüssler Fiorenza, 2:196-217. 2 vols. New York.

Sampley, J. Paul. 1988. "Paul, His Opponents in 2 Corinthians 10–13, and the Rhetorical Handbooks." In *The Social World of Formative Christianity and Judaism*, edited by Jacob Neusner, 162-77. Philadelphia.

Schottroff, Luise. 1988. "Die befreite Eva." In Christine Schaumberger and Luise Schottroff, *Schuld und Macht. Studien zu einer feministischen Befreiungstheologie*. Munich.

———. 1996. "'Gesetzesfreies Heidenchristentum' — und die Frauen? Feministische Analysen und Alternativen." In *Von der Wurzel getragen. Christlich-feministische Exegese in Auseinandersetzung mit Antijudaismus*, edited by Luise Schottroff and Marie-Theres Wacker. Leiden.

Schüngel-Straumann, Helen. 1989. "Mann und Frau in den Schöpfungstexten von Gen 1–3 unter Berücksichtigung der innerbiblischen Wirkungsgeschichte." In *Mann und*

Frau. Grundproblem theologischer Anthropologie, edited by Theodor Schneider, 142-66. Freiburg.

Thrall, Margaret E. 1994. *The Second Epistle to the Corinthians.* Vol. 1. Edinburgh.

Witherington, Ben, III. 1995. *Conflict and Community in Corinth: A Socio-Rhetorical Commentary on 1 and 2 Corinthians.* Grand Rapids.

Translated by Everett R. Kalin

Galatians: On Discomfort about Gender and Other Problems of Otherness

Brigitte Kahl

Difference and Dominance

Galatians, the core document for the Reformation doctrine of justification, is Paul the apostle's most combative writing, and its interpretation continues to be controversial, also in feminist exegesis. From Marcion to Luther and beyond, the letter's antithetical dynamism has been fed into polarizing and hierarchical processes that had severe historical consequences: in the separation of the church from the synagogue, in the Reformation split between Catholicism and Protestantism or between Lutheranism and the peasant movement, and in the West's "conquistador" pattern of culture and dominance in general. Against this background, Galatians, with its severe polemic against circumcision and works of the law, appears not only as evidence for the separation of Jew and Christian (Briggs 1994, 225), but also as one of the foundational sources of Western thinking about and actualizing difference in the form of dominance — by excluding, exploiting, and exterminating the "others" (cf. Castelli 1991, 124ff.; Boyarin 1994, 234).

If Galatians is read in this way, Galatians 3:28, one of the most important biblical declarations about the issue of justice among nations, races, classes, and genders, can only be perceived as a kind of isolated spark, thrown off from a liberating, egalitarian practice in the church before and beside Paul into the dark and forbidding context of Galatians. As a foil to this shining spark, the allegorical verdict of expulsion issued against the "Arab" slave woman Hagar (Gal 4:30), who came to be the ancestress of Islam, would then be the "authentic Pauline" statement in contrast to Galatians 3:26-28: a programmatic anticipation of the European history of power exercised against the other religion, the other gender, against the subjugated of every kind (Briggs 1994, 223ff.).

Hermeneutical Sound Barrier

The interpretation that follows attempts to read the Pauline relationship to the "others" in a different way, in which, first of all, the "synchronic" coherence of the statement is presupposed and the logic of the argument is deciphered through an analysis of the text and context in the literary and sociohistorical setting as a whole. In this reading, Galatians 3:28 appears to be an integral part and a key declaration of Galatians as a whole.

The problems for a socio-literary rereading of the Pauline text, however, go far beyond the questions of synchronic (literary-critical) and diachronic (historical-critical/sociohistorical) methodology. Our ways of reading Paul are predetermined: by Luther's reading, by Augustine, by Constantine, by Marcion, by the failed messianic revolt under Bar Kokhba in 135 C.E., by the Jewish tragedy of 70 C.E. Can we actually imagine a Paul who does not yet think in terms of opposition between Jews and Christians but instead between Jews and Gentiles (Stendahl 1978)? For whom "being a Christian" is a radical messianic variant of Judaism before the destruction of the Second Temple? A Paul who until the time of his execution by Rome shortly before the outbreak of the Jewish revolt uncompromisingly identified himself with the cross, that is, with the side of the losers — the Jewish side — long before he was canonized and inserted into the history of the winners? It was not until the fall of Jerusalem that the Pauline attack on the "works of the law" and on militant Jewish separatism became the perverse sounding board for the Roman triumph over Israel. This Roman triumph gave the words that other tone, whose sound we always also hear to this day, a tone that to a large extent has blotted out the "original tone." The more critically we read our triumphant post-Roman, Western Christian history from the perspective of its losers, the more readily we could be successful in penetrating this "hermeneutical sound barrier" and learning to understand Paul in a new way.

Masculinity Dispute

With a certain degree of justification, one could designate Galatians as the "most phallocentric" document in the New Testament. Nowhere else does "naked manhood" stand so exposed at the center of a highly emotional (5:12!) and deeply theological dispute. Galatians has by far the most frequent references to the two concepts of foreskin and circumcision, and nowhere else does such an extraordinary pairing of words appear as the "gospel of the foreskin" and the "gospel of the circumcision" (2:7). Nevertheless, translations have usually treated this provocative combination of theology and male anatomy as a linguistic faux pas and concealed it with circumlocutions like the "gospel to the Gentiles/the Jews" (e.g., the NIV).

At this point Paul begins to become unreadable. The central question in

Galatians is: Why is it that the non-Jewish men who are accepted into God's people Israel through identification with the Jewish Messiah, Jesus, dare not receive the specific sign of Jewish male identity, circumcision? This question was very likely tied to problems of (male) anatomical gender configuration much more concretely and clearly than we are accustomed to think. In this respect, the Galatian conflict is, first of all, actually a "problem related to masculinity issues" (Fatum 1989, 66). In any case, it is precisely when one reads and takes Galatians seriously as a letter targeting maleness that it gains a startling feminist explosiveness.

Thinking the Other Differently (1:6-9)

In 1:6, immediately after the salutation (1:1-5), Paul omits the customary gracious thanksgiving/prayer section and charges into the Galatians like an angry bull. Just two verses later they are confronted with a twofold anathema (1:8, 9). From the start the situation is at the point of falling apart. Against whom or what is the curse directed? If one goes along with the standard translations and interpretations, the Galatians are falling for "a different gospel — not that there is another gospel" (1:6-7 NRSV). Thus, one could say, they are following a "nongospel," against whose proponents Paul hurls his word invoking God's curse. Since the fundamental conflict of the whole letter involves Paul's battle against the desires of the non-Jewish Galatians to be circumcised (5:2-12; 6:12; cf. 2:3), the countergospel is almost unavoidably identified with some form of "Judaism."

This leads to an antithesis with very problematic historical consequences: on the "right" side stands the gospel about Christ, that is, the doctrine of justification (key word "grace," 1:6), "rightly" represented by Paul, along with the (Protestant) Christians. On the opposite side, marked by the curse, appear works righteousness, the law, and Jews as prototypes of the Occidental Christian "other," who doesn't belong and shouldn't exist. With this almost classic formulation of a repressive identity concept, Galatians 1:6-9 comes to bear the heavy burden of being quotable as a universal formula for liquidation and extermination, the "Christian" way of dealing with "others."

The problem: the Greek text does not say that there is no "other gospel" *(heteron euangelion)*. Rather, it says, literally, that it "*is* not another." The translation of the relative clause, *ho ouk estin allo,* is not very complicated. But theologically, what is said is apparently so unthinkable that commentaries as a rule suppose that Paul fell prey to a slip of the tongue here as well. But what if Paul actually meant what he said? If what he wished to deny was not the existence and legitimacy of "another gospel" but its otherness?

The One Gospel and the Other (1:10–2:21)

In the narrative portion of his writing to the Galatians, Paul quickly makes it clear that there is nothing that concerns him so much as the legitimacy of the "other gospel." To be sure, he himself for about two decades had found himself in the position of the suspicious outsider. His prophetic call to be the messianic evangelist to the Gentiles had abruptly brought him from a dominant status within Judaism (1:13-14) onto the periphery, not only geographically. From then on, his relationship to Jerusalem as the center of Judaism and of the early church remained distant and exceedingly ambivalent (1:17, 18-19; 2:6, 12; 4:25). With one exception: after seventeen years, on the basis of a revelation, Paul sees that it is now actually necessary for him to bring up for discussion in Jerusalem his proclamation of the gospel among the nations/Gentiles (1:10; 2:2), until now legitimated only from heaven. The allusions in 2:1-5 (spying fellow believers; Titus, a Greek, was not compelled to be circumcised) enable us to suspect something that Paul's rhetoric would instead like to conceal: the drama with which the conflicts actually played themselves out over the "other" Pauline foreskin-gospel (2:7), which from the normative perspective in Jerusalem was seriously lacking in legitimacy and authority. At this point, however, a kind of Pentecost miracle occurs. At the apostolic gathering in Jerusalem, the leading Jerusalem authorities "see" (2:7) that this foreskin-gospel has been entrusted (*pepisteumai*, 2:7) with the same divine authority and "grace" (2:9), and given the same effectiveness (*energeō*, 2:8), as the Petrine circumcision-gospel (2:7). Thereupon "the pillars" give Paul and Barnabas the "right hand of fellowship." Correspondingly, Paul and the churches of the uncircumcised accept the obligation to show material solidarity with the "poor" (the collection, 2:9-10).

The fundamental significance of this handshake is hard to overestimate. The opposition that separates humanity and that, in varied ways, is taken both in Greek and in Jewish thinking to be constitutive for cosmic order, the opposition, that is, between the "one" and the "other" (Martyn 1985, 413ff.), the privileged and the underprivileged (Schüssler Fiorenza 1988, 270-71; 1983, 218) — in this particular case between the circumcised and the uncircumcised — is taken away in an exemplary fellowship that develops a way of living that accepts and integrates the differences, thereby allowing them to continue to exist side by side. This unity in diversity, based on the messianic transformation toward an "inclusive Judaism," is for Paul the point at which the truth of the gospel is at stake. The gospel about the Messiah Jesus is "one" only in the duality of a circumcision and foreskin gospel. This makes it clear why Paul attacks his opponents with such vigor right at the beginning. If the Galatians as non-Jews allow themselves to be circumcised, thereby creating a unity in uniformity, instead of practicing their otherness "differently" and in a new way, in togetherness with the circumcised, they deny the fundamental messianic reality (2:21; 5:2-6). Paul's anathema is not directed against "another gospel" but, on the contrary, against a uniformity-based proclamation that functions in an opposite manner (*par' ho:* 1:8, 9), thus denying the *skandalon* of thinking and living "otherness" in a new way. Such denial happened, for example, in the "incident at Antioch" (2:11-21). In Antioch, one of the metropolises of the Greco-Roman world, the Jews *(Ioudaioi)* had eaten together with the non-Jews *(ethnē)*, but then, "for fear of the circumcision faction" (2:12), all of them, without exception, returned to the conventional practice of eating separately. Independent of how exactly one would evaluate the possibilities and boundaries for Jewish-Greek table fellowship in the diaspora, as these were laid down by the Torah, the following holds true: if, within the social structure of a major Hellenistic city, two groups that are ethnically, religiously, and culturally clearly separate — and, again and again, also hostile — come together at a common table, then it is not by chance that for Paul this is the significant sign of a new messianic practice of reconciliation and solidarity. And yet, culturally, socially, and also politically, the participants in this table fellowship found themselves sitting in a very precarious spot. Presumably their eating together had not only provoked the militant (zealot?) advocates of hostility toward other groups and toward Rome, but had also aroused the suspicion of the official Roman peace-ideology or its Hellenistic and Jewish supporters. A peace among nations that did not stand under the mark of Caesar but of a crucified rival king made the "round table" at Antioch into a subversive place within the overall structure of the empire. (On the Roman imperial background of Galatians, see Kahl 2010 for more comprehensive information.)

It is no accident that the first extensive and programmatic statement of Paul's teaching on justification (2:15-21) is found precisely in this context. It delegitimizes an exclusionary interpretation of the law that stands in the way of the coming together of the nations "in Christ" (2:18), an interpretation that has been rendered obsolete through the Messiah Jesus. The teaching on justification provides the justification for enabling the others to continue to be other (Stendahl 1978, 11). It is not a notice of withdrawal from Judaism but a theology that confers equality of status, a theology that has its *Sitz im Leben* at the table at which Jews and non-Jews eat together — and in the kitchen in which, to use contemporary terminology, "kosher" and "nonkosher" food is prepared.

Unfortunately, Paul "forgets" to mention women in his presentation of these conflicts that shaped the early church. In the context of his time, his perspectives and his language are androcentric in character. And yet a critical feminist reading cannot be content simply to expose the patriarchal deficiencies in biblical texts. It also involves laying bare the far-reaching emancipatory ruptures, departures, and rebellious impulses in the androcentric discourse of the "apostle to the nations" (Schottroff 1985, 107). Precisely as interfaces of opposing ways of thinking, the Pauline texts take on significance for today's controversies.

God the Father and "Mother Paul":
The Genesis Story Read in an Other Way (3:1–4:31)

In the form of a proof from Scripture, the two core chapters of Galatians contain the theological foundation for the messianic redefinition of the people of God as the space for the integration of the nations. The Genesis narrative as the primal account of Israel's becoming a people provides the intertextual matrix. Paul begins with the first generation, with Abraham, Sarah, and Hagar, and reactivates two clearly defined narrative patterns, which are lodged in the semantic depth-structure of the Genesis account as a rebellious potentiality for an antigenealogy (Kahl 2004): (a) the "irregular parentage" and (b) the "irregular line of succession among the brothers."

a. In all three progenetrix accounts, especially in the Sarah-Abraham sequence, a woman's barrenness propels the action. This motif, with which the Genesis account highlights masculine impotence for the sake of emphasizing divine fatherhood and contrasts human inability to engender children with God's power as creator, is radicalized by Paul to exclude biological paternity completely.

How does Paul read Genesis? The entire "heritage" proceeding from Abraham is, one could say, concentrated first of all on "the faith gene" (Gal 3:6). In this way all who believe are in principle legitimated as Abraham's descendants and heirs (3:7, 29). Of course, whether or not this faith genealogy "bears fruit" depends on the one "heir" who comes into the world as Messiah Jesus (3:16), the son of Abraham and of a human mother, but without a father, other than God (4:4). Through this, God's creative intervention, the one messianic-Abrahamic "seed-Christ" (3:16), from now on "embodies" the uniqueness and unity of the people of God (= the children of Abraham; 3:29) and the unity and uniqueness of God (3:20) in a new, messianic way in becoming one with the "other" (3:28): "There is no longer Jew or Greek, there is no longer slave or free, there is no longer male and female; for all of you are one in Christ Jesus" (3:26-28).

With this messianic "spermat(he)ology," Paul gives Jewish monotheism a radical, inclusive-universal and antihierarchical definition. Christ becomes the "nucleus" of a fellowship of Abraham's children that is plural in nature, which encroaches on the borders of the old national, religious, social, and gender-based identities. The diversity of (biological) fathers no longer divides people into those who belong and those who don't, into on-the-top and on-the-bottom, since the only thing that still counts is origin from God the Father and (the nonbiological) father Abraham. This attempt to express the ecumenical identity of the people of God genealogically also constitutes far and away the most daring variant of a messianic genealogy. In contrast to Matthew 1 and Luke 3, the patriarchal father-son succession that serves as the backbone for every "orderly" genealogical, social, and political hierarchy is totally eliminated and leveled off. The "phallocentricity" of Galatians is articulated in rigorously antiphallocratic language.

Viewed in this way, it no longer appears accidental that in what follows in chapter 4 mothers dominate: the mother of Jesus (4:4), Jerusalem the mother (4:25-26), Hagar the mother (4:24-25, 31), Sarah the mother (4:31), and . . . Paul the "mother" (4:19)! With few exceptions (Gaventa 1990; Osiek 1992), the provocation of a Paul who depicts himself as a woman in labor, struggling to give birth, is ignored — it doesn't fit any of the current clichés about Paul. While Paul certainly pictures himself elsewhere in paternalistic roles (1 Cor 4:15), the semantic universe in Galatians is apparently no longer a suitable place to use "father" metaphorically. Here, as in the provocative Deutero-Isaiah citation about the mothers who are not "with child," who are infertile and without a husband (Gal 4:27), pictures of women and men are "de-rigidified" and opened up, set free from biologically defined role requirements, set free from patterns of gender and marriage — a substantial effect of the messianic opening and unity in Galatians 3:28 (Schüssler Fiorenza 1988, 263; 1983, 211; Schottroff 1985, 102).

b. Changing identity and exchanging roles are also involved in the Sarah-Hagar allegory (4:21-31). As an additional way of telling the Genesis story, the "irregular line of succession among brothers" comes into play. Since in Genesis 4 Cain, the firstborn, had murdered his second-born brother, Abel, the normative priority of the first over the second is confirmed with respect to none of the numerous pairs of brothers in the Genesis narrative. Again and again, as in the story of Ishmael and Isaac, the "lesser" moves up into the place of the "greater." Since the hierarchy among brothers constitutes a structural element for the patriarchal order, the "exchange of brothers" is no picturesque secondary element. Already here, in the "genetic material" of the people of God, the leveling off of the structures of dominance and the "primogeniture of the other" are anchored (Kahl 1994, 57).

Up to now this element has been used only in a positive sense: according to Paul's own report, the boundary-crossing messianic establishment of fellowship that makes the Galatians, originating in Celtic Gaul, Sarah's children and Abraham's heirs had its beginning precisely in Arabia, the location of Hagar's descendants (Gal 1:17). In this way, the beginning of the Pauline "mission to the Gentiles" is implicitly described as the calling home of the Arab Ishmaelites, those once driven out of Israel and Israel's enemies: the "actual" Hagar. Unfortunately, Paul makes explicit only the negative aspect of his new reading of the Sarah-Hagar story: in an allegorical reactualization Paul applies the picture of his militant enemies ("persecuting," 4:29; in contrast to Gen 21:9 LXX) to the "literary" Hagar and her son. By using Genesis 21:10 he demands that Hagar (= those who are making propaganda against him) be driven out.

Who are these "opponents"? Surely not "the Jews." Paul constantly speaks in Galatians as a Jew (Gal 2:15 and passim), and even for the "Gentiles" the new messianic identity is first and foremost a Jewish identity. They have to forsake their old gods and, along with that, their traditional social and cultural contexts (4:8); they receive Israel's family tree and history, which are literally written on their body

(Gal 3–4); they must not worship the Roman emperor as God. And yet, as Jews, they remain "other," thereby provoking those among their Jewish brothers (and sisters?) who fight against every compromise with respect to "the others" as a falling away from God, because they (according to Paul) still think in terms of the premessianic systems that focus on distinctions.

The undermining of the old polar dichotomies is the real subject of the Sarah-Hagar allegory. All identity markers and perhaps also battle slogans of an exclusive, separatist Judaism, which from a position of superiority fights against the Pauline mission praxis as a betrayal and surrender of what is Jewish to the Gentiles/Rome, are in a "crazy" way located on the "false" side: the Sinai covenant, the biological fatherhood of Abraham (= national identity), present-day Jerusalem, and covenant all fall under the same rubric (*systoicheō*, 4:25) as slavery, non-Israel (Arabia/Hagar), flesh. On the other side, the side of the Spirit, Israel and non-Israel appear together ("we/you," 4:28, 31) under the motherhood of Sarah/of the heavenly Jerusalem as the (biologically) fatherless children of the promise. This subversion of the old distinctions as a sign of the new creation is anchored in the apocalyptic pattern of thought (Martyn 1985, 419-20) just as much as the previously mentioned image of labor (Sutter Rehmann 1995, 251ff.) that Paul used in 4:19. Once again, the other is thought about in another way. "Allegorical" (= speaking in another way) language has specific ways of expressing this (Castelli 1994, 243).

Bear One Another's Burdens (Galatians 5–6)

If one has followed Paul's argument up to this point, the practical problems of life in Galatia begin to take on a clearer shape. If Hagar's children are suddenly Sarah's descendants and Arabs all at once stand there as Jews with an impeccable Jewish genealogy, and the other way around; if, on the other hand, as a Greek one has become a Jew — with all that follows from that down to the inmost realms of life — and yet is not allowed to become a "real" Jew among (circumcised) Jews; if the old identities and classification systems are, in Christ, left behind and central stipulations of the law annulled; then are there any rules for behavior at all that still apply? And, who are "we"? Has everything become acceptable? Presumably the Galatian congregations also found themselves in a quandary — the Galatian men, that is. Being uncircumcised plus being part of Israel — wasn't that a description that fit only women? Were the men as uncircumcised Jews perhaps not real men, but a kind of "third sex" somewhere in the middle? It can be assumed that the conflict in Galatia resulted not only from sociocultural problems of dislocation and unclear ethical norms (Barclay 1988, 73) but was sharpened by a massive "uneasiness between the sexes."

Whether or not circumcision as prescribed by the Jewish law discriminates against women is controversial (Schüssler Fiorenza 1988, 262; 1983, 210-11; Lieu 1994; Schottroff and Wacker 1996, 230-31). It is undoubtedly true, it seems to me, that it represents an additional element of the distinction between male and female being rendered religiously obsolete (Plaskow 1992, 112ff.). If among the messianic people of God the old polarity and hierarchy of "male = without exception circumcised" (cf. Gen 17:10-14) and "female = without exception uncircumcised" no longer applies, but there is instead a new "pluriformity" of male = circumcised, male = uncircumcised, female = uncircumcised, this must have also contained a destabilizing element of the established sexual relationships and identities, especially for men. That in the Western tradition circumcision and being a Jew were put on the same level as being a woman/being other (Boyarin 1994, 230) does not yet characterize the circumstances in the Galatian congregations. There circumcision/law are functioning as a dominant model of identity and normality against which Paul, from a position of his own marginalization, polemicizes: since the Messiah has torn down the walls to the other, it is necessary for the Galatian men to preserve that tiny and psychologically minor — and yet highly significant — cultural, social, and religious piece of non-Jewish otherness, their foreskin. Only in this way can it be remembered, learned, practiced, and demonstrated that on the basis of messianic reality it no longer means anything whether or not one is Jew or Greek, slave or free, male or female (Gal 5:1-12; 3:28).

If one also gives attention to these issues in the background, the *parenesis* in Galatians becomes a fascinating vision of what identity and difference could mean under the conditions of the new creation. First of all, the Galatian believers are not a sphere where there is no authority and where everything goes. The law has not been abolished; rather, it is fulfilled in the one command of love for the neighbor (5:6, 14). The torah of Christ supersedes the old (delimiting) requirements of the Torah of Moses, but puts into effect its essential intention as the law of (the new) creation. What follows from this in terms of "works" and norms for concrete doing and avoiding — Paul even names a series of virtues and vices (5:19-23) — is in total conformity with the Torah, directed, to be sure, to the norm of the Spirit, which in the short section of 5:13–6:11 alone is mentioned thirteen times. The Spirit, from which the Galatians live, should establish the norm by which they live (5:25).

The word at the center of the section is *allēlōn*, "one another." The Greek term, which is a reduplication of *allo* = "somebody/something else," occurs in 5:13–6:10 no fewer than seven times, along with, in 6:4-5, the related conceptual pairing "one's own" — "someone else's/other" *(idion/heteron)*. With that, the initial issue in 1:6-9 and the key issue in 3:28 move explicitly into the center once more: How can one group (Jews) become one with the others (Greeks), if the others continue to be other and if there is no hierarchical authority to declare "what is essential"?

The Pauline answer goes like this: become one and find yourself on the level of the "other." Live out freedom in that "you" render service to another as slaves

(5:13), correct another with an authority that is grounded in the Spirit (6:1) — bearing in mind your own fallibility and accountability (6:5) — and bear one another's burdens (6:2). In these "regulations for the family of faith," vertical authority is ended and replaced by the shared and the individual responsibility of the members of the family (6:10); and, as was the case with the "historic handshake" in Jerusalem, even the "teaching office" is spelled out in horizontal, reciprocal terms as an issue of the material and spiritual sharing of goods (*koinōneō/koinōnia*, 6:6 and 2:9). The messianic transformation with respect to the "one" and the "other" takes place as a with-one-another. Paul, with this normative standard ("canon," 6:16) for identity and action, does not make things easy for the Galatians. Since the old distinctions and hierarchies are surpassed under the sign of the cross and of the new creation, Paul saw that the "simple" way of an acceptance of the generally accepted patterns of identity — Jewish = male = circumcised — was blocked off. Instead of this, he asked something unreasonable of the Galatian men: the scandalous praxis and self-definition under the categories of an inferior model of action and identity — "typically female" (cf. 4:19) and "the moral standards typical of slavery." On the basis of a messianic Judaism, male freedom/dominance is practiced by serving the other, even women, with the kind of service expected of slaves (cf. Schottroff 1994, 304ff.; 1995, 209ff.), renouncing all "phallocratically" based rights (and privileges) of a father. The biological de-virilization of masculinity, the fatherless Pauline genealogy, the "slave" model as the model for action by those who are free — these make a muddle of all patterns of identity and systems of classification. Polarities based on nation, class, and gender are de-hierarchicalized: a new form of living together of the one and the other, of which love, as the fulfilling of the torah of the one God, is the center, love practiced as becoming one in the Messiah Jesus — of the one son and heir of Abraham (5:13; 3:20, 28, 16). This biblically based anti-imperial, anti-Occidental concept of unity is the central theme not only of Galatians 3:26-28 but of Galatians as a whole.

That this model of life and faith was bound to become a stigma, especially for men (6:17), is perfectly clear. Perhaps the Galatians would rather have been "real" Jews, in contrast to the "Gentiles"; perhaps they fell back into their old non- or anti-Jewish identities; perhaps their children later became "real" Christians, in distinction from Judaism. Precisely at this point, the origin of an "exclusive Christianity," Paul, the border-crosser, with his vision of a messianically open, inclusive Judaism, was domesticated and rendered harmless — long after his execution by Rome. And then it could also happen that service (as slaves) went, as a matter of course, from being a task for messianic men to being one for women.

LITERATURE

Barclay, John. 1988. *Obeying the Truth: A Study of Paul's Ethics in Galatians.* Edinburgh.

Boyarin, Daniel. 1994. *A Radical Jew: Paul and the Politics of Identity.* Berkeley, Calif.

Briggs, Sheila. 1994. "Galatians." In *Searching the Scriptures,* edited by Elisabeth Schüssler Fiorenza, 2:218-36. 2 vols. New York.

Castelli, Elizabeth A. 1991. *Imitating Paul: A Discourse of Power.* Louisville.

———. 1994. "Allegories of Hagar: Reading Galatians 4,21-31 with Postmodern Feminist Eyes." In *The New Literary Criticism and the NT,* edited by Elizabeth Struthers Malbon and Edgar V. McKnight, 228-50. Journal for the Study of the New Testament: Supplement Series, vol. 109. Sheffield.

Fatum, Lone. 1989. "Women, Symbolic Universe and Structures of Silence: Challenges and Possibilities in Androcentric Texts." *Studia theologica* 43:61-80.

Gaventa, Beverly R. 1990. "The Maternity of Paul: An Exegetical Study of Galatians 4:19." In *The Conversation Continues: Studies in Paul and John,* edited by Beverly R. Gaventa and Robert R. Fortna, 189-210. Festschrift for J. Louis Martyn. Nashville.

Jankowski, Gerhard. 1990. "Friede über Gottes Israel. Paulus an die Galater. Eine Auslegung." *Texte & Kontexte* 13, no. 3-4:3-120.

Jegher-Bucher, Verena. 1991. *Der Galaterbrief auf dem Hintergrund antiker Epistolographie und Rhetorik. Ein anderes Paulusbild.* Zurich.

Kahl, Brigitte. 1976. *Traditionsbruch und Kirchengemeinschaft bei Paulus. Eine exegetische Studie zur Frage des "anderen Evangeliums."* Berlin.

———. 1987. *Armenevangelium und Heidenevangelium. "Sola scriptura" und die ökumenische Traditionsproblematik im Lichte von Väterkonflikt und Väterkonsens bei Lukas.* Berlin.

———. 1994. "Die Frau am Väterbrunnen. Von der Kirchenmutterschaft Hagars." In *Für Gerechtigkeit streiten. Theologie im Alltag einer bedrohten Welt,* edited by Dorothee Sölle, 53-58. Festschrift for Luise Schottroff. Gütersloh.

———. 2004. "Hagar between Genesis and Galatians: The Stony Road to Freedom." In *From Prophecy to Testament: The Function of the Old Testament in the New,* edited by Craig A. Evans, 219-32. Peabody, Mass.

———. 2010. *Galations Re-Imagined: Reading with the Eyes of the Vanquished.* Minneapolis.

Lieu, Judith. 1994. "Circumcision, Women and Salvation." *New Testament Studies* 40:358-70.

Martyn, J. Louis. 1985. "Apocalyptic Antinomies in Paul's Letter to the Galatians." *New Testament Studies* 31:410-24.

Osiek, Carolyn. 1992. "Galatians." In *The Women's Bible Commentary,* edited by Carol A. Newsom and Sharon H. Ringe, 333-37. London and Louisville.

Plaskow, Judith. 1990. *Standing Again at Sinai: Judaism from a Feminist Perspective.* New York.

———. 1992. *Und wieder stehen wir am Sinai. Eine jüdisch-feministische Theologie.* Lucerne.

Schottroff, Luise. 1985. "Wie berechtigt ist die feministische Kritik an Paulus? Paulus und die Frauen in den ersten christlichen Gemeinden im Römischen Reich." In *Einwürfe* 2, edited by Jürgen Ebach and Friedrich-Wilhelm Marquardt, 94-111. Munich.

———. 1993. "'Freue dich, du Unfruchtbare.' Zion als Mutter in 4 Esra 9–10 und Gal 4,21-31." In *Theologie zwischen Zeiten und Kontinenten,* edited by Theodor Schneider and Helen Schüngel-Straumann, 31-43. Freiburg, Basel, and Vienna.

————. 1994. *Lydias ungeduldige Schwestern. Feministische Sozialgeschichte des frühen Christentum.* Gütersloh.

————. 1995. *Lydia's Impatient Sisters: A Feminist Social History of Early Christianity.* Louisville.

Schottroff, Luise, and Marie-Theres Wacker, eds. 1996. *Von der Wurzel getragen. Christlich-feministische Exegese in Auseinandersetzung mit Antijudaismus.* Leiden, New York, and Cologne.

Schüssler Fiorenza, Elisabeth. 1983. *In Memory of Her: A Feminist Theological Reconstruction of Christian Origins.* New York.

————. 1988. *Zu ihrem Gedächtnis . . . Eine feministisch-theologische Rekonstruktion der christlichen Ursprünge.* Munich.

Stendahl, Krister. 1978. *Der Jude Paulus und wir Heiden. Anfragen an das abendländische Christentum.* Munich.

Strenge, Britta. 1997. "Sara — unser aller Mutter? Versuch über Gal 4,22-26, Bereschit Rabba 53 und Röm 9." *Texte & Kontexte* 20, no. 1-2:73-84.

Sutter Rehmann, Luzia. 1995. *Geh — frage die Gebärerin. Feministisch-befreiungs-theologische Untersuchungen zum Gebärmotiv in der Apokalyptik.* Gütersloh.

Translated by Everett R. Kalin

Ephesians: Community Spirit and Conservative Values as Survival Strategies in the Churches of Asia Minor

Helga Melzer-Keller

The letter to the church in Ephesus is well known especially for its detailed depictions of the church and for its extensive "teaching on marriage" in 5:21-33. The latter has become the basis for the Christian, in particular, the Roman Catholic, understanding of marriage (see Fleckenstein 1994, 16-96). Although this text clearly speaks about the subordination of the wife to her husband, it has enjoyed uninterrupted favor up to the present, especially for use in church weddings, because of its "poetic" language. For a commentary from a feminist perspective, it is therefore advisable not only to provide a running commentary on the entire document, but also to raise a special awareness of the pervasive patriarchal understanding of marriage in that passage.

Introductory Issues

The Letter's Literary Dependence on the Letter to the Colossians

The letter to the church in Ephesus is dependent literarily on the one to the church in Colossae. This relationship is shown both by the letter's formal following of the structure of its model and by parallels in terminology and subject matter (see Gnilka 1971, 7-13; Schnackenburg 1982, 26-30). Nevertheless, the author treats the existing material freely and adds new parts, with which the author pursues his or her own theological goals. For these reasons the author cannot be identical with the author of Colossians.

The Question of Authorship

Since Colossians is not by Paul, the letter dependent on it, Ephesians, cannot be by Paul either. The main support for this, in addition to linguistic and stylistic peculiarities untypical of the way Paul writes, is provided by theological differences from the genuine letters of Paul (see Gnilka 1971, 13-18; Schnackenburg 1982, 20-26).

Nevertheless, the letter purports to be by Paul, so we are dealing with a pseudepigraphic document. The author clearly understands himself or herself to be an heir to Paul's way of thinking, standing in the Pauline tradition. Moreover, by using the pseudonym "Paul," the author claims for his or her own writing the authority of the great apostle.

Consequently, Ephesians was written by an author from the circle of those carrying on the Pauline tradition in Asia Minor. Whether the author was a man or a woman cannot be determined, even if the androcentric language (see Eph 1:5; 6:23) and the table of household duties (Eph 5:21–6:9) make it easier to envision the author's perspective as male.

The recognizable later developments in theological reflection suggest a considerable temporal distance from the apostolic period. Therefore, the end of the first century can be assumed to be the time of writing.

The Addressees

According to Ephesians 1:1, the letter is addressed to "the saints who are in Ephesus and are faithful in Jesus Christ." However, the words "in Ephesus" are lacking in the earliest and best textual witnesses. Besides, several remarks that show that there were no personal relationships between the sender and the addressees (Eph 1:15-16; 3:2) are in conflict with the fact that Paul — in whose name the book was written — personally knew the members of the church in Ephesus very well (see Acts 19:8-10; 20:31). Thus we can assume that the document known today as the "Letter to the Ephesians" was sent at first without any information about the addressees and that at a later time this was perceived to be a lack that had to be dealt with. It is probable that originally the letter was not addressed to a particular church. As a kind of circular letter, it was intended for a larger circle of readers that included the churches in Asia Minor. For simplicity's sake, however, in what follows we shall use the common designation for the addressees.

Contents and Occasion

The letter is divided into two large sections: a theological exposition in Ephesians 1:3–3:21 and, in Ephesians 4:1–6:20, practical admonitions. The constant theme is and remains the one church, made up of Jews and Gentiles, in a mystical union with the exalted Christ as its head.

The author says nothing about the reason for writing the letter. Only indirectly, from the main thematic emphasis, can we surmise what is at stake: the inner unity of the churches and the obligation, evoked by their faith, to live in a way that sets them apart from their non-Christian environment. Apparently the author perceives the churches in Asia Minor to be in danger of expending all their energy in factionalism and quarreling, especially between "Jewish Christians" and "Gentile Christians," and of giving less and less thought to how they live.

The Letter Opening

The Salutation (1:1-2)

The author begins the letter with the salutation that was common in the ancient world (the so-called *praescript*). In structure and wording it corresponds in large measure to the openings of the letters written by Paul himself. In the first part the sender and addressees are named; in the second part a greeting and a blessing are added.

The author, by naming "Paul, an apostle of Jesus Christ by the will of God," as the sender of the letter, emphatically puts himself or herself and the letter under the authority of the great apostle. The importance of this sender is heightened all the more by the omission of the names of any cosenders (in contrast to 1 Cor 1:1; 2 Cor 1:1; Gal 1:2; Phil 1:1; 1 Thess 1:1; and to Col 1:1 as well). The letter is addressed to "the saints (in Ephesus), who are faithful in Christ Jesus"; that is, the baptized who have come to faith in Christ.

The Opening Praise to God (1:3-14)

The salutation is followed by a doxology (the so-called eulogy) praising God as the "Father of our Lord Jesus Christ," who has blessed the Christians (1:3). In what follows the author unfolds what this blessing encompasses, thereby directing the addressees' attention to the saving acts performed by God on their behalf: all the things for which they are indebted to God.

They are first reminded, in 1:4-6a, that "before the foundation of the world" Christians were chosen to lead a holy and blameless life and to be sons of God. Although there is no doubt that this refers to all believers, the author speaks only of "sonship" — clearly revealing his or her androcentric perspective. In 1:6b-8 the author thinks about the redemption God enabled the addressees to receive through the sending of his Son. Finally, the high point of God's saving acts is explained in 1:9-10: God revealed to Christians the "mystery of his will"; that is, he granted them a look into his plans, which remain hidden to all others. The motif used here of an esoteric knowledge granted by God to the chosen is often found in the apocalyptic writings of the early Jewish period (cf. 4 Ezra 14:5-7, for example). What sets the Christians' secret knowledge apart concerns the fulfillment of the world's salvation that has been brought about by God in Christ: heaven and earth have become reconciled with one another in Christ as the head of all (cf. Col 1:16, 20). The ultimate fulfillment of this reign of God, bringing the fullness of salvation, is still to come, and yet, according to Ephesians 1:11-12, the Christians have already become inheritors of God's salvation, for which, once again (cf. 1:4-6a), they have been predestined.

In 1:13-14 the author abruptly switches from first- to second-person plural. The addressees are spoken to directly and reminded of their coming to be Christians, from their hearing of the gospel to their "sealing" in baptism. The Holy Spirit received in baptism is the pledge that they have been appointed heirs of divine salvation (cf. 1:10-11). The final phrase, "to the praise of his glory," is a stylistically appropriate ending for the doxology.

Thanksgiving and Intercession (1:15-23)

The expansive doxology is followed in 1:15-16 by a thanksgiving for the faith the addressees already have and, in 1:17-19, by an intercession that they might grow even more in the knowledge that they have been chosen for salvation. This combination of thanksgiving and intercession — the faith shown to this point is indeed commendable, but its need for ripening still remains — is fully in accord with Paul's letter style (cf. Phil 1:4, 9; Philem 4, 6).

In that God also used in Christ's case the same power shown to the believers whom God chose, this section can lead into a christological confession in Ephesians 1:20-23: the early Christian belief in Christ's resurrection and installation as ruler at God's right hand (cf. Rom 1:3-4; Phil 2:9-11). The background of what is said about Christ's power as ruler in "this age and the age to come" is the idea, stemming from apocalyptic thought, that the present evil age will be replaced by the time of salvation. Indeed, with Christ this time of salvation has already begun in the present age. Since God has put all things "under the feet" of the exalted Christ (a quotation of Ps 8:7 [Eng. 6]), he has become the head over all things. But while the cosmos has been made subject to him, the church is his body. Thus, in contrast to the cosmos, which is full of unholiness, the church is the sphere in which the fullness of salvation is already present, and it is from the church that salvation will also spread throughout every part of the cosmos.

The image of the body or organism must have been known to the document's addressees. With the help of this image, the point is made in ancient literature that the various members of the state or of a particular group belong together like parts of a body and are dependent on one another (for example, Dio Chrysostom, *Orationes* 33.16). In Romans 12:3-8 and 1 Corinthians 12:12-28, Paul had also made use of this idea, saying that the members of the churches addressed by him should consider themselves to be equal members of the body of Christ. What is new in the depiction in Ephesians is that the discussion is not about the members of a local church in their relationship to one another but about *the church* as an abstract reality in its *subjection to its head, Christ* (cf. already Col 1:18). Since in this context the church is also granted a role in bestowing salvation on the world, one can speak of a "hierarchy of redemption" in the order "Christ/the head over all, the church/the body of Christ, the world." This model of the body of Christ is undoubtedly capable of strengthening the self-confidence of Christians, who are apparently threatened by their environment; at the same time, however, this model contains the potential danger of fostering in the church a triumphalistic self-understanding.

Reminding the Recipients of Their New Existence (2:1-10)

After the expansive introductory doxology (Eph 1:3-14) and the christological-ecclesiological creed appended to the thanksgiving and intercession (1:15-23), the author reminds the recipients of the ways they themselves have experienced — and continue to experience — the saving acts of God in Christ.

First, in 2:1-3, the Christians are reminded that before their conversion they lived in sin and were thus in death's power. In this context, the "ruler of the power of the air" refers to the enemy of God, the enemy that according to ancient thought ruled over the region between heaven and earth that is inhabited by spiritual beings and demons.

Set in contrast to this depiction of being "dead through trespasses and sins" is the redemptive work of God, motivated by love, which the recipients have experienced in their own bodies in baptism (2:4-7); they have been made alive with Christ and raised with him, and, with him, they have already been installed into their place in heaven (cf. already Col 2:12; 3:1). Thus, whereas Paul himself clearly spoke about salvation as a future event (cf. Rom 6:5, 8; 1 Thess 5:9), the author of Ephesians thinks instead of salvation as a present reality, effected through baptism. And this saving work of God, already begun in the church, is for all the ages still to come a sign of "the immeasurable riches of God's grace."

On the basis of the Christians' experiences depicted here, fundamental consequences are drawn that follow completely along the line of Paul's teaching on justification (Eph 2:8-10). The addressees are saved not by virtue of their own merit but solely by God's grace and through God's gift of faith (cf. Rom 3:24, 28; 5:1; Gal 2:16); nonetheless, good works are important as a testimony to the believer's new existence.

Extended Descriptions of the Church of Christ

The New Access to God in the Church Made Up
of Jews and Gentiles (2:11-22)

The author's primary interest is discussed in the second part of the letter; "the church" is the theme. First, in Ephesians 2:11-22, the author discusses the unity of those who believe in Christ, those who stem from the people of Israel ("Jewish Christians") and those of non-Jewish origin ("Gentile Christians"). Apparently, in the course of a gradual alienation from Judaism in the congregations that believed in Christ, rivalries sprang up between Christians of Jewish and non-Jewish origins, even within the individual congregations themselves. In 2:11-22 the "Gentile Christians" in particular are addressed. The emphatic use of the second-person plural, as well as the way the argument proceeds, lets us conclude that the author is a Jewish Christian who perceives the difficulties between the two groups springing from the arrogance the "Gentile Christians" show toward the "Jewish Christians" (cf. Rom 11:16-18).

That is why, in Ephesians 2:11-13, the author reminds the "Gentile Christians" that before their baptism they had to live without the covenant promises given to the people of Israel and thus without hope. This was true until they, who were originally far removed from salvation, attained through Christ — unexpectedly and without merit — a share in the saving promises to Israel and became, together with the "Jewish Christians," equals in a new community. This joining of those who were originally Jewish and those who were originally non-Jewish in the community of those who believe in Christ is pictured in 2:14-18 as a peace agreement between two groups of enemies. The law, which was given to Israel alone and was constitutive for Jewish identity, is in this new community no longer the mark of a particular privileged group.

The unity brought about by Christ in the church between the Jewish and the non-Jewish in origin is developed by the author in 2:19-22 by means of an image: the church as the *household of God*. The "Gentile Christians" are no longer homeless but, together with the "Jewish Christians," are coheirs of the saving promises to Israel in the community of the baptized, the church. The image is then developed somewhat differently. Now the church is seen as the *house of God* and a holy temple, that is, as a building. In this image the "Jewish Christians" and "Gentile Christians" are living stones with which the house is built, with Christ as the cornerstone of the whole building (compare this image with 1 Cor 3:9, 11, 16-17; 6:19). In contrast to Paul's metaphorical language, what is new here is the setting up of the church "upon the foundation of the apostles and prophets." So the author is already looking back at the foundational period, interested in connecting the church at the time of writing with the first bearers of the Christian tradition.

Paul as the Proclaimer of the Saving Mystery "Church" (3:1-13)

The author now lets Paul himself speak, as one of those named "apostles," about his role as a proclaimer of the saving mystery "church" (cf. Col 1:24-29). The emphatic "I Paul" with which the message begins in Ephesians 3:1 confers a special weight on the statements that follow (cf. 2 Cor 10:1; Gal 5:2; Philem 19). According to the fictitious setting, Paul is sitting in prison at the time the letter is written. At the conclusion of his presentation in Ephesians 3:13, Paul returns to this time of distress.

In 3:2-7 Paul sets forth his special commission: to him, just as to all the "apostles and prophets" he mentions (3:5), God made known the mystery about the church, the mystery hidden from earlier generations, that the people of non-Jewish origin had also become "coheirs," "fellow members of the body," and "sharers in" God's promise of salvation. Of this good news, this gospel, he is a servant.

3:8-12 develops Paul's appointment and commission further. The high point of Paul's train of thought is the proclamation of "the wisdom of God in its rich variety" to the "rulers and authorities in the heavenly places," the space stretching between heaven and earth, occupied by spiritual beings and demons (see 2:2). The church, whose mystery the apostle proclaims, gains a cosmic significance: in it God's secret plan of salvation for the entire world is revealed. Thus Paul is the inspired revealer of the mystery of salvation hidden in the church.

Intercession for the Believers (3:14-21)

The statements about the church finally lead into an intercessory prayer to God on behalf of the addressees (3:14-19). Its object is to bring to a fuller experience those who have already been incorporated into the church by baptism. Following its solemn opening, the supplication is developed in two stages, in which faith is addressed from the aspects of both life and knowledge: God is asked to use divine power to nurture faith and love in the hearts of the believers (3:16-17) and to lead the believers to a full, all-encompassing knowledge of the mystery of salvation (3:18-19a). In the end, the ultimate goal of faith, love, and knowledge is attaining "all the fullness of God."

In 3:20-21 the supplication concludes with a doxology (the word comes from *doxa*, "honor," "renown," "splendor," "glory"). Doxologies are used in the liturgy, especially at the ends of prayers. They always contain the name of the person being praised, the statement of praise, and a reference to eternity, along with a concluding "Amen." Our doxology contains all these elements. Beyond that, what sets it apart is that in it the church is named as the location of the praise. That makes it clear that the doxology rounds off the entire first section of the letter.

Exhortations for the Christian Life

Christian Life in the Context of the Church (4:1-16)

To the theoretical section of the letter a practical one is now attached, in which the author encourages and admonishes the addressees to live a Christian life. This *parenesis* (from *paraineō,* "to exhort, admonish") begins with a look at the life of the Christians in the church.

In 4:1-6 Paul himself is again put forward as the speaker, in order to draw practical consequences from the knowledge that people of Jewish and non-Jewish origin are called into the one church without distinction (cf. 2:11-22). The attitudes with which "Jewish Christians" and "Gentile Christians" are admonished to show mutual tolerance — humility and gentleness, patience and love — are not in themselves specifically Christian (cf., for example, *Rule of the Community* 4:2-6; Testament of Dan 6:9), but they emerge again and again in New Testament letters as "virtues" necessary for making life together function properly (cf. Col 3:12; Phil 2:3; 2 Tim 2:25; Titus 3:2; James 3:13-14). The emphasis with which the author exhorts the readers to strive for the attitudes mentioned, for the sake of "the unity of the Spirit in the bond of peace," suggests tensions and perhaps even the inclination to split apart. And thus the addressees are once again called to remember how significant the unity is to which they are called: they are *one* body, united by the *one* Spirit, the *one* Lord, the *one* faith, the *one* baptism, the *one* God.

In Ephesians 4:7-10 the author once again reverts to "we" terminology, which links the author with those who are being addressed. Virtually as evidence for the fact that there are no distinctions in the one community, even from God's point of view, the author points out that *all* members of the church have received, even if it is measured out to each person individually, "the grace of Christ" (which apparently has the same meaning as Paul's "gifts" — cf. 1 Cor 12:8-11, 28-31a). To support the author's assertion, a slightly altered quotation of Psalm 68:19 (18) is applied to Christ: he — the one who "descended," that is, the one who became human, who after his resurrection ascended once more into heaven — he, as the exalted one, gave humanity his gifts.

According to Ephesians 4:11, five gifts conveying particular offices are preeminent among all the gifts: the ones received by the apostles and prophets, which come from the church's foundational period (cf. 2:20; 3:5), and the ones received by the evangelists, the pastors, and the teachers, which apparently had not received their importance before the author's time and likely included the tasks of leading and instructing the church. According to 4:12, the officeholders that are mentioned are to "equip" the believers for ministry to the church and for building up the body of Christ.

The goal of this "building activity" is spelled out in 4:13-16. What is decisive is the unity of all in faith and in the maturing of the church into the "perfect man" [*sic*], that is, their growing together that reaches its completion in the body of Christ. This constitutive thought is followed by a sharp attack on tendencies among the recipients to go off in other directions, which are here categorically characterized as false teachings. It becomes clear once again that the author sees that the unity of the church is threatened. To counter that, the author stresses once more what the believers' goal must be: united in *one* body, to grow into Christ as their common head, who holds them together.

Christian Life in a Non-Christian Environment (4:17–5:14)

While the fellowship of believers in Christ has been revealed to the addressees as a new context for living, the societal and social surroundings in which they live continue to be the old ones. In the face of this tension, the author sees his "Gentile" addressees in particular exposed to the constant temptation to abandon their newly received faith. To prevent this, the author ascribes to their fellow Gentiles an ungodly and depraved way of life and urgently sets this before their eyes as a way of deterring them: characteristic of the "Gentiles" are an ignorance of the reality of God arising from a vanity for which they themselves bear the guilt, sexual promiscuity, and greed (cf. Rom 1:21; Gal 5:19; Col 1:21; 3:5).

In contrast to that, there is a description in Ephesians 4:20-24 of the life that those who are now baptized learned to know through missionary preaching and catechetical instruction, an entirely different and incomparably superior life. The believers are urged to put away their "former way of life," renew their "spirit," and clothe themselves "with the new self." The putting off of the old person and the putting on of the new have actually already happened in baptism (cf. Rom 6:6; 13:14; Col 3:9-10). And yet, since this fundamental reorientation has to prove itself again and again in everyday life, the process of becoming new is never fully finished.

What the putting off of the old person and the putting on of the new mean in concrete terms is set forth in Ephesians 4:25–5:2 (cf. Col 3:8-12). Not only prohibitions but also positive injunctions are presented. Many of the standards of behavior that are brought forward are already found in the First Testament. The Christians are not to lie but to speak the truth; they are to keep their anger under control (cf. Ps 4:5[4]); they are not to make room for the devil's enticements; they are not to steal but, instead, are to do good with what they have honorably earned (cf. Prov 28:19-22; Sir 7:15); through their words they are to build others up rather than discourage them. To behave differently would mean grieving the Holy Spirit, with whom they were sealed at baptism. Finally, to summarize all this, a short "vice list" (cf. Rom 1:29; Gal 5:19-21; Col 3:8) is contrasted with a "list of virtues" (cf. Gal 5:22-23). In short, what is involved is replacing bitterness, wrath, anger, slander, and all that is evil with kindness, mercy, and the readiness to forgive. The parenetic material finally reaches its climax in the command to love, with which the Christians are to imitate the love of God and of Christ that they themselves have experienced.

In a second run-through, the author once again warns in Ephesians 5:3-7 against several kinds of behaviors that are allegedly characteristic of the addressees' non-Christian fellow Gentiles but are to have no place among them. About sexual promiscuity and greed — "vices" that carry with them the loss of salvation — the Christians should not even speak (cf. 4:19). They are to refrain from any kind of "obscene, silly and vulgar talk" and not to let that kind of thing lead them to abandon the "Christian" way of life about which they have been reminded.

Through the use of the metaphor of light and darkness, the contrast between the allegedly typical "pagan" and Christian ways of life is set forth one last time in 5:8-14. This dualism is also found in early Jewish writings (e.g., Testament of Levi 19:1; *Rule of the Community* 1:9-10; 2:16; *War Scroll* 1:1, 9; 13:16), but the author binds it tightly to belonging to Christ. As those who did not believe in Christ, the addressees were darkness, but now they are light, and thus should live as "children of light," that is, in kindness, righteousness, and truth. The Christian way of life, defined in this way, is actually capable of exposing the works of darkness — by showing, through the offer of a convincing alternative, the non-Christian way of life to be godless and life-denying. A cry to awake, which may come from an ancient Christian baptismal hymn, rounds out the entire section on the Christian life in a non-Christian environment: the time of darkness is over for the baptized; now the time of light, the time of Christ, is here, and the life they lead is to bear its mark.

The distinction the author makes here between the "pagan" and Christian ways of living must be labeled problematic. For the Christian "virtues" emphasized here — the renunciation of sexual promiscuity and greed, circumspect speech — are by no means specifically Christian. Rather, ancient philosophers quite similarly tried to attract people toward a "virtuous" pattern of life (see, for example, the orations of Dion of Prusa on various questions about virtue: Dio Chrysostom, *Orationes* 62-80). The strongly polarizing way of presenting the issues in Ephesians is, therefore, to be understood as an attempt in the Christian church to make a special push for patterns of behavior that are treated positively even in the non-Christian world, in order to give the church a profile that distinguishes it clearly from its environment and that possesses a certain powerful and inviting aura.

Christian Life within the Church Itself (5:15-20)

In Ephesians 5:15-20 the author turns to the life that believers in Christ live within the church. Once again the addressees are asked to exhibit conduct that is oriented toward the will of God and thus "wise" (cf. Col 4:5). The will of God should not actually be sought in tipsy, wine-induced ecstasy — as it is in the pagan cult of Dionysus, for example — but instead should be expected from God's Spirit. The

Spirit is at work in Christian worship, as the Christians encourage one another in psalms and hymns and spiritual songs, singing and praising the Lord in their hearts and thanking the Lord at all times for everything (cf. Col 3:16-17).

Christian Life in the Household —
the Table of Household Duties (5:21–6:9)

In Ephesians 5:21–6:9, the author turns to Christian behavior within the "household" *(oikos)*, which we are to envision as the smallest economic and social unit of ancient Mediterranean society, as well as the primary system for individual relationships. And yet we have no strict separation between life in the church and life "in the household," since the exhortation to be subject to one another, which opens the passage that follows, brings to a close the series, begun in 5:18, describing patterns of behavior that are filled with, as well as commanded by, the Spirit.

In this section the author goes back to a section from Colossians (Col 3:18–4:1). The Colossians section, along with Ephesians 5:21–6:9 and 1 Peter 2:18–3:7, has since Martin Luther been called a "table of household duties" (*Die Bekenntnis-schriften der evangelisch-lutherischen Kirche* [*Confessional Writings of the Evangelical Lutheran Church*] 523) (*Haustafel* [cf. the *Book of Concord* (2000), 365, which translates *Haustafel* as "Household Chart" rather than using the more common translation employed here; trans.]). In this Colossians passage the various groups that are part of an ancient "household" are directly addressed and instructed about proper relations with one another, and here we find, on the one hand, the head of the household, the paterfamilias, and on the other, his wife, children, and slaves. This unconventional structure shows certain points of contact with ancient writings "on the economy" that, following Aristotle (*Politica* 1.1253b, 1-14) and Xenophon *(Oeconomicus)*, were widely disseminated up to the early imperial period (see Balch 1988, 26-28). Here, in a comparable manner, the inhabitants of the ancient "household" are urged to fulfill the obligations that applied to them. The objective of the economic texts is that the household be managed smoothly and productively. At the same time, they serve to stabilize patriarchal societal structures. There are diverse views on the aim and object of the Christian adaptation of this conservative economic concept in the form of the table of household duties (see Schüssler Fiorenza 1988a, 128-33; 1983, 86-90). Most likely the table of household duties is to be understood as a conscious acknowledgment of the prevailing form of society and its traditional values. Understood in this way, the table of household duties is intended to free the Christian churches from the suspicion — fully grounded, yet detrimental to their public reputation — of undermining, by the way they relate to one another as brothers and sisters, the patriarchal structures of order in Greco-Roman society (cf. Balch 1988, 28-29; Schüssler Fiorenza 1988a, 125; 1983, 84). Even if, compared with the significantly more rigid demands for submission among their non-Christian contemporaries, the table of household duties displays a "more humanizing" character, inasmuch as the responsibility of the head and leader of the household for those who are subordinate household members is emphasized, it adopts a form of society no less based on domination and subordination and it fails to strengthen tendencies — found also in Greco-Roman society — aimed at a higher degree of equality of men and women.

As we have said, the author of Ephesians made use of the table of household duties in Colossians 3:18–4:1 but padded its basic structure by referring to the christological and ecclesiological expositions found in Ephesians up to this point. In the light of this procedure, the question arises about the consequences the expansions have on the patriarchal ideology contained in the table of household duties: Is the patriarchal order broken down or strengthened by the Christology and ecclesiology?

a. The heading (Eph 5:21). What is new in the table of household duties in Ephesians is that, right at the beginning, placed before it like a heading, is a summons to be subject mutually to one another. Apparently, all the groups of people addressed in what follows are to understand their role in the household as a realization of this mutual subjection. In this way the difference between the paterfamilias and those placed under him is definitively in fact formally diminished. And yet, since, in the following explanations, the injunction of subordination is repeated only with reference to wives, children, and slaves, there is no justification for the conclusion that, on the basis of the initial injunction in 5:21, there is already a weakening, or even an abolition, of the patriarchal structure of the household.

b. The instructions about marriage (5:22-33). In Colossians 3:18 wives are instructed to be subject to their husbands, "as is fitting in the Lord." In the Greek the verb "to be subject" *(hypotassō)* sets forth the concept of order and, in the context, intends the acknowledgment of the existing patriarchal order between husbands and wives. The admonition is motivated by pointing out that this is "proper" also in the eyes of God. This rather colorless "explanation" is further developed in Ephesians 5:22-24: the wife is to be subject to her husband because the husband is the head of the wife, just as the church is subject to Christ because Christ is the church's head. For one thing, the concept comes into play here that the husband is over the wife on the basis of the order of creation, since the woman, according to Genesis 2:4b-24, was created only *after* him, *from* him and *for his sake* (cf. 1 Cor 11:3-12; 1 Tim 2:13). Going beyond that, the author draws upon christological/ecclesiological statements from the first part of the letter. Thus the commonly known basis for the superiority of the husband, derived from the order of creation, is superelevated on the basis of Christology. In the end, the headship of the husband over the wife is shown to depend on the mystery of the relationship of Christ to his church. In this way the requirement that the wife be subject becomes all-encompassing: she is to take a subordinate role "in everything."

With respect to the way husbands are to act, Colossians 3:19 says only that they should love their wives and refrain from treating them harshly. This admonition is also substantially expanded in Ephesians 5:25-27 by appeal to christological/ecclesiological statements. Husbands are to love their wives just as Christ loves the church. Thus the way husbands act is supposed to resemble what Christ is doing for the church. Set forth for reflection in this context are the saving acts Christ has already performed for the church: Jesus' death on the cross, the cleansing of the believers in baptism, and the presentation of the church to himself as his spotless bride (cf. 2 Cor 11:2).

In Ephesians 5:28-30 the instructions for husbands are expanded even further. On the basis of paralleling the relationships between husband and wife and Christ and the church, as well as the reference to the church as the body of Christ, it is only logical that the wife can now also be referred to as the body of her husband. From here it is only a small step to compare the love for their wives that is demanded of husbands with their love for their own bodies and to use that to motivate the desired behavior: just as people obviously do not hate their own bodies but instead provide them with nourishment and keep them warm, in the same way men must love their wives as their own bodies and take care of them. And now we have come full circle, referring once again to Christ's love for the church: Christ also takes care of the church in this way, as his own body, and Christ's care can be experienced by individual Christians as members of this body.

In 5:31-32 Christology-ecclesiology finally gains the upper hand with respect to the teaching on marriage. The author quotes Genesis 2:24 here. The First Testament passage, which originally explained the mutual attraction of the sexes (a so-called etiology), was called upon by both Jews and Christians to provide the creation-theological justification for the indissolubility of marriage (cf. Mark 10:7-8 and the parallel in Matt 19:4-6; 1 Cor 6:16). Nevertheless, the author has the passage point to Christ and the church, that is to say, humanity's first marriage is for the author a type representing the relationship between Christ, who is called the new Adam already in Paul (Rom 5:14; 1 Cor 15:45-49), and the church. In this way the mysterious connection of Christ and the church becomes a kind of prototype, to which the marriage partners are to give visible expression by imitating it as they fulfill the corresponding injunctions in the first part of the table of household duties.

After this theological reflection on the unity of Christ and the church, the author presses on in 5:33 to the conclusion of the teaching on marriage. The injunctions to the marriage partners are brought once again to the heart of the matter: husbands are to love their wives and wives are to fear (NRSV "respect") their husbands. The use of the verb "fear" *(phobeō)* is new. Here we are also dealing with an attitude with which subordinates relate to those who are over them (cf. 6:5).

In traditional exegesis the point of view is persistently supported that the relationship between husband and wife becomes truly more profound through its parallel with the relationship between Christ and the church, and the relationship in which the one is over the other is set aside in the spirit of mutual subjection and love. Yet even if the severity of the wife's subjection is to be softened by the manner in which the husband shows himself to be her head, the husband is and remains her "head." It can be inferred from the Christology-ecclesiology of the entire letter that even Christ's deep and dedicated love does not relativize the power inequality between him as the "head" and the church as his "body." So, in reality, all the wife can do is receive, "be taken care of." Aside from that, she is to be subject "in every-thing." So, finally, the patriarchal order is anchored in Christology and ecclesiology. Thereby the hierarchical difference between husband and wife is not relativized, to say nothing of abolished, but is instead transcended and unassail-ably legitimated. Existing patriarchal structures are ideologically reinforced. With that the author goes far beyond the very obvious pragmatism of the table of household duties in Colossians 3:18–4:1. We no longer have here merely an apolo-getic affirmation of the patriarchal order in Greco-Roman society, but fundamen-tal rules of behavior, valid as a matter of principle, which are no longer up for dis-cussion, formally constructed and grounded as they are in the relationship between Christ and the church. On the basis of this religious legitimation of a hi-erarchically structured relationship of the sexes, the norm found in the table of household duties can exhibit the fateful history of its consequences right up into our own times — namely, when women who are married are even today com-pelled to, or feel themselves compelled to, be submissive, and thereby prevented from being equal subjects of their partnership (see Thistlethwaite 1990, 254-56).

c. The admonitions for children and fathers (Eph 6:1-4). In addition to his wife, the next ones who are under the authority of the paterfamilias in the "household" in antiquity are the children. Therefore in 6:1-4 they also are instructed to be obedi-ent to their father, just as he is instructed to exhibit moderation in his dealings with them. In contrast to the instructions on marriage, the author of Ephesians follows the pattern in Colossians more closely here (and in the section that follows).

The demand for obedience directed at the children in 6:1-3 is short and to the point. Its justification is the Decalogue commandment found in Exodus 20:12 and Deuteronomy 5:16. The fathers, on the one hand, are forbidden to provoke their children to anger and, on the other hand, are instructed to bring them up with dis-cipline and with faith in Christ.

d. The admonitions for slaves and masters (Eph 6:5-9). Finally, the obedience also demanded of slaves is motivated in 6:5-8 by telling them that their obedience to their "earthly masters" is to be lived out as obedience to Christ. In addition to that, they are promised a reward in heaven. The "masters," on the other hand, are urged to deal prudently with their slaves, and it is indeed remarkable that in this context reference is made to the irrelevance of social distinctions and the equality of all before God.

Here, the conservative patriarchal character of the table of household duties once again becomes evident, as does the author's preference for basing the argument on Christology. Slavery is accepted, and religious motivation is provided for positioning slaves under existing dependency relationships. Nevertheless, within patriarchal structures that remain untouched, the clear words to the "masters" contain the potential, not to be underestimated, for humanizing the often miserable living conditions of slaves.

But this "inner humanization" of preexisting structures finally depends on the understanding and good will of the "masters." In reality, an analysis of the effects of the tables of household duties down through the ages shows that texts such as Ephesians 6:5-9 served the masters not so much as an impetus for this kind of "inner humanization" of patriarchal social structures but much more as an effective instrument for maintaining such structures and providing them with religious legitimacy.

Christian Life as Warfare against Evil (6:10-20)

The parenetic section of the letter is brought to a conclusion in 6:10-20. The addressees are once again strongly encouraged to resist evil.

The summons to spiritual warfare dominates 6:10-13. The call to put on the armor of God has numerous parallels in the First Testament and in the New Testament letters (cf. Isa 59:17; Wis 5:18; Rom 13:12; 2 Cor 6:7; 10:4; 1 Thess 5:8). In the background here once again is the idea that the reign of Christ has not been fully realized and that especially the space between heaven and earth is still dominated by spiritual beings and demonic forces (cf. Eph 2:2).

The "weapons" God has made available to the Christians for their warfare are described in 6:14-17. They are understood to be the inner attitudes and gifts that come from God: truth and righteousness, the readiness "to proclaim the gospel of peace," faith, salvation, and the Word of God.

But the most effective "weapon," according to 6:18-20, is prayer (cf. Col 4:2-4). Incessant prayer appears to have been a distinctive feature of early Christian life (cf. Luke 18:1; Rom 12:12; 1 Thess 5:17). How highly the author estimates the effectiveness of prayer becomes clear in the injunction to pray for the fictitious sender of the letter, Paul, who expects this to provide more strength for carrying out his work of proclamation.

Conclusion

Some Information and Concluding Greetings (6:21-24)

Shortly before the document's conclusion the author imparts a few pieces of information that contribute to the fiction that this is a genuine letter from Paul. The concluding greeting at the end conforms to the pattern in letters from antiquity.

Addressing the blessing only to the "brothers" is due to the use of androcentric language. Essential elements from the letter's introduction are taken up once more and expanded: the wish is for peace, love, faith, and grace. The motif of permanence forms an open, hopeful prospect.

Summary

In this writing the author of Ephesians addresses the churches of Asia Minor in Paul's name and with his authority. The author apparently saw the inner unity of the churches endangered, especially among Christians of Jewish and non-Jewish origins. For this reason his or her preeminent purpose is to strengthen Christians in the understanding that they form *one* church, whose *one* head is Christ. The author ascribes to the church an actual role in imparting salvation to the cosmos. The behavior of people outside of this church is thoroughly depreciated, and the believers in Christ are emphatically warned against falling back into this kind of behavior. In this way the author strives to further feelings of unity among the addressees and to raise the level of their self-assurance toward the non-Christians among whom they lived. This runs the risk, of course, that the image of the church that is presented can be construed in a narrow, triumphalistic way.

In keeping with the mission of the church in the world, the author demands of the addressees that they live an exemplary life, which is to have its effect also outside the church. One aspect of that, among others, is the adoption of an ethic based on a conservative, patriarchal table of household duties. The problem with all this is the extremely important christological-ecclesiological explanation and motivation of the modes of behavior, especially of women and slaves. For in this way the patriarchal order is ultimately given religious sanction. After surveying the harmful effects that this has had down through the ages, one is quick to take refuge in an interpretation that focuses on the words about mutual submission and surrender, especially with respect to the relationship between husbands and wives. But the only thing that glossing things over like this accomplishes is that the hierarchical model of marriage favored in the table of household duties can keep on having its effect subliminally and in an uncontrolled manner. Only a critical exposure of the structure of the argument found in the table of household duties in Ephesians can, therefore, support the liberation of women from the traditions that are oppressing them.

LITERATURE

Balch, David L. 1988. "Household Codes." In *Greco-Roman Literature and the New Testament: Selected Forms and Genres,* edited by David E. Aune, 25-50. Sources for Biblical Study, vol. 21. Atlanta.

Fischer, Karl Martin. 1973. *Tendenz und Absicht des Epheserbriefes.* Forschungen zur Religion und Literatur des Alten und Neuen Testaments, vol. 111. Göttingen.

Fleckenstein, Karl-Heinz. 1994. *Ordnet euch einander unter in der Furcht Christi. Die Eheperikope in Eph. 5:21-33. Geschichte der Interpretation, Analyse und Aktualisierung des Textes.* Forschung zur Bibel, vol. 73. Würzburg.

Gielen, Marlis. 1990. *Tradition und Theologie neutestamentlicher Haustafelethik. Ein Beitrag zur Frage einer christlichen Auseinandersetzung mit gesellschaftlichen Normen.* Bonner biblische Beiträge, vol. 75. Frankfurt am Main.

Gnilka, Joachim. 1971. *Der Epheserbrief.* Herders theologischer Kommentar, vol. 10. Freiburg im Breisgau.

Johnson, E. Elizabeth. 1992. "Ephesians." In *The Women's Bible Commentary,* edited by Carol A. Newsom and Sharon H. Ringe, 338-42. London and Louisville.

Schnackenburg, Rudolf. 1982. *Der Brief an die Epheser.* Evangelisch-katholischer Kommentar zum Neuen Testament, vol. 10. Neukirchen-Vluyn.

Schüssler Fiorenza, Elisabeth. 1983. *In Memory of Her: A Feminist Theological Reconstruction of Christian Origins.* New York.

———. 1984. *Bread Not Stone: The Challenge of Feminist Biblical Interpretation.* Boston.

———. 1988a. *Brot statt Steine. Die Herausforderung einer feministischen Interpretation der Bibel,* esp. 111-44. Fribourg.

———. 1988b. *Zu ihrem Gedächtnis. Eine feministisch-theologische Rekonstruktion der christlichen Ursprünge.* Munich.

Tanzer, Sarah J. 1994. "Ephesians." In *Searching the Scriptures,* edited by Elisabeth Schüssler Fiorenza, 2:325-48. 2 vols. New York.

Thistlethwaite, Susan B. 1990. "Epheser 5:21-33: Missbrauch führt zu Misshandlung." In *Feministisch gelesen,* edited by Eva Renate Schmidt et al., 1:253-59. 3rd ed. Zurich and Stuttgart.

Translated by Everett R. Kalin

Philippians: Lifting Up Those Who Have Been Put Down

Sheila Briggs

The City of Philippi and the Christian Church in the First Century

Paul addresses his letter to the Christian church in Philippi. The city of Philippi was a Roman colony, in which Roman law and Roman regulations for governing a city were in effect.

From two New Testament documents, Philippians and Acts, we know of a Christian church in Philippi. The historical reliability of Acts has been questioned by many interpreters. In any case, the report in Acts 16 about Paul's missionary activity in Philippi agrees with the statements in Philippians on two significant points. Both sources attest to the leading role women play in the church. In Acts we learn of Lydia, who is described as "a worshiper of God, . . . from the city of Thyatira and a dealer of purple cloth" (Acts 16:14). According to this report, she was part of a prayer meeting for women who were adherents of the Jewish faith (16:13). That raises the question of how this statement is to be understood. If it is understood as a reference to a Jewish community of faith, the word *proseuchē* — here translated as a "prayer meeting" — in common use meant the same as "synagogue." It is striking that there is no mention in this passage of the presence of men at this prayer meeting. Should we take that to mean that only women took part in this prayer meeting? Or did Paul and his fellow apostle Silas direct their attention only to the women? Both explanations are problematic. Beginning with the research of Bernadette Brooten, it is incontrovertible that in many places in antiquity women took part in synagogue life. But Brooten does not regard this passage as evidence that this was a reference to a synagogue of women in which men did not participate. On the other hand, there is hardly any evidence for the physical separation of women and men in the synagogue and no evidence at all for such a separation in the first century or in diaspora Judaism in all of antiquity (cf. Brooten 1982, 139-40 and chapter 6). Why did Paul and Silas direct their attention only to women if there was no separation of the sexes in Jewish worship? An additional difficulty is that in all the excavations in the city of Philippi, no traces have been found of a Jewish congregation or of individual Jews in the first three centuries. It should be remembered that in Acts Lydia is not referred to as a Jew but as a "Godfearer." Godfearers were Gentiles who belonged to the Jewish congregation without full conversion to Judaism. Were the participants in the Jewish prayer meeting primarily or exclusively Godfearers, and were they, like Lydia, not full proselytes or Jews by birth? If Jews were not present, or not present on an ongoing basis, that would explain why there is no evidence of organized congregational life or of individual Jews. Although *proseuchē* means the same as synagogue, neither word points definitively to a Jewish building (cf. Kraemer 1992, 118). Perhaps a small Jewish congregation supported primarily by Godfearers could not afford such a building.

Whether or not any form of Jewish community life existed prior to or alongside of the Christian church, it is important to know how Paul's warning against so-called Judaists in Philippians 3:2-11 is to be understood. There Paul is attacking those who very likely advocated the observation of the Torah in the Christian church. Circumcision, as found in the law, was required for full membership in the Jewish community. Paul's critics were Jewish Christians who made conversion to Judaism a precondition for full membership in the Christian church. It is possible that there also was a Jewish congregation that competed with that of the Christians. Was there a connection between the women's prayer meeting mentioned in Acts and the "Judaists" in Philippians?

Philippians speaks neither of a women's prayer meeting nor of Lydia. The latter should not surprise us since Lydia was not from Philippi. Her profession as a merchant selling purple cloth was the reason she was living in Philippi. The city was located on the Via Egnatia, one of the most important roads for travel in the Roman Empire. Lydia could have left the city for business reasons or she was driven from the city as the Christian church came under persecution, as Philippians intimates.

The Religious and Social Status of Women in Philippi

Even if Acts 16 does not describe historical realities, the text still shows that many of the first Christian women had a prior spiritual home in Judaism. Many Philippian women surely belonged to other Greco-Roman religions before they joined the Christian church. In the light of archaeological and inscriptional finds at the site, Portefaix and Abrahamsen have tried to sketch a picture of the broader world of religious experience of the women in Philippi. They enumerate three religions that in a special way took up the concerns of women, the cults of Diana, Isis, and Dionysus (cf. Portefaix 1988, 75-128; Abrahamsen 1987, 20-23). There is no information in Philippians about the original religious connections of the women mentioned in the letter.

Because of the strong Roman self-consciousness of the colony at Philippi, all religions considered of foreign origin were pushed out to the margins in the first century. Hellenization progressed very slowly, and non-Roman religions took a public form only in the second half of the second century. It is likely that women adherents of the religions named above could be found in the first century, but they were discouraged from coming forward publicly in such a way as to be considered in competition with the Roman cults regulated by the state. Acts 16 reports that the Jewish prayer meeting took place outside the city, and we can assume that those involved thereby acknowledged the boundaries and rules of Roman tolerance.

The emperor cult was the most important of the religions in the colony. Worship was owed above all to Augustus *(divus Augustus)*, but worship was also accorded to Livia *(diva Augusta)*, his wife. In Philippi Livia was worshiped with particular zeal: we know of seven priestesses of Livia from Philippi. These women belonged to the elite, for they had to be Roman citizens by birth, and they had to bear the costs of their office themselves. Precisely in Roman religions, which are essentially more patriarchal, we discover a model for self-assured women. In the political sphere, the historic Livia was among the most important people of her time. She was an adviser of her husband, Augustus, and directed the political development of the empire. As a protectress she could involve herself in Roman politics without holding any public office. She was, therefore, a model for those women who, through their high social status or their access to resources, tried to put others under obligation to them in order in this way to influence political and public life. Although few women of the Roman upper class became members of the Christian church in the first century, they often had in common with women like Lydia a striving for authority and autonomy and respect for their spiritual and organizational capabilities.

There was in antiquity no unified ideology with respect to the sexes. In part this is due to the multiplicity of cultures that existed in the Roman Empire. More important is the significance and function of sexual distinctions in the broad sphere of ancient ideologies, in which allegedly "natural" differences between men and women functioned as a basis for social inequality. People's capabilities and roles, which according to this perspective were predetermined by nature, were determined by their societal status just as strongly as by their gender. That had the consequence that under certain circumstances the designations "male" and "female" did not coincide with a person's biological gender. Women could practice masculine virtues and take on masculine roles without undermining their gender-specific classification. Above all in the area of the household, male functions were taken on by women. Since the household was not confined, as it is today, to one's own family, leading a household enabled a woman to have economic independence and a role in shaping what happened in society. As a rule, a man was the head of the household *(paterfamilias)*, but women (like Lydia) also took on these roles. If a woman took on a position, activity, or authority otherwise understood to be that of a man, it did not lead to a weakening of the broadly held assumption that the nature and ability of a man and a woman are fundamentally different. Rather, in that case, the woman was understood to be a man, both mentally and morally. The empress Livia was a patroness of Jewish women and men. Philo of Alexandria praised Livia for her "masculine" intellect. Usually Philo was an eager supporter of a woman's inferiority and weakness. Therefore he could justify Livia's public intervention on behalf of the Jewish population only with the assumption that she was intellectually a man (cf. Torjesen 1993, 57-87, 105-6).

On the Origin of the Letter to the Church at Philippi

As with all of Paul's letters, the date and place of origin of Philippians cannot be established with certainty. The problem of finding the letter's place and date of origin is intensified by the fact that the text we have contains more than one letter. There is no consensus about whether Philippians is one unified letter or a compilation of more than one, but in more recent research the arguments for the unity of the letter rely primarily on its rhetorical structure. But this argument can be applied to a later redactional reworking of the text as well as to the original version. Therefore such points of departure do not allow us to decide about the historical composition of the letter (cf., among others, Bormann 1995, 87-118). At first glance, Philippians 3:1a appears to be a sentence from the conclusion of a letter, and yet, with a clear change of theme and mood, the letter continues. In the next century Bishop Polycarp wrote a letter to the Christian church in Philippi in which he mentioned that Paul sent "letters" to this church (Polycarp, *To the Philippians* 3.2). Whether he was referring to the Philippians we now have or to other genuine or inauthentic Pauline letters that are now lost cannot be said with any certainty.

The contents of Philippians also point to at least two different letters. We are struck by the discrepancy between the descriptions of Paul's adversaries in Philippians 1:15-17 and 3:2. Paul ascribed to the former "envy," "rivalry," "selfish ambition," and the desire to increase his suffering in prison. Paul leveled no moral accusations at the latter but saw in them the greater danger to the church, because they wanted to introduce into the church of Christ the rite of circumcision prescribed by the Torah. We are well aware from other Pauline letters that Paul found his principal opponents in the second group, among the so-called Judaists.

In my opinion, a division of Philippians is unavoidable, but that says nothing about the number of letters contained in the text, their chronological order, or the context in which each arose. Exegetes often suggest a threefold division of the letter, seeing in Philippians 4 an independent letter of thanksgiving. There is controversy about the assigning of individual verses to the three letters. For a feminist exegesis this problem can be ignored. The majority of interpreters acknowledge Philippians 1:1–3:1a as a unit and as the core of a letter Paul wrote during his imprisonment.

Summary and Structure of the Letter

The following offers an orientation to the letter as a whole, which will provide the context for the passages relevant for a feminist exegesis. The greeting, 1:1-2, is followed by a prayer or prayer report (1:3-11), in which thanksgiving and intercession for the church are interwoven. The intimate connection between Paul and the church shapes his choice of words. He expresses his longing and compassionate love for the congregation (1:8-9). In 1:12-14 Paul shows that it is precisely his imprisonment that has served the spread of the gospel. As he sees it, the reason for the accusation against him, his proclamation about Christ, is known everywhere, and this gives other Christians the courage to preach the gospel with greater boldness. To be sure, the gospel is not always preached with the best of motives (1:15-18).

In 1:19-26 Paul again addresses the church as precisely those who are best equipped to share in his suffering. Here he takes up the principal theme of the textual unit 1:3–3:1, the suffering of Christians as communion with Christ. The apostle's body is the place in which the proclamation about Christ takes place (1:20). His life is of value as a physical presupposition for his mission, while his death would bring him to the goal of his proclamation, the full realization of his union with Christ. For the sake of the Christians in Philippi, Paul sets aside the death for which he longs (1:24-26). Paul's remaining alive thus becomes an obligation for the Philippians to conduct their lives in a manner worthy of Christ (1:27). Paul calls upon the church in 1:27-30 to imitate him and his suffering. According to 1:29, the Christians in Philippi have already suffered because of their faith. The missionary activity of Christians in a Roman colony easily aroused suspicion among the authorities. The refusal to subordinate the worship of Christ to the emperor cult and other forms of Roman religion would be understood as an attack on the authority of the Roman state, an attack that needed to be suppressed.

In 2:1-4 Paul emphasizes a unity of thought and feeling, through which Christians become one soul (*sympsychoi* in 2:2; cf. *mia psychē* in 1:27), which unites them with Christ (2:5). This communion shows itself as Christians devote themselves to the needs of others. This leads to the so-called Christ hymn (2:6-11), which is probably a pre-Pauline composition, used here to call the readers to a readiness to suffer and to humility. This text's expressive force comes from the tension between the divine origin and goal of Christ's existence, on the one hand, and his humbling as a human, on the other. Christ becomes a slave and suffers the kind of execution slaves could expect, death on a cross. Christ's humbling is equated with his obedience to God. God exalts Christ, the obedient slave, and names him the world's Lord. In 2:12-13 Paul teaches the church how to interpret the hymn. Obedience to the apostle is tied to the work of God, which directs the will and work of the Christians. Paul urges the Christians to give a united witness to their faith, to which they are also obligated by Paul's missionary activity among them and his readiness to be offered up (2:14-17). In 2:25-30 he gives a report about Epaphroditus, whom the church has sent to provide Paul also with material support during his imprisonment.

A clear break in the text occurs between 3:1 and 3:2. Paul criticizes his opponents with extraordinary vehemence. The issue is circumcision and, in that context, whether Christians are obligated to observe the Torah. For Paul, circumcision, as a sign of the acceptance of the Jewish law, is "confidence in the flesh" (3:3-4), which is incompatible with Christian faith. Paul wants to reach his goal, attaining the resurrection of the dead, through incorporation into the "power of the resurrection" and into Christ's suffering (3:10-11). He describes the attainment of this goal by using the image of an athletic competition into which he throws himself in order to win the prize (3:13-14). In 3:12–4:1 he desires to strengthen the congregation's ability to endure. From his talk about the "enemies of the cross of Christ" (3:18-19) we can conclude that there already have been clashes between the Philippian Christians and those among whom they lived. In this context it is especially significant that Paul affirms, "But our citizenship is in heaven" (3:20). Membership in the Christian church was a challenging matter for Roman citizens, for they were caught in a conflict of loyalties between the demands of the Roman state and of the church. Paul does not minimize this conflict, but he speaks very explosively of Christians as citizens of a different *politeuma* (country or commonwealth). Anyone who was excluded from the political community also lost the possibility of attaining honor by getting involved in politics. It is not surprising, therefore, that Paul promises the church that Christ intends to transform "our humble body" into "his glorious body" (3:21). Anyone humbled in the earthly *politeuma* can hope for honor in the one in heaven.

In 4:2-3 Paul turns to the leaders of the church in Philippi. First he addresses Euodia and Syntyche, whose conflict with one another he wants settled. This is followed by a repeated call to "Rejoice in the Lord" (4:4; cf. 3:1) and a series of blessings. As part of what might originally have been the conclusion of a letter Paul appends a list of virtues, which draws upon Stoic ideas but which he transforms into Christian admonitions (4:8-9). This is followed in 4:10-20 by thanks for the financial support the church gave him. The text that has come down to us ends with greetings (4:21-23), from which we learn that there were also Christians in the emperor's household. The emperor's household included those involved in governing the Roman Empire. Perhaps this involved slaves and former slaves active in the government who in some cases had attained positions of greater importance.

Focal Points of a Feminist Exegesis

Women with Positions of Leadership in the Early Christian Church

At the beginning of Philippians Paul greets the *episkopoi* and *diakonoi* in the congregation (1:1). Although these words are often translated "bishops" and "deacons," these offices of the later, hierarchically structured church did not yet exist in the middle of the first century. Here we are not dealing with church offices from which women were (increasingly) excluded but with roles in the church that were also open to women (cf. Osiek 1994, 240-41). In Romans 16:1 Paul commends to the recipients Phoebe, who was the *deacon* in the church in Cenchreae. Here Paul uses a masculine word to identify Phoebe. That is an indication that Phoebe, as well as women in Philippi, had the same function as a male deacon. There was still no distinction between the activities of female deaconesses and male deacons. On the basis of the presence of women *diakonoi* in the early church we cannot, however, determine whether or not the ancient sexual ideology had been overcome. We know that women were praised as men if they successfully took on roles, functions, and authority otherwise reserved for men. Nothing more is known about Euodia and Syntyche's special functions in the congregation. They could have belonged to the circle of *episkopoi* and *diakonoi* and were surely important members of the congregation, leading Paul to fear that their conflict could endanger the congregation's unity.

Women as Citizens of a Christian "Country"

Even when women belonged to families that were citizens of the city, it was not often possible for them to be active in the political arena. That was especially true in a Roman colony like Philippi, which was ruled in accord with a strict patriarchal Roman city charter and in which women were systematically excluded from all political offices.

Politeuma is not often used as a designation for the "country," but instead for the largely autonomous community or colony that an ethnic minority could form in a Hellenistic city. The Jewish population of Alexandria, for example, was joined together in a *politeuma* in which they themselves regulated their daily life. Of course, even in the community of an ethnic minority, women were discriminated against. Here rich women had access to public activities and offices (cf. Brooten 1982) denied to other women. The political image of a *politeuma* was especially attractive to the women in Philippi, where even rich upper-class women could occupy no public offices in the city except in the Livia cult. We can deduce from Philippians 3:20 that the Christian church understood the image of citizenship in heaven as a picture countering what they experienced in the political community. This alternate community was one in which being a woman or coming from a lower class was no longer an obstacle to having a share in shaping the common life. In this context, the Christians in Philippi perhaps had the desire to understand the tasks of the *episkopoi* and *diakonoi* as actual offices, in the sense of the public honors bestowed in a polis, honors from which the great majority of Christians were excluded.

The Theology of the Women in the Church at Philippi

Paul felt responsible for the spiritual leadership of the churches that arose out of his missionary activity. Nevertheless, the Pauline churches did not passively accept the apostle's teaching. Rather, they thought their faith through theologically and had forthright discussions with Paul. Can traces of this back-and-forth be discerned in Philippians, and was this theological exchange also shaped by the leading role women played in the congregation? I'm taking up here the Pauline language of corporeality and the influence of Judaism.

In other letters the apostle devotes his attention to the body of Christ and the bodies of Christians. Corporeality was certainly an important theme for him, but in Philippians he puts the emphasis on suffering and humbled bodies. Although in ideological terms women were often equated with corporeality, they had physical experiences with their bodies in that era that could connect them with the Pauline language about suffering and humbled bodies. The dangers of childbirth, exhaustion through frequent pregnancies, and a high death rate among mothers and children were all part of the daily suffering of a woman's body. In addition, men had the legal right to inflict bodily punishment on the women subordinated to them. The bodies of female slaves were at the unrestricted disposal of their masters, and, as sexual property, not subject to the ideal of chastity envisioned for free women. According to antiquity's patriarchal sexual ideology, chastity was the principal virtue for women and the only way for women to gain honor. Coerced unchastity branded her enslavement on the body of the female slave and cut her off from the attainment of any kind of honor.

In Philippians Paul used deeply personal language in speaking about the suffering he experienced in his own body and about the bodies of the Philippians (1:20; 3:21). It is possible that he also drew upon language already in use in the congregation about the transformation and glorification of suffering and humbled bodies through Christ. The women, among them slaves, could have developed this theology of corporeality. It's true, of course, that Paul was speaking of the body in androcentric terms here. Perkins observes that Paul only used images and themes from the world of men's experience: the imagery of military battles (2:25) and athletic competition (1:27; 3:13-14) as well as his concern for circumcision (3:2; 3:5; cf. Perkins 1992, 343). Nevertheless, the images of battle and sport were familiar to the women in Philippi. Many military veterans lived in Philippi, and many women came from families in which the traditions of the Roman army were maintained. They also watched the games in the stadium and could understand the comparison between runners and Christians.

Women who wanted to abandon the gender roles assigned to them were forced, on the basis of the polarization of male and female in antiquity, to become "a man." Early Christian literature contains numerous examples of a woman becoming a man (cf. Vogt 1995, 170-85), which often exposes the male author's devaluing of women. Others appear to be the fantasies of women who longed to have the moral character and freedom associated with "masculinity." In the Acts of Paul the woman apostle Thecla decides to have her hair cut short and to dress like a man. In the account of the martyrdom of Perpetua (around 203 C.E.), before her execution Perpetua dreams that her body is transformed into a man's body and that she defeats a gladiator in battle. A woman's desire to have a man's body meets with misunderstanding among feminists today. Under the ideological conditions of antiquity, it seemed reasonable to women to envision themselves as men, if they no longer wished to fulfill patriarchal expectations. The Philippian women could envision themselves in the role and body of a runner in the stadium.

We have already discussed whether a gathering of Jewish women for prayer like the one envisioned in Acts could have formed the core of the Philippian church. What Acts 16 describes is a completely plausible beginning for a Christian congregation. Judaism in Paul's time consisted of many tendencies that offered various possibilities for the participation of women in Jewish life. In some synagogues women served as officeholders and patronesses. Many ancient sources testify to the appeal Judaism held for women. It is likely that women converted to Judaism more frequently than men, for the requirement of circumcision (of which Paul disapproved) was no obstacle for them!

The image of "Judaists" is given to us in Paul's letters. As Paul depicts them, the Judaists wanted the Jewish Torah imposed on the Christian church as a matter of principle. But which perspective on the law did they advocate? Was it similar to the limited demands that according to Acts 15 were agreed upon for Gentile Christians at the first Christian council in Jerusalem, or to the stricter Torah established later, as we find it in the Mishnah? In Philippians and in other letters Paul asserts that the Judaists primarily demanded of Christians circumcision, but also the observance of the food laws and of the Jewish festivals. Circumcision wasn't an issue for women, and the other requirements would have burdened the women no more than the men. In short, Paul's letters give no grounds for the assertion that the Judaists wanted to impose on the Christians an understanding of the Torah that was hostile to women.

In the controversy about whether the Torah applies to Christians, women undoubtedly took diverse positions. Some found themselves among Paul's critics. Was the strife between Euodia and Syntyche connected to the disagreements about the Torah? The Pauline text lends no support to viewing this conflict as pointless squabbling kindled by the jealous rivalry between two women. The answer to this question depends on whether Philippians 4:2 and 3:2-7 are parts of the same letter. Even if they are, a clear difference between the two passages is not to be overlooked. Paul encouraged *(parakalō)* the two women instead of issuing warnings. Euodia and Syntyche were probably women whose houses provided a place for the church to meet. Perhaps they also gave Paul financial support. It is possible that in the Christian gatherings at their houses they allowed the participation of missionaries and teachers who were not members of the Pauline circle and were considered enemies by Paul. What is certain is that for a long time they had worked together and with Paul. Perhaps they also were a missionary pair like Paul and Barnabas and other men and women enumerated in the Pauline letters (cf. D'Angelo 1990, 65-86, especially pp. 75-76). In any case, we assume that the controversy had a theological basis.

The Enslaved Christ and the Reality of Slaves

The description of Christ as a slave appeared in a society in which slavery was a constant reality. It is certain that the church at Philippi counted among its members women who were slaves and those who had been freed, who were slaveholders and those born free. And so we must ask how the statement about the enslaved Christ affected people most of whom had experienced the impact of slavery on their own bodies (cf. Briggs 1989, 137-53, to which reference is made by Schottroff 1994, 71-75; 1995, 43-46).

According to the hymn, Christ freely surrendered his divine form and his equality with God and took on the form of a slave. He became a human being, humbled himself and became obedient "to the point of death." He endured the form of execution meant for slaves, death on the cross. The significance of Christ's humiliation through enslavement advances to the foreground the insurmountable tension between his divine and human existence. In antiquity, the concept of honor was the touchstone of the ideological separation between free and slave. Freedom denotes a human existence worthy of respect, slavery the opposite. The free person's sense of honor is based on the humiliation of the enslaved. The statement in Philippians 2:6-8 derives its force from its repeated opposition to this ideology, since Christ, whose equality with God makes him worthy of all honor, takes upon himself the humiliating existence of a slave. Even though he accepted the death of a slave on the cross, that does not mean that he exhibited the moral transgressions with which, in the eyes of antiquity, slaves were contaminated. What effect did this image of the enslaved Christ have on the slaves and slave owners in the early Christian church? What follows is not an exact reproduction of the attitudes of Christian slaves and slave owners in the first century. The inner world of the thoughts and feelings of people in the past, with whom we can no longer enter into direct communication, is fundamentally inaccessible to historians. I am undertaking only an intuitive impression of inner perceptions, lost to us, that Christians could have had in the encounter with the enslaved Christ in the hymn in Philippians. For this impression, although it is historically possible, I can offer no proof.

Through Paul's letter to the Philippians slaves were called upon to identify with the enslaved Christ. Christ humbled himself (*etapeinōsen;* 2:8) and received the same body Christians received, a humble body (*sōma tēs tapeinōseōs;* 3:21). Although Philippians equates all people with humbled slaves, slaves will have experienced the formulation most sharply. Slaves could also have believed that their Christian faith conferred on them a dignity that went beyond slavery and that they were consigned to slavery for a limited time, through a stroke of fate and not by nature. They could also have expected being released from slavery. Their salvation through Christ will have changed their existence more than the not-infrequent freeing of slaves. They could also hope that just as God has exalted the humbled Christ, God would also glorify their "humble body" and call them to the honor of heavenly citizenship (3:20-21).

Slaveholders, on the other hand, could interpret these verses in a decidedly different manner. They could have relied on the fact that Christ was an almost fairy tale–like exception among slaves. Slavery was an existence unworthy of him, for, as a being like God, he did not have the defective moral character of a slave. His exaltation was the confirmation that, although in appearance he was a slave, when all was said and done, he never actually was one. Besides, as a slave Christ confirmed that the most important virtue for slaves was obedience.

As an ancient text Philippians could be interpreted by slaves as well as by slaveholders. Feminist exegesis does not need to consider all interpretive possibilities as equally valid theologically. Historically we can also begin with the assumption that the slaves attempted to actualize their understanding of the Christ hymn in Philippians within the social reality of the Christian church. Only gradually, not everywhere and only after passionate arguments, could conventional models of control become established in the thinking of Christianity. Although Euodia and Syntyche are usually pictured as well-to-do women who put their house at the disposal of the congregation, it is possible that they were slaves, for these also could lead a congregation. The Roman author and officeholder Pliny reports that he investigated two female slaves that were designated as *ministrae* in the Christian church (*Epistula* 10.96.8). The Latin word *ministrae* could (but does not have to with certainty) indicate that these female slaves were *diakonoi* in their congregation. From the context it is clear that Pliny took them for women who were leaders in the congregation and who for that reason could supply him with a detailed picture of the Christians. In addition, his report shows the legal practice of interrogating slaves only by means of torture. The Christian slaves in Philippi and elsewhere were exposed to more intense suffering than other members of the church during a persecution.

I would like to emphasize that Philippians, in its original context and also today, is a text that is open. Varied hopes, experiences, and concepts were linked with it then as they are now. We should not expect that an ancient text sees its society's ideological barriers with complete clarity and breaks through them. What is of greatest importance, in my opinion, is that Philippians presupposes the existence of an early Christian church in which women and men humbled by society could become aware that they are people with honor.

LITERATURE

Abrahamsen, Valerie A. 1987. "The Woman at Philippi: The Pagan and Christian Evidence." *Journal of Feminist Studies in Religion* 3:17-30.

———. 1995. *Women and Worship at Philippi: Diana/Artemis and Other Cults in the Early Christian Era*. Portland, Maine.

Bormann, Lukas. 1995. *Philippi: Stadt und Christengemeinde zur Zeit des Paulus*. Leiden.

Briggs, Sheila. 1989. "Can an Enslaved God Liberate? Hermeneutical Reflections on Philippians 2:6-11." *Semeia* 47:137-53.

———. 1994. "Galatians." In *Searching the Scriptures*, edited by Elisabeth Schüssler Fiorenza, 2:228-33. 2 vols. New York.

Brooten, Bernadette J. 1982. *Women Leaders in the Ancient Synagogue*. Chico, Calif.

D'Angelo, Mary Rose. 1990. "Women Partners in the New Testament." *Journal of Feminist Studies in Religion* 6:65-86.

Kraemer, Ross S. 1992. *Her Share of the Blessings: Women's Religions among Pagans, Jews, and Christians in the Greco-Roman World*. Oxford.

Osiek, Carolyn. 1994. "Philippians." In *Searching the Scriptures*, edited by Elisabeth Schüssler Fiorenza, 2:237-49. 2 vols. New York.

Perkins, Pheme. 1992. "Philippians." In *The Women's Bible Commentary*, edited by Carol A. Newsom and Sharon H. Ringe, 343-45. London and Louisville.

Portefaix, Lilian. 1988. *Sisters Rejoice: Paul's Letter to the Philippians and Luke-Acts as Received by First-Century Philippian Women*. Stockholm.

Schottroff, Luise. 1994. *Lydias ungeduldige Schwestern. Feministische Sozialgeschichte des frühen Christentums*. Gütersloh.

———. 1995. *Lydia's Impatient Sisters: A Feminist Social History of Early Christianity*. Louisville.

Torjesen, Karen Jo. 1993. *When Women Were Priests: Women's Leadership in the Early Church and the Scandal of Their Subordination in the Rise of Christianity*. San Francisco.

Vogt, Kari. 1995. "Becoming Male: A Gnostic and Early Christian Metaphor." In *The Image of God: Gender Models in Judeo-Christian Tradition*, edited by Kari Børresen. Minneapolis.

Translated by Everett R. Kalin

Colossians: The Origin of the Table of Household Duties

Angela Standhartinger

Since the beginning of feminist theological interpretation of Colossians, the involvement of the letter in the history of Christian repression has been observed. Colossians 3:18–4:1 is the first and oldest of a series of New Testament texts that call on wives, children, and slaves to be subject to husbands, fathers, and masters. This text, along with Ephesians 5:22–6:9 and 1 Peter 2:18–3:7, is often called a "table of household duties." The term originates with Martin Luther's *Small Catechism,* where he collected them under the heading "*Bible Passages for all kinds of holy orders and walks of life, through which they may be admonished, as through lessons particularly pertinent to their office and duty*" (*Book of Concord* 2000, 365). The tables of household duties, especially within Protestantism, were seen to be a divine command that assigned roles within the family and declared marriage and the family to be the locus of the Christian life's fundamental responsibility. Those who supported slavery used those texts as an alleged divine legitimation, and it was over against those texts that African Americans developed strategies for theological argumentation since the beginning of their struggle for freedom (Martin 1991).

How did the development of such tables of household duties come about in churches in which the distinctions between slave and free, men and women were abolished (Gal 3:28)? How did the demand that wives be subordinate arise in churches that chose women as their leaders, ambassadors, and apostles (Phil 4:2-3; 1 Cor 1:11; Rom 16:1-3, 7)? To investigate the origin of the table of household duties, I wish first to point out some of the theological concerns that led to the writing of Colossians. In this way I would like to make a contribution to a critical revision of lines of development within the Jesus movement (Schottroff 1995, 196-99; 1998, 201-4).

The Sender and Addressees of Colossians

The letter cannot have been written by Paul. The differences in linguistic style and theology are too great, with respect, for example, to its teaching on the church (compare Col 1:24-25; 2:19 with 1 Cor 12:12-31 or Rom 12:4-8) or on baptism and resurrection (compare Col 2:11-12 with Rom 6:3-11). The letter, which purports to have been written by Paul in prison, intimates in some places that Paul's death had been known for a long time (see below).

Many interpreters assume that the letter's principal intention is to do battle with an opposition group or "philosophy" in Colossae that the letter warns against in Colossians 2:4-23. But Colossians is addressed to a much wider circle, which, in addition to the neighboring cities of Laodicea and Hierapolis (2:1; 4:13, 15-16), encompasses all humanity, the whole world (1:5-6, 23, 28; 2:1). The choice of Colossae, an insignificant town in the hinterlands of Asia Minor, as the addressee city demonstrates the unremitting spread of the gospel.

Most of the people named in Colossians are also mentioned in Philemon. But the two letters cannot have been written to the same church, since the relationships between Paul and the congregation depicted in each are in conflict with one another (Col 1:7-8; 2:1-5; Philem, especially v. 22). Most interpreters therefore assume that Colossians displays literary dependence on Philemon. This makes it all the more striking that the only woman mentioned in Philemon, namely, Apphia (→ Philemon), is omitted in Colossians, while another woman, Nympha (4:15), is mentioned.

A Pseudepigraphical Letter

So the letter is not by Paul and, in my view, also not directed to a specific church. Rather, it is directed by someone or a group — I will call the author in what follows "Paula" — to churches that were interested in the letters of Paul and his coworkers. Paula was well acquainted with the theology and language of Paul and his coworkers. Some interpreters have surmised that Paula belonged to the Pauline school (Ludwig 1974). This "school" needs to be envisioned as a shared mission in which there were theological discussions (cf., for example, 1 Cor 1–4; Rom 6; 10) and knock-down, drag-out disputes (Galatians; 1 and 2 Corinthians), both in the churches and with and among the missionaries.

But why did Paula write a letter in the name of Paul and Timothy and not in her own name? Many interpreters surmise that Paula wrote the letter pseudonymously (falsely ascribing it to someone else) in order to confer Paul's authority on her theological perspective and her admonitions (D'Angelo 1994, 313-14, for example). However, the writing of pseudonymous letters does not have to be ascribed to a lack of authority in the second generation. Some philosophical schools, for example, had a perspective different from our own on the right to use another au-thor's name. They published their ideas not in the author's name but under the name of the school's actual spiritual founder (Iamblichus, *Vita Pythagorae* 158 and elsewhere; Seneca, *Epistula* 33.4). Galen traces the origin of pseudonymous writ-ings bearing his name to the publication of manuscripts and other writings he gave to others for private use (Galen, *De libris propriis* 2). Moreover, education in antiquity made use of the art of *ēthopoiia,* that is, embellishing a situation or his-torical figures by putting speeches in their mouths or inventing letters (Theon, *Progymnasmata* 8). What Paul would have said or written if, shortly before his death, he would have composed a letter to newly established churches — this could have been one of the ideas behind Paula's Colossians.

The Passages Framing the Letter (1:1-8 and 4:7-18)

Paula, by making use of Philemon, imitates Paul's way of writing letters. But the thanksgiving (Col 1:3-8) begins with "we" rather than "I" (1:3 and also in 1 and 2 Thessalonians). Who stands behind the "we" is an open question. There are a se-ries of statements about the relationship of Paul and his coworkers to the presum-ably fictitious addressees. Paul and his coworkers have heard of the trust/faith *(pistis)* of the addressees and of their love for all the saints (= Philem 4-5). The prepositional separation of the third part of the triad "faith, love, hope" (cf. 1 Cor 13:13; 1 Thess 1:3) shows that Paula places special emphasis on the hope laid up for them in heaven.

Paula reports that "the word of truth, the gospel" (Col 1:5) has come to the ad-dressees just as to the rest of the world, that it has been "bearing fruit and grow-ing" among them (1:6) just as in the whole world. For a letter that was allegedly written in the 60s C.E., this is a "bold" (to avoid saying "exaggerated") assertion. The combination "bearing fruit and growing" (1:6, 10) breaks the laws of botany. Reversing what we see in nature emphasizes that the gospel must first bear fruit before it can grow and spread. At the conclusion of the thanksgiving (all one sen-tence in Greek), Epaphras is mentioned, from whom the church learned about this.

Epaphras, "our beloved fellow slave" *(syndoulos)* and "faithful minister *(diakonos)* of Christ" (1:7), can hardly be the church's leader, for he is not in Colossae (4:12-14). He is with Paul in prison and, like Paul himself, is fighting for the church in Colossae and the other churches nearby (1:29–2:1). In Epaphras, Paula has created Paul's "double." Both are called "ministers" *(diakonoi)* of God (cf. 1:23, 25). For Paula, Epaphras is not the only "faithful minister" and "beloved fellow slave." Paula characterizes Tychicus in the same way (4:7-8) and says similar things about Onesimus (4:9) and Archippus (4:17). She calls Onesimus a "beloved brother" (cf. Philem 16) and "one of you." That he was or is a slave, as Philemon says, she fails to mention. Standing behind these fictitious reports is no hierarchical concept of achieving God's work but rather a collective perspective that includes the entire church. Not just Epaphras, Tychicus, and Onesimus but all the addressees constitute the "faithful brothers and sisters" (Col 1:2). Epaphras is characterized as a member of the congregation (4:12).

Through the lists of greetings, Paula develops a concept of the church that is different from that in the Pastoral Epistles, for example. And yet, in contrast to the Pauline letters, one is struck by the absence of the call to greet one another and of the transmission of greetings from all the saints (cf. 1 Thess 5:26; 1 Cor 16:19-20; 2 Cor 13:12). Also striking is the fact that, in contrast to Romans 16 or 1 Corinthians 16:19-20, for example, women are hardly ever (with the exception of Col 4:15) mentioned by name. The many (fictitious) reports with which Paula embellishes the list of names in Philemon strengthen the impression that the church is made up only of men and make remembering "well-known" women all but impossible.

And yet, perhaps only by accident, Paula has also contributed to the remembrance of the women in the Pauline churches. At the end of her letter Paula gives two directives: first, once the letter has been read to those in Colossae, it is also to be made available to the church in Laodicea, and second, Paul's — very likely fictitious — letter to Laodicea is to be read to those "in Colossae" (4:16). This shows that Paula wants the letters of the Pauline missionary team to be collected and copied. In her time, and even decades later, this was not something that could be taken for granted, as Acts and the Acts of Thecla show, since they make no reference to any Pauline letters. With this idea of a letter exchange, Paula makes it possible to reconstruct a picture of the Pauline missionary team that shows the group's complexity.

Laying the Theological Foundations (1:9-23)

In 1:9-11 Paula speaks of the prayers that Paul and his coworkers have voiced on the church's behalf. The prayer is that they are granted wisdom (a word that occurs quite often in Colossians), insight, steadfastness, patience, full knowledge of God's will, and lives worthy of God (1:10). Finally, the church is called on to thank God the Father for enabling "us" to share in the inheritance of the saints in the light and for transferring us from the power of darkness into the kingdom of the beloved Son (1:12-13). Salvation and redemption are already a heavenly reality. A similar prayer is uttered by Aseneth after she is received into the heavenly kingdom (Joseph and Aseneth 15:13 [Philonenko edition]). Colossians 1:12-14 is the introduction to one of the letter's best-known passages, the Colossian hymn (1:15-20). This song or poem describes in detail "God's beloved Son." However, the hymn leaves open the identity of the "he" who is the hymn's subject. If we replace the masculine pronouns with feminine pronouns, we discover the original hymn to wisdom upon which the

Colossians hymn is based. Here the praises of wisdom are sung: she is the creator of all that is, the head of the heavenly world, and the beginning of all things. The word "fullness" in 1:19 means "the totality of divine reality" (cf. also 2:9-10), which, coming to dwell in wisdom, reconciles the world with God (D'Angelo 1994, 318). This reworking and interpretation of a wisdom hymn as a hymn about Christ are not unique in the Jesus movement (cf. Phil 2:6-11; John 1:1-18). It occurs here through the alteration of the personal pronouns and the introduction of two lines, "the firstborn from the dead" (Col 1:18c; cf. Rev 1:5) and "by making peace through the blood of his cross" (Col 1:20b). The theological idea this verse contains is that the death of righteous individuals ends the separation between God and God's people, establishing peace, in that, by their blood, the righteous wash away the sins of the people (cf., e.g., 4 Macc 17:22–18:4a). This theology is disturbing today. But in a time in which the cross was not a wall decoration but a cruel instrument of torture and execution, with senseless deaths the order of the day, this is a possible theological interpretation of the deaths of God's friends (Schottroff 1996).

Here in Colossians 1:15-20, as in Philippians 2:6-11, it is a figure as close to God as we can imagine, bearing God's own image, who suffers death on the cross. It is truly God who is the suffering righteous one (2 Cor 5:19). Paula takes up a different theology of the cross in Colossians 2:14-15. Here the cross is the means by which victory over (cosmic) powers hostile to God is achieved. Two different theological conceptions form the background for Paula's assertion that the separation between God and the world has been overcome. The way things are in heaven has already now become a reality for the addressees — all their sins are forgiven in the sight of God (1:14, 21-22; 2:13; 3:13).

Reports about Paul and the Church(es) (1:23–2:7 and 4:2-6)

Bearing the stamp of prayer language and thanksgiving hymns, the beginning of the letter describes the addressees' participation in the new cosmic reality. Paula could have ended the letter right there. Instead, however, a restriction is placed on this reality in 1:23: "provided that you continue securely established and steadfast in . . . faith *(pistis)* . . ." (cf. 2:6). The author, at no loss for words, repeatedly calls for steadfastness (1:11; 2:5-6), patience (1:11), and persistence (4:2), pointing to one of the church's most serious problems. They appear to be splitting apart and turning away, their expectations unfulfilled. Colossians 1:23 proclaims once again (cf. 1:6) that the gospel has already been proclaimed throughout the whole world, and makes reference to the alleged author Paul. But here Paul is (only) one of the ministers *(diakonoi)* of this worldwide proclamation, which is described in the passive voice *(kērychthentos)*, happening all on its own.

In the history of interpretation, a lot of ink has been spilled on Colossians 1:24. Did Paula really want to say that there was something lacking in Christ's suffering? It is in any case clear that the words "in my flesh I am completing what is lacking in Christ's afflictions" are referring to a decisive event. It is certain that the end of the story of Christ's suffering is known to all the addressees. Here we have a hidden reference to the death of Paul. Paul's death, unreported in the New Testament, brought insecurity to his friends. Although Paul must have seen his own impending death on many occasions (2 Cor 11:23-26; Phil 1), he was convinced that he would experience the end of the world and the return of Christ (1 Thess 4:15; Rom 13:11-12). His violent death (1 Clement 5.5-7) must have severely shaken his friends and put them in danger. Was getting baptized still worth it, if the life that was promised has not come? Should one not conclude from Paul's death that such a life was too dangerous? Was it not wiser, therefore, to abandon the sinking ship and make friends with the world once again?

Paula objects to such a view by saying that Paul's death was not meaningless, but happened for the sake of the body of Christ, the church (*ekklēsia* — cf. Col 1:18). Paula develops a new ecclesiology here. In contrast with Paul, she does not speak of many gatherings *(ekklēsiai)* of the saints in various locations but only of one gathering, which is his body (1:24), which is able to grow by holding fast to the head — Christ (2:19). This hierarchical image is taken from the Roman philosophy of the state (Seneca, *De clementia* 3.2.1-3; Q. Curtius Rufus 10.9.1-5). Paula's ecclesiology depicts the relationship between Christ and church as a mirror image of the relationship between the emperor and his body, the Roman Empire (the picture is different in Rom 12:4-8; 1 Cor 12:12-31).

Paula gives another reason for Paul's death, the *oikonomia* (plan/arrangement) of God, which was entrusted to Paul in order to bring "the word of God" to its fulfillment. This promise is more precisely detailed through the process, described in 1:26-27, of the revelation of a long-hidden mystery that has now been revealed to all the saints in heaven and on earth, namely, "Christ in you, the hope of glory." The proclaimer of this event is not Paul alone but "we," a term not more precisely defined (1:28). But Paula emphasizes the difficult battle that Paul is waging for the addressees, their neighboring communities, and all who have not seen (or no longer see) *(heōrakan)* him (1:29–2:1). Battle metaphors are often used in the descriptions of martyrdoms (4 Macc 17:11-16, and in other passages; 2 Tim 4:7). Even if Paul is (now) absent bodily, he is present with the addressees in spirit and sees and rejoices over them (Col 2:5). Paula's letter is, as it were, a letter from heaven with which the dead Paul gives assurance of his spiritual presence. With this letter the author wants to comfort them all and bind them together in love (2:2; cf. 2:19; 3:14-15).

In closing, Paula comments on the situation in which the Pauline missionary team find themselves (4:2-6). The church is to pray that God might open a door for the word, the mystery of Christ, for which Paul is in prison. The expression "open a door" has a double meaning. It means both obtaining one's freedom and missionary success (2 Cor 2:12; Diogenes Laertius 6.86). And yet, the prayer does not ask that Paul obtain his freedom, but that it might be revealed to the imprisoned Paul how he is to speak (Col 4:3). In the second half of the first century numerous philosophers were summoned before imperial courts and sentenced to banishment or death. They discussed defense strategies, and many were of the opinion that the best preparation consisted in being true to themselves and not relying on the assistance of God (Arrian, *Epicteti dissertationes* 1.2.8-9; Philostratus, *Vita Apollonii* 8.12). Paula recommended that addressees be circumspect toward those outside the community and consider carefully how they speak (Col 4:5-6). Then they will know how they are to answer everyone or how they are to defend themselves *(apokrinesthai)*. The church is not called upon to proclaim the gospel.

Admonitions (2:8–3:17)

But Paul's letter (from heaven) is not only meant to console and unite and to call on people not to leave the community. It also contains a long list of admonitions. Already in the personal reports Paula has the fictitious author say, "I am saying this so that no one may deceive you with plausible arguments" (2:4). The call not to let "someone" cause them uncertainty is explained more fully in the second chapter (2:8, 16, 18). Most of the energy devoted to the investigation of Colossians up to now has been focused on the issue of who is meant by this "someone." Some interpreters believe that the word "philosophy" used in 2:8 is the self-designation of the opponents and that it refers to members of an ancient philosophical school. Others see in the "elemental spirits of the universe" *(stoicheia tou kosmou)* referred to in 2:8 and 20 the "rulers and authorities" seen by Paula, according to 2:15, to be stripped of their powers through Christ. These interpreters believe that the opponents, who had gnostic origins, held that their redemption depended on the overcoming of these powers, which in their view had not yet occurred. A third group, focusing on the terms "new moons" and "sabbaths," as well as allusions to food and purity regulations (2:16, 20-23), tries to locate the opponents within Judaism. The translation and interpretation of 2:18 are especially controversial. Is the verse speaking about the worship of angels? Or are hostile powers to be outwitted through worship? Or is it the observation of worship in heaven and the angels that are participating in it that is at issue? Depending on the interpretation, the verse could be speaking about various manifestations of gnostic theology or of magic or of Judaism (mysticism or apocalyptic, for example). A fourth group is of the opinion that the varied allusions represent a typical Hellenistic-Roman religious mix.

In the light of the varied and mutually exclusive interpretations, some interpreters are in fundamental doubt that any concrete opposition group of that period is in view (Hooker 1973). This view is in my opinion correct, for the allusions are vague and the characterizations capable of diverse interpretations. Paula does not see the church in a position of superiority, able to make judgments; rather, she fears that they could be manipulated and exploited.

The author seeks to invigorate the church by encouraging them to "seek the things that are above" (3:2). For Paula baptism brings about a totally new existence, which she describes with three images (2:11-12). In Christ all the addressees have been circumcised with a circumcision "not made with hands." Paula assumes that many in the church do not number themselves among "the circumcision" (cf. also 3:11 and 4:10-11). But the formulation also brings to mind the promise of a circumcision of the heart (Deut 30:6 and elsewhere). In Christ the addressees have put aside the body of the flesh. For many of Paula's contemporaries, this putting off of the flesh is the prerequisite for the soul's ascent to God. Life according to the flesh belongs to the world and has no place in the heavenly sphere. Already in Galatians baptism was understood as a sign of the putting on of the new reality (Gal 3:26-27). In the third image Paula takes up the thought of being buried with Christ in baptism (cf. Rom 6:3-4). But for Paula, with baptism the resurrection has already happened (Col 2:20; 3:1, 3-4).

Beginning with Colossians 3:5, Paula makes a number of suggestions about how this new reality can and should affect the church's life. She calls for putting to death sexual immorality, impurity, passion, evil desire, and greed and for getting rid of anger, wickedness, and evil speech. The vices enumerated here are also found in other vice lists. And yet evil speech is seldom emphasized so strongly (3:8-9). It is especially important for Paula that no one uses words that create uncertainty in others (cf. 2:4). As a contrast to the putting off of the "old self with its practices," Paula sets forth the putting on of the new, renewed self, transformed and qualified for the reality sung about in the hymn (1:15-16). This is given specificity by the use of the well-known baptismal confession, taken from Galatians 3:28, in Colossians 3:11: "where there is no longer Greek and Jew, circumcised and uncircumcised, barbarian, Scythian, slave and free; but Christ is all and in all." Like her elder brother Paul (cf. 1 Cor 12:13), Paula conceals her sisters. The pair "There is not male and female" (Gal 3:28) is absent from Colossians 3:11. All the groups that are named can be represented by men alone. For Paula, this is the reality of Christ, which is at work in all who can be assigned to the groups that are named.

Beginning with 3:12, Paula specifies what putting on the new self means for life in the church. In a list of virtues she brings together the characteristics that work like a mirror into which women look. Taking God as their model, they are to forgive one another, especially when there are causes for complaint (3:13). In love they are to be bound together in one body, a body whose life is shaped by the peace that comes from Christ (3:14-15). Filled with the word of Christ, the addressees are to teach and admonish one another (cf. 1:28) with psalms and hymns and Spirit-filled songs (3:16). In contrast to the worship life in Corinth (1 Cor 14), we notice that Paula does not make a distinction between pneumatic speech and interpretation. But their worship is less disorderly. The worshipers don't all talk at once, but the addressees sing to God "in their hearts."

The "Table of Household Duties" (3:18–4:1)

Colossians 3:18–4:1 forms a self-contained section that is set apart in form from its context. Suddenly the church as a whole is no longer addressed in the plural. Instead, certain social groups, wives, children, and slaves, are singled out and told to be subject to their corresponding groups, husbands, fathers, and masters. These last three groups can be embodied in a single free man in his three separate roles.

The section's content is neither new nor specifically Christian. The individual admonitions appear with regularity in several philosophical and Jewish writings (Schüssler Fiorenza 1988, 305-16; 1983, 251-59). Interpreters are divided over whether a particular theological significance lies behind a limited number of references to the "Lord" (3:18 and elsewhere), and if so, what it is. The composition of the groups and the content of the admonitions belong to the field of ancient economics — there is unity on that issue. In the philosophy of economics, following Aristotle (*Politica* 1.1253b.1-14 and in other passages) and Xenophon (*Oeconomicus*), a number of treatises and tractates are produced discussing the relationship between masters of the house and slaves, sons, and wives, along with an appropriate monetary system. Especially economic treatises that arise in the imperial period regard the household (*oikos*) as the nucleus of the state (Areios Didymos, Stobaios 2.7.26; Josephus, *Contra Apionem* 2.198-210). The peace, security, and welfare of the state, according to the ideology described in these documents, can be guaranteed only through a correct order in the household. The economic treatises are, of course, a discussion of themes and not collections of admonitions. Nor do they address individual groups (although ideologically oriented images of the virtues appropriate to individual groups, especially women, have been preserved; Wagener 1994). For this reason some interpreters believe that the "tables of household duties" are a specifically Christian creation. Others have countered that the argumentation in this text is not really christological or theological. And so they assume that Paula took this text from an ancient source, perhaps modifying it slightly. Many interpreters assign Colossians 3:18–4:1, along with Ephesians 5:22–6:9 and 1 Peter 2:18–3:7, as well as 1 Timothy 2:8-15, 6:1-2, Titus 2:1-10, and others, to a genre whose formal historical characteristics consist in the parenetic transfer of the contents of the philosophy of economics onto the individual groups. To be sure, no additional parallels have been found up to now (which does not mean that there never were any). There is another problem as well. Colossians 3:18–4:1 is usually considered the earliest extant example of the genre "table of household duties." With the exception of the literarily dependent parallel in Ephesians 5:22–6:9, none of the later texts belonging to this genre conforms to the formal pattern of the Colossians text, and these later texts agree in content with the philosophy of economics more strongly than does Colossians 3:18–4:1. This observation is hard to explain in form-historical terms. Some interpreters (for example, Munro 1978) have supposed that the table of household duties in 3:18–4:1 is a later addition (gloss) by another author. In favor of this argument is the fact that this self-enclosed text is unexpected in the context. Moreover, Colossians 3:18–4:1 does not have a word to say about the problem, widespread in the Jesus movement, of relationships involving mixed religions (1 Cor 7:12-23 and elsewhere). The demands are unspecific and unrealistic in the context of husbands or masters who are not believers (in contrast, for example, to 1 Pet 3:1-6). In my opinion this text is not a gloss. The correctly observed gloss-like effects of the text, however, provide some indications of Paula's intentions that lie behind this section.

Under the names of the legendary lawgivers Charondas and Zaleucus, popular philosophical law collections from the first centuries have been preserved, which exhibit important parallels to Colossians 3:18–4:1 in form and content, although to this point they have not really received much attention in discussions about tables of household duties. The "Foreword to the Laws" of Charondas contains a compilation of duties toward God as well as duties of the old and young, subjects and rulers, men and women.[1] The lists of Zaleucus give the duties of slaves toward masters, rulers toward subjects (228.13-16, Thesleff). Most of the social groups of the city and its houses are addressed, and the duties specific to the related groups are listed with imperatives and with some of the reasons given briefly (cf. Col 3:18–4:1). All we can do is conjecture about the intention and use of these lists of laws. Charondas demands that the laws be shared with all the citizens and be recited at city festivals. We can no longer say whether this demand has a historical basis or is a literary fiction.

More can be said about the *Sitz im Leben* of another similar list of laws. On a stele from the second or first century B.C.E. that was found in Philadelphia (in Asia Minor), there is a list of conditions for entering the house of mysteries. It reads:

> To good fortune! . . . The prescriptions given to Dionysus in his sleep, who grants full access to his house for men and women, free and slaves. . . . To this one (i.e., Dionysus) Zeus gave prescriptions for the performance of healings, purifications, and mysteries according to the customs of the ancestors, as they are now written. When they enter this house, men and women, free and slaves should swear by all the gods that they bear no lies against man or woman, perform no poison or evil curses against others. . . . Except for sexual relations with his own wife, a man must not defile another woman, whether free or slave, who has a husband, and a man must not defile a boy or a virgin, nor commend these actions to others. . . . A free woman must keep herself holy and not know anyone except her own husband. . . . The gods will be gracious to those who follow. . . .[2]

1. The text of *Prooimia nomōn* of Charondas (and Zaleucus) can be found in Holger Thesleff, *The Pythagorean Texts of the Hellenistic Period*, Annals of Archaeology and Anthropology 30 (Abo: Abo Akademi, 1965).

2. *Sylloge inscriptionum graecarum*, 2nd ed., 3.985. The translation has been taken from M. Eugene Boring, Klaus Berger, and Carston Colpe, eds., *Hellenistic Commentary to the New Testament* (Nashville: Abingdon, 1995), no. 771, p. 468.

Here also we find once again two social groups related to one another — men and women — along with brief reasons for the admonitions. This inscription has a twofold purpose. First, it obligates men and women to swear on certain feast days that they will keep the injunctions. Second, it reveals to all standing outside the shrine what is happening within. Presumably this serves to protect the community devoted to the mystery. Mystery cults were viewed with suspicion by noninitiates, but especially by Roman officials, since one of the cults' characteristics was keeping things from outsiders. They were suspected — in part not unjustly — of celebrating the abolition of social rules, of rejoicing about women in men's roles, slaves as free, and all kinds of sexual "perversions" (Kraemer 1992, 22-79). So it is no surprise that the introduction of mystery cults into Rome was forbidden for a long time. With the erection of the inscription in Philadelphia, Dionysus guarded the mystery shrine against such suspicions. All who come by are informed that here, also and especially in what happens in secret, "right order" is preserved in everything, that this mystery cult obligates its members to be especially zealous in holding on to their traditional roles.

Now, what did Paula want to achieve by introducing her table of household duties in Colossians? She introduces a kind of table of laws whose contents have been determined by the philosophy of economics (leaving out, it is true, the central issues of a monetary system and of the relationship between the household and the state). This exposes contradictions between the table of household duties, on the one hand, and the particular situation of church and the context of the letter on the other (cf. also McGuire 1990). If the differences between slave and free are abolished when one puts on the new self (3:10-11), then why should slaves submit themselves to their earthly masters? Why does she treat earthly relationships as a central issue at all, since she has described the heavenly reality of the addressees in such detail?

Relationships between different social groups are not discussed at all in Colossians other than in the table of household duties. The only social group discussed both in 3:18–4:1 and in the rest of the letter are the "fellow slaves" Epaphras and Tychicus. This "title," known only from Colossians, is related to Paul's self-designation as a "slave of Christ" (Gal 1:10; Phil 1:1; and elsewhere). At the same time, the section on slaves is the longest in the table of household duties and contains some remarkable comments. In antiquity slaves were not persons with legal standing. But here they are promised an inheritance (Col 3:24). They are also warned about the actions of wrongdoers, and told "there is no partiality" (3:25). What advantage should slaves expect from the standing accorded them as legal persons?

On the literary level, this *parenesis* concerning slaves applies explicitly to Tychicus and Epaphras, the latter of whom is characterized as one of the addressees (4:12). Some things, in my view, support the idea that the *parenesis* concerning slaves is addressed to them and to the whole congregation. Not least among the things that strike us is the appearance of the key word *isotēs* in the admonition to the masters, a context in which it is out of place. *Isotēs* means equality, a concept that the Essenes, for example, used to oppose slavery (Philo, *Quod omnis probus liber sit* 79; cf. also *De specialibus legibus* 1.68). Colossians 4:1 can be translated as follows: "Masters, treat your slaves with justice and equality *(isotēs)*." Perhaps a hint from Paula to read the "table of household duties" against the grain.

Like the stele in Philadelphia, the table of household duties, when it becomes known to those standing on the outside (4:5), announces what is happening on the inside ("in the Lord") — by no means the overthrow of patriarchal social rules but their reinforcement. It was an announcement that, in the light of 3:11, had a calming effect, not least on Roman governors. But there are grounds for the supposition that at least a part of the addressees discovered Paula's cover-up strategies and "blew the cover off" the table of household duties — so strikingly lifted out of its context — in accord with the new reality in Christ, with the abolition of class distinctions and with a church of fellow slaves determined to encourage one another.

Summary

I have tried to reconstruct the interests that led Paula to write Colossians. Whether Paula was a woman or a man can hardly be determined. Many may find the concept of a male author to be more natural. But if we assume that Paula was a woman (or a group of women), then she would have done something typical of many women today. She consoled the friends of Paul who through his death were dejected and robbed of all hope. For her friend Paul she has written a letter from heaven, a testament as it were, with which she explained his death and exhorted the church to stay together. She developed the theology of her friends in a decisive way and rescued them in a severe crisis. But Paula has concealed her own name. And she has — this is her greatest error — concealed her sisters and made their work, their bond with one another, and their steadfastness to a large extent invisible. Still more: she sacrificed them for an easier — indeed, it might have appeared to be the only — way of short-term survival at a threatening time. She has avoided feminine images for God and for the divine reality. She has envisioned the relationship between God, God's Son, and the world in strongly hierarchical terms and seen this as a model for relationships on earth. Through the creation or the incorporation into her letter of the table of household duties, she has come to share the blame for the history of the oppression of women, girls, and slaves. It is possible that she overestimated the critical understanding of her hearers and readers. It is also possible that some of her sisters and brothers saw through her tactics, uncovered the contradictions between the table of household duties and the context, and unmasked the table of household duties as that which it was perhaps meant to be: something written to provide cover and protection to the community in the face of persecution. But others, especially the authors of Ephesians and the Pastoral Epistles, could use her letter as a point of departure and a Pauline legitimation for their writings, which oppressed women and slaves. But it does honor to Paula and her sisters that these authors found that what they wrote was necessary.

LITERATURE

Book of Concord, The. 2000. Edited by Robert Kolb and Timothy J. Wengert. Minneapolis.

Campbell, Douglas A. 1996. "Unravelling Colossians 3:11b." *New Testament Studies* 42:120-32.

D'Angelo, Mary Rose. 1994. "Colossians." In *Searching the Scriptures,* edited by Elisabeth Schüssler Fiorenza, 2:313-24. 2 vols. New York.

Hooker, Morna D. 1973. "Were There False Teachers in Colossae?" In *Christ and Spirit in the New Testament,* edited by Barnabas Lindars and Stephen S. Smalley, 315-31. Cambridge.

Johnson, E. Elizabeth. 1992. "Colossians." In *The Women's Bible Commentary,* edited by Carol A. Newsom and Sharon H. Ringe, 346-48. London and Louisville.

Kraemer, Ross S. 1992. *Her Share of the Blessings: Women's Religions among Pagans, Jews, and Christians in the Greco-Roman World.* New York.

Ludwig, Helga. 1974. "Der Verfasser des Kolosserbriefes. Ein Schüler des Paulus." Ph.D. diss., Göttingen.

Martin, Clarice J. 1991. "The Haustafeln (Household Codes) in African American Biblical Interpretation: 'Free Slaves' and 'Subordinate Women.'" In *Stony the Road We Trod: African American Biblical Interpretation,* edited by Cain H. Felder, 206-31. Minneapolis.

McGuire, Anne. 1990. "Equality and Subordination in Christ: Displacing the Powers of the Household Code in Colossians." In *Religion and Economic Ethics,* edited by Joseph F. Gower, 65-85. Lanham, Md.

Munro, Winsome. 1978. "Col. 3:18–4:1 and Eph. 5:21–6:9: Evidences of a Late Literary Stratum?" *New Testament Studies* 18:434-47.

Orsay, Groupe. 1989. "Lecture féministe des 'codes domestiques.'" *Foi et vie* 88:59-69.

Schottroff, Luise. 1995. *Feministische Exegese. Forschungserträge zur Bibel aus der Perspektive von Frauen,* edited by Silvia Schroer and Marie-Theres Wacker. Darmstadt.

———. 1996. "Kreuz, Opfer und Auferstehung Christi. Geerdete Christologie im Neuen Testament und in feministischer Spiritualität." In *Ihr aber, für wen haltet ihr mich? Auf dem Weg zu einer feministisch-befreiungstheologischen Revision von Christologie,* edited by Renate Jost and Eveline Valtink, 102-23. Gütersloh.

———. 1998. *Feminist Interpretation: The Bible in Women's Perspective.* Minneapolis.

Schüssler Fiorenza, Elisabeth. 1983. *In Memory of Her: A Feminist Theological Reconstruction of Christian Origins.* New York.

———. 1988. *Zu ihrem Gedächtnis . . . Eine feministisch-theologische Rekonstruktion der christlichen Ursprünge.* Munich.

Standhartinger, Angela. 1997. "Studien zur Entstehungsgeschichte und Intention des Kolosserbriefs." Manuscript. Frankfurt am Main.

Wagener, Ulrike. 1994. *Die Ordnung des "Hauses Gottes." Der Ort von Frauen in der Ekklesiologie und Ethik der Pastoralbriefe.* Wissenschaftliche Untersuchungen zum Neuen Testament, 2nd ser., vol. 65. Tübingen.

For Further Reading

MacDonald, Margaret. 2000. *Colossians and Ephesians.* Sacra pagina, vol. 17. Collegeville, Minn.

———. 2007. "Slavery, Sexuality and House Churches: A Reassessment of Colossians 3.18–4.1 in Light of New Research on the Roman Family." *New Testament Studies* 53:94-113.

Maier, Harry O. 2005. "A Sly Civility: Colossians and Empire." *Journal for the Study of the New Testament* 27:323-49.

Müller, Peter, ed. 2009. *Kolosser-Studien.* Biblisch-theologische Studien, vol. 103. Neukirchen-Vluyn.

Standhartinger, Angela. 2000. "The Origin and Intention of the Household Code in the Letter to the Colossians." *Journal for the Study of the New Testament* 79:117-30.

———. 2004. "Colossians and the Pauline School." *New Testament Studies* 50:571-93.

———. 2009. "'. . . wegen der Hoffnung, die für euch im Himmel bereitliegt' (Kol 1,5). Zum Prooemium im Kolosserbrief und seinem politischen Hintergrund." In *Kolosser-Studien,* edited by Peter Müller, 1-22. Biblisch-theologische Studien, vol. 103. Neukirchen-Vluyn.

Translated by Everett R. Kalin

1 Thessalonians: Opposing Death by Building Community

Jutta Bickmann

Introduction

The first letter to the believers in Christ in Thessalonica has up to now stood at the margin of feminist exegesis. The reasons for this are obvious, for the letter offers only a few concrete points of contact for feminist interests.

1 Thessalonians offers no material for the reconstruction of women's history. In the accounts in 1:2–3:13 no individuals in Thessalonica, and, consequently, no women believing in Christ, are mentioned. Moreover, the letter contains no list of greetings, in which women could have been mentioned. To be sure, we proceed on the assumption that the church in Thessalonica had women as members, and yet we cannot reconstruct from 1 Thessalonians the things they were able to do (→ 2 Thessalonians). Only in isolated instances do women exegetes consult 1 Thessalonians, especially 5:12-24, to illumine the meaning of concepts like "coworker for God" (3:2) and those who "labor" among and "have charge of" another person (5:12), terms that are used in other Pauline letters to describe women and their activities (Schüssler Fiorenza 1988, 217, 219, 232; 1983, 171, 169, 181).

Moreover, the arguments of the letter are not clearly related to women or "women's issues." Paul's friendly or hostile attitude toward women cannot be directly addressed on the basis of this text. It is true that there could be an exception to this in what is said in 4:4 about the "vessel" that each person should "take" or "possess in holiness and honor." If "vessel" *(skeuos)* here is to be translated as "wife," we certainly are confronted with a text hostile to women (see below).

Nevertheless, there is value in a feminist analysis of the whole text that goes beyond a hermeneutic of suspicion (contrary to the view of Fatum 1994). For this a methodological approach will be chosen that is oriented to more recent scholarly ways of thinking about literary texts, using "rhetorical criticism" and "reader response criticism," to be more precise. This way of interpretation pays attention to the letter as an act of communication — whereby the ways an ancient letter can communicate are to be looked at separately — and as a relational event between its author and its readers. It seeks to uncover the process of reading and understanding that this text sets in motion and directs for its readers.

Exegetes traditionally reckon 1 Thessalonians, which is probably the earliest Christian writing that has come down to us, among the "minor" Pauline letters, thinking that, in contrast to Romans, 1 and 2 Corinthians, and Galatians, it has no major theology to offer. Those who make such an evaluation are looking for a Pauline theology — in the sense of an elaborate system of thought — that is to be filtered out of the texts. But in this way of thinking, what the author has written is the only place out of which meaning emerges. For this reason, the exegete is concerned about putting himself or herself in the author's position, allowing the reading process — and, with that, the faith community reading the document — to fade away as a place from which meaning arises. But precisely 1 Thessalonians has much to offer from the perspective of how it is read: its theology is to be found primarily on the relational level, and it opens itself to us when we reconstruct from the text the addressees' process of reading (cf. Marxsen 1979; Malbon 1983; Bickmann 1998).

Systematic theological considerations support this exegetical approach. By drawing upon Martin Buber's ideas, feminist Christian theologians, especially Dorothee Sölle and Carter Heyward, have developed a theology that strives to describe not God's being in itself but God as power in relationship and as a source of this power. The interpretation of 1 Thessalonians offered here cannot and does not intend to be a "biblical foundation" for such a theology. But Sölle and Heyward's theology sharpens our awareness that it is theologically meaningful to read biblical texts not only under the aspect of their subject matter but also, or even primarily, under the aspect of the way in which relationship is communicated by them.

The Primary Concern of 1 Thessalonians

How can we describe the process of reading and understanding set in motion by the first letter to the church in Thessalonica? According to my understanding of the text, the individual sections of the letter yield a meaningful whole when one regards 1 Thessalonians as an ancient letter of consolation that operates with early Jewish apocalyptic's understanding of reality.

Offering Consolation in a Situation of Suffering

The original readers of 1 Thessalonians are to find consolation for their separation from members of the church who have died and for their separation from Paul, the church's founder. Various passages indicate that the letter is addressing a situation of suffering. In 2:14, without being specific, the text mentions hostile acts members of the church have experienced at the hands of other residents of Thessalonica: "For you, brothers and sisters, became imitators of the churches of God in Christ Jesus that are in Judea, for you suffered the same things from your own compatriots as they did from the Judeans." In 4:13, the text refers to the death of members of the church, which brings sorrow to those "who are left" (4:15).

There is no way to determine historically whether the deaths of church members are a consequence of the hostile acts of the residents of Thessalonica. The conflict described in Acts 17:1-9 can only have occurred at the time in which Acts was written and therefore offers no historical background for understanding Paul's letter. In no case can we envision as background a systematic persecution of Christians, not even the start of such a thing. One can only assume that the new group experienced hostility and exclusion in their social environment.

Finally, the entire letter contains expressions that signify suffering, tribulation, and death, as in 1 Thessalonians 1:3, 6; 2:2, 9, 15-17; 3:3-5, 7. It is true that they refer primarily to things the letter partners had experienced in the past, but they still let us see the text's interest in helping the readers to interpret experiences of suffering.

Conditions for Effective Consolation

The theological perspective of the consolation offered in 1 Thessalonians is hope for the return of the Lord, the *parousia tou kyriou,* which brings an end to all separation: "and so we will be with the Lord forever" (4:17; 5:10 is similar). And yet, this perspective is formulated only in the last third of the letter, for only then are the readers able to receive it. It is only at this point that they are able to accept and carry out the twofold summons to console one another with these words (4:18; 5:11).

The preceding sections of the letter are meant to create the conditions under which consolation can effectively happen. For, in general, bringing consolation, as a multilayered act of communication, has not done all it can do by offering and providing support for information about something, in this case about an assurance provided by faith. Rather, the goal of offering consolation is enabling one or more others to overcome an experience of limitation or contingency, that is, an experience through which a person's or a group's identity and understanding of reality are fundamentally called into question.

The presupposition for this is a supportive relationship between the consoler and the one needing consolation, in which the one seeking consolation can rely on the consoler to do what is necessary to engender meaning. The one to be consoled must know that in this experience of deep sorrow he or she is taken seriously, must be able to find access to the consoler's understanding of reality, and must recognize that the consoler is capable of providing help.

On the basis of such a relationship consolation can, in principle, occur in two ways. Either the cause of suffering is removed — in this case consolation means altering the situation of the sufferer — or consolation works toward a change the sufferer should make in his or her understanding of reality and involves the summons to make, and support for making, this inner change. In texts from antiquity, both ways of offering comfort are found. Hellenistic philosophy, in its various orientations, essentially advocates a concept of consolation that emphasizes changing oneself. The person, that is, the free man who does not have to work to support himself, can find happiness only when he learns to regard experiences of limitation and contingency as neither good nor bad, but as unimportant *(adiaphora)*. The opposite concept is found in Israel's faith in God. In the face of many experiences of suffering, Psalms and prophetic and wisdom texts emphasize that true consolation consists solely in a change of the situation (e.g., Pss 71:20-21; 86:17; Isa 51:3; 52:9-10; Job 16:2; 21:34). In the face of experiences of limitation and contingency, which are understood as an experience of death, as the absence of the living God, the right to life and happiness is affirmed, and it is formulated as hope that God will intervene on behalf of God's pious ones (Ps 119:50, 52).

The Apocalyptic-Wisdom Perspective of 1 Thessalonians

This hope is also maintained in the texts of early Jewish apocalyptic — one of the directions that wisdom thinking took — texts that are pessimistic about the world and critical of those in power. The Fourth Book of Ezra ($\rightarrow$ 4 Ezra) and the Syriac Apocalypse of Baruch are examples of such texts. The advocates of apocalyptic thought undergo persecution, even as they understand themselves to be faithful to YHWH and the truly wise. They can continue to envision God's intervention into history only as an end to history, as the judgment of the world and, in its wake, the beginning of a new age. At the judgment, expected at any moment, those in power will be shown that their understanding of reality is false, their "knowledge" bringing disaster, while the longing for justice and fullness of life on the part of those presently being persecuted will be fulfilled. Within early Judaism, those who think in apocalyptic terms confer authority on their understanding of reality by seeing it as a direct revelation of God to a wise teacher like Enoch, Baruch, or the "Teacher of Righteousness." This enables the group in question to understand itself to be the suffering righteous and thus a group that opposes society and lives a life of resistance, without needing to minimize the suffering they are experiencing (Sutter Rehmann 1995, 15-18 and elsewhere).

Within the early Jewish apocalyptic-wisdom perspective, 1 Thessalonians interprets the sufferings believers in Christ are experiencing as a sign of the present time of crisis: "In fact, when we were with you, we told you beforehand that we were to suffer persecution; so it turned out, as you know" (1 Thess 3:4). From the beginning, "tribulations" *(thlipseis)* are seen to be part of what it means to believe in Christ (1:6; 2:2, 14). Therefore these tribulations cannot refute the fundamental conviction *(pistis)* that with Jesus the Christ God's eschatological activity has begun (1:9-10). On the contrary, they instead confirm the minority status of the persecuted righteous (3:4), who polemically fence themselves off from the others, the ones without knowledge (cf. esp. 2:14-16).

So in 1 Thessalonians consolation in the face of the death of members of the church does not mean denying the pain that accompanies the experience of death or consoling the mourners with talk about the hereafter. Rather, even in the face of death, consolation means not giving up the hope for God's saving intervention that overcomes the boundary imposed by death. It means keeping this hope alive by speaking with one another about it, thereby interpreting the situation of suffering and in this way already changing it (→ 2 Thessalonians).

The Process of Consolation in 1 Thessalonians

Consolation requires a relationship between those who bring consolation and those who need it, and so 1 Thessalonians devotes considerable space to the establishment of such a relationship. Instead of what is usually found in Greco-Roman letters — a brief recapitulation of the status of the relationship in order to create a cordial context for conversation — the actual introductory section of 1 Thessalonians (1:2–3:13) occupies three of the letter's five chapters. 1:2–2:16 reminds the readers that the history of the church in Thessalonica is a history of their relationship with Paul, and in 2:17–3:10 the experience of separation between the church and the traveling missionary is shown to be a deadly threat to that relationship.

Establishing a Relationship (1:2–2:16)

The history of the relationship in 1:2–2:16 is a sketch of the ideal teacher-pupil relation. On the one side is Paul, the traveling missionary. It is true that the letter's salutation (1:1) names Silvanus and Timothy as cosenders, but the "we" in the letter refers solely to Paul, as the emphatic "that is, I myself, Paul" in 2:18 shows. It is the relationship with him that is being discussed, for he is the one who brings them revealed knowledge, about the *logos* or the *euangelion tou theou*. He knows that he has been commissioned by God to bring people the good news, and he sees himself as a faithful messenger of what has been revealed to him (2:4). At the same time, his commission puts him under obligation to the addressees with whom God establishes salvation-bringing communication through his proclamation. As their teacher, he becomes responsible for them (2:5-8, 12), for only in his person do they gain access to the knowledge that offers salvation in the time of eschatological crisis.

On the other end are the letter's addressees, as Paul's disciples. They have accepted the proclamation of the traveling missionary as God's word and, in the ensuing relationship with him as a teacher, have established a relationship with the true and living God (1:9-10). The letter calls to mind that they have made a wise and fitting decision (2:13).

With its rehearsal of the past, the text seeks to maintain the relationship in its tried and true form, achieving that by the communication the letter itself provides. The sender presents himself as the one commissioned by God to bring what God has revealed and offers the addressees anew the security provided by the relationship they had previously experienced. The letter itself is indirectly designated as the currently available means of communicating revealed knowledge, as the *logos tou theou* proclaimed by Paul.

"Like a Nurse" (2:7)

In 2:1-8 and 2:9-12 Paul uses comparisons from family life to describe his relationship with the addressees: "But we were gentle among you, like a nurse tenderly caring for her own children. So deeply do we care for you that we are determined to share with you not only the gospel of God but also our own selves" (2:7-8); "we dealt with each of you like a father with his children, urging and encouraging you and pleading . . . [with] you" (2:11-12). As a charismatic bearer of revelation commissioned by God, Paul expresses his self-understanding by means of masculine and feminine images in such a way that both roles emphasize his responsible care for the members of the church.

For both images, he and his addressees can call upon ideas from Hellenistic and from early Jewish contexts. Not only the father but also the nurse *(trophos)* is responsible for bringing up and educating especially boys. According to Hellenistic perspectives, she functions as the first teacher, to the extent that from her the child learns how to speak and is introduced to stories and myths. In early Judaism the great significance of women as educators and advisers can be found above all in wisdom texts — it is not without good reason that divine wisdom has the form of a woman (cf. Schroer 1991, 19-20). It is social-historically inappropriate to construe "caring for" or "providing warmth to" *(thalpein* in 2:7) narrowly as "serving as a wet nurse to" or, indeed, to speak of a "nurturer who surrenders herself for the infant" (Holtz 1990, 83).

In any case, with its descriptions of roles, the text remains within the conceptual context of the ancient patriarchal economy, according to which not every father, it is true, but *one particular* father, the paterfamilias, has at his beck and call all the members of the household, among whom are nurses, who are often slaves, or, at the very least, paid workers (on the text's patriarchal potential, cf. Schüssler Fiorenza 1988, 291-92; 1983, 233-34).

Reflecting on Experiences of Death (2:17–3:10)

Beginning with 2:17, the letter no longer deals with the relationship's ideal beginning but deals with a period in which the apostle is involuntarily separated from the church, with various attempts at overcoming the separation. The section serves the overall intention of the letter, to comfort the addressees.

In the first place, the separation from the sender of the letter is interpreted as an experience of death in the time of eschatological crisis. Paul sees himself as "orphaned," robbed of the beloved family receiving his instruction (2:17), and he thus sees himself in "distress and persecution" (3:7). The perpetrator of his suffering and the one who opposed his fruitless attempts to return is "Satan" (2:18), who now, as "tempter" in the midst of the young church, could bring Paul's effort to naught through "persecutions" (3:3, 5). Here is the interpretation offered the letter's readers for understanding their own experiences of suffering: they are painful, they stand in unremitting tension with the joy they had experienced with one another (2:19-20), and they are to be interpreted as experiences of death in this time of eschatological crisis.

Then the text shows how the letter's sender is actively dealing with his experience of death: he cannot "bear" the separation and his sorrow (3:1, 5), and "with great eagerness" he battles to stay in communication with them. Since he cannot overcome the spatial distance between himself and them (2:17-18), the communication continues indirectly — through Timothy, Paul's "brother" and "coworker for God in proclaiming the gospel" (3:2). First of all, this messenger enables Paul to be present with the church by "strengthening" and "encouraging" them. But then he fulfills the same function for Paul, whom he can inform about the continuation of the relationship and to whom, in this way, he can impart an experience of life: "For this reason, brothers and sisters, during all our distress and persecution we have been encouraged about you through your faith. For we now live, if you continue to stand firm in the Lord" (3:7-8).

For the readers of the letter a way is opened to act and live in the face of these experiences of suffering: maintaining the communication between themselves and Paul and continuing to understand how to interpret reality on the basis of revealed knowledge — these are what make opposing death possible. In this way the letter achieves the function of Timothy, the messenger: as antiquity understood it, the letter enables the discussion partners to be present with one another and therefore replaces speaking together directly, even though it does so imperfectly (cf. 3:10). So the offer for a relationship that is found in 1:2–2:16 is continued here: the sender signals his competence in dealing with suffering and commends the epistolary communication as the bearer of active resistance to counterbalance the experience of death.

Strengthening the Church's Identity (4:1-12)

After reconstructing the history of their relationship, the author makes use of his role as the addressees' teacher and endeavors to enable them to overcome their experience of death. Beginning with 4:1, the letter gives instructions, turning first to a series of urgent requests to the addressees (4:1-12). Exegetes offer conflicting interpretations of this section, since its function in this part of the letter appears just as unclear as the origin and meaning of individual admonitions. In my opinion, the text's accent lies on the summons to continue to "do more and more" (4:1, 10) to move ahead on the path to "sanctification" (4:3-4, 7). If they do that, the church is remaining true to what they have already received from Paul (4:1-2, 6, 11), which they are already living out (4:1, 9-10). In this way their identity can be experienced as marking them off from the "outsiders" (4:12), those with no saving relationship to God (4:5-6). Thus the text is trying to strengthen the identity of the addressees as a community of faith (similarly Smith 1995, 84-86).

To make "sanctification" *(hagiasmos)* the distinctive mark of the community of believers means bringing into full effect the relationship with God that the addressees have accepted on the basis of the proclamation of the traveling missionaries. This actualization of what God has given (cf. 4:7) happens through the creation of ideal relationships with the *adelphos,* that is, within the church (4:6, 9-10). 4:1-12 pleads for an ethic of holiness, such as can be found in Leviticus 17–26 and in early Jewish texts. As in those texts, dissimilar admonitions appear next to one another in this section of 1 Thessalonians: warnings against immoral sexual relations (4:3) and against dishonest business practices (4:6), a summons to "brotherly love" and one to self-sufficiency within the community (4:11-12).

In the light of the evident androcentricity of the text, a question arises about the meaning of the admonition in 4:4: "that each one of you know how to take/to possess your own vessel *(to heautou skeuos ktasthai)* in holiness and honor." The word "vessel" *(skeuos)* is rendered in current German translations as *Frau* (wife; cf. 1 Pet 3:7), whom the man being addressed is to "acquire" (Luther), to "seek to win" *(Zürcher Bibel),* or with whom he is to "have sexual relations in a holy and respectful manner" *(Einheitsübersetzung).* So 1 Thessalonians 4:4 is making an appeal for sexual behavior in conformity with proper standards, in opposition to the "sexual immorality" mentioned in 4:3 and to the "lustful passion" running wild outside the church (4:5).

But these translations obscure the sexism that they presuppose in the Pauline text. For the image of "vessel" defines the wife as the sexual object of the husband, whom he uses to his own advantage or acquires through marriage. Holtz sees the sexism, but understands it to be in accord with a "Jewish way of thinking" (1990, 159), thus excusing it by an expedient that reveals its own anti-Judaism. Luise Schottroff, on the other hand, makes a plea for exposing the contempt for women that she also recognizes in the terminology of the text: she finds 4:3-8 to be criticizing the "greed of the man entering into marriage, who uses his power to enrich himself" (1991, 32) by driving up the price of the dowry (4:6).

Schottroff's critique is an attack on what she sees as an obscuring of the text by the translations. Still, the coordination of "vessel" and "wife," which is supported by a few references from rabbinic literature, is by no means persuasive. There are more widely scattered references to "vessel" as "body." They are also found in early Jewish literature (*Hodayot* 4:9; Testament of Naphtali 2:2; 8:6; Apocalypse of Sedrach 11:5, 10-11) and denote the fragility of the human body. In my opinion 1 Thessalonians 4:4 is to be understood in this sense, as an unspecific admonition to use one's perishable body in a way that accords with the call to holiness rather than misusing it. The sexism veiled by the translations mentioned above would in this view be brought from the outside to the (in any case strongly androcentric) text.

The Picture of the Abolition of All Separation (4:13–5:11)

Not until 4:13 does the text address the problem of members of the congregation who have died, who have "fallen asleep through Jesus" (4:14). It describes the basis for hope: God will prove to be true and life-giving for the ones who have died, just as for the living, having already proven to be such for Jesus the Christ (1:9-10; 4:14, 16), so that death, the boundary separating the dead believers in Christ from those who are alive, will be abolished (4:15, 17).

The text spells out this hope as an apocalyptic vision of the return of the *kyrios* (4:16-17). While the end-time event means for those who believe in Christ the beginning of an unending communion, knowledge of which already alters the present (5:5-10), it brings upon those now in authority "sudden destruction" (5:3). They lull themselves into a false sense of security — the slogan "peace and security" is a possible allusion to the ideology of the Pax Romana. The image of the "woes," frequently used in apocalyptic, which connotes, along with terror and inevitability, also the new beginning that has been promised (cf. Sutter Rehmann 1995, 186-96), is in 5:3 employed exclusively in negative terms. The woes merely signal destruction — "and there will be no escape." Even here, the polemic against the others is not given for its own sake. Rather, the text once again strengthens the group of addressees by pointedly separating them from their environment and confirming their understanding of reality.

Summary and Evaluation

Our interpretation has shown with what care the letter to the church in Thessalonica offers the addressees a relationship meant to enable them, in their situation of sorrow, to hold on to their newly acquired identity as believers in Christ and to come to terms with the deaths the community has experienced. We may assume that before the arrival of the missionaries, the addressees had no relationship to the hope Israel knew, and that they were, therefore, fully dependent on the proclamation of the missionaries. Therefore, separation was a fundamental threat to the young community. The letter seeks to come to terms with this, on the one hand, by establishing an exclusive relationship to Paul as a bearer of revelation, in order to create the possibility of experiencing a relationship with God, and, on the other hand, by strengthening the group's identity through drawing up in polemical terms the boundary that separates them from outsiders.

Both ideas have their legitimacy in the way 1 Thessalonians envisions things — both, however, become problematic in the light of how they came to be viewed. When churches like those in Corinth or Galatia no longer acknowledge Paul's claim of exclusive leadership, but rely on their own competence or on other teachers, that's when the way Paul envisions his role runs up against its limits (→ 1 Corinthians; 2 Corinthians; Galatians). Paul's authority as grounded in a direct revelation from God can under no circumstances be applied directly to the way church offices are structured today. The way Christians came to use the strategy of walling off outsiders appears even more problematic. For persecuted minorities, these strategies fulfill the important function of preserving and legitimizing their own claim of worthiness and their own resistance. In the course of the church's history, however, this claim all too often showed itself to be deadly for others, when Christian groups who had come to be in power misused it in order to provide a basis for the oppression of other minorities.

LITERATURE

Bickmann, Jutta. 1998. "Kommunikation gegen den Tod. Studien zur paulinischen Briefpragmatik am Beispiel des ersten Thessalonicherbriefs." Würzburg.

Fatum, Lone. 1994. "1 Thessalonians." In *Searching the Scriptures,* edited by Elisabeth Schüssler Fiorenza, 2:250-62. 2 vols. New York.

Heyward, Carter. 1982. *The Redemption of God: A Theology of Mutual Relation.* Washington, D.C.

—————. 1986. *Und sie rührte sein Kleid an. Eine feministische Theologie der Beziehung.* Stuttgart.

Holtz, Traugott. 1990. *Der erste Brief an die Thessalonicher.* Evangelisch-katholischer Kommentar, vol. 13. 2nd ed. Zurich, Braunschweig, and Neukirchen-Vluyn.

Malbon, Elizabeth Struthers. 1983. "No Need to Have Any One Write? A Structural Exegesis of 1 Thessalonians." *Semeia* 26:57-84.

Marxsen, Willi. 1979. *Der erste Brief an die Thessalonicher.* Zürcher Bibelkommentare Neues Testament, vol. 11, 1. Zurich.

Perkins, Pheme. 1992. "1 Thessalonians." In *The Women's Bible Commentary,* edited by Carol A. Newsom and Sharon H. Ringe, 349-50. London and Louisville.

Schottroff, Luise. 1991. "Frauen und Geld im Neuen Testament. Feministisch-theologische Beobachtungen." In *Geld regiert die Welt. Reader der Projektgruppenbeiträge zur feministisch-befreiungstheologischen Sommeruniversität 1990*, 25-56. Kassel.

Schroer, Silvia. 1991. "Weise Frauen und Ratgeberinnen in Israel — Vorbilder der personifizierten Chokmah." In *Auf den Spuren der Weisheit. Sophia — Wegweiserin für ein weibliches Gottesbild*, edited by Verena Wodtke, 9-23. Freiburg, Basel, and Vienna.

Schüssler Fiorenza, Elisabeth. 1983. *In Memory of Her: A Feminist Theological Reconstruction of Christian Origins*. New York.

————. 1988. *Zu ihrem Gedächtnis. Eine feministisch-theologische Rekonstruktion der christlichen Ursprünge*. Munich.

Smith, Abraham. 1995. *Comfort One Another: Reconstructing the Rhetoric and Audience of I Thessalonians*. Louisville.

Sutter Rehmann, Luzia. 1995. *Geh — frage die Gebärerin. Feministisch-befreiungstheolgische Untersuchungen zum Gebärmotiv in der Apokalyptik*. Gütersloh.

FOR FURTHER READING

Adams, Sean A. 2009. "Evaluating 1 Thessalonians: An Outline of Holistic Approaches to 1 Thessalonians in the Last 25 Years." *Currents in Biblical Research* 8, no. 1:51-70.

Crüsemann, Marlene. 2010. *Die pseudepigraphen Briefe an die Gemeinde in Thessaloniki: Studien zu ihrer Abfassung und zur jüdisch-christlichen Sozialgeschichte*. Stuttgart.

Gupta, Nijay K. 2009. "'Vessel (skeuos)' in 1 Thessalonians 4.4 and the Epistle of Jeremiah: The Strategy of a Pauline Metaphor in Light of the Apostle's Jewish Background, Teaching, and Theology." *Irish Biblical Studies* 27, no. 4:138-55.

Translated by Everett R. Kalin

2 Thessalonians: Hope in God's Just Judgment

Marlene Crüsemann

The second letter to the church in Thessalonica, shorter than 1 Thessalonians, exhibits what is probably the strangest set of circumstances for the composition of a New Testament letter. On the one hand, in its structure and choice of themes, it follows 1 Thessalonians to such an extent that it can be seen that 1 Thessalonians served as its literary model (Wrede 1903). There are extensive verbal agreements. Besides 1 Thessalonians 2:9/2 Thessalonians 3:8, the prescript (1:1 in each case) is especially striking: "Paul, Silvanus, and Timothy, to the church of the Thessalonians in God our Father and the Lord Jesus Christ." No address in other Pauline letters is found twice with almost total agreement in wording. This is important, since 1 Thessalonians itself begins in a highly unusual way (→ 1 Thessalonians): the authors appear to be of equal status; the title "apostle" and other designations are missing; the church is not addressed as people living "in" Thessalonica but, through the use of a genitive construction, as consisting of people, in a virtually complete sense, "from" the inhabitants. On the other hand, the second letter nowhere makes an explicit reference to the first, either to treat it positively or elaborate on it. On the contrary, in 2:2 there is a warning against being perplexed "by a letter, as though from us." Together with 2:15 and the "sign of authenticity" in 3:17, which is lacking in 1 Thessalonians and is meant here to confer Paul's authority on 2 Thessalonians, the intention becomes obvious: 2 Thessalonians would like to be understood to be the only Pauline letter to Thessalonica, replacing the first, which is allegedly spurious (Lindemann 1977). Here, in 2 Thessalonians, true consolation is expressed "during all your persecutions and the afflictions that you are enduring" (1:4). As a postapostolic writing, 2 Thessalonians is most often dated in the last third of the first century C.E.

A Church without Women?

At first glance, the text, formulated in a thoroughly androcentric manner and, in addition, containing no direct or indirect reference to women, offers some resistance to a feminist investigation (Johnson 1992, 352). Stereotypically, "brothers" are addressed throughout the letter (1:3 and elsewhere). There is the suspicion that, with only men in view as actual members of the church, women should essentially be neither mentioned nor given special attention. And yet, the absence of any traces of women is not the same as hostility toward women, just as, by comparison, the presence of topics relating to women's activities does not automatically speak for a feminist perspective (→ 1 Timothy). Thus, "pending proof to the contrary," an inclusive reading suggests itself. "As long as women or feminine points of view are not explicitly excluded, it must be assumed that grammatically androcentric texts are referring both to men and women" (Schüssler Fiorenza 1988, 2). That means that as far as letters are concerned, including those that are pseudepigraphic, both genders are addressed and are the letters' recipients. I would like to recover the contents of 2 Thessalonians in terms of a feminist social history (Schottroff 1994, 75ff.; 1995, 46-51).

The Structure and Contents of the Letter

- 1:1-2. Prescript and introductory greeting from the three supposed authors.
- 1:3-12. Introductory section in the form of the thanksgiving, with which it begins (3-4), followed by a description of the appearance of Jesus and of the judgment of God — in content already part of the letter's main section (5-10), concluding with intercession for the congregation (11-12).
- 2:1-12. The main section of the letter, with its treatment of the problem: Is the day of the Lord already here (1-2)? The events before the day of the Lord and what that day will bring about (3-12). Thanksgiving for the church as God's chosen ones (13-14).
- 2:15–3:16. Admonitions, including an appeal to God for consolation and strength (2:16-17), a request for prayer, along with a statement of what to pray for (3:1-5), a call to do the work needed to support themselves (6-12), a call for obedience (14-15).
- 3:17-18. Conclusion, with a "mark of authenticity."

In what follows, we plan to give greater exegetical attention to important issues on which 2 Thessalonians deviates from or modifies the letter that serves as its model.

An Exemplary Group of Male Coworkers (3:6-12)

With few exceptions (2:5; 3:17), 2 Thessalonians, like 1 Thessalonians, uses the first-person plural to refer to the three stated authors. It is important to note this, lest Paul be too quickly separated from those around him (Beavis 1994, 265). Although the plural is used in many sentences, it is the letter's interpreters who, without the need to do so, often start the process of giving the apostle a leading role, by concentrating on him and by their (un)conscious identification with him as an individual figure. To a large extent, Paul, Silvanus, and Timothy are presented as a group, as a team of men. This impression is strengthened by the fact that they are to serve as a model for all, as a common ethical ideal. This pattern is already set forth in the first letter, in connection with the motif of imitation ($\rightarrow$ 1 Thessalonians), which shows up even more frequently there: "what kind of persons we proved to be among you" (1 Thess 1:5). In 2 Thessalonians the earlier behavior of the missionaries in the church was meant to have had, from the start and primarily, a pedagogical significance: "We wanted to give you in ourselves an example to imitate" (2 Thess 3:9).

According to that last statement, discipleship means imitating what these men did — rather than Jesus. In 3:6, this is explicitly given as a primary point of the apostolic tradition (Vander Stichele 1990). This way of life appears to be important only with respect to a limited area of early Christian life, the problem of work and supporting oneself. But that this is given a relatively extensive treatment shows its importance. In 3:6-12, through association and repetition, the concepts "work" (*ergazō*, vv. 8, 10, 11, 12), "eat" (*phagomai, esthiō*, vv. 8, 10, 12), and "in a disorderly manner" (*ataktōs*, vv. 6, 11) are elaborated upon. The adverb *ataktōs* appears in the New Testament only here; the verb *ataktein* occurs in verse 7; and the adjective *ataktos* in 1 Thessalonians 5:14. Elsewhere, the terminology is frequently used in military contexts, with the meaning "in disarray" (Josephus, *Bellum judaicum* 3.113) or "undisciplined," "without a plan," "disoriented," but it is also used as a parallel to *anomos*/"lawless" (Josephus, *Contra Apionem* 2.151), which is used as a proper noun in 2 Thessalonians (2:8). The addressees are instructed to recognize that these exemplary men have behaved in their midst in a manner that was anything but undisciplined. On the contrary, through hard work they earned their own bread. Accordingly, the order that is to be maintained involves the requirement of gainful employment for all, including even the church's leaders. If the letter's authors identify *their own* activity as that of *ergatai*/"gainfully employed workers," then that has normative character for all who hold office. Moreover, since the reward consists of food rather than money (cf. Matt 10:10), a concept of power is revealed "in which influence in a community and material advancement are radically separated from one another" (Leutzsch 1994, 63). The slogan that sounds so rigid, "Anyone unwilling to work should not eat" (2 Thess 3:10), serves inner-church democratization toward "those at the bottom." Thereby, through the explicit choice of low social status, 2 Thessalonians moves in the broad stream of early Christian witnesses to a church of the poor (Schottroff 1994, 206ff.; 1995, 136-51). It can be assumed that this indication of low status also brought with it sensitivity to women's work, which men themselves found to be demanding and difficult (Rom 16:6, 12).

The Just Judgment — 1:3-12: A Glorious Wonder

A principal theme and a motif of what is written here are the judgment and the apocalyptic battle. Both are absent in 1 Thessalonians 4:13-18 in the depiction of the anticipated parousia, the coming of Jesus Christ. There, with no questions, without battle or judgment, the living and the resurrected dead find fellowship with the Messiah, who comes to gather them to himself. In contrast to this, it is striking that here in this 2 Thessalonians passage Jesus, as the protagonist, carries out in fiery flames the retributive judgment in a cosmic drama. At the same time, this brings rest to the suffering church, since their oppressors are condemned to eternal punishment (vv. 6-9).

In what way could such a scene have become for the readers a desirable vision? First of all, it begins in verse 3 in the form of a thanksgiving and consists in a single Greek sentence that continues until verse 12 and ends in intercession. This thanksgiving confers a positive perspective on the coming judgment. This is supported by the strange statement in verse 5 that this gives "evidence" *(endeigma)* "of God's just judgment and is intended to make you worthy of the kingdom of God, for which you are also suffering." It is making reference to the persecutions and afflictions *(diōgmoi/thlipseis,* v. 4) that have already been mentioned. In this way, the symbols for the justice that is coming are the very sufferings from which the judgment will bring release.

A statement of this kind becomes understandable against the background of the Jewish theology of suffering (Bassler 1984; Perkins 1988, 1234-36). Wolfgang Wichmann (1930) uses this term to characterize a theological perspective emerging from the Jewish War and the destruction of Jerusalem in 70 C.E., a perspective that encounters and interprets the suffering of the Jewish people that these events evoked. It is found in the Syriac Apocalypse of Baruch (2 Baruch 13:1-12; 48:48-50; 52:5-7) and in many other rabbinic writings, especially in the circle of Rabbi Akiba (died about 130 C.E.) and his school (for example, *Genesis Rabbah* on Gen. 8:1). Its consolation consists in an eschatological reversal: the righteous, who now suffer, can be certain that they are already now suffering God's punishments for their few sins, for which on the day of divine judgment they will have already atoned. They will then receive the blessings that come as a reward for their merits. The evildoers, on the contrary, will experience only horrible things, since they will have long since used up through good fortune here and now the benefits of their few merits. The many witnesses to this theology of suffering reveal their value for dealing with the Jewish catastrophe in the everyday experience of the people. Wichmann stressed this at a time in which not a few of his New Testament colleagues used the same sources to draw up anti-Jewish patterns of thought such as "a Jewish morality of merit," "thinking in terms of merits," or even "addiction to merit."

For 2 Thessalonians this means: the present oppression through persecution offers an occasion for joy and hope, since it is to be seen as evidence for God's just judgment. This provides a clear experiential criterion for determining who the righteous are.

What are the specific acts of oppression to which the passage refers? In connection with 2:4, it seems reasonable to imagine conflicts like those for which we have evidence in the first and second centuries in a confrontation with the "loyalty religion" that requires a show of allegiance to Rome. These conflicts can be described as "the persecution of Christians" as well as "the persecution of Jews" (Schottroff 1990, 73ff.). These were situations in which pressure was exerted on members of monotheistic groups, when their loyalty to Roman customs and religion was called into question, often through denunciation. That's what happened in 38 C.E. when the non-Jewish inhabitants of Alexandria wanted to force the Jews to set up a statue of the emperor in the synagogue, thereby setting up a conflict between the Torah and the Roman state, which led to a pogrom (Philo, *In Flaccum* 41-54). At the beginning of the second century, in the province of Bithynia-Pontus in Asia Minor, a kind of test was set before those accused of being Christians, whom Pliny had to interrogate and judge — would they offer sacrifices before statues of the emperor and of the gods, or not (Pliny, *Epistulae ad Trajanum* 10.96)? In particular the synoptic apocalypses are a historical source for persecutions (Schottroff 1990, summary, 94), in this case for events connected with the conquest of Jerusalem by Vespasian. On the basis of the terminology used there, these events are to be seen as parallels to 2 Thessalonians (Holland 1988, 134ff.; Hartman 1990, 480ff.).

Together with other Jews, the Jewish-Christian authors of 2 Thessalonians await the judgment, sure of its coming as compensation for their suffering, at which their Messiah Jesus will execute universal retribution (1:7-9). Instructive in this context are the biblical texts that serve as the basis both for what will happen at the judgment and for the next section, 2:1-12. Since apocalyptic writers quote the Scripture and expand and rewrite it for their time, they choose a "subversive form of resistance": their "visions" are "quotations" (Ebach 1985, 16-17). In this way the context of the quotations often contains the explosive nature of the message in code form. The last chapter of Isaiah (Isa 66) plays the most important role for 2 Thessalonians. A string of direct quotations, as, for example, *en pyri phlogos*/"in flaming fire" (2 Thess 1:8/Isa 66:15 LXX), demonstrates this (Aus 1976, 266ff.). What Isaiah 66 is pointing to is Jerusalem's ultimate shalom, the eschatological birth of peace for Zion, the day of YHWH, on which God judges the earth with fire and sword, the glory and splendor of God among the nations for Israel's sake and thereby for all people. In 2 Thessalonians 1:10-12 the *doxa*/"glory" stands for the wonderful demonstration of the truth of Jesus as the Messiah and of those who belong to him. This yields an amazing correspondence with Isaiah 66:18-20: those from the nations who are saved are those who proclaim the glory of YHWH among all the other nations. They will also bring home the Israelites who are scattered abroad. In what now follows, the connection with Jerusalem is emphasized.

Apocalyptic Decision — 2:1-12 — *Star Wars* or Gospel of the Poor?

The question about the identity of the apocalyptic figures in 2 Thessalonians 2:1-12, their relationships and activities, has to a strong degree captivated and stimulated the imaginations of interpreters down through the centuries. In particular, the enigmatic "power that is restraining" *(to katechon/ho katechōn)* gave rise to an impressive reception history (Trilling 1980, 94ff.). By contrast, feminist examination of the passage more likely voices displeasure and revulsion in the face of a scenario that exhibits alarming parallels to the way war is waged today, in the sense of the final *Star Wars* battle. Mary Ann Beavis speaks of "troops of men" whose war for the "control of the universe," like wars today, reckons with the annihilation of the innocent (1994, 268). Yet such a judgment remains too firmly confined to the surface of traditional exegesis, which considers the imposing mysterious figures too much in isolation or writes them off as apocalyptic speculation, without asking about their significance for an oppressed minority.

The place to begin is with Luise Schottroff's important observation, based on the apocalypses in Matthew, Mark, and Luke, that apocalyptic prophecies are "a theological examination of a present that is experienced as oppressive," "an expression of a *present* taken seriously in every aspect" (1990, 87). How does 2 Thessalonians evaluate its present? According to 2:2, the addressees are letting themselves become shaken in mind *(saleuthēnai)* and alarmed *(throeisthai;* cf. Mark 13:7; Matt 24:6) — in part by the reading of 1 Thessalonians — as though "the day of the Lord is already here," as though the parousia, the return of Jesus and being gathered together with him, is a present reality (2 Thess 2:1). In opposition to this, the text formulates its description of the course of the end events (often labeled by interpreters as a kind of "eschatological timetable"), which, in the face of an acute "expectation that the end is at hand," puts the emphasis on "delay." Thus it lists the following *future* stages that are to occur before Jesus' coming: the rebellion *(apostasia)* and, along with it, the revelation of the "one who practices lawlessness" *(anomia,* v. 3) and his atrocious deeds. But this lawless one is being held back by "what is now restraining him" *(to katechon,* v. 6), and this mysterious element, encompassing all these points, is consistently counted as part of the letter's description of the present.

This, however, is unlikely. With respect to the text's content, its pseudepigraphic nature has up to now been overlooked in the question about determining the time in view. How is it with the writing of a letter that is essentially supposed to have been written at a much earlier time? Statements about the present of the "real" recipients can only occur as prophecies. Thereby one gains the advantage of being able to disguise as a prophecy the unsparing depiction of the present. The mystery about the restraining *katechon* can to a great degree be solved by means of its function in a pseudepigraphic letter: as a figure of the past, it serves to bridge the time from the apostle to the actual present and is really necessary to fill the time of several intervening decades. Through the inclusion of "Do you not re-member?" (2:5-8), what is in the text is clearly seen as a way of filling the gap be-tween the statements about the "lawless one."

The way in which the notion of the delay is worded also ties it to Isaiah 66 (Aus 1977). Using their own translation, the authors cite the verb used in the birth image in Isaiah 66:9, which expresses God's power to shut the womb and slow down the birth process. In the midst of the pains that come when the woman in la-bor is finally able to push, the renewed Zion and its peace will be born quickly (Isa 66:7-9). These very strong pains run their course when the restraint is removed (2 Thess 2:7). Consequently, the text is interested less in the date of the parousia than in how to interpret the present. Accordingly, the present is the time of the most intense labor pains and the arena for the "one who practices lawlessness" (2:3), the "lawless one" (2:8). Most often given the misleading translation "Antichrist" or "the Evil One" (Trilling) in exegesis done in German, these names instead indicate, first of all, extreme hostility to Israel's Torah. Thus the returning Jesus appears as the victor over the enemy of the Torah. With the help of the Scrip-ture citations to which we have already pointed, it also becomes clear that what we have here is a coded designation for a "Gentile ruler" (Holland 1988, 107) who, like Antiochus IV, desecrates the temple and "exalts himself above every so-called god" (2:4/Dan 11:36). At the time the letter was written, that could only mean the repre-sentative of imperial Rome who threatened every other way of worshiping God, including, along with synagogues, house churches as well. The culmination is reached with the occupation of "the temple of God" (universally identified by exe-getes as the temple in Jerusalem), when the "lawless one" declares himself to be god (2 Thess 2:4). This is followed by a time of unrighteousness and bewilderment (2:9-12), during which the addressees can be led to believe what is false and take pleasure in unrighteousness. To counter this, the letter summons the readers to persevere and to stay on the right path.

The attack on the temple in Jerusalem by Vespasian and Titus had already happened, and through the *Judaea Capta* victory coin that was struck immediately thereafter, it had become known in the whole Roman world. 2 Thessalonians, by denouncing something of that kind in its own time, moves close to the Judaism that is faithful to temple and Torah. The letter awaits the appearance of Jesus, bringing liberation that all will see and believe. He is actually the mighty Messiah, but he achieves his victory without weapons (2:8) — he kills the enemy of the To-rah by the breath of his mouth. The letter here is citing Isaiah 11:4 and indirectly but clearly saying why the last judgment is to be awaited with hope: it brings "jus-tice for the poor" and, at long last, "a just judgment on behalf of the meek of the earth," by effecting the downfall of the representative of power and ungodliness. As an expression of the resistance of groups that have been forcibly marginalized, this is by no means to be equated with modern ideas of waging "star wars." These people await the victory of the unarmed Messiah, not plans dreamed up by military strategists (cf. Sutter Rehmann 1995, 120ff., on 1 Cor 15:19-25). The question remains what it meant and means for men to leave to God judgment and retribution for an all-powerful enemy. A renunciation of the personal use of violence, especially as this is advocated by the androcentrically formulated Sermon on the Mount (Matt 5:39-41), implies saying good-bye to the male prerogative of resistance one usually finds in society. It is a call to practice peaceful resistance. For women, however, this still does not provide the formulation of an alternative to the role they are expected to play, continual accommodation and submission to those who are always stronger (Schottroff 1994, 170ff.; 1995, 112-15). They and their diverse experiences of resistance are not in view in 2 Thessalonians.

LITERATURE

Aus, Roger D. 1976. "The Relevance of Jes 66,7 to Revelation 12 and 2 Thessalonians 1." *Zeitschrift für die neutestamentliche Wissenschaft* 67:252-68.

———. 1977. "God's Plan and God's Power: Isaiah 66 and the Restraining Factors of 2 Thess. 2:6-7." *Journal of Biblical Literature* 96:537-53.

Bassler, Jouette M. 1984. "The Enigmatic Sign: 2 Thessalonians 1:5." *Catholic Biblical Quarterly* 56:496-510.

Beavis, Mary Ann. 1994. "2 Thessalonians." In *Searching the Scriptures*, edited by Elisabeth Schüssler Fiorenza, 2:263-71. 2 vols. New York.

Ebach, Jürgen. 1985. "Apokalypse. Zum Ursprung einer Stimmung." In *Einwürfe*, 2, 5-61. Munich.

Hartman, Lars. 1990. "The Eschatology of 2 Thessalonians as Included in a Communication." In *The Thessalonian Correspondence*, edited by Raymond F. Collins, 470-85. Biblotheca ephemeridum theologicarum lovaniensium, vol. 87. Leuven.

Holland, Glenn S. 1988. *The Tradition That You Received from Us: 2 Thessalonians in the Pauline Tradition*. Hermeneutische Untersuchungen zur Theologie, vol. 24. Tübingen.

Johnson, E. Elizabeth. 1992. "2 Thessalonians." In *The Women's Bible Commentary*, edited by Carol A. Newsom and Sharon H. Ringe, 351-52. London and Louisville.

Leutzsch, Martin. 1994. *Die Bewährung der Wahrheit. Der dritte Johannesbrief als Dokument urchristlichen Alltags*. Trier.

Lindemann, Andreas. 1977. "Zum Abfassungszweck des zweiten Thessalonicherbriefes." *Zeitschrift für die neutestamentliche Wissenschaft* 68:35-47.

Perkins, Pheme. 1988. "2 Thessalonians." In *Harper's Bible Commentary*, edited by James L. Mays, 1234-36. San Francisco.

Schottroff, Luise. 1990. "Die Gegenwart in der Apokalyptik der synoptischen Evangelien." In Luise Schottroff, *Befreiungserfahrungen. Studien zur Sozialgeschichte des Neuen Testaments*, 73-95. Theologische Bücherei, vol. 82. Munich.

———. 1994. *Lydias ungeduldige Schwestern. Feministische Sozialgeschichte des frühen Christentums*. Gütersloh.

———. 1995. *Lydia's Impatient Sisters: A Feminist Social History of Early Christianity*. Louisville.

Schüssler Fiorenza, Elisabeth. 1984. *Bread Not Stone: The Challenge of Feminist Biblical Interpretation.* Boston.

——. 1988. *Brot statt Steine. Die Herausforderung einer feministischen Interpretation der Bibel.* Fribourg.

Sutter Rehmann, Luzia. 1995. *Geh — frage die Gebärerin. Feministisch-befreiungstheologische Untersuchungen zum Gebärmotiv der Apokalyptik.* Gütersloh.

Trilling, Wolfgang. 1980. *Der zweite Brief an die Thessalonicher.* Evangelisch-katholischer Kommentar zum Neuen Testament, vol. 14. Neukirchen-Vluyn.

Vander Stichele, Caroline. 1990. "The Concept of Tradition and 1 and 2 Thessalonians." In *The Thessalonian Correspondence,* edited by Raymond F. Collins, 499-504. Biblotheca ephemeridum theologicarum lovaniensium, vol. 87. Leuven.

Wichmann, Wolfgang. 1930. *Die Leidenstheologie: Eine Form der Leidensdeutung im Spätjudentum.* Beiträge zur Wissenschaft vom Alten und Neuen Testament, vol. IV/2, 53. Stuttgart.

Wrede, William. 1903. *Die Echtheit des zweiten Thessalonicherbriefs untersucht.* Leipzig.

For Further Reading

Börschel, Regina. 2001. *Die Konstruktion einer christlichen Identität. Paulus und die Gemeinde von Thessalonich in ihrer hellenistisch-römischen Umwelt.* Bonner biblische Beiträge, vol. 128. Berlin and Vienna.

Brodie, Thomas L., Dennis R. McDonald, and Stanley E. Porter, eds. 2006. *The Intertextuality of the Epistles: Exploration of Theory and Practice.* New Testament Monographs, vol. 16. Sheffield.

Crüsemann, Marlene. 2009. "'Wer nicht arbeiten will, soll auch nicht essen'. Sozialgeschichtliche Beobachtungen zu 2 Thess 3,6-13." In *Essen und Trinken in der Bibel,* edited by Michaela Geiger, Christl M. Maier, and Uta Schmidt, 212-23. Festschrift for Rainer Kessler. Gütersloh.

——. 2010. *Die pseudepigraphen Briefe an die Gemeinde in Thessaloniki. Studien zu ihrer Abfassung und zur jüdisch-christlichen Sozialgeschichte.* Beiträge zur Wissenschaft vom Alten und Neuen Testament, vol. 191. Stuttgart.

Metzger, Paul M. 2005. *Katechon. II Thess 2,1-12 im Horizont apokalyptischen Denkens.* Zeitschrift für die neutestamentliche Wissenschaft und die Kunde der älteren Kirche, Beihefte, vol. 135. Berlin and New York.

Roh, Taesong. 2007. *Der zweite Thessalonicherbrief als Erneuerung apokalyptischer Zeitdeutung.* Novum Testamentum et Orbis Antiquus, vol. 62. Göttingen and Fribourg.

Translated by Everett R. Kalin

Pastoral Epistles: A Tamed Paul — Domesticated Women

Ulrike Wagener

Under the designation "the Pastoral Epistles," that is, "the Shepherd Epistles," the three late New Testament writings 1 and 2 Timothy and Titus (written between 90 and 150 c.e.) have been united since the eighteenth century. This designation points to the structure and content of the writings, which purport to be written by Paul to two of his disciples to give them instructions for their tasks as church leaders. Within the New Testament these three letters attract particular attention because of their polemic against the activities of women and because of a massive theologically supported misogyny (hatred of women). While traditional exegesis has dealt with the so-called women's issue separately, in isolation from the interpretation of the writings as a whole, feminist exegesis is interested in shedding light on the inner connection between the whole theological and ecclesiological point of view of the Pastoral Epistles and their view of how women and men relate to one another. The polemical tone of the Pastorals shows they are part of an ongoing conflict. Through an analysis of the literary strategy and the theology of the Pastorals, I would like to reconstruct the underlying conflict, in order to understand, so far as possible, the women opponents under attack, from whom we have no written testimony of their own. This study is meant to contribute to the reconstruction of the history of women in the early church, since, in the analysis of the Pastoral Epistles' restrictive ideas, an alternative perspective on Christian existence comes into view.

The Pastoral Epistles as Pseudepigraphic Writings

The Pastorals cannot have been written by Paul, as both their language and content show (cf. Roloff 1988; Donelson 1986). We are dealing with pseudepigrapha, that is, writings ascribed to someone not their author. Pseudepigraphy is a widespread phenomenon in ancient literature, arising from an orientation to an earlier period regarded as normative. Ethical teachings in particular are treated as normative in the present by connecting them with an authority in the past. In early Christianity of the second and third generations, writings were ascribed to an apostle in order to confer authority on one's own position in polemic disputes between diverse Christian lines of thought. Pseudepigraphy was readily used with the letter genre in particular, since in antiquity letters were regarded as a substitute for someone's presence and were thus able to provide for the presence of the letter's author. The pseudepigraphic Pastorals make use of this feature of genuine letters: they claim to supply the authoritative word of Paul for their time.

The literary fiction pervades the letters as a whole. They suggest an unbroken connection with the apostle: Paul is the normative origin of the *didaskalia* (teaching) of the Pastorals; they present their theology, ecclesiology, and ethics as Pauline legacy *(parathēkē),* which is to be preserved. The continuity this literary device suggests, however, conceals the Pastorals' actual difference from the apostle. The "Pauline tradition" as it appears in the Pastorals, understood to be specific content that has been handed on, is a new concept in the letters, and it did not exist in this sense before they were written.

The background for the composition of the Pastoral Epistles is probably a fundamental conflict over the correct understanding of Paul's person and proclamation. The Pastorals themselves say followers of Paul have turned away from him and gone over into the camp of his opponents (1 Tim 1:19-20; 2 Tim 1:15; 2:17-18; 4:10, 14-15). This assertion invites us to see behind the polemic of the Pastorals a dispute involving diverse perspectives — each invoking Paul — about the apostle's legitimate heritage. If for a long period the opponents in the Pastorals were sought within Gnosticism, they are in recent years more likely sought in ascetically oriented Christianity, as it appears in the Acts of Paul and Thecla.[1] Thus the Pastorals require a new reading of the authentic Pauline letters, for they have Paul making reference to, modifying, and correcting utterances that, according to the fiction, he himself had made in earlier letters. In this way, the Pastorals fashion a "Paul" who conforms to society, who has a positive relationship to the prevailing social institutions (the state, the family, slavery) and ethical norms. In what has been written on this topic, the "domesticizing" of Paul is usually presented as legitimate or unavoidable. With reference to the opponents battled in the letters, exegetes have for a long time been unable to disentangle themselves from the way the Pastorals look at things, which disqualifies these opponents as heretics. In recent years this bias has been criticized from different sides, including from feminist exegesis. In the same way, we must challenge the androcentricity of earlier reconstructions of the conflict, which think of the false teachers as male and can only conceive of the women being criticized as the addressees. By contrast, an analysis of the letters that

---

1. The thesis that the Pastorals were polemicizing against oral traditions that later ended up in the Acts of Paul and Thecla was proposed by D. R. MacDonald. It is being significantly modified in more recent investigations by Annette Merz (1995b; 2004).

831

does not isolate the instructions for women but looks at them in the context of all the issues under discussion, also gets a clear view of the women in the churches of the Pastorals as individuals, that is, as preachers and teachers.

In the context of early Christian pseudepigraphy, it is a peculiarity of the Pastorals that they not only have a fictitious author but also have two fictitious addressees. The figures of "Timothy" and "Titus" function as exemplary models, serving to make clear what the author thinks of as authentic Christian discipleship. Thus the figures of the apostle's disciples form the connecting link between apostolic beginnings and the present situation: just as they were commissioned by Paul, they in turn are to entrust to "faithful people/men" (*pistoi anthrōpoi,* 2 Tim 2:2) what they heard from him. This is probably a reference to the officeholders in the time of the author, for whom trustworthiness is created through "Paul's" fictitious instruction. Thus the author is making available to his own time two normative authorities. The first is the letters themselves, with their system of Christian ethics conformed to societal norms and a hierarchical model for the church. The second is the office, which also is legitimated as a Pauline institution. Since the functions of a bishop and the fictitious addressees coincide in the letter — their particular task is to instruct and advise the church — Timothy and Titus can be understood to be models for the office of bishop.

In their fundamental theological and ethical stance, the Pastorals can be interpreted as a unit. To be sure, it is not absolutely necessary from the start to consider them as a cohesive body of letters. For what catch the eye are the extensive agreements between 1 Timothy and Titus, with respect to both literary genre and to the themes that are treated. Both are written in conformity with the genre of instructions to officeholders empowered to instruct others. In these epistolary instructions from rulers to their royal or imperial representative, orders are given for tasks in the addressee's sphere of influence, but these orders, bypassing the representative, are meant for the people under the rulers' control. So also the addressees Timothy and Titus, as representatives of "Paul," are given for their tasks as leaders instructions that are really intended for various groups in the church, concerning their role and the behavior appropriate to it. This doubling in 1 Timothy and Titus indicates that the letters originally were to be read individually. That the letters were addressed to different places, Ephesus and Crete, could be understood as an indication of different local circumstances. 2 Timothy is to be assigned to the genre of testaments. "Paul" — shortly before his death as a martyr — calls people to a discipleship modeled on his. The letter contains numerous personal notices that are meant to give plausibility to Paul's presupposed situation as he goes to his death.

Instructions for Church Leaders:
The First Letter to Timothy and the Letter to Titus

The Primary Thematic Model: The Church as the "House of God"

A large amount of traditional material is used in the Pastorals, but it is structured and transformed in accord with a particular theological-ethical model. The design derives its inner stringency from the primary ecclesiological image of the church as *oikos theou*, the "house(hold) of God." The key passage is found in 1 Timothy 3:14-15: "I hope to come to you soon, but I am writing these instructions to you so that, if I am delayed, you may know how one ought to behave in the household of God, which is the church of the living God, the pillar and bulwark of the truth."

The foundation for the ecclesiology and ethics as a whole is laid in this primary image of the *oikos theou*. For ancient societies, the *oikos* is the central social and economic community. According to Greco-Roman thinking, it is hierarchically structured, subject to a head of the house, who leads and, accordingly, has power over the other members of the family (wife, children, slaves). Beginning with Aristotle, a particular literary genre developed about this, namely, economics, which dealt with the issue of how such a "household" was to be run successfully. Consequently, in the Pastorals a patriarchal-hierarchical institution forms both the model for church order and the norm for personal life.

1 Timothy is structured concentrically around 3:14-15. This passage is framed by two larger complexes of instructions on church order: the first part, 2:1–3:13, contains directives for prayer in worship services (2:1–3:1a) and, in two so-called office codes, qualifications for the offices of bishop and deacon (3:1-13). The second part, in 5:1–6:2, gives instructions for dealing with various groups of older and younger men and women in the church (5:1-2), for the office of widow (5:3-16) and the office of elder (5:17-22). It ends with directives for slaves (6:1-3), which lead into a polemic against opponents, just as the church order complexes in general are framed by sections of antiheretical polemic (1:3-11; 4:1-11; 6:3-10). To this is to be added a thanksgiving of "Paul's" in 1:12-17, the subject matter of which is his conversion and his election as an apostle. Through the depiction of Paul as a converted sinner, he becomes not only the model for believers but also the origin and guarantor of "correct doctrine."

In Titus the same themes are also found. Clothed as a directive to "Titus," like that to "Timothy," to order and instruct the church (Titus 1:5; 2:1, 15; 3:1, 8-11), this letter also lists the qualifications for the office of elder or bishop (office code, 1:5-9); gives rules for the behavior of older men and women, young men and women and slaves (2:1-10); and urges obedience to government authorities and participation in social structures (3:1-3). These parenetic sections alternate with antiheretical passages (1:10-16; 3:9-11). Since a commentary on all the material is not possible within the framework of this chapter, the intention in what follows is to use central passages in the text to show how the primary model of the *oikos theou* functions and what consequences that has for the contexts.

Qualifications for the Church Offices of Bishop, Deacon, and Deaconess (1 Timothy 3:1-13; Titus 1:5-9)

1 Timothy deals with various church offices in two passages. First, in the third chapter, the offices of bishop, deacon, and deaconess are treated, with the bishop as the leading officeholder. Then, in the fifth chapter, we see another structure for the offices, which speaks of the offices of widow and elder. While the relationship of bishops and elders to one another is not expressly established in 1 Timothy, Titus 1:5, 7 does make the connection and, indirectly, identifies them with one another. Here we see a process in which differing church orders are coalescing.

The office code in 1 Timothy 3:1-13 does not describe fields of activity but rather the prerequisites for office. To a certain degree the required qualifications are not related to the particular office. Rather, on the one hand, they name universal virtues the author expects of all Christians, such as levelheadedness, dependability, peacefulness, sobriety, hospitality, or, quite generally, honorableness and irreproachability, or, on the other hand, they formulate vices that all are to guard against, such as slander, drunkenness, love of money, and quarrelsomeness (1 Tim 3:2-3, 8, 10-11; Titus 1:7). These are virtues and vices found in Hellenistic philosophy that, first of all, have no specifically Christian background but are portrayed as Christian by the author. In this he is motivated by the concern that the Christian church have a good reputation among non-Christians. The motif found here, an orientation on the non-Christian world in which they live, is also found elsewhere in the New Testament (→ 1 Peter) and in other early Christian writings. But in 1 Timothy it becomes especially critical, since here the reaction of the outsiders is decisive for the Christians' salvation or condemnation. If the way the bishop conducts his office becomes the occasion for vilification by outsiders, he is then in danger of falling into the snare of the devil (1 Tim 3:7).

In some places in the office codes, in addition to the general virtues, special abilities and particular qualifications are named. For the office of bishop, these are, in particular, his aptness to teach (1 Tim 3:2), as well as the fact that he not be a recent convert (3:6) and that he possess "sound" doctrine (Titus 1:9); deacons "must hold fast to the mystery of the faith with a clear conscience" (1 Tim 3:9). In addition, for both offices, there are requirements that relate to marriage and family life. The rule that the bishop and deacon are to be the "husband of one wife" (1 Tim 3:2, 12; Titus 1:6) holds up as norm that they are to be married only once, but it could also be directed against asceticism, since the opponents in the Pastorals clearly abstain from certain foods and practice sexual asceticism (cf. 1 Tim 4:3). In addition, the male candidates for the offices of bishop and deacon must do a good job of being head of the house, which is seen especially in their authority over their children and all subordinate members of the household, the head of the house seeing to it that these remain submissive (1 Tim 3:4, 12; Titus 1:6). With this requirement the author adopts an established *topos* of Hellenistic philosophy of power: since the individual households are regarded as the foundation of the community, good leadership of his own household qualifies the free man for the exercise of political leadership. When, in the introduction to the code pertaining to the bishop, the episcopate is praised as *kalon ergon* (a noble task, 1 Tim 3:1), becoming a bishop is emphasized in favorable terms as an undertaking beneficial for the community. Here it becomes clear how the *oikos* ecclesiology of the Pastorals functions. What serves as the point of comparison for the transfer of the *oikos* model to the church is not the fellowship of Christians as the "family of God" (as in Gal 6:10; Eph 2:19) but the church as a hierarchically organized institution that stands over against the individual believer (1 Tim 3:15) and, as an antitype to the disputes fostered by the opponents, is called *oikonomia theou*, "God's well-ordered economy" (1 Tim 1:4). This order is represented and safeguarded through the one who holds office. What this person does, compared to what the members of the church do, is defined by analogy to the role of the head of the house. This is especially true for the bishop, whose task consists primarily in the instruction and training of the members of the church, who are described as those who hear and learn. In a certain way, of course, the metaphor breaks down. Although the church leader relates to the church with the authoritative functions of the head of the house, his authority is derivative in nature. The actual head of the house is God (cf. 2 Tim 2:21); accordingly the church leader can be called *oikonomos theou* (Titus 1:7), God's steward. The definitive hallmark of a steward at that time was that he could be trusted to do the job in fidelity to the one who assigned him the task. In the transfer of this image to the church, the church leader thus stands in a special relationship of trustworthiness and responsibility toward God and is obligated to give God an account of the fulfilling of the charge. The application of the house metaphor is concentrated on the office and its orderly operation, and in this way it shows the fundamentally hierarchical orientation of the model.

Through its dependence on the role of the head of the house, the first prerequisite for the episcopate is to be male. The diaconate, by contrast, can be occupied by men and women. 1 Timothy 3:11 expressly speaks of women and 3:12 of men in this office. For a long time exegetes had applied 3:11 to wives of the deacons, although nothing in the text points in this direction. Rather, the question arises whether the masculine designation *diakonos* is to be read generically already in 3:8-10. We have evidence for the use of *diakonos* as a title applied to a woman, Phoebe, in Romans 16:1, and a feminine form of the designation for the office (*diakonissa*) is not commonly used until the fourth century. So there is much to favor the view that the code for the deacon in 1 Timothy 3:8-10 first presents stipulations for both genders, in order then, in 3:11-12, to append gender-specific requisites. In doing this the author can only refer to the women deacons as *gynaikes* (women), because there is no feminine designation for the office.

So the author presupposes the existence of women deacons, without having a positive interest in them. Moreover, in a subtle way he emphasizes the men who hold the office. For one thing, he also connects their assumption of office, like that of the bishops, to fulfilling the role of the head of the house, although deacons do not function as teachers and leaders. Through the insertion of verse 12, which applies to male deacons, the positive evaluation of the work of deacons that follows in verse 13 seems disassociated from the women and applied to the men alone. In this respect the concluding affirmation in 3:13 corresponds to the positive characterization of the episcopate in 3:1. As verses that frame the entire office code, they provide the evaluative perspective in which the male officeholders are accorded respect that is withheld from the women.

The Instructions for Prayer at Worship and for the Roles of Men and Women in the Worship Service (1 Timothy 2:1–3:1a)

1 Timothy 2 begins with an emphatic call for all forms of prayer in the worship service (2:1). Prayer for those in authority is specifically mentioned, through which the Christian church is to have assurance of a "quiet and peaceable life" (2:2). Fundamentally, however, the supplication is explicitly applied to all people. This comprehensive orientation for prayer is theologically grounded in God's desire that everyone be saved (2:3-4).

In 2:8, building on this foundation, a short directive is given on how prayer is to be offered during the service by men, who are to avoid anger and arguments. The short exhortation to the men is followed by the considerably longer admonition about women's behavior at worship (2:9–3:1a).

This code for women is constructed in such a way that two exhortations (2:9-12) are connected by chiasm to two biblical justifications (2:13-14). The first exhortation is aimed at seeing to it that women wear no ostentatious clothing or costly jewelry. The author has taken up a so-called polemic against ostentation, a widespread *topos* of Hellenistic philosophy. Probably the author had access to the same or a quite similar form of the *topos* on ostentation adopted by Jewish(-Christians), as we find it in 1 Peter 3:1-6. However, while the *parenesis* in 1 Peter is given a stronger theological basis, the author of the Pastorals bases the argument on Hellenistic concepts of virtue (modesty, reserve, and respectability), which, when applied to women, have a strong sexual connotation. And so the external adornment of women in the worship service is interpreted by the author in a sexual context.

The second exhortation prohibits women from teaching (1 Tim 2:11-12): they must not teach, which in the author's view would represent having authority over men. Here we have the same tradition as in the command for silence in 1 Corinthians 14:33b-36, where it is a later interpolation, though not by the author of the Pastorals. Comparing the two texts makes it possible to discover the specific intention of the teaching prohibition in 1 Timothy. In 1 Corinthians 14:33b-36 the argument rests on the antithesis of the "public" and "private" spheres, which is made analogous to the antithesis between male and female. That is why women should be silent in public worship, and if they want to learn about something, they should ask their husbands at home. By contrast, the exhortation in 1 Timothy is shaped, in form and content, by the contrast "teaching — learning," which is made analogous to "ruling — being subordinate." This shift makes it clear that the author's primary concern is "sound teaching," which he safeguards by making the (male) officeholders the only ones authorized to teach. Also, what the author demands in order to defend against teaching by women is not primarily silence but quietness *(hēsychia)*. It would be a mistake to see here a weakening of the prohibition in comparison to 1 Corinthians. The concept of *hēsychia* points the women to the ideal of "keeping still," which implies the compliant fulfilling of their own subordinate role. And so the teaching prohibition in 1 Timothy 2:11-12 is directed against independent theological thinking and teaching by women, which is characterized as overstepping the boundaries established for the role of women and disavowed as a presumptuous usurpation of authority.

The second part of the *parenesis* concerning women (2:13-14), which provides the basis for the exhortations, takes up early Jewish interpretations of the creation and fall stories in Genesis 2 and 3. The two supporting arguments are connected by chiasm to the two directives in the first part. The teaching prohibition is based on the fact that Adam was created first and Eve second, which is supposed to verify her unalterable position of inferiority. The polemic against ostentation is supported with a sexually oriented interpretation of Genesis 3, which understands Eve's offense to be a sexual act with the serpent (perceived to be male).

Since the author, with the aid of the creation and fall traditions, interweaves the exhortations and their bases by chiasm, he binds them together into a new argumentative complex in which the figure of Eve forms the focal point. In this interweaving, the teaching prohibition and the polemic against ostentation have the goal of repressing the active participation of women in the church's life and worship. The significant rhetorical effort put into the *parenesis* on women, in contrast to the preceding *parenesis* on men in 1 Timothy 2:8, and the emphatically stated teaching prohibition in 1 Timothy 2:12 indicate that women are actually arising here to teach independently during the worship service. The linking with the polemic against ostentation permits the conclusion that these women were well-to-do and economically independent.

The women's wealth forms the basis for their positions of authority and influence. In the context of the social setting of the Pastorals, cities in Asia Minor in the Roman Empire, the aspect of private wealth has a central significance for assuming positions of leadership, since public officeholders essentially pay out of their own means the costs of the tasks they have taken on. On the basis of this financial commitment, members of the cities' upper classes are honored as "benefactors" *(euergetai)*, as numerous inscriptions attest. The terminology of the Pastoral Epistles corresponds exactly to this milieu, when, as shown above, the office of bishop is designated as a beneficial undertaking on behalf of the community (1 Tim 3:1).

The fundamental significance of riches for the assumption of positions of leadership that is shown here applies, of course, to men as well as women. But it is specifically significant for women, since riches are the principal basis for their public influence. While the sphere of public civic activity is solely a male prerogative within conservative philosophic theory, women could in practice make use of the community's substantial financial need and, on the basis of their own financial contributions, assume positions of honor and authority. Against this background, it is plausible that these women saw value in making a public show of their riches. With this as background, the polemic against ostentation, in conjunction with the teaching prohibition, gains a direct plausibility. With this polemic against ostentation the author is taking direct aim at these women's focus on social status and trying to force them back into the restrictive framework of their domestic roles as wives. Thus there is no basis for the assumption that those being addressed are "sexually permissive" women. Instead, the sexualizing interpretation is the tool the author uses to turn back their demands for participation and for taking on particular roles in the church.

Having refused women active participation in the worship service and, with that, in the life of the church, the author concludes by giving his basic conception of a woman's role. She will be saved through childbearing (1 Tim 2:15). These words about salvation appear to offer the woman who has fallen under sin a "way of escape." And yet, the promise of salvation, spoken in the indicative, has an immense prescriptive role: it eliminates a woman's freedom and compels women to fulfill their reproductive role, which is emphasized through a formulaic confirmation (3:1a) of a questionable theological utterance.

We can see here that the restrictive instructions for women derive their strength from applying the household model to the church. In the process, it is not simply a social structure that is applied to the church with the use of the *oikos* model but in particular the way this structure is used ideologically, as can be seen in the literature of economics: while in particular instances women could by all means function as heads of the household, the role of the head of the house is clearly assigned to the husband in the way it is envisioned in economics. Correspondingly, the exercise of the office of leadership in the church is restricted to men, while women are basically assigned a subordinate role: the women should accept this status and be submissive and, above all, not advocate a position of their own or contradict the person who has the office of teacher. At the same time, the ecclesiology of the *oikos theou* also lends support to the patriarchal structures of the private households by requiring the women to carry out their role as wives and to have children. Thus the understanding of the church as the "household of God" does not mean that the church represents an alternative to the private households; rather, it is their structural extension and validation.

Instructions for Old and Young Men and Women: 1 Timothy 5:1-2 and Titus 2:1-10

In the view of the Pastorals, the Christian church is made up of defined groups, to which people are assigned not only by gender but also by age and by their status as slave or free. Thus they are organized according to their status. 1 Timothy 5:1-2 takes up the groups as defined by age and gender, in order to give the church leader instructions for his interaction with them. Thereby we get an indication of that period's philosophical ideal of a gentle but resolute leader. In Titus 2, on the other hand, there are more instructions for the behavior of the groups in the church themselves. As in the office codes, in part, general virtues are listed (2:2-3: prudence, respectability). The basic misogynous attitude becomes evident when Titus gives currency to two beloved ancient clichés, the caricatures of an old woman as a "scandalmonger" and as a slave to drink (2:3).

In Titus 2:3-4 the older women are given the task of instructing younger women, which has been incorrectly interpreted by many exegetes as a mitigation of the prohibition to teach in 1 Timothy 2:12. If one looks at what they are to teach, it becomes clear that the apparent permission granted the women itself has a restrictive function. The older women are to induce the younger women to be submissive to their husbands and to fulfill the obligations that go with their role as wife, mother, and manager of the household. The Pastoral Epistles exhibit here an analogy to a development in the literature of pagan economics. If originally the husband was assigned the task of instructing his (younger) wife and showing her what her tasks involved, the neo-Pythagorean letters concerning women also assign this role to an older woman (cf. Theano to Kalisto, in Städele 1980, letter 174.1). In this way, especially restrictive instructions for women are to be legitimated by the fact that they (allegedly) originate with women, experienced ones at that.

In Titus 2:3-5, as in 1 Timothy 2:15, the "private" side of the *oikos* ecclesiology is instilled: the obligations appropriate to one's role in the ancient household are fully applicable in the Christian church, and this is once again justified on the basis of the reaction of their non-Christian neighbors.

The Offices of Widows and Elders (1 Timothy 5:3-25)

The regulations for the office of widow and of elder take up the major portion of 1 Timothy 5. We have here a structure for offices different from the one presupposed for bishops and deacons in chapter 3. Here the author is making use of a traditional office order that contained instructions for the payment and selection of widows in the church (5:3, 5, 9, 11-12) as well as of elders (5:17). The regulations for widows in 5:3-16 in particular present exegetes with many problems, since the text is full of contradictions and tensions. These can be explained if one starts with the assumption that the tradition about widows being drawn upon here offers a model of Christian existence for women that is entirely different from the one the author of the Pastoral Epistles is setting forth. In the tradition drawn upon here, the word *chēra* (widow) is apparently understood to refer to a woman who remains unmarried by her own choice and whose sexual asceticism forms the basis of a charismatic existence. The First Testament tradition that God is especially concerned about widows and orphans is transferred to this new way of being a widow, a status that is no longer endured but chosen. A special relationship with God that manifests itself in prayer (5:5) becomes the basis for the possession of prophetic gifts by the *chēra* (→ Judith; see Luke 2), assuring her of a highly honored status (1 Tim 5:3). Establishing a regulation for widows that includes their remuneration and formalizes a selection process represents a certain institutionalization process for this charismatic manifestation. But the ascetic orientation persists in the traditional office regulation as a basis for the widows' honored status.

Now the author of the Pastorals stands in barely concealed opposition to this fundamentally ascetic-charismatic institution of widows. He brings his *oikos*-oriented concept of church, with its restrictive consequences for women, into the widow tradition that has an entirely different orientation. For one thing, as in 1 Timothy 2:15 and Titus 2:4-5, he speaks about the primacy of the (private) household tasks for women (1 Tim 5:4, 8), apparently attempting thereby a substantial restriction of the pool of possible candidates. And secondly, he orients the admission requirements for the office of widow to the duties and values of the *oikos*. In this way the author forces the institution of *chēra*, which on the basis of its ascetic character stands outside of the hierarchical structures of the traditional household, into a tension-filled synthesis with his primary view of the church: the office of widow, despite its ascetic orientation, is called upon to confirm the norms and values of the household. At the same time, fitting the office of widow into the *oikos* church is bound up with a fundamental attack on the prestige of the *chēra* in the church. With the requirement that the candidates receive prior attestation with respect to their roles as wife, household manager, and mother (5:9-10), in order that they can be considered honorable members of the church, the office of widow itself is deprived of the ability of conferring an esteemed status. Therewith, the *chērai* — originally highly esteemed as charismatic women offering prayers and as prophetesses *(charismatische Beterinnen und Prophetinnen)* — are denied the honored status and the prestige that had been explicitly conferred on the offices of bishop and deacon.

The background for this desire to impose restrictions might be that in the churches to which the Pastoral Epistles were addressed, the ascetic office of widow possessed a strong attraction for women, since a *chēra's* way of life opened up the possibility of independent religious activity in an accepted form. At least some of the "widows" had financial resources of their own, as can be inferred from the polemic in 5:6. The author's attacks in 5:11-13 against the "younger women" *(neōterai)* in the office of widow show, furthermore, that in spite of the age limit already spelled out in the tradition, young, unmarried women also lived as "widows." The author sees them as thirsty for knowledge, but declares their search for knowledge to be unfruitful (5:13). At the same time, the widows are apparently teaching in the houses, which moves the author to characterize this reproachfully as "saying what they should not say." With this characterization the author complains especially about the women's ethics, which he repudiates on the basis of its hostility to marriage and the family. As in the bishop's code and the *parenesis* concerning slaves, he makes reference to the reaction of the non-Christians among whom they live: if those on the outside slander the Christian church because its young women live without being under the control of a husband, then the women bring guilt upon themselves and are, accordingly, in danger of falling into the clutches of the devil (5:14-15). If in the Pastorals "good works" — understood as fulfilling the roles that prevail in church and society — have, on the one hand, the power to save, that also means the opposite is true: all rebellion against those roles leads to destruction. The "widows," on the contrary, apparently have a totally different understanding of Christian existence. In this respect, it can be assumed that the *chērai* not only have an ethic and views about the basis of authority in the church different from those of the author of the Pastoral Epistles, but that they are also rooted in an alternative, charismatic theology and Christology.

Admonishing the Rich (1 Timothy 6:3-10, 17-19)

While the theme of riches already appears more than once in the admonitions directed at women (1 Tim 2:9–3:1a; 5:5-6), the attitude toward riches once again becomes a theme in chapter 6, this time in its own right. In 6:17-19 (as in 5:5-6), a life lived in reliance on one's own wealth is contrasted with trust in God, which leads to the true life that is to come. The rich are to lay the foundation for that life by giving alms during their life on earth. To be sure, no basic contrast is made between the present life and that in the future: a "pious" life in the present is already sharing in the promise (cf. 4:8); the eschatological future is seen to be in full continuity with life on earth, if the latter has been lived out in accord with the ethic espoused in the Pastoral Epistles.

Thus, while the *parenesis* in 6:17-19 strikes a rather moderate tone and offers the rich a heavenly reward for living a good life, 6:6-10 harshly denounces riches as a temptation and lays bare the threat of losing salvation. This tension can be resolved if one recognizes the inner connection of the attitude toward riches adopted in both passages. In the context of early Christian positions on having and renouncing possessions, the Pastoral Epistles adopt a fundamentally positive attitude toward riches. But since the Christian tradition in general shows a deeply critical attitude toward riches, a basis had to be provided for a more positive attitude toward riches such as that in the Pastorals. Their answer to the question of how the Christian life was to be squared with the possession of earthly goods has clear parallels to the view in the *Shepherd of Hermas* or to the line of reasoning laid out in a later period by Clement of Alexandria: being rich is not fundamentally incompatible with salvation, but it surely exposes Christians to the danger of falling into sin. What is decisive here is not the possession of wealth as such but one's attitude toward it. One's possessions must not become the foundation and orientation of one's life; they are provided instead by setting one's hope on God (1 Tim 6:17). There are two clear marks of this inner attitude that characterize the way you live: living simply and charity. These two elements shape the two passages on riches in 1 Timothy 6:6, 7-10, which describe the ideal of the simple life that is satisfied with the food and clothing necessary for life, and unfold against this background the dangers of an inner attachment to riches; 6:17-19 calls for acts of charity and for generosity as an outward expression of the proper inner attitude, which is characterized by setting your hope on God. That the former passage, because of its threat of judgment, appears very much harsher and more unforgiving, while the latter, in positive terms, appeals to the "reward" awaiting those who live in accord with what is urged, is simply an argumentative strategy. The Pastorals make use of positions considerably more critical of riches in order, by contrast, to emphasize all the more strongly their own, positive ethical exhortations.

Incidentally, these two elements are found again in the passages about women. To oppose making a show of one's one affluence, "good works" are also brought forward in 2:9-10 and 5:10, while 5:5-6, which is analogous to 6:7-10, threatens those living the life of luxury with the loss of salvation. This analogy indicates that we dare not think that the ones called rich in the Pastoral Epistles are all men, as exegetes have frequently done.[2] To be sure, two decisive shifts that have an inner connection are evident in the admonitions about women in comparison with the ethical exhortations about riches. Since the rich women are viewed primarily from the perspective of their gender, and only secondarily with reference to their social status, the *parenesis* about women focuses more on sexual ethics and concludes with a different statement about salvation. That is, the women in 2:9-15, as well as the widows in 5:3-16, are specifically *not* promised a reward in heaven for the charitable use of their financial means; they gain salvation primarily by fulfilling their sexual role (2:15).

2. Cf. the critique given by Wagener 1994, 46, 163.

Admonishing the Slaves (1 Timothy 6:1-2; Titus 2:9-10)

In contrast to the tables of household duties in Colossians and Ephesians, as well as the table of duties for different social groups in 1 Peter, masters and slaves are not both admonished in the Pastorals but only the subordinate group. By taking this course, the Pastorals adopt the perspective of the masters and exhibit an attitude of hostility toward slaves when, as in the treatment of women, they bring up social prejudices and clichés (Titus 2:10: slaves make off with funds). Behind the ethical exhortations stands the question of the consequences of the fact that in the Christian church slaves and masters are *adelphoi*, brothers and sisters (1 Tim 6:2a). While, from the equality proclaimed in the church (Gal 3:28; 1 Cor 12:13; Col 3:11), Christian slaves made the connection to the hope of freedom from slavery (1 Cor 7:15-24), the Pastoral Epistles were drawing the exact opposite conclusion: precisely because their masters were also believers, the slaves were to serve them all the more willingly and eagerly. Support for this is drawn from the fact that the owners were the slaves' benefactors and were loved by God (1 Tim 6:2); moreover, attention is once more drawn to the reaction of their neighbors. The "Paul" of the Pastorals is obviously conscious of correcting here the attitude of the real Paul in Philemon, since he actually makes a verbal appeal to Philemon 16 (cf. Merz 1995a, 8-11). In so doing he deprives the slaves of the Pauline argumentation on which they based their efforts to achieve emancipation.

The Testament of "Paul": The Second Letter to Timothy

2 Timothy gives the impression of being a very personal letter. It contains a great many names of Paul's followers and opponents and an entire series of what appear to be purely private references (2 Tim 1:15-18; 4:9-16). And so, for a long time, interpreters of the letter had very serious reservations about regarding the letter as pseudepigraphic. It is why some exegetes assumed that at least the personal notices had to be authentic (the "fragment hypothesis"). But these reservations merely show how clever and thorough the epistolary fiction executed in this letter really is. 2 Timothy is a testament that offers an admonitory homily clothed in the form of a letter. This genre offers particularly favorable possibilities for the intention of the Pastorals of painting a specific portrait of Paul — the one who follows society's norms. A person's testament is his or her final and thus ultimately valid word, to which special respect and unparalleled significance are ascribed.

"Paul" is portrayed as a prisoner, forsaken by almost everyone, on his way to a martyr's death (4:6-8). In this situation he turns to "Timothy," who is depicted as a faithful disciple (3:10-11). Timothy is challenged to follow Paul also in suffering (2:1-13), to preach the "sound doctrine" passed on by Paul and impress it on the hearers' minds (3:14–4:5). Standing over against the faithful disciple are the apostates. Into the mouth of the dying Paul is put a prophecy about the end-time, in which every imaginable vice and false teaching will arise (3:1-9).

In this passage we once again find a polemic specifically directed against women. Within the antiheretical polemic it is said that the false teachers would slip into houses and in a subversive manner direct their attention especially to women. This brings to mind the reproach against the young "widows" in 1 Timothy 5:13, that they flit from house to house spreading destructive teachings. The ones to whom these teachings are directed are mocked in 2 Timothy 3:6 as "females" and depicted as sinful and "swayed by all kinds of desires." These reproaches are derived from the traditional polemic against heretics and thus have little to say about the concrete behavior of the women being discussed. Then in 3:7 it is mockingly asserted they would "always [be] instructed" and yet "never arrive at a knowledge of the truth." Here the word *manthanein*, "learn," which already played a central role in 1 Timothy 2:11 and 5:13, is taken up again. Apparently learning and gaining knowledge are a central concern for these women. The Pastorals seize on this search for knowledge, used so positively by those they oppose, in order to use irony to disqualify it. Yet knowledge means something quite different for each side. For the Pastorals "knowledge of the truth" *(epignōsis tēs alētheias)* is precisely defined as insight into the truth of the Christian faith, in the sense of orthodoxy. It refers to an attitude of acceptance of this theology and ethic, which is not paradoxical or mysterious but immediately clear. Therefore learning only makes sense for the Pastorals when it "bears fruit," that is, leads to what they consider to be "good works" (cf. 1 Tim 5:10). Therefore, as the Pastorals understand it, a knowledge of the truth can be pursued successfully by gleaning it directly from the way it is lived out, namely, by falling in line with what is laid down in the structures of society and church. A speculative search for knowledge and discussion about the truth are, by contrast, rejected as "wrangling over words" and "senseless controversies" (2 Tim 2:14, 23). They serve no useful purpose but lead only to the destruction of the hearers. And yet it appears that those on the other side, precisely with their theological speculations and discussions, have exerted a not inconsiderable attraction to women. Thus it also could have been unsatisfied desires for intellectual activity and demands for education that made the women open to the teaching of the opponents.

The *Oikos* Ecclesiology in the Pastorals — Hierarchizing and Restricting Women's Participation in the Church

By means of the *oikos* ecclesiology, the Pastorals develop a hierarchical model of the church, which radically restricts the possibilities for participation for freeborn women, as well as for slaves. To achieve that, the letters modify and correct statements in the authentic Pauline letters. One may ask how in the history of the early church it came to this hierarchizing of the church's structures, as well as to the accompanying removal of women from positions of leadership. As far as the Pastoral Epistles are concerned, neither reference to a defensive accommodation to the norms of their environment nor recourse to the necessity of fighting heresy can offer an adequate explanation. For one thing, the growth of the increasingly rigid differentiation of orthodoxy and heresy shows itself to be a development that calls for an adequate explanation. Secondly, the restrictive stance of the Pastoral Epistles clearly crosses the bounds of a defensive apologetic. The defensive-apologetic element is eclipsed by an offensive impulse whose starting point is the transformed inner social structure. Hierarchizing the way offices are structured develops a dynamic of its own, since the representatives of hierarchy in society cultivate interests of their own, which need not be congruent with those of the communities as a whole. In the office codes in the Pastoral Epistles, if the qualifications for church offices, especially that of the bishop, are tied to the authoritarian fulfillment of the role of the head of the household, then the status of the officeholders in the church is thereby determined in a way that corresponds to the status of secular ruling classes. The office of leadership in the church slowly positions itself at the same level as other positions of leadership in society and is, accordingly, granted the attendant social prestige. Here we must once again return to the findings of the literary analysis of the Pastoral Epistles. When the author patterns his letter on the genre of epistolary instructions from rulers, this advances the ruling class's self-confident pride and their view of themselves as authoritative figures distinguished from the rest of the church. Alongside the battle against opponents within the church, such aspirations for prestige naturally also first require gaining acceptance in the larger society. With that in mind, in view of the hierarchical nature of Roman society and the conservative ethos of its ruling classes, what is offered is a self-presentation that gives centrality to the unmistakable rule of Christian officeholders over women, the young, and slaves. By being in this way an advocate of uncontested *patria potestas,* the male ruling classes of Christianity then in the process of establishing itself as orthodox could expect approval and honor from the (male) pagan elite. This awareness of fundamental agreement with the views of society's ruling class finds expression in the Pastoral Epistles in that they, in contrast to 1 Peter, for example, lay out no limits to the orientation to their pagan surroundings but can actually even make eternal salvation or damnation depend on the judgment of those outside the church.

In the further course of the church's history, this ecclesiological and ethical starting point in the Pastoral Epistles had a great effect and left its mark on the theology and structure of the Christian church in many different ways. Since the author's pseudepigraphic strategy was successful, and his writings have been canonized as part of the Pauline corpus, they built and build an essential support for basic positions that are restrictive in the conflicts over the role of women in the church. Thus the history of reception of the Pastoral Epistles in the church also bears responsibility for the fact that the removal of women from positions of leadership and their subordinate role have continued to be central elements in perspectives on church order through the early church period, in the Middle Ages and into the modern era, and, for many Christian women and men, still play a role in shaping identity today.

And yet, both exegesis on the Pastoral Epistles and a look into the history of the church show that the conflict over the sharing of power between the sexes has never ceased, because women again and again have asserted their rights to equal participation. In this respect, the most polemic and restrictive witnesses against women, such as the Pastoral Epistles, are also at the same time always testimonies to their own limits. They demonstrate that the conflict has continued and that the silence of the women could not be definitively accomplished.

LITERATURE

Bassler, Jouette M. 1984. "The Widows' Tale: A Fresh Look at 1 Tim 5:3-16." *Journal of Biblical Literature* 103:23-41.

————. 1996. *1 Timothy, 2 Timothy, Titus.* Nashville.

Dewey, Joanna. 1992. "1 Timothy, 2 Timothy, Titus." In *The Women's Bible Commentary,* edited by Carol A. Newsom and Sharon H. Ringe, 353-61. London and Louisville.

Donelson, Lewis R. 1986. *Pseudepigraphy and Ethical Argument in the Pastoral Epistles.* Hermeneutische Untersuchungen zur Theologie, vol. 22. Tübingen.

Felber, Anneliese. 1994. *Harmonie durch Hierarchie? Das Denken der Geschlechterordnung im frühen Christentum.* Frauenforschung, vol. 26. Vienna.

Hanson, Anthony Tyrell. 1981. "The Domestication of Paul: A Study in the Development of Early Christian Theology." *Bulletin of the John Rylands University Library of Manchester* 63:402-18.

Kidd, Reggie W. 1990. *Wealth and Beneficence in the Pastoral Epistles.* Society of Biblical Literature Dissertation Series, vol. 122. Atlanta.

Korenhof, Mieke. 1989. "1. Timotheus 5:3-16: Witwen — Betschwester, Klatschbase, Ketzerin." In *Feministisch gelesen,* edited by Eva Renate Schmidt et al., 2:238-50. Stuttgart.

Küchler, Max. 1986. *Schweigen, Schmuck und Schleier. Drei neutestamentliche Vorschriften zur Verdrängung der Frauen auf dem Hintergrund einer frauenfeindlichen Exegese des AT im antiken Judentum.* Novum Testamentum et Orbis Antiquus, vol. 1. Göttingen.

MacDonald, Dennis Ronald. 1983. *The Legend and the Apostle: The Battle for Paul in Story and Canon.* Philadelphia.

MacDonald, Margaret Y. 1988. *The Pauline Churches: A Socio-Historical Study of Institutionalization in the Pauline and Deutero-Pauline Writings.* Society for New Testament Studies Monograph Series, vol. 60. Cambridge.

Maloney, Linda M. 1994. "The Pastoral Epistles." In *Searching the Scriptures,* edited by Elisabeth Schüssler Fiorenza, 2:361-80. 2 vols. New York.

Merz, Annette. 1995a. "Die intertextuelle Dimension von Pseudepigraphie und die geschichtliche Verortung der Pastoralbriefe in der Paulustradition am Beispiel von 1 Tim 6:2 und 1 Tim 5:3-16." Lecture, Neuendettelsau, September 24-26, 1995.

———. 1995b. "Das intertextuelle Verhältnis zwischen den Pastoralbriefen und den Paulus- und Theklaakten." Lecture, Heidelberg, December 1995.

Munroe, Winsome. 1983. *Authority in Paul and Peter: The Identification of a Pastoral Stratum in the Pauline Corpus and 1 Peter.* Society of New Testament Studies Monograph Series, vol. 45. Cambridge.

Nürnberg, Rosemarie. 1988. "Non decet neque necessarium est ut mulieres doceant. Überlegungen zum altkirchlichen Lehrverbot für Frauen." *Jahrbuch für Antike und Christentum* 31:57-73.

Pagels, Elaine. 1988. *Adam, Eve, and the Serpent.* New York.

———. 1991. *Adam, Eva und die Schlange. Die Theologie der Sünde.* Reinbek.

Roloff, Jürgen. 1988. *Der erste Brief an Timotheus.* Evangelisch-katholischer Kommentar, vol. 15. Zurich and Neukirchen-Vluyn.

Schottroff, Luise. 1994. "Frauenunterwerfung und Hass auf Frauenbefreiung (1 Tim 2:9-15)." In Luise Schottroff, *Lydias ungeduldige Schwestern. Feministische Sozialgeschichte des frühen Christentums,* 104-19. Gütersloh.

———. 1995. *Lydia's Impatient Sisters: A Feminist Social History of Early Christianity,* 69-78. Louisville.

Schüngel-Straumann, Helen. 1989. *Die Frau am Anfang. Eva und die Folgen.* Freiburg.

Schüssler Fiorenza, Elisabeth. 1983. *In Memory of Her: A Feminist Theological Reconstruction of Christian Origins,* 285-342. New York.

———. 1988. "Der patriarchale Haushalt Gottes und die Frauen-Ekklesia." In Elisabeth Schüssler Fiorenza, *Zu ihrem Gedächtnis . . . Eine feministisch-theologische Rekonstruktion der christlichen Ursprünge,* 343-407. Munich.

Städele, Alfons. 1980. *Die Briefe des Pythagoras und der Pythagoreer.* Beiträge zur klassischen Philologie, vol. 115. Meisenheim.

Thurston, Bonny Bowman. 1989. *The Widows: A Women's Ministry in the Early Church.* Minneapolis.

Verner, David Carl. 1983. *The Household of God and the Social World of the Pastoral Epistles.* Society of Biblical Literature Dissertation Series, vol. 71. Chico, Calif.

Wagener, Ulrike. 1994. *Die Ordnung des "Hauses Gottes." Der Ort von Frauen in der Ekklesiologie und Ethik der Pastoralbriefe.* Wissenschaftliche Untersuchungen zum Neuen Testament, 2nd ser., vol. 65. Tübingen.

For Further Reading

Merz, Annette. 2004. *Die fiktive Selbstauslegung des Paulus. Intertextuelle Studien zur Intention und Rezeption der Pastoralbriefe.* Novum Testamentum et Orbis Antiquus, vol. 52. Göttingen.

Translated by Everett R. Kalin

Philemon: A Reading under Apphia's Critical Eyes

Sabine Bieberstein

When Elizabeth Cady Stanton and other women wanted to participate in an international conference of "abolitionists," the movement to abolish slavery, in London in 1840, with a reference to their gender they were denied official delegate status and assigned the role of silent observers in the gallery. For Cady Stanton, this crucial experience united the fight for the emancipation of slaves with that for the emancipation of women. For me today this experience can still be used to show the neuralgic points of a feminist liberation-theological reading of Philemon.

The oppression of women is not to be separated from various other forms of oppression. Philemon is to be put in the context of the oppression of slaves, both in antiquity and also — and especially — throughout the history of the church up to the present time, to the extent that it has been read and misused as a document justifying slavery. This history of the letter's effect is to be named as a history of injustice and exposed, and it is to be distinguished from an analysis of the function of the letter in the context of slavery in antiquity.

The critical voice of women in the fight for the liberation of the oppressed must be heard. In its struggle to promote a new relationship with the slave Onesimus, the letter's opening section calls on a woman, Apphia, as witness, in that she — along with her husband, Archippus, and an entire house church — is addressed as a recipient, alongside the first addressee, Philemon. In this way, the interaction between Paul and Philemon, construed in the letter corpus as being exclusively between the two men, is forced open. The reading by Philemon occurs, as it were, publicly, before the church's very eyes, and in this way it must also find approval before Apphia's critical judgment.

Power relationships — even in the fight for a "good cause" — must be unmasked. This calls for an analysis of the letter's language and argumentation strategy,

I am very grateful to Regula Grünenfelder, Andrea Jäkle, and Hermann-Josef Venetz for inspiring conversations and constructive critique.

which, through a pronounced use of power terminology, the buildup of emotional pressure, and the creation of a critical public, turn out to be anything but "domination-free" (as many current commentaries assert that they are). With these three facets as a hermeneutic key, Philemon shall be read in what follows from a feminist perspective. In the background stands the hermeneutic of suspicion, developed above all by Elisabeth Schüssler Fiorenza, which in Philemon can expose power relationships in quite diverse ways. In making the analysis I am primarily utilizing the historical critical method's palette of techniques, expanding this repertoire by means of sociohistorical questions, with an eye to the reconstruction of women's history and the situation of slaves.

Apphia and the Reconstruction of Women's History

Philemon is the only New Testament letter that mentions a woman as an addressee in the prescript.[1] Since the fourth century at the latest (Theodore of Mopsuestia, ca. 352-428), she has been thought to be Philemon's wife. It is true that the text does not completely rule out this interpretation, but, on the other hand, neither does it give the interpretation any sign of support. On the contrary, the reasons for denying this view outweigh those that support it. For after the first addressee, Philemon, who is surely to be identified as the "you" (singular) to whom the rest of the letter is addressed, a woman and a man are mentioned, each by name and each with an individual title. There is not a single word that relates Apphia to either of the two men. Even the fact that she is named directly after Philemon does not automatically indicate that she is characterized as his wife. The New Testament example of Prisca and Aquila (Acts 18:26; Rom 16:3; and 1 Cor 16:19), as well as inscriptions that mention married couples, shows that with respect to married couples the order in which the husband and the wife are mentioned is not fixed. So the picture that more likely arises is that of an addressee, next to whom are placed two "witnesses," who are singled out from the larger circle of addressees mentioned in what follows. This latter group is designated as the "church in *your* [sing.] house," in distinction from Romans 16:5 and 1 Corinthians 16:19, for example, where the church in the house of Prisca and Aquila is spoken of as the "church in *their* house." The letter that follows, up to Philemon 24, is addressed to "you" (sing.), so that here as well Apphia does not appear as a coparticipant, sharing responsibility with Philemon.

This makes it clear that the text at least has no interest in identifying Apphia as Philemon's wife. This interpretation is more in keeping with an androcentric way of characterizing women. It involves the danger of reducing women to the func-

---

1. On this section, see the articles by Winter 1984/85; 1987; and 1994, as well as the one by Leutzsch 1994.

tions they perform in a patriarchal household, underestimating their independent role in the early churches and construing their significance as merely derivative.

But what can be said about Apphia? Her name, perhaps of Phrygian origin, is well attested in western Asia Minor. Beyond that, we learn nothing of her origin, her occupation, or her social standing. Since the letter does not even name the place in which the recipients live, we do not get beyond the traditional supposition that it is Colossae (cf. Col 1:7; 4:7-17). The fact that Apphia is named already in the prescript allows us to assume that she has a significant role in the house church that is being addressed. The way she is addressed, "sister," is comparable to the designation "brother" used for the cosender, Timothy (Philem 1), and the addressee Philemon (vv. 7, 20). Paul also uses this designation for another woman, Phoebe (Rom 16:1), the deacon *(diakonos)* and leader *(prostatis)* of the church at Cenchreae. Like Apphia, she is mentioned without reference to a man, and she undertook, also apparently without a man, a trip to Rome on church business.

This sole naming of a woman in the prescript of Philemon opens a "window" into a tradition about women in the early churches, a tradition that has become invisible: just as we can assume that besides Apphia there were other involved and responsible women (and men) in this church, so also we can conclude that there were just such people in all other house churches. This sheds light on the rich relational network in these churches, which in Philemon is also revealed in the mention of Timothy as cosender as well as of other coworkers (Philem 23-24). And it must also correct the image, still prevalent in many places, of Paul as the great "Lone Ranger" of early Christianity. Paul must be understood much more strongly "as a link in a chain. It is the chain of those who taught him hope and of those, who together with him and at times also in critical distance from him and his kind, give form to the new life before God" (Schottroff 1995, 207; 1998, 213).

The fact that Paul addresses Apphia in addition to the principal addressee shows that he sees in her an ally who could intervene in support of his request. As the letter is read, she is present. Paul is confident that first of all she, and then also Archippus, the second person mentioned by name, and the other members of the house church have the competence and influence to work effectively on behalf of a cause about which he apparently receives considerable resistance from Philemon.

The Letter's Purpose and the History of Its Interpretation

How is this purpose to be more precisely understood and evaluated? Traditionally, on the basis of the reference to the separation in verse 15 and the forceful request for the reception of the slave, it was concluded that Onesimus was a fugitive, a runaway slave, who had sought refuge with Paul in order that Paul would intercede on his behalf with his master, Philemon. Because of the obligation Paul imposes upon himself in verses 18-19, it was further assumed that before Onesimus fled he had stolen money or done something else wrong, so that his master incurred damages not only for the loss of his work but also for the theft.

A background for this assertion is the fact that in antiquity the flight of a slave was a punishable offense that ought to be prevented and deterred. There were ingenious public and private measures for capturing runaway slaves, and no limits were put on what the slave owners could do for punishment. Nevertheless, the fugitives could seek asylum in certain places like shrines. Also attested is the case of a (successful) plea by a high-ranking friend of a slave owner on behalf of such a fugitive (cf. Pliny the Younger to Sabinianus, from the time of Trajan [98-117], *Epistulae* 9.21). In the history of Philemon's interpretation, seeing it as a plea by Paul for a fugitive makes it possible to use Philemon as "evidence" for seeing the flight of slaves as unchristian: after he had become a Christian through Paul, Onesimus, according to this view, recognized his "responsibility" and willingly returned to slavery. The consequences of this interpretation, above all in slaveholder societies such as North America, were disastrous (cf. Winter 1994, 302). Moreover, this interpretation continued the injustice endured by slaves, since the perspective of slave owners was adopted and Onesimus was criminalized and written off (examples in Martin 1991, 330-32).

On the basis of a feminist liberation-theological concern, Sara C. Winter (1984/85; 1987; 1994) — adopting a thesis by John Knox (1935) — argues against this interpretation. She shows that the interpretation could not explain how a fugitive could have stayed on with Paul in prison. She maintains that it was never said that Onesimus was a fugitive and, in particular, that the thanksgiving (vv. 4-7), in which the letter's principal themes were otherwise introduced, did not fit this interpretation. Rather, according to Winter, Paul's request was to be understood not as being on behalf of Onesimus but instead to get him back: like Epaphroditus in Philippians 2:25-30, Onesimus was sent to Paul in prison on the church's behalf by Archippus, who was to be seen as the letter's principal addressee and Onesimus's owner. Now Paul wanted to keep him permanently, not, indeed, as his personal servant, as Philemon 13 is commonly understood, but as a coworker for the gospel.

True, Winter's explanation does prevent a misuse of Philemon like the one mentioned above. However, her interpretation cannot explain why a non-Christian slave, of all people — and especially one characterized as "unhelpful" (v. 11) — would have been sent on the church's behalf. And the "sending back" (v. 12) must also be seen as an expression for the return of runaway slaves, as parallel texts from antiquity show (cf. Arzt 1995, 136).

Admittedly, neither perspective can explain every aspect of the letter. It seems to me that the flight of a slave is the more probable background for the letter. In both cases, however, Paul is acting within the slave system. That is shown by the fact that he never infringes on Philemon's right to deal with his slave. It is also shown in the slave terminology we have just indicated above — which Paul used in other places, to be sure, also in the figurative sense and for the relationship with God and Christ.

Paul has repeatedly been reproached for never explicitly demanding that Onesimus be set free. Nevertheless, what is hidden behind the letter's purpose and why Paul argues with such vehemence are to be carefully investigated.

The Letter's Structure and Line of Argument

The letter, with its prescript (address and blessing, vv. 1-3), thanksgiving (vv. 4-7), body (vv. 8-22), and conclusion (greetings and blessing, vv. 23-25), exhibits all the formal elements of Paul's large letters. It is illuminating for an understanding of the line of argument to divide the body of the letter into two parts, based on a new start in verse 17, and, together with the thanksgiving, to interpret this as three interrelated parts of an argument in accord with ancient rhetoric (with proem, argument, and epilogue — Church 1978).

Prescript (vv. 1-3) and Conclusion (vv. 23-25): Support for the Argument

The beginning and end of the letter are related to one another in the sense that through the women and men mentioned in both passages there is a break in the one-on-one relationship between Paul and Philemon and that in each case the blessings are directed toward the whole group of those addressed.

Verse 1 makes it clear that the letter is not from Paul alone: just as Paul names cosenders in all his letters except Romans, here he mentions Timothy as cosender. Mentioned as addressees are three individuals and a house church. Because of that, as well as through the mention of those being greeted in the conclusion of the letter, a public group is established that stands over against the "you" (singular) to whom, from verse 2 on, the letter is directed, and behind which, presumably, is hidden the first person mentioned, Philemon. Before a critical group thus endowed with authority, Philemon will have to give an account of how he deals with Onesimus.

At the same time, this group of people can be understood as a model for an already realized new community that is evoked at the beginning and end of the letter. Pointing to this are the designations "*co*worker," "*fellow* prisoner," and "*fellow* soldier," but especially the forms of address "brother" and "sister," which Paul uses at the beginning for Timothy and Apphia and, in the course of the letter, also for Philemon (vv. 7, 20). This self-designation of members of the churches of Jesus Christ as brothers and sisters points, at the very least, to programmatically formulated relationships that are independent of position, status, and gender (cf. Gal 3:26-29). That these are not self-evident, but that this "discipleship of equals" (Elisabeth Schüssler Fiorenza) has to be fought for, becomes clear in Philemon not with respect to women but with respect to Onesimus, the "slave-become-Christian" in his sought-after, but clearly not self-evident, reception as a "beloved brother" (Philem 16). In this designation, two elements that had already been used for Philemon (vv. 1, 7) are carefully set next to one another, indicating here the new relationship Paul is calling for between Philemon and Onesimus.

Paul calls himself a "prisoner of Jesus Christ." For one thing, this is a reference to his own situation in prison;[2] for another, it is the start of a series of references to this imprisonment that pervade the letter (vv. 9, 10, 13, indirectly also v. 23: "fellow prisoner"). Even if Paul does not call himself an apostle in this letter, as he does in others, he still provides himself with a dignity and authority that are surely hard to oppose.

The Thanksgiving (Proem, vv. 4-7) as the First Part of the Argument

Throughout the thanksgiving Paul takes up themes that he will return to in his argument. The prayers mentioned in verse 4 are taken up again in verse 22 (in this latter verse as prayers of the addressees), and they form brackets around the letter's tripartite argument. To the love for which Paul praises Philemon in verses 5 and 7, he returns in verse 9 and, crucially, in verse 16, where Paul calls on him to make this love tangible by welcoming Onesimus as a beloved brother. Paul also calls in verse 17 for a concrete manifestation of the fellowship that according to verse 6 is intended to act effectively and invokes in verse 14 the goodness likewise mentioned in verse 6. And when Paul gives expression in verse 7 to his joy that the "hearts" of the "saints" have been "refreshed" through Philemon, he also, at the very least, does this to tie the image of the heart with Onesimus in verse 12 and, in verse 20, to request that Philemon "refresh" his own heart — namely, by fulfilling his request.

All in all, Paul allows an extremely positive image of Philemon to emerge. Yet the individual traits are shaped in such a way that they can serve the further argument, in that Philemon must now also act in accord with this image.

The Argument (vv. 8-16) as the Second Part of Making the Case

In verses 8-16 Paul begins to put forward his purpose, but he does it in such a way that it almost has to be filtered out from the letter — so that it is not without reason that the most varied assumptions are offered about the intent and purpose of the letter (see above). Paul resorts to putting the matter in the form of a request, but not without mentioning that he really has the authority to command Philemon to act, and also without failing to refer to his age and his imprisonment. Paul does not specify exactly what he is asking with respect to Onesimus. Never-

---

2. Caesarea, Rome, and Ephesus are under consideration as the place of imprisonment. The first two locations have the support of statements in Acts. Ephesus can be inferred from indirect references in the Pauline letters and is likely the most probable.

theless, the section leads to the statement that Philemon should welcome him back no longer as a slave but as a beloved brother, both in the "flesh" and in the "Lord." This has to be interpreted as a call for a relationship of equals between the (former) master and the (former) slave.

But Paul offers no substantive theological or christological arguments for this new relationship, as he does in Galatians 3:26-29 or in 1 Corinthians 12:12-13. Instead Paul operates on a highly emotional level: the references to his age and his imprisonment (three times in Philem 8-16) make it difficult to refuse his request. In verses 10-13 he connects Onesimus intimately with himself in that he calls him his child, whose "father" he became, and his own "heart." Moreover, he stresses how gladly he would keep him so that he might be of service to him in prison — instead of to Philemon. But when Paul connects Onesimus so intimately with himself, it becomes practically impossible for Philemon to take any action against Onesimus. This, as well as Paul offering himself to Philemon as a model for his brotherly attitude toward Onesimus in verse 16, severely limits the voluntary nature — stressed in verse 14 — of Philemon's action.

The Epilogue (vv. 17-22) as the Third Part of the Argument

With the letter's first imperative verb, verse 17 formulates a clear request: "welcome him as you would welcome me." Once again the fate of Onesimus is connected intimately with the person of Paul, in that Philemon's action over against Onesimus is paralleled with Philemon's relationship with Paul. This intimate tie has in what follows a thoroughly tangible basis: Paul is prepared to pay for any losses that Onesimus has inflicted on Philemon. This is so important to Paul that he writes this with his own hand in the need to demonstrate the letter's authenticity. At the same time, he stresses that Philemon owes him his own self, thus drawing Philemon into a creditor-debtor relationship.

The terminology from the economic sphere used in this section — the relationship between Paul and Philemon is recast into one between "business partners," involving debts and their repayment — makes it impossible to spiritualize the expectation laid on Philemon and points instead to the economic side of the situation. The emancipation of a slave makes sense only when the financial consequences have been taken into account. Perhaps this is also in view when Paul calls on Philemon to receive Onesimus as his "partner," so that more is being asked of Philemon than "merely" the release of his slave (cf. Arzt 1995, 137-38).

Finally, verses 20-21 strengthen the appeal still further, with verse 20 pointing for the third time to the "heart," thereby appealing to the emotions, while verse 21 quite openly reckons with Philemon's acceptance or presupposes it. According to verse 22, Paul is even prepared to personally come and see how Philemon is handling the matter.

Paul appears to reckon with considerable resistance from Philemon and tries to overcome it by using power terminology and simultaneous appeals on the emotional level. In addition, by means of the men and women mentioned in the letter he calls into being a group of people who are set over against Philemon as a critical corrective and as an example to be emulated. Before this group he will have to give an account about his decision with respect to Onesimus.

Reading the Letter under the Eyes of Apphia

I am reading Philemon as a white, western European middle-class woman, a participant in the structural violence of an economic and social system that consciously accepts the exploitation of the South by the North, an ever greater gap between poor and rich, those who have work and those who do not, domestic populations and refugees, etc. Perhaps these inherent constraints are comparable with the entanglements faced by Paul and his brothers and sisters in the churches that found themselves in a social system based on the "self-evident" inequality of the free and slaves. Paul remains to a certain degree within this system: he does not call its utility into question, does not condemn slavery, and also operates with the logic of slavery in that he is constantly negotiating about Onesimus without letting him step forward as an independent individual — with the possible exception of verse 16.

On the other hand, he summons Philemon to act in a way that is obviously not easy for him and that apparently calls into question the laws about the master-slave relationship. In addition, his letter places the problem of Onesimus, the slave (who believes in Christ) — the problem that according to the way the collection of Pauline letters is structured is dealt with "man to man" — in the context of a church that as a critical group of people limits the ways the slave owner (who believes in Christ) can act. This public group of church members is a "counter" to another public group, the state, that grants unlimited power to a slave owner over against a slave. Paul makes use of a house church's network of relationships to achieve what he desires and to conjure up an exemplary new reality.

In the spirit of a creative reconstruction of women's history, let us take the matter one step further. Within this network of relationships, we can think of Apphia as an advocate in the fight against the inhuman structures of slavery, which create constraints from which it is almost impossible for an individual to break out. A reading under the critical eyes of Apphia makes it possible to break down such false constraints and to seek liberating alternatives. She can help us to break open the androcentric way of perceiving "Pauline churches" and to see in them diverse women and men, with their stories and their battles. And not least, she leads us to criticize the traditional designation of "a Letter *of Paul to Philemon*" as improperly restrictive.

Sabine Bieberstein

LITERATURE

Arzt, Peter. 1995. "'. . . einst unbrauchbar, jetzt aber gut brauchbar' (Phlm 11). Das Problem der Sklaverei bei Paulus." In *". . . so lernen die Völker des Erdkreises Gerechtigkeit." Ein Arbeitsbuch zu Bibel und Ökonomie,* edited by Kuno Füssel and Franz Segbers, 132-38. Lucerne.

Church, F. Forrester. 1978. "Rhetorical Structure and Design in Paul's Letter to Philemon." *Harvard Theological Review* 71:17-33.

Knox, John. 1935. *Philemon among the Letters of Paul.* New York.

Leutzsch, Martin. 1994. "Apphia, Schwester!" In *Für Gerechtigkeit streiten. Theologie im Alltag einer bedrohten Welt,* edited by Dorothee Sölle, 76-82. Festschrift for Luise Schottroff. Gütersloh.

Martin, Clarice J. 1991. "The Rhetorical Function of Commercial Language in Paul's Letter to Philemon (Verse 18)." In *Persuasive Artistry: Studies in New Testament Rhetoric in Honour of George A. Kennedy,* edited by Duane Watson, 321-37. Journal for the Study of the New Testament: Supplement Series, vol. 50. Sheffield.

Perkins, Pheme. 1992. "Philemon." In *The Women's Bible Commentary,* edited by Carol A. Newsom and Sharon H. Ringe, 362-63. London and Louisville.

Schottroff, Luise. 1995. "Auf dem Weg zu einer feministischen Rekonstruktion der Geschichte des frühen Christentums." In *Feministische Exegese. Forschungserträge zur Bibel aus der Perspektive von Frauen,* edited by Luise Schottroff, Silvia Schroer, and Marie-Theres Wacker, 175-248. Darmstadt.

———. 1998. "Toward a Feminist Reconstruction of the History of Early Christianity." In *Feminist Interpretation: The Bible in Women's Perspective,* 179-254. Minneapolis.

Winter, Sara C. 1984/85. "Methodological Observations on a New Interpretation of Paul's Letter to Philemon." *Union Seminary Quarterly* 39:203-12.

———. 1987. "Paul's Letter to Philemon." *New Testament Studies* 33:1-15.

———. 1994. "Philemon." In *Searching the Scriptures,* edited by Elisabeth Schüssler Fiorenza, 2:301-12. 2 vols. New York.

FOR FURTHER READING

Arzt-Grabner, Peter. 2003. *Philemon.* Papyrologische Kommentare zum Neuen Testament, vol. 1. Göttingen.

Bieberstein, Sabine. 2000. "Disrupting the Normal Reality of Slavery: A Feminist Reading of the Letter to Philemon." *Journal for the Study of the New Testament* 79:105-16.

DeVos, Craig Steven. 2001. "Once a Slave, Always a Slave? Slavery, Manumission and Relational Patterns in Paul's Letter to Philemon." *Journal for the Study of the New Testament* 82:89-105.

Frilingos, Chris. 2000. "'For My Child, Onesimus': Paul and Domestic Power in Philemon." *Journal of Biblical Literature* 119, no. 1:91-104.

Nicklas, Tobias. 2008. "The Letter to Philemon: A Discussion with J. Albert Harrill." In *Paul's World,* edited by Stanley E. Porter, 201-20. Pauline Studies, vol. 4. Leiden.

Wengst, Klaus. 2005. *Der Brief an Philemon.* Theologischer Kommentar zum Neuen Testament, vol. 16. Stuttgart.

Translated by Everett R. Kalin

856

Hebrews: Strangers in the World

Ulrike Wagener

The so-called letter to the Hebrews occupies a peripheral position in contemporary scholarly and ecclesiastical reception of New Testament scriptures, and this
includes feminist exegesis. Its metaphorical language and its theological concepts
remain strange. In imagery full of cultic sacrifices, Hebrews portrays Christ as the
high priest who through his unique sacrifice has opened the doors to the heavenly
sanctuary. This cultic language and a worldview close to the mystery cults of antiquity contribute to a certain aloofness of today's exegesis with regard to Hebrews; (not only) feminist reception finds a Christology of self-sacrifice offensive,
which in its history of transmission had oppressive effects on women (cf. Schüssler
Fiorenza 1995, 98-107).

In any case, in its interpretation of the life and death of Jesus, Hebrews presents an original theology that differs clearly from other strands of New Testament tradition. Traditionally, this text was categorized as one of the letters of
Paul, but it differs from these considerably in linguistic style and theological
content. Moreover, it is not a genuine letter: Hebrews lacks the introductory prescript (the formula at the beginning of the letter) and the characteristic epistolary elements in its text. Solely the last verses (13:22-25) seem to represent an
epistolary closure. This could originally have been a short note accompanying
the text (Vanhoye 1985, 497). Or this epistolary closure was added later to suggest
that Hebrews was one of Paul's letters (Grässer 1990, 17). The genre of the actual
"letter" suggests that it is an anonymously transmitted sermon (Kittredge 1994,
428). Despite the (secondary) title of "to the Hebrews," the text is addressed to a
Greek-speaking audience. Places of origin and destination are not known; only
the linguistic similarities and the content link it to Philo, thus suggesting that
Alexandria might have been the place of composition. In relation to its date of
composition, there is a debate as to whether Hebrews assumes the continued existence of the temple in Jerusalem or whether that building had already been destroyed. This would indicate a date of composition either before or after 70 C.E.
(cf. the overview in Feld 1985, 14-18). The text does not provide a definite answer

to this question. The time of origin probably lies between 60 and 100 C.E.; a more accurate dating is not possible.

Canonization and the Question of Authorship

The special position of Hebrews goes back to the time of the early church: it is included in the oldest manuscripts of Paul's letters, including the papyrus 𝔓46 (around 200 C.E.). The Eastern church counted it among the Holy Scriptures and assumed it was written by Paul but edited by one of his followers or colleagues. The Western church had reservations about it; the oldest lists of the New Testament canon do not include it. The authorship of Paul remained contested, but eventually the text was included in the New Testament canon at the end of the fourth century owing to the authority of the Eastern church — but the unresolved question of who was the author remained (Vanhoye 1985, 495).

In feminist biblical interpretation Hebrews never gained much attention despite the question of possible female authorship that presented an interesting point of departure for further study. At the beginning of the twentieth century, Adolf von Harnack thought Hebrews had been written by the missionary Priscilla (also called Prisca), who was mentioned in Acts (18:2, 24-26) and in some of Paul's letters (Rom 16:3-5; 2 Tim 4:19) (Harnack 1900). Ruth Hoppin accepted and extended this view (Hoppin 1969). Both argued that precisely the anonymity of the letter supported the view of female authorship. The development of the prohibition of female teaching might have led to the elision of the author's name. In contrast to the Pauline epistles, it was noted that — despite the apparent learning and theological originality of its male or female author — Hebrews did not refer to personal authority. Rather, the text shows apologetic tendencies that seem defensive about assuming authority and a lecturing mode (Hoppin 1969, 22, discussing Heb 13:22). This hesitation to seize the authority of teaching might reflect the growing critique in early Christianity of the role of women as teachers and their authority (1 Cor 14:33-35; 1 Tim 2:12). In addition, in Hebrews we find alternately "I" and "we" in relation to the author; this might indicate that Prisca worked together with her husband Aquila. Such considerations are contested with the argument that in Hebrews 11:32 we find a reference to the author in the grammatical masculine form (most recently D'Angelo 1992). This counterargument is not convincing — as D'Angelo herself points out — since it proves only that the "author either is a man or *pretends* to be one" (emphasis added). Apart from the convention to use the masculine form, a female author could also try to hide behind an apparently masculine subject to avoid the pressure against women in positions of teaching and leadership (Kittredge 1994, 430, 433). While most traditional exegesis without question presupposes male authorship, one has to keep open the possibility that — as in all cases of anonymous and pseudonymous writings of early

Christianity — Hebrews could have been written by a woman. But the concrete case *that* Hebrews was written by a woman cannot be made. Methodically, the literary criteria are missing; we cannot ascertain what "feminine writing" in antiquity ought to look and sound like.

This "disappointing" result leads to the hermeneutical question of the significance of the letter's authorship for today's dealings with the text. The attempt at determining a female author is based on the perception that this will give the writing more authority for women. However, female authorship does not necessarily mean that the text will break with patriarchal thought-structures or contain liberating content (Kittredge 1994, 434). As important as it is for feminist theology and social history to know that women have shaped the development of Christianity and have composed writings, each individual text must be evaluated according to its content and history of interpretation. Moreover, the female or male author of Hebrews clearly intended not to appear in the text. She or he does not claim personal authority but builds entirely on the power of conviction of the text itself and its arguments.

Theme, Literary Character, and Structure

The literary genre of Hebrews suggests that it is not a letter but a sermon; it names itself a "word of exhortation" (Heb 13:22). The text's style is reminiscent of the rhetoric of antiquity, using formal elements with ease (Grässer 1990, 15f.). Hebrews draws on manifold sources: liturgical traditions (formulas of belief and hymns), treatises from the scholarly teaching-traditions of Jewish synagogue communities (chapter 11: on faith in times past), and especially quotations of Scripture that form the basis of argument throughout. The citation and the kind of exegesis are oriented by the Septuagint. Thematically, Hebrews can be characterized as an interweaving of Christology and ecclesiology: Christ is the high priest whose sacrifice provides salvation once and for all and opens the path to the heavenly sanctuary. This mystery requires a community with enduring faith on the journey toward heavenly perfection. The christological explanations thus serve to encourage Christians who are in danger of losing their faith and hope. The situation this encouragement is meant to address can be sketched out in a few remarks. It is clear that the addressees had suffered state persecution, imprisonment, and dispossession, and that they stood firm (10:32-34). It is debated whether the addressees are acutely suffering under these conditions in the present (Lehne 1990, 120), or whether the "fatigue" is the result of a less tense and calmer situation for the churches (cf. de Silva 1996, 109). The latter is contradicted for, according to 13:3, fellow Christians are in jail and being tortured. In any case, the strong bond of the Christian community seems to loosen; some members do not attend services any more (10:25). Also, the choice of the pointedly cultic metaphors could indicate that

the addressees have a need for stronger ritual-cultic representations of the promised salvation, that is, a yearning for a concrete substitute for the cult of the temple.
This need could stem from altercations with Jewish Christians or from accusations
of atheism leveled against Christians by society (Lehne 1990, 120).

The thorough christological argumentation of Hebrews is very systematic,
while the author links the separate parts successfully and intricately through rhetorical means, like theme sentences, literary embedding, and so forth. The exegesis
of Hebrews found several structures of composition (cf. Vanhoye's intricate five-
part model; 1979, 119-47). Several different ways of structuring are possible; mostly
it is ordered into three parts: first, the christological foundation (1:1–5:10); second,
the unfolding of the Christology (5:11–10:39); and third, the consequences for
Christian discipleship (11:1–13:21) (similarly Grässer 1990, 29). Yet, this structure
does not imply a strict separation between a doctrinal and an ethical part, for even
the two first parts directly address and admonish the addressees.

The Christological Foundation: The Superiority and Uniqueness of the Son (1:1–5:10)

This first part begins with a prologue (1:1-4) that introduces a typical contrast
within Hebrews: while God has spoken in many ways in the past through prophets, he now speaks through the one Son. The past is contrasted with the present.
This is the particular thought-structure that explains the soteriological meaning
of Christ in this letter: it interprets Christ against the background of Jewish (salvation) history, dialectically interlinking continuity and discontinuity. Christ is the
fulfillment of Israel's legacy and at the same time the definitive, superior substitute
of this legacy (Lehne 1990, 119-20). This idea is substantiated in the argument by
drawing on Holy Scripture to support Christ's superiority. Simultaneously, in the
parallel positioning of *many* prophets versus the *one* Son, the philosophical assumption that singularity is better than plurality becomes clear (Kittredge 1994,
434).

Both thought structures mentioned above — the contrast of then/now and
many/one — can be criticized from a feminist perspective. While the former binary tends to support anti-Jewish exegesis, the latter "logic of one" leads to a
thinking that continuously excludes the sexual difference. It rests on the equation
of human with man and perpetuates it. This is not a specific problem of Hebrews
but rather points to the fundamental difficulty of an exclusive Christology that is
reduced to male metaphors.

According to 1:2-4, the Son is the preexistent mediator of creation, the reflection of God's glory, the one who cleanses of sin and thus is enthroned at the right
hand of God. Feminist exegesis has shown that — as in other early Christian
hymns — characteristics of the female figure of godly "Sophia" (wisdom) have

here been transferred to the Logos, or rather the Son of God (cf. Schüssler Fio-renza 1995, 113ff., esp. 148).

In three argumentative steps the superiority of the Son is argued: 1:5–2:16 shows his grandeur through a comparison with the angels: "The angels are changeable and transient, but the son remains unchanged for eternity" (Grässer 1990, 82). The angels are servants, but the Son will be enthroned at God's right hand and rule (1:13, citing Ps 110:1). But this heavenly glorification presupposes his earlier descent, according to the christological schema of abasement and exalta-tion (cf. Phil 2:6-11). Christ was placed beneath the angels for a short while in his incarnation; Hebrews arrives at this interpretation by applying Psalm 8, which deals with human dignity in general, to Christ specifically (Heb 2:6-8). The rela-tionship between Christ and his disciples is understood as a close correspondence between the one "Son" and the many "sons." This rests on common descent (2:11) and includes the shared goal of perfection.[1]

This christological model of abasement and exaltation of the "son" is subject to feminist critique for its androcentrism, which postulates sonship as the central metaphor for the relationship between Christ and God as well as that between the faithful and God mediated by Christ (Schottroff 1990, 132-35). Another aspect of this androcentrism is that the effects of such male symbolism on female followers of the community do not come into view at all; in this understanding, the partici-pation of women in Christ's saving act is tantamount to symbolic masculinization.

In addition, feminists debate whether the schema of abasement and exaltation represents a kyrio-centric theology of domination supportive of patriarchal struc-tures or whether it is a critique of patriarchy and kyriarchy.[2] Schottroff empha-sizes positively the solidarity of God as expressed through Christ's becoming hu-man, showing God "as one who descends to the most wretched and shares their lot" (Schottroff 1994, 72; 1995, 44). The notion of a God that becomes a slave sug-gests the possibility of subverting social hierarchies. Schüssler Fiorenza, however, insists on the danger of spiritualization: "rather it (the danger) consists of the proclamation in masculine mythological terminology of Jesus as a godly being, es-chewing his historical being. That the Galilean messenger of Sophia is presented in kyriarchal terms as cosmic ruler and sovereign is comparable to Isis's power and rule over the world" (Schüssler Fiorenza 1995, 149). Schüssler Fiorenza admits that such mythological language might have helped to strengthen the identity of early

---

1. In this instance, Hebrews seems to refer to gnostic-mythical understandings. However, it differs from gnosis by its emphasis on the humanity of Christ: it highlights that Christ became flesh and blood (2:14), that he was similar in everything to his "brothers" (2:17), that is, he had to encoun-ter temptation and suffering (2:18).

2. This discussion thus far has not focused on Hebrews but mainly on Phil 2:6-11; cf. Schottroff 1994, 71-75; 1995, 43-46; Schüssler Fiorenza 1995, 147ff. Schüssler Fiorenza suggests that the term "pa-triarchy" be replaced by "kyriarchy" to point to the many dimensions of domination within family and society.

Christian churches; in the light of reception history, however, it tended to legitimate Christian rule christologically.

In the second argumentative step (3:1–4:13), the significance of Jesus is further developed by comparing him with Moses and by invoking the tradition of the exodus, the journey in the desert and the conquest of the land. This argument serves didactic purposes as well. In the broadening of the son metaphor, Jesus' superiority over Moses is explained by drawing on family or household metaphors (3:1-6):[3] both Jesus and Moses are described as *pistos,* meaning faithful and dependable (3:2, 5). They fulfill their role and task in loyalty toward God, the father and master of the household. But Jesus is positioned above Moses within the household, because he is the son, whereas Moses is only the *therapōn.* This word suggests a servant who is either slave or free; in this case it probably means the steward of the household. Thus, the relation between Moses and Jesus is described as simultaneously corresponding and surpassing.

For didactical purposes this analogy is expanded to include the followers of Moses and Jesus: the loss of faith by the Israelites in the desert becomes — with recourse to Psalm 95 — a warning example for the addressees. The generation of the desert did not remain faithful; they retreated because they became frightened and lost their trust. David A. de Silva (1994; 1996) argues that the relationship between God and his people here is fashioned analogous to Greco-Roman categories of patron-client relationships. The underlying system of values is that of honor and shame: God is understood as the patron and benefactor, whose ability to look after his clients is repeatedly proven and who thus expects them to repay him with loyalty and respect. Lack of faith means either insufficient trust in the abilities of the benefactor or an accusation of insidiousness. It is for this reason that lack of faith represents an insult, an assault on his honor. The Israelites draw the wrath of God because of their fickleness; their lack of faith prevents the fulfillment of the prophecy that they would enter into his "rest" (Heb 3:7-19). The term *katapausis* used here means the arrival in the Promised Land and is seen in eschatological terms as the entry into the final Shabbat. Since the Israelites have thus gambled away their salvation, Hebrews warns its readers not to fail in the same way by abandoning their first faith (4:1-11). This suggests that the writer links the present situation of the addressees to that of the Israelites in the desert: they are in danger of insulting God again by turning away from him as the real benefactor. This would be even more serious in the present because God has sent his final word in Christ (cf. below, 5:11–6:20).

Already in 2:17 and 3:1, Christ is accorded the title "high priest," and in the third argumentative step, 4:14–5:10, this becomes the central thematic concern.

---

3. The usage of the metaphor "house(hold)" and "God's family" can be found in the Synoptic Gospels, occasionally in Paul's letters, but centrally in the deutero-Pauline Pastoral Epistles (→); cf. Wagener 1995.

This section is again structured in terms of the conception of corresponding and surpassing but now in contrast to the priesthood of Levi. The corresponding aspect is seen in that Jesus, like the Levitical high priest, understands the weaknesses of humans because he shared in human existence until death. The superiority over the Levitical priesthood is initially only hinted at with the referral to Psalm 110:4 with the qualification as "priest according to the order of Melchizedek" (Heb 5:6). The didactical gist of the argument is apparent from the outset: the addressees are encouraged, with their sight upon Jesus, to remain faithful because Jesus as their high priest has reached heavenly perfection and because he can sympathize with them on account of his participation in human existence (4:14-15). Jesus is the fount of salvation because he has conquered death: he has learned obedience through the experience of fear of death (5:7-10). As in 2:1-18, 5:1-10 emphasizes Jesus' human existence as prerequisite for his act of salvation.

The Unfolding of the High Priest Christology (5:11–10:18)

Before the high priest Christology is unfolded, the text inserts a detailed admonition (5:11–6:20), its tone veering from a scathing critique of the lack in maturity of the addressees (5:12–6:8) to approval (6:9-10) and encouragement (6:10-20). Having warned the listeners in 3:7-11 with the negative example of the Israelites in the desert against losing their steadfastness in faith, the author again warns of the dangers of "falling away" from faith. For those who have been enlightened and have participated in Christ's meal, there will be no second chance to turn around, because "on their own they are crucifying again the Son of God and holding him up to contempt" (6:6). Here we see again the underlying social model of thinking in terms of honor and shame. The theological statement of the impossibility of a second repentance creates a lot of difficulties for many exegetes and is often de-emphasized (cf. Grässer 1990, 388). It should, however, not be understood in a dogmatic way but rather as a rhetorical device: it is an appeal to feeling, an "argument from *pathos*" that belonged to the rhetorical repertoire of antiquity: the author wants to create fear about the consequence of a falling away from faith (de Silva 1996, 109-10).

High Priest according to the Order of Melchizedek (7:1-28)

The First Testament figure of Melchizedek is introduced to argue for the superiority of Christ above the Levitical priesthood. Melchizedek is without beginning and end, without father and mother, and thus is similar to God's Son. Moreover, he received from Abraham the tithe — thus he is ranked higher than Abraham — and the tithe is simultaneously bestowed on the yet unborn Levi. Psalm 110:4, which speaks of the eternal priesthood of the order of Melchizedek, is drawn upon to argue that God has provided another priesthood that is superior to the Levitical priesthood; through the latter, being inferior, it is therefore not possible to attain perfection (7:11-21).

The New Covenant and Its Worship of God (8:1–10:39)

This part combines two of the typical dualisms of Hebrews: the historical one of "old covenant" and "new covenant" and the geographical one of the spatially conceived "heavenly image" and its "earthly copy."

For the first contrast, Hebrews refers to Jeremiah 31:31-34, where God promises a new covenant whose people have the Torah written on their hearts, where each one of them knows God and all sins are forgiven. This promise of the new covenant that has no cultic resonances in Jeremiah is integrated in Hebrews into a cultic frame of reference. The succession from "old" to "new" covenant is interpreted with the help of middle Platonic notions, namely, the contrast of the heavenly image with its earthly copy (Heb 8:5): whereas during the worship of the "old covenant" the Levitical priests entered a sanctuary made by human hands, Christ, through his death, enters into the heavenly sanctuary itself (9:12, 24). The symbolism equates Christ not only with the sacrificing high priest but also at the same time with the sacrificial animal: as the earthly sanctuary is cleansed by the blood of the sacrificial animal, the heavenly sanctuary requires a better sacrifice to be cleansed (9:22). With this once-and-for-all sacrifice, all other earthly sacrifices on earth become unnecessary. The cult of sacrifices has ended. At the same time, the metaphorical use of the concept of sacrifice is opened up as it is found in other Jewish and Christian texts: in Hebrews the praise of God's name, good deeds, and the participation in the community of the faithful are regarded as "sacrifices" (13:15-16).

The underlying philosophical framework is highly problematic from a feminist perspective (Kittredge 1994, 441). The contrast of "heavenly" and "earthly" correlates in such thought with the dualistic differentiation of "male" and "female": the denigration of the earthly then tends to go hand in hand with the denigration of the "feminine" as well. Hebrews does not make this identification explicitly, but it is there implicitly in the male image of "sons" used to depict Christian existence (see above): femininity has no symbolic space in salvation. The christological concept in Hebrews has been interpreted in diverse ways by feminist theologians. Mary Rose D'Angelo detects feminist traits in the text. She argues that the understanding of Christ as the high priest excludes any perception of Christian office based on "flesh and blood" criteria like race, gender, and class. Moreover, the reestablishment of different classes of priests in Christian churches is fundamentally questionable in view of the emphasis Hebrews places on the "once-

and-for-all" nature of Christ's saving act (D'Angelo 1992). While the assumed end of the cult of sacrifice and the metaphorical or rather spiritual redefining of the terminology of sacrifice in Hebrews are often interpreted positively, Hildegard Cancik-Lindemaier (1991) evaluates this differently: the metaphorical redefinition of the term "sacrifice" is more problematic than actually existing cults of sacrifice: only when animal sacrifices ceased to exist could (within Christianity) the discourse of sacrifice assume prominence and give religious legitimacy to any kind of socially desired acts of "sacrifice" or renunciation.

European and American white female theologians in particular have criticized the christological conception of Christ's sacrificial death as necrophilia, as belittling violence and glorifying suffering (cf. Strobel 1991). As the history of reception shows, the idea of the representative sacrifice has served to stabilize hegemonic structures of power and inequality by channeling violence and by protecting the powerful from the protest of the oppressed (Schüssler Fiorenza 1995, 106). The description of Christ's suffering as obedience to the Father has been called "child abuse by the divine" by Rita Nakashima Brock, who points out that this serves as a symbolic framework legitimizing violence toward women and children. Schüssler Fiorenza (1995, 105) explicitly mentions Hebrews as a negative example of a biblical text that clothes in theological and christological garb the suffering and victimization that are the result of kyriarchal structures of violence. Luise Schottroff asks whether the theology and Christology of Hebrews have to be criticized as "theology of power" and whether the text is a "building block in the building of church hierarchy and societal brutality" (Schottroff 1990, 135). However, she then asserts that it can be read positively as an answer to the experience of suffering of the members of the early church (as can be seen in early Christian martyr narratives): the image of Christ as the almighty and all-encompassing ruler and, at the same time, his human despair and fear of death can become a foundation for courage and hope. In a different context, without concrete links to Hebrews, Schottroff points out that the christological interpretation of the cross embodies a process of appropriation and reversal. While the Roman state uses the cross as an instrument of oppression, Jesus' followers turn this around: they turn the sign of oppression into the sign of their power. Schottroff sees this appropriation as a result of extreme pressure, and she disagrees with the feminist critique that sees an infatuation with "blessed suffering" in this. "What is not seen is that the Roman Empire with its strategy of violent oppression of the nations really does not allow for other ways to express that such lack of freedom and disdain for human beings could no longer be borne. Martyrdom could have been avoided but the price to pay would have been approval of this brutality. One could either be in the ranks of the arena — howling with the mob — or down with the animals" (Schottroff 1996, 111). In this view the theology of the cross provides strength through God's solidarity in suffering and thus serves to provide strength and courage in times of massive political pressure and personal danger.

In my view, one has to distinguish with Schottroff between the reception history of the theology of the cross in the church and the Second Testament interpretation of these texts within their original contexts. However, one should not expect the New Testament texts to be free from androcentrism and misogyny.

The language of Hebrews is by no means positive encouragement throughout. In the added parenetic piece of 10:19-39, following the christological part, one finds — as in 6:4-8 — language invoking threat and fear: for those who have come to know Christ and still fall away from him, there is no salvation, but punishment in God's judgment: "It is a fearful thing to fall into the hands of the living God" (10:31). Hebrews thus creates fear in order to get the addressees to stand firm in the face of the pressure in Roman society to conform and to fear the rulers (cf. de Silva 1996, 116). The text tries to make the addressees immune to the judgment of society that claims that Jesus' death on the cross and the act of following him are a disgrace. Hebrews does this by turning the terms "disgrace" and "honor" on their heads: what is regarded as honor in the eyes of society is disgrace in God's eyes, and what is disgraceful in societal terms is honorable in God's eyes. The text thus develops an alternative model of honor and disgrace that is contrary to society's norms. This is elucidated in the last part of the sermon about faith and Christian existence as a journey.

The Way of Faith (11:1–13:22)

The whole eleventh chapter (11:1-40) is an essay on faith. It is defined initially as "the assurance of things hoped for, the conviction of things not seen" (11:1). This stance is then exemplified with a long series of instances from the history of Israel. The exemplary witnesses of faith share that they only act upon the promises of God and that they are willing to give up worldly security and approval. Abraham, Isaac, and Jacob were wanderers living in tents. The related terms used here, "strangers and foreigners" *(xenoi* and *parepidēmoi),* indicate a lower social status than that of citizens. They give up the honor of worldly citizenship in order to testify that God has provided them with a heavenly home (11:10, 14-16).

Particularly obvious is the contrast between worldly and godly honor in the example of Moses. He forsakes the honor of being the son of Pharaoh's daughter and rather shares the misery of the Israelites because he "considered abuse suffered for the Christ to be greater wealth than the treasures of Egypt" (11:26).

Two women are mentioned by name in the list of the faithful: Sarah, because she trusted God's promise of a child, and Rahab, because she offered hospitality to Israeli spies. Moreover, it says, in summing up: "Women received their dead by resurrection. Others were tortured, refusing to accept release, in order to obtain a better resurrection" (11:35) — referring probably to the martyrdom of the seven brothers and their mother in 2 Maccabees 7.

The inclusion of women in this list of people of faith has been regarded as noteworthy by Ruth Hoppin, who sees this as a possible indication of the female authorship of Hebrews. But if one considers the significance of women in First Testament stories, particularly those of the primordial-parent narratives (Gen 12–50), then this inclusion is not surprising. Rather, many of those figures have been left out (cf. D'Angelo 1992). In addition, there seems to be a linguistic masculinization of the female figures: the text expresses the fact that Sarah, despite her age, will bear a child because of God's promise, in masculine terms, *dynamis eis katabolēn spermatos,* "power to eject sperms." The phrase here is the antique technical term for ejaculation. There are some biological theories from antiquity about a female ejaculation (cf. van der Horst 1996), but for the interpretation of this text a theological tradition, following Genesis 18:11, is more useful than this biological one. According to that text, "it had ceased with Sarah after the manner of women," suggesting menopause. Philo has interpreted this in such a way that Sarah — who stands for virtue and true knowledge in his allegorical exegesis (Philo, *Legum allegoriae* 3.244f.) — has become "virginal" and thus "masculine" (Philo, *De posteritate Caini* 134; *Quaestiones et solutiones in Genesin* 4.15; cf. also D'Angelo 1992). In Paul's typological exegesis, Galatians 4:21-26, Sarah's motherhood is spiritualized as being "according to the promise" and contrasted with Hagar's motherhood "according to the flesh." Thus, there is a theological tradition that reads Sarah's recovered fertility in a figurative sense as "spiritual fertility," which in Hebrews seems to require masculine metaphors.

In Hebrews 12 and 13, the parenetic consequences are drawn from the examples of faithful followers; starting with the imagery of a race in 12:1-3: because of the "cloud of witnesses" (12:1), present female and male followers need to run with perseverance and look to Jesus, who ran ahead. Before discussing the concrete ethical admonitions for everyday life in 13:1-17, 12:4-11 again suggests reasons for the addressees to stand firm in the face of threats and persecutions. It interprets their suffering as the kind of chastisement that God bestows only on "legitimate" sons. Here, too, the intent clearly is to find theological meaning in extremely negative experiences: suffering particularly can thus be understood as a sign of participation in salvation. This argument bases itself on a fatherly educational praxis that quite naturally includes the notion of punishment. Similarly, the patriarchal differentiation between legitimate and illegitimate children (12:8: *nothoi,* children out of wedlock) is presupposed and serves as the theological representation of the relationship between God and Christians (cf. D'Angelo 1992). Within the argument of Hebrews, this serves to encourage and affirm those among the addressed who are persecuted and humiliated. In church history these kinds of statements have poisoned the image of God by portraying God in the image of a father whose love is inseparably intertwined with violence. Such theological imagery has to be rejected today and thoroughly scrutinized in view of its effects throughout history of supporting domestic violence of fathers and husbands.

The metaphors of sacrifice and punishment in Hebrews portray poignantly the theological problem of the "dark side of God": In what way can one think of the experience of injustice and suffering as part of God's work? Feminist exegesis and theology have rightly criticized traditional Christian responses to this question because they tend to degrade God to a violent demon. On the other hand, the theological attempt to bring the experience of injustice and suffering into a connection with God can, when done by those who suffer under them, be an important step against resignation and thus function as an act of survival. But such theological assertions highly risk being easily perverted; they reflect unmistakably the contextuality and confessional nature of every form of God language. When these assertions become generalized and contextless dogmatism, they congeal into the language of hierarchy — against their original intent.

LITERATURE

Cancik-Lindemaier, Hildegard. 1991. "Opfersprache. Religionswissenschaftliche und religionsgeschichtliche Bemerkungen." In *Schrift der Flammen. Opfermythen und Weiblichkeitsentwürfe im 20. Jahrhundert,* edited by Gudrun Kohn-Waechter, 38-56. Berlin.

Casey, Juliana. 1980. *Hebrews.* Wilmington, Del.

D'Angelo, Mary Rose. 1992. "Hebrews." In *The Women's Bible Commentary,* edited by Carol A. Newsom and Sharon H. Ringe, 364-67. London and Louisville.

De Silva, David A. 1994. "Despising Shame: A Cultural-Anthropological Investigation of the Epistle to the Hebrews." *Journal of Biblical Literature* 113:439-61.

―――. 1996. "Exchanging Favor for Wrath: Apostasy in Hebrews and Patron-Client Relationships." *Journal of Biblical Literature* 115:91-116.

Feld, Helmut. 1985. *Der Hebräerbrief.* Erträge der Forschung, vol. 228. Darmstadt.

Grässer, Erich. 1990. *An die Hebräer.* Evangelisch-katholischer Kommentar, vol. 17, 1-3. Zurich, Braunschweig, and Neukirchen-Vluyn.

Harnack, Adolf von. 1990. "Probabilia über die Adresse und den Verfasser des Hebräerbriefs." *Zeitschrift für die neutestamentliche Wissenschaft und die Kunde der älteren Kirche* 1:16-41.

Hopkins, Julie. 1993. *Towards a Feminist Christology: Jesus of Nazareth, European Women, and the Christological Crisis.* Kampen.

―――. 1996. *Feministische Christologie. Wie Frauen heute von Jesus reden können.* Mainz.

Hoppin, Ruth. 1969. *Priscilla, Author of the Epistle to the Hebrews and Other Essays.* New York.

Kittredge, Cynthia B. 1994. "Hebrews." In *Searching the Scriptures,* edited by Elisabeth Schüssler Fiorenza, 2:428-52. 2 vols. New York.

Lehne, Susanne. 1990. *The New Covenant in Hebrews.* Journal for the Study of the New Testament: Supplement Series, vol. 44. Sheffield.

Schottroff, Luise. 1990. "Christus der versuchte Bruder. Hebräerbrief 2,10-18." In Luise Schottroff and Dorothee Sölle, *Hannas Aufbruch. Aus der Arbeit feministischer Befreiungstheologie. Bibelarbeiten, Meditationen, Gebete.* Gütersloh.

———. 1994. *Lydias ungeduldige Schwestern. Feministische Sozialgeschichte des frühen Christentums.* Gütersloh.

———. 1995. *Lydia's Impatient Sisters: A Feminist Social History of Early Christianity.* Louisville.

———. 1996. "Kreuz, Opfer und Auferstehung Christi. Geerdete Christologie im Neuen Testament und in feministischer Spiritualität." In *Ihr aber, für wen haltet ihr mich? Auf dem Weg zu einer feministisch-befreiungstheologischen Revision von Christologie,* edited by Renate Jost and Eveline Valtink, 102-23. Gütersloh.

Schüssler Fiorenza, Elisabeth. 1995. *Jesus: Miriam's Child, Sophia's Prophet; Critical Issues in Feminist Christology.* London.

Strobel, Regula. 1991. "Feministische Kritik an traditionellen Kreuzestheologien." In *Vom Verlangen nach Heilwerden. Christologie in feministisch-theologischer Sicht,* edited by Doris Strahm and Regula Strobel, 52-64. Fribourg and Lucerne.

Van der Horst, Pieter W. 1996. "Sarah's Seminal Emission: Hebrews 11.11 in the Light of Ancient Embryology." In *A Feminist Companion to the Hebrew Bible in the New Testament,* edited by Athalya Brenner, 112-34. Sheffield.

Vanhoye, Albert. 1979. "Literarische Struktur und theologische Botschaft des Hebräerbriefs." *Studien für die Neue Testament Umwelt* 4:119-47.

———. 1980. "Literarische Struktur und theologische Botschaft des Hebräerbriefs." *Studien für die Neue Testament Umwelt* 5:19-49.

———. 1985. "Hebräerbrief." In *Theologische Realenzyklopädie,* 14:494-505. Berlin.

Wagener, Ulrike. 1995. "'Ihr sollt mir Söhne und Töchter sein.' Die Bedeutung von familiärer und häuslicher Symbolik für die Ethik der Geschlechterdifferenz frühchristlicher Schriften." In *Und drinnen waltet die züchtige Hausfrau. Zur Ethik der Geschlechterdifferenz,* edited by Helga Kuhlmann, 112-23. Gütersloh.

Translated by Tina Steiner

James: Conflict about the Way of Justice

Irene Dannemann

The letter of James is a record of theological discussions in early Christian churches at the end of the first century. The text shows a precise knowledge of the Greek translation of the Hebrew Bible, the Septuagint (LXX), which was holy scripture for the authors of James. James grapples with the theology of people who appeal to Paul and with the way life was being lived in the churches.

From the perspective of genre, the letter of James is a "written intervention" (Ahrens 1995, 73). The only thing that points to the letter form is the beginning in James 1:1, the greeting to "the twelve tribes in the Dispersion," the address to several churches outside Palestine that are part of the Jewish tradition.

It is not possible to provide a precise location for James. The clash with merchants or people engaged in business possibly presupposes a city environment, but the defense of farm workers indicates that agricultural work is part of the experience of the churches addressed. The Greek language points to the eastern part of the Roman Empire, thus to Syria, Asia Minor, or Egypt, perhaps also Greece.

It remains unclear who wrote the letter. It is in any case clear that it is not actually by Jesus' brother James himself. The author could have been an individual man, a scribe, a teacher standing within the Jewish tradition, or a woman or group rooted in this tradition. As Standhartinger conclusively shows for the letter to the church in Colossae (→ Colossians), it would accord with the understanding of authorship in antiquity if a group of authors put themselves in this apostle's tradition by alleging that the document originated with James. James was written in the first century, after the Pauline letters, perhaps between 70 and 100 C.E. (Paulsen 1987, 492).

James does not argue directly with Paul's letters themselves; rather, in a later period, the letter battles with people who appeal to Paul and to his authority. Whether these people live in churches founded by Paul, thereby giving us in James a picture of the later history of the Pauline churches, or whether the people lived elsewhere, Paul's ideas having reached them in written or oral form, cannot be decided (Laws 1980, 16-18). James attests the diversity used by early Christianity to settle on its theological emphases and shape the Christian life.

Numerous sayings in James go back to Jesus. In some cases these diverge significantly from the Gospel traditions, especially from Matthew. Particularly clear are the differences with respect to the prohibition against oaths in James 5:12, in contrast to Matthew 5:34-37, as well as in the comment that you will not get what you pray for if you ask wrongly (James 4:3, in contrast to Matt 7:7). Sometimes similar themes are presented in a totally different form, as, for example, the relationship between hearing and doing in James 1:22, in contrast to Matthew 7:21, 24-27, and the warning to the rich in James 5:1-6, in contrast to Matthew 6:19-24. In James we have a record of the orally transmitted Jesus tradition that is independent of the written tradition found in the Gospels, especially in Matthew (Laws 1980, 223-24).

It is difficult to reconstruct the story of women from James, since only a few of the aspects of a woman's life are treated. Only James 1:27; 2:15, 25; and 4:4 mention women explicitly: widows, sisters, the prostitute Rahab, and adulteresses. We learn hardly anything about the women in the churches to which James is addressed.

All the way through, James refers to the people in the churches as "brothers." I am replacing this address with "brothers and sisters," since it is not the men alone who are addressed; rather, we have here a typically androcentric formulation.

The interpretation that follows is dependent on the interpretive work of Professor Elsa Tamez, who teaches in Costa Rica. Its intention is to induce the reader, after a first reading of the letter, to read it once again, the second time organized thematically. This can disabuse the reader of the impression that James is just a stringing together of a bunch of unrelated themes.

The Description of Oppression

Four groups of oppressed people are described in James: widows and orphans (1:27), farm workers (5:1-12), the poor (2:5-6, 15), and the baptized (2:7). Widows and orphans are mentioned together in James 1:27, as they are in the Hebrew Bible (e.g., Exod 22:22; Deut 14:29; 24:17, 19; 27:19; Isa 1:17). The concept of widow in this traditional Jewish combination refers to women without husbands (W. Schottroff 1992, 59-62) who have also done significant work in the church, for example, caring for orphans (L. Schottroff 1990, 230). The widows, who are predominantly poor, are not to be excluded but cared for: *episkeptomai* refers to giving them comprehensive care, not just paying them visits. The widows themselves are not addressed here but appear exclusively as the objects of care provided by others.

The extremely difficult economic situation of orphans in ancient society is obvious. Their care by the church, particularly by the widows, incorporates them into a new family and possibly protects them against becoming slaves. The church is to see to the social integration of orphans and widows, that is, to include them in their community both materially and spiritually.

James 5:1-6 complains against the injustice of depriving those who harvest the crops of their wages. Women have also participated in the harvesting of grain (W. Schottroff 1996, 25). The cries of those withheld wages and of those defrauded of their wages (cf. Deut 24:15) have come before the ears of God like the blood of Abel (Gen 4:10). God is by no means indifferent to this cry. As in Genesis 4, God will actively intervene, and James 2:1-4 summons the addressees to do the same: "Don't give seats of honor in your assembly to those wearing gold rings and fine clothing while you make those with dirty clothing stand off in the corner." The term "assembly" *(synagōgē)* shows how closely Jewish and Christian congregations were still bound together at that time. The expression has an enigmatic significance: it means the assembly of the church for any reason whatsoever (Laws 1980, 99-102), not only their coming together to render justice on issues within the community (against Ahrens 1995, 113-16). All gatherings of the church are to be organized so that the way people are seated does not mirror social distinctions (as Mark 10:35-45 also indicates). James 2:6 reproaches the addressees for despising *(atimazein)* the poor. This is reminiscent of Proverbs 14:21:

> Those who despise their neighbors are sinners,
>> but happy are those who are kind to the poor.

James 2:6 then compares what the church members are doing with what they have experienced: How can you despise the poor? "Is it not the rich who oppress you? Is it not they who drag you into court?" James calls on the addressees to remember that they themselves experience contempt and injustice, since they are powerless against the rich. James 2:5 bases the criticism of the dismissive attitude toward the poor on the fact that those who have nothing have been chosen by God (the destitute, *ptōchoi,* in James 2:2-3, 5-6; cf. L. Schottroff 1978, 26-28).

James 2:15-16 takes up the situation in which "a brother and a sister" (that is, men and women who are members of the church) have no clothing and not enough to eat, while the church ignores its self-evident task of providing them with food and clothing (cf. Matt 25:35-36; Acts 2:44-47). In the light of James's customary usage, the explicit mention of sisters is uncommon and thus striking. It is probably easiest to explain by the assumption that the poverty of the church's women members was especially noticeable (Tamez 1994, 384). James's criticism that the church speaks a blessing over those who are hungry and exposed to the freezing cold ("Go in peace"), without actually doing anything to relieve their poverty, ties in with the social welfare work in early Christian and Jewish congregations (L. Schottroff 1990, 229-42) and shows that this diaconal activity was not self-evident and enduring but had to be taken up again and again.

To denounce the disputes, the pursuit of pleasure, a false attitude toward God, and arrogance in the churches, James 4:4 uses the image of adulterers (*moichalides;* cf. Matt 12:39 and parallels). This calls to mind Ezekiel 16, in which Jerusalem appears as one who has broken the vows of her marriage with God, who has prostituted herself with other gods. James 4:4 polemically uses the image of the whoring wife as a horrifying picture designed to devalue completely an attitude to life, to prayer, and to God that it opposes. By using society's negative attitude toward prostitutes and toward wives who also engage in sexual relationships outside of marriage, this stereotypical image has the effect of evoking hostility toward women.

The addressees also experience injustice when the rich "blaspheme the excellent name that was invoked over you" (2:7). When God's name is spoken over people, they are declared to be God's possession (Deut 28:10; Amos 9:12; Isa 43:7; Jer 14:16) and are seen to be blessed by God (Num 6:27). In James 2:7 the baptismal practice of invoking the name of Jesus on those being baptized probably shines through. Public blaspheming *(blasphēmeō)* of Christians signifies a deadly danger for them, possibly leading to an accusation, a demand to confess, and even execution (cf. Dannemann 1996, 223-33).

Those who are doing business and the rich are named as the oppressors, and the role of women in these groups is barely visible any longer: merchants or those engaged in business who move into the city, want to make a profit, and brag about their success are criticized in James 4:13-17 with the comment that this success can evaporate in an instant. James directs against them a criticism similar to that which Luke 12:13-21 levels at the rich grain growers.

James 5:1-6 says about the expensive clothing and the gold and silver of the rich *(plousioi)* that they will not endure and that they are not treasured in the sight of God (cf. Matt 6:19-21). That the rich live lavishly, withhold the wages of those harvesting the crops, drag people into court (as in James 2:6), and see to it that those doing justice are condemned (at times unto death) is unjust in the eyes of God. By introducing the perspective of God's judgment, James alludes to the experience that justice is not, or not always, achieved in this world. James points out that that does not mean God condones injustice. The focus on the day of judgment is meant to inspire the poor to have hope: God's judgment will not allow the rich and their unrighteous activity to escape unpunished — it will catch up with them. The injustice will not go unpunished.

The Meaning of All This for Real-Life Situations

Poverty was a real problem in the churches. The members included widows, orphans, and people who could not adequately clothe or feed themselves (1:27; 2:15-16). But not everyone was this poor. Some (we cannot say how many) looked down their noses at those without means (2:1-6) and had at least enough to clothe and feed the desperately poor (2:15-16). But in comparison with the really rich, they were also poor; in court they didn't have a chance against them. The lowly (*tapeinos* in 1:9-10; cf. 4:6; see below) belonged to the church, but the rich to whom they were contrasted probably did not. The position of the ones who harvested the crops (5:1-6) remains unclear. Those with beautiful clothes come into the church, are a part of it, or wish to be (2:1-4). Outside of the church are the rich, who take the poor to court or blaspheme them publicly (2:6-13). But they could belong to a different church that is in a controversy with the addressees, a controversy so severe that they are the fiercest of enemies. This picture is unusual, although Acts of Thecla 11–14 says that former coworkers of Paul participated in the accusations against him because they were not in agreement with his preaching.

The rich landowners who were the objects of the prophetic accusations in 5:1-6 and the merchants in 4:13-17 probably were not among those to whom James was addressed. But the merchants and the rich in 2:5-7 could have been members of another Christian church (Tamez 1994, 386-87). The picture emerges from all this that the social structure of the churches James is addressing was not uniform: they were made up of those without possessions and those on the bottom end of the social scale as well as of those who were despised and treated as though they did not have equal rights. The really rich probably were not members, but they were possibly part of other Christian or Jewish groups who did not live with the addressees in friendly coexistence or solidarity. Thus we find in James possible indications of the existence of mutually hostile churches located in the same place.

Militant Patience

James protests injustice and indicates that it will come to an end: God stands on the side of the poor and oppressed. God has chosen them (2:5), hears the cries of the defrauded harvest workers (5:4). The lowly *(tapeinos)* are given God's grace (4:6 quotes Prov 3:34; cf. Luke 1:52; 2 Cor 7:6). They and not the rich are the ones who should boast (James 1:9-12). By means of divine judgment this God is the guarantor of the hope that oppression will end and with it the cries of the victims (5:1-9).

According to James, "militant patience" is to be the fundamental attitude toward life (Tamez 1991, 99; 1994, 389): people are not to become lethargic, apathetic, and passive. And yet they are to accept the wisdom that they cannot change everything, and, with confidence in God, they are also to endure severe suffering (1:5-6). As examples of those who endured a similar fate, James 5:10-11 offers the suffering and the patience of the prophets (cf. Matt 5:12) and of Job. They remained steadfast and did not turn away from God, and God turned to them, full of compassion and mercy. Militant patience does not mean to accept all injustice apathetically or to give up. It is a patience that awaits the right moment, in order once again to spring into action.

The eschatological perspective of gaining the crown of life for a patient and just way of life (James 1:9-12; 2:5) not only depicts an image of hope that lies ahead on the horizon but also offers a present reality. A good, long-lasting life is not only promised for the hereafter, but it can already begin today: in the doing of justice, if people make love of the neighbor the basis of their existence (2:5, 8). Christians should live with the attitude of militant patience: like one who tills the land (*geōrgos,* like the landowner who planted a vineyard in Matt 21:33-41; cf. W. Schottroff 1996, 32-36), they are to wait for the precious crop from the earth and for rain. They should keep on sowing, free of doubt, not caught up in mutual complaining. God's judgment will become for them the perfect harvest (James 5:7-9). With the idea about the coming of Jesus at God's judgment, James is telling the addressees that they must give an account of their deeds before God. In the light of their present reality, in which many attempts at just action fail and in which they are not consistently supported by others, the perspective of judgment is meant to encourage them. To hope for justice and to enlist oneself in its cause is not based on the successes of those engaged in the struggle but in the will of God. Therefore people should not give up but keep on striving, like the farmers who keep on tilling the fields every year. And into God's hands can be placed whatever cannot be brought to completion.

Prayer as an Expression of Unflagging Endurance

James describes prayer as basic to the life of Jewish-Christian communities. Prayer signifies the cry of the defrauded (5:4), signifies people drawing near to God after they have cleansed their hands and purified their hearts (4:7-10). Insufficient trust in God and selfishness are criticized by James 1:6-8 and 4:3-4 as attitudes that doom prayers to failure. That the elders *(presbyteroi)* of the church visit the sick, pray over them, and anoint them with oil in the name of God (5:13-15) does not in any special way lay emphasis on the people holding these offices but serves to lessen the burden and limit the power of the leader of the church. The group of elders has the task of visiting the sick, rather than leaving them alone or even avoiding them. Moreover, James 5:16 says all in the congregation are to confess their sins to and to pray for one another. James 5:16-18 calls for confidence in the effectiveness of prayer, which is greater than we can imagine, and can even work miracles. In prayer people come near to God, God becomes the people's "dear friend," and the church becomes "God's woman-friend" (Tamez 1991, 100).

Concluding Observations

James emphasizes that faith and works belong inseparably together. James 2:20-26 derives this conviction from the Bible by pointing to Abraham and Rahab. According to 2:21-23, Abraham's willingness to sacrifice Isaac (Gen 22) illustrates his God-pleasing action. Thus he becomes the friend of God (James 2:23 combines Gen 15:6 with 2 Chron 20:7 and Isa 41:8). By hospitably welcoming Joshua's two envoys (Josh 2:1-21), the prostitute Rahab shows them her faith, which she confesses in Joshua 2:11. James makes Rahab a model just as much as the patriarch, in this way altering the tradition of the Hebrew Bible, in which Abraham is much more important (cf. the revaluation of Rahab as a progenitrix of Jesus in Matt 1:5). Through the highly original juxtaposition of Abraham and Rahab, with their own theological points (cf. how Paul argues with respect to Abraham in Gal 3 and Rom 4), James 2:24 emphasizes his "not by faith alone": acting justly belongs to faith and to a life pleasing to God. Since Rahab and Abraham did not commit themselves to the God of Israel at the beginning of their lives but only later, James also sees in them a model for people who are just coming to the church (Laws 1980, 138): they can find the way to God by means of righteous deeds.

Convinced that works and faith belong together, James keeps insisting on this in a situation wherein the Pauline hope that righteous deeds will follow faith as a matter of course is no longer manifest in the life of all those Christians who appeal to Paul. James 2:14-26, 3:13-18, and 3:2-12 charge that people are severing the correlation between faith and works that is clearly to be found in the letters of Paul. James's biting statements allow the conclusion that he is polemically raising objections to behavior that is actually occurring. James 2:17 pointedly asserts that a faith without works is dead.

James helps to illustrate how diverse theology looked in early Christianity, with what variety life and faith took shape. The isolated place this writing now occupies in the New Testament canon does not mean that James was not taken seriously in early Christianity. Perhaps at the beginning its interpretation of the central elements of Christian faith and life circulated widely and was very influential (Laws 1980, 20-26, 38). James illustrates that theological and ethical insights and truisms do not always endure: widows and orphans, inadequately clothed and hungry men and women were not effectively supported in all churches. Even the early church had to fight tooth and nail, again and again, to achieve an effective social ministry.

James shows us how time-bound biblical writings are. James takes traditions handed on from the past and applies them to his own time and to churches that are under scrutiny as the document is being written. It raises for us the question of the relationship between faith and justice in our own lives. We cannot hide behind the excuse that we are all sinful and that God will forgive our sins. To counter that view, James stresses that God sees all injustice and is not willing to let it go unnoticed. No, people are going to have to answer for it if in their societies injustice wins.

LITERATURE

Ahrens, Matthias. 1995. *Der Realitäten Widerschein. Oder: Arm und Reich im Jakobusbrief. Eine sozialgeschichtliche Untersuchung.* Berlin.

Dannemann, Irene. 1996. *Aus dem Rahmen fallen. Frauen im Markusevangelium. Eine feministische Re-Vision.* Berlin.

Laws, Sophie. 1980. *A Commentary on the Epistle of James.* Black's New Testament Commentaries. London.

Paulsen, Henning. 1987. "Jakobusbrief." In *Theologische Realenzyklopädie*, 488-95. Berlin.

Schottroff, Luise. 1978. "Den Armen wird das Evangelium gepredigt. Die älteste Tradition über Jesus von Nazareth." In Luise Schottroff and Wolfgang Stegemann, *Jesus von Nazareth*, 9-46. Stuttgart.

———. 1990. "DienerInnen der Heiligen. Der Diakonat der Frauen im Neuen Testament." In *Diakonie — biblische Grundlagen und Orientierungen*, edited by Gerhard K. Schäfer and Theodor Strohm, 222-42. Heidelberg.

Schottroff, Willy. 1992. "Die Armut der Witwen." In *Schuld und Schulden. Biblische Traditionen in gegenwärtigen Konflikten*, edited by Willy Schottroff and Marlene Crüsemann, 54-89. Munich.

———. 1996. "Das Gleichnis von den bösen Weingärtnern (Mk 12,1-9 parr). Ein Beitrag zur Geschichte der Bodenpacht in Palästina." *Zeitschrift des deutschen Palästina-Vereins* 112, no. 1:18-48.

Tamez, Elsa. 1991. "Elemente der Bibel, die den Weg der christlichen Gemeinde erhellen. Eine hermeneutische Übung anhand des Jakobusbriefes." *Evangelische Theologie* 51:92-100.

———. 1994. "James." In *Searching the Scriptures*, edited by Elisabeth Schüssler Fiorenza, 2:381-91. 2 vols. New York.

Translated by Everett R. Kalin

1 Peter: Survival Strategies for Harried Communities

Irene Foulkes

In dealing with a document such as 1 Peter, which reflects and incorporates patriarchal concepts common in Hellenistic society, we will attempt to uncover data within the text, and implications derived from the text, that were significant for women in the communities that first received the letter and also in today's world (cf. commentary on 3:7). Using elements from the text, we will also construct fresh messages, conceived from a feminist perspective (cf. 3:3-4). In this exercise, however, we must take into account our tendency to ethnocentrism and attempt to overcome it by recognizing that social situations similar to those addressed by 1 Peter still exist in many parts of the world, and survival strategies similar to those recommended by this letter may yet be relevant (cf. 3:1-6).

The Author and His Companions

The missionary effort that produced Christian communities in the interior of Asia Minor (1:1) has been associated with Peter and later with a Petrine circle in Rome. Written in Peter's name, this letter mentions colleagues such as "brother" Sylvanus and "son" Mark along with a feminine personage called "the co-elect one in Babylon" (5:12-13). Although many versions gratuitously supply the word "church" as the referent for this enigmatic phrase, the fact that it occurs between the names of two well-known persons raises the question whether the author may indeed be referring to an individual woman, a "sister." If so, we may be justified in taking a clue from Paul's reference to women as companions in missionary journeys: "Do we not have the right to take along a sister as wife, as do the other apostles and the Lord's brothers and Cephas?" (1 Cor 9:5). Since this woman "greets" the recipients of the letter, we may presume that she was already known to them, perhaps, because of having traveled in the region.

Social Status and Christian Women

Certain groups of people are clearly identifiable among the recipients of the letter. Slaves are addressed, but not masters. The term *oiketai* used in 1 Peter 2:18 defines these slaves as workers in the basic economic unit of Hellenistic society, the household *(oikos)*, either a rural estate or an urban production unit. Although slaves are referred to only by generic masculine forms, the presence of slave women in the Christian community is not only a valid inference but is also attested by the well-known letter of Pliny the Younger to the emperor Trajan in 112 C.E. Pliny reports that he has thoroughly investigated the possibility that Christianity was a subversive cult, to the extent of questioning by torture two slave women who were called *ministrae*. It is clear that slave women were welcomed into membership and that neither their sex nor their legal status as slaves constituted a barrier to their functioning in an official capacity within the community.

While most Christians probably represented the lower strata of society, instructions to some women about limiting their indulgence in luxury apparel (3:3-4) suggest that at least a sprinkling of well-off women had joined the Christian community. What would attract women of higher status to an unprestigious group? In the first century, Jewish communities of the diaspora did attract a number of Gentile women, who found there a liberating experience. As a variety of new religious forms and beliefs — Christianity among them — accompanied the widespread movement and mix of peoples in the region, women of means (as well as the general populace) would investigate novel cults, with their promise of communion with a deity and fellowship in a human community. In the dominant sector of society more women than men adopted new religions. For men who exercised power within the established socioeconomic and political structures, it was not in their interest to seek alternative forms of belief or relationships.

Opposition, Antagonism, and Harassment

The basic problem addressed by the letter is the adverse social pressure exercised against believers in an environment hostile to the nonconforming character of the Christian communities. Their withdrawal from peer activities and everyday relations with others (4:4) aroused suspicion and disloyalty (2:13-14) and wrongdoing (2:12). While physical abuse is not mentioned, deviance control mechanisms such as slander and intimidation were used against the believers (3:9, 14, 16; 4:14), who felt threatened by the possibility that open violence might follow. If the Christian faith had taken root largely in a population of resident aliens, as the terms "exiles of the Dispersion" (1:1) and "aliens and exiles" (2:11) may indicate, this dimension of foreignness would have reinforced the suspicions of the local populace. Addressing the anxiety that gripped the Christian community in the face of unjust treatment, the authors aim to strengthen the believers in three areas: their conduct, their theological interpretation of the conflict, and their emotional response to it.

As bearers of the honor of the family or the group, women were particularly singled out for observation, and sharp criticism would target the church if the conduct of women members deviated from the norms of propriety. Reference to traditional codes for the behavior of wives (3:1-6) fits this picture.

If violence should erupt against the Christian community, women would experience it in an additional dimension: sexual violence, almost universally wielded against women apprehended for any type of suspected misdemeanor. The injunction not to be afraid (4:14) would demand of women an additional effort of will and emotional discipline.

Values that strengthen a community under stress are urged on the readers. In-group cohesion must be enhanced by love and service toward each other (4:8-10). Rather than replicating the oppressive attitudes and exploitative actions so common in the rest of society, Christians are to be humble with one another (3:8; 5:5b), and elders responsible for the well-being of the church are not to profit from their charge nor lord it over the group but to lead by personal example (5:1-3). In these exhortations it is not hard to recognize qualities traditionally assigned to women. For the survival and flourishing of the church as it was meant to be (and, by extension, society as it should be), these most human qualities must be fostered in both men and women, not relegated to one gender only. As these passages indicate, the church should be in the forefront of cultural change in this area. At the same time, it is not only the incorporation of these so-called feminine qualities that is essential to the nature of the church but also the recognition that women and men form coequal partnerships, as 3:7 suggests.

An important component for their survival strategy, 1 Peter provides the harried Christians with a theological interpretation of their distress: they "are sharing in Christ's sufferings" (4:13). For centuries women who suffer violence at the hands of husbands, fathers, or other patriarchal figures have been told, supposedly with the authorization of texts such as these, that the only Christian response to their pain is to consider it part of Christ's sufferings and accept it without resistance. Such an interpretation directly contradicts the argument of this letter, which challenges distressed and vulnerable victims of mistreatment to assume a new perspective on this experience that will vindicate their option for Christian faith and enable them to overcome their fear and take on an active role in the face of antagonism (cf. commentary on 3:6b).

The author's reference to "Christ's sufferings" presupposes that these communities are familiar with the traditions of Jesus' life and death. Just as Jesus incurred opposition by announcing and demonstrating the reign of God, Christians in Asia Minor were to realize that their decision to follow Jesus would likewise provoke contradiction. By maintaining this position, both women and men knowingly assumed this consequence, and, to that extent, they were in control of their destiny.

In other words, they were neither hapless victims of their enemies nor helpless pawns of blind fate. By contrast, daughters, wives, and other disenfranchised women victims of male violence today have not made any such choice. They are not in control; violence is inflicted on them simply because the aggressor, by social definition, has the power to treat them violently. (A different situation is envisioned in 2:18-25; see below.)

God the Birther and Nourisher: 1:3; 2:2-3

Referring to God as "Father of our Lord," the author goes on to describe God's relation to Christian believers with maternal imagery: "God has given us a new birth." Although the verb used here can refer to male begetting as well as female birthing, in this verse it depicts the experience of new believers who have been born into the Christian community through God's travail. Even when "seed" is mentioned in connection with new birth (1:23), the metaphor points not to a male progenitor but to "the living word of God." In a vein similar to 1:3, the language of 2:2-3 takes the familiar household scene of a nursing mother and projects it as an image of God as nourisher of newborn believers, infants who will survive and develop only by eagerly feeding on the unadulterated milk offered by the divine Nourisher. Anything less is a threat to survival; the offspring must drink at the breast of God.

"Household Management": 2:18–3:7

Hellenistic moralists stressed the importance of maintaining the hierarchical relation between master and slave, husband and wife, father and children, to insure the proper economic and political functioning of society. The author of 1 Peter incorporates the first of these categories but modifies its form, both by not addressing masters at all and then by speaking directly to the subordinates: slaves and wives. The husband-wife pair appears in reverse order in 3:1-7, and the women addressed are identified as wives of nonbelievers. Instructions for these women echo contemporary documents, while the brief instructions to Christian husbands break new ground.

The letter reflects a situation where people of the subordinate category (slaves, women) have joined a strange new cult on their own initiative, a religious community viewed as potentially subversive because of its emphasis on mutuality, and certainly suspicious because of its demand for exclusive loyalty. The Christian movement called into question the top-down model of strict social control in the patriarchal household, where uniformity of religion, with the choice dictated by the dominant male, was the expected norm.

Interpretation of the domestic code in 1 Peter will to a large extent be determined by one's definition of the overall aim of the letter. What effect does the author attempt to bring about in his audience? Current debate over the author's strategy clarifies the alternatives (cf. Elliott and Balch in Talbert 1986). On the one hand, the submission ethic of the domestic code can be interpreted as a strategy of assimilation to the surrounding culture, that is, some degree of capitulation to non-Christian values and, possibly, the incorporation of those values into the Christian ethos, profoundly altering a previous pattern of more egalitarian relations. Women decry the fact that the Christian church assumed a hierarchical model very early in its history.

An alternative interpretation proposes that the submissive behavior enjoined here is only part of the picture. At the same time that the author wants to help his readers avoid further opposition, he aims at subverting the patriarchal household by introducing new values that unmask its malefic character. He accomplishes this by constructing a new frame of reference — the life and death of Christ — that should enable abused subordinates to discern that God sides with the suffering people and not with oppressive authorities. Instead of passive capitulation to the prevailing power system, we can perceive here an active opposition to evil. In this view, the strategy is twofold: submission is recommended as a survival tactic, but reference to Christ's suffering authorizes victims of patriarchy to condemn it as evil. In this way the author enhances their dignity as persons and thus their prospects for withstanding daily indignities and overt cruelty.

Women who live out their lives in patriarchal systems recognize the expediency motif, knowing that subordinating themselves and their abilities to power figures is often the only way to have any breathing room at all. Whether by personal experience or by observation, we have learned that despotic control over other persons is evil, but seldom has this knowledge been bolstered by exegesis. From elements in 1 Peter, however, a hermeneutical criterion has emerged that enables women to perceive and oppose the evils of patriarchal power systems: the life and death of Christ.

Slave Women and Sexual Servitude: 2:18-25

Because a slave woman's body was owned by her master, her sexuality also belonged to him. Slave women and young boys were required to provide sexual services not only for their owner but also for any other male that he would designate. Assigning slaves to serve as prostitutes was also common practice. When the sexual degradation and pain imposed gratuitously on slaves are brought to light, we can focus on the proposed parallel of Christ's endurance of unjustly inflicted suffering (2:19-21) in a new way, overcoming the limits of interpretations that attribute only male experiences to the Christ figure. An integral part of the human condition assumed by Christ is the sexual servitude imposed on women.

Solidarity in Suffering: 2:20-25

Slaves who conduct themselves correctly and yet suffer battering are told to follow the example of Christ: not having done any wrong, he endured defiance without defiance. Often interpreted as a justification for requiring submission, this text has been preached by power figures to disenfranchised people, including women, as God's plan for them. Agents of the church have willfully ignored the fact that 1 Peter speaks not from power but from the underside of society, where slaves — human beings with no human rights — struggled to survive in a political and economic system that afforded absolutely no hope of change. By converting this last-resort counsel into divine design for all time, Christian interpreters have perpetuated the dehumanization of women and men trapped in no-escape situations. After denouncing this fatal error, however, we must still respond to the suffering of people so ensnared today. In contrast to Christ, whose determined opposition to dehumanizing religious structures provoked their deadly reprisal, these women and men, like the slaves before them, have exercised no choice; the violence they undergo is gratuitous. Only in such extreme cases is reference to the suffering Christ an option, and only for the purpose of strengthening the victim's survival capacity by affirming Christ's solidarity with her. (On the sacrificial theology of 2:24, see commentary on Rom 3:21-26.)

Submission and Independence: 3:1-6

The women addressed here are those whose husbands are not Christians. Exhorting these women to adopt the subordinate behavior demanded by their society, the author suggests that such exemplary conduct might contribute to the husbands' conversion. However, these wives must not forfeit their independence from their husbands in the area of religious adherence, even though wives are expected to submit to their husbands' gods only. In many parts of the world at present, Christian women face reprimands and threats from their husbands, stemming from the suspicion they and other guardians of female morality and male honor cast on a woman who defies convention by declaring religious independence. These women counsel each other to defuse suspicion by adopting model wifely behavior: give in to all other demands and show due deference to the "head of the house." With this conflict-avoidance strategy they attempt to buy a small space for their religious practice, and hope their spouse might look more positively on the Christian message. But success is not guaranteed, so the women urge each other not to be intimidated, not to be afraid.

When the author exhorts women to forgo elaborate hairdos, gold jewelry, and expensive clothes (see comment above on social status), he again echoes his non-Christian contemporaries. Their common concern is that decent wives not bring dishonor to their husbands by appearing to want attention from other men. Repudiating the concept of women as men's property and showcases for a husband's honor, we find elements in this text that can contribute to a fresh, liberating message for women. Consumer culture defines the female body as an object to be shaped, exhibited, and exploited. Invading a woman's own concept of her self/her body, the constant media onslaught causes many women to think of themselves as objects to be adorned and displayed, particularly for men. As women we can reject this depersonalization and claim our right to be agents, not objects, and to conceive of our bodies as the means for carrying out self-directed action in the world. The author of this letter urged women to develop their own personal qualities; women today can claim, as God-given, this esteem for the selfhood of women, this positive assessment of women as persons.

A cryptic reference to "holy women of long ago" (1 Pet 3:5) suggests that stories of Israelite heroines circulated in some form within early Christian circles. We rightfully wonder whether women in the churches were able to do any "rereading" of these stories from their own point of view and for their own needs. An example: the author proposes Sarah as a model of wifely obedience (3:6), but such a role is hardly supported by an attentive reading of the Genesis story. Ironically, in citing her reference to Abraham as "lord" (Gen 18:12), the author ignores the fact that this word is embedded in a derogatory remark about him. The Genesis narrative reveals that relations in this ancient family were far from exhibiting the submission-to-authority model being urged on Christian wives.

Husbands, Cohabit as Coheirs: 3:7

In addressing Christian husbands, the author puts an entirely different focus on the marriage relationship, defying the authority/submission pattern. Two compound words stand out: husband and wife should live-together as heirs-together. These lexical novelties underscore the cultural novelty of a relationship in which men must give honor to the socially defined "weaker" partner, women. More than egalitarian, this relationship takes into account, and compensates for, the social inequality inherent in patriarchal society. The solidarity ethic urged on the community as a whole is thus applied to its most intimate unit in a way that transforms its usual character. Only this kind of transformation would back up the use of "household" as a symbol for the community of the Spirit (1 Pet 2:5), the household of God (4:17). (Cf. Russell 1987, 36-41.)

A key concept in first-century social relations, honor has been defined as the "social acknowledgement of worth" (Malina 1981, 27), that is, the value that a person has in the eyes of others. This type of social ranking was of prime importance in Greco-Roman society, and constant effort was expended by individuals and families to acquire more honor. Because persons of power were in a position to grant honor to another person, the power figure in a marriage — the husband — is instructed to use his advantage to increase the status of his partner, not just in their personal relationship but also in the public eye. The concluding remark of 3:7, "so that nothing may hinder your prayers," adds a stunning, transcendent dimension to this requirement of social transformation: a man's communion with God depends on his achieving a relationship of equality with his wife.

Conclusion

Addressed to harassed and vulnerable communities, 1 Peter stresses survival strategies, some of which reflect the subordinate position of women. A feminist hermeneutic requires that such teaching be understood as part of a specific first-century context and condemns its conversion into a paradigm for all times and places. The theme of Christ's acceptance of suffering must not be used as an argument that would require women to submit to violent treatment. On the contrary, this historical pointer highlights Jesus' active solidarity with the victims of oppression and his denunciation of the evil inherent in patriarchal structures. Within the Christian community, the letter proposes some liberating elements for women, as in the instruction to husbands that promotes a more equal relationship in marriage. Other aspects of the letter, such as the birthing and nourishing metaphors, spur us to pursue new feminine figures for God.

Literature

Achtemeier, Paul J. 1996. *I Peter*. Hermeneia Commentary. Minneapolis.

Balch, David H. 1981. *Let Wives Be Submissive: The Domestic Code in 1 Peter*. Chico, Calif.

Campbell, Barth L. 1998. *Honor, Shame, and the Rhetoric of 1 Peter*. Atlanta.

Malina, Bruce J. 1981. *The New Testament World: Insights from Cultural Anthropology*. Atlanta.

Russell, Letty. 1987. *Household of Freedom: Authority in Feminist Theology*. Philadelphia.

Russell, Letty, and J. Shannon Clarkson. 1996. *Dictionary of Feminist Theologies*. Louisville.

Talbert, Charles H., ed. 1986. *Perspectives on First Peter*. Macon, Ga.

2 Peter: Guideposts for the Godly Life

Irene Foulkes

The author of 2 Peter polemicizes against rival teachers whose doctrine is never defined but whose character and conduct are denounced as scandalous. Called purveyors of heresy (2:1, 14), they are also accused of shameful practices and described as lustful and greedy (2:2-3), insatiable sinners, and slaves of their own adulterous desires (2:14, "eyes full of adultery," i.e., constantly on the lookout for women). Since women are traditionally identified with sex in general, and the sexual sin in particular, this aspect of the polemic demands our attention. While it is men who are attacked here, it is their desire for women that provides grounds for the charges ("ethical misconduct," Bauckham 1983, 255; contra Reicke 1964, 164, "contamination through paganism"). Although the letter nowhere speaks of or to women directly, women are brought in as a negative presence. Centuries of misogyny in Christianity have reinforced this view. Because men continue to treat women as sex objects, we must demand and practice the right to define our own identity as full persons and active subjects, particularly in the church and in relation to religious authority figures.

A catalogue of virtues (1:5-7), similar to lists in Hellenistic popular philosophy, includes qualities that contrast sharply with the patriarchal values that drive people and institutions in the cutthroat world of global capitalism. In the author's eschatological scheme, these qualities are guideposts for the "godly lives" required in the present time (3:11) before the Day of the Lord brings fiery destruction (3:12). In some sense Christian communities thus constitute a foretaste of the renewed creation, to be characterized by justice in all of human society (3:13) that will follow after the fateful day. This utopian vision of 2 Peter can be claimed by women as we strive to live with dignity and promote mutuality and justice in our time.

LITERATURE

Bauckham, Richard J. 1983. *Jude, 2 Peter*. Word Biblical Commentary, vol. 50. Waco, Tex.
Reicke, Bo. 1964. *The Epistles of James, Peter, and Jude*. Anchor Bible. Garden City, N.Y.

Letters of John

Kerstin Ruoff

1 John: Do Not Become Callous . . .

The so-called First Letter of John has little in common with its name: it neither shows itself to be a letter, lacking the classic stylistic elements of that genre, nor designates anyone named John as its author. This writing is actually an anonymous treatise that is strongly dependent, to the point of using individual turns of phrase, on the Gospel of John (→), particularly on the prologue (John 1:1-18) and the farewell discourses (chapters 14–17). Neither sender nor recipients are mentioned; greetings or commendations directed to common acquaintances are lacking, as are references to a prior or an anticipated visit. The document's classification as a letter is tied primarily to the use throughout the document of second-person plural direct address; the joy announced at the beginning (1 John 1:4) also takes up a theme of the classical letter form. Neither manuscript damage nor incongruities in content are present to indicate the forcible removal of names. Rather, the anonymity appears to belong to the literary as well as the theological design of this writing, which will be treated in greater detail (see "A Tradition without Heroes" below).

Nevertheless, already in the earliest list of biblical writings from the New Testament period, the Muratorian Canon (about 200 C.E.), the writing was associated with the name John. Since in antiquity writings were combined in scripture scrolls arranged by author and length, our "letter" has received John's name, as well as its place in the New Testament canon. It is certain that both the letter and the Gospel arose in a church with a common mind-set (cf. O'Day 1992, 374). Yet it is quite unlikely that the three Johannine letters are from the same hand (cf. Hutaff 1994, 406). Contemporaneous with the practical necessity of assigning the writings to a single author for the purpose of bibliographic oversight and preservation, the way the text was read changed through its external assignment to a (male) author. For it unexpectedly ended up in that series of contemporary writings that made use of the pseudepigraphic patronage of a famous authority. Thus the Muratorian

Canon presupposes that we have a direct eyewitness and ear witness of the life of Jesus to thank for the Gospel and first letter. However, it is precisely such authorities and their fragmentation into varied traditions that 1 John, both in form and content, opposes.

In Place of an Obvious Structure

The provisional designation as a "treatise" strengthens expectations of a linear line of thought, which this document fails to satisfy. Again and again it revolves around certain themes without in any way suggesting that it is bringing them to a conclusion, in the sense of having nothing more to say on the subject. Here too, in the modesty of a form that is more occasional and oral, which allows a lot of space for allusions and citations, one can read a theological implication. Apparently our authors find themselves in a dialogue that is not oriented to regulating the community's day-to-day life together, as are broad passages in the Pauline letters, but that endeavors to establish a fundamental consensus about their common faith. That permits the conclusion that the text put forth its message at a time in which the separation between Judaism and the newly emerging Christianity was not complete but still under discussion.

The principal focuses on love, righteousness, and sin, as well as the confession of Jesus as the Christ, which pervade the text, will thus be addressed in the sections that follow. The document's introduction, however, stands apart from the presentation of these themes and merits separate treatment.

With its first words 1 John continues the many-layered interplay between structure and message found in the Gospel with the same name: "what was from the beginning" (1:1) makes use of the words of the prologue with which the Gospel of John opens (John 1:1), in order to present an uninterrupted development from the roots of biblical faith, as we find them in the creation account (Gen 1:1). This is all the more remarkable since exegetes traditionally assign the Johannine community to a Hellenistic milieu, its independence appearing to have been sealed by its exclusion, against its own will, from the synagogue (cf. John 9:22, 34). Countering this view, Luise Schottroff has convincingly explained that the Johannine church bears the stamp of Jewish-Gnostic tradition (Schottroff 1970, 228-96; on 1 John see especially 286-87; Schottroff 1984, especially 97 and 106 n. 16). Thus the first verses make it easier for both groups, Jews and non-Jews, whose separation and coming together are brought to mind in the alternating address to the recipients as "parents" and "children" in 2:12-14, to ally themselves with the writing's message. For with equal right "what was from the beginning" means, along with the foundation laid in Genesis 1:1, the beginning of the Johannine proclamation, "what we have heard, . . . seen, . . . looked at and touched" (1 John 1:1). For their testimony the authors do not refer to the scene between the Risen One and doubting Thomas

(John 20:24-29) that the word "touched" might have called to mind, but to the "*logos* of life." *Logos* is inadequately reproduced by the translation "word," so that it seems more appropriate to use the Greek term. Along with *pneuma* (see 3:24–4:3; 4:6, 13), the concept designates the divine Spirit, a presence of God (also called *hypostasis*), now thought of as male, which takes the place of the feminine *sophia*, wisdom (→ Gospel of John; Wisdom; Proverbs). This *logos* of life is explicitly set at the Father's side (1:2), from whom he went out and revealed himself to the authors. In this formulation knowledgeable contemporaries hear a clear allusion to the wisdom interpretation of Genesis 1 in Proverbs 8:22-31 and Wisdom 8:2-4. At the end of this introductory section, it is made clear that the purpose of the writing's proclamation consists in "having" fellowship with the addressees, which simultaneously includes a fellowship with the Father and with his Son Jesus Christ. The perfect joy in 1:4 is a stylistic element of the letter form, but it also resonates with wisdom overtones, for the recognition of wisdom is accompanied by a life in joy.

Already in this first section, the frames of reference change between the "you" addressed and the "we" doing the writing. As is the case with "our fellowship is with the Father and with his Son Jesus Christ" in 1:3c, it can generally be assumed that the "we" used by the letter's proclaimers also includes the addressees, thereby presupposing their assent.

A Minimum Consensus Is the Greatest Challenge

This external form is especially useful for the intention of the letter since it is striving above all to call the recipients to abide in love (2:5-6, 10, 17, 24, 28; 3:14, 17, 24; 4:12, 16; cf. John 15:4-5), for when that happens Christ is present and, therefore, the Father as well. The model for this is brothers and sisters bound to one another in love (in the masculine designation *adelphoi* for brothers, *adelphai*, "sisters," is self-evidently intended as well, and this should be taken into account in contemporary translations). There is no retreat to be seen here into inwardness, no battening down the hatches against what lies outside. Rather, this requirement presents itself more as mutual regard and tolerance in an obviously tense relationship. Instead of persecuting one another or even trying to kill someone, an issue raised in the reference to Cain (1 John 3:11-12), love between brothers and sisters culminates in being ready to sacrifice life itself for one another (3:16). Viewed so radically, it is a counterpart and an inseparable response to God's love (3:9-11; 4:20-21). The authors preclude the misunderstanding that one could choose like-minded brothers and sisters in the constant address of the recipients as "children" *(teknia)* and simultaneously as beloved *(agapētoi)*, and they also emphasize theologically that the reconciliation they envision includes the entire world (2:2; 4:9-10, 14).

The criterion for love is keeping the commandments (2:3; 5:1-3). What is in

view here, first of all, is the so-called double command of love, which in 5:1 is identified as a self-evident reality. Secondly, this serves as a reminder of the directive
that believers are obliged to keep the law. The promised gift of the Spirit *(pneuma)*
in no way contradicts this but confirms that the obligation is indeed being met
(3:24; 4:13).

For in this way everyone who "does" *(poiein)* righteousness also is numbered
among the children of God (2:29). "Those who are born of God" are further characterized by the fact that they do not sin (3.9; 5:18) but live according to the law
(3:4-10) and confess that Jesus is the Christ (5:1).

The claim of righteous behavior necessarily evokes the question about being
caught up in sin, which is equated with lawlessness *(anomia,* 3:4). All who claim to
be sinless are branded by 1 John as liars, in their own eyes and in God's (1:8-10), so
that attaining perfection by one's own efforts is out of the question. At the same
time, the authors explain that all those who are created by God do not sin (5:18). As
this translation already suggests, the entire creation is spoken of here. Nevertheless, there are also "those who are born of the *diabolos*" (3:7-8); the writing does
not, however, reveal to us how they got that way. Only this much is clear: while
"those who are created/begotten by God" are established in God from the very beginning of their existence, we know nothing about the origin of those who are
born of the *diabolos.* Like Wisdom 1 and 2, 1 John affirms the thoroughgoing goodness of creation, though it can neither deny nor explain the existence of evil. Thus
punishment is not imposed on sin (4:17-21), but it is made the object of intercessory prayer (5:16). To be sure, it is said that there can be a mortal sin, for which an
intercessory prayer is not to be given. But this is neither followed by a call for excommunication nor by a threat about the loss of salvation. The writers also withhold an explanation of the action to which this refers. Taken as a whole, this lack of
clarity shows itself to be intentional.

Since love embraces all those created by God (5:1) and reconciliation applies
to the whole world (4:14), 1 John has no interest in creating a list of virtues (cf., the
contrary approach, the tables of household duties in Col 3:18–4:1 and Eph 5:21–6:9;
→ Pastoral Epistles), for such a list, of necessity, evokes controversy. Righteousness
grows from an attitude that expresses itself in respect for God and the brothers
and sisters.

A Christology of Eloquent Silence

Like the anonymity of the authors, the fact that 1 John nowhere makes a specific
reference to the life of Jesus must also be seen as a theological statement. It is true
that, as in the Pauline letters, Jesus is confessed as and believed to be the Son of
God (1:7; 2:22; 4:15; 5:1, 20). But beyond that we learn nothing about his life and
teaching. There is not even any mention of the resurrection. In its place we have

the promise of eternal life, which the community is already experiencing (2:25; 4:9; 5:11). We encounter the name Jesus solely in the confession formula that he is the Christ or the Son of God, connected with the verbs *homologein* ("agree, acknowledge, confess," 4:15), *pisteuein* ("believe, trust in, acknowledge," 5:1), or *eidenai* ("know, understand," see 5:20). The text withholds all details, even with respect to the basic theological challenges of his scandalous death on the cross and his resurrection. How extraordinarily meager this is can be seen by looking at the Pauline letters (cf. 1 Cor 1:18-29; 15:3-19; Gal 3:13; Phil 2:6-11 and 3:7-12, alluding to Deut 27:26), to say nothing of the Gospels. It is not sufficient to imply that the recipients know the details, making any further elaboration unnecessary, for in the end the proper interpretation of Jesus becomes the stone of stumbling that will later lead to religious separation. Apparently the authors are concerned to show the greatest possible tolerance, to avoid such a separation. They hold firm on the binding nature, for all believers, of the confessions of Jesus as the Christ and as the Son sent by God. Whoever forsakes this fundamental consensus is labeled as the "antichrist" and thus interpreted to be a prophetic sign of the end-time (1 John 2:18, 22; 4:3). We must, of course, be careful to avoid identifying the term with the devil, an identification that did not occur until the Middle Ages. There is no evidence for this in the New Testament period. In the biblical writings the term "antichrist" occurs exclusively in the Johannine letters (see above and 2 John 7). Since it is clearly related to the denial of Christ, it seems to be more helpful to translate the word today "false Christian." This variation preserves the association with the false prophets or "pseudoprophets" (Deut 13:6; 1 Kings 22:21-22; Jer 14:14-16; 23:25-32; Zech 13:2-6). The designation is already found in the polemics in the prophetic writings in the First Testament and can thus be considered a traditional theme. In the New Testament period, it is an essential element of apocalyptic theology and polemics (cf. Matt 24:11, 24; Mark 13:22; 1 Tim 4:1-5; 2 Pet 2:1). As Micah 3:5-11 does with respect to the greed of the clergy, 1 John also stresses that confessing the Father without acting accordingly, in this case by loving all brothers and sisters, is meaningless (3:15-18). Nevertheless, it must be maintained that 1 John threatens no sanctions against those who do not share its confession.

Moreover, the eloquent silence about the appearance of Jesus must be interpreted to mean that the significance of the historical person Jesus and what he did in the past disappears behind a Christology focused on the present. This interpretation is supported by the formulation that Christ has already come in the flesh (4:2). The syntax of the phrase does not place the emphasis on whether Christ has come in the flesh or in some other mode of appearance, but on the declaration that his coming (in the perfect tense) has already occurred, although it has continuing significance for the present (cf. Lieu 1991, 75).

Since the end of the world had not yet occurred, there must have been doubt that Jesus was the Messiah. A way of coming to terms with that was to hope for a return of the Redeemer or to continue to insist that the Messiah had not yet appeared. However, 1 John continues to maintain the view developed in the Gospel of John, that the salvation event, first presented in John as something that is awaited (John 1:9; 6:14), has with Martha's messianic confession (11:27) already become a reality, so that from then on it is spoken of in the perfect tense (12:46; 16:28; 18:37). Thus the Johannine church's hope is not to be sought in a promised messianic future but in the present, which is to be understood as the presence of God (cf. on this the presence of wisdom in the world: Wis 7:27; 8:8; Prov 8:2, 3, 22; Sir 24:6-11).

This certainty allows everyday life to be open to God's intervention. There is confidence in God's help and advocacy (namely, in the *paraklētos,* 1 John 2:1; cf. John 14:16, 26; 15:26; 16:7-15). What's more, the farewell discourses actually demand making requests to God (14:13; 15:7, 16; 16:23-24; similarly, 17:22), since God is thereby glorified or revealed. Let it be noted that in the demand, and in the obvious trust in God this involves, God becomes present and the world is thereby overcome (1 John 5:3-5). Right at the end of the letter the authors take up this ecclesial responsibility by calling to mind the need to ask in a threefold repetition that makes it impossible to ignore (5:14, 15, 16; also already in 3:22). All the variations go back to a quotation of Psalm 2:8, which is also found verbatim in the scene in which Martha makes her messianic confession (John 11:22). While the Synoptic Gospels, in the baptism and transfiguration narratives, take up the traditional adoption formula, "This is my beloved Son" (cf. Matt 3:17; 12:18; 17:5; Mark 1:11; 9:7; Luke 3:22; 9:35; based on Ps 2:7; also Isa 42:1), thereby making Jesus a messianic king, the Johannine church does not apply this title to Jesus and instead puts itself in the place of the one to whom God's promise applies, "Ask of me, and I will give to you" (Ps 2:8). In this way the majestic apex of election is separated from the messianic hope. What remains is the brazen boldness, already now, even here and with precisely this confidence in God, to be God's own partners (cf. 1 John 5:19: "We know that we are God's children").

A Tradition without Heroes: The Strength of the Weak

Instead of the diversity of voices the Gospels represent, in which the different groups and individuals seek to gain a hearing for the appropriate interpretation of Jesus' appearance, the authors of 1 John endeavor to formulate the unifying factors behind this clash of views as the basis for comprehensive and necessary tolerance.

It is in many respects consistent with this that 1 John sends off empty-handed all those who endeavor to investigate its authors and addressees. We learn nothing about where these people are from, where they have settled, or their names. The writing wraps itself in anonymity. And yet precisely in this way it makes itself known.

In the same way, the Wisdom of Solomon relates the history of Israel entirely without names (Wis 10), thereby making it accessible to other traditions, inviting every reader to identify with these nameless ones (cf. Schroer 1996, 111). This generalizing is combined with a vehement critique of kings (Wis 6:1-8; 7:1-6) and with the insistence that God has created the world totally good, indeed as a world without death (Wis 1:14; see on this 1 John 1:5). With the figure of the righteous person and the dialogue between the righteous one and the righteous one's enemy, the Wisdom of Solomon is referring to an even older tradition, which we encounter in an exemplary collection known as the Servant Songs in the book of Isaiah (Isa 42:1-9; 49:1-9; 50:4-9; 52:13–53:12). Before the eyes of a preponderant majority, the righteous one suffers a deadly defeat and, contrary to all expectation, is vindicated by God (Wis 1:16–2:24; 3:1-9; 4:17; 5:1-16; on this cf. Georgi 1988).

It is precisely this knowledge of the power of the weak in the wisdom tradition that 1 John is striving to keep alive. The stylistic device of anonymity is only one part of the evidence. In this way the authors steered clear of a competition typical of the time, which found expression in pseudepigraphy, putting the claim of one's own perspective under the patronage of a well-known figure. With the appeal to diverse traditions and their advocates, a power struggle necessarily arises (we already find one example of this in 1 Cor 1:10-13; the history of the early church provides further evidence). Even on this apparently external level, the circle that we know as the Johannine school allows no veneration of the saints. By insisting on anonymity, it denies any form of co-optation.

What's more, the self-chosen anonymity offers a special opportunity for the traditions of women. Where no female author appears, her authority can be neither doubted nor undermined (on women as letter writers see Hutaff 1994, 407-8). In patriarchy, the expunging of women's names constitutes one strategy, blotting out the theology of outstanding women (the nameless woman who anointed Jesus in Mark 14:3-9, for example), along with the memory of the women who hand it on. But since the authors themselves steer clear of providing names, sexual hierarchy has been rendered ineffective and patriarchy hoisted with its own petard (cf. below, on 2 John).

At the same time, the authors are walking in the footsteps of a legendary figure from the Gospel; the Beloved Disciple, as someone unknown, appears for the community in immediate proximity to Jesus and thereby pushes all others (especially Peter) to the lower ranks (especially John 20:1-8). In an exemplary way the Gospel of John has left unoccupied the most important role among the followers of Jesus, and thereby saved a place for the nameless believers whose trust, even before they are granted sight (John 20:29-30), makes them companions of Jesus who abide in Christ (1 John 2:24-25; 3:23-24; 4:13-17; 5:13, 18-20).

2 John: From One Woman to Another?

The brief letter that was taken into the canon as 2 John and thereby preserved, stands in a close relationship to 1 John. It is true that the dependence relationship of the two texts is disputed and, because of the sheer brevity of the text, incapable of being clarified conclusively. With respect to their content, however, it can be established that, in addition to several points of agreement, the two letters are in conflict with one another on two issues.

First, there is a shift in the time perspective with respect to confessing Christ. 1 John assumes that the coming of the Messiah has already occurred (1 John 4:2), whereas the text we are examining distances itself in verse 7 from those who do not confess that Jesus Christ is coming (present participle) in the flesh. Here the semantic specificity of the words "is coming" always suggests an interpretation oriented to the future, according to which the Christ event is still awaited (or awaited again). The text maintains that those who do not share this confession would pay by losing their own salvation, for they are threatened with not receiving their full reward (v. 8).

Second, while 1 John avoids differences and instead insists on love and reconciliation that embrace all (1 John 2:2), 2 John recommends withholding all social contact from people who do not accept its teaching. This shift accords with a pointed remark at the beginning of the letter: "I was overjoyed to find some of your children walking in the truth, just as we have been commanded" (v. 4). This involves the reproach that the majority of the "children" are not conforming to this expectation, particularly since a twofold repetition restricts mutual love to keeping the commandments (vv. 5-6). While 1 John gives assurance that those who are being addressed do not need instruction (2:7, 14, 21, 24, 27), the authors of 2 John commit the recipients to that which they have agreed to as a "beginning" (v. 6), for they are to "abide" *in it* and not, for example, in God (1 John 3:23-24), in the light (2:10), or in love (4:16). In addition, the supplementing of the law by the gift of the Spirit is omitted (cf. 3:24; 4:13).

Clearly the atmosphere has grown more bitter. The language of the letter's format, in which it is stressed that the author and addressee are "elect," also indicates rivalry. The motif of election is popular in the later pseudepigraphic letters (cf. 1 Tim 5:21; 2 Tim 2:10; Titus 1:1; 1 Pet 1:2; 2:4, 6, 9; also Col 3:12) but absent in 1 John.

It seems rather unattractive to ascribe this, of all letters, to a woman, as its signature suggests we do (cf. Schüssler Fiorenza 1993, 301; 1983, 248). Nevertheless, the fact remains that, regardless of how literally we take this letter's signature, it allows us to conclude that the modification of 1 John we have here probably bears the signature of a woman. For whoever it is that wants to invalidate 1 John, by introducing herself as an "elect sister," she assumes that her readers ascribe authority to women, regardless of whether this identity is assumed or real.

894

The common supposition is that the *kyria* to whom the letter is addressed is a designation for a congregation. But since this term is used in the New Testament only in 2 John, this collective use cannot be substantiated. On the contrary, it seems to me more likely to assume that the "Lady" *(kyria)* of a congregation is addressed here. Bernadette Brooten notes a later example of the use of this title in an inscription from Beth Shearim (Brooten 1982, 76), and, with reference to other instances of this usage (Brooten 1982, 76 n. 17), she asserts that it is not uncommon. The address, in its juxtaposition to the "children" *(teknoi)* envisioned to be dependent on her in some way, also appears to be consistent with her position. Finally, it is unlikely that the patriarchal tradition would hand on such a designation unaltered if it had not at one time appeared to be historically plausible.

The sender also continues to be puzzling. With the use of the definite article, "the elder" introduces himself precisely as if he were known. In a relationship of brothers and sisters, to which the greetings at the end point, this designation would be quite clear, depending on the number of the brothers and sisters. The confusion between a masculine (v. 1, the elder) and a feminine (v. 13, the elect sister) form can perhaps still be explained by the predominance of masculine office designations (like the use of the masculine title *archisynagōgos,* "synagogue leader," for a woman named Rufina; cf. Brooten 1982, 5ff.). So, did the author simply intend to take his or her authority into account in order to show, beyond the relational image, the Jewish-Christian claim for preeminence with respect to their Hellenistic brothers and sisters?

In any case, the title points to a Jewish or Jewish-Christian context (cf. Matt 15:2 par.; 21:23 par.; 26:3, 47, 57 par.; 27:1-3, 12, 20; numerous examples in Acts, esp. 20:17; understood as an office in 1 Tim 3:1; 4:14; 5:17-19; Titus 1:5; 2:2-3; Heb 11:2; James 5:14; 1 Pet 5:1, 5). In addition to the definite article, however, what is astounding is the singular, for the presbytery always consisted of a consultative group, out of which an individual would not be recognizable from the use of the title. So it can at least be excluded from consideration that a person known far beyond some limited region and introducing himself simply as "the elder" could count on being recognized by this name. All by itself, the multiplicity of references that Brooten offers for the feminine use of the term speaks for the fact that the term was all too common (Brooten 1982, 41-55). So, in any case, we are dealing with a stylized designation for the sender and, correspondingly, probably also for the recipient. That the latter uses the feminine speaks for a rich, self-evident women's tradition, the greater part of which requires our reconstruction.

3 JOHN: THE STRUGGLE FOR TOLERANCE

Using the style of a letter of recommendation, 3 John reacts to a situation in the church that, on the basis of the political style used in 2 John (just as, for example, in the Pastoral Epistles; → 1 Peter and 2 Peter), has grown more bitter. Once again the elder speaks (v. 1) and claims, in turning to Gaius, whose behavior is praised (vv. 3-4), to be turning to one of her or his "children" *(tekna)*, likely better understood as "disciples." Gaius is encouraged to receive the brothers and sisters with confidence, even when they are strangers, and to send them on "in a manner worthy of God" (vv. 5-6).

Here reference is made to a practice of hospitality like that which we encounter in the *Didache* at the beginning of the second century (*Didache* 11–13). Clearly this became for many congregations a financial burden they were no longer willing or able to bear, so that it became necessary to diminish the support. The *Didache* regulates this according to solid practical criteria: whoever stays more than two days without self-support is branded as a "false prophet" and excluded from further aid (*Didache* 11.5-6; up to three days, 12.2). Moreover, the *Didache* also sets forth theological qualifications according to which only those who do not contradict the community's own theology (11.1-2), who hold themselves to the Lord's ways and come in his name, are true prophets (11.7; 12.1).

3 John shares with the *Didache* this commitment to the "name" (v. 7) and stresses as corroboration for the trustworthiness of the emissaries that they accept no support from "nonbelievers." However, the conversation is broken off, for a person named Diotrephes, obviously known to sender and recipient alike, refuses to welcome the brothers and sisters and possesses enough authority to stop others from offering assistance by threatening to expel them. This accusation confirms the reproach that the elder makes against him, namely, that he desires to put himself first, for Diotrephes clearly possesses great influence. To oppose him, the author turns to a particular individual. To guard against being slandered, the author announces a visit (v. 10) and defends his or her own trustworthiness as well as that of Demetrius, whom the letter commends (v. 12). All this shows that the author is in a position of weakness, since the majority of those who consider themselves to be orthodox are siding with Diotrephes.

Finally, verse 13 turns to the need to continue the dialogue face-to-face (cf. also 2 John 12). Written communication is clearly no longer up to the task at hand. The areas of discord need to be clarified in personal discussion. Conversations, in contrast to writings, are conditioned by the time and circumstances under which they occur, and this guards against the desire to put truths in a final form by codifying them in writing. The ephemeral nature of oral communication constantly forces the partners to seek reassurance that they understand one another. While something in writing does not necessarily anticipate an answer but is in itself a statement of authority, both partners in a conversation have the same power to continue or to terminate their communication. Whoever wants to speak with someone (3 John 14) is in that way showing a basic step toward tolerance.

The fact that this private letter was received into the canon is astonishing, especially since that was denied to the *Didache*, a considerably more salient writing theologically. Thus the evidence for its inclusion in the New Testament is later than that for the two preceding Johannine letters, assuming that the witnesses number them as we do. Presumably the provocative situation found in 2 John needed to be straightened out, and the attempt is embodied in 3 John. In contrast to a theology of the elect, who appear to be certain of their orthodoxy, we find in 3 John a document of the weak and excluded, who, despite that, seek to stay in fellowship. Following the path set out in 1 John, the reality that God is truly present is revealed by associating with these weak ones.

LITERATURE

Brooten, Bernadette. 1982. *Women Leaders in the Ancient Synagogue: Inscriptional Evidence and Background Issues.* Chico, Calif.

Georgi, Dieter. 1988. "Frau Weisheit oder das Recht auf Freiheit als schöpferische Kraft." In *Verdrängte Vergangenheit, die uns bedrängt. Feministische Theologie in der Verantwortung für die Geschichte,* edited by Leonore Siegele-Wenschkewitz, 243-67. Munich.

Hutaff, Margaret D. 1994. "The Johannine Epistles." In *Searching the Scriptures,* edited by Elisabeth Schüssler Fiorenza, 2:406-27. 2 vols. New York.

Lieu, Judith. 1991. *The Theology of the Johannine Epistles.* Cambridge.

O'Day, Gail R. 1992. "1, 2, and 3 John." In *The Women's Bible Commentary,* edited by Carol A. Newsom and Sharon H. Ringe, 374-75. London and Louisville.

Schottroff, Luise. 1970. *Der Glaubende und die feindliche Welt. Beobachtungen zum gnostischen Dualismus und seiner Bedeutung für Paulus und das Johannesevangelium.* Neukirchen.

———. 1984. "'Mein Reich ist nicht von dieser Welt.' Der johanneische Messianismus." In *Gnosis und Politik,* edited by Jacob Taubes, 97-108. Vol. 2 of *Religionstheorie und Politische Theologie.* Munich et al.

Schroer, Silvia. 1996. *Die Weisheit hat ihr Haus gebaut. Studien zur Gestalt der Sophia in den biblischen Schriften.* Mainz.

Schüssler Fiorenza, Elisabeth. 1983. *In Memory of Her: A Feminist Theological Reconstruction of Christian Origins.* New York.

———. 1993. *Zu ihrem Gedächtnis . . . Eine feministisch-theologische Rekonstruktion der christlichen Ursprünge.* 2nd ed. Gütersloh.

FOR FURTHER READING

Klauck, Hans-Josef. 1991. *Der erste Johannesbrief.* Evangelisch-katholischer Kommentar zum Neuen Testament, vol. 23, 1. Neukirchen.

———. 1992. *Der zweite und dritte Johannesbrief.* Evangelisch-katholischer Kommentar zum Neuen Testament, vol. 23, 2. Neukirchen.

Translated by Everett R. Kalin

Jude: The Implications of Feminist Reading

Ruth Anne Reese

The book of Jude does not say anything about women, and only a few women have commented on the book. I am a woman, white, middle class, American (though living in Britain for some time), reading the book of Jude (over and over again as part of my Ph.D. research). In a situation where a biblical book says nothing specific about women and where few women have commented, what is a feminist reading of such an epistle? This is a crucial question because in this context a feminist reading is not one that focuses on the role of women in the book nor is it one that explores the modern interpretation of the book by women (both valid and practiced ways of feminist reading). So, what is feminist reading? First, what is reading? and then what makes reading distinctly feminist?

Reading is an act of interpretation. It is putting together marks on the page to make meaning and expand communication. It is the processes (both rational and irrational) used to come to understanding. Reading is also participation. When we read we participate in a shared code, language. It is this participation, this living in language, that allows us to interpret and to discuss our interpretations with others.

Feminists read differently than other readers. Reading, for most feminists, is an overtly political and ethical act. Feminist politics demands value and care for women and their relationships. Feminist ethics demands justice. While feminists are continually discussing and reworking their ideas of both the political and the ethical, most would agree that feminists have made a dual effort to value women and oppose women's oppression. Reading is an opportunity to act on these commitments. When feminists choose to make female characters the sole focus of their study, they emphasize the inherent value of women. They exercise care for the characters portrayed and for the effect these characters have on women today. Another type of feminist reading notes the patriarchal nature of ancient texts and points out the devalued place of women in this worldview. This is an appeal for justice toward women.

Feminist readings can be interpretative acts of value and justice embodied in care and truthfulness, particularly when these acts are performed for the liberation of women. I want to demonstrate this with a reading of the Epistle of Jude. This is only one feminist way of reading the epistle. There are others. As we read the text of Jude, I will comment on the *reader* and her possible response to this text and on her *location*. I will develop this theme of location and response a little more fully after the commentary section.

The translation that follows is my own. The epistle begins with these words: "Jude, a servant of Jesus Christ and brother of James, to the called who are beloved by God the Father and kept by Jesus Christ; may mercy, peace, and love be multiplied to you." The reader is immediately aware who the letter is from, Jude, and to whom it is addressed, a group of people who are named (i.e., distinguished or set apart) as people who are loved by God and who are kept by Jesus. The use of the second-person pronoun, "you," invites all readers to identify themselves with this chosen group.

The next paragraph reads: "Beloved, while having all zeal to write to you about our common salvation, it was necessary to write to you, calling you to contend diligently for the faith once for all delivered to the saints. For certain people *(anthrōpoi)* have slipped in secretly, those written long beforehand into this judgment, ungodly people. They change the grace of our God into a license and deny the only master and our lord Jesus Christ."

In this paragraph another group of people is introduced. Three important characteristics are outlined in this description. First, this group is secret — it is hidden, undercover. Second, this group, in contrast to the beloved group, is called "ungodly." Third, this group is accused of perverting two of the fundamental elements of Christian faith — God's grace and the acknowledgment of the position of Jesus Christ. This group of people, identified as the ungodly or as "these people," is a sharp contrast to those who are called beloved and kept. But allow me also to enumerate some characteristics of the beloved.

First, the beloved are not doing anything. They exist in a passive state of being loved and being kept. They are being encouraged to contend for the faith, but they are not yet doing that. On the other hand, the ungodly are actively turning God's grace into a license and denying the position of Jesus Christ.

Second, the text lures its readers to identify themselves with the beloved. Part of the allure of such an identity comes from the knowledge of safety. If one is loved and kept by God and Jesus, one must be safe from accusation.

There is a tension at the beginning of this text. The description of the people involved in this situation creates an explosive "us (the beloved) and them (the ungodly)" drama. The implication is that it is far better to be on the good side than on the bad side. In this case, being on the good side means being loved and kept by God and Jesus.

The "us and them" division is heightened in the next twelve verses. There has been a great deal of dispute over the wording of Jude 5, and I myself choose to follow the more difficult reading of the UBS second edition.[1] The reading there is *hapax panta hoti Iēsous.* (For a full and well-reasoned account of the variants in this verse, I recommend Osburn 1981.) Verses 5-7 are one sentence, which reads as follows:

> But I want you to remember, you who already know these things once for all, that Jesus saved a people out of Egypt, the second time destroyed those who did not believe, and the angels who did not keep their place but abandoned their own habitation he kept for a great judgment day in eternal bonds and darkness, just as Sodom and Gomorrah and those cities around in like manner to these gave themselves up to fornication and followed after other flesh, these are set forth as an example of suffering by eternal fire.

At the beginning of these verses the beloved, you, are given a task. The beloved must remember what they already know. This is followed by three elliptical references to ancient texts, but these references are difficult. The first one is unclear. When is the second time that Jesus saved people out of Egypt? The second is so brief as to be elusive. Who are these angels and when did Jesus keep them in chains? And the third is distorted. Why are Sodom and Gomorrah depicted as undergoing judgment of *eternal* fire? There is a conflict of memory between the memory of the readers, who should already know these things, and the memory of the author. These examples are his memory and not the memory of the reader.

Verse 8 continues: "And also in like manner these dreamers defile the flesh, reject lordship, and blaspheme glories." In Greek the last part of verse 8 reads *sarka men miainousin kyriotēta de athetousin doxas de blasphēmousin.* The translation of these phrases is problematic, and the meaning is not easy to determine.

These people are named as people who defile, reject, and blaspheme, and they do these things in the same way as the examples given in the previous verses. Unfortunately, the connection between verses 5-7 and 8 is not immediately clear, and even after much study commentators still disagree about the connection. The reader's failure to draw a clear connection raises tension between the reader's identification with the beloved, who are supposed to remember and therefore agree with the author, and the failure to remember. Whose memory should be trusted?

Verse 9 continues: "But Michael, the archangel, when disputing with the devil, arguing about the body of Moses, did not dare to bring a judgment of blasphemy but said, 'May the Lord rebuke you.'"

Again this is a story that the modern reader, at least, has trouble recalling since it is not extant. Richard Bauckham provides a reconstruction in his Word commentary on Jude. How does one obey a command to remember when the things recounted are not shared?

---

1. UBS: United Bible Series, 2nd ed. (London et al., 1987).

Verse 10: "But these blaspheme what they do not understand, and they know physically like the speechless animals, in these things they are destroyed."

This verse points to further characteristics of these people. They slander things they don't understand. Their knowledge is instinctive and destructive.

Verse 11 pronounces prophetic woes against these ungodly people: "Woe to these, they have gone the way of Cain, given themselves up to the error of Balaam's wages, and destroyed themselves in the rebellion of Korah."

How have these people done these things? The reader is not told. What is the way (or road) of Cain? Is it his murderous anger toward his brother or his wandering after God marked him? In what way can these people participate in the road of Cain? What was the error in Balaam's wages? As far as the story in Numbers is concerned, Balaam received only that which he was promised and which God gave him permission to take. Are both Balaam and the ungodly accused unjustly? How do these people destroy themselves by joining in the rebellion of Korah? These are important questions because if these people do the things of which they are accused, then they could not be secret, as the beginning of the epistle indicates. Murder, profiteering, and group rebellion are not solitary and secret activities.

These people are then described in metaphors in verses 12-13: "These are those stains fearlessly feasting together with you in your love feasts, they shepherd themselves, they are waterless clouds driven by the wind, they are uprooted, fruitless autumnal trees twice dead, they are wild waves of the sea foaming up their shame, they are wandering stars for whom the darkness of darkness has been kept."

These metaphors communicate the worthlessness of these people. Everything about them is dead or damaged. There is nothing in them which would bring true hope or life to the people they associate with. The pitch of the text rises as the next two verses recount a prophecy against these people.

Verses 14-15: "But Enoch the seventh from Adam prophesied, saying, 'Behold, the Lord came with his holy myriads to make a judgment against all these and to convict all souls of all their ungodly deeds which they did in an ungodly manner and of all the violence which these sinners spoke against him.'" The writer portrays the people he is speaking of as perpetrating ungodly actions, violence, and language misuse. The author identifies these people with a quotation from the apocryphal book of Enoch, thus lending the authority of another voice to the judgment against them.

In verse 16, the voice of the ungodly is further identified: "These are querulous murmurers proceeding according to their own desires, and their mouth speaks excessively, they marvel at faces for profit."

These people are portrayed as argumentative and complaining. They are selfish and do what they want. They talk at length, and use their capacity for wonder in order to profit themselves.

Verse 17 begins with a strong contrast to the twelve previous verses while verse 18 gives further details about the people who have slipped secretly into the presence of the beloved. These verses read: "But you, beloved, remember the words which were spoken beforehand by the apostles of our Lord Jesus Christ who said to you that in the last times there would be mockers who acted according to their own ungodly desires."

Verse 17 begins with the words: "But you, beloved." After all of the characterization of the ungodly, the focus of the text returns to the beloved. Once again they are instructed to remember. This time they are to remember the prediction of Christ. The very things Jude has described in the earlier section were anticipated by Jesus. There is only one final thing to say about these people.

Verse 19: "These are those who cause division, physical, not having the spirit."

In a summary, the ungodly have been characterized by Jude either directly or through association as dreamers, as people who defile the flesh, reject authority, and blaspheme glories (v. 8). They talk about things they don't understand, and the knowledge they have is based on instinct (v. 10). They have followed after the likes of Cain, Balaam, and Korah (v. 11). They have failed to provide hope or possibility of life consistent with their position (vv. 12-13). They have acted profanely, spoken against the Lord with violence and thus abused language (v. 15). They argue and complain and do what they like and profit by their wonder (v. 16). They divide people, and do not possess the spirit (v. 19). This is the portrait of the ungodly.

Verses 20-21 are another contrast: "But you, beloved, build each other up in your most holy faith, pray in the Holy Spirit, keep yourselves in the love of God, looking for the mercy of our Lord Jesus Christ into eternal life."

The beloved are never described beyond their identity as loved, called, and kept. Instead, they are given instructions. Each time I come to this part of the epistle, I am surprised. I expect an instruction, but not this one. What I expect is judgment, excommunication, rejection of the other, an end. But the instructions in the text are much different. They are directed at the beloved. It is the beloved who are expected to act, and their actions are to be directed toward themselves, not toward the other. They are to encourage, to pray, to locate themselves within God's love, and to look for mercy.

Along with verse 5, the two verses that follow present some of the most significant and difficult textual variants. I have chosen to follow the Nestle-Aland reading. Verses 22-23 give further instructions: "Have mercy on some who are doubting, save some, snatching them out of the fire, but on some have mercy with fear, hating also the garment defiled by the flesh."

The beloved are to practice mercy and salvation. They are to practice this for people who doubt, for people who are being destroyed, and for those who are dirty.

The epistle ends with verses 24-25: "Now to the one who is able to guard you and to stand you without stumbling before his glory, faultless with exuberant joy, to the only God our savior through Jesus Christ our Lord be glory, honor, strength and power from all the ages and now and into all ages. Amen."

The text ends here with a description of a God who is able (but is he willing?) to guard you, the beloved. The secure position of the beloved is called into question in the end. What distinguishes the beloved from the ungodly? It is not the name. It is not enough to say, "I am one of the beloved," or even "I am one of the ungodly." The distinguishing factor is what these groups of people do. In this text, the beloved are those who build each other up, pray, and keep themselves in God's love while looking for Jesus' mercy. It is this last phrase that is most interesting. The beloved are responsible for remaining in God's love. The actions identify the position.

This change, from the secure, confident beloved who might be able to judge the ungodly and fight against them to the beloved who must work to keep themselves within God's love, forces the beloved to contemplate their position perhaps even more than the ungodly. After all, it is the beloved to whom the letter is addressed (while the ungodly may be listening in, and might even identify themselves as the beloved); the author's real hope is to persuade the people he is addressing. And in this case, he wants to persuade them to look after themselves and in the process reach out a hand to those who can be saved.

Location is important. Where are you reading this text from? What position are you taking? Do you identify with the beloved? With the ungodly? With the author? Are you reading from a position where you are an outsider (neither beloved nor ungodly)? The position from which one reads will be part of the reader's response to a text. I have tried to read, in this one instance, by identifying myself with the beloved. I did this for two reasons. First, because the text invites the reader to do so with the use of the second-person plural pronoun, and second, because I think that people of faith, when reading sacred letters, generally identify themselves with the recipient of the letter (they read the text as if it were addressed to them). And my choice of location — for it is a choice — affected my reading. I asked questions of the author, and challenged the accuracy of his memory. And while I wondered about his portrayal of the ungodly, in the end I came to accept it. This is partly because of my location as a reader. If I had to identify myself differently, I would have asked different questions and had different resistances.

But while location is chosen, it is also given. I may choose to identify myself as one of the beloved, but I have no choice in my identity as woman or as white. These are given. And so I ask myself, would I have read differently if I was identified differently? If I were a man or a person of color or a European, would I read differently? Undoubtedly. In my reading I want to assert that which stands in common with feminist ethics. It does not allow the beloved to dominate the ungodly; rather, the beloved are confronted with their own need to act. It encourages mutual support, a recognition of and active participation in spirituality, and mercy toward the self and others. There is a movement against oppression and toward just action. There is the recognition that humanity must struggle together toward the common goal of staying within God's love. Feminist reading acknowledges difference, acknowledges the validity of our given location and our choice.

Jude is not about women, and (up to now) not many women have written on it, but continued reflection by women and feminists will open further doors in the text. And then readers will see more and different readings of the book, and these readings may challenge old readings or may challenge us, so that we ask again where we are standing as we read. Are we standing against oppression and for the encouragement of humanity, and women in particular?

LITERATURE

Bauckham, Richard J. 1983. *Jude, 2 Peter.* Word Biblical Commentary, vol. 50. Waco, Tex.

Cole, Eve Browning, and Susan Coultrap-MacQuin, eds. 1992. *Explorations in Feminist Ethics: Theory and Practice.* Bloomington, Ind.

Flax, Jane. 1990. *Thinking Fragments: Psychoanalysis, Feminism, and Postmodernism in the Contemporary West.* Berkeley, Calif.

Osburn, Carol D. 1981. "The Text of Jude 5." *Biblica* 62, no. 1:107-15.

Revelation: Inspirations from Patmos

Luzia Sutter Rehmann

In everyday language, in literature, and in the mass media, people often speak of the "Apocalypse," or "apocalyptic times," in the sense of the end of the world. At the end of the twentieth century many people began to realize with dread that they were able to destroy themselves and all life on Earth. Dread finds its tongue in the name "apocalypse." It may be that the last book of the New Testament fascinates so many women and men for that very reason. The difficult history of its interpretation, burdened in part by church institutions and in part from free-church communities, has set countless seals on the text, which is already so enigmatic, so unwieldy. In what follows I will not concentrate on attacking the existing approaches, but will sketch new ways of access that are being opened in feminist-liberation-theological discussions.

Introduction

Revelation was written in Asia Minor, on the island of Patmos, toward the end of the first century (1:9). Since there was probably a Roman penal colony on the island, scholars generally assume that John was an exile when he wrote his book. While it is true that Emperor Domitian did not order any persecutions of Christians, he kept strict watch over the religious lives of his subjects, especially those religions that were not tied to a single people, land, and language.

Magic, astrology, soothsaying, and prophecy were criminalized because attempts to predict the future were often connected to criticism of the state and agitation for uprisings (MacMullen 1966, 148-49). Ultimately we can only guess whether John had been exiled for life, deported by force, or sentenced to the quarries on Patmos (cf. Collins 1984, 102-3). According to John, he had come to Patmos "because of the word of God and the testimony of Jesus" (1:9). Everything John describes is seen from a "jailhouse perspective" (Schüssler Fiorenza 1985, 198); that is, his is a perception acutely alive to violence and injustice.

The early adherents of the Messiah Jesus regarded themselves as Jewish and were for a long time regarded by officialdom as Jewish also. It took several more centuries until the boundaries were defined between Christian and Jewish communities. John makes no distinction between an old and a new Israel and calls the Jesus followers "Jews" (2:9; 3:9). He emphasizes Jewish tradition by citing the prophetic books and the Torah and writing in an anti-Roman vein corresponding to Jewish experience in his time. The frequent formula about "following God's commandments and holding fast to the testimony about Jesus" belongs in this same context. The first part means observing the Torah, including a life according to Jewish practice (cf. Acts 15:23-29). Testimony about Jesus refers to readiness for martyrdom.

It may be that in Smyrna the internal Jewish conflict was so severe that the Jesus Jews had been expelled from the Jewish community (Rev 2:9). The message for Philadelphia begins with the "key of David" and the door that no one can again close (3:7). The Messiah Jesus is the door that no one can close. He is the mediator and gives access to God, so that no one can separate those who cling to Jesus Messiah from God. They have not abandoned the covenant with the Jewish God, even if individual Jewish communities might exclude them.

Revelation belongs within the broad current of apocalyptic literature from which only the book of Daniel was placed in the canon. But apocalyptic passages and ways of thinking are found in many biblical writings. Apocalyptic theology has been assailed as containing many anti-Jewish prejudices (Sutter Rehmann 1995). For instance, it allegedly calculates the time of the end, luridly depicts the end-time events (fantasy, speculation), and is pessimistic and shaped by a deterministic view of history. The state of research is quite disparate as well (cf. Zager 1989). So to this day, no satisfying definition of apocalyptic has been developed. "Apocalypse" refers to the literary genre of revelatory writings, whereas "apocalyptic" describes, in addition, the world of religious imagination, the theology whose perspective shapes thought and perception. Apocalyptic writings — such as the books of Daniel, Enoch, Baruch, 4 Esdras, and Revelation — are about coming to understand and to get a grip on the addressees' time here and now, which is difficult and makes for suffering. Most of them arise from a profound, all-encompassing political-religious crisis — a turning point and moment of decision. I do not consider apocalyptic writing as "consolatory literature," but rather as a complex type of liberation theology, since it closely analyzes the situation of the addressees and names it (often using mythic imagery and names), and its starting point is the experience of suffering of human beings.

For apocalyptic eschatology, the present is the moment of decision in which it is up to us whether the reign of God will break in or continue to be delayed. God is thus dependent on our cooperation. We cannot force it — but it would be in vain to wait for the reign of God until it falls into our laps. The metaphor of childbirth, which occurs frequently especially in apocalyptic literature, is a vivid example of this attitude: the time for bearing a child must be completed (we can do nothing about it), but for the birth itself we need all our strength, our persistence, and our endurance, if the birth is to be successful (cf. Sutter Rehmann 1995).

Feminist Criticism

The seer develops his analysis of the situation of injustice and his images of hope in letters to seven congregations in Asia Minor and in a whole series of visions. Feminine metaphors are central — the whore of Babylon (chapters 17; 18), the bride of the Lamb (chapters 19–22), and the woman in labor (12:1-6, 13-17). Yet feminist critique begins at this very point, for John does not seem to know any concrete, flesh-and-blood women. Women's experiences of life and of suffering either are not described or are negatively evaluated (Kitzberger 1994). The only concrete woman seems to be the prophet Jezebel (2:20), but as the seer's rival she is the object of his disparagement and opposition. He accuses her of seducing her followers into fornication and the eating of flesh sacrificed to idols.

In 14:4 women appear for the first time, but only in the formulation "those who have not defiled themselves with women." The true followers of the Lamb must therefore be men. This is an irritating idea for women. Susan Garrett (1992) also criticizes the fact that John divides women into bad and good, and she therefore describes Revelation as misogynistic.

While Ingrid R. Kitzberger (1994) seems to proceed on the assumption that Christian women suffered more in the endangered communities than the men did, since they were subject to the men, I can find nothing about that in Revelation. It contains very little information about Christian community life. The relations of believers to one another appear to be "brotherly" (22:9), but they do not play a very big role. This is a lamentable finding (so Schaumberger and Schottroff 1988, 99). But nothing can be deduced from it regarding the oppression of women. Many of the everyday activities John tells us about could have been done by women or men. For example, there were male and female harpists, male and female musicians, male and female flautists, trumpeters, artists (18:22-23). Those who wash their clothing (the image refers to women's daily life) are called blessed (7:14; 22:14) — the reference is to those who overcome, who are prepared to be martyrs. Martyrdom was experienced by a great many women as well (cf. Musurillo 1972). In the ancient church tradition, those condemned to martyrdom were regarded (during their imprisonment, and even if they were set free) as priests, mediators close to God. Precisely this trace, which leads to imprisonment, must be taken very seriously in Revelation.

Method of Interpretation

1. *Location in time and place.* To understand John's message we have to try to recognize the situation of the communities addressed. Locating them in time and space is therefore important. John probably wrote twenty to thirty years after the destruction of Jerusalem by the Roman army. That trauma is present in Revelation (18:8; 21:10). The anti-Roman polemic can also be understood in light of the political situation of the Jewish people after this devastating war. The addressees of Revelation had had bitter experiences of Rome's crushing power. One indication of it could well be the deportation of the seer.

2. *Language.* The language of Revelation enchants, sparkles, blinds painfully, and fascinates. Adela Yarbro Collins sees a certain analogy between the schizophrenic's hallucinations and the visions in Revelation. The seer is said to be in danger of withdrawing from empirical reality, of distancing himself from the painful experiences of the everyday world (1984, 55). Consequently, one often encounters psychological questions about whether John was mentally ill. I prefer to ask: Is Revelation as open and elusive as life itself, which likewise cannot be nailed down to a single meaning and once-for-all explanations? Does John write this way because he is fighting for justice out of love for humanity, whose misery he has to contemplate? Elisabeth Schüssler Fiorenza emphasizes John's evocative language, with which he writes so poetically and creatively, fashioning a new structure of plausibility (1985). He interprets shattered reality anew for the threatened Christians of Asia Minor by developing a language that opens outward. With his linguistic poetry he reaches the readers at their intuitive, emotional level. Again and again readers dive down into abyss, fly into the open heaven. I begin to perceive colors; dream images arise. As if in a "magical eye" (Baccei 1994), contours begin to dissolve and new forms present themselves. Internal ears and eyes are opened to the nuanced dynamic of images. John speaks quite frequently of opening: 3:7-8, 20; 4:1; 5:2, 9; 6:1-2; 10:2, 8; 15:5; 19:11. Again and again we see opened doors and gates of heaven, open seals, opened abysses, open books. In this way John succeeds in holding imaginative spaces for survival ajar.

3. *Apocalyptic.* To be able to understand John, we have to take the apocalyptic worldview seriously. *Apokalyptein* means to open, to uncover, to reveal. John uncovers for his addressees their own distressed situation by giving a name to their suffering. That suffering consists of persecution for their witness to Christ or of catastrophes that should effect repentance. Here he is in line with the ancient prophetic interpretations of the people's misfortunes, and he also poses the question of the responsibility for suffering and its cause. But he does not only proceed analytically, naming the status quo. He also uncovers concealed perspectives on action and reveals unsuspected visions of the closeness of God; he proclaims to the powers that build on violence that their end is near.

In Christian history of interpretation, the rhetoric of the end has often been politically misused as threats of punishment of those who are already oppressed. In this interpretative perspective hope for God's new world on earth is consigned to oblivion and beyond. But God's new world in the apocalyptic rhetoric of Revelation is a world beyond violence, not beyond nature. Therefore speaking of a change of time can offer release to people who are under emotional or physical pressure. When John describes the coming change as a fundamental turning point and end of the present violence, John opens the horizon for a new heaven and new earth to come into view. He sticks a foot in the door of the fatalism that accepts injustice and suffering as inevitable. Behind that door, which Jesus Messiah has opened, appears a world without injustice and the misuse of power. Here we must take note of the therapeutic power of apocalyptic language: images, metaphors, and poetic turns create, open up spaces in a world where everything seems to have its price, where nothing will ever change. John speaks a language that opens up ways to enter upon, a disclosing language that reveals conditions, broadens horizons, and leaves behind dividing walls; in addition, he lays relationships open as well with his apocalyptic perceptions.

4. *Reflected mythology.* The rule of ancient rhetoric is fundamental here: *microcosm and macrocosm* correspond and are analogously constructed: as in heaven, so on earth. For the readers of Revelation, this means that it is not enough to know what the symbols could mean when they appear in other myths. That is, so to speak, only the theoretical background. If we recognize mythical features, we must pay attention to John's *reflected mythology;* that is, we have to ask ourselves *how* he arranges the mythical material for his specific addressees. We have to ask the *social-historical* question about how the reality of their lives might have looked. Only then can we try to understand how the symbols and the reality of the addressees could have corresponded to one another. The symbols present the macrocosm, and the reality projected into heaven represents the microcosm of human life. John not only sees into the hearts of the communities, where what is murky and what is clear are both hidden, where he makes out conflicts and strength, but from 4:1 onward he begins to draw major lines, to unfold connections. As if in a drive-in movie theater with a gigantic projection screen (the heavens), John sees macrocosmically. Angels, monsters, the Lamb, riders, and female figures appear, and a grand dynamic ensues on this heavenly screen. And he begins to perceive the earth transforming itself and the coming-to-be of a new creation.

Outline of the Book

The Seven Letters: Chapters 1–3

Chapters 2–3 contain the so-called letters addressed to communities in Asia Minor: Ephesus (2:1-7), Smyrna (2:8-11), Pergamum (2:12-17), Thyatira (2:18-28), Sardis (3:1-5), Philadelphia (3:7-12), and Laodicea (3:14-21).

These chapters not only describe the problems in the communities but also open action perspectives and sketch visions of a better life. At various points it becomes obvious that the communities are under pressure and suffer from persecution. The Greek term *thlipsis* means distress, suffering, persecution (compare Matt 24:21 and Acts 11:19). The execution of Antipas is mentioned in Revelation 2:13. John himself is said to be in banishment on the island of Patmos (1:9). It is possible that these sufferings arose out of conflicts with the Jewish communities under Roman pressure (2:9; 3:7, 9) and have to be understood as consequences of some Roman punitive measures (1:9; 2:10, 13).

John is to be considered Jewish (1:3; 2:9). In the manner of ancient prophetic tradition, he attempts to give a theological analysis of his people's suffering and depicts the part they played in it by naming the consequences of their own guilt. He depicts their wrong behavior in concepts rich in tradition: fornication (2:21) and eating flesh sacrificed to idols (2:14) — the prophetic metaphors for going astray from the good ways of Torah. If they stop doing this and return to God, their sufferings will also come to an end. Like the prophets, John is convinced that wholehearted observance of the Torah and practice of the faith, as well as bearing witness to Jesus Messiah (1:2), are an action perspective in the present time of violence. Fornication is taught especially by the prophet Jezebel (2:20). She seems to have been an influential rival of John, for which reason he wants to denigrate her. The metaphor of "repenting of fornication" opens the horizon of the theme of freedom from patriarchal marriage; and "not eating flesh sacrificed to idols" leads us to Christian communities on the borders of the Roman Empire, on the fringes of civilization (cf. 18:4-5).

John interprets the sufferings that have been experienced in apocalyptic terms, that is, that the end of the time of injustice is near; God is coming to prosecute unrighteousness and let the earth and its inhabitants experience justice. John hopes for God's justice, and he refers his visions to that hope (2:7: eating of the tree of life; 2:10: receiving the crown of life; 2:17: eating of the hidden manna and receiving a stone with a new name; 3:4: wearing white garments and standing in the book of life; 3:8: a door is opened that no one can close; 3:12: becoming a pillar in God's temple; 3:20-21: eating and reigning with Jesus Messiah).

The New Song: Chapters 4 and 5

The seer beholds an opened door into heaven. He is invited to seize this opportunity and to look closely at what is about to happen (4:1-2). He sees a throne, comparable to the vision in Ezekiel 1. In Revelation 4:8 the cherub-like "beings" sing a hymn of praise. The twenty-four elders cast down their crowns — that is, they set aside their venerability — for to God alone belong praise, honor, and power (4:11).

Pablo Richard (1996, 102) calls a vision "the restoration of the collective consciousness of the community." Thus these two chapters represent a founding of the community. Here are unifying visions, songs, common celebration. This retroactive assurance of community is also accomplished through a "reconstruction of heaven" (Richard 1996, 102). Heaven is not to be understood in fundamentalist fashion. It means a dimension of fulfilled life, beyond violence and injustice, where God's nearness can be perceived. Reconstructing heaven and making it visible mean apprehending and appreciating the world of the saints, the poor, the persecuted. Thus the hope for resurrection is set free. The new song (5:9) expresses this hope for God's justice. The murdered Messiah has purchased the freedom of his people from all nations with his blood. These songs of the poor and the tortured run through the whole book and are part of the spiritual power of the "heavenly" community.

The Seven Seals: Chapters 6 and 7

In chapters 6 and 7 we find the first of the three sets of visions made up of seven images each. This first vision is about the opening of the book closed with seven seals. Only the Lamb is worthy to break the seals (5:9). With each seal that is opened, an image appears: the first four produce the images of the apocalyptic riders representing battle, slaughter, injustice, and death (through the sword, famine, and pestilence). These are frightful images that follow one another in a grand, breathless dynamic. They can be read as an analysis of the unjust condition of the world order of the time. Then opening the book would require great strength: whoever really wants to know how the world functions must have the courage to face the wild riders and not turn away.

The fifth seal represents a break and interrupts the sequence. Instead of a further analysis of injustice, we see those who have been slain (6:9). The victims emerge from silence and invisibility. They interrupt the sequences of violence with their cry to God: "How long will it be before you judge?" Their demand of justice, in the tradition of the Psalms, is a protest against the riders and the violence they bring with them.

The opening of the seventh seal can be read as support for this demand: the earth enters into solidarity with those who are suffering. She is unwilling to continue to be a stage for violence. Her quaking is a sign of its life. She presses toward the new life that she desires to bring forth from herself, as a mother brings forth her child. Sun, moon, and stars, together with the earth, demonstrate the nearness of the new. They interrupt human-created violence. The rulers are quite aware of what that means. They fear judgment because they know their own crimes. They implore the earth to shelter them, but the earth is not willing to be an accomplice of the rulers; she does not cooperate with them (6:15-17). She holds her breath, so to speak: we have to hear the silence in the next verse (7:1). Not a breath of air moves. This is an enormous contrast to the agitated images of the riders.

The seventh seal is not opened until 8:1. In that interval, no violence, no noise, and no outcry rule. Here is a Sabbath-like, jubilant mood, filled only by songs of praise (7:10). The concluding dialogue between one of the elders and the seer sketches an impressive vision of God's nearness to human beings (7:13-17).

The Seven Trumpets: Chapters 8–11

Now, after the seer has witnessed the opening of the book and has withstood the images, there begins a new series of visions, with seven angels blowing trumpets. A blast of the trumpet announces the last opportunity for turning around. The horrors that follow are seen as opportunities for penance that are not grasped (9:20-21). The individual trumpets are associated with gruesome events, each of which slays a third of the living creatures affected by it. The narrative perspective is now turned toward the cosmos, which reflects God's wrath, and no longer toward the powers of wickedness (the riders in 6:3-8). Here attention is drawn to the earth's prophetic task. The seer is summoned by the trumpets to behold how the earth is being destroyed and to turn around. I do not read these trumpet blasts as evoking these horrible things, since that would make God responsible for the destruction of the realm of the living, but rather as attempts to draw attention to the misery that exists. Only after four trumpets have sounded does the seer enter into the events. He begins then to see and to hear (8:13). Only now does he perceive what is happening. Now he understands the shriek of the eagle flying by as a cry of woe over humanity (8:13). Only when the fifth trumpet sounds does he see with eyes of understanding: now it is not merely fire that is falling from heaven, but a star. The earth is now no longer simply being burned up; the underworld is opening up and releasing smoke from its maw — no, not smoke, but locusts! — no, not a swarm of locusts, but an army of warriors (9:1-12)! Little by little, the seer's perception sharpens. John learns to see and lets us share in the learning process, so that we, too, can begin to see. The earth is destroyed? Burned up? Why, what has happened? How much any theology falls short if it tries to interpret the destructions as God's punishment! John teaches us not to look away until we understand: it is devilish war that brings about destruction.

The seventh trumpet is delayed, increasing the tension. The seer receives a commandment to prophesy that is similar to the one given to Ezekiel (Ezek 3:1-3).

Two witnesses are sent out; both are killed and rise again (Rev 11:11). This resurrection causes many to fear God (11:11). Those who can now see can also hear the voice that addresses the risen ones. I consider this emphasis on seeing and hearing to be central to Revelation. Living in the fear of God means not only living according to Acts 15:28 (keeping free of meat sacrificed to idols, blood, and sexual immorality), but also understanding which powers are inimical to life and which ones cause it to flourish; it means seeing and hearing with understanding the things that are happening around me. The many who can now see and hear are people from the "great city" (Rev 11:8). John also calls this great city the place where "their Lord was crucified." Hence this description seems to apply to the city of Jerusalem.

Before the seventh trumpet sounds, the earth again quakes. She senses the nearness of the good life and works in cooperation to bring it forward, so that a great many more people learn to fear God (11:13).

The sounding of the seventh trumpet in 11:15 brings us to a first climax in the book of Revelation. Now God's time has come, the time of judgment and justice, the time when his menservants and maidservants can breathe a sigh of relief. Again the earth quakes, and the heavens are opened.

The Great Signs: Chapters 12–16

Chapter 12 begins with a great sign: a very pregnant woman crowned with stars, standing on the moon. There are a multitude of depictions of women standing on the moon, but scarcely any of them is of a pregnant woman, certainly not one giving birth.

But we understand this woman's message only if we are aware of the threat to her and of her actions as a struggle for new life. The woman is giving birth; she cries out and is in pain (12:2). Only now does the seer perceive the other sign: a fearsome dragon is tormenting the pregnant woman because it intends to devour her child (12:4). The birth is successful, but the child is torn from the woman (12:5). She can flee, but without her child. In the wilderness she finds a place prepared for her by God, that is, a community in solidarity with her (12:6).

The dragon, with its many heads and horns, represents a fearful threat. This is a woman-torturing, child-devouring monster. The depiction of this experience of violence suffered by a pregnant woman makes us aware of the fate of women who are captured, persecuted, or affected by war. In 12:13-17 the theme of flight (cf. 18:4) is taken up again.

In 12:7 Michael, the fighting angel, appears for the first and only time. He and his angelic army fight against the dragon and throw it down from heaven. This victory is celebrated exuberantly (12:10-12), and yet this short-lived policy has severe consequences for the earth and the sea (12:12) as well as for the woman's progeny (12:17). Nor does this victory create peace, for more beasts appear (13:1, 11). They tempt people to place a symbol on their hands and foreheads, a sign that is necessary if they are to be able to buy and sell (13:17). The dragon gives these beasts their strength (13:2). They are a kind of extension of the devouring power of the dragon. John shows two possible ways of dealing with the dragon. While the violent casting down of the dragon from heaven only creates new violence and causes more beasts to arise, the woman's strategy seems to be preferable: she herself departs from heaven and withdraws to the margins of civilization, where she finds a place prepared for her by God (12:6). This strategy is nonviolent and moves toward an end to complicity; it aims to starve the dragon by taking away its nourishment. That John wishes to proceed in a nonviolent manner is evident in 13:10: "If you take captive, into captivity you go; if you kill by the sword, by the sword you must be killed" (author's translation).

The beasts from the sea and from the deep cause all their worshipers to put signs on their foreheads or right hands to demonstrate their adherence. Anyone who does not worship the image of the beast (13:15) is killed. Anyone who does not bear the sign cannot buy or sell, and thus is excluded from a society founded on trade and exchange.

It is again clear how important it is to see and hear — to be able simply to perceive and to think — when, in the next chapter, the other beast arises. The Lamb is also a beast, but of a different kind. One must be able to see the difference between the Lamb and the dragon's beasts. The worshipers of the Lamb also bear a sign on their foreheads. How can we distinguish these worshipers from the others? In 14:3, John hears them singing. The beast's adherents did not sing. They want to buy and sell, not sing. The worshipers of the Lamb sing a new song: "And I heard a voice from heaven like the sound of many waters and like the sound of loud thunder" (14:2). The worshipers of the Lamb can hear and understand these heavenly voices, so that only they can learn a new song.

What is this song about? The singers have all been redeemed from the earth (14:3); they are arisen, they have died and been made new. They are transformed from agents of the beast to followers of the Lamb. The earth protects, in her womb, those who have been brought to violent death until God calls them back (20:12-13; cf. 4 Esdras). This is — for those who can see — the transformative purchase that creates life, redemption (in contrast to Rev 13:7). The new song sings of this transformative release, of this purchase, which is so different from the buying and selling in terms of the beast.

The pouring out of the bowls of wrath (in 16:1-2) causes painful sores, life in the sea is killed, waters turn to blood, the sun scorches the people, the realm of the beast and the Euphrates dry up. Life on earth becomes more and more impossible. But who beholds it? Who cares?

The earth is altered into a battlefield: *Harmagedōn* (16:16). It is a dreadful transformation, and yet the people "cursed the name of God . . . and did not turn around" (16:9, 21). The earth, however, reacts with an earthquake (16:18). Earthquakes, the trembling and shaking of the earthly womb, where the dead are preserved, are metaphors for giving birth, for the labor of the earth. She cooperates with God, she hurries to bring forth the new life, hastening to shake off the systems of oppression and violence.

The End of the Great City: Chapters 17–19

Chapter 17 begins with a description of the great whore who sits on many waters. The kings of the earth committed *porneia*, fornication, with her. She is seated on a beast with seven heads and ten horns. This is, then, the same beast figure as the dragon (12:3) or the beast from the sea (13:1). The beast is explained (17:7-14). It is full of royal power, ruling power, future and past. It will make war on the Lamb. Because it will lose, it will turn against the whore and hate her, make her desolate and naked, and tear and burn her flesh (17:16). This seems to me not so much God's judgment as, rather, the tragic consequence of exploitation, which the kings have perpetrated on the city. One day they will altogether devour and destroy it. This is God's will only insofar as it has been made possible by an interruption in the violence (17:17). The heavens and the saints will rejoice at it (18:20). It was, after all, they who cried out for God's justice (cf. 6:10). Those who made themselves immensely rich are outraged at the destruction of their world: the kings (18:9), the merchants (18:11), and the shipowners (18:19).

The profiteers of the great city have thus not yet been explicitly "punished." They lose the sources of their wealth, the place where they had been able to carry out their schemes. At the same time, the basis for their sins has been withdrawn from them. The city is shaken by plagues (18:8) and its destruction is announced (18:21). The saints are to leave the city so as not to share in its end (18:4).

The city has usually been associated with Rome. But the image is somewhat enigmatic, and cities similar to Rome could also be intended. Even Jerusalem could be included, since it had for a long time to endure plundering to enrich foreign powers. The end of the city is also the end of its exploitation, the beginning of a new era (19:2). Only now can the new city, the new Jerusalem (21:2), come to be. Hence a great multitude rejoices when the violence is interrupted. A festal mood akin to that of the Sabbath reigns, expressing a great sense of relief. The one who had gone out with the white horse (6:2) completes his justifying work (19:11-21). He is the king of kings, and so the kings of the earth finally encounter the limits to their power. The kings' flesh is offered as food. The whole hierarchy they had built up for themselves is "fed" with it (19:18). The beast and the kings themselves, with their violent and destructive armies, are thrown into the lake of fire (19:20).

The New Jerusalem: Chapters 20–22

Now there is commotion in heaven and on earth (20:11), and the motif of opening is given its full significance. The books are opened; that is, the stories of each individual are heard and tested before God. The sea gives up its dead (20:13). The precondition for judgment, after all, is that the dead must be released from their chambers. The opening of the earth's womb (cf. 4 Esdras) is here indicated by the references to the sea and the realm of the dead *(ho hadēs),* both of which give back their dead. Death's preservative function is thus made unnecessary, and death is thrown into the lake of fire (Rev 20:14).

Now, finally, John's addressees can breathe easily: the old, violent world order has passed away (21:1). But what is now visible is not nothingness, the beyond as such; rather, a new creation is seen. The work of justice, unrolling slowly, developing in stages, is at the same time a work of creation, the transformation of the earth, indeed, of the whole cosmos. In place of the great city, which has fallen, the holy city now shines (21:2). The bridal metaphors of 19:7 are taken up again: the new city is adorned like a bride for her husband. Her adornment is that there will be no more violent death, no more suffering, neither crying nor pain (21:4). God will dwell in this city. A close relationship is portrayed: the thirsty receive the water of life at no cost, and they will become children of God (21:7).

The new Jerusalem is described in 21:10-27. The city is built of precious stones and comes down out of heaven from God. It is thus a union of earth and heaven: the stones come from within the earth; they are the earth's treasures, preserved for the new creation. In the bride figure of the holy city is glimpsed the Jewish princess Sabbath: "But there is no more expressive image that reflects [the Sabbath's] sweetness and the longing with which it is awaited than its being called 'bride' in the Bible and in the synagogue. It is cherished in the hearts of the Jewish people as a beloved bride and as 'lovely princess Sabbath'" (Lazarus 1898).

The new creation blooms with justice and shalom and promises rest to the weary (cf. 14:13).

In 22:1-5 the seer beholds the river of the water of life that emerges from the throne of God and of the Lamb. Revelation closes with 22:6-21. We hear once again from John the seer (22:8); the angel who showed him all these things (22:9); Jesus, who sent the angel (22:16); the Spirit; and the Bride herself (22:17). These five "I's" are the authoritative voices that stand behind this book.

Thematic Cross Sections

"Whore" and Bride

The sharp and sometimes even pornographic metaphors of a people or a city as an immoral woman (cf. Ezek 23; Hos 2:1-2; 5:3; Isa 23:15-18; Nah 3:4) wound women and seem unacceptable. But in my opinion John is not writing pornographically. Babylon is called "mother of *pornai* and of earth's abominations" (Rev 17:5). Renate Kirchhoff warns us against translating *pornē* simply as whore or prostitute, since these negatively weighted moral concepts produce a narrowing of perspective (Kirchhoff 1994, 65). In Jewish texts *pornē* describes the "forbidden woman," that is, a woman who has sexual intercourse contrary to the rules, in the sense of the Jewish purity laws. Revelation links to the tradition that uses *porneia* as a metaphor for the worship of and sacrifice to idols. But *porneia, porneuō,* and *pornē* are used in Revelation in the dominant sense of the words as well as metaphorically. Therefore it certainly seems appropriate to investigate the situation of the *pornē* Babylon in social-historical terms. In 17:1–19:4, John portrays a great city as *pornē*. But it is striking that we hear nothing of a payment she received from her johns. Quite the contrary; those who commit fornication with her also get rich from her. The kings, the merchants, and the seafarers (18:3, 9, 11, 15, 19) exploit Babylon in every way. Thus Babylon seems to be in the situation of an enslaved prostitute from whose earnings her masters live, or a woman who lives in a condition that is not protected by any law. How would our perception of "Babylon" change if we were to see the city as the object of exploitation?

Babylon is thrown into the sea like a millstone (18:21) because she is supposed to have deceived all the nations through sorcery (18:23). More than once she is said to be drunk with blood (17:6), but her johns are also drunk on blood. In 17:1, 15 it is said that she sits on "waters." Here we get a glimpse of a realistic experience in the author's own time, as regards places where johns made contact with prostitutes: "Corinth had numerous baths that served men, but women also, as assignation sites. The women working there also prostituted themselves. . . . Athenaios attests the common custom — in Corinth also — that slave women who worked in the baths also performed sexual services for the guests. Prostitutes could also seek clients in the guest houses that were often attached to baths" (Kirchhoff 1994, 46). She is depicted as richly adorned: clothed in fine linen, purple and scarlet, adorned with gold, jewels, and pearls (18:17). She is thus to be compared with the new city Jerusalem (19:8; 21:11-12). But the *pornē* Babylon is altogether a woman who lives contrary to the rules, whereas Jerusalem is the true bride, adorned for the husband who is meant for her (21:2).

This division of women, devised from an androcentric point of view, into "permitted" and "not permitted" requires a feminist critique. Nevertheless, it is worthwhile to go into detail and to examine the behavior of the "johns": they not only exploit Babylon, they also let her fall as soon as they are under threat; they project the threat onto her and punish her (17:16). This seems to me to be a realistic depiction of the completely insecure work situation in which prostitutes in John's time (and again today) find themselves in many respects. The seer's critique is not so much addressed to the women engaged in prostitution; rather, it is directed to those who have to do with the *pornē:* the Jewish-Christian men who "prostitute themselves with them" and do not repent (see below).

On a macrocosmic level the city reveals the exploitative rulers, with their violence and cold-bloodedness that drive the city into misery. In this connection I see the rejoicing of the heavens and the saints (18:20) as equally part of the prophetic task of the city to make injustice visible (18:5).

On a microcosmic level this image is significant for the way of life of both women and men. For women I see an exciting prospect in reflecting on the situation of the exploited *pornē* and developing a social-historical analysis. John's advice to withdraw from this city (18:4) could also be read as an encouragement to withdraw from patriarchal role models and compulsions, from roles that make women accomplices.

Susan Garrett critiques the perspective on women expressed by men's control of female sexuality. Virgins were under male control, which John applauds in them (they are pure and obedient), while the whores escape male control but are downgraded morally (Garrett 1992, 377). I want to counter that critique to the extent that it likewise succumbs to an androcentric perspective: the virgins — that is, the unmarried women who lived in Christian communities — were in fact no longer under male control. They belonged to themselves; that is, they felt themselves to be God's temples rather than their husbands' vessels (cf. Wire 1990; Sutter Rehmann 1994). As is evident from the apocryphal Acts, women fought vehemently to get free from their patriarchal bonds (as betrothed, wives, concubines). But they were harshly punished for it: Thecla, for example, is condemned to death by her own mother, and later is in fact placed in the fire (Schneemelcher 1989, 216-24).

When John refers to the wife of the Lamb (19:7 and 21:9), he does not call her virgin, but *nymphē*, bride (21:2). Thus the subject is not her virginity, but her decision for the Lamb. I can see nothing here about male control over female sexuality. John speaks of a woman *(gynē)*, who prepares herself for her wedding and clothes herself with shining, pure linen. *She* prepares and dresses herself; that is, she is perceived as active, autonomous in her doing. (She could, after all, be described as being dressed or prepared for her marriage.) The white linen is explained in 19:8 as the righteous deeds of the saints, thus surrounding the bride with an ethical context. I like the idea that the efforts of many together to effect justice yield a textile, a finely woven garment that is the precondition for the new life (the new city). Here the work of women weavers finds an echo as metaphor for work for the realm of God.

It seems, then, that John knew unmarried virgins and widows (women who declined to remarry), and because of them he could recommend a strategy for resistance and liberation to both women and men. If we retain the reading indicated above, we will have to recognize both the micro- and macrodimensions of such statements. Not entering into a patriarchal marriage in order to become the bride of the Lamb then means, macrocosmically, maintaining a religious union with the God of the Torah and the people Israel, and following God's Messiah, Jesus (12:17). Microcosmically this decision is expressed in freedom from marriage or not entering into a second marriage (cf. Mark 10:6-9; 12:25). We can see the same twofold dimension in the metaphor of adultery and *pornē:* macrocosmically it criticizes idolatry, distancing oneself from the practices of Jewish life (eating flesh sacrificed to idols). Microcosmically we can only surmise that problems must have arisen that John addresses in terms of *porneia,* fornication.

I must here leave unresolved whether John is addressing the problem of mixed marriages, or whether he understands marriage itself as an institution of Roman patriarchy that should be undermined. In any case, John has nothing to say about the patriarchal family. There are no living children in Revelation. Children are only mentioned as the offspring of Jezebel and all those who commit adultery with her (Rev 2:23). In a second instance, the star-crowned woman gives birth to a child, a son (12:4, 5), who, however, is snatched away and vanishes, being taken to God. This tends to strengthen the notion that John is writing for a brotherhood made up of unmarried persons.

Male Sexuality

John's compatriots are called upon to follow the Lamb as *parthenoi,* virgin-like. This is explained as "not defiling themselves with women" (14:4). But "defiling oneself with women" is also what the *pornos,* the fornicator, does.

When Paul speaks of *porneuō* in 1 Corinthians 10:8, he is referring to the Israelites' unlawful intercourse with Moabite women (Num 25). According to Kirchhoff (1994), it is in Paul's interest to interpret Genesis 2:24 ("therefore a man leaves his father and his mother and clings to his wife, and they become one flesh") as a marital relationship. In using *pornē* (1 Cor 6:12-20) Paul implies that a man is forbidden to have sexual intercourse with anyone but his own wife: "Genesis 2:24 serves to parallel the relationship of the Christian man to the *pornē* with (his relationship to his wife and) his relationship to the Lord. For this purpose he derives from Genesis 2:24b, c a rule that applies to all relationships that are called *kollasthai:* A man who unites himself to X . . . necessarily becomes one with X. Therefore this applies both to the relationship to the *pornē* and to that with his wife and also to that with the Lord" (Kirchhoff 1994, 165-66).

But what constitutes the unlawfulness of *porneuein* in Revelation? In 2:4 it says: "But I have this against you, that you have abandoned the love you had at first." The angel of the community at Ephesus is accused of infidelity. In 2:14 the community angel at Pergamum is reproached for having permitted an interpretation that allowed the eating of meat sacrificed to idols and *porneia.* If he continues to pursue this way of life, the logical consequence will be war, injustice, violence. The same is the problem in Thyatira (2:20-21), while there is praise for those in Sardis (3:4) who have not soiled (14:4) their clothes.

This behavior of people in Ephesus, Pergamum, Thyatira, and Sardis is in line with the behavior of the *pornē* Babylon. Probably this is about conflicts over the practices of Jewish life, which for Christian communities at that time consisted of keeping the food and marriage laws (Acts 15:28-29). But in view of the major role assumed by the imposing image of the *pornē* Babylon, we have to ask ourselves whether John is anxious about the uncontrolled sexuality of his fellows. In Revelation 12:1-6 John encourages the women to withdraw into the desert and live celibate lives, and he suggests to the men that they should live virginal lives as well (14:4).

Those who are companions of the *pornē* Babylon participate in her sins. They become one flesh with her. The adherents of the *pornē* become *pornoi,* while the followers of the Lamb become lambs (7:17); that is, they live, in accordance with the Jewish traditions of martyrdom, in closeness to God. But the suffering of the martyrs evokes God's wrath on the unrighteous, for it is God alone who gives life and can take it away (cf. 4 Macc 13:13-14; 16:25). The fundamental strength of the martyrs is often expressed as *hypomonē:* endurance (Rev 1:9; 2:2, 3; 3:10). Luise Schottroff understands *hypomonē* as "the attitude of men and women martyrs in Jewish and Christian tradition." Martyrs take on themselves sufferings like persecution, conflicts with society and the authorities that can lead even to pogroms and executions, "because they expect God's reign to come on earth and draw consequences for their whole lives from that hope" (Schaumberger and Schottroff 1988, 105). The metaphor of the Lamb reveals the close association with martyrdom and refers to the sacrificial lamb that is slain so that its blood may effect redemption (1:5; cf. Rom 8:36). John's Lamb-Christology should be considered in relation to male sexuality, for the Lamb, *to arnion,* neither evokes a masculine image nor arouses any desire for identification on the part of men. Lamb-Christology seems to me relatively gender-neutral and not well suited to exclude women from the priestly office since, demonstrably, women are capable of martyrdom. Talk about the Lamb and his bride plays with an alienating effect as regards the sexuality of this ill-matched pair. The bride is certainly not a metaphorical sheep, but clearly a human person.

John does not speak of eunuchs (as does, for example, Matt 19:12), but the Lamb on Zion is accompanied by virginal followers (Rev 14:1-4). We may find it irritating that the roles of male and female disciples are differently described: unmarried Christian women can identify with the Bride. They are encouraged to abandon an exploitative situation and take an active role in leading their lives as brides of the Lamb. Virginal male Christians, on the other hand, who have arisen with the Lamb, receive the role of the *aparchē,* the first followers of their leader.

The Woman in Labor

In 12:1-6, 13-17 we encounter a woman about to give birth, under threat and fleeing to the desert. This passage is the center of Revelation, and deciphering it is central to the discovery of women's experience in Revelation and the unfolding of John's message from its very center.

The star-crowned woman has mythical features, and consequently she is often compared to Isis, the Queen of Heaven. But we must take into account how John presents this mythical material to his addressees and reflects it in his apocalyptic perspective. This woman is not a goddess, even though she may remind us of one. She seems not to be evaluated as either good or bad. At the beginning she is powerfully described: as the mistress of the stars of heaven, pregnant and beautiful. Later we see her on the earth, robbed of her divine emblems and of her newborn child. The dragon torments her in order to obtain her baby. She is not tortured by her labor pains, but she is by the dragon so that her labors start and her baby is no longer safe in her womb. He continues to pursue her on earth, because his hunger is not satisfied. At last, the woman finds "a place prepared by God" (12:6) where she experiences solidarity with a desert community (12:6) and is strengthened.

This woman is traditionally compared to the people Israel, which has brought forth the Messiah, or to the "true" Israel, the church, which is threatened but cannot be destroyed. These interpretations involve a number of difficulties. From a feminist perspective it is problematic that they make the woman and her experiences of life and suffering invisible. The woman is pregnant, is in pain, gives birth under the most difficult circumstances (comparable to giving birth in captivity), but she is strong enough to find an escape, and this is where God wants her to be, in safety, in a community on the margins of civilization. All these actions on the part of the woman are swept away by an allegorical interpretation (in which the woman = Israel). This allegorizing method of reading makes major parts of Revelation appear sterile and dogmatic.

The woman's flight into the wilderness can be seen as a strategy of liberation. John appeals to women: stop feeding the woman-torturing, child-devouring dragon, thereby keeping him alive. In doing this John sets the murderous world economic order of the Pax Romana in relationship to the exploitation of women as vessels for reproduction who have to produce heirs and workers for their husbands and families and soldiers for the state. The woman's role seems highly attractive. But face-to-face the dragon, beauty, and the ability to give birth are shown to be vulnerable and painful exploitation. The apocryphal Acts of the Apostles and the many Acts of the martyrs show that, in fact, this path into the desert was chosen by many women in the first Christian centuries.

It is true that the apocryphal Acts were written quite a bit later than Revelation was, and yet there is no reason not to see the desert community to which the persecuted woman flees as a community of Christian ascetics. For John tirelessly denounces *porneia*, and his comment on the fall of Babylon is that it will no longer know any music or any light, no millstones, none of the things having to do with a wedding; in short, there will be no more marriages there (18:21-24). Stevan L. Davies (1980) thinks that the apocryphal Acts were written by communities of women, groups like those in Acts 6:1-6, 9:36-42, and 1 Timothy 5:3-16: widows and virgins who have joined together in a Christian life free of marriage. The woman in labor is structurally part of a series of visions with angels at their center (Rev 5:2; 7:2; 10:1-3; 18:1-2; 19:17). These angels are often described in much the same terms as the woman in labor: surrounded with a cloud, a rainbow on the head, a face like the sun, the earth illuminated by its shining radiance, etc. The verb *krazein*, "crying out," unites these angelic visions, including 12:1-2. In the other angelic visions we hear also about the strong voice of angels, and we learn what they have cried. But the woman in labor does not speak; she gives birth. She brings a new, integral life into the world and cannot be restrained. She withstands the unequal combat with the seven-headed monster, thus becoming a model of endurance and resistance *(hypomonē)*.

In this impressive vision John expresses the apocalyptic hope for an end to violence. The life-giving power will conquer the life-destroying power. It will not be long before the son (the future generation) will take power. When he comes, his companions will share in his power (2:26-27). Then the consequences of complicity will be visible to all (19:15). This is genuinely apocalyptic language. The powerless people who live on the margins place their hopes in God, the life-creating power. God will come and demand justice for them. This is the same tradition and language as in the Psalms, the Prophets, and Job. The vision of resurrection arises out of these hopes. It may not be, it cannot be, that death sets a seal on the injustice people have experienced. The resurrection for judgment is a vision of hope, resting on the unremitting demand for justice. We find that hope here as well. It empowers the tortured mother and strengthens her (clothed with the sun, crowned with the stars) and gives the wings of the eagle (12:14).

Creation Spirituality

John was not living on the island of Patmos of his own free will, and yet his place of exile became a source of power for his visions. The heat must have been great on the tiny island: southwest of the largest town is a region called Braza, from *brazein* (to cook). Patmos was, in fact, an island rich in trees, not hilly, and easily reached by ship. As a result, it was repeatedly deforested, and the result was that its water sources dried up; its major river ran dry (cf. Schmidt 1949). John probably had this bled-dry landscape before his eyes, and it inspired his vision as a counterexperience. The vision of God's closeness in 7:13-17 can tell us a lot about his life in Patmos: when God is present, he and his companions experience no more heat. Hunger and thirst come to an end. They will discover sources of water in which they can revive themselves. Even the description of the gleaming, newly built city culminates in the picture of a wealth of water and trees (22:2). Whoever wants to enter that city must wash his or her clothes, and so receive power over the trees of life (22:14). And: "Let everyone who is thirsty come. Let anyone who wishes take the water of life as a gift!" (22:17).

John dreams with his eyes open. He sees the barren cliffs vibrating in the heat and the creatures' thirst. The earth and its inhabitants cry out for the water of life.

"And I saw a new heaven and a new earth" (21:1). The risen inhabitants of the earth will dwell in an earth transformed.

Scholars frequently speak of a dualistic worldview in apocalyptic literature. A theory of two worlds, based on the notion of a material and a spiritual, immaterial world, has served as an interpretive model for many apocalyptic texts. The old, mortal creation in which are physical bodies, sickness, and death must be overcome. This dualistic model for interpretation and its application must, however, be revised (cf. Sutter Rehmann 1995). In apocalyptic books (e.g., 4 Esdras), in fact, the earth is often presented as being like a mother. She nourishes her children, suffers and rejoices with them. She gives birth to new life out of her own self; she also gives from within herself treasures such as metals and gemstones (Rev 21:11-23). The earth takes the dead into her womb and delivers them when God's time comes (14:3; 20:12-13). She is involved in the new creation as subject and thus cannot be dismissed as an object to be overcome.

The earth is mistreated by the ruling powers, and yet she seizes every opportunity to support God's life-giving will: for example, when she offers the "kings of the earth" no refuge from God's wrath (6:15-17). In 14:3, however, her cooperation with God is hinted at. She releases the 144,000 innocent dead from her earthly womb where she has sheltered them, to live a new life before God. The character of earth as subject is clearest in 12:16: "But the earth came to the help of the woman; she opened her mouth and swallowed the river that the dragon had poured from his mouth."

All creation is involved in the process of transformation into a new earth and a new heaven. John does not think of the resurrection as something individual, but rather as a cosmic event. The whole cosmos suffers under the subjection by the kings, but it rejoices when God is coming. Even an eagle is capable of commiserating with the inhabitants of the earth in their wretched condition (8:13). The frequent earthquakes are clear signs that the earth is alive. They advance the process of redemption, which is what the image of the earth giving birth signals: as the earth is in labor, trembling, shaking off the dragon, beasts, and kings, as she cooperates with the new life to come, resurrection must be near (Sutter Rehmann 1995). The earthquakes open her womb, disclose what is in the abyss, and set free what the sea had taken.

The apocalyptic vision of a redeemed, resurrected community (the new Jerusalem, 21:10-11; God's new world, 21:1) does not lead us to retreat from the world, although it does call us to withdraw from the world's power centers and inspires our passionate engagement on behalf of altered relationships here and now.

It is not death that is to be eliminated, but killing, murdering, lying, and exploitation. So-called natural death, which belongs to life, is not a subject that interests John. On the contrary: in the traditions of martyrdom, death is part of life. Mortality is accepted, but not injustice and violence.

Again and again John sees and hears the dead who have been slaughtered. He sees them at the throne of God and hears their singing: in 5:9, 7:9, 14:1-5, 15:3, and 19:1-8. The Jewish sages say that even the dead sing God's praise: "And all the dead rest on the Sabbath day, and they come, host upon host, and sing before the Holy One, blessed be He, and they come and cast themselves down in prayer in the synagogues, to confirm what is spoken (in the Scriptures): Let the faithful exult in glory . . . (Ps 149:5). And on every Sabbath and New Moon they emerge living from their graves and come and receive the visage of the Shekinah (that is, of God) and cast themselves down before him" (Grözinger 1982, 25).

In Revelation 7:9-10 the white-clad multitude sings God's greatness, honor, and power. For the political rulers of the time, however, that had to sound like disloyalty, as a rejection of the respect and honor due to themselves. We can imagine this singing as a demand for justice, much as Allan Boesak said of the liberation movement of the blacks in South Africa, where many sang in the prisons even though singing was forbidden there (Boesak 1988, 65).

LITERATURE

Baccei, Tom. 1994. *Das magische Auge. Dreidimensionale Illusionsbilder.* Munich.

Boesak, Allan. 1987. *Comfort and Protest: Reflections on the Apocalypse of John of Patmos.* Edinburgh and Philadelphia.

——. 1988. *Schreibe dem Engel Südafrikas. Trost und Protest in der Apokalypse des Johannes.* Stuttgart.

Collins, Adela Yarbro. 1984. *Crisis and Catharsis: The Power of the Apocalypse.* Philadelphia.

Davies, Stevan L. 1980. *The Revolt of the Widows: The Social World of the Apocryphal Acts.* London and Amsterdam.

Garrett, Susan R. 1992. "Revelation." In *The Women's Bible Commentary,* edited by Carol A. Newsom and Sharon H. Ringe, 377-82. London and Louisville.

Green, Elizabeth. 1996. "Die Wehen der Schöpfung und die Töchter Gottes." *Schlangenbrut* 52:27-30.

Grözinger, Karl Erich. 1982. *Musik und Gesang in der Theologie der frühen jüdischen Literatur. Talmud, Midrasch, Mystik.* Tübingen.

Kirchhoff, Renate. 1994. *Die Sünde gegen den eigenen Leib. Studien zu* porne *und* porneia *in 1 Kor 6,12-20.* Göttingen.

Kitzberger, Ingrid Rosa. 1994. "Wasser und Bäume des Lebens — eine feministisch-intertextuelle Interpretation von Apk 21/22." In *Weltgericht und Weltvollendung. Zukunftsbilder im Neuen Testament,* edited by Hans-Josef Klauck, 206-24. Freiburg, Basel, and Vienna.

Lazarus, Nahida Ruth. 1898. *Das jüdische Haus. Culturstudien über das Judentum.* 2nd ed. Berlin.

——. 1993. *Das jüdische Haus. Culturstudien über das Judentum.* In Pnina Navé Levinson, *Esther erhebt ihre Stimme,* 97-98. Gütersloh.

MacMullen, Ramsay. 1966. *Enemies of the Roman Order.* Cambridge.

Musurillo, Herbert, ed. 1972. *The Acts of the Christian Martyrs.* Oxford.

Richard, Pablo. 1996. *Apokalypse. Das Buch von Hoffnung und Widerstand.* Lucerne.

Schaumberger, Christine, and Luise Schottroff. 1988. *Schuld und Macht. Studien zu einer feministischen Befreiungstheologie.* Munich.

Schmidt, Johanna. 1949. "Patmos." In *Paulys Realencyclopädie.* 36th half-volume. Waldsee.

Schneemelcher, Wilhelm, ed. 1989. *Neutestamentliche Apokryphen.* Vol. 2. Tübingen.

Schüssler Fiorenza, Elisabeth. 1985. *The Book of Revelation.* Philadelphia.

Sutter Rehmann, Luzia. 1994. "'Und ihr werdet ohne Sorgen sein . . . Gedanken zum Phänomen der Ehefreiheit.'" In *Für Gerechtigkeit streiten,* edited by Dorothee Sölle, 88-95. Gütersloh.

———. 1995. *Geh, frage die Gebärerin. Feministisch-befreiungstheologische Untersuchungen zum Gebärmotiv in der Apokalyptik.* Gütersloh.

Wire, Antoinette Clark. 1990. *The Corinthian Women Prophets.* Minneapolis.

Zager, Werner. 1989. *Begriff und Wertung der Apokalypse in der neutestamentlichen Forschung.* Frankfurt, Berlin, New York, and Paris.

For Further Reading

Levine, Amy-Jill. 2010. *A Feminist Companion to the Apocalypse of John.* Feminist Companion to the New Testament and Early Christian Literature. London and New York.

Translated by Linda M. Maloney

The Story of Thecla: Apostle between Fiction and Reality

Anne Jensen

The account of an early Christian apostle named Thecla is written formally as an act of an apostle but is no longer included in the canonical books of the New Testament. It is one of the writings called apocryphal, that is, "hidden," scriptures. This is most unfortunate, as this narrative never was a secret and most certainly was not a heretical text, but a well-read and highly esteemed document in the first century of Christianity. Thecla was regarded with the same respect as the apostles and other biblical figures (cf. Albrecht 1986, 239ff.). This short work is of particular interest for theological and historical research on women because here a woman is obviously accepted and described as an apostle. This is in clear contrast to canonical scriptures like the Pastoral Letters that aim to silence women in the public sphere. The figure of Thecla caused controversy already in the second century: Tertullian, who argued for female subservience, indignantly observed that women of Carthage would use this female apostle and martyr to legitimate their own activities as Christian teachers (*De baptismo* 17).

In its version existing today, the Thecla story, which, according to Tertullian, came from a presbyter in Asia Minor, is integrated into the story of Paul. There certainly was a separate oral tradition of Thecla that survived independently even after its incorporation into the Acts of Paul, as is indicated in handed-down manuscripts. Of Paul's story a few severely damaged fragments are almost all that remains, whereas Thecla's story is available in many complete manuscripts. This too testifies to her significance.

The Acts of Thecla (in Greek: *praxeis*, Latin: *acta*, German: *Akten* or *Geschichten*) is structured as "martyrologies" in analogy to the other acts or stories of apostles. The story of Thecla even consists of two very different martyrdoms. Although Thecla does not die in them, she was, according to early Christian understanding, no less a martyr than those who died during the persecutions. The women and men who survived martyrdom were highly esteemed in the Christian communities. In particular, they had the right to readmit the so-called *lapsi*, those who did not remain steadfast in persecution, into the community. Normally this was the right of the bishop.

The Martyrdom in Iconium

The first story of martyrdom the Acts of Thecla narrates takes place in Iconium. There, Onesiphorus and his wife Lectra (2 Tim 1:16) await the apostle Paul. When he arrives, he delivers a long sermon at their house. He pronounces beatitudes and concentrates on the ideal of abstinence, suggesting that this is the essence of the Christian message: Paul preaches "the word of God of abstinence and resurrection" (Acts of Thecla 5). The theology in this writing is confused, and although it is not spelled out as such, one can feel the presence of the fundamental elements of patristic virginity-propaganda: marriage is an old institution rendered obsolete by Christ; it is possible now on earth to anticipate the life of the angels and the life of resurrection by means of abstinence.

Thecla hears the apostle's sermon from the window of her house and is deeply fascinated. The shocked mother, Theocleia, calls the fiancé Thamyris, but they fail to change Thecla's mind. Thamyris agrees to lay charges against Paul in a court of law. The crowd is incensed by the apostle: "Away with the magician! He has ruined all our women!" (15). Paul gives testimony before the court but without mentioning the ideal of abstinence. When he is taken to prison, Thecla follows him there at night. (Indeed, Christians visited their imprisoned sisters and brothers often in jail.) In the trial she is standing with Paul before the judge, and the interest is focused entirely on her and her refusal to get married. The mother wants her burned at the stake. Paul is merely sent into exile, but Thecla is bound to the stake but is rescued by a cloudburst.

This whole story is logically not very stringent. The disappointed fiancé wants to win his bride back and does not want her to die. The judgment is pronounced by the mother, not the governor. The sermon on virginity is at the core of the asceticism that is behind this narrative; it emerges once again in the last episode of this first part: Paul is hiding with the family of Onesiphorus in a graveyard, where they fast for days. Thecla finds them there and confronts Paul with an unusual decision: "I will cut off my hair and follow you wherever you go." He answered: "The time is evil and you are attractive. You could be tested worse than you have been and you may not stand firm but give in to despair." Thecla said: "Give me first Christ's seal for then no test will come upon me." Paul replied: "Thecla, have patience, then you will receive the water" (25).

This passage is puzzling. The renunciation of the adornment of hair (later the "tonsure") has a clear ascetic motive: it is a renunciation of erotic attractiveness. But this seems not to be enough protection for the apostle. The delay of the baptism is difficult to explain in New Testament times. So this passage may be more a literary product of the ascetic environment than a historical reminiscence.

The Martyrdom in Antioch

The second part of the account is set in Antioch (it remains unclear whether it is Syrian or Pisidian Antioch). The Thecla we meet here is completely different. In Iconium she did not speak a single time, but now she is the heroine of the story from beginning to end. At first glance, this episode also starts with a story about chastity like that of Thecla and Thamyris above, and like those we encounter in similar versions in the five noncanonical Acts of Apostles (Acts of Peter, Acts of Paul, Acts of Andrew, Acts of Thomas, and Acts of John). As she arrives in Antioch, a Syrian named Alexander falls in love with her and tries to get close to her via Paul. The apostle pretends not to know her — and vanishes from the story. And then the following remarkable episode takes place:

> Because he was a powerful man, he embraced her on the street. But she did not allow this, instead she searched for Paul. And she shouts loudly: "Do not rape a foreigner, do not rape the servant of God! I am the first among Iconians but they exiled me from the city because I did not want to marry Thamyris." She grabs Alexander, tears his robes, throws down the wreath from his head and makes him into a laughing stock. He takes her before the governor, on the one hand because he loved her, on the other, because he was ashamed that something like this had happened to him. She admitted what she had done and the governor sentenced her to death in the arena. The women grew angry and shouted: "Despicable judgment! Godless judgment!" But Thecla only asked the governor to be allowed to remain chaste until she had to face the animals. A rich woman, Tryphaina, whose daughter had died, took her into custody and found solace in Thecla's company. (26-27)

If one looks more closely at this narrative, it is clear that this is not a classic example of the refusal to marry as in other stories of chastity, but a normal defense against sexual assault that certainly would not have fetched the death penalty. The official charge against Thecla further on reads very differently: "Desecration of the temple" (28). This charge explains the real conflict between Christianity, which Thecla, the woman apostle, proclaims, and the inherited religion of goddesses and gods. Thecla's plea "to be allowed to remain chaste until she had to face the animals" does not express her fear of Alexander's renewed attempts at seduction, but the very real fear of being forced into prostitution. Given Thecla's charge of offending the local religion, the judge had the competence to impose just such a sentence. But instead of sending her to a public prison, he accepts Tryphaina's offer of custody.

The name of a Queen Tryphaina is historically attested, but the identity of Thecla's protector is not clear. A strong bond develops between the two women, because Tryphaina had lost her daughter Falconilla early on. The daughter appears to her mother in a dream: "Mother, take this foreign woman, the abandoned Thecla, in my place so that she can pray for me and I can go to the place of the righteous" (28).

A little later, the martyr does fulfill this plea: "She did not hesitate to raise her voice: 'My God, Son of the Highest in the Heaven, grant her according to her will that her daughter Falconilla may live in eternity'" (29).

Their contemporaries were convinced that martyrs commanded a very special charismatic authority. The motif of saving intercession for the dead can also be found in the Martyrdom of Perpetua and Felicitas.

The departure to the arena the following morning is tumultuous, owing to Tryphaina's protests, but finally the soldiers arrive and take a very composed Thecla away. As at the earlier sentencing (27: "Despicable judgment! Godless judgment!"), a large group of women protest, showing their solidarity with Thecla: "May the city fall because of this crime! Kill all of us women, Proconsul! Sickening performance! Despicable judgment!" (32). Later in the course of this martyrdom, they are even going to try to numb the animals with fragrant herbs.

Thecla is confronted first with bears and lions, then with many other animals. She prays with her arms wide open, then sees a pool of water full of seals and exclaims: "Now is the moment to wash myself." As she plunges in she speaks these words: "In the name of Christ Jesus I baptize myself on my last day" (34).

This passage also is puzzling because we know of no other self-baptism in early Christian literature. However, Christians hoped that baptism would give them strength in the hour of torture (cf. the Martyrdom of Perpetua and Felicitas: there the catechumens are baptized in prison). In the understanding of early Christianity, one already became a Christian through conversion; baptism was the seal of this conversion.

The fighting in the arena intensifies. But when Thecla is to be bound between two bulls to be torn apart, a surprising change occurs: Tryphaina collapses and is feared to be dead. This could incite the wrath of the emperor, as she is a relative of the court. The animal fight is stopped abruptly at Alexander's pleas, and Thecla is freed. The governor is surprised by the miracle of her survival, which Thecla, the woman apostle, explains in the following manner: "I am a servant of the living God. This is what happened: I believed in the one in whom God delights, His Son. Because of him, none of the animals attacked me. He alone is the condition of salvation and the foundation of eternal life. Because he is the shelter for the weary in a storm, he refreshes the downhearted and he is the shield for the hopeless. In one word: Who does not believe in him, will not live, but will be dead in eternity" (37).

This testimonial speech is the counterpart to the apostle Paul's speech in Iconium (17). Thecla is now in fact an apostle only. She stays another week with

Tryphaina, who, with many of her servants, converts to Christianity. Then Thecla leaves for Myra to find Paul: "She took male and female servants, girded up and altered her dress into men's robes and went to Myra. There she found Paul, preaching God's word, and she went up to him. He was frightened when he saw her and the people with her because he feared that she was faced with another test. She noticed and said: 'I have had the bath, Paul. The One who works with you preaching the good news also worked with me and washed me'" (40).

This is one of the few passages that link the first and the second stories (Paul's refusal to baptize — Thecla's self-baptism). For the journey she arranged her clothes like "men's robes." Together with the one about the short hair, this passage is sometimes read in connection to the *topos* of female praise: "She was like a man," found in patristic literature. Or it is seen as an expression of female self-esteem, to be equal to men. Textually though, it seems that the change of dress is rather a measure of practicality when traveling.

After Thecla has given an account of her rescue to the church in Myra, she takes her leave: "Thecla stood up and said to Paul: 'I will go to Iconium.' Paul responded: 'Go forth and teach the word of God!' Tryphaina sent her many clothes and gold so that she could give 'a part' to Paul for the ministry among the poor" (41). From being the apostle's pupil she has become an equal, in this instance almost superior, colleague. She will be only a short time in Iconium to visit her mother once more (Thamyris is already dead). Thecla's path leads to Seleucia — and here the account ends: "She enlightened many through the word of God and passed away gently" (43).

Only her prayer that she speaks at her homecoming in the house of Onesiphorus, where Paul had preached, remains to be added: "My God and God of this house in which I saw the light; Christ Jesus, you Son of God, you were my helper in prison, my helper in the fire and my helper among the animals: you are God and to you be honor and glory for ever. Amen" (42).

Examining the Original Tradition

The opinion, found occasionally in scholarly reports, that the author of the Acts of Paul simply invented Thecla has not gained much ground. The kernel of the story has to be regarded as historical. But of what does this kernel consist? Without doubt, it is the martyrdom Thecla endured during her work as an apostle. But is her refusal to marry the reason, as the written version seems to suggest? Here I have my doubts. It is true that the opposition of female and male Christians toward marriage, family, and bourgeois life was the cause for many conflicts. And doubtlessly it was a great achievement of women Christians to find ways of life that provided them with a materially secured existence and a respected social position outside marriage.

Turning away from matrimony is seen as a beacon of emancipation, particularly in American feminist literature. An example of this is the interpretation of the chastity stories in the extracanonical Acts of the Apostles that we have already mentioned. "Chastity as Autonomy" is Virginia Burrus's programmatic title. Stevan L. Davies has suggested, because of this motif, that all five extracanonical Acts of the Apostles were written by women. In a somewhat toned-down version, Dennis R. MacDonald and Virginia Burrus maintain that these stories emanate from a circle of women. More precisely, they suggest that at the beginning of the tradition these stories were told by women storytellers. Ross S. Kraemer disagrees with this interpretation because the women converted by the apostles were not always very autonomous. Sheila E. McGinn assumes a male editor for the Acts of Thecla, who "domesticated" the popular story of Thecla that originated from a woman (McGinn 1994, 805). An individual or collective female authorship of the oral version of the Thecla story is quite possible but in my opinion not conclusive. It is certain, however, that the editor tried to change the story of Thecla into a story of Paul — luckily with little success!

More important than the authorship, it seems to me, is the reception of the story, which moved beyond the circle of women into the mainstream of the Christian community. In my investigation I tried to separate the two levels of tradition that are entangled in the written account. My conclusion is that the original oral tradition tells of a female apostle who suffers as a martyr. This is particularly clear in the second part of the narrative where there are no ascetic motifs. Thecla is not a preacher for chastity but a "servant of God" in the propagation of the good news.

The secondary layer is that of the editorial work, integrating the account of Thecla into the Acts of Paul. The presbyter mentioned by Tertullian could have been the one who turned the story of Thecla's martyrdom, according to the fashion of the time, into a small edifying novel by giving the first part, with Paul's sermon on abstinence and Thecla's refusal of marriage, an ascetic-erotic tinge. The first part expresses the theology and social practices of ascetic-oriented circles. The connection between the two parts is only very superficial.

How do we deal with this story today? Should we include it in the canon? This would give too much weight to the canon. A canon with open boundaries is preferable. Yes, in view of the boundless amount of allegedly normative traditions in Catholicism, Martin Luther was right at the time to call attention to the normative origin with his principle of *sola Scriptura*. But by now, in contrast, the dangers and limitations of such exclusive fixation on Scripture have become plain. Philomène, an early Christian thinker, and her followers have argued that God can speak through all scriptures and not only through the biblical canon, as long as one knows how to read correctly.

LITERATURE

Albrecht, Ruth. 1986. *Das Leben der heiligen Makrina auf dem Hintergrund der Thekla-Traditionen. Studien zu den Ursprüngen des weiblichen Mönchtums im 4. Jahrhundert in Kleinasien.* Forschungen zur Kirchen- und Dogmengeschichte, vol. 38. Göttingen.

Burrus, Virginia. 1987. *Chastity as Autonomy: Women in the Stories of the Apocryphal Acts.* Studies in Women and Religion, vol. 23. Lewiston, N.Y., and Queenston, Ontario.

Cooper, Kate. 1992. "Apostles, Ascetic Women, and Questions of Audience: New Reflections on the Rhetoric of Gender in the Apocryphal Acts." *SBL Seminar Papers,* 147-53.

Davies, Stevan L. 1980. *The Revolt of the Widows: The Social World of the Apocryphal Acts.* Carbondale and Edwardsville, Ill.

Jensen, Anne. 1992. *Gottes selbstbewusste Töchter. Frauenemanzipation im frühen Christentum?* Freiburg.

Kraemer, Ross S. 1976. *Ecstatics and Ascetics: Studies in the Function of Religious Activities for Women in the Greco-Roman World.* Princeton.

MacDonald, Dennis R. 1983. *The Legend and the Apostle: The Battle for Paul in Story and Canon.* Philadelphia.

———. 1984. "The Role of Women in the Production of the Apocryphal Acts of Apostles." *Iliff Review* 40, no. 4:21-38.

McGinn, Sheila E. 1994. "The Acts of Thecla." In *Searching the Scriptures,* edited by Elisabeth Schüssler Fiorenza, 2:800-828. 2 vols. New York.

Nauerth, Claudia, and Rüdiger Warns. 1981. *Thekla. Ihre Bilder in der frühchristlichen Kunst.* Göttinger Orient-Forschungen, 2nd ser., vol. 3. Wiesbaden.

Schottroff, Luise. 1995. "Frauengeschrei. Frauenwiderstand und Frauensolidarität in den Theklaakten." *Schlangenbrut* 50:5-8.

"Die Theklaakten (in: Die Paulusakten)." 1989. In *Neutestamentliche Apokryphen,* edited by V. Wilhelm Schneemelcher, vol. 2, *Apostolisches, Apokalypsen und Verwandtes.* 5th ed. Tübingen.

Thekla die Apostolin. Ein apokrypher Text neu entdeckt. 1995. Translated and commented on by Anne Jensen. Freiburg.

FOR FURTHER READING

Bremmer, Jan N., ed. 1996. *The Apocryphal Acts of Paul and Thecla.* Kampen.

Davis, Stephen J. 2001. *The Cult of Saint Thecla: A Tradition of Women's Piety in Late Antiquity.* Oxford.

Translated by Tina Steiner

Acts of Xanthippe, Polyxena, and Rebecca; or, Three Women and Two Lionesses

Irene Dannemann

The text of the Acts of Xanthippe, Polyxena, and Rebecca (shortened to Acts of Xanthippe; abbreviated Acts Xant) is available only in the Greek original and in a hard-to-get English translation.[1] In what follows, therefore, a summary of the contents of this text will first be offered and then the themes that are most important from a feminist perspective will be addressed and interpreted. These are the following:

- the married Xanthippe's sexual refusal,
- the unmarried Polyxena's freedom from marriage,
- violent attacks on the protagonists,
- women as pray-ers, not as proclaimers,
- the picture of women, men, and apostles.

Following that, I shall turn to the questions of who wrote this text and when, with what intention and for which group.

The Content

The work tells how three women, Xanthippe, Polyxena, and Rebecca, became Christians.

The story begins with Xanthippe (1-22), the wife of Probus, a ruler ("king") of Spain. As one of her husband's slaves becomes ill and pins his hope for healing on Paul alone, Xanthippe hears of Paul for the first time. She longs for his teaching and his God. She draws back from Probus, sighs and prays all night long. Probus is mortified at the change in her (1-6). As Paul comes into the city shortly after this,

---

1. The English text is found in the *Ante-Nicene Fathers (ANF)*, vol. 10. The translations of direct quotes in this article are taken from the *ANF* [trans.].

Xanthippe recognizes him, and Probus takes him into his house. Paul does not baptize Xanthippe right away, although she requests it. After a while Probus wants to be rid of Paul because so many people are coming into his house (7-10), but Xanthippe doesn't want the church to meet elsewhere (10). But Probus throws Paul out of the house and locks his wife in her room, while the influential ex-prefect Philotheus invites Paul into his house (11). Xanthippe learns of this from slaves in her house, and that evening, after bribing the guard at the door of her house, she heads in that direction. Demons waylay her, pursuing her with light-ning and fiery torches. Xanthippe becomes afraid and reproaches herself that, on the way to baptism and to salvation, she has been overtaken by her sins. Then, sud-denly, Paul and a handsome young man are at her side, and the demons disappear. Xanthippe asks Paul: "Master, why hast thou left me solitary? Even now make haste to seal me, so that if death come upon me I may depart to him who is full of compassion and has no arrogance" (12-13). Thereupon Paul baptizes her in the house of Philotheus and gives her the Eucharist *(eucharistia)*. On the next day Je-sus appears to her and speaks to her. She faints, having forgotten to eat because of her intense longing for Christ (14-16).

After her husband, Probus, has a dream, which the wise men Barandus and Gnosteas interpret for him as a sign of the victory of Jesus Christ, who marks those who come to him with the impregnable breastplate of baptism and makes them invincible, the three wish to be baptized (17-18). They throw themselves at the feet of Xanthippe, who is in prayerful song, and ask her to pray for them. She immedi-ately sends them to Paul, and Probus is baptized by Paul the next day. Thereupon Xanthippe prepares for a celebration at her house. In the process she is attacked in a dark corner by a demon, disguised as an actor she knows, into whose face she hurls an iron lamp stand, obliterating all its features. The demon cries out, "O vio-lence, from this destroyer even women have received power to strike us" (21).

Now Polyxena, Xanthippe's beautiful younger sister, enters the story (22-42). In Xanthippe's bedroom Polyxena sits with her sister, who is reading the prophets. As Xanthippe and Polyxena's nurse head off to be with Paul, Polyxena stays behind in the room, and she is carried off by the enemy of the man she wants to marry. In this hopeless situation she quotes Psalm 142:4. She is carried off to a ship that is go-ing to sail to Babylon. But the lack of a favorable wind prevents it from making headway. As Peter is sailing by, he prays, at the behest of a voice from heaven, for Polyxena, the poor, troubled soul on ship. The ship lands in Greece, where the apostle Philip awaits Polyxena on shore. He has her taken to a house for safe keep-ing, but she flees, because 8,000 armed men lined up by the man who abducted her want to capture her again (Acts Xant 23-25). She ends up lost in a wilderness and is threatened by a lioness. She beseeches the lioness, "[T]ear me not until I re-ceive baptism." The lioness spares her and brings her to a road along which the apostle Andrew is traveling. She runs up to him and implores him to baptize her. They go to a spring, where they meet Rebecca, a Jewish slave sold into this area.

She calls Andrew a prophet and an apostle. The lioness, impressed as she was by Polyxena's prayer, speaks to Andrew on behalf of the two women, and he baptizes them both and asks them to pray for him. Polyxena tells Andrew that she and Rebecca want to follow him, but he denies the request and charges them to stay. Then the two women go to the lioness in the mountains, and Rebecca says, "It is indeed better for us to live with wild beasts and perish of hunger than to be compelled by Greeks and idolaters to fall into the filth of marriage" (26-31). They travel with a donkey driver who became a Christian through Philip. He wants to bring them to the sea so that they can reach Spain, but a prefect abducts Polyxena (31-34). While Rebecca escapes and goes to the house of an old woman, the imprisoned Polyxena is to be brought to the bed of the prefect. But she so impresses her captors that they report that she is ill. She is visited by the prefect's son, who tells her about Paul's preaching in Antioch and about Thecla. He asks about her god and wants to flee with Polyxena. But their conversation is reported to the prefect, who has them thrown to the wild beasts. But in the arena a lioness licks the soles of Polyxena's feet, whereupon the prefect and the city come to faith (36-37).

As Onesimus is sailing to Spain, he comes to the harbor in which Polyxena, Rebecca, and the prefect's son are looking for a ship bound for Spain. Onesimus takes the three on board, and another attempt to abduct Polyxena is averted (38-39). In Spain Paul, Xanthippe, and Probus greet the new arrivals. The two sisters are so happy to see one another. Paul persuades Polyxena's abductor to stop pursuing her and baptizes him along with the man who wanted to marry her. The entire city rejoices (40-42). "From that time forward [Polyxena] left not at all the blessed Paul in her fear of temptations" (42).

Married Xanthippe's Sexual Refusal

The social consequences of Xanthippe's sexual refusal are described. It means her withdrawal from her husband, with whom she not only no longer shares a bed but also no longer eats (the association of these two items is also found in the Acts of Thomas 82-89, 95-96, 98, 103). She tells her husband "No," directly, to his face, or informs him through others. She breaks free of the well-trodden paths, and when she refuses to come to supper, Probus reacts with rage: "Think not in bed also thou wilt keep away from me" (Acts Xant 12). But he accepts her decision, for it is nowhere reported that he forced his way into her room or compelled her to come to his bed. Xanthippe refuses sexual contact with Probus but does not withdraw from him fundamentally. She continues her relationship with him and brings him into contact with Paul. When Probus wants Paul to baptize him, he hears him preach. Paul rejects extramarital sexual contact but emphasizes the unity of marriage (20; cf. 1 Cor 7:1-16, 25-40). Probus quickly asks, "Why then has Xanthippe withdrawn from me?" and Paul, as in 1 Corinthians 7:32-34, 37-38, 40, explains that some, with more foresight than others, shed all desires of the flesh. Probus returns home unbaptized, eats nothing and cannot get to sleep (Acts Xant 20), and receives baptism the next day (21). Probus takes hold of the situation where the change in Xanthippe most radically affects his day-to-day existence. Paul does not defend and support Xanthippe (Davies 1980, 111-12), by calling on Probus, for example, to accept his wife's decision about their sexual relationship, but instead leaves it to the couple to solve this problem themselves. The conversation between Probus and Paul reads like a discussion about 1 Corinthians 7 and that chapter's effects. Acts of Xanthippe 20 shows both Paul's restrained method of argumentation when his preaching on the theme of sexuality is attacked, and the explosiveness his thoughts carry for churches and marriages. Xanthippe denies her husband sexual relations but stays with him rather than leaving him (41). Whether or not they, after they eat together again (21-22), possibly also share a bed, is an open question. Perhaps what is in view is a solution like that in 1 Corinthians 7:5, where, to be sure, sex is not seen as a positive energy for life.

Xanthippe's refusal of sex and the way in which Probus comes to terms with it can be interpreted in two ways. (1) Married Christian women should be encouraged to use this kind of pressure so that their husbands also seek baptism — encouraged under the assumption that then table and bed fellowship can be discussed in a new way. (2) Control over their own body is depicted as a possible and good way for women to act. Xanthippe acts independently and, on her own and on the basis of her own needs, seeks the Christian God. And yet she does not in this way become an autonomous person, nor does she alienate herself from her social context (as is asserted by Burrus 1987, 2, 59-60, but with reference to the depictions of women in the apocryphal Acts of the Apostles), but remains attached to her husband and their common household. Before their encounter with Christianity, Proclus is already prepared to accede to the desires of his wife (5) — on this view, Christian faith changes nothing about the way the married couple relate to one another.

Probus sees Xanthippe's sexual refusal as putting her marriage with him in question (6), and this causes him to be greatly troubled. Xanthippe appears to have no problem with life without sex. She desires baptism and thinks a great deal about God and about her sins — these thoughts control her life. To be sure, her decision about her sexuality leads to a crisis with her husband, in which she remains steadfast in her decision. And in this way she breaks out of the role expected of her as a good housewife and prospective mother. Married Christian women are shown here a wife who is not caught up in her customary societal roles as a hard-working housewife, submissive wife, and prospective mother but prays, reads the Bible, and goes to church meetings every day. The self-determination over her own body that Xanthippe lives out in sexual abstinence is an expression of new accents for Christian women's own lives.

In the groups and churches in which the Acts of Xanthippe was recounted, the picture of Xanthippe emboldened women to hold on to their own faith under-standings and to live in accord with them, even if conflicts in their marriages arose thereby (Davies 1980, 110-14). Husbands were called upon to support their wives and to leave them alone, and both partners were encouraged to stay together.

The Unmarried Polyxena's Freedom from Marriage

Polyxena's role is entirely different from Xanthippe's. She is the younger woman who marries neither the man who wants to wed her nor her abductor from Spain, and neither of these men has any sexual contact with her. Even the planned sexual assault by the prefect who had her abducted in Greece is thwarted (36). Polyxena remains unmarried, and at the end of the story she wishes to leave her family and follow Paul (42).

Her behavior can be interpreted as "freedom from marriage" (Sutter Rehmann 1994 coins this phrase): Polyxena changes her life, decides to devote her-self to an unmarried itinerant life with Paul, and thereby decides for a way of life like that of Thecla. It is said of Thecla that after a time with Paul she goes her own way and becomes an independent teacher and proclaimer of the word of God (Acts of Paul and Thecla 41 and 43). Analogously (since the Acts of Paul and Thecla were known), the readers of the Acts of Xanthippe possibly envisioned a similar perspective for Polyxena: a life as a woman proclaimer independent of a man. Polyxena lives an independent life; unfortunately we do not know whether her sister Xanthippe, with whom she has an important relationship, supports her in this or not. Polyxena leaves her sister — perhaps because those around her would not permanently accept her new way of life (this is the view of Burrus 1987, 59-60, about the heroines of the apocryphal Acts of the Apostles). From the flow of the narrative, it is easy to envision that Rebecca stays with her and travels with her.

Xanthippe and Polyxena present two very different ways of life for women. Rebecca's life is depicted less clearly. She is unmarried and speaks of marriage quite disparagingly (Acts Xant 35). We read nothing about her sexuality, but as a slave, she is surely no longer a virgin. Rather, she has experienced sex in a manner over which she likely had no say at all (on the sexuality of women slaves, cf. Dannemann 1996, 135-38, 212-18). She joins Polyxena and speaks of her as a "sister" (35).

Brutal Attacks on the Protagonists

We read of many such attacks by men or demons in the Acts of Xanthippe. When attacked, the women defend themselves: as Xanthippe is attacked out on the street, she begins a loud lament and she prays. Paul and a "beautiful youth" appear, so the demons disappear (13).[2] Later, Xanthippe defends herself against the attack of a demon by becoming aggressive — to the demon's horror, through Christ "even women have received power to strike us" (21). Xanthippe successfully drives this demon away. Polyxena impresses her guards at the prefect's house so much by her speech that they lie for her. Because with her prayer she reminds the son of the prefect of Thecla, he undertakes a great risk for the prisoner (36). Even in the battle on the island, Polyxena does not remain passive. Rather, she jumps into the sea when she sees the numerical superiority of her attackers. A ship's captain rescues her, and the crew flees with her (39).

Thus the women defend themselves in quite different ways, and each time they succeed. Resistance by women on the most diverse levels is seen as entirely natural, as a fully legitimate way for women to act, enabling them to protect themselves.

The attacks on Xanthippe and Polyxena are not generally depicted as sexual attacks. In the Acts of Thomas 42-46, 62-64, there is a much more drastic portrayal of how women are threatened sexually by men or demons. But whether that means that in the Acts of Xanthippe no attack on the women's sexual integrity is in view, is not possible to decide: rapes are often a self-evident part of bodily attacks on women (Schottroff 1994, 175; 1995, 115, assumes Acts Xant 21 to be an intended rape). The reserved presentation in the Acts of Xanthippe can mean that the groups that used that document were not confronted with sexual threats or that they did not want to deal with this theme because it was dangerous.

When the attacks occur, the women are not so well protected by their male companions that nothing will happen to them and they can feel secure. This situation also occurs in the Bible: Abraham does not protect Sarah from the pharaoh, but God delivers her (Gen 12:10-20). The Acts of Xanthippe conveys the image that women should defend themselves and can trust one another and God, but that they cannot rely on men, not even the apostles (Davies 1980, 66-69). In that respect this text shows an image completely different from that shown by the church fathers: while in their writings women are dangerous for men, the Acts of Xanthippe describes men as a danger for women (Davies 1980, 116 says the same thing with respect to the apocryphal Acts of the Apostles in general).

In reaction to the brutal attacks by men, the Acts of Xanthippe shows several different forms of solidarity among women: Polyxena is strengthened by remembering Xanthippe (23, 26); the foreigner Polyxena, unfamiliar with the area, and the runaway slave Rebecca join forces in order to survive (29-42); an old woman harbors Rebecca, who had fled the prefect's soldiers (as Tryphaina does for Thecla in the Acts of Paul and Thecla 27-39), and comforts her in her sorrow and concern for Polyxena (35).

---

2. In the Hypostasis of the Archons 92.19–93.10, Norea speaks of a rape by the archons, when she calls on God for help. Thereupon the angel Eleleth appears, and the attackers withdraw.

Women as Pray-ers, Not as Proclaimers

The prayers of Xanthippe and Polyxena take up a lot of space in the Acts of Xanthippe. Many of them are longer than a discourse or even any prayer of an apostle. It is striking how Xanthippe wrestles with God even before she has heard Paul. She has heard about Paul's healings and sermons, but knows neither his name nor the name of his God. She herself sets out to find this God through prayer and asks God to illumine her lack of knowledge (2-3). She does not wait for the authority of a Paul but begins on her own the journey to this God. Such an independent way was also chosen by Thecla, as she baptizes herself in the arena (Acts of Paul and Thecla 34). Xanthippe formulates her deepest needs in her prayers and asks God for help. She never expresses her fears and her longing to Paul. She awaits compassion and understanding from God (Acts Xant 13), not from Paul.

Polyxena also prays again and again — often in her prayers remembering her sister Xanthippe (from whom she was violently separated) and the last time they were together (23 and 26), when Xanthippe read aloud from the Bible for Polyxena and herself. This remembered evening is the counterimage to the horrors of her abduction, and she seeks consolation in remembering it, especially as long as she is all alone and Rebecca has not yet joined her.

On three occasions Polyxena herself also speaks up and tells others about her God and her faith: to the donkey driver, himself a Christian (31-32); to her guards in the prefect's house (36); and to the prefect, who had condemned her to the arena (37). But Polyxena does not speak this way before large groups, in contrast, for example, to Lucius, a disciple of Paul's, who preaches publicly before their departure from Greece, while Polyxena appears to speak only within the group (38). When the lioness does not attack Polyxena in the arena but lies at her feet, the prefect summons her and his son to the palace to learn about Christ. Polyxena does not speak publicly in the arena — and yet the entire city is won for the Christian faith (37). As with Thecla, a lioness saves a condemned woman in the arena (cf. Acts of Paul and Thecla 33). But in contrast to Thecla, women in the Acts of Xanthippe do not publicly take the role of preachers, not even in a church gathering. That can mean that the Acts of Xanthippe arose in a time in which women could not preach to men (any longer). With reserve the Acts of Xanthippe criticizes this practice and its justification in women's failure to be called and, ultimately, their inferiority (Davies 1980, 64-66, 104). The picture of Polyxena opens up a few times in the direction of a proclamation by her. And if her comparison with Thecla (Acts Xant 36) also applies to the conclusion of the story, then the perspective flashes into view that perhaps Polyxena later will actually become an independent preacher. But this is only hinted at, with none of the clarity we find in Acts of Paul and Thecla 42-43.

The Picture of Women, Men, and Apostles

In the entire account, it is the women who drive the action forward. They find all kinds of new ways to encounter an apostle, to get baptized, and to survive. In this regard we hear far less about Rebecca than about the two women from Spain, Xanthippe and Polyxena. She is still present during Polyxena's return (38), but the Jewish former slave goes unmentioned at the group's reception in Spain.

The men in Acts of Xanthippe are always described in relation to one of the women protagonists. Probus is fully occupied with reacting to the changes in his wife. He is more of a marginal figure who embodies the relational network in the life of the protagonist. Polyxena's abductors and the man who wants to marry her are independent actors, but they are totally unsuccessful in their efforts (according to Burrus 1987, 75, writing about the most important male characters in the apocryphal Acts of the Apostles). Polyxena remains unmarried and independent. In the course of the conflict over accepting the Christian faith, it is not the male figures who propel the action; rather, they follow Xanthippe and Polyxena's example. Perhaps the relationship between men and women reaches its symbolic climax when the two wise men fall on their knees before Xanthippe as she is praying (19): the men realize their dependence on the intercession of women.

Four apostles appear in the Acts of Xanthippe: Paul, Peter, Philip, and Andrew. They do not stand in the foreground of the text, are not its protagonists, but primarily react to the requests of the women protagonists. And their actions in this regard are not exactly praiseworthy. Paul twice rejects Xanthippe's requests for baptism (8, 11). He puts her off, even though he sees her faith, and she actually comforts and encourages him (9). He shows no such hesitation over Probus's baptism. The meeting of the ship on which Peter is traveling with the one on which Polyxena is being abducted comes off as a kind of caricature of the apostle: instead of trying to come to her aid, he is content to offer a prayer and sail by (24). The apostle Philip appears only in a marginal episode recounting his activity in Greece (25), but he leaves Polyxena unbaptized. Andrew attempts to distance himself from Polyxena and baptizes her and Rebecca only after the lioness, speaking in a human voice, advocates baptizing women. By forbidding them to accompany him (28-30), he denies them his protection — and we are dealing here with a woman from Spain who had never been to Greece and a fugitive woman slave.

In the Acts of Xanthippe the women protagonists appear in an unfamiliar way — they are the principal figures, while husbands, suitors, or abductors appear only on the margin. The apostles don't make a good impression, for they react to the women with hesitation, sometimes even rejecting the women's attempts to be baptized or instructed or to accompany them. The Acts of Xanthippe criticizes this apostolic behavior (Davies 1980, 67). The document wants to keep women from having overly high expectations of the apostles, namely, to seek from them understanding or effective assistance (Davies 1980, 68).

The interest of the Acts of Xanthippe concentrates on the women figures and their decisions and motives, not on the lives of the men or apostles, who do not appear in a good light. True, the apostles have brought people to faith, but they often leave the sympathetically portrayed women protagonists in the lurch. This portrayal is diametrically opposed to the negative view of women in the church fathers, who describe women either as ignorant and unendingly burdened with the sins peculiar to their gender or as an unattainable perfect ideal (Davies 1980, 103). In the Acts of Xanthippe the men have to rely on the initiative and even the intercession of the women.

The Acts of Xanthippe as a Text

The Acts of Xanthippe was probably written in the middle of the third century.[3] This dating is dependent on a comparison with the other acts of apostles with which the work is acquainted: the Acts of Paul and Thecla, the Acts of Paul, the Acts of Peter, possibly also the Acts of Andrew, the Acts of Thomas, and the Acts of Philip ("Acts of Xanthippe" [Greek] 1893, 47-52; Davies 1980, 6-10; Jensen 1995, 68). By contrast, situations or persons in the Acts of Xanthippe are practically never picked up in other writings ("Acts of Xanthippe" [Greek] 1893, 43-47 cites the few reminiscences). Xanthippe and Polyxena are honored as saints on September 23 ("Acts of Xanthippe" [Greek] 1893, 43-47).

It is unclear where the Acts of Xanthippe was written. The Greek language and the good acquaintance with the Acts of Paul and Thecla point to the eastern part of the Roman Empire (Davies 1980, 10-11).

The Acts of Xanthippe is a novel written with humor and suspense. Like many acts of apostles, it is modeled on the Greek novel (it is designated as a "novel" by Jensen 1995, 68, a "romantic novel" by Davies 1980, 86, 109), in which two young people fall in love, are separated by unfortunate circumstances, and do actually get back together and celebrate their love match (Standhartinger 1995, 231-37). And yet, the Acts of Xanthippe differs from the Greek romantic novel, for Xanthippe and Probus live a newly defined form of marriage as missionaries, and Polyxena does not marry at all. Instead, she becomes a companion of Paul's, and possibly Rebecca goes along with her. Polyxena remains more independent than Xanthippe and, like Thecla, chooses an itinerant form of life.

Describing the literature as "popular light fiction" (Schneemelcher 1989, 76) is an attempt to trivialize and write it off and stands in contradiction to the strongly reflective prayers in the Acts of Xanthippe and to the complex and unusual women figures portrayed in the text. The message of the Acts of Xanthippe is: listen to this

---

3. This is the date given by "Acts of Xanthippe" (Greek) 1893, 53-54; Jensen 1995, 67 dates it in the second half of the third century; Davies 1980, 10 opts for 190-225, because it does not betray definite knowledge of the Acts of Philip; Schneemelcher 1989, 77 dates it in the sixth century.

story about two Spanish women who became Christians, were baptized by an apostle, and as Christian women lived two very diverse lives. This writing's concentration on women and the bad impression the men give make it reasonable to assume that it was produced by women for women (cf. Davies 1980, 50, 63-64, 73, 102-9; Burrus 1987, 76-77). The ecclesiastical authorities cannot have found congenial the often almost ironic pictures of Paul, Peter, and Andrew, as well as the ineffective protection offered by Philip. Nor could they have enjoyed the peripheral role of Xanthippe's husband Probus, who is always merely reacting to Xanthippe, and who perhaps even has to accept the permanent asexuality of his marriage.

The Acts of Xanthippe does not contain a picture of women that is useful to men, for it shows women to be unwilling to "go along to get along" in society and the family. The women's self-determination and the stereotypical picture of men are the strongest arguments that the Acts of Xanthippe could not have arisen without the participation of such strong women and was written for women to stimulate them to imitate these exemplary women.

Literature

"Acts of Xanthippe" (English). 1965. Translated by W. A. Craigie. In *The Ante-Nicene Fathers,* edited by Allan Menzies, 10:205-17. 5th ed. Grand Rapids.

"Acts of Xanthippe" (Greek). 1893. In *Apocrypha Anecdota: A Collection of Thirteen Apocryphal Books and Fragments,* edited by Montague Rhodes James M. A., 43-85. Cambridge et al.

Burrus, Virginia. 1987. *Chastity as Autonomy: Women in the Stories of Apocryphal Acts.* Lewiston, N.Y., and Queenston, Ontario.

Dannemann, Irene. 1996. *Aus dem Rahmen fallen. Frauen im Markusevangelium. Eine feministische Re-Vision.* Berlin.

Davies, Stevan L. 1980. *The Revolt of the Widows: The Social World of the Apocryphal Acts.* Carbondale and Edwardsville, Ill.

Jensen, Anne. 1995. *Thekla — Die Apostolin. Ein apokrypher Text neu entdeckt.* Translation and Commentary. Freiburg, Basel, and Vienna.

Schneemelcher, Wilhelm, ed. 1989. *Neutestamentliche Apokryphen in deutscher Übersetzung.* Vol. 2, *Apostolisches, Apokalypsen und Verwandtes.* 5th ed. Tübingen.

Schottroff, Luise. 1994. *Lydias ungeduldige Schwestern. Eine feministische Sozialgeschichte des frühen Christentums.* Gütersloh.

———. 1995. *Lydia's Impatient Sisters: A Feminist Social History of Early Christianity.* Louisville.

Standhartinger, Angela. 1995. *Das Frauenbild im Judentum der hellenistischen Zeit. Ein Beitrag anhand von "Joseph und Aseneth."* Leiden, New York, and Cologne.

Sutter Rehmann, Luzia. 1994. "'Und ihr werdet ohne Sorge sein. . . .' Gedanken zum Phänomen der Ehefreiheit im frühen Christentum." In *Für Gerechtigkeit streiten. Theologie im Alltag einer bedrohten Welt,* 88-95. Festschrift for Luise Schottroff. Gütersloh.

Translated by Everett R. Kalin

Gospel of Mary: Mary Magdalene as
Beloved Disciple and Representative of Jesus

Judith Hartenstein and Silke Petersen

Introduction

Tradition and Attestation

The Gospel of Mary (GMary) is a short writing the title of which corresponds to those of the canonical Gospels. However, it does not include the life of Jesus but rather conversations between Jesus and his women and men disciples, as well as conversations among the disciples themselves following his departure. Not only is it not a canonical Gospel, but it also belongs to a theological orientation whose writings were banned. For this reason this gospel, though relatively widely circulating for a couple of centuries, was subsequently so utterly suppressed that even its existence was unknown. Today, fragments of three ancient manuscripts are available: barely half of it, translated into Coptic, has been preserved as the first writing contained in Codex BG (= Berolinensis Gnosticus). This manuscript includes eight pages from the middle and end of the writing, while ten further pages (pp. 1-6, 11-14) are missing. This codex was discovered at the end of the nineteenth century in Egypt and brought to Berlin, but through a series of unfortunate events took over fifty years to be published. In addition to the Gospel of Mary, this manuscript contains a portion of the Acts of Peter along with the Apocryphon of John and the Sophia of Jesus Christ, two writings attested also in the library of Nag Hammadi (→ Gospel of Thomas). Thus Codex BG, and with it the Gospel of Mary, are often thought of in connection with these codices. In addition, two papyrus fragments of the gospel exist in Greek (found in Egypt); these contain no additional text and are both believed to derive from the third century. Particularly for an apocryphal writing, these three manuscripts represent a relatively widespread and very early attestation.

Genre, Contents, and Structure

Following the missing pages, the gospel opens with a conversation between Jesus and his disciples in which fundamental questions regarding the nature of the world, sin, etc., are discussed. Presumably this represents a post-Easter conversation, for later, following Jesus' departure, his death is presupposed in a remark by the disciples. Most likely in the lost pages, at the outset of the gospel, an appearance of Jesus after his resurrection is reported.

Writings in which an appearance of the Risen One frames an extended dialogue with his disciples were disseminated in the second century; among them were included, for example, the Apocryphon of John and the Sophia of Jesus Christ. In such writings Jesus is instructing his disciples about fundamental questions of existence. In most cases the material has a very different character from the words of Jesus known from the canonical Gospels.

In the Gospel of Mary the dialogue is brought to a close by several concluding instructions of Jesus; among other things, he exhorts his disciples to mission. Following this he departs for good. Those left behind are sad and fearful about the tasks awaiting them, but Mary comforts them. This leads to a discussion about Jesus' words. In this context, Peter asks Mary to pass on to them things Jesus said that only she knows since she was particularly close to Jesus. Mary complies with this request and reports a vision and an extended conversation with Jesus. Mary's narration of this conversation with Jesus constitutes most of the second half of the gospel, part of which are four of those missing pages.

At the end of Mary's long speech, a discussion resumes among the disciples. Mary is attacked by Andrew and Peter, who dispute that she has really quoted words of Jesus. They are shocked by the novelty of the teaching and consider it impossible that Jesus has granted special instruction to a woman. Mary defends herself and is supported by Levi in doing so; at the end of the writing the disciples set out in mission.

The gospel is clearly divided into two main parts: first, the conversation between Jesus and his disciples, and second, the conversation between Jesus and Mary, narrated by Mary. Both sections are connected — and at the end concluded — by discussions among the disciples. What is unusual in this structure is Mary's long speech: writings about conversations with Jesus following his resurrection typically end with his disappearance and a short report on the further doings and fate of the disciples. This untypical structure shows already the powerful role of Mary.

Time and Place of Composition

The extant manuscripts attest to the composition of the Gospel of Mary no later than the end of the second century c.e. Since the canonical Gospels are presupposed, it can have been written no earlier than the beginning of that century. We tend to date it in the second half, since it presumes a differentiated exegetical tradition and in form and content itself builds on other Gnostic writings. (King 1994, 628 dates this gospel from the first half of the second century.)

It is possible that Egypt is the place of composition (Pasquier 1983, 13f.), since the gospel was already widely distributed there as early as the beginning of the third century. The fact that all the extant manuscripts of it were found in Egypt may be due to climatic conditions and does not thereby rule out composition in another place, such as Syria.

Translation[1]

Pages 1-6 are missing.

Conversation of Jesus with His Disciples

(BG p. 7, 1-19, 5) ". . . will matter then be destroyed or not?" The Savior said, "All natures, all formations, all creatures, exist in and with one another, and they will be resolved again into their own roots. For the nature of matter is resolved into the (roots) of its nature alone. *Let whoever has ears hear!*"[2] (NH: "He who has ears to hear, let him hear.")

Peter said to him, "Since you have explained everything to us, tell us this also: What is the sin of the world?" The Savior said, "There is no sin, but it is you who make sin when you do the things that are like the nature of adultery, which is called 'sin.' That is why the Good came into your midst, *to those of every nature, to restore them into their roots.*" (NH: "to the [essence] of every nature, in order to re-

---

1. [In the absence of a generally accessible, complete German translation of this gospel, the German authors have provided their own translation here, following the BG Codex (8502, I). The pagination indicated follows the BG text, while the headings are their own. Rather than retranslating their translation, I have reproduced here the translation by George W. MacRae and R. McL. Wilson (edited by Douglas M. Parrott, introduced by Karen L. King) given in *The Nag Hammadi Library in English,* third and completely revised edition, James M. Robinson, general editor (San Francisco: HarperSanFrancisco, 1978), pp. 542ff. (abbreviated henceforth NH). Where the German translation differs significantly from the English, however, I have provided my own translation of the German in italics. I have also translated the section headings given by the German authors.] [Translator's note.]

2. [As noted above, I have *italicized* places where the text departs from NH and moves into my own translation of the German text instead. In those cases, I place the Nag Hammadi text (referred to in note 1) in parentheses following the translation given by the authors. Because of the authors' concerns throughout for gender inclusivity, changing the published English is appropriate even though the meaning may be substantially the same.] [Translator's note.]

store it to its root.") Then he continued and said, "That is why you [become sick] and die, [*because you love* (BG p. 8) *what will betray you.*] (NH: "for [. . . , p. 8] of the one who.") *Let the one who* understands understand. Matter gave birth to a passion that has no equal, which proceeded from (something) contrary to nature. Then there *arose* a disturbance in the whole body. That is why I said to you, 'Be of good courage,' and if you are discouraged (be) encouraged in the presence of the different forms of nature. *Let whoever has ears hear.*"

Concluding Decrees of Jesus

When the blessed one had said this, he *kissed* (NH: greeted) them all, saying, "Peace be with you. *Bring forth my peace.* (NH: 'Receive my peace to yourselves.') Beware that no one lead you astray, saying, 'Lo here!' or 'Lo there!' For the Son of Man is within you. Follow after him! Those who seek him will find him. Go then and preach the gospel of the kingdom. Do not [BG, p. 9] lay down any rules beyond what I appointed for you, and do not give a law like the lawgiver lest you be constrained by it."

Jesus' Departure and Mary's Consolation

When he had said this, he departed. But they were grieved. They wept greatly, saying, "How shall we go to the *peoples* (NH: Gentiles) and preach the gospel of the kingdom of the Son of Man? If they did not spare him, how will they spare us?" Then Mary stood up, *kissed* (NH: greeted) them all, and said to her *brothers* [and sisters][3] (For "brothers and sisters" NH has *brethren*), "Do not weep and do not grieve nor be irresolute, for his grace *will be with all of you* (NH: [will be with] you entirely) and will protect you. But rather let us praise his greatness, for he has prepared us [*Greek: united us*] and made us *human* (NH: into men)."

Mary Transmits Words of Jesus

When Mary *had* said this, she turned their hearts [*Greek: minds*] to the Good, and they began to discuss the words of the [Savior]. [BG page 10] Peter said to Mary, "Sister, we know that the Savior loved you more than the rest of women. Tell us the words of the Savior which you remember — which you know (but) we do not, nor

---

3. Presumably other women and men are assumed to be present in addition to Mary and the male disciples mentioned by name. But if a contrast between Mary and the men may be intended, the translation needs to be only "brothers."

have we heard them." Mary answered and said, "What is hidden from you I will proclaim to you." And she began to speak to them these words: "I," she said, "I saw the Lord in a vision and I said to him, 'Lord, I saw you today in a vision.' He answered and said to me, 'Blessed are you, that you did not waver at the sight of me. For where the mind is, there is the treasure.' I said to him, 'Lord, now *(tell me)*, does he who sees the vision see it through the soul or through the spirit?' The Savior answered and said, 'He does not see through the soul nor the spirit, but the mind which [is] between the two — that is [what] sees the vision and it is [. . .]' (BG pp. 11-14 missing).

. . . [BG p. 15] it. And desire *said*, 'I did not see you descending, but now I see you ascending. *But* why do you lie, *you who* (NH: since you) belong to me?' The soul answered and said, 'I saw you, *(but)* you did not see me nor *notice* me. I served you as a garment, and you did not *recognize* me.' When it had said this, it went away rejoicing *even more* greatly.

"Again it came to the third power, which is called ignorance. [It (the power)] questioned the soul, saying, 'Where are you going? *You were seized in wickedness; in fact, you were seized while judging* (NH: In wickedness are you bound. But you are bound, do not judge!).' And the soul said, 'why do you judge me although I have not judged? I was *seized* (NH: bound) though I have not *seized* (NH: bound). I was not recognized. But I have recognized that *everything* (NH: the All) is being dissolved, both *what belongs to the earth* (BG p. 16) *and what belongs to heaven* (NH: the earthly [things] [p. 16] and the heavenly).'

"When the soul had *destroyed* (NH: overcome) the third power, it went upwards and saw the fourth power, (which) took seven forms. The first form is darkness, the second desire, the third ignorance, the fourth is the excitement of death, the fifth is the kingdom of the flesh, the sixth is the foolish wisdom of flesh, the seventh is the wrathful wisdom. These are the seven powers of wrath. They ask*ed* the soul, 'Whence do you come, slayer of *human beings* (NH: men), or where are you going, *destroyer of places* (NH: conqueror of space)?' The soul answered and said, 'What *seized* (NH: binds) me has been slain, and what surround*ed* me has been *destroyed* (NH: overcome) and my desire has [been] ended, and ignorance has died. In a world I (BG p. 17) was released from a world, and in *one form* (NH: a type) from a *superior form* (NH: heavenly type), and (from) the fetter of oblivion which is transient. From this time forth I will *receive* (NH: attain to) rest *from* time, *from* the *moment, from* the aeon, in silence.'"

Conversations among the Disciples

When Mary had said this, she fell silent, since it was to this point that the Savior had spoken with her. But Andrew answered and said to the *brothers (and sisters)*, "Say what you *are thinking* about what she has said. I *for one* do not believe that the

Savior has said this. For certainly these teachings are strange ideas." Peter answered and spoke concerning these same things. He questioned them about the Savior: "Did he really speak with a woman without our knowledge and not openly? Are *even* we to turn and all listen to her? Did he *choose her over* us?"

(BG p. 18) Then Mary wept and said to Peter, "My brother Peter, what do you think? Do you think that I thought this up myself in my heart, or that I am lying about the Savior?" Levi answered and said to Peter, "Peter, you have always been hot-tempered. Now I see you contending against the woman like the adversaries [*Greek: like her adversary*]. But if the Savior made her worthy, who are you indeed to reject her? Surely the Savior knows her very well. That is why he loved her more than us. Rather let us be ashamed and put on the perfect human being and *bring it forth for us/ourselves* (NH: acquire it for ourselves) as he commanded us, and preach the gospel, not laying down any other rule or other law beyond what the Savior said." When (BG p. 19) [*Levi had said this*] they began to go forth [to] proclaim and to preach [*Greek: When Levi had said this, he began to go forth and to preach*].

The Gospel according to Mary[4]

Unity and Use of Theological Traditions

Internal Coherence

The Gospel of Mary does not make a very unified first impression. The individual sections differ both thematically and in their similarity to the canonical Gospels. In addition, we find interlocking levels of narrative: conversations among the group are interposed with descriptions of events from the past. Mary reports on a conversation with Jesus in which Jesus' contribution is portrayed as a further dialogue, namely, between the soul and various powers. This section concerning the ascent of the soul seems particularly out of place, the more so since the missing pages keep us from seeing how it was integrated into the conversation between Mary and Jesus.

Because of the obvious differences in material, various models have been developed to explain the emergence of this gospel through multiple layers of redaction or through the piecing together of originally autonomous sections (Till and Schenke 1972, 26; Wilson 1956, 240; Pasquier, 1983, 8-9). None of these models is convincing, however; each tends to create more problems than it solves. Furthermore, in its present form the gospel is a meaningfully constructed text. Even if traditions were worked over along the way, they have now been integrated into the framework of the text as a whole and must be interpreted accordingly (King 1994, 626-27; Hartenstein 1997, 112-13).

---

4. Manuscripts of antiquity normally place the title at the end of the writing.

A narrative coherence exists, first, through the consistent setting: in the preserved text the group of disciples is assembled throughout. Jesus comes to them (presumably at the beginning) and later departs again; and it is in their midst that Mary unfolds her account. Even when reference is made to past events, the scenery remains the same. A unity of subject matter exists, further, in that both Mary in her words of comfort following Jesus' departure and Levi in his defense of Mary at the end refer back to Jesus' final instructions. For instance, there is constant reference to the Son of Man (or the perfected human being) established within the disciples. And Levi expressly repeats Jesus' prohibition against enacting laws, connecting this with the call to mission. All the conversations among the disciples are related to Jesus' instructions in this way; only at the very end are his directives put into action. In the concluding dialogue, Mary's speech is also engaged along with these earlier instructions of Jesus. A final connection is thematic: in Jesus' teachings at the beginning, the dissolution and resolution of all things to their roots and their essence is explained; it is to be understood as a disintegration and restoration. In the account of the soul's ascent repeated by Mary, this theme is developed further. The soul reascends to its origin and is able to defeat the powers precisely because it comes from on high itself.

The Relationship of the Gospel of Mary to the Canonical Gospels and to Gnostic Ideas

Persons appear in this gospel who are known from other Christian traditions, for instance, from the canonical Gospels. Furthermore, the greatest portion of the text is presented as Jesus' words. Nevertheless, there are only relatively few parallels to sayings of Jesus handed down from other sources; his teaching is very different from that found in the documents more familiar to us. Correspondences with the Synoptic Gospels consist primarily in the final instructions of Jesus, which are very nearly a compilation of known sayings of Jesus, albeit with some differences (for enumeration of the parallel texts, cf. Puech 1990, 313f.; King 1994, 609). Both in the differences and in the combining of the sayings, the gospel's theological concerns become evident. The entire section thus appears as a skillful reworking of earlier tradition through which an entirely new, original meaning emerges.

This can be detailed through two examples: the promise of Jesus' peace is similar to promises in the Johannine farewell discourses ("My peace I give you," John 14:27; cf. also John 20:19, 21, 26; Luke 24:36). In the Gospel of Mary as well, Jesus speaks of his peace, but he does not bestow it upon his disciples; rather he challenges them to bring it forth. This implies that Jesus' peace is an entity that has already been established in the disciples and for which they can and ought to concern themselves.

A similar tendency for reworking is manifest in the statement about the Son of Man within. The juxtaposition of the false views that refer outward and the presence within corresponds to Luke 17:21, but there refers to the reign of God (cf. also Mark 13:21; Matt 24:23; Gospel of Thomas 113; the meaning of the Lukan text is disputed; it is probably to be understood not as "within you" but as "among you"). In Luke 17:23-24, however, there follows a partially parallel statement about the Son of Man. The record in the Gospel of Mary can be understood as a combination of both statements through which a specific interpretation of the image of the Son of Man is found. In the Gospel of Mary the Son of Man is not a future figure and not exclusively identified with Jesus, but rather stands for authentic humanity made possible for the disciples through Jesus, yet which they themselves must also bring into reality. Both Mary and Levi take up this image and emphasize partly Jesus' contribution and partly the necessity of one's own effort. But they speak only of "humanity," or of the "perfect human being" — the expression "Son of Man" may have been used earlier (in the gospel) only to correspond to the New Testament usage.

It is precisely these differing formulations of true humanity in the Gospel of Mary that show that the author had various forms of expression at her or his disposal. To build on Jesus traditions like those in the canonical Gospels is just one of those possibilities and appears to have been chosen quite consciously. This leads to the conclusion that this gospel presupposes such traditions, and indeed probably in the form of Gospels. (Evidence for this comes primarily through the presumed combining of Luke 17:21 and 23-24, which presumably were found in this form only in Luke. But there are echoes of other Gospels as well.) Yet the Gospel of Mary does not merely presuppose them; it also manifests a sovereign freedom making possible the new combination of sayings. Also, this tradition appears to have considerable significance, for the text clearly strives to correspond with it.

Yet the Gospel of Mary does not make use solely of canonical Gospel traditions but also uses typical Gnostic terminology and reworks Gnostic conceptions. This becomes particularly clear in Mary's speech: for example, in the section about the soul's ascent and in Jesus' praise of Mary for not wavering. Being unwavering is a characteristic of true Gnostics and is depicted as an ideal in Gnostic treatises.

The conception of the soul's ascent or its heavenly journeys is widespread in ancient religious texts. In the Gospel of Mary as well as in other Gnostic texts (e.g., First Apocalypse of James, NHC V: 3 p. 33-36; Irenaeus, *Adversus haereses* 1.21.5), this ascent is always a return that hostile powers attempt to prevent. The texts assume that part of the human being has a heavenly origin but is trapped in the world, shackled to the body, and ignorant of its own origin. Liberation from this condition is made possible through knowledge (= *gnōsis*). The knowledge of one's condition represents simultaneously one's redemption from it: for instance, in the Gospel of Mary, simply the reference to the provenance of the soul is sufficient to overcome the powers. Mary's silence at the end of her speech corresponds to the silence the soul has reached at the goal of its ascent: by mentioning Mary's silence, the author shows her fulfilling the soul's path of ascent. In reporting the soul's liberation from its incapacity for knowledge, she too is herself freed from this incapacity and from the world.

The Gospel of Mary is the writing of an individual or group that cherished differing religious traditions of which what we consider Christian is only one. Yet to connect these was apparently not considered a problem; rather, everything is traced directly or indirectly back to Jesus himself — indeed, explicitly to the Jesus of the canonical Gospels (Hartenstein 1997, 263ff.).

Mary's Role in the Gospel of Mary

Mary as Jesus' Representative

Although Mary has no further name in the gospel, Mary Magdalene is unambiguously meant. She is addressed by Peter as "sister" and as the most important of the female disciples. This status, clearly hers also in the canonical Gospels, is granted her without dispute. But in this gospel her role goes far beyond that of a leader of the group of female disciples. Even in the structure of the gospel she is to a great extent made parallel to Jesus, and in the second half of the text takes over his role in instructing the others. This finding is all the more significant in that this sort of role does not emerge in other texts comparable to the Gospel of Mary. But the parallelism between Mary and Jesus extends also to details of their portrayal, as when she, like Jesus, kisses everyone, comforts them (behavior that normally belongs to appearances of the Risen One), and reinforces his injunctions.

In this gospel's portrayal, Mary moves into the place otherwise occupied only by the Redeemer. She is the one who mediates to the others revelations previously unknown to them. One difference remains, however: even Mary is passing on words of Jesus. Despite all parallelism, she is thus not equal to him but ultimately always refers back to him. But following Jesus' departure she is nevertheless his representative for the other disciples and the source of his teaching. Even later, she can still mediate authentic yet previously unknown sayings. In the discussion at the end, this status of Mary is attacked but is defended by reference to Jesus' choice. Even her conversation with Jesus shows her special worthiness, above all in Jesus' naming her as blessed.

To present this role of Mary is one of the concerns of this gospel. Its point of departure is the canonical Gospels' Easter stories, particularly Mary Magdalene's encounter with the Risen One in John 20:14-18. In this story too Mary is instructed about Jesus' ascent to the Father (John 20:17); this could have been the motivation for making Mary the one who conveys knowledge about the soul's ascent. In contrast to the canonical Gospels, "seeing the Lord" (John 20:18) does not function in the Gospel of Mary as proof of his resurrection; this gospel is much more concerned with gaining access to knowledge from beyond through a vision of the Risen One. Nevertheless, such visions are not accessible to people of all times (thus Pagels 1981, 51-52); rather, in Gnostic texts they are limited to the circle of Jesus' disciples.

The Dispute with Peter

The conflict between Mary and Peter depicted in this gospel is not the account of an actual dispute. Rather, this is a literary fiction in which the conflict is portrayed favoring Mary. The text shows no interest in representing Peter's position fairly; instead he is to be shown in the wrong.

Peter is not consistently a negative figure in this gospel. He takes part in the conversation with Jesus by at least asking one question. Even his request to Mary for instruction speaks well of him — in the world of the Gospel of Mary! But already in the formulation of this request the later conflict is intimated. The request is phrased in such a way that the later attack is prepared but not yet explicitly uttered. Yet above all it makes possible the refutation of Peter on the basis of his own words.

In his request to Mary, Peter regards her as the most important of the (female) disciples of Jesus and at the same time establishes her special relationship with Jesus. This status emerges from the canonical Gospels and is generally accepted. Peter, however, limits Mary's privileged position when he says that the Lord loved her more than the other *women* and thereby excludes himself and the other male disciples. Nevertheless, Mary seems to be superior to Peter in regard to the knowledge received from the Redeemer; otherwise, of course, he would not be able to request that she say something unknown even to him. Thus in his request, Peter's stance is still open to subsequent developments. Nevertheless, following Mary's speech, Peter categorically denies that Jesus could have given special instruction to a woman and thereby privilege her over against everyone else. Here the limits of Peter's insight come into view. His objection, however, is not only jealous and petty, but it is also undercut by the facts previously established (by Peter himself!): if Mary had a particularly close relationship with Jesus, then special instruction to her is conceivable and plausible, even if this special status was primarily over against the other women. The only possible alternative, however, namely, that Mary was lying, is impossible for a woman Jesus accepted as leader of the female disciples. Thus the portrayal of Peter before and after Mary's speech clearly places him in the wrong.

In contrast, Levi brings the insight of the gospel to expression by saying, "He loved her more *than us*," and thereby including also the male disciples. According to this assertion, Mary is loved not only more than the other women but also more than all other disciples. This privilege is Jesus' decision and thus reveals Mary's gifts.

Even Andrew's objection that Mary's depiction contradicts the rest of Jesus' teaching is undercut within the gospel itself. In the overall structure, Jesus gives instructions at the beginning that for all intents and purposes correspond to what Mary passes on as Jesus' words. Admittedly, the text is preserved in too fragmentary a form to establish this more precisely.

These points reveal the Gospel of Mary as a defense, both artful and clear, of Mary and her position — even today the text conveys this appeal. It works as a confirmation for those readers who treasure Mary highly. They are strengthened in their position precisely through the ineffectual attacks on Mary. Yet the gospel is confirming and assuring not solely in reference to the position of Mary. What is said here also promises redemption and ascent for all who follow Mary's words.

Historical Evaluation

No conclusions as to the historical figure of Mary Magdalene can be drawn from this gospel. It does not provide its own access to traditions from the time of Jesus but rather reworks traditions familiar to us from the canonical texts. In the process, a thoroughly distinctive means of viewing the Christian tradition emerges through the new juxtaposition of familiar themes and texts.

Even if implications for the historical Mary Magdalene are absent, the Gospel of Mary is nevertheless not without relevance for the question of women in early Christendom. The way Mary Magdalene and other persons are portrayed in this gospel opens access for us into the threads of discussion and disputed questions about women in the second century c.e. Here two themes are particularly interesting: first, the portrayal of Mary as an apostle; and second, Peter and Andrew's hostility to her.

Mary as an Apostle

The gospel proceeds on the basis of the special relationship between Jesus and Mary Magdalene, in order to make plausible the Redeemer's communicating more to Mary than to the others. These secret revelations are passed on to the others by Mary, who thereby rises to become a mediator of the tradition and guarantor of the tradition of a Christian-Gnostic group, and is equipped with apostolic authority. Other currents in early Christendom invoked Peter, John, James, or Thomas; remarkably, in the Gospel of Mary a woman is endowed with this apostolic function. Among the church fathers, too, various citations can be found for Gnostic groups that invoked Mary: the Greek church father Origen reports in his treatise in opposition to Celsus (an educated non-Christian who in the middle of the second century wrote a treatise against Christians) that Celsus knew of several Gnostic groups that invoked women: Marcellians invoking Marcellina, Carpocratians invoking Salome, others invoking Mary and yet others Martha (cf. *Contra Celsum* 5.62). Hippolytus reports in his *Refutation of All Heresies* that the Naasseners appeal to Mariamne (= Mary Magdalene) and James (5.7.1; 10.9.3). He uses the same Greek word *(paradidōmi)* that Paul uses when he speaks of the words of Jesus or teachings of the early church handed down to him (1 Cor 11:2; 15:3). The image of Mary Magdalene as a central apostolic figure through whose transmission special knowledge is handed down is not an isolated instance here. Not only the Gospel of Mary but also the remarks of the church fathers show that Gnostic groups appealed to Mary Magdalene as a witness to the tradition.

The Dispute between Mary and Peter: Historical Background

The conflict between Peter and Mary permeating the second half of the Gospel of Mary has close parallels in other Gnostic writings. In addition to this gospel, the Gospel of Thomas (→ Gospel of Thomas) and the Pistis Sophia (a later Gnostic writing) report attacks by Peter against Mary. These texts, as well as others, reveal a lively debate about women in the second and third centuries C.E., whereby the arguments are placed in the mouths of the disciples themselves: the debated questions of later periods are presented in the form of a discussion among persons in the circle around Jesus. In the Gospel of Mary, Mary is attacked because of her teaching: a woman whose knowledge is superior to that of men and to whom they are to listen seems shocking. It is possible that the portrayal revolves concretely around the question of the legitimacy of women's public teaching.[5]

In various texts Peter is the counterpart of Mary. From today's perspective the connection between Peter and ecclesial Christendom (and Roman orthodoxy) lies close at hand. However, this connection appears problematic for the second century since at this point the boundaries between orthodoxy and heresy were just emerging. Thus the Gospel of Mary and the other texts show Peter not in the first instance as representative of ecclesial Christendom but rather as an enemy of women. Mary and Peter are symbolic figures of the debate between women and men. Various texts from the second and third centuries attest that the dispute regarding an appropriate role for women was taken in the most diverse directions among Christians. Both in Gnostic and in non-Gnostic groups these questions were debated vigorously and with the most diverse outcomes (see "The Story of

---

5. Jesus' final instruction, prohibiting the issuance of laws, which Levi takes up again and relates to the preaching of the gospel, fits into this context. Only Jesus' ordinances are valid, and that they are not to be supplemented by the disciples is declared emphatically. This is directed most likely against other Christian groups where rules are followed that do not go back to Jesus and could apply, for example, to the exclusion of women from proclaiming. It is unlikely that the prohibition of creating laws has an anti-Jewish intent.

Thecla" above). Within this diversity, the Gospel of Mary takes a clear position for women: it confirms the legitimacy of apostolic leadership on the part of women (King 1994, 632).

The conflict between Peter and Mary can be read in this text against the backdrop of the New Testament references permeating this gospel also in other ways. Even though no New Testament text exists as a direct source, in the resurrection reports Mary and Peter appear indirectly in conflict with one another to the extent that various texts ascribe the initial encounter with the Risen One to each of them. (The appearance of the Risen One legitimizes apostolic authority, as the Pauline assertions in 1 Corinthians 9 and 15 reveal.) The Gospel of Mary takes the vision of the Risen One in John 20 as its point of departure; in her vision Mary receives otherworldly knowledge about the soul's ascent that she passes on to the others. This primacy of Mary sets off the conflict of the legitimacy of her proclamation that is resolved in her favor.

Just as the Gospel of John traces its tradition back to the Beloved Disciple, the Gospel of Mary appeals to Mary Magdalene. In both texts the authors refer to a person in the circle of disciples whom they portray standing in a sort of rivalry with Peter in order to establish their own position departing from the usual "Peter line."

In the Gospel of Mary the direct debate between Peter and Mary results in a stronger differentiation from Peter. The community of this gospel stands farther away from Petrine Christianity than does that of the Gospel of John. Both nevertheless invoke persons who through the special love of Jesus for them are lifted out from the circle of other disciples. This love of Jesus gives the Christians invoking the Beloved Disciple or Mary Magdalene, as "heirs" of these two placing themselves in their tradition, a legitimation of their special relationship to Jesus and his proclamation.

Even as we read the Johannine writings as witnesses to a specifically Johannine Christianity, the Gospel of Mary is a recovered witness to an early Christian community that invoked Mary Magdalene.

LITERATURE

Hartenstein, Judith. 1997. "Die zweite Lehre. Erscheinungen des Auferstandenen als Rahmenerzählungen frühchristlicher Dialoge." Ph.D. diss., Humboldt-Universität, Berlin.

King, Karen L. 1994. "The Gospel of Mary Magdalene." In *Searching the Scriptures,* edited by Elisabeth Schüssler Fiorenza, 2:601-34. 2 vols. New York.

Lührmann, Dieter. 1988. "Die griechischen Fragmente des Mariaevangeliums POx 3525 und PRyl 463." *Neues Testament* 30:321-38.

Marjanen, Antti. 1996. *The Woman Jesus Loved: Mary Magdalene in the Nag Hammadi Library and Related Documents.* Nag Hammadi and Manichaean Studies, vol. 40. Leiden.

Pagels, Elaine. 1979. *The Gnostic Gospels.* New York.

——. 1981. *Versuchung durch Erkenntnis. Die Gnostischen Evangelien.* Frankfurt.

Pasquier, Anne. 1983. *L'Evangile selon Marie (BG 1).* Bibliothèque Copte de Nag Hammadi, Section Textes, vol. 10. Quebec.

Puech, Henry Charles. 1990. "Das Evangelium der Maria." Edited by Beate Blatz. In *Neutestamentliche Apokryphen in deutscher Übersetzung,* vol. 1, *Evangelien,* edited by Wilhelm Schneemelcher, 313-15. 6th ed. Tübingen.

Schröter, Jens. 1999. "Zur Menschensohnvorstellung im Evangelium nach Maria." In *Ägypten und Nubien in spätantiker und christlicher Zeit. Akten des 6. Internationalen Koptologenkongresses, Münster, July 20-26, 1996,* edited by Stephen Emmel et al., 178-88. Wiesbaden.

Till, Walter C., and Hans-Martin Schenke. 1972. *Die gnostischen Schriften des koptischen Papyrus Berolinensis 8502.* Texte und Untersuchungen zur Geschichte der altchristlichen Literatur, vol. 60. 2nd ed. Berlin.

Wilson, Robert McL. 1956. "The New Testament in the Gnostic Gospel of Mary." *New Testament Studies* 57, no. 3:233-43.

Wilson, Robert McL., and George W. MacRae. 1979. "The Gospel according to Mary." In *Nag Hammadi Codices V, 2-5 and VI with Papyrus Beronlinensis 8502, 1 and 4,* edited by Douglas M. Parrott, 453-71. Nag Hammadi Studies, vol. 11. Leiden.

FOR FURTHER READING

Boer, Esther de. 1997. *Mary Magdalene — beyond the Myth.* London.

Hartenstein, Judith. 2003. "Das Evangelium nach Maria." In *Nag Hammadi Deutsch 2. Band: NHC V,2–XIII,1, BG 1 und 4,* edited by Hans-Martin Schenke, Hans-Gebhard Bethge, and Ursula Ulrike Kaiser, 833-44. Berlin and New York.

——. 2007. "Mary Magdalene the Apostle: A Re-interpretation of Literary Traditions?" *lectio difficilior* 1; http://www.lectio.unibe.ch.

King, Karen L. 2003. *The Gospel of Mary of Magdala: Jesus and the First Woman Apostle.* Santa Rosa, Calif.

Mohri, Erika. 2000. *Maria Magdalena. Frauenbilder in Evangelientexten des 1. bis 3. Jahrhunderts.* Marburger Theologische Studien, vol. 63. Marburg.

Petersen, Silke. 1999. *"Zerstört die Werke der Weiblichkeit!" Maria Magdalena, Salome und andere Jüngerinnen Jesu in christlich-gnostischen Schriften.* Nag Hammadi and Manichaean Studies, vol. 48. Leiden.

Tuckett, Christopher. 2007. *The Gospel of Mary.* Oxford Early Christian Gospel Texts. Oxford.

Translated by Lisa E. Dahill

Gospel of Thomas: Early Christian
Traditions about Women Disciples of Jesus;
or, Mary Magdalene Becomes Male

Judith Hartenstein and Silke Petersen

Introduction

*The Story of the Document's Discovery,
the Nature of the Text, and Its Place of Origin*

In the vicinity of the village of Nag Hammadi in Upper Egypt, a buried collection of ancient codices was discovered by chance at the end of 1945. The codices originate in the fourth century c.e.; the texts contained within them, which are in Coptic, are translations of earlier Greek versions. The majority of the texts can be assigned to an ancient religious movement called Gnosticism. Gnosticism (from the Greek word *gnōsis,* "knowledge") apparently arose about the same time as Christianity but was not dependent on Christianity (the time of origin and dependency relationship are both topics of scholarly controversy). In the second and third centuries Gnosticism and Christianity related to one another in varied ways and intermingled. A series of Christian Gnostic writings arose. Through the battle against Gnosticism as a heretical movement by anti-Gnostic Christian authors, the majority of Gnostic texts were lost. The ideas of this religious movement had to be reconstructed almost entirely from what the church fathers wrote against them. Since the discovery at Nag Hammadi, a greater number of original Gnostic writings are available for the first time, including the Gospel of Thomas (Gos Thom). The existence of the Gospel of Thomas was known about earlier, since it was mentioned by several church fathers. Moreover, at the end of the nineteenth century, three Greek papyrus fragments were found in Egypt (Oxyrhynchus Papyri 1, 654, and 655), which could be assigned to the Gospel of Thomas only after the Coptic version was known. The title "The Gospel of Thomas" stands (as is usual) at the end of the text and designates it as a gospel. But the Gospel of Thomas, in contrast to Matthew, Mark, Luke, and John, contains no narratives and no account of the death and resurrection of Jesus. Rather, it is a collection of sayings of Jesus and short conversations between Jesus and his disciples. The first sentence of the gospel gives the heading for the document: "These are the hidden words that the living Jesus spoke and Didymos Judas Thomas wrote them down. And he said, 'Whoever finds the meaning of these words will not taste death.'" Then follow shorter and longer sayings (aphorisms, parables, brief dialogues), without a discernible organizing principle and with no temporal perspective.

The reference to Thomas and the form of his name, Didymos Judas Thomas, support eastern Syria as the place of origin for the gospel, for other writings in which Thomas is important also originated there.

The Date of the Gospel and Its Relationship to the Synoptic Gospels

The date of the Gospel of Thomas is disputed. The earliest papyrus fragment can be dated at the end of the second century, so the gospel must have arisen before that time. Scholars have proposed dates between 50 and 150 for its origin. What is decisive is how one evaluates the relationship between this gospel and the Synoptics. About half of the sayings in the Gospel of Thomas have close parallels in the Synoptics. The (widely discussed) question is whether the Gospel of Thomas is dependent on the Synoptics or if it contains independent, perhaps actually older, traditions. Many American scholars consider the Gospel of Thomas to be independent and date it in the first century (e.g., Patterson 1993); many European scholars support its dependence and a date in the second century (e.g., Schrage 1964). Both views have far-reaching consequences for the picture of the historical Jesus, and that is why the issue is so controversial.

The division among scholars already points to the fact that there is no all-inclusive solution to the problem. Several sayings likely did arise independently, but others show dependence, in that they incorporate redactional elements from the Synoptic Gospels. It appears to make sense to speak here about influence on the Gospel of Thomas by the texts of Matthew, Mark, and Luke (cf. Schröter 1997). We have only one single complete manuscript from the fourth century, and that a translation, and therefore it is probable that through repeated copying and through translation the text has been brought in line with the text of the Synoptics. Moreover, it is conceivable that even after some sayings became fixed in a written form in one of the Synoptics, they continued to be circulated orally and then incorporated into the Gospel of Thomas. Because this gospel is a collection of sayings, it is also conceivable that there was a gradual growth of the writing, in which, thus, older sayings stand next to more recent ones. So the question of dependence can be different for each individual saying. Basically we must reckon with the possibility that the Gospel of Thomas contains old traditions not dependent on the Synoptics.

Theological Tendencies

The Gospel of Thomas and Gnosticism

Like the questions about the date and dependence of the Gospel of Thomas, the question of its theological orientation is also contested. Attempts have failed to locate the gospel within a Gnostic movement of which we are already aware, and it is debated whether the text is Gnostic at all. The gospel does not contain any description of Gnostic mythology, and only a few sayings presuppose with some probability Gnostic mythological views (49, 50; perhaps 2, 24, 28, 83, 84). But also clear is a proximity to basic ideas found in Gnostic groups (but not there alone!) — the saving function of knowledge (1, 2, 5, 18, 46); renunciation of the world (27, 56, 80, 110, perhaps 42) and the world's blindness (28); renunciation of the body and of reproduction (7, 29, 79, 87, 112); the difference between the sexes as a problem (22, 114); rest as the ideal state (50, 60, 90). It is certain that the gospel was treasured, read, and transmitted in Gnostic groups, but that does not mean it is always and exclusively to be seen in this context. Most of the collection betrays no sign of a specific Gnostic origin. It is therefore not appropriate to read parts of the Gnostic myth into sayings that offer no grounds for this in the text. Presumably the gospel did receive mythological interpretations in the course of its use among Gnostics, but the background for its origin is more likely to be found in the context of wisdom literature (Davies 1983, 36-61). In this regard, wisdom and Gnosticism are not to be seen as alternatives; rather, the Gospel of Thomas can offer an insight into the wisdom roots of Gnosticism (Patterson 1993, 106-10).

Social Radicalism

While the Gnostic character of the Gospel of Thomas can be disputed, it is clearly a Christian writing. Just as we speak about Synoptic and Johannine tradition or Christianity, it is also appropriate to speak of Thomas Christianity or Thomas tradition. What is specific to Thomas Christianity manifests itself as a renunciation of the world and in a life that, while it does indeed take place in the world for a while (in saying 42 Jesus says, "Become passers-by"), does not want to live by the world's values. Patterson calls the dominant behavior of Thomas Christians social radicalism (1993, 4), comparable to the behavior Theissen (Theissen 1973) describes for earliest Christianity. This social radicalism entails homelessness, willful poverty, begging, cutting family ties, relativizing piety and purity, and the depreciation of officialdom. While the Synoptic Gospels tend to domesticize this tradition of the Jesus movement, Thomas Christianity continues the tradition of social radicalism (Patterson 1993, 4). Patterson's view of the Gospel of Thomas presents itself as a point of departure for the interpretation of the sayings that are important here.

The Renunciation of Family and Motherhood

One aspect of social radicalism is the renunciation of family. Several sayings in the Gospel of Thomas express hostility to the family. Saying 99 tells the story of the true relatives of Jesus (cf. Mark 3:31-35; Matt 12:46-50; Luke 8:19-21): "The disciples said to him, 'Your siblings and your mother are standing outside.' He said to them, 'Those here who do the will of my father, they are my siblings and my mother. It is they who will enter the kingdom of my father.'"

Unique to Thomas's version of this saying (in comparison with the Synoptic texts) is the expression "enter the kingdom of my father" at the end. Through the phrase "enter the kingdom," this saying is connected with sayings 22 and 114 (see below), and it puts the story of Jesus' true relatives in the context of the concept of kingdom in the Gospel of Thomas. Aside from the parables, the term "kingdom" appears especially in sayings that call for "being different" and that name values not accepted by society as presuppositions for participating in the kingdom: "If you do not fast as regards the world, you will not find the kingdom" (27; cf. 46, 49, 54). The kingdom is something for outsiders in the Gospel of Thomas. And it is not to be found in the future or in another place, but here and now (3, 113) and in the presence of Jesus (82).

Connected with the renunciation of family ties (16, 31, 55, 79, 99, 101, 105), the radical attitude of the Gospel of Thomas also involves renunciation of Jesus' earthly mother and of motherhood in general. In this regard, the theme of saying 79 is the renunciation of motherhood as such: "A woman in the crowd said to him, 'Blessed are the womb that carried you and the breasts that nourished you.' He said to her, 'Blessed are those who have heard the word of the father and have truly kept it. For there will be days when you will say, "Blessed are the womb that has not conceived and the breasts that have not given milk."'"

This saying combines two sections that are known to us from Luke's special material (Luke 11:27-28 and 23:29). The combination of the two texts causes a shift in their meaning: the second half of the saying occurs in an eschatological context in Luke, while in Thomas the ascetic significance becomes more important. Through the addition of the second saying, the beginning is also cast in a new light. The blessing of Jesus' mother has a more critical tone than it has in its Lukan context. While the Lukan version still allows the statement "Blessed rather are those who hear the word of God and obey it" to be read as something superior, rather than directly opposed, to the praise spoken of Mary, a reading favorable to Mary is no longer possible in Thomas. Through the denial of the blessing in the appended saying, the praise of motherhood at the beginning is clearly denied by Jesus, and it is set in clear opposition to hearing and obeying the word.

An additional saying hostile to the family is transmitted in the Gospel of Thomas in two versions, in saying 55 (cf. Matt 10:37-38, parallel to Luke 14:26-27): "Jesus said, 'Whoever does not hate his father and his mother cannot become a disciple of mine. And whoever does not hate his brothers and sisters and take up his cross as I do will not be worthy of me,'" and in saying 101: "Whoever does not hate his father and his mother as I do cannot become a disciple of mine. And whoever does not love his father and his mother as I do cannot become a disciple of mine. For my mother . . . , but my true mother gave me life."

Possible ways of filling in the gap at the end of the text include: "For my mother [has deceived me] . . . ," or "For my mother, [who has given birth to me, has destroyed me]. . . ."[1] It is not possible to say with certainty how the text read. Nevertheless, through the "but" in the final sentence it becomes clear that the last two lines are understood as contrasts. Here the "normal" mother and the true mother are contrasted. From this ending of the text, its beginning can be understood as well. The demand to love father and mother is no watering down of the earlier demand to hate these persons. The apparently contradictory statements do not refer to the same persons. In the first statement the earthly parents are in view, in the second the true parents. Through the twofold "as I do" that Thomas adds here — in contrast to the Synoptic versions and also to the doublet in saying 55 — the text is at the same time an indication of how to live and a self-attestation of Jesus (on the identity of Jesus and the disciples, cf. 108). His earthly parents (Mary and Joseph), whom he rejects, are contrasted with his true parents, whom he loves. The father Jesus loves, his true father, is God. Who his heavenly mother is supposed to be is less clear. Perhaps the Holy Spirit is in view, who is also thought to be feminine in other writings from Syria (in the Gospel of Philip 17, for example).

Women in Parables

The Gospel of Thomas contains numerous parables, some of which are known from the Synoptic tradition, others transmitted only in Thomas. By comparison with the parallels, we can establish some peculiarities of the parables in the Gospel of Thomas. Allegorical tendencies are often missing, and the parables occasionally give the impression, based on their form, of being more original (Gos Thom 64, 65). Frequently we find in the image of comparison in the parables about the kingdom a person and not a thing. So, for example, saying 96 says, "The Kingdom of the Father is like a woman. She took a bit of yeast, [concealed] it in some dough, and made it into huge loaves." (By contrast, it says in Matthew 13:33: "The kingdom of heaven is like yeast that a woman took. . . .") Exegetes continue to debate vigorously whether or not there is a particular understanding of parables in the Gospel of Thomas, and what that could look like.

In addition to saying 96, a woman plays the major role in another parable,

---

1. These are the suggestions offered by the Berlin Working Circle in the Appendix to the Aland Synopsis (1996, 543 n. 141).

saying 97: "Jesus said, 'The kingdom of the father is like a woman who is carrying a jar filled with meal. While she was walking on the path, very far from home, the handle of the jar broke and the meal emptied out behind her on the path. She did not know it; she had noticed no accident. When she reached her house, she set the jar down on the floor and found it empty.'"

This parable is connected to the previous one, about the woman with the yeast, through the woman as the one taking the action and through the words "dough" (saying 96) and "meal" (saying 97) that tie the two parables together thematically. Such verbal connections are typical of the Gospel of Thomas.

In the parable of the woman with the jar, it is first of all difficult to understand the level on which the image is operating. How can her meal escape from the jar without her noticing it? It is conceivable that the text is talking about a jar with the handle turned down to the bottom: when the handle breaks, a hole is opened at the bottom of the jar for the meal to trickle out. How to interpret the parable presents even greater difficulties. There is nothing in the text to suggest that something positive is to be made of the scattered meal. On the contrary, what is stressed is the woman's ignorance and, at the end, the jar's emptiness. At first blush neither of these fits with the reign of God — elsewhere in Gnostic texts ignorance and emptiness are precisely concepts devoid of positive content.

And yet the parable can be understood against the background of the Gospel of Thomas's social radicalism. Daily life and business activities are evaluated critically in Thomas. The reign of God is often contrasted with "ordinary" life — to find the one means to give up the other. Thus, in saying 76 a merchant sells all his merchandise to obtain a pearl, thus giving up his calling. In Matthew 13:45-46, by contrast, a merchant is looking for pearls from the start; by buying them he fulfills his calling. In saying 8 a fisherman is called wise for choosing one large fish out of a net of small ones and throwing all the small ones back — he, too, is failing to practice his calling.

By the world's standards the woman with the jar of meal also fails to do what she is supposed to do. Now she cannot bake any bread or use the meal for anything else. In distinction from the texts we have just used for comparison, however, what happened here is not the result of a decision on the woman's part; it just happened. Her ignorance is actually stressed in the text. Perhaps that is meant to express the fact that the coming of God's reign happens in a hidden manner. It is there even if we do not know it and do not recognize it (cf. Gos Thom 113). But how can an interpretation tie together social radicalism and the woman's ignorance? And the image of the jar's emptiness remains puzzling too.

Women Disciples of Jesus in the Gospel of Thomas

Salome

Saying 61 contains a short conversation between Jesus and Salome, in which she identifies herself as a disciple: "Jesus said, 'Two will rest on a bed: the one will die, the other will live.' Salome said, 'Who are you, man, as from whom have you come up onto my bed and eaten from my table?' Jesus said to her, 'I am the one who is out of the same. I was given some of the things of my father.' (Salome said,) 'I am your disciple.' (Jesus said,) 'Therefore I say, if someone becomes the <same>,[2] s/he will be filled with light, but if s/he becomes separated, s/he will be filled with darkness.'" A saying of Jesus known also from Luke 17:34 is the starting point for the short dialogue, in which an attempt is made to interpret it and to come to terms with its provocative assertion. Salome and Jesus are reclining together at the table. After Jesus' provocative statement, Salome asks Jesus who he is, that he would say such a thing (questions about Jesus' nature occur also in Gos Thom 24, 37, 43, 52, 91). Jesus' answer consists of two parallel statements. He is "from the one who is out of the same," that is, he comes from the sameness and unity of the divine world. And he has a part in everything that belongs to that world. In the Gospel of Thomas Jesus and the Father belong together intimately; just like the Father (3, 37, 50), Jesus is designated as "living" (1, 52, 59, 111).

Salome responds to this self-assertion, "I am your disciple." In the Coptic text the words "Salome said" are missing before her answer is given. But it is clear that she is the one making the statement, because the feminine article occurs before the word for disciple *(mathētēs)*. It is not absolutely necessary to add "Jesus said" before the next statement (it would also be conceivable that Salome is continuing to speak or the author is making a comment). But it is in keeping with the style of the Gospel of Thomas to conclude dialogues with a saying of Jesus.

The saying at the end, like the one at the beginning, is constructed as a contrast; it repeats and interprets the statement Jesus makes at the beginning. The contrast "light-darkness" is also used elsewhere in the Gospel; light belongs to the heavenly realm, and in this world there is darkness (24, 50, 77, 83). The people who live, who are like God, are full of light; those, on the other hand, who die are separated from God and full of darkness. As a disciple of Jesus, Salome is drawn into the divine sameness; she belongs to Jesus, to the divine light, and she will live.

---

2. The Coptic text has "destroyed." Presumably we have a scribal error here in which one letter is miswritten for a similar one. The Coptic word for "undivided" appears earlier in the saying.

Mary Magdalene

A Mary is mentioned in two sayings of the Gospel of Thomas. On the basis of parallel traditions in other Gnostic writings (the Gospel of Philip, the Gospel of Mary, the Sophia of Jesus Christ, the Pistis Sophia), it is clear that Mary Magdalene is in view rather than Jesus' mother, who appears in Thomas in quite different contexts and is not referred to as Mary (see above).

Mary Magdalene has a special relationship to Jesus and to the other disciples. In saying 21 she asks Jesus about his disciples: "Mary said to Jesus, 'Whom are your (male and female) disciples like?' . . ."

Jesus gives a long and puzzling answer, the meaning of which we cannot go into here. It is another aspect of the saying that holds our interest. In all customary German translations, the question reads, "Whom are your (male) disciples like?" This is in keeping with the traditional androcentric usage, which gives the impression that a woman is asking about a group of men. In our inclusive reading, by contrast, a woman stands vis-à-vis a group of men *and women*. This translation has two different consequences for our understanding of the text. On the one hand, it becomes clear that in Thomas there are also women disciples, which is also clear in saying 61. On the other hand, however, the contrast "a woman/a group of men" disappears in this translation. Perhaps this contrast was intended here (and in other texts), and it is no longer obvious. Nevertheless, the translation "(male and female) disciples" is to be preferred, since nothing speaks against women being involved. The formulation's unnaturalness is important, in order to keep on bringing to a conscious level the question of the presence or absence of women.

In another text in the Gospel of Thomas, the final saying (114), the discipleship of women becomes the explicit theme: "Simon Peter said to him, 'Let Mary leave us, for women are not worthy of life.' Jesus said, 'Look, I will drag her in order to make her male, so that she too may become a living male spirit resembling you. For every woman who makes herself male will enter the kingdom of heaven.'"

One aspect of this saying is a particular source of controversy, what "to make her male" could mean. Understandably, some exegetes have reacted to the phrase critically (Lagrand 1980, 106; Meyer 1985, 561, for example). We can only think about the validity of this criticism after an attempt to understand the saying.

There are a great many parallels in antiquity to the expression "to make male" or "to become male," including in non-Christian traditions. It is clear that we are not dealing here with a specifically Gnostic choice of words but with an "element of the *koiné* culture from the period near the end of antiquity: on a generally accepted scale of values 'male' and 'female' stand in opposition to one another. At that time, 'to become male' always designates a development leading from a lower to a higher stage of moral and intellectual perfection" (Vogt 1985, 434). Thus, in the first century Philo of Alexandria can say, "For progress is indeed nothing else than the giving up of the female gender by changing into the male, since the female gender is material, passive, corporeal and sense perceptible, while the male is active, rational, incorporeal, and more akin to mind and thought" (*Questions and Answers on Exodus* 1.8).

In antiquity the category "gender" is used abstractly and is spiritualized. The following statement has come to us from Origen: "For indeed sex is no distinction in the presence of God, but a person is designated either a man or a woman according to the diversity of spirit. How many out of the sex of women are counted among the strong men before God, and how many of the men are reckoned among slack and sluggish women?" *(In Jesu Nave homiliae xxvi)*. Through that kind of use of language, "to become male" is actually depicted as a task for both sexes, but the higher value of the male over the female hardly appears accidental.

The interpretation of saying 114 in the Gospel of Thomas has produced differing results. Some see the saying as a call for asceticism — more precisely, a renunciation of sexuality and of producing children — by women, who in this way, through surrendering their ability to bring children into the world, become men's equals (Schrage 1964, 167-68, among others). But the gospel offers no direct calls to avoid sexuality. What is clear, by comparison, is the rejection of having children (79) and family ties. These tendencies also create the background for the statement in saying 114.

A comparison with other sayings in the gospel can help this interpretation: mentioned in saying 114 as the goal of "making male" is entering the kingdom of heaven. This phrase, "to enter into the kingdom," is used in two other sayings. In saying 99 it became clear that the presupposition for entering the kingdom was spiritual; family ties were a hindrance. Jesus devalues the family and thereby attacks the social structure of (ancient) society. The rejection of family ties called for in saying 99, for the sake of a spiritual relationship as the way of "entering the kingdom," is not isolated in the Gospel of Thomas. Rather, it is part of the world-denying ethic of Thomas Christianity.

An additional saying speaks of "entering the kingdom," and it is connected with saying 114 in yet another way. In saying 22 we read: "Jesus saw little children being suckled. He said to his disciples, 'These being suckled are like those who enter the kingdom.' They said to him, 'Shall we enter the kingdom as little ones?' Jesus said to them, 'When you make the two one, and when you make the inside like the outside and the outside like the inside, and the above like the below, that is, when you make the male and the female into a single one, so that the male not be male and the female not female; . . . then will you enter the kingdom.'"

The statement of Jesus that little children are like those who "enter the kingdom" is misunderstood at first. It is not the children's being little that is to be striven for, as the disciples assume, but that they are unaffected by the distinctions made in this world. The fundamental distinctions of this world, the dualistic way of thinking (the two), with its differentiation between inner and outer, above and below, should be eliminated, and, with that, the fundamental distinction between male and female will be eliminated. The connection of this saying with 114 lies on various levels; common to both are the theme: "male and female," the goal: "entering the kingdom," and the connection with Mary (the immediately prior saying, number 21, is the only one in the gospel besides 114 that mentions Mary).

Saying 114 is also to be read against the background of the rejection and elimination of the world's distinctions, as they are formulated in saying 22. In 114 to become male means "to become a living spirit that can enter the kingdom of God," just as in 22 the male-femaleness/androgyny enables one to enter the kingdom of God. The divergent formulation in saying 114 is not an "error in reasoning on Thomas's part" (Leipoldt 1967, 76), nor is the saying a later addition (Davies 1983, 152-53; Meyer 1985, 561). Rather, it emerges from its connection with the conflict between Mary and Peter and the location of the saying at the end of the gospel. The issue here is that Peter's demand that Mary be sent away is rejected, since Jesus adjudges her to be capable of becoming the equal of males. For this reason the process to which one is to aspire is expressed here from the perspective of a change for a woman. As in the two sayings discussed above, a turning away from the world's structures is sought, in this case from the usual gender role assigned to a woman.

The placing of saying 114 at the end of the gospel gives this text special importance. The question that is raised here is whether everything said in the previous 113 sayings also applies to women, or whether women are excluded from the community to which the gospel is addressed. The general validity of the saying becomes clear through the repetition of its central statement. The first time, the statement is applied to Mary: "I shall drag her in order to make her male." The second time, the statement is generalized: "every woman who makes herself male." What is stated in Mary's case, by way of example, applies to all women, even in the absence of Jesus' direct leading.

Jesus' retort to Peter's demand is, on the one hand, a positive one for women — they are included, the Gospel of Thomas applies to them in like measure. On the other hand, it is negative: women dare not remain as they are, but they must "be made male" under the leading of Jesus. The equality of women presupposes a change on their part, not on the part of men (a problem still with us today).

What is maddening about this saying is its assertion that women must first become what men already are inherently. The essential problem is the way it is stated, equating male with perfect and losing sight of the fact that men are not inherently perfect. At first glance, this way of speaking in 114 is much inferior to what the gospel says in saying 22, which calls on men as well as women to change. And yet, ultimately, both sayings, as well as many other texts from the same period, are promoting the ideal of an asexual spirituality that, operating on the basis of the stereotypical connection between women and sexuality, always expects the greater change from women. To the ancient mind, the androgynous person is intellectual and asexual. This becomes clear in something said by Clement of Alexandria: "For souls, themselves by themselves, are equal. Souls are neither male nor female, when they no longer marry nor are given in marriage. And is not woman translated into man, when she is become equally unfeminine, and manly, and perfect?" (*Stromata* 6.100.3). The antithesis male-female is denied in order to be reestablished in the statement that follows, now on the metaphorical level.

This use of male and female shows that gender ascriptions are constructed. What male and female mean is not established outside of our everyday reality; rather, it is constructed anew, again and again, in the process of "doing gender." The metaphorical use of male and female does not occur apart from social realities but presupposes and influences them.

Therefore, a reading of the text should not stay only on the metaphorical level, but it should also raise the question about the practical implications of "becoming male." In his reflections on the last saying in Thomas, Patterson asks under what circumstances women could undertake the itinerant life called for in the gospel, and he remarks that dressing as a man could have provided women a certain degree of protection (1993, 155).

There are several examples of women in men's clothing in ancient texts. The apocryphal Acts of the Apostles (see the Acts of Thecla [commonly known as the Acts of Paul (and Thecla)]) offer examples closest to our text. Even if they are later than the Gospel of Thomas, they stand in a certain proximity to Gnosticism and some of the characters exhibit a lifestyle not tied to a particular locality. Moreover, they offer interesting information about the problems Christian women experienced gaining acceptance in a male-oriented environment. The best-known example of an itinerant woman preacher is Thecla. She is reported to have had her hair shorn on all sides (Acts of Paul 25) and to have sown "her garment into a man's outer garment" (40) in order to travel with Paul. These and similar stories from other Acts (cf. Acts of Thomas 114, 129; Acts of Philip 95, 125) can enable us to imagine how "to make yourself male" could have been understood by women.

The criticism of saying 114's chauvinism mentioned at the beginning of this section is modified in the context of the parallels we have mentioned. On the positive side, it should be stressed that we have clear evidence here for the acceptance of women disciples of Jesus (cf. Patterson 1993, 154). The one-sided emphasis on the saying's hostility to women, given this background for the saying, is not justified, particularly since the maddening formulation is not a rarity in ancient texts, as has been shown.

The Conflict between Mary Magdalene and Peter
in the Gospel of Thomas and in the Gospel of Mary

An attack by Peter against Mary is reported in both writings. However, while in the Gospel of Mary this is directed at Mary's special authority and position of leadership (→ Gospel of Mary), in the Gospel of Thomas, Peter creates a controversy over her (and the other women's) participation in hearing Jesus, and thus belonging to the circle of Jesus' followers at all. Mary is vindicated in both texts, but the argument is structured in different ways.

The origin of the conflict between these two individuals in the Gospel of Mary can be explained in connection with stories of Jesus' postresurrection appearances in the New Testament (→ Gospel of Mary). It is difficult to say how it arose in the Gospel of Thomas. A general dependence of the Gospel of Thomas on the Synoptics is unlikely, and even on the assumption that the gospel presupposes the canonical Gospels, the origin of a Mary-Peter conflict and the role of Peter as an enemy of women do not become easier to explain.

Historically speaking, there actually was a discussion about the exclusion of women. Either it was a dispute within Thomas Christianity about the participation of women, whereby the intention of excluding women was ascribed to Peter, seen in the tradition as the leading male disciple; or the conflict had its roots in actual disputes between historical individuals in the earliest Christian communities.

LITERATURE

Aland, Kurt, ed. 1996. *Synopsis quattuor evangeliorum,* 517-46. 15th ed. Stuttgart.

Blatz, Beate. 1990. "Das koptische Thomasevangelium." In *Neutestamentliche Apokryphen,* vol. 1, *Evangelien,* edited by Edgar Hennecke and Wilhelm Schneemelcher, 93-113. Tübingen.

Buckley, Jorunn Jakobsen. 1985. "An Interpretation of Logion 114 in the Gospel of Thomas." *Novum Testamentum* 27:245-72.

Davies, Stevan L. 1983. *The Gospel of Thomas and Christian Wisdom.* New York.

Lagrand, James. 1980. "How Was the Virgin Mary 'Like a Man'?" *Novum Testamentum* 22:97-107.

Layton, Bentley, ed. 1989. *Nag Hammadi Codex II, 2-7,* vol. 1. Nag Hammadi Studies, vol. 20. Leiden.

Leipoldt, Johannes. 1967. *Das Evangelium nach Thomas. Koptisch und Deutsch.* Texte und Untersuchungen zur Geschichte der altchristlichen Literatur, vol. 101. Berlin.

Meyer, Marvin W. 1985. "Making Mary Male: The Categories 'Male' and 'Female' in the Gospel of Thomas." *New Testament Studies* 31:554-70.

Patterson, Stephen J. 1993. *The Gospel of Thomas and Jesus.* Sonoma, Calif.

Petersen, Silke. 1999. *"Zerstört die Werke der Weiblichkeit!" Maria Magdalena, Salome und andere Jüngerinnen Jesu in christlich-gnostischen Schriften.* Nag Hammadi and Manichaean Studies, vol. 48. Leiden, Boston, and Cologne.

Schrage, Wolfgang. 1964. *Das Verhältnis des Thomasevangeliums zur synoptischen Tradition und zu den koptischen Evangelienübersetzungen.* Beihefte zur Zeitschrift für neutestamentliche Wissenschaft und die Kunde der älteren Kirche, vol. 29. Berlin.

Schröter, Jens. 1997. *Erinnerung an Jesu Worte.* Wissenschaftliche Monographien zum Alten und Neuen Testament 76. Neukirchen.

Theissen, Gerd. 1973. "Wanderradikalismus." *Zeitschrift für Theologie und Kirche* 70:245-71.

Vogt, Kari. 1985. "'Männlichwerden' — Aspekte einer urchristlichen Anthropologie." *Concilium* 21:434-42.

FOR FURTHER READING

Hartenstein, Judith. 2007. "Nackt auf fremdem Land (Die Kinder auf dem Feld). EvThom 21,1-4." In *Kompendium der Gleichnisse Jesu,* edited by Ruben Zimmermann, 878-82. Gütersloh.

Losekam, Claudia. 2007. "Einssein statt Getrenntsein (Zwei auf einem Bett). EvThom 61 (vgl. Q 17,34f.)." In *Kompendium der Gleichnisse Jesu,* edited by Ruben Zimmermann, 889-903. Gütersloh.

Petersen, Silke. "Die Frau auf dem Weg (Vom Mehlkrug). EvThom 97." In *Kompendium der Gleichnisse Jesu,* edited by Ruben Zimmermann, 916-20. Gütersloh.

Plisch, Uwe-Karsten. 2007. *Das Thomasevangelium. Originaltext mit Kommentar.* Stuttgart.

Standhartinger, Angela. 2007. "Einssein an Gottes Brust (Stillkinder). EvThom 22." In *Kompendium der Gleichnisse Jesu,* edited by Ruben Zimmermann, 883-87. Gütersloh.

Uro, Risto. 2003. *Thomas: Seeking the Historical Context of the Gospel of Thomas.* London.

Translated by Everett R. Kalin

Shepherd of Hermas: Being Enticed into Conversion in the Erotic Church of Sophia

Ulrike Auga

As I read, the ambiguity of the text entices me into making ever-new subjective and risk-laden decisions that alter me and enable the world to be changed.

On the Challenge of Reading This Text

This sizable writing, written in Rome about 140-145 C.E., documents a variety of Christianity hard to find elsewhere, in which women and female images occupy a wider than usual range. The Shepherd of Hermas is an outsider who calls into question traditional evaluations of content and form.

Hermas wants to save the threatened church through a re-vision. He offers his informative and educational program for leading the members of the church to *radical conversion (metanoia)* and to the dynamic task of building the church together. Various characteristics of Christianity in Rome at the time the book was written can be discerned: (1) cultural and theological diversity; (2) a strong Jewish tradition; (3) a theological position mediating between the impossibility of being forgiven for those sins committed after baptism (Heb 6:4-6) and ethical indifference, through the granting of one (but *only one*) *second chance for conversion*. The customary translation "repentance" does not accord with the author's intention (Ernst 1996, 63-65).

In German commentaries, Hermas is accused of being without a coherent theology (Dibelius 1923, 423), of being trite and unliterary (Brox 1991, 5.21 and repeatedly).

Through the use of historical criticism, feminist exegesis comprehends the significance of the female characters for the soteriology of Hermas (Smith 1979), uses sociological models to demonstrate social fragmentation with respect to carrying out certain functions in the church and to demonstrate an increasing stress on qualifications to do such tasks (Osiek 1983; 1990), and emphasizes the liminal (borderline) and transformational character of the feminine symbolism (Osiek 1992) and genre (Osiek 1986; Humphrey 1995).[1]

The *allegory and allegorizing*[2] that Hermas uses, like the writing itself, find themselves at the moment in a period of scholarly rehabilitation (cf. the introduction in Kurz 1993, 28-65). Hermas leads into a bizarre world of images made up of raptures and visions with *personifications*,[3] which contain encoded messages whose solutions the author either undertakes himself *(vertically explicit allegorical expressions)* or leaves to the reader. It seems to me that it will be possible, with the aid of literary critical methods, to decipher *(vertically implicit)* additional allegorical images (Ernst 1996, 13-55) in an allegorical reading process. Here we will introduce those that show that the writing contains a sophia ecclesiology and finds itself on the edge of a de-eroticizing process in the church.

In accord with allegory, Hermas takes the readers into a dynamic of an allegorical vision and its interpretation. It is his strategy, through constant motivation, (self-)correction with a risk-laden call for decision, intentional repetition (Henne 1990, 19-21), and a gradual increase in specificity, to create the capacity to achieve conversion, to *entice*, as it were, to beguile into the process of salvation and growth. Hermas is himself caught up in this development of the *horizontal allegorical progression*, in which he absolutely expects a lot of criticism from his hearers. But he does not ask too much of those whom he calls to renewal; rather, he instructs them in the reading of allegory (Quilligan 1979).[4]

1. The text appeared in the German original under the name of Ulrike Ernst. A current debate revolves around the designation of the whole text as an apocalypse, pseudoapocalypse, or allegory. There is a consensus about the allegorical nature of individual texts.

2. To simplify, *allegory* can be understood as descriptive or narrative material for which, next to the first *(initial)* meaning, another *(allegorical)* is *also intended*, which is not blended with the first. The allegorical meaning can be given explicitly or is implicitly assumed. *Allegorizing* (an allegorical method of interpretation) is a reading strategy that is used here only for allegorical texts.

3. An *allegorical personification* is a particular kind of allegory in which the allegorical person, through the discrepancy between form and meaning, has a second dimension of meaning. It is to be distinguished from a one-dimensional personification, which lacks a second meaning.

4. The process of bringing the readers to awareness begins with the tension between initial and allegorical levels. The readers are recruited to make subjective vertical statements, but they must let themselves be led by the *horizontal progression* of the allegory, which is predetermined by the structure of the text. In this interplay of allegory and vertical as well as horizontal allegorizing, the interaction between author, text, and reader becomes clear as a *positive enticing*. The readers are themselves participants in the allegory in that they must at any given time make their own subjective (ethical) decision. The obvious goal is a growth of the readers in the act of self-definition through constantly deciding anew.

Controversial Presuppositions

One witness is the Bible manuscript Codex Sinaiticus (as far as Mandates 4.3.6); in the fourth century it placed the Shepherd of Hermas after Barnabas, subsequent to the books of the New Testament. The presence of Hermas in that codex testifies also to the significance of the original Greek text of this work. In the second and third century, it was widely accepted as belonging to the New Testament canon and was greatly loved well into the Middle Ages. Its unexplained rejection (Wilson 1995, 51-72) confronts us with the problem of the canon.

I do not number the text as a unit with 114 chapters, but employ the usual outward division, with its indication of five Visions (hereafter Vis), twelve Mandates (commandments; hereafter Man), and ten Similitudes (parables; hereafter Sim). The author, of course, has no interest in a precise differentiation of literary genres. The entire book is written from the first-person perspective of Hermas, with many passages of dialogue, and it is supplied with autobiographical details that blend into the fictional account. Hermas is the only author of the different parts as well as the step-by-step producer of the whole text. The "masterful inconsistencies" (Snyder 1968, 6) are not the product of various authors (against Osiek 1983), but are there because the author wants them to be exactly like that.

Contents

Vision 1: The prehistory begins with the depiction of the sale of Hermas as a slave to a woman named Rhoda in Rome. He meets her again later as a freedman and, encountering her in various contexts, falls in love with her, for which she in turn reproaches him from heaven. Later an older woman *(presbytera)* appears to him and summons Hermas and his family to conversion.

Vision 2: A year later he sees the older woman, who commissions him to hand on the contents of a little book, which he at first cannot understand. Hermas's children have betrayed him, and he is to live with his wife as with a "sister." Christianity is informed of one final opportunity for conversion and of persecution. A man explains that the old woman is not the Sibyl but the church. Hermas, Clement, and Grapte are to proclaim her words in Rome and beyond.

Vision 3: The older woman shows Hermas the building of a tower. Then she reveals the allegorical vision: "The tower that you see being built is I myself, the church" (Vis 3.3.3; cf. Sim 9.13.1). The individual stones (living and dead Christian men and women, with and without positions of leadership) must be worked on and sorted. Seven women appear, representing virtues that are to be fulfilled. Hermas asks for the interpretation of the three forms in which the woman appears. Her becoming younger, more beautiful, and happier signifies the positive transformation of the members of the church.

Vision 4: Hermas encounters a sea monster, which is subdued through Hermas's faith. The woman, who now appears as a virgin in a wedding dress, interprets this as a reference to the persecutions.

Vision 5: A shepherd figure, from which the book derives its name, appears as a new bringer of revelations. This angel of conversion has been sent by the holiest angel of all (Jesus Christ). He commands Hermas to write down his commandments and parables, which then follow in the Mandates and Similitudes.

Mandates 1-12: These commandments are meant to provide the church with a more specific ethic in its process of transformation. With reference to Vision 3, the following are treated: faith, love for God, and restraint (1); simplicity (2); truth (3); desire and conduct in marriage (4); patience, outbursts of temper (5); faith in the works of the righteous angel and fear of the evil angel (6); liberating reverence before God instead of fear of the devil (7); refraining from doing evil (8); double-mindedness (9); getting rid of sadness and putting on joyfulness (10); false prophecy (11); good and evil desire (12).

Similitude 1: Parables 1-5 continue speaking about the ethic, with the aid of pictorial examples. Those who serve God will dwell in the city that is on the other side. In the alien city on this side they are to use the prosperity God has given them for helping the poor.

Similitude 2: The image of the vine that grows up around the elm tree imparts an original social message. As the poor members of the church need the material support of the better-off, the latter are dependent on the ideal gifts of the former.

Similitudes 3 and 4: Just as in winter it is impossible to tell the leafless trees apart, so also on earth the righteous and the unrighteous cannot be recognized outwardly. In the summer-like woods of the world to come, you will be able to tell the dead and living trees apart.

Similitude 5: True fasting means following God. The pictorial account about the servant of the owner of the vineyard (cf. Matt 21:33-46 and parallels) shows that Hermas assumes that there is an extra reward for good works that go beyond what God expects. In addition, the true servant is identified christologically as the Son of God in whom the Holy Spirit dwells.

Similitude 6: Similitudes 6-9 deal with the theme of conversion. By means of two shepherds, who represent avenging angels, the unequal relationship between the time of harmful enjoyment and the punishment that follows is made clear. But Hermas also names a useful and saving pleasure.

Similitude 7: As his family's representative, Hermas endures torments for their sins.

Similitude 8: Different branches of a willow tree stand for diverse groups of Christians. They are used to demonstrate the necessity of conversion.

Similitude 9: This, the most comprehensive parable in the entire book, gives specificity to the vision of the tower in Vision 3 in its reflection on the church. Hermas looks at twelve mountains before the building of the tower begins, in which he now takes part. He describes the rock, with its door to the tower, six supervisors of the building project and various builders, as well as twelve allegorically personified virtue-virgins, who are responsible for the inclusion and exclusion of the stones (members of the church) in the tower (the church). After the inspection of the construction site ends, the building's owner gives the Shepherd the task of purifying the building and then leaves. The virtue-virgins remain to oversee the project. Twelve beautiful, wild women clothed in black (vices) bring back the stones that had been thrown away. The tension mounts, for the Shepherd does not have time to explain something to Hermas until the next day. In a crucial scene, before Hermas learns the solution, he has to prove himself for a night in the midst of the twelve virgins (Sim 9.10.6–11.8).

Similitude 10: Once more the chief angel (God's Son) and the Shepherd (Vis 5) summon Hermas, and through him all believers, to timely conversion and to good deeds. The virgins (virtues, positive energies) will live with Hermas if he purifies his house (himself, his family, and church).

Non-Allegorical Feminine Figures and Their Contribution to the Understanding of the Social and Religious Situation of the Church

Women occupy Hermas's attention in his daily life, in which reality and vision merge. Despite their diversity, he always experiences them as crucial figures in his search for salvation (Smith 1979, 104-32), but also, at the same time, as a challenge to his ethical behavior, whereby any failure on his part would threaten his salvation. A tension arises between a positive erotic energy, which Hermas experiences as a salvation-bringing force, and the fear of being excluded from salvation by overstepping the boundary of sexual honor of the female figures he meets. Do we encounter here a (still conscious) ethical dilemma of the (early) *kyrial* Christian theology and church, a solution to which is once again sought through the progressive suppression of eroticism and feminine elements?

Rhoda

The changing relationships in which Hermas is entangled with the wealthy Christian woman Rhoda, someone unknown to the writing's hearers, give the whole book its start. The prehistory begins: "The one who raised me sold me to a certain Rhoda at Rome. Many years later, I became reacquainted with her and began to love her as a sister. After some time, as she was bathing in the river Tiber, I saw her, gave her my hand, and brought her out of the river. Seeing her beauty, I thought in my heart: 'How happy I would be if I had such a wife, both in regard to beauty and manner.' I wanted only this, nothing more" (Vis 1.1.1-2). In a few sentences the author Hermas sketches his struggle. The text implies, first of all, that the woman exercising control over him releases him from slavery and thus enables his social advancement. The *domina* (mistress)–slave relationship, however, is also at the same time a commonly used expression between lovers in the Roman literature of the period (Leutzsch 1989, 168 n. 65, with the references).

As Hermas encounters her again, he feels that he is her equal. The description of the relationship as one between a brother and a sister is important in the writing and is used repeatedly (his wife shall be a sister to him; sleeping like a brother among the virgins). The address "Sister-Brother" implies an *egalitarian* love relationship, which, however, does not basically need to exclude erotic, even sexual, encounters, since these words of address are used in the description of nonincestuous heterosexual relationships in the literature of love (Leutzsch 1989, 168 n. 64, with the references; cf. Gen 26:7; 1 Cor 9:5; Song 4:9-10; 5:1; Tob 7:13-15; 8:4, 7; Jubilees 27:14, 17). It cannot be determined to what degree in Hermas we are dealing with a specifically Christian form of address or one that alludes to the nearness of the end-time.

Bathing scenes also occur in the First Testament (2 Sam 11:2), in the deuterocanonical First Testament literature, as well as in imperial non-Christian literature (cf. the references in Hilhorst 1988, 691-92). It is true that "to want to have as a wife" can contain a sexual allusion (1 Cor 5:1; John 4:18); nonetheless, Rhoda is not described as a seductress. Hermas himself immediately adds the qualification that he had not compromised the woman's honor. That he had in fact done that with his thoughts, he reveals in his self-criticism that emerges from the mouth of Rhoda in a vision Hermas receives from heaven: "'God . . . is angry with you because you have sinned against me.' I answered her, 'Have I sinned against you? How? Or when did I say a shameful thing to you? Have I not always considered you as a goddess? Have I not always honored you as a sister? Why do you malign me, woman, with these evil and unclean charges?' Laughing she said to me, 'The evil desire arose in your heart . . .'" (Vis 1.1.6b-8a). Hermas struggles with the issue of to what extent sexual lust excludes one from salvation. When he raises this in the context of the warning against amassing possessions (Vis 1.1.8-9), the possibilities for the most diverse forms of love that are addressed are not distinguished on the basis of their eroticism or sexuality but on the basis of the virtue-destroying desire to carry them out.

Hermas's Wife

Hermas really does fail as a paterfamilias, since his children's betrayal of their parents during the persecutions of Christians and the excesses of his wife add to his concern about salvation (Smith 1979, 83-86). When his wife is first mentioned, her offense is also spelled out, as well as her altered relationship to Hermas in the future. "But communicate this message to all your children and to your wife who from now on will be as a sister to you. She does not hold her tongue, with which she does evil" (Vis 2.2.3). Her "offence with her tongue" is not a gender-specific reproach directed against women but is, first of all, a part of First Testament Jewish *parenesis* as well as of the exhortations found in the surrounding culture (cf. James 1:26; 3:5-6, 8; 1 Tim 5:13; Leutzsch 1989, 173). This is all the clearer to Hermas since Grapte, Rhoda, and especially the woman revealer are introduced as active speakers or teachers.

From the author's language as well as the mention of his sexual abstinence, it can be concluded that the term "Sister" for his wife is intended to provide a new definition of their relationship, including their sexual interaction (Brox 1991, 98). In Rome in the second century, only women of the upper class, in contrast to the major part of the population, could be in control of their own sexuality (Schottroff 1980, 92-93). Moreover, the married woman was restricted to the role of mother and wife. Sexual sensitivity and restraint on the part of Hermas and the acknowledgment of his wife as his "Sister" thus signify here refraining from the utilization of negative power in the relationship.

Grapte

Hermas knows women as equal church members who act independently in a church governed by brothers and sisters sharing power. "So you will write two little books and send one to Clement and one to Grapte. . . . Grapte will admonish the widows and orphans" (Vis 2.4.3). According to Similitude 9.26.2, caring for the widows and orphans is the special ministry of the deacons. It can therefore be conjectured that Grapte is a female deacon, or in any case plays a particular, prominent role in the church. Further assertions remain speculative (that she is Clement's wife, or a member of a community of widows or virgins; cf. a summary of the suggestions in Smith 1979, 87-89).

Hermas does not offer a systematic order for the organization of his church (as the *Didache,* for example, does). He uses the term *ekklēsia* synonymously for the individual congregation and the church at large. When he mentions groups of people with specific responsibilities, the issue is not one of hierarchy but of ethical behavior. The monarchical episcopate (the hegemony of one bishop over male or female colleagues — the papacy emerged later from the hegemony of the Roman bishop) has not yet been established. Hermas names members of a leadership team for the church, such as male and female elders and bishops, as well as shepherds (all three at times referring to the same groups of people), and, beyond this, male and female deacons and teachers. To these are added positions such as female and male apostles, prophets, and martyrs. In the original Greek text, these designations are given in the plural, which has the same form in all the genders of the noun. A verbal inclusion of women in or exclusion from these functions is not present in Hermas. Since specific role designations are documented for the early church's life (woman teacher, Prisca, Acts 18:26; woman apostles, Junia, Rom 16:7, and Mary, Gospel of Mary; woman deacon, Phoebe, Rom 16:1-2; woman prophet, 1 Cor 11:5; Acts 21:9; cf. 1 Tim 3:11), and Grapte is explicitly named, it can be concluded on linguistic grounds that the functional designations in Hermas also include women (Leutzsch 1989, 161) and that the non-gender-specific address *adelphoi* for members of the church is to be understood as an address to sisters and brothers.

Allegorical Female Figures and the Significance of Their Polysemy (Ambiguity) for a Sophia Ecclesiology

The Wisdom Figure of the Woman-Revealer and Her Allegorical Interpretation Signifying the Church

In the appearances of the woman-revealer and in the building of the tower (the women and the tower are both identified as the church), it is shown how salvation can be assured through the "erotic" church (Vis 1–4). The woman who here makes her appearance stands in the tradition of the postexilic Sophia, personified as a woman (Osiek 1992, 55-74; Humphrey 1995, 119-49).

This wisdom figure is accorded particular honor as Lady Church, for she is the Lady *(Herrin)* standing alongside the owner of the tower *(Bauherr,* namely, Jesus Christ). The preexistence of Wisdom (Prov 8:22-31; Sir 1:4; 24:3-9) corresponds to the preexistence of the church (cf. 2 Clement 14.1-2). She is also a wise, angry teacher, preacher, and adviser (Prov 1:20-33; 8:1-21). As Mother Wisdom she can address women and men of the church as "Children" *(tekna* — Vis 3.9.1).

The woman first appears after Rhoda, from heaven, had accused Hermas of sinning against her (Vis 1.1.1–2.1). Hermas sees a dignified old woman with a book in her hands. Through a circle of motivation, criticism, and acceptance she gets him to confront the decision for conversion (Vis 1.1.1–3.2). Wisdom admonishes and calls for a decision to accept the invitation to eat at her table (Prov 9:1-6); in Hermas the church calls for conversion, without which exclusion from salvation results. Quite suddenly the woman is introduced as the revealer. She maintains this role until, beginning with Vision 5, it is assumed by the Shepherd. On the basis of the most horrible revelations in the book, Hermas at first understands only that God's creative power is to be extolled, for with wisdom and providence God has created the world and the holy church (Vis 1.1.3-4). Like the origins of the "wise woman," whose image flowed into that of the wisdom figure, wisdom, and with that the church, is independent of class and social strata. The revealer speaks to Hermas, who, despite his socially liminal status, does not belong intellectually or materially to the upper classes and who, in his allegorical personification, also stands for the empirical church. One year later Hermas is transported to the same place, where he sees the woman (Vis 1.1–3.4). She charges him to bring a message to the elect *(eklektoi)*.

In a dream a man enlightens Hermas: "'The elder lady from whom you received the little book — who do you think she is?' I answered: 'The sybil [*sic*].' 'Wrong,' he said. 'Then who is she?' I asked. 'The church,' he said" (Vis 2.4.1). She is old, for she is older than everything else, and the world was created for her sake. The characterization of the figure must give the hearers an occasion to mistake her for the Sibyl, a popular figure from time immemorial (Levine 1994, 98-108). Hermas brings us to the interpretation of the allegorical person. The woman is the church, the addressees are the church, and Hermas is the church. Hermas imparts its messages through the multiplicity of differing and overlapping images (polysemy — Henne 1989, 131-35). Beginning with Vision 3, the woman church stands beside herself as the tower church and reveals the code (cf. 4 Ezra 10:27): "The tower that you see being built is I myself, the church" (Vis 3.3.3a). Then the elder woman shows Hermas seven women, who are virtues (3.8.7). The admonitory address of the elder woman is composed in the style of a wisdom address (3.8.11b–9.10). Like wisdom, the woman changes her form, for first she was old and sitting in a chair, the second time younger and standing, and finally, on the third occasion, young and beautiful and joyful. The three forms in which the woman appears are now interpreted by a man as references to the condition of the church (3.11-13), which does not need to be harmonized with the first interpretive direction. At first it related to the preexistent church, which in its original and final form is ideal. The transformation into the three figures takes us in another direction, which mirrors the empirical church of one's experience. Thus the two ways in which the church appears are united in one figure.

In Vision 4 Hermas is met by the elder woman as a fully rejuvenated virgin in Roman bridal dress. She is the empirical church, entirely transformed into the ideal church. Hermas, who was an erring Christian, has through conversion become a revelation recipient, prophet, and teacher. Can he, by proving himself until the end-time, actually become a transcendent bridegroom? In the Wisdom of Solomon, advice-dispensing Sophia appears in Hellenistic form as Solomon's bride and life-companion and, at the same time, also the beloved wife of God (Wis 7–9), which does not go without erotic allusions. Is the Sophia church thus the bride of wisdom's pupil Hermas, with whom he lives in earthly syzygy (companionship — cf. *Didache* 11.11), in analogy to the heavenly syzygy between Christ and the church? Hermas is also an allegorical personification of the empirical church, the elder lady the allegorical personification of the ideal church. The preexistent unity, which flies apart in the world, begins its unification with an eye to the future. Wisdom and the empirical church, which will then coincide with the ideal church, will enter into an eternal marriage.

The Personified Virtue-Women

The positive view of life that is imparted by the ethic of Hermas is striking, with its concern for basic attitudes more than for commandments. Sadness is a vice (Vis 3.1.9; Sim 9.15.3, for example) and, like doubt, to be avoided. People, like transcendent figures, and even commandments, plants, mountains, and places can be happy, for joy is a virtue (Sim 9.15.2) and enjoyment can be beneficial. "Every act is luxury for a person that is done with pleasure. . . . But there are also luxuries that save. Many luxuriate in doing good, carried away by their own pleasure" (Sim 6.5.5, 7). Hermas makes his appeal much more frequently with happiness and the motivation that follows from doing good and from the nearness of salvation than with the threat of punishment. But he also speaks of the power that people need for this: "it is not possible to keep these commandments without these young women" (Sim 10.3.1). These virgins are "powers of the Son of God" (Sim 9.13.2) and arise from God's loving care (Man 12.6.4; Sim 9.13.7). The virtues are not just requirements, but they are also the effective resources through which it becomes possible to fulfill the commandments. Through the equipping of the woman wisdom (the church) with the virtues (commandments and effective resources), an image emerges in which Hermas experiences erotic love as a source of power. For once, strangely enough, Hermas does not ask anything. "She [Lady Church] looked at me smiling and said to me: 'Do you see seven women around the tower?' 'I see them, lady,' I said. 'The tower is being sustained by them according to God's command'" (Vis 3.8.2). Then Hermas experiences the ways they work, which are identical with their names. Like faith and her daughter restraint, as well as simplicity, knowledge, innocence, reverence, and love, which are each daughters of one another, they must be faithfully observed (Vis 3). We are still dealing here with *simple personifications* rather than allegorical ones, for the seven women merely stand for the characteristic to which they point, but do not act as actual persons. Lady Church, which has her model in personified Wisdom, does not build a house but a tower. Proverbs 9:1 says,

> Wisdom has built her house,
> she has hewn her seven pillars.

The seven pillars are now seven virtue-women, and what are being hewn are the stones, that is, the Christians who are being enticed to conversion. That Wisdom herself is one of the seven virtues can be explained from the image's polysemy.

In Similitude 9 the women play a more important role in the building of the tower than they do in Vision 3. The tower is built by the six supervisors of the building project and the *twelve virgins.* As they appear they are really *allegorical personifications,* for what they do is important rather than just the transferred significance of their names. "The young women who cared for the tower ran up to him [the tower's owner, Jesus Christ] and kissed him, and began to walk with him around the tower" (Sim 9.6.2). Twelve vice-women take away the stones (Christians) rejected for the building of the tower (9.9.5). After the tower is finished, the Shepherd leaves the scene without explaining the revelation and entrusts Hermas to the virgins (9.11.1-7). When it is announced that the Shepherd will not return in the evening, Hermas asks where he is to stay. The virgins answer, "You will sleep with us as a brother and not as a husband, for you are our brother, and besides, we are going to *live* with you because we *love* you so much" (9.11.3). Hermas stated that he was ashamed to stay with them. And this is what happened next: "The one who seemed most prominent among them began to *kiss* and embrace me, and when the others saw her embracing me, they too began to kiss me, lead me around the tower, and *play* with me" (9.11.4). Then Hermas loses his inhibitions and says, "It was as if I had *become young again,* and I too began to play with them. Some were dancing, some moving rhythmically, some singing. Keeping silence, I walked with them around the tower and was *very happy* with them" (9.11.5). But as evening comes, Hermas still wants to go home, but they restrain him. So he spends the night with them and sleeps beside the tower on their outstretched garments. The virgins have him lie in their midst, "and they did nothing but pray. So I also prayed with them unceasingly" (9.11.7). The next morning the Shepherd returns and asks the virgins if they had done anything to him, whereupon he gives assurances about the night's platonic joy.

Amazingly, the Woman-Church-Wisdom disappears from the story completely in Vision 4, after she has been replaced by the Shepherd. And so the allegorical virgins in Similitude 9 are now actively involved in building the tower, and wisdom is no longer mentioned as an individual virtue. Certain attributes of the woman appear to be transferred to the twelve, who now themselves portray a polysemic figure of wisdom (Ernst 1996, 104-10). The interconnection of virtues as a characteristic of wisdom is common. In Wisdom 8:7 it says, "her [wisdom's] labors are virtues; for she teaches self-control and prudence, justice and courage." The fusion of virtues and "spirits" also reminds one of Hermas (Wis 7:22-23). If the twelve virgins signify wisdom, it can be assumed that the twelve vice-women correspond to Lady-foolishness, wisdom's polar opposite, who lures people into apostasy. Even the otherwise unexplained pattern of the Shepherd can be a polysemic form of wisdom. Now and again wisdom has "clearly androgynous tendencies, appearing at one moment as a young man from heaven, and then as a celestial virgin" (Benz 1969, 576-77). In Vision 3 the Shepherd is called a young man and immediately replaces Lady Wisdom. But the virgins must retain traits that are characteristic of wisdom, so that Hermas can form a transcendent union with Sophia.

This sheds light on Similitude 9.10.6–11.8: as allegorical virtue-virgins typifying wisdom, they want to dwell with Hermas forever, just as in the past wisdom desired to dwell with Israel (1 Enoch 42:1-2; cf. Sir 24:3-7). Wisdom says of herself,

then I was beside [God] as a beloved,
and I was daily [God's] delight,
  rejoicing before [God] always,
rejoicing in [God's] inhabited world
  and delighting in the human race. (Prov 8:30-31)

Wisdom, in the form of the twelve, played with the human figure Hermas (cf. the way he is repeatedly addressed: *anthrōpe*) in the sight of God. Solomon desires wisdom as his beloved companion. "I loved [wisdom] and sought her from my youth; I desired to take her for my bride" (Wis 8:2). The relationship is characterized throughout with erotic elements. The erotic allusions in the night scene may well also touch on pagan materials (Luschnat 1973/74, 53-70; Hilhorst 1988, 695-97, with the parallels from *Corpus Hermeticum*), but only the assumption of the reworking of wisdom material explains their use.

It is the key passage leading up to the great interpretation in Similitude 9.11.9–31.2. After the night of preparation, the Shepherd not only interprets the revelation but from then on also speaks of the kingdom of God. In his close relationship with the virtues, Hermas is affirmed; what is more, he may still enter into a very special love-relationship with wisdom. Is the connection that is hinted at in the last meeting with the church, dressed as a bride, now confirmed? In his encounter with wisdom, Hermas, like Solomon, prays (Wis 8:21). Hermas experiences love and *erotic power* as a religious force that created in him, standing for the empirical church, a positive *transformation*. Now in Similitude 9 the women from Vision 3 have to be called virgins, for with their change in status Hermas emphasizes that the boundary between eroticism and sexuality cannot be crossed at a religious site (Leutzsch 1989, 183). With respect to that, it must be explicitly said that the female figures, who here are in control of what occurs, do not impinge on Hermas's integrity. Hermas has no desire to resolve for his sophia church the tension between a warning against being excluded from salvation through those sexual transgressions that destroy integrity and the recognition that access to salvation includes erotic energy.

Literature

Baudrillard, Jean. 1992. *Von der Verführung. Mit einem Essay von Laszlo F. Földenyi.* Munich.

Benz, Ernst. 1969. *Die Vision. Erfahrungsformen und Bilderwelt.* Stuttgart.

Brox, Norbert. 1991. *Der Hirt des Hermas.* Kommentar zu den Apostolischen Vätern, vol. 7. Göttingen.

Dibelius, Martin. 1923. *Der Hirt des Hermas.* Handbuch zum Neuen Testament, Ergänzungsband. Die apostolischen Väter, vol. 4. Tübingen.

Ernst, Ulrike. 1996. "Das Bild der Kirche in der III. Vision und dem IX. Gleichnis des Hirten des Hermas." Master's thesis, Berlin.

Henne, Philippe. 1989. "La polysémie allégorique dans le Pasteur d'Hermas." *Ephemerides theologicae lovanienses* 65, no. 1:131-35.

————. 1990. "Le pasteur d'Hermas." *Connaissance des Pères de L'Eglise* 38:18-25.

Hilhorst, Antoon. 1988. "Hermas." In *Reallexikon für Antike und Christentum*, 14:682-701.

Humphrey, Edith McEwan. 1995. *The Ladies and the Cities, Transformation, and Apocalyptic Identity in Joseph and Aseneth, 4 Ezra, the Apocalypse, and the Shepherd of Hermas*. Sheffield.

Kurz, Gerhard. 1993. *Metapher, Allegorie, Symbol*. 3rd ed. Göttingen.

Lampe, Peter. 1989. *Die stadtrömischen Christen in den ersten beiden Jahrhunderten. Untersuchungen zur Sozialgeschichte*. 2nd ed. Tübingen.

Leutzsch, Martin. 1989. *Die Wahrnehmung sozialer Wirklichkeit im "Hirten des Hermas."* Göttingen.

Levine, Amy-Jill. 1994. "The Sibylline Oracles." In *Searching the Scriptures*, edited by Elisabeth Schüssler Fiorenza, 2:99-108. 2 vols. New York.

Lindemann, Andreas, and Henning Paulsen, eds. 1992. *Die Apostolischen Väter. Griechisch-deutsche Parallelausgabe auf Grundlage der Ausgaben von Franz Xaver Funk, Karl Bihlmeyer and Molly Whittaker*. Tübingen.

Luschnat, Otto. 1973/74. "Die Jungfrauenszene in der Arkadienvision des Hermas." *Theologia Viatorum* 12:53-70.

Madsen, Debora L. 1994. *Rereading Allegory: A Narrative Approach to Genre*. New York.

Osiek, Carolyn. 1983. *Rich and Poor in the Shepherd of Hermas: An Exegetical-Social Investigation*. Washington, D.C.

————. 1986. "The Genre and Function of the Shepherd of Hermas." *Semeia* 36:113-21.

————. 1990. "The Early Second Century through the Eyes of Hermas: Continuity and Change." *Biblical Theology Bulletin* 20:116-22.

————. 1992. "The Social Function of Female Imagery in Second Century Prophecy." *Vetera Christianorum* 29:55-74.

Quilligan, Maureen. 1979. *The Language of Allegory: Defining the Genre*. Ithaca, N.Y., and London.

Schottroff, Luise. 1980. "Frauen in der Nachfolge Jesu in neutestamentlicher Zeit." In *Traditionen der Befreiung. Sozialgeschichtliche Bibelauslegungen 2: Frauen in der Bibel*, edited by Willy Schottroff, 91-133. Munich.

————. 1991. "Women as Disciples of Jesus in New Testament Times." In *Let the Oppressed Go Free*. Louisville.

Schroer, Silvia. 1996. *Die Weisheit hat ihr Haus gebaut. Studien zur Gestalt der Sophia in den biblischen Schriften*. Mainz.

Smith, Martha M. 1979. "Feminine Images in the Shepherd of Hermas." Ph.D. diss., Durham.

Snyder, Graydon F. 1968. *The Shepherd of Hermas: A New Translation and Commentary*. London, Camden, and Toronto.

Staats, Reinhart. 1986. "Hermas." In *Theologische Realenzyklopädie*, 100-108. Berlin.

Wilson, Christian J. 1995. *Five Problems in the Interpretation of the Shepherd of Hermas: Authorship, Genre, Canonicity, Apocalyptic, and the Absence of the Name "Jesus Christ."* Lewiston, N.Y., Queenston, and Lampeter, Ontario.

Translated by Everett R. Kalin

Gospel of Peter: A Female Disciple
of the Lord and Her Female Friends

Caroline Vander Stichele

We can no longer restrict ourselves to the Christian writings that were accepted into the canon if we want to understand the role women played in early Christianity. Feminist research wants to break through the walls that prevent us from making use of the "other" side of the story (Schüssler Fiorenza 1994, 8). It would, however, be naïve to think that this other, more "heretical" side of Christian history would necessarily be a better abode for women. One of the texts that make this clear is the Gospel of Peter (hereafter Gos Pet).

The so-called Gospel of Peter is essentially a fragmentary text that is part of a manuscript from the eighth century; it was discovered in Akhmim (Egypt) during excavations in 1886-87. Two different divisions of the text are in use. In one version the text is divided into sixty verses; in the other into fourteen chapters. In agreement with Hennecke-Schneemelcher (1987), we are using both divisions in what follows. The text was identified as a fragment of the Gospel of Peter primarily on the basis of 7:26 and 14:60, in which the first-person singular is used; in 14:60 this person refers to himself as "I, Simon Peter." The preserved fragment begins in the middle of the passion narrative and ends with the return of the disciples to their homes immediately after the discovery of the empty tomb by the women. The last sentences of the fragment resemble the beginning of John 21, in which the disciples gather by the Sea of Tiberias.

An important point of discussion concerns the relationship of this text fragment to the canonical Gospels. There are various tendencies in the current discussion. The view advocating a direct dependence of the Gospel of Peter on the canonical Gospels (cf. Zahn 1893; Kirk 1994) could at the beginning reckon with considerable agreement. On this issue people have by now become much more cautious. The agreements with the Gospels are, of course, recognized, but we have

---

This essay was originally written in Dutch and translated into German by Gabriele Merks-Leinen, M.A.

gotten a better view of the differences, which make a direct dependence more problematic. According to Schaeffer (1991, 182), the Gospel of Peter more likely goes back to traditions that are orally, rather than literarily, dependent on the canonical Gospels. Brown (1994, 1334) also thinks it more likely that Peter is a free harmonization of remembrances and traditions that go back to the canonical Gospels. Other authors assume that it goes back to an independent tradition. According to Koester (1990, 240), Mark and John, as well as the Gospel of Peter, have used and reworked, independently of one another, the same earlier passion narrative. Finally, other exegetes favor a combination of the two views. Thus Crossan (1995, 223-24) takes the position that three different layers have to be distinguished: the original layer, which he calls the Cross Gospel; a canonical layer, stemming from the canonical Gospels; and a redactional layer.

In what follows I shall discuss in greater detail the only text in the gospel in which women appear, the account of the discovery of the empty tomb in 12:50–13:57. After a sketch of the preceding context, I shall analyze the account itself and then discuss its relationship to the parallel accounts in the canonical Gospels. I am using the translation found in Hennecke-Schneemelcher (1987, 187-88; for the Greek text of Gos Pet 12:50–13:57, cf. K. Aland, *Synopsis Quattuor Evangeliorum*).

The Preceding Context (1:1-11:49)

Our text fragment of the Gospel of Peter begins with the account of the end of Jesus' trial before Pilate and reports about Jesus' crucifixion and burial. The scribes, Pharisees, and elders ask the soldiers to guard the tomb for three days (8:30). Pilate gives them Petronius, the centurion, along with soldiers. Together with them, the elders and scribes also go to the tomb (8:31). A stone is laid before the entrance and sealed. But in the night "in which the Lord's day dawned" (9:35), the stone begins to roll away on its own, the tomb opens, and two men enter. The guards see three men come out, "and two of them sustaining the other, and a cross following them" (10:39). The guards decide to tell Pilate what they have seen and heard. Then they see the heavens opening and someone coming down and entering the tomb (11:44). The soldiers tell Pilate what has happened, and he commands them to say nothing (11:49). Then follows the women's visit to the tomb (12:50–13:57).

When we look more closely at the relationship between the account of the empty tomb and its preceding context, we can see that references to a narrator who speaks in the first person ("I" and "we") precede as well as follow (cf. 7:26-27 and 14:59-60) the account. The "I" is equated with Peter in 14:60 and the "we" with "the twelve disciples of the Lord" in 14:59. Nowhere in the manuscript, however, is "the Lord" identified. The names "Jesus" and "Christ" do not occur.

The passage that precedes the visit of the women shows striking similarities with Matthew's version of the burial, above all the motif of the guarding of the tomb (Matt 27:62-66). But there are also striking differences. Thus, for example, not only the guards but also the elders and scribes are at the tomb. More importantly, the resurrection itself is described, something that occurs in none of the canonical Gospels.

Nowhere in the preceding or following context are the women named. Their role is apparently restricted to the discovery of the empty tomb. They don't appear to be aware of what has occurred at the tomb, as reported in the prior section. They are, however, well aware (Gos Pet 12:53) of where the tomb is and that the entrance is blocked by a large stone (8:32; 9:37).

The Visit of the Women to the Tomb (12:50-13:57)

In 12:50 a new person appears on the stage. She is introduced as Mary Magdalene and as "a woman disciple of the Lord" *(mathētria tou kyriou)*. What else is said of her sounds more negative. Out of fear, she has not done at the tomb "what women are wont to do for those beloved of them who die" (12:50). This fear is specifically identified as "fear of the Jews." A similar motive, though not specifically identified as such, moves the other (male) disciples to hide themselves after Jesus' death (Setzer 1994, 123). But there the motivation for the action of the disciples is stated thus: "For we were sought after by them [namely, the Jews, elders, and priests in v. 25] as evildoers and as persons who wanted to set fire to the temple" (7:26).

In 12:51 Mary Magdalene takes her women friends *(philas)* with her to the tomb. These women are not identified by name. It is even unclear whether or not they also can be understood to be disciples. Beginning with 12:52, it is no longer Mary Magdalene but all the women together who are the subject of the action and appear as a single person in the story. The fear of the Jews is mentioned again and ascribed to all the women, but this time specified as fear of being seen. It is the women who now speak: "Although we could not weep and lament on that day when he was crucified, yet let us now do so at his sepulcher. But who will roll away for us the stone also that is set on the entrance to the sepulcher, that we may go in and sit beside him and do what is due? — For the stone was great, — and we fear lest anyone see us. And if we cannot do so, let us at least put down at the entrance what we bring for a memorial of him and let us weep and lament until we have again gone home" (12:52b-54).

The words of the women are partly a repetition of what the narrator has already told us in the preceding verses. First, the women could not do what was expected of them when he died. This is specified in 12:52 and 12:54 as "weep[ing] and lament[ing]," and in 12:54 also as "put[ting] down at the entrance what we bring for a memorial of him." Second, it is suggested that the women were not present at the crucifixion. In the preceding context they are actually not mentioned. Despite their absence, they appear to know that a stone was rolled in front of the tomb (8:32–

9:34), but not that this was later rolled aside (9:37). The stone is a problem because the women not only want to go to the tomb (12:52) but also to enter it: "that we may go in and sit beside him and do what is due" (*ta opheilomena,* 12:53). The remark in 12:54, that the stone was great, sounds strange. The past tense *(ēn)* can indicate that this is more likely a comment of the narrator than of the women. The fear of being seen is once again mentioned; but it is suggested for the first time that the women have something with them. Yet it remains unclear what it actually is.

As the women reach the tomb, they find it already open but do not enter. "So they went and found the sepulcher opened. And they came near, stooped down and saw there a young man *(neaniskos)* sitting in the midst of the sepulcher, comely and clothed with a brightly shining robe" (13:55). He is sitting there in the tomb, where they actually want to go. His words are given in 12:56: "Wherefore are ye come? Whom seek ye? Not him that was crucified? He is risen and gone. But if ye believe not, stoop this way and see the place where he lay, for he is not here. For he is risen and is gone thither whence he was sent." In the three questions the young man asks, there is a shift from the subject (the women) to the object (the crucified one). Then comes the announcement that he is risen and gone. There is an allusion to the women's possible lack of faith. So that this lack of faith should not become a reality, it has to be prevented by reference to the fact that the place where he had lain is empty and the explanation that he has gone to the place from which he had been sent. The women's reaction is given in 13:57: "Then the women fled affrighted." Here the people are expressly described as "women" *(gynaikes).* Once more their fear is mentioned, but this time without an object. They flee. We can draw the following conclusions from this analysis. The role of women in the Gospel of Peter is reduced to 12:50–13:57. Only one of them, Mary Magdalene, is mentioned by name. She is described as a woman disciple. The other women are introduced only as her women friends. There are four references to the women's fear. It is specified to be fear of the Jews and fear of being seen. The women go to the tomb to do what women "are wont to do" (12:50) and "what is due" (12:53). To weep and lament is a part of that. And yet the women do not do what they had set out to do, namely, to go in, sit, weep, and lament. The object of their intentions is already gone. Thus, the women appear to fail. They were already failing from the start in that they did not do what was expected of them, and now, at the end, they appear to fail again.

A Comparison with the Canonical Narratives about the Empty Tomb

The account of the discovery of the empty tomb by the women in the Gospel of Peter shows striking agreements with, as well as differences from, the parallel narratives in the canonical Gospels. Not only Brown (1994) but also Crossan (1995) assumes that this account has been influenced by the canonical tradition. Total independence actually seems to me unlikely as far as this account is concerned. In it-self, however, that does not yet imply direct literary dependence. More important for me, however, is the question whether the role of the women in this gospel is different from their role in the canonical tradition. In the light of the differences between the Synoptic tradition and John, I shall first concentrate on the accounts from the Synoptic Gospels, that is, on Mark 16:1-8, Matthew 28:1-10, and Luke 24:1-12, and after that go into John 20:1-18.

As for how the first three Gospels relate to one another, I assume that Matthew and Luke are dependent on Mark in this account. Like the Gospel of Peter, the Synoptics report the visit of several women to the tomb, Mary Magdalene among them. In both cases the women are afraid, but for different reasons. In the Synoptics, their fear is evoked by the appearance of a heavenly messenger and not by the Jews, as in the Gospel of Peter. The content of the message imparted in this gospel is closest to that in Mark and Matthew. But an important difference is that the women in Peter are not given a task. The situation is different in Luke, in that, while the women do not receive a task there either, they actually do tell the disciples what has happened. The flight of the women clearly corresponds to Mark 16:8, where, however, it is also reported that they are silent. They obviously do not fulfill their role as women messengers in Mark. In the Gospel of Peter, by contrast, they are not even given a task. With reference to the Synoptic Gospels, however, the agreements with Mark are the greatest.

In the light of the notable differences between the Gospel of John and the Synoptics, I would also like to point out briefly the agreements between John and the Gospel of Peter. What is striking, first of all, is that in the two Gospels Mary Magdalene is the only woman explicitly named. In both cases she decides to go to the tomb. An additional element in Peter is the fear of the Jews. And yet this element is not completely absent in John. In John 19:38 it is said that Joseph of Arimathea was a disciple secretly, "because of his fear of the Jews." The same expression occurs also in 20:19, where the disciples keep the doors locked "for fear of the Jews." However, John does not say Mary Magdalene was afraid, not even of the Jews.

A parallel between John and the Gospel of Peter consists in the fact that no explicit reason is given for Mary's trip to the tomb, although the Gospel of Peter does suggest that she wants to go to the tomb to do what she should have done earlier. This negative motive lets her appear as a woman disciple who has failed in her gender-specific role. She has, finally, not done "what women are wont to do for those beloved of them who die" (Gos Pet 12:50). We find an additional striking parallel with John in Gospel of Peter 13:55, where it is said that the women stooped down and saw, which is also said of Mary Magdalene in John 20:11-12 (cf. also "the other disciple" in John 20:5 and Peter in Luke 24:12).

I conclude this comparison with the canonical Gospels with an overview of the most important differences. In the Gospel of Peter the fear of the women is specified as fear of the Jews and as fear to be seen. The women had been present neither at the crucifixion nor at the burial; they appear only in the account of the discovery of the empty tomb. Mary Magdalene and the other women had failed to do what was expected of them as women, and they try to make up for this by visiting the tomb. The young man suggests possible unbelief on their part. They receive on their way no message for the (other) male disciples.

The cumulative effect of these differences is that, in light of the background of the preceding context, the account in the Gospel of Peter is of only secondary importance. The "News" is not actually imparted again in this account; this occurred, rather, in the prior account, in which the resurrection event itself is described. In this account only male witnesses are mentioned explicitly, namely, the soldiers, the centurion, and the elders (Gos Pet 10:38). The empty tomb narrative only reinforces what has happened and does not have any independent significance. Consequently, the women are demoted from first- to second-grade (female) witnesses.

Conclusions

What a comparison between the narrative of the empty tomb in Peter and those in the canonical Gospels makes clear is that the role of women is diminished. In case this was not what the author intended, at the very least the way he treated the traditions at his disposal has a negative effect. A continuity emerges here between the Gospel of Peter and the canonical Gospels, in which we can identify a similar development from Mark via Matthew and Luke to John. In this way there is a gradual reduction of the unique and important role played by the women in Mark 16:1-8. There, in verse 7, a young man says to the women that they are to go to the male disciples, "above all" to Peter; in Luke 24:12 Peter himself visits the tomb; in John 20:2-10 he is the first to enter the tomb; in the Gospel of Peter, "I, Peter" literally has the last word.

This ambiguity with reference to the witness of the women can perhaps be explained as part of the controversy over belief in the resurrection. The emphasis on fear of the Jews among Jesus' disciples in the Gospel of Peter appears to presuppose an anti-Jewish apologetic interest. As a reaction to Jews who deny the resurrection, the Gospel of Peter asserts that Jews witnessed Jesus' resurrection and intentionally denied it (Setzer 1994, 116-25). In this way attention is shifted from the women to the men who were present at the tomb. It is possible that a controversy over the questionableness of the testimony of the women who discovered the empty tomb plays a role in this shift (Setzer 1997, 270).

That this testimony was actually preserved, on the other hand, points to the fact that it was an established tradition that could not simply be eliminated (Setzer 1997, 262). Above all, the decisive role played by Mary Magdalene is clearly uncontested in this tradition, insofar as she is always mentioned. Her role is thereby to be compared with that of Peter among the male disciples (Schottroff 1990, 141; 1993,

175). That she is called a "woman disciple" in the Gospel of Peter strengthens this further, and makes it clear that, despite the tendency to minimize her significance, she was nevertheless seen as a woman disciple in later tradition.

LITERATURE

Brown, Raymond E. 1994. *The Death of the Messiah: From Gethsemane to the Grave; A Commentary on the Passion Narratives in the Four Gospels.* 2 vols. New York.

Crossan, John Dominic. 1995. *Who Killed Jesus?* San Francisco.

Hennecke, Edgar, and Wilhelm Schneemelcher, eds. 1987. *Neutestamentliche Apokryphen.* Vol. 1, *Evangelien.* 5th ed. Tübingen.

Kirk, Alan. 1994. "Examining Priorities: Another Look at the Gospel of Peter's Relationship to the New Testament Gospels." *New Testament Studies* 40:572-95.

Koester, Helmut. 1990. *Ancient Christian Gospels: Their History and Development.* London and Philadelphia.

Schaeffer, Susan E. 1991. *The "Gospel of Peter," the Canonical Gospels, and Oral Tradition.* New York.

Schottroff, Luise. 1990. "Maria Magdalena und die Frauen am Grabe Jesu (1982)." In Luise Schottroff, *Befreiungserfahrungen. Studien zur Sozialgeschichte des Neuen Testaments,* 134-59. Munich.

———. 1993. "Mary Magdalene and the Women at Jesus' Tomb." In *Let the Oppressed Go Free: Feminist Perspectives on the New Testament.* Louisville.

Schüssler Fiorenza, Elisabeth. 1994. "Transgressing Canonical Boundaries." In *Searching the Scriptures,* edited by Elisabeth Schüssler Fiorenza, 2:1-14. 2 vols. New York.

Setzer, Claudia. 1994. *Jewish Responses to Early Christians: History and Polemics, 30-150 CE.* Minneapolis.

———. 1997. "Excellent Women: Female Witness to the Resurrection." *Journal of Biblical Literature* 116:259-72.

Zahn, Theodor. 1893. *Das Evangelium des Petrus.* Erlangen and Leipzig.

Translated by Everett R. Kalin

Protevangelium of James: God's Story Goes On

Bettina Eltrop and Claudia Janssen

The Protevangelium of James (hereafter Prot Jas) is generally counted as one of the apocryphal infancy gospels, and is also known by the name "Birth of Mary." It is predominately (about 75 percent of the preserved text) the story of Mary's conception, birth, and childhood, up until her marriage, and of the virgin birth of her son, Jesus. This writing's interest in Mary is often ascribed to the apologetic intention of the message of the Protevangelium of James: there were "attacks by Jews against the assertion that Jesus was born of a virgin," the opponents alleging that Jesus was an illegitimate child (Rebell 1992, 126; Schaberg 1994, 719-20). The Protevangelium of James reacted to these accusations by a broad unfolding of Mary's undefiled status, bringing forward all kinds of pertinent events. This gives us a way of reading the Gospels that leaves no doubt about the purity and innocence of Mary and about the legitimacy of her son's origin. Others view the document differently, criticizing the assessment that it is a defense against outside attacks on the virginity of Mary. These critics hold that the primary motivation of the work is neither christological nor mariological; rather, it is a (salvation)-historical document (Allen 1991). We will interpret the document in the context of its own time and place, that is, in the framework of disputes in early Christianity about its being part of Judaism. But we also want to take a critical look at the picture of Mary that is given here, with its emphasis on her virginity. We invite the document's readers to set aside for a time their glasses colored by the Mariology in the church's history and find delight in the fullness of biblical images and traditions that is offered in the Protevangelium of James.

In Conversation with Biblical Traditions (1–4)

The Protevangelium of James describes itself as the "Histories of the Twelve Tribes of Israel" (1:1). The reference to First Testament traditions and the verbal quotation of many passages are striking. The stories and quotations from the First Testament are treated in a manner similar to that used with sections taken from the texts of the Gospels in the New Testament. They are quoted in free form, often fragmentarily, and inserted into the context of new stories. Gaps that were discovered within the traditions being handed down, gaps that clearly evoked questions, were filled in the new accounts. The traditions that were handed down were in this way given currency for one's own situation. This way of dealing with the biblical traditions corresponds to what is known in Jewish scriptural interpretation as midrash: "Midrash rests on the rabbinic conviction that the bible can be made to speak to this very day. If it is our text, then it can and must answer our questions and share our values; when we struggle with it, it will yield meaning" (Plaskow 1992, 82; cf. Stemberger 1977, 83ff.).

The Protevangelium of James was written about 150 C.E., in a time of inner-Christian controversy in which some churches and theologians, like Marcion, fought vigorously to distance themselves from their Jewish roots (materials available in Schottroff 1996, 240-42; Allen 1991, 516-17). In opposition to these tendencies, the Protevangelium of James sees Christianity rooted in the Jewish tradition, appeals to the common roots, and skillfully brings Old and New Testament traditions together. A salvation-historical model in which Christianity supersedes Judaism as the chosen people cannot be found here anymore than it can in the Gospel of Luke (against Allen 1991; → Gospel of Luke). The connection is made, in the first place, through the characters in the story, in whom figures from the Hebrew Bible and the Gospels come alive. Thus Joachim embodies Abraham (Prot Jas 1:3), Elijah, Moses (Prot Jas 1:4 — Exod 24:18; 34:28; 1 Kings 19:8), Elkanah (Prot Jas 1:1-2 — 1 Sam 1:21), Joachim (Dan 13 [Susanna]), and Zechariah (Prot Jas 4:2 — Luke 1:13). Present anew in Anna are the barren Sarah (Prot Jas 2:2-4 — Gen 18) and Elizabeth (Luke 1), Hannah (Prot Jas 4:1 — 1 Sam 1 and 2) and Judith (Prot Jas 2:1-2 and Jth 8:6; 10). Mary's being turned over to God in the temple calls to mind the story of Samuel (Prot Jas 7 and 8 — 1 Sam 1 and 2); during her pregnancy she repeats the words of Rebekah (Prot Jas 17:2 — Gen 25:23). Zechariah's story (Prot Jas 24) copies that of Zechariah in 2 Chronicles 24. This list could be expanded extensively; the biblical references can only be hinted at in this restricted space.

People who heard these stories immediately had in view the images and events of the biblical stories they knew: the fateful experiences of childless foremothers and forefathers, the fortunate turn of events for Israel in the account about Judith, the story of Susanna and the Hannah-Samuel tradition, the fate of Zechariah in 2 Chronicles. They not only hear these stories as accounts of events from the past, but they also draw from them insights and perspectives offering hope for their own present situation. In this way the Protevangelium of James aligns itself with conversations with the biblical tradition that make it applicable in the present, something that can also be documented within the Hebrew Bible itself (Butting 1994).

The Temple as a Source of Hope (7–16; 23–24)

The Jerusalem temple plays a major role in the Protevangelium of James. Already in the first chapter, the account of the "Histories of the Twelve Tribes" begins with Joachim coming to the temple to bring an offering (cf. also chapter 5). Mary is consecrated for service in the temple and at age three brought there to live and grow. And when at age twelve she has to forsake the temple as her permanent place of residence, the connection with it nevertheless continues: she is chosen to weave a curtain for it.

The Protevangelium of James also ends in the temple and in this way again connects with biblical traditions. The account of the martyrdom of Zechariah and the hope to go up once again to Jerusalem (23–24) calls to mind the conclusion of the Hebrew Bible (Allen 1991, 513). With the establishment of the canon after 70 C.E., the martyrdom of Zechariah and, following on that, the hope of the return to Jerusalem and the rebuilding of the temple are placed at the end of the scriptures (2 Chron 36:23). This hope of a return to Jerusalem is also expressed in this concluding notice of the Protevangelium of James (25:1): "Now I, James, who wrote this history, when a tumult arose in Jerusalem on the death of Herod, withdrew into the wilderness until the tumult in Jerusalem ceased." It is surely not too much of a stretch to see in these words an important indication of the situation and the hopes of the community in which the Protevangelium of James is recounted. They find themselves in the diaspora (Egypt is quite likely the place of writing, although Syria is also discussed), but hold on to their hope for Jerusalem and the temple. To the city and its temple they attach their longings and hopes, their stories of liberation and their lament over what has been lost.

Traditional Accounts about Mary (5–6; 17–20)

At the center of what the Protevangelium of James is interested in recounting stands Mary, a girl, a woman around whom additional stories about women are told or retold. A major portion of the text tells about her life: her parents and their desire for a child; her conception, birth, and childhood; her growing up as a virgin in the temple and her time in Joseph's house after she reaches twelve years of age. From the beginning, Mary herself is pictured as a miraculous and eagerly awaited child, her parents as pious Jews. She grows up in complete purity — until she is three she lives at home, in a "sanctuary," surrounded only by likewise undefiled daughters of the Hebrews (cf. Joseph and Aseneth), and then in the temple in Jerusalem. At her birth, a midwife stands by at Anna's side. The description of the birth reports things known to women (cf. Gen 25:19-26; 35:16-19; Ruth 4:13-17; Luke 1; Soranus, *Gynecology* 26.70; cf. Janssen 1998). It is mentioned, for instance, that Mary was given her name in the presence of women and that Anna nursed her for half a year. At the birth of Jesus two midwives also play an important role. In chapters 18 and 19 it is reported how Joseph sought a midwife in Bethlehem, for the delivery was close at hand. The midwife is present at the delivery and utters a word of praise. It is assumed to be self-evident that she will report afterward what she had experienced, without receiving a summons to do so.

The multiplicity of stories about women permits the assumption that, to a high degree, things women know and traditions told by women have been incorporated into this writing. An example can clarify that further: by means of the motif of the barren woman, the stories of the foremothers Sarah, Rachel and Leah, Rebekah, Hannah, and Elizabeth are linked with Anna's lot in the Protevangelium of James. Knowledge about the persistence of God's help in the history of God's people and of God's partiality toward women finds expression here (→ Gospel of Luke; Janssen 1998). It is, of course, unique in stories with this motif that in the Protevangelium of James the barren woman (Anna) gives birth to a girl (Mary).

The Protevangelium of James fills in gaps that can be seen in the infancy narratives of the Gospels of Matthew and Luke, gaps that had probably occasioned many questions and diverse interpretations: How is it conceivable that Jesus comes from God or the Holy Spirit? What is the significance of the wondrous conception — is Mary really above reproach with respect to adultery? What was the birth like — did Mary have pain in childbirth as all women do? Doubt with respect to the wondrous conception can come as a reaction to attacks from outside (cf. Origen, *Contra Celsum* 1.39), but also just through Matthew 1:18-25 alone and differences between the two accounts in the Gospels. By their own interpretations and a new arrangement of the materials from texts at their disposal, the authors attempted to explain to themselves and their community how to interpret these matters so difficult to understand. A good example of how they proceeded is found in Protevangelium of James 11:2-3. Here the angel proclaims to Mary that she will conceive through God's word. "When she heard this she doubted in herself and said: 'Shall I conceive of the Lord, the living God, [and bear] as every woman bears?'" Then the angel gives a more precise explanation: "Not so, Mary, for a power of the Lord shall overshadow you. . . ." Questions and correctives are tied together here and the "proper" interpretation supplied.

According to the interpretation of the authors, the conception takes place through the word and power of God, and it provides no support for the idea that Jesus' origin might be illegitimate (cf. Schaberg 1994, 718). To make it entirely clear that Mary had not committed adultery, the order of events concerning the conception of Jesus, the trial on the charge of adultery — in accord with Numbers 5 — and the wondrous birth is painted in broad detail. The beginning of the Protevangelium of James, with numerous reminiscences of the story of Susanna (Dan 13), is already signaling that in what follows the story concerns the suspicion of adultery, to which an innocent young woman has been exposed. Mary's "undefiled status" after Jesus' birth is actually "proven" through a gynecological examination by a midwife named Salome. She establishes that the hymen is intact and that Mary is still a virgin. In this way any lingering doubt about the possibility of sexual intercourse is removed — and actually made subject to divine punishment: the midwife's hand is consumed by fire, since she does not want to believe that Mary is still a virgin and puts this to the test. "The flaming hand warns the reader: it is dangerous to doubt Mary's virginity" (Schaberg 1994, 723). As Salome prayed to God, she was healed.

How the Tradition Is Carried Forward in This Writing

Even though the Protevangelium of James positions itself within the history of Israel, many of the things it describes diverge from Jewish practices known to us. It is to be questioned, for example, whether Mary could have grown up in the temple in the manner indicated. Mary's precocious ability to walk and the fact that her steps number precisely seven show her to be a miraculous child. Here, as with the description of her first birthday, Hellenistic customs and motifs appear to have gained entrance. It is interesting to see how unabashedly these are woven into the account. It is not treated as a problem that in the Jewish tradition one's birthday was not celebrated.

It is striking, furthermore, that in comparison with the Gospel texts from which the Protevangelium of James draws its material, prophetic traditions are largely lacking. According to information in the Protevangelium of James, Mary comes from a rich family. Her advocacy of the poor as found in the Gospel of Luke is set aside. The Magnificat, Mary's song of praise, is completely absent and therewith also its political vision about the downfall of the rich and powerful and the exaltation of the lowly. Nor is the adoration of the shepherds mentioned. The lack of a place in the inn as a sign of Jesus' poverty is reinterpreted. In the Protevangelium of James, Jesus is born in a cave simply because the family is traveling, not because they can find no place in the inn. It is also not by reason of poverty that Jesus is laid in a manger; no, he is being hidden from Herod's murderous soldiers. The Protevangelium of James has a primary interest in cultic themes. Questions about purity and events occurring in the surroundings of the temple are extensively discussed. Additionally, the mixing of Hellenistic and Jewish traditions leaves the impression that the resistance to Hellenistic-Roman traditions and customs had been given up in various areas (cf., by contrast, the naming of John in Luke 1:57-66, for example, in intentional opposition to a Hellenistic-Roman practice; cf. Eltrop 1996; 1997).

Undefiled and under Control — Women in the Protevangelium of James

The changes the Protevangelium of James undertakes involve thoroughgoing losses compared with the New Testament tradition. Even the inclusion of traditions handed on by women and the multiplicity of women who are mentioned do not make the Protevangelium of James a writing favorable to women. On the contrary! It has no interest in the life of women who do not stand in the immediate context of their reproductive capabilities and of questions about their sexuality. The emphasis on virginity here also fails to offer women any perspectives for an autonomous and independent life, in contrast to ascetically oriented movements in early Christianity. From many "acts" of apostles and reports of female Christian martyrs that arose at the same time as the Protevangelium of James, it is clear that the practice of living free of marriage ties enabled women, outside of the ordered life of patriarchy, to have a way of life that assured them of freedom and independence (cf. Sutter Rehmann 1994). That the Magnificat was not picked up in the Protevangelium of James shows that it wanted to impart a picture of women that no longer made prophetic-political discourse part of the lives of women or girls. In contrast to the Gospel of Luke, Mary and Elizabeth do not appear as virgins who powerfully proclaim the gospel.

Visions of an empowerment of women are not given in the Protevangelium of James. They live in the background as wives or "undefiled" daughters and virgins, whose sexuality can be controlled. In contrast to men, they do not appear in public. The only apparent life lived outside of normal social and religious paths, that of Mary, is depicted in such a way that it soon becomes clear that she also moves within the way things are ordered. By and large she appears to be passive, with little self-awareness. She moves from the protection her parents provide to that of the priests in the temple and, thereafter, to Joseph's. She willingly yields to her fate and fulfills the tasks laid upon her. The picture of Mary given in the Protevangelium of James became the foundation for many later mariological sketches that take as their starting point Mary's perpetual virginity and undefiled status (even though the picture of her in the Protevangelium of James does not speak of this). Especially through the reference to Eve, who, according to Protevangelium of James 13:1 (in accord with 1 Tim 2:14 and in opposition to Gen 3), is depicted as the only one who is deceived (while Adam is cleared), the Protevangelium of James has a decisive role in the development of a tradition that exalts Mary over all other women and their sexuality.

Finally, we would like to esteem the Protevangelium of James primarily as an important document within the discussion process over the identity of early Christianity in the time of upheaval after the Bar Kokhba revolt. It deserves a great deal of credit for keeping alive the memory of the matriarchs and patriarchs and of the other biblical traditions about women in which the community recounting the events in the Protevangelium of James felt itself rooted.

LITERATURE

Allen, John L., Jr. 1991. "The Protoevangelium of James as an Historia: The Insufficiency of the Infancy Gospel Category." *SBL Seminar Papers,* 508-17.

Berendts, Alexander. 1895. *Studien über Zacharias-Apokryphen und Zacharias-Legenden.* Leipzig.

Butting, Klara. 1994. *Die Buchstaben werden sich noch wundern. Innerbiblische Kritik als Wegweisung feministischer Hermeneutik.* Berlin.

Eltrop, Bettina. 1996. *Denn solchen gehört das Himmelreich. Kinder im Matthäusevangelium. Eine feministisch-sozialgeschichtliche Untersuchung.* Stuttgart.

———. 1997. "Die Niedrigen werden erhöht. Die Vorgeschichte im Lukasevangelium." In *Lukas entdecken. Arbeits- und Lesebuch zum Lukasevangelium,* edited by Katholisches Bibelwerk, 22-23. Stuttgart.

Hennecke, Edgar, and Wilhelm Schneemelcher, eds. 1959. *Neutestamentliche Apokryphen in deutscher Übersetzung.* Vol. 1, *Evangelien.* 3rd ed. Tübingen.

Janssen, Claudia. 1998. *Elisabet und Hanna — zwei widerständige alte Frauen in neutestamentlicher Zeit. Eine sozial geschichtliche Untersuchung.* Mainz.

Plaskow, Judith. 1990. *Standing Again at Sinai: Judaism from a Feminist Perspective.* San Francisco.

———. 1992. *Und wieder stehen wir am Sinai. Eine jüdisch-feministische Theologie.* Lucerne.

Rebell, Walter. 1992. *Neutestamentliche Apokryphen und apostolische Väter.* Munich.

Schaberg, Jane. 1994. "The Infancy of Mary of Nazareth." In *Searching the Scriptures,* edited by Elisabeth Schüssler Fiorenza, 2:708-27. 2 vols. New York.

Schirmer, Eva. 1988. *Eva — Maria: Rollenbilder von Männern für Frauen.* Offenbach am Main.

Schneider, Gerhard, ed. 1995. *Evangelia infantiae apocrypha: (griechisch, lateinisch, deutsch) = Apokryphe Kindheitsevangelien.* Freiburg im Breisgau.

Schottroff, Luise. 1996. "'Gesetzesfreies Heidenchristentum' — und die Frauen? Feministische Analysen und Alternativen." In *Von der Wurzel getragen. Christlich-feministische Exegese in Auseinandersetzung mit Antijudaismus,* edited by Luise Schottroff and Marie-Theres Wacker, 227-45. Leiden, New York, and Cologne.

Stemberger, Günter. 1977. *Geschichte der jüdischen Literatur. Eine Einführung.* Munich.

Sutter Rehmann, Luzia. 1994. "'Und ihr werdet ohne Sorge sein . . .' Gedanken zum Phänomen der Ehefreiheit im frühen Christentum." In *Für Gerechtigkeit streiten. Theologie im Alltag einer bedrohten Welt,* edited by Dorothee Sölle, 88-95. Festschrift for Luise Schottroff. Gütersloh.

Vielhauer, Philipp. 1978. "Art. Kindheitsevangelien." In *Geschichte der urchristlichen Literatur. Einleitung in das Neue Testament, die Apokryphen und die apostolischen Väter,* 665-79. Berlin and New York.

Translated by Everett R. Kalin

Contributors' Vitae

AUGA, ULRIKE (NÉE ERNST), Protestant theologian and scholar of culture, spent several years-long research leaves in Johannesburg, South Africa; Bamako; Bali; and Jerusalem. Since 2008 she has held the chair of Theology and Gender Studies at the Seminar for Religious Studies at the Humboldt University in Berlin. Her work focuses on the intersection of intercultural theology, gender research, queer theory, and postcolonial theory. She studies the regulation of religious and secular knowledge of gender, collective bodies and life, that is, the relation of biopolitics and religion, and is preparing a "critical biotheology." In 2011 her gender-theoretical and postcolonial reading of the Shepherd of Hermas was published. Recent publications include the following: *Intellektuelle — zwischen Dissidenz und Legitimierung. Eine kulturkritische Theorie im Kontext Südafrikas,* 2nd ed. (Münster et al.: LIT, 2010); "Ausschluss oder Anschlüsse? Theologie — Geschlechtertheorie — Religionswissenschaft," in *Frau — Gender — Queer, Gendertheoretische Ansätze in der Religionswissenschaft,* ed. Susanne Lanwerd and Márcia E. Moser (Würzburg, 2009); "Undoing Gender: Nationalisms, Emerging Communities and Gender in View of Globalization; Also a Gender Based Reading of the Palestinian Declaration of Independence and the Charter of the Islamic Resistance Movement (Hamas)," in *Gender in Conflicts: Palestine — Israel — Germany,* ed. Ulrike Auga and Christina von Braun (Berlin et al.: LIT, 2006); "Wahrheit und Versöhnung oder maskuline Versöhnung am Kap? Religiöse Legitimierung nationaler Geschlechterformation," in *Erlöser: Fantasmen und Figurationen männlicher Herrschaft,* GenderCodes. Transkriptionen zwischen Wissen und Geschlecht (Bielefeld, 2007), 197-210; "Sexuelle Rechte und Menschenrechte. Probleme der interkulturellen Debatte," *Zeitschrift für Germanistik* 17, no. 2 (2008): 357-69.

BAIL, ULRIKE, Ph.D., Privatdozentin (adjunct professor), German Studies and Protestant Theology at the University of Tübingen. She obtained her doctorate in 1997; her dissertation title was "Gegen das Schweigen klagen. Eine intertextuelle Studie zu Psalm 6, Psalm 55 und 2 Samuel 13" (Gütersloh, 1998); habilitation in 2003 at the Ruhr-Universität in Bochum (*"Die verzogene Sehnsucht hinkt an ihren Ort."*

Literarische Überlebensstrategien nach der Zerstörung Jerusalems im Alten Testament
[Gütersloh, 2004]). In 2004/5 she was guest professor for feminist theology at the
Humboldt University, Berlin; she is currently private scholar and author in theology
and the recipient of several awards. Recent publications include the following: "Der
Fall Isebel(s) oder: Ein Fenstersturz, eine abwesende Leiche und ein Zitat," in
Körperkonzepte im Ersten Testament. Aspekte einer Feministischen Anthropologie, ed.
Hedwig-Jahnow-Forschungsprojekt (Stuttgart, 2003), 80-93; "Hautritzen als
Körperinszenierung der Trauer und des Verlustes im Alten Testament," in *"Dies ist
mein Leib." Leibliches, Leibeigenes und Leibhaftiges bei Gott und den Menschen,* ed.
Jürgen Ebach et al., Jabboq 9 (Gütersloh, 2006), 54-80; "Ein Wort als Grenze:
Schibbolet. Bemerkungen zu Ri 12,1-7," in *Dem Tod nicht glauben. Sozialgeschichte
der Bibel. Festschrift für Luise Schottroff zum 70. Geburtstag,* ed. Frank Crüsemann et
al. (Gütersloh, 2004), 293-311; "Biblical-Theological Perspectives on Violence be-
tween Brothers and Sisters: The Rape of Tamar (2 Sam 13)," in *When "Love" Strikes:
Social Sciences, Ethics, and Theology on Family Violence,* ed. Annmie Dillen (Leuven–
Dudley, Mass., 2009), 297-315; with Frank Crüsemann, Marlene Crüsemann, Erhard
Domay, Jürgen Ebach, Claudia Janssen, Hanne Köhler, Helga Kuhlmann, Martin
Leutzsch, and Luise Schottroff, eds., *Bibel in gerechter Sprache,* 2nd ed. (Gütersloh
2006; 3rd ed. 2007), cotranslator of the book of Psalms.

BAUER-LEVESQUE, ANGELA, Ph.D., is Academic Dean and Harvey H. Guthrie Jr. Professor of Bible, Culture and Interpretation at Episcopal Divinity School in Cambridge, Massachusetts, where she has taught since 1994. She holds a master of divinity from the University of Hamburg (1986) and a Ph.D. from Union Theological
Seminary in New York (1993). In her teaching and writing she has emphasized various aspects of social location (gender, race, sexual identity) and their impact on biblical hermeneutics and interpretation. Her publications include the following: *Gender in the Book of Jeremiah: A Feminist-Literary Reading* (Peter Lang, 1999); *The
Indispensable Guide to the Old Testament* (Pilgrim Press, 2009); with Elizabeth
Margill, *Seeing God in Diversity: Exodus and Acts* (Morehouse, 2006); as well as various essays in anthologies, including "The Book of Jeremiah" in *The Queer Bible
Commentary* (SCM, 2006).

BAUMANN, GERLINDE, Ph.D., b. 1962, adjunct professor, studied Protestant theology
at the universities of Tübingen, Hamburg, and Göttingen; her research foci are feminist theology, systematic theology, and First Testament; she was active from 1990 to
2003 in the research project "Hedwig Jahnow"; her Ph.D. dissertation was on the history of the tradition around the figure of Wisdom in Proverbs 1–9 (1996); her habilitation focused on violence in Nahum 1:2-8 (2005). Since 2005 she has been research
fellow at the Department of Theology of the University of Pretoria, South Africa.
She was a parish minister from 2006 to 2009. Since 2009 she has been a private translator and author, adjunct professor at the University of Marburg. She is translator of
Proverbs, Nahum, Habakkuk, and Zephaniah for *Bibel in gerechter Sprache.* Recent

publications include the following: *Gottesbilder der Gewalt im Alten Testament verstehen* (Understanding images of a violent God in the Old Testament) (Darmstadt: Wissenschaftliche Buchgesellschaft, 2006); "Gottes Gewalt im Wandel. Motivik und Theologie von Nahum 1,2-8 — eine intertextuelle Studie" (The changing character of God's violence: Motifs and theology in Nahum 1:2-8 — an intertextual study), Wissenschaftliche Monographien zum Alten und Neuen Testament, vol. 18 (Neukirchen-Vluyn, 2005); *Love and Violence: The Imagery of Marriage for YHWH and Israel in the Prophetic Books* (Collegeville, Minn.: Liturgical Press, 2003); "Trendy Monotheism: Ancient Near Eastern Models and Their Value in Elucidating 'Monotheism' in Ancient Israel," *Old Testament Essays* 19, no. 1 (2006): 9-25; "Die 'Männlichkeit' JHWHs. Ein Neuansatz im Deutungsrahmen altorientalischer Gottesvorstellungen," in *Sozialgeschichte der Bibel,* ed. Frank Crüsemann et al., Festschrift für Luise Schottroff zum 70. Geburtstag (Gütersloh, 2004), 197-213.

BICKMANN, JUTTA, b. 1964, received her Ph.D. in theology from the University of Münster in 1997 with a study on 1 Thessalonians. She teaches Roman Catholic religious instruction and Latin at a secondary school. At present she is enrolled in professional training as Gestalt therapist and is offering Gestalt counseling.

BIEBERSTEIN, SABINE, b. 1962, received her Ph.D. in 1997 from the University of Fribourg, Switzerland, with the study *Verschwiegene Jüngerinnen — vergessene Zeuginnen. Gebrochene Konzepte im Lukasevangelium* (Fribourg and Göttingen, 1998). After working in parish ministry, adult education, and biblical-pastoral ministry in Roman Catholic dioceses and parishes, she was called to the Catholic University of Eichstätt-Ingolstadt (Germany) Faculty of Religious Pedagogy and Formation. Her research focuses on the Gospel of Luke, the Epistle to the Galatians, and the development of resurrection hope. Her recent publications include the following: "'Töchter Gottes in Christus Jesus' (Gal 3,26)? Überlegungen zum neutestamentlichen Befund," in *Töchter (Gottes). Studien zum Verhältnis von Kultur, Religion und Geschlecht,* ed. Joachim Kügler and Lukas Bormann, Bayreuther forum transit, vol. 8 (Münster, 2008), 83-100; with Sabine Kutzelmann and Dorothea Egger, *Prophetinnen — Apostelinnen — Diakoninnen. Frauen in den paulinischen Gemeinden,* Werkstatt Bibel, vol. 5 (Stuttgart, 2003); with Klaus Bieberstein, "Auferweckt gemäss der Schrift. Das Ringen um Gottes Gerechtigkeit und die Hoffnung auf die Auferweckung der Toten," *Bibel und Kirche* 64 (2009): 70-77; ed., *Frauen und Geld,* Frauen-BibelArbeit, vol. 21 (Stuttgart, 2008); with Luzia Sutter Rehmann and Ulrike Metternich, eds., *Sich dem Leben in die Arme werfen. Auferstehungserfahrungen* (Gütersloh, 2002).

BIETENHARD, SOPHIA, Ph.D., b. 1960, studied in Berne, Paris, Atlanta, and Jerusalem in preparation for teaching and ministry; Ph.D. from the University of Berne with a dissertation on the figure of Joab in 2 Samuel and 1 Kings. She is engaged as teacher in middle schools and in adult education, and is currently teaching and doing research in the training of teachers in the school system of Berne. Recent publications include the following: "Michal und die Frau am Fenster. Ein Beitrag zur Motiv- und Redaktionsgeschichte von II Sam 6, 20-23," *Theologische Zeitschrift* 55 (1999): 3-25; "Freedom, Liberation and Context as Hermeneutical Tasks," in *Feminist Interpretation of the Bible and the Hermeneutics of Liberation,* Journal for the Study of the Old Testament: Supplement Series, vol. 374 (Sheffield, 2003), 126-36; with Silvia Schroer, eds., *Feminist Interpretation of the Bible and the Hermeneutics of Liberation,* Journal for the Study of the Old Testament: Supplement Series, vol. 374 (Sheffield, 2003).

BRENNER, ATHALYA, Ph.D., b. 1943 in Israel; B.A. in Biblical Studies and English Literature, University of Haifa, Israel; M.A. in Biblical Studies, Hebrew University Jerusalem; Ph.D. in Near Eastern Studies, Manchester, U.K. From 1992 to 1997 she was professor of feminism and Christianity at the Catholic University of Nijmegen, Netherlands; from 1992 to 1996, guest professor at the Technion, Haifa; from 1997 to 2008, professor of Hebrew Bible/Old Testament at the University of Amsterdam. In 2002 she received an honorary doctorate from the Catholic Theological Faculty, University of Bonn. She is the author of numerous books and articles. Being a member of the editorial boards of *Biblical Interpretation,* Brown Judaic Studies, and *Journal for the Study of the Old Testament,* she is the compiler/editor of the *Feminist Companion to the Bible,* 1st and 2nd ser., 19 vols. (Sheffield Academic Press, now Continuum); The Bible in the 21st Century (BCT) Series, 5 vols. (Continuum/T. & T. Clark), and the Amsterdam Studies in Bible and Religion, n.s. (Sheffield Phoenix Press).

BRIGGS, SHEILA, Associate Professor of Religion and Gender Studies at the College of Letters, Arts and Sciences of the University of Southern California. Her research and teaching areas include feminist theology, particularly nineteenth- and twentieth-century German theology, early Christianity, theories of history, and modern liberation movements.

BUTTING, KLARA, Ph.D., b. 1959. Following fifteen years of work in ministry, she is a private scholar and a lecturer at the University of Bochum. For more than twenty-five years she has been the director of Erev-Rav, a network of European Christians. The name Erev-Rav — the "mixed multitude" of non-Jewish origin that fled with Israel from Egypt (Exod 12:38) — identifies programmatically a theology of liberation in the context of Europe as the aim of the network's efforts, part of which are the organization of international conferences as well as a publishing house that, among others, publishes the journal *Junge Kirche.* She translated for *Bibel in gerechter Sprache* the books of Joel and Esther. Recent publications include the following: *Prophetinnen gefragt. Die Bedeutung der Prophetinnen im Kanon aus Tora und Prophetie* (Wittingen, 2001); *Der das Licht und die Finsternis schuf. Glauben heute, biblisch — politisch — spirituell* (Wittingen, 2007). She is author and coeditor of the series Die Bibel erzählt. See *Hiob* (vol. 1), *Esther* (vol. 2), *Markus* (vol. 3), *1 Samuel* (vol. 4), *2 Samuel* (vol. 5) (Wittingen, 2003-9).

CRÜSEMANN, MARLENE, Ph.D., b. 1953, studied Protestant theology at the Universities of Göttingen and Heidelberg, and wrote her doctoral dissertation on the composition of 1 and 2 Thessalonians. She is a private scholar working on New Testament exegesis and social-historical as well as feminist interpretation of the Bible; coeditor and cotranslator (2 Corinthians, 1 and 2 Thessalonians) of *Bibel in gerechter Sprache* (Gütersloh, 2006; 3rd ed. 2007). Other recent publications include the following: "Irredeemably Hostile to Women: Anti-Jewish Elements in the Exegesis of the Dispute about Women's Right to Speak (1 Cor. 14:34-35)," *Journal for the Study of the New Testament* 79 (2000): 19-36; "Trost, *charis* und Kraft der Schwachen. Eine Christologie der Beziehung nach 2 Kor," in *Die pseudepigraphen Briefe an die Gemeinde in Thessaloniki. Studien zu ihrer Abfassung und zur jüdisch-christlichen Sozialgeschichte*, ed. Marlene Crüsemann and Jochum-Bortfeld, Beiträge zur Wissenschaft vom Alten und Neuen Testament (Stuttgart, 2010), 111-37; with Carsten-Jochum Bortfeld, eds., *Christus und seine Geschwister. Christologie im Umfeld der Bibel in gerechter Sprache* (Gütersloh, 2009).

DANNEMANN, IRENE, Ph.D., b. 1962, works in parish ministry in Bad Vilbel near Frankfurt am Main. She was a coworker in the research project "Feminist Liberation Theology" at the University of Kassel where she received her Ph.D. with a dissertation on the "wicked" women in the Gospel of Mark (*Aus dem Rahmen fallen. Frauen im Markus-Evangelium. Eine feministische Re-Vision* [Berlin, 1996]). She translated the Gospel of Mark for *Bibel in gerechter Sprache*.

ELTROP, BETTINA, Ph.D., b. 1961, is married with three children. She studied Catholic theology and biology in Bonn, holds a Ph.D. from the University of Kassel under the direction of Luise Schottroff on "children in the Gospel of Matthew," and is currently editor at the Katholisches Bibelwerk e.V. Stuttgart.

ENGELMANN, ANGELIKA, Ph.D., b. 1950, studied Protestant theology in Greifswald and Leipzig, served in parish ministry in Dresden, and subsequently was active in religious and congregational pedagogy as well as adult education. From 1995 to 2005 she was professor of theology at the Protestant College of Social Work in Dresden, and since 2006 has taught Christian religion at a high school and a medical college in Dresden.

EXUM, J. CHERYL, Ph.D., is professor of Biblical Studies at the University of Sheffield and a director of Sheffield Phoenix Press, for which she is the editor of two series: Bible in the Modern World and Hebrew Bible Monographs. She is the author of numerous scholarly works on literary, feminist, and cultural interpretation of the Bible, and her works include *Tragedy and Biblical Narrative: Arrows of the Almighty; Fragmented Women: Feminist (Sub)versions of Biblical Narratives; Plotted, Shot, and Painted: Cultural Representations of Biblical Women; Was sagt das Richterbuch den Frauen?* and *The Song of Songs: A Commentary.*

FANDER, MONIKA, Ph.D., b. 1956, studied Catholic theology and biology at Münster; from 1982 to 1989 she was research assistant in New Testament exegesis at the Catholic Faculty at Münster; she received her Ph.D. in 1989 with the dissertation "Women in the Gospel of Mark"; since 1989 she has held various teaching positions in areas of "feminist exegesis" at Protestant and Catholic faculties in Germany and Switzerland. Since 1993 she has been director of an educational institute in Singen on Lake Constance. Her recent publications center on christological themes and the infant narratives of the New Testament. With U. Bechmann she has edited *Grundbegriffe zum Alten und Neuen Testament (99 Wörter Theolgie konkret)* (Munich, 2003) and is the author of "'Mein Gott, mein Gott, warum hast Du mich verlassen?' (Mk 15,34). (Kriegs)Traumatisierung als Thema das Markusevangeliums," in *Christologie und Lebensbezug,* ed. E. Moltmann-Wendel and R. Kirchhoff (Göttingen, 2005), 116-56.

FELD, GERBURGIS, b. 1958, holds an academic degree ("Diplom") in Catholic theology and an M.A. in classical languages. She teaches at a secondary school in Hamm. Her continuing research focuses on Levitical prescriptions of purity/impurity, on evolution, and on *metanoia.* Recent publications include the following: "Was heist gut lehren? Die Hermeneutik des Unbehagens in Lehr- und Lernprozessen," *Bibel und Kirche* 56, no. 1 (2001): 162-64; "Reinheit/Unreinheit," in *Wörterbuch der Feministischen Theologie,* ed. Elisabeth Gössmann and Helga Kuhlmann, 2nd ed. (Gütersloh, 2002); "Der schamhafte Gott," in FAMA 2003; "Menstruation," available at www.wibilex.de.

FISCHER, IRMTRAUD received her Ph.D. in 1988 and her habilitation in 1993. Since 2004 she has been University Professor for Old Testament Biblical Studies and, since 2007, Vice-Rector for Research and Continuing Education at the Karl-Franzens Universität Graz. From 1997 to 2004 she was full professor for Old Testament and Theological Women's Studies at the Catholic Theological Faculty at Bonn, and from 1994 to 1997 she was assistant professor in Graz. She held guest professorships in Marburg, Bamberg, Vienna, and in the "Theologisches Studienjahr Jerusalem." She is a member of the editorial board of *Biblical Interpretation* and author of numerous contributions to proceedings, journals, and anthologies. She was a member of the advisory board of *Bibel in gerechter Sprache.* Among her recent publications are *Gotteslehrerinnen. Weise Frauen und Frau Weisheit im Alter Testament* (Stuttgart, 2006); *Gottesstreiterinnen. Biblische Erzählungen über die Anfänge Israels,* 3rd ed. (Stuttgart, 2006); *Women Who Wrestled with God: Biblical Stories of Israel's Beginnings,* trans. Linda M. Maloney (Collegeville, Minn., 2005; also French translation); *Rut,* Herders theologischer Kommentar zum Alten Testament, 2nd ed. (Freiburg im Breisgau, 2005); *Gotteskünderinnen. Zu einer geschlechterfairen Deutung des Phänomens der Prophetie und der Prophetinnen der Hebräischen Bibel* (Stuttgart, 2002; also French translation); *Genderfaire Exegese. Gesammelte Beiträge zur Reflexion des Genderbias und seiner Auswirkungen in der Übersetzung und Auslegung biblischer Texte, exuz 14* (Münster, 2004).

FOULKES, IRENE, Ph.D., professor emerita, holds the Ph.D. degree in theoretical linguistics from Georgetown University. Born in the United States, she is a citizen of Costa Rica where she taught until 2001 as professor for New Testament at Universidad Biblica Latinoamericana San José. Some recent publications include the following: "Primera Corintios," in *Comentario Biblico Latinoamericano* (Estella, Spain: Verbo Divino, 2003), 817-58; "Los códigos de deberes domésticos en Colosenses 3.18–4,1 y Efesios 5,22–6,9," *Revista de Interpretación Biblica Latinoamericana*, no. 55 (2006): 41-62; "Praxis exegética feminista: conceptos, instrumentos, procedimientos," *Alternativitas*, no. 36 (2008): 39-58.

GERBER, CHRISTINE, Ph.D., b. 1963 in Hamburg, is professor of New Testament in the Department of Theology at the University of Hamburg. Her areas of study are Paul and his school (commentary on Ephesians), Hellenistic Judaism (Flavius Josephus), methodology of exegesis, and feminist theology/gender studies in the interpretation of the Second Testament. She is one of the translators of *Bibel in gerechter Sprache*. Recent publications include the following: *Paulus und seine "Kinder." Studien zur Beziehungsmetaphorik der paulinischen Briefe*, Beihefte zur Zeitschrift für die neutestamentliche Wissenschaft, vol. 136 (Berlin et al., 2005); "In Bewegung. Zur Frage der Geschlechterdifferenz und zu feministischen Diskursen in den Bibelwissenschaften," *Theologische Literatur Zeitung* 130 (2005): cols. 1365-86; with Benita Joswig and Silke Petersen, eds., *Gott heisst nicht nur Vater. Zur Rede über Gott in den Übersetzungen der Bibel in gerechter Sprache*, Biblisch-theologische Schwerpunkte, vol. 32 (Göttingen, 2008), her contribution is "'Gott Vater' und die abwesenden Väter. Zur Übersetzung von Metaphern am Beispiel der Familienmetaphorik," 145-61.

GNADT, MARTINA S., b. 1957, minister, is director of the unit on adult education of the Landeskirchenamt of the Protestant Church of Kurhessen-Waldeck in Kassel. One major area of her work is to integrate the diverse approaches, how they are worked out and discussed, with women's and men's work, with family-formation and education for seniors, and to create new projects resulting from that work. Another area is to advance intergenerational learning; cf. her "Die Eltern haben saure Trauben gegessen, und den Kindern werden die Zähne stumpf . . . ? Über den schwierigen, aber möglichen Umgang mit Schattenseiten unserer (Familien-) Geschichte," in *Familienbande*, ed. Sabine Bieberstein et al., Frauenbibelarbeit, vol. 23 (Stuttgart, 2009), 49ff.

HABERMANN, RUTH, b. 1954, minister, is currently chaplain to the students at Goethe University in Frankfurt. She has many years of teaching experience at colleges and academies and additional training in person-focused counseling (MBSR) and meditation (different traditions: Theravada, Zen, and Vipassana). Her particular interest in her work with students is the all-transforming, revolutionary power of mindfulness. She lives in Frankfurt am Main.

HARTENSTEIN, JUDITH, Ph.D., b. 1964 in Bonn, studied Protestant theology and received her Ph.D. in Berlin with a dissertation on the appearances of the Risen One in the apocryphal gospels primarily from the discoveries at Nag Hammadi. She served as curate in Essen, and as research assistant in New Testament studies in Marburg, where she completed her habilitation with a dissertation on persons in the Gospel of John. Currently she is lecturer in Marburg and a minister of the Protestant Church of the Rhineland. Together with Silke Petersen she translated the Gospel of John for *Bibel in gerechter Sprache;* in addition she translated the First Epistle of John. Recent publications include the following: *Charakterisierung im Dialog. Maria Magdalena, Petrus, Thomas und die Mutter Jesu im Johannesevangelium im Kontext anderer frühchristlicher Darstellungen,* Novum Testamentum et Orbis Antiquus/Studien zur Umwelt des Neuen Testaments, vol. 64 (Göttingen, 2007) (habilitation dissertation); *Mary Magdalene the Apostle: A Re-interpretation of Literary Traditions?* lectio difficilior 1/2007 (http://www.lectio .unibe.ch); "Women in John's Gospel," *Theology Digest* 53 (2005): 127-31 (translation of "Frauen im Johannesevangelium," *Bibel und Kirche* 59, no. 3 [2004]: 131-36); "Das Evangelium nach Maria," in *Nag Hammadi Deutsch,* vol. 2 (Berlin et al., 2003), 833-44; with Silke Petersen and Angela Standhartinger, eds., *"Eine gewöhnliche und harmlose Speise"? Von den Entwicklungen frühchristlicher Abendmahlstraditionen* (Gütersloh, 2008).

HÄUSL, MARIA, Ph.D., b. 1964 in Waging am See, Upper Bavaria, studied Catholic theology in Munich; she received her Ph.D. in 1993 with a dissertation on Abishag and Bathsheba in 1 Kings 1 and 2; habilitation in 2002 with a study of the book of Jeremiah. She was Aigner-Rollett-Guestprofessor for women's and gender studies at Graz University during the winter term of 2004-5; since 2006 she has been professor for biblical theology (Catholic) at the Technical University of Dresden. Her feminist-theological research foci are the city of Zion/Jerusalem as a female figure (including in deuterocanonical texts); translation of the book of Jeremiah for *Bibel in gerechter Sprache;* pregnancy, birth, and the beginning of life; the construction of alienness and identity in postexilic texts (Ezra/Nehemiah). Recent publications include the following: "Auf den Leib geschrieben. Körperbilder und -konzeptionen im Alten Testament," *Biblische Anthropologie. Neuere Einsichten aus dem Alten Testament,* ed. Chr. Frevel, Quaestiones disputatae, vol. 237 (Freiburg, 2010), 134-63; "Geburt — Kampf um Leben und gegen den Tod. Atl. Vorstellungen und Rituale für Mutter und Kind am Anfang des Lebens," in *An den Schwellen des Lebens — Zur Geschlechterdifferenz in Ritualen des Übergangs,* ed. Bernhard Heininger, Geschlecht — Symbol — Religion, vol. 5 (Münster, 2008), 119-34; "Gott als Vater und Mutter und die Sohnschaft des Volkes in der Prophetie: Rezeption mythischer Vorstellungen," in *Mythisches in biblischer Bildsprache. Gestalt und Verwandlung in Prophetie und Psalmen,* ed. H. Irsigler, Quaestiones disputatae, vol. 209 (Freiburg, 2004), 258-89; *Bilder der Not. Weiblichkeits- und Geschlechtermetaphorik im Buch Jeremia,* Herders biblische Studien, vol. 37 (Freiburg, 2003); "Geschlechterordnung, symbolische Ordnung, Götterordnung — Forschung zur Geschlechterdifferenz in der alttestamentlichen Exegese," in *Wahrnehmung der Geschlechterdifferenz in religiösen Symbolsystemen,* ed. B. Heininger, Geschlecht — Symbol — Religion, vol. 1 (Münster, 2003), 15-25.

JANSSEN, CLAUDIA, Ph.D., b. 1966, studied Protestant theology at Kiel and Marburg; Ph.D. 1996; habilitation in 2004 with dissertation on the resurrection of the body in 1 Corinthians 15. Since 2004 she has been lecturer in New Testament at the University of Marburg and director of studies at the Frauenstudien- und -bildungszentrum of the Evangelische Kirche Deutschlands at Hofgeismar. She is one of the coeditors of *Bibel in gerechter Sprache* (2006) and *Sozialgeschichtliches Wörterbuch zur Bibel* (2009). Her primary areas of research are the theology of Paul and social-historical and feminist interpretation of the Bible. Recent publications include the following: *Anders ist die Schönheit der Körper. Paulus und die Auferstehung in 1 Kor 15* (Gütersloh, 2005); with Ulrike Bail, Marlene Crüsemann, Frank Crüsemann, Erhard Domay, Jürgen Ebach, Hanne Köhler, Helga Kuhlmann, Luise Schottroff, and Martin Leutzsch, eds., *Bibel in gerechter Sprache,* for which she translated the Epistle to the Romans (Gütersloh, 2006); with Frank Crüsemann, Kristian Hungar, Rainer Kessler, and Luise Schottroff, eds., *Sozialgeschichtliches Wörterbuch zur Bibel* (Gütersloh, 2009); with Benita Joswig, eds., *Erinnern und aufstehen — antworten auf Kreuzestheologien* (Mainz, 2000); with Luise Schottroff and Beate Wehn, eds., *Paulus. Umstrittene Traditionen — lebendige Theologie. Eine feministische Lektüre* (Gütersloh, 2001).

JENSEN, ANNE, Ph.D., b. 1941 in Hamburg, studied theology in Toulouse and Tübingen, Ph.D. 1984, habilitation 1992. From 1980 until 1997 she was research associate at the Ecumenical Institute Tübingen, directed by Hans Küng, and from 1997 to 2008 director of the Institut für Ökumenische Theologie, Ostkirchliche Orthodoxie und Patrologie of the Unversity of Graz, Austria. Died August 13, 2009. Recent publications include the following: *God's Self-Confident Daughters: Early Christianity and the Liberation of Women* (Louisville: Westminster John Knox, 1996); *Frauen im frühen Christentum* (Berne et al., 2002); with Michaela Sohn-Kronthaler, eds., *Formen weiblicher Autorität. Erträge historisch-theologischer Frauenforschung* (Münster, 2002); with G. Larentzakis, eds., *Diakonat und Diakonie in frühchristlicher und ostkirchlicher Tradition* (Graz, 2008).

JOST, RENATE, Ph.D., b. 1955, professor of Women's Studies in Theology/Feminist Theology at the Augustana-Hochschule at Neuendettelsau; she studied Protestant theology in Bethel, Göttingen, Marburg, and at Union Theological Seminary, New York. From 1984 to 1988 she was in parish ministry in Frankfurt; research associate in Old Testament at the university in that city from 1989 to 1993; director of studies at the Frauenstudien- und -bildungszentrum of the Evangelische Kirche Deutschlands; Ph.D. in 1994 with a dissertation on "the queen of heaven" in Jeremiah, habilitation in 2003. Translator of the book of Ruth in *Bibel in gerechter Sprache.* Among her recent publications are the following: *Gender, Sexualität und Macht in der Anthro-*

pologie des Richterbuches, Beiträge zur Wissenschaft vom Alten und Neuen Testament, vol. 164 (Stuttgart, 2006); *Frauenmacht und Männerliebe, Egalitäre Utopien* (Stuttgart, 2006); with Klaus Raschzok, eds., *Gender — Religion — Kultur: Biblische, interreligiöse und ethische Aspekte* (Stuttgart, 2009); with Gisela Matthiae, Claudia Janssen, Annette Mehlhorn, and Antje Röckemann, eds., *Feministische Theologie. Initiativen, Kirchen, Universitäten — Eine Erfolgsgeschichte* (Gütersloh, 2008); with Marcel Nieden, eds., *Hexenwahn* (Stuttgart, 2004).

KAHL, BRIGITTE, Dr. Sc.theol., graduated from Humboldt University in Berlin. As a professor of New Testament at Union Theological Seminary in New York and an associate professor in the Religion Department of Columbia University, her work's major focus has been examining the relationship between the New Testament and the Roman Empire, especially with regard to Pauline texts. Her "critical reimagination" uses ancient art and architecture to illuminate constructs of gender and power relevant for biblical interpretation. She is the translator of Galatians for *Bibel in gerechter Sprache.* Among her recent publications are the following: *Galatians Reimagined: Reading with the Eyes of the Vanquished; Paul in Critical Contexts* (Minneapolis: Fortress, 2009); "Acts of the Apostles: Pro(to)-Imperial Script and Hidden Transcripts," in *In the Shadow of Empire: Reclaiming the Bible as History of Faithful Resistance,* ed. Richard A. Horsley (Louisville: Westminster John Knox, 2008), 137-56; "Fratricide and Ecocide: Re-reading Gen 2–4," in *Earth Habitat: Eco-Justice and the Church's Response,* ed. D. Hessel and L. Rasmussen (Minneapolis: Fortress, 2001); "Reading Galatians and Empire at the Great Altar of Pergamon," *Union Seminary Quarterly Review* 59 (2005): 21-43; "Hagar between Genesis and Galatians: The Stony Road to Freedom," in *From Prophecy to Testament,* ed. Craig A. Evans (Peabody, Mass.: Hendrickson, 2004).

KARRER-GRUBE, CHRISTIANE, Ph.D., b. 1960, studied Protestant theology in Munich, and was a minister of the Evangelisch-Lutherische Kirche in Bavaria; from 1994 to 2002 she was lecturer in Old Testament at the Universities of Munich and Kiel; Ph.D in 1999. She lives in Utrecht, Netherlands. Recent publications include the following: *Ringen um die Verfassung Judas,* Beihefte zur Zeitschrift für die alttestamentliche Wissenschaft, vol. 308 (Berlin, 2001); "Von der Rezeption zur Redaktion: Eine intertextuelle Analyse von Jeremia 13,14-26," in *Sprachen — Bilder — Klänge. Dimensionen der Theologie im Alten Testament und in seinem Umfeld. Festschrift für Rüdiger Bartelmus zu seinem 65. Geburtstag,* ed. Christiane Karrer-Grube et al., Alter Orient und Altes Testament, vol. 359 (Münster, 2009), 14-26; "Grenz-Überschreitung. Zum Körperkonzept in der Erzählung über Jephtas Tochter," in *Körperkonzepte im Ersten Testament. Aspekte einer feministischen Anthropologie,* ed. Hedwig-Jahnow-Forschungsprojekt (Stuttgart, 2003), 94-123.

KASSEL, MARIA, b. 1931, studied Catholic theology and German studies; until 1992 she was professor at the Catholic Theological Faculty, University of Münster, but retired since then. She developed a depth-theological psychology that she later joined with feminist research especially in the area of traditional religious symbolism. She published books and journal articles. For a number of years she was guest professor at the C. G. Jung Institute in Zurich. She is working on a depth-psychological-feminist-theological hermeneutics. Recent publications include the following: *Das Evangelium — eine Talentenschmiede? Tiefenpsychologische Revision eines verinnerlichten christlichen Kapitalismus,* Forum Theologie und Psychologie, vol. 1 (Münster, 2001); *Das Auge im Bauch. Erfahrungen mit tiefenpsychologischer Spiritualität,* rev. ed. (Stuttgart, 2006); see http://www.opus-magnum.de/index.php?area=vbcmsarea_content&contentid=85; *Traum, Symbol, Religion: Tiefen psychologische und feministische Analyse,* rev. ed. (Stuttgart, 2009); see http://www.opus-magnum.de/index.php?area=vbcmsarea_content&contentid=195.

KATO, KUMIKO, b. 1965 in Tokyo in a Roman Catholic family. She received her B.A. and M.A. in Religious Studies from the University of Tokyo. From 1992 to 1996 she studied in Paderborn, Germany. Since 1996 she has been an instructor at the University of the Sacred Heart, Tokyo, and other colleges. Her primary foci of research are the wisdom literature of the Hebrew Bible and the history of religion of ancient Israel. She has published widely in Japanese.

KIRCHHOFF, RENATE, Ph.D., b. 1960, is professor of New Testament and Dean of the Department of Theology and Diaconia at the University of Applied Sciences, Freiburg, Germany. Her areas of research are Pauline theology, interpretations of the death of Jesus in the New Testament, exegesis and reception of miracle texts, hermeneutics of biblical texts. She translated the letter of James for *Bibel in gerechter Sprache.* Recent publications include the following: *Christologie im Lebensbezug* (Gütersloh, 2005); "'Nur uninteressante Fragen haben eine endgültige Antwort' — Jesus als Lehrer im Markusevangelium," in *Evangelische Hochschulperspektiven* 1, ed. W. Schwendemann (Freiburg, 2005); "Was lernten die verschiedenen Anfängerinnen und Anfänger im Glauben bei Paulus?" *Pädagogik und Theologie* 2 (2001): 153-61.

LAMB, REGENE, b. 1960 in Brazil and studied Protestant theology in São Leopoldo. For several years she was research fellow in the University of Kassel's Project on Feminist Liberation Theology. From 2001 to 2006 she taught at the Methodist Institute in Porto Velho, Rondonia/Brazil. She is active in adult education and a member of the Ecumenical Center for Biblical Interpretation (CEBI). Since 2006 she has been a parish minister in the Lutheran church in Cachoeira do Sul, RS.

LEE, KYUNG SOOK, Ph.D., b. 1948 in Korea, studied at Ewha Women's University in Seoul (1966-73), and Protestant theology at the University of Göttingen (1974-81); she received her doctorate in Old Testament studies in 1981. She is the cofounder of the *Ewha Journal of Feminist Theology;* since 2008, she has been dean of the Graduate School at Ewha Women's University. Among her recent publications is a commentary on the book of Kings in the Global Bible Commentary, edited by D. Patte et al. (Nashville: Abingdon, 2004).

LOEWENCLAU, ILSE VON, Ph.D., b. 1924, studied classical philology in Berlin and was awarded the doctorate in 1949, then studied Protestant theology and served as parish minister in Falkensee. She taught First Testament studies at the Sprachenkonvikt (a Protestant theological seminary with emphasis on ancient languages) in Berlin. She retired in 1984 and taught in the United States of America at Newton, Mass., 1985, and Bangor, Maine, 1987-88, and in 1986 at the Kirchliche Hochschule in Bielefeld, Germany.

MAIER, CHRISTL, Ph.D., b. 1962, M.Div. University of Tübingen, 1994, Ph.D. Humboldt University, Berlin, with a dissertation entitled "Die 'fremde Frau' in Proverbien 1–9." She was research fellow in the Marburg Hedwig Jahnow Project on Feminist Hermeneutics. She completed her habilitation in 2000 in Berlin with a dissertation entitled "Jeremia als Lehrer der Tora." From 2003 to 2006 she was associate professor of Old Testament at Yale Divinity School, New Haven, Conn. Since 2007, she has been professor of Old Testament at Philipps-University in Marburg. She serves on the editorial board of *lectio difficilior,* a feminist Internet journal. Her areas of specialization are wisdom literature, prophecy, Jerusalem in the First Testament, and feminist exegesis. She is the cotranslator of the book of Psalms for *Bibel in gerechter Sprache.* Among her recent publications are the following: *Daughter Zion, Mother Zion: Gender, Space, and the Sacred in Ancient Israel* (Minneapolis: Fortress, 2008); "Psalm 87 as a Reappraisal of the Zion Tradition and Its Reception in Galatians 4:26," *Catholic Biblical Quarterly* 69 (2007): 473-86; "Beziehungsweisen — Körperkonzept und Gottesbild in Ps 139," in *Körperkonzepte im Ersten Testament: Aspekte einer feministischen Anthropologie,* Hedwig-Jahnow-Forschungsprojekt (Stuttgart: Kohlhammer, 2003), 172-88; "'Frau Weisheit hat ihr Haus gebaut': Sozialgeschichtliche und feministische Aspekte weisheitlicher Theologie," in *Theologie des Alten Testaments aus der Perspektive von Frauen,* ed. Manfred Oeming (Münster: LIT-Verlag, 2003), 223-41; "Göttin," in *Wissenschaftliches Bibellexikon,* ed. Klaus Koenen and Michaela Bauks, http://www.wibilex.de.

MELZER-KELLER, HELGA, Ph.D., b. 1967 in Wolfsburg. From 1986 to 1991 she studied Catholic theology in Würzburg; she engaged in doctoral studies beginning in 1991 with successful completion in 1997. From 1995 to 1997 she worked as an academic associate in the section of Introductory and Biblical and Auxiliary Sciences at the University of Würzburg. Currently she is an academic associate in the department of New Testament Studies at the University of Bamberg in relation to the Deutsche Forschungsgemeinschaft project on the "History of the Research of the Q-Source" and instructs in a number of adult education institutions.

MÜLLNER, ILSE, Ph.D., is professor of Catholic Theology and Biblical Theology, particularly First Testament, at the University of Kassel. Born in 1966 in Vienna, Austria, she received her doctorate from Westfälische-Wilhelms-Universität Münster, where she was also an academic associate; subsequently lecturer at the University of Essen. Since 2004 she has been at Kassel. Her centers of research are the books of Samuel, Job, and Joel, narratology, violence, feminist exegesis, and canonical interpretation of Scripture. Among her recent publications are *Das hörende Herz. Weisheitsliteratur in der hebräischen Bibel* (Stuttgart, 2006); "Prophetic Violence: The Marital Metaphor and Its Impact on Female and Male Readers," in *Prophetie in Israel*, ed. Irmtraud Fischer, Konrad Schmid, and Hugh G. M. Williamson, Altes Testament und Moderne, vol. 11 (Münster, 2003), 199-204; "Dialogische Autorität. Feministisch-theologische Überlegungen zur kanonischen Schriftauslegung," *lectio difficilior* 2 (2005), http://www.lectiounibe.ch/d/index/htm; "Didaktische Aspekte der personifizierten Weisheit in Spr 1/9," in *"Gott bin ich, kein Mann!" Beiträge zur Hermeneutik der biblischen Gottesrede (Festschrift für Helen Schüngel-Straumann)*, ed. Ilona Riedel-Spangenberger and Erich Zenger (Paderborn, 2006), 215-25; "Bad Women: Isebel, Atalja, die Macht und das Böse," in *Hat das Böse ein Geschlecht? Theologische und religionswissenschaftliche Verhältnisbestimmungen*, ed. Helga Kuhlmann and Stefanie Schäfer-Bossert (Stuttgart, 2006), 151-61.

PETERMANN (BATMARTHA), INA JOHANNE, b. 1956, studied Protestant theology and Judaistic studies; had study leave at the Leo Baeck College in London, was academic associate in Old Testament in Heidelberg and Marburg, and curate in Schwalbach (in the Taunus region, Germany). She earned her Ph.D. with a dissertation on the book of Ruth (unpublished), and has written various publications on questions of exegesis and feminist theology. Since 2008 she has been a parish minister in Büdingen (Hessia).

PETERSEN, SILKE, Ph.D., b. 1965 in Hamburg, studied Protestant theology, received in 1993 the degree of master of theology. From 1994 to 1997 she was academic associate at the Institute for New Testament Studies in the Department of Protestant Theology in the University of Hamburg; she received her Ph.D. in 1998. From 1998 to 1999 she held a postgraduate fellowship of the Deutsche Forschungs Gemeinschaft at the University of Würzburg and its Interdisciplinary Graduate College, where her major focus was on the perceptions of gender differences in religious symbol systems; from 1999 until 2003 she was university assistant at the University of Hamburg and completed her habilitation in 2005; currently she is adjunct professor at that university. Together with Judith Hartenstein she translated the First and Second Epistles of John and the Gospel of John for *Bibel in gerechter Sprache*. Further publications include the following: *"Zerstört die Werke der Weiblichkeit!" Maria Magdalena, Salome und andere Jüngerinnen Jesu in christlich-gnostischen Schriften*, Nag Hammadi and Manichaean Studies, vol. 48 (Leiden, Boston, and Cologne, 1999); *Brot, Licht und Weinstock. Intertextuelle Analysen johanneischer Ich-bin-Worte*, Supplements to Novum Testamentum, vol. 127 (Leiden and Boston, 2008); with Christine Gerber and Benita Joswig, "'Warum und inwiefern ist Judas ein "Daimon"?' Überlegungen zum Evangelium des Judas (Codex Tchacos 44, 21)," *Zeitschrift für Antikes Christentum/Journal of Ancient Christianity* 13 (2009): 108-26; with Judith Hartenstein and Angela Standhartinger, eds., *"Eine gewöhnliche und harmlose Speise?" Von den Entwicklungen frühchristlicher Abendmahlstraditionen* (Gütersloh, 2008); with Christine Gerber and Benita Joswig, eds., *Gott heisst nicht nur Vater. Zur Rede über Gott in den Übersetzungen der "Bibel in gerechter Sprache,"* Biblisch-theologische Schwerpunkte, vol. 32 (Göttingen, 2008).

RAKEL, CLAUDIA, Ph.D. Until 2004, she was academic associate to the chair of Old Testament and Women's Studies in Theology at the University of Bonn. Her doctorate, obtained in 2003, was on the book of Judith. She now teaches in Gelsenkirchen, in the Ruhr district of Germany. For *Bibel in gerechter Sprache* she translated the Second Book of Chronicles, the book of Judith, and the Prayer of Manasseh. Recent publications include the following: *Judit — Über Schönheit, Macht und Widerstand im Krieg. Eine feministisch-intertextuelle Lektüre,* Beihefte zur Zeitschrift für die alttestamentliche Wissenschaft, vol. 334 (Berlin and New York, 2003); "Und Sara lachte . . . Genderforschung im Alten Testament," in *Gender Talks. Geschlechterforschung an der Universität Bonn,* ed. Sabine Sielke and Anke Ortlepp, Transcription 1 (Frankfurt am Main, 2004), 41-61; "Feste der Errettung als Einspruch gegen den Krieg," *Jahrbuch Biblische Theologie* 18 (2003): 169-201; with Irene Leicht and Stefanie Rieger-Goertz, eds., *Arbeitsbuch Feministische Theologie. Inhalte, Methoden, Materialien für Hochschule, Erwachsenenbildung und Gemeinde* (Gütersloh, 2003).

RAPP, URSULA, Dr. theol., studied Catholic theology in Vienna and Jerusalem. She was senior assistant to the professor of First Testament Exegesis and coordinated Gender Studies at the University of Lucerne, Switzerland. Her doctorate was awarded by the University of Graz, Austria; her dissertation was on Miriam. Her habilitation is focused on women in the book of Sirach. She cooperated in the production of *Bibel in gerechter Sprache,* translating the books of Obadiah, Esdras, and Nehemiah. She is married and has three children. Recent publications include the following: *Mirjam. Eine feministisch-rhetorische Lektüre der Mirjamtraditionen in der hebräischen Bibel,* Beihefte zur Zeitschrift für die alttestamentliche Wissenschaft 317 (Berlin and New York, 2002); "'Söhne' sind auch Töchter, aber 'Töchter' sind keine Söhne. Zum Begriff 'Tochter' im Ersten Testament und seiner Übersetzung in der 'Bibel in gerechter Sprache,'" in *Töchter (Gottes). Studien zum Verhältnis von Kultur, Religion und Geschlecht,* ed. Joachim Kügler and Lukas Bormann, Bayreuther forum Transit, vol. 8 (Münster, 2008), 46-64; "Weibliche Unreinheit und die Verwerfung der Gleichgültigkeit. Religionskritik an, in und mit der Geburtstora in Lev 12," in *Kritik an, in und mit biblischen Texten — Beiträge des IBS 2007 in Vierzehnheiligen,* ed. Joachim Kügler and Ulrike Bechmann, Bayreuther Forum Transit 9 (Münster, 2009), 182-99; "Zippora. Das Verschwinden einer Ehefrau," in *Die Tora, die Bibel und die Frauen,* vol. 1, ed. Irmtaud Fischer et al. (Stuttgart: Kohlhammer et al., 2009);

with Luzia Sutter Rehmann and Ulrike Metternich, eds., *Zum Leuchten bringen. Biblische Texte vom Glück* (Gütersloh, 2006).

Reese, Ruth Anne, Ph.D., teaches New Testament at Asbury Theological Seminary in Wilmore, Kentucky. She is the author of two books: *Writing Jude: The Reader, the Text, and the Author in Constructs of Power and Desire* (Brill, 2000), and *2 Peter and Jude,* Two Horizons New Testament Commentary (Grand Rapids: Eerdmans, 2007).

Richter Reimer, Ivoni, Ph.D., b. 1959 in Brazil, studied theology at the Lutheran Theological Faculty of the University of São Leopoldo (RS); she undertook doctoral studies from 1985 to 1990, successfully completing them in 1990 in Kassel with Luise Schottroff and a dissertation entitled *Frauen in der Apostelgeschichte des Lukas: Eine feministisch-theologische Exegese* (Gütersloh, 1992), English translation: *Women in the Acts of the Apostles: A Feminist Liberation Perspective* (Fortress Press, 1995). She has numerous publications in German and Portuguese in the areas of New Testament and feminist exegesis. She currently teaches in the masters and doctoral programs of the Catholic University in Goiânia. She is the coordinator of a research group on the Jesus movement and the beginnings of *ekklesia* in feminist perspective as well as of "Research and Studies in Religion and Holy Scriptures." She is married and has two sons. Among her recent publications are the following: "Matos, Keila, Aggression and Silence: Violation of Human Rights of Women as a Bible Hermeneutical Challenge," in *Lieblingsfrauen der Bibel und der Welt. Ausgewählt für Luise Metzler zum 60. Geburtstag,* ed. Christina Duncker and Katrin Keita (Norderstedt: Books on Demand GMBH, 2009), 73-87; *Milagre das Mãos: curas e exorcismos de Jesu em seu contexto historico-cultural* (São Leopoldo: Oikos; Goiânia: Ed. da UCG, 2008); *Imaginários da Divindade: textos e interpretações* (São Leopoldo: Oikos; Goiânia: Ed. da UCG, 2008); *Grava-me como selo sobre seu coração: teologia biblica feminista* (São Paulo [Paulinas], 2006); with João O. Souza, *O Sagrado na vida: subsídios para aulas de Teologia* (Goiânia: Ed. da UCG, 2008).

Ruoff, Kerstin, b. 1967. Her postsecondary education included German studies, Protestant theology, and pedagogy in Munich, Marburg, and Frankfurt am Main; she was academic associate in New Testament with Professor Dr. Georgi in Frankfurt. She was engaged by the Odenwaldschule in Ober-Hambach to administer the curriculum of interdisciplinary courses for senior grades, to organize individualized learning. She is the educational coordinator of didactics in the seminar established by the secondary liberal-arts schools of Heppenheim (Hessia) as well as of the advancement of highly gifted students within the school district through, inter alia, integration with the Ministry of Culture of Hessia. Since 2009 she has taught at Campus Klarenthal in Wiesbaden. Recent publications include *Spiel mir das Lied vom Leben! Inszenierender Unterricht* (2010).

Schmidtgen, Beate, Ph.D., b. 1966, studied in Heidelberg, Marburg, and Berne and received her doctorate from the University of Basel with a dissertation entitled "Die Stadt als Frau im Buch Jesaja." She was a research fellow in the Marburg Research Project "Hedwig Jahnow"; for *Bibel in gerechter Sprache* she translated the book of Haggai and, with Matthias Millard, the book of Isaiah. She is active in adult education as a teacher and, since 2005, has shared with her partner-in-marriage the ministry of a parish in Lörrach within the Protestant Regional Church of Baden. They have three children.

SCHOLZ, SUSANNE, Ph.D., is a professor in Old Testament at Perkins School of Theology at Southern Methodist University in Dallas, Texas. Her research focuses on the epistemologies and sociologies of biblical hermeneutics, feminist biblical hermeneutics, and cultural and literary critical methodologies. Among her recent publications are the following: *Sacred Witness: Rape in the Hebrew Bible* (Minneapolis: Fortress, 2010); *Introducing the Women's Hebrew Bible* (Edinburgh: T. & T. Clark, 2008); *Biblical Studies Alternatively: An Introductory Reader* (Upper Saddle River, N.J.: Prentice-Hall, 2003). For *Bible in gerechter Sprache,* she provided the translation of First Maccabees. She can be reached at www.womensHebrewBible.com.

SCHOTTROFF, LUISE, Ph.D., b. 1934 in Berlin, began her studies in Protestant theology in 1951, received her doctorate in 1960 from the University of Göttingen, and her habilitation in 1969, University of Mainz. She was professor of New Testament in Mainz, Kassel, and Berkeley, California, until 2004. Her work is focused chiefly on the social history of early Christianity and, in connection with that, on a feminist and liberation-theological interpretation and hermeneutics of the New Testament that is committed to the Christian-Jewish dialogue. She is one of the coeditors of *Bibel in gerechter Sprache,* ed. Ulrike Bail et al. (Gütersloh: Gutersloher Verlagshaus, 2006; 3rd ed. 2007) and provided the translation of Matthew and 1 Corinthians; with Frank Crüsemann et al., she coedited *Sozialgeschichtliches Wörterbuch zur Bibel* (Gütersloh, 2009). Further recent publications include the following: *Die Gleichnisse Jesu* (Gütersloh, 2005; 2nd ed. 2007); ET: *The Parables of Jesus* (Minneapolis: Augsburg Fortress, 2006); with Andrea Bieler, *Das Abendmahl — Essen, um zu leben* (Gütersloh, 2007); ET: *The Eucharist: Bodies, Bread, and Resurrection* (Minneapolis: Fortress, 2007); with Dorothee Sölle, *Jesus von Nazareth* (Munich, 2000; 6th ed. 2007; ET, Louisville, 2002).

SCHROER, SYLVIA, Ph.D., b. 1958, is a Catholic theologian. Since 1997 she has been professor of Old Testament and Biblical Environment at the Faculty of Theology of the University of Berne, Switzerland. For years she has worked to make the primary focus of her research, the iconography of the ancient Orient, creative and fruitful for feminist exegesis. She is the founder and editor of the first Internet journal of feminist exegesis in Europe, the *lectio difficilior* (www.lectio.unibe.ch). Her work and research deal chiefly with the Old Testament and ancient Oriental image-symbolism; history of religion of Israel/Palestine; women's history in Israel/Palestine and environment; wisdom theology; biblical theology of creation and anthropology; zoological theology. Among her recent publication are the following: *Die Ikonographie Palästinas/Israels und der Alte Orient. Eine Religionsgeschichte in Bildern*, 2 vols. (Fribourg, CH, 2005 and 2008); *Images and Gender: Contributions to the Hermeneutics of Reading Ancient Art*, Orbis biblicus et orientalis, vol. 220 (Fribourg and Göttingen, 2006); with Thomas Staubli, *Die Körpersymbolik der Bibel* (Darmstadt: Wissenschaftliche Buchgesellschaft, 1998), ET: *Body Symbolism of the Bible* (Minneapolis: Fortress, 2001); with Othmar Keel, *Eva — Mutter alles Lebendigen. Frauen und Göttinnenidole aus dem Alten Orient*, 2nd ed. (Fribourg, 2008); with Sophia Bietenhard, eds., *Feminist Interpretation of the Bible and the Hermeneutics of Liberation*, Journal of the Study of the Old Testament: Supplement Series, vol. 374 (Sheffield: Sheffield University Press, 2003).

Schüngel-Straumann, Helen, Ph.D., b. 1940 in St. Gallen, Switzerland. For her secondary education, she enrolled in the evening curriculum of a liberal arts school (Gymnasium) in Zurich; she studied theology in Tübingen, Paris, and Bonn. She was the first layperson to be awarded the degree of Ph.D. in Old Testament by the Catholic Faculty of Theology at the University of Bonn (1969). Since 1987 she has been professor of biblical theology at the University of Kassel. She founded the Helen Straumann Foundation for Feminist Theology (located in Basel) (www.feministische-theologie.de), and since 2002 has been developing a feminist-theological library at the Center for Gender Studies at the University of Basel. Since 2009 she has resided in Basel, Switzerland. Recent publications include the following: *Anfänge Feministischer Exegese*, Gesammelte Beiträge, mit einem orientierenden Nachwort und einer Auswahlbibliographie (Münster, 2002); *Das Buch Tobit*, Herders theologischer Kommentar zum Alten Testament (Freiburg: Herder, 2000); "Eva, die Frau am Anfang," in *Geschlechterstreit am Beginn der europäischen Moderne*, ed. Gisela Engel (Königstein and Taunus, 2004), 28-37; *Theologie von Frauen für Frauen? Chancen und Probleme der Rückbindung feministischer Theologie an die Praxis. Beiträge zum internationalen Kongress anlässlich des 20-jährigen Gründungs-jubiläum der European Society of Women in Theological Research*, ed. Irmtraud Fischer (Münster, 2007): two contributions: pp. 86-101 and 227-60; with Elisabeth Gössmann et al., eds., *Wörterbuch der Feministischen Theologie*, 2nd ed. (Gütersloh, 2002).

Seifert, Elke, Ph.D., b. 1961, studied Protestant theology in Marburg and Tübingen. Her doctoral dissertation is entitled *Tochter und Vater im Alten Testament;* it was published in 1997 by Neukirchener Verlag, Neukirchen-Vluyn. Her research is focused chiefly on women's paid work and on sexual violence to women and girls. She participates in the work of a consulting office for the prevention of sexual abuse of girls and is a coworker in the Research Project "Hedwig Jahnow." Since 1995 she has been minister of a parish in Hasselroth/Niedermittlau.

Standhartinger, Angela, b. 1964, studied Protestant theology in Frankfurt am Main, Munich, and Heidelberg. Her doctoral dissertation is entitled *Das Frauenbild im Judentum in der hellenistischen Zeit. Ein Beitrag anhand von 'Joseph und Aseneth',*

Arbeiten zur Geschichte des antiken Judentums und des Urchristentums, vol. 26 (Leiden: Brill, 1995). Her habilitation dissertation was published by Brill also, in 1999, and is entitled *Studien zur Entstehungsgeschichte und Intention des Kolosser-briefs*, Supplements to Novum Testamentum, vol. 94. Since 2000 she has been professor of New Testament in Marburg. She translated Ephesians and Colossians for *Bibel in gerechter Sprache*. Recent publications include the following: "The Epistle to the Congregation in Colossae and the Invention of the 'Household Code,'" in *A Feminist Companion to the Deutero-Pauline Epistles*, ed. Amy-Jill Levine (London: Continuum, 2003), 88-97; "Colossians and the Pauline School," *New Testament Studies* 50 (2004): 571-93; "'Nicht wenige der vornehmen griechischen Frauen' (Apg 17,12). Aspekte zum Religionswechsel von Frauen im Spiegel der jüdischen und christlichen Adaptionen des antiken Liebesromans in Joseph und Asenet und den Theklaakten," in *Ehrenmord und Emanzipation. Die Geschlechterfrage in Ritualen von Parallelgesellschaften*, ed. Bernhard Heininger, Geschlecht-Symbol-Religion, vol. 6 (Berlin: Lit, 2009), 145-69; "'For Freedom . . . Freed'? Hagar in Galatians," *Theology Digest* 50, no. 1 (2003): 43-51; with Judith Hartenstein and Silke Petersen, eds., *"Eine gewöhnliche und harmlose Speise"? Von den Entwicklungen frühchristlicher Abendmahlstraditionen* (Gütersloh, 2008).

STROTMANN, ANGELIKA, b. 1956, in Osnabrück, studied philosophy, theology, and sociology in Frankfurt am Main and was awarded the doctoral degree in 1990 with a dissertation entitled "'Mein Vater bist du!' (Sir 21:10): Zur Bedeutung der Vaterschaft Gottes in frühjüdischen Schriften." From 2002 to 2008 she was professor of biblical theology and religious education in Heidelberg; since 2008 she has been professor of New Testament at the University of Paderborn. Her research is focused chiefly on wisdom Christology in the New Testament and wisdom writings in the First Testament, New Testament, and Judaism. She is coeditor and one of the authors of the Festschrift for Johannes Beutler, S.J., *Israel und seine Heilstraditionen im Johannes-evangelium* (Paderborn, 2004). She participated in the translation for *Bibel in gerechter Sprache* (Sirach and Philemon). Further publications include the following: "Biblische Intertextualität. Die Taufe Jesu im Markusevangelium," in *Intertextualität und Bildung — didaktische und fachliche Perspektiven*, ed. R. Olsen, H.-B. Petermann, and J. Rymarczyk (Frankfurt am Main, 2006), 301-23; "Die göttliche Weisheit als Nahrungsspenderin, Gastgeberin und sich selbst anbietende Speise. Mit einem Ausblick auf Joh 6," in *"Eine gewöhnliche und harmlose Speise"? Von den Entwicklungen frühchristlicher Abendmahlstraditionen*, ed. J. Hartenstein, S. Petersen, and A. Standhartinger (Gütersloh, 2008), 131-56.

SUTTER REHMANN, LUZIA, b. 1960, Ph.D. and Dr. habil. She is titular professor of New Testament in the Protestant Faculty of Theology of the University of Basel and a director of studies of the working group for contemporary issues of the Reformed parish in Biel, Switzerland. Her research is focused primarily on the social history of early Christianity, liberation-theological interpretation of the New Testament. For

Bibel in gerechter Sprache she translated the Gospel of Luke. Recent publications include the following: articles "Ehe," "Abtreibung," "Braut," "Jungfrau," "Sexualität," and "Mann/Frau," in *Sozialgeschichtliches Wörterbuch zur Bibel*, ed. F. Crüsemann et al. (Gütersloh, 2009); "Abgelehnte Tischgemeinschaft in Tobit, Ester, Judit. Ein Plädoyer für Differenzierung," in *lectio difficilior* 1/2008, an electronic journal edited by Sylvia Schroer and Tal Ilan; "To Turn the Groaning into Labor: Romans 8:22-23," in *A Feminist Companion to Paul*, ed. Amy-Jill Levine (London and New York, 2004), 78-84; *Konflikte zwischen ihm und ihr. Sozial geschichtliche und exegetische Untersuchungen zur Nachfolgeproblematik von Ehepaaren* (Gütersloh, 2002); with Sabine Bieberstein and Ulrike Metternich, eds., *Sich dem Leben in die Arme werfen. Auferstehungserfahrungen*, 4th ed. (Gütersloh, 2002).

TAMEZ, ELSA, professor emerita of Universidad Biblica Latinoamericana in San José, Costa Rica, and adviser to the United Bible Society on translating the Scriptures. Her doctoral degree was awarded by the Université de Lausanne, Switzerland; she studied literature and linguistics at the Universidad Nacional in Costa Rica. She is the author of numerous books and articles. Among her recent publications, translated also into English and other languages, are the following: *When the Horizons Close: Rereading Ecclesiastes* (Maryknoll, N.Y., 2000); *Jesus and Courageous Women* (New York, 2001); *Struggles for Power in Early Christianity: A Study of the First Letter of Timothy* (Maryknoll, N.Y.: Orbis, 2007); with Mary John Mananzan and Mercy Amba Oduyoye, eds., *Women Resisting Violence: Spirituality for Life* (Eugene, Oreg.: Wipf and Stock, 2004); editor of *Through Her Eyes: Women's Theology from Latin America* (Eugene, Oreg.: Wipf and Stock, 2006); her last publication, available thus far only in Spanish, is about the epistle of James: *No discriminéis a los pobres. Lectura latinoamericana de la Carta de Santiago* (2008). Professor Tamez is married and has two sons.

ULRICH, KERSTIN, b. 1961 in Berlin; studied Protestant theology in Berlin and Marburg. From 1990 until 1996 she was academic associate in the area of Old Testament at Philipps-Universität Marburg and research fellow in the Hedwig Jahnow Research Project. From 1996 to 1998, she was curate, and from 1998 until 2007 she was minister in the Protestant Church of the Rhineland with primary responsibility for congregational and family formation in Mühlheim, Ruhr. Since 2007 she has taught religion at the primary and secondary level in a private school and a special education school in Neukirchen-Vluyn with a focus on "emotional and social development." She holds the office of honorary pastor, is married, and has two daughters. Recent publications include the following: translations of the lectionary readings from the book of Joshua in Erhard Domay and Hanne Köhler, eds., *Der Gottesdienst. Liturgische Texte in gerechter Sprache*, vol. 4, *Die Lesungen* (Gütersloh, 2001), 84, 446-48, 500; "Landnahme," in *Grundbegriffe zum Altern und Neuen Testament. 99 Wörter Theologie konkret*, ed. Ulrike Bechmann and Monika Fander (Munich, 2003), 107f.

VANDER STICHELE, CAROLINE, Ph.D., studied theology at the Faculteit der Godge-leerdheit Leuven/Belgium. Her 1992 doctoral dissertation was on authenticity and integrity in 1 Corinthians 11:2-16. She currently teaches biblical studies at the Universiteit van Amsterdam. Recent publications include the following: "Murderous Mother, Ditto Daughter: Herodias and Salome at the Opera," *lectio difficilior: European Electronic Journal for Feminist Exegesis* 2 (2001), http://www.lectio.unibe.ch; "Apocalypse, Art and Abjection: Images of the Great Whore," in *Culture, Entertainment, and the Bible,* ed. G. Aichele, Journal for the Study of the Old Testament: Supplement Series, vol. 309 (Sheffield: Sheffield Academic Press, 2000), 114-38; with Todd Penner, *Contextualizing Gender in Early Christian Discourse: Thinking beyond Thecla* (London: T. & T. Clark, 2009); with Todd Penner, "Script(ur)ing Gender in Acts: The Past and Present Power of Imperium," in *Mapping Gender in Ancient Religious Discourses,* ed. T. Penner and C. Vander Stichele, Biblical Interpretation Series, vol. 84 (Leiden: Brill, 2007), 231-66; with Todd Penner, "Mastering the Tools or Retooling the Masters? The Legacy of Historical-Critical Discourse," in *Her Master's Tools? Feminist and Postcolonial Engagements of Historical-Critical Discourse,* ed. T. Penner and C. Vander Stichele, Global Perspectives on Biblical Scholarship (Atlanta, 2005), 1-29.

WACKER, MARIE-THERES, Ph.D. b. 1952, studied Catholic theology in Bonn, Tübingen, and Jerusalem; was awarded the doctoral degree in 1981 with a dissertation on the Ethiopic version of the book of Enoch, habilitation in 1995 on *Figurationen des Weiblichen im Hoseabuch.* From 1996 until 1998, she was professor of biblical theology at the University of Cologne, and since 1998 she has been professor for Old Testament and Theological Women's Studies at the Catholic Theological Faculty of the University of Münster. She is a member of the editorial board of *Concilium,* an international theological journal. She translated the book of Baruch and the Letter of Jeremiah for *Bibel in gerechter Sprache.* Among her recent publications are the following: *Von Göttinnen, Göttern und dem einzigen Gott. Studien zum biblischen Monotheismus aus feministisch-theologischer Sicht* (Münster, 2004); "Feminist Criticism and Related Aspects," in *The Oxford Handbook of Biblical Studies,* ed. John Rogerson and Judith Lieu (Oxford, 2006), 634-54; "'Nomadische' Zugänge zur Hebräischen Bibel. Ein feministisch-exegetisches Gespräch mit Rosi Braidotti," in *Citizenship-Biographien-Institutionen. Perspektiven lateinamerikanischer und deutscher Theologinnen auf Kirche und Gesellschaft,* ed. Virginia R. Azcuy and Margit Eckholt (Münster, 2009), 193-206; with Stefanie Rieger-Goertz, eds., *Mannsbilder. Kritische Männerforschung und theologische Frauenforschung im Gespräch* (Münster, 2006) (to which she contributed a study on Adam); with Hille Haker and Susan Ross, eds., *Women's Voices in World Religions,* Concilium (2006): 3.

WAGNER, ULRIKE, Ph.D., b. 1960, exegete and social ethicist, studied Protestant theology, history, and philosophy in Münster and one year, 1984-85, at Pittsburgh Theological Seminary; awarded the doctoral degree in New Testament by the Protestant

Theological Faculty in Münster. Since 2001 she has been professor of professional ethics at the Police Academy in Villingen-Schwenningen. Her work and research are focused on the culture and ethics state monopoly on force, peace and conflict studies, conflict management, ethic-didactics, social-historical and feminist exegesis, gender-relations and community-structures, New Testament ethics of peace and commerce. She is among the translators of *Bibel in gerechter Sprache*. Recent publications include the following works: "Die Kinder Gottes und der antike Haushalt. Familienbilder und Gemeindemodelle in den paulinischen und deuteropaulinischen Briefen," in *Jahrbuch für Internationale Germanistik* 36, no. 1 (2004): 75-94; "Verschwenderische Fülle oder haushälterische Vernunft? Oikonomia Gottes, christliche Existenz und Geschlechterdifferenz im frühen Christentum," in *Haushalt, Hauskult, Hauskirche. Zur Arbeitsteilung der Geschlechter in Wirtschaft und Religion*, ed. E. Klinger, S. Böhm, and T. Franz (Würzburg, 2004), 75-109; "An Timotheus: Erster und Zweiter Brief. Brief an Titus," in *Bibel in gerechter Sprache*, ed. Ulrike Bail et al. (Gütersloh, 2006), 2185-2202; "Phoebe. Römer 16," in *Die besten Nebenrollen. 50 biblische Randfiguren*, ed. M. Keuchen, H. Kuhlmann, and H. Schroeder-Wittke, Festschrift für Martin Leutzsch zum 50. Geburtstag (Münster and Hamburg, 2006), 266-71; with M. Oeming and F. Crüsemann the article "Friede/Krieg," and with R. Kessler the article "Militär," in *Sozialgeschichtliches Wörterbuch zur Bibel*, ed. F. Crüsemann et al. (Gütersloh, 2009), 170-76 and 386-89.

The Translators

Dahill, Lisa E., is Associate Professor of Worship and Christian Spirituality at Trinity Lutheran Seminary, Columbus, Ohio. A former chair of the Bonhoeffer Group of the American Academy of Religion, she is the author of *Reading from the Underside of Selfhood: Bonhoeffer and Spiritual Formation,* Princeton Theological Monograph Series (Wipf and Stock, 2009), and translator of *Conspiracy and Imprisonment, 1940-1945,* Dietrich Bonhoeffer Works, vol. 16 (Fortress, 2006).

Kalin, Everett R., is Christ Seminary–Seminex Professor Emeritus of New Testament at Pacific Lutheran Theological Seminary (PLTS) in Berkeley, California. Prior to coming to PLTS, he taught at Concordia Seminary, St. Louis, and at Christ Seminary–Seminex. The translator of five previous books, he resides in Oakland, California.

Lukens, Nancy, is Professor Emerita of German and Women's Studies at the University of New Hampshire, a freelance translator, mother of Hanna Lukens and partner of Martin Rumscheidt. Her work focuses on twentieth-century German resistance movements, German women writers, East German literature, translation and cultural studies. She cotranslated Dorothee Sölle's *Mystery of Death* (2007), Dietrich Bonhoeffer's *Sanctorum Communio* (1998) and *Letters and Papers from Prison* (2010), and translated his *Fiction from Tegel Prison* (2000).

Maloney, Linda M., is a priest of the Episcopal Diocese of Vermont. She received her Ph.D. from Saint Louis University and her Th.D. from Eberhard-Karls Universität Tübingen. She has taught at the Graduate Theological Union and was academic editor for Liturgical Press from 1995 to 2010. She is the translator of more than thirty books and articles.

Rumscheidt, Barbara (1941-2003), received the degree of Bachelor of Education from McGill University, and the degrees of Master of Theological Studies and Master of Theology from Atlantic School of Theology, Halifax, Nova Scotia. She taught for several years in the schools of the Protestant School Board of Greater Montréal and was lecturer at AST. She is the author of *No Room for Grace: Pastoral Theology and Dehumanization in the Global Economy* (Eerdmans, 1998).

RUMSCHEIDT, MARTIN, is an ordained minister of the United Church of Canada; he received his Ph.D. from McGill University and the D.D. *(honoris causa)* from Victoria University, Toronto. He taught historical theology from 1970 until his retirement in 2002 at the University of Windsor (Ontario); Atlantic School of Theology, Halifax, Nova Scotia; and Charles University, Prague. Together with Barbara Rumscheidt and Nancy Lukens, he translated several books in feminist theology and biblical interpretation. He lives with his partner, Nancy Lukens, in New Hampshire.

STEINER, TINA, received her Ph.D. from the University of Cape Town. She teaches in the English Department at Stellenbosch University in South Africa. Her research and teaching interests include themes such as translation, migration, diaspora, and the Indian Ocean as a conceptual and spatial concept in relation to contemporary African fiction. She is the author of *Translated People, Translated Texts: Language and Migration in Contemporary African Fiction* (St. Jerome, 2009).

Index of Authors